Robert Williams Buchanan

The Poetical Works of Robert Buchanan

Robert Williams Buchanan

The Poetical Works of Robert Buchanan

ISBN/EAN: 9783743324961

Manufactured in Europe, USA, Canada, Australia, Japa

Cover: Foto ©ninafisch / pixelio.de

Manufactured and distributed by brebook publishing software (www.brebook.com)

Robert Williams Buchanan

The Poetical Works of Robert Buchanan

THE POETICAL WORKS
OF
ROBERT BUCHANAN

WITH A PORTRAIT OF THE AUTHOR

London
CHATTO & WINDUS, PICCADILLY
1884

Contents.

EARLY POEMS.

	PAGE
PASTORAL PICTURES :	
1. Down the River	1
2. The Summer Pool	3
3. Up the River	4
4. Snow	6
TO THE LUGGIE	7
FRA GIACOMO	8
CHARMIAN	9
CLOUDLAND	9
CUCKOO SONG	12
THE WHITE DEER	12
CONVENT-ROBBING	13
THE BALLAD OF THE WAYFARER	15
IN SPRING-TIME	16
THE FISHERMAN	16
THE CHURCHYARD	16
SEA-WASH	17
EARTH AND THE SOUL	17
A CURL	18
LOVE AND TIME	20

UNDERTONES.
(1864.)

POET'S PROLOGUE—To David in Heaven	21
THE UNDERTONES :	
1. Proteus ; or, a Prelude	24
2. Ades, King of Hell	26
3. Pan	30
4. The Naiad	35
5. The Satyr	36
6. Venus on the Sun-Car	39
7. Selene the Moon	40
8. Iris the Rainbow	41
9. Orpheus the Musician	42
10. Polypheme's Passion	43
11. Penelope	52
12. Sappho : on the Leucadian Rock	54
13. The Syren	54
14. A Voice from Academe	58
15. Pygmalion the Sculptor	59
16. Antony in Arms	65
17. Fine Weather on the Digentia	65
18. Fine Weather by Baiae	70
19. The Swan-Song of Apollo	73
POET'S EPILOGUE—To Mary on Earth	74

IDYLS AND LEGENDS OF INVERBURN.
(1865.)

THE LOWLAND VILLAGE	76
WILLIE BAIRD	77
LORD RONALD'S WIFE	83
POET ANDREW	84
WHITE LILY OF WEARDALE-HEAD	90
THE ENGLISH HUSWIFE'S GOSSIP	93
THE FAËRY FOSTER-MOTHER	98
THE GREEN GNOME	99
HUGH SUTHERLAND'S PANSIES	100
THE DEAD MOTHER	105
THE WIDOW MYSIE (an Idyl of Love and Whisky)	106
THE MINISTER AND THE ELFIN	110
VILLAGE VOICES :	
1. January Wind	111
2. April Rain	112
3. Summer Moon	112
4. December Snow	113

LONDON POEMS.
(1866-70.)

BEXHILL, 1866	113
THE LITTLE MILLINER ; OR, LOVE IN AN ATTIC	115
LIZ	119
THE STARLING	124
JANE LEWSON	125
LANGLEY LANE (a Love Poem)	135
EDWARD CROWHURST ; OR, 'A NEW POET'	136
ARTIST AND MODEL (a Love Poem)	147
NELL	149
ATTORNEY SNEAK	152
BARBARA GRAY	155
THE BLIND LINNET	157

CONTENTS.

'TIGER BAY' (a Stormy Night's Dream): PAGE
  1. The Tigress 157
  2. [illegible] 158
  3. — 159
THE CITY ASLEEP 159
UP IN AN ATTIC 160
TO THE MOON 161
SPRING SONG IN THE CITY . . . 162
IN LONDON, MARCH 1866 . . . 163
A LARK'S FLIGHT 163
DE BERNY 165
THE WAKE OF TIM O'HARA . . . 166
KITTY KEMBLE 168
THE SWALLOWS 173
TOM DUNSTAN; OR, THE POLITICIAN . 174
O'MURTOGH 175
THE BOOKWORM 176
THE LAST OF THE HANGMEN . . . 177
LONDON, 1864 180
THE MODERN WARRIOR 183
PAN: EPILOGUE 185
L'ENVOI TO LONDON POEMS . . . 185

MISCELLANEOUS POEMS.
(1866-70.)

THE DEATH OF ROLAND 186
THE GIFT OF EOS 192
CLARI IN THE WELL 196
SERENADES 197
IN THE GARDEN 198
THE ASRAI (Prologue to the Changeling) . 200
THE CHANGELING (a Legend of the Moonlight):
  1. The Asrai 201
  2. The Changeling's Birth . . . 202
  3. His Mortal Life 203
  4. His Sorrow and Sin . . . 203
  5. The Battle-Field 204
  6. The Abbot Paul 204
TO CLARI (with the Preceding Poem) . . 206

NORTH COAST, AND OTHER POEMS.
(1867-68.)

MEG BLANE:
  1. Storm 207
  2. Dead Calm 211
  3. A Troubled Deep 214
  4. 'And the Spirit of God moved upon the Waters' 217
THE BATTLE OF DRUMLIEMOOR (Covenant Period) 221
THE NORTHERN WOOING . . . 223
AN ENGLISH ECLOGUE 227
A SCOTTISH ECLOGUE 229
THE SCAITH O' BARTLE 232
THE GLAMOUR 241
SIGURD OF SAXONY (Mediæval) . . 244
A POEM TO DAVID 246
HAKON 247

SONNETS
WRITTEN BY LOCH CORUISK, ISLE OF SKYE.
(1870.)

CORUISKEN SONNETS: PAGE
  1. Lord, is it Thou? . . . 248
  2. We are Fatherless . . . 248
  3. We are Children . . . 248
  4. When we are all Asleep . . 249
  5. But the Hills will bear Witness . 249
  6. Desolate! 249
  7. Lord, art Thou here? . . 250
  8. God is Beautiful . . . 250
  9. The Motion of the Mists . . 250
  10. Coruisk 250
  11. But Whither? . . . 251
  12. God is Pitiless . . . 251
  13. Yes, Pitiless 251
  14. Could God be Judged? . . 251
  15. The Hills on their Thrones . 251
  16. King Blaabhein . . . 252
  17. Blaabhein in the Mists . . 252
  18. The Fiery Birth of the Hills . 252
  19. The Changeless Hills . . 252
  20. O Mountain Peak of a God . 253
  21. God the Image . . . 253
  22. The Footprints . . . 253
  23. We are Deathless . . . 253
  24. A Voice in the Whirlwind . 254
  25. Cry of the Little Brook . . 254
  26. The Happy Hearts of Earth . 254
  27. Father, forgive Thy Child . 254
  28. God's Loneliness . . . 255
  29. The Cup of Tears . . . 255
  30. The Light of the World . . 255
  31. Earth's Eldest Born . . 255
  32. What Spirit cometh? . . 256
  33. Stay, O Spirit! . . . 256
  34. Quiet Waters . . . 256

THE BOOK OF ORM.
(1870.)

INSCRIPTION (To F. W. C.) . . . 257
PROEM (to Book of Orm and Political Mystics) 257
THE BOOK OF THE VISIONS SEEN BY ORM THE CELT 257
1. FIRST SONG OF THE VEIL:
  1. The Veil Woven . . . 258
  2. Earth the Mother . . . 259
  3. Children of Earth . . . 259
  4. The Wise Men . . . 260
2. THE MAN AND THE SHADOW:
  1. The Shadow 261
  2. The Rainbow . . . 266
3. SONGS OF CORRUPTION:
  1. Phantasy 268
  2. The Dream of the World without Death 269
  3. Soul and Flesh . . . 272
4. THE SOUL AND THE DWELLING . . 273
5. SONGS OF SEEKING:
  1. 275
  2. Quest 276

		PAGE
3.	The Happy Earth	276
4.	O Unseen One!	277
5.	World's Mystery	277
6.	The Cities	278
7.	The Priests	278
8.	The Lamb of God	278
9.	Doom	279
10.	God's Dream	279
11.	Flower of the World	280
12.	O Spirit	280

6. THE LIFTING OF THE VEIL:
    1. Orm's Vision 280
    2. The Face and the World . . . 281
    3. Orm's Awakening 284

7. THE DEVIL'S MYSTICS:
    1. The Inscription without . . . 284
    2. The Tree of Life 284
    3. The Seeds 285
    4. Fire and Water; or, a Voice of the Flesh 286
    5. Sanitas 286
    6. The Philosophers 287
    7. The Devil's Prayer 287
    8. Homunculus; or, the Song of Deicides 287
    9. Roses 288
    10. Hermaphroditus 289
    11. After 289
    12. His Prayer 290

8. THE VISION OF THE MAN ACCURST . 290

POLITICAL MYSTICS.
(1871.)

TITAN AND AVATAR (a Choral Mystic):
  1. Ode of Nations 295
  2. The Avatar's Dream 297
  3. The Elemental Quest 301
  4. The Elemental Doom 303
THE FOOL OF DESTINY (a Choric Drama) . 307
THE TEUTON MONOLOGUE (1870) . . 330
THE REPLY 333
THE CITY OF MAN 334

SONGS OF THE TERRIBLE YEAR.
(1870.)

ODE TO THE SPIRIT OF AUGUSTE COMTE (1871) 335
A DIRGE FOR KINGS 337
THE PERFECT STATE 338
THE TWO VOICES (January 1871) . . 339
ODE BEFORE PARIS (December 1870) . 340
A DIALOGUE IN THE SNOW (before Paris, December 1870) 341
THE PRAYER IN THE NIGHT . . . 343
THE SPIRIT OF FRANCE 344
THE APOTHEOSIS OF THE SWORD (Versailles, 1871) 345
THE CHAUNT BY THE RHINE (1871) . . 347

SAINT ABE AND HIS SEVEN WIVES.
A TALE OF SALT LAKE CITY.

	PAGE
DEDICATION: TO OLD DAN CHAUCER	349

APPROACHING UTAH.—THE BOSS'S TALE:
  1. Passing the Ranche 350
  2. Joe Wilson goes a-courting . . 350
  3. Saint and Disciple 351
  4. The Book of Mormon 352
  5. Joe ends his Story—First Glimpse of Utah 355

THE CITY OF THE SAINTS:
  1. Among the Pastures—Summer Evening Dialogue 356
  2. Within the City—St. Abe and the Seven 361
  3. Promenade—Main Street, Utah . 364
  4. Within the Synagogue—Sermonizeth the Prophet 367
  5. The Falling of the Thunderbolt . 369
  6. Last Epistle of St. Abe to the Polygamists 371

THE FARM IN THE VALLEY—SUNSET (1871) 377

WHITE ROSE AND RED.
A LOVE STORY.

DEDICATION 380
INVOCATION ('Know'st thou the Land?') . 380

1. THE CAPTURE OF EUREKA HART:
    1. Natura Naturans 381
    2. Eureka 383
    3. The Capture 385
    4. Thro' the Wood 387
    5. The Red Tribe 388

2. RED ROSE:
    1. Erycina Ridens 390
    2. Log and Sunbeam 390
    3. Nuptial Song 392
    4. Arretez! 392
    5. The Farewell 393
    6. The Paper 396

3. WHITE ROSE:
    1. Drowsietown 397
    2. After Meeting 399
    3. Phœbe Anna 402
    4. Nuptial Song 404

4. THE GREAT SNOW:
    1. The Great Snow 405
    2. The Wanderer 407
    3. Retrospect: the Journey . . . 411
    4. The Journey's End 415
    5. Face to Face 417
    6. Pauguk 419
    7. The Melting of the Snow . . . 421
    8. The Last Look 422

EPILOGUE 423

CONTENTS.

FACES ON THE WALL.
(1876.)
	PAGE
LONE HOUSE	424
STORM AND CALM	424
WITHOUT AND WITHIN	425
NAPOLEON	425
ABRAHAM LINCOLN	425
WALT WHITMAN	425
O FACES!	425
TO TRIFLERS	426
THE WANDERERS	426
THE WATCHER OF THE BEACON	426
'AND THE SPIRIT OF GOD MOVED UPON THE WATERS'	426

BALDER THE BEAUTIFUL.
A SONG OF DIVINE DEATH.

PROEM TO ——. (A Song of a Dream)	427
1. THE BIRTH OF BALDER:	
1. Balder's Birth-Song	429
2. His Growth and Godhead	432
2. THE FINDING OF BALDER:	
1. Frea in the Wood	433
2. The Shadow in the Wood	434
3. Full Godhead	438
4. The Man by the Ocean	440
3. THE HEAVENWARD JOURNEY:	
1. The Goddesses	442
2. The Fruit of Life	445
3. The City of the Gods	446
4. The Voice of the Father	448
5. Balder's Return	448
4. BALDER'S RETURN TO EARTH:	
1. 'Balder is here'	451
2.	453
3. All Things Blest by Balder	454
4. The Cry from the Ground	455
5. The Shadow on the Earth	456
6. On the Heights—Evening	458
7. The Vow of Balder	459
5. BALDER'S QUEST FOR DEATH:	
1.	460
2.	461
3. The Fight of Ships	462
4. Ydun	463
6. BALDER AND DEATH:	
1. The Altar of Sacrifice	465
2. Balder and Death	467
3. 'O Death, pale Death'	468
4. Death Sings	468
5.	469
6. The Last Prayer	470
7. The First Snowflake—Falling of the Snow	471

7. THE COMING OF THE OTHER:	PAGE
1.	473
2. The Light on the Snow	473
3. The Face and the Voice	474
4. 'Wake, Balder! Wake!'	475
5. The Birth and Death	476
6. The Paracletes	477
7.	478
8.	479
8. THE TWILIGHT OF THE GODS:	
1.	480
2.	481
3. The Bridge of Ghosts	481
4. 'Behold, I am Risen'	482
5. Alfader	484
6. The Brethren	486
7. Father and Son	488
8. Twilight	489
9. 'A Cross and a Lily'	490
9. THE LAST BLESSING:	
1. The Waking of the Sea	491
2. From Death to Life	491

MISCELLANEOUS POEMS AND BALLADS.
(1878-83.)

DEDICATION (To Harriett)	493
THE STRANGE COUNTRY	493
THE BALLAD OF JUDAS ISCARIOT	494
THE LIGHTS OF LEITH	496
THE WEDDING OF SHON MACLEAN (a Bagpipe Melody)	500
HANS VOGEL (an Episode of the Franco-Prussian War)	503
PHIL BLOOD'S LEAP (a Tale of the Gold-Seekers)	504
THE FAËRY REAPER (Ireland)	508
THE 'MIDIAN-MARA'	510
O'CONNOR'S WAKE (an Irish Fiddle Tune)	512
HIGHLAND LAMENT	515
JAMES AVERY	515
THE DEVIL'S PEEPSHOW (Old Style)	517
DAYBREAK (Fragment)	519
EUPHROSYNE; OR, THE PROSPECT	519
STANLEY FARM	521
ON A YOUNG POETESS'S GRAVE	521
LOVE IN WINTER (a Genre Picture)	522
WILL O' THE WISP (a Ballad written for Clari, on a Stormy Night)	523
GIANT DESPAIR:	
1. His Death	526
2. After	527
THE MOUNTAIN WELL	528
THE SONG OF THE SHEALING	529
THE SECRET OF THE MERE	529
MNEMOSYNE; OR, THE RETROSPECT	531
VANITY FAIR	532

Early Poems.

PASTORAL PICTURES.

I.

DOWN THE RIVER.

How merry a life the little River leads,
Piping a vagrant ditty free from care ;
Now rippling as it rustles through the reeds
And broad-leaved lilies sailing here and
  there,
Now lying level with the clover meads
And musing in a mist of golden air !
Bearing a pastoral peace where'er it' goes,
Narrow'd to mirth or broaden'd to repose :
Through copsy villages and tiny towns,
By belts of woodland singing sweet,
Pausing where sun and shadow meet
Without the darkness of the breezy downs,
Bickering o'er the keystone as it flows
'Neath mossy bridges arch'd like maiden
  feet ;
And slowly widening as it seaward grows,
Because its summer mission grows complete.

Run seaward, for I follow !
      Let me cross
My garden-threshold ankle-deep in moss.
Sweet Stream, your heart is beating and I
  hear it,
As conscious of its pleasure as a girl's :
O little River, whom I love so well,
Is it with something of a human spirit
You twine those lilies in your sedgy curls ?
Take up the inner voice we both inherit,
O little River of my love, and tell !

The rain has crawled from yonder mountain-side,
And passing, left its footprints far and wide.

The path I follow winds by cliff and scar,
Purple and dark and trodden as I pass,
The foxglove droops, the crocus lifts its
  star,
And bluebells brighten in the dewy grass.
Over deep pools the willow hangs its hair,
Dwarf birches show their sodden roots and
  shake
Their melting jewels on my bending brows,
The mottled mavis pipes among their
  boughs
For joy of five unborn in yonder brake.
The River, narrow'd to a woody glen,
Leaps trembling o'er a little rocky ledge,
Then broadens forward into calm again
Where the gray moor-hen builds her nest
  of sedge ;
Caught in the dark those willow-trees have
  made,
Lipping the yellow lilies o'er and o'er,
It flutters twenty feet along the shade,
Halts at the sunshine like a thing afraid,
And turns to kiss the lilies yet once more.

Those little falls are lurid with the rain
That ere the day is done will come again.
The River falters swoll'n and brown,
Falters, falters, as it nears them,
Shuddering back as if it fears them,
Falters, falters, falters, falters,
Then dizzily rushes down.

But all is calm again, the little River
Smiles on and sings the song it sings for
  ever.
Here at the curve it passes tilth and farm,
And faintly flowing onward to the mill
It stretches out a little azure arm
To aid the miller; aiding with a will,
And singing, singing still.

B

Sweet household sounds come sudden on
   mine ear :
The waggons rumbling in the rutted lanes,
The village clock and trumpet Chanticleer,
The flocks and cattle on the marish-plains,
With shouts of urchins ringing loud and
   clear;
And lo! a Village, breathing breath that
   curls
In foam-white wreaths through ancient
   sycamores!
A hum of looms comes through the cottage
   doors.
I stumble on a group of country girls
Faring afield thro' deep and dewy grass ;
Small urchins rush from sanded kitchen-
   floors
To stare with mouths wide open as I pass.

  But yonder cottage where the woodbine
   grows,
Half cottage and half inn, a pretty place,
Tempts ramblers with the country cheer it
   shows;
Entering, I rob the threshold of a rose,
And meet the welcome on a mother's face.
Come, let me sit. The scent of garden
   flowers
Flits through the casement of the sanded
   room,
Hitting the sense with thoughts of summer
   hours
When half the world has budded into bloom.
Is that the faded picture of our host
Shading the plate of pansies where I sit—
That lean-limb'd stripling straighter than a
   post,
Clad in a coat that seems a sorry fit?
I drink his health in this his own October,
That bites so sharply on the thirsty tongue ;
And here he comes, but not so slim and sober
As in the days when Love and he were
   young.
'Hostess!' I fill again and pledge the glory
Of that stout angel answering to my call,
Who changed him from the shadow on the
   wall
Into the rosy tun of sack before me!

  Again I follow where the river wanders,
The landscape billows into hills of thyme ;
Over the purple heights I slowly climb ;
Till in a glen of birchen-trees and boulders
I halt, beneath a heathery mountain ridge
Clothed on with amber cloud from head to
   shoulders.

  I wander on and gain a mossy bridge,
And watch the angling of a shepherd boy ;
Below the little river glimmers by,
Touched with a troubled sense of pain or
   joy
By some new life at work in earth and sky.
The marshes there steam mist from hidden
   springs,
Deep-hidden in the marsh the bittern calls,
And yonder swallow oils its ebon wings
While fluttering o'er the falls.
Below my feet the little budding flower
Thrusts up dark leaves to feel the coming
   shower :
I'll trust these weather-signs and creep apart
Beneath this crag until the rain depart,—
'Twill come again and go within an hour.

The moist soft wind has died and fallen now,
The air is hot and hush'd on flower and tree,
The leaves are troubled into sighs, and see!
There falls a heavy drop upon my brow.
The cloudy standard is above unfurl'd ;
The aspen fingers of the blinded Rain
Feel for the summer eyelids of the world
That she may kiss them open once again.
Darker and darker, till with one accord
The clouds pour forth their hoard in gusts
   of power,
A sunbeam rends their bowels like a sword
And frees the costly shower!

  Fluttering around me and before me,
Stretched like a mantle o'er me,
The rushing shadows blind the earth and
   skies,
Dazzling a darkness on my gazing eyes
With troublous gleams of radiance, like the
   bright
Pigments of gold that flutter in our sight,
When with shut eyes we strain
Our aching vision back upon the brain.

  Across the skies and o'er the plain
Fast fly the swollen shadows of the Rain ;
Blown duskly by,
From hill to hill they fly,
O'er solitary streams and windy downs,
O'er trembling villages and darkened towns!

I crouch beneath the crag and watch the mist
Move on the skirts of yonder mountains gray
Until it bubbles into amethyst
And softly melts away.
The thyme-bells catch their drops of silver dew,
And quake beneath the load;
The squadron'd pines that shade the splashing road
Are glimmering with a million jewels too.
And hark! the Spirit of the Rain
Sings to the Summer sleeping,
Pressing a dark damp face against the plain,
And pausing, pausing, not for pain,
Pausing, pausing, ere the low refrain,
Because she cannot sing for weeping.
She flings her cold dim arms about the Earth,
That soon shall wear the blessing she has given,
Then brightens thro' her tears in sunny mirth
And flutters back to heaven.

A fallen sunbeam trembles at my feet,
And as I sally forth the linnets frame
Their throats to answer yonder laverock sweet.
The jewell'd trees flash out in emerald flame.
The bright drops fall with throbs of peaceful sound,
And melt in circles on the shallow pools
That glisten on the ground.
Last, Iris issues from her cloudy shrine,
Trembling alone in heaven where she rules,
And arching down to kiss with kisses sweet
The bright green world that flashes at her feet,
Runs liquid through her many hues divine.

II.
THE SUMMER POOL.

THERE is a singing in the summer air,
The blue and brown moths flutter o'er the grass,
The stubble bird is creaking in the wheat,
And perch'd upon the honeysuckle hedge
Pipes the green linnet. Oh, the golden world!
The stir of life on every blade of grass,
The motion and the joy on every bough,
The glad feast everywhere, for things that love
The sunshine, and for things that love the shade!

Aimlessly wandering with weary feet,
Watching the wool-white clouds that wander by,
I come upon a lonely place of shade,—
A still green Pool, where with soft sound and stir
The shadows of o'erhanging branches sleep,
Save where they leave one dreamy space of blue,
O'er whose soft stillness ever and anon
The feathery cirrhus blows. Here unaware
I pause, and leaning on my staff I add
A shadow to the shadows; and behold!
Dim dreams steal down upon me, with a hum
Of little wings, a murmuring of boughs,—
The dusky stir and motion dwelling here,
Within this small green world. O'ershadowed
By dusky greenery, tho' all around
The sunshine throbs on fields of wheat and bean,
Downward I gaze into the dreamy blue,
And pass into a waking sleep, wherein
The green boughs rustle, feathery wreaths of cloud
Pass softly, piloted by golden airs:
The air is still,—no birds sing any more,—
And, helpless as a tiny flying thing,
I am alone in all the world with God.

The wind dies—not a leaf stirs—on the Pool
The fly scarce moves; Earth seems to hold her breath
Until her heart stops, listening silently
For the far footsteps of the coming Rain!

While thus I pause, it seems that I have gained
New eyes to see; my brain grows sensitive
To trivial things that, at another hour,
Had passed unheeded. Suddenly the air
Shivers, the shadows in whose midst I stand
Tremble and blacken—the blue eye o' the Pool
Is closed and clouded; with a sudden gleam,
Oiling its wings, a swallow darteth past,
And weedling flowers beneath my feet thrust up

Their leaves to feel the fragrant shower. Oh hark!
The thirsty leaves are troubled into sighs,
And up above me, on the glistening boughs,
Patters the summer Rain!

      Into a nook,
Screen'd by thick foliage of oak and beech,
I creep for shelter; and the summer shower
Murmurs around me. Oh, the drowsy sounds!
The pattering rain, the numerous sigh of leaves,
The deep, warm breathing of the scented air,
Sink sweet into my soul—until at last
Comes the soft ceasing of the gentle fall,
And lo! the eye of blue within the Pool
Opens again, while with a silvern gleam
Dew-diamonds twinkle moistly on the leaves,
Or, shaken downward by the summer wind,
Fall melting on the Pool in rings of light!

III.
UP THE RIVER.

BEHIND the purple mountains lies a lake,
Steadfast thro' storm and sunshine in its place;
Asleep 'neath changing skies, its waters make
A mirror for the tempest's thunder-face;
Thence—singing songs of glee,
Fluttering to my cottage by the sea,
 By bosky glen and grove,
Past the lone shepherd, moveless as the rock
Whence stretch'd at length he views his scatter'd flock,—
Cometh the little River that I love.

To-day I'll bid farewell to books,
And by the River loved so well,
Thro' ferny haunts and flowery nooks,
Thro' stony glen and woody dell,
The rainy river-path I'll take,
Till by the silent-sleeping lake
 I hear the shepherd's bell.
The summer bleats from every rocky height,
The bluebell banks are dim with dewy light,
 The heavens are clear as infants' eyes above;
This is no day—you, little River, know it!—
 For sage or poet
  To localise his love.

In rippling cadence, calm and slow,
Sing, little River, as I go,
Songs of the mountains whence you flow!

The grassy banks are wet with dew that flashes
Silverly on the Naiad-river's lashes—
The Naiad-river, bright with sunken suns,
Who murmureth as she runs.
Yonder the silver-bellied salmon splashes
Within the spreading circle of blue shade
That his own leaps have made:
And here I stoop, and pluck with tender care
A lily from the Naiad's sedgy hair.
And curling softly over pebble,
Weaving soft waves o'er yellow sands,
Singing her song in tinkling treble,
The mountain Lady thro' the farmer's lands
Slides to the sea, with harvest-giving hands.

Here freckled cowslips bloom unsought,
 Like yellow jewels on her light green train;
 And yonder, dark with dreaming of the rain,
Grows the wood-violet like a lowly thought.
Lightly the mountain Lady dances down,
Dressed maidenly in many a woodland gem;—
Lo, even where the footprint of the clown
Has bruised her raiment-hem,
Crimson-tipp'd daisies make a diadem.

The little River is the fittest singer
To sound the praises of a day so fair.
The dews, suck'd up thro' pores of sunshine, linger
As silver cloudlets in mid-air;
And over all the sunshine throws
Its golden glamour of repose.
The Silence listens, in a dream,
To hear the ploughman urge his reeling team,
The trout, that flashes with a sudden gleam,
And musical motions heaved by hills that bound
The slumberous vales around.
I loiter onward slowly, and the whole
Sweet joy is in my happy fancies drowned.
The sunshine meets the music. Sight and sound
 Are wedded by the Soul.
—Sing, little River, this sweet morn,
Songs of the hills where thou wert born!

For, suddenly, mine eyes perceive
The purple hills that touch the sky;
Familiar with the stars of eve,
Against the pale blue West they lie,
Netted in mists of azure air,
With thread-like cataracts here and there.
Oh hark! Oh hark!
The shepherd shouts, and answering sheep-
 dogs bark;
And voices, startling Echo from her sleep,
Are blown from steep to steep.

At yonder falls, the trembling mountain
 Lady
Clings to the bramble high above me
 lying,
With veil of foam behind her swift feet
 flying,
And a lorn terror in her lifted voice,
Ere springing to the rush-friezed basin
 shady,
That boils below with noise.
Then, whirling dizzily for a moment's
 space,
She lets the sun flash brightly on her face,
And lightly laughs at her own terror past,
And floateth onward fast!

Thus wandering onward, ankle deep in
 grass,
Scaring the cumbrous black cock as I pass,
I came upon two shepherd boys, who wade
For coolness in the limpid waves,
And with their shade
Startle the troutling from its shallow caves.

Let me lie down upon the bank, and
 drink!
The minnows at the brim, with bellies
 white
Upturned in specks of silvery light,
Flash from me in a shower, and sink.
Below, the blue skies wink
Thro' heated golden air—a clear abyss
Of azure, with a solitary bird
Steadfastly winging thro' the depths un-
 stirred.
The brain turns dizzy with its bliss;
And I would plunge into the chasms cool,
And float to yonder cloud of fleecy wool,
That floats below me, as I kiss
The mountain Lady's lips with thirsty
 mouth.

What would parch'd Dives give amid his
 drouth
For kisses such as this?

Sing, little River, while I rest,
Songs of your hidden mountain nest,
And of the blue sky in your breast!

The landscape darkens slowly
With mountain shadows; when I wander
 on,
The tremulous gladness of the heat seems
 gone,
And a cool awe spreads round me, sweet
 and holy,—
A tender, sober-suited melancholy.
The path rough feet have made me winds
 away
O'er fenny meadows to the white highway,
Where the big waggon clatters with its
 load,
And pushing onward, to the ankles wet
In swards as soft as silken sarcenet,
I gain the dusty road.

The air is hotter here. The bee booms by
With honey-laden thigh,
Doubling the heat with sounds akin to heat;
And like a floating flower the butterfly
Swims upward, downward, till its feet
Cling to the hedgerows white and sweet.
A black duck rises clumsily with a cry,
And the dim lake is nigh.
The road curves upward to a dusty rise,
Where fall the sunbeams flake on flake;
And turning at the curve, mine eyes
Fall sudden on the silent lake,
Asleep 'neath hyacinthine skies.

Sing, little River, in your mirth,
Sing to thyself for joy the earth
Is smiling on your humble worth;
And sing for joy that earth has given
A place of birth so near to heaven!
Sing, little River, while I climb
These little hills of rock and thyme;
And hear far-off your tinkling chime!
 The cataracts burst in foamy sheen;
The hills slope blackly to the water's brim,
And far below I see their shadows dim;
 The lake, so closely hemmed between
Their skirts of heather and of grass,
Grows black and cold beneath me as I pass.

The sunlight fades on mossy rocks,
And on the mountain sides the flocks
  Are split like streams ;—the highway dips
Down, narrowing to the path where lambs
Lay to the udders of their dams
  Their soft and pulpy lips.
The hills grow closer ; to the right
The path sweeps round a shadowy bay,
Upon whose slated fringes, white
  And crested wavelets play.
All else is still. But list, oh list !
Hidden by boulders and by mist,
A shepherd whistles in his fist ;
From height to height the far sheep bleat
In answering iteration sweet.
Sound, seeking Silence, bends above her,
Within some haunted mountain grot ;
Kisses her, like a trembling lover—
So that she stirs in sleep, but wakens not !

Along this rock I 'll lie,
With face turn d upward to the sky.
A dreamy numbness glows within my
    brain—
It is not joy and is not pain—
'Tis like the solemn, sweet imaginings
That cast a shade on Music's golden wings.
With face turned upward to the sun,
I lie as indolent as one
Who, in a vision sweet, perceives
Spirits thro' mists of lotus leaves ;
  And now and then small shadows move
Across me, cast by clouds so small
Mine eyes perceive them scarce at all
  In the unsullied blue above.
I hear the streams that burst and fall,
The straggling shepherd's frequent call,
  The kine low bleating as they pass,
The dark lake stirring with the breeze,
The melancholy hum of bees,
  The very murmur of the grass.

IV.
SNOW.

I WANDER forth this chill December dawn :
John Frost and all his elves are out, I see,
As busy as the elfin world can be,
Clothing a world asleep with fleecy lawn.
'Mid the deep silence of the evening hours
They glimmered duskly down in silent
    showers,
And featly have they laboured all night long,
Cheering their labour with a half-heard
    rhyme—
Low as the burthen of a milkmaid's song
When Echo moans it over hills of thyme.

There is a hush of music on the air—
The white-wing'd fays are faltering every-
    where ;
And here and there,
Made by a sudden mingling as they fall,
There comes a softer lullaby than all,
Swept in upon the universal prayer.
Mine eyes and heart are troubled with a
    motion
Of music like the moving waves of ocean,
When, out of hearing, o'er the harbour bars
They sigh toward the moon and jasper stars.
The tiny squadrons waver down and thicken,
Gathering numbers as they fly,
And nearing earth their thick-set ranks they
    quicken,
And swim in swarms to die !

But now the clouds are winnowèd away :
The sky above is gray as glass ; below
The feeble twilight of the dreamy day
Nets the long landskip hush'd beneath the
    snow.
The arrowy frosts sting keenly as I stray
Along the rutted lane or broad highway,
Past wind-swept hedges sighing sharp and
    clear,
Where half the sweetly changeful year
The scented summer loves to gleam and
    glow.
The new-lain snowy carpet, ankle-deep,
Crumbles beneath my footsteps as I pass,
Revealing scanty blades of frozen grass ;
On either side the chirping sparrows leap,
And here and there a robin, friendly now,
From naked bough to bough.
That snow-clad homestead in the river's arm
Is haunted with the noisy rooks that fly
Between its leafless beeches and the sky,
And hailing fast for yonder fallow farm,
A solitary crow is plunging by.
Light muffled winds arising high among
White mountains brooding in their winter
    rest,
Bear from the eastern winter to the West
The muttered diapason of a song
Made by the thunder on a mountain's breast.

The sun is hanging in a purple globe,
'Mid yellow mists that stir with silver breath;
The quiet landskip slumbers, white as death,
Amid its naked fields and woody wolds,
Wearing the winter as a stainless robe
Low-trailing in a fall of fleecy folds.
By pasture-gates the mottled cattle swarm,
Thick'ning the misty air, with piteous eyes
Fixed ever on the tempest-breeding skies,
And watch the lingering traces of the storm.
A feeble sunbeam kisses and illumes
Yon whitened spire that hints a hidden town,
And flickering for a space it darkens down
Above the silence of forgotten tombs.

I gain the shoulder of the woodland now,
A fledgling's flutter from a small hill's brow.
I see the hamlet, half a mile below,
With dripping gables and with crimson panes,
And watch the urchins in the narrow lanes
Below the school-house, shouting in the snow.
The whitened coach comes swiftly round the road
With horns to which a dozen hills reply,
And rattling onward with its laughing load,
Halts steaming at the little hostelry.
Hard by the lonely woodman pants and glows,
And, wrapt in leather stockings to the thigh,
Toils with an icicle beneath his nose.
In yonder field an idle farm-boy blows
His frozen fingers into tingling flame ;
The gaunt old farmer, as he canters by,
Reins in to greet the country clowns by name ;
That chestnut pony in the yellow fly
Draws the plump parson and his leaner dame.

I loiter down the road, and feel the ground
Like iron 'neath my heel ; the windless air
Seems lying in a swound.
Frost follows in its path without a sound,
And plies his nimble fingers everywhere,
Under my eyelids and beneath my hair.
Yon mountain dons once more its helm of cloud,
The air grows dark and dim as if in wonder ;
Once more the heaven is winnow'd, and the crowd
Of silken fays flock murmurously under
A sky that flutters like a wind-swept shroud.

Through gloomy dimbles, clad with new-fall'n snow,
Back to my little cottage home I go.
But once again I roam by field and flood,
Stung into heat where hoar-frosts melt and bite,
What time the fog-wrapt sun drops red as blood,
And Eve's white star is tingling into sight.

TO THE LUGGIE.[1]

OH, sweet and still around the hill
  Thy silver waters, Brook, are creeping ;
Beneath the hill, as sweet and still,
  Thy weary Friend lies sleeping :
A laurel leaf is in his hair,
  His eyes are closed to human seeming,
And surely he hath dreams most fair,
  If he, indeed, be dreaming.

O Brook ! he smiled, a happy child,
  Upon thy banks, and loved thy crying,
And, as time flew, thy murmur grew
  A trouble purifying ;
Till, last, thy laurel leaf he took,
  Dream-eyed and tearful, like a woman,
And turned thy haunting cry, O Brook !
  To speech divine and human.

O Brook ! in song full sweet and strong,
  He sang of thee he loved so dearly ;
Then softly creep around his sleep,
  And murmur to him cheerly ;
For though he knows no fret or fear,
  Though life no more slips strangely through him,
Yet he may rest more sound to hear
  His friend so close unto him.

And when at last the sleepers cast
  Their swathes aside, and, wondering, waken,
Let thy Friend be full tenderly
  In silvern arms uptaken.
Him be it then thy task to bear
  Up to the Footstool, softly flowing,—
Smiles on his eyes, and in his hair
  Thy leaf of laurel blowing !

---

[1] See 'The Luggie and other Poems,' by the late David Gray.

FRA GIACOMO.

I.

ALAS, Fra Giacomo,
  Too late! but follow me . . .
Hush! draw the curtain—so!
  She is dead, quite dead, you see.
Poor little lady! she lies,
  All the light gone out of her eyes!
But her features still wear that soft,
  Gray, meditative expression,
Which you must have noticed oft,
  Thro' the peephole, at confession.
How saintly she looks, how meek!
  Though this be the chamber of death,
I fancy I feel her breath,
  As I kiss her on the cheek.
Too holy for *me*, by far!—
  As cold and as pure as a star,
Not fashioned for kissing and pressing,
  But made for a heavenly crown! . . .
Ay, Father, let us go down,—
  But first, if you please, your blessing.

II.

. . . Wine? No! Come, come, you must!
  Blessing it with your prayers,
You'll quaff a cup, I trust,
  To the health of the Saint upstairs.
My heart is aching so!
  And I feel so weary and sad,
Through the blow that I have had!
  You'll sit, Fra Giacomo? . . .

III.

Heigho! 'tis now six summers
  Since I saw that angel and married her—
I was passing rich, and I carried her
  Off in the face of all comers . . .
So fresh, yet so brimming with Soul!
  A sweeter morsel, I swear,
Never made the dull black coal
  Of a monk's eye glitter and glare . . .
Your pardon—nay, keep your chair!—
  A jest! but a jest! . . . Very true,
It is hardly becoming to jest,
  And that Saint upstairs at rest—
Her Soul may be listening, too!
  To think how I doubted and doubted,
Suspected, grumbled at, flouted

That golden-hair'd Angel, and solely
  Because she was zealous and holy!—
Night and noon and morn
  She devoted herself to piety—
Not that she seemed to scorn,
  Or shun, her husband's society;
But the claims of her Soul superseded
  All that I asked for or needed,
And her thoughts were far away
  From the level of lustful clay,
And she trembled lest earthly matters
  Interfered with her *aves* and *paters*!
Sweet dove! she so fluttered, in flying
  To avoid the black vapours of Hell,
So bent on self-sanctifying,—
  That she never thought of trying
To save her poor husband as well!
  And while she was named and elected
For place on the heavenly roll,
  I (beast that I was) suspected
Her manner of saving her Soul—
  So half for the fun of the thing,
What did I (blasphemer!) but fling
  On my shoulders the gown of a monk,
(Whom I managed for.that very day
  To get safely out of the way),
And seat me, half-sober, half-drunk,
  With the cowl drawn over my face,
In the Father Confessor's place . . .
  Eheu! benedicite!
In her beautiful sweet simplicity,
  With that pensive gray expression,
She sighfully knelt at confession,—
  While I bit my lips till they bled,
And dug my nails in my palm,
  And heard, with averted head,
The horrible words come calm—
  Each word was a serpent's sting;
But, wrapt in my gloomy gown,
  I sat like a marble thing
As she uttered *your* name. SIT DOWN!

IV.

More wine, Fra Giacomo?
  One cup—as you love me! No?
Come, drink! 'twill bring the streaks
  Of crimson back to your cheeks.
Come! drink again to the Saint,
  Whose virtues you loved to paint,
Who, stretched on her wifely bed,
  With the soft, sweet, gray expression
You saw and admired at confession—
  Lies *poisoned*, overhead!

V.

Sit still—or, by God, you die!
Face to face, soul to soul, you and I
Have settled accounts, in a fine
Pleasant fashion, over our wine—
Stir not, and seek not to fly—
Nay, whether or not, you are mine!
Thank Montepulciano for giving
Your death in such delicate sips—
'Tis not every monk ceases living
With so pleasant a taste on his lips—
But lest Montepulciano unsurely should kiss,
Take this!—and this!—and this!

VI.

... Raise him; and cast him, Pietro,
Into the deep canal below:
You can be secret, lad, I know ...
And hark you, then to the convent go—
Bid every bell of the convent toll,
And the monks say mass, for your mistress's
    soul.

CHARMIAN.

Cleo. Charmian!
Char. Madam?
Cleo. Give me to drink mandragora!
     Antony and Cleopatra.

In the time when water-lilies shake
Their green and gold on river and lake,
When the cuckoo calls in the heart o' the
    heat,
When the Dog-star foams and the shade is
    sweet;
Where cool and fresh the River ran,
I sat by the side of Charmian,
And heard no sound from the world of
    man.

All was so sweet and still that day!
The rustling shade, the rippling stream,
All life, all breath, dissolved away
Into a golden dream;
Warm and sweet the scented shade
Drowsily caught the breeze and stirred,
Faint and low through the green glade
Came hum of bee and song of bird.
Our hearts were full of drowsy bliss,
And yet we did not clasp nor kiss,
Nor did we break the happy spell
With tender tone or syllable.

But to ease our hearts and set thought free,
We pluckt the flowers of a red rose-tree,
And leaf by leaf, we threw them, Sweet,
Into the River at our feet,
And in an indolent delight
Watch'd them glide onward, out of sight.

Sweet, had I spoken boldly then,
How might my love have garner'd thee!
But I had left the paths of men,
And sitting yonder, dreamily,
Was happiness enough for me!
Seeking no gift of word or kiss,
But looking in thy face, was bliss!
Plucking the rose-leaves in a dream,
Watching them glimmer down the stream,
Knowing that eastern heart of thine
Shared the dim ecstasy of mine!

Then, while we linger'd, cold and gray
Came Twilight, chilling soul and sense;
And you arose to go away,
Full of a sweet indifference!
I missed the spell—I watch'd it break,—
And such come never twice to man:
In a less golden hour I spake,
And did *not* win thee, Charmian!

For wearily we turned away
Into the world of everyday,
And from thy heart the fancy fled
Like the rose-leaves on the River shed;
But to me that hour is sweeter far
Than the world and all its treasures are:
Still to sit on so close to thee,
Were happiness enough for me!
Still to sit on in a green nook,
Nor break the spell by word or look!
To reach out happy hands for ever,
To pluck the rose-leaves, Charmian!
To watch them fade on the gleaming River,
And hear no sound from the world of man!

CLOUDLAND.

Under green branches I lie,
Pensive, I know not why;
All is dead calm down here;
But yonder, tho' heaven smiles clear,
Bright winds blow, and silent and slow
The vaporous Clouds sail by.

For the branches, that here and there
Grow yellow in autumn air,
Are parted ; and through the rent
Of a flower-enwoven tent,
The round blue eye of the peaceful sky
Shows tearless, quiet, and fair.

Face upward, calmly I rest
As the leaf that lies dead on my breast ;
And the only sound I hear
Is a rivulet tinkling near,
And falling asleep in the woodland deep
Like a fluttering bird in a nest.

My mood would be full of grace
As an eremite's peaceful face,
And I should slumber away
The delicate dreamful day,
Save for Shapes that swim thro' the silence dim
Of the blue ethereal space !

I close my eyes in vain,
In a pensive, poetic pain :
Even then, to the gurgling glee
Of the Brook I cannot see,
Silent and slow they glide and they go
O'er the bright still blank of the brain !

With a motion wind-bequeath'd,
Fantastically wreathed,
They disturb my Soul,—as the beat
Of the pale Moon's silvern feet
Broke the sleep forlorn of the Sea new-born,
Till it audibly stirr'd and breathed.

White as a flock of sheep,
Slender and soft and deep,
With a radiance mild and faint
As the smile of a pictured Saint,
Or the light that flies from a mother's eyes
On the face of a babe asleep !

Yonder with dripping hair,
Is Aphrodite the fair,
Fresh from the foam, whose dress
Enfleeces her loveliness,
But melts like mist from the limbs sun-kiss'd
That are kindling unaware !

One, like a Titan cold,
With banner about him roll'd,
Bereft of sense, and hurl'd
To the wondrous under-world,
And drifting down, with a weedy crown,
Some miraculous River old.

One like a bank of snows,
Which flushes to crimson, and glows ;
One like a goddess tall
In a violet robe ;—and all
Have a motion that seems like the motion of dreams,—
A dimly disturb'd repose ;—

A motion such as you see
In the pictured divinity
By the touch of an artist thrown
On a Naiad sculptured in stone,
For ever and ever about to quiver
To a frighten'd flush, and flee !

Beautiful, stately, slow,
The pageants changefully grow ;
And in my bewilder'd brain
Comes the distinct refrain
Of the stately speech and the mighty reach
Of Songs made long ago.

Into my heart there throng
Rich melodies worshipp'd long :
The epic of Troy divine,
Milton's majestical line,
The palfrey pace and the glittering grace
Of Spenser's magical song.

Do whatever I may,
I cannot shake them away ;
They are haunting voices that move
Like the wondrous shapes above ;
Stately and slow they come and they go,
Like measured words when we pray.

When the troublous motion sublime
Of the Clouds and the answering rhyme,
Ceasing, leave now and again
A pause in the hush'd heart, *then*
The brook bursts in with a pastoral din,
A gurgling lyrical chime !

Oh ! sweet, very sweet, to lie
Pensive, I know not why,
And to fashion magical swarms
Of poet-created Forms
In the pageants dumb that go and come
Above in a windless sky !

For yonder, a dark Ship furls
Sails by an Island of pearls,
And crafty Ulysses steers
Through the white-tooth'd waves, and hears
The liquid song of the syren throng,
That beckon through golden curls.

Tis faded away, and lo!
The Grecian tents, like snow,
And a brazen Troy afar,
Whence Helen glitters a star;
And the tents reveal the glimmering steel
Of the gathering Greeks below!

In fierce, precipitate haste
From a golden gate are chased
A shadowy Adam and Eve;
And within the Gate they leave,
Doth a sunbeam stand like the angel's brand,
To illumine the azure waste.

The sunbeam fading, behold
A huge Tree tipp'd with gold,
And a naked Eve beneath,
With the apple raised to her teeth;
While round and round the Snake coils,
    wound
In many a magical fold.

Oppress'd with fanciful fears,
Trembling with unshed tears,
I droop my eyes, until
The notes of the lyrical rill
Are shaken like rain on my eyelids twain,
And another pageant appears.

Far, far away, snow-white,
Full of a silvern light,
Beauteous, and yet so small
They are scarce perceived at all,
See Una guide her Lamb, by the side
Of the mounted Red-Cross Knight.

Then, to meet a far foe, speeds
The Knight over azure meads,
While threatening Dragons, hordes
Of Satyrs, and traitor swords,
Assail the Maid, but tremble afraid
At the milk-white Lamb she leads!

And she wanders undismay'd
Through vistas of sun and shade;
Over a mountain's brow
She shines like a star; and now

She fading is seen in the depths dark-green
Of a mimical forest glade,—

Which, opening flower-like, shows
A Garden of crimson repose,
Of lawns ambrosial,
Streams that flash as they fall,
In the innermost fold an arbour of gold
Like the yellow core of a rose.

On the verge of this fairy land
Doth mailèd Sir Guyon stand,
And bending his bloody plume
'Neath portals of snowy bloom,
He enters the place with a pallid face,
Breathless, and sword in hand.

Oh! is it not sweet, sweet, sweet,
To lie in this green retreat,
In a beautiful dim half-dream
Like a god on a hill; and seem
A part of the fair strange shapes up there,—
With the wood-scents round my feet?

But shadows lengthen around,
And the dew is dim on the ground;
And hush'd, to list to the tune
Of the coming stars and moon,
The brook doth creep thro' the umbrage
    deep
With cooler, quieter sound.

Homeward;—but when the pale
Moon filleth her silver sail,
I shall sit alone with a book
'Neath another heaven, and look
On the spiritual gleam and the cloudy dream
Of Milton's majestical tale;

Or wandering side by side
With Una, through forests wide,
Watch her beauty increase
To heavenly patience and peace,
While the Lamb of light licks her hand
    snow-white,
And watches her face, meek-eyed!

Or, 'mid trumpets murmuring loud,
The waving of banners proud,
And the rattle of horses' hooves,
See the Grecian host—as it moves
Its glittering powers to the Trojan towers,
That dissolve away, as a Cloud!

CUCKOO SONG.

O KITTY BELL, 'twas sweet, I swear,
  To wander in the spring together,
When buds were blowing everywhere,
  And it was golden weather!
And down the lanes beside the farm
  You roam'd beside me, tripping lightly,—
Blushing you hung upon my arm,
  And the small gloved hand press'd tightly! . . .
And the orchis sprang
  In the scented meadow,
And the throstle sang
  In the greenwood shadow;
And your eyes were bright
  With happy dew,—
Could I doubt a light
  So divinely blue,
When you kiss'd and sighed
'I will be true'? . . .
    Cuckoo!
Though far and wide
  The brown bird cried—
      '*Cuckoo! cuckoo! cuckoo!*'

O Kitty Bell, the cry seem'd sweet,
  For you were kind, and flowers were springing;
The dusty willow in the heat
  Its woolly bells were swinging,
And in its boll the linnet brown
  Finish'd her nest with wool and feather,
And *we* had thoughts of nestling down,
  In the farm by the mill, together. . . .
And over the hill
  The breeze was blowing,
And the arms of the mill
  Kept coming and going;
And who but Love
  Was between us two,
When around and above
  The flittermice flew,
And as night drew nigh,
You swore to be true? . . .
    Cuckoo!
I heard the cry
From woods hard by—
      '*Cuckoo! cuckoo! cuckoo!*'

O Kitty Bell, 'tis spring again,
  But all the face of things looks iller;
The nests are built in wood and lane,
  But *you* are nested with the miller.
And other lovers kiss and swear,
  While I behold in scorn and pity,
For 'all,' I cry, 'is false and fair,'
  And curse the cuckoo and Kitty. . . .
And over the hill
  The breeze is blowing,
And the arms of the mill
  Keep coming and going;
And the hidden bird
  Is singing anew
The warning I heard
  When I trusted you;
And I sicken and sigh,
  With my heart thrill'd through . . .
    Cuckoo!
Wherever I fly
I hear the cry—
      '*Cuckoo! cuckoo! cuckoo!*'

THE WHITE DEER.

THE hunter leaps from slumber,
  And quits his cottage door;
Days and nights without number,
  Forth he has fared before.

Still the old quest is sorest,
  The hunter's heart is cold;
He seeks the deer of the forest
  With mystical horns of gold.

Dim as a dream it glimmers
  Through the dark forest glades,
Passes with starlight tremors,
  Trances the sight and fades.

By the dim quiet fountain
  Lies the print of its form;
Up mid the cloud of the mountain
  Cries its voice in the storm!

Not a bullet or arrow
  Hath reached its bosom yet,
And though the ways are narrow,
  It steps through noose and net.

The hunter's cheek is sickly,
  Time hath silvered his hair,
His weary breath comes quickly,
  He trembleth in despair.

Many a one before him
　Hath been a hunter here,
Then, with the sad sky o'er him,
　Died in quest of the deer.

See, the day is dying!
　See, the hunter is spent!
Under the dark trees lying;
　Perishing ill content.

Ev'n as his sad eyes darken,
　Stirs the boughs of the glade,
He gathers his strength to hearken,
　Peering into the shade.

And lo, with a soft light streaming,
　Stainless and dimly bright,
Stands with its great eyes gleaming
　The mystical deer, snow-white!

Closer it comes up creeping,
　With burning beautiful eyes—
Then, as he falls back sleeping,
　Touches his lips and flies!

II.

The live foot ever fleeing,
　It comes to the dying and dead—
Oh, hope in the darkness of being!
　Methinks I hear thy tread.

Around, above me, and under,
　God's forest is closing dim;
I chase the mystical wonder,
　Footsore and weary of limb.

Down in the dim recesses,
　Up on the heights untrod,
Eluding our dreams and guesses,
　Slips the secret of God.

Only seen by the dying,
　In the last spectral pain;
Just as the breath is flying—
　Flashing and fading again.

White mystery, might I view thee!
　Bright wonder, might we meet!
Ever as I pursue thee,
　I see the print of thy feet.

Ever those feet are roaming,
　Ever we follow in quest;
While thou hauntest the gloaming
　Never a soul shall rest.

CONVENT-ROBBING.

(OLD STYLE.)

MAY MARGARET felt a cold cloud come down on her—
They made her a nun and put a black gown on her;
　Young Roland went white
　Thro' the winter moonlight,
Looming tall in the breath of the frost every night,
And gazed at the Convent, and plann'd how to win her there,
And his cheek gather'd dew till the dawn, and grew thinner there.

'A ruse, ho, a ruse!' cried his brother, Clerk John, to him,—
When in vain both the monks and the leeches had gone to him,—
　'Cease to fume and to frown,
　Close thine eyes, lie thee down,
Stretch thee straight on a bier in thy chilly death-gown;
The great bell shall ring, and thy house gather gloom in it,
While I'll to the Convent, and beg thee a tomb in it!'

The Convent bell tolls, hung with black are the porches there,
Come tall black pall-bearers and pages with torches there,
　Then the bier,—and thereon
　The pale youth dead and gone!
And behind, grim as Death, weeping sore, goes Clerk John!
And the chapel is dark, as the bearers pace slow in it,
And all the black nuns stands with lights in a row in it.

Ah! chill is the chapel, the great bell chimes weary there,
Black bearers, black nuns, and black pages look dreary there;
　The youth lies in death,
　Not a syllable saith;
But the tiny frost-cloud on his lips is his breath!—

And the shroud round his limbs hath bright
   armour of steel in it
And his hand, gloved in mail, grips the
   sword it can feel in it!

Ho, she screameth,—May Margaret! kneels
   by the side of him!—
'White Mary above, be the guardian and
   guide of him!
     They plighted us twain,
     Yet we parted in pain,
And ah! that so soon I should clasp him
   again!'
Wan, wan, is her cheek, with dim torch-
   light the while on it—
Does she dream?.. Has the face changed?
   .. and is there a smile on it?

She holds his cold hand to her heart, and
   doth call on him,
Drop by drop, warm and scented, her tender
   tears fall on him;
     The nuns, sable-gown'd,
     Chanting low, stand around;
Clerk John bites his lips, with his eyes on
   the ground..
'Dear heart, that we meet but in woe such
   as this again!'
Then she kisses his lips!—Does she dream?
   .. Did he kiss again?

Who opens the door with a terrible shout
   at once?—
A great wind sweeps in, and the lights are
   blown out at once!
     The Abbess screams low,
     Moan the nuns in a row,
Thro' the porch sweeps the wind and the
   sleet and the snow,
But the moon thro' the quaint-colour'd win-
   dows is beaming now,—
And wonderful shapes round the bier gather
   gleaming now!—

The sable pall-bearers and pages are new-
   arrayed,
In armour that glitters like golden dew
   arrayed!
     How chill the moon glows!
     How it blows! how it snows!
Yet May Margaret's cheek is as red as a
   rose!

And 'a miracle,'
   holy now,
For shiningly vest[
   now!

He draweth May M
   cheek to him,
She kisses him softl
   to him;
     The nuns sa
     Shiver disma
As he lifteth the g
   ground,
And turneth it de
   her,—
And a mantle of er
   cover her!

On the floor of th
   sound hollow r
Clerk John and th
   now ...
     Hark! is it f
     Of horses' fo
Or the wild wind w
   sleet?
Down the aisles of t
   die away,
While fast in the sn
   hie away!

'Saints,' crieth th
   your dole on u
To take our sweet
   on us!'
     And the nur
     Murmur slyl
'Ah! would he m
And they look at tl
   sin on them,
And the moon blus
   ing in on them

Ay, fast in the snov
   now!
Young Roland's wa
   covers now!
     To the bowe
     For the brid:
And the jolly old pr
'May all who love
   'win such kiss
Die such death,—a
   such as this is,

THE BALLAD OF THE WAYFARER.
(OLD STYLE.)

O'ER the cheerless common,
  Where the bleak winds blow,
Wanders the wan Woman ;
  Waysore and weary,
Through the dark and dreary
  Drift-bed of the Snow.
On her pale pinch'd features snowing 'tis and sleeting,
By her side her little Son runs with warm heart beating,
Clinging to her wet robe, while she wails repeating :
' Further, my child, further—further let us go ! '

Fleet the Boy doth follow,
  Wondering at her woe ;
On, with footfall hollow,
  O'er the pathway jagged
  Crawls she wet and ragged, .
    Restless and slow.
' Mother ! ' now he murmurs, mid the tempest's crying,
' Mother, rest a little—I am faint with flying—
Mother, rest a little ! ' Still she answers sighing,
' Further, child, and faster—further let us go !

  But now she is sitting
    On a stone, and lo !
  Dark her brows are knitting,
    While the Child, close clinging
    To her raiment wringing,
      Shivers at the snow.
' Tell me of my *father !* for I never knew him
Is he dead or living, are we flying to him ? '
' Peace, my child ! ' she answers, and the voice thrills through him ;
' When we wander further—further !—thou shalt know.'

  (Wild wind of December,
    Blow, wind, blow !—)
  ' Oh, but I remember !
    In my mind I gather
    Pictures of my father,
      And a gallant show.

Tell me, mother, tell me—did we always wander?
Was the world once brighter? In some town out yonder
Dwelt we not contented ? ' Sad she seems to ponder,
Sighing ' I will tell thee—when we further go.'

  'Oh, but Mother, listen !
    We were rich, I know !
  (How his bright eyes glisten !)
    We were merry people,
    In a town with a steeple,
      Long, long ago ;
In a gay room dwelling, where your face shone brightly,
And a brave man brought us food and presents nightly.
Tell me, 'twas my father ? ' Now her face looms whitely,
While she shivers moaning, ' Peace, let us go ! '

  How the clouds gather !
    How the winds blow !
  ' *Who* was my father?
    Was he Prince or Lord there,
    With a train and a sword there ?
      Mother, I *will* know !—
I have dreamt so often of those gallant places ;
There were banners waving—I could see the faces—
Take me to my father ! ' cries he with embraces,
While she shivers moaning, ' No, child, no ! '

  While the child is speaking,
    Forth the moon steals slow,
  From the black cloud breaking,
    Shining white and eerie
    On the wayside weary,
      Shrouded white in snow.
On the heath behind them, 'gainst the dim sky lying,
Looms the Gallows blackly, in the wild wind sighing.
To her feet the woman springs ! with fierce shriek crying—
' See ! Oh, God in heaven ! . . . Woe, child, woe ! '

(Blow, wind of December,
      Blow, wind, blow!—)
'*Thou* canst not remember—
Thou wert but a blossom
   Suckled on my bosom,
      Years, years ago!
Thy father stole to feed us; our starving
      faces stung him;
In yonder town behind us, they seized him
      and they hung him!
They murdered him on Gallows-Tree, and
      to the ravens flung him!
Faster, my child, faster—faster let us go!'

IN SPRING-TIME.

SWEET, sing a song of the May to me,
   Sweeten the lingering hours!
Soft comes her whisper each day to me,
See, thro' the green and the gray, to me;
   'Thrills the faint flame of the flowers.
For the spell of the winter is ended,
   The rainbow is seen thro' the showers,
And the May, by fair spirits attended,
   Shall smile up the skies, and be ours. . .
Afar away yonder her foot cometh slow to
      us—
She steals up the south, with her cheeks all
      aglow, to us!
The blue waters tremble! the rain singeth
      low to us!
Green stir the blossoming bowers!

THE FISHERMAN.

THE sea is moaning, the little one cries,
In child-bed sorrow the Mother lies,
And the Fisher fisheth afar away
In the morning gray.

The drift is dark as the dawn appears:
Is it the moan of the wind he hears—
Is it the splash of the ocean foam,
Or a cry from home?

He fisheth there that the babe may eat—
The wind is whistling in shroud and sheet;
He looketh down from the side of his bark
On the waters dark.

Sees he the gleam of the foam-flake there,
Or a white, white face in its floating hair?—
Sea-weeds salt that are shoreward drifted,
Or arms uplifted?

His heart is heavy, his lips are set,
He sighs as he draggeth in his net—
A goodly gift from the waters wild
To Mother and Child!

The Dawn gleams cold as he homeward flies
The boat is laden, the new-born cries,
But the wraith of the mother fades far away
In the morning gray!

THE CHURCHYARD.

(A GENRE PICTURE.)

How slowly creeps the hand of Time
   On the old clock's green-mantled face!
Yea, slowly as those ivies climb,
   The hours roll round with patient pace;
The drowsy rooks caw on the tower,
   The tame doves hover round and round;
Below, the slow grass hour by hour
   Makes green God's sleeping ground.

All moves, but nothing here is swift;
   The grass grows deep, the green boughs
      shoot;
From east to west the shadows drift;
   The earth feels heavenward underfoot;
The slow stream through the bridge doth
      stray
   With water-lilies on its marge,
And slowly, piled with scented hay,
   Creeps by the silent barge.

All stirs, but nothing here is loud:
   The cushat broods, the cuckoo cries;
Faint, far up, under a white cloud,
   The lark trills soft to earth and skies;
And underneath the green graves rest;
   And through the place, with slow footfalls,
With snowy cambric on his breast,
   The old gray Vicar crawls.

And close at hand, to see him come,
   Clustering at the playground gate,
The urchins of the schoolhouse, dumb
   And bashful, hang the head and wait;
The little maidens curtsey deep,
   The boys their forelocks touch meanwhile,
The Vicar sees them, half asleep,
   And smiles a sleepy smile.

Slow as the hand on the clock's face,
  Slow as the white cloud in the sky,
He cometh now with tottering pace
  To the old vicarage hard by ;
Smothered it stands in ivy leaves,
  Laurels and yews make dark the ground ;
The swifts that built beneath the eaves
  Wheel in still circles round.

And from the portal, green and dark,
  He glances at the church-clock old—
Gray soul ! why seek *his* eyes to mark
  The creeping of that finger cold?
He cannot see, but still as stone
  He pauses, listening for the chime,
And hears from that green tower intone
  The eternal voice of Time.

SEA-WASH.

WHEREFORE so cold, O Day,
  That gleamest far away
O'er the dim line where mingle heaven and ocean,
  While fishing-boats lie netted in the gray,
And still smooth waves break in their shoreward motion—
  Wherefore so cold, so cold?
O say, dost thou behold
A Face o'er which the rock-weed droopeth sobbing,
A Face just stirred within a sea-cave old
By the green water's throbbing ?

Wherefore, O Fisherman,
  So full of care and wan,
This weary, weary morning shoreward flying
  While stooping downward, darkly thou dost scan
That which below thee in thy boat is lying?
  Wherefore so full of care !
What dost thou shoreward bear
Caught in thy net's moist meshes, as a token?
Ah ! can it be the ring of golden hair
Whereby my heart is broken?

Wherefore so still, O Sea ?
  That washest wearilie
Under the lamp lit in the fisher's dwelling,
  Holding the secret of thy deeps from me,
Whose heart would break so sharply at the telling?

Wherefore so still, so still?
  Say, in thy sea-cave chill
Floats she forlorn with foam-bells round her breaking,
  While the wet Fisher lands and climbs the hill
To hungry babes awaking?

EARTH AND THE SOUL.

'CHILD of my bosom, babe of my bearing ;
  Why dost thou turn from me now thou art old?
Why, like a wild bird for passage preparing,
  Shrink from my touch with a tremor of cold ?'
'Mother, I dread thee ! mother, I fear thee !
  Darkness and silence are hid in thy core ;
Deep is thy voice, and I tremble to hear thee ;
  Let me begone, for thou lov'st me no more !'

'Love thee not, dearest one, son of my splendour,
  Love thee not ? How shall I smile thee a sign ?
See my soft arms, they are kindly and tender !
  See my fond face, flushing upward to thine !'
'Mother, thy face looketh dreadful and ghastly !
  Mother, thy breath is as frost on my hair !
Hold me not, stay me not, time speedeth fastly,
  Look, a kind Hand beckons softly up there !'

'Child, yet a while ere thy cruel feet fare on !
  See, in my lap lie the flowers of the May ;
See, in my hair twine the roses of Sharon ;
  See, on my breast gleam the gems of Cathay !'
'Mother, I know thou art queenly and splendid,
  Yet is there death in the blush of thy bloom ;
Touch me not, mother—my childhood is ended,
  Dark is thy shadow and dreadful thy doom.'

'Child, 'twas I bare thee! child, 'twas I fashioned
Those gleaming limbs, and those ringlets of light,
Made thee a spirit sublime and impassioned,
Read thee the Book of the stars night by night,
Led thy frail feet when they failed sorrow-laden,
Whispered thee wonders of death and of birth,
Made thee the heir of the garden of Aiden,
Child, it was I, thy poor mother, the Earth!'

'Mother, I know it! and oh, how I loved thee,
When on thy bosom I leapt as a child,
Shared each still pleasure that filled thee and moved thee,
Thrilled to the bliss of thy face when it smiled.
Yea, but I knew not thy glory was fleeing,
Not till that night thou didst read me the scroll,
Sobbed in my ear the dark secret of Being;
Mother, I wept—thy fair creature, the Soul!'

'Child, wherefore weep? Since the secret is spoken,
Lie in mine arms—I will rock thee to rest;
Ne'er shall thy slumber be troubled and broken,
Low will I sing to thee, held to my breast.
Oh, it is weary to wander and wander;
Child of my fashioning, stay with me here.'
'Mother, I cannot; 'tis brighter up yonder;
Dark is thy brow with the shadow I fear!'

'Child, yet one kiss! yet one kiss, ere thou flyest!'
'Nay, for thy lips have the poison of death!'
'Child, one embrace!' 'Nay, all vainly thou criest;
I see thy face darken, I shrink at thy breath.'
'Go, I have wept for thee, toiled for thee, borne with thee,
Pardoned thee freely each taint and each stain.

Take the last love of my bosom forlorn with thee—
Seek the great Void for a kinder in vain!'

'Mother, I go; but if e'er I discover
That which I seek in those regions untrod,
I will come back to thee; softly bend over
Thy pillow, and whisper the secret of God.'
'Child, thou wilt find me asleep in black raiment,
Dead by the side of the infinite Sea;
Drop one immortelle above me for payment
Of all the wild love I have wasted on thee!'

A CURL.*

(A BOY'S POEM.)

SEE! what a treasure rare
  I hold with fingers aglow!
  —'Tis full of the bright
  Subdued sunlight
Which shone in the scented hair
  Of a maiden I once held fair;
  And I puzzle my brains to know
If the heart of the beautiful girl
Hath kept the light of the Long Ago,
As long as the yellow curl?

What matter? Why, little or none!
  She is nought to me now, understand;
  But I feel less sad
  Than tearfully glad,
And a passionate thrill hath run
Through my veins, like a flash of the sun,—
  That with so unheeding a hand
I can grasp a small part of the gold
Which dazzled my wits, when I planned and planned
For the love of that maiden, of old.

See! I crush it with finger and thumb,
  Half in cruelty, half in jest.—
  As she lies asleep,
  Doth a shudder creep
Thro' her heart, and render it numb?
Doth a sorrowful whisper come

---

* As these verses bear a certain superficial resemblance, *in subject*, to Mr. Tennyson's Poem, 'A Ringlet,' it may be as well to state that they appeared in print several years before the publication of 'Enoch Arden, and other Poems.'

From afar, while her lord is at rest
By her side, and none else are by?
Doth she shiver away from her husband's
    breast,
And hide her face, and cry?

Is her heart quite withered and sere?
Are the pledges forgotten yet,
    That, with blushing face,
    In a secret place,
She breathed in my burning ear,
In the morning of the year,
When, after long parting, we met
By the Sea, on the shadowy lawn,
And spake till the sunset faded to jet,
And moon and stars made a dawn?

As she lies in her wifely place,
  The wings of her white soul furled,
    Does the cheek at rest
    On her husband's breast
Grow scorch'd with the hot disgrace
Of the kisses I rain'd on her face,
When the mists of the night upcurled
From the ocean that night of June,
And make a glamour, wherein the world
Seemed close to the stars and moon?

By this ringlet of yellow hair,
  Still full of the light forlorn
    Of that parting spot!
    Hath she quite forgot
The passionate love she bare,
And the hope she promised to share,
When the ringlet of gold was shorn,
And the flowers felt the sun on the soil,
And the firefly stars went out in the morn,
And I hurried back to my toil?

I could crush it under my heel!
  Hath she forgotten the clear
    Vision of fame
    That died, when her shame
Made my wild brain totter and reel?
Hath she a heart to feel?—
False to her vows in a year!
False and hollow as Hell!
False to the voice that warned in her ear!
And false to her God as well!

This curl that she gave to me
Fell over her brow of snow,
    So 'twas near the bright
    Spiritual light

That burned in the brain—and see!
I am kissing it tenderly!
  She is asking for mercy, I know;
So I kiss it again and again,
  For I know some charm makes the wild
    kiss glow
Like fire thro' the woman's brain!

She cannot choose but atone!
  By the brow where this curl once gleam'd!
    She must in sin thought,
    Against him who bought
The heart already mine own,
And left me weeping alone.
'Tis a charm, and my loss is redeemed!
And the sin 'gainst her lord will be—
  To remember how close to the stars we
    seemed
That night in the mists by the Sea!

She will look on her husband's face,
  She will kiss him on the cheek—
    She will kiss, she will smile;
    And all the while,
In thought no other may trace,
She'll be back in that perfumed place,
  Hearing the words that I speak,
Vowing the vow I believe,
While the sunset dies with a purple streak,
'Neath the whitening star of eve.

And the voice of the waves will bar
  All sweeter sounds from her ears,
    She'll be under the moon
    Of that night of June,
And the motion of moon and star
Will trouble her from afar;
  And then, when the silver spheres
Fade fitfully out of the skies,
  And the red dawn breaks, she will wake
    in tears,
And shrink from her husband's eyes!.

And in time, when again and again
  I have kissed the magical gold,
    Those same gross eyes
    Will be open and wise,
And his heart will be feverish pain,
And a doubt will arise in his brain;
  And ere she is grown very old,—
He will know she is frail as foam,—
  He will see the light of that night in her
    cold
Face,—and my curse strikes home!

For perchance in her yearning she may
  Be bewildered and brought to blame,
    By a new delight
    So like that night
With its mimical glamour of day,
That she cannot shake it away ;
  And following it once more,
She will take a path of shame,
  While the man blushes red at his darken'd
    door
As the children utter her name.

See ! my passionate lips are warm
  On the curl, in a cruel bliss—
    In day or mirk
    The charm would work !—
While she dreams of that night till her form
Is caught in the eddies of storm !
There's a devil impels me to kiss,
And my blood boils to and fro ;
  She asks for mercy ! shall mercy like this
Be given my darling ? . . . No !

With the world, as it ebbs and flows,
  My heart is in jarring tune ;
    Let the memory
    Of her beauty be
Furled in a soft repose
Round my heart, like the leaves of a rose.
The faith, which has faded too soon,
I bury with this last cry ;
  For the curl, still bright with that night
    of June,
Lo ! I tenderly put it by !

LOVE AND TIME.

This is the place, as husht and dead
  As when I saw it long ago ;
Down the dark walk with shadows spread
  I wander slow.

The tangled sunlight, cold and clear,
  Steals frost-white through the boughs
    around.
There is no warmth of summer here,
  No summer sound.

Darnel and nettle, as I pass,
  Choke the dim ways, and in the bowers
Gather the weeds and the wild grass
  Instead of flowers.

O life ! O time ! O days that die !
  O days that live within the mind !
Here did we wander, she and I,
  Together twined.

We passed out of the great broad walk,
  Beyond the emerald lawns we strayed,
We lingered slow in tender talk
  Along the shade.

And then the great old maze we found,
  And smiling entered it unseen,
Half sad, half glad, went round and round
  Thro' windings green.

In the bright centre of the maze
  A rose-bush grew, a dial gleam'd ;
She pluck'd a rose . . . with blissful gaze
  Watch'd it, and dreamed.

O life ! O time ! O days divine !
  O dreams that keep the soul astir !
That hour eternity was mine,
  Looking at her !

This is the place. I wander slow.
  Dark are the shades of shrub and tree,
The dial stands, the leaves lie low,
  But where is she ?

O life ! O time ! O birds and flowers !
  O withering leaves upon the bough !
Alas, she measures not her hours
  With roses now.

The dial stands—the dark days roll—
  From year to year the roses spring—
Eternity is in my soul,
  Remembering.

The dial stands—the summer goes—
  All changeth, nothing dieth, here !
And all reneweth like a rose,
  From year to year.

Undertones.
(1864.)

POET'S PROLOGUE.
TO DAVID IN HEAVEN.

'Quo diversus abis?'
'Quem Di diligunt, adolescens moritur.'

I.

Lo! the slow moon roaming
Thro' fleecy mists of gloaming,
Furrowing with pearly edge the jewel powder'd sky!
Lo, the bridge moss-l den,
Arch'd like foot of maiden,
And on the bridge, in silence, looking upward, you and I!
Lo, the pleasant season
Of reaping and of mowing—
The round still moon above,—beneath, the river duskily flowing!

II.

Violet colour'd shadows,
Blown from scented meadows,
Float o'er us to the pine-wood dark from yonder dim corn-ridge;
The little river gushes
Thro' shady sedge and rushes,
And gray gnats murmur o'er the pools, beneath the mossy bridge;—
And you and I stand darkly,
O'er the keystone leaning,
And watch the pale mesmeric moon, in the time of gleaners and gleaning.

III.

Do I dream, I wonder?
As, sitting sadly under
A lonely roof in London, thro' the grim square pane I gaze?
Here of you I ponder,
In a dream, and yonder
The still streets seem to stir and breathe beneath the white moon's rays.
By the vision cherish'd,
By the battle braved,
Do I but dream a hopeless dream, in the city that slew you, David?

IV.

Is it fancy also,
That the light which falls so
Faintly upon the stony street below me as I write,
Near tall mountains passes
Thro' churchyard weeds and grasses
Barely a mower's mile away from that small bridge, to-night?
And, where you are lying,—
Grass and flowers above you—
Is mingled with your sleeping face, as calm as the hearts that love you?

V.

Poet gentle-hearted,
Are you then departed,
And have you ceased to dream the dream we loved of old so well?
Has the deeply cherish'd
Aspiration perish'd,
And are you happy, David, in that heaven where you dwell?
Have you found the secret
We, so wildly, sought for,
And is your soul enswath'd, at last, in the singing robes you fought for?

VI.

In some heaven star-lighted,
Are you now united
Unto the poet-spirits that you loved, of English race?
Is Chatterton still dreaming?
And, to give it stately seeming,
Has the music of his last strong song passed into Keats's face?
Is Wordsworth there? and Spenser?
Beyond the grave's black portals,
Can the grand eye of Milton *see* the glory he sang to mortals?

VII.

You at least could teach me,
Could your dear voice reach me

Where I sit and copy out for men my soul's
  strange speech,
Whether it be bootless,
  Profitless, and fruitless,—
The weary aching upward strife to heights
  we cannot reach,
The fame we seek in sorrow,
The agony we forego not,
The haunting singing sense that makes us
  climb—whither we know not.

VIII.

Must it last for ever,
  The passionate endeavour,
Ay, have ye, there in heaven, hearts to throb
  and still aspire?
In the life you know now,
Render'd white as snow now,
Do fresher glory-heights arise, and beckon
  higher—higher?
Are you dreaming, dreaming,
Is your soul still roaming,
Still gazing upward as we gazed, of old in
  the autumn gloaming?

IX.

Lo, the book I hold here,
In the city cold here!
I hold it with a gentle hand and love it as I
  may;
Lo, the weary moments!
Lo, the icy comments!
And lo, false Fortune's knife of gold swift-
  lifted up to slay I.
Has the strife no ending?
Has the song no meaning?
Linger I, idle as of old, while men are reap-
  ing or gleaning?

X.

Upward my face I turn to you,
I long for you, I yearn to you,
The spectral vision trances me to utt'rance
  wild and weak;
It is not that I mourn you,
To mourn you were to scorn you,
For you are one step nearer to the beauty
  singers seek.
But I want, and cannot see you,
I seek and cannot find you,
And, see! I touch the book of songs you
  tenderly left behind you!

XI.

Ay, me! I bend above it,
With tearful eyes, and love it,
With tender hand I touch the leaves, but
  cannot find you there!
Mine eyes are haunted only
By that gloaming sweetly lonely,
The shadows on the mossy bridge, the
  glamour in the air!
I touch the leaves, and only
See the glory they retain not—
The moon that is a lamp to Hope, who
  glorifies what we gain not!

XII.

The aching and the yearning,
The hollow, undiscerning,
Uplooking want I still retain, darken the
  leaves I touch—
Pale promise, with much sweetness
Solemnizing incompleteness,
But ah, you knew so little then—and now
  you know so much!
By the vision cherish'd,
By the battle bravéd,
Have you, in heaven, shamed the song, by
  a loftier music, David?

XIII.

I, who loved and knew you,
In the city that slew you,
Still hunger on, and thirst, and climb, proud-
  hearted and alone:
Serpent-fears enfold me,
Syren-visions hold me,
And, like a wave, I gather strength, and
  gathering strength, I moan;
Yea, the pale moon beckons,
Still I follow, aching,
And gather strength, only to make a louder
  moan, in breaking!

XIV.

Tho' the world could turn from you,
This, at least, I learn from you:
Beauty and Truth, tho' never found, are
  worthy to be sought,
The singer, upward-springing,
Is grander than his singing,
And tranquil self-sufficing joy illumes the
  dark of thought.

This, at least, you teach me,
In a revelation :
That gods still snatch, as worthy death, the
soul in its aspiration.

XV.

And I think, as you thought,
Poesy and Truth ought
Never to lie silent in the singer's heart on
earth ;
Tho' they be discarded,
Slighted, unrewarded,—
Tho', unto vulgar seeming, they appear of
little worth,—
Yet tender brother-singers,
Young or not yet born to us,
May seek there, for the singer's sake, that
love which sweeteneth scorn to us!

XVI.

While I sit in silence,
Comes from mile on mile hence,
From English Keats's Roman grave, a voice
that sweetens toil !
Think you, no fond creatures
Draw comfort from the features
Of Chatterton, pale Phaethon, hurled down
to sunless soil ?
Scorch'd with sunlight lying,
Eyes of sunlight hollow,
But, see ! upon the lips a gleam of the
chrism of Apollo !

XVII.

Noble thought produces
Noble ends and uses,
Noble hopes are part of Hope wherever she
may be,
Noble thought enhances
Life and all its chances,
And noble self is noble song,—all this I
learn from thee !
And I learn, moreover,
'Mid the city's strife too,
That such faint song as sweetens Death can
sweeten the singer's life too !

XVIII.

Lo, my Book !—I hold it
In weary hands, and fold it
Unto my heart, if only as a token I aspire ;

And, by song's assistance,
Unto your dim distance,
My soul uplifted is on wings, and beckon'd
higher, nigher.
By the sweeter wisdom
You return unspeaking,
Though endless, hopeless, be the search, we
exalt our souls in seeking.

XIX.

Higher, yet, and higher,
Ever nigher, ever nigher,
To the glory we conceive not, let us toil
and strive and strain !—
The agonizëd yearning,
The imploring and the burning,
Grown awfuller, intenser, at each vista we
attain,
And clearer, brighter, growing,
Up the gulfs of heaven wander,
Higher, higher yet, and higher, to the
Mystery we ponder !

XX.

Yea, higher yet, and higher,
Ever nigher, ever nigher,
While men grow small by stooping and the
reaper piles the grain,—
Can it then be bootless,
Profitless and fruitless,
The weary aching upward search for what
we never gain ?
Is there not awaiting
Rest and golden weather,
Where, passionately purified, the singers
may meet together ?

XXI.

Up ! higher yet, and higher,
Ever nigher, ever nigher,
'Thro' voids that Milton and the rest beat
still with seraph-wings ;
Out thro' the great gate creeping
Where God hath put his sleeping—
A dewy cloud detaining not the soul that
soars and sings,
Up ! higher yet, and higher,
Fainting nor retreating,
Beyond the sun, beyond the stars, to the far
bright realm of meeting !

XXII.

O Mystery! O Passion!
  To sit on earth, and fashion,
What floods of music visibled may fill that
  fancied place!
To think, the least that singeth,
  Aspireth and upspringeth,
May weep glad tears on Keats's breast and
  look in Milton's face!
When human power and failure
  Are equalized for ever,
And the one great Light that haloes all is
  the passionate bright endeavour!

XXIII.

But ah, that pale moon roaming
  Thro' fleecy mists of gloaming,
Furrowing with pearly edge the jewel-
  powder'd sky,
And ah, the days departed
  With your friendship gentle-hearted,
And ah, the dream we dreamt that night,
  together, you and I!
Is it fashion'd wisely,
  To help us or to blind us,
That at each height we gain we turn, and
  behold a heaven behind us?

THE UNDERTONES.

Thou Fame! who makest of the singer's Life,
Faint with the sweetness of its own desire,
A statue of Narcissus, still and fair
For evermore, and lending evermore
Over its beauteous image mirrorèd
In the swift current of our human days,
Eternally in act to clasp and kiss!
O Fame, teach thou this flesh and blood to love
Some beauteous counterpart, and while it bends,
Tremulously gazing on the image, blow
Thy trump aloud, and freeze it into stone!

I.
PROTEUS:
OR, A PRELUDE.

1.

INTO the living elements of things
  I, Proteus, mingle, seeking strange dis-
  guise:
I track the Sun-god on an eagle's wings,
  Or look at horror thro' a murderer's eyes,
In shape of hornèd beast my shadow glides
  Among broad-leavèd flowers that blow 'neath
  Afric tides.

2.

Lo! I was stirring in the leaves that shaded
  The Garden where the Man and Woman
  smiled:
I saw them later, raimentless, degraded,
  The apple sour upon their tongues; be-
  guiled
By the sweet wildness of the Woman's tears,
  I dropt in dew upon her lips, and stole
Under her heart, a stirring human Soul,
  The blood within her tingling in mine ears;
And as I lay, I heard a voice that cried
  'Lo, Proteus, the unborn, shall wake
  to be
Heir of the Woman's sorrow, yet a guide
  Conducting back to immortality—
The spirit of the leaves of Paradise
  Shall lift him upward, to aspire and rise!'
Then sudden, I was conscious that I lay
  Under a heaven that gleam'd afar away:—
I heard the Man and Woman weeping,
  The green leaves rustling, and the Serpent
  creeping,
The roar of beasts, the song of birds, the
  chime
Of elements in sudden strife sublime,
  And overhead I saw the starry Tree,
  Eternity,
Put forth the blossom Time.

3.

A wind of ancient prophecy swept down,
  And wither'd up my beauty – where I lay
On Paris' bosom, in the Trojan town;
  Troy vanish'd, and I wander'd far away,—
Till, lying on a Virgin's breast, I gazed
  Thro' infant eyes, and saw, as in a dream,
The great god Pan whom I had raised and
  praised,
Float huge, unsinew'd, down a mighty
  stream,
With leaves and lilies heap'd about his head,
  And a weird music hemming him around,
While, dropping from his nerveless fingers
  dead,
A brazen sceptre plunged with hollow
  sound:
A trackless Ocean wrinkling tempest-wing'd
Open'd its darkness for the clay unking'd:

Moreover, as he floated on at rest,
With lips that flutter'd still in act to speak,
An eagle, swooping down upon his breast,
Pick'd at his songless lips with golden beak.

4.

There was a sound of fear and lamentation,
The forests wail'd, the stars and moon grew pale,
The air grew cloudy with the desolation
Of gods that fell from realmless thrones like hail ;
But as I gazed, the great God Pan awaking,
Lookt in the Infant's happy eyes and smiled,
And smiling died ; and like a sunbeam breaking
From greenwood olden, rose a presence mild
In exhalation from the clay, and stole
Around the Infant in an auriole—
When, gladden'd by the glory of the child,
Dawn gleam'd from pole to pole.

5.

And, lo ! a shape with pallid smile divine
Wander'd in Palestine ;
And Adam's might was stately in his eyes,
And Eve's wan sweetness glimmer'd on his cheek,
And when he open'd heavenly lips to speak,
I heard, disturbing Pilate into sighs,
The rustle of those leaves in Paradise !
Then all was dark, the earth, and air, and sky,
The sky was troubled and the earth was shaken,
Beasts shriek'd, men shouted, and there came a cry—
'My God, I am forsaken !'
But even then I smiled amid my tears,
And saw in vision, down the future years,
What time the cry still rung in heaven's dark dome,
The likeness of his smile ineffable,
Serenely dwell
On Raphael, sunn'd by popes and kings at Rome,
And Dante, singing in his Tuscan cell !

6.

Suddenly, from the vapours of the north,
Ice-bearded, snowy-visaged, Strength burst forth,
Brandishing arms in death :
'Twas Ades, frighted from his seat in Hell
By that pale smile of peace ineffable,
That with a sunny life-producing breath,
Wreathed summer round the foreheads of the Dead,
And troubled Hell's weird silence into joy.
And with a voice that rent the pole he said,
' Lo, I am Thor, the mighty to destroy !'
The accents ran to water on his mouth,
The pole was kindled to a fiery glow,
A breath of summer floated from the south
And melted him like snow.

7.

Yea thus, thro' change on change,
Haunted for ever by the leafy sound
That sigh'd the Woman and the Man around,
I, Proteus, range.
A weary quest, a power to climb and soar,
Yet never quit life's bitterness and starkness,
A groping for God's hand amid the darkness.
The day behind me and the night before,
This is my task for evermore !
I am the shadow of the inspiration
Breath'd on the Man; I am the sense alone,
That, generation upon generation,
Empowers the sinful Woman to atone
By giving angels to the grave and weeping
Because she knows not whither they are going ;
I am the strife awake, the terror sleeping,
The sorrow ever ebbing, ever flowing.
Mine are the mighty names of power and worth
The seekers of the vision that hath fled,
I bear the Infant's smile about the earth,
And put the Cross on the aspirant's head,
I am the peace on holy men who die,
I waft as sacrifice their fleeting breath—
I am the change that is not change, for I
Am deathless, being DEATH.

8.

For, evermore I grow
Wiser, with humbler power to feel and know;
For, in the end I, Proteus, shall cast
All wondrous shapes aside but one alone,
And stand (while round about me in the Vast
Earth, Sun, Stars, Moon, as snowflakes melt at last,)

A Skeleton that, shadow'd by the Tree,
  Eternity,
Holds in his hands the blossom Time full
  blown,
And kneels before a Throne.

II.

ADES, KING OF HELL.

1.

BENEATH the caves where sunless loam
  Grows dim and reddens into gold ;
'Neath the fat earth-seams, where the
  cold
Rains thicken to the flowery foam
  Fringing blue streams in summer zones ;
Beneath the spheres where dead men's
  bones
Change darkly thro' slow centuries to marl
  and glittering stones ;—

2.

Orb'd in that rayless realm, alone,
  Far from the realm of sun and shower,
  A palpable god with godlike power,
I, Ades, dwelt upon a throne ;
  Much darkness did my eyelids tire ;
But thro' my veins the hid Sun's fire
Communicated impulse, hope, thought, pas-
  sion, and desire.

3.

Eternities of lonely reign,
  Full of faint dreams of day and night
  And the white glamour of starry light,
Oppress'd my patience into pain ;
  Upward I sent a voice of prayer
  That made a horror in the air :
And ' Ades craves a queen, O Zeus ! ' shook
  heaven unaware.

4.

The gods stopt short in full carouse,
  And listen'd. On the streams of Hell
  The whole effulgent conclave fell
As in a glass. With soft-arch'd brows,
  And wings of dewy-tinctured dye,
  Pale Iris listen'd blushingly ;
And Heré sought the soul of Zeus with
  coldly eager eye.

5.

Then the clear hyaline grew cold
  And dim before the Father's face ;
  Gray meditation clothed the place ;
And rising up Zeus cried, ' Behold ! '—
  And on Olumpos' crystal wall,
  A kingly phantom cloudy and tall,
Throned, sceptred, crown'd, was darkly
  apparition'd at the call.

6.

' Behold him ! ' Zeus the Father cried,
  With voice that shook my throne for-
    lorn :
Pale Hermes curl'd his lips in scorn,
And Iris drew her bow aside :
  Artemis paled and did not speak ;
  Sheer fear flush'd Aphrodité's cheek ;
And only owl-eyed Pallas look'd with pitying
  smile and meek.

7.

A weary night thro' earth and air
  The shadow of my longing spread,
  And not a goddess answeréd.
All nature darken'd at my prayer ;
  Which darkness earth and air did
    shroud,
No star rain'd light, but, pale and proud,
With blue-edged sickle Artemis cut her slow
  path thro' cloud.

8.

And when the weary dark was done,
  Beyond my sphere of realm upsprang,
  With smile that beam'd and harp that
    sang,
Apollo piloting the Sun ;
  And conscious of him shining o'er,
  I watch'd my black and watery floor
Wherein the wondrous upper-world is
  mirror'd evermore.

9.

When lo, there murmur'd on my brain,
  Like sound of distant waves, a sound
  That did my godlike sense confound
And kiss'd my eyelids down in pain ;
  And far above I heard the beat
  Of musically falling feet,
Hurl'd by the echoes of the earth down to
  my brazen seat.

10.

And I was 'ware that overhead
  Walk'd one whose very motion sent
  A sweet immortal wonderment
Thro' the deep dwellings of the Dead,
  And flush'd the seams of cavern and mine
To gleams of gold and diamond shine,
And made the misty dews shoot up to kiss her feet divine.

11.

By Zeus, the beat of those soft feet
  Thrill'd to the very roots of Hell,
  Troubling the mournful streams that fell
Like snakes from o t my brazen seat :
  Faint music reach'd me strange and slow,
  My conscious Throne gleam'd pale as snow,
A beauteous vision vaguely fill'd the dusky glass below.—

12.

When I beheld in that dark glass
  The phantom of a lonely maid,
  Who gather'd flowers in a green glade
Knee-deep in dewy meadow-grass,
  And on a riverside. Behold,
  The sun that robed her round with gold,
Mirror'd beneath me raylessly, loom'd white and round and cold.

13.

Soft yellow hair that curl'd and clang
  Throbb'd to her feet in softest showers,
  And as she went she gather'd flowers,
And as she gather'd flowers she sang :
  It floated down my sulphurous eaves,
  That melody of flowers and leaves,
Of vineyards, gushing purple wines, and yellow slanted sheaves.

14.

Darkling I mutter'd, ' It were choice
  Proudly to throne in solemn cheer
  So fair a queen, and ever to hear
Such song from so divine a voice !'
  And with the wish I upward breathed
  A mist of fire that swiftly seethed
Thro' shuddering earth-seams overhead, and round her warm knees wreathed.

15.

Whereon the caves of precious stones
  Grew bright as moonlight thrown on death,
  And red gold brighten'd, and the breath
Drew greenness moist from fleshless bones;
  And every cave was murmuring :
  ' O River, cease to flow and sing,
And bear the tall bride on thy banks to the footstool of thy king !'

16.

Then writhed the roots of forest trees
  In tortuous fear, till tremblingly
  Green leaves quaked round her. A sharp cry
Went upward from the Oreades ;
  Low murmurs woke in bower and cave,
  With diapason in the wave :
The River eddied darkly round, obeying as a slave.

17.

Half stooping downward, while she held
  A flower in loosening fingers light ;
  The quick pink fading from the white
Upon her cheek ; with eyes that welled
  Dark pansy thoughts from veins that dart
  Like restless snakes round the honied heart,
And balmy breath that mildly blew her rose-red lips apart,—

18.

She listen'd—stately, yet dismay'd ;
  And dimly conscious of some change
  That made the whispering place seem strange
And awful, far from human aid ;
  And as the moaning Stream grew near,
  And whirl'd unto her with eddies clear,
She saw my shadow in his waves and shrank away in fear.

19.

'Small River, flowing with summer sound,
  Strong River, solemn Ades' slave,
  Flow unto her with gentle wave,
And make an isle, and hem her round.'
  The River, sad with gentle worth,
  Felt backward to that cave of earth
Where, troubled with my crimson eyes, he shudder'd into birth.

20.

Him saw she trembling ; but unseen,
　Under long sedges lily-strew'd,
　Round creeping roots of underwood,
　Low down beneath the grasses green
　Whereon she waited wondering-eyed,
　My servant slid with stealthy tide :—
Then like a fountain bubbled up and foam'd
　　on either side.

21.

And shrinking back she gazed in fear
　On his wild hair, and lo, an isle—
　Around whose brim waves rose the while
　She cried, 'O mother Ceres, hear!'
　Then sprang she wildly to and fro,
　Wilder than rain and white as snow.
'O honour'd River, grasp thy prize, and to
　　the footstool flow!'

22.

One swift sunbeam with sickly flare
　On white arms waving high did gleam,
　What time she shriek'd, and the strong
　　Stream
Leapt up and grasp'd her by the hair.
　And all was dark. With wild heads
　　bow'd
　The forest murmur'd, and black cloud
Split spewmy on the mountain tops with fire
　　and portent loud!

23.

Then all was still as the Abyss,
　Save for the dark and bubbling water,
　And the far voice. 'Bear Ceres' daughter
　Unto the kingly feet of Dis!'
　Wherefore I rose upon my throne,
　And smote my kingdom's roof of stone ;
Earth moan'd to her deep fiery roots—Hell
　　answer'd with a groan.

24.

When swiftly waving sulphurous wings
　The Darkness brooded down in fear
　To listen. I, afar, could hear
　The coming River's murmurings ;
　My god-like eyes with flash of flame
　Peer'd up the chasm. As if in shame
Of his slave-deed, darkly and slow, my
　　trembling servant came.

25.

The gentleness of summer light,
　This stream, my honour'd slave pos-
　　sessed :
　The blue flowers mirror'd in his breast,
　And the meek lamps that sweeten night,
　Had made his heart too mild to
　　bear
　With other than a gentle care,
And slow sad solemn pace, a load so violet-
　　eyed and fair!

26.

Him saw I, as, thro' looming rocks,
　He glimmer'd like a serpent gray
　Whose moist coils hiss ; then, far
　　away,
　Lo, the dim gleam of golden locks,
　Lo, a far gleam of glinting gold,
　Floating in many a throbbing fold,
What time soft ripples panted dark on
　　queenly eyelids cold.

27.

Silently, with obeisance meet,
　In gentle arms escorting well
　The partner of eternal Hell,
　Thus flow'd, not halting, to my feet
　The gracious River with his load :
　Her with dark arm-sweep he bestow'd
On my great footstool--then again, with
　　sharp shriek, upward flow'd.

28.

So fair, so fair, so strangely fair,
　Dark from the waters lay my love ;
　And lo, I, Ades, stoop'd above,
　And shuddering touch'd the yellow hair
　That made my beaded eyeballs close—
　Awful as sunshine. Cold as snows,
Pale-faced, dank-lidded, proud, she lay in
　　wonderful repose.

29.

And all the lesser Thrones that rise
　Around me, shook. With murmurous
　　breath,
　Their Kings shook off eternal death,
　And with a million fiery eyes
　Glared red above, below, around,
　And saw me stooping fiery-crown'd ;
And the white faces of the damn'd arose
　　without a sound.

30.

As if an awful sunbeam, rife
   With living glory, pierced the gloom,
   Bringing to spirits blind with doom
   The summers of forgotten life,—
     Those pallid faces, mad and stern,
     Rose up in foam, and each in turn
Roll'd downward, as a white wave breaks,
   and seem'd to plead and yearn.

31.

What time this horror loom'd beyond,
   Her soul was troubled into sighs:
   Stooping, throned, crown'd, I touch'd
     her eyes
With dim and ceremonial wand;
   And looking up, she saw and knew
   An awful love which did subdue
Itself to her bright comeliness and gave her
   greeting due!

32.

'Welcome!'—The rocks and chasms and
   caves,
   The million thrones and their black
     kings,
   The very snakes and creeping things,
The very damn'd within the waves,
   Groan'd 'welcome;' and she heard—
     with light
   Fingers that writhed in tresses bright,—
But when I touch'd her to the soul, she
   slowly rose her height.

33.

While shadows of a reign eterne
   Quench'd the fine glint in her yellow
     hair,
   She rose erect more hugely fair,
And, dark'ning to a queenhood stern,
   She gazed into mine eyes and thence
   Drew black and subtle inference,
Subliming the black godhead there with
   sunnier, sweeter sense.

34.

Low at her feet, huge Cerberus
   Crouch'd groaning, but with royal look
   She stooping silenced him, and took
   The throne sublime and perilous
     That rose to hold her and upstream'd
     Vaporous fire: the dark void scream'd,
The pale Eumenides made moan, with eyes
   and teeth that gleam'd.

35.

Behold, she sits beside me now,
   A weighty sorrow in her mien,
   Yet gracious to her woes – a queen;
   The sunny locks about her brow
     Shadow'd to godhead solemn, meet;
     Throned, queen'd; but round about
     her feet,
Sweeten'd by gentle grass and flowers, the
   brackish waves grow sweet.

36.

And surely, when the mirror dun
   Beneath me mirrors yellowing leaves,
   And reapers binding golden sheaves,
   And vineyards purple in the sun,
     When fulness fills the plenteous year
     Of the bright upper-world, I hear
The voice among the harvest-fields that
   mourns a daughter dear.

37.

'Lo, Ceres mourns the bride of Dis,'
   The old Earth moans; and rocks and
     hills,
   'Persephoné;' sad radiance fills
The dripping horn of Artemis
   Silverly shaken in the sky;
   And a great frost-wind rushing by—
'Ceres will rob the eyes of Hell when seed-
   time draweth nigh.'

38.

And in the seed-time after snow,
   Down the long caves, in soft distress,
   Dry corn-blades tangled in her dress,
   The weary goddess wanders slow—
     The million eyes of Hell are bent
     On my strange queen in wonderment,—
The ghost of Iris gleams across my waters
   impotent!

39.

And the sweet Bow bends mild and
   bland
   O'er rainy meadows near the light,
   When fading far along the night
   They wander upward hand-in-hand;
     And like a phantom I remain,
     Chain'd to a throne in lonely reign,
Till, sweet with greenness, moonlight-kiss'd,
   she wanders back again.

40.

But when afar thro' rifts of gold
And caverns steep'd in fog complete,
I hear the beat of her soft feet,
My kingdom totters as of old ;
And, conscious of her sweeter worth,
Her godhead of serener birth,
Hell, breathing fire thro' flowers and leaves,
feels to the upper-earth.

III.

PAN.

IT is not well, ye gods, it is not well!
Yea, hear me grumble—rouse, ye sleepers, rouse
Upon thick-carpeted Olumpos' top—
Nor, faintly hearing, murmur in your sloth
' 'Tis but the voice of Pan the malcontent!'
Shake the sleek sunshine from ambrosial locks,
Vouchsafe a sleepy glance at the far earth
That underneath ye wrinkles dim with cloud,
And smile, and sleep again !
                ME, when at first
The deep Vast murmur'd, and Eternity
Gave forth a hollow sound while from its voids
Ye blossom'd thick as flowers, and by the light
Beheld yourselves eternal and divine,—
ME, underneath the darkness visible
And calm as ocean when the cold Moon smoothes
The palpitating waves without a sound,—
Me, ye saw sleeping in a dream, white-hair'd,
Low-lidded, gentle, aged, and like the shade
Of the eternal self-unconsciousness
Out of whose law YE had awaken'd—gods
Fair-statured, self-apparent, marvellous,
Dove-eyed, and inconceivably divine.

Over the ledges of high mountains, thro'
The fulgent streams of dawn, soft-pillowĕd
On downy clouds that swam in reddening streaks
Like milk wherein a crimson wine-drop melts,
And far beyond the dark of vague low lands,
Uprose Apollo, shaking from his locks
Ambrosial dews, and making as he rose
A murmur such as west winds weave in June.

Wherefore the darkness in whose depth I sat
Wonder'd : thro' newly-woven boughs, the light
Crept onward to mine eyelids unaware,
And fluttering o'er my wrinkled length of limb
Like tremulous butterflies above a snake,
Disturb'd me,—and I stirr'd, and open'd eyes,
Then lifted up my eyes to see the light,
And saw the light, and, seeing not myself,
Smiled !
Thereupon, ye gods, the woods and lawns
Grew populously glad with living things.
A rod of stone beneath my heel grew bright,
Writhing to life, and hissing drew swift coils
O'er the upspringing grass ; above my head
A birch unbound her silver-shimmering hair,
Brightening to the notes of numerous birds;
And far dim mountains hollow'd out themselves
To give forth streams, till down the mountain-sides
The loosen'd streams ran flowing. Then a voice
Came from the darkness as it roll'd away
Under Apollo's sunshine-sandall'd foot,
And the vague voice shriek'd ' Pan !' and woods and streams,
Sky-kissing mountains and the courteous vales,
Cried 'Pan!' and earth's reverberating roots
Gave forth an answer, ' Pan !' and stooping down
His fiery eyes to scorch me from my trance,
Unto the ravishment of his soft lyre
' Pan !' sang Apollo : when the wide world heard,
Brightening brightlier, till thro' murmurous leaves
Pale wood-nymphs peep'd around me whispering ' Pan !'
And sweeter faces floated in the stream
That gurgled to my ankle, whispering ' Pan !'
And, clinging to the azure gown of air
That floated earthward dropping scented dews,
A hundred lesser spirits panted ' Pan !'
And, far along an opening forest-glade,
Beating a green lawn with alternate feet,
' Pan !' cried the satyrs leaping. Then all sounds

Were hush'd for coming of a sweeter sound;
And rising up, with outstretch'd arms, I,
Pan,
Look'd eastward, saw, and knew myself a
god.

It was not well, ye gods, it was not well!
Star-guiders, cloud-compellers—ye who
stretch
Ambrosia-dripping limbs, great-statured,
bright,
Silken and fair-proportion'd, in a place
Thick-carpeted with grass as soft as sleep;
Who with mild glorious eyes of liquid depth
Subdue to perfect peace and calm eterne
The mists and vapours of the nether-world,
That curl up dimly from the nether-world
And make a roseate mist wherein ye lie
Soft-lidded, broad-foreheaded, stretch'd
supine
In awful contemplations—ye great gods,
Who meditate your forms and find them
fair—
Ye heirs of odorous rest—it was not well!—
For, with Apollo sheer above, I, Pan,
In whom a gracious godhead lived and
moved,
Rose, glorious-hearted, and look'd down;
and lo,
Goat-legs, goat-thighs, goat-feet, uncouth
and rude,
And, higher, the breast and bowels of a
beast,
Huge thews and twisted sinews swoll'n like
cords,
And thick integument of bark-brown skin—
A hideous apparition masculine!
But in my veins a new and natural youth,
In my great veins a music as of boughs
When the cool aspen-fingers of the Rain
Feel for the eyelids of the earth in spring,
In every vein quick life; within my soul
The meekness of some sweet eternity
Forgot; and in mine eyes soft violet-thoughts
That widen'd in the eyeball to the light,
And peep'd, and trembled chilly back to the
soul
Like leaves of violets closing.

                    By my lawns,
My honey-flowing rivers, by my woods
Grape-growing, by my mountains down
whose sides

The slow flocks thread like silver streams at
eve,
By the deep comfort in the eyes of Zeus
When the soft murmur of my peaceful dales
Blows like a gust of perfume on his cheek,
There where he reigns, cloud-shrouded—by
meek lives
That smoothe themselves like wings of doves
and brood
Over immortal themes for love of me—
I swear it was not well.
                  Ay, ay, ye smile;—
Ye hear me, garrulous, and turn again
To contemplation of the slothful clouds
That curtain ye for sweetness. Hear me,
gods!
Not the ineffable stars that interlace
The azure panoply of Zeus himself,
Have surer sweetness than my hyacinths
When they grow blue in gazing on blue
heaven,
Than the white lilies of my rivers when
In leafy spring Selené's silver horn
Spills paleness, peace, and fragrance.—And
for these,
For all the sensible or senseless things
Which swell the sounds and sights of earth
and air,
I snatch some glory which of right belongs
To ye whom I revile: ay, and for these,
For all the sensible or senseless things
Which swell the sounds and sights of earth
and air,
I will snatch fresher glory, fresher joy,
Robbing your rights in heaven day by day,
Till from my dispensation ye remove
Darkness, and drought that parches thirsty
skins,
The stinging alchemy of frost, the agues
That rack me in the season of wet winds—
Till, bit by bit, my bestial nether-man
Peels off like bark, my green old age shoots
up
Godhead apparent, and I know myself
Fair—as becomes a god!
                  Ay, I shall do!
Not I alone am something garrulous, gods!
But the broad-bosom'd earth, whose count-
less young
Moan 'Pan!' most piteously when ye
frown
In tempests, or when Thunder, waving
wings,

Groans crouching from your lightning spears, and then
Springs at your lofty silence with a shriek !
Not I alone, low horror masculine,
But earthquake-shaken hills, the dewy dales,
Blue rivers as they flow, and boughs of trees,
Yea, monsters, and the purblind race of men,
Grow garrulous of your higher glory, gods ;
Yearning unto it moan my name aloud,
Climbing unto it shriek or whisper ' Pan !'
Till from the far-off verdurous depths, from deep
Impenetrable woods whose wondrous roots
Blacken to coal or redden into gold,
I, stirring in this ancient dream of mine,
Make answer—and they hear.
       In Arcady
I, sick of mine own envy, hollow'd out
A valley, green and deep ; then pouring forth
From the great hollow of my hand a stream
Sweeter than honey, bade it wander on
In soft and rippling lapse to the far sea.
Upon its banks grew flowers as thick as grass,
Gum-dropping poplars and the purple vine,
Slim willows dusty like the thighs of bees,
And, further, stalks of corn and wheat and flax,
And, even further, on the mountain sides
White sheep and new-yean'd lambs, and in the midst
Mild-featured shepherds piping. Was not this
An image of your grander ease, O gods ?
A faint sweet picture of your bliss, O gods ?
They thank'd me, those sweet shepherds, with the smoke
Of crimson sacrifice of lambkins slain,
Rich spices, succulent herbs that savour meats ;
And when they came upon me ere aware,
Walk'd sudden on my presence where I piped
By rivers lorn my mournful ditties old,
Cried ' Pan !' and worshipp'd. Yet it was not well,
Ye gods, it was not well, that I, who gave
The harvest to these men, and with my breath
Thicken'd the wool upon the backs of sheep,
I, Pan, should in these purblind mortal forms
Witness a loveliness more gently fair,

Nearer to your dim loveliness, O gods !
Than my immortal wood pervading self,—
Carelessly blown on by the rosy Hours,
Who breathe quick breath and smile before they die—
Goat-footed, horn'd, a monster—yet a god.

By wanton Aphrodité's velvet limbs,
I swear, ye amorous gods, it was not well !—
Down the long vale of Arcady I chased
A wood-nymph, unapparell'd and white-limb'd,
From gleaming shoulder unto foot a curve
Delicious, like the bow of Artemis :
A gleam of dewy moonlight on her limbs ;
Within her veins a motion as of waves
Moon-led and silver-crested to the moon ;
And in her heart a sweetness such as fills
Uplooking maidens when the virgin orb
Witches warm bosoms into snows, and gives
The colourable chastity of flowers
To the tumultuous senses curl'd within.
Her, after summer noon, what time her foot
Startled with moonlight motion milk-blue stalks
Of hyacinths in a dim forest glade,—
Her saw I, and, uplifting eager arms,
I rush'd around her as a rush of boughs,
My touch thrill'd thro' her, she beheld my face,
And like a gnat it stung her, and she fled.

Down the green glade, along the verdurous shade,
She screaming fled and I pursued behind :
By Zeus, it was as though the forest moved
Behind her, following ; and with shooting boughs,
And bristling arms and stems, and murmurous leaves,
It eddied after her—my underwood
Of bramble and the yellow-blossom'd furze
Flung its thick growth around her waist, my trees
Dropt thorns before her, and my growing grass
Put forth its green and sappy oils and slid
Under her feet ; until, with streaming hair
Like ravell'd sunshine torn 'mid scars and cliffs,
Pale, breathless, and long-throated like a swan,

With tongue that panted 'tween the foamy
   lips
As the red arrow in a tulip's cup,
She, coming swiftly on the river-side,
Into the circle of a sedgy pool
Plunged knee-deep, shrieking. Then I,
   thrusting arms
To grasp her, touch'd her with hot hands
   that clung
Like burrs to the soft skin; while, writhing
   down
Even as a fountain lessens gurglingly,
She cried to Artemis, 'Artemis, Artemis,
Sweet goddess, Artemis, aid me, Artemis!'
And o'er the laurels on the river-side,
Dark and low-fluttering, Daphne's hidden
   soul
Breathed fearful hoar-frost, echoing 'Arte-
   mis';
When lo, above the sandy sunset rose
The silver sickle of the green-gown'd witch
Which flicker'd thrice into a pallid orb,
And thrice flash'd white across the forest
   leaves,
And—lo, the change ye wot of: melting
   limbs
Black'ning to oozy sap of reeds, white hands
Waving aloft and putting forth green shoots,
The faint breath-bubbles circling in a pool,
Last, the sharp voice's murmur dying away
In the low lapping of the rippling pool,
The melancholy motion of the pool,
And the faint undertone of whispering reeds.

By Latmos and its shepherd, was it well?
By smooth-chinn'd Syrinx, was it well, O
   gods?
Yet mark. What time the pallid sickle
   wax'd
Blue-edged and luminous o'er the black'ning
   west,
I, looming hideous in the smooth pool,
   stooped
And pluck'd seven wondrous pipes of brittle
   reeds
Wherein the wood-nymph's soul still flutter'd
   faint;
And these seven pipes I shaped to one,
   wherein
I, Pan, with ancient and dejected head
Nodding above its image in the pool,
And large limbs stretch'd their length on
   shadowy banks,

Did breathe such weird and awful ravish-
   ment,
Such symmetry of sadness and sweet sound,
Such murmurs of deep boughs and hollow
   cells,
That neither bright Apollo's hair-strung lute,
Nor Heré's queenly tongue when her red
   lips
Flutter to intercession of love-thoughts
Throned in the counsel-keeping eyes of Zeus,
Nor airs from heaven, blow sweetlier. Hear
   me, gods!
Behind her veil of azure, Artemis
Turn'd pale and listen'd; mountains, woods,
   and streams,
And every mute and living thing therein,
Marvell'd, and hush'd themselves to hear
   the end—
Yea, far away, the fringe of the green sea
Caught the faint sound and with a deeper
   moan
Rounded the pebbles on the shadowy shore.
Whence, in the season of the pensive eve,
The earth plumes down her weary, weary
   wings;
The Hours, each frozen in his mazy dance,
Look scared upon the stars and seem to
   stand
Stone-still, like chisell'd angels mocking
   Time;
And woods and streams and mountains,
   beasts and birds,
And serious hearts of purblind men, are
   hush'd;
While music sweeter far than any dream
Floats from the far-off silence, where I sit
Wondrously wov'n about with forest
   boughs—
Through which the moon peeps faintly, on
   whose leaves
The unseen stars sprinkle a diamond dew—
And shadow'd in some water that not flows,
But, pausing, spreads dark waves as smooth
   as oil
To listen!
     Am I over-garrulous, gods?
Thou pale-faced witch, green-kirtled,—thou
   whose light
Troubles the beardless shepherd where he
   sleeps
On Latmos,—am I over-garrulous?
Nay, then, pale huntress of my groves, I
   swear

D

The lily and the primrose 'neath thy heel
Savour as fair as thee, as pure as thee,
Drinking the lucid glamour of thy speed ;
And on the cheeks of marriageable maids
Dwelleth a pallor enviably sweet,
Sweet as thy sweetest self, yet robb'd from thee.
Snow-bosom'd lady, art thou proud?—Then hark . . .
When last in the cool quiet of the night
Thou glimmeredst dimly down with thy white nymphs
And brush'd these dewy lawns with buskin'd foot,
I, Pan the scorn'd, into an oak-tree crept,
And holding between thumb and finger— thus—
A tiny acorn, dropt it cunningly
In the small nest beneath thy snow-heap'd breasts,
And thou didst pause in tumult, cried aloud,
Then redden'd like a rose from breast to brow,
Sharp-crimson like a rose from breast to brow,
And trembled, aspen-hearted, timorous
As new-yean'd lambs, and with a young doe's cry
Startled amazed from thine own tremulous shade
Faint-mirror'd in the dark and dewy lawn !

Ha, turn your mild grand eyes, O gods, and hear !
Why do I murmur darkly, do ye ask?
What do I seek for, yearn for?—Why, not much.
I would be milky-limb'd and straight and tall
And pleasant-featured, like Apollo there !
I would be lithe and fair as Hermes is ;
And, with that glittering sheath of god-like form,
Trust me, could find for it a wit as keen
As that which long ago did prick and pain
The thin skin of the Sun-God. I would be
Grand and fine-statured as becomes a god,
A sight divine conceived harmoniously,
A stately incarnation of my sweet
Pipings in lonely places. There's the worm !

Ay, ay, the mood is on me—I am aged,
White-bearded, and my very lifted hands
Shake garrulously—and ye hear, and smile.
By the faint undertone of this blind Earth,
Swooning towards the pathway of the Sun
With flowery pulses, leafy veins, whene'er
She hears in intercession of new births
My voice miraculous melancholy old,—
I swear not I alone, a sensible god,
Shall keep these misproportions, worse than beast's ;
While woods and streams, and all that dwell therein,
And merest flowers, and the starr'd coils of snakes,
Yea, purblind mortal men, inhale from heaven
Such dews as give them heavenly seemliness,
Communicably lovely as the shapes
That doze on high Olumpos.
                                           Is it well ?
Ye who compel the very clouds to forms
Beauteous and purely beauteous, ere my rain
Rends their white vestments into flowers to make
My peaceful vales look lovely,—gods, great gods,
I ask ye, is it well ?—Ye answer not.
But Earth has answer'd, and all things that grow,
All things that live, all things that feel or see
The interchanges of the sun and moon ;
And with a yearning palpable and dumb,
Yet conscious of some glory yet unborn,
Of unfulfillèd mysteries, I, Pan, Prophesy.
                          In the time to come,—in years
Across whose vast I wearily impel
These ancient, blear'd, and humble-lidded eyes,—
Some law more strong than I, yet part of me,
Some power more piteous, yet a part of me,
Shall hurl ye from Olumpos to the depths,
And bruise ye back to that great darkness whence
Ye blossom'd thick as flowers ; while I—I, Pan –
The ancient haunting shadow of dim earths,
Shall slough this form of beast, this wrinkled length,
Yea, cast it from my feet as one who shakes
A worthless garment off ; and lo, beneath,
Mild-featured manhood, manhood eminent,
Subdued into the glory of a god,

Sheer harmony of body and of soul,
Wondrous, and inconceivably divine.

Wherefore, ye gods, with this my prophecy
I sadden those sweet sounds I pipe unseen.
From dimly lonely places float the sounds
To haunt the regions of the homeless air,
Whatever changeful season ye vouchsafe
To all broad worlds which, hearing, whisper,
 'Pan!'
And thence they reach the hearts of lonely men,
Who wearily bear the burthen and are pain'd
To utterance of fond prophetic song,
Who singing smile, because the song is sweet,
Who die, because they cannot sing the end.

It is my care to keep the graves of such
Thick-s'rewn and deep with grass and precious flowers
Such as ye slumber on; and to those graves,
In sable vestments, ever comes the ghost
Of my forgot and dumb eternity,
Mnemosyne; but what she broods on there
I know not, nor can any wholly know,
Mortal or god. The seasons come and go,
In their due season perish rocks and trees,
In their due season are the streams drain'd dry;
Earth dumbly changes, and those lonely men,
Less blind than purblind mortals, sing and die;
But still, with hooded and dejected head,
Above those graves ponders Mnemosyne;
While I remain to pipe my ditties old,
And my new prophecy, in ancient woods
And by the margins of unfortunate pools,—
My wondrous music dying afar away
Upon the fringes of the setting sun.

IV.

THE NAIAD.

1.

DIAN white-arm'd has given me this cool shrine,
Deep in the bosom of a wood of pine:
 The silver-sparkling showers
 That close me in, the flowers
That prink my fountain's brim, are hers and mine;
And when the days are mild and fair,
And grass is springing, buds are blowing,
Sweet it is, 'mid waters flowing,
Here to sit, and know no care,
 'Mid the waters flowing, flowing, flowing,
 Combing my yellow, yellow hair.

2.

The ounce and panther down the mountain-side
Creep thro' dark greenness in the eventide;
 And at the fountain's brink
 Casting great shades they drink,
Gazing upon me, tame and sapphire-eyed;
 For, awed by my pale face, whose light
 Gleameth thro' sedge and lilies yellow,
 They, lapping at my fountain mellow,
 Harm not the lamb that in affright
 Throws in the pool so mellow, mellow, mellow,
 Its shadow small and dusky-white.

3.

Oft do the fauns and satyrs, flusht with play,
Come to my coolness in the hot noon-day.
 Nay, once indeed, I vow
 By Dian's truthful brow,
The great god Pan himself did pass this way,
 And, all in festal oak-leaves clad,
 His limbs among these lilies throwing,
 Watch'd the silver waters flowing,
 Listen'd to their music glad,
 Saw and heard them flowing, flowing, flowing,
 And ah! his face was worn and sad!

4.

Mild joys around like silvery waters fall;
But it is sweetest, sweetest far of all,
 In the calm summer night,
 When the tree-tops look white,
To be exhaled in dew at Dian's call,
 Among my sister-clouds to move
 Over the darkness earth bedimming,
 Milky-robed thro' heaven swimming,
 Floating round the stars above,
 Swimming proudly, swimming, proudly swimming,
 And waiting on the Moon I love.

5.

So tenderly I keep this cool green shrine,
Deep in the bosom of a wood of pine;

Faithful thro' shade and sun,
  That service due and done
May haply earn for me a place divine
  Among the white-robed deities
    That thread thro' starry paths, attending
My sweet Lady, calmly wending
Thro' the silence of the skies,
  Changing in hues of beauty never ending,
Drinking the light of Dian's eyes.

V.

THE SATYR.

1.

THE trunk of this tree,
  Dusky-leaved, shaggy-rooted,
  Is a pillow well suited
To a hybrid like me,
  Goat-bearded, goat-footed;
For the boughs of the glade
  Meet above me, and throw
A cool pleasant shade
  On the greenness below;
Dusky and brown'd
  Close the leaves all around;
And yet, all the while,
  Thro' the boughs I can see
A star, with a smile,
  Looking at me.

2.

Full length I lie,
  On this mossy tree-knot,
With face to the sky,
  The vast blue I see not;
And I start in surprise
  From my dim half-dream,
  With the moist white gleam
Of the star in mine eyes:
  So strange does it seem
  That the star should beam
From her crystal throne
  On this forest nook
  Of all others, and look
Upon me alone:
Ay, that yonder divine
  Soft face
  Should shine
On this one place;
And, when things so fair
Till the earth and air,
Should choose to be,
Night after night,
The especial light
  Of a monster like me!

3.

Why, all day long,
  I run about
With a madcap throng,
  And laugh and shout.
Silenus grips
  My ears, and strides
On my shaggy hips,
  And up and down
  In an ivy crown
Tipsily rides;
And when in a doze
  His eyelids close,
Off he tumbles, and I
Can his wine-skin steal,
I drink—and feel
  The grass roll—sea-high!
Then with shouts and yells,
  Down mossy dells,
I stagger after
  The wood-nymphs fleet,
Who with mocking laughter
  And smiles retreat;
And just as I clasp
  A yielding waist,
  With a cry embraced,
——Gush! it melts from my grasp
Into water cool,
  And—bubble! trouble!
  Seeing double!
I stumble and gasp
  In some icy pool!

4.

All suborn me,
Flout me, scorn me!
Drunken joys
  And cares are mine,
Romp and noise,
  And the dregs of wine;
And whene'er in the night
  Diana glides by
  The spot where I lie,
With her maids green-dight,
  I must turn my back
In a rude affright,
  And blindly fly
  From her shining track!

Or if only I hear
  Her bright foot-fall near,
    Fall with face to the grass,
  Not breathing for fear
    Till I feel her pass.

5.

I am—
  I know not what:
Neither what I am,
  Nor what I am not—
I seem to have rollick'd,
  And frolick'd,
In this wood for ay,
  With a beast's delight
Romping all day,
  Dreaming all night!
Yet I seem
  To remember awaking
Just here, and aching
  With the last forsaking
    Tender gleam
Of a droll strange dream.—
When I lay at mine ease,
  With a sense at my heart
    Of being a part
Of the grass and trees
And the scented earth,
  And of drinking the bright
    Subdued sunlight
With a leafy mirth:
Then behold, I could see
  A wood-nymph peeping
Out of her tree,
  And closer creeping,
Timorously
  Looking at me!
And still, so still,
I lay until
  She trembled close to me,
    Soft as a rose to me,
  And I leapt with a thrill
    And a shout, and threw
Arms around her, and press'd her,
Kiss'd her, caress'd her,—
  Ere she scream'd, and flew.

6.

Then I was 'ware
  Of a power I had—
To drink the air,
    Laugh and shout,
    Run about,

  And be consciously glad—
So I follow'd the maiden
  'Neath shady eaves,
Thro' groves deep-laden
  With fruit and leaves,
Till, drawing near
  To a brooklet clear,
I shuddering fled
  From the monstrous shape
There mirrorëd—
Which seem'd to espy me,
  And grin and gape,
And leap up high
  In the air with a cry,
    And fly me!

7.

Whence I seem to have slowly
  Grown conscious of being
A thing wild, unholy,
  And foul to the seeing.—
But ere I knew aught
  Of others like me,
I would lie, fancy-fraught,
In the greenness of thought,
  Beneath a green tree;
And seem to be deep
  In the scented earth-shade
'Neath the grass of the glade,
  In a strange half-sleep:
When the wind seem'd to move me,
  The cool rain to kiss,
The sunlight to love me,
  The stars in their bliss
To tingle above me;
And I crept thro' deep bowers
That were sparkling with showers
  And sprouting for pleasure,
And I quicken'd the flowers
  To a joy without measure—
Till my sense seem'd consuming
  With warmth, and, upspringing,
I saw the flowers blooming,
  And heard the birds singing!

8.

Wherever I range,
  Thro' the greenery,
That vision strange,
  Whatsoever it be,
Is a part of me
Which suffers not change.—

The changes of earth,
  Water, air, ever-stirring,
    Disturb me, conferring
My sadness or mirth :
  Wheresoever I run,
I drink strength from the sun ;
The wind stirs my veins
  With the leaves of the wood,
The dews and the rains
    Mingle into my blood.
I stop short
  In my sport,
    Panting, and cower,
While the blue skies darken
  With a sunny shower ;
And I lie and hearken,
  In a balmy pain
    To the tinkling clatter,
    Pitter, patter,
  Of the rain
On the leaves close to me,
  And sweet thrills pass
Thro' and thro' me,
  Till I tingle like grass.
When lightning with noise
  Tears the wood's green ceiling,
When the black sky's voice
  Is terribly pealing,
I hide me, hide me, hide me,
  With wild averted face,
    In some terror-stricken place,
While flowers and trees beside me,
  And every streamlet near,
Darken, whirl, and wonder,
Above, around, and under,
And murmur back the thunder
  In a palpitating fear !

9.

Ay ; and when the earth turns
  A soft bosom of balm
To the darkness that yearns
  Above it, and grows
    To dark, dewy, and calm
      Repose,—
I, apart from rude riot,
Partake of the quiet
  The night is bequeathing,
  Lie, unseen and unheard,
    In the greenness just stirr'd
      By its own soft breathing—
And my heart then thrills
  With a strange sensation
Like the purl of rills
  Down moonlit hills
    That loom afar,
With a sweet sensation
Like the palpitation
  Of yonder star !

10.

Thro' yonder bough
  Her white ray twinkles ;
And on my brow
  She silently sprinkles
    A dewy rain,
    That lulls my brain
To a dream of being
  Under the ground,
Blind to seeing,
  Deaf to sound,
Drinking a dew
  That drops from afar,
And feeling unto
  The sweet pulse of a star,
Who is beckoning me
  Though I cannot see !
And of suddenly blooming
  Up into the air,
And, swooning, assuming
  The shape I wear !
While all fair things
  Fly night and day from me,
Wave bright wings,
  And glimmer away from me !

11.

—She shines above me,
  And heareth not,
Though she smiles on this spot
And seems to love me.
Here I lie aloof,
  Goat-footed, knock-kneed,
  A monster, indeed,
From horns to hoof ;
And the star burns clearly
  With pearl-white gleam—
Have I merely
  Dream'd a dream ?

12.

—Did she hear me, I wonder ?—
  She trembles upon
    Her throne—and is gone !
The boughs darken under,

Then thrill, and are stirr'd
By the notes of a bird,
The green grass brightens
With pearly dew,
And the whole wood whitens
As the dawn creeps thro'.—
'Hoho!'—that shout
Flung the echoes about
The boughs, like balls!
  Who calls?—
'Tis the noisy rout
Of my fellows upspringing
From sleep and dreaming,
To the birds' shrill singing,
The day's soft beaming:
And they madly go
To and fro,
Though o' nights they are dumb.
Hoho! hoho!
I come! I come!
Hark!—to the cry
They reply:
'Ha, there, ha!'
'Hurrah!'—'hurrah!'
And startling afraid.
At the cries,
In the depths of the glade
Echo replies—
'Ho, there!'—'ho, there!'—
By the stream below there
The answer dies.

VI.

VENUS ON THE SUN-CAR.

1.

TELL me, thou many-finger'd Frost,
Coming and going like a ghost
  In leafless woods forsaken—
O Frost that o'er him lying low
Drawest the garment of the snow
  From silver cloud-wings shaken,
And round bare boughs with strange device
Twinest fantastic leaves of ice—
  When will Adon waken?
Lo, dawn by dawn I rise afar
Beside Apollo in his car,
  And, far below us wreathing,
Thy fogs and mists are duskly curl'd
Round the white slumber of the world,
  Like to its own deep breathing;
But crimson thro' the mist our light
Foameth and freezeth, till by night
  Snow-bosom'd hills we fade on—
The pallid god, at my desire,
Gives unto thee a breath of fire
  To reach the lips of Adon.

2.

Tell me, thou bare and wintry World,
Wherein the wingèd flowers are curl'd
  Like pigmy spirits dozing—
O World, within whose lap he lies,
With thy quick earth upon his eyes,
  In dim unseen reposing,
Husht underneath the wind and storm,
Still rosy-lipt in darkness warm—
  Are Adon's eyes unclosing?
Lo, dawn by dawn I rise afar
Beside Apollo in his car,
  Thro' voids of azure soaring,
And gazing down on regions dead,
With golden hair dishevellèd,
  And claspèd hands imploring.
Wonderful creatures of the light
Hover above thee, hanging bright
  Faint pictures glen and glade on:
The pallid god, at my desire,
Hideth in glimmering snows his fire,
  To reach the sleep of Adon.

3.

Tell me, thou spirit of the Sun,
Radiant-lock'd and awful one,
  Strong, constant, unforsaking—
Sun, by whose shadier side I sit
And search thy face, and question it,
  Conferring light and taking—
Whose fiery westward motion throws
The shadow-hours on his repose,—
  Is my Adon waking?
Lo, dawn by dawn I rise afar
Beside thee in thy flaming car,
  Thou ever-constant comer!
And flashing on the clouds that break
Around our path thy sunbeams make
  A phantom of the summer.
O breathe upon the Moon, that she
May use her magic witchery
  When snowy hills we fade on,
That, in the dark, when thou art gone,
She speed the resurrection,
  And stir the sleep of Adon!

4.

Tell me, O silver-wingëd Moon,
That glidest to melodious tune
   Ice-sparkling skies on skies up,—
O Moon, that to the sunset gray,
Drinking faint light that fades away,
   Liftest immortal eyes up,
And walking on, art thro' the night
Troubled to pain by that strange light,—
   When will Adon rise up?
Lo, dawn by dawn I rise afar
Beside Apollo in his car,
   Imploring sign or token
But night by night such pale peace beams
Upon his slumber, that it seems
   Too beauteous to be broken!
O gentle goddess, be not cold—
But, some dim dawn, may we behold
   New glory hill and glade on,
The leaves and flowers alive to bliss,
And, somewhat pale with thy last kiss,
   The smiling face of Adon!

VII.
SELENE THE MOON.

1.

I HIDE myself in the cloud that flies
   From the west and drops on the hill's gray
      shoulder,
And I gleam through the cloud with my
      panther-eyes,
   While the stars turn paler, the dews grow
      colder;
I veil my naked glory in mist,
   Quivering downward and dewily glistening,
Till his sleep is as pale as my lips unkist,
   And I tremble above him, panting and
      listening.
As white as a star, as cold as a stone,
   Dim as my light in a sleeping lake,
With his head on his arm he lieth alone.
   And I sigh 'Awake!
Wake, Endymion, wake and see!'
And he stirs in his sleep for the love of me;
   But on his eyelids my breath I shake:
      'Endymion, Endymion!
      Awaken, awaken!'
And the yellow grass stirs with the mystic
      moan,
   And the tall pines groan,
And Echo sighs in her grot forsaken
      The name of Endymion!

2.

A foamy dew from the Ocean old,
   Whence I rise with shadows behind me
      flying,
Drops from my sandals and glittereth cold
   On the long spear-grass where my love is
      lying;
My face is dim with departed suns,
   And my eyes are dark from the depths of
      ocean,
A starry shudder throughout me runs,
   And my pale cloud stirs with a radiant
      motion,
When the darkness wherein he slumbers
      alone
Ebbs back from my brightness, as black
      waves break
From my shining ankle with shuddering tone;
   And I sigh 'Awake!
Wake, Endymion, wake and hear!'
And he stirs in his sleep with a dreamy fear,
   And his thin lips part for my sweet sake:
      'Endymion, Endymion!
      Awaken, awaken!'
And the skies are moved, and a shadow is
      blown
   From the Thunderer's throne,
And the spell of a voice from Olumpos shaken
      Echoes 'Endymion!'

3.

Then under his lids like a balmy rain
   I put pale dreams of my heavenly glory;—
And he sees me lead with a silver chain
   The tamed Sea-Tempest white-tooth'd and
      hoary;
And he sees me fading thro' forests dark
   Where the leopard and lion avoid me in
      wonder,
Or ploughing the sky in a pearly bark,
   While the earth is dumb with my beauty
      under!
Then he brightens and yearns where he lies
      alone,
   And his heart grows dumb with a yearning
      ache,
And the thin lips part with a wondering moan,
   As I sigh 'Awake!
Wake, Endymion, wake and see
All things grow bright for the love of me,
With a love that grows gentle for thy sweet
      sake!
      Endymion, Endymion!

Awaken, awaken!'
And my glory grows paler, the deep woods groan,
And the waves intone,
Ay, all things whereon my glory is shaken
Murmur 'Endymion!'

4.

Ah! The black earth brightens, the Sea creeps near
When I swim from the sunset's shadowy portal;
But he will not see, and he will not hear,
Though to hear and see were to be immortal:
Pale as a star and cold as a stone,
Dim as my ghost in a sleeping lake,
In an icy vision he lieth alone,
And I sigh 'Awake!
Wake, Endymion, wake and be
Divine, divine, for the love of me!'
And my odorous breath on his lids I shake:
'Endymion, Endymion!
Awaken, awaken!'
But Zeus sitteth cold on his cloud-shrouded throne
And heareth my moan,
And his stern lips form not the hope-forsaken
Name of Endymion.

VIII.

IRIS THE RAINBOW.

1.

'MID the cloud-enshrouded haze
Of Olumpos I arise,
With the full and rainy gaze
Of Apollo in mine eyes;
But I shade my dazzled glance
With my dripping pinions white
Where the sunlight sparkles dance
In a many-tinctured light:
My foot upon the woof
Of a fleecy cloudlet small,
I glimmer thro' the roof
Of the paven banquet-hall,
And a soft pink radiance dips
Thro' the floating mists divine,
Touching eyes and cheeks and lips
Of the mild-eyed gods supine,
And the growing glory rolls
Round their foreheads, while I stain,
With a blush like wine, the bowls
Of transparent porcelain:
Till the whole calm place has caught
A deep gleam of rosy fire—
When I darken to the thought
In the eyes of Zeus the Sire.

2.

Then Zeus, arising, stoops
O'er the ledges of the skies,
Looking downward, thro' the loops
Of the starry tapestries,
On the evident dark plain
Speck'd with wood and hill and stream,
On the wrinkled tawny main
Where the ships, like snowflakes, gleam;
And with finger without swerve,
Swiftly lifted, swiftly whirl'd,
He draws a magic curve
O'er the dark low-lying world;
When with waving wings display'd,
On the Sun-god's threshold bright
I upleap, and seem to fade
In a flash of golden light;
But I plunge thro' vapours dim
To the dark low-lying land,
And I tremble, float, and swim,
On the strange curve of the Hand:
From my wings, that drip, drip, drip,
With cool rains, shoot jets of fire,
As across green capes I slip
With the thought of Zeus the Sire.

3.

Thence, with drooping wings bedew'd,
Folded close about my form,
I alight with feet unview'd
On the ledges of the storm;
For a moment, cloud-enroll'd,
Mid the murm'rous rain I stand,
And with meteor eyes behold
Vapoury ocean, misty land;
Till the thought of Zeus outsprings
From my ripe mouth with a sigh,
And unto my lips it clings
Like a shining butterfly;
When I brighten, gleam, and glow
And my glittering wings unfurl,
And the melting colours flow
To my foot of dusky pearl;
And the ocean mile on mile
Gleams thro' capes and straits and bays,

And the vales and mountains smile,
 And the leaves are wet with rays,—
While I wave the humid Bow
 Of my wings with flash of fire,
And the Tempest, crouch'd below,
 Knows the thought of Zeus the Sire.

IX.
ORPHEUS THE MUSICIAN.

I SAT of old beside a stream new-born
 From loamy loins of mountains cold,
And it was garrulous of dreams forlorn
 And visions old :

Wherefore the legends of the woods and caves
 With that faint melody were blended ;
And as the stream slid down to ocean-waves,
 I comprehended.

Into a dreary silence dim and deep
 I sank with drowsy sighs and nods :
Then sang—my blue eyes dark and wise from sleep—
 The birth of gods.—

A gleaming shoulder cut the stream, and lo !
 I saw the glistening Naiad rise :
She floated, like a lily white as snow,
 With half-closed eyes.

And suddenly, thronging the boughs around,
 Came forest faces strange and glad,
That droopt moist underlips and drank the sound
 Divinely sad.

Far down the glade, where heavy shadows slept,
 Stole, purple-stainëd by the vine,
Silenus,—thro' whose blood my music crept
 Like wondrous wine :

Tiptoe, like one who fears to break a spell,
 He came, with eyeballs blank as glass—
Not drawing breath till, at my feet, he fell
 Prone on the grass.

Then, leaning forkëd chin upon his hand,
 He listen'd, dead to tipsy strife,
And lo ! his face grew smooth and soft and bland
 With purer life

Goat-footed fauns and satyrs one by one,
 With limbs upon the greensward thrown,
Gather'd, and darken'd round me in the sun,
 Like shapes of stone :

Between the sunset and the green hillside
 Quaint pigmy spirits linger'd bright,
Till heaven's one star swam dewy, opening wide
 To the delight,—

While sunlight redden'd, dying, and below
 All heark'd—like shapes upon a cup,
By skiëd Heré, in the ambrosial glow,
 Held rosily up.

Then twilight duskly gloam'd upon the place,
 Full of sweet odour and cool shade,
But music made a lamp of every face
 In the forest-glade :

Till swiftly swam, in showers of pearly beams,
 Selené to her azure arc,
Scattering silence, light, and dewy dreams
 On eyelids dark.

The music sadden'd, and the greenwood stirr'd,
 The moonlight clothed us in its veil,
As stooping down the dove-eyed goddess heard,
 Smiled, and grew pale :

For as they listen'd, satyrs, nymphs, and fauns
 Conceived their immortality—
Yea, the weird spirits of the woods and lawns,
 Gross, vile, to see—

Whence her pure light disturb'd them, and they strove
 To shake away the sweet strange charm ;
But the light brighten'd, shaken from above
 With pearly arm.

They could not fly, they could not cry nor speak,
 It held them like a hand of strength,—
They hid their faces, wild, abash'd and weak,
 And writhed full length.

The Naiad lifted up her dewy chin,
 And knew, and saw the light with love,
Made peaceful by a purity akin
 To hers above,

And countless beauteous spirits of the shade
  Knew their own souls and felt no fear;
While Echo, nestling in her thyme-cave, made
  An answer clear.

Till, when I ceased to sing, the satyr-crew
  Rush'd back to riot and carouse;
Self-fearful faces blushingly withdrew
  Into leafy boughs;

Lastly, Silenus to his knees upcrept,
  Rubb'd eyelids swollen like the vine,
Stared blankly round him, vow'd that he had slept,
  And bawl'd for wine.

X.
POLYPHEME'S PASSION.

Ho, Silenus!—no one here!
  The kitchen empty, the flocks in stalls,
  The red fire flickering over the walls,
And—a young kid spitted—dainty cheer!
Ho, Silenus!—tipsy old reveller,
Soft-zone-unloosener, bright-hair-disheveller,
Where are you hiding, you tipsy old hound you,
With your beard of a goat and your eyes of a lamb?

SILENUS.
Ho, Cyclops!

POLYPHEME.
He mocks me! Where are you, confound you?

SILENUS.
Patience, sweet master, here I am!—

POLYPHEME.
Rise! or with my great fist I'll put an end to thee;
The dregs of my great flagon have been warming thee—
Thou'rt drunk, sow-ears. I find there's no reforming thee,
Tho' six round moons I've tried to be a friend to thee.
Once more divinely warming those old veins,
  Chirping like grasshoppers at every pore,
Foaming as warm as milk among thy brains,
  Gushing like sunshine in thine heart's dry core,
Runs the pink nectar of my vines. It stains,
  Flowing from that bald head, this grassy floor—
Too sweet for earth to drink, unmeet for thee,
Fit only to be quaff'd by gods like me!

SILENUS.
Cyclops!

POLYPHEME.
Jump up, then, quickly. Nay, no more.
Follow me to this rocky eminence,
Cool-cushion'd with the yellow moss, from whence
We can at ease behold
The cloud-stain'd greenness of the ocean sleek,
Rounding its glassy waves into the creek,
Speckled with sparkling jewels manifold,
And, far away, one melting patch of gold.
Now, sit!—Nay, nearer, higher—here, above
My shoulder. Turn thy face to mine, Silenus!
Fear not:—being fill'd with the sweet milk of Venus,
Thou'rt a fit counsellor for one in love;
And, as I'm in a talking humour, why—
Suppose we chat a little at our leisure.

SILENUS.
With pleasure!
The subject?

POLYPHEME.
    One alone beneath the sky,
Old man, is worthy of the conversation
And serious consideration
Of such a god as I!
Now, guess the name of that sweet thing?

SILENUS.
    With ease.
Bacchus, the god to whom these aged knees
Bend gloriously impotent so often,
And in whose luscious pool
I dip hot mouth and eyes, and soak and soften
The yoke of thy strong rule.

POLYPHEME.
A thing a thousand times more beautiful!

SILENUS.
I know no thing more beautiful than he
When, dripping odours cool,
 Deep-purpled, like a honey-bosom'd flower
 For which the red mouth buzzes like a bee,
 He bursts from thy deep caverns gushingly,
 And throws his pleasure round him in a
  shower,
And sparkles, sparkles, like the eyes that see,
In sunshine, murmuring for very glee
And bursting beaded bubbles until sour
Lips tremble into moist anticipation
Of his rich exultation!

POLYPHEME.
Has little Bacchus, whom ye praise so, power
 To unnerve these mighty limbs, make this
  one Eye
Rain impotent tears, hurl this gigantic bulk
Down on its stubborn knees—nay, make me
  skulk
And fume and fret, and simper oaths,
 and sigh,
Like tiny mortal milking-maids who sulk
 In dairies, frothing yellow like their
  cream?
Could Bacchus, once let loose to fight and
  fly,
 Do all these things to sinewy Polypheme?

SILENUS.
Assuredly!

POLYPHEME.
  By this right hand, you lie!—
I am a god, great-statured, strong, and born
 Out of Poseidon's nervy loins divine!
I laugh the wrath of Zeus himself to scorn;
And when I rise erect on Aetna's horn
 My shadow on the faint sea-hyaline
Falls like a cloud wherein the winds drop
  still
And white-wing'd ships move slowly without
  will.
Shall bulk so wondrous and so grand as mine
Yield to the miserable god of wine?

SILENUS.
Certainly not.

POLYPHEME.
  Never!—by Pallas' spear,
At whose sharp touch the plump god leaps
 and flies,
While startled Revel shrieks with haggard
 eyes!
Never, by Hermes, whom the drunken
 fear,
But whose quick fingers pilfer not the wise!

SILENUS.
Whom shall we praise, O Cyclops?

POLYPHEME.
  Thou shalt hear—
Tell me, didst thou ever see a,—
Ever see a, ever hear a,—'
Either far away or near, a—
Nymph so sweet as Galatea?

SILENUS.
Never!

POLYPHEME.
'Tis false, old man! she is not fair;—
Those weeds that under ocean rot at ease
Into dark dreams o' the flowery earth, and
 there
Put purples in the sea-nymph's sunny hair
Are fairer: she is changeable as these.
She is as wanton as the perfumed fays
 That dimple on the windless sea and dally,
 Musically,
With the puff'd sails of ships becalm'd for
 days.

SILENUS.
True, Cyclops, she is fickle; and by her
Whose amorous breath blew the Greek host
 to Troy,
I have seen fairer!

POLYPHEME.
  Dotard! Driveller!
Not her the false Idalian shepherd-boy,
 With silken string, like a tame heifer,
  led—
Nay, not lush Aphrodite, whose blue eyne,
 Pink-lidded, smiled on their unhallow'd
  bed—
Is half so fair, so precious, so divine,
As Galatea!

SILENUS.
Exactly what I said.

POLYPHEME.
Her voice hath gentle sweetness, borrowëd
From soft tide-lispings on the pebbly sand,
'Tis like the brooding doves in junipers ;
White as a shell of ocean is her hand,
Wherein, with rosy light, the pink blood
  stirs !
Her hair excels the fruitage of the beech
Wherein the sun runs liquid gleam on gleam ;
Her breasts are like two foaming bowls of
  cream,
A red straw-berry in the midst of each !
And the soft gold-down on her silken chin
Is like the under side of a ripe peach—
A dimple dipping honeyly therein !

SILENUS.
Her eyes—

POLYPHEME.
Profane them not !—For their sweet fire is
Wondrous and various as the Bow
Drawn over rainy ledges dripping low
By many-colour'd Iris—
From whose bright end, plunged the dark
  waters under,
Woven with the tapestries of her sea-cave,
And dying hue by hue on the green wave,
They may have drunk a portion of their
  wonder.
But oh, what tongue can tell
Their glory inexpressible ?
You seem to see the music of the ocean
Folded within them, as within a shell,
And gently stirring with a violet motion,
Until it drops unto the lips, and there
Flutters in perfumed accents on the air ;
Nor this alone. They change as the sea
  changes,
In hues as various as the ringdove's dyes :
Whatsoever sweet and strange is'
Flashes across them with a quick surprise.
Now, in their troubled orbs rise multiform
Wild pictures of sky-tempest and sea-storm ;
And her wild eyes droop brightly on her breast
Till it is troubled like a thing distrest ;
But in their softest mood
You watch the pale soul tremulously brood
On those bright orbs whose fire the dark
  sea cools,
And there it trembles, as the moonlight flows
On seas just stirr'd by their own deep repose,
And throbbing, throbbing, into silver pools !

SILENUS.
O eloquent Cyclops, pause, and breathe a
  space !—
Few eyes save thine, few eyes of earth, have
  plainly
Seen this immortal Galatea's face ;
For she thou lovest is of that fair race
Whom mortal vision dreams of, but seeks
  vainly—
For they comb and they comb
  Their yellow locks,
  Under the foam,
  Among weedy rocks !
  And they sing unseen
  In their sea-caves green,
And gaze at the white sun overhead
  Whose pale ray saddens their dripping
    curls,
Or the moon that glimm'ring in ocean's
  bed
  Leaves her light for ever in pools of
    pearls !

POLYPHEME.
Chirrup not, wine-sponge !—Am not I a
  god?
Cannot this eye peer to Olumpos' helm ?
Does not the great sea, trembling at my nod,
Hush itself humbly around this my realm ?

SILENUS.
It does, O Cyclops !

POLYPHEME.
          Save, of course, when I
Hurl rocks and trees down on the shudder-
  ing ships,
And, while I loom above the waves, my lips
Roar terrible defiance at the sky.

SILENUS.
Precisely.

POLYPHEME.
    Ask not, then, the when and how ;
But turn thine ancient gaze
On the broad wonder of my brow,
Thence drop it, in a natural amaze,
Down the steep mountain to my sinewy feet,
Round which the lambs, as small as snow-
  flakes, bleat ;
Now, tell me—am I fair ?

SILENUS.
                    Most fair!
POLYPHEME.
          Thy fears
Lie to my strength a hollow lie, Silenus!

SILENUS.
By all the love that there exists between us,
By doves that perch on Bacchus' vine-
    wreath'd ears,
I swear thou art most beautiful!

POLYPHEME.
              Again:
Have those blurr'd eyeballs noticed that of
    late
Mine air has grown more solemn, more
    sedate,
More bountiful to those I hold in chain
To watch my flocks, and more compassion-
    ate;
As if I struggled underneath the weight
Of some indefinite pain?
That I have learn'd to tremble and to blush,
To droop this eyelid modestly, to flush
All over at the tiniest whispering sound,
To pick small dainty steps upon the ground
As if I saw and seeing fear'd to crush
Some crawling insect or the crimson-crown'd
Small daisy-flower that, whensoe'er I pass,
Shuts up its little leaves upon the grass
And thinks the shadowy eve has stolen down!

SILENUS.
Cyclops!—These things I saw, but fear'd to
    question;
Nay, with a blush I own it—do not frown!—
I set thy trouble down as indigestion.
For neither dainty kids, nor lambs stall-
    fed,
Nor sucking-swine with pippins in their
    teeth,
Nor ox-thighs with green herbs engarlanded,
Nor foamy curds wherein hot apples seethe
Nay, not the parsley-flavour'd tongues of
    sheep,
Could tempt o' late thy dainty appetite;
But lying on the mountain out of sight
Of melancholy thou hast drunken deep;
While down among the yellow pastures
    moaning

With lambs new-yean'd, where thy cool
    streamlets run,
We saw thee loom above us, mighty one!
And heard thee, like the monstrous seas
    intoning,
Melodiously groaning!

POLYPHEME.
Ay me! ay me!
SILENUS.
              Be calm, sweet Polypheme!
The eagle poised o'er yonder cropping lamb
Flew scared, at that big cry.

POLYPHEME.
                    Ay me! I am
Lost, swallow'd up, absorbed into a dream!
Thro' the swift current of my frame gigantic
Eddies a frantic
Consuming fire. I am not what I seem.
For Galatea I refuse all food,
For Galatea I grow weak and wild
And petulant-featured as a sickly child;
For Galatea I, in desperate mood,
Seek out green places in this solitude,
And close my eyes, and think I am a curl
Tingling, tingling, lightly
Against the snow-heap'd bosom swelling
    whitely!

SILENUS.
One should not break his heart for any girl.

POLYPHEME.
Ay me! I close my eyes in a sweet woe,
And dream that I am little, fair, and sweet,
For a small goddess's embraces meet,
Nor huge, nor rough. It was not always so!
Of old, Silenus, this great awful Me
Was swoll'n with glory at the contemplation
Of its enormity in yonder sea;
I revell'd in the roar and consternation,
When, grasping rocks with frantic acclama-
    tion,
Round this frowning, Ætna-crowning head
    I whirl'd them,
Tremendously, stupendously, and hurl'd
    them
On the passing fleets below;
And from under came the thunder of vessels
    crush'd asunder,
And the shriek, faint and weak, of the
    mortals in their wonder,

And the sea rolled underneath, and the winds
    began to blow,
And above the desolation, drunk with rage,
    I took my station,
With my waving arms expanded and my
    crimson eye aglow,
And to earth's reverberation,
Roar'd 'Ho! ho! ho!'

SILENUS.

Cyclops! sweet Cyclops!—

POLYPHEME.

                  Fear not!
I am as weak as the eagle's callow young;
Yet listen, mild old man, and interfere not.
One summer day, when earth and heaven
    rung
With thunders, and the hissing lightning
    stung
With forkëd meteor tongue
The green smooth living ocean till it
    shriek'd—
I stood aloft on Ætna's horn and wreak'd
My cruel humour with a monstrous glee:
When lo! from out the rainy void did flit
Bright Iris, and with tremulous foot alit
On this my mountain, touching even me
With her faint glory: for a moment, she
Paused shudd'ring high above me: then
    with fleet
Footstep slid downward till she reach'd my
    feet;
And there, with many-tinctured wings
    serene,
She waved the seas to silence, and, beguiled
By her mild message, the dark ocean
    smiled—
A palpitating lapse of oily green,
With silvery glimmers here and there be-
    tween
The shadows of the clouds that, dewy and
    mild,
Parted and flutter'd:—when, with radiant
    head
Plunging among the mountain mists, she
    fled.
But, as the vapours fleam'd away, behold!
I saw far down upon the brown sea-strand
A nymph who held aloft in pearly hand
A white-tooth'd comb, and comb'd her locks
    of gold
Over a dank and ship-wreck'd sailor-lad,—
On whose sad eyelids a faint radiance lay,
Robb'd from some little homestead far away,
Some silent hearth that wearily would wait,
For that faint smile which left it desolate,
And hush itself and watch and yearn and
    pray.
Oh! tenderly she comb'd her locks of gold,
Over that gently-sleeping sailor-lad,
Stretch'd 'mid the purple dulse and rock-
    weed cold;
And all the while she sang a ditty sad,
To deep division of the wave that roll'd
Up to her feet, like a huge snake that springs
At two bright butterflies with golden wings:

    Marinere, O Marinere,
      Waken, waken!
      Sleep-o'ertaken,
Look upon me, with no fear,
Look, and see, and hear:
Underneath the white-tooth'd waves,
Sleep your comrades in their caves;
Coral grottoes are their bed,
Purple plants stir overhead,
All around black weeds are twined,
Frozen still without a wind;
And the sea-nymphs in distress
Pluck dark flowers all odourless,
Growing deep in caverns clear,
Gently to bestrew their bier.
    Under the sea
    They sleep—ah me!
    They have slept for many a year.

    Marinere, O Marinere,
      Wake not, wake not,
      Slumber break not,
Close your eyelids with no fear,
Do not see, nor hear!
Far above the silence deep,
Where your gentle comrades sleep,
Rolls the sea and foams the storm,
Horrors thicken, terrors swarm,
And the sea-nymphs, lightning-led,
Flash about white-garmented;
But below the Storm-god's frown,
Sleep the shipwreck'd fathoms down—
Ocean-flowers are on the bier,
Foam-bells hang in every ear!
    Under the sea
    They sleep—ah me!
    They shall sleep for many a year.

SILENUS.

That was the song she sang?

POLYPHEME.

It was. But ill
Those tender accents fill
This rocky breast, whose distant roar
Frightens those white waves seaward from
   the shore.
For they trembled, tinkling, twining,
For melodious combining,
While her yellow locks fell shining
   To her knees,
While the Storm, with bright eyes glistening,
Thro' its cloud-veil looking at her,
Hung breathlessly and listening
   On the seas :
And in the sun she sat her,
While her voice went pitter-patter,
Pitter-patter, like the clatter
   Of bright rain on boughs of trees !
   Then ho ! with my great stride,
   Down the steep mountain side,
I sprang unto her, with mine arms extended!
   Her bright locks gleam'd afraid,
   Like a sunbeam trapt in shade,
In my deep shadow, and the music ended ;
   And she rose erect to fly,
   Panting, moaning, and her cry
Met the lifted cry of Ocean, and they blended!
   While earth reel'd under,
   Downward I bore,
   With step of thunder,
   On to the shore ;
   And in shrieking amaze,
   With eyes fasten'd in fear—
   Like a star's firm gaze
   When a cloud draws near—
On the horror that came
   With an eye of flame,
She leapt to the water,
   All woebegone ;
   And her bright locks shone
And tript and distraught her,
   But the water caught her
   And push'd her on !
From billow to billow,
   With wild locks streaming
   And tangling oft ;
From billow to billow,
   Dark-green, or gleaming
   Like doves' wings soft,
From billow to billow,
   Panting and screaming,
   With white hands beaming
   And waving aloft !
Then, coming hideous
   On to the tide,
I spurn'd the perfidious
   Foam aside,
And follow'd her, dashing
   Thro' storm sublime,
Flashing, crashing,
Splashing-splashing
   On the seaweed's slippery slime !
The billows clomb up,
With flash of foam up,
   My loins and thighs ;
Till they gleâm'd and fleam'd,
   With clangor and anger,
And around me upstream'd
   With their wild white eyes !
Till panting, choking,
Dripping and soaking,
With nostrils smoking,
I halted, spitting,
   Spurting, chin-deep,
And saw her sitting
   Where gulls were flitting
   Far out on the deep ;
And all around her with gentle motion
One smooth soft part of the murmurous
   ocean
   Had gone to sleep !
Then waving her hands,
   And shaking her locks,
To the ocean sands,
   To the purple rocks
Under the foam,
   To the sea-caves brown,
She sank to her home,
   Down ! down ! down ! down !
And the sea grew black
   In her shining track,
   And the waters green
Darken'd afar ;
   And the one thing seen
Was the steadfast star
Of my round Eye red,
   Rolling immense
   With a pain intense
In my rocky head,
Mid the white foam wreathing
Around wind-led,
And the great sea scething

Down to deep breathing,
Like a monster panting, on its sandy bed !

SILENUS.

Most musical Cyclops !

POLYPHEME.

Hush !—Unto the beach
I wearily strode, with great head bow'd, and dragg'd
Foot-echoes after me ; and with no speech,
On yonder shore, weedy and wet and cragg'd,
I stood, and in an agony of pain
Look'd out with widening eyeball on the main.
Lo ! far away a white wind glided dim
O'er the cloud-cover'd bright'ning ocean-rim,
And violet shadows here and there were trail'd
Over the waters : then behold the sun
Flasht pale across the waste, and one by one,
Like sea-gulls dripping rain, rose ships white-sail'd.
All else was silence, save monotonous moan
Of the broad-chested billows, till the warm
Light kindled all things, and I, loomed alone—
The one huge cloud remaining of the storm ;
And in the awfulness of that strange hour
A change came over my big throbbing breast,
And the soft picture of the calm had power
To move my mountainous bulk with vague unrest !—

SILENUS.

Weep not, O Cyclops—lest thy tears should roll
Down oceanward and brain the grazing sheep !

POLYPHEME.

Ay me, ay me, the passion in my soul !
Ay me, her glory haunts me, and I weep !—
O, I would give away the world to be
As soft, as sweet, as fleecy-limb'd as she,
As tiny and as tender and as white
As her mild loveliness !
With two soft eyes such as mere men possess,
Two pretty little dewy eyes, that might
Interpret me aright !

SILENUS.

Amazement !—Polypheme, whom vast Poseidon
Spawn'd upon Thoosa in the salted brine,
Thou who canst strangle fleets, and sit astride on
Ætna and roar thine origin divine !
Wrong not thyself, thy beauty, and thy sire !
See ! where thy mighty shadow stretches wide
Down the steep mountain side,
And see ! that eyeball of immortal fire !
Had wanton Helen, Paris' love-sick toy,
Beheld thee, Polypheme,
Hill-haunting Echo had not found a theme
In ruin and the ten years' war of Troy !

POLYPHEME.

And is it so ?

SILENUS.

By Ganymede bright eyed,
By—by—

POLYPHEME.

Enough—let us return. I stood,
When she had flown, in meditative mood ;
Then, raising up my resinous hands, I cried:
' O thou from whose huge loins I darkling came,
King of all ocean and its wondrous races,
Return, return, the nymph to my embraces,
Or, thro' thy lips ooze-dripping, name her name !'
And o'er the sands did a low murmur creep,
Whispering ' Galatea ;' and, deep-pain'd,
I vaguely knew, like one who dreams in sleep,
She was a goddess of the sacred deep,
Not to be lightly woo'd or roughly gain'd.

SILENUS.

O pitiful ! and you—

POLYPHEME.

In the dim birth
Of the strange love that stirs my hid blood's fountains,
As unborn earthquakes trouble springs in mountains,
I look'd abroad upon the fair green earth ;
And lo, all things that lived, all things that stirr'd,
Unto the very daisy closing up
In my great shade its crimson-tippĕd cup,
And the small lambs, and every little bird
Seem'd to abhor and dread, avoid and fear me ;

E

And in an agony of hate for all,
I cried ' How can a thing so sweet, so small,
So gentle, love me—or be happy near me?'
Whereon I sadly clomb the cliffs and made
A looking-glass of yonder ocean, where
Startled by my long shade
The silver-bellied fishes rose afraid;
But with a lover's hand I smooth'd my hair
To sleekness, parting it with care,
And husht the rugged sorrow of my brow—
Then, stooping softly o'er the dimpled mirror,
I shaped my face to a sweet smile—as now I

SILENUS.

O agony ! help, help, ye gods ! O terror !
Hide me !

POLYPHEME.

What ails thee ? Ha !

SILENUS.

                O Ocean's child—
Cyclops ! My heart, with admiration rent,
Fainted and cried with its deep ravishment
Because you look'd so beauteous when you
    smiled !

POLYPHEME.

Thou liest !—and (ay me) you shrunk in fear
As silly younglings shrink at something
    hateful ;
Yet tremble not :—to a lorn lover's ear,
Ev'en flattery so base as thine is grateful.
Ay me, ay me—I am
A great sad mountain in whose depths doth
    roam
My small soul, wandering like a gentle lamb
That bleats from place to place and has no
    home;
But prison'd among rocks
Can just behold afar
A land where honey-flowing rivers are
And gentle shepherds with their gentle flocks:
For even so my timid soul looks round
On beauteous living things—that creep and
    seem,
To this vast Eye, like insects on the ground—
From whose companionship 'tis shut and
    bound
Within this mountain of a Polypheme !

SILENUS.

Most melancholy Cyclops, be consoled !

POLYPHEME.

My heart is like those blubbery crimson blots
That float on the dank tide in oozy spots ;
It is as mild as patient flocks in fold.
I am as lonely as the snowy peak
Of Dardanos, and, like an eagle, Love
Stoops o'er me, helpless, from its eyric above,
And grasps that lamb, my Soul, within its
    beak.
Nay, on the margin of the waters where
She comes and goes like a swift gull, I sit
Above these flocks, and rake my little wit
To pipe upon the misty mountain air
Ditties as tender as a shepherd man,
Perch'd on a little hillock, half asleep,
Surrounded by his silly stainless sheep,
Pipes with mild pleasure and no definite plan
In fields Arcadian.   [*He sings.*

    White is the little hand of Galatea,
        That combs her yellow locks with dainty
            care ;
    Bright is the fluttering hand of Galatea,
        When tangled, like a dove, in sunny
            hair.
    Sweet is Galatea—sweet is Galatea—
        Ay, so sweet !
    Complete is Galatea, from her feathery
        fingers fair
    To her small white mice of feet !
    The billows huge and hoar cease to rumble
        and to roar,
    When the white hands wave above them,
        like doves that shine and soar,
    And, as gentle, from the shore, I adore, and
        implore Galatea !

    Ho, that these limbs were meet for Galatea
        With soft pink kisses sweetly to enfold !
    Ho, had I two small eyes, that Galatea
        Might there my gentle gentle heart
            behold !
    Dear is Galatea—dear is Galatea—
        Ay, so dear !
    No peer has Galatea, but her bosom is so
        cold
        And her eyes so full of fear !
    When the great seas wildly rise, there is
        terror in her eyes,
    And she trembles in sweet wonder, like a
        bird that storms surprise,—
    And before my tender cries, and my sighs,
        swiftly flies Galatea !

Under the white sea-storm sits Galatea,
  While overhead the sea-birds scream in flocks,
In deep-green darkness sitteth Galatea,
  Combing out sunshine from her golden locks!
Fair sits Galatea—fair sits Galatea—
  Ay, so fair!
Ho, there sits Galatea, in the shade of purple rocks,
  Mid the fountain of her hair!
Ho, would I were the waves, on whose crest the tempest raves,
So might I still the tempest that my raging bulk outbraves,
For the dark-green stillness laves, and enslaves, and encaves Galatea!

SILENUS.

Comfort, O Cyclops, comfort! There is sure
Some remedy for such a wound as this:
Red wine, I say again: the plump God's kiss
Is sweeter far than honey, rich and pure.

POLYPHEME.

Alas, not he whose temples Artemis
Bound with weird herbs and poison-snakes that hiss
But sting not—wise Asclepios—could cure!
For evermore, Silenus, when my brain
Lies in a dream just conscious of its pain,
And my full heart throbs tenderly and rockingly,
Far out upon the bosom of the main
She flashes up, green-kirtled, and laughs mockingly.
Thrice has her smile enticed me to the chin
Thro' the great waves that round me bite and bark,
And gleam'd away and left me in the dark.
Alas, that I must woo and never win!
Alas that I am foul while she is fair!
Alas, that this red Eye, my only one,
Like a brown lizard looking on the sun,
Turns green in her bright mist of yellow hair!

SILENUS.

Majestic Cyclops! Heir of the huge Sea!
God-like,—like those great heavens that oversheen us!
One-eyed, like the bright Day! Wilt thou by me,
Thy servant, be advised?

POLYPHEME.
Speak on, Silenus.

SILENUS.
Behold!—Beneath the many-tinctured west hid,
Fades Phoibos crimson-crested,
And the faint image of his parting light
On the deep Sea broad-breasted
Fades glassily; while down the mountain height
Behind us, slides the purple shadow'd Night.
Come in!—and from your cellar iced by springs
Drag forth the god of wine,
And listen to him as he chirps and sings
His songs delicious, dulcet, and divine:
Throned in the brain, magnificently wise,
And blowing warmly out thro' kindled eyes
All vapours vapid, vague, and vain.
Seek the god's counsel, Cyclops, I beseech thee;
'Tis he alone, if once his magic reach thee,
Can cure Love's panting heat or shivering pain.

POLYPHEME.
He cannot make me fair!

SILENUS.
Phoo!—He will teach thee
To lift thy dreamy gaze from the soft sod,
And rise erect, big-hearted, self-reliant,
On Ætna's horn—with leathern lungs defiant—
No minnow-hearted grampus of a god!
And—then in the quick flush and exultation
Of that proud inspiration,
Wine in his nostrils, Polypheme will be
In Polypheme's own estimation
A match for any girl on land or sea.
Then, furiously, gloriously rash,
Grasp Opportunity, that, passing by
On the sheet-lightning with a moment's flash,
Haunts us for ever with its meteor eye;
And—grasp the thing thou pantest for in vain,
Ay, hold her fast, and for a space entreat her—
But, if she still be deaf to thy sad pain,
Why, hearken to the mad god in thy brain,
And make a meal of trouble—that is, eat her!

XI.
PENELOPE.

WHITHER, Ulysses, whither dost thou roam,
Rolled round with wind-led waves that render dark
The smoothly-spinning circle of the sea?
Lo, Troy has fallen, fallen like a tower,
And the mild sunshine of degenerate days
Sleeps faintly on its ruins. One by one,
Swift as the sparkle of a star, the ships
Have dipt up moistly from the under-world,
And plumëd warriors, standing in their prows,
Stretching out arms to wives and little ones
That crowd with seaward faces on the beach,
Have flung their armour off and leapt and swam
Ere yet the homeward keels could graze the sand.
And these—the gaunt survivors of thy peers—
Have landed, shone upon by those they love,
And faded into happy happy homes;
While I, the lonely woman, hugging close
The comfort of thine individual fame,
Still wait and yearn and wish towards the sea;
And all the air is hollow of my joy:
The seasons come and go, the hour-glass runs,
The day and night come punctual as of old;
But thy deep strength is in the solemn dawn,
And thy proud step is in the plumëd noon,
And thy grave voice is in the whispering eve;
And all the while, amid this dream of thee,
In restless resolution oceanward,
I sit and ply my sedentary task,
And fear that I am lonelier than I know.

Yea, love, I am alone in all the world,
The past grows dark upon me where I wait,
With eyes that hunger seaward and a cheek
Grown like the sampler coarse-complexionëd.
For in the shadow of thy coming home
I sit and weave a weary housewife's web,
Pale as the silkworm in the cone; all day
I sit and weave this weary housewife's web,
And in the night with fingers swift as frost
Unweave the weary labour of the day.
Behold how I am mock'd!—Suspicion
Mumbles my name between his toothless gums;
And while I ply my sedentary task,
They come to me, mere men of hollow clay,
Gross-mouth'd and stain'd with wine they come to me,
And whisper odious comfort, and upbraid
The love that follows thee where'er thou art,
That follows, and perchance, with thy mo'st cheek,
Dips on the dozy bottom of the world.
They come, Ulysses, and they seek to rob
Thy glory of its weaker wearier half.
They tell me thou art dead; nay, they have brought
To these cold ears that bend above the web
Whispers that thou, no wiser than thy peers,
Hast pluckt upon the windy plain of Troy
A flower thou shrinest in a distant land,
A chamber'd delicacy drowsy-eyed,
Pink-lidded, wanton, like the queen who wit :h'd
The fatal apple out of Paris' palm.

And I—and I—ah me, I rise my height,
In matron majesty that melts in tears,
And chide them from me with a tongue that long
Hath lost the trick of chiding: what avails?
They heed me not, rude men, they heed me not;
And he thou leftest here to guard me well,
He, the old man, is helpless, and his eyes
Are yellow with the money-minting lie
That thou art dead. O husband, what avails?
They gather on me, till the sense grows cold
And huddles in upon the steadfast heart;
And they have dragged a promise from my lips
To choose a murderer of my love for thee,
To choose at will from out the rest one man
To slay me with his kisses in the dark,
Whene'er the weary web at which I work
Be woven: so, all day, I weave the web;
And in the night with fingers like a thief's
Unweave the silken sorrow of the day.

The years wear on. Telemachus, thy son,
Grows sweetly to the height of all thy hope:
More woman-like than thee, less strong of limb,
Yet worthy thee; and likest thy grave mood,

When, in old time, among these fields, thine
  eye
Would kindle on a battle far away,
And thy proud nostrils, drinking the mild
  breath
Of tanned haycocks and of slanted sheaves,
Swell suddenly, as if a trumpet spake.
Hast thou forgotten how of old he loved
To toy with thy great beard, and sport with
  thee,
And how, in thy strong grasp, he leapt and
  seem'd
A lambkin dandled in a lion's paw?
But change hath come, Troy is an old wife's
  tale,
And sorrow stealeth early on thy son,
Whom sojourn with my weeping woman-
  hood
Hath taught too soon a young man's gentle-
  ness.
Behold now, how his burning boy-face turns
With impotent words beyond all blows of
  arm
On those rude men that rack thy weary wife !
Then turns to put his comfort on my cheek,
While sorrow brightens round him—as the
  grey
Of heaven melts to silver round a star !

Return, Ulysses, ere too late, too late :
Return, immortal warrior, return :
Return, return, and end the weary web !
For day by day I look upon the sea
And watch each ship that dippeth like a gull
Across the long straight line afar away
Where heaven and ocean meet ; and when
  the winds
Swoop to the waves and lift them by the hair,
And the long storm-roar gathers, on my
  knees
I pray for thee. Lo, even now, the deep
Is garrulous of thy vessel tempest-tost ;
And on the treeless upland gray-eyed March,
With blue and humid mantle backward
  blown,
Plucks the first primrose in a blustering
  wind.
The keels are wheel'd unto the ocean sand
And eyes look outward for the homeward
  bound.
And not a marinere, or man or boy,
Scum'd and salt-blooded from the boisterous
  sea,
Touches these shores, but straight I summon
  him,
And bribe with meat and drink to tell good
  news,
And question him of thee. But what avails?
Thou wanderest ; and my love sits all alone
Upon the threshold of an empty hall.

My very heart has grown a timid mouse,
Peeping out, fearful, when the house is still.
Breathless I listen thro' the breathless dark,
And hear the cock counting the leaden hours,
And, in the pauses of his cry, the deep
Swings on the flat sand with a hollow clang ;
And, pale and burning-eyed, I fall asleep
When, with wild hair, across the weary wave
Stares the sick Dawn that brings thee not
  to me.

Ulysses, come ! Ere traitors leave the
  mark
Of spread wine-dripping fingers on the
  smooth
And decent shoulders that now stoop for
  thee !
I am not young or happy as of old,
When, awed by thy male strength, my face
  grew dark
At thy grave footfall, with a serious joy,
Or when, with blushing backward-looking
  face,
I came a bride to thine inclement realm,
Trembling and treading fearfully on flowers.
I am not young and beauteous as of old ;
And much I fear that when we meet thy face
May startle darkly at the work of years,
And turn to hide a disappointed pang,
And then, with thy grave pride, subdue itself
Into such pity as is love stone-dead.
But thou, thou too, art old, dear lord—thy
  hair
Is threaded with the silver foam—thy heart
Is weary from the blows of cruel years ;
And there is many a task thy wife can do
To soothe thy sunset season and make calm
Thy journey down the slow descent to Sleep.

Return, return, Ulysses, ere I die !
Upon this desolate, desolate strand I wait,
Wearily stooping o'er the weary web—
An alabaster woman, whose fix'd eyes
Stare seaward, whether it be storm or calm,
And ever, evermore, as in a dream,

I see thee gazing hither from thy ship
In sunset regions where the still seas rot,
And stretching out great arms whose
   shadows fall
Gigantic on the glassy purple sea ;
And ever, evermore, thou lingerest,
And evermore thy coming far away
Aches on the burning heartstrings,—ever-
   more
Thou comest not, and I am tired and old.

XII.
SAPPHO:
ON THE LEUCADIAN ROCK.

1.

O sweet, sweet, sweet!
While the Moon, with her dove's eyes fair,
And her beautiful yellow hair,
   And the Sea-Snake coiling round her sil-
      vern feet,
Walk'd dumbly up above in the jewell'd air
   Waving her luminous wings,
To sit upon this crag above the sea
Clasp'd close, so close, to thee,
   Pale with much yearning, while the mur-
      murings
Of the great waters seem'd to waft to me
   The name of Phaon,
   To whisper Phaon, Phaon,
Phaon, Phaon, Phaon, with deep intonin ,
   Hushfully, hushfully moaning !

2.

O bliss, bliss, bliss !
Though the Moon look'd pale in the sky,
On thy passionate heart to lie,
   To cling to thy burning lips with kiss on
      kiss,
Faintly watching the butterfly stars swim by
   In the track of that queenly Moon ;
And in a dream, clasp'd close, so close, to
   thee,
To list and seem to be
   A portion of the faint monotonous tune
Made for its mistress by the serpent sea,
   That whisper'd Phaon,
   Phaon, Phaon, Phaon,
Phaon, Phaon, Phaon, while Dian darken-
   ing
   Stoop'd hushfully, hushfully, harkening !

3.

O pain, pain, pain !
While the Moon, in a sky as clear
As of old, walks on, and I hear
   Her palpitating foot on the living main,
While, under her feet, the green sea-snake
   creeps near
   Hissing with scales that gleam,
To stand upon this crag beside the sea
And dream, and dream, of thee—
   With clench'd white hands, set teeth, and
      robes that stream
Behind me in the wind, while audibly
   The waves moan Phaon,
   Shriek Phaon, Phaon, Phaon,
Phaon, Phaon, Phaon, with deep intoning,
   Mournfully, mournfully, moaning !

4.

O rest, rest, rest !—
While the Moon with her virgin light
Thro' eternities of night
   Dumbly paces on to the east from the
      west,—
To mingle with the waves that under the
   height
   Murmur along the shore,
To mix my virgin love, my agony,
Into the serpent sea
   That Dian seeks to silence evermore,
To cling to those white skirts and moan of
   thee,
   O Phaon, Phaon,
   Restless for love of Phaon,
Phaon, Phaon, Phaon, with ceaseless motion
   Soothed by the soother of Ocean !

XIII.
THE SYREN.

AH, kiss me, Sweetest, while on yellow sand
   ' Murmurs the breaking billow,
And smoothe my silken ringlets with thy
   hand,
   And make my breast thy pillow ;
And clasp me, Dearest, close to lip and cheek
   And bosom softly sighing,
While o'er the green sea, in one orange streak,
   The summer day is dying !
Kiss, kiss, as one that presses to his mouth
   A vine-bunch bursting mellow,

In this lone islet of the sleepy south
  Fringëd with smooth sands yellow :
A twilight of fresh leaves endusks us round,
  Flowers at our feet are springing,
And wave on wave breaks smoothly to the sound
  Of my sweet singing !

EUMOLPUS.

Is it the voice of mine own Soul I hear?
  Or some white sybil of the spherëd ocean?
And are these living limbs that lie so near,
  Stirring around me with a serpent-motion?
Is this a tress of yellow yellow hair,
  Around my finger in a ring enfolden?
Whose face is this, so musically fair,
  That swoons upon my ken thro' vapours golden?
What sad song withers on the odorous air?
  Where am I, where?
Where is my country and that vision olden?

THE SYREN.

I sang thee hither in thy bark to land
  With deftly warbled measure,
I wove a witch's spell with fluttering hand,
  Till thou wert drunken, Dearest, with much pleasure.
At hush of noon I had thee at my knee,
  And round thy finger pink I wound a curl,
And singing smiled beneath with teeth of pearl,
Of what had been, what was, and what should be
  Sang dying ditties three !
And lo ! thy blood was ravish'd with the theme,
And lo ! thy face was pale with drowsy dream,
While stooping low, with rich lips tremulous,
  I kiss thee thus !—and thus !

EUMOLPUS.

Thy kisses trance me to a vision wan
  Of what hath been and neverm re will be.
O little fishing-town Sicilian,
  I can behold thee sitting by the sea !
O little red-tiled town where I was born !
  O days ere yet I sail'd from mortal ken !
Why did I launch upon the deep forlorn,
  Nor fish in shallow pools with simple men?
It was a charm ; for while I rockt at ease
  Within our little bay,
There came a melody across the seas
  From regions far away ;
And ah ! I fell into a swooning sleep,
  And all the world had changed before I knew,—
And I awoke upon a glassy deep
  With not a speck of land to break the view,
And tho' I was alone, I did not weep,
  For I was singing too !
I sang ! I sang ! and with mine oars kept time
  Unto the rude sweet rhyme,
And went a-sailing on into the west
  Blown on by airs divine,
Singing for ever on a wild-eyed quest
  For that immortal minstrel feminine ;
And night and day went past, until I lost
  All count of time, yet still did melodise ;
. And sun and stars beheld me from their skies ;
And ships swam by me, from whose decks storm-tost
  Rude seamen gazed with terror-glazëd eyes.
And still I found not her for whom I sought,
  Yet smiled without annoy,
To ply the easy oar, and take no thought,
  And sing, was such sweet joy !—
Then Tempest came, and to and from the sky
  I rose and fell in that frail bark of mine,
While the snake Lightning, with its blank bright eye,
  Writhed fierily in swift coils serpentine
  Along the slippery brine ;
And there were days when dismal sobbing Rain
  Made melancholy music for the brain,
And hours when I shriek'd out and wept in woe
  Prison'd about by chilly still affright,
While all around dropt hushëd flakes of Snow
  Melting and mingling down blue chasms of night.
Yet evermore, I heard that voice sublime
  Twining afar its weirdly woven song,
And ev r, ever more, mine oars kept time,
  And evermore I utterëd in song
  My yearnings sad or merry, faint or strong.
Ah me ! my love for her afar away,
  My yearning and my burning night and day !
In dreams alone, I met her in still lands,
  And knelt in tears before her,
And could not sing, but only wring mine hands,
  Adore her and implore her !

She glisten'd past me as a crane that sails
Above the meeting of the ocean-gales,
  With waft of broad slow wing to regions new;
And tho' I follow'd her from place to place,
She held her veil dew-spangled to her face,
  And I could merely feel her eyes of blue
    Steadfastly gazing thro'!
Wherefore my heart had broken quite,—but then
I would awake again,—
To see the oily water steep'd in rest
  While, glistering in many-colour'd flakes
Harming me not, lay brooding on its breast
  Leviathan and all the ocean-snakes,
And on the straight faint streak afar the round
  Moist eye of morning lookt thro' dewy air,
And all was still, a joyous calm profound,—
And I would break the charm with happy sound
    To find the world so fair!
And lo! I drank the rain-drops and was glad,
  And smote the bird of ocean down and ate;
And ocean harm'd me not, and monsters sad
  That people ocean and the desolate
Abysses spared me,—charm'd by the song
  warbled wildly as I went along.
Yet day and night sped on, and I grew old
  Before I knew; and lo!
My hands were wither'd, on my bosom cold
  There droopt a beard of snow,—
And raising hands I shriek'd, I cried a curse
  On that weird voice that twinëd me from home;
And echoes of the awful universe
  Answer'd me; and the deep with lips of foam
Mock'd me and spat upon me; and the things
  That people ocean rose and threaten'd ill,
Yea also air-born harpies waving wings,
  Because I could not sing to charm them still.
I was alone, the shadow of a man,
  Haunting the trackless waste of waves forlorn,
Blown on by pitiless rains and vapours wan,
Plaining for that small town Sicilian,
  Where, in the sweet beginning, I was born!

THE SYREN.

Ah, weep not, Dearest! lean upon my breast,
  While sunset darkens stilly,
And Dian poises o'er the slumberous west
  Her silver sickle chilly;
The eyes of heaven are opening, the leaves
  Fold dark and dewy round the closing roses,
In lines of foam the breaking billow heaves,
  Each thing that gladdens and each thing that grieves
    Dip slow to sweet reposes.

EUMOLPUS.

O voice that lured me on, I know thee now!
  O melancholy eyes, how bright ye beam!
O kiss, thy touch is dewy on my brow!
  Sweet Spirit of my dream!

THE SYREN.

Name thy love, and I am she,
Name thy woe, and look on me,
Name the weary melody
That led thee hither o'er the sea,—
Then call to mind my ditties three
Of what hath been, what is, and what shall be!

EUMOLPUS.

Ah woe! ah woe!
I see thee and I clasp thee, and I know!
Sing to me, Sweetest, while the shadows grow—
    Sing low! sing low!
Oh, sweet were slumber now, at last, at last,
For I am sick of wandering to and fro,
And ah! my singing-days are nearly pass'd—
    Sing low! sing low! sing low!

THE SYREN.

Love with wet cheek, Joy with red lips apart,
  Hope with her blue eyes dim from looking long,
Ambition with thin hand upon his heart—
    Of which shall be the song?
Of one, of one,
Who loved till life was done,
  For life with him was loving, tho' she slew
    his love with wrong.
Then, on a winter day,
When all was lost and his young brow was gray,
He knelt before an Altar pilëd proud
With bleachëd bones and fruits and garlands gay,
    And cried aloud:—

'Have I brought Joy, and slain her at thy feet?
Have I brought Peace, for thy cold kiss to kill,
Have I brought Youth crownèd with wild-flowers sweet,
With sandals dewy from a morning hill,
For thy gray solemn eyes to fright and chill?
Have I brought Scorn the pale and Hope the fleet,
And First-Love in her lily winding-sheet?
And art thou pitiless still?
O Poesy, thou nymph of fire,
Grandest of that fair quire
Which in the dim beginning stoop'd and fell,—
So beauteous yet so awful, standing tall
Upon the mountain-tops where mortals dwell,
Seeing strange visions of the end of all,
And pallid from the white-heat glare of Hell!
Is there no prophecy, far-seeing one,
To seal upon these lips that yearn to sing?
Can nought be gain'd again? can nought be won?
Is there no utterance in this suffering,
Is there no voice for any human thing?'
Then, smiling in the impotence of pain,
His sweet breath at the Altar did he yield,—
While she he loved, afar across the main,
Stoop'd down to break a weary people's chain,
And crown a hero on a battle-field!

EUMOLPUS.

Ah no! ah no!
So sad a theme is too much woe!
Sing to me sweetlier, since thou lovest me so—
Sing low; sing low!

THE SYREN.

Sisters we, the syrens three,
Fame and Love and Poesy!
In the solitude we sit,
On the mountain-tops we flit,
From the islands of the sea
Luring man with melody;
Sisters three we seem to him
Foating over waters dim,—
Syrens, syrens three, are we—
Fame and Love and Poesy!

EUMOLPUS.

Ah woe! ah woe!
That is the song I heard so long ago!
That is the song
That lured me long:
Those were the three I saw, with arms of snow
And ringlets waving yellow, beckoning,
While on the violet deep I floated slow,
With little heart to sing;
And lo! they faded as I leapt to land,
And their weird music wither'd on the air,
And I was lying drowsy on the sand
Smiling and toying with thy yellow hair!

THE SYREN.

Sisters we, the syrens three,
Fame and Love and Poesy,
Sitting singing in the sun,
While the weary marinere
Passes on or faints in fear,—
Sisters three, yet only one,
When he cometh near!
Charmèd sight and charmèd sound
Hover quietly around,
Mine are dusky bowers and deep,
Closèd lids and balmy sleep,
Kisses cool for fever'd cheeks and warmth for eyes that weep!

EUMOLPUS.

Sing low! sing low!
Thou art more wondrous fair than mortals know.
Bringest thou, Beautiful, or peace or woe?
Close up each eyelid with a warm rich kiss
And let me listen while the sunlights go.
I cannot bear a time so still as this,
Unbroken by thy voice's fall and flow.
Sing to me, Beautiful! Sing low, sing low, sing low!

THE SYREN.

Love with wet cheek, Joy with red lips apart,
Hope with her blue eyes dim from looking long,
Ambition with thin hand upon his heart—
Of which shall be the song?
Ah, woe! ah, woe!
For Love is dead and wintry winds do blow.
Yea, Love is dead; and by her funeral bier
Ambition gnaws the lip and sheds no tear;

And in the outer chamber Hope sits wild,
  Watching the faces in the fire and weeping;
And at the threshold Joy the little child
  With rosy cheeks runs leaping,
And stops,—while in the misty distance
    creeping
Down western hills the large red sun sinks
    slow—
To see Death's footprints on the still white
    snow.
Ah, Love has gone, and all the rest must go.
  Sing low! sing low! sing low!

        EUMOLPUS.

It is a song that slays me. Sing no more.

        THE SYREN.

Ah, Sweet, the song is o'er!—
The ocean-hum is hush'd, 'tis end of day,
  The long white foam fades faintly,
The orange sunset dies into the gray
  Where star on star swims saintly.
Hast thou not sung? and is not song enough?
  Hast thou not loved? and is not loving all?
Art thou not weary of the wayfare rough,
  Or is there aught of life thou wouldst recall?
Ah no, ah no!
The life came sweetly—sweetly let it go!
  Mine are dusky bowers and deep,
  Closèd eyes and balmy sleep,
Kisses cool for fever'd cheeks and warmth
  for eyes that weep!

        EUMOLPUS.

Thou art the gentle witch that men call
    Death!
Ah, Beauteous, I am weary, and would
    rest!

        THE SYREN.

Lie very softly, Sweet, and let thy breath
  Fade calmly on my breast!
  Call me Love or call me Fame,
    Call me Death or Poesy,
  Call me by whatever name
    Seemeth sweetest unto thee:—
I anoint thee, I caress thee;
With my dark reposes bless thee,
I redeem thee, I possess thee!
I can never more forsake thee!
  Slumber, slumber, peacefully,
  Slumber calm and dream of me,
Till I touch thee, and awake thee!

        EUMOLPUS.

Diviner far than song divine can tell!
Thine eyes are dim with dreams of that
    awaking!
Yea, let me slumber, for my heart is
    breaking
With too much love. Farewell! farewell!
    farewell!

        THE SYREN.

Charmèd sight and charmèd sound
  Close the weary one around!
  Charmèd dream of charmèd sleep
Make his waiting sweet and deep!
  Husht be all things! Let the spell
  Duskly on his eyelids dwell!

        EUMOLPUS.

Farewell! farewell! farewell!

        THE SYREN.

O melancholy waters, softly flow!
  O Stars, shine softly, dropping dewy
    balm!
O Moon walk on in sandals white as snow!
  O Winds, be calm, be calm!
For he is tired with wandering to and fro,
  Yea, weary with unrest to see and know.
    O charmèd sound
    That hoverest around!
O voices of the Night! Sing low! sing low!
    sing low!

XIV.

A VOICE FROM ACADEME.

OVER this azure poplar glade
The sunshine, fainting high above,
Ebbs back from woolly clouds that move
Like browsing lambs and cast no shade;
And straight before me, faintly seen
Thro' emerald boughs that intervene,
The visible sun turns white and weaves
Long webs of silver thro' the leaves.
The grassy sward beneath my foot
Is soft as lips of lambs and beeves.
How cool those harebells at the root
Of yonder tree, that dimly dance
Thro' dews of their own radiance!

Yonder I see the river run,
Half in the shade, half in the sun;

And as I near its shallow brink
The sparkling minnows, where they lie
With silver bellies to the sky,
Flash from me in a shower and sink.
I stand in shadows cool and sweet,
But in the mirror at my feet
The heated azure heavens wink.

All round about this shaded spot,
Whither the sunshine cometh not,
Where all is beautiful repose—
I know the kindled landskip glows;
And further, flutter golden showers
On proud Athenai white with towers,
And catching from the murmurous sea,
[Stain'd with deep shadows as of flowers
And dark'ning down to purple bowers
Thro' which the sword-fish darts in glee,]
A strife that cometh not to me.

For in this place of shade and sound,
Hid from the garish heat around,
I feel like one removed from strain
And fever of the happy brain—
Where thoughts thrill fiery into pain:
Like one who, in the pleasant shade
The peaceful pulseless dead have made,
Walking in silence, just perceives
The gaudy world from which he went
Subdue itself to his content,
Like that white globe beyond the leaves!

XV.
PYGMALION THE SCULPTOR.
Materiem superabat opus.

1. SHADOW.

UPON the very morn I should have wed
Death put his silence in a mourning house;
And, coming fresh from feast, I saw her lie
In stainless marriage samite, white and cold,
With orange blossoms in her hair, and gleams
Of the ungiven kisses of the bride
Playing about the edges of her lips.

Then I, Pygmalion, kiss'd her as she slept,
And drew my robe across my face whereon
The midnight revel' linger'd dark, and pray'd;
And the sore trouble hollow'd out my heart
To hatred of a harsh unhallow'd youth
As I glode forth. Next, day by day, my soul
Grew conscious of itself and of its fief
Within the shadow of her grave: therewith,
Waken'd a thirst for silence such as dwells
Under the ribs of death: whence slowly grew
Old instincts that had tranced me to tears
In mine unsinew'd boyhood, sympathies
Full of faint odours and of music faint
Like buds of roses blowing;—till I felt
Her voice come down from heaven on my soul,
And stir it as a wind that droppeth down
Unseen, unfelt, unheard, until its breath
Troubles the shadows in a sleeping lake.

And the voice said, 'Pygmalion,' and 'Behold,'
I answer'd, 'I am here;' when thus the voice:
'Put men behind thee—take thy tools, and choose
A block of marble white as is a star,
Cleanse it and make it pure, and fashion it
After mine image: heal thyself: from grief
Comes glory, like a rainbow from a cloud.
For surely life and death, which dwell apart
In grosser human sense, conspire to make
The breathless beauty and eternal joy
Of sculptured shapes in stone. Wherefore thy life
Shall purify itself and heal itself
In the long toil of love made meek by tears.'

I barr'd the entrance-door to this my tower
Against the hungry world, I hid above
The mastiff-murmur of the town, I pray'd
In my pale chamber. Then I wrought, and chose
A rock of marble white as is a star,
And to her silent image fashion'd clay,
And purified myself and heal'd myself
In the long toil of love made meek by tears.

2. THE MARBLE LIFE.

THE multitudinous light oppress'd me not,
But smiled subdued, as a young mother smiles,
When fearful lest the sunbeam of the smile
Trouble the eyelids of the babe asleep.

As Ocean murmurs when the storm is past
And keeps the echoed thunders many days,

My solitude was troublous for a time:
Wherefore I should have harden'd; but the
   clay
Grew to my touch, and brighten'd, and
   assumed
Fantastic images of natural things,
Which, melting as the fleecy vapours melt
Around the shining cestus of the moon,
Made promise of the special shape I loved.
Withdrawing back, I gazed. The unshaped
   stone
Took outline in the dusk, as rocks unhewn
Seen from afar thro' floating mountain mists
Gather strange forms and human lineaments.
And thus mine eye was filled with what I
   sought
As with a naked image, thus I grew
Self-credulous of the form the stone would
   wear,
And creeping close I strove to fashion clay
After the vision. Day and night, I drew
New comfort from my grief; my tears became
As honey'd rain that makes the woodbine
   sweet,
Until my task assumed a precious strength
Wherewith I fortified mine inner ear
Against the pleadings of the popular tongue
That babbled at my door; and when there
   dawn'd
A hand as pure as milk and cold as snow,
A small white hand, a little radiant hand,
That peep'd out perfect from the changing
   mass,
And seem'd a portion of some perfect shape
Unfreed, imprison'd in the stone,—I wept
Warm tears of utter joy, and kiss'd the
   hand,
As sweet girl-mothers kiss the newly born,
Weak as a mother. Then I heard no more
The murmurous swarm beneath me, women
   and men;
But, hoarded in my toil, I counted not
The coming and the going of the sun:
Save when I swoon'd to sleep before the
   stone,
And dream'd, and dreaming saw the perfect
   shape
Emblazon'd, like the rainbow in a stream,
On the transparent tapestry of sleep.

   Ah me, the joy, the glory, and the dream,
When like a living wonder senseless stone
Smiles to the beating of a heart that hangs
Suspended in the tumult of the blood!
To the warm touch of my creating hand
The marble was as snow; and like the snow
Whereon the molten sunshine gleams as
   blood,
It soften'd, glow'd, and changed. As one
   who stands
Beneath the cool and rustling dark to watch
The shadow of his silently beloved
Cross o'er the lighted cottage blind and feel
The brightness of the face he cannot see,
So stood I, trembling, while the shape
   unborn
Darken'd across the white and milky mass
And left the impress of its loveliness
To glorify and guide me. As I wrought
The Past came back upon me, like the ghost
Of the To-Come. Whate'er was pure and
   white,
Soft-shining with a snow-like chastity,
Came back from childhood, and from that
   dim land
Which lies behind the horizon of the sense,
Felt though forgotten; vanishings divine
Of the strange vapours many-shaped and fair
Which moisten sunrise when the eye of
   heaven
Openeth dimly from the underworld:
Faint instincts of the helpless babe that
   smiles
At the sweet pictures in its mother's eyes
And lieth with a halo round its head
Of beauty uncompleted: memories
Of young Love's vivid heaven-enthronèd
   light,
By whose moist rays the pensive soul of
   youth
Was troubled at the fountains, like a well
Wherein the mirror'd motion of a star
Lies dewy and deep;—and, amid all, there
   dwelt
A vaguer glory, deeper sense of power,
Scarce conscious of itself yet ruling all,
Like the hid heart which rocks the jaded
   blood,
Brightens the cheek, throbs music to the
   brain.
Yet dwells within the breast scarce recog-
   nised,
Save when our pulses warn us and in fear
We pause to listen.—Even so at times
Those visions tranced me to a dumb dismay,
And, sudden music thronging in mine ears,

I hearken'd for that central loveliness
Whose magic guided and created all.

Then languor balmier than the blood i'
      the veins
When youth and maiden mingle and the
      moon
Breathes on the odorous room wherein they
      lie
Chamber'd as in a folded rose's leaves,
Oppress'd me, and a lover's rapture fill'd
My soul to swooning. Lo, I kiss'd the stone,
And toy'd with the cold hand, and look'd
      for light
In the dim onward-looking marble eyes,
And smooth'd the hair until it seem'd to
      grow
Soft as the living ringlets tingling warm
Against a heaving bosom. At her feet
I knelt, and tingled to the finger-tips
To gaze upon her breathless loveliness—
Like one who, shuddering, gazes on a shrine
From human eyes kept holy,
                          Then at last
Fair-statured, noble, like an awful thing
Frozen upon the very verge of life,
And looking back along eternity
With rayless eyes that keep the shadow
      Time,
She rose before me in the milky stone,
White-limb'd, immortal; and I gazed and
      gazed
Like one that sees a vision, and in awe
Half hides his face, yet looks, and seems to
      dream.

3. THE SIN.

BLUE night. I threw the lattice open wide,
Drinking the odorous air; and from my
      height
I saw the watch-fires of the town and heard
The gradual dying of the murmurous day.
Then, as the twilight deepen'd, on her limbs
The silver lances of the stars and moon
Were shatter'd, and the shining fragments
      fell
Resplendent at her feet. The Cyprian star
Quiver'd to liquid emerald where it hung
On the ribb'd ledges of the darkening hills,
Gazing upon her; and, as in a dream,
Methought the marble, underneath that
      look,
Stirr'd—like a bank of stainless asphodels
Kiss'd into tumult by a wind of light.

Whereat there swam upon me utterly
A drowsy sense wherein my holy dream
Was melted, as a pearl in wine: bright-eyed,
Keen, haggard, passionate, with languid
      thrills
Of insolent unrest, I watch'd the stone,
And lo, I loved it: not as men love fame,
Not as the warrior loves his laurel wreath,
But with prelusion of a passionate joy
That threw me from the height whereon I
      stood
To grasp at Glory, and in impiousness
Of sweet communing with some living Soul
Chamber'd in that cold bosom. As I gazed,
There was a buzz of revel in mine ears,
And tinkling fragments of a song of love,
Warbled by wantons over wine-cups, swam
Wildly within the brain.—Then I was
      shamed
By her pale beauty, and I scorn'd myself,
And standing at the lattice dark and cool
Watch'd the dim winds of twilight enter in,
And draw a veil about that loveliness
White, dim, and breathed on by the common
      air.

But, like a snake's moist eye, the dewy star
Of lovers drew me; and I watched it grow
Large, soft, and tremulous; and as I gazed
In fascinated impotence of heart,
I pray'd the lifeless silence might assume
A palpable life, and soften into flesh,
And be a beautiful and human joy
To crown my love withal; and thrice the
      prayer
Blacken'd across my pale face with no word.
But thro' the woolly silver of a cloud
The cool star dripping emerald from the
      baths
Of Ocean brighten'd in upon my tower,
And touch'd the marble forehead with a
      gleam
Soft, green, and dewy; and I said 'the prayer
Is heard!'
            The live-long night, the breathless
      night
I waited in a darkness, in a dream,
Watching the snowy figure faintly seen,
And ofttimes shuddering when I seem'd to
      see

Life, like a taper burning in a skull,
Gleam thro' the rayless eyes : yea, wearily
I hearken'd thro' the dark and seem'd to hear
The low warm billowing of a living breast,
Or the slow motion of anointed limbs
New-stirring into life ; and, shuddering,
Fearing the thing I hoped for, awful eyed,
On her cold breast I placed a hand as cold
And sought a fluttering heart.—But all was still,
And chill, and breathless ; and she gazed right on
With rayless orbs, nor marvell'd at my touch:
White, silent, pure, ineffable, a shape
Rebuking human hope, a deathless thing,
Sharing the wonder of the Sun who sends
His long bright look thro' all futurity.

When Shame lay heavy on me, and I hid
My face, and almost hated her, my work,
Because she was so fair, so human fair,
Yea not divinely fair as that pure face
Which, when mine hour of loss and travail came,
Haunted me, out of heaven. Then the Dawn
Stared in upon her : when I open'd eyes,
And saw the gradual Dawn encrimson her
Like blood that blush'd within her,—and behold
She trembled—and I shriek'd !
                With haggard eyes,
I gazed on her, my fame, my work, my love !
Red sunrise mingled with the first bright flush
Of palpable life—she trembled, stirr'd, and sigh'd—
And the dim blankness of her stony eyes
Melted to azure. Then, by slow degrees,
She tingled with the warmth of living blood :
Her eyes were vacant of a seeing soul,
But dewily the bosom rose and fell,
The lips caught sunrise, parting, and the breath
Fainted thro' pearly teeth.
                I was as one
Who gazes on a goddess serpent-eyed,
And cannot fly, and knows to look is death.
O apparition of my work and wish !
The weight of awe oppress'd me, and the air
Swung as the Seas swing around drowning men.

4. Death in Life.

About her brow the marble hair had clung
With wavy tresses, in a simple knot
Bound up and braided ; but behold, her eyes
Droop'd downward, as she wonder'd at herself,
Then flush'd to see her naked loveliness,
And trembled; stooping downward ; and the hair
Unloosening fell, and brighten'd as it fell,
Till gleaming ringlets tingled to the knees
And cluster'd round about her where she stood
As yellow leaves around a lily's bud,
Making a fountain round her such as clips
A Naiad in the sunshine, pouring down
And throwing moving shadows o'er the floor
Whereon she stood and brighten'd.
                          Wondering eyed,
With softly heaving breast and outstretch'd arms,
Slow as an eyeless man who gropes his way,
She thrust a curving foot and touch'd the ground,
And stirr'd ; and, downcast-lidded, saw not me.
Then as the foot descended with no sound,
The whole live blood grew pink within the veins
For joy of its own motion. Step by step,
She paced the chamber, groping till she gain'd
One sunlight-slip that thro' the curtain'd pane
Crept slant—a gleaming line on wall and floor ;
And there, in light, she pausing sunn'd herself
With half-closed eyes ; while flying gleams of gold
Sparkled like flies of fire among her hair,
And the live blood show'd brightlier, as wine
Gleams thro' a curd-white cup of porcelain.

   There, stirring not, she paused and sunn'd herself,
With drooping eyelids that grew moist and warm,
What time, withdrawn into the further dark,
I watch'd her, nerveless, as a murderer stretch'd
Under a nightmare of the murder'd man.

And still she, downcast-lidded, saw me not ;
But gather'd glory while she sunn'd herself,
Drawing deep breath of gladness such as
 earth
Breathes dewily in the sunrise after rain.

Then pray'd I, lifting up my voice aloud,
'O apparition of my work and wish !
Thou most divinely fair as she whose face
Haunted me, out of heaven ! Raise thine
 eyes !
Live, love, as thou and I have lived and
 loved !
Behold me—it is I—Pygmalion.
Speak, Psyche, with thy human eyes and
 lips,
Speak, to Pygmalion, with thy human soul !'

And still she, downcast-lidded, saw me not,
But gather'd glory as she sunn'd herself.
Yet listen'd murmuring inarticulate speech,
Listen'd with ear inclined and fluttering lids,
As one who lying on a bed of flowers
Hearkeneth to the distant fall of waves,
That cometh muffled in the drowsy hum
Of bees pavilion'd among roses' leaves
Near to the ears that listen. So she stood
And listen'd to my voice, framing her lips
After the speech; nay, when the sound had
 ceased,
Still listen'd, with a shadow on her cheek—
Like the Soul's Music, when the Soul has
 fled,
Fading upon a dead Musician's face.

But, stooping in mine awe, with out-
 stretch'd arms,
I crept to her ; nor stirr'd she, till my breath
Was warm upon her neck : then raised she
 eyes
Of dewy azure, ring in ring of blue
Less'ning in passionate orbs whereon my
 face
Fell white with yearning wonder ; when a
 cry
Tore her soft lips apart, the gleaming orbs
Widen'd to silvery terror, and she fled,
With yellow locks that shone and arms that
 waved,
And in the further darkness cower'd and
 moan'd,
Dumb as a ringdove that with fluttering
 wings
Watches a serpent in the act to spring.

What follow'd was a strange and wondrous
 dream
Wherein, half conscious, wearily and long
I wooed away her fears with gentle words,
Smooth gestures, and sweet smiles,—with
 kindness such
As calms the terror of a new-yean'd lamb,
So pure, it fears its shadow on the grass ;
And all the while thick pulses of my heart
Throng'd hot in ears and eyelids,—for my
 Soul
Seem'd swooning, deaden'd in the sense,
 like one
Who sinks in snows, and sleeps, and wakes
 no more.

Yet was I conscious of a hollow void,
A yearning in the tumult of the blood,
Her presence fill'd not, quell'd not ; and I
 search'd
Her eyes for meanings that they harbour'd
 not,
Her face for beauty that disturb'd it not.
'Twas Psyche's face, and yet 'twas not her
 face,
A face most fair, yet not so heavenly fair,
As hers who, when my time of travail came,
Haunted me, out of heaven. For its smile
Brought no good news from realms beyond
 the sun,
The lips framed heavenly nor human speech,
And to the glorious windows of the eyes
No Soul clomb up—to look upon the stars,
And search the void for glimpses of the peaks
Of that far land of morning whence it comes.

Then, further, I was conscious that my
 face
Had lull'd her fears ; that close to me she
 came
Tamer than beast, and toy'd with my great
 beard,
And murmur'd sounds like prattled infants'
 speech,
And yielding to my kisses kissed again.
Whereat, in scorn of my pale Soul, I cried,
' Here will I feast in honour of this night !'
And spread the board with meats and fruits
 and wine,
And drew the curtain with a wave of arm
Bidding the sunlight welcome : lastly,
 snatch'd
A purple robe of richness 'rom the wall,

And flung it o'er her while she kiss'd and
smiled,
Girdling the waist with clasp and cord of
gold.

    Then sat we, side by side. She, queenly
stoled,
Amid the gleaming fountain of her hair,
With liquid azure orbs and rosy lips
Gorgeous with honey'd kisses; I, like a
man
Who loves fair eyes and knows they are a
fiend's,
And in them sees a heav'n he knows is hell.
For, like a glorious feast, she ate and drank,
Staining her lips in crimson wine, and
laugh'd
To feel the vinous bubbles froth and burst
In veins whose sparking blood was meet
to be
A spirit's habitation. Cup on cup
I drain'd in fulness—careless as a god—
A haggard bearded head upon a breast
In tumult like a sun-kist bed of flowers.

    But ere, suffused with light, the eyes of
Heaven
Widen'd to gaze upon the white-arm'd
Moon,
Stiller than stone we reign'd there, side by
side.
Yea, like a lonely King whose Glory sits
Beside him,—impotent of life but fair,—
Brightly apparellëd I sat above
The tumult of the town, as on a throne,
Watching her wearily; while far away
The sunset dark'd like dying eyes that shut
Under the waving of an angel's wing.

    5. SHADOW.

THREE days and nights the vision dwelt
with me,
Three days and nights we dozed in dreadful
state,
Look'd piteously upon by sun and star;
But the third night there pass'd a homeless
sound
Across the city underneath my tower,
And lo! there came a roll of muffled wheels,
A shrieking and a hurrying to and fro
Beneath, and I gaz'd forth. Then far below
I heard the people shriek 'A pestilence!'

But, while they shriek'd, they carried forth
their Dead,
And flung them out upon the common ways,
And moaning fled : while far across the hills
A dark and brazen sunset ribb'd with black
Glared, like the sullen eyeballs of the plague.

    I turn'd to her, the partner of my height :
She, with bright eyeballs sick with wine,
and hair
Gleaming in sunset, on a couch asleep.
And lo! a horror lifted up my scalp,
The pulses plunged upon the heart, and fear
Froze my wide eyelids. Peacefully she lay
In purple stole array'd, one little hand
Bruising the downy cheek, the other still
Clutching the dripping goblet, and the light,
With gleams of crimson on the ruinous hair,
Spangling a blue-vein'd bosom whence the
robe
Fell back in rifled folds; but dreadful
change
Grew pale and hideous on the waxen face,
And in her sleep she did not stir, nor dream.
Therefore, it seem'd, Death pluck'd me by
the sleeve,
And, sweeping past, with lean forefinger
touch'd
The sleeper's brow and smiled; when,
shrinking back,
I turn'd my face away, and saw afar
The brazen sullen sunset ribb'd with black
Glare on her, like the eyeballs of the
plague!

    O apparition of my work and wish!
Shrieking I fled, my robe across my face,
And left my glory and my woe behind,
And sped, thro' pathless woods, o'er moon-
lit peaks,
Toward sunrise ;—nor have halted since
that hour,
But wander far away, a homeless man,
Prophetic, orphan'd both of name and fame.
Nay, like a timid Phantom evermore
I come and go with haggard warning eyes;
And some, that sit with lemans over wine,
Or dally idly with the glorious hour,
Turn cynic eyes away and smile aside;
And some are saved because they see me
pass,
And, shuddering, yet constant to their task,
Look up for comfort to the silent stars.

XVI.

ANTONY IN ARMS.

Lo, we are side by side!—One dark arm furls
  Around me like a serpent warm and bare;
The other, lifted 'mid a gleam of pearls,
Holds a full golden goblet in the air:
Her face is shining through her cloudy curls
  With light that makes me drunken unaware,
And with my chin upon my breast I smile
Upon her, darkening inward all the while.

And thro' the chamber curtains, backward roll'd
  By spicy winds that fan my fever'd head,
I see a sandy flat slope yellow as gold
  To the brown banks of Nilus wrinkling red
In the slow sunset; and mine eyes behold
  The West, low down beyond the river's bed,
Grow sullen, ribb'd with many a brazen bar,
Under the white smile of the Cyprian star.

A bitter Roman vision floateth black
  Before me, in my dizzy brain's despite;
The Roman armour brindles on my back,
  My swelling nostrils drink the fumes of fight:
But then, she smiles upon me!—and I lack
  The warrior will that frowns on lewd delight,
And, passionately proud and desolate,
I smile an answer to the joy I hate.

Joy coming uninvoked, asleep, awake,
  Makes sunshine on the grave of buried powers;
Ofttimes I wholly loathe her for the sake
  Of manhood slipt away in easeful hours:
But from her lips mild words and kisses break,
  Till I am like a ruin mock'd with flowers;
I think of Honour's face—then turn to hers—
Dark, like the splendid shame that she confers.

Lo, how her dark arm holds me!—I am bound
  By the soft touch of fingers light as leaves:
I drag my face aside, but at the sound
  Of her low voice I turn—and she perceives
The cloud of Rome upon my face and round
  My neck she twines her odorous arms and grieves,
Shedding upon a heart as soft as they
Tears 'tis a hero's task to kiss away!

And then she loosens from me, trembling still
  Like a bright throbbing robe, and bids me 'go!'—
When pearly tears her drooping eyelids fill,
  And her swart beauty whitens into snow;
And lost to use of life and hope and will,
  I gaze upon her with a warrior's woe,
And turn, and watch her sidelong in annoy—
Then snatch her to me, flush'd with shame and joy!

Once more, O Rome! I would be son of thine—
  This constant prayer my chain'd soul ever saith—
I thirst for honourable end—I pine
  Not thus to kiss away my mortal breath.
But comfort such as this may not be mine—
  I cannot even die a Roman death:
I seek a Roman's grave, a Roman's rest—
But, dying, I would die upon her breast!

XVII.

FINE WEATHER ON THE DIGENTIA.

HORATIUS COGITABUNDUS.

I.

FAVONIUS changes with sunny kisses
  The spring's ice-fetters to bands of flowers,
And the delicate Graces, those thin-skinn'd Misses,
  Are beginning to dance with the rosy Hours;
The Dryades, feeling the breeze on their bosoms,
Thro' tuby branches are blowing out blossoms;
The naked Naiad of every pool,
Lest the sunshine should drive her to playing the fool,
Lies full length in the water and keeps herself cool;

Pan is piping afar, 'mid the trees,
His ditty dies on the dying breeze,
While a wood-nymph leaneth her head on
    his knees,
In a dream, in a dream, with her wild eyes
    glistening,
Her bosom throbbing, her whole soul list-
    ening !
In fact, 'tis the season of billing and cooing,
Amorous flying and fond pursuing,
Kissing, and pressing, and mischief-doing ;
And pleasant it is to take one's tipple
    In the mild warm breath of the spicy South,
    And deftly to fasten one's lips to the mouth
Of a flasket warmer than Venus' nipple !
Pleasant, pleasant, at this the season
When folly is reason and reason treason,
When nought is so powerful near or far
    As the palpitating
    Titillating
Twinkle, twinkle, of the Cyprian star !

2.

But what has a shaky quaky fellow,
Full of the sunshine but over-mellow,
To do with the beautiful Lesbian Queen,
The pink-eyed precious with locks of yellow,
The goddess of twenty and sweet eighteen,
Whose double conquest o'er Pride and Spleen
In the Greek King's bed put a viper green
And darken'd the seas with the Grecian force?
    Nothing, of course !
Well, even I have of joy my measure
And can welcome the newborn Adonis with
    pleasure ;
For since at Philippi, worst of scrapes,
    I saved my skin for the good of the nation,
    And made my pious asseveration
To scorn ambition and cultivate grapes,
I've found by a curious convolution
    Of physical ailments and heavenly stars,
    And of wisdom wean'd on the blood-milk
    of Mars,
That my pluck is surpass'd by my elocution—
    And learnt, in fine,
    That rosy wine
And sunshine agree with my constitution !
                  (*Bibit.*)

3.

Pleasant it is, I say, to sit here,
    Just in the sunshine without the threshold,
    And, with fond fingers and lips, caress old
Bacchus' bottle, the source of wit, here !

Drowsily hum the honey-bees,
Drowsily murmur the birds in the trees,
Drowsily drops the spicy breeze,
Drowsily I sit at mine ease.

4.

An idle life is the life for me,—
Idleness spiced by philosophy !
I care not a fig for the cares of business,
Politics fill me with doubt and dizziness,
Pomps and triumphs are simply a bore to
    me,
Crude ambition will come no more to me,
I hate the vulgar popular cattle,
And I modestly blush at the mention of
    battle.
No !—Here is my humble definition
Of a perfectly happy and virtuous condition :
A few fat acres aroundabout,
    To give one a sense of possession ; a few
Servants to pour the sweet Massic out ;
Plenty to eat and nothing to do ;
A feeling of cozy and proud virility ;
    A few stray pence ;—
    And the tiniest sense
Of self-conserving responsibility !

5.

For, what is Life?—or, rather ask here,
    What is that fountain of music and motion
We call the Soul ?—As I sit and bask here,
    I confess that I haven't the slightest notion.
Yet Plato calls it eternal, telling
How its original lofty dwelling
Was among the stars, till, fairly repining
At eternally turning a pivot and shining,
    Heaven it quitted
    To dwell unpitied
In a fleshly mansion of wining and whining;
Aristotle, I don't know why,
Believes that, born up above in the sky
The moment that Body is born on the earth,
'Tis married to Body that moment of birth ;
Hippo and others, whose heads were a
    muddle,
Affirm 'tis compounded of water—puddle !
Fire, not a few, with Democritus, swear ;
While others—chameleons—reduce it to Air;
Water and fire, cries Hippocrates !
No, water and earth, cries Xenophanes !
Earth and fire, cries Parmenides !
Stop ! cries Empedocles,—all of these !

Ennius follow'd Pythagoras, thinking
The transmigration of spirits a truth ;—
A doctrine I choose to apply in sooth
To the spirit that lies in the wine I'm drinking ;
Speculation, muddle, trouble,
Some see obliquely, others double,
    While under their noses,
    Which smell not the roses,
Truth placidly bursts like a spangled bubble.

6.

Altogether, they puzzle me quite,
They all seem wrong and they all seem right.
The puzzle remains an unsatisfied question ;
But Epicurus has flatly tried
To prove that the soul is closely allied
To wine, and sunshine, and good digestion.
For without any prosing, head-racking, or preaching,
That's the construction I put on his teaching!
'Tis simple : the Soul and the Body are one,
Like the Sun itself and the light of the Sun,
Born to change with all other creations,
Homunculi, qualities, emanations,
To pass thro' wondrous and strange gradations ;
And if this be the case, our best resource
Is to make the most of our time, of course,
Nor grumble and question till hoary and hoarse.
And I slightly improve upon Epicurus,
Who shirk'd good living, as some assure us,
And assert, from experience long and rare,
That body and soul can be perfectly snug,
    With sunshine, fresh air,
    And no physical care,
In a garden that never requires to be dug.

7.

I, Quintus Horatius Flaccus, am learning
From the tuneful stars in my zenith turning,
From my bachelorhood, which is wide awake,
That the sum of good is a life of ease,
A friend or two, if the humour please,
And not a tie it would pain you to break.
Call me selfish, indolent, vain,
But I don't and won't see the virtue of pain,
Be it of body or be it of brain ;
Philippi finish'd my education,
For it taught me the doctrine of self-preservation.

I hate the barking of Scylla's dogs,
    Round Charybdis your sailor may spin,
    but not I :—
In short, I am one of those excellent hogs
That grunt in the Grecian epicure's sty.
Day by day, my delight has grown wider
Since I learnt that wine is a natural good,
And the stubborn donkey called Fortitude
Has a knack of upsetting the bile of its rider.
All creeds that vex one are mere vexation ;
But I firmly believe, and no man dare doubt me,
In Massic taken in moderation,
And I like to dwell where no fools can flout me—
    Sans physical care,
    In the sunny air,
And to sing—when I feel the fresh world about me !
                              (*Bibit.*)

8.

Bear witness, Flower!—One's sense perceives
The rich sap lying within your leaves,
Which lusciously swoon to a soft blood-red
As the sunlight woos them from overhead !
Now, here is a parallel worth inspection
Of body and blood in perfect connexion
With what some call Soul, that obscure abstraction
Which I have proved to my satisfaction
To be Body in lesser or greater perfection.
The perfect parts of the perfect flower
Were nourish'd by sunshine for many an hour,
Till the sunshine within them o'erflowing— hence
The juice whose odorous quintessence,
Though sweetly expressing the parts and the whole,
Is simply a part of the whole, and still
Inseparate from the general will.
The Flower is the Body, the Scent is the Soul !
See ! I press a thorn in the milky stalk :
The small thing droops o'er the garden walk,
The soft leaves shiver, the sap runs dry,
And never more will the flower's mild eye
Drink the breath of the moon—it will linger, and die.
But the scent of the flower, some would cry, is the sweeter ;
    True, but the scent, every moment, grows less,

And, further observing, they would confess,
That the flower, as a flower, is the incompleter !
Well, between my fingers I sharpl press
The delicate leaves, and thro' every vein
The perfect anatomy shrinks with pain,
  And the flower with its odorous quintessence
Will never, 'tis clear, be perfection again.
  Bah ! I pluck it, I pluck it, and cast it hence,
As Death plucks humanity body and brain !
But the odour has not yet flown, you cry,
It sweetens the air, tho' the flower doth die !
Of course ; and the feelers and stem and leaves,
And the sap and the odour it interweaves,
  No longer perfect and gastronomic,
Are in common resolving themselves, one perceives,
  Back to first principles—say atomic ;
And whatever destination your fine
Hard-headed philosophers choose to assign
To the several parts, they are reft of their power,
  And, so far as concerns its true functions —to scent
  The soft air, and look fair—and its first sweet intent,
'Tis clear that the whole is no longer a Flower.

9.

Take that bulky and truly delectable whole,
  The egotistic disciple of Bacchus,
With small hare's-eyes and gray hairs on his poll,
  Myself—good Quintus Horatius Flaccus !
There's a Body ! There's a Soul !
Many a year, over Rome's dominions,
Has he vaunted his Epicurean opinions :
He may be wrong, he may be right,
So he roars his creed in no mad heroics,—
Since down in the grave, where all creeds unite
Even Epicureans are changed to Stoics.
(*Bibit.*)

10.

Humph, the grave !—not the pleasantest prospect, affirms
  This quiet old heart starting up with a beat—

Well, 'tis rather hard that liquor so sweet
Goes simply to flavour a meal for worms !
After all, I'm a sensible man,
To render my span
As happy and easeful as ever I can.
To-morrow may mingle, who knows, who knows,
  The Life that is Dream with the Death that is Sleep,
And the grass that covers my last repose
  May make a sward where the lambkins leap
Round a mild-eyed mellifluous musical boy
Who pipes to his flock in a past >ral joy,
While the sun that is shining upon him there
Draws silver threads thro' his curly hair,
And Time with long shadows stalks past the spot,
And the Hours pass by, and he sees them not!
Instead of moping and idly rueing it,
Now, this is the pleasantest way of viewing it !—
To think, when all is over and done,
Of insensately feeling one's way to the sun,
Of being a part of the verdure that chases
The mild west-wind into shady places,
While one's liver, warming the roots of a tree,
Creeps upward and flutters delectably
In the leaves that tremble and sigh and sing,
And the breath bubbles up in a daisy ring,
And the heart, mingling strangely with rains and snows,
Bleeds up thro' the turf in the blood of a rose.

11.

Which reminds me, here, that the simile drawn
From the flower that is withering on the lawn,
May, by a stretch of the thought, apply
To the universe—ocean, earth, air, and sky ;
And dividing the whole into infinite less,
First principles, atomies numberless,
We find that the sum of the universe strange
Suffers continual mystical change ;
While the parts of the whole, tho' their compounds range
Thro' all combinations from men down to daisies,
Are eternal, unchangeable, suffer no phases.
So that Death, to the dullest of heads so unsightly,
Is (here I improve Epicurus slightly)

Is but the period of dissolution
Into some untraceable constitution
Of the several parts of the Body and Soul,—
And the total extinction of Man as a whole.
As to Time—mere abstraction ! With even
   motion
Like waves that gathering foamy speech
Grow duskily up on a moonlit beach,
And seem to increase the huge bulk of the
   ocean,
Hours roll upon hours in the measureless sea
   Of eternity :
      Never ceasing, they seem increasing ;
But the parts of the Infinite, changing never,
Increase not, tho' changing, the Whole, the
   For Ever.
Time ? Call it a compound, if you please,
A divisible drop in eternal seas,
An abstract figure, by which we men
Try to count our sensations again and again,
And then you will know, perceiving we
   must
Nourish some compound with dust of dust,
And seeing how short our sensations and
   powers,
     Why I am one,
     Who sits in the sun,
Whose Time is no limited number of hours,
But wine ever-present, in nectarine showers.

12.

O Mutability, dread abstraction,
Let me be wise in the satisfaction
Of my moderate needs in a half-inaction !
While Propertius grows love-sick and weary
   and wan,
While thou, Virgil, singest of arms and the
   man,
While assassins on Cæsar sharpen their eyes,
   While Agrippa stands grimly on blood-
     stained decks,
   While Mæcenas flirts with the female sex,
Teach me to sport and philosophize !
   O Mutability, lasting ever,
   Changing ever, yet changing never,
Teach me, O teach me, and make me
   wise !—
In the dreadful depth of thy eyeballs dumb,
   Strange meanings flutter and pass to
     nought,
   And beautiful images fade as they come,
     Thro' an under-trouble of shady thought !

13.

Yonder, yonder, the River doth run,
From sun to shade, and from shade to sun,
   Shaking the lilies to seed as it flows,
   Under the willow-trees taking a doze,
And waking up in a flutter of fun !
Could you look at the leaves of yonder tree !
The wind is stirring them as the sun is stir-
   ring me !
The woolly clouds move quiet and slow,
   In the pale blue calm of the tranquil skies,
And their shades that run on the grass below
   Leave purple dreams in the violet's eyes !
The vine droops over my head with bright
   Clusters of purple and green—the rose
   Breaks her heart on the air—and the
     orange glows
Like golden lamps in an emerald night.*
While I sit, with the stain of the wine on
   my lip,
Shall nature and I part fellowship ?
No, by Bacchus ! This view from the thres-
   hold of home
Is as glad to the core, and as sorrow-
   despising,
As Aphrodité when fresh from the foam
That still on her bosom was falling and
   rising,
While the sunshine crept thro' her briny
   hair
And mingled itself with the shadows there,
And her deepening eyes drank their azure
   from air,
And she blush'd a new beauty surpassingly
   fair !

14.

'Tis absurd to tell me to ruffle a feather,
Because there may soon be a change of
   weather.
When the Dog-Star foams, I will lie in the
   shade,
And watch the white sun thro' an emerald
   glade ;
When winter murmurs with rain and storm,
I will watch my hearth smile to itself, and
   keep warm ;
And for Death, who having fulfilled his task
   Leaves his deputy Silence in houses of
     mourning,—

---

* Golden lamps in a green night.—ANDREW MARVEL.

Well, I hope he no troublesome questions
    will ask,
  But knock me down, like an ox, without
    warning.
Like the world, I most solemnly promise
    devotion
  To pleasure commingled of light, music,
    motion.
I like (as I said) to sit here in my mirth,
  To be part of the joy of the sweet-smelling
    earth,
To feel the blood blush like a flower with its
    glee,
  To sing like a bird, to be stirr'd like a tree,
Drowsily, drowsily, sit at mine ease,
  While the odd rhymes buzz in my brain like
    bees,
And over my wine-cup to chirp and to nod,
    Ay to sit—till I fall ·
    Like that peach from the wall—
Self-sufficient, serene, happy-eyed,—like a
    GOD!   (*Bibit.*)

15.

Ay, crop the corn with the crooked sickle,
  Sow harvest early and reap too late,
Prove Fortune friendly or false or fickle,
  Blunder and bother with aching pate,
Attempting to conquer chance or fate,
Struggle, speculate, dig, and bleed,
Reap the whirlwind of Venus' seed,
O senseless, impotent human breed!
What avails! what avails! Were ye less
    intent
  On your raking and digging, perchance
    ye'd behold
The fleecy vapours above you roll'd
Round the dozing Deities dead to strife,
With their mild great eyes on each other bent
Enchanging a wisdom indifferent
To the native honours of death and life.
Sober truths of a pleasure divine
Keep them supine!
The grand lazy fellows have nothing to do
With the hubble and trouble of me or of you,
The stars break around them in silver foam,
And they calmly amuse themselves, some-
    times, by stealing
A peep at us pigmies, with much the same
    feeling
With which, from the candour and quiet of
    home,
I glance at the strife of political Rome.

Serene, happy-eyed, self-sufficient, they rest
On the hill where the blue sky is leaning her
    breast:—
Jove seated supreme in the midst, at his side
  Apollo the Sun and Selene the Moon,
Juno half dozing, her foot of pride
  On the neck of Venus the drowsy-eyed,
  And Pallas humming the spheric tune.

16.

Flash!
Lightning, I swear!—there's a tempest
    brewing!
Crash!
Thunder, too—swift-footed lightning pur-
    suing!
The leaves are troubled, the winds drop
    dead,
The air grows ruminant overhead—
Splash!
That great round drop fell pat on my nose.
Flash! crash! splash!—
I must run for it, I suppose.
O what a flashing and crashing and
    splashing,
The earth is rocking, the skies are riven—
Jove in a passion, in god-like fashion,
  Is breaking the crystal urns of heaven.

XVIII.

FINE WEATHER BY BAIAE.

Virgil to Horace.

1.

Sweet is soft slumber, Horace, after toil,
To him who holds the glebe and ploughs
    the fruitful soil,
Sweet to salt-blooded mariners, on decks
    washed red with storm,
Deep sleep wherein past tempest and green
    waves
    Make shadows multiform;

2.

Sweet 'tis to Cæsar, when the red star, grown
Swart with war's dust, doth fade, to loll
    upon a throne
Dispensing gifts, while on his lips a crafty
    half-smile dies,
And the soft whispers of approving Rome
    Fan his half-closèd eyes!

3.

Sweet to Tibullus, sick and out of tune,
What time his elegies like wolves howl at the moon,
Comes Pity loos'ning Delia's zone as breezes part a cloud ;
And sweet to thee a wine-cup rough with sleep,
    After the tawny crowd.

4.

And further, sweetly comes a scroll from thee,
To Virgil where he dwells at Baiae near the sea—
For, sick with servile snakes of state that twine round Cæsar's foot,
He welcomes thy moist greeting and thy thought
    Poetically put.

5.

Such alternation of unrest and rest,
All fitful peace and passion of the yearning breast,
Deepen the meanings flashing swift in Joy's pink-lidded eyne,
And help the Hours to juggle with the fruits
    Of easy creeds like thine.

6.

The time-glass runs, the seasons come and go,
After the rain, the flowers, after the flowers, the snow ;
This Hour is pale and olive-crown'd, that splash'd with rebel-mud—
This, flusht to gaze on Cæsar's laurell'd brows,
    That, drunk with Cæsar's blood !

7.

Shall merest mortal man with drowsy nod
Sit under purple vine and doze and ape the god?
Wave down the everlasting strife of earth and air and sea?
And, like a full-fed fruit that gorges light,
    Grow rotten on the tree?

8.

Leave the grand mental war that mortals keep?
Eat the fat ears of corn, yet neither sow nor reap?
Loll in the sunshine, sipping sweets, what time the din of fights
Quenches the wind round Troy, and very gods
    Feel dizzy on their heights?

9.

Nay, friend !—For such a man each hour supplies
Portents that mock his ease, affright his languid eyes ;
The very elements are leagued to goad him blood and brain,
The very Sun sows drouth within his throat
    Until it raves for rain !

10.

Methinks I see thee sitting in the sun,
Whose kisses melt thy crusty wrinkles one by one :
Thy lips droop darkly with a worm of thought, half sad, half wroth,
Which stirs the chrysalis mouth, then, ripe with wine,
    Bursts like a golden moth.

11.

Unfaith is with thee, Horace. Sun and wind
Disturb the tranquil currents of thy heart and mind ;
In midst of Joy, comes pigmy doubt, prick-pricking like a flea,
Till, wide awake, you rack your brains to prove
    Your perfect bliss to me.

12.

O better far, if Man would climb, to range
Thro' sun and thunder-storm tempestuous paths of change,
To mingle with the motion huge of earth and air and main,
And lastly, fall upon a bed of flowers
    When wearied down by pain.

13.

Deep, deep, within Man's elemental parts—
Earth, water, fire, and air that mix in human hearts,—
Subsists Unrest that seeketh Rest, and flashes into gleams
That haunts our soul to action, and by night
    Disturb our sleep with dreams.

14.

And thus we fashion with a piteous will
The gods in drowsy mildness seated on a hill,
The day before them evermore, the starry night behind,—
Inheritors of the divine repose
    We seek and cannot find.

15.

Woe, woe, to him, who craving that calm boon
Falleth to sleep on beds of poppy flowers too soon!
The elements shall hem him in and fright his shrieking soul,
And, since he asks for light, Lightning itself
    Shall scorch his eyes to coal!

16.

My Horace!—I am here beside the deep,
Weaving at will this verse for Memory to keep:
I share the sunshine with my friend, and like a lizard bask;
But I, friend, doubt this summer joy,—and you
    Shall answer what I ask.—

17.

Bluff March has blown his clarion out of tune,
Gone is the blue-edged sickle of the April moon;
Faded hath fretful May behind a tremulous veil of rain,—
But I would the boisterous season of the winds
    And snows were here again!

18.

For I am kneeling on the white sea-sand,
Letting the cold soft waves creep up and kiss my hand;
A golden glare of sunshine fills the blue air at my back,
And swims between the meadows and the skies,
    Leaving the meadows black.

19.

All is as still and beautiful as sleep:
Nay, all *is* sleep—the quiet air, the azure deep;
The cool blue waves creep thro' my fingers with a silver gleam,
As, lost in utter calm, I neither think
    Nor act, but only dream.

20.

This is the poetry of Heart's repose,
For which my spirit yearn'd thro' drifting winds and snows—
Only the tingling coolness on my hand seems part akin
To that bleak winter warring when the dream
    Of peace arose within.

21.

What time I dream'd of this, the winds, cast free,
Swoop'd eagle-like and tore the white bowels of the sea;
The winter tempest moved above, and storm on storm did frown;—
I saw the awful Sea bound up in cloud
    And then torn hugely down.

22.

Within my blood arose the wild commotion,
My soul was battling abroad with winds and ocean;
But in the centre of the wrath, all nature, sea and sky,
Call'd out aloud for peace divine as this,
    And lo, I join'd the cry.

23.

And calm has come, and June is on the deep,
The winds are nested, and the earth takes mellow sleep;
Yet, friend, my soul, though husht in awe, feels peace so still is pain,—
And the monotonous yearning voice within
    Calls out for war again!

24.

For hark! into my dream of golden ease
Breaketh the hollow murmur of untroubled seas;
And behold, my blood awakens with a thrill and sinks and swells,
As when low breezes die and rise again
    On beds of asphodels.

25.

Ay, now, when all is placid as a star,
My soul in incompleteness longs for active
    war;
Amid its utter happiness, it sighs imperfectly
In answer to the beautiful unrest
    Within the sleeping sea.

26.

Unsatisfied, I hunger on the land,
Only subdued by this bright water on my
    hand;
The beating heart within my breast for
    louder utterance yearns—
I listen, and the sympathetic sea
    Its endless moan returns.

27.

Quiet, monotonous, breathless, almost
    drown'd,
Inaudibly audible, felt scarce heard, cometh
    the sound,
Monotonous, so monotonous, but oh! so
    sweet, so sweet,
When my bid heart is throbbing forth a
    voice,
    And the two voices meet.

28.

The void within the calm for which I
    yearned,
Until this moment was imperfectly dis-
    cerned;
But now I feel to the roots of life an inner
    melody,
That harmonises my unquiet heart
    With the unquiet sea.

29.

Hear I the crawling movements of the main?
Or hear I dim heart-echoes dying in the
    brain?
Is there but one impatient moan, and is it
    of the sea?
And, if two voices speak, which voice
    belongs
    To ocean, which to me?

30.

The sounds have mingled into some faint
    whole,
Inseparate, trembling o'er the fibres of my
    soul;
And the cool waves have a magic all my
    swooning blood to quell;
The sea glides thro' and thro' me, and my
    soul
    Keeps sea-sound like a shell.

31.

Ah, the monotonous music in my soul,
Enlarging like the waves, murmuring with-
    out control!—
Is it that changeful nature can rest not night
    nor day?
And is the music born of this lorn Man,
    Or Ocean,—Horace, say?

32.

Is there a climbing element in life
Which is at war with rest, alternates strife
    with strife,
Whereby we reach eternal seas upon whose
    shores unstirr'd
Ev'n Joy can sleep,—because no moan like
    this
    Within those waves is heard?

XIX.

THE SWAN-SONG OF APOLLO.

1.

O Lyre! O Lyre!
Strung with celestial fire!
Thou living soul of sound that answereth
    These fingers that have troubled thee so
    long,
With passion, and with music, and with
    breath
    Of melancholy song,—
    Answer, answer, answer me,
    With thy withering melody!
    For the earth is old, and strange
    Mysteries are working change,
    And the Dead who slumber'd deep
    Startle troubled from their sleep,
    And the ancient gods divine,
    Pale and haggard o'er their wine,
Fade in their ghastly banquet-halls, with
    large eyes fixed on mine!

2.

Ah me! ah me!
The earth and air and sea

Are shaken; and the great pale gods sit still,
  The roseate mists 'around them roll away:—
Lo! Hebe listens in the act to fill,
  And groweth wan and gray;
    On the banquet-table spread,
    Fruits and flowers grow sick and dead,
    Nectar cold in every cup
    Gleams to blood and withers up;
    Aphrodité breathes a charm,
    Gripping Pallas' bronzèd arm;
    Zeus the Father clenches teeth,
    While his cloud-throne shakes beneath;
The passion-flower in Heré's hair melts in a snowy wreath!

3.

  Ah, woe! ah, woe!
  One climbeth from below,—
A mortal shape with pallid smile divine,
  Bearing a heavy Cross and crown'd with thorn,—
His brow is moist with blood, his strange sweet eyne
  Look piteous and forlorn:
    Hark, O hark! his cold foot-fall
    Breaks upon the banquet-hall!
    God and goddess start to hear,
    Earth, air, ocean, moan in fear;
    Shadows of the Cross and Him
    Dark the banquet-table dim,
    Silent sit the gods divine,
    Old and haggard over wine,
And slowly to thy song they fade, with large eyes fixed on mine!

4.

  O Lyre! O Lyre!
  Thy strings of golden fire
Fade to their fading, and the hand is chill
  That touches thee; the great bright brow grows gray—
I faint, I wither, while that conclave still
  Dies wearily away!
    Ah, the prophecy of old
    Sung by us to smilers cold!—
    God and goddess droop and die,
    Chilly cold against the sky,
    There is change and all is done,
    Strange look moon and stars and sun!
    God and goddess fade, and see!
    All their large eyes look at me!
While woe! ah, woe! in dying song, I fade,
  I fade, with thee!

POET'S EPILOGUE.

TO MARY ON EARTH.

'Simplex munditiis.'

1.

So! now the task is ended; and to-night,
Sick, impotent, no longer soul-sustain'd,
Withdrawing eyes from that ideal height
Where, in low undertones, those Spirits plain'd,
Each full of special glory unattain'd,—
I turn on you, Sweet-Heart, my weary sight.—
Shut out the darkness, shutting in the light:
So! now the task is ended. What is gain'd?

2.

First, sit beside me. Place your hand in mine.
From deepest fountain of your veins the while
Call up your Soul; and briefly let it shine
In those gray eyes with mildness feminine.
Yes, smile, Dear!—you are truest when you smile.

3.

My heart to-night is calm as peaceful dreams.—
Afar away the wind is shrill, the culver
Blows up and down the moors with windy gleams,
The birch unlooseneth her locks of silver
And shakes them softly on the mountain streams,
And o'er the grave that holds my David's dust
The Moon uplifts her empty dripping horn:
Thither my fancies turn, but turn in trust,
Not wholly sadly, faithful though forlorn.
For you, too, ove him, mourn his life's quick fleeting;
We think of him in common. Is it so?—
Your little hand has answer'd, and I know
His name makes music in your heart's soft beating;
And——well, 'tis something gain'd for him and me—
Him, in his heaven, and me, in this low spot,
Something his eyes will see, and joy to see—
That you, too, love him, though you knew him not.

4.

Yet this is bitter. We were boy and boy,
Hand link'd in hand we dreamt of power
 and fame,
We shared each other's sorrow, pride, and
 joy,
To one wild tune our swift blood went and
 came,
Eyes drank each other's hope with flash of
 flame.
Then, side by side, we clomb the hill of life,
We ranged thro' mist and mist, thro' storm
 and strife ;
But then,——it is so bitter, now, to feel
That his pale Soul to mine was so akin,
Firm-fix'd on goals we each set forth to win,
So twinly conscious of the sweet Ideal,
So wedded (God forgive me if I sin !)
That neither he, my friend, nor I could steal
One glimpse of heaven's divinities—alone,
And flushing seek his brother, and reveal
Some hope, some joy, some beauty, else
 unknown ;
Nor, bringing down his sunlight from the
 Sun,
Call sudden up, to light his fellow's face,
A smile as proud, as glad, as that I trace
In your dear eyes, now, when my work is
 done.

5.

Love gins in giving. What had I to give
Whereof his Poet-Soul was not possest?
What gleams of stars he knew not, fugitive
As lightning-flashes, could I manifest?
What music fainting from a clearer air?
What lights of sunrise from beyond the grave?
What pride in knowledge that he could not
 share?—
Ay, Mary, it is bitter ; for I swear
He took with him, to heav'n, no wealth I
 gave.

6.

No, Love, it is not bitter ! Thoughts like
 those
Were sin these songs I sing you must adjust.
Not bitter, ah, not bitter !—God is just ;
And, seeing our one-knowledge, just God
 chose,
By one swift stroke, to part us. Far above
The measure of my hope, my pride, my
 love,
Above our seasons, suns and rains and
 snows,—
He, like an exhalation, thus arose ;
Hearing in a diviner atmosphere
Music we only *see*, when, dewy and dim,
The stars thro' gulfs of azure darkness swim,
Music we seem to see, but cannot hear.
But evermore, my Poet, on his height,
Fills up my Soul with sweetness to the brim,
Rains influence, and warning, and delight ;
And *now*, I smile for pride and joy in him !

7

I said, Love gains by giving. And to know
That I, who could not glorify my Friend,
Soul of my Soul, although I loved him so,
Have power and strength and privilege to
 lend
Glimpses of heav'n to Thee, of hope, of bliss!
Power to go heavenward, pluck flowers and
 blend
Their hues in wreaths I give you with a kiss—
You, Love, who climb not up the heights
 at all !
To think, to think, I never could upcall
On his dead face, so proud a smile as this !

8.

Most just is God : who bids me not be sad
For his dear sake whose name is dear to thee,
Who bids me proudly climb and sometimes
 see
With joy a glimpse of him in glory clad ,
Who, further, bids your life be proud and
 glad,
When I have climb'd and seen, for joy in me.
My lowly-minded, gentle-hearted Love !
I bring you down his gifts, and am sustain'd :
You watch and pray—I climb—he stands
 above.
So, now the task is ended, what is gain'd?

9.

This knowledge.—Better in your arms to rest,
Better to love you till my heart should break,
Than pause to ask if he who would be blest
Should love for more than his own loving's
 sake.
So closer, closer still ; for (while afar,
Mile upon mile towa·d the polar star,
Now in the autumn time our Poet's dust
Sucks back thro' grassy sods the flowers it
 thrust

To feel the summer on the outer earth)
I turn to you, and on your bosom fall.
Love grows by giving. I have given my all.
So, smile—to show you hold the gift of worth.
10.
Ay, all the thanks that I on earth can render
To him who sends me such good news from God,
Is, in due turn, to thy young life to tender
Hopes that denote, while blossoming in splendour,
Where an invisible Angel's foot hath trode.

So, Sweet-Heart, I have given unto thee,
Not only such poor song as here I twine,
But Hope, Ambition, all of mine or me,
My flesh and blood, and more, my soul divine.
Take all, take all! Ay, wind white arms about
My neck and from my breath draw bliss for thine:
Smile, Sweet-Heart, and be happy—lest thou doubt
How much the gift I give thee makes thee mine!

Idyls and Legends of Inverburn.
(1865.)

Fly to the city, Spirit of the Spring,
Breathe softly on the eyes of those who read,
And make a gentle picture of the scene
Wherein these men and women come and go :
The clachan with its humming sound of looms,
The quaint old gables, roofs of turf and thatch,
The glimmering spire that peeps above the firs,
The stream whose soft blue arms encircle all,—
And in the background heathery norland hills,
Hued like the azure of the dew-berrie,
And mingling with the regions of the rain !

THE LOWLAND VILLAGE.

SEVEN pleasant miles by wood, and stream, and moor,
Seven miles along the country road that wound
Uphill and downhill in a dusty line,
Then from the forehead of a hill, behold—
Lying below me, sparkling ruby-like—
The village!—quaint old gables, roofs of thatch,
The glimmering spire that peep'd above the firs,
The sunset lingering orange-red on all,
And nearer, tumbling thro' a mossy bridge,
The river that I knew ! No wondrous peep
Into the faëry land of Oberon,
Its bowers, its glowworm-lighted colonnades
Where pigmy lovers wander two by two,
Could weigh upon the city wanderer's heart
With peace so pure as this ! Why, yonder stood,
A fledgling's downward flight beyond the spire,
The gray old manse, endear'd by memories
Of Jean the daughter of the minister;
And in the cottage with the painted sign,
Hard by the bridge, how many a winter night
Had I with politicians sapient-eyed
Discuss'd the county paper's latest news
And read of toppling thrones !—And nought seem'd changed !
The very gig before the smithy door,
The barefoot maiden with the milking pail
Pausing and looking backward from the bridge,
The last rook wavering homeward to the wood,
All seem'd a sunset-picture, every tint
Unchanged, since I had bidden it farewell.
My heart grew garrulous of olden times,
And my face sadden'd, as I saunter'd down.
Then came a rural music on my ears,—
The waggons in the lanes, the waterfall
With cool sound plunging in its wood-nest wild,
The rooks amid the windy rookery,
The shouts of children, and more far away
The crowing of a cock. Then o'er the bridge
I bent, above the river gushing down

Thro' mossy boulders, making underneath
Green-shaded pools where now and then a
    trout
Sank in the ripple of its own quick leap ;
And like some olden and familiar tune,
Half humm'd aloud, half tinkling in the
    brain,
Troublously, faintly, came the buzz of looms.
And here I linger'd, nested in the shade
Of Peace that makes a music as she grows ;
And when the vale had put its glory on
The bitter aspiration was subdued,
And Pleasure, tho' she wore a woodland
    crown,
Look'd at me with Ambition's serious eyes.
Amid the deep green woods of pine, whose
    boughs
Made a sea-music overhead, and caught
White flakes of sunlight on their highest
    leaves,
I foster'd solemn meditations ;
Stretch'd on the sloping river banks, fresh
    strewn
With speedwell, primrose, and anemone,
I watch'd the bright king-fisher dart about,
His quick small shadow with an azure gleam
Startling the minnows in the pool beneath ;
Or later on the moors, where far away
Across the waste the sportsman with his gun
Stood a dark speck across the azure, while
The heath-hen tower'd with beating wings
    and fell.
I caught the solemn wind that wander'd down
With thunder-echoes heaved among the hills.
Nor lack'd I, in the balmy summer nights,
Or on the days of rain, such counterpoise
As books can give. The honey-languaged
    Greek
Who gently piped the sweet bucolic lay,
The wit who raved of Lesbia's loosen'd zone
And loved divinely what was less than earth,
Were with me ; others, of a later date :
The eagle-eyed comedian divine ;
The English Homer, not the humpback'd
    one
Who sung Belinda's curl at Twickenham,
But Chapman, master of the long strong line;
Moreover, those few singers who have lit
The beacon-lights of these our latter days—
Chief, young Hyperion, who setting soon
Sent his pale look along the future time,
And the tall figure on the hills, that stoopt
To see the daisy's shadow on the grass.

WILLIE BAIRD.

' An old man's tale, a tale for men gray-hair'd,
Who wear, thro' second childhood, to the Lord.

'TIS two-and-thirty summers since I came
To school the village lads of Inverburn.

My father was a shepherd old and poor,
Who, dwelling 'mong the clouds on norland
    hills,
His tartan plaidie on, and by his side
His sheep-dog running, redden'd with the
    winds
That whistle southward from the Polar seas:
I follow'd in his footsteps when a boy,
And knew by heart the mountains round our
    home ;
But when I went to Edinglass, to learn
At college there, I look'd about the place,
And heard the murmur of the busy streets
Around me, in a dream ;—and only saw
The clouds that snow around the mountain-
    tops,
The mists that chase the phantom of the
    moon
In lonely mountain tarns,—and heard the
    while,
Not footsteps sounding hollow to and fro,
But winds sough-soughing thro' the woods
    of pine.
Time pass'd ; and day by day those sights
    and sounds
Grew fainter,—till they troubled me no more.

O Willie, Willie, are you sleeping sound?
And can you feel the stone that I have placed
Yonder above you ? Are you dead, my doo ?
Or did you see the shining Hand that parts
The clouds above, and becks the bonnie
    birds,
Until they wing away, and human eyes,
That watch them till they vanish in the blue,
Droop and grow tearful ? Ay, I ken, I ken,
I'm talking folly, but I loved the child !
He was the bravest scholar in the school !
He came to teach the very dominie—
Me, with my lyart locks and sleepy heart !

O weel I mind the day his mother brought
Her tiny trembling tot with yellow hair,
Her tiny poor-clad tot six summers old,

And left him seated lonely on a form
Before my desk. He neither wept nor gloom'd ;
But waited silently, with shoeless feet
Swinging above the floor ; in wonder eyed
The maps upon the walls, the big black board,
The slates and books and copies, and my own
Grey hose and clumpy boots ; last, fixing gaze
Upon a monster spider's web that fill'd
One corner of the whitewash'd ceiling, watch'd ,
The speckled traitor jump and jink about,
Till he forgot my unfamiliar eyes,
Weary and strange and old. 'Come here, my bairn !'
And timid as a lamb he seed'ed up.
'What do they call ye?' 'Willie,' coo'd the wean,
Up-peeping slyly, scraping with his feet.
I put my hand upon his yellow hair,
And cheer'd him kindly. Then I bade him lift
The small black bell that stands behind the door
And ring the shouting laddies from their play.
'Run, Willie !' And he ran, and eyed the bell,
Stoop'd o'er it, seem'd afraid that it would bite,
Then grasp'd it firm, and as it jingled gave
A timid cry—next laugh'd to hear the sound—
And ran full merry to the door and rang,
And rang, and rang, while lights of music lit
His pallid cheek, till, shouting, panting hard,
In ran the big rough laddies from their play.

Then rapping sharply on the desk I drove
The laddies to their seats, and beckon'd up
The stranger—smiling, bade him seat himself
And hearken to the rest. Two weary hours
Buzz-buzz, boom-boom, went on the noise of school,
While Willie sat and listen'd open-mouthed;
Till school was over, and the big and small
Flew home in flocks. But Willie stay'd behind.

I beckon'd to the mannock with a smile,
And took him on my knee and crack'd and talk'd.

First, he was timid ; next, grew bashful ; next,
He warm'd and told me stories of his home,
His father, mother, sisters, brothers, all ;
And how, when strong and big, he meant to buy
A gig to drive his father to the kirk ;
And how he long'd to be a dominie :
Such simple prattle as I plainly see
You smile at. But to little children God
Has given wisdom and mysterious power
Which beat the mathematics. *Quærere Verum in sylvis Academi*, Sir,
Is meet for men who can afford to dwell
For ever in a garden, reading books
Of morals and the logic. Good and weel !
Give me such tiny truths as only bloom
Like red-tipt gowans at the hallanstone,
Or kindle softly, flashing bright at times,
In fuffing cottage fires !

      The laddie still
Was seated on my knee, when at the door
We heard a sound of scraping : Willie prick'd
His ears and listened, then he clapt his hands—
'Hey ! Donald, Donald, Donald !' [See ! the rogue
Looks up and blinks his eyes—he kens his name !]
'Hey, Donald, Donald !' Willie cried. At that
I saw beneath me, at the door, a Dog—
The very collie dozing at your feet,
His nose between his paws, his eyes half closed.
At sight of Willie, with a joyful bark
He leapt and gamboll'd, eying *me* the while
In queer suspicion; and the mannock peep'd
Into my face, while patting Donald's back—
'It's Donald ! he has come to take me home !'

An old man's tale, a tale for men gray-hair'd,
Who wear, thro' second childhood to the grave !
I'll hasten on. Thenceforward Willie came

Daily to school, and daily to the door
Came Donald trotting; and they homeward
  went
Together—Willie walking slow but sure,
And Donald trotting sagely by his side.
[Ay, Donald, he is dead! be still, old man!]

What link existed, human or divine,
Between the tiny tot six summers old,
And yonder life of mine upon the hills
Among the mists and storms? 'Tis strange,
  'tis strange!
But when I look'd on Willie's face, it seem'd
That I had known it in some beauteous
  life
That I had left behind me in the north.
This fancy grew and grew, till oft I sat—
The buzzing school around me—and would
  seem
To be among the mists, the tracks of rain,
Nearing the awful silence of the snow.
Slowly and surely I began to feel
That I was all alone in all the world,
And that my mother and my father slept
Far, far away in some forgotten kirk—
Remember'd but in dreams. Alone at nights,
I read my Bible more and Euclid less.
For, mind you, like my betters, I had been
Half scoffer, half believer; on the whole,
I thought the life beyond a useless dream,
Best left alone, and shut my eyes to themes
That puzzled mathematics. But at last,
When Willie Baird and I grew friends, and
  thoughts
Came to me from beyond my father's grave,
I found 'twas *pleasant* late at e'en to read
My Bible—haply, only just to pick
Some easy chapter for my pet to learn—
Yet night by night my soul was guided on
Like a blind man some angel hand convoys.

I cannot frame in speech the thoughts that
  fill'd
This gray old brow, the feelings dim and
  warm
That soothed the throbbings of this weary
  heart!
But when I placed my hand on Willie's head,
Warm sunshine tingled from the yellow hair
Thro' trembling fingers to my blood
  within;
And when I look'd in Willie's stainless eyes
I saw the empty ether floating gray
O'er shadowy mountains murmuring low
  with winds!
And often when, in his old-fashion'd way,
He question'd me, I seem'd to hear a voice
From far away, that mingled with the cries
Haunting the regions where the round red sun
Is all alone with God among the snow!

Who made the stars? and if within his
  hand
He caught and held one, would his fingers
  burn!
If I, the gray-hair'd dominie, was dug
From out a cabbage garden such as *he*
Was found in? if, when bigger, he would
  wear
Gray homespun hose and clumsy boots like
  mine,
And have a house to dwell in all alone?
Thus would he question, seated on my knee,
While Donald (wheesht, old man!) stretch'd
  lyart limbs
Under my chair, contented. Open-mouth'd
He hearken'd to the tales I loved to tell
About Sir William Wallace and the Bruce,
And the sweet lady on the Scottish throne,
Whose crown was colder than a band of ice,
Yet seem'd a sunny crown whene'er she
  smiled;
With many tales of genii, giants, dwarfs,
And little folk that play at jing-a-ring
On beds of harebells 'neath the silver moon;
Stories and rhymes and songs of Wonder-
  land:
How Tammas Ercildoune in Elfland dwelt,
How Galloway's mermaid comb'd her golden
  hair,
How Tammas Thumb stuck in the spider's
  web,
And fought and fought, a needle for his
  sword,
Dyeing his weapon in the crimson blood
Of the foul traitor with the poison'd fangs!

And when we read the Holy Book, the
  child
Would think and think o'er parts he loved
  the best;
The draught of fish, the Child that sat so
  wise
In the great Temple, Herod's cruel law
To slay the bairns, or—oftenest of all—
The crucifixion of the Good Kind Man

Who loved the weans and was a wean him-
  self.
He speir'd of Death! and were the sleepers
  cold
Down in the dark wet earth? and was it
  God
That put the grass and flowers in the kirk-
  yard?
What kind of dwelling-place was heaven
  above?
And was it full of flowers? and were there
  schools
And dominies there? and was it far away?
Then, with a look that made your eyes
  grow dim,
Clasping his wee white hands round
  Donald's neck,
'Do doggies gang to heaven?' he would ask;
'Would Donald gang?' and keek'd in
  Donald's face,
While Donald blink'd with meditative gaze,
As if he knew full brawly what we said,
And ponder'd o'er it, wiser far than we!
But how I answer'd, how explain'd these
  themes
I know not. Oft I could not speak at all.
Yet every question made me think of things
Forgotten, puzzled so, and when I strove
To reason puzzled me so much the more,
That, flinging logic to the winds, I went
Straight onward to the mark in Willie's way.
Took most for granted, laid down premises
Of Faith, imagined, gave my wit the reins,
And oft on nights at e'en, to my surprise,
Felt palpably an angel's glowing face
Glimmering down upon me, while mine eyes
Dimm'd their old orbs with tears that came
  unbid
To bear the glory of the light they saw!

So summer pass'd. Yon chestnut at the
  door
Scatter'd its burnish'd leaves and made a
  sound
Of wind among its branches. Every day
Came Willie, seldom going home again
Till near the sunset: wet or dry he came:
Oft in the rainy weather carrying
A big umbrella, under which he walk'd—
A little fairy in a parachute
Blown hither, thither, at the wind's wild
  will.
Pleased was my heart to see his pallid cheeks
Were gathering rosy-posies, that his eyes
Were softer and less sad. Then, with a
  gust,
Old Winter tumbled shrieking from the hills,
His white hair blowing in the wind.

              The house
Where Willie's mother lives is scarce a mile
From yonder hallan, if you take a cut
Before you reach the village, crossing o'er
Green meadows till you reach the road again;
But he who thither goes along the road
Loses a reaper's mile. The summer long
Wee Willie came and went across the fields:
He loved the smell of flowers and grass, the
  sight
Of cows and sheep, the changing stalks of
  wheat,
And he was weak and small. When winter
  came,
Still caring not a straw for wind or rain
Came Willie and the collie; till by night
Down fell the snow, and fell three nights and
  days,
Then ceased. The ground was white and
  ankle-deep;
The window of the school was threaded o'er
With flowers of hueless ice—Frost's unseen
  hands
Prick'd you from head to foot with tingling
  heat.
The shouting urchins, yonder on the green,
Play'd snowballs. In the school a cheery
  fire
Was kindled every day, and every day
When Willie came he had the warmest seat,
And every day old Donald, punctual, came
To join us, after labour, in the lowe.

Three days and nights the snow had
  mistily fall'n.
It lay long miles along the country-side,
White, awful, silent. In the keen cold air
There was a hush, a sleepless silentness,
And mid it all, upraising eyes, you felt
God's breath upon your face; and in your
  blood,
Though you were cold to touch, was flaming
  fire,
Such as within the bowels of the earth
Burnt at the bones of ice, and wreath'd them
  round
With grass ungrown.

One day in school I saw,
Through threaded window-panes, soft snowy flakes
Fall with unquiet motion, mistily, slowly,
At intervals; but when the boys were gone,
And in ran Donald with a dripping nose,
The air was clear and gray as glass. An hour
Sat Willie, Donald, and myself around
The murmuring fire, and then with tender hand
I wrapt a comforter round Willie's throat,
Button'd his coat around him close and warm,
And off he ran with Donald, happy-eyed
And merry, leaving fairy prints of feet
Behind him on the snow. I watch'd them fade
Round the white curve, and, turning with a sigh,
Came in to sort the room and smoke a pipe
Before the fire. Here, dreaming all alone,
I sat and smoked, and in the fire saw clear
The norland mountains, white and cold with snow
That crumbled silently, and moved, and changed,—
When suddenly the air grew sick and dark,
And from the distance came a hollow sound,
A murmur like the moan of far-off seas.

I started to my feet, look'd out, and knew
The winter wind was whistling from the clouds
To lash the snow-clothed plain, and to myself
I prophesied a storm before the night.
Then with an icy pain, an eldritch fear,
I thought of Willie; but I cheer'd my heart,
'He's home, and with his mother, long ere this!'
While thus I stood the hollow murmur grew
Deeper, the wold grew darker, and the snow
Rush'd downward, whirling in a shadowy mist.
I walk'd to yonder door and open'd it.
Whirr! the wind swung it from me with a clang,
And in upon me with an iron-like crash
Swoop'd in the drift! With pinch'd sharp face I gazed
Out on the storm! Dark, dark, was all! A mist,
A blinding, whirling mist, of chilly snow,
The falling and the driven; for the wind
Swept round and round in clouds upon the earth,
And birm'd the deathly drift aloft with moans,
Till all was dreadful darkness. Far above
A voice was shrieking, like a human cry!

I closed the door, and turn'd me to the fire,
With something on my heart—a load—a sense
Of an impending pain. Down the broad lum
Came melting flakes that hiss'd upon the coal;
Under my eyelids blew the blinding smoke,
And for a time I sat like one bewitch'd,
Still as a stone. The lonely room grew dark,
The flickering fire threw phantoms of the snow
Along the floor and on the walls around;
The melancholy ticking of the clock
Was like the beating of my heart. But, hush!
Above the moaning of the wind I heard
A sudden scraping at the door; my heart
Stood still and listen'd; and with that there rose
An awsome howl, shrill as a dying screech,
And scrape-scrape-scrape, the sound beyond the door!
I could not think—I could not breathe—a dark,
Awful foreboding gript me like a hand,
As opening the door I gazed straight out,
Saw nothing, till I felt against my knees
Something that moved and heard a moaning sound—
Then, panting, moaning, o'er the threshold leapt
Donald the dog, alone, and white with snow.

Down, Donald! down, old man! Sir, look at him!
I swear he knows the meaning of my words,
And tho' he cannot speak, his heart is full!
See now! see now! he puts his cold black nose
Into my palm and whines! he knows, he knows!
Would speak, and cannot, but he minds that night!

The terror of my heart seem'd choking me.
Dumbly I stared and wildly at the dog,

G

Who gazed into my face and whined and
  moan'd,
Leap'd at the door, then touched me with
  his paws,
And lastly, gript my coat between his teeth,
And pull'd and pull'd—whiles growling,
  whining whiles—
Till fairly madden'd, in bewilder'd fear,
I let him drag me through the banging door
Out to the whirling storm. Bareheaded,
  wild,
The wind and snow-drift beating on my face
Blowing me hither, thither, with the dog,
I dash'd along the road. What follow'd
  seem'd
An eerie, eerie dream!—a world of snow,
A sky of wind, a whirling howling mist
Which swam around with hundred sickly
  eyes;
And Donald dragging, dragging, beaten,
  bruised,
Leading me on to something that I fear'd—
An awful something, and I knew not what!
On, on, and farther on, and still the snow
Whirling, the tempest moaning! Then I
  mind
Of groping blindly in the shadowy light,
And Donald by me burrowing with his nose
And whining. Next a darkness, blank and
  deep!
But then I mind of tearing thro' the storm,
Stumbling and tripping, blind and deaf and
  dumb,
And holding to my heart an icy load
I clutch'd with freezing fingers. Far away—
It seem'd long miles on miles away—I saw
A yellow light—unto that light I tore—
And last, remember opening a door
And falling, dazzled by a blinding gleam
Of human faces and a flaming fire,
And with a crash of voices in my ears
Fading away into a world of snow.

When I awaken'd to myself, I lay
In my own bed at home. I started up
As from an evil dream and look'd around,
And to my side came one, a neighbour's wife,
Mother to two young lads I taught in school.
With hollow, hollow voice I question'd her,
And soon knew all: how a long night had
  pass'd
Since, with a lifeless laddie in my arms,
I stumbled horror-stricken, swooning, wild

Into a ploughman's cottage: at my side,
My coat between his teeth, a dog; and how
Senseless and cold I fell. Thence, when the
  storm
Had pass'd away, they bore me to my home.
I listen'd dumbly, catching at the sense;
But when the woman mention'd Willie's
  name,
And I was fear'd to phrase the thought that
  rose,
She saw the question in my tearless eyes
And told me—he was dead.

     'Twould weary you
To tell the thoughts, the fancies, and the
  dreams
That weigh'd upon me, ere I rose in bed,
But little harm'd, and sent the wife away,
Rose, slowly drest, took up my staff and went
To Willie's mother's cottage. As I walk'd,
Though all the air was calm and cold and
  still,
The blowing wind and dazzled snow were
  yet
Around about. I was bewilder'd like!
Ere I had time to think I found myself
Beside a truckle bed, and at my side
A weeping woman. And I clench'd my
  hands,
And look'd on Willie, who had gone to sleep.

In death-gown white, lay Willie fast asleep,
His blue eyes closed, his tiny fingers clench'd,
His lips apart a wee as if he breathed,
His yellow hair kaim'd back, and on his face
A smile—yet not a smile—a dim pale light
Such as the snow keeps in its own soft wings.
Ay, he had gone to sleep, and he was sound!
And by the bed lay Donald watching still,
And when I look'd, he whined, but did not
  move.

I turn'd in silence, with my nails stuck deep
In my clench'd palms; but in my heart of
  hearts
I pray'd to God. In Willie's mother's face
There was a cold and silent bitterness—
I saw it plain, but saw it in a dream,
And cared not. So I went my way, as grim
As one who holds his breath to slay himself.
What follow'd that is vague as was the rest:
A winter day, a landscape hush'd in snow,
A weary wind, a small white coffin borne

On a man's shoulder, shapes in black, o'er all
The solemn clanging of an iron bell,
And lastly me and Donald standing both
Beside a tiny mound of fresh-heap'd earth,
And while around the snow began to fall
Mistily, softly, thro' the icy air,
Looking at one another, dumb and cold.

And Willie's dead!—that's all I comprehend—
Ay, bonnie Willie Baird has gone before:
The school, the tempest, and the eerie pain,
Seem but a dream,—and I am weary like.
I begged old Donald hard—they gave him me—
And we have lived together in this house,
Long years, with no companions. There's no need
Of speech between us! Here we dumbly bide,
But ken each other's sorrow,—and we both
Feel weary. When the nights are long and cold,
And snow is falling as it falleth now,
And wintry winds are moaning, here I dream
Of Willie and the unfamiliar life
I left behind me on the norland hills!
'Do doggies gang to heaven?' Willie ask'd;
And ah! what Solomon of modern days
Can answer that? Yet here at nights I sit,
Reading the Book, with Donald at my side;
And stooping, with the Book upon my knee,
I sometimes gaze in Donald's patient eyes—
So sad, so human, though he cannot speak—
And think he knows that Willie is at peace,
Far far away beyond the norland hills,
Beyond the silence of the untrodden snow.

LORD RONALD'S WIFE.

I.

LAST night I toss'd upon my bed,
Because I knew that she was dead:
The curtains were white, the pane was blue,
    The moon peep'd through,
    And its eye was red—
'I would that my love were awake!' I said.

II.

Then I rose and the lamp of silver lit,
    And over the rushes lightly stept,
Crept to the door and open'd it,
    And enter'd the room where my lady slept;
And the silver lamp threw a feeble ray
    Over the bed on which she lay,
And sparkled on her golden hair,
Smiled on her lip and melted there,
And I shudder'd because she look'd so fair;—
For the curtains were white and the pane was blue,
    And the moon look'd through,
    And its eye was red:
'I will hold her hand, and think,' I said.

III.

And at first I could not think at all,
    Because her hand was so thin and cold;
The gray light flicker'd along the wall,
    And I seem'd to be growing old;
I look'd in her face and could not weep,
    I hated the sound of mine own deep breath,
Lest it should startle her from the sleep
    That seem'd too sweet and mild for death.
I heard the far-off clock intone
    So slowly, so slowly—
Afar across the courts of stone,
The black hound shook his chain with a moan,
    As the village clock chimed slowly,
    slowly, slowly.
I pray'd that she might rise in bed,
    And smile and say one little word,
'I long to see her eyes!' I said ..
    I should have shriek'd if she had stirr'd.

IV.

I never sinn'd against thee, Sweet!
    And yet last night, when none could see..
I know not.. but from head to feet,
    I seem'd one scar of infamy:
Perhaps because the fingers light
I held had grown so worn and white,
Perhaps because you look'd so fair,
With the thin gray light on your golden hair!

V.

You were warm, and I was cold,
    Yet you loved me, little one, I knew—
I could not trifle—I was old—
    I was wiser, carefuller, than you;
I liked my horse, I liked my hound,
I liked to hear the trumpet sound,

Over my wine I liked to chat,
  But soberly, for I had mind :
You wanted that, and only that,
  You were as light as is the wind.
At times, I know, it fretted me—
  I chid thee mildly now and then—
No fault of mine—no blame to thee—
  Women are women, men are men.
At first you smiled to see me frown,
  And laughing leapt upon my knee,
And kiss'd the chiding shadow down,
  And smooth'd my great beard merrily;
But then a change came o'er you, Sweet!
  You walk'd about with pensive head;
You tried to read, and as you read
  Patted your small impatient feet :—
'She is wiser now!' I smiling said . .
And ere I doubted—you were dead.

VI.

All this came back upon my brain
  While I sat alone at your white bedside,
And I remember'd in my pain
  Those words you spoke before you died—
For around my neck your arms you flung,
  And smiled so sweet though death was near—
'I was so foolish and so young!
  And yet I loved thee!—kiss me, dear!'
I put aside your golden hair,
  And kiss'd you, and you went to sleep
And when I saw that death was there,
  My grief was cold, I could not weep;
And late last night, when you were dead,
  I did not weep beside your bed,
For the curtains were white, and the pane was blue,
    And the moon look'd through,
    And its eye was red—
'How coldly she lies!' I said.

VII.

Then loud, so loud, before I knew,
  The gray and black cock scream'd and crew,
And I heard the far-off bells intone
    So slowly, so slowly,
The black hound bark'd, and I rose with a groan,
    As the village bells chimed slowly, slowly, slowly.
I dropp'd the hand so cold and thin,
  I gazed, and your face seem'd still and wise,
And I saw the damp dull dawn stare in
  Like a dim drown'd face with oozy eyes;
And I open'd the lattice quietly,
And the cold wet air came in on me,
  And I pluck'd two roses with fingers chill
From the roses that grew at your window-sill,
I pluck'd two roses, a white and a red,
Stole again to the side of your bed,
Raised the edge of your winding fold,
  Dropp'd the roses upon your breast,
  Cover'd them up in the balmy cold,
That none might know—and there they rest!
And out at the castle-gate I crept
Into the woods; and then . . I wept!
But to-day they carried you from here,
  And I follow'd your coffin with tearless cheek—
They knew not about the roses, dear!—
  I would not have them think me weak.

VIII.

And I am weary on my bed
Because I know you are cold and dead;
And I see you lie in darkness, Sweet!
With the roses under your winding-sheet;
The days and nights are dreary and cold,
And I am foolish, and weak, and old.

POET ANDREW.

O Loom, that loud art murmuring,
  What doth he hear thee say or sing?
Thou hummest o'er the dead one's songs,
    He cannot choose but hark,
His heart with tearful rapture throngs,
    But all his face grows dark.

O cottage Fire, that burnest bright,
  What pictures sees he in thy light?
A city's smoke, a white white face,
    Phantoms that fade and die,
And last, the lonely burial-place
    On the windy hill hard by.

'Tis near a year since Andrew went to sleep—
A winter and a summer. Yonder bed
Is where the boy was born, and where he died,
And yonder o'er the lowland is his grave:
The nook of grass and gowans where in thought

I found you standing at the set o' sun . .
The Lord content us—'tis a weary world.
　These five-and-twenty years I've wrought
　　and wrought
In this same dwelling ;—hearken ! you can
　　hear
The looms that whuzzle-whazzle ben the
　　house,
Where Jean and Mysie, lassies in their teens,
And Jamie, and a neighbour's son beside,
Work late and early.　Andrew who is dead
Was our first-born ; and when he crying
　　came,
With beaded een and pale old-farrant face,
Out of the darkness, Mysie and mysel
Were young and heartsome ; and his smile,
　　be sure,
Made daily toil the sweeter.　Hey, his kiss
Put honey in the very porridge-pot !
His smile strung threads of sunshine on the
　　loom !
And when he hung around his mother's neck,
He deck'd her out in jewels and in gold
That even ladies envied ! . . Weel ! . . in time
Came other children, newer gems and gold,
And Andrew quitted Mysie's breast for mine.
So years roll'd on, like bobbins on a loom ;
And Mysie and mysel' had work to do,
And Andrew took his turn among the rest,
No sweeter, dearer ; till, one Sabbath day,
When Andrew was a curly-pated tot
Of sunny summers six, I had a crack
With Mister Mucklewraith the Minister,
Who put his kindly hand on Andrew's head,
Call'd him a clever wean, a bonnie wean,
Clever at learning, while the mannikin
Blush'd red as any rose, and peeping up
Went twinkle-twinkle with his round black
　　een ;
And then, while Andrew laugh'd and ran
　　awa',
The Minister went deeper in his praise,
And prophesied he would become in time
A man of mark.　This set me thinking, sir,
And watching,—and the mannock puzzled
　　me.

　Would sit for hours upon a stool and draw
Droll faces on the slate, while other lads
Were shouting at their play ; dumbly would
　　lie
Beside the Lintock, sailing, piloting,
Navies of docken-leaves a summer day ;

Had learn'd the hymns of Doctor Watts by
　　heart
And as for old Scots songs, could lilt them
　　a'—
From Yarrow Braes to Bonnie Bessie Lee—
And where he learn'd them, only Heaven
　　knew ;
And oft, altho' he feared to sleep his lane,
Would cowrie at the threshold in a storm
To watch the lightning,—as a birdie sits,
With fluttering fearsome heart and dripping
　　wings,
Among the branches.　Once, I mind it weel,
In came he, running, with a bloody nose,
Part tears, part pleasure, to his fluttering
　　heart
Holding a callow mavis golden-bill'd,
The thin white film of death across its een,
And told us, sobbing, how a neighbour's son
Harried the birdie's nest, and how by chance
He came upon the thief beside the burn
Throwing the birdies in to see them swim,
And how he fought him, till he yielded up
This one, the one remaining of the nest ;—
And 'O the birdie's dying !' sobb'd he sore,
'The bonnie birdie's dying !'—till it died ;
And Andrew dug a grave behind the house,
Buried his dead, and cover'd it with earth,
And cut, to mark the grave, a grassy turf
Where blew a bunch of gowans.　After that,
I thought and thought, and thick as bees
　　the thoughts
Buzz'd to the whuzzle-whazzling of the
　　loom—
I could make naething of the mannikin !
But by-and-by, when Hope was making hay,
And web-work rose, I settled it and said
To the good wife, ' 'Tis plain that yonder lad
Will never take to weaving—and at school
They say he beats the rest at all his tasks
Save figures only : I have settled it :
Andrew shall be a minister—a pride
And comfort to us, Mysie, in our age :
He shall to college in a year or twa
(If fortune smiles as now) at Edinglass.'
You guess the wife open'd her een, cried
　　' Foosh !'
And call'd the plan a silly senseless dream,
A hopeless, useless castle in the air ;
But ere the night was out, I talk'd her o'er,
And here she sat, her hands upon her knees,
Glow'ring and heark'ning, as I conjured up,
Amid the fog and reek of Edinglass

Life's peaceful gloaming and a godly fame.
So it was broach'd, and after many cracks
With Mister Mucklewraith, we plann'd it a',
And day by day we laid a penny by
To give the lad when he should quit the
 field.

And years wore on ; and year on year was
 cheer'd
By thoughts of Andrew, drest in decent
 black,
Throned in a Pulpit, preaching out the
 Word,
A house his own, and all the country-side
To touch their bonnets to him. Weel, the lad
Grew up among us, and at seventeen
His hands were genty white, and he was tall,
And slim, and narrow-shoulder'd : pale of
 face,
Silent, and bashful. Then we first began
To feel how muckle more he *knew* than we,
To eye his knowledge in a kind of fear,
As folk might look upon a crouching beast,
Bonnie, but like enough to rise and bite.
Up came the cloud between us silly folk
And the young lad that sat among his books
Amid the silence of the night ; and oft
It pain'd us sore to fancy he would learn
Enough to make him look with shame and
 scorn
On this old dwelling. 'Twas his *manner*,
 sir !
He seldom lookt his father in the face,
And when he walkt about the dwelling,
 seem'd
Like one superior ; dumbly he would steal
To the burnside, or into Lintlin Woods,
With some new-farrant book,—and when I
 peep'd,
Behold a book of jingling-jangling rhyme,
Fine-written nothings on a printed page,
And, press'd between the leaves, a flower
 perchance,
Anemone or blue forget-me-not,
Pluckt in the grassy woodland. Then I
 look'd
Into his drawer, among his papers there,
And found—you guess?—a heap of idle
 rhymes,
Big-sounding, like the worthless printed
 book :
Some in old copies scribbled, some on scraps
Of writing paper, others finely writ

With spirls and flourishes on big white
 sheets.
I clench'd my teeth, and groan'd. The
 beauteous dream
Of the good Preacher in his braw black dress,
With house and income snug, began to fade
Before the picture of a drunken loon
Bawling out songs beneath the moon and
 stars,—
Of poet Willie Clay, who wrote a book
About King Robert Bruce, and aye got fou,
And scatter'd stars in verse, and aye got fou,
Wept the world's sins, and then got fou,
 again,—
Of Ferguson, the feckless limb o' law,—
And Robin Burns, who gauged the whisky-
 casks
And brake the seventh commandment. So
 at once
I up and said to Andrew, ' You're a fool !
You waste your time in silly senseless verse,
Lame as your own conceit : take heed ! take
 heed !
Or, like your betters, come to grief ere long !'
But Andrew flusht and never spake a word,
Yet eyed me sidelong with his beaded een,
And turn'd awa', and, as he turn'd, his
 look—
Half scorn, half sorrow—stang me. After
 that,
I felt he never heeded word of ours,
And tho' we tried to teach him common-
 sense
He idled as he pleased ; and many a year,
After I spake him first, that look of his
Came dark between us, and I held my
 tongue,
And felt he scorn'd me for the poetry's sake.
This coldness grew and grew, until at last
We sat whole nights before the fire and spoke
No word to one another. One fine day,
Says Mister Mucklewraith to me, says he,
' So ! you've a Poet in your house !' and
 smiled ;
' A Poet? God forbid !' I cried ; and then
It all came out : how Andrew slyly sent
Verse to be paper ; how they printed it
In Poet's Corner ; how the printed verse
Had ca't a girdle in the callant's head ;
How Mistress Mucklewraith they thought
 half daft
Had cut the verses out and pasted them

In albums, and had praised them to her friends,
I said but little; for my schemes and dreams
Were tumbling down like castles in the air,
And all my heart seem'd hardening to stone.
But after that, in secret stealth, I bought
The papers, hunted out the printed verse,
And read it like a thief; thought some were good,
And others foolish havers, and in most
Saw naething, neither common-sense nor sound—
Words pottle-bellied, meaningless, and strange,
That strutted up and down the printed page,
Like bailies made to bluster and look big.

'Twas useless grumbling. All my silent looks
Were lost, all Mysie's flyting fell on ears
Choke-full of other counsel; but we talk'd
In bed o' nights, and Mysie wept, and I
Felt stubborn, wrothful, wrong'd. It was to be!
But mind you, though we mourn'd, we ne'er forsook
The college scheme. Our sorrow, as we saw
Our Andrew growing cold to homely ways,
And scornful of the bield, but strengthen'd more
Our wholesome wish to educate the lad,
And do our duty by him, and help him on
With our rough hands—the Lord would do the rest,
The Lord would mend or mar him. So at last,
New-clad from top to toe in homespun cloth,
With books and linen in a muckle trunk,
He went his way to college; and we sat,
Mysie and me, in weary darkness here;
For tho' the younger bairns were still about,
It seem'd our hearts had gone to Edinglass
With Andrew, and were choking in the reek
Of Edinglass town.

It was a gruesome fight,
Both for oursel's at home, and for the boy,
That student life at college. Hard it was
To scrape the fees together, but beside,
The lad was young and needed meat and drink.
We sent him meal and bannocks by the train,
And country cheeses; and with this and that,
Though sorely push'd, he throve, though now and then
With empty wame: spinning the siller out
By teaching grammar in a school at night.
Whiles he came home: weary old-farrant face
Pale from the midnight candle; bringing home
Good news of college. Then we shook awa'
The old sad load, began to build again
Our airy castles, and were hopeful Time
Would heal our wounds. But, sir, they plagued me still—
Some of his ways! When here, he spent his time
In yonder chamber, or about the woods,
And by the waterside,—and with him books
Of poetry, as of old. Mysel' could get
But little of his company or tongue;
And when we talkt, atweel, a kind of frost,—
My consciousness of silly ignorance,
And worse, my knowledge that the lad himsel'
Felt sorely, keenly, all my ignorant shame,
Made talk a torture out of which we crept
With burning faces. Could you understand
One who was wild as if he found a mine
Of golden guineas, when he noticed first
The soft green streaks in a snowdrop's inner leaves?
And once again, the moonlight glimmering
Thro' watery transparent stalks of flax?
A flower's a flower! . . . But Andrew snoov'd about,
Aye finding wonders, mighty mysteries,
In things that ilka learless cottar kenn'd.
Now, 'twas the falling snow or murmuring rain;
Now, 'twas the laverock singing in the sun,
And dropping slowly to the callow young;
Now, an old tune he heard his mother lilt;
And aye those trifles made his pallid face
Flush brighter, and his een flash keener far,
Than when he heard of yonder storm in France,
Or a King's death, or, if the like had been,
A city's downfall.

He was born with love
For things both great and small: yet seem'd to prize
The small things best. To me, it seem'd indeed

The callant cared for nothing for itsel',
But for some special quality it had
To set him thinking, or at least bestow
A tearful sense he took for luxury.
He loved us in his silent fashion weel ;
But in our feckless ignorance we knew
'Twas when the humour seized him—with a
  sense
Of some queer power we had to waken up
The poetry—ay, and help him in his rhyme!
A kind of patronising tenderness,
A pitying pleasure in our Scottish speech
And homely ways, a love that made him note
Both ways and speech with the same curious
  joy
As fill'd him when he watch'd the birds and
  flowers.

He was as sore a puzzle to us then
As he had been before. It puzzled us,
How a big lad, down-cheek'd, almost a man,
Could pass his time in silly childish joys . . .
Until at last, a hasty letter came
From Andrew, telling he had broke awa'
From college, pack'd his things, and taken
  train
To London city, where he hoped (he said)
To make both fortune and a noble fame
Thro' a grand poem, carried in his trunk ;
How, after struggling on with bitter heart,
He could no longer bear to fight his way
Among the common scholars ; and the end
Bade us be hopeful, trusting God, and sure
The light of this old home would guide him
  still
Amid the reek of evil.

          Sae it was !
We twa were less amazed than you may
  guess,
Though we had hoped, and fear'd, and
  hoped, so long !
But it was hard to bear—hard, hard, to bear !
Our castle in the clouds was gone for good ;
And as for Andrew—other lads had ta'en
The same mad path, and learn'd the bitter
  task
Of poverty and tears. She grat. I sat,
In silence, looking on the fuffing fire,
Where streets and ghaistly faces came and
  went,
And London city crumbled down to crush
Our Andrew; and my heart was sick and cold.

Ere long, the news across the country-side
Speak quickly, like the crowing of a cock
From farm to farm—the women talkt it o'er
On doorsteps, o'er the garden rails ; the men
Got fu' upon it at the public-house,
And whisper'd it among the fields at work.
A cry was quickly raised from house to
  house,
That all the blame was mine, and canker'd
  een
Lookt cold upon me, as upon a kind
Of upstart. 'Fie on pride !' the whisper said,
'The fault was Andrew's less than those who
  taught
His heart to look in scorn on honest work,—
Shame on them !—but the lad, poor lad,
  would learn !'
O sir, the thought of this spoil'd many a web
In yonder—tingling, tingling, in my ears,
Until I fairly threw my gloom aside,
Smiled like a man whose heart is light and
  young,
And with a future-kenning happy look
Threw up my chin, and bade them wait and
  see . . .
But, night by night, these een lookt London-
  ways,
And saw my laddie wandering all alone
'Mid darkness, fog, and reek, growing afar
To dark proportions and gigantic shape—
Just as the figure of a sheep-herd looms,
Awful and silent, thro' a mountain mist !

You may be ken the rest. At first, there came
Proud letters, swiftly writ, telling how folk
Now roundly call'd him 'Poet,' holding out
Bright pictures, which we smiled at wearily—
As people smile at pictures in a book,
Untrue but bonnie. Then the letters ceased,
There came a silence cold and still as frost,—
We sat and hearken'd to our beating hearts,
And pray'd as we had never pray'd before.
Then lastly, on the silence broke the news
That Andrew, far awa', was sick to death,
And, weary, weary of the noisy streets,
With aching head and weary hopeless heart,
Was coming home from mist and fog and
  noise
To grassy lowlands and the caller air.

  'Twas strange, 'twas strange !—but this,
  the weary end
Of all our bonnie biggins in the clouds,

Came like a tearful comfort. Love sprang up
Out of the ashes of the household fire,
Where Hope was fluttering like the loose
　white film ;
And Andrew, our own boy, seemed nearer
　now
To this old dwelling and our aching hearts
Than he had ever been since he became
Wise with book-learning. With an eager
　pain,
I met him at the train and brought him
　home ;
And when we met that sunny day in hairst,
The ice that long had sunder'd us had
　thaw'd,
We met in silence, and our een were dim.
Ah !—I can see that look of his this night !
Part pain, part tenderness—a weary look
Yearning for comfort such as God the Lord
Puts into parents' een. I brought him here,
Gently we set him down beside the fire,
And spake few words, and hush'd the noisy
　house ;
Then eyed his hollow cheeks and lustrous
　een,
His clammy bueless brow and faded hands,
Blue vein'd and white like lily-flowers. The
　wife
Forgot the sickness of his face, and moved
With light and happy footstep but and ben,
As though she welcomed to a merry feast
A happy guest. In time, out came the truth :
Andrew was dying : in his lungs the dust
Of cities stole unseen, and hot as fire
Burnt—like a deil's red een that gazed at
　Death.
Too late for doctor's skill, tho' doctor's skill
We had in plenty ; but the ill had ta'en
Too sure a grip. Andrew was dying, dying :
The beauteous dream had melted like a mist
The sunlight feeds on : a' remaining now
Was Andrew, bare and barren of his pride,
Stark of conceit, a weel-belovëd child,
Helpless to help himsel', and dearer thus,
As when his yaumer*—like the corn-craik's
　cry
Heard in a field of wheat at dead o' night—
Brake on the hearkening darkness of the
　bield.

And as he nearer grew to God the Lord,

　　* *Yaumer*, a child's cry.

Nearer and dearer ilka day he grew
To Mysie and mysel'—our own to love,
The world's no longer. For the first last
　time,
We twa, the lad and I, could sit and crack
With open hearts—free-spoken, at our ease ;
I seem'd to know as muckle then as he,
Because I was sae sad.

　　　　　　　Thus grief, sae deep
It flow'd without a murmur, brought the
　balm
Which blunts the edge of worldly sense and
　makes
Old people weans again. In this sad time,
We never troubled at his childish ways ;
We seem'd to *share* his pleasure when he sat
List'ning to birds upon the eaves ; we felt
Small wonder when we found him weeping
　o'er
His old torn books of pencill'd thoughts and
　verse ;
And if, outbye, I saw a bonnie flower,
I pluckt it carefully and bore it home
To my sick boy. To me, it somehow seem'd
His care for lovely earthly things had
　changed—
Changed from the curious love it once had
　been,
Grown larger, bigger, holier, peacefuller ;
And though he never lost the luxury
Of loving beauteous things for poetry's sake,
His heart was God the Lord's, and he was
　calm.
Death came to lengthen out his solemn
　thoughts
Like shadows to the sunset. So we ceased
To wonder. What is folly in a lad
Healthy and heartsome, one with work to
　do,
Befits the freedom of a dying man. . .
Mother, who chided loud the idle lad
Of old, now sat her sadly by his side,
And read from out the Bible soft and low,
Or lilted lowly, keeking in his face,
The old Scots songs that made his een so
　dim !
I went about my daily work as one
Who waits to hear a knocking at the door,
Ere Death creeps in and shadows those that
　watch ;
And seated here at e'en i' the ingleside,

I watch'd the pictures in the fire and smoked
My pipe in silence; for my head was fu'
Of many rhymes the lad had made of old
(Rhymes I had read in secret, as I said),
No one of which I minded till they came
Unsummon'd, murmuring about my ears
Like bees among the leaves.

                        The end drew near.
Came Winter moaning, and the Doctor said
That Andrew couldna live to see the Spring;
And day by day, while frost was hard at work,
The lad grew weaker, paler, and the blood
Came redder from the lung. One Sabbath day—
The last of winter, for the caller air
Was drawing sweetness from the barks of trees—
When down the lane, I saw to my surprise
A snowdrop blooming underneath a birk,
And gladly pluckt the flower to carry home
To Andrew. Ere I reach'd the bield, the air
Was thick wi' snow, and ben in yonder room
I found him, Mysie seated at his side,
Drawn to the window in the old arm-chair,
Gazing with lustrous een and sickly cheek
Out on the shower, that waver'd softly down
In glistening siller glamour. Saying nought,
Into his hand I put the year's first flower,
And turn'd awa' to hide my face; and he . .
. . He smiled . . and at the smile, I knew not why,
It swam upon us, in a frosty pain,
The end of a' was come at last, and Death
Was creeping ben, his shadow on our hearts.
We gazed on Andrew, call'd him by his name,
And touch'd him softly . . and he lay awhile,
His een upon the snow, in a dark dream,
Yet neither heard nor saw; but suddenly,
He shook awa' the vision wi' a smile,
Raised lustrous een, still smiling, to the sky,
Next upon us, then dropt them to the flower
That trembled in his hand, and murmur'd low,
Like one that gladly murmurs to himsel'—
'Out of the Snow, the Snowdrop—out of Death
Comes Life;' then closed his eyes and made a moan,
And never spake another word again.

. . And you think weel of Andrew's book?
  You think
That folk will love him, for the poetry's sake,
Many a year to come? We take it kind
You speak so weel of Andrew!—As for me,
I can make naething of the printed book;
I am no scholar, sir, as I have said,
And Mysie there can just read print a wee.
Ay! we are feckless, ignorant of the world!
And though 'twere joy to have our boy again
And place him far above our lowly house,
We like to think of Andrew as he was
When, dumb and wee, he hung his helpless arms
Round Mysie's neck; or—as he is this night—
Lying asleep, his face to heaven—asleep,
Near to our hearts, as when he was a bairn,
Without the poetry and human pride
That came between us to our grief, langsyne!

WHITE LILY OF WEARDALE HEAD.

THE ELVES.

ALL day the sunshine loves to dwell
  Upon the pool of Weardale Well;
  But when the sunbeams shine no more
The Monk stalks down the moonlit dell:
  His robe is black, his hair is hoar,
    He sits him down by Weardale Well;
  He hears the water moan below,
  He sees a face as white as snow,
  His nightly penance there is done,
  And he shall never see the sun.

THE MONK.

Hear them, old Anatomy!
Down the glade I see them flee—
White-robed Elfins, three times three!

THE ELVES.

Night by night, in pale moonlight,
  The Monk shall tell his story o'er,
And the grinning Gnome with teeth of white
  Hearkeneth laughing evermore;
  His nightly penance thus is done—
And he shall never see the sun!

THE GNOME.

Ever new and ever old,
Comrade, be thy story told,
While the face as white as snow
Sighs upon the pool below.

THE MONK.

'I love the sunshine,' said
White Lily of Weardale-head.

And underneath the greenwood tree,
  She wander' free, she wander'd bold ;
The merry sun smiled bright to see,
  And turn'd her yellow hair to gold :
Then the bee, and the moth, and the butterfly
  Hunting for sweets in the wood-bowers fair,
Rose from the blooms as she wander'd by,
  And played in the light of her shining hair.
She sat her down by Weardale Well,
  And her gleaming ringlets rustled and fell,
Clothing her round with a golden glow,
  And her shadow was light for the pool below;
Then the yellow adder fold in fold
  Writhed from his lair in the grass and roll'd
With glittering scales in a curl o' the gold :
  She stroked his head with her finger light,
And he gazed with still and glistening eye;
  And she laught and clapt her hands of white,
And overhead the sun went by
Thro' the azure gulfs of a cloudless sky ;
'All things that love the sun, love me,
And O but the sun is sweet to see,
And I love to look on the sun,' said she.

But the Abbess gray of Lintlin Brae
Hated to look on the light of day ;
She mumbled prayers, she counted beads,
  She whipt and whipt her shoulders bare,
She slept on a bed of straw and reeds,
  And wore a serk of horse's hair.
By candle-light she sat and read,
  And heard a song from far away,
She cross'd herself and raised her head—
  'Who sings so loud ?' said the Abbess gray.
I, who sat both early and late
A shadow black at the Abbey gate,
'Mater sacra, it is one
Who wanders evermore in the sun,

A little maiden of Weardale-head,
Whose father and mother have long been dead,
But she loves to wander in greenwood bowers,
Singing and plucking the forest flowers.'
The Abbess frown'd, half quick, half dead,
'There is a sin !' the Abbess said.

I found her singing a ditty wild,
  Her gleaming locks around her roll'd ;
I seized her while she sang and smiled,
  And dragged her along by the hair of gold:
The moth and butterfly, fluttering,
  Follow'd me on to Lintlin Brae,
The adder leapt at my heart to sting,
  But with sandall'd heel I thrust it away ;
And the bee dropt down ere I was 'ware
On the hand that gript the yellow hair,
And stang me deep, and I cursed aloud,
And the sun went in behind a cloud !

THE ELVES.

Nightly be his penance done !
He shall never see the sun !

THE MONK.

The cell was deep, the cell was cold,
It quench'd the light of her hair of gold ;
One little loop alone was there,
  One little eye-hole letting in
A slender ray of light as thin
  As a tress of yellow hair.

'Oh for the sunshine !' said
White Lily of Weardale-head ;
And in the dark she lay,
  Reaching her fingers small
To feel the little ray
  That glimmer'd down the wall.

And while she linger'd white as snow
She heard a fluttering faint and low ;
And stealing thro' the looplet thin
The moth and butterfly crept in—
With golden shadows as they flew
  They waver'd up and down in air,
Then dropping slowly ere she knew,
  Fell on her eyes and rested there :
And O she slept with balmy sighs,
  Dreaming a dream of golden day,
The shining insects on her eyes,
  Their shadows on her cheeks, she lay ;

And while she smiled on pleasant lands,
  On the happy sky and wood and stream,
I, creeping in with outstretch'd hands,
  Murder'd the things that brought the dream.
She woke and stretch'd her hands and smiled,
  Then gazed around with sunless eyes,
Her white face gloom'd, her heart went wild,
  She sank with tears and sighs.
'Oh for the sunshine!' said
White Lily of Weardale-head.

And while she lay with cries and tears,
There came a humming in her ears ;
And stealing through the looplet thin
The yellow honey-bee crept in,
And hover'd round with summer sound
  Round and around the gloomy cell ;
  Then softly on her lips he fell,
And moisten'd them with sweetness found
  Among the flowers by Weardale Well ;
And O she smiled and sang a song,
  And closed her eyelids in the shade,
And thought she singing walkt among
  The lily-blooms in the greenwood glade.
I heard the song and downward crept,
  And enter'd cold and black as sin,
And slew, although she raved and wept,
  The bee that brought the sweetness in:
'Oh for the sunshine!' said
White Lily of Weardale-head.

And while she lay as white as snow
She heard a hissing sad and low ;
And writhing through the looplet thin
The little yellow snake crept in :
His golden coils cast shadows dim,
  With glistening eye he writhed and crept,
And while she smiled to welcome him,
  Into her breast he stole, and slept ;
And O his coils fell warm and sweet
  Upon her heart and husht its beat,
And softest thrills of pleasure deep
Ran through her, though she could not sleep,
  But lay with closëd eyes awake,
  Her little hand upon the snake—
'All things that love the sun, love me,
And O but the sun is sweet to see !
And I long to look on the sun,' said she.

Then down, on sandall'd foot, I crept,
  To kill the snake that heal'd the pang,

But up, with waving arms, she leapt,
  And out across the threshold sprang,
And up the shadowy Abbey stairs,
  Past the gray Abbess at her prayers,
Through the black court with leap and run,
Out at the gate, and into the sun !
There for a space she halted, blind
  With joy to feel the light again,
But heard my rushing foot behind
  And sped along the Abbey lane ;
The sunshine made her strong and fleet,
As on she fled by field and fold,
Her shining locks fell to her feet
  In ring on ring of living gold ;
But the sun went in behind a cloud,
  As I gript her by the shining locks,
I gript them tight, I laught aloud,
  The echoes rang through woods and rocks ;
Moaning she droopt, then up she sprang,
The adder leapt at my heart and stang,
And like a flash o' the light she fell
Into the depths of Weardale Well !
The adder stang with fatal fang,
Around I whirl'd and shriek'd and sprang,
  Then fell and struggled, clenching teeth ;
Then to the oozy grass I clang,
  And gazed upon the pool beneath ;
The white death-film was on mine eye,
  Yet look'd I down in agony ;
And as I look'd in throes of death,
In shining bubbles rose her breath
And burst in little rings of light,
  And upward came a moaning sound ;
But suddenly the sun shone bright,
  And all the place was gold around,
And to the surface, calm and dead,
Uprose White Lily of Weardale-head :
Her golden hair around her blown
Made gentle radiance of its own ;
Her face was turn'd to the summer sky
  With smile that seem'd to live and speak,
The golden moth and butterfly,
  With glowing shadows, on her cheek ;
And lying on her lips apart
  The honey-bee with wings of gold,
And sleeping softly on her heart
  The yellow adder fold in fold ;
And as I closed mine eyes to die,
Overhead the sun went by
Through the azure gulfs of a cloudless sky !

THE ELVES.

All day the sunshine loves to dwell
Upon the sleep of Weardale Well;
All day there is a gentle sound,
And little insects pause and sing,
The butterfly and moth float round,
The bee drops down with humming wing,
And all the pool lies clear and cold,
Yet glittering like hair of gold.
All day the Monk in hollow shell
Lies dumb among the Abbey-tombs,
While, in the grass and foxglove-blooms,
The adder basks by Weardale Well;
But the adder stings his heart by night:
His tale is told, his penance done,
His eyes are dark, they long for light,
Yet they shall never see the sun!

THE ENGLISH HUSWIFE'S GOSSIP.

A ploughman's English wife, bright-eyed, sharp-speech'd,
Plump as a pillow, fresh as clothes new-bleach'd :
The firelight dancing ruddy on her cheeks,
Irons Tom's Sunday linen as she speaks.

At three-and-forty, simple as a child,
Soft as a sheep yet curious as a daw,
Wise, cunning, in a fashion of his own,
Queer, watchful, strange, a puzzle to us all :—
That's John!

My husband's brother—seven years
Younger than Tom. When we were newly wed,
John came to dwell with Tom and me for good,
And now has dwelt beside us twenty years,
But now, at forty-three, is breaking fast,
Grows weaker, brain and body, every day.
At times he works, and earns his meat and drink,
At times is sick, and lies and moans in bed,
Beside the noisy racket up and down
He makes when he is glad. A natural!
Man-bodied, but in many things a child;
Unfinish'd somewhere— where, the Lord knows best

Who made and guards him ; wiser, craftier,
Than Tom, or any other man I know,
In tiny things few men perceive at all ;
No fool at cooking, clever at his work,
Thoughtful when Tom is senseless and un-kind,
Kind with a grace that sweetens silent-ness,—
But weak when other working-men are strong,
And strong where they are weak. An angry word
From one he loves,—and off he creeps in pain—
Perhaps to ease his tender heart in tears.
But easy-sadden'd, sir, is easy-pleased!
Give him the babe to nurse, he sits him down,
Smiles like a woman, and is glad at heart.

Crazed? There's the question! Mister Mucklewraith,
Your friend—and John's as well—will answer 'No!'
And often has he scolded when I seem'd
To answer 'Yea.' Of late the weary limbs
Have tried the weary brain, that every day
Grows feebler, duller ; yet the Minister
Still stands his friend and helps him as he can.
'Tender of heart,' says Mister Mucklewraith,
'Tender of heart, goodwife, is wise of head:
If John is weak, his heart is to be blamed;
And can the erring heart of mortal be
O'er gentle?' Hey, 'tis little use to talk!
The Minister is soft at heart as he!

Talk of the . . . John! and home again so soon?
The children are at school, the dinner o'er,
Tom still is busy working at the plough.
Weary?—then sit you down and rest awhile.
John fears all strangers— is ashamed to speak—
But stares and counts his fingers o'er as now,
Yet—trust him!—when you vanish he will tell
The colour of your hair, your hat, your clothes,
The number of the buttons on your coat—
Eh, John ?—he laughs—as sly as sly can be!

Now, run to Tom—as quickly as you can—
Say he is wanted by the gentleman
[Tom knows the name] from Mister Mucklewraith's.

Off, like an arrow from a bow, you see!
That's nothing! John would run until he dropt
For me, and need no thanking but a smile,
Would work and work his fingers to the bone,
Do aught I asked, without or in the house,—
And just because I cheer him merrily
And speak him kindly. Tom he little likes,
And would not budge a single step to serve,
For Tom is rough, and says I humour him,
And mocks him for his silly childish ways.
And Tom has reason to be wroth at times!
But yesterday John sat him on a stool,
And ripp'd the bellows up, to find from where
The wind came! slowly did it bit by bit,
As sage as Solomon, and when 'twas done
Just scratch'd his head, still puzzled, creeping off
To some still corner in the meadow, there
To think the puzzle out in peace alone!
There is his weakness—curiosity!
Those watchful, prying, curious eyes of his,
That like a cat's see better in the dark,
Are ne'er at rest; his hands and eyes and ears
Are eager getting knowledge,—when 'tis got,
Lord knoweth in what corner of his head
He hides it, but it ne'er sees light again!

Oft he reminds me of a painter lad
Who came to Inverburn a summer since,
Went poking everywhere with pallid face,
Thought, painted, wander'd in the woods alone,
Work'd a long morning at a leaf or flower,
And got the name of clever. John and he
Made friends—a thing I never could make out;
But, bless my life! it seem'd to me the lad
Was just a John who had learnt to read and paint!

He buys a coat: what does he first, but count
The pockets and the buttons one by one—
A mighty calculation sagely summ'd;
Our eldest daughter goes to Edinglass,
Brings home a box—John eyes the box with greed,
And next, we catch him in the lassie's room,
The box wide open, John upon the floor,
And in his hand a bonnet, eyed and eyed,
Turn'd o'er and o'er, examined bit by bit,
Like something wondrous as a tumbled star!
Our youngest has a gift—a box of toys,
A penny trumpet—not a wink for John
Till he has seen the whole, or by and by
He gives the child a sixpence for the toy,
And creeps away and cuts it up to bits
In wonder and in joy. It makes me cry
For fun to watch his pranks, the natural!
But think not, sir, that he was ever so :—
Nay! twenty years ago but few could tell
That he was simpler than the rest of men—
His step was firm, he kept his head erect,
Could hold his tongue, because he knew full well
That he was not so clever as the rest.—
Now, when his wits have gone so fast asleep,
He thinks he is the wisest man of men!
Yet, sir, his heart is kindly to the core,
Tho' sensitive to touch as fly-trap flowers:
He loves them best that seem to think him wise,
Consult him, notice him, and those that mock
His tenderness he never will forgive.
Money he saves to buy the children gifts—
Clothes, toys, whate'er he fancies like to please—
And many of his ways so tender are,
So gentle and so good, it fires my blood
To see him vex'd and troubled. Just a child!
He weeps in silence, if a little ill;
A cold, a headache—he is going to die;
But then, again, he can be trusted, sir!
(Ye cannot say the like of many men!)
Tell him a secret,—torture, death itself,
Would fail to make him whisper and betray.

Nay, sit you down—and smoke? Ay, smoke your fill:
Both John and father like their cutty-pipe;
Tom will be here as fast as he can come;
And I can chat and talk as well as work.

John, simple as he is, has had his cares:
They came upon him in his younger days

When he was tougher-hearted, and I think
They help'd to make him silly as he is :
Time that has stolen all his little wits,
By just a change of chances, might have
    made
Our John another man and strengthen'd
    him ;
The current gave a swirl, and caught the
    straw,
And John was doom'd to be a natural !
Oft when he sits and smokes his pipe and
    thinks,
I know by his downcast eyes and quivering
    lips
His heart is aching ; but he ne'er complains
Of *that*—the sorest thought he has to bear.
I know he thinks of Jessie Glover then ;
But let him be, till o'er his head the cloud
Passes, and leaves a meekness and a hush
Upon the heart it shadow'd. Jessie, sir ?—
She was a neighbour's daughter in her teens,
A bold and forward huzzie, tho' her face
Was pretty in its way : a jet-black eye,
Red cheeks, black eyebrows, and a comely
    shape
The petticoat and short-gown suited well.
In here she came and stood and talk'd for
    hours
[Her tongue was like a bell upon a sheep—
Her very motion seem'd to make it jing]
And, ere I guess'd it, John and she were
    friends.
She pierced the silly with her jet-black eye,
Humour'd him ever, seem'd to think him
    wise,
Was serious, gentle, kindly, to his face,
And, ere I guess'd, so flatter'd his conceit
That, tho' his lips were silent at her side,
He grew a mighty man behind her back,
Held up his head in gladness and in pride,
And seem'd to have an errand in the world.
At first I laugh'd and banter'd with the rest—
'How's Jessie, John ?' and ' Name the
    happy day ;'
And, 'Have ye spoken to the minister ?'
Thinking it just a joke ; and when the lass
Would sit by John, her arm about his neck,
Holding his hand in hers, and humour him,
Yet laugh her fill behind the silly's back,
I let it pass. I little liked her ways—
I guess'd her heart was tough as cobbler's
    wax—
Yet what of that ?—'Twas but a piece of fun.

A piece of fun !—'Twas serious work to
    John !
The huzzie lured him with her wicked eyes,
And danced about him, ever on the watch,
Like pussie yonder playing with a mouse.
I saw but little of them, never dream'd
They met unknown to me ; but by and by
The country-side was ringing with the talk
That John and she went walking thro' the
    fields,
Sat underneath the slanted harvest sheaves
Watching the glimmer of the silver moon,
Met late and early—courted night and day—
John earnest as you please, and Jess for fun.
I held my peace awhile, and used my eyes !
New bows and ribbons upon Jessie's back,
Cheap brooches, and a bonnet once or twice,
Proved that the piece of fun paid Jessie well,
And showed why John no longer spent his
    pence
In presents to the boys. I saw it all,
But, pitying John, afraid to give him pain
I spake to Jessie, sharply bade her heed,
Cried 'shame' upon her, for her heartless-
    ness.
The huzzie laugh'd and coolly went her way,
And after that came hither nevermore
To talk and clatter. But the cruel sport
Went on, I found. One day, to my surprise,
Up came a waggon to the cottage door,
John walking by the side, and while I stared
He quickly carried to the kitchen here,
A table, chairs, a wooden stool, a broom,
Two monster saucepans, and a washing tub,
And last, a roll of blankets and of sheets.
The waggon went away, here linger'd John
Among the things, and blushing red says he,
'I bought them all at Farmer Simpson's
    sale—
Ye'll keep them till I need them for myself !'
And then walk'd out. Long time I stood
    and stared,
Puzzled, amazed ; but by-and-by I saw
The meaning of it all. Alas for John !
The droll beginning of a stock in trade
For marriage stood before me! Jessie's eyes
And lying tongue had made him fairly
    crazed,
And ta'en the little wits he had to spare.
With flashing face, set teeth, away I ran
To Jessie—found her washing at a tub,
Covered with soap-suds—and I told her all ;
And for a while she could not speak a word

For laughter. 'Shame upon ye, shame, shame, shame!
Thus to misuse the lad who loves ye so!
Mind, Jessie Glover, folks with scanty brains
Have hearts that can be broken!' Still she laugh'd!
While tears of mirth ran down her crimson cheeks
And mingled with the frothy suds of soap;
But, trust me, sir, I went not home again
Till Jessie's parents knew her wickedness;
And last, I wrung a promise from her lips
From that day forth to trouble John no more,
To let him know her fondness was a joke,
Pass by him in the street without a word,
And, though perhaps his gentle heart might ache,
Shake him as one would shake a drunken man
Until his sleepy wits awoke again.

I watch'd that Jessie Glover kept her word.
That night, when John was seated here alone,
Smoking his pipe, and dreaming as I guess'd
Of Jessie Glover and a wedding ring,
I stole behind him silently and placed
My hand upon his shoulder: when he saw
The shadow on my face, he trembled, flush'd,
And knew that I was sad. I sank my voice,
And gently as I could I spake my mind,
Spake like a mother, told him he was wrong,
That Jessie only was befooling him
And laugh'd his love to scorn behind his back,
And last, to soothe his pain, I rail'd at her,
Hoping to make him angry. Here he sat,
And let his pipe go out, and hung his head,
And never answer'd back a single word.
'Twas hard, 'twas hard, to make him understand!
He could not, would not! All his heart was wrapt
In Jessie Glover; and at twenty-three
A full-grown notion thrusts its roots so deep,
'Tis hard indeed to drag it up without
Tearing the heart as well. Without a word,
He crept away to bed. Next morn, his eyes
Were red with weeping—but 'twas plain to see
He thought I wrong'd both Jessie and himself.

That morning Jessie pass'd him on the road:
He ran to speak—she toss'd her head and laugh'd—
And sneering pass'd him by. All day he wrought
In silence at the plough—ne'er had he borne
A pang so quietly. At gloaming hour
Home came he, weary: here was I alone:
Stubborn as stone he turn'd his head away,
Sat on his stool before the fire and smoked;
Then while he smoked I saw his eyes were wet:
'John!' and I placed my hand upon his arm.
He turn'd, seem'd choking, tried in vain to speak,
Then fairly hid his face and wept aloud,—
But never wept again.

The days pass'd on.
I held my tongue, and left the rest to time,
And warn'd both father and the boys. My heart
Was sore for John! He was so dumb and sad,
Never complaining as he did of old,
And toiling late and early. By-and-by,
'Jenny,' says he, as quiet as a lamb,
'Ye'll keep the things I bought at Simpson's sale—
I do not need them now!' and tried to smile,
But could not. Well, I thank'd him cheerily,
Nor seem'd to see his heart was aching so:
Then after that the boys got pence from John,—
The smaller playthings, and the bigger clothes:
He eased his heart by spending as of old
His money on the like.

Well may you cry
Shame, shame on Jessie! Heartless, graceless lass!
I could have whipt her shoulders with a staff!—
But One above had sorer tasks in store.
Ere long the village, like a peal of bells,
Rang out the tale that Jessie was a thief,
Had gone to Innis Farm to work a week,
And stolen Maggie Fleming's watch and chain—
They found them in her trunk with scores of things

From poorer houses. Woe to Jessie then
If Farmer Fleming had unkindly been,
Nor spared her for her sickly father's sake!
The punishment was spared—she kept the shame!
The scandal rose, with jingling-jangling din,
And chattering lasses, wives, and mothers join'd.
At first she saw not that the sin was guess'd;
But slowly, one by one, her lassie friends,
Her very bosom-gossips, shook her off:
She heard the din, she blush'd and hid her face,
Shrinking away and trembling as with cold,
Like Eve within the garden when her mouth
Was bitter with the apple of the Tree.

One night, when John returned from work and took
His seat upon the stool beside the fire,
I saw he knew the truth. For he was changed!
His look was dark, his voice was loud, his eyes
Had lost their meekness; when we spoke to him,
He flush'd and answer'd sharply. He had heard
The tale of Jessie's shame and wickedness,—
What thought he of it all? Believe me, sir,
He was a riddle still: in many things
So peevish and so simple, but in one—
His silly dream of Jessie Glover's face—
So manly and so dumb,—with power to hide
His sorrow in his heart and turn away
Like one that shuts his eyes when men pass by
But looks on Him. 'Twas natural to think
John would have taken angry spiteful joy
In Jessie's fall,—for he was ever slow
Forgetting and forgiving injuries;
But no! his voice was dumb, his eyes were fierce,
Yet chiefly when they mention'd Jessin scorn,
He seem'd confused and would not understand,
Perplext as when he breaks the children's toys.

Now, bold as Jessie was, she could not bear
The shame her sin had brought her, and whene'er
We met she tingled to the finger-tips;
And soon she fled away to Edinglass
To hide among the smoke. It came to pass,
The Sabbath after she had flitted off,
That Mister Mucklewraith (God bless him!) preach'd
One of those gentle sermons low and sad
Wherewith he gathers wheat for Him he serves:
The text—let him who is sinless cast the first
Stone at the sinner; and we knew he preach'd
Of Jessie Glover. Hey! to hear him talk
Ye would have sworn that Jessie was a saint,
An injured thing for folk to pet and coax!
But tho' ye know 'twas folly, springing up
Out of a heart so kindly to the core,
Your eyes were dim with tears while hearkening—
He spake so low and sadly. John was there.

And early down the stairs came John next day
Drest in his Sabbath clothes. 'I'm going away,'
He whispers, 'for a day or maybe two—
Don't be afraid if I'm away at night,
And do not speak to Tom;' and off he ran
Ere I could question. When the evening came,
No sign of John! Night pass'd, and not a sign!
Tom sought him far and near without avail.
The next night came, and we were sitting here
Weary and pensive, wondering, listening,
To every step that pass'd, when in stept John,
And sat beside the fire, and when we ask'd
Where he had been, he snapt us short and crept
Away to bed.

But by-and-by, I heard
The truth from John himself—a truth indeed
That was and is a puzzle, will remain
A puzzle to the end. And can ye guess
Where John had been? Away in Edinglass,
At Jessie Glover's side, holding her hand
And looking in her eyes!

'Jessie!' he said;
And while she stared stood scraping with his shoes,
And humm'd and haw'd and stammer'd out a speech,
Whose sense, made clear and shorten'd, came to this:

H

The country folk that call'd her cruel names
And mock'd her so, had done the same by him !
He did not give a straw for what they said !
He did not give a straw, and why should she?
And tho' she laugh'd before, perchance when folk
Miscall'd her, frighten'd her from home and friends,
She'd turn to simple John and marry him ?
For he had money, seven pound and more,
And yonder in his home, to stock a house,
The household things he bought at Simpson's sale ;
John Thomson paid him well, and he could work,
And, if she dried her eyes and married him,
Who cared for Tom and Jennie, and the folk
That thought them crazed ? . . John, then and now ashamed,
Said that she flung her arms about his neck,
And wept as if her heart was like to break,
And told him sadly that it could not be.
He scratch'd his head, and stared, and answer'd nought—
His stock of words was done, but last, he forced
His money in the weeping woman's hand,
And hasten'd home as fast as he could run.

He feels it still ! it haunts him night and day !
Ay, silly tho' he be, he keeps the thought
Of Jess still hidden in his heart ; and now,
Wearing away like snowdrift in the sun,
If e'er he chance to see, on nights at home,
One of the things he bought at Simpson's sale
(I keep them still, tho' they are worn and old,)
His eyes gleam up, then glisten,—then are dark.

THE FAËRY FOSTER-MOTHER.

I.

BRIGHT Eyes, Light Eyes ! Daughter of a Fay !
I had not been a married wife a twelvemonth and a day,
I had not nurst my little one a month upon my knee,
When down among the blue-bell banks rose elfins three times three,
They gript me by the raven hair, I could not cry for fear,
They put a hempen rope around my waist and dragg'd me here,
They made me sit and give thee suck as mortal mothers can,
Bright Eyes, Light Eyes ! strange and weak and wan !

II.

Dim Face, Grim Face ! lie ye there so still?
Thy red red lips are at my breast, and thou may'st suck thy fill ;
But know ye, tho' I hold thee firm, and rock thee to and fro,
'Tis not to soothe thee into sleep, but just to still my woe?
And know ye, when I lean so calm against the wall of stone,
'Tis when I shut my eyes and try to think thou art mine own ?
And know ye, tho' my milk be here, my heart is far away,
Dim Face, Grim Face ! Daughter of a Fay !

III.

Gold Hair, Cold Hair ! Daughter to a King !
Wrapt in bands of snow-white silk with jewels glittering,
Tiny slippers of the gold upon thy feet so thin,
Silver cradle velvet-lined for thee to slumber in,
Pigmy pages, crimson-hair'd, to serve thee on their knees,
To bring thee toys and greenwood flowers and honey bags of bees,—
I was but a peasant lass, my babe had but the milk,
Gold Hair, Cold Hair ! raimented in silk !

IV.

Pale Thing, Frail Thing ! dumb and weak and thin,
Altho' thou ne'er dost utter sigh thou'rt shadow'd with a sin ;
Thy minnie scorns to suckle thee, thy minnie is an elf,
Upon a bed of rose's-leaves she lies and fans herself ;

And though my heart is aching so for one
  afar from me,
I often look into thy face and drop a tear
  for thee,
And I am but a peasant born, a lowly cotter's
  wife,
Pale Thing, Frail Thing! sucking at my life!

V.

Weak Thing, Meek Thing! take no blame
  from me,
Altho' my babe may fade for lack of what I
  give to thee;
For though thou art a stranger thing, and
  though thou art my woe,
To feel thee sucking at my breast is all the
  joy I know,
It soothes me tho' afar away I hear my
  daughter call,
My heart were broken if I felt no little lips
  at all!
If I had none to tend at all, to be its nurse
  and slave,
Weak Thing, Meek Thing! I should shriek
  and rave!

VI.

Bright Eyes, Light Eyes! lying on my knee!
If soon I be not taken back unto mine own
  countree,
To feel my own babe's little lips, as I am
  feeling thine,
To smoothe the golden threads of hair, to
  see the blue eyes shine,—
I'll lean my head against the wall and close
  my weary eyes,
And think my own babe draws the milk with
  balmy pants and sighs,
And smile and bless my little one and sweetly
  pass away,
Bright Eyes, Light Eyes! Daughter of a Fay!

THE GREEN GNOME.

A MELODY.

Ring, sing! ring, sing! pleasant Sabbath
  bells!
Chime, rhyme! chime, rhyme! through the
  dales and dells!
Rhyme, ring! chime, sing! pleasant Sab-
  bath bells!
Chime, sing! rhyme, ring! over fields and
  fells!

And I gallop'd and I gallop'd on my palfrey
  white as milk,
My robe was of the sea-green woof, my serk
  was of the silk,
My hair was golden yellow, and it floated
  to my shoe,
My eyes were like two harebells bathed in
  shining drops of dew;
My palfrey, never stopping, made a music
  sweetly blent
With the leaves of autumn dropping all
  around me as I went;
And I heard the bells, grown fainter, far
  behind me peal and play,
Fainter, fainter, fainter, fainter, till they
  seem'd to die away;
And beside a silver runnel, on a lonely heap
  of sand,
I saw the green Gnome sitting, with his
  cheek upon his hand;
Then he started up to see me, and he ran
  with cry and bound,
And drew me from my palfrey white, and
  set me on the ground:
O crimson, crimson, were his locks, his face
  was green to see,
But he cried, 'O light-hair'd lassie, you are
  bound to marry me!'
He claspt me round the middle small, he
  kissed me on the cheek,
He kissed me once, he kissed me twice—I
  could not stir or speak;
He kissed me twice, he kissed me thrice—
  but when he kissed again,
I called aloud upon the name of Him who
  died for men!

Ring, sing! ring, sing; pleasant Sabbath
  bells!
Chime, rhyme! chime, rhyme! through the
  dales and dells!
Rhyme, ring! chime, sing! pleasant Sab-
  bath bells!
Chime, sing! rhyme, ring! over fields and
  fells!

O faintly, faintly, faintly, calling men and
  maids to pray,
So faintly, faintly, faintly, rang the bells
  afar away;
And as I named the Blessed Name, as in
  our need we can,
The ugly green green Gnome became a tall
  and comely man!

His hands were white, his beard was gold,
 his eyes were black as sloes,
His tunic was of scarlet woof, and silken
 were his hose ;
A pensive light from Faëryland still linger'd
 on his cheek,
His voice was like the running brook, when
 he began to speak :
'O you have cast away the charm my step-
 dame put on me,
Seven years I dwelt in Faëryland, and you
 have set me free !
O I will mount thy palfrey white, and ride
 to kirk with thee,
And by those sweetly shining eyes, we twain
 will wedded be !'

Back we gallop'd, never stopping, he before
 and I behind,
And the autumn leaves were dropping, red
 and yellow, in the wind,
And the sun was shining clearer, and my
 heart was high and proud,
As nearer, nearer, nearer, rang the kirk-
 bells sweet and loud,
And we saw the kirk before us, as we trotted
 down the fells,
And nearer, clearer, o'er us, rang the wel-
 come of the bells !

Ring, sing ! ring, sing ! pleasant Sabbath
 bells !
Chime, rhyme ! chime, rhyme ! through the
 dales and dells !
Rhyme, ring ! chime, sing ! pleasant Sab-
 bath bells !
Chime, sing ! rhyme, ring ! over fields and
 fells !

HUGH SUTHERLAND'S PANSIES.

The aged Minister of Inverburn,
A mild heart hidden under features stern,
Leans in the sunshine on the garden-rale,
Pensive, yet happy, as he tells this tale,—
And he who listens sees the garden lie
Blue as a little patch of fallen sky.

'THE lily minds me of a maiden brow,'
Hugh Sutherland would say ; ' the marigold
Is full and sunny like her yellow hair,
The full-blown rose her lips with sweetness
 tipt ;
But if you seek a likeness to her eyes—
Go to the pansy, friend, and find it there !'
'Ay, leeze me on the pansies !' Hugh would
 say—
Hugh Sutherland, the weaver—he who
 dwelt
Here in the white-wash'd cot you fancy so—
Who knew the learnëd names of all the
 flowers,
And recognised the lily, tho' its head
Rose in a ditch of dull Latinity !

Pansies ? You praise the ones that grow
 to-day
Here in the garden : had you seen the place
When Sutherland was living ! Here they
 grew,
From blue to deeper blue, in midst of each
A golden dazzle like a glimmering star,
Each broader, bigger, than a silver crown ;
While here the weaver sat, his labour done,
Watching his azure pets and rearing them,
Until they seem'd to know his step and
 touch,
And stir beneath his smile like living things !
The very sunshine loved them, and would
 lie
Here happy, coming early, lingering late,
Because they were so fair.

     Hugh Sutherland
Was country-bred—I knew him from the
 time
When on a bed of pain he lost a limb,
And rose at last, a lame and sickly lad,
Apprenticed to the loom—a peevish lad,
Mooning among the shadows by himself.
Among these shadows, with the privilege
Of one who loved his flock, I sought him
 out,
And gently as I could I won his heart ;
And then, tho' he was young and I was old,
We soon grew friends. He told his griefs
 to me,
His joys, his troubles, and I help'd him on ;
Yet sought in vain to drive away the cloud
Deep pain had left upon his sickly cheek,
And lure him from the shades that deepen'd
 it.
Then Heaven took the task upon itself
And sent an angel down among the flowers !
Almost before I knew the work was done,
I found him settled in this but and ben,

Where, with an eye that brighten'd, he had found
The sunshine loved his garden, and begun
To rear his pansies.

Sutherland was poor,
Rude, and untutor'd; peevish, too, when first
The angel in his garden found him out;
But pansy-growing made his heart within
Blow fresh and fragrant. When he came to share
This cottage with a brother of the craft,
Only some poor and sickly bunches bloom'd,
Vagrant, though fair, among the garden-plots;
And idly, carelessly, he water'd these,
Spread them and train'd them, till they grew and grew
In size and beauty, and the angel thrust
Its bright arms upward thro' the bright'ning sod,
And clung around the sickly gardener's heart.
Then Sutherland grew calmer, and the cloud
Was fading from his face. Well, by-and-by,
The country people saw and praised the flowers,
And what at first had been an idle joy
Became a sober serious work for fame.
Next, being won to send a bunch for show,
He gained a prize—a sixth or seventh rate,
And slowly gath'ring courage, rested not
Till he had won the highest prize of all.
Here in the sunshine and the shade he toil'd
Early and late in joy, and, by-and-by,
Rose high in fame; for not a botanist,
A lover of the flowers, poor man or rich,
Came to the village, but the people said
'Go down the lane to Weaver Sutherland's,
And see his pansies!'

Thus the summers pass'd,
And Sutherland grew gentler, happier;
The angel God had sent him clung to him:
There grew a rapturous sadness in his tone
When he was gladdest, like the dewiness
That moistens pansies when they bloom the best;
And in his face there dawn'd a gentle light
Like that which softly clings about a flow'r,
And makes you love it. Yet his heart was glad
More for the pansies' sakes than for his own:
His eye was like a father's, moist and bright,
When they were praised; and, as I said, they seem'd
To make themselves as beauteous as they could,
Smiling to please him. Blessings on the flowers!
They were his children! Father never loved
His little darlings more, or for their sakes
Fretted so dumbly! Father never bent
More tenderly above his little ones,
In the still watches of the night, when sleep
Breathes balm upon their eyelids! Night and day
Poor Hugh was careful for the gentle things
Whose presence brought a sunshine to the place
Where sickness dwelt: this one was weak and small,
And needed watching like a sickly child;
This one so beauteous, that it shamed its mates
And made him angry with its beauteousness.
'I cannot rest!' cried Hughie with a smile,
'I scarcely snatch a moment to myself—
They plague me so!' Part fun, part earnest, this:
He loved the pansies better than he knew.
Ev'n in the shadow of his weaving-room
They haunted him and brighten'd on his soul:
Daily while busy working at the loom
The humming seem'd a mystic melody
To which the pansies sweetly grew and grew—
A leaf unrolling soft to every note,
A change of colours with the change of sound;
And walking to the door to rest himself,
Still with the pleasant murmur in his ears,
He saw the flowers and heard the melody
They make in growing! Pleasure such as this,
So exquisite, so lonely, might have pass'd
Into the shadowy restlessness of yore;
But wholesome human contact saved him here,
And kept him fresh and meek. The people came
To stir him with their praise, and he would show

The medals and the prizes he had got—
As proud and happy as a child who gains
A prize in school.
     The angel still remain'd
In winter, when the garden-plots were bare,
And deep winds piloted the wandering snow:
He saw its gleaming in the cottage fire,
While, with a book of botany on his knee,
He sat and hunger'd for the breath of spring.
The angel of the flowers was with him still!
Here beds of roses sweeten'd all the page;
Here lilies whiter than the falling snow
Crept gleaming softly from the printed lines;
Here dewy violets sparkled till the book
Dazzled his eyes with rays of misty blue;
And here, amid a page of Latin names,
All the sweet Scottish flowers together grew
With fragrance of the summer.

       Hugh and I
Were still fast friends, and still I help'd him on;
And often in the pleasant summer-time,
The service over, on the Sabbath day,
I join'd him in the garden, where we sat
And chatted in the sun. But all at once
It came upon me that the gardener's hand
Had grown less diligent; for tho' 'twas June
The garden that had been the village pride
Look'd but the shadow of its former self;
And ere a week was out I saw in church
Two samples fairer far than any blown
In Hughie's garden—blooming brighter far
In sweeter soil. What wonder that a man,
Loving the pansies as the weaver did—
A skilful judge, moreover—should admire
Sweet Mary Moffat's sparkling pansy-eyes?

The truth was out. The weaver play'd the game
(I christen'd it in sport that very day)
Of ' Love among the Pansies!' As he spoke,
Telling me all, I saw upon his face
The peevish cloud that it had worn in youth;
I cheer'd him as I could, and bade him hope:
'You both are poor, but, Sutherland, God's flowers
Are poor as well!' He brighten'd as I spoke,
And answer'd, 'It is settled! I have kept
The secret till the last, lest "nay" should come
And spoil it all; but "ay" has come instead,
And all the help we wait for is your own!'

Even here, I think, his angel clung to him.
The fairies of his garden haunted him
With similes and sympathies that made
His likes and dislikes, though he knew it not.
Beauty he loved if it was meek and mild,
And like his pansies tender ev'n to tears;
And so he chose a maiden pure and low,
Who, like his garden pets, had love to spare,
Sunshine to cast upon his pallid cheek,
And yet a tender clinging thing, too weak
To bloom uncared for and unsmiled upon.

Soon Sutherland and she he loved were one,—
And bonnily a moon of honey gleam'd
At night among the flowers! Amid the spring
That follow'd, blossom'd with the other buds
A tiny maiden with her mother's eyes.
The little garden was itself again,
The sunshine sparkled on the azure beds;
The angel Heaven had sent to save a soul
Stole from the blooms and took an infant shape;
And wild with pleasure, seeing how the flowers
Had given her their choicest lights and shades,
The father bore his baby to the font
And had her christen'd PANSY.

       After that
Poor Hugh was happy as the days were long,
Divided in his cares for all his pets,
And proudest of the one he loved the best.
The summer found him merry as a king,
Dancing the little one upon his knee
Here in the garden, while the plots around
Gleam'd in the sun, and seem'd as glad as he.

But moons of honey wane, and summer suns
Of wedlock set to bring the autumn in!
Hugh Sutherland, with wife and child to feed,
Wrought sore to gain his pittance in a world
His pansies made so fair. Came Poverty
With haggard eyes to dwell within the house;

When first she saw the garden she was glad,
And, seated on the threshold, smiled and span.
But times grew harder, bread was scarce as gold,
A shadow fell on Pansy and the flowers;
And when the strife was sorest, Hugh received
An office—lighter work and higher pay—
To take a foreman's place in Edinglass.
'Twas hard, 'twas hard, to leave the little place
He loved so dearly; but the weaver look'd
At Mary, saw the sorrow in her face,
And gave consent,—happy at heart to think
His dear ones would not want. To Edinglass
They went, and settled. Thro' the winter hours
Bravely the weaver toil'd; his wife and child
Were happy, he was heartsome—tho' his taste
Was grassy lowlands and the caller air.

The cottage here remain'd untenanted,
The angel of the flowers forsook the place,
The sunshine faded, and the pansies died.

Two summers pass'd; and still in Edinglass
The weaver toil'd, and ever when I went
Into the city, to his house I hied—
A welcome guest. Now first, I saw a change
Had come to Sutherland: for he was pale
And peevish, had a venom on his tongue,
And hung the under-lip like one that doubts.
Part of the truth I heard, and part I saw—
But knew too late, when all the ill was done!
At first, poor Hugh had shrunk from making friends,
And pored among his books of botany,
And later, in the dull dark nights he sat,
A dismal book upon his knee, and read:
A book no longer full of leaves and flowers,
That glimmer'd on the soul's sweet consciousness,
Yet seem'd to fill the eye,—a dismal book,—
Big-sounding Latin, English dull and dark,
And not a breath of summer in it all.
The sunshine perish'd in the city's smoke,
The pansies grew no more to comfort him,
And he began to spend his nights with those
Who waste their substance in the public-house:
The flowers had lent a sparkle to his talk,
Which pleased the muddled wits of idle men;
Sought after, treated, liked by one and all,
He took to drinking; and at last lay down
Stupid and senseless on a rainy night,
And ere he waken'd caught the flaming fire,
Which gleams to white-heat on the face and burns
Clear crimson in the lungs.

But it was long,
Ere any knew poor Hughie's plight; and, ere
He saw his danger, on the mother's breast
Lay Pansy withering—tho' the dewy breath
Of spring was floating like a misty rain
Down from the mountains. Then the tiny flower
Folded its leaves in silence, and the sleep
That dwells in winter on the flower-beds
Fell on the weaver's house. At that sad hour
I enter'd, scarcely welcomed with a word
Of greeting: by the hearth the woman sat
Weeping full sore, her apron o'er a face
Haggard with midnight watching, while the man
Cover'd his bloodshot eyes and cursed himself.
Then leaning o'er, my hand on his, I said—
'She could not bear the smoke of cities, Hugh!
God to His Garden has transplanted her,
Where summer dwells for ever and the air
Is fresh and pure!' But Hughie did not speak;
I saw full plainly that he blamed himself;
And ere the day was out he bent above
His little sleeping flower, and wept, and said:
'Ay, sir! she wither'd, wither'd like the rest,
Neglected!' and I saw his heart was full.
When Pansy slept beneath the churchyard grass
Poor Hughie's angel had return'd to Heaven,
And all his heart was dark. His ways grew strange,
Peevish, and sullen; often he would sit
And drink alone; the wife and he grew cold,
And harsh to one another; till at last
A stern physician put an end to all,
And told him he must die.

No bitter cry,
No sound of wailing rose within the house
After the Doctor spoke, but Mary mourn'd
In silence, Hughie smoked his pipe and set
His teeth together, at the ingleside.
Days pass'd; the only token of a change
Was Hughie's face—the peevish cloud of care
Seem'd melting to a tender gentleness.
After a time, the wife forgot her grief,
Or could at times forget it, in the care
Her husband's sickness brought. I went to them
As often as I could, for Sutherland
Was dear to me, and dearer for his sin.
Weak as he was he did his best to toil,
But it was weary work! By slow degrees,
When May was breathing on the sickly bunch
Of mignonette upon the window-sill,
I saw his smile was softly wearing round
To what it used to be, when here he sat
Rearing his flowers; altho'. his brow at times
Grew cloudy, and he gnaw'd his under lip.
At last I found him seated by the hearth,
Trying to read: I led his mind to themes
Of old langsyne, and saw his eyes grow dim:
'O sir,' he cried, 'I cannot, cannot rest!
Something I long for, and I know not what,
Torments me night and day!' I saw it all,
And sparkling with the brilliance of the thought,
Look'd in his eyes and caught his hand, and cried,
'Hugh, it's the pansies! Spring has come again,
The sunshine breathes its gold upon the air
And threads it through the petals of the flowers,
Yet here you linger in the dark!' I ceased
And watch'd him. Then he trembled as he said,
'I see it now, for as I read the book
The lines and words, the Latin seem'd to bud,
And they peep'd thro'.' He smiled, like one ashamed,
Adding in a low voice, ' I long to see
The pansies ere I die!'

What heart of stone
Could throb on coldly, Sir, at words like those?

Not mine, not mine! Within a week poor Hugh
Had left the smoke of Edinglass behind,
And felt the wind that runs along the lanes,
Spreading a carpet of the grass and flowers
For June the sunny-hair'd to walk upon.
In the old cottage here he dwelt again:
The place was wilder than it once had been,
But buds were blowing green around about,
And with the glad return of Sutherland,
The angel of the flowers came back again.
The end was near and Hugh was wearied out,
And like a flower was closing up his leaves
Under the dropping of the gloaming dews.

And daily, in the summer afternoon,
I found him seated on the threshold there,
Watching his flowers, and all the place, I thought,
Brighten'd when he was nigh. Now first I talk'd
Of heavenly hopes unto him, and I knew
The angel help'd me. On the day he died
The pain had put its shadow on his face,
The words of doubt were on his tremulous lips:
'Ah, Hughie, life is easy!' I exclaim'd,
'Easier, better, than we know ourselves:
'Tis pansy-growing on a mighty scale,
And God above us is the gardener.
The fairest win the prizes, that is just,
But all the flowers are dear to God the Lord:
The Gardener loves them all, He loves them all!'
He saw the sunshine on the pansy-beds
And brighten'd. Then by slow degrees he grew
Cheerful and meek as dying man could be,
And as I spoke there came from far-away
The faint sweet melody of Sabbath bells.
And 'Hugh,' I said, 'if God the Gardener
Neglected those he rears as you have done
Your pansies and your Pansy, it were ill
For we who blossom in His garden. Night
And morning He is busy at His work.
He smiles to give us sunshine, and we live:
He stoops to pluck us softly, and our hearts
Tremble to see the darkness, knowing not
It is the shadow He, in stooping, casts.
He pluckt your Pansy so, and it was well.
But, Hugh, though some be beautiful and grand,

Some sickly, like yourself, and mean and
　　poor,
He loves them all, the Gardener loves them
　　all!'
Then later, when he could no longer sit
Out on the threshold, and the end was near,
We set a plate of pansies by his bed
To cheer him. 'He is coming near,' I said,
'Great is the garden, but the Gardener
Is coming to the corner where you bloom
　　So sickly!' And he smiled, and moan'd,
　　'I hear!'
And sank upon his pillow wearily.
His hollow eyes no longer bore the light,
The darkness gather'd round him as I said,
'The Gardener is standing at your side,
His shade is on you and you cannot see:
O Lord, that lovest both the strong and
　　weak,
Pluck him and wear him!' Even as I
　　pray'd,
I felt the shadow there and hid my face;
But when I look'd again the flower was
　　pluck'd,
The shadow gone: the sunshine thro' the
　　blind
Gleam'd faintly, and the widow'd woman
　　wept.

THE DEAD MOTHER.

I.

As I lay asleep, as I lay asleep,
Under the grass as I lay so deep,
As I lay asleep in my cotton serk
Under the shade of Our Lady's Kirk,
I waken'd up in the dead of night,
I waken'd up in my death-serk white,
And I heard a cry from far away,
And I knew the voice of my daughter May:
'Mother, mother, come hither to me!
Mother, mother, come hither and see!
Mother, mother, mother dear,
Another mother is sitting here:
My body is bruised, and in pain I cry,
On straw in the dark afraid I lie,
I thirst and hunger for drink and meat,
And mother, mother, to sleep were sweet!'
I heard the cry, though my grave was deep,
And awoke from sleep, and awoke from
　　sleep.

II.

I awoke from sleep, I awoke from sleep,
Up I rose from my grave so deep!
The earth was black, but overhead
The stars were yellow, the moon was red;
And I walk'd along all white and thin,
And lifted the latch and enter'd in,
And reach'd the chamber as dark as night,
And though it was dark my face was white:
'Mother, mother, I look on thee!
Mother, mother, you frighten me!
For your cheeks are thin and your hair is
　　gray!'
But I smiled, and kiss'd her fears away,
I smooth'd her hair and I sang a song,
And on my knee I rock'd her long:
'O mother, mother, sing low to me—
I am sleepy now, and I cannot see!'
I kiss'd her, but I could not weep,
And she went to sleep, she went to sleep.

III.

As we lay asleep, as we lay asleep,
My May and I, in our grave so deep,
As we lay asleep in the midnight mirk,
Under the shade of our Lady's Kirk,
I waken'd up in the dead of night,
Though May my daughter lay warm and
　　white,
And I heard the cry of a little one,
And I knew 'twas the voice of Hugh my
　　son:
'Mother, mother, come hither to me!
Mother, mother, come hither and see!
Mother, mother, mother dear,
Another mother is sitting here:
My body is bruised and my heart is sad,
But I speak my mind and call them bad;
I thirst and hunger night and day,
And were I strong I would fly away!'
I heard the cry, though my grave was deep,
And awoke from sleep, and awoke from
　　sleep!

IV.

I awoke from sleep, I awoke from sleep,
Up I rose from my grave so deep,
The earth was black, but overhead
The stars were yellow, the moon was red;
And I walk'd along all white and thin,
And lifted the latch and enter'd in.

'Mother, mother, and art thou here?
I know your face, and I feel no fear;
Raise me, mother, and kiss my cheek,
For oh I am weary and sore and weak.'
I smooth'd his hair with a mother's joy,
And he laugh'd aloud, my own brave boy;
I mised and held him on my breast,
Sang him a song, and bade him rest.
'Mother, mother, sing low to me—
I am sleepy now and I cannot see!'
I kiss'd him, and I could not weep,
As he went to sleep, as he went to sleep.

V.

As I lay asleep, as I lay asleep,
With my girl and boy in my grave so deep,
As I lay asleep, I awoke in fear,
Awoke, but awoke not my children dear,
And heard a cry so low and weak
From a tiny voice that could not speak;
I heard the cry of a little one,
My bairn that could neither talk nor run,
My little, little one, uncaress'd,
Starving for lack of the milk of the breast;
And I rose from sleep and enter'd in,
And found my little one pinch'd and thin,
And croon'd a song and hush'd its moan,
And put its lips to my white breast-bone;
And the red, red moon that lit the place
Went white to look at the little face,
And I kiss'd and kiss'd, and I could not weep,
As it went to sleep, as it went to sleep.

VI.

As it lay asleep, as it lay asleep,
I set it down in the darkness deep,
Smooth'd its limbs and laid it out,
And drew the curtains around about;
Then into the dark, dark room I hied
Where he lay awake at the woman's side,
And though the chamber was black as night,
He saw my face, for it was so white;
I gazed in his eyes, and he shriek'd in pain,
And I knew he would never sleep again,
And back to my grave went silently,
And soon my baby was brought to me;
My son and daughter beside me rest,
My little baby is on my breast;
Our bed is warm and our grave is deep,
But he cannot sleep, he cannot sleep!

THE WIDOW MYSIE.

AN IDYL OF LOVE AND WHISKY.

Tom Love, a man 'prepared for friend or foe,
Whisker'd, well-featured, tight from top to toe.'

O WIDOW MYSIE, smiling, soft, and sweet!
O Mysie, buxom as a sheaf of wheat!
O Mysie, Widow Mysie, late Monroe,
Foul fall the traitor-face that served me so!
O Mysie Love, a second time a bride,
I pity him who tosses at your side—
Who took, by honied smiles and speech misled,
A beauteous bush of brambles to his bed!

You saw her at the ploughing match, you ken,
Ogling the whisky and the handsome men:
The smiling woman in the Paisley shawl,
Plump as a partridge, and as broad as tall,
With ribbons, bows, and jewels fair to see,
Bursting to blossom like an apple-tree,
Ay, that was Mysie,—now two score and ten,
Now Madam Love of Bungo in the Glen!
Ay, that was Mysie, tho' her looks no more
Dazzle with beams of brightness as of yore!—
The tiny imps that nested in her eyes,
Winning alike the wanton and the wise,
Have ta'en the flame that made my heart forlorn
Back to the nameless place, where they were born.

O years roll on, and fair things fade and pine!—
Twelve sowings since and I was twenty-nine:
With ploughman's coat on back, and plough in hand,
I wrought at Bungo on my father's land,
And all the neighbour-lassies, stale or fair,
Tried hard to net my father's son and heir.
My heart was lightsome, cares I had but few,
I climb'd the mountains, drank the mountain dew,
Could sit a mare as mettlesome as fire,
Could put the stone with any in the shire,

THE WIDOW MYSIE.

Had been to college, and had learn'd to dance,
Could blether thro' my nose like folks in France,
And stood erect, prepared for friend or foe,
Whisker'd, well-featured, tight from top to toe.

'A marriageable man, for every claim
Of lawful wedlock fitted,' you exclaim?
But, sir, of all that men enjoy or treasure,
Wedlock, I fancied, was the driest pleasure.
True ; seated at some pretty peasant's side,
Under the slanted sheaves I loved to bide,
Lilting the burthen of a Scottish tune,
To sit, and kiss perchance, and watch the moon,
Pillow'd on breasts like beds of lilies white
Heaving and falling in the pale moonlight ;
But rather would have sat with crimson face
Upon the cutty-stool with Jean or Grace,
Than buy in kirk a partner with the power
To turn the mother-milk of Freedom sour.

I loved a comely face, as I have said,
But sharply watch'd the maids who wish'd to wed,—
I knew their arts, was not so cheaply won,
They loved my father's Siller, not his Son.
Still, laughing in my sleeve, I here and there
Took liberties allow'd my father's heir,
Stole kisses from the comeliest of the crew,
And smiled upon the virgin nettles too.
So might the game have daunder'd on till this,
And lasted till my father went to bliss,—
But Widow Mysie came, as sly as sin,
And settled in the 'William Wallace' Inn.

The Inn had gone to rack and loss complete
Since Simpson drown'd himself in whisky neat ;
And poor Jock Watt, who follow'd in his shoes,
Back'd by the sourest, gumliest of shrews,
(The whisky vile, the water never hot,
The very sugar sour'd by Mistress Watt,)
Had found the gossips, grumbling, groaning, stray
To Sandie Kirkson's, half a mile away.
But hey ! at Widow Mysie's rosy face,
A change came o'er the spirits of the place,

The fire blazed high, the shining pewter smiled,
The glasses glitter'd bright, the water boil'd,
Grand was the whisky, Highland born and fine,
And Mysie, Widow Mysie, was divine !

O sweet was Widow Mysie, sweet and sleek !
The peach's blush and down were on her cheek,
And there were dimples in her tender chin
For Cupids small to hunt for kisses in ;
Dark-glossy were her ringlets, each a prize,
And wicked, wicked were her beaded eyes ;
Plump was her figure, rounded and complete,
And tender were her tiny tinkling feet !
All this was nothing to the warmth and light
That seem'd to hover o'er her day and night ;—
Where'er she moved, she seem'd to soothe and please
With pleasant murmurs as of humble-bees ;
Her small plump hands on public missions flew
Like snow-white doves that flying croon and coo ;
Her feet fell patter, cheep, like little mice ;
Her breath was soft with sugar and with spice ;
And when her finger - so !—your hand would press,
You tingled to the toes with loveliness,
While her dark eyes, with lessening zone in zone,
Flasht sunlight on the mirrors of your own,
Dazzling your spirit with a wicked sense
That seem'd more heavenly-born than innocence !

Sure one so beauteous and so sweet had graced
And cheer'd the scene, where'er by Fortune placed ;
But with a background of the pewter bright,
Whereon the fire cast gleams of rosy light,
With jingling glasses round her, and a scent
Of spice and lemon-peel where'er she went,
What wonder she should to the cronies seem
An angel, in a cloud of toddy steam ?
What wonder, while I sipt my glass one day,
She, and the whisky, stole my heart away ?

She was not loath!—for, while her comely face
Shone full on other haunters of the place,
From me she turn'd her head and peep'd full sly
With just the corner of her roguish eye,
And blush'd so bright my toddy seem'd to glow
Beneath the rosy blush and sweeter grow;
And once, at my request, she took a sip,
And nectar'd all the liquor with her lip.
'Take heed! for Widow Mysie's game is plain,'
The gossips cried, but warn'd me all in vain:
Like sugar melting at the toddy's kiss,
My very caution was dissolved in bliss,
Fear died for ever with a mocking laugh,
And Mysie's kisses made his epitaph.

Kisses? Ay, faith, they follow'd score on score,
After the first I stole behind the door,
And lingered softly on these lips of mine
Like Massie whisky drunk by bards divine.
But O! the glow, the rapture, and the glee,
That night she let me draw her on my knee—
When bliss thrill'd from her to my fingertips,
Then eddied wildly to my burning lips,
From which she drank it back with kisses fain,
Then blush'd and glow'd and breathed it back again—
Till, madden'd with the ecstasy divine,
I clasp'd her close and craved her to be mine,
And thrilling, panting, struggling up to fly,
She breathed a spicy 'Yes' with glistening eye,
And while my veins grew fire, my heart went wild,
Fell like a sunbeam on my heart, and smiled!

The deed thus done, I hied me home, you say,
And rued my folly when I woke next day?
Nay! all my business was to crave and cry
That Heaven would haste the holy knot to tie,
Though 'Mysie lass,' I said, 'my gold and gear
Are small, and will be small for many a year,
Since father is but fifty years and three,
And tough as cobbler's wax, though spare and wee!'

'Ah, Tam,' she sigh'd, 'there's nothing there to rue—
The gold, the gear, that Mysie wants is you!'
And brightly clad, with kisses thrilling through me,
Clung like a branch of trembling blossoms to me.

I found my father making up his books,
With yellow eyes and penny-hunting looks.
'Father,' I said, 'I'm sick of single life,
And will, if you are willing, take a wife.'
'Humph,' snapt my father, '(six and four are ten,
And ten are twenty)—Marry? who? and when?'
'Mistress Monroe,' I said, 'that keeps the inn.'
At that he shrugg'd his shoulders with a grin:
'I guess'd as much! the tale has gone the round!
Ye might have stay'd till I was underground!
But please yourself—I've nothing to refuse,
Choose where you will—you're old enough to choose;
But mind,' he added, blinking yellow eye,
'I'll handle my own guineas till I die!
Frankly I own, you might have chosen worse,
Since you have little siller in your purse—
The Inn is thriving, if report be true,
And Widow Mysie has enough for two!'

'And if we wait till he has gone his way,
Why, Mysie, I'll be bald, and you'll be gray,'
I said to Mysie, laughing at her side.
'Oh, let him keep his riches,' she replied,
'He's right! there's plenty here for you and me!
May he live long; and happy may he be!'
'O Mysie, you're an angel,' I return'd,
With eye that glisten'd dewily and yearn'd.
Then running off she mixed, with tender glee,
A glass of comfort—sat her on my knee—
'Come, Tam!' she cried, 'who cares a fig for wealth—
Ay, let him keep it all, and here's his health!'
And added, shining brightly on my breast,
'Ah, Tam, the siller's worthless—Love is best!'

O Widow Mysie, wert thou first sincere,
When tender accents trembled on mine ear,
Like bees that o'er a flower will float and fleet,
And ere they light make murmurs soft and sweet?
Or was the light that render'd me unwise,
Guile's—the sly Quaker with the downcast eyes?
O Widow Mysie, not at once are we
Taught the false scripture of Hypocrisy!
Even pink Selfishness has times, I know,
When thro' his fat a patriot's feelings glow;
Falsehood first learns her nature with a sigh,
And nurses bitterly her first-born Lie!

Days pass'd; and I began, to my amaze,
To see a colder light in Mysie's gaze;
Once when, with arm about her softly wound,
I snatch'd a kiss, she snapt and flusht and frown'd;
But oftener her face a shadow wore,
Such as had never darken'd it before;
I spoke of this, I begg'd her to explain,—
She tapt my cheek, and smiled, and mused again.
But, in the middle of my love-alarm,
The Leech's watch went 'tick' at Bungo Farm;
My father sicken'd, and his features cold
Retain'd the hue, without the gleam, of gold.

Then Mysie soften'd, sadden'd, and would speak
Of father's sickness with a dewy cheek;
When to the Inn I wander'd, unto me,
Lightly, as if she walk'd on wool, came she,
And 'Is he better?' 'Is he changed at all?'
And 'Heaven help him!' tenderly would call.
'So old—so ill—untended and alone!
He is your father, Tam,—and seems my own!'
And musing stood, one little hand of snow
Nestling and fluttering on my shoulder—so!
But father sicken'd on, and then one night,
When we were sitting in the ingle-light,
'O Tam,' she cried, 'I have it!—I should ne'er
Forgive myself for staying idly here,
While he, your father, lack'd in his distress
The love, the care, a daughter's hands possess—
He knows our troth—he will not say me nay;
But let me nurse him as a daughter may,
And he may live, for darker cases mend,
To bless us and to join us in the end!'
'But, Mysie——' 'Not a word, the thing is plann'd,'
She said, and stopt my mouth with warm white hand.
She went with gentle eyes that very night,
Stole to the chamber like a moonbeam white;
My father scowl'd at first, but soon was won—
The keep was carried, and the deed was done.

O Heaven! in what strange Enchanter's den
Learnt she the spells wherewith she conquer'd men?
When to that chamber she had won her way,
The old man's cheek grew brighter every day;
She smooth'd the pillows underneath his head,
She brought sweet music roundabout his bed,
She made the very mustard-blisters glow
With fire as soft as youthful lovers know,
The very physic bottles lost their gloom
And seem'd like little fairies in the room,
The very physic, charm'd by her, grew fine,
Rhubarb was nectar, castor-oil was wine.
Half darkly, dimly, yet with secret flame
That titillated up and down his frame,
The grim old man lay still, with hungry eye
Watching her thro' the room on tiptoe fly;—
She turn'd her back—his cheek grew dull and dim!
She turn'd her face—its sunshine fell on him!
Better and better every day grew he,
Colder and colder grew his nurse to me,
Till up he leapt, with fresher new life astir,
And only sank again—to kneel to her!

'Mysie!' I cried, with flushing face, too late
Stung by the pois'nous things whose names I hate,
Which in so many household fires flit free,
The salamanders, Doubt and Jealousy,—

'Mysie!'—and then, in accents fierce and bold,
Demanded why her looks had grown so cold?
She trembled, flush'd, a tear was in her eye,
She dropt her gaze, and heaved a balmy sigh,
Then spoke with tender pauses low and sad:
Had I a heart? She knew full well I had.
Could I without a conscience-qualm behold
My white-hair'd father, weak, untended, old,
Who had so very short a time to live,
Reft of the peace a woman's hands can give?
'Mysie!' I shriek'd, with heart that seem'd to rend,
With glaring eyes, and every hair on end.
Clasping her little hands, 'O Tam,' she cried,
'Save for my help your father would have died;
Bliss! to have saved your filial heart that sorrow!
But for my help, why, he may die to-morrow.
Go, Tam!—this weak warm heart I cannot trust
To utter more—be generous! be just!
I long have felt—I say it in humility—
A sort of—kind of—incompatibility!
Go, Tam! Be happy! Bless you! Wed another!
And I shall ever love you!—as a mother!'

Sir, so it was. Stunn'd, thunder-stricken, wild,
I raved, while father trembled, Mysie smiled;
O'er all the country-side the scandal rang,
And ere I knew, the bells began to clang;—
And shutting eyes and stopping ears, as red
As ricks on fire, I blushing turn'd and fled.
Twelve years have pass'd since I escaped the net,
And father, tough as leather, lingers yet,
A gray mare rules, the laugh has come to me,
I sport, and thank my stars that I am free!
If Mysie likes her bargain ill or well,
Only the Deil, who won it her, can tell;
But she, who could so well his arts pursue,
May learn a trick to cheat her Teacher too.

THE MINISTER AND THE ELFIN.

I.

'O WHO among you will win for me
The soul of the Preacher of Woodilee?
For he prays, he preaches, he labours sore,
He cheats me alike of rich and poor,
And his cheek is pale with a thought divine,
And I would, I would that he were mine?'
'O surely *I* will win for thee
The Minister of Woodilee;
Round and around the elfin tree,
Where we are fleeting in company,
The Minister of Woodilee,
Laughing aloud, shall dance with me!'

II.

The Minister rode in the white moonshine,
His face was pale with his thought divine,
And he saw beneath the greenwood tree
As sweet a maiden as well could be:
My hair of gold to my feet fell bright,
My eyes were blue, and my brow was white,
My cheeks were fresh as the milk of kine
Mingled with drops of red red wine,
And they shone thro' my veil o' the silk with gleam
Like a lover's face thro' a thin light dream;
But the sickness of death was in mine ee,
And my face was pallid and sad to see,
And I moaned aloud as the man came near,
And I heard him mutter a prayer in fear!

III.

But the Minister, when he look'd on me,
Leapt down and set my head on his knee,
Wet my lips with the running stream,
And I open'd my eyes as in a dream,
I open'd my eyes and look'd on him,
And his head whirl'd round and his cheek grew dim!
I kiss'd him twice, I kiss'd him thrice,
Till he kiss'd again with lips of ice,
Till he kiss'd again with lips of stone,
And clasp'd me close to his cold breast-bone;
And tho' his face was weary and sad,
He laugh'd aloud and seem'd mad, so mad.
Then up to my feet I leapt in glee,
And round and round and around went we,
Under the moonlit greenwood tree!

IV.

He leapt on his steed and home rode he,
The Minister of Woodilee ;
And when at the door of the manse he rein'd,
With blood his lips were damp'd and stain'd,
And he pray'd a prayer for his shame and sin,
And dropt a tear as he enter'd in,
But the smile divine from his face had fled,
When he laid him down on his dying bed.

V.

'O thanks, for thou hast won for me
The Minister of Woodilee,
Who nevermore, O nevermore,
Shall preach and pray and labour sore,
And cheat me alike of rich and poor,
For the smile divine no more wears he—
Hasten and bring his soul to me!'

VI.

Oh, off I ran his soul to win,
And the gray gray manse I enter'd in,
And I saw him lying on his bed,
With book and candle at his head ;
But when he turn'd him, weary and weak,
A smile and a tear were on his cheek,
And he took my hand and kiss'd it thrice,
Tho' his lips were clammy cold as ice.
'O wherefore, wherefore, dost thou
One who has stolen thy soul from bliss?'
Then over his face so pale with pain
The thought divine came back again,
And 'I love thee more for the shame,' he said,
'I love thee more on my dying bed,
And I cannot, cannot love thee less,
Tho' my heart is wae for its wickedness ;
I love thee better, I love thee best,
Sweet Spirit that errest and wanderest ;
Colder and colder my blood doth run,
I pray for thee, pray for thee, little one!'
Then I heard the bell for the dying toll,
And I reach'd out hands to seize his soul,
But I trembled and shriek'd to see as he died
An angel in white at his bedside!
And I fled away to the greenwood tree,
Where the elves were fleeting in company,
And I hate my immortality,
And 'twere better to be a man and dee!

VILLAGE VOICES.

I.

JANUARY WIND.

I.

THE wind, wife, the wind ; how it blows, how it blows ;
It grips the latch, it shakes the house, it whistles, it screams, it crows,
It dashes on the window-pane, then rushes off with a cry,
Ye scarce can hear your own loud voice, it clatters so loud and high ;
And far away upon the sea it floats with thunder-call,
The wind, wife, the wind, wife ; the wind that did it all!

II.

The wind, wife, the wind ; how it blew, how it blew ;
The very night our boy was born, it whistled, it scream'd, it crew ;
And while you moan'd upon your bed, and your heart was dark with fright,
I swear it mingled with the soul of the boy you bore that night ;
It scarcely seems a winter since, and the wind is with us still,—
The wind, wife ; the wind, wife ; the wind that blew us ill!

III.

The wind, wife, the wind ; how it blows, how it blows!
It changes, shifts, without a cause, it ceases, it comes and goes ;
And David ever was the same, wayward, and wild, and bold—
For wilful lad will have his way, and the wind no hand can hold ;
But ah! the wind, the changeful wind, was more in the blame than he ;
The wind, wife ; the wind, wife, that blew him out to sea!

IV.

The wind, wife; the wind ; now 'tis still, now 'tis still ;
And as we sit I seem to feel the silence shiver and thrill,

'Twas thus the night he went away, and we
   sat in silence here,
We listen'd to our beating hearts, and all
   was weary and drear;
We long'd to hear the wind again, and to
   hold our David's hand—
The wind, wife; the wind, wife, that blew
   him out from land!

V.

The wind, wife, the wind; up again, up
   again!
It blew our David round the world, yet
   shriek'd at our window-pane;
And ever since that time, old wife, in rain,
   and in sun, and in snow,
Whether I work or weary here, I hear it
   whistle and blow,
It moans around, it groans around, it
   comes with scream and cry—
The wind, wife; the wind, wife; may it
   blow him home to die!

II.

APRIL RAIN.

I.

SHOWERS, showers, nought but showers,
   and it wants a week of May,
Flowers, flowers, summer flowers, are hid
   in the green and the gray;
Green buds and gray shoots cover their
   sparkling gear,
They stir beneath, they long to burst, for
   the May is so near, so near,—
While I spin and I spin, and the fingers of
   the Rain
Fall patter, pitter, patter, on the pane.

II.

Showers, showers, silver showers, murmur
   and softly sing,
Flowers, flowers, summer flowers, are
   swelling and hearkening;
It wants a week of May, when my love and
   I will be one,
The flowers will burst, the birds will sing,
   as we walk to church in the sun.
So patter goes my heart, in a kind of
   pleasant pain,
To the patter, pitter, patter of the Rain.

III.

SUMMER MOON.

I.

SUMMER Moon, O Summer Moon, across
   the west you fly,
You gaze on half the earth at once with
   sweet and steadfast eye;
Summer Moon, O Summer Moon, were I
   aloft with thee,
I know that I could look upon my boy who
   sails at sea.

II.

Summer Moon, O Summer Moon, you
   throw your silver showers
Upon a glassy sea that lies round shores of
   fruit and flowers,
And on the blue tide's silver edge drop
   blossoms in the breeze,
And the shadow of the ship lies dark near
   shades of orange-trees.

III.

Summer Moon, O Summer Moon, now
   wind and storm have fled,
Your light creeps thro' a cabin-pane and
   lights a flaxen head:
He tosses with his lips apart, lies smiling in
   your gleam,
For underneath his folded lids you put a
   gentle dream.

IV.

Summer Moon, O Summer Moon, his head
   is on his arm,
He stirs with balmy breath and sees the
   moonlight on the Farm,
He stirs and breathes his mother's name, he
   smiles and sees once more
The Moon above, the fields below, the
   shadow at the door.

V.

Summer Moon, O Summer Moon, across
   the lift you go,
Far south you gaze and see my Boy, where
   groves of orange grow!
Summer Moon, O Summer Moon, you turn
   again to me,
And seem to have the smile of him who
   sleeps upon the sea!

IV.
DECEMBER SNOW.

I.

The cold, cold snow! the snow that lies so white!
The moon and stars are hidden, there is neither warmth nor light—
I wonder, wife—I wonder, wife—where Jeanie lies this night?

II.

'Tis cold, cold, cold, since Jeanie went away,
The world has changed, I sit and wait, and listen night and day,
The house is silent, silent, and my hair has grown so gray—
'Tis cold, cold, cold, wife, since Jeanie went away.

III.

And tick! tick! tick! the clock goes evermore,
It chills me, wife—it seems to keep our bairn beyond the door;
I watch the firelight shadows as they float upon the floor,
And tick! tick! tick! wife, the clock goes evermore!

IV.

'Tis cold, cold, cold!—'twere better she were dead,
Not that I heed the Minister, and the bitter things he said,—
But to think my lassie cannot find a place to lay her head—
'Tis cold, cold, cold, wife—better she were dead!

V.

The cold, cold snow! the snow that lies so white!
Beneath the snow her little one is hidden out of sight,
But up above, the wind blows keen, there's neither warmth nor light,
I wonder, wife—I wonder, wife—where Jeanie lies this night!

London Poems.
(1866-70.)

Greift nur hinein in's volle Menschenleben!
Ein jeder lebt's, nicht vielen ist's bekannt,
Und wo ihr's packt, da ist's interessant.
Faust—Vorspiel auf dem Theater.

BEXHILL, 1866.

Now, when the catkins of the hazel swing
Wither'd above the leafy nook wherein
The chaffinch breasts her five blue speckled eggs,
All round the thorn grows fragrant, white with may,
And underneath the fresh wild hyacinth-bed
Shimmers like water in the whispering wind;
Now, on this sweet still gloaming of the spring,
Within my cottage by the sea, I sit,
Thinking of yonder city where I dwelt,
Wherein I sicken'd, and whereof I learn'
So much that dwells like music on my brain.

A melancholy happiness is mine!
My thoughts, like blossoms of the muschatel,
Smell sweetest in the gloaming; and I feel
Visions and vanishings of other years,—
Faint as the scent of distant clover meadows—
Sweet, sweet, though they awaken serious cares—
Beautiful, beautiful, though they make me weep.

The good days dead, the well-belovèd gone
Before me, lonely I abode amid
The buying, and the selling, and the strife
Of little natures; ye there still remain'd

I

Something to thank the Lord for.—I could live!
On winter nights, when wind and snow were out,
Afford a pleasant fire to keep me warm;
And while I sat, with homeward-looking eyes,
And while I heard the humming of the town,
I fancied 'twas the sound I used to hear
In Scotland, when I dwelt beside the sea.
I knew not how it was, or why it was,
I only heard a sea-sound, and was sad.
It haunted me and pain'd me, and it made
That little life of penmanship a dream!
And yet it served my soul for company,
When the dark city gather'd on my brain,
And from the solitude came never a voice
To bring the good days back, and show my heart
It was not quite a solitary thing.

The purifying trouble grew and grew,
Till silentness was more than I could bear.
Brought by the ocean murmur from afar,
Came silent phantoms of the misty hills
Which I had known and loved in other days;
And, ah! from time to time, the hum of life
Around me, the strange faces of the streets,
Mingling with those thin phantoms of the hills,
And with that ocean-murmur, made a cloud
That changed around my life with shades and sounds,
And, melting often in the light of day,
Left on my brow dews of aspiring dream.
And then I sang of Scottish dales and dells,
And human shapes that lived and moved therein,
Made solemn in the shadow of the hills.
Thereto, not seldom, did I seek to make
The busy life of London musical,
And phrase in modern song the troubled lives
Of dwellers in the sunless lanes and streets.
Yet ever I was haunted from afar,
While singing; and the presence of the mountains
Was on me; and the murmur of the sea
Deepen'd my mood; while everywhere I saw,
Flowing beneath the blackness of the streets,
The current of sublimer, sweeter life,
Which is the source of human smiles and tears,

And, melodised, becomes the strength of song.

Darkling, I long'd for utterance, whereby
Poor people might be holpen, gladden'd, cheer'd;
Bright'ning at times, I sang for singing's sake.
The wild wind of ambition grew subdued,
And left the changeful current of my soul
Crystal and pure and clear, to glass like water
The sad and beautiful of human life;
And, even in the unsung city's streets,
Seem'd quiet wonders meet for serious song,
Truth hard to phrase and render musical.
For ah! the weariness and weight of tears,
The crying out to God, the wish for slumber,
They lay so deep, so deep! God heard them all;
He set them unto music of His own;
But easier far the task to sing of kings,
Or weave weird ballads where the moon-dew glistens,
Than body forth this life in beauteous sound.
The crowd had voices, but each living man
Within the crowd seem'd silence-smit and hard:
They only heard the murmur of the town,
They only felt the dimness in their eyes,
And now and then turn'd startled, when they saw
Some weary one fling up his arms and drop,
Clay-cold, among them,—and they scarcely grieved,
But hush'd their hearts a time, and hurried on.

'Twas comfort deep as tears to sit alone,
Haunted by shadows from afar away,
And try to utter forth, in tuneful speech,
What lay so musically on my heart.
But, though it sweeten'd life, it seem'd in vain.
For while I sang, much that was clear before—
The souls of men and women in the streets,
The sounding sea, the presence of the hills,
And all the weariness, and all the fret,
And all the dim, strange pain for what had fled—
Turn'd into mist, mingled before mine eyes,
Roll'd up like wreaths of smoke to heaven, and died:

The pen dropt from my hand, mine eyes
   grew dim,
And the great roar was in mine ears again,
And I was all alone in London streets.

Hither to pastoral solitude I came,
Happy to breathe again serener air
And feel a purer sunshine ; and the woods
And meadows were to me an ecstasy,
The singing birds a glory, and the trees
A green perpetual feast to fill the eye
And shimmer in upon the soul ; but chief,
There came the murmur of the waters,
   sounds
Of sunny tides that wash on silver sands,
Or cries of waves that anguish'd and went
   white
Under the eyes of lightnings. 'Twas a bliss
Beyond the bliss of dreaming, yet in time
It grew familiar as my mother's face ;
And when the wonder and the ecstasy
Had mingled with the beatings of my heart,
The terrible City loom'd from far away
And gather'd on me cloudily, dropping dews,
Even as those phantoms of departed days
Had haunted me in London streets and
   lanes.
Wherefore in brighter mood I sought again
To make the life of London musical,
And sought the mirror of my soul for shapes
That linger'd, faces bright or agonised,
Yet ever taking something beautiful
From glamour of green branches, and of
   clouds
That glided piloted by golden airs.

And if I list to sing of sad things oft,
It is that sad things in this life of breath
Are truest, sweetest, deepest. Tears bring
   forth
The richness of our natures, as the rain
Sweetens the smelling brier ; and I, thank
   God,
Have anguish'd here in no ignoble tears—
Tears for the pale friend with the singing lips,
Tears for the father with the gentle eyes
(My dearest up in heaven next to God)
Who loved me like a woman. I have
   wrought
No garland of the rose and passion-flower,
Grown in a careful garden in the sun ;
But I have gather'd samphire dizzily,
Close to the hollow roaring of a Sea.

Far away in the dark
   Breaketh that living Sea,
Wave upon wave ; and hark !
   These voices are blown to me ;
For a great wind rises and blows,
   Wafting the sea-sound near,
But it fitfully comes and goes,
   And I cannot always hear ;
Green boughs are flashing around,
   And the flowers at my feet are fair,
And the wind that bringeth the ocean-sound
   Grows sweet with the country air.

THE LITTLE MILLINER ;

OR, LOVE IN AN ATTIC.

With fairy foot and fearless gaze
   She passes pure through evil ways ;
She wanders in the sinful town,
   And loves to hear the deep sea-music
Of people passing up and down.

Fear nor shame nor sin hath she,
   But, like a sea-bird on the Sea,
Floats hither, thither, day and night :
   The great black waters cannot harm her,
Because she is so weak and light !

My girl hath violet eyes and yellow hair
A soft hand, like a lady's, small and fai.
A sweet face pouting in a white straw
   bonnet,
A tiny foot, and little boot upon it ;
And all her finery to charm beholders
Is the gray shawl drawn tight around her
   shoulders,
The plain stuff-gown and collar white as
   snow,
And sweet red petticoat that peeps below.
But gladly in the busy town goes she,
Summer and winter, fearing nobodie ;
She pats the pavement with her fairy feet,
With fearless eyes she charms the crowded
   street ;
And in her pocket lie, in lieu of gold,
A lucky sixpence and a thimble old.

We lodged in the same house a year ago :
She on the topmost floor, I just below,—
She, a poor milliner, content and wise,
I, a poor city clerk, with hopes to rise ;
And, long ere we were friends, I learnt to
   love
The little angel on the floor above.

For, every morn, ere from my bed I stirr'd,
Her chamber door would open, and I heard,—
And listen'd, blushing, to her coming down,
And palpitated with her rustling gown,
And tingled while her foot went downward slow,
Creak'd like a cricket, pass'd, and died below;
Then peeping from the window, pleased and sly,
I saw the pretty shining face go by,
Healthy and rosy, fresh from slumber sweet,—
A sunbeam in the quiet morning street.
All winter long, witless who peep'd the while,
She sweeten'd the chill mornings with her smile;
When the soft snow was falling dimly white,
Shining among it with a child's delight,
Bright as a rose, though nipping winds might blow,
And leaving fairy footprints in the snow!

And every night, when in from work she tript,
Red to the ears I from my chamber slipt,
That I might hear upon the narrow stair
 el low 'Good evening,' as she pass'd me there.
And when her door was closed, below sat I,
And hearken'd stilly as she stirr'd on high,—
Watch'd the red firelight shadows in the room,
Fashion'd her face before me in the gloom,
And heard her close the window, lock the door,
Moving about more lightly than before,
And thought, 'She is undressing now!' and oh!
My cheeks were hot, my heart was in a glow!
And I made pictures of her,—standing bright
Before the looking-glass in bed-gown white,
Upbinding in a knot her yellow hair,
Then kneeling timidly to say a prayer;
Till, last, the floor creak'd softly overhead,
'Neath bare feet tripping to the little bed,—
And all was hush'd. Yet still I hearken'd on,
Till the faint sounds about the streets were gone;
And saw her slumbering with lips apart,
One little hand upon her little heart,

The other pillowing a face that smiled
In slumber like the slumber of a child,
The bright hair shining round the small white ear,
The soft breath stealing visible and clear,
And mixing with the moon's, whose frosty gleam
Made round her rest a vaporous light of dream.

How free she wander'd in the wicked place,
Protected only by her gentle face!
She saw bad things—how could she choose but see?—
She heard of wantonness and misery;
The city closed around her night and day,
But lightly, happily, she went her way.
Nothing of evil that she saw or heard
Could touch a heart so innocently stirr'd,—
By simple hopes that cheer'd it through the storm,
And little flutterings that kept it warm.
No power had she to reason out her needs,
To give the whence and wherefore of her deeds;
But she was good and pure amid the strife,
By virtue of the joy that was her life.
Here, where a thousand spirits daily fall,
Where heart and soul and senses turn to gall,
She floated, pure as innocent could be,
Like a small sea-bird on a stormy sea,
Which breasts the billows, wafted to and fro,
Fearless, uninjured, while the strong winds blow,
While the clouds gather, and the waters roar,
And mighty ships are broken on the shore.

And London streets, with all their noise and stir,
Had many a pleasant sight to pleasure her.
There were the shops, where wonders ever new,
As in a garden, changed the whole year through.
Oft would she stand and watch with laughter sweet
The Punch and Judy in the quiet street;
Or look and listen while soft minuets
Play'd the street organ with the marionettes;

Or joined the motley group of merry folks
Round the street huckster with his wares
  and jokes.
Fearless and glad, she join'd the crowd that
  flows
Along the streets at festivals and shows.
In summer time, she loved the parks and
  squares,
Where fine folk drive their carriages and
  pairs ;
In winter time her blood was in a glow,
At the white coming of the pleasant snow ;
And in the stormy nights, when dark rain
  pours,
She found it pleasant, too, to sit indoors,
And sing and sew, and listen to the gales,
Or read the penny journal with the tales.

  Once in the year, at merry Christmas
    time,
She saw the glories of a pantomime,
Feasted and wonder'd, laugh'd and clapp'd
  aloud,
Up in the gallery among the crowd,
Gathering dreams of fairyland and fun
To cheer her till another year was done ;
More happy, and more near to heaven, so,
Than many a lady in the tiers below.

  And just because her heart was pure and
    glad,
She lack'd the pride that finer ladies had :
She had no scorn for those who lived
  amiss,—
The weary women with their painted bliss ;
It never struck her little brain, be sure,
She was so very much more fine and pure.
Softly she pass'd them in the public places,
Marvelling at their fearful childish faces ;
She shelter'd near them, when a shower
  would fall,
And felt a little frighten'd, that was all,
And watch'd them, noting as they stood
  close by
Their dress and fine things with a woman's
  eye,
And spake a gentle word if spoken to,—
And wonder'd if their mothers lived and
  knew ?

  Her look, her voice, her step, had witchery
And sweetness that were all in all to me !
We both were friendless, yet, in fear and
  doubt,
I sought in vain for courage to speak out.
Wilder my heart could ne'er have throbb'd
  before her,
My thoughts have stoop'd more humbly to
  adore her,
My love more timid and more still have
  grown,
Had Polly been a queen upon a throne.
All I could do was wish and dream and sigh,
Blush to the ears whene'er she pass'd me by,
Still comforted, although she did not love
  me,
Because—her little room was just above me!

  'Twas when the spring was coming, when
    the snow
Had melted, and fresh winds began to blow,
And girls were selling violets in the town,
That suddenly a fever struck me down.
The world was changed, the sense of life
  was pain'd,
And nothing but a shadow-land remain'd ;
Death came in a dark mist and look'd at
  me,
I felt his breathing, though I could not see,
But heavily I lay and did not stir,
And had strange images and dreams of *her*.
Then came a vacancy : with feeble breath,
I shiver'd under the cold touch of Death,
And swoon'd among strange visions of the
  dead,
When a voice call'd from Heaven, and he
  fled ;
And suddenly I waken'd, as it seem'd,
From a deep sleep wherein I had not
  dream'd.

  And it was night, and I could see and hear,
And I was in the room I held so dear,
And unaware, stretch'd out upon my bed,
I hearken'd for a footstep overhead.

  But all was hush'd. I look'd around the
    room,
And slowly made out shapes amid the
  gloom.
The wall was redden'd by a rosy light,
A faint fire flicker'd, and I knew 'twas night,
Because below there was a sound of feet
Dying away along the quiet street,—

When, turning my pale face and sighing low,
I saw a vision in the quiet glow :
A little figure, in a cotton gown,
Looking upon the fire and stooping down,
Her side to me, her face illumed, she eyed
Two chestnuts burning slowly, side by side,—
Her lips apart, her clear eyes strain'd to see,
Her little hands clasp'd tight around her knee,
The firelight gleaming on her golden head,
And tinting her white neck to rosy red,
Her features bright, and beautiful, and pure,
With childish fear and yearning half demure.

Oh, sweet, sweet dream ! I thought, and strain'd mine eyes,
Fearing to break the spell with words and sighs.

Softly she stoop'd, her dear face sweetly fair,
And sweeter since a light like love was there,
Brightening, watching, more and more elate,
As the nuts glow'd together in the grate,
Crackling with little jets of fiery light,
Till side by side they turn'd to ashes white,—
Then up she leapt, her face cast off its fear
For rapture that itself was radiance clear,
And would have clapp'd her little hands in glee,
But, pausing, bit her lips and peep'd at me,
And met the face that yearn'd on her so whitely,
And gave a cry and trembled, blushing brightly,
While, raised on elbow, as she turn'd to flee,
'*Polly!*' I cried,—and grew as red as she !

It was no dream !—for soon my thoughts were clear,
And she could tell me all, and I could hear :
How in my sickness friendless I had lain,
How the hard people pitied not my pain ;
How, in despite of what bad people said,
She left her labours, stopp'd beside my bed,
And nursed me, thinking sadly I would die ;
How, in the end, the danger pass'd me by ;
How she had sought to steal away before
The sickness pass'd, and I was strong once more.

By fits she told the story in mine ear,
And troubled all the telling with a fear
Lest by my cold man's heart she should be chid,
Lest I should think her bold in what she did ;
But, lying on my bed, I dared to say,
How I had watch'd and loved her many a day,
How dear she was to me, and dearer still
For that strange kindness done while I was ill,
And how I could but think that Heaven above
Had done it all to bind our lives in love.
And Polly cried, turning her face away,
And seem'd afraid, and answer'd 'yea' nor 'nay ;'
Then stealing close, with little pants and sighs,
Look'd on my pale thin face and earnest eyes,
And seem'd in act to fling her arms about
My neck, then, blushing, paused, in fluttering doubt,
Last, sprang upon my heart, sighing and sobbing,—
That I might feel how gladly hers was throbbing !

Ah ! ne'er shall I forget until I die
How happily the dreamy days went by,
While I grew well, and lay with soft heart-beats,
Heark'ning the pleasant murmur from the streets,
And Polly by me like a sunny beam,
And life all changed, and love a drowsy dream !
'Twas happiness enough to lie and see
The little golden head bent droopingly
Over its sewing, while the still time flew,
And my fond eyes were dim with happy dew !
And then, when I was nearly well and strong,
And she went back to labour all day long,
How sweet to lie alone with half-shut eyes,
And hear the distant murmurs and the cries,
And think how pure she was from pain and sin,—
And how the summer days were coming in !
Then, as the sunset faded from the room,
To listen for her footstep in the gloom,

To pant as it came stealing up the stair,
To feel my whole life brighten unaware
When the soft tap came to the door, and when
The door was open'd for her smile again !
Best, the long evenings !—when, till late at night,
She sat beside me in the quiet light,
And happy things were said and kisses won,
And serious gladness found its vent in fun.
Sometimes I would draw close her shining head,
And pour her bright hair out upon the bed,
And she would laugh, and blush, and try to scold,
While ' Here,' I cried, ' I count my wealth in gold ! '
Sometimes we play'd at cards, and thrill'd with bliss,
On trumping one another with a kiss.
And oft our thoughts grew sober and found themes
Of wondrous depth in marriage plans and schemes ;
And she with pretty calculating lips
Sat by me, cautious to the finger-tips,
Till, all our calculations grown a bore,
We summ'd them up in kisses as before !

Once, like a little sinner for transgression,
She blush'd upon my breast, and made confession :
How, when that night I woke and look'd around,
I found her busy with a charm profound,—
One chestnut was herself, my girl confess'd,
The other was the person she loved best,
And if they burn'd together side by side,
He loved her, and she would become his bride ;
And burn indeed they did, to her delight,—
And had the pretty charm not proven right ?
Thus much, and more, with timorous joy, she said,
While her confessor, too, grew rosy red,—
And close together press'd two blissful faces,
As I absolved the sinner, with embraces.

And here is winter come again, winds blow,
The houses and the streets are white with snow ;
And in the long and pleasant eventide,
Why, what is Polly making at my side ?
What but a silk-gown, beautiful and grand,
We bought together lately in the Strand !
What but a dress to go to church in soon,
And wear right queenly 'neath a honey-moon !
And who shall match her with her new straw bonnet,
Her tiny foot and little boot upon it,
Embroider'd petticoat and silk-gown new,
And shawl she wears as few fine ladies do ?
And she will keep, to charm away all ill,
The lucky sixpence in her pocket still !
And we will turn, come fair or cloudy weather,
To ashes, like the chestnuts, close together !

LIZ.

The crimson light of sunset falls
  Through the gray glamour of the murmuring rain,
And creeping o'er the housetops crawls
  Through the black smoke upon the broken pane,
Steals to the straw on which she lies,
  And tints her thin black hair and hollow cheeks,
Her sun-tann'd neck, her glistening eyes,—
  While faintly, sadly, fitfully she speaks.
But when it is no longer light,
  The pale girl smiles, with only One to mark,
And dies upon the breast of Night,
  Like trodden snowdrift melting in the dark.

I.

Ah, rain, rain, rain !
It patters down the glass, and on the sill,
And splashes in the pools along the lane—
  Then gives a kind of shiver, and is still :
  One likes to hear it, though, when one is ill.
Rain, rain, rain, rain !
  Ah, how it pours and pours !
Rain, rain, rain, rain !
  A dismal day for poor girls out-o'-doors !

II.

Ah, don't ! That sort of comfort makes me cry.
And, Parson, since I'm bad, I want to die.
  The roaring of the street
  The tramp of feet,
  The sobbing of the rain,
  Bring nought but pain ;

They're gone into the aching of my brain;
  And whether it be light,
  Or dark dead night,
Wherever I may be, I hear them plain!
I'm lost and weak, and can no longer bear
To wander, like a shadow, here and there—
  As useless as a stone—tired out—and sick!
  So that they put me down to slumber quick,
It does not matter where.
No one will miss me; all will hurry by,
  And never cast a thought on one so low;
  Fine gentlemen miss ladies when they go,
But folk care nought for such a thing as I.

III.

'Tis bad, I know, to talk like that—too bad!
Joe, though he's often hard, is strong and true—
[And there's the baby, too!—
But I'm so tired and sad.
I'm glad it was a boy, sir, very glad.
A man can fight along, can say his say,
  Is not look'd down upon, holds up his head,
And, at a push, can always earn his bread:
Men have the best of it, in many a way.
But ah! 'tis hard indeed for girls to keep
  Decent and honest, tramping in the town,—
  Their best but bad—made light of—beaten down—
Wearying ever, wearying for sleep.
If they grow hard, go wrong, from bad to badder,
Why, Parson dear, they're happier being blind:
They get no thanks for being good and kind—
The better that they are, they feel the sadder!

IV.

Nineteen! nineteen!
  Only nineteen, and yet so old, so old;—
  I feel like fifty, Parson—I have been
So wicked, I suppose, and life's so cold!
Ah, cruel are the wind, and rain, and snow,
  And I've been out for years among them all:
  I scarce remember being weak and small
Like baby there—it was so long ago.

It does not seem that I was born. I woke,
  One day, long, long ago, in a dark room,
  And saw the housetops round me in the smoke,
  And, leaning out, look'd down into the gloom,
Saw deep black pits, blank walls, and broken panes,
  And eyes, behind the panes, that flash'd at me,
And heard an awful roaring, from the lanes,
  Of folk I could not see;
Then, while I look'd and listen'd in a dream,
  I turn'd my eyes upon the housetops gray,
And saw, between the smoky roofs, a gleam
  Of silver water, winding far away.
That was the River. Cool and smooth and deep,
  It glided to the sound o' folk below,
  Dazzling my eyes, till they began to grow
Dusty and dim with sleep.
Oh, sleepily I stood, and gazed, and hearken'd!
  And saw a strange, bright light, that slowly fled,
  Shine through the smoky mist, and stain it red,
And suddenly the water flash'd,—then darken'd;
And for a little time, though I gazed on,
  The river and the sleepy light were gone;
But suddenly, over the roofs there lighten'd
  A pale, strange brightness out of heaven shed,
And, with a sweep that made me sick and frighten'd,
  The yellow Moon roll'd up above my head;—
And down below me roar'd the noise o' trade,
And ah! I felt alive, and was afraid,
  And cold, and hungry, crying out for bread.

V.

All that is like a dream. It don't seem *true!*
  Father was gone, and mother left, you see,
  To work for little brother Ned and me;
And up among the gloomy roofs we grew,—
Lock'd in full oft, lest we should wander out,
  With nothing but a crust o' bread to eat,

While mother char'd for poor folk round
    about,
Or sold cheap odds and ends from street
    to street.
Yet, Parson, there were pleasures fresh and
    fair,
To make the time pass happily up there :
A steamboat going past upon the tide,
    A pigeon lighting on the roof close by,
    The sparrows teaching little ones to fly,
The small white moving clouds, that we
    espied,
    And thought were living, in the bit of
      sky—
    With sights like these right glad were
      Ned and I ;
And then, we loved to hear the soft rain
    calling,
    Pattering, pattering, upon the tiles,
And it was fine to see the still snow falling,
    Making the housetops white for miles on
      miles,
And catch it in our little hands in play,
And laugh to feel it melt and slip away !
But I was six, and Ned was only three,
And thinner, weaker, wearier than me ;
    And one cold day, in winter time, when
      mother
Had gone away into the snow, and we
    Sat close for warmth and cuddled one
      another,
He put his little head upon my knee,
And went to sleep, and would not stir a limb,
But look'd quite strange and old ;
And when I shook him, kiss'd him, spoke
    to him,
He smiled, and grew so cold.
Then I was frighten'd, and cried out, and
    none
    Could hear me ; while I sat and nursed
      his head,
Watching the whiten'd window, while the
    Sun
Peep'd in upon his face, and made it red.
And I began to sob ;—till mother came,
Knelt down, and scream'd, and named the
    good God's name,
And told me he was dead.
And when she put his night-gown on, and,
    weeping,
    Placed him among the rags upon his bed,
I thought that brother Ned was only sleep-
    ing,
And took his little hand, and felt no fear.
But when the place grew gray and cold
    and drear,
And the round Moon over the roofs came
    creeping,
    And put a silver shade
All round the chilly bed where he was laid,
I cried, and was afraid.

VI.

Ah, yes, it's like a dream ; for time pass'd
    by,
And I went out into the smoky air,
Fruit-selling, Parson — trudging, wet or
    dry—
    Winter and summer—weary, cold, and
      bare.
And when old mother laid her down to die,
And parish buried her, I did not cry,
And hardly seem'd to care ;
I was too hungry, and too dull ; beside,
    The roar o' streets had made me dry as
      dust—
It took me all my time, howe'er I tried,
    To keep my limbs alive and earn a crust ;
I had no time for weeping.
And when I was not out amid the roar,
Or standing frozen at the playhouse door,
Why, I was coil'd upon my straw, and
    sleeping.
Ah, pence were hard to gain !
Some girls were pretty, too, but I was plain :
Fine ladies never stopp'd and look'd and
    smiled,
    And gave me money for my face's sake.
That made me hard and angry when a child;
    But now it thrills my heart, and makes
      it ache !
The pretty ones, poor things, what could
    they do,
    Fighting and starving in the wicked town,
    But go from bad to badder—down, down,
      down—
Being so poor, and yet so pretty, too?
Never could bear the like of that—ah, no !
Better have starved outright than gone so
    low !

VII.

But I've no call to boast. I might have
    been
As wicked, Parson dear, in my distress,
But for your friend – you know the one I
    mean ?—

The tall, pale lady, in the mourning dress,
Though we were cold at first, that wore
   away—
     She was so mild and young,
     And had so soft a tongue,
And eyes to sweeten what she loved to say.
She never seem'd to scorn me—no, not she ;
And (what was best) she seem'd as sad as
   me !
Not one of them that make a girl feel base,
And call her names, and talk of her disgrace,
And frighten one with thoughts of flaming
   hell,
     And fierce Lord God with black and
       angry brow ;
But soft and mild, and sensible as well ;
And oh, I loved her, and I love her now.
She did me good for many and many a
   day—
     More good than pence could ever do, I
       swear,
For she was poor, with little pence to
   spare—
     Learn'd me to read, and quit low words,
       and pray.
And, Parson, though I never understood
How such a life as mine was meant for good,
And could not guess what one so poor and
   low
     Would do in that sweet place of which
       she spoke,
And could not feel that God would let me
   go
Into so bright a land with gentlefolk,
I liked to hear her talk of such a place,
     And thought of all the angels she was
       best,
Because her soft voice soothed me, and her
   face
     Made my words gentle, put my heart at
       rest.

VIII.

Ah, sir ! 'twas very lonesome. Night and
   day,
     Save when the sweet miss came, I was
       alone,—
Moved on and hunted through the streets
   of stone,
And even in dreams afraid to rest or stay.
Then, other girls had lads to work and strive
   for ;
     I envied them, and did not know 'twas
       wrong,

And often, very often, used to long
For some one I could like and keep alive for.
   Marry ? Not they !
     They can't afford to be so good, you know ;
But many of them, though they step astray,
   Indeed don't mean to sin so much, or go
Against what 's decent. Only—'tis their way.
And many might do worse than that, may be,
   If they had ne'er a one to fill a thought—
It sounds half wicked, but poor girls like me
   Must sin a little, to be good in aught.

IX.

So I was glad when I began to see
   Joe Purvis fancied me ;
And when, one night, he took me to the play,
   Over on Surrey side, and offer'd fair
   That we should take a little room and
     share
Our earnings, why, I could not answer
   'Nay !'
And that's a year ago ; and though I'm
   bad,
I've been as true to Joe as girl could be.
I don't complain a bit of Joe,'dear lad,
   Joe never, never meant but well to me ;
And we have had as fair a time, I think,
   As one could hope, since we are both so
     low.
Joe likes me—never gave me push or blow,
   When sober : only, he was wild in drink.
But then we don't mind beating when a man
   Is angry, if he likes us and keeps straight,
Works for his bread, and does the best he
   can ;—
'Tis being left and slighted that we hate.

X.

And so the baby 's come, and I shall die !
   And though 'tis hard to leave poor baby
     here,
Where folk will think him bad, and all's
   so drear,
The great LORD GOD knows better far
   than I.
Ah, don't !—'tis kindly, but it pains me so !
You say I'm wicked, and I want to go !
'GOD's kingdom,' Parson dear? Ah nay,
   ah nay !
That must be like the country—which I
   fear :
I saw the country once, one summer day,
   And I would rather die in London here

XI.

For I was sick of hunger, cold, and strife,
  And took a sudden fancy in my head
To try the country, and to earn my bread
Out among fields, where I had heard one's life
Was easier and brighter. So, that day,
I took my basket up and stole away,
Just after sunrise. As I went along,
  Trembling and loath to leave the busy place,
I felt that I was doing something wrong,
  And fear'd to look policemen in the face.
And all was dim : the streets were gray and wet
After a rainy night : and all was still ;
I held my shawl around me with a chill,
And dropt my eyes from every face I met ;
Until the streets began to fade, the road
  Grew fresh and clean and wide,
Fine houses where the gentlefolk abode,
  And gardens full of flowers, on every side.
That made me walk the quicker—on, on, on—
As if I were asleep with half-shut eyes,
And all at once I saw, to my surprise,
The houses of the gentlefolk were gone,
  And I was standing still,
Shading my face, upon a high green hill,
  And the bright sun was blazing,
And all the blue above me seem'd to melt
  To burning, flashing gold, while I was gazing
On the great smoky cloud where I had dwelt.

XII.

I'll ne'er forget that day. All was so bright
  And strange. Upon the grass around my feet
The rain had hung a million drops of light;
  The air, too, was so clear and warm and sweet,
It seem'd a sin to breathe it. All around
  Were hills and fields and trees that trembled through
A burning, blazing fire of gold and blue ;
  And there was not a sound,
Save a bird singing, singing, in the skies,
And the soft wind, that ran along the ground,
  And blew so sweetly on my lips and eyes.
Then, with my heavy hand upon my chest,
  Because the bright air pain'd me, trembling, sighing,
I stole into a dewy field to rest,
  And oh, the green, green grass where I was lying
Was fresh and living—and the bird sang loud,
Out of a golden cloud—
And I was looking up at him and crying !

XIII.

How swift the hours slipt on!—and by and by
The sun grew red, big shadows fill'd the sky,
  The air grew damp with dew,
  And the dark night was coming down, I knew.
Well, I was more afraid than ever, then,
  And felt that I should die in such a place,—
So back to London town I turn'd my face,
And crept into the great black streets again ;
And when I breathed the smoke and heard the roar,
Why, I was better, for in London here
My heart was busy, and I felt no fear.
I never saw the country any more.
And I have stay'd in London, well or ill—
  I would not stay out yonder if I could.
For one feels dead, and all looks pure and good—
I could not bear a life so bright and still.
All that I want is sleep,
Under the flags and stones, so deep, so deep!
God won't be hard on one so mean, but He,
  Perhaps, will let a tired girl slumber sound
  There in the deep cold darkness under ground ;
And I shall waken up in time, may be,
Better and stronger, not afraid to see
  The great, still Light that folds Him round and round !

XIV.

See ! there's the sunset creeping through the pane—
How cool and moist it looks amid the rain !
I like to hear the splashing of the drops
  On the house-tops,
And the loud humming of the folk that go
Along the streets below !
I like the smoke and noise—I am so bad—
  They make a low one hard, and still her cares. . . .

There's Joe! I hear his foot upon the
　　stairs !—
He must be wet, poor lad !
He will be angry, like enough, to find
　　Another little life to clothe and keep.
But show him baby, Parson—speak him
　　kind—
And tell him Doctor thinks I'm going to
　　sleep.
A hard, hard life is his ! He need be strong
And rough, to earn his bread and get along.
I think he will be sorry when I go,
　　And leave the little one and him behind.
I hope he'll see another to his mind,
To keep him straight and tidy. Poor old
　　Joe !

THE STARLING.

I.

The little lame tailor
　　Sat stitching and snarling—
Who in the world
　　Was the tailor's darling?
To none of his kind
Was he well-inclined,
　　But he doted on Jack the starling.

II.

For the bird had a tongue,
　　And of words good store,
And his cage was hung
　　Just over the door.
And he saw the people,
　　And heard the roar,—
Folk coming and going
　　Evermore,—
And he look'd at the tailor,—
　　And swore.

III.

From a country lad
　　The tailor bought him,—
His training was bad,
　　For tramps had taught him ;
On alehouse benches
　　His cage had been,
While louts and wenches
　　Made jests obscene,—
But he learn'd, no doubt,
　　His oaths from fellows
Who travel about
　　With kettle and bellows,
And three or four,
　　The roundest by far
That ever he swore,
　　Were taught by a tar.
And the tailor heard—
　　'We'll be friends !' said he,
'You're a clever bird,
　　And our tastes agree—
We both are old,
　　And esteem life base,
The whole world cold,
　　Things out of place,
And we're lonely too,
　　And full of care—
So what can we do
　　But swear?

IV.

'The devil take you,
　　How you mutter !—
Yet there's much to make you
　　Swear and flutter.
You want the fresh air
　　And the sunlight, lad,
And your prison there
　　Feels dreary and sad,
And here I frown
　　In a prison as dreary,
Hating the town,
　　And feeling weary:
We're too confined, Jack,
　　And we want to fly,
And you blame mankind, Jack,
　　And so do I !
And then, again,
　　By chance as it were,
We learn'd from men
　　How to grumble and swear ;
You let your throat
　　By the scamps be guided,
And swore by rote—
　　All just as I did !
And without beseeching,
　　Relief is brought us—
For we turn the teaching
　　On those who taught us !'

V.

A haggard and ruffled
　　Old fellow was Jack,
With a grim face muffled
　　In ragged black,

And his coat was rusty
  And never neat,
And his wings were dusty
  With grime of the street,
And he sidelong peer'd,
  With eyes of soot,
And scowl'd and sneer'd,—
  And was lame of a foot!
And he long'd to go
  From whence he came;—
And the tailor, you know,
  Was just the same.

VI.

All kinds of weather
  They felt confined,
And swore together
  At all mankind;
For their mirth was done,
  And they felt like brothers,
And the swearing of one
  Meant no more than the other's;
'Twas just a way
  They had learn'd, you see,—
Each wanted to say
  Only this—' Woe's me!
I'm a poor old fellow,
  And I'm prison'd so,
While the sun shines mellow,
  And the corn waves yellow,
  And the fresh winds blow,—
And the folk don't care
  If I live or die,
But I long for air,
  And I wish to fly!'
Yet unable to utter it,
  And too wild to bear,
They could only mutter it,
  And swear.

VII.

Many a year
  They dwelt in the city,
In their prisons drear,
  And none felt pity,
And few were sparing
  Of censure and coldness,
To hear them swearing
  With such plain boldness;
But at last, by the Lord,
  Their noise was stopt,—
For down on his board
  The tailor dropt,

And they found him dead,
  And done with snarling,
And over his head
  Still grumbled the Starling;
But when an old Jew
  Claim'd the goods of the tailor,
And with eye askew
  Eyed the feathery railer,
And, with a frown
  At the dirt and rust,
Took the old cage down,
  In a shower of dust,—
Jack, with heart aching,
  Felt life past bearing,
And shivering, quaking,
  All hope forsaking,
    Died, swearing.

JANE LEWSON.

Clasping his knee with one soft lady-hand,
  The other fingering his glass of wine,
Black-raimented, white-hair'd, polite, and bland,
  With mellow voice discourses Doctor Vine:
He warms, with deep eyes stirr'd to thoughtful light,
  And round about his serious talk the while,
Kindly, yet pensive—worldly wise, yet bright,
  Like bloom upon the blackthorn, blows his smile.

All, strong and mighty are we mortal men!
Braving the whirlwind on a ship at sea,
Facing the grim fort's hundred tongues of fire,
Ay, and in England, 'neath the olive branch,
Pushing a stubborn elbow through the crowd,
To get among the heights that keep the gold;
But there is might and might,—and in the one
Our dames and daughters shame us. Come, my friend,
My man of sinews,—conscious of your strength,
Proud of your well-won wrestles with the world,—
Hear what a feeble nature can endure!

A little yellow woman, dress'd in black,
With weary crow's-feet crawling round the eyes,

And solemn voice, that seem'd a call to
   prayer ;
Another yellow woman, dress'd in black,
Sad, too, and solemn, yet with bitterness
Burn'd in upon the edges of her lips,
And sharper, thinner, less monotonous
   voice ;
And last, a little woman auburn-hair'd,
Pensive a little, but not solemnised,
And pretty, with the open azure eyes,
The white soft cheek, the little mindless
   mouth,
The drooping childish languor. There they
   dwelt,
In a great dwelling of a smoky square
In Islington, named by their pious friends,
And the lean Calvinistic minister—
The Misses Lewson, and their sister Jane.

Miss Sarah, in her twenty-seventh year,
Knew not the warmer passions of her sex,
But groan'd both day and night to save her
   soul ;
Miss Susan, two years younger, had regrets
Her sister knew not, and a secret pain
Because her heart was withering—whence
   her tongue
Could peal full sharp at times, and show a
   sting ;
But Jane was comely—might have cherish'd
   hopes,
Since she was only twenty, had her mind
Been hopefuller. The elders ruled the
   house.
Obedience and meekness to their will
Was a familiar habit Jane had learn'd
Full early, and had fitted to her life
So closely, 'twas a portion of her needs.
She gazed on them, as Eastern worshippers
Gaze on a rayless picture of the sun.
Her acts seem'd other than her own ; her
   heart
Kept melancholy time to theirs ; her eyes
Look'd ever unto them for help and light ;
Her eyelids droop'd before them if they chid.
A woman weak and dull, yet fair of face !
Her mother, too, had been a comely thing—
A bright-hair'd child wed to an aged man,
A heart that broke because the man was
   hard,—
Not like the grim first wife, who brought
   the gold,
And yielded to his melancholy kiss

The melancholy virgins. Well, the three,
Alone in all the world, dwelt in the house
Their father left them, living by the rents
Of certain smaller houses of the poor.
And they were stern to wring their worldly
   dues—
Not charitable, since the world was base,
But cold to all men, save the minister,
Who weekly cast the darkness of his blessing
Over their chilly table.

                   All around
The life of London shifted like a cloud,
Men sinned, and women fell, and children
   cried,
And Want went ragged up and down the
   lanes ;
While the two hueless sisters dragg'd their
   chain
Self-woven, pinch'd their lives complexion-
   less,
Keeping their feelings quiet, hard, and pure.
But Jane felt lonesome in the world ; and
   oft,
Pausing amid her work, gazed sadly forth
Upon the dismal square of wither'd trees,
The dusty grass that grew within the
   rails,
The garden-plots where here and there a
   flower
Grew up, and sicken'd in the smoke, and
   died ;
And when the sun was on the square, and
   sounds
Came from the children in the neighbouring
   streets,
She thought of happy homes among the
   fields,
And brighter faces. When she walk'd
   abroad,
The busy hum of life oppress'd her heart
And frighten'd her : she did not raise her
   eyes,
But stole along,—a sweet shape clad in
   black,
A pale and pretty face, at which the men
Stared vacant admiration. Far too dull
To blame her gloomy sisters for the shape
Her young days took, she merely knew the
   world
Was drear ; and if at times she dared to
   dream
Of things that made her colour come and go,

And dared to hope for cheerier, sunnier
    days,
She grew the wanner afterwards, and felt
Sad and ashamed. The dull life that she
    wore,
Like to a gloomy garment, day by day,
Was a familiar life, the only life
She clearly understood. Coldly she heard
The daily tale of human sin and wrong,
And the small thunders of the Sunday nights
In chapel. All around her were the streets,
And frightful sounds, and gloomy sunless
    faces.
And thus with tacit dolour she resign'd
Her nature to the hue upon the cheeks
Of her cold sisters. Yet she could not pray
As they pray'd, could not wholly feel and
    know
The blackness of mankind, her own heart's
    sin ;
But when she tried to get to God, and
    yearn'd
For help not human, she could only cry,
Feeling a loveless and a useless thing,
Thinking of those sweet places in the fields,
Those homes whereon the sun shone pleasantly,
And happy mothers sat at cottage doors
Among their children.

    Save for household work,
She would have wasted soon. From week
    to week
The burthen lay on her,—the gloomy twain
Being too busy searching for their souls,
And begging God above to spare the same.
Yet she was quiet thus, content and glad
To silent drudgery, such as saved her heart
From wilder flutterings. The Sabbath day
Was drearest : drest in burial black, she sat
Those solemn hours in chapel, listening,
And scarcely heeding what she heard, but
    watching
The folk around, their faces and their dress,
Or gazing at the sunshine on the floor ;
And service over, idly pined at home,
And, looking from the window at the
    square,
Long'd for the labour of the coming day.
Her sisters watch'd her warily, be sure ;
And though their hearts were pure as pure
    could be,
They loved her none the better for her face.

Love is as cunning as disease or death,
No doctor's skill will ward him off or cure,
And soon he found this pale and weary girl,
Despite the cloud of melancholy life
That rain'd around her. In no beauteous
    shape,
In guise of passionate stripling iris-eyed,
Such as our poets picture in their songs,
Love came ;—but in a gloomy garb of one
Whom men call'd pious, and whose holy
    talk
Disarm'd the dragons. 'Twere but idle,
    friend,
To count the wiles by which he won his way
Into her heart ; how she vouchsafed him all
The passion of a nature not too strong ;
How, when the first wild sunshine dazzled
    her,
The woman loved so blindly, that her
    thoughts
Became a secret trouble in the house ;
And how at last, with white and frighten'd
    face,
She glided out into the dark one night,
And vanish'd with no utterance of farewell.

The sisters gave a quick and scandall'd
    cry,
And sought a little for the poor flown bird;
Then, thinking awful things, composed
    their hearts
In silence, pinch'd their narrow natures
    more,
And waited. 'This is something strange,'
    they thought,
'Which God will clear ; we will not think
    the worst,
Although she was a thing as light as straw.'
Nor did they cry their fear among their
    friends,
Hawking a secret shame, but calmly waited,
Trusting no stain would fall upon their chill
And frosty reputations. Weeks pass'd by ;
They pray'd, they fasted, yellowing more
    and more,
They waited sternly for the end, and heard
The timid knock come to the door at last.

It was a dark and rainy night ; the streets
Were gleaming watery underneath the
    lamps,
The dismal wind scream'd fitfully without,
And made within a melancholy sound ;

And the faint knock came to the door at last.
The sisters look'd in one another's faces,
And knew the wanderer had returned again,
But spoke not; and the younger sister rose,
Open'd the door, peer'd out into the rain,
And saw the weary figure shivering there,
Holding a burthen underneath her shawl.
And silently, with wan and timid look,
The wanderer slipt in. No word of greeting
Spake either of the sisters, but their eyes
Gleam'd sharply, and they waited. White and cold,
Her sweet face feebly begging for a word,
Her long hair dripping loose and wet, stood Jane
Before them, shivering, clasping tight her load,
In the dull parlour with the cheerless fire.
Till Susan, pointing, cried in a shrill voice,
'What are you carrying underneath your shawl,
Jane Lewson?' and the faint despairing voice,
While the rain murmur'd and the night-wind blew,
Moan'd, 'It's my *Baby!*' and could say no more,
For the wild sisters scream'd and raised their hands,
And Jane fell quivering down upon her knees,
The old shawl opening show'd a child asleep,
And, trebling terror with a piteous cry,
The child awaken'd.

              Pointing to the door,
With twitching lips of venom, Susan said—
'Go!' and the elder sister echo'd her
More sadly and more solemnly. But Jane,
Clinging to Sarah's skirts, implored and moan'd,
'Don't turn me out! my little girl will die!
I have no home in all the world but here;
Kill me, but do not drive from the house!'
'Jane Lewson,' Susan cried, as white as death,
'Where is the father of this child?' and Jane
Moan'd, 'Gone, gone, gone;' and when she named his name,
And how, while she who spake in sickness lay,
He secretly had fled across the seas,
They shiver'd to the hair. Holding her hand
Upon her heart, the elder sister spake
In dull monotonous voice—'Look up! look up!
Perhaps 'tis not so ill as we believed
Are you a wedded woman?' The reply
Was silentness and heavy drooping eyes,
Yet with no blush around the quivering lids;
And Sarah, freezing into ice, spake on
In dull monotonous voice—' Your sin has brought
Shame on us all, but they who make their beds
Must sleep upon them; go away, bad woman!
The third of what our father left is yours,
But you are not our sister any more.'
Still moaning, shuddering, the girl begg'd on,
Nor ceased to rock the babe and still its cries,
'Kill me, but do not drive me from the house!
Put any pain upon me that you please,
But do not, do not, drive me forth again
Into the dreadful world! I have no friends
On all the earth save you!' The sisters look'd
At one another, and without a word
Walk'd from the room.

              Jane sat upon the floor,
Soothing the child, and did not rise, but waited;
The agony and terror dried her tears,
And she could only listen, praying God
That He would soften them; and the little one
Look'd in her face and laugh'd.

              A weary hour
Pass'd by, and then, still white, and stern, and cold,
The sisters enter'd, and the elder one
Spake without prelude: 'We have talk'd it o'er,
Jane Lewson, and have settled how to act;
You have a claim upon us: will you take
The third of what our father left, and find
Another home?' But Jane cried, 'Do not, do not,
Drive me away;' I have no friends save you;
And I am sorry.' Trembling, for her heart
Was not all cold, the elder icicle

Resumed: 'Take what is left you, and be gone,
And never see our faces any more;
Or if you will, stay with us here, but only
On these conditions: For the infant's sake,
And for the sake of our good name, our friends
Must never know the miserable child
Is yours; but we will have it given out
That, being lonely and unwedded here,
We have adopted a poor tenant's child,
With view to bring it up in godliness.'
Jane answer'd, with a feeble thrill of hope,
'Anything, anything,—only leave me not
Alone in the dark world.' 'Peace!' Susan said,
'You do not understand: the child herself
Must never know Jane Lewson is her mother:
Neither by word nor look nor tender folly,
Must you reveal unto the child her shame,
And yours, and ours!' Then, with a bitter cry,
And a wild look, Jane cried, 'And must my babe
Not know me?' 'Never,' Sarah Lewson said:
'For the babe's sake, for yours, for ours, the shame
Must not be utter'd. See, you have your choice:
Take what our father gave you, and depart,
Or stay on these conditions. We are firm.
We have decided kindly, not forgetting
You were our sister, nor that this poor child
Is blameless, save that all the flesh is sin,
But not forgetting, either, what we owe
To God above us.' Weeping o'er the child,
Not rising yet, Jane answer'd, 'I will stay;
Yes, gladly, for the little baby's sake,
That folk may never call it cruel names.'
And the stern sisters took from off the shelf
The great old Bible, placed it in her hands
And made her kiss it, swearing before God
Never to any one in all the world,
Not even to the child itself, to tell
She was its sinful mother. Wi'd and dazed,
She sware upon the Book. 'That is enough,'
Said Sarah; 'but, Jane Lewson, never again
Speak to us of the evil that has pass'd;
Live with us as you used to do, and ask
The grace of God, who has been kinder far
Than you deserved.'

Thus, friend, these icicles
Dealt their hard measure, deeming that they did
A virtuous and a righteous deed; and Jane,
The worn and mindless woman, sank again
Into submission and house-drudgery,
Comforted that she daily saw her child,
And that her shame was hidden from the world,
And that the child would never suffer scorn
Because a sinner bore it. But her heart
Was a bruised reed, the little sunny hue
Had gone from all things; and whene'er she pray'd,
She thought the great cold God above her head
Dwelt on a frosty throne and did not hear.

II.

Yet He, the Almighty Lord of this our breath,
Did see and hear, and surely pitied too,
If God can pity,—but He works as God,
Not man, and so we cannot understand.

No whisp'r of reproach, no spoken word,
Troubled with memories of her sinfulness
The suffering woman; yet her daily life
Became a quiet sorrow. In the house
She labour'd with her hands from morn to night,
Seeing few faces save the pensive ones
Whose yellow holiness she bow'd before;
And tacitly they suffer'd her to sink
Into the household drudge.—with privilege
Upon the Sabbath day to dress in black,
Sit in the sunless house or go to prayer,—
So idle, that her thoughts could travel back
To shame and bitterness. Her only joy
Was when she gave her little girl the breast,
(They dared not rob her weary heart of that.)
When, seated all alone, she felt it suck,
And, as the little lips drew forth the milk,
Felt drowsily resign'd, and closed her eyes,
And trembled, and could feel the happy tears.

There came a quiet gathering in the house,
And by the gloomy minister the child
Was christen'd; and the name he gave to her

K

Was 'Margaret Lewson.' For the sisters said,
'Her mother being buried, as it were,
The girl shall take our name.' And Jane sat by,
And heard the pious lie with aching heart,
And ever after that her trouble grew.

Soon, when the sound of little feet were heard
In the dull dwelling, and a baby-voice
Call'd at the mother's heart, Jane thrill'd and heard,
But even as she listen'd the sweet sounds
Would seem to die into the cloud that hid
The great cold God above her. Margaret
Grew to a little wildling, quick and bright,
Black-eyed, black-hair'd, and passionate and quick,
Not like its mother; fierce and wild when chid,
So that the gloomy sisters often thought,
'There is a curse upon it;' yet they grew
To love the little wildling unaware,
Indulged it in their stern and solemn way,
More cheer'd than they believed by its shrill laugh
Within the dismal dwelling. But the child
Clung most to Jane, and though, when first it learn'd
To call her by her Christian name, the sound
Bruised the poor suffering heart, that wore away;
And all the little troubles of the child,
The pretty joys, the peevish fits, the bursts
Of passion, work'd upon her nature so,
That all her comfort was to snatch it up,
And cover it with kisses secretly.
Wilful and passionate, yet loving too,
Grew Margaret,—an echo in a cave
Of human life without; clinging to Jane,
Who never had the heart to fondle it
Before her sisters; not afraid at times
To pinch the thin, worn arms, or pull the hairs
Upon the aching head, but afterwards
Curing the pain with kisses and with tears.
So that as time wore on the mother's heart
Grew tenderer to its trouble than before.

Then later, when the little girl went forth
To school hard by, the motion and the light
Hied from the house; and all the morning hours
The thin face came and went against the panes,
Looking out townward,—till the little shape
Appear'd out of the cloud, and pale eyes grew
Dim to its coming. As the years went on,
The mother, with the agony in her heart
She could not utter, quietly subdued
Her nature to a listening watchfulness:
Her face grew settled to expectant calm,
Her vision penetrated things around
And gazed at something lying far beyond,
Her very foot linger'd about the house,
As if she loiter'd hearkening for a sound
Out of the world. For Margaret, as she grew,
Was wilder and more wilful, openly
Master'd the gloomy virgins, and escaped
The pious atmosphere they daily breathed
To gambol in a freer, fresher air;
And Jane would think, ''Twill kill me, if my child
Should turn out wicked.' Mindless though she was,
And feeble, yet the trouble made her sense
Quick, sharp, and subtle to perceive and watch.
A little word upon the girlish tongue
Could sting her,—nay, a light upon the face,
A kindling of the eye, a look the child
Wore when asleep, would trouble her for days,
Carrying strangest import. So she waited,
Watching and listening,—while the young new life
Drew in the air, and throve, absorbing hues
Out of a thousand trivial lights and shades
That hover'd lightly round it. Still to Jane
The habit of submission clung: she watch'd
The wiser sterner faces oftentimes,
Trembling for confirmation of her fears;
And nightly pray'd that God, who was so just,
So hard to those who went astray at all,
Would aid her sisters, helping them to make
The little Margaret better as she grew,—
Waking her secret trouble evermore
With countless, nameless acts of help and love,
And humble admonition,—comforted
By secret fondlings of the little arms,

Or kisses on the tiny, wilful mouth
Apart in childish slumber.
                  Thus the years
Pass'd over her like pensive clouds, and melted
Into that dewy glimmer on the brain,
Which men call Memory. Wherefore recount
The little joys and sorrows of the time:
The hours when sickness came, and thought itself
Tick'd like a death-watch,—all the daily hopes
And impulses and fears? Enough to tell,
That all went onward like a troubled stream,
Until the sisters, worn and growing old,
Felt the still angel coming nearer, nearer,
Scattering sleep-dust on uplooking eyes;
And Jane, though in her prime, was turning gray;
And Margaret was a maiden flower full-blown.

    A passion-flower!—a maiden whose rich heart
Burn'd with intensest fire that turn'd the light
Of the sweet eyes into a warm dark dew;
One of those shapes so marvellously made,
Strung so intensely, that a finger-press,
The dropping of a stray curl unaware
Upon the naked breast, a look, a tone,
Can vibrate to the very roots of life,
And draw from out the spirit light that seems
To scorch the tender cheeks it shines upon;
A nature running o'er with ecstasy
Of very being, an appalling splendour
Of animal sensation, loveliness
Like to the dazzling panther's; yet, withal,
The gentle, wilful, clinging sense of love,
Which makes a virgin's soul. It seem'd, indeed,
The gloomy dwelling and the dismal days,
Gloaming upon her heart, had lent this show
Of shining life a melancholy shade
That trebled it in beauty. Such a heart
Needed no busy world to make it beat:
It could throb burningly in solitude;
Since kindly Heaven gave it strength enough
To rock the languid blood into the brains
Of twenty smaller natures.

                  Then the pain,
The wonder, deepen'd on the mother's heart,—
Her mother, her worn mother, whom she knew not
To be her mother. As she might have watch'd
A wondrous spirit from another world,
Jane Lewson watch'd her child. Could this fair girl,—
This wild and dazzling life, be born of her?—
A lightning flash struck from a pensive cloud
The wan still moon is drinking? Like a woman
Who has been sick in darkness many days,
And steps into the sunshine, Jane beheld
Her daughter, and felt blind. A terror grew
Upon her, that the smother'd sense of pride
Lack'd power to kill. She pray'd, she wept, she dream'd,
And thought, if Margaret's had been a face
More like the common faces of the streets,
'Twould have been better. With this feeling, grew
The sense of her own secret. Oftentimes
A look from Margaret brought the feeble blush
Into the bloodless cheek;—creeping away
Into her chamber, Jane would wring her hands,
Moaning in pain, 'God help me! If she knew!
Ah, if she knew!' And then for many days
Would haunt the dwelling fearfully, afraid
To look on what she loved,—till once again,
Some little kindness, some sweet look or tone,
A happy kiss, would bring her courage back
And cheer her.

                Nor had Margaret fail'd to win
The hard-won sisters; oft their frosty eyes
Enlarged themselves upon her and grew thaw'd—
In secret she was mistress over both—
And in their loveless way, they also felt
A frighten'd pleasure in the beauteous thing
That brighten'd the dull dwelling.

                    Oftentimes,
The fiery maiden-nature flashing forth

In wilful act or speech or evil looks,
Deepen'd Jane's terror. Margaret heeded
        not
The sisters' pious teachings, did not show
A godly inclination,—nay, at times
Mock'd openly. Ah, had she guess'd the
        pain,
The fear, the agony, such mockings gave
Her mother, her worn mother, whom she
        knew not
To be her mother! In her secret heart
Jane deem'd her own deep sorrows all had
        come
Because she had not, in her dreary youth,
Been godly ; and as such flashes as she
        saw
Gleam from her girl, seem'd wicked things
        indeed ;
And at such times the weary woman's eyes
Would seek the sunless faces, searching
        them
For cheer or warning.

     In its season came
That light which takes from others what it
        gives
To him or her who, standing glorified,
Awaits it. 'Tis the old, sad mystery :
No gift of love that comes upon a life
But means another's loss. The new sweet
        joy,
That play'd in tender colours and mild fire
On Margaret's cheek, upon the mother's
        heart
Fell like a firebrand.

     For to Jane, her friend,
Her dearest in the household from the first,
Her mother, her worn mother, whom she
        knew not
To be her mother, Margaret first told
The terror—how she loved and was beloved ;
And seated at Jane's feet, with eyes upturn'd,
Playing with the worn fingers, she exclaim'd,
' I love him, Jane! and you will love him
        too !
I will not marry any other man !'
And suddenly Jane felt as if the Lord
Had come behind her in the dark and
        breathed
A burning fire upon her. For she thought,
' My child will go away, and I shall die !'
But only murmur'd, 'Marry, Margaret ?

You are too young to marry !'——and her
        face
Was like a murder'd woman's.

     And the pain,
The agony, deepen'd, when the lover's face
Came smiling to the dwelling, young and
        bright
With pitiless gladness. Jane was still, and
        moan'd,
' My child will go away, and I shall die !'
And look'd upon her sisters, and could see
They pitied her ; but their stern faces said,
' This is God's will! the just God governs
        all !
How should we cross such love ?' adding,
' Beware,—
For our sakes, for your own, but chief of all
For her sake whom you love, remember
        now!
Pray, and be silent !' And the wounded
        heart
Cried up to God again, and from the sky
No answer came ; when, crush'd beneath
        her pain,
The woman sicken'd, lay upon her bed,
And thought her time was come.

     Most tenderly
Her daughter nursed her ; little fathoming
The meaning of the wild and yearning look
That made the white face sweet and beau-
        tiful ;
For Jane was saying, ' Lord, I want to die!
My child would leave me, or my useless life
Would turn a sorrow to her, if I stay'd :
Lord, let me die !' Yea, the dull nature
        clung
Still into silence, with the still resolve
Of mightier natures. Thinking she would
        die,
Jane lay as in a painless dream, and watch'd
The bright face stir around her, following
The shape about the room, and praying still
For strength—so happy in her drowsy
        dream,
That she went chill at times, and felt that
        thoughts
So tranquil were a sin. A darker hour
Gloam'd soon upon her brain. She could
        not see
The face she loved ; murmur'd delirious
        words ;

And in the weary watches of the night,
Moaning and wringing hands, with closèd eyes,
Cried 'Margaret! Margaret!' Then the sisters sought
To lead the girl away, lest she should hear
The secret; but she conquer'd, and remain'd;
And one still evening, when the quiet fire
Was making ghosts that quiver'd on the floor
To the faint time-piece ticking, Jane awoke,
Gazed long and strangely at the shining face,
Waved her thin arms, cried, 'Margaret! Margaret!
Where are you, Margaret? Have you gone away?
Come to your mother!' The wild cry of pain
Startled the maiden, but she only thought
The fever'd woman raved. Twining her arms
Around Jane's neck, she murmur'd, 'I am here!'
Weeping and kissing; but the woman sigh'd
And shiver'd, crying feebly, 'Let me die!
My little girl has gone into the town,
And she has learn'd to call me wicked names,
And will not come again!'

When, wearied out,
Jane sank to troubled sleep, her child sat still,
Thinking of those strange words; and though at last
She shut them from her thought as idle dream,
Their pain return'd upon her. The next day
She spake unto the sisters of the same,
Adding, in a low voice, 'She talk'd of me,
And moan'd out loudly for a little child—
Has she a child?' The first quick flash of fear
Died from the yellow visages unseen,
And they were calm. 'Delirium!' Sarah said;
'But you, my child, must watch her sick-bed less—
You are too young, too weak, to bear such things.'

And this time Margaret did not say a word,
But yielded, thinking, 'It is very strange!—
There is a mystery, and I will watch:
Can Jane have had a child?'

That very da..
The dark mists roll'd from the sick woman<u>d</u> brain,
And she awoke, remembering nought, and saw
The sisters watching her. Two days they watch'd;
And spake but very little, though they saw
The wan eyes wander with a hungry look,
Seeking the face they loved. Then Sarah took
Jane's hand, and spake more gently, sisterly,
(Such natures, friend, grow kinder as they age,)
Than she had done for many years, and told
Of those wild words utter'd while she was ill;
Jane moan'd and hid her face; but Sarah said,
'We do not blame you, and perchance the Lord
Spake through you! We have thought it o'er, and pray'd:
Now listen, Jane. Since that unhappy night,
We have not spoken of your shame, yet know
You have repented.' With her face still hid,
Jane falter'd, 'Let me die!' but Sarah said,
'We do not think, Jane Lewson, you will live;
So mark me well. If, ere you go away,
You feel that you could go more cheerfully,
If you are certain that it is not sin,
Poor Margaret shall know she is your child;
We will not, now you die, deny you this;
And Margaret will be silent of the shame,—
And, lest you break your oath upon the Word,
Our lips shall tell her.' Still Jane Lewson hid
Her face; and all was quiet in the room,
Save for a shivering sound and feeble crying.
But suddenly Jane lifted up her face,
Beauteous beyond all beauty given to joy,
And quickly whispering, press'd the chilly hand—
'I will not speak! I will not hurt my child

So cruelly !—the child shall never know !
And I will go in silence to my grave,
Leaving her happy,—and perhaps the Lord
'Will pardon me !' Then, for the first last
   time,
The sisters look'd on Jane with different
   eyes,
Admiring sternly, with no words of praise,
Her they had scorn'd for feebleness so long.

Even then the watchers in the chamber
   heard
A sound that thrill'd them through,—a rust-
   ling dress,
A deep hard breathing as of one in pain ;
And pointing with her hand Jane scream'd
   aloud ;
And turning suddenly the sisters saw
A face as white as marble, yet illumed
By great eyes flashing with a terrible flame
That made them quail. And in a dangerous
   voice,
As low as a snake's hissing, Margaret said,
'I have heard all !' Then the great eyes
   were turn'd
On Jane, and for a moment they were
   cold ;
But all at once the breathless agony
Of recognition struck upon her heart,
The bosom heaved and moan'd, the bright
   tears burst,
And Margaret flung herself upon the bed,
Clasping her shivering mother ; and at first
Jane shrank away,—but soon the wondrous
   love
Master'd her,—she could smile and kiss and
   cry—
And hear the dear wild voice cry, 'Mother,
   mother !'
And see the bright face through her tears,
   and feel
That Love was there.

    After the first strange bliss
Of meeting, both were stiller. Jane could
   weep,
And bear to feel so happy. Margaret
Clang to her mother, breathed her bliss upon
   her,
Fondling the silver'd tresses, covering
The thin hard hand with kisses and with
   tears,
Trying to say a thousand merry things
That died in sobs and tears, and only say-
   ing,
For all the utterance of her speechful heart,
'Mother, my mother !' Suddenly her
   shame
Came back upon the woman, and she
   turn'd
To seek her sisters' faces piteously,
But they had stolen from the happy room ;
Whereon again she murmur'd, 'Let me die!
I am a wicked woman, Margaret !
Why did you listen ?' But a second burst
Of love and blissful pain, and bitter things
Hurl'd at the cruel sisters, answer'd her ;
And more tears flow'd, and more fond kisses
   brush'd
The tears away,—until at last Jane cried,
'Dear, I could go away not weeping now—
God is so gentle with me !'

    But He, who drew
Thus from His cloud at last and look'd so
   kind,
Will'd that Jane Lewson should not die so
   soon.
The agony did not kill her, and the joy
Sent a fresh life into her languid blood
And saved her. So that soon she rose from
   bed,
To see the sunshine on her daughter's face,
To see the sunless sisters, who again
Look'd cold as ever.

    But a burning fire
From Margaret scorch'd them to the heart,
   because
They loved the girl ; she heap'd upon their
   heads
Rage and reproaches, mockery and scorn,
Until they cried, 'You are a wicked girl !
Jane Lewson's shame is on you. After this
We cannot dwell together any more.'
And Margaret would have answer'd fiercelier
   still,
But that her feeble mother, piteously
Gazing at them to whom in spite of all
Her heart was humble, begg'd her on her
   knees
For silence; and, thus conquer'd, Margaret
Answer'd her aunts with kisses and with
   tears
Shower'd on her mother's face,

　　　　That evening,
Margaret held her mother round the neck,
And led her to her lover in the house,
And with her lips set firm together, saying,
'This is my dear, dear mother,' told him all,
Concealing nothing. For a time, the man
Look'd startled and appall'd; but being made
Of clay not base, he smiling spake at last,
And stooping softly, kiss'd the thin worn hand—
'She is my mother, too,—and we will dwell
　　Together!'

　　　　And they dwelt together,—leaving
The dismal dwelling in the smoky square,
To dwell within a cottage close to town;
But Jane lived with them only for a year,
And then, because the heart that had been used
To suffering so long could not endure
To be so happy, died; worn out and tired, ·
Kissing her child; and as her dying thoughts
Went back along the years, the suffering seem'd
Not such a thankless suffering after all,
But like a faded garment one has learn'd
To love through habit;—and the woman cried
On her stern sisters with her dying breath.

LANGLEY LANE.

A LOVE POEM.

In all the land, range up, range down,
　Is there ever a place so pleasant and sweet,
As Langley Lane, in London town,
　Just out of the bustle of square and street?
Little white cottages, all in a row,
　Gardens, where bachelors'-buttons grow,
Swallows' nests in roof and wall,
　And up above the still blue sky,
Where the woolly-white clouds go sailing by,—
　I seem to be able to see it all!

For now, in summer, I take my chair,
　And sit outside in the sun, and hear
The distant murmur of street and square,
　And the swallows and sparrows chirping near;
And Fanny, who lives just over the way,
Comes running many a time each day,
　With her little hand's-touch so warm and kind;
And I smile and talk, with the sun on my cheek,
And the little live hand seems to stir and speak,—
　For Fanny is dumb and I am blind.

Fanny is sweet thirteen, and she
　Has fine black ringlets, and dark eyes clear,
And I am older by summers three,—
　Why should we hold one another so dear?
Because she cannot utter a word,
Nor hear the music of bee or bird,
　The water-cart's splash, or the milkman's call.
Because I have never seen the sky,
Nor the little singers that hum and fly,—
　Yet know she is gazing upon them all.

For the sun is shining, the swallows fly,
　The bees and the blue-flies murmur low,
And I hear the water-cart go by,
　With its cool splash-splash down the dusty row;
And the little one, close at my side, perceives
Mine eyes upraised to the cottage eaves,
　Where birds are chirping in summer shine,
And I hear, though I cannot look, and she,
Though she cannot hear, can the singers see,—
　And the little soft fingers flutter in mine.

Hath not the dear little hand a tongue,
　When it stirs on my palm for the love of me?
Do I not know she is pretty and young?
　Hath not my soul an eye to see?
'Tis pleasure to make one's bosom stir,
To wonder how things appear to her,
　That I only hear as they pass around;

And as long as we sit in the music and
  light,
She is happy to keep God's sight,
And *I* am happy to keep God's sound.

Why, I know her face, though I am
    blind—
  I made it of music long ago :
Strange large eyes, and dark hair twined
  Round the pensive light of a brow of
    snow ;
And when I sit by my little one,
And hold her hand, and talk in the sun,
  And hear the music that haunts the
    place,
I know she is raising her eyes to me,
And guessing how gentle my voice must
    be,
  And *seeing* the music upon my face.

Though, if ever Lord God should grant me
    a prayer,
  (I know the fancy is only vain,)
I should pray : Just once, when the weather
    is fair,
  To see little Fanny and Langley Lane ;
Though Fanny, perhaps, would pray to
    hear
  The voice of the friend that she holds so
    dear,
The song of the birds, the hum of the
    street,—
It is better to be as we have been,—
Each keeping up something, unheard, un-
    seen,
  To make God's heaven more strange and
    sweet.

Ah ! life is pleasant in Langley Lane !
  There is always something sweet to
    hear ;
Chirping of birds, or patter of rain ;
  And Fanny, my little one, always near ;
And though I am weak, and cannot live
    long,
And Fanny, my darling, is far from strong,
And though we can never married be,—
What then ?—since we hold one another so
    dear,
For the sake of the pleasure one cannot
    hear,
  And the pleasure that only *one* can see?

EDWARD CROWHURST;

OR, 'A NEW POET.'

I.

Potts, in his dusty chamber, writes,
  A dilettante lord to please :
A ray of country sunshine lights
  The foggy region ruled by these ;
Flock, kind advisers, critics sage,
  To damn the simple country clown,—
The mud of English patronage
  Grows round his feet, and keeps him down.

' THIS little mean-faced duodecimo,
  "Poems by Edward Crowhurst, La-
    bourer,"
This coarsely-printed little book of rhymes,
  Contains within the goodliest gift of song
The gods have graced us with for many a
    day :
A crystal clearness, as of running brooks,
A music, as of green boughs murmuring,
A peeping of fresh thoughts in shady
    places
Like violets new-blown, a gleam of dew-
    drops,
A sober, settled, greenness of repose,—
And lying over all, in level beams,
Transparent, sweet, and unmistakable,
The light that never was on sea or land.

' Let all the greater and the lesser lights
Regard these lines upon a Wood in
    Spring,
Or those which follow, call'd " the Barley-
    Bird,"
And then regard their laurels. Melody
More sweet was never blown through pas-
    toral pipe
In Britain, since the Scottish Ramsay died.
Nor let the squeamish dreamers of our
    time,
Our rainbow bards, despise such song as
    this,
Wealthy in images the poor man knows,
And household chords that make the women
    weep.
Simply yet subtly, Edward Crowhurst
    works :
Singing of lowly truths and homely things—
Death snatching up a cotter's child at
    play,

Light flashing from far worlds on dying
        eyes
That never saw beyond their native fields,
The pathos and the power of common life;
And while, perchance, his deeper vein runs
        on
Less heeded, by a random touch is waken'd
A scent, a flower-tint, a wave of wings,
A sense of rustling boughs and running
        brooks,
Touch'd by whose spell the soul is stirr'd,
        and eyes
Gaze on the dark world round them, and
        are dim.

'This Mister Crowhurst is a poor young
        man,
Uneducated, doom'd to earn his bread
By working daily at the plough; and yet,
Sometimes in midst of toil, sometimes at
        night,
Whenever he could snatch a little time,
Hath written down (he taught himself to
        write!)
His simple verses. Is it meet, we ask,
A nature so superb should languish thus?
Nay, he deserves, if ever man deserved,
The succour of the rich and high in place,
The opportunity to labour less,
And use those truly wondrous gifts of his
In modest competence; and therewithal,
Kindness, encouragement, and good ad-
        vice,
Such as the cultured give. Even now, we
        hear,
A certain sum of money is subscribed,
Enough to furnish well his present needs.
Among the donors, named for honour
        here,
We note the noble Earl of Chremiton,
Lord Phidippus, Lord Gnathos, Lady Dee,
Sir Charles Toroon. But more must yet
        be done.
We dare to put the case on public grounds,
Since he who writes so nobly is, indeed,
A public benefactor,—with a claim
On all who love to listen and to look,
When the fresh Saxon Muse, in homespun
        gear,
The free breeze blowing back her loosen'd
        hair,
Wanders barefooted through the dewy
        lanes

And sings aloud, till all the valleys ring
For pleasure, and the echoes of the hills
Make sweet accord!'
                —*Conservative Review.*

II.

AFTER TEN YEARS.

A homely matron, who has once been fair,
    In quiet suffering old, yet young in years;
Soft threads of silver in her auburn hair,
    'And lines around the eyes that tell of tears;
But on her face there trembles peaceful light,
That seems a smile, and yet is far less bright,—
To tell of watchings in the shade and sun,
And melancholy duty sweetly done.

What, take away my Teddy? shut him up
Between stone walls, as if he was a thief?
You freeze my blood to talk of such a thing!
Why, these green fields where my old man
        was born,
The river, and the woodland, and the lanes,
Are all that keep him living: he was ever
O'er fond of things like those; and now,
        you see,
Is fonder of them than he was before,
Because he thinks so little else is left.
Mad? He's a baby! Would not hurt a
        fly!
Can manage him as easy as our girl!
And though he was a poet and went wrong,
He could not help his failings. Ah, True
        Heart,
I love him all the deeper and the dearer!
I would not lose him for the whole wide
        world!

It came through working lonely in the
        fields,
And growing shy of cheerful company,
And worrying his wits with idle things
He saw and heard when quiet out o' doors.
For, long ere we were wedded, all the place
Knew Teddy's ways: how mad he was for
        flowers
And singing birds; how often at the plough
He used to idle, holding up his head
And looking at the clouds; what curious
        stuff
He used to say about the ways of things;
How week-days he was never company,
Nor tidy on a Sunday. Even then
Folk call'd him stupid: so did I myself,

At first, before his sheepishness wore off;
And then, why I was frighten'd for a time
To find how wondrous brightly he could look
And talk, when with a girl, and no one by.
Right soon he stole this heart of mine away,
So cunningly I scarcely guess'd 'twas gone,
But found my tongue at work before I knew,
Sounding his praises. Mother shook her head;
But soon it was the common country talk
That he and I were courting.

                    After that
Some of his sayings and his doings still
Seem'd foolish, but I used to laugh and say,
'Wait till we marry! I shall make him change!'
And it was pleasant walking after dark,
In summer, wandering up and down the lanes,
And heark'ning to his talk; and pleasant, too,
In winter, to sit cuddling by the fire,
And whispering to the quiet firelight sound
And the slow ticking of the clock. Ere long,
I grew to care for many things he loved.
He knew the names of trees, and birds, and flowers,
Their races and their seasons; named the stars,
Their comings and their goings; and could tell
Strange truths about the manners of the clouds.
Set him before a hedgerow in a lane,
And he was happy all alone for hours.
The woods and fields were full of joy to him,
And wonders, and fine meanings ever new.
How, at the bottom of the wayside well,
The foul toad lies and purifies the drink;
How twice a year red robin sings a song,
Once when the orchis blows its bells in spring,
Once when the gold is on the slanted sheaves;
How late at night the common nightingale
Comes in the season of the barley-sowing,
Silently builds her nest among the boughs,
And then sings out just as the roses blow,
And it is sweet and pleasant in the moon.
Why, half his courtship lay in talk like that,
And, oh! the *way* he talk'd fill'd high my heart

With pleasure. Then, o' quiet winter nights,
With wild bright eyes and voice that broke for joy,
He often read aloud from books of songs;
One I remember, that I liked the best,
A book of pictures and of love-tales, call'd
'The Seasons.' I was young, and did not think:
I only felt 'twas fine. Yet now and then
I noticed more, and took a sober fit,
And tried to make him tidy in his clothes,
And could not, though I tried; and used to sigh
When mother mutter'd hints, as mothers will,
That he should work more hard and look ahead,
And save to furnish out a house for me. . . .
For Teddy smiled, poor lad, and work'd more hard,
But save . . . not he! Instead of laying by,
Making a nest to rear the young ones in,
He spent his hard-won cash in buying books,—
Much dusty lumber, torn and black and old,
Long sheets of ballads, bundles of old rhyme,—
And read them, one by one, at home o' nights,
Or out aloud to me, or at the plough.
I chid at first, but quickly held my tongue,
Because he look'd so grieved; and once he said.
With broken voice and dew-light in his eyes,
' Lass, I 'm a puzzle to myself and you,
But take away the books, and I should die!'
His back went bare for books, his stomach starved
To buy them,—nay, he pawn'd his jacket once,
To get a dreary string of solemn stuff
All about Eve and Adam. More and more
He slacken'd at his toil; and soon the lad,
Who turn'd the cleanest furrow, when he pleased,
Of all the ploughmen, let his work go spoil,
And fairly led an idle thriftless life
In the green woods and on the river side.

And then I found that he himself made verse
In secret,—verse about the birds and flowers,
Songs about lovers, rhymes about the stars,
Tales of queer doings in the village here,—
All writ on scraps of paper out-o'-doors,
And hidden in an old tin coffee-pot
Where he had kept his cash. The first I heard
Was just a song all about him and me,
And cuddling in the kitchen while 'twas snowing;
He read it to me, blushing like a girl,
And I was pleased, and laugh'd, and thought it fine,
And wonder'd where he learn'd to make the words
Jingle so sweetly. Then he read me more,
Some that I liked, some that I fancied poor;
And, last of all, one morn in harvest-time,
When all the men were working in the fields,
And he was nearly ragged, out it came—
'They're reaping corn, and corn brings gold, my lass;
But I will reap gold, too, and fame beside,—
I'm going to print a Book!'

      I thought him mad!
The words seem'd dreadful—such a fool was I;
And I was puzzled more when he explain'd:
That he had sent some verses by the post
To a rich man who lived by selling songs
Yonder in London city; that for months
No answer came, and Teddy strain'd his eyes
Into the clouds for comfort; that at last
There came a letter full of wondrous praise
From the great man in London, offering
Poor Teddy, if he sent him verse enough
To make a pretty little printed book,
To value it in money. Till I die,
I'll ne'er forget the light on Teddy's face—
The light, the glory, and the wonder there:
He laugh'd, and read the letter out aloud,
He leapt and laugh'd and kiss'd me o'er and o'er,
And then he read the letter o'er again,
And then turn'd pale, and sank into a chair,
And hid his bright face in his hands, and cried.

Bewilder'd though I was, my heart was glad
To see his happy looks, and pleased beside
That fine folk call'd him clever. I said nought
To mother—for I knew her ways too well—
But waited. Soon came other wondrous news:
The scraps of verse had all been copied out
On fine white sheets, written in Teddy's hand,
Big, round, and clear, like print; and word had come
That they were read and praised by other folk,
Friends of the man in London. Last of all,
One night, when I was ironing the clothes,
And mother knitting sat beside the fire,
In Teddy came—as bright and fresh and gay
As a cock starling hopping from the nest
On May-day; and with laughing eyes he cried,
'Well, mother, when are Bess and I to wed?'
'Wed?' mother snapt, as sour as buttermilk,
'Wed? when the birds swim, and the fishes fly,
And the green trees grow bread and cheese and butter
For lazy loons that lie beneath and yawn!'
Then Teddy laugh'd aloud, and when I frown'd
And shook my head to warn him, laugh'd the more;
And, drawing out his leathern ploughman's pouch,
'See, mother, see!' he cried,—and in her lap
Pour'd thirty golden guineas!

      At the first,
I scream'd, and mother look'd afraid to touch
The glittering gold,—and plain enough she said
The gold, she guess'd, was scarcely honest gain;
Then Teddy told her all about his book,
And how those golden guineas were the price
The great rich man in London put upon 't.

She shook her head the more ; and when he read
The great man's letter, with its words of praise,
Look'd puzzled most of all; and in a dream,
Feeling the gold with her thin hand, she sat,
While Teddy, proud dew sparkling in his eyes,
Show'd me in print the little song he made
Of cuddling in the kitchen while 'twas snowing,—
'And, Bess,' he cried, ' the gold will stock a house,
But little 'tis I care about the gold :
This bit of printed verse is sweeter far
Than all the shining wealth of all the world!'
And lifted up the paper to his mouth
And kiss'd the print, then held it out at length
To look upon 't with sparkling, happy eyes,
And folded it and put it in his pouch,
As tenderly and carefully, I swear,
As if it were a note upon a bank
For wealth untold. Why linger o'er the tale?—
Though now my poor old man is weak and ill,
Sweet is the telling of his happy time.
The money stock'd a house, and in a month
We two were man and wife.

     Teddy was proud
And happy,—busy finishing the book
That was his heart's delight ; and as for me,
My thoughts were merry as a running brook,
For Teddy seem'd a wise man after all ;
And it was spring-time, and our little home
Was hung with white clematis, porch and wall,
And wall-flower, candituft, and London pride,
All shining round a lilac bush in bloom,
Sweeten'd the little square of garden ground;
And cozy as a finch's mossy nest
Was all within ; the little sleeping-room
And red-tiled kitchen ; and, made snug and fine
By chairs and tables cut of bran-new deal,
The little parlour,—on the mantel-piece

Field-flowers and ferns and bird's-egg necklaces,
Two pretty pictures pasted on the walls,
(The portraits of one Milton and one Burns,)
And, in the corner Teddy loved the best,
Three shelves to keep the old, black, thumb-mark'd books.

    And if my heart had fever, lest the life
Begun so well was over-bright to last,
Teddy could cheer me ; for he placed his arm
Around me, looking serious in his joy,
When we were wed three days ; and ' Bess,' he said,
' The Lord above is very kind to me ;
For He has given me this sweet place and you,
Adding the bliss of seeing soon in print
The verse I love so much.' Then, kissing me,
' I have been thinking of it all,' he said,
' Holpen a bit by lives of other folk,
Which I have read. Now, many men like me
Grow light o' head and let their labour go ;
But men can't live by writing verses, Bess.'
' Nay, nay,' cried I, ''twere pity if they could,
For every man would try the easier task,
And who would reap the fields or grind the corn?'
And Teddy smiling, said, ''Tis so! 'tis so!
Pride shall not puff my wits, but all the day
I will toil happily in the fields I love ;
And in the pleasant evenings 'twill be fine
To wander forth and see the world with you,
Or read out poems in the parlour here,
Or take a pen and write, for ease o' heart,
Not praise, not money.' I was glad ten-fold,—
Put all my fears aside, and trusted him,—
And well he kept his word.

      Yet ill at ease,
Restless and eager, Teddy waited on,
Until the night a monster parcel came
From London : twelve brown volumes, all the same,
Wide-printed, thin, and on the foremost page,
' Poems by Edward Crowhurst, Labourer.'
The happiest hour my Teddy ever knew !

He turn'd the volumes o'er, examined each,
Counted the sheets, counted the printed lines,
Stared at his name in print, held out the page
At arm's length, feasting with his mouth and eyes.
I wonder'd at his joy, yet, spite o' me,
I shared it. 'Twas so catching. The old tale !
A little thing could make my Teddy's heart
Gay as a bunch of roses, while a great
Went by unheeded like a cannon-ball.
The glowworm is a little common grub,
Yet what a pretty gleam it often sheds ;
And that same poor, small, common-looking book,
Set on our table, kept around its leaves
A light like sunshine.

When his joy grew cool,
Teddy took up a book to read it through ;
And first he show'd me, next the foremost page,
A bit of writing called the 'Author's Life,'
Made up of simple things my man had told—
How he was but a lowly labourer,
And how the green fields work'd upon his heart
To write about the pretty things he saw—
All put together by a clever man
In London. For a time he sat and read
In silence, looking happy with his eyes ;
But suddenly he started up and groan'd,
Looking as black as bog-mud, while he flung
The book upon the table ; and I gript
His arm, and ask'd what ail'd him. ' Bess,' he said,
' The joy o' this has all gone sudden sour,
All through the cruel meddling of a fool :
The story of my life is true enough,
Despite the fine-flown things the teller sticks
Around it—peacock's feathers stuck around
The nest of some plain song-bird; but the end
Is like the garlic flower,—looks fine at first,
But stinks on peeping nearer. Bess, my lass,
I never begg'd a penny in my life,
I sought the help of no man, but could work,
What then ? what then ? O Bess, 'tis hard, 'tis hard !
They make me go a-begging, book in hand,
As if I were a gipsy of the lanes
Whistling for coppers at an alehouse door !'

I, too, was hurt, but tried to comfort him ;
'Twas kindly meant, at least, I thought and said ;
But Teddy clench'd his teeth, and sat him down,
And wrote, not rudely, but as if in grief,
To him in London. Till the answer came,
The printed poems cheer'd him, though the book
Had lost a scent that ne'er would come again ;
And when the answer came, 'twas like the words
A mother murmurs to a silly child—
A smiling, pitying, quiet kind of tone,
That made him angrier than violent speech ;
And at the end a melancholy hint
About ingratitude. Teddy must trust
In those who had his fortune most at heart,
Nor rashly turn his friends to enemies,
Nor meddle with the kindly schemes of those
Who knew the great world better far than he.
Oh, Teddy's eyes were dim with bitter dew !
' Begging is begging, and I never begg'd !
Shame on me if I ever take their gold !'
I coax'd him to be silent ; and though soon
The bitter mood wore off, his gladness lost
The look of happy pride it wore of old.

'Twas happy, happy, in the little home,
And summer round about on wood and field,
And summer on the bit of garden ground.
But soon came news, like whiffs of colour'd smoke,
Blown to us thickly on the idle wind,
And smelling of the city. For the land
Was crying Teddy's praises ! Every morn
Came papers full of things about the Book,
And letters full of cheer from distant folk ;
And Teddy toil'd away, and tried his best
To keep his glad heart humble. Then, one day,
A snirking gentleman, with inky thumbs,
Call'd, chatted, pried with little fox's eyes
This way and that, and when he went away
He wrote a heap of lying scribble, styled
'A Summer Morning with the Labourer Bard !'
Then others came : some, mild young gentlemen,
Who chirp'd, and blush'd, and simper'd, and were gone ;

Some, sallow ladies wearing spectacles,
And pale young misses, rolling languid eyes,
And pecking at the words my Teddy spake
Like sparrows picking seed ; and, once or twice,
Plump merry gentlemen who talk'd no stuff,
But chatted sensibly of common things,
And made us feel at home. Ay, not a day
But Teddy must be sent for, from the fields,
To meet with fine-clad strangers from afar.
The village folk began to open eyes
And wonder, but were only more afraid
Of Teddy, gave him hard suspicious looks,
And shunn'd him out-o'-doors. Yet how they throng'd,
Buzzing like humble bees at swarming time,
That morn the oil'd and scented gentleman
(For such we thought him) brought a little note
From Lord Fitztalbot of Fitztalbot Tower,
Yonder across the moorland. 'Twas a line
Bidding my Teddy to the Tower, and he
Who brought it was the footman of my lord.
Well, Teddy went, was many hours away,
And then return'd with. cat's-claws round his lips.
' See ! ' Teddy cried, and flung a little purse
Of money in my lap ; and I, amazed,
Counted ten golden guineas in my palm,
Then gazed at Teddy, saw how pale he was,
And ask'd what ail'd him. ' 'Tis the money, lass,'
He answer'd, groaning deep. ' He talk'd, and seem'd
Right kindly ; ask'd about my home, and you ;
Spoke of the poems, smiled, and bow'd farewell ;
And, dropping that same money in my hat,
Bade me go dine below. I burn'd like fire,
Felt choking, yet was fearful to offend,
And took the money, as I might have took
A blazing cinder, bow'd, and came away.
O Lord! O Lord! this comes of yonder loon,
Who sent the book a-begging !' Then he talk'd—
How fiercely and how wildly, clenching hands :
' Was not a poet better than a lord ?
Why should the cruel people use him so ?
Why would the world not leave his home in peace ?'

And last, he vow'd to send the money back
But I, though shamed and troubled, thought him wrong,
And vow'd my lord was kind, and meant us well,
And won him o'er at last to keep the purse.
And ah ! we found it useful very soon,
When I lay in, and had a dreadful time,
And brought our girl. Then Teddy put aside
All grief and anger ; thought of us alone ;
Forgot, or nearly, all the praise and blame
Of loveless strangers ; and was proud and glad,
Making fond rhymes about the babe and me.

Ah ! had the folk but let my man alone,
All would be happy now. He loved his work,
Because it kept him in the fields ; he loved
The babe and me ; and all he needed more,
To keep his heart content, was pen and ink,
And now and then a book. And as for praise,
He needed it no more than singing birds ;
And as for money, why, he wanted none ;
And as for prying strangers in the house,
They brought a clumsy painful sense of pride
That made him restless. He was ever shy
Of company—he loved to dream alone—
And the poor life that he had known so long
Was just the kind of life he suited best.
He look'd a fine straight man in homespun gear,
But ne'er seem'd easy in his Sunday coat.

What should his fine friends do at last, but write,
Bidding my man to London,—there to meet
A flock o' gentlefolk, who spent their days
In making books ! – Though here we dwell so near,
That northward, far away, you see the sky
Black with the smoky breathing of the city,
We ne'er had wander'd far away from home,
Save once or twice, five miles to westward yonder,
To Kersey Fair. Well, Teddy fix'd to go ;
And seeing him full bent, I held my tongue.
And off he set, one day, in Sunday black,
A hazel staff over his shoulder flung,
His bundle swinging,—and was sped by train

To London town. Two weeks he stay'd
  away ;
And, when he came from London, he was
  changed.
His eyes look'd wild, his cheek was pale,
  his step
Unsteady ; when he enter'd, I could smell
Drink in his breath. Full pain'd, and sick
  at heart,
I question'd him ; but he was petulant,
And snapt me short ; and when I brought
  the child,
He push'd her from him. Next day, when
  he rose,
His face was pallid ; but his kindly smile
Came back upon it. Ere the day was out,
He told me of his doings, of the men
And places he had seen, and when, and how.
He had been dull in dwellings of the rich,
Had felt ashamed in great grand drawing-
  rooms,
And angry that the kindly people smiled
As if in pity ; and the time, he said,
Would have gone drearily, had he lack'd
  the cheer
He chanced to find among some jovial folk
Who lived by making books. Full plain I
  saw
That something had gone wrong. His
  ways were strange,
He did not seem contented in his home,
He scarcely glinted at the poor old books
He loved so dearly. In a little time,
Teddy grew more himself, at home, a-field,
And though, from that day forward, he
  began
To take a glass and smoke a pipe at night,
I scarcely noticed. Thus the year wore
  on ;
And still the papers praised him far away,
And still the letters came from distant folk.

And Teddy had made friends : folk who
  could talk
About the things he loved, and flatter him,
Ay, laugh aloud to see him drink his glass,
And clap his back, and shake him by the
  hand,
How wild soc'er he talk'd. For by degrees
His tongue grew freer, he was more at ease
With strangers. Oft he spent the evening
  hours
With merry-makers in the public-house,

And totter'd home with staring, dazzled
  eyes.
The country people liked him better now,
And loved to coax him out to drink at
  night,
And, gaping, heark'd to the strange things
  he said.
Ah, then my fear grew heavy, though his
  heart
Was kindly still, his head still clear and
  wise,
And he went wastering only now and then.

But soon his ways grew better, for his
  time
Was spent in finishing another book.
Yet then I found him changed in other
  things ;
For once or twice when money as before
Was sent or given him, he only laugh'd,
And took it, not in anger. And, be
  sure,
Money grew needful in the little home—
Another babe was coming. Babe and
  book
Were born together, but the first was born
Quiet and breathless. 'Twould be idle
  talk
To speak about the book. What came of
  that,
Was much the same as what had come
  before :
The papers praised it over all the land,
But just a shade more coolly ; strange folk
  wrote,
But not so oft. Yet Teddy was in glee,
For *this* time fifty golden guineas came
From the rich man in London.

      Once again,
They coax'd him up to London ; once
  again,
Home came he changed,—with wilder words
  of wit,
And sharper sayings, on his tongue. He
  toil'd
Even less than ever : nay, his idle friends,
Who loved to drain the bottle at his side,
Took up his time full sorely. We began
To want and pinch : more money was sub-
  scribed,
And taken :—till at last my man grew sick
Of working in the open fields at all

And just as work grew hardest to his
 mind,
The Lord Fitztalbot pass'd him on the
 road,
And turn'd his head away. A change had
 come,
As dreadful as the change within himself.
The papers wrote the praise of newer men,
The strange folk sent him letters scarce at
 all ;
And when he spake about another book,
The man in London wrote a hasty ' No ! '
And said the work had little chance to sell.
Those words were like a sunstroke. Wild
 and scared,
My Teddy stared at London—all his
 dreams
Came back upon him—and with bitter
 tongue
He mock'd and threaten'd. 'Twas of no
 avail !
His fine-day friends like swallows wing'd
 away,
The summer being o'er ; the country folk
Began to knit their foreheads as of old,
Save one or two renown'd as ne'er-do-
 wells ;
And, mad with pride, bitten with shame
 and fear,
Teddy drank deeper at the public-house.

Teddy to blame? Teddy to blame? Ah,
 nay !
The blame be theirs who broke his simple
 pride
With money, beggar'd him against his will.
The blame be theirs who flatter'd him from
 home,
And led him out to make his humble ways
An idle show. The blame be theirs who
 smiled
Whenc'er he play'd a wrong and foolish
 part,
Because he had skill to write a bit of verse.
The blame be theirs who spoil'd him like a
 child,
And, when the newness of his face was
 gone,
Turn'd from him scornfully and smiled else-
 where.
Teddy to blame !—a silly, ignorant man,
Not learn'd, not wise, not cunning in the
 world !

But hearken how I changed him yet once
 more,
One day when he was sick and ill with
 pain.
I spake of all our early courting days,
Full low and tender, of the happy time
When I brought forth our girl, and of the
 words
He spake when we were happy ; last of all,
' Teddy,' I said, ' let people be unkind,
The whole world hard, you cannot heal
 your pain
Wastering, idling ; think of merrier days,
Of me, and of our girl, and drink no more.'
He gazed at me full long, his bosom rose
And flutter'd, and he held my hand in his,
And shivering, moaning, sank into a chair ;
And, looking at the bookshelf at his side,
And at the common-looking thumb-mark'd
 books,
He promised, promised, with his poor
 cheeks wet,
And his voice broken, and his lips set firm.

True Heart, he kept his word. The
 public-house
Knew him no longer ; in the fields he toil'd
Lonely once more ; and in the evenings
Read books and wrote,—and all he wrote,
 I know,
Was sad, sad, sad. Bravely he work'd all
 day,
But not so cheerfully. And no man cared
To brighten him with goodly words. His
 face
Was stale with gentlefolk, his heart too
 proud
To mix with coarse, low men. Oft in the
 fields
They saw him turn his poor eyes London-
 wards,
And sigh ; but he was silent of the pain
That grew upon him. Slowly he became
The sadden'd picture of his former self :
He stood at ploughtail looking at the
 clouds,
He watch'd the ways of birds and trees and
 flowers ;
But all the little things he learn'd and
 loved
Had ta'en a sadder meaning. Oftentimes,
In spite of all he did to hide his heart,
I saw he would have been a happy man

If any one had praised him as of old;
But he was never sent for from the fields,
No strangers wrote to cheer him, and he
 seem'd
All, all, forgotten. Still, as true as steel,
He held his promise to our girl and me,
Though oft, I know, the dreadful longing
 came
To fly to drink for comfort. Then, one
 night,
I heard a stirring in the dark: our girl
Crept close to me, and whisper'd in mine
 ear—
'Hark! father's crying!'

     O 'tis terrible
To hear a strong man weep! I could not
 bear
To find him grieving so, but crept unto
 him,
And put my arms about him, on his neck
Weeping, 'O Teddy, Teddy, do not so!
Cheer up, for you will kill me if you cry.
What do you long for? Why are you so
 sad?'
And I could feel him crush his hot tears
 down,
And shake through every limb. 'O lass!'
 he cried,
'I cannot give a name to what I want;
I cannot tell you why I grow so sad;
But I have lost the pleasure and the peace
The verses brought me. I am sick and
 changed,—
I think too much of other men,—I seem
Despised and useless. If I did not feel
You loved me so, and were so kind and
 true,
When all the world is cruel, I should fall
And wither. All my strength is gone
 away,
And I am broken!'

     'Twas but little cheer
That I could give him: *that* was grief too
 deep
For foolish me to understand or cure.
I made the little parlour bright o' nights,
Coax'd him to read aloud the books he
 loved,
And often he was like himself again,
Singing for ease o' heart; and now and
 then,

A poem printed in a newspaper,
Or something kind from people in the
 world,
Help'd me a little. So the time wore on;—
Till suddenly, one night in winter time,
I saw him change. Home came he white
 and pale,
Shivering, trembling, looking wild and
 strange,
Yet speaking quietly. 'My head feels
 queer—
It aches a bit!' he said; and the next day
He could not rise from bed. Quiet he
 lay,
But now and then I saw him raise his
 hand
And hold his forehead. In the afternoon,
He fell to troubled sleep, and, when he
 woke,
He did not seem to know me. Full of
 fear,
I sent for Doctor Barth. When Doctor
 came,
He found poor Teddy tossing on his bed,
Moaning and muttering and clenching
 teeth,
And Doctor said, 'The ill is on the brain—
Has he been troubled lately?' and I cried,
'Ay, much, much troubled! He has fretted
 sore
For many months!'

     'Twas sad, 'twas sad, to see
My strong man suffer on his dull sick-bed,
Not knowing me, but crying out of things
That haunted him. I will not weary you,
By telling how the Doctor brought him
 round,
And how at last he rose from bed, the
 ghost
Of his old self, and something gone away
That never would return. Then it was
 plain
That he could work no more: the Light
 had fled,
Which keeps a man a man despite the
 world
And all its cruel change. To fright the wolf,
I took in washing at the cottage here;
And people sent us money now and then,
And pitying letters reach'd us from the
 world,
Too late! too late!

             L

Thank the good God above,
Who made me strong and willing, I could keep
The little house above us, though 'twas dear,
And ah! I work'd more hard because I knew
Poor Teddy's heart would break outright elsewhere.
Yet Teddy hardly seem'd to comprehend
All that had happen'd. Though he knew me well,
And spake full sensibly of many things,
He lack'd the power to speak of one thing long.
Sometimes he was as merry as a bird,
Singing wild songs he learn'd by heart when young;
Sometimes he wish'd to wander out a-field,
But easy 'twas to lead his wits away
To other things. And he was changeful ever,
Now laughing and now crying; and at times
He wrote strange notes to poets that were dead,
And named himself by all their names in turn,
Still making verse, which I had sense to see
Was wild, and strange, and wrong—not like the verse
He made of old. One day for hours he sat,
Looking upon the bit of garden ground,
And smiling. When I spoke, he look'd and laugh'd.
'Surely you know me, Teddy?' I exclaim'd;
And up he raised his head, with shrill thin voice
Saying, 'Yes, you are Queen Elizabeth,
And I am Shakespeare;' and again he smiled
Craftily to himself; but when I hung
Around his neck, and wept, and ask'd again,
He turn'd upon me with so pale a look,
So wan, so sharp, so full of agony,
'Twas clear the cloud was lifted for a moment,

'Twas clear he knew that he was Teddy Crowhurst,
And that the light of life had gone away.

And oft, in sunny weather, he and I
Had walks in quiet places,—in the lanes,
And in the woods, and by the river side;
And he was happy, prying as of old
In little mossy nests, or plucking flowers,
Or dropping pebbles at the water-brim,
To make the speckled minnows start and fly
In little gleams of light. Ne'er had he been
More cunning in the ways and looks of things,
Though memory fail'd him when he tried for names.
The sable streaks upon the arum-flower
Were strange to him as ever; a lark singing
Made his eyes misty as it used to do;
The shining sun, the waving of green boughs,
The rippling of the river down the dell,
Were still true pleasure. All the seasons brought
Something to charm him. Staring on the snow,
Or making great snow-houses like a boy,
He was as busy when the boughs were bare,
As carrying home a bough of scented May
Or bunch of yellow lilies from the pond.
What had been pleasure in his younger days
Came back to keep him quiet in the world.
He gave much love to trees and birds and flowers,
And, when the mighty world was all unkind,
The little, gentle, speechless things were true.

True Heart, I never thought that he could bear
To last so long; but ten slow years have fled
Since the first book that brought the trouble and pain
Was printed,—and within the parlour there
Teddy is sitting, busy as a bee.
Doing? He dreams the world that knows him not

Rings with his praises, and for many an hour
Sits busy with the verse of later years,
Marks, copies, and arranges it with care,
To go to some great printer that he thinks
Is waiting ; and from time to time he eyes
The books they printed, numbering the lines,
Counting the pages. Sometimes he is Burns,
Sometimes John Milton, sometimes other men,
And sometimes—always looking saddest then—
Knows he is Teddy Crowhurst. Thin he is,
And worn, and feeble,—wearing slowly down
Like snowdrift; and at times, when Memory
Comes for a moment like a mirror flash'd
Into his eyes, he does not groan and weep,
But droops the more, and seems resign'd and still.
True Heart, I fear the end is near at last !
He sits and hearkens vacantly and dreams,
He thrills at every knocking at the door,
Stilly he waits for light that never comes,
That never will return until the end.
And oft at evening, when my work is done,
And the dark gathers, and he holds my hand,
The waiting grows intenser, and becomes
The sense o' life itself. Take Teddy hence !
Show me the man will draw my hand away !
I am a quiet comfort to his pain ;
For though his thoughts be far away from here,
I know he feels my hand; and ah ! the touch
Just keeps his heart from breaking. 'Tis my joy
To work where I can watch him through the day,
And quiet him, and see he wants for nought.
He loves to sit among his books and flowers,
And wears away with little pain, and feels
The quiet parlour is a pleasant place ;
And there—God bless him !—in a happy time

Teddy will feel the darkness pass away,
And smile farewell upon his wife and girl,
And Light that he has lost will come again
To shine upon him as he goes to sleep.

ARTIST AND MODEL:

A LOVE POEM.

The scorn of the nations is bitter,
But the touch of a hand is warm.

Is it not pleasant to wander
  In town on Saturday night,
While people go hither and thither,
  And shops shed cheerful light ?
And, arm in arm, while our shadows
  Chase us along the panes,
Are we not quite as cozy
  As down among country lanes ?

Nobody knows us, heeds us,
  Nobody hears or sees,
And the shop-lights gleam more gladly
  Than the moon on hedges and trees ;
And people coming and going,
  All upon ends of their own,
Though they work a spell on the spirit,
  Make it more finely alone.

The sound seems harmless and pleasant
  As the murmur of brook and wind ;
The shops with the fruit and the pictures
  Have sweetness to suit my mind ;
And nobody knows us, heeds us,
  And our loving none reproves,—
I, the poor figure-painter !
You, the lady he loves !

And what if the world should scorn you
  For now and again, as you do,
Assuming a country kirtle,
  And bonnet of straw thereto,
Or the robe of a vestal virgin,
  Or a nun's gray gabardine,
And keeping a brother and sister
  By standing and looking divine ?

And what if the world, moreover,
  Should silently pass me by,
Because at the dawn of the struggle,
  I labour some stories high !

Why, there's comfort in waiting, working,
  And feeling one's heart beat right,—
And rambling alone, love-making,
  In London on Saturday night.

For when, with a blush Titianic,
  You peep'd in that lodging of mine,
Did I not praise the good angels
  For sending a model so fine?
When I was fill'd with the pureness
  You brought to the lonely abode,
Did I not learn to love you?
  And—did Love not lighten the load?

And haply, indeed, little darling,
  While I yearn'd and plotted and plann'd,
And you watch'd me in love and in yearning
  Your heart did not quite understand
All the wonder and aspiration
  You meant by your loveliness,
All the faith in the frantic endeavour
  Your beautiful face could express!

For your love and your beauty have thriven
  On things of a low degree,
And you do not comprehend clearly
  The drift of a dreamer like me;
And perchance, when you look'd so divinely,
  You meant, and meant only, to say:
'How sad that he dwells in a garret!
  And lives on so little a day!'

What of that? If your sweetness and beauty,
  And the love that is part of thee,
Were mirror'd in wilder visions,
  And express'd much more to me,
Did the beautiful face, my darling,
  Need subtler, loftier lore?—
Nay, beauty is all our wisdom,—
  We painters demand no more.

Indeed, I had been no painter,
  And never could hope to rise,
Had I lack'd the power of creating
  The meanings for your sweet eyes;
And what you were really thinking
  Scarcely imported, in sooth,—
Since the truth we artists fail for,
  Is the truth that *looks* the truth.

Your beautiful face was before me,
  Set in its golden hair;
And the wonder and love and yearning
  Were shining sublimely there!
And your eyes said—' Work for glory!
  Up, up, where the angels call!'
And I understood, and I labour'd,
  And I love the face for it all!

I am talking, you think, so strangely!
  And you watch with wondering eyes!—
Could I utter one half of the yearning
  Your face, even now, implies!
But the yearning will not be utter'd,
  And never, ah! never can be,
Till the work of the world is over,
  And we see as immortals see.

Yet bless thee for ever and ever,
  For keeping me humble and true,
And would that my Art could utter
  The wisdom I find in you.
Enough to labour and labour,
  And to feel one's heart beat right,
And to wander unknown, love-making,
  In London on Saturday night!

You think: 'How dearly I love him!
  How dearly he loves me!
How sweet to live on, and love him,
  With children at my knee!
With the useless labour over,
  And comfort and leisure won,
And clever people praising
  The work that he has done!'

I think: 'How dearly I love her!
  How dearly she loves me!
Yet the beauty the heart would utter
  Endeth in agony;
And life is a climbing, a seeking
  Of something we never can see!
And death is a slumber, a dreaming
  Of something that may not be!'

And your face is sweetly troubled,
  Your little hand stirs on mine own,
For you guess at a hidden meaning,
  Since I speak in so tender a tone;
And you rain the yearning upon me
  You brought to my help before,
And I ask no mightier wisdom,—
  We painters demand no more.

And we shall live, my darling,
 Together till we grow old,
And people will buy my pictures,
 And you will gather the gold,
And your loveliness will reward me,
 And sanctify all I do,
And toiling for Love's sake, darling,
 I may toil for Fame's sake, too.

Ah, dearest, how much you teach me,
 How much of hope and of light,
Up yonder, planning and painting,
 And here on Saturday night;
And I turn sad eyes no longer
 From the pageant that passes around,
And the vision no more seems weary,
 And the head may yet be crown'd!

And I ask no more from mortals
 Than your beautiful face implies,—
The beauty the artist beholding
 Interprets and sanctifies.
Who says that men have fallen,
 That life is wretched and rough?
I say, the world is lovely,
 And that loveliness is enough.

So my doubting days are ended,
 And the labour of life seems clear;
And life hums deeply around me,
 Just like the murmur here,
And quickens the sense of living,
 And shapes me for peace and storm,—
And dims my eyes with gladness
 When it glides into colour and form!

His form and His colour, darling,
 Are all we apprehend,
Though the meaning that underlies them
 May be utter'd in the end;
And I seek to go no deeper
 Than the beauty and wonder there,
Since the world can look so wondrous,
 And your face can look so fair.

For ah! life's stream is bitter,
 When too greedily we drink,
And I might not be so happy
 If I knew quite all you think;
And when God takes much, my darling,
 He leaves us the colour and form,—
The scorn of the nations is bitter,
 But the touch of a hand is warm.

NELL.

She gazes not at her who hears,
 But, while the gathering darkness cries,
Stares at the vacancy through tears,
 That burn upon her glistening eyes,
Yet do not flow. Her hair falls free
 Around a face grown deathly thin;
Her elbow rests upon her knee,
 And in her palms she props her chin.

SEE, Nan! his little face looks pinch'd with fright,
His little hands are clench'd together tight!
Born dead, that's comfort! quiet too; when one
 Thinks of what kill'd him! Kiss him, Nan, for me.
Thank God, he never look'd upon the sun
 That saw his father hang'd on gallows-tree.
O boy, my boy! you're better dead and sleeping,
Kill'd by poor mother's fear, and shame, and weeping:
She never loved another living man,
But held to father all thro' right and wrong—
Ah, yes! I never turn'd against him, Nan,
 I stuck by him that stuck by me so long!

You're a kind woman, Nan! ay, kind and true!
God will be good to faithful folk like you!
You knew my Ned?
 A better, kinder lad never drew breath—
We loved each other true, though never wed
In church, like some who took him to his death:
A lad as gentle as a lamb, but lost
 His senses when he took a drop too much—
Drink did it all—drink made him mad when cross'd—
He was a poor man, and they're hard on such.
O Nan! that night! that night!
 When I was sitting in this very chair,
Watching and waiting in the candle-light,
 And heard his foot come creaking up the stair,
And turn'd, and saw him standing *yonder*, white

And wild, with staring eyes and rumpled hair!
And when I caught his arm and call'd, in fright,
He push'd me, swore, and to the door he pass'd
To lock and bar it fast!
Then down he drops just like a lump of lead,
Holding his brow, shaking, and growing whiter,
And—Nan!—just then the light seem'd growing brighter,
And I could see the hands that held his head,
All red! all bloody red!
What could I do but scream? He groan'd to hear,
Jump'd to his feet, and gripp'd me by the wrist;
'Be still, or I shall kill thee, Nell!' he hiss'd.
And I was still, for fear.
'They're after me—I've knifed a man!' he said.
'Be still!—the drink—drink did it—he is dead!'
And as he said the word, the wind went by
With a whistle and cry—
The room swam round—the babe unborn
seem'd to scream out, and die!

Then we grew still, dead still. I couldn't weep—
All I could do was cling to Ned and heark—
And Ned was cold, cold, cold, as if asleep,
But breathing hard and deep.
The candle flicker'd out—the room grew dark—
And—Nan!—although my heart was true and tried,—
When all grew cold and dim,
I shudder'd—not for fear of them outside,
But just afraid to be alone with *him*.
For winds were wailing—the wild rain cried,—
Folk's footsteps sounded down the court and died—
What could I do but clasp his knees and cling?
And call his name beneath my breath in pain?
Until he threw his head up, listening,
And gave a groan, and hid his face again;

'Ned! Ned!' I whisper'd—and he moan'd and shook—
But did not heed or look!
'Ned! Ned! speak, lad! tell me it is not true!'
At that he raised his head and look'd so wild;
Then, with a stare that froze my blood, he threw
His arms around me, crying like a child,
And held me close—and not a word was spoken—
While I clung tighter to his heart and press'd him—
And did not fear him, though my heart was broken—
But kiss'd his poor stain'd hands, and cried, and bless'd him!

Then, Nan, the dreadful daylight, coming cold
With sound o' falling rain,—
When I could *see* his face, and it look'd old,
Like the pinch'd face of one that dies in pain;
Well, though we heard folk stirring in the sun,
We never thought to hide away or run,
Until we heard those voices in the street,
That hurrying of feet.
And Ned leap'd up, and knew that they had come.
'Run, Ned!' I cried, but he was deaf and dumb!
'Hide, Ned!' I scream'd, and held him—
'hide thee, man!'
He stared with bloodshot eyes, and hearken'd, Nan!
And all the rest is like a dream—the sound
Of knocking at the door—
A rush of men—a struggle on the ground—
A mist—a tramp—a roar;
For when I got my senses back again,
The room was empty—and my head went round!
The neighbours talk'd and stirr'd about the lane,
And Seven Dials made a moaning sound;
And as I listen'd, lass, it seem'd to me
Just like the murmur of the great dark Sea,
And Ned a-lying somewhere, stiff and drown'd!

God help him? God *will* help him! Ay,
   no fear!
It was the drink, not Ned—he meant no
   wrong;
So kind! so good!—and I am useless here,
   Now he is lost that loved me true and
   long.
Why, just before the last of it, we parted,
And Ned was calm, though I was broken-
   hearted;
And ah, my heart *was* broke! and ah, I
   cried
And kiss'd him,—till they took me from his
   side;
And though he died *that way*, (God bless
   him!) Ned
Went through it bravely, calm as any
   there:
They've wrought their fill of spite upon his
   head,
And—there's the hat and clothes he used
   to wear!

. . . That night before he died,
I didn't cry—my heart was hard and dried;
But when the clocks went 'one,' I took my
   shawl
To cover up my face, and stole away,
And walk'd along the silent streets, where all
   Look'd cold and still and gray,—
Only the lamps o' London here and there
   Scatter'd a dismal gleaming;
And on I went, and stood in Leicester
   Square,
Ay, like a woman dreaming:
But just as 'three' was sounded close at
   hand,
I started and turn'd east, before I knew,—
Then down Saint Martin's Lane, along the
   Strand,
And through the toll-gate, on to Water-
   loo.
How I remember all I saw, although
   'Twas only like a dream!—
The long still lines o' lights, the chilly
   gleam
Of moonshine on the deep black stream
   below;
While far, far, far away, along the sky
   Streaks soft as silver ran,
And the pale Moon look'd paler up on
   high,
And little sounds in far-off streets began!

Well, while I stood, and waited, and look'd
   down,
And thought how sweet 'twould be to drop
   and drown,
Some men and lads went by,
And turning round, I gazed, and watch'd
   'em go,
Then felt that they were going to see him die,
   And drew my shawl more tight, and fol-
   low'd slow.
 · How clear I feel it still!
The streets grew light, but rain began to
   fall;
I stopp'd and had some coffee at a stall,
   Because I felt so chill;
A cock crew somewhere, and it seem'd a
   call
To wake the folk who kill!
The man who sold the coffee stared at
   me!
I must have been a sorry sight to see!
More people pass'd—a country cart with
   hay
Stopp'd close beside the stall,—and two or
   three
Talk'd about *it!* I moan'd, and crept
   away!

Ay, nearer, nearer to the dreadful place,
   All in the falling rain,
I went, and kept my shawl upon my face,
   And felt no grief or pain—
Only the wet that soak'd me through and
   through
Seem'd cold and sweet and pleasant to
   the touch—
It made the streets more drear and silent,
   too,
And kept away the light I fear'd so much.
Slow, slow the wet streets fill'd, and all
   seem'd going,
Laughing and chatting, the same way,
And grayer, sadder, lighter, it was grow-
   ing,
Though still the rain fell fast and dark-
   en'd day!
Nan!—every pulse was burning—I could
   feel
My heart was made o' steel—
As crossing Ludgate Hill, I saw, all
   blurr'd,
Saint Paul's great clock and heard it
   slowly chime,

And hadn't power to count the strokes I heard,
But strain'd my eyes and *saw* it wasn't time.
Ah! then I felt I dared not creep more near,
But went into a lane off Ludgate Hill,
And sitting on a doorstep, I could hear
The people gathering still!
And still the rain was falling, falling,
And deadening the hum I heard from *there;*
And wet and stiff, I heard the people calling,
And watch'd the rain-drops glistening down my hair,
My elbows on my knees, my fingers dead,—
My shawl thrown off, now none could see,— my head
Dripping and wild and bare.
I heard the crying of a crowd of men,
And next, a hollow sound I knew full well,
For something gripp'd me round the heart!
—and then
There came the solemn tolling of a bell!
O God! O God! how could I sit close by,
And neither scream nor cry?
As if I had been stone, all hard and cold,
I listen'd, listen d, listen'd, still and dumb,
While the folk murmur'd, and the deathbell toll'd,
And the day brighten'd, and his time had come. . . .
. . . Till—Nan!—all else was silent, but the knell
Of the slow bell!
And I could only wait, and wait, and wait,
And what I waited for I couldn't tell,—
At last there came a groaning deep and great—
Saint Paul's struck 'eight'—
I scream'd, and seem'd to turn to fire, and fell!

God bless him, live or dead!
Oh, he was kind and true—
They've wrought their fill of spite upon his head—
Why didn't they be kind, and take *me* too?
And there's the dear old things he used to wear,
And here's a lock o' hair!

And Ned! my Ned!
Is fast asleep, and cannot hear me call;—
God bless you, Nan, for all you've done and said,
But don't mind *me!* My heart is broke, that's all!

ATTORNEY SNEAK.

Sharp like a tyrant, timid like a slave,
 A little man, with yellow, bloodless cheek:
A snappish mingling of the fool and knave,
 Resulting in the hybrid compound—Sneak.

PUT execution in on Mrs. Hart—
If people will be careless, let them smart:
Oh, hang her children! just the common cry!
Am I to feed her family? Not I.
I'm tender-hearted, but I dare be just,—
I never go beyond the law, I trust;
I've work'd my way, plotted and starved and plann'd,
Commenced without a penny in my hand,
And never howl'd for help, or dealt in sham—
No! I'm a man of principle, I am.

What's that you say? Oh, *father* has been here?
Of course, you sent him packing? Dear, oh, dear!
When one has work'd his weary way, like me,
To comfort and respectability,
Can pay his bills, and save a pound or two,
And say his prayers on Sunday in a pew,
Can look the laws of England in the face,
'Tis hard, 'tis hard, 'tis shame, and 'tis disgrace,
That one's own father—old and worn and gray—
Should be the only hindrance in his way.
Swore, did he? Very pretty! Threaten'd? Oh!
Demanded money? You, of course, said 'No'?
'Tis hard—my life will never be secure—
He'll be my ruin some day, I am sure.

I don't deny my origin was low—
All the more credit to myself, you know;
Mother (I never saw her) was a tramp,
Father half tramp, half pedlar, and whole scamp,
Who travell'd over England with a pack,
And carried me about upon his back,
Trudging from door to door, to feasts and fairs,
Cheating the silly women with his wares,
Stealing the farmers' ducks and hens for food,
Pilfering odds and ends where'er he could,
And resting in a city now and then,
Till it became too hot,—and off again.
Beat me? No, he knew better. I confess
He used me with a sort of tenderness;
But would have warp'd my nature into sin,
Had I been weak, for lack of discipline.
Why, even now, I shudder to the soul,
To think how oft I ate the food he stole,
And how I wore upon my back the things
He won by cheats and lawless bargainings.
Oh, he had feelings, that I freely say;
But, without principle, what good are they?
He swindled and he stole on every hand,
And I was far too young to reprimand;
And, for the rest, why, he was circumspect,
And might have been committed for neglect.

Ah! how I managed, under stars so ill,
To thrive at all, to me is mystery still.
In spite of father, though, I got along,
And early learn'd to judge the right from wrong;
At roadsides, when we stopp'd to rest and feed,
He gave me lessons how to write and read,
I got a snack of schooling here and there,
And learn'd to sum by instinct, as it were.
Then, latterly, when I was seventeen,
All sorts of evil I had heard and seen;
Knew father's evil ways, bemoan'd my fate,
Long'd to be wealthy, virtuous, and great;
Swore, with the fond ambition of a lad,
To make good use of what poor gifts I had.

At last, tired, sick, of wandering up and down,
Hither I turn'd my thoughts,—to London town;
And finally, with little doubt or fear,
Made up my mind to try my fortune here.
Well, father stared at first, and shook his head;
But when he found I held to what I said,
He clasp'd me tight, and hugg'd me to his heart,
And begg'd and pray'd tha I would not depart;
Said I was all for whom he had to care,
His only joy in trudging here and there;
Vow'd, if I ever left him, he would die,—
Then, last of all, of course, began to cry.
You know how men of his position feel?
Selfish, at best, even when it is real!
I tried to smooth him over, and, next day,
I pack'd what things I had, and ran away.

I need not tell you all my weary fight,
To get along in life, and do aright—
How often people, when I sought a place,
Still push'd my blessed father in my face;
Until, at last, when I was almost stark,
Old Lawyer Hawk made me his under-clerk;
How from that moment, by avoiding wrong,
Possessing principle, I got along;
Read for the law, plotted, and dream'd, and plann'd,
Until—I reach'd the height on which I stand.

'Twas hard, 'twas hard! Just as my business grows,
In father pops his miserable nose,
Steps in, not sober, in a ragged dress,
And worn tenfold with want and wickedness;
Calls me hard names because I wish'd to rise;
Here, in the office, like a baby cries;
Smothers my pride with shame and with disgrace,
Till, red as fire, I coax'd him from the place.
What could I do under so great a blow?
I gave him money, tried to make him go;
But ah! he meant to rest, I plain could see,
His ragged legs 'neath my mahogany!
No principle! When I began complaining,
How he would be my ruin by remaining,
He turn'd upon me, white and wild, and swore,
And would have hit me, had I utter'd more!

'Tommy,' he dared to say, 'you've done amiss;
I never thought to see you come to this.
I would have stopp'd you early on the journey,
If I had ever thought you'd grow attorney,
Sucking the blood of people here in London;
But you have done it, and it can't be undone.
And, Tommy, I will do my best to see
You don't at all disgrace yourself and me.'

I rack'd my brains, I moan'd and tore my hair,
Saw nothing left but ruin and despair;
Father at hand, why, all would deem me low:
'Sneak's father? humph!'—the business would go.
The labour of long years would come to nought!
At last I hit upon a happy thought:
Why should not father, if he pleased to be,
Be decent and respectable like me;
He would be glad and grateful, if a grain
Of principle were settled in his brain.
I made the offer,—proud he seem'd and glad,—
There rose a hope he'd change to good from bad,
Though, 'Tommy, 'tis a way of getting bread
I never thought to come upon,' he said;
And so I placed him in the office here,
A clerk at five and thirty pounds a year.

I put it to you, could a man do more?
I felt no malice, did not close my door,
Gave him the chance to show if he was wise:
He had the world before him, and could rise.

Well, for a mon h or more, he play'd no tricks,
Writ-drawing, copying, from nine to six,
Not smart, of course, or clever, like the rest,
But trying, it appear'd, to do his best;
But by and by he changed—old fire broke out—
He snapp'd when seniors order'd him about—

Came late to office, tried to loaf and shirk—
Would sit for precious hours before his work,
And scarcely lift a pen, but sleepily stare
Out through the window at the empty air,
And watch the sunshine lying in the lane,
Or the bluebottles buzzing on the pane,
And look as sad and worn and grieved and strange
As if he ne'er had had a chance to change;
Came one day staggering in a drunken fit;
Flatly refused one day to serve a writ.
I talk'd, appeal'd, talk'd of my honest name,
He stared, turn'd pale, swore loud, and out it came:
He hated living with that monkey crew,
Had tried his best and found it would not do;
He could not bear, forsooth, to watch the tears
Of people with the Law about their ears,
Would rather steal his meals from place to place,
Than bring the sorrow to a poor man's face—
In fact, you see, he hated all who pay,
Or seek their moneys in the honest way;
Moreover, he preferr'd a roadside crust,
To cleanly living with the good and just:
Old, wild, and used to roaming up and down,
He could not bear to stagnate in a town;
To stick in a dark office in a street,
Was downright misery to a man with feet;
Serving the law was more than he could bear,
Give him his pack, his freedom, and fresh air.

Mark that! how base, ungrateful, gross, and bad!
His want of principle had made him mad.
I gave him money, sent him off by train,
And trusted ne'er to see his face again.

But he came back. Of course. Look'd wan and ill,
More ragged and disreputable still.
Despairing, groaning, wretchedest of men,
I granted him another trial then.
Still the old story—the same vacant stare
Out through the window at the empty air,

More watching of the sunshine in the lane,
And the bluebottles buzzing on the pane,
Then more of tipsiness and drunken dizziness,
And rage at things done in the way of business.
I saw the very office servants sneer,
And I determined to be more severe.
At last, one winter morn, I went to him,
And found him sitting, melancholy, grim,
Sprawling like any schoolboy on his seat,
And scratching drawings on a foolscap sheet:
Here, an old hag, with half-a-dozen chits,
Lash'd with a cat-o'-nine-tails, labell'd
'WRITS;'
There, a young rascal, ragged as a daw,
Drinkin a cup of poison, labell'd 'LAW;'
Elsewhere, the Devil, looking o'er a pile
Of old indictments with a crafty smile,
And sticking Lawyers on an office file!
And in a corner, wretchedly devised,
A shape in black, that kick'd and agonised,
Strung by a pauper to a gallows great,
And underneath it written, 'TOMMIE'S FATE!'
I touch'd his arm, conducted him aside,
Produced a bunch of documents, and cried:
'Now, father, no more nonsense! You must be
No more a plague and a disgrace to me—
If you won't work like others, you must quit;
See, here are two subpœnas, there a writ,
Serve these on Such-a-one and So-and-so.
Be sharp,—and mind your conduct, or you go.'
He never said a word, but with a glare
All round him, drew his thin hand through his hair,
Turn'd white, and took the paper silently,
Put on his hat, and peep'd again at me.
Then quietly, not like a man in ire,
Threw all the precious papers on the fire!
And turning quickly, crying with a shout,
'You, and your documents, be *damn'd!*'
went out.

He came again! Ay, after wandering o'er
The country as of old, he came once more.
I gave him money, off he went; and then,
After a little year, he came again;
Ay, came, and came, still ragged, bad, and poor,
And he will be my ruin, I am sure.
He tells the same old tale from year to year,
How to his heart I ever will be dear;
Or oft into a fit of passion flies,
Calls me ungrateful and unkind,—then cries,
Raves of his tenderness and suffering,
And mother's too——and all that sort of thing!
He haunts me ever like a goblin grim,
And—to be candid—I'm afraid of him;
For, ah! all now is hopeless, to my cost,—
Through want of principle the man is lost.

—That's Badger, is it? He must go to Vere,
The Bank of England clerk. The writ is here.
Say, for his children's sake, we may relent,
If he'll renew at thirty-five per cent.

BARBARA GRAY.

A mourning woman, robed in black,
Stands in the twilight, looking back;
Her hand is on her heart, her head
Bends musingly above the Dead,
Her face is plain, and pinch'd, and thin,
But splendour strikes it from within.

I.

'BARBARA GRAY!
Pause, and remember what the world will say,'
I cried, and turning on the threshold fled,
When he was breathing on his dying bed;
But when, with heart grown bold,
I cross'd the threshold cold,
Here lay John Hamerton, and he was dead.

II.

And all the house of death was chill and dim,
The dull old housekeeper was looking grim,
The hall-clock ticking slow, the dismal rain
Splashing by fits against the window-pane,
The garden shivering in the twilight dark,
Beyond, the bare trees of the empty park,
And faint gray light upon the great cold bed,
And I alone; and he I turn'd from,—dead

III.

Ay, 'dwarf' they called this man who sleeping lies;
No lady shone upon him with her eyes,
No tender maiden heard his true-love vow,
And pressed her kisses on the great bold brow.
What cared John Hamerton? With light, light laugh,
He halted through the streets upon his staff;
Halt, lame, not beauteous, yet with winning grace
And sweetness in his pale and quiet face;
Fire, hell's or heaven's, in his eyes of blue;
Warm words of love upon his tongue thereto;
Could win a woman's Soul with what he said,
And I am here; and here he lieth dead.

IV.

I would not blush if the bad world saw now
How by his bed I stoop and kiss his brow!
Ay, kiss it, kiss it, o'er and o'er again,
With all the love that fills my heart and brain.

V.

For where was man had stoop'd to me before,
Though I was maiden still, and girl no more?
Where was the spirit that had deign'd to prize
The poor plain features and the envious eyes?
What lips had whisper'd warmly in mine ears?
When had I known the passion and the tears?
Till he I look on sleeping came unto me,
Found me among the shadows, stoop'd to woo me,
Seized on the heart that flutter'd withering here,
Stung it and wrung it with new joy and fear,
Yea, brought the rapturous light, and brought the day,
Waken'd the dead heart, withering away,
Put thorns and roses on the unhonour'd head,
That felt but roses till the roses fled!
Who, who, but he crept unto sunless ground,
Content to prize the faded face he found?
John Hamerton, I pardon all—sleep sound, my love, sleep sound!

VI.

What fool that crawls shall prate of shame and sin?
Did he not think me fair enough to win?
Yea, stoop and smile upon my face as none,
Living or dead, save he alone, had done?
Bring the bright blush unto my cheek, when ne'er
The full of life and love had mantled there?
And I am all alone; and here lies he,—
The only man that ever smiled on me.

VII.

Here, in his lonely dwelling-house he lies,
The light all faded from his winsome eyes:
Alone, alone, alone, he slumbers here,
With wife nor little child to shed a tear!
Little, indeed, to him did nature give;
Nor was he good and pure as some that live,
But pinch'd in body, warp'd in limb,
He hated the bad world that loved not him!

VIII.

Barbara Gray!
Pause, and remember how he turn'd away;
Think of your wrongs, and of your sorrows. Nay!
Woman, think rather of the shame and wrong
Of pining lonely in the dark so long;
Think of the comfort in the grief he brought.
The revelation in the love he taught.
Then, Barbara Gray!
Blush not, nor heed what the cold world will say;
But kiss him, kiss him, o'er and o'er again,
In passion and in pain,
With all the love that fills your heart and brain!
Yea, kiss him, bless him, pray beside his bed,
For you have lived, and here your love lies dead.

THE BLIND LINNET.

τί γὰρ ἔδει μ' ὁρᾶν,
ὅτῳ γ' ὁρῶντι μηδὲν ἦν ἰδεῖν γλυκύ ;
SOPH. ŒD. TYR.

I.

THE sempstress's linnet sings
  At the window opposite me ;—
It feels the sun on its wings,
  Though it cannot see.
Can a bird have thoughts? May be.

II.

The sempstress is sitting,
  High o'er the humming street,
The little blind linnet is flitting
  Between the sun and her seat.
All day long
She stitches wearily there,
And I know she is not young,
And I know she is not fair ;
For I watch her head bent down
  Throughout the dreary day,
And the thin meek hair o' brown
  Is threaded with silver gray ;
And now and then, with a start
  At the fluttering of her heart,
She lifts her eyes to the bird,
And I see in the dreary place
The gleam of a thin white face.
And my heart is stirr'd.

III.

Loud and long
The linnet pipes his song !
For he cannot see
  The smoky street all round,
But loud in the sun sings he,
  Though he hears the murmurous sound;
For his poor, blind eyeballs blink,
  While the yellow sunlights fall,
And he thinks (if a bird can think)
  He hears a waterfall,
Or the broad and beautiful river
  Washing fields of corn,
Flowing for ever
  Through the woods where he was born;
And his voice grows stronger,
  While he thinks that he is there,
And louder and longer
  Falls his song on the dusky air,
And oft, in the gloaming still,
  Perhaps (for who can tell?)
The musk and the muskatel,
  That grow on the window sill,
Cheat him with their smell.

IV.

But the sempstress can see
  How dark things be ;
How black through the town
  The stream is flowing ;
And tears fall down
  Upon her sewing.
So at times she tries,
  When her trouble is stirr'd
To close her eyes,
  And be blind like the bird.
And *then*, for a minute,
  As sweet things seem,
As to the linnet
  Piping in his dream !
For she feels on her brow
  The sunlight glowing,
And hears nought now
  But a river flowing—
A broad and beautiful river,
  Washing fields of corn,
Flowing for ever
  Through the woods where she was born—
And a wild bird winging
  Over her head, and singing !
And she can smell
The musk and the muskatel
  That beside her grow,
And, unaware,
She murmurs an old air
  That she used to know !

'TIGER BAY:

A STORMY NIGHT'S DREAM.

I.

THE TIGRESS.

A DREAM I had in the dead of night :
  Darkness—the Jungle—a black Man sleeping—
Head on his arm, with the moon-dew creeping
Over his face in a silvern light :

The Moon was driving, the Wind was crying ;
  Two great lights gleam'd, round, horrid, and red,
  Two great eyes, steadfast beside the bed
Where the man was lying.
      Hark ! hark !
    What wild things cry in the dark ?
    Only the Wind as it raves,
    Only the Beasts in their caves,
    Where the Jungle waves.

The man slept on, and his face was bright,
  Tender and strange, for the man was dreaming—
  Coldly the light on his limbs was gleaming,
On his jet-black limbs and their folds of white ;—
Leprous-spotted, and gaunt, and hated,
  With teeth protruding and hideous head,
  Her two eyes burning so still, so red,
The Tigress waited.
      Hark ! hark !
    The wild things cry in the dark ;
    The Wind whistles and raves,
    The Beasts groan in their caves,
    And the Jungle waves.

From cloud to cloud the cold Moon crept,
  The silver light kept coming and going—
  The Jungle under was bleakly blowing,
The Tigress watch'd, and the black Man slept.
  The Wind was wailing, the Moon was gleaming :
  He stirr'd and shiver'd, then raised his head :—
Like a thunderbolt the Tigress sped,
And the Man fell screaming—
      Hark ! hark !
    The wild things cry in the dark ;
    The wild Wind whistles and raves,
    The Beasts groan in their caves,
    And the Jungle waves.

II.
'RATCLIFFE MEG.

Then methought I saw another sight :
  Darkness—a Garret—a rushlight dying—
  On the broken-down bed a Sailor lying,
Sleeping fast, in the feeble light ;—
The Wind is wailing, the Rain is weeping
  She croucheth there in the chamber dim,
  She croucheth there with her eyes on him
As he lieth sleeping—
      Hark ! hark !
    Who cries outside in the dark ?
    Only the Wind on its way,
    Only the wild gusts astray,
    In Tiger Bay.

Still as a child the Sailor lies :—
  She waits—she watches—is she human ?
  Is she a Tigress ? is she a Woman ?
Look at the gleam of her deep-set eyes !
Bloated and stain'd in every feature,
  With iron jaws, throat knotted and bare,
  Eyes deep sunken, jet black hair,
Crouches the creature.
      Hark ! hark !
    Who cries outside in the dark ?
    Only the Wind on its way,
    Only the wild gusts astray,
    In Tiger Bay.

Hold her ! scream ! or the man is dead ;
  A knife in her tight-clench'd hand is gleaming ;
  She will *kill* the man as he lieth dreaming !
Her eyes are fixed, her throat swells red.
The Wind is wailing, the Rain is weeping ;
  She is crawling closer—O Angels that love him !
  She holds her breath and bends above him,
While he stirreth sleeping.
      Hark ! hark !
    Who cries outside in the dark ?
    Only the Wind on its way,
    Only the wild gusts astray
    In Tiger Bay.

A silken purse doth the sleeper clutch,
  And the gold peeps through with a fatal glimmer !
  She creepeth near—the light grows dimmer—
Her thick throat swells, and she thirsts to touch.
She looks—she pants with a feverish hunger—
She dashes the black hair out of her eyes—

She glares at his face . . . he smiles and sighs—
And the face looks younger.
  Hark! hark!
  Who cries outside in the dark?
  Only the Wind on its way,
  Only the wild gusts astray
    In Tiger Bay.

She gazeth on,—he doth not stir—
  Her fierce eyes close, her brute lip quivers;
  She longs to strike, but she shrinks and shivers:
The light on his face appalleth her.
The Wind is wailing, the Rain is weeping:
  Something holds her—her wild eyes roll;
  His Soul shines out, and she fears his Soul,
Tho' he lieth sleeping.
  Hark! hark!
  Who cries outside in the dark?
  Only the Wind on its way,
  Only the wild gusts astray
    In Tiger Bay.

III.

INTERCESSION.

I saw no more, but I woke,—and prayed:
  'God! that made the Beast and the Woman!
God of the tigress! God of the human!
Look to these things whom Thou hast made!
Fierce and bloody and famine-stricken,
  Knitted with iron vein and thew—
  Strong and bloody, behold the two!—
We see them and sicken.
  Mark! mark!
  These outcasts fierce of the dark;
  Where murmur the Wind and the Rain,
  Where the Jungle darkens the plain,
    And in street and lane.'

God answer'd clear, 'My will be done!
  Woman-tigress and tigress-woman—
  I made them both, the beast and the human,
But I struck a spark in the brain of the one.
And the spark is a fire, and the fire is a spirit;
  Tho' ye may slay it, it cannot die—
  Nay, it shall grow as the days go by,
For my Angels are near it—
  Mark! mark!
  Doth it not burn in the dark?
  Spite of the curse and the stain,
  Where the Jungle darkens the plain,
    And in street and lane.'

God said, moreover: 'The spark shall grow—
  'Tis blest, it gathers, its flame sha lighten,
Bless it and nurse it—let it brighten!
'Tis scatter'd abroad, 'tis a Seed I sow.
And the Seed is a Soul, and the Soul is the Human;
  And it lighteth the face with a sign and a flame.
Not unto beasts have I given the same,
But to man and to woman.
  Mark! mark!
  The light shall scatter the dark:
  Where murmur the Wind and the Rain,
  Where the Jungle darkens the plain,
    And in street and lane.'

. . . So faint, so dim, so sad to seeing,
  Behold it burning! Only a spark!
  So faint as yet, and so dim to mark,
In the tigress-eyes of the human being.
Fan it, feed it, in love and duty,
  Track it, watch it in every place,—
  Till it burns the bestial frame and face
To its own dim beauty.
  Mark! mark!
  A spark that grows in the dark;
  A spark that burns in the brain;
  Spite of the Wind and the Rain,
  Spite of the Curse and the Stain;
  Over the Sea and the Plain,
    And in street and lane.

THE CITY ASLEEP.

Still as the Sea serene and deep,
  When all the winds are laid,
The City sleeps—so still, its sleep
  Maketh the soul afraid.

Over the living waters, see!
  The Seraphs shining go,—
The Moon is gliding hushfully
  Through stars like flakes of snow.

In pearl-white silver here and there
  The fallen moon-rays stream ;
Hark ! a dull stir is in the air,
  Like the stir of one in dream.

Through all the thrilling waters creep
  Deep throbs of strange unrest,
Like washings of the windless Deep
  When it is peacefullest.

A little while—God's breath will go,
  And hush the flood no more ;
The dawn will break—the wind will blow,
  The Ocean rise and roar.

Each day with sounds of strife and death
  The waters rise and call ;
Each midnight, conquer'd by God's breath,
  To this dead calm they fall.

Out of His heart the fountains flow,
  The brook, the running river,
He marks them strangely come and go,
  For ever and for ever.

Till darker, deeper, one by one,
  After a weary quest,
They, from the light of moon and sun,
  Flow back, into His breast.

Love, hold my hand ! be of good cheer !
  For His would be the cost,
If, out of all the waters here,
  One little drop were *lost*.

Heaven's eyes above the waters dumb
  Innumerably yearn ;
Out of His heart each drop hath come,
  And thither *must* return.

UP IN AN ATTIC.

'Do you *dream* yet, on your old rickety sofa, in the dear old ghastly bankrupt garret at No. 66?'—*Gray to Buchanan* (see *The Life of David Gray*).

  HALF of a gold-ring bright,
    Broken in days of old,
  One yellow curl, whose light
    Gladden'd my gaze of old ;
  A sprig of thyme thereto,
    Pluckt on the mountains blue,
  When in the gloaming-dew
    We roamed erratic ;

Last, an old Book of Song,—
  These have I treasured long,
    Up in an Attic.

Held in one little hand,
  They gleam in vain to me :
Of Love, Fame, Fatherland,
  All that remain to me !
Love, with thy wounded wing,
  Up the skies lessening,
  Sighing, too sad to sing !
Fame, dead to pity !
Land,—that denied me bread !
Count me as lost and dead,
  Tomb'd, in the City.

Daily the busy roar,
  Murmur and motion here ;
Surging against its shore,
  Sighs a great Ocean here !
But night by night it flows
Slowly to strange repose,
Calm and more calm it grows
  Under the moonshine :
Then, only then, I peer
On each old souvenir
  Shut from the sunshine.

Half of a ring of gold,
  Tarnish'd and yellow now,
Broken in days of old,
  Where is thy fellow now?
Upon the heart of *her*?
Feeling the sweet blood stir,
Still (though the mind demur)
  Kept as a token?
Ah ! doth her heart forget?
Or, with the pain and fret,
  Is *that*, too, broken?

Thin threads of yellow hair,
  Clipt from the brow of her,
Lying so faded there,—
  Why whisper *now* of her?
Strange lips are press'd unto
The brow o'er which ye grew,
Strange fingers flutter through
  The loose long tresses.
Doth she remember still,
Trembling, and turning chill
  From his caresses?

Sprig from the mountains blue
 Long left behind me now,
Of moonlight, shade, and dew,
 Wherefore remind me now?
Cruel and chill and gray,
Looming afar away,
Dark in the light of day,
 Shall the Heights daunt me?
My footsteps on the hill
Are overgrown,—yet still
 Hill-echoes haunt me!

Book of Byronic Song,
 Put with the dead away,
Wherefore wouldst *thou* prolong
 Dreams that have fled away?
Thou art an eyeless skull,
Dead, fleshless, cold, and null,
Complexionless, dark, dull,
 And superseded;
Yet, in thy time of pride,
How loudly hast thou lied
 To all who heeded!

Now, Fame, thou hollow Voice,
 Shriek from the heights above!
Let all who will rejoice
 In those wild lights above!
When all are false save you,
Yet were so beauteous too,
O Fame, canst *thou* be true,
 And shall I follow?
Nay! for the song of Man
Dies in his throat, since Pan
 Hath slain Apollo!

O Fame, thy hill looks tame,
 No vast wings flee from thence,—
Were *I* to climb, O Fame,
 What could I see from thence?
Only, afar away,
The mountains looming gray,
Crimson'd at close of day,
 Clouds swimming by me;
And in my hand a ring
And ringlet glimmering,—
 And no one nigh me!

Better the busy roar,
 Best the mad motion here!
Surging against its shore,
 Groans a great Ocean here.

O Love,—thou wouldst not wait!
O Land,—thou art desolate!
O Fame,—to others prate
 Of flights ecstatic!
Only, at evenfall,
Touching these tokens small,
I think about you all,
 Up in an Attic!

TO THE MOON.

The wind is shrill on the hills, and the plover
 Wheels up and down with a windy scream;
The birch has loosen'd her bright locks over
 The nut-brown pools of the mountain stream;
Yet here I linger in London City,
 Thinking of meadows where I was born—
And over the roofs, like a face of pity,
 Up comes the Moon, with her dripping horn.

O Moon, pale Spirit, with dim eyes drinking
 The sheen of the Sun as he sweepeth by,
I am looking long in those eyes, and thinking
 Of one who hath loved thee longer than I;
I am asking my heart if ye Spirits cherish
 The souls that ye witch with a harvest call?—
If the dream must die when the dreamer perish?—
 If it be idle to dream at all?

The waves of the world roll hither and thither,
 The tumult deepens, the days go by,
The dead men vanish—we know not whither,
 The live men anguish—we know not why;
The cry of the stricken is smother'd never,
 The Shadow passes from street to street;
And—o'er us fadeth, for ever and ever,
 The still white gleam of thy constant feet.

M

The hard men struggle, the students ponder,
  The world rolls round on its westward way;
The gleam of the beautiful night up yonder
  Is dim on the dreamer's check all day;
The old earth's voice is a sound of weeping,
  'Round her the waters wash wild and vast,
There is no calm, there is little sleeping,—
  Yet nightly, brightly, thou glimmerest past!

Another summer, new dreams departed,
  And yet we are lingering, thou and I;
I on the earth, with my hope proud-hearted,
  Thou, in the void of a violet sky!
Thou art there! I am here! and the reaping and mowing
  Of the harvest year is over and done,
And the hoary snow-drift will soon be blowing
  Under the wheels of the whirling Sun.

While tower and turret lie silver'd under,
  When eyes are closed and lips are dumb,
In the nightly pause of the human wonder,
  From dusky portals I see thee come;
And whoso wakes and beholds thee yonder,
  Is witch'd like me till his days shall cease,—
For in his eyes, wheresoever he wander,
  Flashes the vision of God's white Peace!

SPRING SONG IN THE CITY.

Who remains in London,
  In the streets with me,
Now that Spring is blowing
  Warm winds from the sea;
Now that trees grow green and tall,
  Now the Sun shines mellow,
And with moist primroses all
  English lanes are yellow?

Little barefoot maiden,
  Selling violets blue,
Hast thou ever pictured
  Where the sweetlings *grew*?—
Oh, the warm wild woodland ways,
  Deep in dewy grasses,
Where the wind-blown shadow strays,
  Scented as it passes!

Pedlar breathing deeply,
  Toiling into town,
With the dusty highway
  Thou art dusky brown,—
Hast thou seen by daisied leas,
  And by rivers flowing,
Lilac ringlets which the breeze
  Loosens lightly blowing?

Out of yonder waggon
  Pleasant hay-scents float,
He who drives it carries
  A daisy in his coat:
Oh, the English meadows, fair
  Far beyond all praises!
Freckled orchids everywhere
  Mid the snow of daisies!

Now in busy silence
  Broods the nightingale,
Choosing his love's dwelling
  In a dimpled dale;
Round the leafy bower they raise
  Rose-trees wild are springing;
Underneath, thro' the green haze,
  Bounds the brooklet singing.

And his love is silent
  As a bird can be,
For the red buds only
  Fill the red rose-tree,—
Just as buds and blossoms blow
  He'll begin his tune,
When all is green and roses glow
  Underneath the Moon!

Nowhere in the valleys
  Will the wind be still,
Everything is waving,
  Wagging at his will:
Blows the milkmaid's kirtle clean,
  With her hand prest on it!
Lightly o'er the hedge so green
  Blows the ploughboy's bonnet!

Oh, to be a-roaming
  In an English dell!
Every nook is wealthy,
  All the world looks well,
Tinted soft the Heavens glow,
  Over Earth and Ocean,
Brooks flow, breezes blow,
  All is light and motion!

IN LONDON, MARCH 1866.

To-day the streets are dull and dreary,
   Heavily, slowly the Rain is falling,
I hear around me, and am weary,
   The people murmuring and calling ;
The gloomy room is full of faces,
   Firelight shadows are on the floor,
And the deep Wind cometh from country places,
   And the Rain hath a voice I would hear no more.
     Ah! weary days of windy weather!
       And will the Rain cease never, never!
     A summer past we sat together,
       In that lost life that lives for ever!

Ah! sad and slow the Rain is falling,—
   And singing on seems sad without him.
Ah! wearily the Wind is calling!
   Would that mine arms were round about him!
For the world rolls on with air and ocean
   Wetly and windily round and round,
And sleeping he feeleth the sad still motion,
   And dreameth of *me*, though his sleep be sound!
     Ah! weary days of windy weather!
       And will the Rain cease never, never!
     A summer past we sat together,
       In that lost life that lives for ever!

I sing, because my heart is aching,
   With hollow sounds around me ringing :
Ah! nevermore shall he awaking
   Yearn to the Singer and the Singing!
Yet sleep, my father, calm and breathless,
   And if thou dreamest, dream on in joy!
While over thy grave walks Love the deathless,
   Stir in the darkness, and bless thy boy!
     Ah! weary days of windy weather!
       And will the Rain cease never, never!
     A summer past we sat together,
       In that lost life that lives for ever!

A LARK'S FLIGHT.

In the quiet City park,
Between the dawn and the dark,
   Loud and clear,
   That all may hear,
Sings the Lark.

Beyond the low black line
   Of trees the dawn peeps red,—
Clouds blow woolly and fine
   In the ether overhead,
Out of the air is shaken
   A fresh and glistening dew,
And the City begins to awaken
   And tremble thro' and thro';
See! (while thro' street and lane
   The people pour again,
And lane and alley and street
   Grow hoarse to a sound of feet,)
Here and there
   A human Shape comes, dark
Against the cool white air,
   Flitting across the park—
While over the dew-drench'd green,
   Singing his 'Hark! Oh, hark!'
Hovering, hovering, dimly seen,
   Rises the Lark.

'Mystery! Oh, mystery!'
   Clear he lilts to lightening day.
'Mystery! Oh, mystery!
   Up into the air with me,
   Come away, come away!'

Who is she that, wan and white,
   Shivering in the chilly light,
Shadeth weary eyes to see
   Him who makes the melody?
She is nameless, she is dull,
   She has ne'er been beautiful,
She is stain'd in brain and blood,
   Gross with mire, and foul with mud,—
Thing of sorrow, what knows *she*
   Of the mighty mystery?

The Lark sings sad and low,—
   'The City is dull and mean—
There is woe! there is woe!
   Never a soul is clean;
The City is dark, the wrong is deep;
   Too late to moan, too late to weep!
Tired, tired I sleep, sleep!'

Who is he, the stooping one,
   Smiling coldly in the sun,
Arms behind him lightly thrown,
   Pacing up and down alone?
'Tis the great Philosopher,
   Smoothly wrapt in coat of fur,
Soothly pondering, man-wit wise,
   At his morning exercise.

He has weigh'd the winds and floods,
He is rich in gather'd goods,
He is crafty, and can prove
God is Brahma, Christ, nor Jove ;
He is mighty, and his soul
Flits about from pole to pole,
Chasing signs of God about,
In a pleasant kind of doubt ;—
What, to help the mystery,
Sings the Lark to such as he?

The Lark cries:
  'Praise to Nature's plan !
Year on year she plies
  Her toil of sun and skies,
    Till the beast flowers up in Man,
Lord of effect and cause,
  Proud as a King can be ;
But a Voice in the cloud cries, "Pause!"
  And he pauses, even he,
  On the verge of the Mystery.'

Oh, loud and clear, that all may hear,
  Rising higher, with 'Hark ! Oh, hark!'
Higher, higher, higher, higher,
Quivering as the dull red fire
  Of dawn grows brighter, cries the Lark :
And they who listen there while he
  Singeth loud of Mystery,
Interpret him in under-tone
  With a meaning of their own,
Measuring his melody
By their own soul's quality.

Tall and stately, fair and sweet,
Walketh maiden Marguerite,
Musing there on maid and man,
In her mood patrician ;
To all she sees her eyes impart
The colour of a maiden heart ;
Heart's chastity is on her face,
She scents the air with nameless grace,
And where she goes with heart astir,
Colour and motion follow her.

What should the Singer sing
  Unto so sweet a thing,
    But, 'Oh, my love loves me !
And the love I love best is guarding the nest,
  While I cheer her merrily,—
Come up high ! come up high ! to a cloud
    in the sky !
And sing of your love with me !'

Elbows on the grassy green,
Scowling face his palms between,
Yonder gaunt Thief meditates
Treason deep against his mates ;
For his great hands itch to hold
Both the pardon and the gold.
Still he listens unaware,
Scowling round with sullen stare,
Gnawing at his under-lip,
Pond'ring friends and fellowship,
Thinking of a friendly thing
Done to him in suffering,
And of happy days and free
Spent in that rough companie :
Till he seeks the bait no more,—
And the Lark is conqueror.

For the Lark says plain,
  'Who sells his pal is mean :
    Better hang than gain
    Blood-money to save one's skin—
A whip for the rogue who'd tell,'
  He hears the Singer say,—
'Better the rope and the cell—
Better the devils of Hell ! ,
  Come away ! come away !'

O Lark ! O Lark !
  Up, up, for it is light—
The Souls stream out of the dark,
  And the City's spires gleam bright ;
The living world is awake agan,
  Each wanders on his way,
The wonderful waters break again
  In the white and perfect Day.
Nay ! nay ! descend not yet,
  But higher, higher, higher !
Up thro' the air, and wet
  Thy wings in the solar fire !
There, hovering in ecstacy,
Sing, 'Mystery ! Oh, mystery !'

O Lark ! O Lark ! hadst thou the might
  Beyond the cloud to wing thy way,
To sing and soar in ceaseless flight,
  It might be well for men this day.
Beyond that cloud there is a zone,
  And in that zone there is a land,
And in that land, upon a throne,
  A mighty Spirit sits alone,
    With musing cheek upon His hand.

And all is still and all is sweet
Around the silence of His seat,—
  Beneath, the waves of wonder flow,—
And melted on His shining feet
  The years flash down as falling snow.

O Lark! O Lark!
Up! for thy wings are strong;
While the Day is breaking,
And the City is waking,
  Sing a song of wrong—
Sing of the weak man's tears,
Of the strong man's agony;
The passion, the hopes, the fears,
The heaped-up pain of the years,
  The human mystery.
O Lark! we might rejoice,
Could'st reach that distant land,
For we cannot hear His voice,
And we often miss His hand!
And the lips of each are Ice
To the kiss of sister and brother;
And we see that one man's vice
Is the virtue of another.
Yea, each that hears thee sing
  Translates thy song to speech,
And, lo! the rendering
  Is so different with each!
The gentle are oppress'd,
The foul man fareth best;
Wherever we seek, our gain
Is full of a poisonous pain.
In one soft note and long
Gather our sense of wrong;
Rise up, O Lark! from the sod,
Up, up, with soundless wings,—
Rise up to God! rise up, rise up, to God!
Tell Him these things!

DE BERNY.

You knew him slightly. We, who knew him well,
Saw something in his soul you could not see—
A strength wherein his very vices throve,
A power that darken'd much the outer man,
Strange, yet angelically innocent.
His views were none of ours; his morals—well,
Not English morals at the best; and yet
We loved him and we miss him;—the old haunts

Seem dull without that foolish full-grown child;
The world goes on without him:—London throngs
With sport and festival; and something less
Than poor De Berny haunts us everywhere—
The buying and the selling, and the strife
Of little natures.

    What a man was that!—
Just picture him as you perceived him, Noel,
Standing beyond his circle. Spare and tall,
Black-bearded and black-eyed; a sallow face,
With lines of idle humour round the lips;
A nose and eyebrow proudly curved; an eye
Clear as a child's. But thirty summers old!
Yet wearied out, save only when he warm'd
His graces in the sunshine. What an air
Was his, when, cigarette in mouth, and hands
Thrust in the pockets of his pantaloons,
He took his daily walk down Regent Street,
Stared at the pretty girls, saluted friends,
And, pleased as any lady, stopp'd to study
The fashions in the windows of the shops!
Did he not walk as if he walk'd on thrones,
With smiles of vacant patronage for all?
And who could guess he had not breakfasted,
Had little chance of dining, since his purse
Held just the wherewithal to buy a loaf—
Change from the shilling spent in purchasing
The sweet post-prandial cigar!

    He lived—
Ah! Heaven knew *how*—for 'twas a mystery!
While the sun shone, he saunter'd in the sun;
But late at night sat scribbling, by the light
Of a wax-candle. Wax? De Berny's way;
For, mark, this wanderer let his body suffer,
Hunger'd and pinch'd, rather than bate a jot
Of certain very useless luxuries:
Smoked nought but real Havannah, 'tis averr'd,
And sat at night within his dingy lodging,
Wrapt, king-like, in a costly dressing-gown
His mother gave him; slippers on his feet;
His cat, Mignonne, the silken-hair'd Chinese,
Seated upon his shoulder, purring low;
And something royal in his look, despite
His threadbare pantaloons!

A clever man!
A nature sparkling o'er with *jeux d'esprit!*
Well read in certain light philosophies
Down from Voltaire; and, in his easy way,
A sceptic—one whose heart belied his brain.
Oft, leaning back and puffing his cigar,
Pushing his wan white fingers through his hair—
His cat Mignonne, the velvet-paw'd Chinese,
Rubbing her soft white cheek against his beard,
And purring her approval—he would sit,
Smiling his sad, good-humour'd, weary smile,
And lightly launch his random, reckless shafts
At English thrift, the literary cant,
The flat, unearnest living of the world,
And (last and lightest) at the tender sex,
Their little virtue and their mighty vows.

This was the man whose face went pale with pain,
When that shrill shriek from Poland fill'd his ear;
This was the man who pinch'd himself to send
A mite to Garibaldi and the Cause;
Who cried, or nearly cried, o'er Lamartine,
And loved the passionate passages of Sand;
Who would have kiss'd the ground beneath the feet
Of any shape called 'Woman,' plain or fair;
Gave largess royal to children in the streets;
Treated an unclean beggar seeking alms
To a clean shirt, and sent him off amazed;
And when he heard sweet voice or instrument,
Breath'd passionate breath, like one that drinks with pain
An atmosphere too heavenly rare and sweet.
Pleasure? Ah me! what pleasure garner'd he,
Who fasted oftener than ate; who pawn'd
His coat to serve a neighbour, and was cold;
Whose only little joy was promenading
On sunny summer days in Regent Street?
His talk? Why, how he talk'd, as I have said;
Incubus could not prove his neighbours worse,
Or himself blacker, or the cold world colder;

His jests so oft too broad for decent ears,
His impiousness so insolently strong,
His languid grace so callous unto all
Save the sad sunshine that it flutter'd in.
Yet, Noel, I could swear that Spirits—those
Who see beneath the eyes, and hear the breathing
The Soul makes as it stirs within the breast—
Bent not unlovingly, not angrily,
Above that weary, foolish, full-grown Child!
Weary—of what? Weary, I think, for want
Of something whose existence he denied;
Not sick of life, since he had never felt
The full of living—wearied out, because
The world look'd falsehood, and his turn was truth.

Well, late one morning in the summer time,
They found him lying in his easy-chair,
Wrapt royally in the costly dressing-gown
His mother gave him, slippers on his feet,
And something royal in his look,—cold, dead!
A smell of laudanum sicken'd all the air
Around him; on the table at his side
A copy of De Musset's *Elle et Lui*;
And close at hand a crumpled five-pound note,
On which was written in his round clear hand
'*Pour Garibaldi. Vive la Liberté!*'

THE WAKE OF TIM O'HARA.
(SEVEN DIALS.)

To the Wake of O'Hara
  Came company;
All St. Patrick's Alley
  Was there to see,
  With the friends and kinsmen
  Of the family.
On the long deal table lay Tim in white,
And at his pillow the burning light.
Pale as himself, with the tears on her cheek,
The mother received us, too full to speak;
But she heap'd the fire, and on the board
Set the black bottle with never a word,
While the company gather'd, one and all,
Men and women, big and small,
Not one in the Alley but felt a call
  To the Wake of Tim O'Hara.

At the face of O'Hara,
    All white with sleep,
Not one of the women
    But took a peep,
And the wives new-wedded
    Began to weep.
The mothers gather'd round about,
And praised the linen and lying-out,—
For white as snow was his winding-sheet,
And all was peaceful, and clean, and sweet;
And the old wives, praising the blessèd dead,
Were thronging around the old press-bed,
Where O'Hara's widow, tatter'd and torn,
Held to her bosom the babe new-born,
And stared all round her, with eyes forlorn,
    At the Wake of Tim O'Hara.

For the heart of O'Hara
    Was good as gold,
And the life of O'Hara
    Was bright and bold,
And his smile was precious
    To young and old!
Gay as a guinea, wet or dry,
With a smiling mouth, and a twinkling eye!
Had ever an answer for chaff and fun;
Would fight like a lion, with any one!
Not a neighbour of any trade
But knew some joke that the boy had made;
Not a neighbour, dull or bright,
But minded *something*—frolic or fight,
And whisper'd it round the fire that night,
    At the Wake of Tim O'Hara!

    'To God be glory
      In death and life,
    He's taken O'Hara
      From trouble and strife!'
Said one-eyed Biddy,
    The apple-wife.
'God bless old Ireland!' said Mistress Hart,
Mother to Mike of the donkey-cart;
'God bless old Ireland till all be done,
She never made wake for a better son!'
And all join'd chorus, and each one said
Something kind of the boy that was dead;
And the bottle went round from lip to lip,
And the weeping widow, for fellowship,
Took the glass of old Biddy and had a sip,
    At the Wake of Tim O'Hara.

    'Then we drank to O'Hara,
      With drams to the brim,

While the face of O'Hara
    Look'd on so grim
In the corpse-light shining
    Yellow and dim,
The cup of liquor went round again,
And the talk grew louder at every drain;
Louder the tongues of the women grew!—
The lips of the boys were loosening too!
The widow her weary eyelids closed,
And, soothed by the drop o' drink, she
    dozed;
The mother brighten'd and laugh'd to hear
Of O'Hara's fight with the grenadier,
And the hearts of all took better cheer,
    At the Wake of Tim O'Hara.

    Tho' the face of O'Hara
      Lookt on so wan,
    In the chimney-corner
      The row began—
    Lame Tony was in it,
      The oyster-man;
For a dirty low thief from the North came
    near,
And whistled 'Boyne Water' in his ear,
And Tony, with never a word of grace,
Flung out his fist in the blackguard's
    face;
And the girls and women scream'd out for
    fright,
And the men that were drunkest began to
    fight,—
Over the tables and chairs they threw,—
The corpse-light tumbled,—the trouble
    grew,—
The new-born joined in the hullabaloo,—
    At the Wake of Tim O'Hara.

    'Be still! be silent!
      Ye do a sin!
    Shame be his portion
      Who dares begin!'
'Twas Father O'Connor
    Just enter'd in!—
All look'd down, and the row was done—
And shamed and sorry was every one;
But the Priest just smiled quite easy and
    free—
'Would ye wake the poor boy from his
    sleep?' said he;
And he said a prayer, with a shining face,
Till a kind of a brightness filled the place;

The women lit up the dim corpse-light,
The men were quieter at the sight,
And the peace of the Lord fell on all that night
 At the Wake of Tim O'Hara!

KITTY KEMBLE.

'All the world's a stage.'

Draw softly back the curtains of the bed—
Aye, here lies Kitty Kemble cold and dead:
Poor Kitty Kemble, if I steal a kiss,
Who deems the deed amiss?

Cold bloodless cheek whereon there lingers faint
The crimson dye of a life's rouge and paint;
Cold lips that fall, since thy false rows of teeth
No longer prop the toothless gums beneath;
Cold clammy brow that lies there bald and bare
No longer screen'd and shadow'd by false hair;
Poor Kitty Kemble! is it truly *thou*
On whom I look so very sadly now?
Lightest of ladies, is thy mortal race
Run out indeed, thy luminous laughing face
Turn'd to this mindless mask of marble dead?
And even thy notes of tinkling laughter fled,
Which, when all other charms to please were past,
Stay'd with thee till the last?

God bless thee, Kitty Kemble!—and God love thee!
Warm be the kindred earth that lies above thee—
Lightest of ladies, never sad or sage,
A glad coquette at sixty years of age,
And even with thy last expiring breath
Flirting thy fan at thy lean Lover, Death!

Tho' nature made you volatile and witty,
Your parents were most vulgar people, Kitty;
Hard work was daily yours, and trouble maybe
To mind the wretched house and nurse the baby,
While to the third-class Theatre hard by
Your father and your mother both did hie,
Mother as dresser, while with surly mien
Toil'd father as a shifter of the scene;
And thus it happen'd that you early grew
Familiar with the British drama too,
And thro' the dusty stage-door you would steal
With father's midday beer or evening meal,
Until that blissful day when to your glee
The keen-eyed ballet-master noticed thee,
And quickly, being a bright and clever girl,
You learnt from him to dance and twist and twirl,
Leaping ere long before the garish lights,
A smiling spangled creature in pink tights.
Aye, Kitty, and the common scandal says
The ballet-master in those early days,
Finding you quick and rapidly advancing,
Taught you love's dalliance as well as dancing!
But you were very clever; and ere long
Were brightest, smartest of the ballet throng;
No lighter trimmer leg was to be seen
When you were only rising seventeen,
And from the stalls to your sweet guileless eyes
Ogles and nods and smiles began to rise.
Then later, like a wise girl and a pretty,
You chose to bless a close man from the City,
Quiet, respectable, and most demure
With a stiff salary and prospects sure;
And him, my dear, you used for your ambition
Still bent of course to better your position.
For tho' so light and merry, you were ever
Ambitious, Kitty, quick and bright and clever;
And now you got your educated lover
To hear you read the British drama over,
To criticise your clever imitations
Of the tall leading lady's declamations,
And to correct your tone, and guide your tongue,
Whenever you pronounced your English wrong;
And tho' the fellow was in soul a bore,
And had no intellect to help you more,
You got in this Bohemian sort of college
Some gleams of grace and scraps of solid knowledge;

KITTY KEMBLE.

And while your silly sisters took repose
You grew grammatical, as grammar goes.

O Kitty, what a lavish little elf
Thou wast, yet economic of thyself!
So free, so merry, and innocent of guile;
And yet at heart so *busy*, all the while
You danced and dallied with those sparkling eyes,
In weighty speculations how to rise!
Yes, Kitty, and you rose; ere long you made
The prettiest, wittiest sort of chambermaid
(That saucy female elf of the stage-inn,
Chuck'd by each handsome guest beneath the chin;
A nymph oft carrying a warming-pan,
And sweetheart of the comic waiting-man)
Or haply, on extravaganza nights,
As a slim fairy prince in trunks and tights,
You pertly spake a dozen lines or so,
While just behind you, glaring in a row,
Your sillier sisters of the ballet stood,
With spleen and envy raging in their blood!
Thus, Kitty Kemble, on and up you went,
Merry, yet ill content;
And soon you cast, inflated still with pride,
Your City man aside,
Cut him stone dead to his intense annoy,
And, like a maiden coy,
Dropt, blushing crimson, in the arms scarce vital
Of an old man of title!
A sad dyspeptic dog, the worn and yellow
Wreck of a handsome fellow,
And tho' the lord of boundless rolls and lands,
Just a mere puppet in your pretty hands.

O Kitty Kemble, how you coaxed and teased him,
Nursed him and pain'd him, petted him and pleased him,
Drove him nigh crazy, made his slow blood start
With the glad beating of your burning heart,
Until he vowed, you managed him so neatly,
To marry you completely;
And with this view transmitted you, poor fool,
To a French boarding-school;

And there you taught, I fear, your power being such,
More than you learnt, tho' what you learnt was much!
O you were still and patient as a mouse,
Much as your spirit hated the strict house,
The teachers grim, the insipid simpering misses,
The walks—so different from the coulisses!

There learning patiently did you abide,
Till one fine morning your protector died,
And once again, alas! as in times past,
On the hard world your gentle lot was cast.
But, Kitty, what a change in you was made
By those few seasons wintering in the shade;
In like a common moth you crept full sly,
But *out* you came a perfect butterfly!
A pretty little sparkling wench,
Prattling so prettily in French,
Or dashing off, with fingers white,
Gay little scraps of music bright;
Merry and wicked, and not wise,
With babies dancing in her eyes,
Most apt at quoting saw and joke
From Shakespeare and less famous folk,
Making the ignorant listener stare
With charming *mots* from Molière!

But, Kitty Kemble, 'tis not given to me
To write in full your fair biography.
About this very time from English sight
Your pretty little figure vanished quite;
And dainty rivals came and conquered here,
And the false world forgot you quite, I fear.
I think your next appearance in our view
Was in a blaze of splendour bright and new,
When, after many years of preparation,
Provincial trial, trouble, and vexation,
Out you emerged on the astonish'd City,
The town's delight, the beaux', the critics', Kitty!
The brightest wonder human eye could see
In good old Comedy:
A smile, a voice, a laugh, a look, a form,
To take the world by storm!
A dainty dimpling intellectual treasure
To give old stagers pleasure!
A rippling radiant cheek—a roguish eye—
That made the youngsters sigh!
And thus beneath a tinsel'd pasteboard Star
At once you mounted your triumphant car,

O'er burning hearts your chariot wheels were
   driven,
Bouquets came rolling down like rain from
   heaven,
And on we dragged you, Kitty, while you
   stood
Roguish and great, not innocent and good,
The Queen Elect of all Light Womanhood !

Yes, Kitty Kemble, let the preacher cry
His word of ' Vanity, O Vanity !'
But those, I think, were happy, happy days.
Indeed, yours was a life that throve with
   praise,
And brighten'd ; passionate and eager ;
   made
To love the lamp-light and to hate the
   shade ;
To play with happiness and drink the beam
Till it suffused your substance gleam by
   gleam,
Making of elements past your control
The smiling semblance of a living Soul.
In sooth, you were a summer creature, one
Who never really throve save in the sun ;
And take away its perfect self-content,
Your very beauty grew indifferent.
Further, you did not crave for love or fame,
Or that still colder shadow—a good name ;
You were not even avaricious (tho'
'Twas sweet, of course, to see the guineas
   grow).
Nay, Kitty, all your care and your delight
Was to gleam past upon the public sight,
To gleam, to smile, to sparkle, and depart
Ere sympathy could reach your little heart ;
To let the flaming footlights underneath
Light up your rouge, whiten your spotless
   teeth,
And to those eyes, so luminous and bright,
Dart beams of glorious artificial light ;
To feel your bright and lissom body free
In brightly-hued theatric drapery ;
And on your skin, as white as morning milk,
The clinging satin and the slippery silk.
In private life 'twas your delight to be
The beauty of Bohemian revelry ;
To the smart little literary man
Whispering wicked jests behind your fan,
And not at all too nice in modesty
As to reject a dinner *vis-à-vis*
At Kew or Richmond, freely sipping port
With hirsute critics of the heavier sort,

And oft enough on such a holiday
Opening at last your own small purse to
   pay !
Beneath your beauty, rouged, and ring'd,
   and pearled,
You were at heart the woman of the world,
Not quite forgetting yet (tho' well content
Quite to forget) your very low descent ;
And having gained your little life's en-
   deavour,
You could, I know, have deemed it bliss
   for ever.

For ever, Kitty Kemble ? Ah, my child !
(Surely thou art a child at last ?)
When days and nights are glad and wild,
   They whirl the quicklier past !
To Sorrow's faintest funeral symphony
Time lingers darken'd steps dejectedly
With sad eyes heavenward ; but how fleet
   he flies
When Revel sings and Mirth doth melo-
   dize !
Thy merry laughter and thy gay delight
Quicken'd the Greybeard's footsteps day and
   night,
And Kitty, suddenly, to thy surprise,
The cruel crowsfeet gather'd 'neath thine
   eyes.

But paint is bright, and powder pearly
   white,
And many merry years, in that fierce light
Which beats on thrones and faces like to
   thine,
Thy ways were witching and thy lot divine.
Thy life was surely glad. The need was
   fled
Long since of choosing lovers for thy bread
Or thine advancement, and thou now wert
   free
To pick at will thy male society.
All that is dark. We laymen cannot tell
What amatory happiness befell ;
We only know for certain Cupid's dart
Ne'er struck so deadly deep into thy heart,
As to befool our Kitty into passion
Of the mad vulgar fashion.
We only know thou, Kitty, ever wert
Lightest of ladies, delicate and pert,
Clever and quick, and horribly well read.
And as the happy seasons o'er thee fled
Thy bust swelled out, thy body fresh and fair

Grew plumper, and thou didst assume thine
   air,
Round, roguish, royal, dazzling, plump, and
   good,
Of most delicious demi-matronhood.
I think we loved thee even better then
Than ever, Kitty ; all the older men,
I know, adored thee! and thou wert
   supreme,
Yea, grand above all modern guess or
   dream,
In wanton Widows, those we love to see
In unctuous Shakespearian comedy.
Great wast thou also, Kitty, great and true,
As the bold Beatrice in 'Much Ado' ;
And all the mighty Town went raving mad
To see thy ' Lady Teazle.'

      Wild and glad
Rolled the years onward, and thy little
   heart
(Tho' certainly thy stoniest, toughest part)
Was just enough at least to *act* with.
Well !
At forty summers still thy fortune fell
On pleasant places ; for a little yet
The fickle British public loved its pet.
True, here and there, thy features, still so
   pretty,
Were sharpening into shrewish lines, my
   Kitty ;
And nose and chin, though still most soft
   and sweet,
Seem'd slowly journeying on the way to
   meet !
A certain shrillness in the voice's tone,
Which from the very first had been thine
   own,
But rather pleased the ear than otherwise
When thou hadst fleeter feet and younger
   eyes,
Grew harsher and more harsh upon the ear.
Never, indeed, in any earlier year
Hadst thou performed so perfectly as now,
And yet the cruel British Critic's brow
Grew cloudy. Vain were trick of tone or
   smile
To hide the artful, artificial style,
The superficial tones, the airs capricious,
That in thy younger days had been delicious.
O Kitty, all thy being's constant pain
To win the heart once more was wholly vain;
Most vain, most piteous ! Thy familiar airs

Were met by only vacant shrugs and stares,
Thy tricks, thy jokes, thy jests, thy wanton
   ways,
Awakened only pity and amaze ;
And presently, when thou didst rashly try
A fair young part, as in the days gone by,
Down on thee came the cruel Critic's blud-
   geon,
Out spoke at last the oracular Curmudgeon,
Hinting out openly, in accents cold,
That thou wert *passée*, past thy prime, and
   old,
The ghost of loveliness and lightness, fit
To play old women,—better still to quit
The Stage for ever. O poor thing ! poor
   thing !
The cruel knife cut deep enough to bring
The sad blood from your very heart at last;
You winced, you smirked, you struggled,
   and at last
You seem'd to triumph ; and the bitter truth
That thou hadst spent thy previous years
   of youth
Was taken home indeed to thy fair breast,
And there, like to a very viper's nest,
It bred and flourish'd. Kitty, tho' thy face
Was merry still in many a public place,
Thy shrill laugh loud, thy manner brazen
   bold,
Black was thy soul and piteously cold.
Anon into the country thou didst fare,
And spend a brighter, happier season there;
Bearing about with thee from year to year
The shadow of thine earlier triumphs here.
That passed, like all the rest. Ah me ! ah
   me !
Even the provinces deserted thee,
As we had done ; so our poor Kitty came
To be the lonely ghost of a great name—
A worn and wanton woman, not yet sage
Nor wearied out, tho' sixty years of age,
Wrinkled and rouged, and with false teeth
   of pearl,
And the shrill laughter of a giddy girl ;
Haunting, with painted cheek and powder'd
   brow,
The private boxes, as spectator now ;
Both day and night, indeed, invited out
To private picnic and to public rout,
Because thy shrill laugh and thy ready joke
Ever enlivened up the festal folk ;
Nor did such people woo thy service less
Because of tales of thy past wickedness

Oh, thou wert very clever, keen, and bright,
Most gay, most scandal-loving, and most
    light !
Still greatly given to French literature,
And foreign feuilletons not over pure ;
Still highly rouging up thy cheek so dead
Into a ghostly gleam of rosy red :
Still ever ready talking with a man,
To tap his naughty knuckles with thy fan
Coquettishly, and meanwhile with thy dim
Yet lustrous eyes to smile and ogle him !
Yet ever with a lurking secret sense
Of thine own beauty's utter impotence,
With hungry observation all the while
To catch the covert sneer or lurking smile—
A helpless fear, a pang, a sharp distress,
Curdling thy choicest mirth to bitterness.

Sad years, my child, sad years of lonely
    gloom !
Nor let the hasty Moralist assume
Neglect and age and agony could be
GOD's ruthless instruments to chasten thee.
Nay, Kitty Kemble, tho' thy spirit grew
Still bitterer as the seasons flash'd and flew,
Thy bright face ne'er one moment turned
    away
From the glad gaudy world of every day,
I know religion never moved thy thought,
Comfort in God was neither found nor
    sought.
Still thou wert happiest, happiest and best
By the old gaslight, rouged and gaily drest,
At each new play thy well-known face was
    seen,
Merry and quick, yet hiding secret spleen ;
At each new brilliant *débutante's* success
Thy soul did wince for very bitterness ;—
And all the taste of thy departed power
Was gall and wormwood on thy soul each
    hour ;
And never, Kitty, till thy latest breath,
Didst thou remember God, the Soul, and
    Death.

Yet very quietly, one wintry day,
Death's pale and unseen footsteps past thy
    way,
And as Death swiftly sail'd upon the air,
He lightly breathed one breath upon thee
    there
As a reminder ;—after that thy face
Changed very strangely ; shrivell'd in its
    place ;

One helpless eyelid fluttered, and thy faint
Dark cheek contracted underneath thy
    paint ;
And after that same day thy speech was
    ne'er
Quite constant to thy thought, or wholly
    clear ;
And ev'n thy very thought at times would
    seem
Suddenly to dissolve away in dream !

Yet, Kitty Kemble, to the last we found
    thee
Constant to the old haunts of life around
    thee,
Still in the public gaslight thou wert seen,
Tho' now upon a staff compelled to lean,
Thine eyes still black and quick, thy tones
    and words
Still gay, thy laugh shrill as a mocking
    bird's !
Ah ! but I think thy heavenly Sire was near
His daughter's dwelling-place at last, my
    dear !
That quiet day I looked upon thee last,
I had called at midday as thy porch I
    passed,
Found thee 'from home,' and past the quiet
    door
Away was turning, when, from the first floor,
Thy quick voice called me ; and upstairs I
    went,
To find my lady lying indolent,
Pillow'd in state upon her stately bed,
A pretty ribbon'd night-cap on her head,
While on her hollow cheeks' false hectic
    bloom
Strange shade fell sadly from the darken'd
    room.
And there upon thy pillow, partly read,
Feydeau's last fever-piece ; around thee
    spread
Old playbills, pink and yellow, white and
    green,
Whereon in mighty capitals was seen
Thine own triumphant name. Alas ! alas !
Shall I forget till life and memory pass
Thy look of blended pleasure, pride, and
    pain,
Thy eager laughter, garrulous and vain,
Thy tremulous, feverish voice and fretful
    glee,
As thou didst prattle, pointing out to me,

With a lean, palsied finger, dead and cold,
Thy mighty triumphs in the days of old?
And suddenly (my child, shall I forget?—
The voice, the tone, the look, all linger yet!)
The feverish emotion grew too much;
And with a passionate, spasmodic clutch,
Thou didst against my shoulder wildly press
Thy cheek, once warm with life and loveliness,
And moaning madly over thy lost years
Hysterically break to bitterest tears!
What comfort could I give? ere, once more gay,
Thou with light hand didst sweep the tears away,
And break, with fretful wish and eager will,
To laughter sadder still;
Prattling, in thy most artificial tone,
Words to make Angels moan!

And here's the end of all. And on thy bed
Thou liest, Kitty Kemble, lone and dead;
And on thy clammy cheek there lingers faint
The deep dark stain of a life's rouge and paint;
And, Kitty, all thy sad days and thy glad
Have left thee lying for thy last part clad,
Cold, silent, on the earthly Stage; and while
Thou liest there with dark and dreadful smile,
The feverish footlights of the World flash bright
Into thy face with a last ghastly light;
And while thy friends all sighing rise to go,
The great black Curtain droppeth, slow, slow, slow.

God help us! We spectators turn away;
Part sad, we think, part merry, was the Play.
God help the lonely player now she stands
Behind the darken'd scenes with wondering face,
And gropes her way at last, with clay-cold hands,
Out of the dingy place,
Turning towards Home, poor worn and weary one,
Now the last scene is done.

THE SWALLOWS.

I.

O Churchyard in the city's gloom,
    What charm to please hast thou,
That, seated on a broken tomb,
    I muse so oft, as now?
The dreary autumn wind goes murmuring by,
And in the distant streets the ragged urchins cry.

Thou holdest in thy sunless land
    Nought I have seen or known,
No lips I ever kissed, no hand
    That ever clasped mine own;
And all is still and dreary to the eye,—
The broken tombs, dark walls, roofed by a sunless sky.

Now to the murmur that mine ears
    Catch from the distant lanes,
Dimming mine eyes with dreamy tears,
    Slow, low, my heart refrains;
And the live grass creeps up from thy dead bones,
And crawls, with slimy stains, over thy gray gravestones.

The cries keep on, the minutes pass,
    Mine eyes are on the ground,
The silent many-fingered grass
    Winds round, and round, and round:
I seem to see it live, and stir, and wind,
And gaze, until a weight is heavy on my mind.

II.

O Churchyard in the shady gloom,
    What charm to please hast thou,
That, seated on a broken tomb,
    I muse so oft, as now?
Haply because I learn, with sad content,
How small a thing can make the whole world different!

Among the gravestones worn and old,
    A sad sweet hour I pass,
Where thickest from thy sunless mould
    Upsprings the sickly grass;

For, though the earth holds no sweet-smell-
    ing flower,
The Swallows build their nests up in thy
    square gray tower.

While, burthened by the life we bear,
    The dull and creeping woe,
The mystery, the pain, the care,
    I watch thy grasses grow,
Sighing, I look to the dull autumn skies,
And, lo! my heart is cheered, and tears are
    in mine eyes.

For here, where stillness, death, and
    dream,
    Brood above creeping things,
Over mine eyes with quick bright gleam
    Shine little flashing wings,
And a strange comfort takes thy shady air,
And the deep life I breathe seems sweetened
    unaware!

TOM DUNSTAN; OR, THE POLITICIAN.

'How long, O Lord, how long?'

I.

Now poor Tom Dunstan's cold,
    Our shop is duller;
Scarce a tale is told,
    And our talk has lost its old
Red-republican colour!
Though he was sickly and thin,
    'Twas a sight to see his face,—
While, sick of the country's sin,
    With bang of the fist, and chin
Thrust out, he argued the case!
He prophesied men should be free!
    And the money-bags be bled!
' She's coming, she's coming!' said he;
' Courage, boys! wait and see!
    Freedom 's ahead!'

II.

All day we sat in the heat,
    Like spiders spinning,
Stitching full fine and fleet,
    While old Moses on his seat
Sat greasily grinning;
And here Tom said his say,
    And prophesied Tyranny's death;
And the tallow burned all day,
    And we stitch'd and stitch'd away
In the thick smoke of our breath.
Weary, weary were we,
    Our hearts as heavy as lead;
But ' Patience! she's coming!' said he;
' Courage, boys! wait and see!
    Freedom 's ahead!'

III.

And at night, when we took here
    The rest allowed to us,
The Paper came, with the beer,
    And Tom read, sharp and clear,
The news out loud to us;
And then, in his witty way,
    He threw the jests about:
The cutting things he'd say
    Of the wealthy and the gay!
How he turn'd 'em inside out!
And it made our breath more free
    To hearken to what he said—
' She's coming! she's coming!' said he;
' Courage, boys! wait and see!
    Freedom 's ahead!'

IV.

But grim Jack Hart, with a sneer,
    Would mutter, ' Master!
If Freedom means to appear,
    I think she might step *here*
A little faster!'
Then, 'twas fine to see Tom flame,
    And argue, and prove, and preach,
Till Jack was silent for shame,—
    Or a fit of coughing came
O' sudden, to spoil Tom's speech.
Ah! Tom had the eyes to see
    When Tyranny should be sped:
' She's coming! she's coming!' said he
' Courage, boys! wait and see!
    Freedom 's ahead!'

V.

But Tom was little and weak,
    The hard hours shook him;
Hollower grew his cheek,
    And when he began to speak
The coughing took him.
Ere long the cheery sound
    Of his chat among us ceased,

And we made a purse, all round,
  That he might not starve, at least.
His pain was sorry to see,
  Yet there, on his poor sick-bed,
'She's coming, in spite of me!
Courage, and wait!' cried he;
  '*Freedom*'s ahead!'

VI.

A little before he died,
  To see his passion!
'Bring me a Paper!' he cried,
And then to study it tried,
  In his old sharp fashion;
And with eyeballs glittering,
  His look on me he bent,
And said that savage thing
  Of the Lords o' the Parliament.
Then, dying, smiling on me,
'What matter if *one* be dead?
She's coming at last!' said he;
'Courage, boy! wait and see;
  Freedom's ahead!'

VII.

Ay, now Tom Dunstan's cold,
  The shop feels duller;
Scarce a tale is told,
And our talk has lost the old
  Red-republican colour.
But we see a figure gray,
  And we hear a voice of death,
And the tallow burns all day,
  In the thick smoke of our breath;
Ay, while in the dark sit we,
Tom seems to call from the dead—
'She's coming! she's coming!' says he;
'Courage, boys! wait and see!
  Freedom's ahead!'

How long, O Lord! how long
  Must thy Handmaid linger—
She who shall right the wrong,
Make the poor sufferer strong?
  Sweet morrow, bring her!
Hasten her over the sea,
  O Lord! ere Hope be fled!
Bring her to men and to me! . . .
O Slave, pray still on thy knee,
  'FREEDOM'S *ahead!*'

O'MURTOGH.

(NEWGATE, 18—)

'It's a sight to see a bold man die!'

TO-NIGHT we drink but a sorrowful cup ..
Hush! silence! and fill your glasses up.
Christ be with us! Hold out and say:
'Here's to the Boy that died this day!'

Wasn't he bold as the boldest here?
Red coat or black did he ever fear?
With the bite and the drop, too, ever free?
He died like a man. . . . I was there to see!

The gallows was black, our cheeks were white
All underneath in the morning light;
The bell ceased tolling swift as thought,
And out the murdered Boy was brought.

There he stood in the daylight dim,
With a Priest on either side of him;
Each Priest look'd white as he held his book,
But the man between had a brighter look!

Over the faces below his feet
His gray eye gleam'd so keen and fleet:
He saw us looking; he smiled his last . . .
He couldn't wave, he was pinioned fast.

This was more than one could bear,
For the lass who loved him was with us there;
She stood in the rain with her dripping shawl
Over her head, for to see it all.

But when she met the Boy's last look,
Her lips went white, she turned and shook;
She didn't scream, she didn't groan,
But down she dropt as dead as stone.

He saw the stir in the crowd beneath,
And I saw him tremble and set his teeth;
But the hangman came with a knavish grace
And drew the nightcap over his face.

Then I saw the Priests, who still stood near,
Pray faster and faster to hide their fear;
They closed their eyes, I closed mine too,
And the deed was over before I knew.

The crowd that stood all round of me
Gave one dark plunge like a troubled sea ;
And I knew by that the deed was done,
And I opened my eyes and saw the sun.

The gallows was black, the sun was white,
There he hung, half hid from sight ;
The sport was over, the talk grew loud,
And they sold their wares to the mighty crowd.

We walked away with our hearts full sore,
And we met a hawker before a door,
With a string of papers an arm's-length long,
A dying speech and a gallows song.

It bade all people of poor estate
Beware of O'Murtogh's evil fate ;
It told how in old Ireland's name
He had done red murther and come to shame.

Never a word was sung or said
Of the murder'd mother, a ditch her bed,
Who died with her newborn babe that night,
While the blessed cabin was burning bright.

Nought was said of the years of pain,
The starving stomach, the madden'd brain,
The years of sorrow and want and toil,
And the murdering rent for the bit of soil.

Nought was said of the murther done
On man and woman and little one,
Of the bitter sorrow and daily smart
Till he put cold lead in the traitor's heart.

But many a word had the speech beside :
How he repented before he died ;
How, brought to sense by the sad event,
He prayed for the Queen and the Parliament !

What did we do, and mighty quick,
But tickle that hawker's brains with a stick;
And to pieces small we tore his flam,
And left him quiet as any lamb !

Pass round your glasses ! now lift them up!
Powers above, 'tis a bitter cup !
Christ be with us !   Hold out and say :
' Here's to the Boy that died this day ! '

Here's his health !—for bold he died ;
Here's his health !—and it's drunk in pride:
The finest sight beneath the sky
Is to see how bravely a MAN can die.

THE BOOKWORM.

WITH spectacles upon his nose,
  He shuffles up and down ;
Of antique fashion are his clothes,
  His napless hat is brown.
A mighty watch, of silver wrought,
  Keeps time in sun or rain
To the dull ticking of the thought
  Within his dusty brain.

To see him at the bookstall stand
  And bargain for the prize,
With the odd sixpence in his hand
  And greed in his gray eyes !
Then, conquering, grasp the book half blind,
  And take the homeward track,
For fear the man should change his mind,
  And want the bargain back !

The waves of life about him beat,
  He scarcely lifts his gaze,
He hears within the crowded street
  The wash of ancient days.
If ever his short-sighted eyes
  Look forward, he can see
Vistas of dusty Libraries
  Prolonged eternally.

But think not as he walks along
  His brain is dead and cold ;
His soul is thinking in the tongue
  Which Plato spake of old ;
And while some grinning cabman sees
  His quaint shape with a jeer,
He smiles,—for Aristophanes
  Is joking in his ear.

Around him stretch Athenian walks,
  And strange shapes under trees ;
He pauses in a dream and talks
  Great speech, with Socrates.
Then, as the fancy fails—still mesh'd
  In thoughts that go and come—
Feels in his pouch, and is refresh'd
  At touch of some old tome.

The mighty world of humankind
　Is as a shadow dim,
He walks through life like one half blind,
　And all looks dark to him ;
But put his nose to leaves antique,
　And hold before his sight
Some press'd and withered flowers of Greek,
　And all is life and light.

A blessing on his hair so gray,
　And coat of dingy brown !
May bargains bless him every day,
　As he goes up and down ;
Long may the bookstall-keeper's face,
　In dull times, smile again,
To see him round with shuffling pace
　The corner of the lane !

A good old Ragpicker is he,
　Who, following morn and eve
The quick feet of Humanity,
　Searches the dust they leave.
He pokes the dust, he sifts with care,
　He searches close and deep ;
Proud to discover, here and there,.
　A treasure in the heap !

THE LAST OF THE HANGMEN.

A GROTESQUE.

What place is snugger and more pretty
Than a gay green Inn outside the City,
To sit in an arbour in a garden,
With a pot of ale and a long churchwarden !

Amid the noise and acclamation,
He sits unknown, in meditation ;
'Mid church-bells ringing, jingling glasses,
Snugly enough his Sunday passes.

BEYOND the suburbs of the City, where
Cheap stucco'd villas on the brick-field stare,
Where half in town, half country, you espy
The hay-cart standing at the hostelry,—
Strike from the highway down a puddly lane,
Skirt round a market-garden, and you gain
A pastoral footpath, winding on for miles
By fair green fields and over country stiles ;
And soon, as you proceed, the busy sound
Of the dark City at your back is drowned,
The speedwell with its blue eye looks at you,
The yellow primrose glimmers through the dew ;
Out of the sprouting hedgerow at your side,
Instead of the town sparrow starveling-eyed,
The blackbird whistles and the finches sing;
Instead of smoke, you breathe the pleasant Spring ;
And shading eyes dim from street dust you mark,
With soft pulsations soaring up, the LARK,
Till o'er your head, a speck against the gleam,
He sings, and the great City fades in dream !

Five miles the path meanders ; then again
You reach the road, but like a leafy lane
It wanders now ; and lo ! you stand before
A quaint old country Inn, with open door,
Fresh-watered troughs, and the sweet smell of hay.

And if, perchance, it be the seventh day—
Or any feast-day, calendar'd or not—
Merry indeed will be this smiling spot ;
For on the neighbouring common will be seen
Groups from the City, romping on the green ;
The vans with gay pink curtains empty stand,
The horses graze unharness'd close at hand;
Bareheaded wenches play at games in rings,
Or, strolling, swing their bonnets by the strings ;
'Prentices, galloping with gasp and groan,
On donkeys ride, till out of breath, or thrown ;
False gipsies, with pale cheeks by juice stain'd brown,
And hulking loungers, gather from the town.
The fiddle squeaks, they dance, they sing, they play,
Waifs from the City casting care away,
And with the country smells and sights are blent
Loud town-bred oaths and urban merriment.

N

Ay; and behind the Inn are gardens
    green,
And arbours snug, where families are seen
Tea-drinking in the shadow; some, glad
    souls,
On the smooth-shaven carpet play at bowls;
And half-a-dozen, rowing round and round,
Upon the shallow skating-pond are found,
And ever and anon will one of these
Upset, and stand there, wading to the
    knees,
Righting his crank canoe! Down neigh-
    bouring walks
Go 'prentice lovers in delightful talks;
While from the arbour-seats smile plea-
    santly
The older members of the company;
And plump round matrons sweat in Paisley
    shawls,
And on the grass the crowing baby sprawls.

Now hither, upon such a festal day,
I from my sky-high lodging made my way,
And followed straggling feet with summer
    smile;
'Jog on,' I sung, 'and merrily hent the
    stile,'
Until I reached the place of revelry;
And there, hard by the groups who sat at
    tea,
But in a quiet arbour, cool and deep,
Around whose boughs white honeysuckles
    creep,
A Face I saw familiar to my gaze,
In scenes far different and on darker days:—
An aged man, with white and reverent hair,
Brow patriarchal yet deep-lined with care,
His melancholy eye, in a half dream,
Watching the groups with philosophic
    gleam;
Decent his dress, of broadcloth black and
    clean,
Clean-starch'd his front, and dignified his
    mien.
His right forefinger busy in the bowl
Of a long pipe of clay, whence there did roll
A halo of gray vapour round his face,
He sat, like the wise Genius of the place;
And at his left hand on the table stood
A pewter-pot, filled up with porter good,
Which ever and anon, with dreamy gaze
And arm-sweep proud, he to his lips did
    raise.

'Twas Sunday; and in melancholy swells
Came the low music of the soft church-bells,
Scarce audible, blown o'er the meadows
    green,
Out of the cloud of London dimly seen—
Whence, thro' the summer mist, at in-
    tervals,
We caught the far-off shadow of St. Paul's.

Silent he sat, unnoted in the crowd,
With all his greatness round him like a
    cloud,
Unknown, unwelcomed, unsuspected quite,
Smoking his pipe like any common wight;
Cheerful, yet distant, patronising here
The common gladness from his prouder
    sphere.
Cold was his eye, and ominous now and
    then
The look he cast upon those merry men
Around him; and, from time to time, sad-
    eyed,
He rolled his reverent head from side to
    side
With dismal shake; and, his sad heart to
    cheer,
Hid his great features in the pot of beer.

When, with an easy bow and lifted hat,
I enter'd the green arbour where he sat,
And most politely him by name did greet,
He went as white as any winding-sheet!
Yea, trembled like a man whose lost eyes
    note
A pack of wolves upleaping at his throat!
But when, in a respectful tone and kind,
I tried to lull his fears and soothe his
    mind,
And vowed the fact of his identity
Was as a secret wholly safe with me—
Explaining also, seeing him demur,
That *I* too was a public character—
The GREAT UNKNOWN (as I shall call him
    here)
Grew calm, replenish'd soon his pot of beer
At my expense, and in a little while
His tongue began to wag, his face to smile;
And in the simple self-revealing mode
Of all great natures heavy with the load
Of pride and power, he edged himself more
    near,
And poured his griefs and wrongs into mine
    ear.

'Well might I be afraid, and sir to you !
They'd tear me into pieces if they knew,—
For quiet as they look, and bright, and smart,
Each chap there has a tiger in his heart !
At play they are, but wild beasts all the same—
Not to be teased although they look so tame ;
And many of them, plain as eye can trace,
Have got my 'scutcheon figured on the face.
It's all a matter of mere destiny
Whether they go all right or come to me :
Mankind is bad, sir, naturally bad !'

And as he shook his head with omen sad,
I answered him, in his own cynic strain :

'Yes, 't is enough to make a man complain.
This world of ours so vicious is and low,
It always treats its Benefactors so.
If people had their rights, and rights were clear,
You would not sit unknown, unhonour'd, here ;
But all would bow to you, and hold you great,
The first and mightiest member of the State.
Who is the inmost wheel of the machine?
Who keeps the Constitution sharp and clean ?
Who finishes what statesmen only plan,
And keeps the whole game going? You're the Man !
At one end of the State the eye may view
Her Majesty, and at the other—*you* ;
And of the two, both precious, I aver,
They seem more ready to dispense with *her !*'

The Great Man watched me with a solemn look,
Then from his lips the pipe he slowly took,
And answered gruffly, in a whisper hot :

'I don't know if you're making game or not !
But, dash my buttons, though you put it strong,
It's my opinion you're more right than wrong !

There's not another man this side the sea
Can settle off the State's account like me.
The work from which all other people shrink
Comes natural to me as meat and drink,—
All neat, all clever, all perform'd so pat,
It's quite an honour to be hung like that !
People don't howl and bellow when they meet
The Sheriff or the Gaoler in the street ;
They never seem to long in their mad fits
To tear the Home Secretary into bits ;
When Judges in white hats to Epsom Down
Drive gay as Tom and Jerry, folk don't frown ;
They cheer the Queen and Royal Family,
But only let them catch a sight of *me*,
And like a pack of hounds they howl and storm !
And that's their gratitude ; 'cause I perform,
In genteel style and in a first-rate way,
The work they're making for me night and day !
Why, if a mortal had his rights, d' ye see,
I should be honour'd as I ought to be —
They'd pay me well for doing what I do,
And touch their hats whene'er I came in view.
Well, after all, they do as they are told ;
They're less to blame than Government, I hold.
Government *sees* my value, and it knows
I keep the whole game going as it goes,
And yet it holds me down and makes me cheap,
And calls me in at odd times like a sweep
To clean a dirty chimney. Let it smoke,
And every mortal in the State must choke !
And yet, though always ready at the call,
I get no gratitude, no thanks at all.
Instead of rank, I get a wretched fee,
Instead of thanks, a sneer or scowl may-be,
Instead of honour such as others win,
Why, I must hide away to save my skin.
When I am sent for to perform my duty,
Instead of coming in due state and beauty,
With outriders and dashing grays to draw
(Like any other mighty man of law),
Disguised, unknown, and with a guilty cheek,
The gaol I enter like an area sneak !

And when all things have been perform'd
    with art
(With my young man to do the menial
    part)
Again out of the dark, when none can see,
I creep unseen to my obscurity!'

His vinous cheek with virtuous wrath was
    flushed,
And to his nose the purple current rushed,
While with a hand that shook a little now,
He mopp'd the perspiration from his brow,
Sighing ; and on his features I descried
A sparkling tear of sorrow and of pride.
Meantime, around him all was mirth and
    May,
The sport was merry and all hearts were
    gay,
The green boughs sparkled back the merri-
    ment,
The garden honeysuckle scatter'd scent,
The warm girls giggled and the lovers
    squeezed,
The matrons drinking tea look'd on full
    pleased.
And far away the church-bells sad and slow
Ceased on the scented air. But still the
    woe
Grew on the Great Man's face—the smiling
    sky,
The light, the pleasure, on his fish-like eye
Fell colourless ;—at last he spoke again,
Growing more philosophic in his pain :

  'Two sorts of people fill this mortal
    sphere,
Those who are hung, and those who just
    get clear ;
And I'm the schoolmaster (though you may
    laugh),
Teaching good manners to the second half.
Without my help to keep the scamps in awe,
You'd have no virtue and you'd know no
    law ;
And now they only hang for blood alone,
Ten times more hard to rule the mob have
    grown.
I've heard of late some foolish folk have
    plann'd
To put an end to hanging in the land ;
But, Lord ! how little do the donkeys know
This world of ours, when they talk non-
    sense so !

It's downright blasphemy ! You might as
    well
Try to get rid at once of Heaven and Hell !
Mankind is bad, sir, naturally bad,
Both rich and poor, man, woman, sad, or
    glad !
While some to keep scot-free have got the
    wit
(Not that they're really better—devil a
    bit !),
Others have got my mark so plain and fair
In both their eyes, I stop, and gape, and
    stare.
Look at that fellow stretch'd upon the
    green,
Strong as a bull, though only seventeen ;
Bless you, I know the party every limb,
I've hung a few *fac-similes* of him !
And cast your eye on that pale wench who
    sips
Gin in the corner ; note her hanging lips,
The neat-shaped boots, and the neglected
    lace :
There's baby-murder written on her face !—
Tho' accidents may happen now and then,
I know my mark on women and on men,
And oft I sigh, beholding it so plain,
To think what heaps of labour still remain !'

  He sigh'd, and yet methought he smackt
    his lips,
As one who in anticipation sips
A feast to come. Then I, with a sly thought,
Drew forth a picture I had lately bought
In Regent Street, and begged the man of
    fame
To give his criticism on the same.
First from their case his spectacles he took,
Great silver-rimm'd, and with deep search-
    ing look
The picture's lines in silence pondered he.

  ' This is as bad a face as ever I see !
This is no common area-sneak or thief,
No stealer of a pocket-handkerchief,
No ! deep's the word, and knowing, and
    precise,
Afraid of nothing, but as cool as ice.
Look at his ears, how very low they lie,
Lobes far below the level of his eye,
And there's a mouth, like any rat-trap's
    tight,
And at the edges bloodless, close, and white.

'Who *is* the party? Caught, on any charge?
There's mischief near, if he remains at
    large!'

    Gasping with indignation, angry-eyed,
'Silence! 'tis very blasphemy,' I cried;
'Misguided man, whose insight is a sham,
These noble features you would brand and
    damn,
This saintly face, so subtle, calm, and high,
Are those of one who would not wrong a
    fly—
A friend of man, whom all man's sorrows
    stir,
'Tis Mr. Mill, the great Philosopher!'

    Then for a moment he to whom I spake
Seemed staggered, but, with the same
    ominous shake
O' the head, he, rallying, wore a smile half
    kind,
Pitying my simplicity of mind.

    'Sir,' said he, 'from my word I will not
    stir—
I've seen that look on many a murderer;
But don't mistake—it stands to common
    sense
That education makes the difference!
I've heard the party's name, and know that
    he
Is a good pleader for my trade and me;
And well he may be! for a clever man
Sees pretty well what others seldom can,—
That those mark'd qualities which make
    him great
In *one* way, might by just a turn of fate
Have raised him in *another!* Ah, it's sad—
Mankind is bad, sir, naturally bad!
It takes a genius in our busy time
To plan and carry out a bit of crime
That shakes the land and raises up one's
    hair;
Most murder now is but a poor affair—
No art, no cunning, just a few blind blows
Struck by a bullet-headed rough who knows
No better. Clever men now see full plain
That crime don't answer. Thanks to *me*,
    again!
Ah, when I think what would become of
    men
Without my bit of schooling now and
    then,—

To teach the foolish they must mind their
    play,
And keep the clever under every day,—
I shiver! As it is, they're kept by me
To decent sorts of daily villany—
Law, money-lending, factoring on the land,
Share-broking, banking with no cash in
    hand,
And many a sort of weapon they may use
Which never brings their neck into the
    noose;
For if they're talented they can invent
Plenty of crime that gets no punishment,
Do lawful murder with no sort of fear
As coolly as I drink this pot of beer!'

    The Great Man paused and drank; his
    face was grim,
Half buried in the pot; and o'er its rim
His eye, like the law's bull's-eye, flashing
    bright
To deepen darkness round it, threw its light
On the gay scene before him, and it seemed
Rendered all wretched near it as it gleamed.
A shadow fell upon the merry place,
Each figure grew distorted, and each face
Spake of crime hidden and of evil thought.
Darkling I gazed, sick-hearted and dis-
    traught,
In silence. Black and decent at my side,
With reverend hair, sat melancholy-eyed
The Patriarch. To my head I held my
    hand,
And ponder'd, and the look of the fair land
Seemed deathlike. On the darkness of my
    brain
The voice, a little thicker, broke again:

    'Ah, things don't thrive as they throve
    once,' he said,
'And I'm alone now my old woman's
    dead.
I find the Sundays dull. First, I attend
The morning service, then this way I wend
To take my pipe and drop of beer; and
    then,
Home to a lonely meal in town again.
'Tis a dull world!—and grudges me my
    hire—
I ought to get a pension and retire.
What living man has served his country so?
But who's to take my place I scarcely
    know!

Well, Heaven will punish their neglect
   anon :—
'They'll know my merit, when I'm dead
   and gone!'

He stood upon his legs, and these, I
   think,
Were rather shaky, part with age, part
   drink,
And with a piteous smile, full of the sense
Of human vanity and impotence,
Grimly he stood, half senile and half sly,
A sight to make the very angels cry ;
Then lifted up a hat with weepers on—
(Worn for some human creature dead and
   gone)
Placing it on his head (unconsciously
A little on one side) held out to me
His right hand, and, though grim beyond
   belief,
Wore unaware an air of rakish grief—
Even so we parted, and with hand-wave
   proud
He faded like a ghost into the crowd.

Home to the mighty City wandering,
Breathing the freshness of the fields of
   Spring,
Hearing the Lark, and seeing bright winds
   run
Between the bending rye-grass and the sun,
I mused and mused ; till with a solemn
   gleam
My soul closed, and I saw as in a dream,
Apocalyptic, cutting heaven across,
Two mighty shapes—a Gallows and a Cross.
And these twain, with a sea of lives that
   clomb
Up to their base and struck and fell in foam,
Moved, trembled, changed ; and lo! the
   first became
A jet-black Shape that bowed its head in
   shame
Before the second, which in turn did change
Into a luminous Figure, sweet and strange,
Stretching out mighty arms to bless the
   thing
Which hushed its breath beneath Him
   wondering.
And lo ! those visions vanished with no
   word
In brightness ; and like one that wakes I
   heard

The church bells chime and the cathedrals
   toll,
Filling the mighty City like its Soul.

Then, like a spectre strange and woe-
   begone,
Uprose again, with mourning weepers on,
His hat a little on one side, his breath
Heavy and hot, the gray-hair'd Man of
   Death,
Tottering, grog-pimpled, with a trembling
   pace
Under the Gateway of the Silent Place,
At whose sad opening the great Puppet
   stands
The rope of which he tugs with palsied
   hands.

Christ help me! whither do my wild
   thoughts run ?
And Christ help *thee*, thou lonely aged one!
Christ help us all, till all 's that dark grows
   clear—
Are those indeed the Sabbath bells I hear?

LONDON, 1864.

I.

WHY should the heart seem stiller,
   As the song grows stronger and surer ?
Why should the brain grow chiller,
   And the utterance clearer and purer ?
To lose what the people are gaining
   Seems often bitter as gall,
Though to sink in the proud attaining
   Were the bitterest of all.
I would to God I were lying
   Yonder 'mong mountains blue,
Chasing the morn with flying
   Feet in the morning dew !
Longing, and aching, and burning
   To conquer, to sing, and to teach,
A passionate face upturning
   To visions beyond my reach,—
But with never a feeling or yearning
   I could utter in tuneful speech !

II.

Yea ! that were a joy more stable
   Than all that my soul hath found,—
Than to see and to know, and be able
   To utter the seeing in sound ;

For Art, the Angel of losses,
  Comes, with her still, gray eyes,
Coldly my forehead crosses,
  Whispers to make me wise ;
And, too late, comes the revelation,
  After the feast and the play,
That she works God's dispensation
  By cruelly taking away :
By burning the heart and steeling,
  Scorching the spirit deep,
And changing the flower of feeling,
  To a poor dried flower that may keep !
What wonder if much seems hollow,
  The passion, the wonder dies ;
And I hate the angel I follow,
  And shrink from her passionless eyes,—
Who, instead of the rapture of being
  I held as the poet's dower—
Instead of the glory of seeing,
  The impulse, the splendour, the power—
Instead of merrily blowing
  A trumpet proclaiming the day,
Gives, for her sole bestowing,
  A pipe whereon to play !
While the spirit of boyhood hath faded,
  And never again can be,
And the singing seemeth degraded,
  Since the glory hath gone from me,—
Though the glory around me and under,
  And the earth and the air and the sea,
And the manifold music and wonder,
  Are grand as they used to be !

III.

Is there a consolation
  For the joy that comes never again ?
Is there a reservation ?
  Is there a refuge from pain ?
Is there a gleam of gladness
  To still the grief and the stinging ?
Only the sweet, strange sadness,
  That is the source of the singing.

IV.

For the sound of the city is weary,
  As the people pass to and fro,
And the friendless faces are dreary,
  As they come, and thrill through us,
    and go ;
And the ties that bind us the nearest
  Of our error and weakness are born ;
And our dear ones ever love dearest
  Those parts of ourselves that we scorn ;
And the weariness will not be spoken,
  And the bitterness dare not be said,
The silence of souls is unbroken,
  And we hide ourselves from our Dead !
And what, then, secures us from madness?
  Dear ones, or fortune, or fame ?
Only the sweet singing sadness
  Cometh between us and shame.

V.

And there dawneth a time to the Poet,
  When the bitterness passes away,
With none but his God to know it,
  He kneels in the dark to pray ;
And the prayer is turn'd into singing,
  And the singing findeth a tongue,
And Art, with her cold hands clinging,
  Comforts the soul she has stung.
Then the Poet, holding her to him,
  Findeth his loss is his gain :
The sweet singing sadness thrills through
    him,
  Though nought of the glory remain ;
And the awful sound of the city,
  And the terrible faces around,
Take a truer, tenderer pity,
  And pass into sweetness and sound ;
The mystery deepens to thunder,
  Strange vanishings gleam from the
    cloud,
And the Poet, with pale lips asunder,
  Stricken, and smitten, and bow'd,
Starteth at times from his wonder,
  And sendeth his Soul up aloud !

THE MODERN WARRIOR.

O WARRIOR for the Right,
  Though thy shirt of mail be white
As the snows upon the breast of The Adored,
  Though the weapon thou mayest claim
  Hath been temper'd in the flame
Of the fire upon the Altar of the Lord,
  Ere the coming of the night,
  Thy mail shall be less bright,
And the taint of sin may settle on the
    Sword !

For the foemen thou must meet
Are the phantoms in the street,
And thine armour shall be foul'd in many a
    place,

And the shameful mire and mud,
With a grosser stain than blood,
Shall be scatter'd 'mid the fray upon thy face;
And the helpless thou dost aid
Shall shrink from thee dismayed,
Till thou comest to the knowledge of things base.

Ah, mortal, with a brow
Like the gleam of sunrise, thou
May'st wander from the pathway in thy turn,
In the noontide of thy strength
Be stricken down at length,
And cry to God for aid, and live, and learn;
And when, with many a stain,
Thou arisest up again,
The lightning of thy look will be less stern.

Thou shalt see with humbler eye
The adulteress go by,
Nor shudder at the touch of her attire;
Thou shalt only look with grief
On the liar and the thief,
Thou shalt meet the very murtherer in the mire—
And to which wouldst thou accord,
O thou Warrior of the Lord!
The vengeance of the Sword and of the Fire?

Nay! batter'd in the fray,
Thou shalt quake in act to slay,
And remember *thy* transgression and be meek;
And the thief shall grasp thy hand,
And the liar blushing stand,
And the harlot if she list shall kiss thy cheek;
And the murtherer, unafraid,
Shall meet thee in the shade,
And pray thee for the doom thou wilt not wreak.

Yet thou shalt help the frail
From the phantoms that assail,
Yea, the strong man in his anger thou shalt dare;
Thy voice shall be a song
Against wickedness and wrong,
But the wicked and the wronger thou shalt spare.

And while thou lead'st the van,
The ungrateful hand of man
Shall smite thee down and slay thee unaware.

With an agonisëd cry
Thou shalt shiver down and die,
With stainëd shirt of mail and broken brand;
And the voice of men shall call,
'He is fallen like us all,
Though the weapon of the Lord was in his hand;'
And thine epitaph shall be,
'He was wretched ev'n as we;'
And thy tomb may be unhonoured in the land.

But the basest of the base
Shall bless thy pale dead face
And the thief shall steal a bloody lock of hair;
And over thee asleep,
The adulteress shall weep
Such tears as she can never shed elsewhere,
Shall bless the broken brand
In thy chill and nerveless hand,
Shall kiss thy stainëd vesture with a prayer.

Then, while in that chill place
Stand the basest of the base,
Gather'd round thee in the silence of the dark,
A white Face shall look down
On the silence of the town,
And see thee lying dead with those to mark,
And a voice shall fill the air,
'Bear my Warrior lying there
To his sleep upon my Breast!' and they shall heark.

Lo, then those fallen things
Shall perceive a rush of wings
Growing nearer down the azure gulfs untrod,
And around them in the night
There shall grow a wondrous light,
While they hide affrighted faces on the sod,
But ere again 'tis dark,
They shall raise their eyes, and mark
White arms that waft the Warrior up to God!

PAN: EPILOGUE.

'Pan, Pan is dead!'—E. B. BROWNING.

THE broken goblets of the Gods
  Lie scatter'd in the Waters deep,
Where the tall sea-flag blows and nods
  Over the shipwreck'd seamen's sleep;
The gods like phantoms come and go
  Amid the wave-wash'd ocean-hall,
Above their heads the bleak winds blow;
  They sigh, they shiver to and fro—
    'Pan, Pan!' those phantoms call.

O Pan, great Pan, thou art not dead,
  Nor dost thou haunt that weedy place,
Tho' blowing winds hear not thy tread,
  And silver runlets miss thy face;
Where ripe nuts fall thou hast no state,
  Where eagles soar, thou now art dumb,
By lonely meres thou dost not wait;—
  But *here* 'mid living waves of fate
    We feel thee go and come!

O piteous one!—In wintry days
  Over the City falls the snow,
And, where it whitens stony ways,
  I see a Shade flit to and fro;
Over the dull street hangs a cloud—
  It parts, an ancient Face flits by,
'Tis thine! 'tis thou! Thy gray head bowed,
  Dimly thou flutterest o'er the crowd,
    With a thin human cry.

Ghost-like, O Pan, thou glimmerest still,
  A spectral Face with sad dumb stare;
On rainy nights thy breath blows chill
  In the street-walker's dripping hair;
Thy ragged woe from street to street
  Goes mist-like, constant day and night;
But often, where the black waves beat,
  Thou hast a smile most strangely sweet
    For honest hearts and light!

Where'er thy shadowy vestments fly
  There comes across the waves of strife,
Across the souls of all close by,
  The gleam of some forgotten life:
There is a sense of waters clear,
  An odour faint of flowery nooks;
Strange-plumaged birds seem flitting near

The cold brain blossoms, lives that hear
  Ripple like running brooks.

And as thou passest, human eyes
  Look in each other and are wet—
Simple or gentle, weak or wise,
  Alike are full of tender fret;
And mean and noble, brave and base
  Raise common glances to the sky;—
And lo! the phantom of thy Face,
While sad and low thro' all the place
    Thrills thy thin human cry!

Christ help thee, Pan! canst *thou* not go
  Now all the other gods are fled?
Why dost thou flutter to and fro
  When all the sages deem thee dead?
Or, if thou still must live and dream,
  Why leave the fields of harvest fair—
Why quit the peace of wood and stream—
And haunt the streets with eyes that gleam
    Through white and holy hair?

L'ENVOI TO LONDON POEMS.

I DO not sing for Maidens. They are roses
  Blowing along the pathway I pursue:
No sweeter things the wondrous world discloses,
  And they are tender as the morning dew.
Blessed be maids and children: day and night
  Their holy scent is with me as I write.

I do not sing for School-boys or Schoolmen.
  To give them ease I have no languid theme
When, weary with the wear of book and pen,
  They seek their trim poetic Academe;
Nor can I sing them amorous ditties, bred
Of too much Ovid on an empty head.

I do not sing aloud in measured tone
  Of those fair paths the easy-soul'd pursue;
Nor do I sing for Lazarus alone,
  I sing for Dives and the Devil too.
Ah! would the feeble song I sing might swell
As high as Heaven, and as deep as Hell!

I sing of the stain'd outcast at Love's feet,—
　Love with his wild eyes on the evening
　　light;
I sing of sad lives trampled down like wheat
　Under the heel of Lust, in Love's despite;
I glean behind those wretched shapes ye see
　In the cold harvest-fields of Infamy.

I sing of death-beds (let no man rejoice
　Till that last piteous touch of all is
　　given!);
I sing of Death and Life with equal voice,
　Heaven watching Hell, and Hell illumed
　　by Heaven.
I have gone deep, far down the infernal
　　stair—
And seen the spirits congregating there.

I sing of Hope, that all the lost may hear;
I sing of Light, that all may feel its ray;
I sings of Soul, that no one man may fear;
I sing of God, that some perchance may
　　pray.
Angels in Hosts have praised Him loud and
　　long,
But Lucifer's shall be the harvest song.

Oh, hush a space the sounds of voices light
　Mix'd to the music of a lover's lute.
Stranger than dream, so luminously bright,
　The eyes are dazzled and the mouth is
　　mute,
Sits Lucifer; singing to sweeten care,
He twines *immortelles* in his hoary hair!

Miscellaneous Poems.
(1866–70.)

THE DEATH OF ROLAND.

De Karlemane et de Rolant,
Et d'Olivier, et des vassaus,
Qui moururent à Rainscevaux!

I.

DEAD was Gerard the fair, the girl-mouth'd,
　the gay,
Who jested with the foe he slung his sword
　to slay;
Dead was the giant Guy, big-hearted, small
　of brain;
Dead was the hunchback Sanche, his red
　hunch slit in twain;
Dead was the old hawk Luz, and sleeping
　by his side
His twin-sons, Charles the fleet, and Pierre
　the serpent-eyed;
Dead was Antoine, the same who swore to
　speak no word
Till five score heathen heads fell by his
　single sword;
Dead was the wise Gerin, who gript both
　spear and pen;
Sansun was dead, Gereir was dead!—dead
　were the mighty men!

II.

Then Roland felt his sense return, and
　stirr'd, and cried,
Felt down if Adalmar lay safe against his
　side,
And smiled most quietlie, for joy the Sword
　was there;
With heavy-mailed hand brush'd back his
　bloody hair,
And lying prone upon his back, beheld on
　high
The stars like leopard-spots strewn in the
　sapphire sky.
He turn'd his head, and lo! the large hills
　looming dim,
In the wan west the Moon with red and
　wasting rim;
Then sighing sore, swung round his head
　as in a swoon,
And met the hunchback's eyne, glazèd
　beneath the Moon.
Chill was the air, and frosty vapours to and
　fro,
Like sheeted shapes, in dim moonshine,
　were stealing slow;
And Roland thought, because his wound
　had made him weak,

The cold shapes breathed alive their breath
  upon his cheek.
Crawling unto his knees, shivering in the
  cold,
He loosed his helm, and dimly gleaming
  down it roll'd ;
And darkly his dim eyes distinguish'd things
  around,—
The mute and moveless shapes asleep upon
  the ground,
A helm glittering dim, a sword-hilt twink-
  ling red,
A white steed quivering beside a warrior
  dead,
And in one moonlit place, a ring on a white
  hand,
When Roland thought, 'Gerard! the
  brightest of the band!'
And no one stirr'd ; behind, the hills
  loom'd large and dim ;
And in the west the waning Moon with red
  and wasting rim.

III.

Then Roland cried aloud, 'If living man
  there be
Among these heaps of slain, let that man
  answer me!'
And no soul spake. The wind crept chilly
  over all,
And no man felt it creep, or heard the
  leader call.
'Ho, Olivier! Gerin! speak, an' ye be not
  slain!'
The voices of the hills echoed the cry
  again,—
Only a heathen churl rose cursing on his
  side,
And spat at him who spake, and curl'd his
  limbs, and died.
Then Roland's mighty heart was heavy
  with its woes,—
When fitfully, across the fields, faint ra-
  diance rose,
First a faint spark, and then a gleam, and
  then a glare,
Then smoke and crimson streaks that
  mingled in the air,
And as the thick flame clear'd, and the
  black smoke swam. higher,
There loom'd beyond a Shape like one girt
  round with fire!

And Roland cried aloud, because his joy
  was great,
And brandish'd Adalmar, and fell beneath
  the weight,
But lying prone strain'd eyes, and, gazing
  through the night,
Still saw the glittering Shape circled with
  spectral light.
He seem'd in a dark dream, he could not
  think at all,
Until his heart rose up, and he had strength
  to crawl :
Then, like a bruisèd worm weary he slipt
  and slow,
Straining his fever'd eyes lest the sweet
  ghost should go,
And oft he paused to breathe, feeling his
  pulses fail,
'Mong heathens foul to smell and warriors
  clad in mail,
But coming near the gleam beheld the godly
  man,
Turpin the Archbishop, unhelm'd and gaunt
  and wan,—
Gripping with skinny hand the ivory Cross
  sat he,
Clad head to heel in frost-white mail and
  propt against a tree.

IV.

And when on hands and knees the stricken
  Chief came near,
The Bishop raised the Cross, and knew his
  comrade dear ;
And Roland's heart swell'd up, and tears
  were on his cheek,
He touch'd the blessèd Cross, and smiled
  and did not speak ;
While, 'Glory be to God!' the Bishop
  faintly said,
'Thou livest, kinsman dear, though all the
  rest be dead!
For while I linger'd here and listen'd for a
  sound,
And in the dim red Moon beheld the dead
  around,
Thinking I heard a cry, I sought to cry again,
But all my force had fled, and I was spent
  with pain ;
When, peering round, I saw this heathen
  at my heel,
And search'd his leathern scrip and gat me
  flint and steel,

Then crawl'd, though swooning-sick, and found his charger gray,
And searching in the bags found wither'd grass and hay,
And made a fire, a sign for thee, whoe'er thou wert,
But fainted when it blazed, for I am sorely hurt;
And waken'd to behold thee near, wounded and weak,
The red fire flaming on thy face, thy breath upon my cheek.'

V.

Then those brave Chiefs wrung hands, and as the crimson flare
Died out, and all was dark, the Bishop said a prayer;
And shadows loom'd out black against the frosty shine,
While Turpin search'd his pouch and murmur'd, ' Here is wine ! '
And Roland on his elbows raised himself and quaff'd,
Yea, till his head reel'd round, a great and goodly draught,
And quickly he felt strong, his heart was wild and light,
He placed his dear Sword softly down, and rose his height,
Loosening his mail, drew forth the shirt that lay beneath,
And took the blood-stain'd silk and tore it with his teeth,
Dressing the Bishop's wounds with chilly hand and slow,
Then, while the Bishop pray'd, bound up his own wide wound alsoe.

VI.

Then Roland search'd around, dipping his hands in blood,
Till in a henchman's pack he found a torch of wood,
And taking flint and steel, blew with his mouth, and lo !
The torch blazed bright, and all grew crimson in the glow.
Then into Turpin's hands he set that beacon bright
Who glittering like fire, sat looming in its light,
And crept across the mead, into the dark again,
And felt the faces of the dead, seeking the mighty men.

VII.

Blest be thy name, White Mary, for thy breath and might,
Like vapour cold, did fill the nostrils of thy knight !
Yea, all his force came back, his red wound ceased to bleed,
And he had hands of strength to do a blessèd deed !
For one by one he found each well-belovèd head,
Sought out the mighty Chiefs, among the drifts of dead,
Softly unloosed their helms, let the long tresses flow,
Trail'd them to Turpin's feet and set them in a row;
And underneath the tree the pine-torch blazing bright
Lit shapes in silvern mail and faces snowy white:
Sansun, who grasp'd his sword with grip that ne'er unloosed;
Gerin, with chin on breast, as if he breathed and mused ;
Great Guy, with twisted limbs, and bosom gash'd and bare,
And blood-clots on his arms the frost had frozen there ;
Old Luz, his skinny hands filled with a foeman's beard ;
Charles with his feet lopp'd off, Pierre with his green eye spear'd ;
Sanche, the fierce woman's foe, and round his neck, behold !
A lock of lady's hair set in a ring of gold ;
Antoine, with crafty smile, as if new fights he plann'd ;
Gerard, still smiling on the ring that deckt his hand ;
And, brightest of the host, our Roland's comrade dear,
The iron woman-shape, the long-lock'd Olivier,
Who gript the bladeless hilt of Durandal his pride,
And held it to his kissing lips, as when he droop'd and died.

VIII.

And Turpin raised the torch, counted them,
  one by one:
'Ah, woe is me, sweet knights, for now your
  work is done!'
Then, reaching with the Cross, he touch'd
  their brows and cried:
'White Mary take your souls, and place
  them at her side,
White Mary take your souls, and guard
  them tenderlie,—
For ye were goodly men as any men that
  be!'
And Roland stooping touch'd the brow of
  Olivier,
Smoothing the silken hair behind the small
  white ear,
And cried, 'Ah, woe is me, that we should
  ever part!'
And kiss'd him on the clay-cold lips, and
  swoon'd, for ache of heart.

IX.

Then Turpin dropt the torch, that flamed
  upon the ground,
But drinking blood and dew, died out with
  drizzlie sound;
He groped for Roland's heart, and felt it
  faintly beat,
And, feeling on the earth, he found the
  wine-flask sweet,
And fainting with the toil, slaked not his
  own great drouth,
But, shivering, held the flask to Roland's
  gentle mouth:
E'en then, his Soul shot up, and in its shirt
  of steel
The Corse sank back, with crash like ice
  that cracks beneath the heel!

X.

The frosty wind awaken'd Roland from his
  swound,
And, spitting salt foam from his tongue, he
  look'd around,
And saw the Bishop dear lying at length
  close by,—
Touch'd him, and found him cold, and
  utter'd a great cry: .
'Now, dead and cold, alas! lieth the noblest
  wight

For preaching sermons sweet and wielding
  sword in fight;
His voice was as a trump that on a moun-
  tain blows,
He scatter'd oils of grace and wasted
  heathen-foes,—
White Mary take his soul, to join our com-
  rades dear,
And let him wear his Bishop's crown in
  heaven above, as here!'

XI.

Now it grew chiller far, the grass was moist
  with dew,
The landskip glimmer'd pale, the frosty
  breezes blew,
The many stars above melted like snow-
  flakes white,
Behind the great blue hills the East was
  laced with light,
The dismal vale loom'd clear against a
  crimson glow,
Clouds spread above like wool, pale steam
  arose below,
And on the faces dead the frosty Morning
  came,
On mighty men of mark and squires un-
  known to fame,
And golden mail gleam'd bright, and broken
  steel gleam'd gray,
And cold dew filled the wounds of those
  who sleeping lay;
And Roland, rising, drank the dawn with
  lips apart,
But scents were in the air that sicken'd his
  proud heart!
Yea, all was deathly still; and now, though
  it was day,
The Moon grew small and pale, but did
  not pass away,
The white mist wreath'd and curl'd over the
  glittering dead;
A cock crew, far among the hills, and
  echoes answer'd.

XII.

Then peering to the East, through the thick
  vaporous steam,
He spied a naked wood, hard by a running
  stream;

Thirsting full sore, he rose, and thither did
    he hie,
Faintly, and panting hard, because his end
    was nigh ;
But first he stooping loosed from Turpin's
    fingers cold
The Cross inlaid with gems and wrought
    about with gold,
And bare the holy Cross aloft in one weak
    hand,
And with the other trail'd great Adalmar his
    brand.
Thus wearily he came into the woody place,
And stooping to the stream therein did dip
    his face,
And in the pleasant cold let swim his great
    black curls,
Then swung his head up, damp with the
    dim dewy pearls ;
And while the black blood spouted in a
    burning jet,
He loosed the bandage of his wound and
    made it wet,
Wringing the silken folds, making them
    free from gore,
Then placed them cool upon the wound,
    and tighten'd them once more.

XIII.

Eastward rose cloudy mist, drifting like
    smoke in air,
Ghastly and round the Sun loom'd with a
    lurid glare,
High overhead the Moon shrivell'd with
    sickle chill,
The frosty wind dropp'd down, and all was
    deathlier still,
When Roland, drawing deep the breath of
    vapours cold
Beheld three marble steps, as of a Ruin
    old,
And at the great tree-bolls lay many a
    carven stone,
Thereto a Dial quaint, where slimy grass
    had grown ;
And frosted were the boughs that gather'd
    all around,
And cold the runlet crept, with soft and
    soothing sound,
And sweetly Roland smiled, thinking,
    'Since death is nigh,
In sooth, I know no gentler place where
    gentle man could die !'

XIV.

Whereon he heard a cry, a crash of
    breaking boughs,
And from the thicket wild leapt one with
    painted brows ;
Half-naked, glistening grim, with oily limbs,
    he came,
His long-nail'd fingers curl'd, his bloodshot
    eyes aflame,
Shrieking in his own tongue, as on the
    Chief he flew,
'Yield thee thy sword of fame, and thine
    own flesh thereto !'
Then Roland gazed and frown'd, though
    nigh unto his death,
Sat still, and drew up all his strength in one
    great breath,
Pray'd swiftly to the Saints he served in
    former days,
With right hand clutch'd the Sword he was
    too weak to raise,
And in the left swung up the Cross !—and,
    shrieking hoarse,
Between the eyebrows smote the foe with
    all his force,
Yea, smote him to the brain, crashing
    through skin and bone,
And prone the heathen fell, as heavy as a
    stone,—
While gold and gems of price, unloosen'd
    by the blow,
Ev'n as he fell rain'd round the ringlets of
    the foe ;
But Roland kiss'd the Cross, and, laughing,
    backward fell,
And on the hollow air the laugh rang heavy,
    like a knell.

XV.

And Roland thought : 'I surely die ; but,
    ere I end,
Let me be sure that *thou* art ended too, O
    friend !
For should a heathen hand grasp thee when
    I am clay,
My ghost would grieve full sore until the
    Judgment Day !'
Then to the marble steps, under the tall
    bare trees,
Trailing the mighty Sword, he crawl'd on
    hands and knees,
And on the slimy stone he struck the blade
    with might—

The bright hilt sounding shook, the blade
flash'd sparks of light;
Wildly again he struck, and his sick head
went round,
Again there sparkled fire, again rang hollow
sound;
Ten times he struck, and threw strange
echoes down the glade,
Yet still unbroken, sparkling fire, glitter'd
the peerless blade!

XVI.

Then Roland wept, and set his face
against the stone—
'Ah, woe! I shall not rest, though cold be
flesh and bone!'
And sickness seized his soul to die so cheer-
less death;
When on his naked neck he felt a touch,
like breath,—
And did not stir, but thought, 'O God,
that madest me,
And shall my sword of fame brandish'd by
heathens be?
And shall I die accursed, beneath a
heathen's heel?
Too spent to slay the slave whose hated
breath I feel!'
Then, clenching teeth, he turn'd to look
upon the foe,
His bright eyes growing dim with coming
death; and lo!
His life shot up in fire, his heart arose
again,
For no unhallow'd face loom'd on his dying
ken,
No heathen-breath he felt,—though he
beheld, indeed,
The white arch'd head and round brown
eyes of Veillintif, his Steed!

XVII.

And pressing his moist cheek on his who
gazed beneath,
Curling the upper lip to show the large
white teeth,
The white horse, quivering, look'd with
luminous liquid eye,
Then waved his streaming mane, and
utter'd up a cry;
And Roland's bitterness was spent—he
laugh'd, he smiled,

He clasp'd his darling's neck, wept like a
little child;
He kiss'd the foam-fleck'd lips, and clasp'd
his friend and cried:
'Ah, nevermore, and nevermore, shall we
to battle ride!
Ah, nevermore, and nevermore, shall we
sweet comrades be,
And Veillintif, had I the heart to die for-
getting thee?
To leave thy brave bright heart to break, in
slavery to the foe?
I had not rested in the grave, if it had
ended so!
Ah, never shall we conquering ride, with
banners bright unfurl'd,
A shining light 'mong lesser lights, a
wonder to the world!'

XVIII.

And Veillintif neigh'd low, breathing on
him who died,
Wild rock'd his strong sad heart beneath
his silken side,
Tears roll'd from his brown eyes upon his
master's cheek,
While Roland, gathering strength, though
wholly worn and weak,
Held up the glittering point of Adalmar the
brand,
And at his comrade's heart drave with his
dying hand;
And the black blood sprang forth, while
heavily as lead,
With shivering, silken side, the mighty
Steed fell dead.
Then Roland, for his eyes with frosty film
were dim,
Groped for his friend, crept close, and
smiled, embracing him;
And, pillow'd on his neck, kissing the pure
white hair,
Clasp'd Adalmar the brand, and tried to
say a prayer:
And that he conquering died wishing all
men to know,
Set firm his lips, and turn'd his face towards
the foe,
Then closed his eyes, and slept, and never
woke again.

Roland is dead, the gentle knight! dead is
the crown of men!

THE GIFT OF EOS.

Not in a mist of loveless eyes dies he,
  Who loveth truly nobler light than theirs ;
To him, nor weariness nor agony,
  Purblind appeals, nor prayers ;
To him, the priceless boon
  To watch from heights divine till all be done ;
Calm in each dreamy rising of the Moon,
  Glad in each glorious coming of the Sun.

CHORUS OF HOURS.

1.

Lo ! here at the portal, awaiting new light,
We linger with pinions dripping dew-light,
Our faces shadow'd, our heads inclining,
The bright star-frost on our tresses shining ;
Our eyes turn'd earthward in vigil holy,
Sinking our voices and singing slowly.

2.

The dark Earth sleepeth to our intoning,
The Ocean only is gleaming and moaning :
Our eyelids droop in a still devotion,
Yet we see the skies in the glass of Ocean,—
The void, star-lighted, is mirror'd faintly,
Slow slides the shade of Selene saintly.

3.

Eos ! Eos ! thou canst not hear us,
Yet we feel thee breathing in slumber near us :
Dark is thy cloud-roof'd temple solemn,
Shadows deepen round arch and column ;
But a quiet light streams round thee, lying
In the feeble arms of thy love undying.

4.

Eos ! Eos ! thy cheek faint-gleaming
Sendeth a joy through the old man's dreaming ;
His white hair poureth in frosty showers
Round a wreath fresh-woven of lily flowers,
And the flowers are fading and earthward snowing,
Save those thou breathest against unknowing !

TITHONOS.

What low, strange music throbs about my brain?
  I hear a motion as of robes—a moaning.

EOS.

'Tis the three sisters and their shadowy train,
Beating the right foot solemnly, and intoning.
Ah ! weary one, and have thy dreams been ill,
That thou upheavest thus a face so pale?

TITHONOS.

Methought that I was dead, and cold, and still,
  Deep in the navel of a charmèd dale !
Ah, love, thy gift doth heavy burthen bring,
  Now I grow old, grow old,
And these weird songs the sisters nightly sing
  Haunt me with memories strange and manifold ;
For every eve, when Phoibos fades away
  Yonder across Parnassos' snow-tipt height,
These halls feel empty, and the courts grow gray,
The sisters lose the radiance of the day,
  And thy bright hair fades to a silvern light ;
And nothing seems that is not sad though sweet !
But Heaven, this East, yea, and the earth below
Are silenced to the ditties these repeat,
  Sinking their voices sad and singing slow :
Yea, Ocean moans with many waters ! sleep
Is troublous even upon eyes that weep !
The monsters of the earth are in their lairs
  Moonlit and cold ; the owl sits still and stares
Through woody nooks with round white eye ; the wind
  Breatheth and gropeth blind ;
The burthen and the mystery and the dream,
  The sense of things that are and yet may be,
The strife between what is and what doth seem,
  Is weary then on all, and most on me !

EOS.

It is enough to know thou canst not die,
  Like those of whom thou 'plainest, drowsy one !

TITHONOS.

The seasons come and go, the moments fly
  Like snow-flakes falling, melting in the sun.
Nothing abideth—all must change the earth
Puts on fresh raiment every dawn of day—
What seems most precious turns to little worth—
Our love, whose face was an auroral birth,
  Steps in the shade an instant,—and is clay.
Is it enough to know I cannot die?
Further than deathless life, can I implore?
Ah, but to know, as the slow years sweep by,
That life is worthy to be lived, is more.
Wherefore the burthen and the dream below?
Wherefore the happiness, the hope, the woe?
Wherefore the slimy sense of evil things
  That draws the adder round the young man's eyes?
Wherefore the yearnings and imaginings,
  The songs of bards, the broodings of the wise?
Have the gods written only on their scroll:
'Man striveth merely for a little space,—
Then there is slumber, and the death-bells toll,
The children cry, the widow hides her face,
The foolish dream is o'er,
And all is done for ever evermore?'
Oh, wherefore life at all, if life be such,—
A joy, a weariness, a growing gray!
If life be more, how may man live too much?

EOS.

Nothing, be sure, can wholly pass away.

HOURS.

Crow's-nest on a yew-tree, swing slow in sad weather,
A lock o' wet hair pastes thy brown sides together!—
Blood-red were her lips till she paled and grew thin,
As the pink under-eyelid of snakes was her skin.
Crow's-nest on a yew-tree that grows on a tomb,
The little black fledglings croak low in the gloom;
O maiden below, canst thou hear how they cry?
Dost thou stir in thy sleep as the adder goes by?
A worm crawl'd away with the little gold ring
He placed on thy finger that summer morning;
Then thy hand became bone, then was turn'd into clay,
While thy heart wither'd slowly; but cheerly, to-day
Thy fingers are leaves on the tree, in whose shade
He sits with as tender a maid!

TITHONOS.

Of death, corruption, change, and mystery,
  They chant their chime to which the old world sleeps!
Why not for ever stand they bright and free,
  Flinging a glad song over dales and deeps,
As morn by morn they do, when from my breast
  With rosy footsteps thou dost bright'ning go,
Blue-wingèd, to Parnassos?

EOS.

  Be at rest!
The sense of things is dark on these also!
And e'en immortal gods grow pale at times
To hear their world-old rhymes.
Yea, Zeus the Sire himself beholds and hears,
Stares vacantly into the blue profound,
What time a rainbow drawn from all earth's tears
Fades on Olumpos with a weeping sound!

TITHONOS.

What then remains, my soul, if this be so?

EOS.

Around my neck I wind thy beard of gray,
And kiss thy quivering eyelids till they glow,
And thy face lightens on me, and I say,
'Look in mine eyes and know!'

O

HOURS.

O clod of green mould, that wast lately a man,
Time was thou wert footsore and weary and wan,
When thy brain was as fire, when thine eyes were as lead,
When thy hair was as white as the bones of the dead!
Dust in the urn, on a shelf, in a shrine,
Hast thou ears, hast thou eyes, canst thou feel, or divine?
Bones in the ground, can ye guess what ye be?
Brain, in the midst of the bones, canst thou see?
Corse, in a clod-gown clammy with dew,
Skull, with a hole where the arrow went through,
Do ye dream, are ye troubled, remember ye there
The life and the light that ye were?

TITHONOS.

Thine eyes are lit with passion strong enew
To melt a mortal's heart to fiery dew!
The burthen and the wonder and the dream,
Yea, all I am or was, and all I seem,
Are dwarf'd within these liquid orbs of thine
To the blue shadow of a love divine!
Yea, sweetest, love is surest, truest, best!
And dearest, knowing it must last for long!

EOS.

Now, close thine eyes, lean heavy on my breast,
And let my lips rain over thee in song!—
Thou wert a mortal who with fearless eyes
Dared seek the love of an immortal thing;
Plead low thou didst, and strive and agonise,
Yet time ebb'd on, and little peace did bring;
And the immortal joy seem'd far away,
Lessening and lessening to a speck of gold
Against the gates of sunrise,—till that day
I came upon thee where thou sleeping lay,
Breathed smoothness on thy wrinkled forehead old,
And woke thee to these wondrous halls, from whence
Thou seest the glimmering tract of earth below,
And tranced thee to nuptials so intense
Thy flesh and blood seem'd melting off like snow,
Leaving thy soul in its eternal hues
Clear, strong, and pale, as yonder crystal sphere
That swings above my threshold, sprinkling dews
Immortal over all who enter here!—
And still thy corporal semblance ages on,
Thy hair dries up, thy bones grow chill and bare.
A little while, my love, and all is gone,
Drunk by the lips of a diviner air!

TITHONOS.

Ah woe! ah woe!—and I am lost for aye!

EOS.

Nothing, be sure, can wholly pass away!
And nothing suffers loss if love remains!
The motion of mine air consumes thy clay,
My breath dries up the moisture of thy veins;
Yet have I given thee immortal being,
Thereto immortal love, immortal power,
Consuming thy base substance till thy seeing
Grows clearer, brighter, purer, hour by hour;—
Immortal honour, too, is thine, for thou
Hast sought the highest meed the gods can give—
Immortal Love hath stoop'd to kiss thy brow!
Immortal Love hath smiled, and bade thee live!
Wherefore the gods have given thee mighty meed,
And snatch'd thee from the death-pyres of thy race,
To wear away these weary mortal weeds
In a serener and a purer place,—
Not amid warriors on a battle plain,
Not by the breath of pestilence or woe,
But here, at the far edge of earth and main,
Whence light and love and resurrection flow—
And I upon thy breast, to soothe the pain!

Immortal life assured, what mattereth
That it be not the old fond life of breath!
Immortal life assured, the soul is free—
It is enough to be!
For lo! the love, the dream, to which is given
Divine assurance by a mortal peace,
Mix with the wonders of supremest heaven,
Become a part of that which cannot cease,
And being eternal must be beauteous too,
And being beauteous, surely must be glad!
O love, my love, thy wildest dreams were true,
Though thou were footsore in thy quest, and sad!
Not in a mist of hungry eyes dies he
Who loveth purely nobler light than theirs;
For him nor weariness nor agony,
Purblind appeals, nor prayers;
But circled by the peace serene and holy
Of that divinest thought he loved so long,
Pensive, not melancholy,
He mingles with those airs that made him strong,—
A little loath to quit
The old familiar dwelling-house of clay,
Yet calm, as the warm wind dissolveth it,
And leaf by leaf it droppeth quite away.
To him the priceless boon
To watch from heights serene till all be done;
Calm in each dreamy rising of the Moon,
Glad in each glorious coming of the Sun!

HOURS.

The stars are fading away in wonder,
Small sounds are stirring around and under,
Far away, from beneath the ocean,
We hear a murmur of wheels in motion,
And the wind that brings it along rejoices,—
Our hearts beat quicker, we lift our voices!

EOS.

It is Apollo! Hitherward he urges
His four steeds, steaming odorous fumes of day;
Along his chariot-wheels the white sea surges,
As up he drives his fiery-footed way.

TITHONOS.

Ye brighten, O ye columns round about!
Ye melt in purple shades, arches and towers!
Cloud-roof, thou partest, and white hands slip out,
Scattering pearls and flowers!
Brighter and brighter, blazing red and gold,
Purple and amethyst, that float and fly!—
While, creeping in, a dawn-wind fresh and cold
Pours silver o'er the couch whereon I lie!
Afar the coming of Apollo grows!
His breath lifts up my hair! my pulses beat!
My beard is moist with dews divinely sweet,
My lap is fill'd with sparkling leaves of rose,
Wherein my fingers, wither'd and sere,
Grope palsiedly in joy!—Afar I hear
The low, quick breathing that the earth is making—
Eastward she turns her dewy side, awaking.
But thou! but thou!
Insufferably brightening!
Thy feet yet bathed in moist still shade, thy brow
Glistening and lightening,
Thy luminous eyes enlarging, ring in ring
Of liquid azure, and thy golden hair
Unfolding downward, curl on curl, to cling
Around thy naked feet rose-tipt and bare!
Thy hands stretch'd out to catch the flowers down-flowing,
Thy blushing look on mine, thy light green vest
In balmy airs of morning backward blowing
From one divine white breast!
The last star melts above thee in the blue,
The cold moon shrinks her horn, as thou dost go
Parnassos-ward, flower-laden, dripping dew,
Heralding him who cometh from below!

HOURS.

1.

Our hearts beat quicker, we lift our voices,
The east grows golden, the earth rejoices,

White clouds part with a radiant motion,
Moist sails glimmer beneath on Ocean,
And downward tripping, the sweet Immortal
Blushingly pauses without the portal!

2.

Eos! Eos! the sound from under
Deepens in music and might and wonder:
Thou standest now on Parnassos' mountain,
Thy feet drip pearls from the sacred fountain,
And the Sisters nine, to thy bright skirt clinging,
Greet thee with smiling and mystic singing!

3.

Eos! Eos! all earth beholds thee,
The light of the sunrise there infolds thee,
A cry comes up from the earth below thee,
Mountains and forests and waters know thee,
Fresh airs thy robe are backward blowing,
Under thy footprints flowers are growing!

4.

Eos! Eos! the sound is louder!
Behinds teams radiance fiercer and prouder!
A moment thou blushest, and glad we view thee,
Then Apollo the Fire-God speeds unto thee,
Speeding by with a smile he hails thee,—
And the golden cloud of his breathing veils thee!

CLARI IN THE WELL.

O MY fountain of a maiden,
  Sweet to hear and bright to see,
Now before mine eyes love-laden
  Dancing, thrilling, flashing free,—
Still thy sparkling bliss a moment, sit thee
  down, and look at me.

Gaze into my face, my dearest!
  Through thy gleaming, golden hair;
Meet mine eyes—ah! thine are clearest
  When my image floateth there;
Now, they still themselves, like waters when
  the windless skies are fair.

In those depths of limpid azure
  See my baby likeness beam!
Deep blue with reflected pleasure
  From some heavenly dome of dream,
Crystal currents of thy spirit swim around
  it, glance, and gleam!

Hold my hand, and heark'ning to me
  For a space, be calm and cold.
While that liquid look flows through me
  And I love thee twenty-fold,
I am smiling at a story thy dead mother
  often told.

When thou wast a little blossom
  Blown about thy village home,
Thou didst on that mother's bosom
  Put a question troublesome:
'Mother, please, where did you find me?
  whence do little children come?'

And the dame with bright beguiling
  Kiss'd her answer first, my dear!
But, still prest, she answer'd smiling—
  ' In the orchard Well so clear,
Thou wert seen one sunny morning, sleeping, and we brought thee here.'

With a look as grave as this is
  Thou didst ponder thoughts profound;
On the next day with fond kisses
  Clinging mother's neck around—
' Mother! mother! I've been looking in the
  Well where I was found!

' Bright and clear it is! but—mother!'
  (Here thine eyes look'd wonderingly)
' In the well there is *another*—
  Just the very same as me!—
And it is awake and moving—and its pretty
  eyes can see!

' When I stretch my arms unto it,
  Out its little arms stretch too!
Apple-blossoms red I threw it,
  And it broke away from view—
Then again it look'd up laughing through
  the waters deep and blue!'

Then thy gentle mother kiss'd thee,
  Clari, as I kiss thee now,
With a wondering fondness bless'd thee,
  Smooth'd the bright hair from thy brow—
Saying, ' 'Tis a little Sister, happy-eyed and
  sweet as thou!

'Underneath the deep pure water
  Dwell its parents in green bowers—
Yes, it is their little daughter,
  Just the same as thou art ours;
And it loves to lie there, looking at the
  pleasant orchard flowers.

'Every day, while thou art growing,
  Thou wilt find thy Sister fair—
Even when the skies are snowing
  And the water freezes there,
Break the blue ice,—through the water with
  a cold cheek she will stare!

'As thou changest, growing taller,
  She will change, through all the years—
Well thou may'st thy Sister call her,
  She will share thy hopes and fears,
She will wear the face *thou* wearest, sweet
  in smiles and sad in tears.

'Ah, my darling! may'st thou ever
  See her look as kind and bright,
Find her woeful-featured never
  In the pleasant orchard light—
May you both be glad and happy, when
  your golden locks are white!'

Golden locks!—what, *these* grow hoary?
  Wrinkles mar a face like this?
Break the charm of the old story
  With the magic of a kiss—
Here thou art, my deep-eyed darling, as
  thou wast,—a thing of bliss.

Does she love thee? does she miss thee?
  Thy sweet Sister in the well?
Does she mourn because I kiss thee—
  Fearing what she cannot tell?—
For you both are link'd together by a truth
  and by a spell.

Darling, be my love and duty
  Judged by *her!* and prove me so;
When upon her mystic beauty
  Thou perceivest shame or woe;
When she changes into sadness, may God
  judge, and strike me low!

Thou and thy sweet Sister move in
  A diviner element,
Clear as light, more sweet to love in
  Than my world so turbulent;
Holy waters bathe and bless you, peaceful,
  bright, and innocent.

And within those eyes of azure
  See! my baby image beam,
Deep blue with reflected pleasure
  From some heavenly dome of dream,
Crystal currents of thy spirit swim around
  it, glance, and gleam.

O my fountain of a maiden,
  Be thy days for ever blest,
Dancing in mine eyes love-laden,
  Lying smiling on my breast,—
Brighter than a fount, in motion, deeper
  than a well, at rest.

SERENADES.

SLEEP on thine eyes, peace in thy breast,
White-limb'd lady, be at rest!
Near the room wherein you lie,
Broods the owl with luminous eye.

Midnight comes; all fair things sleep,
While all dark things vigil keep;
Round thy bed thy scented bower
Foldeth like a lily-flower.

All so still around thee lies,
Peace in thy breast, sleep on thine eyes!
All without is dark as death,
But thy lover wakeneth.

Underneath thy bower I pace,
Star-dew sparkling on my face;
All around me, swift of flight,
Move the creatures of the night.

Hark, the great owl cries again
With an echo in the brain;
And the dark earth in her sleep
Stirs and trembles, breathing deep.

Sleep on thine eyes, peace in thy breast!
Fold thy hands and take thy rest;
All the night, till morning break,
Spirits walk and lovers wake!

II.

Sleep sweet, belovèd one, sleep sweet!
  Without here night is growing,
The dead leaf falls, the dark boughs meet,
  And a chill wind is blowing.

Strange shapes are stirring in the night,
To the deep breezes wailing,
And slow, with wistful gleams of light,
The storm-tost moon is sailing.

Sleep sweet, belovèd one, sleep sweet!
Fold thy white hands, my blossom!
Thy warm limbs in thy lily sheet,
Thy hands upon thy bosom.
Though evil thoughts may walk the dark,
Not one shall near thy chamber;
But shapes divine shall pause to mark,
Singing to lutes of amber.

Sleep sweet, belovèd one, sleep sweet!
Though, on thy bosom creeping,
Strange hands are laid, to feel the beat
Of thy soft heart in sleeping.
The brother angels, Sleep and Death,
Stoop by thy couch and eye thee;
And Sleep stoops down to drink thy breath,
While Death goes softly by thee!

IN THE GARDEN.

HE.

SEEST thou two waifs of cloud on the dim blue
Wandering in the melancholy light?
Methinks they seem like spirits bright and true,
Blending their gentle breaths, and born anew,
In the still rapture of this heavenly night!
See! how the flowering stars their path bestrew,
Till the moon turns, and smiles, and looks them through,
And breathes upon them, when with bosoms white
They blend on one another, and unite.
Now they are gone, they vanish from our view,
Lost in that radiance exquisitely bright! . . .
O love! my love! methinks that thou and I
Resemble those thin waifs in Heaven astray;
We meet, we blend, grow bright!

SHE.

And we must die!

HE.

Nay, sweet, for Love can never pass away!

SHE.

Are *they* not gone? and, dear, shall we not go?
O Love is Life, but after Life comes Death!

HE.

No flower, no drop of rain, no flake of snow,
No beauteous thing that blossometh below,
May perish, though it vanish ev'n as breath!
The bright moon drinks those wanderers of the west,
They melt in her warm breathing, and are blest.
We see them not, but in that light divine
Upgather'd, they are happy, and they shine:
Not lost, but vanish'd, grown ev'n unawares
A part of a diviner light than theirs!

NIGHTINGALES SING.

Through our throats the raptures rise,
In the scented air they swim;
From the skies,
With their own love-lustre dim,
Gaze innumerable eyes!—
Sweet, O sweet,
Thrills the music from each throat,
Thick and fleet,
Note on note,
Till in ecstasy we float!

SHE.

How vast looks Heaven! how solitary and deep!
Dost thou believe that Spirits walk the air,
Treading those azure fields, and downward peep
With great sad eyes when Earth is fast asleep?

HE.

One spirit, at least, immortal LOVE, is there!

A SHOOTING STAR.

Swift from my bliss, in the silence above,
I slip to thy kiss, O my star! O my love!

SPIRITS IN THE LEAVES.

Who are these twain in the garden-bowers?
They glide with a rapture rich as ours.
Touch them, feel them, and drink their sighs,
Brush their lips and their cheeks and eyes!

How their hearts beat! how they glow!
Brightly, lightly, they come and go;
Upward gazing they look in bliss,
Save when softly they pause, to kiss.

Kiss them also, and share the light
That fills their breathing this golden night.
Touch them! clasp them! round them twine,
Their lips are burning with breath divine.

HE.

Love, tread this way with rosy feet;
And resting on the shadowy seat
'Neath the laburnum's golden rain,
Watch how with murmurous refrain
The fountain leaps, its basin dark
Flashing with many a starry spark.
With such a bliss, with such a light,
With such an iteration bright,
Our souls upbubbling from the clay,
Leap, sparkle, blend in silvern spray,
Gleam in the Moon, and, falling still,
Sink duskily with tremulous thrill,
Together blent with kiss and press,
In dark surcease of happiness.
Yet there they pause not, but, cast free
After deep pause of ecstasy,
Heavenward they leap, together clinging,
And like the fountain flash, upspringing!

THE FOUNTAIN LEAPING.

Higher, still higher!
  With a trembling and gleaming
  Still upward streaming,
In the sparkling fire
Of a dim desire;
Still higher, higher,
  With a bright pulsation
  Of aspiration,—
Higher!

Higher, still higher!
  To the lights above me;
They gleam, they love me,
They beckon me nigher,
And my waves aspire,
Still higher, higher;—
  But I fall down failing,
  Still wildly wailing—
Higher!

NIGHTINGALES SING.

Deeper now our raptures grow;
Softlier let our voices croon!
Yet more slow,
Let our happy music flow,
Sweet and slow, hush'd and low,
Now the dark cloud veils the Moon.
Sweet, O sweet!
Watch her as our wild hearts beat! . .
See! she quits the clasping cloud,
Forth she sails on shining feet,
Smiling, with her bright head bow'd!
Pour the living rapture loud!
Thick and fleet,
Sweet, O sweet,
Now the notes of rapture crowd!

SHE (*to herself*).

And *this* is Love!—Until this hour
I never lived; but like a flower
Close prest i' the bud, with sleeping senses
I drank the dark dim influences
Of sunlight, moonlight, shade, and dew.
At last I open, thrilling thro'
With Love's strange scent, which seemeth part
Of the warm life within my heart,
Part of the air I breathe . . . O bliss!
Was ever night so sweet as this?
It is enough to breathe, to be,
As if one were a flower, a tree,
A leaf o' the bough, just stirring light
With the warm breathing of the night!

SPIRITS IN THE LEAVES.

Whisper! what are they doing now?
He is kissing her white, white brow,
Turning it softly to the light,
Like a beautiful tablet marble white.

The Moon is shining upon it—lo!
Whiter it is than driven snow.
He kisseth again and speaketh gay;
Whisper, whisper! what doth he say?

III.

For ever and ever! for ever and ever!
  As the fount that upleaps, as the breezes
    that blow,
      Love thou me!
For ever and ever, for ever and ever,
  While the nightingales sing and the rose
    garlands glow,
      Love I thee!
For ever and ever, with all things to prove
  us,
In this world, in that world that bendeth
  above us,
Asleeping, awaking, in earth, as in Heaven,
By this kiss, this other, by thousands un-
  given,
By the hands which now touch thee, the
  arms that enfold thee,
By the soul in my eyes that now swoons to
  behold thee,
By starlight, by moonlight, by scented rose-
  blossoms,
By all things partaking the joy of our
  bosoms,
By the rapture within us, the rapture around
  us,
By God who has made us and Love who
  hath crown'd us,
One sense and one soul we are blent, ne'er
  to sever.
For ever and ever! for ever and ever!
More kisses to seal it * * * * For ever and
  ever!

    THE WOOD ECHOES.
      For ever and ever!

THE ASRAI.

(PROLOGUE TO THE CHANGELING.)

'Tis midnight, and the light upon my desk
Burns dim and blue, and flickers as I read
The gold-clasp'd tome, whose stainèd yellow
  leaves
Feel spongy to the touch yet rough with
  dust,
When Clari, from her chamber overhead,
Her bright hair flowing brighter from the
  brush,
Steals in, and peeps, and sits upon my
  knee,
And winds her gentle arms around my
  neck,
Then sidelong peeping, on the page antique
Rains her warm looks, and kisses as I read.

'Before man grew of the four elements,
The Asrai grew of three—fire, water, air—
Not earth,—they were not earthly. That
  was ere
The opening of the golden eye of day:
The world was silvern,—moonlight mystical
Flooded her silent continents and seas,—
And in green places the pale Asrai walked
To deep and melancholy melody,
Musing, and cast no shades.

            'These could not die
As men die; Death came later; pale yet
  fair,
Pensive yet happy, in the lonely light
The Asrai wander'd, choosing for their
  homes
All gentle places—valleys mossy deep,
Star-haunted waters, yellow strips of sand
Kissing the sad edge of the shimmering
  sea,
And porphyry caverns in the gaunt hill-
  sides,
Frosted with gems and dripping diamond
  dews
In mossy basins where the water black
Bubbled with wondrous breath. The world
  was pale,
And these were things of pallor; flowers
  and scents,
All shining things, came later; later still,
Ambition, with thin hand upon his heart,
Crept out of night and hung the heights of
  heaven
With lights miraculous; later still, man
  dug
Out of the caves the thick and golden glue
That knits together the stone ribs of earth;
Nor flowers, nor scents, the pallid Asrai
  knew,
Nor burning aspiration heavenward,
Nor blind dejection downward under earth
After the things that glitter. Their desires
Shone stationary—gentle love they felt
For one another—in their sunless world
Silent they walked and mused, knowing no
  guile,
With lives that flow'd within as quietly

As rain-drops dripping with bright measured
  beat
From mossy cavern-caves.'

     O Love! My love!
How thy heart beats! how the fond kisses
  rain!
We cannot love like those—ours is a pain,
A tumult, a delirium, a dream.
O little one of four sweet elements,
Fire on thy face, and moisture in thine
  eyes,
Thy white breast heaving with the balmy
  air,
And in thy heart and on thy kissing mouth
The warmth, the joy, the impulse, and
  delight
Of the enamour'd gentle-hearted earth
Bright with the flowery fulness of the sun!

THE CHANGELING.

A LEGEND OF THE MOONLIGHT.

I.

THE ASRAI.

'O LET him smile as Mortals may,
 And be like Mortals fair,
And let him tread the wondrous way
 Of golden earth and air;
And let the sun's celestial ray
Shine on his sense from day to day,
 Far from these waters wan,
Strew flowers and fruits upon his way,
 And make him blest,—like Man!'

Who prays? Who cries? Who is kneeling
  by night
Down in the Mere in the pale moonlight,
Where pensive Spirits come and go
In gleaming raiments as white as snow,
Walking with silent and solemn tread
That darkling bottom of silvern sands?
Like an azure heaven, far overhead,
The surface smooth of the Mere expands,
Strewn thick with glimmers of starry dew
Reflected down from the ether blue
Those Spirits behold not.

     Strangely fair,
With flashing fingers and flowing hair,
Her face upturned in the rippling rays,
Down in the Mere the Spirit prays;
And on her bosom there waking lies
Her Asrai babe with glittering eyes,—
Silent, as white as a marble stone,
It lies, but utters a feeble moan.

For ere of the earth, and the air, and the
  dew,
 And the fire, that fuseth all these to one,
Bright Man was fashion'd, and lived and
  grew,
 And walked erect in the shining sun,
When the sun itself was eyeless and dark,
 And the earth was wrapped in a starry
    night,
And the only lights that the eyes might
    mark
 Were the cold still spheres of a moon
    snow-white;
Ev'n then, of the dew and the crystal air,
 And the moonray mild, were the Asrai
    made;
And they walked and mused in the midnight
    air,
 But they had no souls and they cast no
    shade.
They knew no hunger and mad desire,
 No bitter passion of mortal birth,
For they were not fashion'd, like Man, from
  fire,
 They were not leavened, like Man, with
    earth—
Cold they were as the pale moonbeam,
Cold and pure as a vestal's dream.
Serene they dwelt in a silvern world,
 Where throbbing waters stole dusky-
    white,
Washing the feet of dark capes star-pearl'd,
 And arch'd by rainbows of rippling light.

And when to the pœan of living things,
 To the cry of the new-born worlds
    around,
Out rolled the Sun, like a shape with
  wings,
 Mighty with odour, and flame, and
    sound;
As the dim dew shaken from Earth's dark
  hair,
While she woke and gladdened supremely
  fair,

In the glorious gleam of the natal ray,
The pallid Asrai faded away!
And when with the sunlight's fiery breath
   Bright Man was moulded, and stood
     supreme,
Royal, the monarch of life and death,
Shadow'd with slumber and dower'd with
   dream,
Their trace was lost; on the human shore
Those sad pale Spirits were seen no more!

. . . Yet far away in the darkened places,
   Deep in the mountains and under the
     meres,
A few fair Spirits with sunless faces
   Lingered on with the rolling years,
And listened, listened, luminous-eyed,
   While the generations arose and died,
And watch'd, watch'd, with sad surprise,
   The gleaming glory of earth and skies,
Beyond their darkness. But ever, by night,
When the moon arose with her gentle light,
The Asrai, hidden from human seeing,
Drank the moonlight that was their being,—
Stirring about with a stealthy tread
On the mountain side, on the water's bed,
Or singing low and clasping hands,
Shadowless moving on shining sands.

But Earth with the snows of time was gray,
   When one of this race so meek and mild,
An Asrai mother, knelt down to pray,
   To heaven uplifting her little child;
For the Asrai with passionless chilly kiss
   Still mingled darkly as mortals do,
And on their bosoms bare babes like this,
   With hair soft golden and eyes of blue,
Like the eyes of stars!

              And she cried that night—
' Blessed indeed is the beauteous light,
   And blessed are those sun-phantoms fair,
For the light turns golden on their hair,
   And their faces are flowers and their breath
     is a fire,
And they move about with a sweet desire
In the amber day; and each night they lie
   Quietly smiling beneath the sky,
Till the rubies of morning again are shaken
   Upon their eyelids, and they awaken!'
And she prayed moreover—'Could this
   thing be!
Could the child I nurse upon my knee,
My own pale little one, blend with clay,
   And grow a thing of divinest day,
Like those fair mortals!'

             Then out of the air
There came in answer unto her prayer
A gentle voice; and it whispered, '*Rise!*
Steal from the water, and under the skies
Find a dead Mother, and on her bed
A new-born Babe that is also dead;
Blend thy Babe with the mortal clay,
And the thing shall be as thou hast prayed—
Thy Child shall walk in the golden day,
   Shall find a Soul, and cast a Shade!'

II.

THE CHANGELING'S BIRTH.

She rises up from the depths of the Mere
And floats away on the surface clear,
Like a swan she sails to the shadowy
   sands,
And soon on the moonlit earth she stands.
Moonbeam-like in the moonbeams bright,
   A space she lingers upon the shore,
Then steals along through the dusky light
   Up the hill and across the moor.
She sees a light that flashes afar
Through the dark like a crimson star,
Now it glimmers, and now is gone,
For shadows come and go thereon.
It comes from the shepherd's dwelling lone,
   Rudely fashioned of turf and stone;
And the sheep dog barks, and the sheep o'
   the fold
Huddle together in wintry cold;
But within the hut the light burns low,
And mortals whispering come and go;
For there on the wretched truckle bed
The wife of the shepherd lieth dead,
And her babe new born by her side doth lie
Closing its eyes with a last faint cry.

. . . The Spirit trembles, as on her hair
   Flasheth the firelight's crimson glare;
Trembles and fades; but she draweth near,
   Eager to see, eager to hear.
Close to the window-pane she flees,
And looketh in!

              In the room she sees,
None stir: 'tis empty; but on the bed
The child and mother are lying dead.

The light burns low ; the clock ticks slow ;
Spectral shadows come and go ;
From the room without a murmur creeps
Of whispered words, and one that weeps.

O Moon ! still Moon !
Sweet and white as a lily in June,
In the garden of heaven bend thy brows
And waft thy breathing into the house !
For the pallid creature of thy breath
The cottage window openeth,
And stealeth in. Like a moonray bright,
   Holding her own babe in her hands,
And bending above that bed, snow white
   She stands !

Find a dead Mother, and on her bed
A new-born Babe that is also dead.
Blend thy Babe with the mortal clay
And the thing shall pass as thou hast
   prayed:
Thy child shall walk in the golden day,
Shall find a Soul, and shall cast a Shade.

O Moon ! still Moon !
The wonderful spell is woven soon !
Breathe again on her hair and eyes,
As she creepeth out, and under the skies
Listens ! O hark ! from within is blown
A child's low murmur, an infant's moan !
Shadows darken across the pane,
   For the peasants gather wondering-eyed—
The child of the shepherd lives again,
   Smiling awake by the corpse's side.

III.

His Mortal Life.

Weary to tell and weary to hear
Were the mortal life for many a year
Of that changeling child ; but he grew on
   earth,
Knowing nought of his mystic birth,
And ever waxed more strong and fair,
With the glory of daylight on eyes and
   hair.

And the poor pale Mother Spirit smiled
From far away on her happy child,
Thinking, 'He thrives, and the golden
   hours
Fill his lap with their fruit and flowers,

And he feels the sun, and he drinks its
   light,
Growing on to a mortal's height.'
And ever nightly unseen she came
   And kiss'd him asleep, to her heart's
     desire,
Though his breath met hers with the fever'd
   flame
Of a fatal fire.

She watched him still with a hunger keen,
   Stronger than mortal mothers know ;
She hover'd o'er him, unheard, unseen,
   Wherever his feet might come and go,
In the sunless hours ; and all the day
She marked his motion from far away,
And heard his voice, through the shine and
   the shower,
Like the voice of a bird !

       But there came an hour
When the Shepherd who called him son lay
   dead,
And when he was buried the Changeling
   said—
'I will take my staff, and will leave this
   place,
And seek new fortunes—God give me grace
That I prosper well !' And away he went,
Humming an old tune, well-content,
Hopeful and fearless, merry and gay,
Over the hills and far away ;
And all alone !

IV.

His Sorrow and Sin.

       Yet not alone,
For step by step, and stone by stone,
Where'er he rested—fleet as wind,
His Spirit Mother came behind ;
Creeping to darkness all the day,
But ever in the cold moonray
Finding his footprints, kissing them,
And often where his raiment hem
Had brushed the warm dew from the grass,
Strewing pale flowers. Thus did she pass
Till brazen city gates by night
She saw him enter. Still and white,
She followed.

       Weary to tell and hear
Were the Changeling's doings for many a
   year,

But the Spirit saw as the time fled on
That his cheek grew paler, his bright eye shone
Less happy and bright; for he dwelt, behold!
Where men and women were heaping gold
And counting gems; and a yellow gleam
Shadowed the sight and darkened the dream
Of his gentle face; and by lamplight now
He read and pondered with pallid brow
O'er parchment scrolls, and tomes which told
Of mystic manners of finding gold.

Then, even then, across him came
So strange a change, so fierce a flame,
That he, forgetting fever-fraught
All things but that one thing he sought,
Was wrapt all round with light of dread!
And ever tossing on his bed
He named a woman's name, and cried
That God would bring her to his side,
His and none other's; and all day
He fevered in the hot sunray
Behind her footprints. Ne'ertheless
His thirst was turned to bitterness,
His love to pain; and soon by night
The Spirit saw him standing white,
Transfigured in a dumb despair,
And his wild shriek rose on the air,
While from a far off bridal room
Came wafted through the summer gloom
The sound of harps and lutes!

                   Then came
Long days and nights of sin and shame.
For in his agony the Man
Kept hideous orgies, and his wan
Wild features gleamed in ghastly mirth,
While naked women-snakes of earth
Twined round him fawning; and he drew
Dark curtains, shutting out the blue,
And the sweet sun; and all the nights,
In feverish flash of ghastly lights,
He slew pure sleep with sounds of sin.
Then the pale Mother peeping in
Beheld his mad distorted face,
And knew it not!

                 Time sped apace,
And lo! he changed, and forth again
He fared, amid a mighty train,
A Warrior now; and to the sound
Of martial strains his head swam round,
His heart kept time; while overhead
Strange suns of sorrow glimmered red.

. . . Weary to tell and weary to hear
The Changeling's doings for many a year!
Weary to tell how the Spirit dim
Moaning in misery followed him,
For whene'er she gazed on his features now,
On the bearded chin and the branded brow,
She shuddered, and often, when she crept
Into the tent where the warrior slept,
  She saw on his hand a blood-red stain.

And she kissed the stain again and again
With her cold pure lips,—but it would not go!

V.

THE BATTLE-FIELD.

One night she walked with a foot of snow
Thro' a battle-field; and the Moon on high
Swam thro' the film of a starry sky,
And the breath of the Moon, like hoar-frost shed,
Gleamed on the dreadful drifts of dead.
Then she saw *him* standing amid it all
Living and bloody, ghastly and tall,
With a hand on his moaning horse's mane!
And his face was awful with hate and pain,
And his eyes were mad—for beneath him lay,
Quivering there in the pale moonray,
A wounded foe—while with red right hand
He held in the air a bloody brand
To cleave him down!
                 Before his look
One moment the Spirit Mother shook;
He could not hear her, he could not see,
But she shriek'd aloud in her agony!
He glared all round him like one in dread
Of a voice from heaven or a ghost from the dead,
And he sheathed his sword with a shudder soon,
Alone in the light of the lonely Moon . . .
O Moon! immortal Moon!

VI.

THE ABBOT PAUL.

Fourscore years have come and gone,
  Since the Asrai Mother knelt down and prayed,

Since the boon was gained, and her little one
Found a soul and cast a shade ;
And now by the side of the same still Mere,
A mighty Monastery stands,
And morn and even its bell rings clear,
Tinkling over the silver sands ;
And the Asrai as they come and go
Hear the sounds in the waters below,
And ever to them the sweet sounds seem
Like distant music heard in a dream,
And they pause and smile, and they murmur ' Hark,'
With uplifted fingers !

    Old, old, old,
With hoary hair and beard snow-white,
With vacant vision and senses cold,
Crawling out to feel the light—
Like a man of marble, gaunt and tall,
Heavy with years, is the Abbot Paul.
Fourscore years have slowly shed
Their snows on the mighty Abbot's head—
But not so white are his thoughts within,
That tell of a long dark life of sin.
Ever he totters and grows to the ground,
And ever by night he hears a sound
Of voices that whisper his name and weep ;
And he starteth up in his nightly sleep
With a touch like a hand upon his hair,
And he looketh around in a sick despair,
But he seeth nought. And he prayeth low :
' Pity me, God ; and let me go
Out of the sunlight,—shaking away
This form fire-fashioned out of clay !'
And often his dark beads counteth he :
' Maria Madonna, come for me !
For I am sick of the sinful light.'

Now ever he readeth low each night
In a parchment scroll, with pictures quaint
Of many a shining-headed Saint
Smiling, each 'mid his aureole,
O'er the dark characters of the scroll ;
And ever when he totters abroad
He bears this parchment scroll of God
Against his heart ; or in the sun
He spells its letters one by one
With dim dark eyes, as he creepeth slow.

. . 'Tis a summer even. The sun sinks low,
And the light of its solemn setting lies
Golden and crimson on the skies,
Purple over the brow of the hill,
And violet dim on the waters still
Of the glassy Mere. In the zenith blue,
Already, dim as drops of dew,
Twinkle the stars !

    In his great arm-chair,
Carried out to the open air,
On the edge of a promontory sweet,
With the waters rippling at his feet,
Sits the Abbot Paul ; and his fingers cold
Still grip that parchment holy and old.
Behind his chair there standeth grim
With cold black eyeball fix'd on him,
A serving-monk.

    The air is chill,
The light is low, but he readeth still,
Mumbling the sacred words aloud ;
And ever his weary neck is bowed
At the names of Mary and every Saint ;
While ever fainter and more faint
His voice doth grow, as he murmureth :
' Holy of Holies, drink my breath !
For I am sick of the sinful light !'

. . . The sun hath sunken out of sight
In the cloudy west afar away—
Chilly it groweth, chilly and gray—
But who is this with steps so still
Coming yonder across the hill ?
Over the peaks with a silvern tread
Flashing, then rising overhead
In the open heaven of a golden June ?

O Moon ! white Summer Moon !

Down the mountain and into the Mere
The pale ray falleth, so silvern clear,
And it creepeth silently over all,
Till it shineth full on the Abbot Paul,
Where he sits and prays. O see ! O see !
Sadder, stiller, groweth he,
But his eyes still burn with a dying gleam ;
While faint, far off, as in a dream,
He hears a murmur, he sees a light.

Silently, coldly, marble white,
Pale and pure as the moonray dim,
Smiling, outstretching her arms to him,
His Spirit Mother upriseth now !

A light not human is on his brow,
A light no human is in his eyes—
Fold by fold, like a dark disguise,

The mortal dress is dropping away ;
Silently, slowly, sinks the clay ;
His eyes see clear by some mystic spell,
And he knoweth the gentle presence well.

'O Mother ! Mother !'

                She answereth low :
' Come from the gleam of the golden glow,
From the wicked flush of the fever'd strife,
Back to the mystical moonlight life !
Thy heart is heavy, thy sense is drear,
Weary with wandering many a year—
Come from the sorrows of the Sun !
My own pale darling, my little one !'

'O Mother ! Mother !'

                Her arms so dim
Are round his neck, and she kisseth him !
She smoothes his hair with a gentle hand,
And she sings a song of the moonlight land.
He listens and listens, but still in a dream
Looking afar off his dark eyes gleam,
Beyond her, through her, at some strange
    thing
There on the hilltops, beckoning ! . . .

Dead in his chair lies the Abbot Paul,
But a Shape stands by him, stately and tall,
And another Shape upon her knee
Is looking up in her agony.

' O Mother ! Mother !' the tall Shape cries,
Gazing on her with gentle eyes—
'O Mother, Mother, I cannot stay—
A voice is summoning me away—
Up the shining track of the sun,
  Past the sphere of the spectral moon,
Further, higher, my path must run—
I have found a Soul, and thou hast thy
    boon ;
And the Soul is a scourge, and the scourge
    a fire,

And it shoots me onward to strive and
    soar,
For this is the end of thy heart's desire—
  I rest not, stay not, for evermore.
O kiss me, Mother, before I go !'

They kiss each other, those shapes of snow,
They cling in the moonlight, they kiss each
    other—
'Child, my child !' and 'Mother ! Mother !'

Silently, swiftly, through the air
Riseth one like a meteor fair,
Riseth one with a last wild cry,
  While the other sinks in a silent swoon,
And whiter, brighter, over the sky,
  Burneth the light of that night of June !

O Moon ! sad Summer Moon !

TO CLARI.

WITH THE PRECEDING POEM.

THOUGH on the dullest dust we tread,
Our days are closed about with dread ;
Before our footsteps and behind
Burns the white Light that keeps us blind.

If Life were all, if Love were clay,
If the great Dream could pass away,
If thou or I could cease to be,
That Light would fade, and we should *see*:

Yea, see and know, and swiftly pass,
Like shapes from a magician's glass ;—
But girt by godhead we remain,
Though human systems wax and wane.

Enough ! we fear not, thou and I,
Knowing we were not born to die,
Because, at every step we tread,
Our days are closed about with dread.

North Coast, and other Poems.
(1867-68.)

MEG BLANE.

I.
STORM.

' LORD, hearken to me !
  Save all poor souls at sea !
Thy breath is on their cheeks,—
  Their cheeks are wan wi' fear ;
Nae man speaks,
  For wha could hear ?
The wild white water screams,
  The wind cries loud ;
The fireflaught gleams
  On tattered sail and shroud !
Under the red mast-light
  The hissing surges slip ;
Thick reeks the storm o' night
  Round him that steers the ship,—
And his een are blind,
  And he kens not where they run.
LORD, be kind !
  Whistle back Thy wind,
For the sake of CHRIST Thy Son ! '

. . . And as she prayed she knelt not on her knee,
But, standing on the threshold, looked to Sea,
Where all was blackness and a watery roar,
Save when the dead light, flickering far away,
Flash'd on the line of foam upon the shore,
And showed the ribs of reef and surging bay !
There was no sign of life across the dark,
No piteous light from fishing-boat or bark,
Albeit for such she hush'd her heart to pray.
With tattered plaid wrapt tight around her form,
She stood a space, spat on by wind and rain,
Then, sighing deep, and turning from the Storm,
  She crept into her lonely hut again.

'Twas but a wooden hut under the height,
  Shielded in the black shadow of the crag :
One blow of such a wind as blew that night
  Could rend so rude a dwelling like a rag.
There, gathering in the crannies overhead,
Down fell the spouting rain heavy as lead,—
  So that the old roof and the rafters thin
Dript desolately, looking on the surf,
While blacker rain-drops down the walls of turf
  Splash'd momently on the mud-floor within.
There, swinging from the beam, an earthen lamp
  Waved to the wind and glimmered in the damp,
And shining in the chamber's wretchedness,
  Illumed the household things of the poor place,
And flicker'd faintly on the woman's face
  Sooted with rain, and on her dripping dress.
A miserable den wherein to dwell,
  And yet she loved it well.

' O Mither, are ye there ? '
A deep voice filled the dark ; she thrill'd to hear ;
With hard hand she pushed back her wild wet hair,
And kissed him. 'Whisht, my bairn, for Mither's near.'
Then on the shuttle bed a figure thin
  Sat rubbing sleepy eyes ;
A bearded man, with heavy hanging chin,
  And on his face a light not over-wise.
' Water ! ' he said ; and deep his thirst was quelled
Out of the broken pitcher she upheld,

And yawning sleepily, he gazed around,
And stretched his limbs again, and soon
   slept sound.
Stooping, she smooth'd his pillow 'neath
   his head,
Still looking down with eyes liquid and
   mild,
And while she gazed, softly he slumbered,
   That bearded man, her child.
And a child's dreams were his; for as he
   lay,
He uttered happy cries as if at play,
And his strong hand was lifted up on
   high
As if to catch the bird or butterfly;
And often to his bearded lips there came
   That lonely woman's name;
And though the wrath of Ocean roared
   so near,
   That one sweet word
   Was all the woman heard,
   And all she cared to hear.

Not old in years, though youth had passed
   away,
And the thin hair was tinged with silver
   gray,
Close to the noontide of the day of life,
She stood, calm featured like a wedded
   wife;
And yet no wedded wife was she, but one
   Whose foot had left the pathways of the
   just,
Yet meekly, since her penance had been
   done,
   Her soft eyes sought men's faces, not the
   dust.
Her tearful days were over: she had found
Firm footing, work to do upon the ground;
The Elements had welded her at length
   To their own truth and strength.

This woman was no slight and tear-strung
   thing,
Whose easy sighs fall soft on suffering,
But one in whom no stranger's eyes would
   seek
   For pity mild and meek.
Man's height was hers—man's strength and
   will thereto,
   Her shoulders broad, her step man-like
   and long;

'Mong fishermen she dwelt, a rude, rough
   crew,
   And more than one had found her hand
   was strong.
And yet her face was gentle, though the sun
   Had made it dark and dun;
   Her silver-threaded hair
Was combed behind her ears with cleanly
   care;
And she had eyes liquid and sorrow-fraught,
   And round her mouth were delicate lines,
   that told
She was a woman sweet with her own
   thought,
Though built upon a large, heroic mould.

   Who did not know Meg Blane?
What hearth but heard the deeds that Meg
   had done?
   What fisher of the main
But knew her, and her little-witted son?
For in the wildest waves of that wild coast
Her black boat hover'd and her net was lost,
And lonely in the watery solitude
The son and mother fished for daily food.
When on calm nights the herring hosts
   went by,
   Her frail boat followed the red smacks
   from shore
And steering in the stern the man would lie
   While Meg was hoisting sail or plying
   oar;
Till, a black speck against the morning sky,
   The boat came homeward, with its silver
   store.
And Meg was cunning in the ways of
   things,
   Watching what every changing lineament
Of wind and sky and cloud and water
   meant,
Knowing how Nature threatens ere she
   springs.
She knew the clouds as shepherds know
   their sheep,
   To eyes unskilled alike, yet different
   each;
She knew the wondrous voices of the Deep;
   The tones of sea-birds were to her a
   speech.
Much faith was hers in GOD, who was her
   guide;
   Courage was hers such as GOD gives to
   few,

For she could face His terrors fearless-eyed,
    Yet keep the still sane woman's nature true.
Lives had she snatched out of the waste by night,
    When wintry winds were blowing;
To sick-beds sad her presence carried light,
    When (like a thin sail lessening out of sight)
Some rude, rough life to the unknown Gulf was going;
    For men who scorned a feeble woman's wail
Would heark to one so strong and brave as *she*,
    Whose face had braved the lightning and the gale,
        And ne'er grown pale,
Before the shrill threat of the murderous Sea.

Yet often, as she lay a-sleeping there,
    This woman started up and blush'd in shame,
Stretching out arm embracing the thin air,
    Naming an unknown name;
There was a hearkening hunger in her face
If sudden footsteps sounded on her ear;
And when strange seamen came unto the place
She read their faces in a wretched fear;
And finding not the object of her quest,
Her hand she held hard on her heaving breast,
And wore a white look, and drew feeble breath,
    Like one that hungereth.

It was a night of summer, yet the wind
    Had wafted from God's wastes the rain-clouds dank,
Blown out Heaven's thousand eyes and left it blind,
Though now and then the Moon gleamed moist behind
    The rack, till, smitten by the drift, she sank.
        But the Deep roared;
Sucked to the black clouds, spumed the foam-fleck'd main,
While lightning rent the storm-rack like a sword,
And earthward rolled the gray smoke of the Rain.

'Tis late, and yet the woman doth not rest,
But sitteth with chin drooping on her breast:
Weary she is, yet will not take repose;
Tired are her eyes, and yet they cannot close;
She rocketh to and fro upon her chair,
    And stareth at the air!

Far, far away her thoughts were travelling:
    They could not rest—they wandered far and fleet,
As the storm-petrels o'er the waters wing,
    And cannot find a place to rest their feet;
And in her ear a thin voice murmuréd,
    ' If he be *dead*—be *dead!* '
Then, even then, the woman's face went white
And awful, and her eyes were fixed in fear,
For suddenly all the wild screams of night
    Were hushed: the Wind lay down; and she could hear
Strange voices gather round her in the gloom,
Sounds of invisible feet across the room,
    And after that the rustle of a shroud,
        And then a creaking door,
    And last the coronach, full shrill and loud,
Of women clapping hands and weeping sore.

Now Meg knew well that ill was close at hand,
    On water or on land,
Because the Glamour touched her lids like breath,
And scorch'd her heart: but in a waking swoon,
Quiet she stayed,—not stirring,—cold as death,
    And felt those voices croon;
Then suddenly she heard a human shout,
The hurried falling of a foot without,
Then a hoarse voice—a knocking at the door—
    ' *Meg, Meg! A Ship ashore!* '

P

Now mark the woman! She hath risen her height,
Her dripping plaid is wrapt around her tight,
Tight clenchëd in her palm her fingers are
Her eye is steadfast as a fixëd star.
One look upon her child—he sleepeth on—
One step unto the door, and she is gone:
Barefooted out into the dark she fares,
    And comes where, rubbing eyelids thick with sleep,
The half-clad fishers mingle oaths and prayers,
    And look upon the Deep.

    . . . Black was the oozy lift,
    Black was the sea and land;
Hither and thither, thick with foam and drift,
    Did the deep Waters shift,
Swinging with iron clash on stone and sand.
Faintlier the heavy Rain was falling,
Faintlier, faintlier the Wind was calling,
    With hollower echoes up the drifting dark!
While the swift rockets shooting through the night
Flash'd past the foam-flecked reef with phantom light,
    And showed the piteous outline of the bark,
Rising and falling like a living thing,
    Shuddering, shivering,
While, howling beastlike, the white breakers there
Spat blindness in the dank eyes of despair.
Then one cried, 'She has sunk!'—and on the shore
Men shook, and on the heights the women cried;
But, lo! the outline of the bark once more!
    While flashing faint the blue light rose and died.
Ah, GOD, put out Thy hand! all for the sake
Of little ones, and weary hearts that wake
    Be gentle! chain the fierce waves with a chain!
Let the gaunt seaman's little boys and girls
Sit on his knee and play with his black curls
    Yet once again!

And breathe the frail lad safely through the foam
Back to the hungry mother in her home!
And spare the bad man with the frenzied eye;
Kiss him, for CHRIST'S sake, bid Thy Death go by—
    He hath no heart to die!

Now faintlier blew the wind, the thin rain ceased,
The thick cloud cleared like smoke from off the strand,
For, lo! a bright blue glimmer in the East,—
    GOD putting out His hand!
And overhead the rack grew thinner too,
    And through the smoky gorge
The Wind drave past the stars, and faint they flew
    Like sparks blown from a forge!
And now the thousand foam-flames o' the Sea
    Hither and thither flashing visibly;
And gray lights hither and thither came and fled,
Like dim shapes searching for the drownëd dead;
And where these shapes most thickly glimmer'd by,
Out on the cruel reef the black hulk lay,
And cast, against the kindling eastern sky,
    Its shape gigantic on the shrouding spray.

Silent upon the shore, the fishers fed
    Their eyes on horror, waiting for the close,
When in the midst of them a shrill voice rose:
    'The boat! the boat!' it said.
Like creatures startled from a trance, they turned
To her who spake; tall in the midst stood she,
With arms uplifted, and with eyes that yearned
    Out on the murmuring Sea.
Some, shrugging shoulders, homeward turned their eyes,
    And others answered back in brutal speech;

But some, strong-hearted, uttering shouts and cries,
  Followed the fearless woman up the beach.
A rush to seaward—black confusion—then
A struggle with the surf upon the strand—
'Mid shrieks of women, cries of desperate men,
  The long oars smite, the black boat springs from land!
    Around the thick spray flies;
The waves roll on and seem to overwhelm.
  With blowing hair and onward-gazing eyes
The woman stands erect, and grips the helm. . . .

Now fearless heart, Meg Blane, or all must die!
Let not the skill'd hand thwart the steadfast eye
The crested wave comes near,—crag-like it towers
Above you, scattering round its chilly showers:
One flutter of the hand, and all is done!
Now steel thy heart, thou woman-hearted one!
  Softly the good helm guides;
Round to the liquid ridge the boat leaps light,—
Hidden an instant,—on the foaming height,
Dripping and quivering like a bird, it rides.
Athwart the ragged rift the Moon looms pale,
  Driven before the gale,
And making silvern shadows with her breath,
Where on the sighing Sea it shimmereth;
And, lo! the light illumes the reef; 'tis shed
  Full on the wreck, as the dark boat draws nigh.
A crash!—the wreck upon the reef is fled;
  A scream!—and all is still beneath the sky,
    Save the wild waters as they whirl and cry.

II.

DEAD CALM.

DAWN; and the Deep was still. From the bright strand,
Meg, shading eyes against the morning sun,
Gazed seaward. After trouble, there was peace.

Smooth, many-coloured as a ring-dove's neck
Stretch'd the still Sea, and on its eastern rim
The dewy light, with liquid yellow beams,
Gleamed like a sapphire. Overhead, soft airs
To feathery cirrus flecked the lightening blue,
Beneath, the Deep's own breathing made a breeze;
And up the weedy beach the blue waves crept,
Falling in one thin line of cream-white foam.

Seaward the woman gazed, with keen eye fixed
On a dark shape that floated on the calm,
Drifting as seaweed; still and black it lay,—
The outline of a lifeless human shape:
And yet it was no drownèd mariner,
For she who looked was smiling, and her face
Looked merry; still more merry when a boat,
With pale and timorous fishermen, drew nigh;
And as the fearful boatmen paused and gazed,
A boat's length distant, leaning on their oars,
The shape took life—dash'd up a dripping head,
Screaming—flung up its limbs with flash of foam,
And, with a shrill and spirit-thrilling cry,
Dived headlong, as a monster of the main
Plunges deep down when startled on its couch
Of glassy waters. 'Twas the woman's child,
The witless water-haunter—Angus Blane.

For Angus Blane, not fearful as the wise
Are fearful, loved the Ocean like a thing

Born amid algæ of the slimy ooze,
A child, he sported on its sands, and crept
Splashing with little feet amid the foam ;
And when his limbs were stronger, and he reached
A young man's stature, the great Gulf had grown
Fair and familiar as his mother's face.
Far out he swam, on windless summer days,
Floating like fabled mermen far from land,
Plunging away from startled fishermen
With eldrich cry and wild phantasmic glare,
And in the untrodden halls below the sea
Awaking wondrous echoes that had slept
Since first the briny Spirit stirred and breathed.
On nights of summer in the gleaming bay
He glistened like a sea-snake in the moon,
Splashing with trail of glistening phosphor-fire,
And laughing shrill till echo answer'd him,
And the pale helmsman on the passing boat,
Thinking some Demon of the waters cried,
Shivered and prayed. His playmates were the waves,
The sea his playground. On his ears were sounds
Sweeter than human voices. On his sense,
Though sadden'd with his silent life, there stole
A motion and a murmur that at times
Brake through his lips, informing witless words
With strange sea-music. In his infancy,
Children had mocked him : he had shunned their sports,
And haunted lonely places, nurturing
The bright, fierce, animal splendour of a soul
That ne'er was clouded by the mental mists
That darken oft the dreams of wiser men.
Only in winter seasons he was sad ;
For then the loving Spirit of the Deep
Repulsed him, and its smile was mild no more ;
And on the strand he wandered ; from dark caves
Gazed at the Tempest ; and from day to day
Moaned to his mother for the happy time

When swifts are sailing on the wind o' the South,
And summer smiles afar off through the rain,
Bringing her golden circlet to the Sea.

And as the deepening of strange melody,
Caught from the unknown shores beyond the seas,
Was the outspreading of his life to her
Who bare him ; yea, at times, the woman's womb
Seemed laden with the load of him unborn,
So close his being clave unto her flesh,
So link'd was his strange spirit with her own.
The faint forebodings of her heart, when first
She saw the mind-mists in his infant eyes,
And knew him witless, turned as years wore on
Into more spiritual, less selfish love
Than common mothers feel ; and he had power
To make her nature deeper, more alive
Unto the supernatural feet that walk
Our dark and troubled waters. Thence was born
Much of her strength upon the Sea, her trust
In the Sea's MASTER ! thence, moreover, grew
Her faith in visions, warnings, fantasies,
Such as came ever thronging on her heart
When most her eyes looked inward—to the place
Fraught with her secret sorrow.

     As she gazed,
Smiling, the bearded face of Angus rose
Nearer to shore, and panting in the sun,
Smiled at the fishers. Then the woman turned,
And took, with man-like step and slow, a path
That, creeping through the shadows of the cliffs,
Wound to the clachan. In the clear, bright dawn
Lay Thornock glittering, while, thin and blue,
Curl'd peat-smoke from the line of fisher-huts
That parted the high shingle from the land.

The tide was low: amid the tangled weeds
The many-colour'd rocks and sparkling
  pools,
Went stooping men and women, seeking
  spoil,
Treasure or drift-wood floating from the
  wreck;
Beyond, some stood in fish-boats, peering
  down,
Seeking the drownèd dead; and, near at
  hand,
So near, a tall man might have waded
  thither
With a dry beard, the weedy reef loom'd
  red,
And there the white-fowl ever and anon
Rose like a flash of foam, whirl'd in the
  air,
And, screaming, settled. But not thither-
  ward
Now look'd Meg Blane. Along the huts
  she went—
Among the rainy pools where played and
  cried
Brown and barefooted bairns—among the
  nets
Stretch'd steaming in the sun—until she
  reached
The cottage she was seeking. At the door,
Smoking his pipe, a grizzly Fisher sat,
Looking to sea. With him she spake
  awhile,
Then, with a troubled look, enter'd the
  hut,
And sought the inner chamber.

      Faint and pale
Light glimmer'd through a loop-hole in the
  wall,
A deep white streak across the sand-strewn
  floor,
All else in shadow; and the room was still,
Save for a heavy breathing, as of one
In quiet sleep. Within the wall's recess,
On the rude bed of straw the sleeper lay,
His head upon his arm, the sickly light
Touching his upturn'd face; while Meg
  drew near,
And gazed upon him with a stranger's eyes,
Quiet and pitying. Though his sleep was
  sound,
His dreams were troubled. Throwing up
  his arms,
He seem'd to beckon, muttering; then his
  teeth
Clench'd tight, a dark frown wrinkled on
  his brow,
And still he lay like one awaiting doom;
But suddenly, in agony supreme,
He breathed like one who struggles, sinks,
  and drowns;
Strangling, with wavering arms and quiver-
  ing limbs,
And screaming in his throat, he fought for
  life;
Till, half-awakening with the agony,
His glazèd eyes he opened, glaring round,
While Meg drew shivering back into the
  shade;
Again, with deeper breath, as if relieved,
He dropp'd his bearded face upon his arm,
And dream'd again.

      Then Meg stole stilly forth,
And in the outer chamber found a lamp,
And lit the same in silence, and returned
On tiptoe to the sleeper. As she went,
White as a murdered woman's grew her
  face,
Her teeth were clench'd together; and her
  eyes
With ring on ring of widening wonder
  glared
In fever'd fascination upon him
Who slumbered. Closer still she crept,
Holding the lamp aloft, until his breath
Was hot upon her cheek,—so gaunt, so
  white,
It seemed her time was come. Yet in her
  look
Was famine. As one famish'd looks on food
After long agony, and thinks it dream,
She gazed and gazed, nor stirred, nor
  breathed, nor lived,
Save in her spirit's hunger flashing forth
Out of her face; till suddenly the man,
Half-opening his eyes, reached out his arms
And gript her, crying, 'Silence! pray to
  GOD!
She's sinking!' then, with shrill and awful
  groan,
Awakened.

      And the woman would have fled,
Had he not gript her. In her face he
  gazed,

Thrusting one hand into his silvered hair,
Seeking to gather close his scattered thoughts,
And his eye brightened, and he murmured low,
'Where am I? Dead or living? Ah, I live!
The ship? the ship?' Meg answered not, but shrank
Into the shadow; till she saw the mists
Pass from his bearded face and leave it clear,
And heard his voice grow calmer, measured now
By tranquil heart-beats. Then he asked again,
'The ship? How many live of those aboard?'
And when she answered he alone was saved,
He groaned; but with a sailor's fearless look,
'Thank GOD for that!' he said; 'and yet He might
Have spared a better man. Where am I, friend?'
'On the north coast,' said Meg, 'upon the shore
At Thornock.'

  Could the seaman, while she spake,
Have marked the lurid light on that pale face,
All else,—the Storm, the terrible fight for life,—
Had been forgotten; but his wearied eye
Saw dimly. Grasping still her quivering wrist,
He question'd on; and, summoning strength of heart,
In her rude speech she told him of the storm:
How from the reef the rending Ship had rolled
As aid drew nigh; how, hovering near its tomb,
The fishers from the whirling waters dragged
Two drownèd seamen, and himself, a corpse
In seeming; how by calm and tender care,
They wound his thin and bloody thread of life
Out of the slowly-loosening hands of Death.

III.
A TROUBLED DEEP.

THEN, with strange trouble in her eyes, Meg Blane
Stole swiftly back unto her hut again,
Like one that flyeth from some fearful thing;
Then sat and made a darkness, covering
Her face with apron old, thinking apart;
And yet she scarce could think, for ache of heart,
But saw dead women and dead men go by,
And felt the wind, and heard the waters cry,
And on the waters, as they washed to shore,
Saw one Face float alone and glimmer hoar
Through the green darkness of the breaking brine.

  And Meg was troubled deep, nor could divine
The wherefore of her trouble, since 'twas clear
The face long wearied for at last was near,
Since all her waiting on was at an end.
Ay, Meg was dull, and could not comprehend
How GOD put out His breath that day, and blew
Her lover to her feet before she knew,
Yet misted the dull future from her sight;
Wherefore she stared stark down on her delight
As on a dead face washing in from sea.
But when she understood full certainly
The thing had come according to her prayer,
Her strength came back upon her unaware,
And she thank'd GOD, albeit the pleasure seemed
Less absolute a bliss than she had dreamed
When it was a sweet trouble far away;
For she was conscious how her hair was gray,
Her features worn, her flesh's freshness gone,
Through toiling in the sun and waiting on;
And quietly she murmur'd, weeping not,
'Perchance—for men forget—he hath forgot!'

  And two long days she was too dazed and weak
To step across the sands to him, and speak;

But on the third day, pale with her intent,
She took the great hand of her son, and went,
Not heeding while the little-witted one,
Mouth'd at the sea and muttered in the sun,
And firmly stepping on along the shore,
She saw, afar off at the cottage door,
The figure of her shipwrecked mariner;
When, deeply troubled by a nameless fear,
She lingered, and she lingered, pale and wan.

Then, coming near, she noted how the man
Sat sickly, holding out his arm to please
A fisher child he held between his knees,
Whose eyes looked on the mighty arm and bare,
Where ships, strange faces, anchors, pictured were,
Prick'd blue into the skin with many a stain;
And, sharply marking the man's face, Meg Blane
Was cheered and holpen, and she trembled less,
Thinking, 'His heart is full of kindliness.'
And, feeling that the thing if to be done
Must be done straight, she hastened with her son,
And, though she saw the man's shape growing dim,
Came up with sickly smile and spake to him,
Pausing not, though she scarce could hear or see—
'Has Angus Macintyre forgotten me?'
And added quickly, 'I am Maggie Blane!'

Whereat the man was smit by sudden pain
And wonder—yea, the words he heard her speak
Were like a jet of fire upon his cheek;
And, rising up erect, 'Meg Blane!' he cried,
And, white and chilly, thrust the bairn aside,
And peered upon the woman all amazed,
While, pressing hard upon her heart, she gazed
Blankly at the dim mist she knew was he.

For a short space both stood confusedly,
In silence; but the man was first to gain
Calmness to think and power to speak again;

And, though his lips were bloodless and prest tight,
Into his eyes he forced a feeble light,
Taking her shivering hand, naming her name
In forced kind tones, yet with a secret shame;—
Nor sought to greet her more with touch or kiss.
But she, who had waited on so long for this,
Feeling her hand between his fingers rest,
Could bear no more, but fell upon his breast,
Sobbing and moaning like a little bairn.

Then, with her wild arms round him, he looked stern,
With an unwelcome burden ill at ease,
While her full heart flowed out in words like these—
'At last! at last! O Angus, let me greet!'[1]
God's good! I ever hoped that we would meet!
Lang, lang hae I been waiting by the Sea,
Waiting and waiting, praying on my knee;
And God *said* I should look again on you,
And, though I scarce believed, God's word comes true,
And He hath put an end to my distress!'—
E'en as she spoke, her son plucked at her dress,
Made fierce grimaces at the man, and tried
To draw her from the breast whereon she cried;
But looking up, she pointed to her child,
And look'd into her lover's eyes, and smiled.
'God help him, Angus! 'Tis *the Bairn!*'
she said;—
Nor noted how the man grew shamed and red,
With child and mother ill at ease and wroth,
And wishing he were many a mile from both.

For now Meg's heart was wandering far away,
And to her soul it seemed but yesterday
That, standing inland in a heathery dell,
At dead of night, she bade this man farewell,
And heard him swear full fondly in her ear
Sooner or late to come with gold and gear,

[1] *To greet;* Anglicè, to weep.

And marry her in church by holy rite;
And at the memory a quiet light,
Rose-like and maiden, came upon her face,
And softened her tall shape to nameless grace,
As warm winds blowing on a birk-tree green
Make it one rippling sheet of radiant sheen.

But soon from that remembrance driven again
By the man's silence and his pallid pain,
She shivered for a moment as with cold,
And left his bosom, looking grieved and old,
Yet smiling, forcing a strange smile, and seeking
For tokens in his face more sweet than speaking.
But he was dumb, and with a pallid frown,
Twitching his fingers quick, was looking down.
'What ails thee, Angus?' cried the woman, reading
His face with one sharp look of interceding;
Then, looking downward too, she paused apart,
With blood like water slipping through her heart,
Because she thought, 'Alas, if it should be
That Angus cares no more for mine and me,
Since I am old and worn with sharp distress,
And men like pretty looks and daintiness;
And since we parted twenty years have past,
And that, indeed, is long for a man's love to last!'

But, agonised with looking at her woe,
And bent to end her hope with one sharp blow,
The troubled man, uplifting hands, spake thus,
In rapid accents, sharp and tremulous:
'Too late, Meg Blane! seven years ago I wed
Another woman, deeming you were dead,—
And I have bairns!' And there he paused, for fear,

As when, with ghostly voices in her ear,
While in her soul, as in a little well
The silver moonlight of the Glamour fell,
She had been wont to hark of nights alone,
So stood she now, not stirring, still as stone,
While in her soul, with desolate refrain,
The words, '*Too late!*' rang o'er and o'er again;
Into his face she gazed with ghastly stare;
Then raising her wild arms into the air,
Pinching her face together in sharp fear,
She quivered to the ground without a tear,
And put her face into her hands, and thrust
Her hair between her teeth, and spat it forth like dust.

And though, with pity in his guilty heart,
The man spake on and sought to heal her smart,
She heard not, but was dumb and deaf in woe;
But when, in pain to see her grieving so,
Her son put down his hand, and named her name,
And whispered, 'Mither! mither! let us hame!'
She seized the hand, and smoothed her features wan,
And rose erect, not looking at the man,
But, gazing down, moved slowly from the spot.

Over this agony I linger not.
Nor shall I picture how on that sad shore
They met and spoke and parted yet once more,
So calmly that the woman understood
Her hope indeed had gone away for good.
But ere the man departed from the place
It seemed to Meg, contemplating his face,
Her love for him had ne'er been so intense
As it had seemed when he was far from thence;
And many a thing in him seemed littlehearted
And mean and loveless; so that ere they parted
She seemed unto her sorrow reconciled.
And when he went away, she almost smiled,
But bitterly, then turned to toil again,
And felt most hard to all the world of men.

IV.

'And the Spirit of God moved upon the waters.'

LORD, with how small a thing
Thou canst prop up the heart against the
  grave!
    A little glimmering
      Is all we crave!
    The lustre of a love
      That hath no being,
The pale point of a little star above
    Flashing and fleeing,
      Contents our seeing.
The house that never will be built; the gold
    That never will be told;
The task we leave undone when we are
  cold;
The dear face that returns not, but is lying,
Lick'd by the leopard, in an Indian cave;
The coming rest that cometh not, till, sigh-
  ing,
We turn our tremulous gaze upon the
  grave.
    And, Lord, how should we dare
      Thither in peace to fall,
    But for a feeble glimmering even *there*—
Falsest, some sigh, of all?
We are as children in Thy hands indeed,
And Thou hast easy comfort for our need,—
The shining of a lamp, the tinkling of a
  bell,
      Content us well.

And even when Thou bringest to our eyes
  A thing long-sought, to show its worth-
  lessness,
Anon we see another thing arise,
And we are comforted in our distress;
And, waiting on, we watch it glittering,
Till in its turn it seems a sorry thing;
    And even as we weep
Another rises, and we smile again!
Till, wearied out with watching on in vain,
    We fall to sleep.

And oft one little light that *looks* divine
  Is all some strong Soul seeks on mortal
  ground;
    There are no more to shine
    When that one thing is found.
If it be worthless, then what shall suffice?
The lean hand grips a speck that was a
  spark,
    The heart is turned to ice,
    And all the world is dark.
Hard are Thy ways when that one thing is
  sought,
Found, touch'd, and proven nought.
Far off it is a mighty magic, strong
    To lead a life along.
But, lo! it shooteth thitherward, and now
  Droppeth, a rayless stone, upon the
  sod.—
The world is lost: perchance not even
  Thou
    Survivest it, Lord God!

    In poverty, in pain,
    For weary years and long,
One faith, one fear, had comforted Meg
  Blane,
  Yea, made her brave and strong;
A faith so faint it seemed not faith at all,
Rather a trouble and a dreamy fear,—
A hearkening for a voice, for a footfall,
  She never hoped in sober heart to hear:
    This had been all her cheer!
    Yet with this balm
      Her Soul might have slept calm
    For many another year.
    In terror and in desolation, she
      Had been sustained,
    And never felt abandoned utterly
      While that remained.
Lord, in how small and poor a space can
  hide
The motives of our patience and our pride,—
The clue unto the fortunate man's distress,
The secret of the hero's fearlessness!
What had sustained this Woman on the
  sea
    When strong men turned to flee?
    Not courage, not despair,
    Not pride, not household care,
    Not faith in Thee!
Nought but a hungry instinct blind and
  dim—
    A fond pathetic pain:
A dreamy wish to gaze again on him
  She never wholly hoped to see again!

Not all at once,—not in an hour, a day
  Did the strong Woman feel her force
  depart,
Or know how utterly had passed away
    The strength of her sad heart.

It was not Love she missed, for Love was
 dead,
 And surely had been dead long ere she
 knew ;
She did not miss the man's face when it fled,
 As passionate women do.
She saw him walk into the world again,
 And had no pain ;
She shook him by the hand, and watched
 him go,
 And thought it better so.
She turned to her hard task-work as of old,
 Tending her bearded child with love ten-
 fold,
Hoisted the sails and plied the oar,
 Went wandering out from shore,
 And for a little space
 Wore an unruffled face,
Though wind and water helped her heart
 no more.
But, mark : she knelt less often on her
 knees,
 For, labour as she might,
 By day or night,
She could not toil enough to give her ease.
And presently her tongue, with sharper
 chimes,
 Chided at times ;
And she who had endured such sharp dis-
 tress
Grew peevish, pain'd at her own peevish-
 ness ;
 And though she did not weep,
 Her features grew disfigur'd, dark, and
 dead,
And in the night, when bitterest mourners
 sleep,
 She feverishly tossed upon her bed.

Slowly the trouble grew, and soon she found
 Less pleasure in the fierce yet friendly
 Sea ;
The wind and water had a wearier sound,
 The moon and stars were sick as corpse-
 lights be ;
Then more and more strange voices filled
 her ear,
 And ghostly feet came near,
And strange fire blew her eyelids down, and
 then
 Dead women and dead men
Dripping with phosphor, rose, and ere she
 wist

Went by in a cold mist ;
Nor left her strengthen'd in her heart and
 bold,
 As they had done of old ;
But ever after they had stolen away
 She had no heart to pray :
 Bitter and dull and cold,
Her Soul crawl'd back into the common
 day.

Out of the East by night
 Drew the dark drifting cloud ;
The air was hushed with snow-flakes
 wavering white,
 But the seas below were loud ;
And out upon the reef the rapid light
 Rose from a shipwrecked bark
 Into the dark !
Pale stood the fishers, while the wind wail'd
 by,
Till suddenly they started with one cry,
And forth into the foam the black boat
 flew,
And fearless to their places leapt the crew.
Then one called out, ' *Meg Blane !*'
But Meg stood by, and trembled and was
 dumb,
Till, smit unto the heart by sudden pain,
Into her hair she thrust her fingers numb,
 And fell upon the sands,
Nor answer'd while the wondering fishers
 called,
But tore the slippery seaweed with her
 hands,
 And screamed, and was appalled.

For, lo ! the Woman's spiritual strength
 Snapt like a thread at length,
And tears, ev'n such as suffering women
 cry,
 Fell from her eyes anon ;
And she knew well, although she knew not
 why,
The charm she had against the deep was
 gone !
 And after that dark hour,
 She was the shadow of a strong
 Soul dead,
 All terrible things of power
 Turned into things of dread,
And all the peace of all the world had
 fled.

Then only in still weather did she dare
  To seek her bread on Ocean, as of old,
And oft in tempest time her shelf was bare,
  Her hearth all black and cold ;
Then very bitterly, with heart gone wild,
    She clung about her child,
And hated all the earth beneath the skies,
Because she saw the hunger in his eyes.
For on his mother's strength the witless
    wight
      Had leant for guide and light,
And food had ever come into his hand,
And he had known no thought of suffer-
    ing ;
Yea, all his life and breath on sea and land
    Had been an easy thing.
And now there was a change in his sole
    friend
      He could not comprehend.
Yet slowly to the shade of her distress
His nature shaped itself in gentleness !
And when he found her weeping, he too
    wept,
And, if she laughed, laughed out in com-
    pany ;
Nay, often to the fisher-huts he crept,
And begged her bread, and brought it
    tenderly,
Holding it to her mouth, and till she ate
Touching no piece, although he hungered
    sore.
And these things were a solace to her fate,
But wrung her heart the more.

Thus to the bitter dolour of her days
In witless mimicry he shaped his ways !
They fared but seldom now upon the Sea,
  But wandered 'mid the marshes hand in
    hand,
Hunting for faggots on the inland lea,
  Or picking dulse for food upon the
    strand.
Something had made the world more sad
    and strange,
But easily he changéd with the change.
For in the very trick of woe he clad
His features, and was sad since she was sad,
Yea, leant his chin upon his hands like her,
  Looking at vacancy ; and when the Deep
  Was troublous, and she started up from
    sleep,
He too awoke, with fearful heart astir ;
And still, the more her bitter tears she shed

Upon his neck, marking that mimic-woe,
The more in blind deep love he fashionéd
His grief to hers, and was contented so.

But as a tree inclineth weak and bare
Under an unseen weight of wintry air,
Beneath her load the weary Woman bent,
And, stooping double, waver'd as she went ;
And the days snow'd their snows upon her
    head
      As they went by,
    And ere a year had fled
      She felt that she must die.

Then like a thing whom very witlessness
  Maketh indifferent, she lingered on,
Not caring to abide with her distress,
    Not caring to be gone ;
But gazing with a dull and darkening eye,
    And seeing Dreams pass by.
Not speculating whither she would go,
But feeling there was nought she cared to
    know,
    And melting even as snow.
Save when the man's hand slipped into her
    own,
    And flutter'd fondly there,
And she would feel her life again, and
    groan,
'O GOD ! when I am gone, how will he
    fare ? '
And for a little time, for Angus' sake,
    Her hopeless heart would ache,
And all life's stir and anguish once again
    Would swoon across her brain.

  ' O bairn, when I am dead,
    How shall ye keep frae harm ?
    What hand will gie ye bread ?
    What fire will keep ye warm ?
  How shall ye dwell on earth awn' frae
    me ?'—
      ' O Mither, dinna dee ! '

  ' O bairn, by nigh or day
    I hear nae sounds ava',
    But voices of winds that blaw,
    And the voices of ghaists that say
      "Come awa ! come awa ! "
  The LORD that made the Wind, and made
    the Sea,
  Is sore on my son and me,
  And I melt in His breath like snaw,'—
      ' O Mither, dinna dee !

'O bairn, it is but closing up the een,
    And lying down never to rise again.
Many a strong man's sleeping hae I seen,—
    There is nae pain!
I'm weary, weary, and I scarce ken why;
    My summer has gone by,
And sweet were sleep, but for the sake o' thee.'—
    'O Mither, dinna dee!'

When summer scents and sounds were on the Sea,
    And all night long the silvern surge plash'd cool,
Outside the hut she sat upon a stool,
And with thin fingers fashion'd carefully,
While Angus leant his head against her knee,
    A long white dress of wool.
'O Mither,' cried the man, 'what make ye there?'
    'A blanket for our bed!'
'O Mither, it is like the shroud folk wear
    When they are drown'd and dead!'
And Meg said nought, but kiss'd him on the lips,
And look'd with dull eye seaward, where the moon
Blacken'd the white sails of the passing ships,
Into the Land where she was going soon.

And in the reaping-time she lay abed,
And by her side the dress unfinishëd,
And with dull eyes that knew not even her child
She gazed at vacancy and sometimes smiled;
And ever her fingers work'd, for in her thought
Stitching and stitching, still the dress she wrought;
And then a beldame old, with blear-eyed face,
For CHRIST and Charity came to the place,
And stilly sewed the woollen shroud herself,
And set the salt and candle on a shelf.
And like a dumb thing crouching moveless there,
    Gripping the fingers wan,
Marking the face with wild and wondering stare,
    And whining beast-like, watch'd the witless man.

Then like a light upon a headland set,
In winds that come from far-off waters blowing,
    The faint light glimmered—fainter—fainter yet!
But suddenly it brighten'd, at its going;
And Meg sat up, and, lo! her features wore
The stately sweetness they had known of yore;
And delicate lines were round her mouth, mild rest
    Was in her eyes, though they were waxing dim;
And when the man crept close unto her breast,
    She brighten'd kissing him.
    And it was clear
She had heard tidings it was sweet to hear,
And had no longer any care or fear.
'I gang, my bairn, and thou wilt come to me!'
    'O Mither, dinna dee!'
But as he spake she dropt upon the bed,
And darken'd, while the breath came thick and fleet:
'O Jessie, see they mind my Bairn!' she said,
    And quiver'd,—and was sleeping at God's Feet.

When on her breast the plate of salt was laid,
    And the corse-candle burned with sick blue light,
The man crouch'd, fascinated and afraid,
    Beside her, moaning through the night;
And answered not the women who stole near,
    And would not see nor hear;
And when a day and night had come and gone,
Ate at the crusts they brought him, gazing on;
And when they took her out upon a bier,
He followed quietly without a tear;
And when on the hard wood fell dust and stone,
He murmur'd a thin answer to the sound,
And in the end he sat, with a dull moan,
    Upon the new-made mound.

Last, as a dog that mourns a master dead,
    The man did haunt that grave in dull dumb pain;

Creeping away to beg a little bread,
  Then stealing back again;
And only knaves and churls refused to give
The gift of bread or meal that he might live—
  Till, pale and piteous-eyed,
He moan'd beneath a load too hard to bear.
  'Mither!' he cried,—
And crawled into the Dark, to seek her *there*.

THE BATTLE OF DRUMLIE-MOOR.

(COVENANT PERIOD.)

BAR the door! put out the light, for it gleams across the night,
  And guides the bloody motion of their feet;
Hush the bairn upon thy breast, lest it guide them in their quest,
  And with water quench the blazing of the peat.
Now, Wife, sit still and hark!—hold my hand amid the dark;
  O Jeanie, we are scatter'd—e'en as sleet!

It was down on Drumliemoor, where it slopes upon the shore,
  And looks upon the breaking of the bay,
In the kirkyard of the dead, where the heather is thrice red
  With the blood of those asleep beneath the clay;
And the Howiesons were there, and the people of Glen Ayr,
  And we gathered in the gloom o' night— to pray.

How! Sit at home in fear, when God's Voice was in mine ear,
  When the priests of Baal were slaughtering His sheep?
Nay! there I took my stand, with my reap-hook in my hand,
  For bloody was the sheaf that I might reap;
And the Lord was in His skies, with a thousand dreadful eyes,
  And His breathing made a trouble on the Deep.

Each mortal of the band brought his weapon in his hand,
  Though the chopper or the spit was all he bare;
And not a man but knew the work he had to do,
  If the Fiend should fall upon us unaware.
And our looks were ghastly white, but it was not with affright,—
  The Lord our God was present to our prayer.

Oh, solemn, sad, and slow, rose the stern voice of Monroe,
  And he curst the curse of Babylon the Whore;
We could not see his face, but a gleam was in its place,
  Like the phosphor of the foam upon the shore;
And the eyes of all were dim, as they fixed themselves on him,
  And the Sea filled up the pauses with its roar.

But when, with accents calm, Kilmahoe gave out the psalm,
  The sweetness of God's Voice upon his tongue,
With one voice we praised the Lord of the Fire and of the Sword,
  And louder than the winter wind it rung;
And across the stars on high went the smoke of tempest by,
  And a vapour roll'd around us as we sung.

'Twas terrible to hear our cry rise deep and clear,
  Though we could not see the criers of the cry,
But we sang and gript our brands, and touched each other's hands,
  While a thin sleet smote our faces from the sky;
And, sudden, strange, and low, hissed the voice of Kilmahoe,
  'Grip your weapons! Wait in silence! They are nigh!'

And heark'ning, with clench'd teeth, we could hear, across the heath,
  The tramping of the horses as they flew,
And no man breathed a breath, but all were still as death,

And close together shivering we drew;
And deeper round us fell all the eyeless
    gloom of Hell,
And—the Fiend was in among us ere we
    knew!

Then our battle-shriek arose, mid the
    cursing of our foes—
No face of friend or foeman could we
    mark;
But I struck and kept my stand (trusting
    God to guide my hand),
And struck, and struck, and heard the
    hell-hounds bark;
And I fell beneath a horse, but I reached
    with all my force,
And ript him with my reap-hook through
    the dark.

As we struggled, knowing not whose hand
    was at our throat,
Whose blood was spouting warm into our
    eyes,
We felt the thick snow-drift swoop upon us
    from the lift,
And murmur in the pauses of our cries;
But, lo! before we wist, rose the curtain of
    the mist,
And the pale Moon shed a glimmer from
    the skies.

O God! it was a sight that made the hair
    turn white,
That wither'd up the heart's blood into
    woe,
To see the faces loom in the dimly lighted
    gloom,
And the butcher'd lying bloodily below;
While melting, with no sound, fell so peace-
    fully around
The whiteness and the wonder of the
    Snow!

Ay, and thicker, thicker, poured the pale
    Silence of the Lord,
From the hollow of His hand we saw it
    shed,
And it gather'd round us there, till we
    groan'd and gasp'd for air,
And beneath was ankle-deep and stainèd
    red;
And soon, whatever wight was smitten down
    in fight
Was *buried* in the drift ere he was dead!

Then we beheld at length the troopers in
    their strength,
For faster, faster, faster up they streamed,
And their pistols flashing bright showed
    their faces ashen white,
And their blue steel caught the driving
    Moon, and gleamed.
But a dying voice cried, 'Fly!' And be-
    hold, e'en at the cry,
A panic fell upon us, and we screamed!

Oh, shrill and awful rose, 'mid the splashing
    blood and blows,
Our scream unto the Lord that let us die;
And the Fiend amid us roared his defiance
    at the Lord,
And his servants slew the strong man
    'mid his cry;
And the Lord kept still in Heaven, and the
    only answer given
Was the white Snow falling, falling, from
    the sky.

Then we fled! the darkness grew! 'mid the
    driving cold we flew,
Each alone, yea, each for those whom he
    held dear;
And I heard upon the wind the thud of
    hoofs behind,
And the scream of those who perish'd in
    their fear,
But I knew by heart each path through the
    darkness of the strath,
And I hid myself all day,—and I am
    here.

Ah! gathered in one fold be the holy men
    and bold,
And beside them the accursed and the
    proud;
The Howiesons are there, and the Wylies
    of Glen Ayr,
Kirkpatrick, and Macdonald, and Mac-
    leod.
And while the widow groans, lo! God's
    Hand around their bones
His thin ice windeth whitely, as a shroud

On mountain and in vale our women will
    look pale,
And palest where the ocean surges boom:
Buried 'neath snow-drift white, with no holy
    prayer or rite,

Lie the loved ones they look for in the gloom;
And deeper, deeper still, spreads the Snow on vale and hill,
And deeper and yet deeper is their Tomb!

THE NORTHERN WOOING.

Skies are dusky, winds are keen,
Round Lallan Farm this Hallowe'en.

All is dark across the night,
But see! one glimmer of pink light!

What are those that in the air
Flit against the window-glare?

Falling flakes of snow they seem,
Or night-moths gather'd by the gleam.

Round and round they wind and wind,—
Tiny shades against the blind.

Child, *wish* now! while thou canst see!
'Tis the faëry companie!

Once a year, on Hallowe'en,
Are the faëry people seen.

Thus round happy farms they fly,
While the peat-fire blazes high.

Lad and lass, to-night beware!
There is magic in the air!

. . . . .

'Ah, bairns, my bairns, forbear on Hallow Night
To mock the faëry people and their night,
For though ye deem these things are all untrue,
Yourselves may be the first to see and rue!
Hark! now the winds a moment cease to roar,
A sound like some one breathing at the door!
And hark again! faint pattings on the pane
Of little finger-taps, like fluttering rain!
Ay! 'tis the faëry people hovering nigh:
Draw back the blind to peep, and they will fly!

But serve them solemnly, with charm and spell,
And the old customs that they love so well,
And they will show you all you wish to see,—
Your true love's face, his country and degree,—
All, all a lass with pleasure asks and learns,
Down to the number of her unborn bairns!

'Ay, please the fays! 'tis easy if ye will;
But woe be yours if they should wish you ill:
Your jo will take to drink, or drown at sea,
Or find another sweeter companie;
Your cheeks will droop, your looks will lose their light;
Ye'll marry an old man, and freeze at night!
In vain, in vain ye try to change your fate,
When *they* have fix'd your lot and future mate:
In vain ye seek to frown and turn aside,—
They make your heart consent in spite of pride.
'Twas so with me, when I was young and gay,
Though I was loth to hearken and obey.
They led me to their choice by spells and charms;
They closed my een, and drew me to his arms!
Or grandfather had ne'er prevailed on me
To droop my pride, and smile as low as he!

'For, though I say it, bairns, my face was fair,
And I was Farmer Binnie's child and heir;
A widowed father's pet, I ruled the place,
Right proud, be sure, of fortune and of face.
My hair was golden then, like Maggie's here,
And I had een as sly, yet crystal clear,
And I could look as bright when pleased and fain,
Or toss my curls with just as sweet disdain!
What wonder, then, if half the country-side
Looked love into my face, and blush'd and cried,
Bleating behind me, like a flock of sheep
Around a shepherd-lass, who, half asleep,

Counts them in play, leads them with pretty
 speech,
Rates all alike, and scarce kens each from
 each?
One found me coy, another found me gleg,
Another skittish as the gray mare Meg;
Just as the humour took me, I was wild
Or gentle,—one day cross, the next day
 mild;
But cared no more for handsome Jamie
 West,
When he came o'er the heather in his
 best,
Jingling his silver spurs at our fire-end,
In breeks so tight 'twas near his death to
 bend,
Than for the grim old Laird of Glumlie
 Glen,
Who rode on solemn sheltie now and then
Over the moors,—and, making mouths at
 me,
With father cracked of crops o'er barley-
 bree,—
While Jock the groom, who knew I loved
 such fun,
Ginger'd the sheltie for a homeward run!

'Yet oft I tried to picture in my brain
What kind of laddie in the end would gain,
And vainly sought 'mong those around to
 find
The substance of the shadow in my mind.
But, bairns, in vain I pictured; and anew
Will you and children's children picture
 too:—
The bonnie shadow flies, and in its place
The chilly substance steals to our embrace.
I swore he should be stately, dark, and
 tall,—
His hair was fiery-red and he was small!
I swore he should be rich in gold and
 lands,—
His fortune was the strength of his two
 hands!
I swore he should be meek and ruled by
 me,—
The De'il himself is easier led than he!'

. . . . .

Round the happy farm they flee,—
Faëry folk in companie.

Near the peat-blaze range in ring;
Fiddler, twang the fiddle-string.

In the great tub duck the head
After apples rosy red!

Slyly let each pair by turn
Watch the magic chestnuts burn!

Love who never loved before,—
Kiss me quick behind the door!

Lad and lass, to-night beware!
There is magic in the air!

. . . . .

'O bairns, we gathered round the blazing
 peat,
And lad and lass sat close and whispered
 sweet,
While ancient women spake of wonders
 seen
On many a long-forgotten Hallowe'en,
And old men nodded snowy polls the while,
Passing the snuff-box round with sceptic
 smile.
Tall in the midst my father had his place,
Health and a golden harvest in his face;
And, hand in his, full rosy and full sly,
Surrounded by my silly sheep sat I.
Loud rang the laughter! fearless grew the
 fun!
Happy and warm at heart was every one!
The old, old shepherd, worn with rain and
 wind,
Blink'd in the ingle-nook with eyes half
 blind,
While at his feet his tired old dog slept
 deep,
And, starting, dream'd of gathering the
 sheep.

'James West was there, the Laird, and
 many more,
Wooers both old and young, and rich and
 poor;
And, though I say it, bairns, that night I
 smiled
My sweetest, and their wits were fairly
 wild.
Braw with new ribbons in my hair lint-light,
Clean as a guinea, newly minted, bright,
I sat and hearkened to their silly speech,
Happy, and with a careless smile for each;
And yet, though some were fine and fair to
 see,
Not one had power to steal my heart from
 me.

'Oh, Hallowe'en in those old times, I vow,
Was thrice as merry, thrice as sweet, as now!
The benches drawn aside, the supper o'er,
Fresh sand was strewn upon this very floor;
The fiddle played—the fiddler gave a squeal—
Up stood the folk, and father led the reel!
The lads loup'd up and kick'd the beam for fun!
The crimson lassies screamed to see it done!
Meantime the old men, with contented look,
Smoked clean new cutties in the chimney nook,
And thought of days when they were young and gay,
And pleased the lassies, too, with feats of play,
Yet one was there, my bairns, amid the throng,
Who, though his years were young, his limbs full strong,
Danced not that night; but pale and gloomy, stayed
Among the gaffers, in the chimney shade,—
Hugh Scott his name, an orphan lad, whose hand
Guided the ploughshare on my father's land,
But one my father prized and trusted best
For cunning and for skill o'er all the rest.
Full well I knew the rogue esteemed me sweet,
But I was gentry, and his masters' meat!
And oft I smiled on him full fond and free,
As ne'er I smiled on those who courted me,
Pleased that my smiles sank sweet to his heart's core,
But certain *he* would never hope for more.

'There in the chimney shadow, pale and sad,
Clad in his clothes of Sabbath, sat the lad:
In vain to catch his look, the lassies leered,
In vain the old folk saw his sulks, and sneered,
But aye his dim and melancholy e'e
Turned flashing in the shade and followed me.

Whene'er I danced with some fine wooer there,
I saw his fist clench and his eyeballs glare,—
Red as a rick on fire I watched him grow
Whene'er my partner whispered light and low,
And had a kiss been stolen in his sight,
I swear he would have ta'en revenge in fight.
Half pleased, half careless, to increase his ill,
I marked him kindly, as a lassie will,
And sent him many a smile of tender light
To cheer him in his nook, that Hallow night.

'Louder the fiddler, gay with many a glass,
Shouted to stir the hearts of lad and lass!
Faster and faster on his strings he skirled!
Faster and faster round the dancers whirled!
Close by, the young folks duck'd for apples red,
Splashing, with puffing cheek and dripping head,
Into the washing-bine, or, in a ring,
With gaping mouths, they played at cherry-string.
But in the parlour, from the turmoil free,
Father sat now with antique companie—
Cronies who mixed their tumblers strong and deep
Twelve times, and toddled, sober, off to sleep.

'But, bairns, 'twas near the hour when ghaists are said
To rise white-sheeted from their kirkyard bed,
When the owl calls, and blinks his e'eball white'
In ruins, where the fairies flit by night.
And now my heart beat fast and thick for fear,
Because the time of spells and charms was near,
And I was bent that very night to fly
Out o'er the meadow to the kiln,—and try
The twining charm, the spell of fairy fate,
And hear the name of him that I should mate.'

. . . .

Lad and lass, to-night beware!
There is magic in the air!

Winds are crying shrill, and, hark
Ghosts are groaning in the dark.

Q

Who will dare this Hallow Night
Leave the happy ingle-light?

Who will dare to stand alone,
While the fairy thread is thrown?

Who this night is free from fear?
Let her ask,—and she shall hear!

. . . . .

'Dark, dark was all, as shivering and alone
I set my foot upon the threshold-stone,
And, trembling close, with twitching fingers caught
The great horn-lanthorn from the stables brought,
And leant against the door to keep it wide,
And peer'd into the solemn gloom, and sighed.
Black was the lift, and faintly fell the rain,
The wind was screeching like a sprite in pain;
And, while I paused, pinching my e'en to mark,
The wind swung-to the door, and left me in the dark!

'O bairns! what would my foolish heart have gi'en
To let the fairies be, that Hallowe'en!
But I had sworn, and all the lassies knew,
And I was shamed, and fain must see it through.
Oh! where were all my boasts, my laughter light,
Now I was there alone amid the night?
While faintly ben the farm the fiddle cried,
And far away the sound of dancing died.

'Thud, thud against my breast my wild heart leapt,
As out across the misty yard I crept,
Holding the lanthorn up;—its flickering ray
Made darkness doubly deep along the way.
Then in my ears I seem'd to hear strange screams,
And fearful faces flashed with lightning-gleams,
And, as I wandered, fingers sharp and wee
Pinched me and pulled my garter o'er the knee.

Out of the yard, across the field, the dew
Still drizzling damply in my face, I flew,
Till, breathless, panting hard against the wind,
Fearful to look before me or behind,
I reached the kiln,—and, standing dizzy there,
Heard softer voices round me in the air,
A sound like little feet along the gloom,
And hummings faint as of a fairy loom.
Then setting down the lanthorn on the ground
I entered in, nor paused to look around.
But faint and fast began to say the charm
All northern lassies know, and reached my arm,
Casting the twine, and catching one end tight—
Flinging the other loose into the night.
O bairns! O bairns! scarce had I uttered thrice
The secret spell, with lips as cold as ice,
When through my blood a sick'ning shudder spread,
For ghaistly fingers tighten'd at the thread!
Then in a hollow voice, to know my doom,
"Who holds? who holds?" I cried into the gloom;—
And ere the echo of my voice had died,
"Hugh Scott! Hugh Scott!" a hollow voice replied:
And, screaming out, and covering up my face,
Kicking the lanthorn o'er, I fled the place,
Stumbling and tripping, flew across the field,
Till, white as any lamb, I reached the bield,
And crept up to my room, and hid my head,
Moaning, among the blankets of the bed!'

. . . . .

Lightly soon shall rise the sun!
Fays, begone! your work is done.

Fiddler, put your tools away,
Take a nap among the hay.

Lads and lassies, flush'd and red,
Yawn no more, but off to bed.

Maiden, thou hast heard and seen
Wonders strange at Hallowe'en.

Thou hast wish'd to hear and see—
And thy fate is fixed for thee.

Sad or merry, ill or well,
Fairy looms have spun the spell.

In among the blankets creep—
Dream about him in your sleep.

Wake and smile with heart resigned!
Kiss and cuddle, and be kind!

. . . . .

'Oh, bitter was my heart, my wits amazed;
Wildly I pondered like a lassie crazed:
Hugh Scott my mate! Hugh Scott, of all around!
A pauper lad, a tiller of the ground!
When wealthy men came lilting o'er the lea,
In shining braws, and sought to marry me!
"Nay, nay!" I cried, and frowning raised my face,
"No force shall make me choose a lot so base:
The spirits of the air but wish this night
To try my heart, and fill my soul with fright;
Yet they shall know full soon they rate me ill,—
I fear them not, nor shall I work their will!"
But as I spoke, I shook, and unaware
Keek'd o'er my shoulder at the glass, and there,
In the faint lamplight burning by the bed,
His face, a moment mirror'd, flash'd and fled!

'O bairns!—what further tale have I to tell?
How could I fight against a fate so fell?
Strive as I might, awaking or asleep,
I found my eyes in fascination deep
Follow Hugh Scott, and, till my heart went wild,
He haunted me from spot to spot, and smiled.
Then, unaware, to notice I began
That he was trim and stout, and like a man,
That there were tender tones upon his tongue,
And that his voice was sweet whene'er he sung.
Nay, more, full soon his manners seemed to me
More fine than those of loftier degree,
And as for gold, though he was humble, still
He had a fortune in his farming skill.
Ay, bairns! before another Hallow Night
The fairies to their wish had worked me quite;
And, since his heart had ever favoured Hugh,
Full easily they won my father too—
And when at last Hugh craved me to be his,
I—fell upon his heart and blush'd for bliss!

'Ah! heed not, bairns, though grandfather should swear
That, when I tried the spell, *himsel'* was there,
And, when I saw the phantom in the room,
Again, was near me, keeking through the gloom;
And that his craft and cunning were the charms
Which cheated me and drew me to his arms.
Nay! nay! right solemnly, with song and spell,
And the old customs that they love so well,
Serve the good fays this night—be bold! be brave!
And though they may not give you *all* ye crave,
Be sure that you will find, as I have found,
Their choice right wise, and all their counsels sound,
And bless for many a year the love and light
They spin for happy hearts, on Hallow Night.'

AN ENGLISH ECLOGUE.

'He crept close to Creation's brim, and heard a roar like water.'

TIMOTHY.

WELL, here's the cuckoo come again, after the barley sowing,
Down on the duck-pond in the lane the white-weed is a-blowing,
The gorse has got its coat of gold, and smells as sweet as clover,
The lady-smocks are blowing bold, the primroses nigh over,

On field and fold all things look fair, and
  lambkins white are leaping,
The speckled snakes crawl here and there,
  —but Holy Tommie's sleeping.

JACOB.

Ah, him that used to work with Crewe!
  Crewe told me how he blundered.
He used to preach. I heard him too.
  LORD! how he groaned and thundered!
The women shrieked like sucking-swine,
  the men roared out like cattle,
But seem'd to think it mighty fine!

TIMOTHY.

All trash and stuff and tattle!
He lost his head through meddling so with
  things that don't concern us;
When questioning too close we go, 'tis little
  GOD will learn us;
To squeeze the crops 'tis hard enough from
  His dry ground about us,
But sowing t'other world is stuff, — it gets its
  crops without us!

JACOB.

That's where it lies! We get no *good* by
  asking questions, neighbour:
'Tis Parsons cook our Sunday food, while
  we are hard at labour;
This world needs help upon its way, for
  men feed one another,
And why do we give Parsons pay?—if not
  to manage t'other?

TIMOTHY.

You're right! No man as grunts and grides
  at this here world has thriven;
Mutton won't drop in our insides though
  we do gape at heaven!
Why, Tommie's cheek was ruddy red, as
  rosy as an apple,
Till Methodism filled his head, and he was
  seen at chapel,
Found out that he'd received a call, grew
  dismal, dull, and surly,
Read tracts at work, big tracts and small,
  went praying late and early,
And by and by began, poor fool, to argue
  with the doubting,
And though he'd scarcely been to school,
  began his public spouting.
I wasn't blind—and soon I found how he
  let matters go here,—

While he was tilling heavenly ground things
  suffered down below here:
Through want of feed, the hens did die, the
  horses next grew useless,
For lack o' milking by and by the very cows
  grew juiceless;
And when I sought him out, and swore in
  rage and consternation,
Why, Tommie sigh'd, and snivell'd sore,
  and talk'd about *salvation*!
'Salvation's mighty well,' says I, right mad
  with my disaster,
'I want to save my property; so find
  another master!'
He didn't grumble or resist, though he
  seemed broken-hearted,
But slipped a tract into my fist the morning
  he departed;
Ay, got a place next day with Crewe, who
  knew the lad was clever,
But dawdled as he used to do, and preached
  as much as ever.

JACOB.

But Crewe soon sent him packing too—he's
  just the sort of fellow;
Why, ev'n when Parson calls, old Crewe
  grunts, grumbles, and looks yellow!

TIMOTHY.

He got another master, though, but soon
  began to tire him;
His wages sank and sank, and so no farmer
  here would hire him;
And soon, between that world and this,
  poor Tommie grew more mournful,
His worldly ways went all amiss—the coun-
  try folk looked scornful—
And last the blessed Methodists grew tired,
  and would not hear him,
And wouldn't heed his talk inspired, and
  shrank from sitting near him.

JACOB.

With Methodists 'tis just the way. Give me
  the High Church, neighbour.

TIMOTHY.

'Why don't you be a man?' said they,
  'keep clean and do your labour?'
And what d'ye think that Tommie cried?—
  'I don't play shilly-shally;
If I'm to serve my LORD and Guide, 'twill
  be continually:

ou think that you can cheat and scoff from
    Sunday on to Sunday,
 nd put the LORD ALMIGHTY off by howl-
    ing out on one day;
 ut if you seek salvation, know, your
    feelings must be stronger.'
 nd holy Tommie would not go to chapel
    any longer.
 earned sense? Not he! Reformed? Pooh,
    pooh! but moped and fretted blindly,
 ecause the precious praying crew had used
    him so unkindly.
 lis back grew bare, his life grew sore, his
    brain grew dreadful airy,
 le thought of t'other world the more 'cause
    this seemed so contrary;
 Vent wandering on the river-side, and in
    the woods lay lurking,
 iaped at the sky in summer-tide when other
    men were working,
 nd once (I saw him) watch'd the skies,
    where a wild lark was winging,
 Vith tears a-shining in his eyes,—because
    the lark was singing!
 ast harvest-time to me he came, and begged
    for work so sadly,
 how'd for his former ways such shame,
    and look'd so sick and badly,
 had not heart to give him pain, but put
    him out a-reaping,
 ut, LORD! the same tale o'er again—he
    worked like one half-sleeping,
 Be off!' says I, 'you lazy lout,' and all the
    rest stood sneering.
 Master,' says he, 'you're right, I doubt,—
    the LORD seems hard o' hearing!
 thought I could fulfil full clear the call
    that I had gotten,
 ut here's another harvest here, and all my
    life seems rotten.
 he Methodists are dull as stone, the High
    Church folk are lazy,
 nd even when I pray alone, the ways of
    Heaven seem hazy.
 eligion don't appear to me to keep a lad
    from sad things,
 nd though the world is fine to see, 'tis full
    of cruel bad things.
 Vhy, I can't walk in woodland ways, and
    see the flowers a-growing,
 nd on the light green meadows gaze, or
    watch the river flowing,
 ut even here, where things look fine, out
    creeps the speckled adder,

Or snakes crawl in the golden shine, and all
    creation's sadder.
The better I have seemed to grow, the worse
    all things have gone with me,
It beats me out and out, and so—I wish the
    LORD was done with me!'
And after these same words were said,
    Tommie grew paler, stiller,
And by and by he took to bed, and quickly
    he grew iller:
And when the early new-year rain was
    yellowing pool and river,
He closed his eyes, and slipt his chain, and
    fell to sleep for ever.

JACOB.

'Tis clear enough, he'd lost his wit—the
    chapel set it turning.

TIMOTHY.

Now, this is how I look at it, although I've
    got no learning:
In this here world, to do like him is nothing
    but self-slaughter,—
He crept close to Creation's brim, and
    heard a roar like water,
His head went round, his limbs grew stiff,
    his blood lost life and motion,—
Like one who stands upon a cliff and sees
    the roaring Ocean. . . .
But there's the Parson at his gate, with
    Doctor Barth, his crony;
Some of these days the old chap's weight
    will kill that precious pony!
Ah, *he's* the man whose words don't fail to
    keep one sage and steady!
Wife, here be Parson! Draw some ale, and
    set the table ready.

A SCOTTISH ECLOGUE.

'The Lord on *him* forgot to *put His mark.*'

SANDIE.

O LORD above, swift is Thy wrath and deep!
And yet by grace Thou sanctionest Thy
    sheep;
And blest are they who till the day o' doom
Like haddocks bear the marking of Thy
    thoomb;
And curst, in spite of works and prayers,
    are they
On whom Thy mark has ne'er been printed
    sae.

For while the non-elected lie beneath,
And fast in flaming fire, and gnash their
  teeth,
Above their heads, where streams of honey
  spring,
Thine Elders stand in shining sarks, and
  sing,
Blessing Thy Name for present gifts and
  past . . .
O wife, John Galloway is gone, at last !

JEANIE.

Dead? Weel, we all are bound to GOD's
  abode,
And John has started first upon the road.
A Christian man and kind was John, in-
  deed,
And free of siller unto folk in need :
Ay, many a hearth will want now John is
  cold !
But GOD will give him back his gifts
  tenfold.

SANDIE.

O Jeanie Gourlay ! keep thy clapper still ;
It talks o' things you understand but ill :
I doubt, I sorely doubt, John Galloway
Is 'neath the oxter * o' the De'il this day !
True, in the way of sinful flesh, his mind
Was charitable, and his heart was kind ;
But Light he lacked as long as he drew
  breath,
And lost the Eldership before his death ;
And he had many a ghostly whispering
To tell he was a miserable thing,
Doom'd by the Wisdom of the Just to be
Condemn'd with those who graceless live
  and dee.
Ay, grace, I fear, John Galloway was
  denied,
Though loud and oft for grace he groaned
  and cried.
'Sandie,' he used to say, ' I fear, I fear
I have no right among the holy here ;
I fear, I fear that I am in the dark—
The LORD on me forgot to put His mark !
I canna steel my heart to folk who sin,
I canna put my thoughts to discipline ;
Oft when I pray, I hear Him whisper plain,
"Jock Galloway, pray awa', but 'tis in
  vain ;"—

* Armpit.

Nae sweet assurance ar
  De'il,
Nae happy faith, like tha
I long for GOD, I beg H
But fear He hath to wrat

JEANIE.

Poor man ! his strife was
  mind,
Nae man can *tell* wh
  destined ;
Ev'n Sandie Gourlay ma
Hath liberty to catch wit

SANDIE

Oh, blasphemy ! Thou
  cease !
The *sign* o' grace is perfe
Such as the LORD, in spi
Vouchsafes to men like
  Ross.
But Galloway ever was a
A whining thing who d
  deep.
Why, mind ye, when
  himsel'—
A heretic, a rogue, a ma
Averring written Scriptu
And doubting GOD, stre
  to dee,
John by the sinner knelt a
'LORD GOD,' he said,
  hairs !
Be kind unto him ! Tak
And bought the coffir
  fee.
'Sandie,' he said, when
  grave,
'I doubt I am less holy
My blood is water, I am
O LORD, it broke my
  pain !
I thought—I dared to
  GOD,
Poor Caird should nev
  road ;
I thought—ay, dared t
  forgi'e !—
The LORD was crueller
Forgetting GOD is just,
What folk should burn i
  blest.'

† The re

Such was his nature, neither strong nor deep,—
Unlike the stern strong shepherds of His sheep.
We made an Elder of John Galloway!
Large seemed his heart, he ne'er was known to stray;
But he had little strength or wrath severe—
He soften'd at the sinful pauper's tear;
He push'd his purse and pleaded like a fool
For every lassie on the cuttie-stool.

JEANIE.

Where had the parish bairns sae kind a friend?

SANDIE.

Bairns? did he teach them *grace*, and make them *mend*?
At Sunday School what lad or lass had care
For fear of flaming Hell, if John was there,—
Questioning blushing brats upon his knees,
And slyly slipping in their hands—bawbees?*
Once while he talked to me o' life and death,
I smelt the smell o' whisky in his breath.
'Drinking again, John Galloway?' I said;
As gray as this pipe-reek, he hung his head.
'O Sandie, Sandie!' he replied, 'I ken
I am indeed the weakest man of men.
Strange doubts torment me daily, and, alas!
I try to drown them in the poison'd glass.
By fits I fear, and in my soul I say,
LORD, *is* Thy mark on poor John Galloway?
And sorely troubled, stealing slyly out,
I try in drink to drown the imp o' Doubt.'
Woman, is this the man ye would defend?
Nay, wheesht awhile, and hearken to his end.
When he fell sick in Martinmas, his fears
Grew deeper far; I found him oft in tears;
Though from the Prophets of God's wrath I read,
He hearken'd, but was little comforted,

* Halfpence.

And even 'Revelations' had no power
To soothe the pangs of his departing hour.
A week before he left this vale of woe,
He at his window sat, and watched the Snow
Falling and falling down without a sound,
Poured slowly from GOD's hand upon the ground:
'See, Sandie, how it snaws!' I heard him say;
'How many folk are cold, cold, cold this day!
How many want the fire that's warming me!
How many starve!—and yet—why should it be?'
And when I took the Book, explained, and read,
He only gave a groan and shook his head.
'Clearer and clearer I perceive my sin,
How I to grace may never enter in;
That Book is for the strong, but I am weak,'
And trembled, and a tear was on his cheek.

JEANIE.

Poor man! poor man! small peace on earth he found.

SANDIE.

The day he died, he called the Elders round,
Shook hands, and said, 'Friends, though I gang from here,
Down under earth, all will at last be clear.
Too long have I been dwelling in the dark,
The LORD on me forgot to put His mark,
GOD help me!' And, till he was cold as clay,
His foolish lips had little more to say;
Yet after we had laid him down in dust,
Weak to the last we found him, and unjust;
For when his will was read, unto our shame,
No holy man was mentioned in the same!
But he had left what little gold he had
To Caird's sick widow and her lass and lad!

THE SCAITH O' BARTLE.

Fathoms deep the ship doth lie,
   Wreath'd with ocean weed and shell,
Still and deep the shadows lie,
   Dusky as a forest dell :
Tangled in the twisted sail,
   With the breathing of the Sea,
Stirs the Man who told this tale,
   Staring upward dreamilie.

I LAID him here, and scarcely wept ; but look !
His grave is green and wild and like a wave,
And strewn with ocean-shells instead of flowers.

   You saw him long ago, on board the *Erne*,
Cod-fishing in Newfoundland, and (you mind?)
We drank a gill, all three, the very day
Before the *Erne* went down off Fitful Head,
And all the crew were drown'd but brother Dan.
Strange, that a man who faced so many a storm,
And stood on splitting planks and never quail'd,
And swam to save his life a dozen times,
Should ever die ashore ! Why, from the first,
We twins were meant for sailors :—GOD Himself
Planted a breeze in both our brains to blow
Our bodies up and down His calms and storms.
Never had wilder, stormier year been known
Here in the clachan, than the very year
When Dan and I were born ;—waters and winds
Roar'd through the wintry season, and the sounds
And sights weigh'd on our Highland mother's heart,
Giving her whims and moods in which the clay
Beneath her heart was fashion'd ; and in March
The Scaith came down the valley, screaming past
Her ears the very hour that we were born.

When other boys were mumping at the school,
I went as cabin-lad on board a whaler,
And Dan took up his canvas-bag, tied up
His serk and comb and brush, with two or three
Big home-baked bannocks and a lump of cheese,
Kiss'd mother, (that's her grave beside his own,)
And walk'd to Aberdeen, where soon he found
A berth on board a brig—the *Jessie Gray*,
Bound south for Cadiz. After that for years
We drifted up and down ;—and when we met
Down in the Forth, and journey'd home together,
We both were twenty, Dan was poor as ever,
But I had saved. How changed he look'd! how fine !
Brown cheek and bit o' whisker, hands like steel,
A build as sturdy as a mountain fir's,—
Ay, every inch a sailor ! Then, the tales
We had for one another !—tales of storms
And sights on land, pranks play'd and places seen !—
But, ' Bob, I'm tired of being on the seas,
The life's a hard one at the best,' says Dan ;
And I was like a fool and thought the same.
So home we came, found father dead and gone,
And mother sorely push'd ; and round her neck
We threw our arms, and kiss'd her, and she cried,
And we cried too, and I took out my pay
And pour'd it in her lap ; but Dan look'd grieved,
And, glancing from the pay to mother, cried,
' I'll never, never go to sea again !'

'Tis thirty years ago, and yet right well
I mind it all. How pleasant for a time
Was life on land : the tousling with the girls,
The merry-making in the public-house,
The cosy bed on winter nights. We work'd—

I at the fishing, Dan at making nets—
And kept old mother for a year and more.
But ere the year was out, the life grew dull:
We never heard the wind blow, but we
    thought
Of sailing on the sea,—we got a knack
Of lying on the beach and listening
To the great waters. Still, for mother's
    sake,
Ashore we had to tarry. By and by,
The restlessness grew worse, and show'd
    itself
In other ways,—taking a drop too much,
Fighting and cutty-stooling—and the folk
Began to shake their heads. Amid it all,
One night when Dan was reading out
    God's Book,
(That bit about the Storm, where Peter tries
To walk on water, and begins to sink,)
Old mother sigh'd and seem'd to go to
    sleep;
And when we tried to wake her, she was
    dead.

With sore, sore hearts we laid poor
    mother down ;
And walk'd that day up yonder cliffs, and
    lay
A hearkening to the Sea that wash'd be-
    neath :
Far, far away we saw a sail gleam wet
Out of a rainy spot below the line
Where sky and water meet ; the Deep was
    calm,
And overhead went clouds whose shadows
    floated
Slowly beneath, and here and there were
    places
Purple and green and blue, and close to
    land
The red-sail'd fish-boats in a violet patch.
I look'd at brother Dan, Dan look'd at
    me,—
And that same morning, off we went
    again !

No rest for us on land from that day
    forth,
We grew to love the waters ; they became
Part of our flesh and blood ; the Sea, the
    Sea,
The busy whistling round the foam-girt
    world,
Was all our pleasure. Now and then we
    met,—
Once in a year or two, and never came
To Scotland but we took a journey here
To look on mother's grave, and spend a day
With old companions. But we never
    thought
Of resting long, and never hoped to die
Ashore, like mother : we had fix'd it, Jack,
That we must drown some day. At last,
    by luck,
We ran together. Dan had got a place
As captain of a brig, and, press'd by him,
They made me mate. Ten years we sail'd
    together,
From Liverpool to New South Wales and
    back ;
And we were lads no more, but staid, strong
    men,
Forty and upward,—yet with kibble arms,
Brown cheeks, and cheerful hearts. Then
    the ill wind
That blows no good to anyone began,
And brought us back to Scotland, to this
    place
Where we were born and bred.

                        Now, mark you, Jack,
Even a sailor is but flesh and blood,
Though out upon the water he can laugh
At women and their ways ; a run on shore,
A splash among the dawties and the drink,
Soon tires, soon tires—then hey ! away
    again
To the wild life that's worthy of a man !
At forty, though, a sailor should be wise,
And 'ware temptation : whole a sailor, free,
But only half a sailor, though afloat,
When wedded. Don't you guess ? Though
    Dan was old,
His head was turn'd, while in the clachan
    here,
And by a woman,—Effie Paterson,
The daughter of a farmer on the hills,
And only twenty. Bonnie, say you ? Ay ;
As sweet a pout as ever grew on land ;
But soft and tender, with a quiet face
That needed the warm hearth to light it up,
And went snow-pallid at a puff of wind
Or whiff of danger. When I saw the trap,
I tried my best to wheedle Dan away,
Back to the brig ; but, red as ricks on fire,
He glinted with those angry eyes of his,

And linger'd. Then, 'twas nearly time to sail;
I talk'd of going, and it all came out:
He meant to *marry*, Jack !—and not content
With marrying, he meant to stop ashore!

Why, if a lightning flash had split our craft,
I should have wonder'd less. But, ' Bob,' says he,
' I love this lassie as I never thought
'Twas in my heart to love; and I have saved;
And I am tired of drifting here and there
On yonder waters: I have earn'd my rest,
And mean to stop ashore until I die.'
'Twas little use to argue things with Dan
When he had settled aught within his mind;
So all I said was vain. What could I do
But put a sunny face upon it all,
And bid him hasten on the day, that I
Might see his wedding, and be off again?

Yet soon I guess'd, before the wedding day,
That Effie did not care a cheep for Dan,
But scunner'd at his brave rough ways and tales
Of danger on the deep. His was a voice
Meant for the winds, with little power to whisper
The soft sleek things that make the women blush,
And tingle, and look sweet. Moreover, Dan
Was forty, and the lassie but a child.
I saw it all, but dared not speak my thought!
For Dan had money, Effie's folks were poor,
And Dan was blind, and Effie gave consent,
And talk was no avail. The wedding guests
Went up to Effie's home one pleasant day,
The minister dropp'd in, the kirk-bells rang,
And all was over. 'Twas a summer morn,
The blue above was fleck'd with feathery down,
The Sea was smooth, and peaceful, and the kirk
Stood mossy here upon the little hill,
And seem'd to smile a blessing over all.

And Effie? Ah! keep me from women, Jack!
Give them a bit o' sunshine—and they smile,
Give them a bit o' darkness—and they weep;
But smiles and tears with them are easy things,
And cheat ye like the winds. On such a day,
With everybody happy roundabout,
Effie look'd happy too; and if her face
Flush'd and was fearful, that was only joy;
For when a woman blushes, who can tell
Whether the cause be gladness, pride, or shame?
And Dan (God bless him!) look'd as young as you,
Trembled and redden'd lass-like, and I swear,
Had he not been a sailor, would have cried.
So I was cheer'd, next day, when off I went
To take his post as captain of the brig,
And I forgot my fears, and thought them wrong,
And went across the seas with easy heart,
Thinking I left a happy man behind.

But often, out at sea, I thought of Dan,
Wonder'd if he was happy. When the nights
Were quiet, still, and peaceful, I would lie
And listen to the washing of the waves,
And think: 'I wonder if this very light
Is dropping far away on poor old Dan?
And if his face looks *happy* in it, while
He sleeps by Effie's side?' On windy nights
I used to think of Dan with trouble and fear;
And often, when the waves were mountains high,
And we were lying-to before the wind,
The screaming surges seem'd to take the shape
Of this old clachan, and I seem'd to hear
Dan calling me; and I would drink the salt,
And pace the deck with all my blood on fire,
Thinking—' If Dan were driving on out here,
Dashing and weather-beaten, never still,
He would be happier!'

　　　　　　　Ay! though the Storm
Roll'd on between us, voices came from Dan
To tell me he was lonely on the land.
Often, when I was sailing in the ship,
He crept about these caves and watch'd the Moon
Silv'ring the windless places of the sea,
And thought of me! or on the beach he lay,
And wearied to the breaking of the waves!
Or out from land he row'd his boat, and gazed
Wistfully eastward! or on windy nights
He speel'd yon cliffs above the shore, and set
His teeth together in the rain and wind,
Straining eyes seaward, seeking lights at sea,
And pacing up and down upon the brink
As if he trode the decks! Why, things like those
Saved him from sinking, salted all his blood,
And soothed his heartache. Wind and wave are far
More merciful than a young woman's heart!

Why, had she been a bickering hizzle, fill'd
With fire and temper, stubborn as a whin,
And cushlingmushling o'er a cheerless fire,
Dan might have brought her round : *that* was the work
He understood full well ; and, right or wrong,
He would have been the Skipper to the end.
But though a man who has been train'd at sea,
Holding a hard strong grip on desperate men,
Can sink his voice and play a gentle part
In sunny seasons, he has little power
To fight with *women's* weapons. Dan, be sure,
Loved Effie with a love the deeper far
And tenderer because he had been bred
On the rough brine ; but when, from day to day,
He met a weary and a waning face,
That tried to smile, indeed, but could not smile,
And saw the tears where never tears should be,
Yet never met an angry look or word,

What could he do? He loved the lass too well
To scold ; tried soothing words, but they were spent
Upon a heart where the cold crancreuch grew ;
And, when the sorrow grew too sharp to bear,
Stole sicken'd from the dwelling. Plain he saw
The lass was dreary, though she kept so still,
And loved him not, though nothing harsh was said,
But fretted, and grew thin, and haunted him
With a pale face of gentleness and grief.
O Jack, Jack, Jack! of all the things accurst,
Worse than a tempest and the rocks ahead,
Is misty weather, not a breath of wind,
And the low moaning of some unseen shore !
Homeless and sad and troubled by her face,
If Dan had let his heart and brain keep still,
Let the sick mildew settle on his soul,
He would have shrunk into a wretched thing
The rains might beat on, and the winds might lash,
And ne'er have had the heart to stand erect,
And set his teeth, and face them, and subdue.
What could he do, but try to ease his heart
By haunting yonder beach, and glorying
In stormy seasons, thinking of the life
He used to lead, with ocean-sound for ever
Making a second life within his blood,
Thinking of me, and feeling that his soul
Was soothed a bit by his old friend the Sea?

And Effie, as the dawn look'd down each day,
Turn'd from the happy shining of the sun,
In wanrest and in tears ; and poor old Dan
Dree'd bitterly the dreary life on land.
No stanchgrass ever heal'd a wound so deep !

'Twas comfort dwelling in so wild a place,
So near to open water ; but for that,
I do not think he could have borne to dwell
Pining ashore. His trouble grew and grew:
No corsy-belly warm'd at Effie's fire,
No doctor's watch tick'd by the jizzen-bed,

No sound of tiny footfalls fill'd the house
With happy cheer ; the dull and lifeless
    mood
Grew on the wife ; her sense of shame
    seem'd gone ;
She paid no heed to dress, or to the house,
But faded, like a pale-faced, listless flower,
Grown in a weedy garden. Then, indeed,
To see all household goods neglected so,
The crowsfeet gathering round Effie's eyes,
The ingleside so cheerless and so cold,
Dan clench'd his fists, and storm'd with
    thunder-voice ;
But Effie only trembled, and was still,
Or threw her apron o'er her face and wept ;
And Dan, who never in his life could bear
To see a woman weep, pleaded and
    begg'd,—
Without avail. Then many and many a
    night
He roam'd the silent cliffs till peep of day,
Or join'd the fishers, out upon the sea ;
And many and many a night he thought he
    heard
My voice a-calling him. One night of storm,
When the sky murmur'd, and the foam-
    fleck'd sea
Flash'd in the fireflaught round the shadowy
    cliffs,
He fix'd to run away ;—but could not go,
Until he gazed on Effie's face once more ;
And when he stole into her room unheard,
He saw her sleeping with a happy smile,
So still, so sweet, so bonnie in her dream,
So like the shining lass she used to be,
That his heart sank, he swaver'd forth again,
And lay upon the waterside and wept,
And tho' the wind was whistling in his eyes,
Tho' the still fireflaught flash'd upon the
    foam,
He felt too weak, too timid, and too sad,
To quit her in the little cottage here,
And dree again the dangers of the deep.

The house is yonder—ay, the slated
    house,
With little patch of garden. Mark the pool
Of water at the door. Beyond you see
The line of boats, drawn high and dry, and
    yonder
The dull, green water, with the purple stain
Out eastward, and the sunlight slanting
    through

Upon a sail. Mark how the clachan lies
Down in the gully, with the barren hills,
Where never ran-tree waves its silver hair,
On either side. Look backward, now !
    The glen,
Hollow'd between the hills, goes inland, far
As eye can see—with yellow pools of rain,
And cattle looking shadowy in the mists
Upon the slopes. How still and dull looks
    all !
'Tis plain you gather, with a sailor's eye,
The danger. When the rains have lasted
    long,
The yellow Waters (rightly christen'd here
The Scaith o' Bartle) gather up the glen,
Suck in the strength of flying mist and cloud,
And, bursting from the hollows where they
    meet,
Rush seaward, with a roaring like the sea,
O'erwhelming all. Thrice has the mischief
    come
In one-and-twenty years.

                            When I came home,
A month ago, and walk'd across the hills
From Cardy town, I paused on yonder cliffs,
And saw the clachan lying at my feet,—
The setting sun shining upon the house
Where Dan was dwelling. Nought was
    alter'd there !
The very smacks and fish-boats just the
    same
As when I quitted. While I stood and
    gazed,
I saw a stooping figure with a staff,
Standing hard by me on the cliffs, and gazing
Silently seaward. As I look'd, he turn'd,
And though the face was haggard, worn,
    and old,
And every hair upon the head was gray,
And the fresh life about the limbs was lost,
I knew old Dan, and, shouting blithely, ran
To hug him to my heart ; and he turn'd
    white,
Shaking like straw in wind, to find 'twas *me*.
Then, when the shock was over, and we
    talk'd,
He brighten'd,—as an icicle turns bright
When shone on. But my heart was shock'd
    and sore !
He was the ghost of what he once had been ;
His voice was broken, and his welcome
    seem'd

Like one's who, sinking on his pillow, smiles
To see a face he loves before he dies;
And when his air grew cheerier, and at last
His love for me came lighter on his look,
His cheeriness seem'd sadder far than all.
Swavering down the path, he took my arm,
Leant heavily on his staff, as if he dream'd,
Talk'd of old times, and friends alive and dead,
Until we halted at his cottage door;
And, while he lifted up the latch, he cast
His eyes to windward, read the weather signs,
After old habit, ere he enter'd in.

Effie was there,—changed too; she welcomed me,
Moved but and ben the house with a light step,
And smiled a bit:—all women have a smile,
A happiness, a kind of second self,
Kept for fresh faces. Yet I saw full soon
The bield was homeless; little love was there;
Ah, that was common talk aroundabout!
The first flush faded soon from Effie's face,
Leaving it dull and wan; she moved about
Like a sick lassie risen from a dream;
And oft, when we were seated in the lowe,
She started, and her colour went and came;
And though her features wore a kind of fear,
There was a light of youth there: she would keek
At Dan, whose eyes were fix'd upon the fire,
Hang o'er her knitting, breathing deep, and then
Hearken and hearken, till the soft bright blush
Died by degrees, her face became composed
To pallor, and the light had gone away,
Leaving her sick and soopit once again.

At last, when we were smoking in the bield
One dull day in November, Dan arose
And took his stick, and, beckoning me, went out:
I follow'd; and he never spake a word,
But gript me by the arm, and walk'd along,
Until we left the clachan far behind,
And took a pathway winding up the hills.
For many weeks, at intervals, the rain
Had fallen; and the hills were dreeping damp,
And down their sides ran many streams new-born,
Making an eerie murmur. Far away
Ben Callachan was glimmering through a mist,
And all round Bartle rose a vaporous steam
Silent and white, with cattle here and there
Dismally looming. Still and dull was all—
So still, so chill; only the faint sharp stir
That is a sound, but seems a click within
The ear itself;—save when from far away
A cow would low, and echoes faint and far
Died inland, or when, blowing on the wind,
A cry came from the sea, whose waves we saw
Beyond us, breaking in a shadowy cloud,
With gleams of glittering foam. But Dan walk'd on,
Scarce heeding ought; and yet his sailor's eye
Took in the signs, and glinted up and down
With the old cunning; but his heart was full,
His voice was broken like a weeping wean's,
And as we went along he told me all.

All that you guess! but somewhat more
—a thought
Of later growth, a nettle in his heart—
That Effie was not true, as wives should be;
And that her fairest thoughts were fallen things
That clung around a fresh young lover's knees.
I stared at Dan, and hearken'd in amaze!
His grip was tight upon my arm, his face
White as the snow on Callachan, his voice
Shrill as a sea-gull's shriek; and all at once
He waved his arms, turn'd his wild face away,
And cried aloud with a full heart—'O God!
Why did I ever cease to sail the Sea?'

I tried to argue with him—he was dumb!
And yet I saw, had I been daft enough
To echo him, he would have hated me.
He only half believed the things he said,
And would have turn'd in wrath on any man
Who could believe them true, and say the same.
He loved the braxie still, as few can love,

Save the Good Shepherd, who has love for all !
Could not have tholed to hear another's thoughts
Condemn her! blamed himself for all his grief!
And gladly would have died beneath her feet,
To win one word, one kiss, one shining look,
To show his love had not been quite in vain!

But on we fared, so fill'd with our own thoughts,
We scarcely saw how far away we wander'd,
How mirk all grew, how close the gathering clouds
Drew to the hill-tops, while the cattle raised
Their heads into the dismal air and cried.
Then, suddenly, there came a lightning gleam
That for a moment lighted up the hills,
The far-off cliffs, and the far flash of foam,
And faded,—to a sound as if the earth
And heavens were torn asunder. Soon the storm
Deepen'd—the thunder and the lightning came
Ofter than dark or silence ; and I felt
Far less myself on those dull endless heights,
Than seeing, hearing, from my ship at sea.
But Dan said little ; only, as the drops
Of rain began to fall, he led the way
Into a mountain shieling, roof'd with turfs,
Where we in shelter crouch'd, and still talk'd on
Of his dull ingleside, his darken'd days,
The terror and the pain he had to dree.
And 'All I care for now is ended, Bob!
I want to die, but not to leave the lass
Untended and unhappy. After all,
I cannot blame her for her crancreuch face,—
She is so young—mid-eild is past with me—
Be sure that she would love me if she could!'
And then he glower'd out on the dark, and groan'd,
'Would I were in my grave!—would I were doom'd
Among the waves!—would I were far out yonder,
Praying and sinking in a boat at sea!'

And I was silent ; but the elements
Made answer. With a clash like iron fell
The headlong torrent of the soot-black clouds,
Drowning the thunders with its dreesome cry,
Birming above, around, and smiting earth
With strength of stone. Never for many a year
Had such a fall been known : it seem'd the Lord
Unlocking all His waters to destroy
The bad world o'er again. No rainbow there
To promise sunshine and a speedy end!
For 'twas the Black Rain, which had once or twice
Gone southward, making frighted Elders groan,
And which old wives in Bartle often call
The 'Deil's rain,' thinking Satan flies himself,
Dropping the dreadful blackness from above.
Silent we waited, watching, and the air
Was full of a great roar—the sods beneath
Seem'd shaking—and the rain-wash forced a way
Through the thick turf above our heads, and fell
Upon us, splashing, as with watery ink,
Our hands and faces. But I saw Dan's eye
Had kindled. He was younger. For the sounds
Quicken'd his sense of life, brought up his strength,
And minded him of former fearsome days
Upon the Ocean ; and his other self—
The sickly self that lived the life on land—
Forsook him. Then there was a lull, a pause—
Not broken by the further fall of rain,
Nor by the thunder-claps, but by a sign
More terrible than all—a roar, a groan,
A motion as of waters, and a sound
Like the dread surging of an angry Sea.

And Dan threw up his arms, screaming aloud,
'THE SCAITH! THE SCAITH!'—and groan'd, and rush'd away,—
I following close behind him in the mirk.

And on he tore, until he gain'd a craig,
Above the glen, yonder between the hills;
And cattle huddled round him, lowing loud,
And the Scaith thicken'd, and the murmur grew,
While we gazed down. The mists hung round the heights,
The rain still fell, but faintly,—and below,
Roaring on seaward, snatching in its course
Boulders and trees and cattle, rush'd the Scaith,
A blacken'd yellow wash of waters, foaming
Where'er it touched the feet of stone or steep,
And dizzily whirling round the great tree-roots
To twist them from their beds. White, scared, and stunn'd,
Dan groan'd, and sank upon his knees, and sobbed.
Done was the thunder; but the waters made
Another thunder, and the fireflaught came
Fainter and fainter. Then we heard from far
A sound more awful—shrieks of living men,
Children and women; while the thinning clouds
Parted to westward, brightening at the rims,
And rays of misty sunset slanted down
On Bartle, and the Scaith had seized its prey.

'Effie!' cried Dan; and sped along the hills,
And would have rush'd right downward to his death
Had I not gript him. But we found a way
O'er the hillside, and gain'd the northern height
Above the clachan. Jack, until I die,
That hour will haunt me! For the village lay
Naip-deep beneath the moaning rain-dyed flood,
And bields sank shatter'd, and the sunset cold
Gleam'd upon Bartle and the sea beyond;
And on the slopes on either side there gather'd
Women and men: some screeching as they saw
The Scaith drink up their houses and their goods,
Some crying for the friends they could not see,
Some sitting still, and looking on their bairns,
As if they had gone wild. Then Dan glared round,
Seeking for Effie,—but he saw her not;
And the damp sunset gleaming on his face,
Grimed with the rain-drops, show'd it ghastly pale,
But he was cool as he had often been
On gruesome nights at sea. 'She is not here!'
He whispered; 'yet she cannot but be saved.
Perchance she gathers with the folk that stand
Waving their arms yonder across the flood:
Oh! would my eyes were young that I might see.'
That way *I* gazed; but all that I could see
Were mists beyond the clachan; down below,
The wildly washing waters; here and there,
Women and children screaming on the roofs,
While punts and skiffs were gliding here and there,
Piloting slowly through the rocks and walls,
To succour those unsaved; at intervals
A leafless tree-top peering through the water,
While frighted birds lit on its twigs, or wheel'd
Around it crying. Then, 'A boat! a boat!'
Dan cried; but he was crying to the air:
The folk around him heard and made a stir,—
But some scarce raised their wild and watery eyes,
And some stopp'd moaning, look'd at him who cried,
And then again sat rocking to and fro,
Gazing straight downward, and with eerie groans
Bewailing their own sorrow.

         Then the place
Blacken'd in gloaming—mists rose from the flood—
The sky turn'd black, with neither stars nor moon,

And down below, flashing from place to place,
The lights, like corpse-lights warning folk of death,
Flitted and faded, showing where the boats
Still moved about upon their weary work
And those who grieved were stiller all around;
The solemn moaning of the Scaith was hush'd,
Your ears could hear the sobbing of the Sea;
And only now and then a hollow splash
Spake plain of walls that yielded and slipt down
Into the waters. Then a light came near,
And to the water's edge a fishing-boat
Brought a dead fisher, and a little child
Who cried for 'mither'; and as he who row'd
Handed the bairn to hungry outstretch'd arms,
And landed with the corpse, old Dan leapt in,
Snatching the lanthorn from the fisher's hand,
Push'd off ere I could follow, and had flown
Into the darkness . . .

    Jack,—I never again
Saw poor old Dan, alive! Yet it was well
His woes were ended; for that very day,
Ere the Scaith came, Effie had crept from home,—
Ay, with a man;—and ere I knew the truth
Why, she was out upon the ocean waves,
And fleeing with the loon to Canada.
Ill winds pursue her! God will find her out!
He sent His water down to free old Dan,
And He is after her across the Deep!

 Next dawning, when the Scaith was part subdued,
And sinking slowly through the seams of earth,
Pouring in bright brown burns to join the sea,
Fouling with mud the line of breaking foam,
'Twas a most piteous sight to see the folk,
With spade and mattock, digging at the graves
Of their own dwellings; taking what was saved
With bitter thankless faces. Fallen walls,
And trees uprooted from the waste hill-sides,
And boulders swept from far along the glen,
And household lumber gather'd everywhere,
Mingled in ruin; and the frailer bields
Were swept away for ever. As for me,
I had my work in hand. I took a spade
And waded through the thick and muddy pools,
('Twas still waist-deep,) right onward to the place
Where Dan had dwelt. For something drew me there,
Foremost of all. The bield was standing still,
Though doors and windows had been beaten in;
And as I splash'd along the passage, bits
Of household lumber tripped me; but I went
Right on to Effie's room, and there the flood
Was lying black and cold;—and there lay Dan.

 Washing upon the water, with his face
Drawn downward, his hands clench'd, his long gray hair
Rippling around him—stiff, and cold, and dead
And when I turn'd his face up to the light,
I did not scunner much—it look'd so strong,
So seaman-like, and fine. I saw it all!
How he had drifted thither in the dark,
And found the water low around the bield,
But slowly rising; how he fought his way,
Search'd but and ben, and last, in Effie's room,
Stood ghastly in the lanthorn light, and saw
The place was empty; how, while there he stood,
Staring in horror, with an eldritch cry
The wild SCAITH struck the crashing window panes,
Dash'd down the lanthorn, gript him in the dark,

Roar'd in his ears, and while it struck him
  down,
Out of his nostrils suck'd the breath of life.
Jack, Jack, we know there comes to men
  who drown
A sudden flashing picture of the past,—
And ah! how pitiful, how pitiful,
In that last minute did the picture come:
A vision of the sounding Sea afar,
A ghaistly ship upon it,—Effie's face,
Coming and going like to floating foam,—
The picture of the kirk upon the hill,
And sunshine smiling on the wedding
  guests,—
The shadowy cliffs where he had paced in
  pain,
The waves, the sun, the moon, the thought
  of me,
All thicken'd on him as he scream'd her
  name,
And struggled with the cruel Scaith, and
  died!

Ay! God Almighty's water, e'en ashore,
More merciful than women, found him out;
And here he lies, but should have lain else-
  where.
Had Scots law, and the blethering woman's
  tongues,
Not hinder'd me,—I would have ta'en a
  boat,
And sewn his body in a sheet, with stones
Fasten'd beneath his soles to sink him
  down,
And row'd out yonder, westward, where the
  sun
Dips red beneath the straight blue water
  line,
Then said a prayer, and softly sent him
  down
Where he could sleep in peace, and hear
  for ever
The washing of the waters through the
  depths:
With flag-flowers o'er his head, great weeds
  all round,
And white salt foam-bells hanging in his
  ears,
His would have been a sailor's sleep indeed!
But as it is, he slumbers here on land, ·
In shade of Bartle Kirk, 'mong country
  loons
And fishermen that shrink at open Sea.

THE GLAMOUR.

The hills close round her—everywhere
Strange voices deepen in the air;
The pain, the hope, the agony,
Flash to a sense of mystery;
The shapes of earth and air and skies
Catch glamour in her weary eyes;
Worn with the pain, worn with the pain,
She would lie down, and sleep again!

O Lord my God, draw not Thy hand away—
The sleep-stoure fills my eyes—I feel my
  grave—
And I would reach a painless end, like those
Thy glamour ne'er hath troubled. I have
  been
O'er long a shadow on the paths of men,
O'er long a screeching bird in happy bields,
O'er long a haunted wanderer day and
  night.
Lord, let me die! Lord, let me die! Lord
  God,
Pity and spare me! Draw Thy hand away!
Thy breath is on me in the mirk, and ah!
I sicken sore, while yonder through the pane
Corpse-candles, blowing blue against the
  wind,
Flit slowly to the kirkyard, down Glen-Earn.

What had I done, that Thou shouldst
  pick me out,
To breathe Thy glamour on? I was a lass
Happy and heartsome, till that dreesome
  day
I walk'd from kirk by moonlight down the
  glen,
And saw Maccaskill of Craig-Dhonil pass,
Sewn to the middle in his winding-sheet,
And waving hairy arms until I swoon'd;—
And ere a year was run Maccaskill died;
And then I kenn'd I had the bitter gift
My father and my father's father had.
Yet I was young, and felt a kind o' pride,
To see so far into Thy mysteries,—
To ken when man or wife was doom'd to
  die;
To see the young life in a lassie's wame,
Although her snood was whole; to prophesy
Tempests and human losses. Many a man
Then turn'd away; but Kenneth married
  me—

Kenneth Macdonald, sheep-herd on the hills,
A holy man and kind ; and for a time
The glamour came no more, and I was gay,
Feeling the young bairn underneath my breast
Breathe softly with the rocking of my heart.
But in the winter gloaming, when the drift
Was thick around the door, and winds were blowing,
And I was lying on the jizzen-bed,
And Jean the howdie wash'd my paps with salt,
I saw a strange thing lying on her knee—
A span-long body in a blood-stain'd sowe—
And scream'd and cried, 'Jean, Jean, the bairn will die !'
And so it was. For while old mother slipt
Out to the kitchen lowe, where Kenneth sat,
To drop a cinder through the wee white sark,
The bairn came dead into the chilly mirk ;
And in the snowy dawning I beheld
The span-long body of my sweet first-born,
Wrapt in its sowe, upon the howdie's knee.

But *Angus* lived—my white-faced sickly bairn,
The last I bore ; for, ere I rose from bed,
I heard, one gloaming dark, from but the house,
A sound of sawing, hewing with an adze,
Mix'd with a sound of weeping, clapping hands ;
And all the bield was empty,—and I knew
A shell was being made for some one near ;
And ah ! before the moon was full again
Just as the season of the lambing came,
My bonnie man was sheeted in the house,
And stiff, and cold ; and I was left alone,
Shadow'd and sad, with hot tears dropping down
On Angus, pulling feebly at my breast.

I never bedded with another man,
Never bare wean again ; but I could earn
Both food and drink, and all my pride and joy
Was Angus. Lord, he was the bonniest bairn
The sweetest, gentlest, ever wrought in flesh,
To gladden mother's eyes. The very day

That he was born, I call'd the minister,
Who gave him baptism, that the glamour ne'er,
Might come on him or his ; and ah ! he grew,
Pale like a lily—for this solemn world
O'er gentle ; and the glamour brought no fear
To mirk our dwelling. Nay, for many a year,
The eerie light seem'd gone away from me,
For never ghaist or burial cross'd my path,
Corpse-light or wraith. Then Angus on the hills
Grew sheep-herd, like his father, though he lack'd
His father's fearless heart ; and, as he grew,
Turn'd weaker, whiter—bonnie still, but thin
And bloodless ; and he lack'd the heart to face
Darkness and danger : ringing of a bell
At midnight, sudden footsteps in the dark,
A hand placed on his shoulder suddenly,
Would strike him down into a swooning fit,
Dreesome to see ; and when his eighteenth year
Was o'er, he sometimes sicken'd at my face,
And shiver'd though he knew me. All at once
The glamour came across my Soul again.
One night, while we were seated in the bield,
I heard a wailing come from but the house,
And horror gript me. 'Mother !' Angus cried,
Glow'ring full fear'd into my burning eyes,
'What ails thee?' 'Wheesht !' I whisper'd ; 'hear ye nought ?'
'Nought ! Angus said. And then I heard a sound
Of groans, and clapping hands ; and suddenly
I saw my Angus shrink until he grew
As small as any babe new-born, and turn,
Swift as the fireflaught, to himself again ?—
And while I scream'd, and fell upon his neck,
Weeping, and kissing him, and moaning low,
He sicken'd at my face, and swoon'd away.

For, though I hid the trouble from my bairn,
Long had he known his mother was a seer,

Whose eyes were troubled by mysterious
    things ;
And every shade he saw upon my face
Distraught him, lest I saw before his path
Mishap or death. My white-faced, fearful
    bairn !
My drooping Angus, with his soft, wide
    eyes,
And fluttering mouth! Alone upon the
    hills,
He trembled—fear'd the lightning and the
    storm—
Tholed not to lie within the dark alone—
And would have wither'd in his bairndom's
    time,
Had I not cheer'd him with a smiling face.

Lord, Thou wert sore upon me ! I was
    lone,
And Angus was my pleasure. I was
    haunted,
And Angus was my help. Yet, once again,
Thy glamour struck me, and I knew, I
    knew,
Angus must die. Hard, hard, both day
    and night,
I tried to cheat myself and hope, and smiled
On Angus, till his heart grew still once more.
But it was all in vain. Thrice Angus
    shrunk,
Three several gloamings, seated in his chair.
And I kept down my fear, and did not
    scream ;
And oft I heard the wailing in the house,
And sounding of the kirk-bells down Glen-
    Earn
At midnight. Then I sicken'd and grew
    thin,
And hunger'd o'er my bairn, and pray'd,
    and pray'd,—
And what to me was light of sun or star
If Angus went away ?

    . . . It was a night
Quiet and cold. The moon and stars were
    out,
The moon-dew glittering on the hills.
    Alone,
I sat, awaiting Angus. It grew late,
And Angus came not ; and the low winds
    blew,
And the clock tick'd, and ah ! my heart was
    dark.

Then, last, I took my cloak, and wander'd
    forth,
To see if he was coming down the Glen,
And took the cold wet pathway in the moon
Until I reach'd the foot of Cawmock Craig,
And saw the straight rock rise into the lift,
Its side all dark, but on its top the Moon
Shining full bright and chilly. As I stood,
I heard a shout, and saw, far, far above,
A figure dark between me and the lift,
Threading the narrow paths around the
    Craig
Whence many a man hath fallen and been
    slain ;
And even then—Lord, Lord !—Thy glamour
    dropt
Upon me, and I saw before my face
The wraith of Angus wrapt in bloody sowe
Gliding before me in the ghaistly light.
Shrill as an owl, I screech'd !—and up above
My Angus heard, and sicken'd, and swam
    round,
And, swooning on the sharp edge of the
    Craig,
Dash'd downward to his death !—

    . . . O bonnie, bonnie
Look'd Angus, lying in his sowe asleep,
Quiet like moonlight on his face, his hair
Kaim'd back and shining round his cold
    white ears.
And yonder in the cold kirkyard he lies ;
And, Lord, I want to slumber at his side,
And cheer him in the darkness of the
    grave,—
For he was ever fearful, weak, and pale—
A young man with a white bairn's timorous
    soul.
And, Lord, I think that Thou at last art
    kind,
For oft the white wraith, glimmering at my
    side,
Hath waved its arms, and moan'd, and
    look'd like *me* :
And I have watched it ever, not afraid,
But sad and smiling, and what dress I
    wore
The wraith hath worn ; and when I turn'd
    my gown
And let the grey hairs hang all down my
    neck,
The wraith too, turn'd its gown, and loos'd
    its hair ;

And yonder, yonder, yonder through the pane
The blue corpse-candles, blowing in the wind,
Flit slowly to the kirkyard, down Glen-Earn.

SIGURD OF SAXONY.

(MEDIÆVAL.)

The sedgy shores of this enchanted lake
Are dark with shadows of the swans which make
    Their nests along its marge ;
And on the hither side, where silver waves
Curl with low music into hollow caves,
    Waiting for that bright barge
Which beareth sleepers to the silent land,
I, Sigurd, in my ghostly sorrow, stand.

I stand alone beneath heaven's silent arch,
Shaded both night and day by clouds that march
    And countermarch above ;
A sombre suit of perfect mail I wear,
A gloomy plume, that troubles the thin air
    To murmurs if I move ;
My sword is red and broken ; and my shield
Bears a gold anchor on a sable field.

This is a place where mortals find not speech ;
Save the small murmurous waves that crawl the beach,
    All is as still as death :
I hear my heart against my ribs of stone,
Like to a wild bird in the net, make moan ;
    My slow and frozen breath
Curls like a vapour o'er the silent spot ;
My shadow seeks my feet, and moveth not.

Nought can redeem her. Wherefore I seek grace
To join her in her distant dwelling-place
    Of pastoral repose ;
And I would make this heart that aches and grieves
As white and perfect as a lily's leaves
    And fragrant as a rose,

That with a stainless spirit I may take
The solemn barge across the enchanted lake.

For, having worn her stainless badge in fight,
Thrice conquering in her name, by day and night
    I rode with vizor down,
Meeting and slaying honourable foes,
Wounded in flesh, giving and taking blows
    To compass her renown.
Thus, warring a sweet war without reprieve,
I, Sigurd, wore her badge upon my sleeve.

Armèd from head to heel, with spear in hand,
I cried her praises through the wondering land,
    And few her praise refused ;
Then flushing with my victory complete,
I hastened back and knelt me at her feet,
    Battered, and maimed, and bruised ;
And then I wooed her in a secret place,
With light upon me from her shining face.

She bathed my bloody brow, with red wounds striped,
And with a kerchief white as snow she wiped
    The foam from off my mouth ;
She set my unhelmed head upon her knee,
And wound white arms about me tenderly,
    And slaked the thirsty drouth
That ebbed in sluggish fire through blood and brain,
From a full cup of cool white porcelain.

Wherefore my soul again was strong. I caught
The voiceless music of her form and thought.
    I knelt upon my knee,
Saying, 'I love thee more than life or fame ;
I love thee only less than my good name,
    Which is a part of thee ;
And I adore thy beauty undefiled !'
Whereat she looked into mine eyes and smiled.

I wooed her night and day with virtuous deeds,
And that humility which intercedes

With ladies for true men.
I took her lily of a hand in mine,
Drinking her breath, as soft as eglantine,
And wooing well; and then
She toyed with my great beard, and gave consent:
So down the flowery path of love we went.

Twined closely, down the soft descent of love
We wandered on, with golden stars above,
And many flowers below,
Until we came to this dark lake or sea,
Which openeth upon eternity,
And could no farther go;
For beyond life and death, and these dark skies,
The place of sleep, the Silent Valley, lies.

Here on the beach we stood, and hand in hand
Waited to wander to that silent land,
And all the shore was dark;
Saying, 'We yearn to see the Happy Vale,
And hand in hand together we will sail
In the enchanted barque.'
Too late to turn: one passage we must take
Across the gleaming silence of the lake.

She said, 'The waters make such threatening moan,
Neither can pass across their waste alone;
We cannot, cannot part;
We will together cross these waves of death.'
But the dark waves grew darker, and the breath
Came colder from the heart;
And by each face a quiet cloud was worn,
Small as the shadow of a lamb new born.

Then in the distant waves we could behold
A radiance like the blowing autumn gold
Of woodland forests deep;
And my sweet lady trembled, growing white
As foam of ocean on a summer night,
When the wild surges leap;
And falling very cold upon my breast,
She faltered, 'I am weary,—let me rest.'

I laid her down upon a flowery bed,
And put soft mosses underneath her head,
And kissed her, and she slept;
And the air brightened round her, as the far
Blue ether burns like silver round a star.
And round her slumber crept
A trouble of the air, and silver clear
The ghostly light upon the lake grew near.

Yea, nearer, nearer grew the light, and soon,
Shaped like the sickle of the early moon,
The barge drew shoreward slow—
A vapour and a radiance all around,
A gleaming of fair faces, and a sound
Of flutes and lute-strings low.
And round my lady crept a shadowy crowd,
Fading and brightening like a moonlit cloud.

They clustered with a ghostly light around
My lady dear, and raised her from the ground,
And bare her to the barque:
Whereon I would have followed, but a hand
Held me like iron to the hated land.
Then all again was dark;
And from the breathing darkness came a hum
Of voices sweet, 'Thy time has not yet come.'

And then I shrieked in utter agony;
While fading far away upon the sea,
I saw the light again;
And with a cry into the waves I sprung,
And sought to follow, but the waters clung
About me like a chain;
And thrice I fought amid their rage and roar,
And thrice they hurled me bleeding on the shore.

Long have I waited here, alone, alone,
Hearing the melancholy waves make moan
Upon the pebbly beach:
With eyes upon the pitiless stars above
Here have I waited in my homeless love,
Pale, patient, deaf to speech,
With the salt rheum upon me, pale and bent,
And breathless as a marble monument.

This lonely watching would invite despair
Did I not oft catch glimpses of my fair
    Lady, so sadly lost,
Making, with radiance round her like a star,
A luminous pathway on the hill afar,
    Then fading like a ghost;
What time I shout aloud, and at the shout
Pause, shuddering at the echoes round about.

Twice has the barge returned: once for a bent
Old servitor, who, down the soft descent
    That leads to this dim land,
Had wandered from the towns that lie behind,
And, groping in the cold, had fall'n stone-blind
    Upon the shifting sand;
Once for a little gold-haired child astray,
Who, wandering hither, fell to sleep at play.

Twice has the mystic barge returned, and twice
Have I been frozen to the earth in ice,
    Helpless to move or speak;
Thrice have I fought with the relentless roar
Of water, and been flung upon the shore
    Battered, and maimed, and weak;
But now I wait with quiet heart and brain,
Grown patient with unutterable pain.

And I *will* wait. To slay myself were sin,
And I, self-slaughter'd, could not hope to win
    My solitary boon;
But if the barge should come again, and leave
Me still in lonely watch without reprieve,
    Under the silver moon
I will lie down upon my back and rest,
With mailèd hands crossed praying on my breast;

And fall to slumber on a bed of weeds,
A knight well worn in honourable deeds,
    Yet lost to life, and old;
And haply I may dream before I wake
That I am floating o'er the pathless lake
    In that bright barge of gold;
And, waking, I may see with sweet surprise
Light shining on me from my lady's eyes.

A POEM TO DAVID.*

I.

I WOULD not be lying yonder,
  Where thou, belovéd, art lying,
Though the nations should crown me living,
  And murmur my praises dying.

Better this fierce pulsation,
  Better this aching brain,
Than dream, and hear faintly above me
  The cry of the wind and the rain;

Than lie in the kirkyard lonely,
  With fingers and toes upcurled,
And be conscious of never a motion
  Save the slow rolling round of the world.

I would not be lying yonder,
  Though the seeds I had sown were springing!
I would not be sleeping yonder,
  And be done with striving and singing!

For the eyes are blinded with mildew,
  The lips are clammy with clay,
And worms in the ears are crawling,—
  But the brain is the brain for aye!

The brain is warm and glowing,
  Whatever the body be;
It stirs like a thing that breatheth,
  And dreams of the Past and To be!

Ay! down in the deep damp darkness
  The brains of the dead are hovelled!
They gleam on each other with radiance,
  Transcending the eye that is shrivelled!

Each like a faint lamp lighteth
  The skull wherein it dwelleth!
Each like a lamp turneth brighter
  Whenever the kirk-bell knelleth!

I would not be lying yonder
  Afar from the music of things,
Not were my green grave watered
  By the tears of queens and kings.

* David Gray, Author of *The Luggie*, and *other Poems*.

If the brain like a thing that breatheth
Is full of the Past and To be,
The silence is far more awful
Than the shriek and the agony ;

And the hope that sweetened living
Is gone with the light of the sun,
And the struggle seems wholly over,
And nothing at all seems done ;

And the dreams are heavy with losses,
And sins, and errors, and wrongs,
And you cannot hear in the darkness
If the people are singing your songs !

There's only the slow still rolling
Of the dark world round and round,
Making the dream more wondrous,
Though it render the sleep more sound.

'T is cold, cold, cold and weary,
Cold in a weary place :
The sense of the sin is present
Like the gleam of a demon's face !

What matter the tingling fingers
That touch the song above you?
What matter the young man's weeping,
And longing to know you and love you?

Nought has been said and uttered,
Nought has been seen or known,—
Detraction, the adder above you,
Is sunned on the cold grave-stone.

II.

Yet 't is dark here, dark,
And the voices call from below !
'T is so dark, dark, dark,
That it seems not hard to go !

'T is dark, dark, dark,
And we close our eyes and are weary !
'T is dark, dark, dark,
And the waiting seems bitter and dreary !

And yonder the sun is shining,
And the green, long grass hath grown,
And the cool kirk-shade looks pleasant,
And you lie so alone, so alone !

The world is heartless and hollow,
And singing is sad without you,
And I think I could bear the dreaming
Were mine arms around about you ;

Were thy lips to mine, belovéd,
And thine arms around me too,
I think I could lie in silence,
And dream as we used to do !

The flesh and the bones might wither,
The blood be dried like dew,
The heart might crumble to ashes,
Till dust was dust anew ;

And the world with its slow still motion
Might roll on its heavenward way,—
And our brains upon one another
Would gleam till the Judgment Day !

HAKON.

HAKON of Thule, ere he died,
Summoned a Priest to his bed-side.

' Ho, Priest ! ' with blackening brow quoth he,
' What comfort canst thou cast to me ?'

The young Priest, with a timorous mouth,
Told of the new gods of the South,—

Of Mary Mother and her Child,
And holy Saints with features mild ;

Of those who hate and those who love,
Of Hell beneath and Heaven above.

Then Hakon laughed full loud and shrill—
' Serve thy puny gods who will ! '

Then, roaring to his benchman red,
' Slit me the throat o' the Priest,' he said ;

' His red heart's blood shall flow before,
As steaming sacrifice to Thor !

' Bring me my mighty drinking-cup :
With fiery wine now fill it up ! '

Then, though so faint his life's blood ran,
' Let me die standing, like a man ! '

He swore, and staggered to his legs,
And drained the goblet to the dregs.

' Skaal be to the gods ! ' he said—
His great heart burst, and he was dead !

Sonnets

WRITTEN BY LOCH CORUISK,* ISLE OF SKYE.

(1870.)

Late in the gloaming of the year,
I haunt the melancholy Mere;
A Phantom I, where phantoms brood,
In that soul-searching solitude.
Hiding my forehead in the dim
Hem of His robe, I question Him!

CORUISKEN SONNETS.

I.

LORD, IS IT THOU?

LORD, is it Thou? GOD, do I touch indeed
Thy raiment hem, that rolls like vapour dark?
O homeless Spirit, that fleest us in our need,
Pause! answer! while I kneel, remain and mark. . .
Father! . . . Ere back they bear me, cold and stark,
Across Thy darken'd threshold,—ere I plead
For love no longer, pity me, and hark!
Surviving the long tale of craft and creed,
The dumb Hills gather round me, gaunt and gray,—
The Waters utter their monotonous moan,—
The immemorial Heavens, with no groan,
Bend dim eyes down, as on their natal day:
Cold are all these as snow, and still as stone;
But *I* have found a voice—to plead, to pray.

II.

WE ARE FATHERLESS.

I FOUND Thee not by the starved widow's bed,
Nor in the sick-rooms where my dear ones died;

In Cities vast I hearken'd for Thy tread,
And heard a thousand call Thee, wretched-eyed,
Worn out, and bitter. But the Heavens denied
Their melancholy Maker. From the Dead!
Assurance came, nor answer. Then I fled
Into these wastes, and raised my hands, and cried:
'The seasons pass—the sky is as a pall—
Thin wasted hands on withering hearts we press—
There is no God—in vain we plead and call,
In vain with weary eyes we search and guess—
Like children in an empty house sit all,
Cast-away children, lorn and fatherless.'

III.

WE ARE CHILDREN.

CHILDREN indeed are we—children that wait
Within a wondrous Dwelling, while on high
Stretch the sad vapours and the voiceless sky;
The House is fair, yet all is desolate
Because our Father comes not; clouds of fate
Sadden above us—shivering we espy
The passing rain, the cloud before the gate,
And cry to one another, 'He is nigh!'
At early morning, with a shining Face,
He left us innocent and lily-crown'd;

---

* For a detailed description of Loch Coruisk, see the writer's Prose Works, Volume v.

And now 'tis late—night cometh on apace—
 We hold each other's hands and look
   around,
Frighted at our own shades! Heaven send
   us grace!
 When He returns, all will be sleeping
   sound.

IV.
WHEN WE ARE ALL ASLEEP.

WHEN He returns, and finds the World so
   drear—
 All sleeping,—young and old, unfair and
   fair,
Will He stoop down and whisper in each
   ear,
 'Awaken!' or for pity's sake forbear,—
Saying, 'How shall I meet their frozen
   stare
 Of wonder, and their eyes so full of fear?
How shall I comfort them in their de-
   spair,
 If they cry out, "Too late! let us sleep
   here"?'
Perchance He will not wake us up, but
   when
 He sees us look so happy in our rest,
Will murmur, ' Poor dead women and
   dead men!
 Dire was their doom, and weary was their
   quest.
Wherefore awake them unto life again?
 Let them sleep on untroubled—it is best.'

V.
BUT THE HILLS WILL BEAR WITNESS.

BUT ye,—ye Hills that gather round this
   day,
 Ye Mountains, and ye Vapours, and ye
   Waves,
Ye will attest the wrongs of men of clay,
 When, in a World all hush'd, sits on our
   graves
The melancholy Maker. From your
   caves
 Strange echoes of our old lost life shall
   come;
With still eyes fixed on your vast archi-
   traves,
 Nature shall speak, though mortal lips be
   dumb.

Then God will cry: 'Sadly the Waters
   fall,
 Sadly the Mountains keep their snowy
   state,
The Clouds pass on, the Winds and Echoes
   call,
 The World is sweet, yet wearily I wait.
'Though all is fair, and I am Lord of all,
 Without my Children I am desolate.'

VI.
DESOLATE!

DESOLATE! How the Peaks of ashen gray,
 The smoky Mists that drift from hill to
   hill,
The Waters dark, anticipate this day
 That sullen desolation. Oh, how still
The shadows come and vanish, with no
   will!
 How still the Waters watch the heaven's
   array!
How still the melancholy vapours stray,
 Mirror'd below, and drifting on, fulfil
Thy mandate as they mingle!—Not a
   sound,
 Save that deep murmur of a torrent near,
Deepening silence. Hush! the dark pro-
   found
 Groans, as some gray crag loosens and
   falls sheer
To the abyss. Wildly I look around,
 O Spirit of the Human, are Thou *here*?

VII.
LORD, ART THOU HERE?

LORD, art Thou here? far from the cities
   zones,
 Brooding in melancholy solitude;
Hushing Thy breath to awful undertones,
 Darkening Thy face, if mortal foot in-
   trude.
Father, how shall I meet Thee in this
   mood?
 How shall I ask Thee why Thou dwell'st
   with stones,
While far away the world, like Lazarus,
   groans,
 Sick for Thy healing. Father, if Thou
   be'st good,

And wise, and gentle, oh come down, come
    down!
Come like an Angel with a human face,
Pass through the gates into the hungry
    Town,
Comfort the weary, send the afflicted
    grace,
Shine brighter on the Graves where we lay
    down
Our dear ones, cheer them in the narrow
    place!

VIII.
GOD IS BEAUTIFUL.

OH, Thou art beautiful! and Thou dost
    bestow
Thy beauty on this stillness—still as
    sheep
The Hills lie under Thee; the Waters
    deep
Murmur for joy of Thee; the voids below
Mirror Thy strange fair Vapours as they
    flow;
And now, afar upon the barren height,
Thou sendest down a radiant look of light
So that the still Peaks glisten, and a glow
Rose-colour'd tints the little snowy cloud
That poises on the highest peak of all.
Oh, Thou art beautiful!—the Hills are
    bowed
Beneath Thee; on Thy name the soft
    Winds call—
The monstrous Ocean trumpets it aloud,
The Rains and Snows intone it as they
    fall.

IX.
THE MOTION OF THE MISTS.

HERE by the sunless Lake there is no air,
    Yet with how ceaseless motion, like a
    shower
Flowing and fading, do the high Mists
    lower
Amid the gorges of the Mountains bare.
Some weary breathing never ceases there,—
    The barren peaks can feel it hour by
    hour;
The purple depths are darken'd by its
    power;
A soundless breath, a trouble all things
    share

That feel it come and go. See! onward
    swim
The ghostly Mists, from silent land to
    land,
From gulf to gulf; now the whole air
    grows dim—
Like living men, darkling a space, they
    stand.
But lo! a Sunbeam, like the Cherubim,
Scatters them onward with a flaming
    brand.

X.
CORUISK.

I THINK this is the very stillest place
    On all God's earth, and yet no rest is
    here.
The Vapours mirror'd in the black loch's
    face
Drift on like frantic shapes and dis-
    appear;
A never-ceasing murmur in mine ear
Tells me of Waters wild that flow and
    flow.
There is no rest at all afar or near,
Only a sense of things that moan and go.
And lo! the still small life these limbs
    contain
I feel flows on like those, restless and
    proud;
Before that breathing nought within my
    brain
Pauses, but all drifts on like mist and
    cloud;
Only the bald Peaks and the Stones remain,
Frozen before Thee, desolate and bowed.

XI.
BUT WHITHER?

AND whither, O ye Vapours! do ye
    wend?
Stirred by that weary breathing, whither
    away?
And whither, O ye Dreams! that night
    and day
Drift o'er the troublous life, tremble, and
    blend
To broken lineaments of that far Friend,
Whose strange breath's come and go ye
    must obey?

O sleepless Soul! In the world's waste
   astray,
Whither? and will thy wanderings ever
   end?
All things that be are full of a quick pain;
   Onward we fleet, swift as the running
   rill,—
The vapours drift, the mists within the
   brain
Float on obscuringly and have no will.
Only the bare Peaks and the Stones remain;
   These only,—and a God sublimely still.

XII.
GOD IS PITILESS.

OH, Thou art pitiless! They call Thee
   Light,
   Law, Justice, Love; but Thou art
   pitiless.
What thing of earth is precious in Thy
   sight,
   But weary waiting on and soul's distress?
When dost Thou come with glorious
   hands to bless
The good man that dies cold for lack of
   Thee?
When bring'st Thou garlands for our
   happiness?
Whom dost Thou send but Death to set us
   free?
Blood runs like wine—foul spirits sit and
   rule—
   The weak are crushed in every street and
   lane—
He who is generous becomes the fool
   Of all the world, and gives his life in
   vain.
Wert Thou as good as Thou art beautiful,
   Thou couldst not bear to look upon such
   pain.

XIII.
YEA, PITILESS.

YEA, Thou art pitiless—Thou dost permit
   The Priest to use Thee as a hangman's
   cord—
Thou proppest up the Layman's shallow
   wit,
   Driving the Beggar from the laden board—
Thou art the easy text of those who hoard
   Their gifts in secret chests for Death to see.

'Mighty and strong and glorious Valleys
   Lord!'
The Prophet cries, gone mad for lack of
   Thee!
While good men dying deem Thy grace a
   dream,
While sick men wail for Thee and mad
   blaspheme,
A thousand forms of Thee the foolish
   preach—
Fair stretch Thy temples over all the lands,
   In each of these some barbarous Image
   stands,
And men grow atheists in the shrine of
   each.

XIV.
COULD GOD BE JUDGED.

CAN I be calm, beholding everywhere
   Disease and Anguish busy, early and
   late?
Can I be silent, nor compassionate
The evils that both Soul and Body bear?
Oh, what have sickly Children done, to
   share
Thy cup of sorrows? yet their dull, sad
   pain
Makes the earth awful;—on the tomb's
   dark stair
Moan Idiots, with no glimmer in the
   brain.
No shrill Priest with his hangman's cord
   can beat
Thy mercy into these—ah nay, ah nay!
The Angels Thou hast sent to haunt the
   street
Are Hunger and Distortion and Decay.
Lord! that mad'st Man, and send'st him
   foes so fleet,
Who shall judge *Thee* upon Thy judg-
   ment-day?

XV.
THE HILLS ON THEIR THRONES.

GHOSTLY and livid, robed with shadow,
   see!
Each mighty Mountain silent on its
   throne,
From foot to scalp one stretch of livid
   stone,
Without one gleam of grass or greenery.

Silent they take the immutable decree—
    Darkness or sunlight come,—they do not stir;
Each bare brow lifted desolately free,
    Keepeth the silence of a death-chamber.
Silent they watch each other until-doom;
    They see each other's phantoms come and go,
Yet stir not. Now the stormy hour brings gloom,
    Now all things grow confused and black below,
Specific through the cloudy Drift they loom,
    And each accepts his individual woe.

XVI.

KING BLAABHEIN.

MONARCH of these is Blaabhein. On his height
    The lightning and the snow sleep side by side,
Like snake and lamb; he waiteth in a white
    And wintry consecration. All his pride
Is husht this dimly-gleaming autumn day—
    He broodeth o'er the things he hath beheld—
Beneath his feet the Rains crawl still and gray,
    Like phantoms of the mighty men of eld.
A quiet awe the dreadful heights doth fill,
    The high clouds pause and brood above their King;
The torrent murmurs gently as a rill;
    Softly and low the winds are murmuring;
A small black speck above the snow, how still
    Hovers the Eagle, with no stir of wing!

XVII.

BLAABHEIN IN THE MISTS.

WATCH but a moment—all is changed! A moan
    Breaketh the beauty of that noonday dream;
The hoary Titan darkens on his throne,
    And with an indistinct and senile scream
Gazes at the wild Rains as past they stream,
    Through vaporous air wild-blowing on his brow;
All black, from scalp to base there is no gleam,
    Even his silent snows are faded now.
Watch yet!—and yet!—Behold, and all is done—
    'Twas but the shallow shapes that come and go,
Troubling the mimic picture in the eye.
    Still and untroubled sits the kingly one.
Yonder the Eagle floats—there sleeps the Snow
    Against the pale green of the cloudless sky.

XVIII.

THE FIERY BIRTH OF THE HILLS.

O HOARY Hills, though ye look aged, ye
    Are but the children of a latter time—
Methinks I see ye in that hour sublime
    When from the hissing cauldron of the Sea
Ye were upheaven, while so terribly
    The Clouds boiled, and the Lightning scorched ye bare.
Wild, new-born, blind, Titans in agony,
    Ye glared at heaven through folds of fiery hair! . . .
Then, in an instant, while ye trembled thus
    A Hand from heaven, white and luminous,
Pass'd o'er your brows, and husht your fiery breath;
    Lo! one by one the still Stars gather'd round,
The great Deep glass'd itself, and with no sound
    A cold Snow fell, and all was still as death.

XIX.

THE CHANGELESS HILLS.

ALL power, all virtue, is repression—ye
    Are stationary, and God keeps ye great;
Around your heads the fretful winds play free;
    Ye change not—ye are calm and desolate.
What seems to us a trouble and a fate
    Is but the loose dust streaming from your feet
And drifting onward—early ye sit and late,
    While unseen Winds waft past the things that fleet.

So sit for ever, still and passionless
As He that made you!—thought and soul's
    distress
  Ye know not, though ye contemplate the
    strife;
Better to share the Spirit's bitterest aches—
Better to be the weakest Wave that breaks
  On a wild Ocean of tempestuous Life.

XX.
O MOUNTAIN PEAK OF A GOD.

FATHER, if Thou imperturbable art,
  Passive as these, lords of a lonely
    land—
If, having laboured, Thou must sit apart—
  If having once open'd the Void, and
    planned
This tragedy, Thou must impassive stand
Spectator of the scenic flow of things,
  Then I—a drop of dew, a grain of
    sand—
Pity Thy lot, poor palsied King of Kings.
Better to fail and fail, to shriek and shriek,
  Better to break, like any Wave, and
    go,—
Impotent godhead, let Thy slave be weak!—
  Yea, do not freeze my Soul, but let it
    flow—
Oh, wherefore call to Thee, a mountain
    Peak
Impassive, beautiful, serene with snow?

XXI.
GOD THE IMAGE.

IMPASSIVE, beautiful, and desolate,
  Is this the Lord my God, whom I en-
    treat?
Powerless to stay the ravages of fate—
  Jove with his right hand palsied, Jove
    effete,
Fetter'd by frost upon a stony seat—
O dreadful apparition! Can this be?
  Yonder He looms, where never a heart
    doth beat,
In the cold ether of theology.
Come down! come down! O Souls that
    wander there!
  Cold are the snows, chill is the dreadful
    air—
Come down! come down into the Valleys
    deep;
Leave the wild Image to the stars, that
    rise
  Around about it with affrighted eyes;
Come to green under-glooms, and sink,
    and sleep.

XXII.
THE FOOTPRINTS.

COME to green under-glooms,—and in your
    hair
  Weave nightshade, foxglove red, and
    rank wolfsbane,
And slumber and forget Him; if in vain
Ye try to slumber off your sorrow there,
Arise once more and openly repair
  To busy haunts where men and women
    sigh,
And if all things but echo back your care,
  Cry out aloud, 'There is no God!' and
    die.
But if upon a day when all is dark,
Thou, stooping in the public ways, shalt
    mark
  Strange luminous footprints as of feet
    that shine—
Follow them! follow them! O soul be-
    reaven!
God had a Son—He hath pass'd that way
    to heaven:
  Follow, and look upon the Face divine!

XXIII.
WE ARE DEATHLESS.

YET hear me, Mountains! echo me, O
    Sea!
  Murmur an answer, Winds, from out
    your caves;
Cry loudly, Torrents, Mountains, Winds,
    and Waves—
Hark to my crying all, and echo me—
All things that live are deathless—I and
    ye.
  The Father could not slay us if He would;
  The Elements in all their multitude
Will rise against their Master terribly,
If but one hair upon a human head
  Should perish! . . . Darkness grows on
    crag and steep,

A hollow thunder fills the torrent's bed;
   The wild Mists moan and threaten as they creep;
And hush! now, when all other cries are fled,
   The warning murmur of the white-hair'd Deep.

XXIV.
A VOICE IN THE WHIRLWIND.

I HEARD a Whirlwind on the mountain peak
   Pause for a space its furious flight and cry—
'There is no Death!' loudly it seemed to shriek;
   'Nothing that is, beneath the sun, shall die.'
The frail sick Vapours echoed, drifting by—
   'There is no Death, but change early and late;
Powerless were God's right Hand, full arm'd with fate,
   To slay the meanest thing beneath the sky.'
Yea, even as tremulous foam-bells on the sea,
   Coming and going, are all things of breath;
But evermore, deathless, and bright, and free,
   We re-emerge, in spite of Change or Death.
Hearken, O Mountains! Waters, echo me!
   O wild Wind, echo what the Man-Wind saith!

XXV.
CRY OF THE LITTLE BROOK.

CHRIST help me! whither would my dark thoughts run,
   I look around me, trembling fearfully;
The dreadful silence of the Silent One
   Freezes my lips, and all is sad to see.
Hark! hark! what small voice murmurs 'God made *me!*'
It is the Brooklet, singing all alone,
Sparkling with pleasure that is all its own,
   And running, self-contented, sweet, and free.
O Brooklet, born where never grass is green,
   Finding the stony hill and flowing fleet,
Thou comest as a Messenger serene,
   With shining wings and silver-sandall'd feet;
Faint falls thy music on a Soul unclean,
   And, in a moment, all the World looks sweet!

XXVI.
THE HAPPY HEARTS OF EARTH.

WHENCE thou hast come, thou knowest not, little Brook,
   Nor whither thou art bound. Yet wild and gay,
Pleased in thyself, and pleasing all that look,
   Thou wendest, all the seasons, on thy way;
The lonely glen grows gladsome with thy play,
   Thou glidest lamb-like through the ghostly shade;
To think of solemn things thou wast not made,
   But to sing on, for pleasure, night and day.
Such happy hearts are wandering, crystal clear,
   In the great world where men and women dwell;
Earth's mighty shows they neither love nor fear,
   They are content to be, while I rebel,
Out of their own delight dispensing cheer,
   And ever softly whispering, 'All is well!'

XXVII.
FATHER, FORGIVE THY CHILD.

OH SING, clear Brook, sing on, while in a dream
   I feel the sweetness of the years go by!
The crags and peaks are softened now, and seem
   Gently to sleep against the gentle sky;
Old scenes and faces glimmer up and die,
   With outlines of sweet thought obscured too long;
Like boys that shout at play far voices cry;
   Oh sing! for I am weeping at the song.

I know not what I am, but only know
  I have had glimpses tongue may never
    speak ;
No more I balance human joy and woe,
  But think of my transgressions, and am
    meek.
Father! forgive the child who fretted
    so,—
  His proud heart yields,—the tears are on
    his cheek !

XXVIII.
GOD'S LONELINESS.

WHEN, in my strong affection, I have
    sought
To play at Providence with men of clay,
How hath my good come constantly to
    nought,
  How hath my light and love been cast
    away,—
  How hath my light been light to lead
    astray,
How hath my love become of sorry worth,
How feeble hath been all my soul's
    essay
To aid one single man on all God's earth !
Father in Heaven, when I think these
    things,
  Helpless Thou seemest to redeem our
    plight—
Thy lamp shines on shut eyes—each Spirit
    springs
To its own stature still in Thy despite—
While haggard Nature round Thy footstool
    clings,
  Pale, powerless, sitt'st Thou, in a Lonely
    Light.

XXIX.
THE CUP OF TEARS.

MY God ! my God ! with passionate appeal,
  Pardon I crave for these mad moods of
    mine,—
Can I remember, with no heart to feel,
  The gift of Thy dear Son, the Man
    Divine—
  My God ! what agonies of love were
    Thine,
Sitting alone, forgotten, on Thy height,
Pale, powerless, awful in that Lonely Light,
  While 'neath Thy feet the cloudy hyaline
Rain'd blood upon the darkness,—where
    Thine Own
  Held the black Cup of all earth's tears,
    and cried !
Ev'n then, tho' Thou wert conscious of his
    groan,
  Pale in that Lonely Light Thou did'st
    abide,
Nor dared, even then, tho' shaken on Thy
    throne,
  To reach Thy hand and dash the Cup
    aside.

XXX.
THE LIGHT OF THE WORLD.

ON the dark waters of man's thought still
    gleams
Softly and silvernly, from night to night,
That starlight Legend, though its substance
    seems
  Consuming in the melancholy light
It sheddeth. Father, do I see aright?
Is it a truth or most divine of dreams?
  That He, Thy Child, walk'd once in rai-
    ment white
With mortal men, and mused by Syrian
    streams?
O Life that puts our noblest life to shame,
  Was it a Star, or light to lead astray?
Thought's waves grow husht beneath that
    silvern flame,
  Our hopes pursue it and our doubts obey ;
And whether truth or phantom, it became
  The sweetest sphere that lights the
    World's black way.

XXXI.
EARTH'S ELDEST BORN.

BUT He, the only One of mortal birth
  Who raised the Veil and saw the Face
    behind,
While yet He wander'd footsore on the
    earth,
  Beheld His Father's Eyes,—that they
    were kind.
Here in the dark I grope, confused, pur-
    blind ;
I have not seen the glory and the peace ;
But on the darken'd mirror of the mind
  Strange glimmers fall, and shake me till
    they cease—

Then, wondering, dazzled, on Thy name I
    call,
And, like a child, reach empty hands and
    moan,
And broken accents from my wild lips fall,
    And I implore Thee in this human
    tone ;—
If such as I can follow Him at all
Into Thy presence, 'tis by love alone.

XXXII.
WHAT SPIRIT COMETH?

WHO cometh wandering hither in my need?
    What gentle Ghost from Heaven cometh
    now?—
Oh, I am broken to the rod indeed—
Father, my earthly father, is it thou?
The stooping shape with piteous human
    brow,
The dear quaint gesture, and the feeble
    pace,
The weary-eyed, world-worn, belovëd face,
    Ev'n as they wildly faded, meet me now.
A gentle voice flows softly, saying plain :
    'From death comes light, from pain
    beatitude ;
Chide not at loss, for out of loss comes
    gain ;
Chide not at grief, for 'tis the Soul's best
    food—
Out of my death-chamber, out of wrong
    and pain,
Cometh a life and odour. God is good.'

XXXIII.
STAY, O SPIRIT !

FATHER, my earthly father, stay, oh stay !
I know thou wert a man as others be ;
Sore were thy feet upon the World's cold
    clay,
And thou didst stumble oft, and on thy
    knee
Knelt little ; but thy gentle heart gleamed
    free
In cloud and shadow, giving its best cheer;
Thou had'st an open hand, and laugh'd
    for glee
When happy men or creatures dumb played
    near.
But in thy latter years God's scourge was
    sore
Upon thee—weary were thy wrongs and
    dire,—
Yet blessings on thee—until all was o'er,
    Cheery thou wert beside a cheerless fire—
Till one red dawn the mark was on the
    door,
And thou wert dead to all the world's
    desire.

XXXIV.
QUIET WATERS.

O RAINBOW, Rainbow, on the livid height,
    Softening its ashen outlines into dream,
Dewy yet brilliant, delicately bright
As pink wild-roses' leaves, why dost thou
    gleam
So beckoningly? Whom dost thou invite
    Still higher upward on the bitter quest?
What dost thou promise to the weary sight
    In that strange region whence thou is-
    suest?
Speakest thou of pensive runlets by whose
    side
Our dear ones wander sweet and gentle-
    eyed,
In the soft dawn of some diviner Day?
Art thou a promise? Come those hues and
    dyes
From heavenly Meads, near which thou
    dost arise,
Iris'd from Quiet Waters, far away !

The Book of Orm.

(1870.)

'This also we humbly beg,—that Human things may not prejudice such as are Divine, neither at from the unlocking of the Gates of Sense, and the kindling of a greater Natural Light, any-ing of incredulity or intellectual night may arise in our minds towards DIVINE MYSTERIES.'—TUDENT'S PRAYER, BACON.

'To vindicate the ways of God to man.'—MILTON.

'God's Mystery will I vindicate, the Mystery of the Veil and of the Shadow; yea, also Death d Sorrow, God's divine Angels on all earths; and I will vindicate the Soul, that the Soul may ndicate the Flesh; and all these things shall vindicate Evil, proving God's mercy to His creatures, eat and small.'—A RUNE FOUND IN THE STARLIGHT.

INSCRIPTION.

To F. W. C.

LOWERS pluckt upon a grave by moonlight, pale
nd suffering, from the spiritual light
hey grew in: these, with all the love and
blessing
hat prayers can gain of God, I send to thee!

PROEM.

(TO BOOK OF ORM AND POLITICAL MYSTICS.)

/HEN in these songs I name the Name of God,
 mean not Him who ruled with brazen rod
he rulers of the Jew; nor Him who calm
t reigning on Olympus; nay, nor Brahm,
siris, Allah, Odin, Balder, Thor,
hough these I honour, with a hundred more);
lenu I mean not, nor the Man Divine,
he pallid Rainbow lighting Palestine;
or any lesser of the gods which Man
ath conjured out of Night since Time began.
mean the primal Mystery and Light,
he most Unfathomable, Infinite,
he Higher Law, Impersonal, Supreme,
he Life in Life, the Dream within the Dream,

The Fountain which in silent melody
Feeds the dumb waters of Eternity,
The Source whence every god hath flown and flows,
And whither each departs to find repose.

THE BOOK OF THE VISIONS SEEN BY ORM THE CELT.

THERE is a mortal, and his name is Orm,
Born in the evening of the world, and looking
Back from the sunset to the gates of morning.

And he is aged early, in a time
When all are aged early,—he was born
In twilight times, and in his soul is twilight.

O brother, hold me by the hand, and hearken,
For these things I shall phrase are thine and mine,
And all men's,—all are seeking for a sign.

Thou wert born yesterday, but thou art old,
Weary to-day, to-morrow thou wilt sleep—
Take these for kisses on thy closing eyelids.

S

I.

FIRST SONG OF THE VEIL.

How God in the beginning drew
Over his face the Veil of blue,
Wherefore no soul of mortal race
Hath ever look'd upon the Face:
Children of earth whose spirits fail
Heark to the First Song of the Veil.

I.

THE VEIL WOVEN.

In the beginning,
　Ere Man grew,
The Veil was woven
　Bright and blue;
Soft mists and vapours
Gather'd and mingled
Over the black world
　Stretched below,
While winds of heaven
Blew from all places,
Shining luminous,
　A starry snow.
Blindly, dumbly,
　Darken'd under
Ocean and river,
　Mountain and dale,
While over his features,
Wondrous, terrible,
The beautiful Master
　Drew the Veil:
Then starry, luminous,
Rolled the Veil of azure
O'er the first dwellings
　Of mortal race;
—And since the beginning
No mortal vision,
Pure or for sinning,
Hath seen the Face

Yet mark me closely!
Strongly I swear,
Seen or seen not,
　The Face is *there*!
When the Veil is clearest
　And sunniest,
Closest and nearest
　The Face is prest;
But when, grown weary
With long downlooking,
The Face withrawing
　For a time is gone,

The great Veil darkens,
And ye see full clearly
Glittering numberless
　The gems thereon.
For the lamp of his features
Divinely burning,
Shines, and suffuses
　The Veil with light,
And the Face, drawn backward
With that deep sighing
Ye hear in the gloaming,
　Leaveth the Night.

Thus it befell to men
Graveward they journeyed,
From waking to sleeping,
　In doubt and in fear,
Evermore hoping,
Evermore seeking,
Nevermore guessing
　The Master so near:
Making strange idols,
Rearing fair Temples,
Crying, denying,
Questioning, dreaming,
Nevermore certain
　Of God and His grace,—
Evermore craving,
To look on a token,
　To gaze on a Face.

Now an Evangel,
　Whom God loved deep,
Said, 'See! the mortals,
　How they weep!
They grope in darkness,
They blunder onward
　From race to race,
Were it not better,
Once and for ever,
　To unveil the Face?'
God smiled.

He said—'Not yet?
Much is to remember,
　Much to forget;
Be thou of comfort!
How should the token
　Silence their wail?'

And, with eyes tear-clouded,
He gazed through the luminous,
Star-inwrought, beautiful,
　Folds of the Veil.

II.
EARTH THE MOTHER.

BEAUTIFUL, beautiful, she lay below,
  The mighty Mother of humanity,
Turning her sightless eyeballs to the glow
  Of light she could not see,
Feeling the happy warmth, and breathing slow
  As if her thoughts were shining tranquilly.
Beautiful, beautiful the Mother lay,
  Crownèd with silver spray,
The greenness gathering hushfully around
  The peace of her great heart, while on her breast
The wayward Waters, with a weeping sound,
  Were sobbing into rest.
For all day long her face shone merrily,
And at its smile the waves leapt mad and free:
But at the darkening of the Veil, she drew
  The wild things to herself, and husht their cries.
Then, stiller, dumber, search'd the deepening Blue
With passionate blind eyes;
And went the old life over in her thought,
Dreamily praying as her memory wrought
The dimly guessed at, never utter'd tale,
  While, over her dreaming,
  Deepen'd the luminous,
  Star-inwrought, beautiful,
Folds of the wondrous Veil.

For more than any of her children of clay
The beautiful Mother knows—
  She is so old!
Ye would go wild to hearken, if this day
Her dumb lips should unclose,
  And the tale be told:
  Such unfathomable things,
  Such mystic vanishings,
She knoweth about God—she is so old.

For oft, in the beginning, long ago,
Without a Veil looked down the Face ye know,
And Earth, an infant happy-eyed and bright,
Look'd smiling up, and gladden'd in its sight.

But later, when the Man Flower from her womb
Burst into brightening bloom,
In her glad eyes a golden dust was blown
Out of the Void, and she was blind as stone.

And since that day
She hath not seen, nor spoken,—lest her say
Should be a sorrow and fear to mortal race,
And doth not know the Lord hath hid away,
But turneth up blind orbs—to feel the Face.

III.
CHILDREN OF EARTH.

So dumbly, blindly,
So cheerly, sweetly,
The beautiful Mother
  Of mortals smiled;
Her children marvell'd
And looked upon her—
Her patient features
  Were bright and mild;
And on her eyeballs
  Night and day,
A sweet light glimmer'd
  From far away.
Her children gather'd
  With sobs and cries,
To see the sweetness
  Of sightless eyes;
But though she held them
  So dear, so dear,
She could not answer,
  She could not hear.
She felt them flutter
  Around her knee,
She felt their weeping,
Yet knew not wherefore—
  She could not see.
'O Mother! Mother
  Of mortal race!
Is there a Father?
Is there a Face?'
She felt their sorrow
  Against her cheek,—
She could not hearken,
  She could not speak;
With thin lips fluttering,

With blind eyes tearful,
  And features pale,
She clasp'd her children,
  And looked in silence
    Upon the Veil.

Her hair grew silvern,
  The swift days fled,
Her lap was heavy
  With children dead;
To her heart she held them,
  But could not warm them—
The life within them
  Was gone like dew.
Whiter, stiller,
  The Mother grew.

The World grew hoary,
The World was weary,
The children cried at
  The empty air:
'Father of mortals!'
The children murmured,
'Father! Father!
  Art Thou there?'
Then the Master answer'd
  From the thunder-cloud:
'I am God the Maker!
I am God the Master!
I am God the Father!'
  He cried aloud.
Further, the Master
  Made sign on sign—
Footprints of his spirits,
  Voices divine;
His breath was a water,
  His cry was a wind.

But the people heard not,
The people saw not,—
Earth and her children
  Were deaf and blind.

IV.
THE WISE MEN.

'CALL the great philosophers!'
Call them all hither,—
  The good, the wise!'
Their robes were snowy,
Their hearts were holy,
  They had cold still eyes.
To the mountain-summits
Wearily they wander'd,
Reaching the desolate
  Regions of snow,
Looming there lonely,
They searched the Veil wonderful
With tubes fire-fashion'd
  In caverns below . . .
God withdrew backward,
And darker, dimmer,
  Deepen'd the day:
O'er the philosophers
Looming there lonely
  Night gather'd gray.
Then the wise men gazing
Saw the lights above them
Thicken and thicken,
  And all went pale—
Ah! the lamps numberless,
The mystical jewels of God,
The luminous, wonderful,
  Beautiful lights of the Veil!

Alas for the Wise Men!
The snows of the mountain
  Drifted about them,
And the wind cried round them,
As the lights of wonder
  Multiplied!
The breath of the mountain
Froze them into stillness,—
  They sighed and died.
Still in the desolate
  Heights overhead,
Stand their shapes frozen,
  Frozen and dead.
But a weary few,
Weary and dull and cold,
Crept faintly down again,
  Looking very old;
And when the people
Gather'd around them,
The heart went sickly
  At their dull blank stare—
'O Wise Men answer!
Is there a Father?
Is there a beautiful
  Face up there?'
The Wise Men answer'd and said:
'Bury us deep when dead—
  We have travelled a weary road,
We have seen no more than ye.
'Twere better not to be—
  There is no God!'

And the people, hearkening,
Saw the Veil above them,
And the darkness deepen'd,
And the Lights gleamed pale.
Ah! the lamps numberless,
The mystical jewels of God,
The luminous, wonderful,
Beautiful Lights of the Veil!

II.

THE MAN AND THE SHADOW.

On the high path where few men fare,
Orm meeteth one with hoary hair,
And speaketh, solemn and afraid,
Of that which haunteth him—a Shade.
Slowly, with weary feet and weak,
They wander to a mountain peak;
And to the man with hoary hair
A Bridge of Spirits riseth fair,
Whereon his Soul with gentle moan
Passeth unto the Land Unknown.

I.

THE SHADOW.

O AGED Man who, clad in pilgrim's garb,
With staff of thorn and wallet lying near,
Sittest among the weeds of the wayside,
Gazing with hollow eyeballs, in a dream,
On that which sleeps—a Shadow—at thy feet!
Hearest thou?

    By the fluttering of thy lips,
I know thou hearest; yet, with downcast eyes,
Thou broodest moveless, letting yonder sun
Make thee a Dial, worn and venerable,
To show the passing hour. All things around
Share stillness with thee; for behold they keep
The gloaming of the year. To russet brown
The heather fadeth; on the treeless hills,
O'er rusted with the slow-decaying bracken,
The sheep crawl slow with damp and red-stain'd wool;
Keen cutting winds from the Cold Clime begin
To frost the edges of the cloud—the Sun
Upriseth slow and silvern—many Rainbows
People the desolate air with flowers that fade
Through pallor unto tears;—and though these flash
Ever around thee, here thou sittest alone,—
Best Dial of them all, old, moveless, dumb,
Ineffably serene with aged eyes,
Still as a stone,—yet with some secret spell
Pertaining to the human, some faint touch
Of mystery in that worn face, to show
Thy wither'd flesh is scented with a Soul.

Nay, then, with how serene and sad a light
Thy face, strange gleams of spiritual pain
Fading there, turneth up to mine! Yea, smile!
Tender as sunlight on the autumn hills,
Cometh that kindly lustre! Aye, thy hand—
Something mysterious streameth from thy palm—
Spirit greets spirit—scent is mixed with scent—
Sweet is the touch of hands. Behold me,—Orm,
Thy brother!

    Brother, we are surely bound
On the same journey,—and our eyes alike
Turn up and onward: wherefore, now thou risest,
Lean on mine arm, and let us for a space
Pursue the path together. Ah, 'tis much,
In this so weary pilgrimage, to meet
A royal face like thine; to touch the hand
Of such a soul-fellow; to feel the want,
The upward-crying hunger, the desire,
The common hope and pathos, justified
By knowledge and gray hairs. Come on! come on!
Up yonder! Slowly, leaning on my strength,
And I will surely pick my steps with thine,—
While at our backs the secret Shadows creep,
And imitate our motions with no sound.

Dost thou remember more than I? *My Soul
Remembereth no beginning.*

    One still day,
I saw the Hills around me, and beheld
The Hills had shadows,—for beyond their rim

The fiery Sun was setting;—then I saw
My Ghost upon the gr und, and as I ran
Eastward, the melancholy semblance ran
Before my footsteps; and I felt afraid.

Could I have shaken off this grievous thing,
Much had been spared me. Since that day
    I ran,
And saw it run before me in the sun,
It hath been with me in the day and night,
The sunlight and the starlight—at the board
Hath joined me, darkening the festal cup—
Hath risen black against the whitening wall
On lonely midnights, when by the wind's
    shriek
Startled from terrible visions seen in dream,
Rising upon my couch, and with quick
    breath
Lighting the lamp, I hearkened—it hath
    track'd
My footsteps into pastoral churchyards,
And suddenly, when I was very calm,
Look'd darkly up out of the gentle graves,
So that I clench'd my teeth, or should have
    scream'd;
And still behind me—see !—it creeps and
    creeps,
Dim in the dimness of this autumn day.

  Higher! yet higher! Though the path
    is steep,
And all around the withering bracken rusts,
Up yonder on the crag, a mossy spring,
Frosted with silver, glistens, and around
Grasses as green as hedgerows in the May
Cushion the lichen'd stones.

       Here let us pause:
Here, where the grass gleams emerald, and
    the spring
Upbubbling faintly seemeth as a sound,
A drowsy hum, heard in the mind itself—
Here, in this stillness, let us pause and
    mark
The many-colour'd Picture. Far beneath
Sleepeth the glassy Ocean like a sheet
Of liquid mother-o'-pearl, and on its rim
A Ship sleeps, and the shadow of the ship;
Astern the reef juts darkly, edged with foam,
Through the smooth brine: oh, hark, how
    loudly sings
A wild, weird ditty to a watery tune,
The fisher among his nets upon the shore;

And yonder, far a
Are running, dwa
    mice,
Along the yellow s
The immeasurable
Against the fields
The rayless cresce
Lies like a reaper's
The immeasurable
From bourne to
    thyme and he
To leafless slope
    slopes
Of granite to the d
Where, with a silv
Pausing, the white
    Snow
On the heights ur
    bound.

  O perishable I
How wondrous an
    and think!
What magic mixed
Wherein, upon a c
A heaven pink-tint
The dim Star of th
In palpitating silve
Her image, puttin
Bathes liquid, like
What magic? W
    Brother,
What strange Ma
    tints,
Pouring the water
The crystal air li
    heavens
With luminous jew
Look'd down, and
    clod,
And lifted thee, an
Colour'd thee wit
    blood
Ran ruby, poured
    air
Through eyes that
The flesh-tints of t
To make thee won
Knitted thy limbs
    blew
Into thy hollow he
Then to the inner
Withdrawing, left

The living apparition of a Man,—
A mystery amid the mysteries,—
A lonely Semblance, with a wild appeal
To which no form that lives, however dear,
Hath given a tearless answer,—a Shape, a Soul,
Projecting ever as it ageth on
A SHADE which is a silence and a sleep.

Yet not companionless, within this waste
Of splendour, dwellest thou—here by thy side
I linger, girdled for the road like thee,
With pilgrim's staff and scrip; and through the vales,
Below, a Storm of people like to thee
Drifts with thee westward darkly, cloud on cloud,
Uttering a common moan, and to our eyes
Casting one common shadow; yet each Soul
Therein now seeketh, with a want like thine,
The inevitable bourne. Nor those alone,
Thy perishable brethren, share thy want,
And wander haunted through the world ;
but Beasts,
With that dumb hunger in their eyes, project
Their darkness—by the yeanling Lambkin's side
Its shade plays, and the basking Lizard hath
Its image on the flat stone in the sun,—
And these, the greater and the less, like thee
Shall perish in their season: in the mere
The slender Water-Lily sees her shape,
And sheddeth softly on the summer air
Her last chill breathing; and the forest Tree
That, standing glorious for a hundred years,
Lengthens its shadow daily from the sun,
Fulfilleth its own prophecy at last,
And falleth, falleth. Art thou comforted?
Nay, then,—behold the Shadows of the Hills,
Attesting these are perishable too,
And cry no more thou art companionless.

How, like a melancholy bell, thy voice
Echoes the word! 'Companionless!' Thine eyes
Suffer with light and tears, and wearily
Thou searchest all the picture beautiful
For vanished faces. Still, 'companionless!'
O Brother, let me hold thy hand again—
Spirit greets spirit—scent is mixed with scent—
Sweet is the touch of hands. Look on me!
Orm!
Thy Brother!
And no nearer? O 'tis sad
That here, like dumb Beasts, yearning with blank eyes,
Wringing each other's hands, pale, passionate,
Full of immortal likeness, wild with thirst
To mingle, yet we here must stand asunder,
Two human Shapes, two Mansions built apart,
Two pale Men,—and two Ghosts upon the ground!

Tread back my footsteps with me in thy mind:
I have wander'd long and far, and O I have seen
Strange visions ; for my Soul resembles not
The miserable souls of common men—
Mere Lamps to guide the Body to the board
And lustful bed—say, rather, 'tis a Wind
Prison'd in flesh, and shrieking to be free
To blow on the high places of the Lord!
Hither and hither hath its pent-up struggle
Compelled my footsteps—o'er the snowy Steeps,
Through the green Valleys—into huts of hinds
And palaces of princes. It hath raved
Loud as the wind among the pines for rest,
Answered by all the winds of all the world
Gather'd like howling wolves beneath the Moon;
And it hath lain still as the air that broods
On meres Coruisken on dead days of frost,
In supreme moments of unearthly bliss,
Feeling the pathos and exceeding peace
Of thoughts as delicate and far removed
As starlight. But in stormy times and calm,
In pain or pleasure, came the Shadow too,
Meeting the Soul in its superbest hour,
And making it afraid.

    These twain have dwelt
Together, haunting one another's bliss,—

The Wind, that would be on the extremest peaks,
And the strange Shadow of the prison-house,
Wherein 'tis pent so very cunningly.
Nay, how they mock each other! 'Shade accursed,'
The Wind moans, 'yet a little while, and thou
Shalt perish with the poor and mean abode
That casts thee—follow and admonish that,—
To *me* thine admonition promiseth
The crumbling of the ruin chain'd wherein
I cry for perfect freedom.' Then methinks
The wild Shade waves its arms grotesque and says,
In dumb show, 'Peace, thou unsubstantial Wind!
Bred of the peevish humour of the flesh,
Born in the body and the cells o' the brain;
With these things shalt thou perish,—foul as gas
Thou senseless shalt dissolve upon the air,
And none shall know that thou hast ever been.'
Thus have they mock'd each other morn and mirk
In speech not human. When I lay at night,
Drunk with the ichor of the form I clasp'd,
How hath the sad Soul, mocking the brute bliss,
The radiant glistening play o' the sense, withdrawn
Unto the innermost chamber of the brain,
And moan'd in shame; while in the taper light,
The Shades, with clasping arms and waving hair,
Seem'd saying, 'Gather roses while thou mayst,
O royal purple Body doom'd to die!
And hush, O Wind, for *thou* shalt perish too!'

I saw a Hind at sunrise—dumb he stood,
And saw the Dawn press with her rosy feet
The dewy sweetness from the fields of hay,
Felt the World brighten—leaves and flowers and grass
Grow luminous—yet beside the pool he stood,
Wherein, in the gray vapour of the marsh,
His mottled oxen stood with large blank eyes
And steaming nostrils: and his eyes like theirs
Were empty, and he humm'd a surly song
Out of a hollow heart akin to beast's:
Yea, sun nor star had little joy for him,
Nor tree nor flower,—to him the world was all
Mere matter for a ploughshare. On the hill
Above him, with loose jerkin backward blown
By winds of morning, and his white brow bare
Like marble, stood a Singer—one of those
Who write in heart's-blood what is blotted out
With ox-gall; and his Soul was in his eyes
To see the coming of the beautiful Day,
His lips hung heavy with beauty, and he looked
Down on the surly clod among the kine,
And sent his Soul unto him through his eyes,
Transfiguring him with beauty and with praise
Into the common pathos. Of such stuffs
Is mankind shapen, both, like thee and me,
Wear westward, to the melancholy Realm
Where all the gather'd Shades of all the world
Lie as a cloud around the feet of God.

This darkens all my seeking. O my friend!
If the whole world had royal eyes like thine,
I were much holpen; but to look upon
Eyes like the ox-herd's, blank as very beast's,
Shoots sorrow to the very roots of life.
Aye! there were hope indeed if each Man seemed
A Spirit's habitation,—but the world
Is curst with these blank faces, still as stone,
And darkening inward. Have these dumb things Souls?
If they be tenantless, dare thou and I
Christen by so sublime a name the Wind
Bred in the wasting body?

Yestermorn,	A Man-beast swung and glimmer'd down
away	at me
blue with its foul	With little eyes and shining ivory teeth.
·hted hall,	Laugh with me! Brute-beast and the small-
w'd Philosopher,	eyed King
inch of yellow hair,	Seem'd brethren—face, eyes, mouth, and
s and a voice	lips the same—
f two bones. 'O	Only the brute-beast was the happier,
	Since never nameless trouble filled his eyes,
sness we name the	Because his ghost upon the glimmering
	grass
f all the life o' the	Beneath him quivered, while he poised
	above
·flesh shoots forth	With philosophic swing by claws and tail.
f thy tints	'O Soul the Flower of all the life o' the
scented bloom of	World,
	O perfect Flower and scented bloom of
ighill in the sun!'	things!'
imortal? How I	O birth betoken'd in that windy hour,
	When, sloughing off the brute, we stand
secret roots,	and groan,
der of the flower!	First frighten'd by the Shadow that has
	chased
that same. city of	Our changes up through all the grooves of
	Time!
of flesh and blood,	Lift up thine eyes, old man, and look on
) the little eyes	me:
the golden crown,	Like thee, a dark point in the scheme of
e in open court,	things,
prinkling him with	Where the dumb Spirit that pervadeth all—
	Grass, trees, beasts, man—and lives and
en of his kingdom	grows in all—
	Pauses upon itself, and awe-struck feels
·s solemnly,	The shadow of the next and imminent
roval, all the while	Transfiguration. So, a living *Man!*
Monkey; yet at	That entity within whose brooding brain
	Knowledge begins and ends—that point in
adow of his throne,	time
sarcophagus	When Time becomes the Shadow of a
of the fountain'd	Dial,—
	That dreadful living and corporeal Hour,
ole, and the more	Who, wafted by an unseen Hand apart
on the tomb close	From the wild rush of temporal things that
	pass,
nger'd. Then me-	Pauses and listens,—listening sees his face
	Glassed in still waters of Eternity,—
narvellous land,	Gazes in awe at his own loveliness,
æval growth	And fears it,—glanceth with affrighted eyes
·kness—underwood	Backward and forward, and beholds all
ing thick with mon-	dark,
	Alike the place whence he unconscious
·e me, by his tail	came,

And that to which he conscious drifteth on,—
Yet seeth before him, wheresoe'er he turn,
The Shadow of himself, presaging doom.

II.

THE RAINBOW.

THE OLD MAN SPEAKS.

Mine eyes are dim. Where am I? Is this Snow
Falling in the cold air? All darkeneth,—
As if between me and the light there stood
Some shape that lived. My God, is this the end?

ORM.

Not yet! not yet! Look up! Thou livest yet!
'Tis but a little faintness, and will pass.

OLD MAN.

Pass? All things pass. The light, the morning dew,
The power that plotted and the foot that clomb;
And delicate bloom of life upon the flesh
Fading like peach-bloom 'neath a finger-press.
O God, to blossom like a flower in a day,
Then wear a winter in slow withering. . . .
Why not with sun-flash, Lord, or bolt of fire? . . .
Where am I?

ORM.

On the lonely heights of Earth;
Beneath thee lies the Ocean, and above thee
The Hills stand silent in the setting Sun.

OLD MAN.

What forms are these that come and change and go?

ORM.

Desolate Shadows of the gathering Rain.

OLD MAN.

What sound is that I hear?

ORM.

The homeless Wind
Shivering behind the Shadows as they glide,
And moaning.

OLD MAN.

Ah!

ORM.

Some phantom of the brain
Appalleth thee! Cling to me! Courage!

OLD MAN.

Hark!
Dost thou not hear?

ORM.

What?

OLD MAN.

Voices of the shapes
That yonder, with their silvern robes wind-blown,
All faint and shadowless against the light,
Beckon me. Hush! They sing a lullaby!
They are the spirits that so long ago
Sung round my cradle,—and they sing the same,—
Though I am grown the ghosts of that fair time.
No! faces! These are faces I remember!
A fair face that, sweet in its golden hair—
And lower, see! a little pale-faced child's,
Sad as a star. 'Father!' A voice cried 'Father!'
Lift me up! Look! How they are gathering!
All sing! All beckon!

ORM.

. . . 'Tis the end indeed.
Within his breast the life-blood of the heart
Swells like a breaking wave, as, clinging round me,
He yearneth, fascinated yet afraid,
With wild dim eyes that look on vacancy!

OLD MAN.

What gleameth yonder in the brightening air?

ORM.

The Spirit of the Rainbow hovering faint
Amid the wind-blown shadows of the Rain.

OLD MAN.

Shadows! I see them—all the Shadows—see!
Uprising from the wild green sea of graves

That beats forlorn about the shores of
   earth.
Shadows—behold them!—how they gather
   and gather,
More and yet more, darker and darker yet ;
Drifting with a low moan of mystery
Upward, still upward, till they almost touch
The bright dim edge of the Bow, but there
   they pause,
Struggling in vain against a breath from
   heaven,
And blacken. Hark! their sound is like a
   Sea!
Above them, with how dim a light divine,
Burneth the Bow,—and lo! it is a Bridge,
Dim, many-colour'd, strangely brightening,
Whereon, all faint and fair and shadowless,
Spirits like those, with faces I remember,
With a low sound like the soft rain in
   spring,
With a faint echo of the cradle song,
Coming and going, beckon me! I come!
Who holds me? Touch me not. O help!
   I am called!
Ah!   . [*Dies.*

ORM.

Gone! Dead! Something very cold
   past by
And touched my cheek like breath ; even
   then, O God,
My comrade heard Thy summons, and
   behold!
Here lieth, void and cold and tenantless,
His feeble habitation. Poor gray hairs,
Thin with long blowing in the windy cold,
At last ye sadden ruin! poor sweet lips,
Ye are dewless, ye are silent! poor worn
   heart,
No more shalt thou, like to a worn-out
   watch,
Tick feebly out the time!

                       O Shadow sad,
Monitor, haunter, waiter till the end,
Brother of that which darkeneth at my feet,
Hast thou too fled, and dost thou follow
   still
The Spirit's quest divine? Nay, thou dark
   Ghost!
Thy work is done for ever—thou art
   doom'd—
A breath from heaven holds thee to the
   ground ;

And here unto the ruin thou art chained,
Moveless, and dark, no more the ghost of
   life,
But dead, the Shadow of a thing of stone.

Thus far, no further, Shadow!—but, O
   brother,
O Spirit, where art *thou*? From what far
   height
Up yonder, pausing for a moment's space,
Lookest thou back thy blessing? Art thou
   free?
Dost thou still hunger upward seeking rest,
Because some new horizon, strange as ours,
Shuts out the prospect of the place of
   peace?
Art thou a wave that, having broken once,
Gatherest up a glorious crest once more,
And glimmerest onward,—but to break
   again ;
Or dost thou smooth thyself to perfect
   peace
In tranquil sight of some Eternal Shore?

From the still region whither thou hast
   fled,
No answer cometh ; but with dewy wings
Brightening before it dieth, how divine
Burneth the Rainbow, at its earthliest edge
Now fading like a flower! Is it indeed
A Bridge whereon fair Spirits come and go?
O Brother, didst thou glide to peace that
   way?
Silent—all silent—dimmer, dimmer yet,
Hue by hue dying, creeping back to
   heaven—
O let me too pass by it up to God!
Too late—it fadeth, faint and far away!

The Shadows gather round me—from the
   ground
My dark familiar looketh silently.
O Shadows, be at peace, for ye shall rest,
Yea, surely ye shall cease ; for now, as ever,
Out of your cloudy being springs serene
The Bow of Mystery that spans the globe!

The beautiful Bow of thoughts ineffable,
Last consequence of this fair cloud of flesh!
The dim miraculous Iris of sweet Dream!
Rainbow of promise! Colour, Light, and
   Soul!

That comes, dies, comes again, and ever
    draws
Its strangest source from tears—that lives,
    that dies—
That is, is not—now here, now faded
    wholly—
Ever assuring, ever blessing us,
Ever eluding, ever beckoning ;
Born of our essence, yet more strange than
    we,
As human, yet more beautiful tenfold,—
Rising in earth out of our cloudy being,
Touching forlornest places with its tints,
Strewing the Sea with opal, scattering
    roses
Across the hollow pathways of the Wind,
Fringing the clouds with flowers of crimson
    fire,
And melting, melting (whither our wild
    eyes
Follow imploring, whither our weak feet
Totter for ever), melting far away,
Yonder ! upon the dimmest peak of Heaven !

III.
SONGS OF CORRUPTION.

Songs of Corruption, woven thus,
With tender thoughts and tremulous,
Sitting with a solemn face
In an island burying-place,
While weary waves broke sad and slow
O'er weedy wastes of sand below,
And stretch'd on every side of me
The rainy grief of the gray Sea.

I.
PHANTASY.

IF thou art an Angel,
    Who hath seen thee,
O Phantasy, brooding
Over my pale wife's sleeping?
    In the darkness
    I am listening
For the rustle of thy robe ;
Would I might feel thee breathing,
Would I might hear thee speaking,
    Would I might only touch thee
        By the hand !

    She is very cold,
My wife is very cold,
    Her eyes are withered,
Her breath is dried like dew ;—
The sound of my weeping
    Disturbeth her not ;
Thy shadow, O Phantasy,
    Lieth like moonlight
    Upon her features,
And the lines of her mouth
    Are very sweet.

    In the night
I heard my pale wife moaning,
    Yet did not know
    What made her afraid.
    My pale wife said,
    'I am very cold,'
And shrank away from thee,
    Though I saw thee not ;
And she kissed me and went to sleep,
And gave a little start upon my arm
When on her living lips
    Thy freezing finger was laid.

    What art thou—
    Art thou God's Angel?
    Or art thou only
    The chilly night-wind,
    Stealing downward
From the regions where the sun
Dwelleth alone with his shadow
    On a waste of snow ?
Art thou the water or earth?
Or art thou the fatal air ?
    Or art thou only
    An apparition
    Made by the mist
Of mine own eyes weeping ?

    She is very cold,
    My wife is very cold !
    I will kiss her,
And the silver-haired mother will kiss
    her,
And the little children will kiss her ;
And then we will wrap her warm,
And hide her in a hollow space ;
And the house will be empty
    Of thee, O Phantasy,
Cast on the unhappy household
    By the strange white clay.

Much I marvel, O Phantasy,
    That one so gentle,

So sweet, when living,
Should cast a Shadow as vast as thine;
For, lo! thou loomest
Upward and heavenward,
Hiding the sunlight
Blackening the snow,
And the pointing of thy finger
Fadeth far away
On the sunset-tinged edges,
Where Man's company ends,
And God's loneliness begins.

II.
THE DREAM OF THE WORLD WITHOUT DEATH.

Now, sitting by her side, worn out with weeping,
Behold, I fell to sleep, and had a vision,
Wherein I heard a wondrous Voice intoning:

Crying aloud, 'The Master on His throne
Openeth now the seventh seal of wonder,
And beckoneth back the angel men name Death.

And at His feet the mighty Angel kneeleth,
Breathing not; and the Lord doth look upon him,
Saying, 'Thy wanderings on earth are ended.'

And lo! the mighty Shadow sitteth idle
Even at the silver gates of heaven,
Drowsily looking in on quiet waters,
And puts his silence among men no longer.

. . . . .

The world was very quiet. Men in traffic
Cast looks over their shoulders; pallid seamen
Shivered to walk upon the decks alone;

And women barred their doors with bars of iron,
In the silence of the night; and at the sunrise
Trembled behind the husbandmen afield.

I could not see a kirkyard near or far;
I thirsted for a green grave, and my vision
Was weary for the white gleam of a tombstone.

But hearkening dumbly, ever and anon
I heard a cry out of a human dwelling,
And felt the cold wind of a lost one's going.

One struck a brother fiercely, and he fell,
And faded in a darkness; and that other
Tore his hair, and was afraid, and could not perish.

One struck his aged mother on the mouth,
And she vanished with a gray grief from his hearthstone.
One melted from her bairn, and on the ground
With sweet unconscious eyes the bairn lay smiling.
And many made a weeping among mountains,
And hid themselves in caverns, and were drunken.

I heard a voice from out the beauteous earth,
Whose side rolled up from winter into summer,
Crying, 'I am grievous for my children.'
I heard a voice from out the hoary ocean,
Crying, 'Burial in the breast of me were better,
Yea, burial in the salt flags and green crystals.'

I heard a voice from out the hollow ether,
Saying, 'The thing ye cursed hath been abolished—
Corruption, and decay, and dissolution!'

And the world shrieked, and the summertime was bitter,
And men and women feared the air behind them;
And for lack of its green graves the world was hateful.

. . . . .

Now at the bottom of a snowy mountain
I came upon a woman thin with sorrow,
Whose voice was like the crying of a seagull.

Saying, 'O Angel of the Lord, come hither,
And bring me him I seek for on thy bosom,
That I may close his eyelids and embrace him.

, I curse thee that I cannot look upon him!
I curse thee that I know not he is sleeping!
Yet know that he has vanished upon God!

'I laid my little girl upon a wood-bier,
And very sweet she seemed, and near unto me;
And slipping flowers into her shroud was comfort.

'I put my silver mother in the darkness,
And kissed her, and was solaced by her kisses,
And set a stone, to mark the place, above her.

'And green, green were their quiet sleeping-places,
So green that it was pleasant to remember
That I and my tall man would sleep beside them.

'The closing of dead eyelids is not dreadful,
For comfort comes upon us when we close them,
And tears fall, and our sorrow grows familiar;

'And we can sit above them where they slumber,
And spin a dreamy pain into a sweetness,
And know indeed that we are very near them.

'But to reach out empty arms is surely dreadful,
And to feel the hollow empty world is awful,
And bitter grow the silence and the distance.

'There is no space for grieving or for weeping;
No touch, no cold, no agony to strive with,
And nothing but a horror and a blankness!'

. . . . .

Now behold I saw a woman in a mud-hut
Raking the white spent embers with her fingers,
And fouling her bright hair with the white ashes.

Her mouth was very bitter with the ashes;
Her eyes with dust were blinded; and her sorrow
Sobbed in the throat of her like gurgling water.

And all around the voiceless hills were hoary,
But red light scorched their edges; and above her
There was a soundless trouble of the vapours.

'Whither, and O whither,' said the woman,
'O Spirit of the Lord, hast Thou conveyed them,
My little ones, my little son and daughter?

'For, lo! we wandered forth at early morning,
And winds were blowing round us, and their mouths
Blew rose-buds to the rose-buds, and their eyes

'Looked violets at the violets, and their hair
Made sunshine in the sunshine, and their passing
Left a pleasure in the dewy leaves behind them; .

'And suddenly my little son looked upward,
And his eyes were dried like dew-drops; and his going
Was like a blow of fire upon my face.

'And my little son was gone. My little daughter
Looked round me for him, clinging to my vesture;
But the Lord had drawn him from me, and I knew it

'By the sign He gives the stricken, that the lost one
Lingers nowhere on the earth, on hill or valley,
Neither underneath the grasses nor the tree-roots.

'And my shriek was like the splitting of an ice-reef,
And I sank among my hair, and all my palm
Was moist and warm where the little hand had filled it.

'Then I fled and sought him wildly, hither and thither—
Though I knew that he was stricken from me wholly
By the token that the Spirit gives the stricken.

'I sought him in the sunlight and the starlight,
I sought him in great forests, and in waters
Where I saw mine own pale image looking at me.

'And I forgot my little bright-haired daughter,
Though her voice was like a wild-bird's far behind me,
Till the voice ceased, and the universe was silent.

'And stilly, in the starlight, came I backward
To the forest where I missed him ; and no voices
Brake the stillness as I stooped down in the starlight,

'And saw two little shoes filled up with dew,
And no mark of little footsteps any farther,
And knew my little daughter had gone also.'

. . . . .

But beasts died ; yea, the cattle in the yoke,
The milk-cow in the meadow, and the sheep,
And the dog upon the doorstep : and men envied.

And birds died ; yea, the eagle at the sungate,
The swan upon the waters, and the farm-fowl,
And the swallows on the housetops : and men envied.

And reptiles ; yea, the toad upon the roadside,
The slimy, speckled snake among the grass,
The lizard on the ruin : and men envied.

The dog in lonely places cried not over
The body of his master ; but it missed him,
And whined into the air, and died, and rotted.

The traveller's horse lay swollen in the pathway,
And the blue fly fed upon it ; but no traveller
Was there ; nay, not his footprint on the ground.

The cat mewed in the midnight, and the blind
Gave a rustle, and the lamp burnt blue and faint,
And the father's bed was empty in the morning.

The mother fell to sleep beside the cradle,
Rocking it, while she slumbered, with her foot,
And wakened,—and the cradle there was empty.

I saw a two-years' child, and he was playing ;
And he found a dead white bird upon the doorway,
And laughed, and ran to show it to his mother.

The mother moaned, and clutched him, and was bitter,
And flung the dead white bird across the threshold ;
And another white bird flitted round and round it,

And uttered a sharp cry, and twittered and twittered,
And lit beside its dead mate, and grew busy,
Strewing it over with green leaves and yellow.

. . . . .

So far, so far to seek for were the limits

Of affliction; and men's terror grew a homeless
Terror, yea, and a fatal sense of blankness.

There was no little token of distraction,
There was no visible presence of bereavement,
Such as the mourner easeth out his heart on.

There was no comfort in the slow farewell,
Nor gentle shutting of belovëd eyes,
Nor beautiful broodings over sleeping features.

There were no kisses on familiar faces,
No weaving of white grave-clothes, no last pondering
Over the still wax cheeks and folded fingers.

There was no putting tokens under pillows,
There was no dreadful beauty slowly fading,
Fading like moonlight softly into darkness.

There were no churchyard paths to walk on, thinking
How near the well-beloved ones are lying.
There were no sweet green graves to sit and muse on,

Till grief should grow a summer meditation,
The shadow of the passing of an angel,
And slepping should seem easy, and not cruel.

Nothing but wondrous parting and a blankness.

. . . . . .

But I awoke, and, lo! the burthen was uplifted,
And I prayed within the chamber where she slumbered,
And my tears flowed fast and free, but were not bitter.

I eased my heart three days by watching near her,
And made her pillow sweet with scent and flowers,
And could bear at last to put her in the darkness.

And I heard the kirk-bells ringing very slowly,
And the priests were in their vestments, and the earth
Dripped awful on the hard wood, yet I bore it.

And I cried, 'O unseen Sender of Corruption,
I bless Thee for the wonder of Thy mercy,
Which softeneth the mystery and the parting.

'I bless Thee for the change and for the comfort,
The bloomless face, shut eyes, and waxen fingers,—
For Sleeping, and for Silence, and Corruption.'

III.
SOUL AND FLESH.

My Soul, thou art wed
  To a perishable thing,
But death from thy strange mate
Shall sever thee full soon,
If thou wilt reap wings
Take all the Flesh can give:

The touch of the smelling dead,
The kiss of the maiden's mouth,
The sorrow, the hope, the fear,
That floweth along the veins:
Take all, nor be afraid;
Cling close to thy mortal Mate!

So shalt thou duly wring
Out of thy long embrace
The hunger and thirst whereof
The Master maketh thee wings,—
The beautiful, wondrous yearning,
The mighty thirst to endure.

Be not afraid, my Soul,
To leave thy Mate at last,
Thou ye shall learn in time
To love each other well;
But put her gently down
In the earth beneath thy feet.

And dry thine eyes and hasten
To the imperishable springs;
And it shall be well for thee
In the beautiful Master's sight,
If it be found in the end
'Thou hast used her tenderly.

IV.

THE SOUL AND THE DWELLING.

A House miraculous of breath
The royal Soul inhabiteth.
Alone therein for evermore,
It seeks in vain to pass the door;
But through the windows of the eyne
Signalleth to its kin divine. . . .
This is a song Orm sang of old
To Oona with the locks of gold.

Come to me! clasp me!
Spirit to spirit!
Bosom to bosom!
Tenderly, clingingly,
 Mingle to one! . . .

Now, from my kisses
Withdrawing, and blushing,
Why dost thou gaze on me?
Why dost thou weep?
Why dost thou cling to me,
Imploring, adoring?
What are those meanings
 That flash from thine eyes?

Pitiful! pitiful!
Now I conceive thee!—
Yea, it were easier
Striking two swords,
To weld them together,
Than spirit with spirit
To mingle, though rapture
 Be perfect as this.
Shut in a tremulous
Prison, each spirit
Hungers and yearns—
Never, ah never,
Belovèd, belovèd,
Have these eyes look'd on
 The face of thy Soul.

Ours are two dwellings,
Wondrously beautiful,
Made in the darkness
 Of soft-tinted flesh:
In the one dwelling,
Prison'd I dwell,
And lo! from the other
 Thou beckonest me!
I am a Soul!
Thou art a Soul!
These are our dwellings!
 O to be free!

Beauteous, belovèd,
Is thy dear dwelling;
All o'er it blowing
The roses of dawn—
Bright is the portal,
The dwelling is scented
 Within and without;
Strange are the windows,
So clouded with azure,
The faces are hidden
 That look from within.

Now I approach thee,
Sweetness and odour
Tremble upon me—
Wild is the rapture!
Thick is the perfume!
Sweet bursts of music
 Thrill from within!
Closer, yet closer!
Bosom to bosom!
Tenderly, clingingly,
 Mingle to one. . . .
Ah! but what faces
 Are those that look forth! ; . .

Faces? What faces? As I speak they die
And all my gaze is empty as of old.
O love! the world was fair, and everywhere
Rose wondrous human dwellings like mine own,
And many of these were foul and dark with dust,
Haunted by things obscene, not beautiful,
But most were very royal, meet to serve
Angels for habitation. All alone
Brooded my Soul by a mysterious fire
Dim-burning, never-dying, from the first
Lit in the place by God; the winds and rains
Struck on the abode and spared it; day and night
Above it came and went; and in the night
My Soul gazed from the threshold silently,
And saw the congregated lamps that swung
Above it in the dark and dreamy blue;
And in the day my Soul gazed on the earth,
And sought the dwellings there for signs,
 and lo!

T

None answer'd ; for the Souls inhabitant
Drew coldly back and darken'd ; and I said,
'In all the habitations I behold,
Some old, some young, some fair, and
some not fair,
There dwells no Soul I know.' But as I
spake,
I saw beside me in a dreamy light
Thy habitation, so serene and fair,
So stately in a rosy dawn of day,
That all my Soul look'd forth and cried,
'Behold,
The sweetest dwelling in the whole wide
world!'
And thought not of the inmate, but gazed
on,
Lingeringly, hushfully ; for as I gazed
Something came glistening up into thine
eyes,
And beckon'd, and a murmur from the
portal,
A murmur and a perfume, floated hither,
Thrill'd through my dwelling, making every
chamber
  Tremble with mystical,
  Dazzling desire!

  ... Come to me! close to me!
  Bosom to bosom!
  Tenderly, clingingly,
   Mingle to one!
  Wildly within me
  Some eager inmate
  Rushes and trembles,
  Peers from the eyes
  And calls in the ears,
  Yearns to thee, cries to thee!
  Claiming old kinship
  In lives far removed!..
  Vainly, ah vainly!
  Pent in its prison
  Must each miraculous
   Spirit remain,—
  Yet inarticulate,
  Striving to language
  Music and memory,
   Rapture and dream!

Rapture and dream! Belovëd one, in vain
My spirit seeks for utterance. Alas,
Not yet shall there be speech. Not yet,
not yet,
One dweller in a mortal tenement

Can know what se
Within the neigl
 beloved,
The mystery, the r
For God's face,
 upon
The poorest Soul's
Soul-haunted worl
 dwelt
Beside me, close
 souls,
We mingled—flesh
 we knew
All joys, all unrese
Yea, not a sunbear
But touched the c
 me swear
I never knew tha
 sound,
All light was insuff
In its strange cha
 vain—
We saw each other
When I was gla
 neighbour
Were dark and dra
And sometimes, wi
 world,
My Soul was lookin
I saw the neighbc
 lit,
The happy window
As if a feast were b
Yet were there p
 gleams,
Low sounds, from t
I knew not ; and]
 these
In a mysterious pai
The frail fair mar
 dwelt
Totter'd and tremb
 drous flesh
A dim sick glimmer
Grew fainter, fainte
The Spirit seemed t
Stood still and dim
Up in the window
 linger'd,
First seen, last seen
So different, more b
Than all that I ha
 aloud

'Stay! stay!' but at the one despairing
    word
The spirit faded, from the hearth within
The dim fire died with one last quivering
    gleam—
The house became a ruin; and I moaned
'God help me! 'twas herself that look'd at
    me!
First seen! I never knew her face be-
    fore!..
Too late! too late! too late!'

    . . . Yea, from my forehead
    Kiss the dark fantasy!
    Tenderly, clingingly,
        Mingle to one!
    Is not this language?
    Music and memory,
        Rapture and dream?—
    O in the dewy-bright
        Day-dawn of love,
    Is it not wondrous,
    Blush-red with roses,
    The beautiful, mystical
        House of the Soul!
    Lo in my innermost
    Chambers is floating
    Soft perfume and music
        That tremble from *thee*. . . .
    Ah, but what faces
    Are these, that look forth?

. . . Sit, still, Belovëd, while I search thy
    looks
For memories. O thou art beautiful!
Crownëd with silken gold,—soft amber
    tints
Coming and going on thy peach-hued
    flesh,—
Thy breath a perfume,—thy blue eyes twain
    stars—
Thy lips like dewy rosebuds to the eye,
Though living to the touch. O royal
    abode,
Flooded with music, light, and precious
    scent,
Curtainëd soft with subtle mystery!
Nay, stir not, but gaze on, still and
    serene,
Possessing me with thy superb still sweep
Of eyes ineffable—sit still, my queen,

And let me, clinging on thee, court the
    ways
Wherein I know thee. Nay, even now,
    Belovëd,
When all the world like some vast tidal
    wave
Withdraws and leaves us on a golden
    shore
Alone together—when thou most art
    mine—
When the winds blow for us, and the soft
    stars
Are shining for us, where we dream apart,—
Now our two dwellings in a dizzy hour
Have mingled their foundations—clinging
    thus
And hungering round me in mine ecstasy,—
Belovëd, do I know thee? Hath my
    Soul
Spoken to thine the imperial speech of
    Souls,
Perfect in meaning and in melody?
Tell me, Belovëd, while thou sittest so,
Mine own, my queen, my palace of de-
    lights,
What lights are these that pass and come
    again
Within thee? Is the Spirit looking forth,
Or is it but the glittering gleams of
    time
Playing on vacant windows? Can I swear
Thou thinkest of me now at all? Behold
Now all thy beauty is suffused with bright-
    ness—
Thou blushest and thou smilest. Tell me
    true,
Thou then wast far within, and with that
    cry
I woke thee out of dream. O speak to
    me!—
Soul's speech, Belovëd! Do not smile that
    way—
A flood of brightness issues from thy
    door,
But mine is scarcely bright. Lovest thou
    me,
Belovëd, my belovëd? Soul belovëd,
Do I possess thee? Sight and scent and
    touch
Are insufficient. Open! let me in
To the strange chambers I have never
    seen!
Heart of the rose, unopen! or I die!

T 2

V.
SONGS OF SEEKING.

Songs of Seeking, day by day
Sung while wearying on the way,—
Feeble cries of one who knows
Nor whence he comes, nor whither goes.
Yet of his own free will doth wear
The bloody Cross of those who fare
Upward and on in sad accord,—
The footsore Seekers of the Lord.

I.

O THOU whose ears incline unto my singing,
Woman or man, thou surely bearest thy burden,
And I who sing, and all men, bear their burdens.

Even as a meteor-stone from suns afar,
I fell unto the ways of life and breathed,
Wherefore to much on earth I feel a stranger.

I found myself in a green norland valley,
A place of gleaming waters and gray heavens,
And weirdly woven colours in the air.

A basin round whose margin rose the mountains
Green-based, snow-crown'd, and windy saeters midway,
And the thin line of a spire against the mountains.

Around were homes of peasants rude and holy,
Who look'd upon the mountains and the forests,
On the waters, on the vapours, without wonder;

Who, happy in their labours six days weekly,
Were happy on their knees upon the seventh.
But I wonder'd, being strange, and was not happy.

For I cried: 'O Thou Unseen, how shall I praise Thee—
How shall I name Thee glorious whom I know not—
If Thou art as these say, I scarce conceive Thee.

'Unfold to me the image of Thy features,
Come down upon my heart, that I may know Thee;'—
And I made a song of seeking, on a mountain.

II.
QUEST.

As in the snowy stillness,
   Where the stars shine greenly
     In a mirror of ice,
The Reindeer abideth alone,
And speedeth swiftly
   From her following shadow
     In the moon,—
I speed for ever
From the mystic shape
That my life projects,
And my Soul perceives;
And I loom for ever
Through desolate regions
Of wondrous thought,
And I fear the thing
That follows me,
And cannot escape it '
   Night or day.

Doth Thy wingèd lightning
   Strike, O Master!
The timid Reindeer
   Flying her shade?
Will Thy wrath pursue me,
Because I cannot
Escape the shadow
   Of the thing I am?

I have pried and pondered,
   I have agonised,
I have sought to find Thee,
   Yet still must roam,
Affrighted, fleeing Thee,
Chased by the shadow
Of the thing I am,
Through desolate regions
Of wondrous thought!

III.
THE HAPPY EARTH.

SWEET, sweet it was to sit in leafy Forests,
In a green darkness, and to hear the stirring
Of strange breaths hither and thither in the branches;

And sweet it was to sail on crystal Waters,
Between the dome above and the dome
    under,
The Hills above me and the Hills beneath
    me;

And sweet it was to watch the wondrous
    Lightning
Spring flashing at the earth, and slowly
    perish
Under the falling of the summer Rain.

I loved all grand and gentle and strange
    things,—
The wind-flower at the tree-root, and the
    white cloud,
The strength of Mountains, and the power
    of Waters.

And unto me all seasons utter'd pleasure:
Spring, standing startled, listening to the
    skylark,
The wild flowers from her lap unheeded
    falling;

And Summer, in her gorgeous loose apparel,
And Autumn, with her dreamy drooping
    lashes;
And Winter, with his white hair blown
    about him.

Yea, everywhere there stirred a deathless
    beauty,
A gleaming and a flashing into change,
An under-stream of sober consecration.

Yet nought endured, but all the glory
    faded,
And power and joy and sorrow were inter-
    woven;
There was no single presence of the Spirit.

IV.
O UNSEEN ONE!

BECAUSE Thou art beautiful,
Because Thou art mysterious,
Because Thou art strong,
Or because Thou art pitiless,
    Shall my Soul worship Thee,
    O Thou Unseen One?

As men bow to monarchs,
As slaves to their owners,
    Shall I bow to Thee?
As one that is fearful,
As one that is slavish,
    Shall I pray to Thee?

Wert Thou a demigod,
Wert Thou an angel,
    Lip-worship might serve;
To Thee, most beautiful,
Wondrous, mysterious,
    How shall it avail?

Thou art not a demigod,
Thou art not a monarch,—
    Why should I bow to Thee?
I am not fearful,
I am not slavish,—
    Why should I pray to Thee?

O Spirit of Mountains!
Strong Master of Waters!
Strange Shaper of Clouds!
When these things worship Thee
    I too will worship Thee,
    O Maker of Men!

V.
WORLD'S MYSTERY.

THE World was wondrous round me—
    God's green World—
A World of gleaming waters and green
    places,
And weirdly woven colours in the air.

Yet evermore a trouble did pursue me—
A hunger for the wherefore of my being,
A wonder from what regions I had fallen.

I gladdened in the glad things of the
    World,
Yet crying always, 'Wherefore, and oh,
    wherefore?
What am I? Wherefore doth the World
    seem happy?'

I saddened in the sad things of the World,
Yet crying, 'Wherefore are men bruised
    and beaten?
Whence do I grieve and gladden to no
    end?'

VI.
THE CITIES.

I TOOK my staff and wandered o'er the mountains,
And came among the heaps of gold and silver,
The gorgeous desolation of the Cities.

My trouble grew tenfold when I beheld
The agony and burden of my fellows,
The pains of sick men and the groans of hungry.

I saw the good man tear his hair and weep;
I saw the bad man tread on human necks
Prospering and blaspheming: and I wondered.

The silken-natured woman suns and breast bond-slave;
The gross man foul'd an earth I in high places;
The innocent were seen, porlang: and I wondered.

The gifts of earth are given to the base;
The monster of the Cities spurned the martyr;
The martyr died, denying: and I wondered.

VII.
THE PRIESTS.

THREE Priests in divers vestments passed and whispered:
'Worship the one God, stranger, or thou diest;
Yea, worship, or thy tortures shall be endless.'

I cried, 'Which God, O wise ones, must I worship?'
And neither answer'd, but one showed a Picture,
A fair Man dying on a Cross of wood.

And this one said, 'The others err, O stranger!
Repent, and love thy brother,—'tis enough!
The Doom of Dooms is only for the wicked.'

I turned and cried unto him, 'Who is wicked?'
He vanish'd, and within a house beside me
I heard a hard man bless his little children.

My heart was full of comfort for the wicked,
Mine eyes were cleared with love, and everywhere
The wicked wore a piteousness like starlight.

I felt my spirit foul with misconceivings,
I thought of old transgressions and was humble;
I cried, 'O God, whose doom is on the wicked!

'Thou art not He for whom my being hungers!
The Spirit of the grand things and the gentle,
The strength of mountains and the power of waters!'

And lo! that very night I had a Vision.

VIII.
THE LAMB OF GOD.

1.

I SAW in a vision of the night
The Lamb of God, and it was white;
White as snow it wander'd through
Silent fields of harebell-blue,
Still it wandering fed, and sweet
Flower'd the stars around its feet.

2.

I heard in vision a strange voice
Cry aloud, 'Rejoice! rejoice!
Dead men rise and come away,
Now it is the Judgment Day!'
And I heard the host intone
Round the footstool of the Throne.

3.

Then the vision pained my sight,
All I saw became so bright—
All the Souls of men were there,
All the Angels of the air;
God was smiling on His seat,
And the Lamb was at His feet.

4.

Then I heard a voice—' 'Tis done!
Blest be those whom God hath won!'
And the loud hosannah grew,
And the golden trumpets blew,
And around the place of rest
Rose the bright mist of the Blest.

5.

Then suddenly I saw again,
Bleating like a thing in pain,
The Lamb of God;—and all in fear
Gazed and cried as it came near,
For on its robe of holy white
Crimson blood-stains glimmer'd bright.

6.

O the vision of the night;
The Lamb of God! the blood-stains bright!
In quiet waters of the skies
It bathed itself with piteous eyes—
Vainly on its raiment fell
Cleansing dews ineffable!

7.

All the while it cried for pain,
It could not wash away the stain—
All the gentle blissful sky
Felt the trouble of its cry—
All the streams of silver sheen
Sought in vain to make it clean.

8.

Where'er it went along the skies
The Happy turned away their eyes;
Where'er it past from shore to shore
All wept for those whose blood it bore—
Its piteous cry filled all the air,
Till the Dream was more than I could bear.

9.

And in the darkness of my bed
Weeping I awakenèd—
In the silence of the night,
Dying softly from my sight,
Melted that pale Dream of pain
Like a snow-flake from thy brain.

IX.
DOOM.

MASTER, if there be Doom,
 All men are bereaven!
If, in the universe,
One Spirit receive the curse,
Alas for Heaven!
If there be Doom for one,
Thou, Master, art undone.

Were I a Soul in heaven,
Afar from pain,
Yea, on Thy breast of snow,
At the scream of one below
I should scream again.
Art Thou less piteous than
The conception of a Man?

X.
GOD'S DREAM.

I HEAR a voice, 'How should God pardon sin?
How should He save the sinner with the sinless?
That would be ill: the Lord my God is just.'

Further I hear, 'How should God pardon lust?
How should He comfort the adulteress?
That would be foul: the Lord my God is pure.'

Further I hear, 'How should God pardon blood?
How should the murtherer have a place in heaven
Beside the innocent life he took away?'

And God is on His throne; and in a dream
Sees mortals making figures out of clay,
Shapen like men, and calling them God's angels.

And sees the shapes look up into His eyes,
Exclaiming, 'Thou didst ill to save this man;
Damn Thou this woman, and curse this cut-throat, Lord!'

God dreams this, and His dreaming is the world;
And thou and I are dreams within His dream;
And nothing dieth God hath dreamt or thought.

XI.
FLOWER OF THE WORLD.

WHEREVER men sinned and wept,
I wandered in my quest;
At last in a Garden of God
I saw the Flower of the World.

This Flower had human eyes,
Its breath was the breath of the mouth;
Sunlight and starlight came,
And the Flower drank bliss from both.

Whatever was base and unclean,
Whatever was sad and strange,
Was piled around its roots;
It drew its strength from the same.

Whatever was formless and base
Pass'd into fineness and form;
Whatever was lifeless and mean
Grew into beautiful bloom.

Then I thought, 'O Flower of the World,
Miraculous Blossom of things,
Light as a faint wreath of snow
Thou tremblest to fall in the wind.

'O beautiful Flower of the World,
Fall not nor wither away;
He is coming—He cannot be far—
The Lord of the Flow'rs and the Stars.

And I cried, 'O Spirit divine!
That walkest the Garden unseen,
Come hither, and bless, ere it dies,
The beautiful Flower of the World.'

XII.
O SPIRIT!

WEARY with seeking, weary with long waiting,
I fell upon my knees, and wept, exclaiming,
'O Spirit of the grand things and the gentle!

'Thou hidest from our seeking—Thou art crafty—
Thou wilt not let our hearts admit Thee wholly—
Believing hath a core of unbelieving—

'A coward dare not look upon Thy features,
But museth in a cloud of misconceiving;
The bravest man's conception is a coward's.

'Wherefore, O wherefore, art Thou veil'd and hidden?
The world were well, and wickedness were over,
If Thou upon Thy throne were one thing certain.'

And lo! that very night I had a Vision.

VI.
THE LIFTING OF THE VEIL.

Thou who the Face Divine wouldst see,
Think,—couldst thou bear the sight, and be?
O waves of life and thought and dream,
Darkening in one mysterious Stream,
Flow on, flow loudly; nor become
A glassy Mirror sad and dumb,
Whereon for evermore might shine
The dread peace of the Face Divine!—
Children of earth whose spirits fail,
Beware the Lifting of the Veil!

I.
ORM'S VISION.

MY Soul had a vision,
And in my Soul's vision
The Veil was lifted,
 And the Face was there!

There was no portent
Of fire or thunder,
The wind was sleeping,
Above and under
 All things lookt fair.
And the change came softly
 Unaware.
On a golden morrow
The Veil was lifted,
And yea! the ineffable Face was there.

My Soul saw the vision
 From a silent spot—
Nay, of its likeness
 Ask me not—
How should my Soul fathom
 The formless features?
Gaze at the Master
 How should it dare?
Only I flutter'd
 To my knees and mutter'd
 A moan, a prayer—

Silent, ineffable,
Gazing downward,
   The Face was there!

This let me whisper:
It stirred not, changed not,
Though the world stood still, amazed;
But the Eyes within it,
Like the eyes of a painted picture,
Met and followed
   The eyes of each that gazed.

II.
THE FACE AND THE WORLD.

THEN my Soul heard a voice
   Crying—'Wander forth
O'er hill and valley,
   O'er the earth—
Behold the mortals
   How they fare—
Now the great Father
   Grants their prayer;
Now every spirit
   Of mortal race,
Since the Veil is lifted,
   Beholds the Face!

I awoke my body,
And up the mountains,
With the sweet sun shining
   I wander'd free—
And the hills were pleasant,
Knee-deep in heather,
And the yellow eagle
   Wheel'd over me—
And the streams were flowing,
And the lambs were leaping
   Merrily!

But on the hill-tops
The shepherds gather'd,
Up-gazing dreamily
   Into the silent air,
And close beside them
The eagle butcher'd
The crying lambkin,
   But they did not see, nor care.
I saw the white flocks of the shepherds,
Like snow wind-lifted and driven,
   Blow by, blow by!
And the terrible wolves behind them,
As wild as the winds, pursuing
   With a rush and a tramp and a cry!

I passed the places
   Of ice and snow,
And I saw a Hunter
   Lying frozen,—
His eyes were sealèd—
   He did not know;
Drinking his heart's-blood,
Not looking upward,
Sat the soot-black raven
   And the corby crow.

Then I knew they linger'd,
Though the Veil was lifted,
   Death and Decay,
And my Spirit was heavy
   As I turned away;
But my Spirit was brighter
As I saw below me
The glassy Ocean
   Glimmering,
With a white sail dipping
Against the azure
   Like a sea-bird's wing—
And all look'd pleasant,
   On sea and land,
The white cloud brooding,
And the white sail dipping,
And the village sitting
   On the yellow sand.

And beside the waters
My Soul saw the fishers
Staring upward,
   With dumb desire,
Though a mile to seaward,
With the gulls pursuing,
Shot past the herring
   With a trail like fire;
Though the mighty Sea-snake
With her young was stranded
In the fatal shallows
   Of the shingly bay—
Though their bellies hunger'd—
   What cared they?

Hard by I noted
Little children,
Toddling and playing
   In a field o' hay—
The Face was looking,
But they were gazing
At one another,
   And what cared *they*?

But one I noted,
A little Maiden,
Look'd up o' sudden
    And ceased her play,
And she dropt her garland
    And stood upgazing,
With hair like sunlight,
    And face like clay.

All was most quiet
    In the air,
Save the children's voices
And the cry of dumb beasts,—
'Twas a weary Sabbath
    Everywhere—
Each soul an eyeball,
    Each face a stare ;—
And I left the place,
    And I wander'd free,
And the Eyes of the Face
    Still followed me !

At the good Priest's cottage
The gray-hair'd grandsire
Lay stiff in the garden—
    For his Soul had fled—
And I cried in passing,
'Oh ye within there,
Come forth in sorrow
    And bury your dead.'
With his flock around him
Praying bareheaded,
The pale Priest, kneeling
    All gaunt and gray,
Answer'd, 'Look upward !
Leave the dead to heaven !
God is yonder !
    Behold, and pray !'

I was sick at heart
    To hear and see,
And to feel the Face
    Still following me,
And all seemed darkening,
    And my heart sank down,—
As I saw afar off
    A mighty Town—
When with no warning,
    Slowly and softly
The beautiful Face withdrew,
And the whole world darken'd,
And the silence deepen'd,
And the Veil fell downward
    With a silver glimmer of dew.

And I was calmer
As, slowly and sweetly,
    Gather'd above me
    Mysterious Light on Light,—
And weary with watching
I lay and slumber'd
    In the mellow stillness
    Of the blessèd night.

. . When my Soul awaken'd
    In the lonely place,
The Veil was lifted,
    And, behold ! the Face—
And sick, heart-weary,
    Onward I ran,
Through fields of harvest
Where the wheat hung wither'd,
    Unreapt by man ;
And a ragged Idiot
Went gibbering gaily
    Among the wheat,
In moist palms rubbing
    The ears together ;
And he laugh'd, and beckon'd
    That I should eat.

At the city gateway
The Sentinels gather'd,
Fearful and drunken
    With eyes like glass—
Look up they dared not,
Lest, to their terror,
Some luminous Angel
    Of awe should pass ;
And my Soul passed swiftly
    With a prayer,
And entered the City :—
Still and awful
    Were street and square,
'Twas a piteous Sabbath
    Everywhere—
Each soul an eyeball,
    Each face a stare.

In pale groups gather'd
    The Citizens,
The rich and poor men,
The lords, the lepers
    From their loathsome dens.
There was no traffic,
The heart of the City
    Stood silently ;
How could they barter,

How could they traffic,
  With the terrible Eyes to see.
Nay! each man brooded
  On the Face alone:
Each Soul was an eyeball,
  Each Shape was a stone;
And I saw the faces,
  And some were glad,
And some were pensive,
  And some were mad;
But in all places,
  Hall, street, and lane,—
'Twas a frozen pleasure,
  A frozen pain.

I passed the bearers
  Of a sable bier,
They had dropped their burthen
  To gaze in fear;
From under the trappings
  Of the death-cloth grand,
With a ring on the finger,
  Glimmer'd the corpse's
    Decaying hand.
I passed the bridal,
  Clad bright and gay,
    Frozen to marble
    Upon its way.

Freely I wandered
  Everywhere—
No mortal heeded
  The passing footstep,
Palace and hovel
  Were free as the mountain air.
Aye! softly I entered
  The carven court of stone,
And the fountains were splashing,
  And the pale King sitting
    Upon his jewell'd throne—
And before him gather'd
  The Frail and Sickly,
    The Poor and Old;
And he open'd great coffers,
  And gave thence freely
    Fine gear and gold,—
Saying, ''Tis written,
  Who giveth freely
Shall in sooth be bless'd
  Twenty-fold!'
But he look'd not upward,
  And seem'd unconscious

Of the strange Eyes watching
  O'er sea and land;
Yet his eyelids quiver'd,
  And his eyes look'd sidelong,
And he hid in his bosom
  A blood-stained hand;
But the beggar people
  Let the gold and raiment
    Lie all unheeded;
While with no speech,
  Upward they lifted
Their wild pale features,
  For the Face was mirror'd
    In the eyes of each.

With the Face pursuing
  I wandered onward,
    Heart-sick, heart-sore,
And entered the fretted
  Cathedral door;
And I found the people
  Huddled together,
    Hiding their faces
    In shame and sin,
For through the painted
  Cathedral windows
The Eyes of Wonder
  Were looking in!
And on the Altar,
  The wild Priest, startled,
Was gazing round him
  With sickly stare,
And his limbs were palsied,
  And he moaned for mercy,
    More wonder-stricken
    Than any there.

Then I fell at the Altar,
  And wept, and murmur'd,
' My Soul, how fares it,
  This day, with *thee*?
Art thou contented
  To live and see,
Or were it better
  Not to be?'
And my pale Soul whisper'd:
' Like a band that holdest
  And keepeth from growing
    A goodly tree,—
A terror hath me—
  I feel not, stir not—
'Twere surely better
  Not to be!'

Then a rush of visions
  Went wildly by!
My Soul beheld the mortle World,
  And the luminous Face on high.
And methought, affrighted,
  That the mortal race
Built cover'd cities
  To hide the Face;
And gather'd their treasures
  Of silver and gold,
And sat amid them
  In caverns cold;
And ever nightly,
  When the Face of Wonder
Withdrew from man,
  Many started,
And hideous revel
  Of the dark began.
And men no longer
  Knew the common sorrow,
The common yearning,
  The common love,
But each man's features
  Were turn'd to marble,
Changelessly watching
  The Face above—
A nameless trouble
  Was in the air—
The heart of the World
  Had no pulsation—
'Twas a piteous Sabbath
  Everywhere!

' III.

ORM'S AWAKENING.

I AWOKE. And rising,
  My Soul look'd forth—
'Twas the dewy darkness,
  And the Veil was glittering
  Over the earth;
But afar off eastward
  The Dawn was glimmering,
All silver pale,
  And slowly fading
With a mystic tremor,
  The Lights gleam'd beautiful
  In the wondrous Veil
Yea, Dawn came cheerily,
  And the hill-tops brighten'd,
And the shepherds shouted,
  And a trumpet blew,
And the misty Ocean

Caught silver tremors,
  With the brown-sail'd fish-boats
  Glimmering through—
And the City murmur'd
  As I ran unto it,
And my heart was merry,
  And my fears were few;
And singing gaily
  The lark rose upward,
Its brown wings gleaming
  With the morning dew!

VII.

THE DEVIL'S MYSTICS.

A scroll antique, with weeds behung,
Writ in a mystic pagan tongue,
Wash'd to Orm's feet by the wan Main
After long nights of wind and rain:
Translating this at dead of night,
The Celt beholds with dazzled sight
Strange gods stalk past, and in their train,
Supreme, the King of Sin and Pain.

I.

THE INSCRIPTION WITHOUT.

THE Moral Law: all Evil is Defect;
The limb deform'd for common use of life
Defect,—but haply in the line of growth.

II.

THE TREE OF LIFE.

THE Master said:
  'I have planted the Seed of a Tree,
It shall be strangely fed
With white dew and with red,
  And the Gardeners shall be three—
  Regret, Hope, Memory!'

The Master smiled:
  For the Seed that He had set
Broke presently through the mould,
With a glimmer of green and gold,
  And the Angels' eyes were wet—
  Hope, Memory, Regret.

The Master cried:
  'It liveth—breatheth—see!
Its soft lips open wide—
It looks from side to side—

'How strange they gleam on me,
 The little dim eyes of the Tree!'

The Master said:
'After a million years,
 The Seed I set and fed
 To itself hath gathered
 All the world's smiles and tears—
 How mighty it appears!'

The Master said:
'At last, at last, I see
 A Blossom, a Blossom o' red
 From the heart of the Tree is shed.
 Fairer it seems to be
 Than the Tree, or the leaves o' the Tree.'

The Master cried:
'O Angels, that guard the Tree,
 A Blossom, a Blossom divine
 Grows on this greenwood of mine;
 What may this Blossom be?
 Name this Blossom to me!'

The Master smiled;
For the Angels answered thus:
'Our tears have nourish'd the same,
 We have given it a name
 That seemeth fit to us—
 We have called it *Spiritus*.'

The Master said:
'This Flower no Seed shall bear
 But hither on a day
 My beautiful Child shall stray,
 And shall snatch it unaware,
 And wreath it in his hair.'

The Master smiled:
''The Tree shall never bear—
 Seedless shall perish the Tree,
 But the Flower my Child's shall be;
 He will pluck the Flower and wear,
 'Till it withers in his hair!'

III.
THE SEEDS.

WHEN all that puzzles sense was planned,
 When the first seeds of being fell,
 In reverence bent, *I* stood at hand,
 And heard a part of the spell:
'Grow, Seed! blossom, Brain!
 Deepen into power and pain!'

Shoots of the seed, I saw them grow,
 Green blades of vegetable sheen,
 They darken'd as with wind, and so
 The Earth's black ball grew green—
'Grow, Seed! blossom, Brain!
 Deepen, deepen, into pain!'

Then starry-bright out of the ground
 The firstling flowers sprang dewy-wet;
 I pluckt one, and it felt no wound—
 There was no pain as yet.
'Grow, Seed! blossom, Brain!
 Deepen, deepen, into pain!'

Next in His Hand He lifted thus
 Bright bubbling water from the spring—
 And in that crystal tremulous
 Quicken'd a living thing.
'Grow, Seed! blossom, Brain!
 Deepen, deepen, into pain!'

And suddenly I ere I was 'ware,
 (So fast the dreadful spell was tried),
 O'er Earth's green bosom everywhere
 Crawl'd living things, and cried.
'Grow, Seed! blossom, Brain!
 Deepen, deepen, into pain!'

On every grass-blade glittering bright
 A shining Insect leapt and played,
 By every sea, on every height,
 A Monster cast its shade—
'Grow, Seed! blossom, Brain!
 Deepen, deepen, into pain!'

The most was lingering in the least,
 The least became the most anon;
 From plant to fish, from fish to beast,
 The Essence deepen'd on.
'Grow, Seed! blossom, Brain!
 Deepen, deepen, into pain!'

And deeper still in subtle worth
 The Essence grew, from gain to gain,
 And subtler grew, with each new birth,
 The creature's power of pain.
'Grow, Seed! blossom, Brain!
 Deepen, deepen, into pain!'

Paler I saw the Master grow,
 Faint and more faint His breathing fell,
 And strangely, lower and more low,
 He mutter'd o'er the spell:

'Grow, Seed! blossom, Brain!
Deepen, deepen, into pain!'

Now the deep murmur of the Earth
　Was mingled with a painful cry,
The yeanling young leapt up in mirth,
　But the old lay down to die.
'Grow, Seed! blossom, Brain!
Deepen, deepen, into pain!'

When standing in the perfect light
　I saw the first-born Mortal rise—
The flower of things he stood his height
　With melancholy eyes.
'Grow, Seed! blossom, Brain!
Deepen, deepen, into pain!'

From all the rest he drew apart,
　And stood erect on the green sod,
Holding his hand upon his heart,
　And looking up at God!
'Grow, Seed! blossom, Brain!
Deepen, deepen, into pain!'

He stood so terrible, so dread,
　With right hand lifted pale and proud,
God feared the thing He fashionëd,
　And fled into a cloud.
'Grow, Seed! blossom, Brain!
Deepen, deepen, into pain!'

And since that day He hid away
　Man hath not seen the Face that fled,
And the wild question of that day
　Hath not been answerëd.
'Grow, Seed! blossom, Brain!
Deepen, deepen, into pain!'

And since that day, with cloudy face,
　Of His own handiwork afraid,
God from His heavenly hiding-place
　Peers on the thing He made.
'Grow, Seed! blossom, Brain!
Deepen, deepen, into pain!'

O Crown of things, O good and wise,
　O mortal Soul that would'st be free,
I weep to look into thine eyes—
　Thou art so like to *me!*
'Grow, Seed! blossom, Brain!
Deepen, deepen, into pain!'

IV.

FIRE AND WATER ; OR, A VOICE
OF THE FLESH.

' Two white arms, a moss pillow,
　A curtain o' green ;
Come love me, love me,
　Come clasp me unseen ! '

As red as a rose is,
　I saw her arise,
Fresh waked from reposes,
　With wild dreamy eyes.

I sprang to her, clasp'd her
　I trembled, I prest,
I drank her warm kisses,
　I kiss'd her white breast.

With a ripple of laughter,
　A dazzle of spray,
She melted, she melted,
　And glimmer'd away!

Down my breast runs the water,
　In my heart burns the fire,
My face is like crimson
　With shame and desire!

V.
SANITAS.

DREAMILY, on her milk-white Ass,
Rideth the maiden Sanitas—
With zone of gold her waist is bound,
Her brows are with immortelles crown'd
Dews are falling, song-birds sing,
It is a Christian evening—
Lower, lower, sinks the sun,
The white stars glimmer, one by one!

Who sitteth musing at his door?
Silas, the Leper, gaunt and hoar ;
Though he is curst in every limb,
Full whitely Time hath snowed on him—
Dews are falling, song-birds sing,
It is a Christian evening—
The Leper, drinking in the air,
Sits like a beast, with idiot stare.

How pale! how wondrous! doth she pass,
The heavenly maiden Sanitas ;
She looketh, and she shuddereth,
She passeth on with bated breath—

Dews are falling, song-birds sing,
It is a Christian evening—
His mind is like a stagnant pool,
She passeth o'er it, beautiful!

Brighter, whiter, in the skies,
Open innumerable eyes;
The Leper looketh up and sees,
His aching heart is soothed by these—
Dews are falling, song-birds sing,
It is a Christian evening—
He looketh up with heart astir,
And every Star hath eyes like her!

Onward on her milk-white Ass
Rideth the maiden Sanitas.
The boughs are green, the grain is pearl'd,
But 'tis a miserable world—
Dews are falling, song-birds sing,
It is a Christian evening—
All o'er the blue above her, she
Beholds bright spots of Leprosy.

VI.
THE PHILOSOPHERS.

WE are the Drinkers of Hemlock!
Lo! we sit apart,
Each right hand is uplifted,
Each left hand holds a heart;
At our feet rolls by the tumult,
O'er our heads the still stars gleam—
We are the Drinkers of Hemlock!
We drink and dream!

We are the Drinkers of Hemlock!
We are worn and old,
Each hath the sad forehead,
Each the cup of gold.
In our eyes the awe-struck Nations
Look, and name us wise, and go—
We are the Drinkers of Hemlock!
We drink and know!

We are the Drinkers of Hemlock!
Silent, kingly, pure;
Who is wise if we be foolish?
Who, if we die, shall endure?
The Bacchanals with dripping vine-leaves,
Blushing meet our eyes, and haste—
We are the Drinkers of Hemlock!
Bitter to taste!

We are the Drinkers of Hemlock!
Spirits pure as snow;
White star-frost is on our foreheads—
We are weary, we would go.
Hark! the world fades with its voices,
Fades the tumult and the cry—
We are the Drinkers of Hemlock!
We drink and die!

VII.
THE DEVIL'S PRAYER.

FATHER which art in Heaven,—not here
below;
Be Thy name hallowed, in that place of
worth;
And till Thy Kingdom cometh, and we
know,
Be Thy will done more tenderly on
Earth;
Since we must live—give us this day our
bread;
Forgive our stumblings—since Thou
mad'st us blind;
If we offend Thee, Sire, at least forgive
As tenderly as we forgive our kind;—
Spare us temptation,—human or divine;
Deliver us from evil, now and then;
The Kingdom, Power, and Glory all are
Thine
For ever and for evermore. Amen.

VIII.
HOMUNCULUS; OR, THE SONG OF DEICIDES.

1.

Now all the mystic Lamps that shed
Light on the living world are fled;
Now the swart digger rinses gold,
Under a starless heaven and cold;
Now every God, save one, is dead,
Now that last God is almost sped;
Cold falls the dew, chill rise the tides,
To this still Song of Deicides.

2.

Homunculus! Homunculus!
Not ever shalt thou conquer us!
Zeus, Astaroth, Brahm, and Menu,
With all the gods, white, black, and blue,

Are fallen, and while I murmur thus,
Strong, and more strong, Homunculus
Upon a Teuton Jackass rides,
Singing the Song of Deicides.

3.

It seems but yesterday the dim
And solitary germ of him
Glimmer'd most strangely on my sense,
While, with my microscope intense,
I search'd a Beast's brain-cavern dark :—
A germ—a gleam—a cell—a spark—
Grown to Homunculus, who rides
To my sad Song of Deicides.

4.

Oh had I then so far foreseen,
This day of doom had never been,
For with a drop of fire from Hell
I would have killed the feeble Cell.
Too late! too late! for slow and strange
He has passed the darker sphere of change,
Lo! he emerges—shouts—derides,
Singing the Song of Deicides!

5.

Black is his raiment, top to toe,
His flesh is white and warm below,
All through his silent veins flow flee
Hunger, and Thirst, and Venery;
But in his eye a still small flame,
Like the first Cell from which he came,
Burns round and luminous,—as he rides
To my still Song of Deicides!

6.

With Obic Circle he began,
Swift through the Phallic rites he ran,
He watch'd until his head went round
The Memphian Sphinx's stare profound;
All these by turn he overcast,
And suck'd the Orphic Egg at last;
Now laughing low he westward strides,
Singing the Song of Deicides!

7.

He drives the Gods o' the north to death—
The Sanctus Spiritus is breath—
He plucks down Thammuz from his joy,
And kneads him to a huswife's toy;
He stares to shame the Afric spheres;
He strikes—he overturns—he sneers—
Over the fallen Titans strides,
And squeaks the Song of Deicides!

8.

Homunculus! Homunculus
Wretched, degenerate, impious!
He will not stay, he will not speak—
Another blow! another shriek!
Lo! where he hacketh suddenly
At the red Cross of Calvary!
All darkens—faintly moan the tides—
Sing low the Song of Deicides!

9.

Gigantic, in a dark mist, see!
Loometh the Cross of Calvary;
With rayless eyes the Skeleton
Quivers through all its bones thereon.
Deep grows the mist, faint falls the wind,
The bloodshot sun setteth behind . . .
A crash! a fall—The Cross he strides,
Singing the Song of Deicides!

10.

Now he hath conquered godhead thus,
Whither will turn Homunculus?
I am the only God let be—
All but my fiends believe in me;
(Though all the Angels deem me prince,
My kith and kin I can't convince.)
Christ help me now! Hither he rides,
Singing my song of Deicides!

11.

Silent I wait—(how stand the odds?)
I am the Serpent of the Gods,—
Wait!—draw the forkèd tongue in slow,
Hoard up my venom for the blow.
Crouch in my cave—of all the host
I know he feareth me the most—
Then strike and crush that thing accurst
I should have stifled at the first! . . .
All Earth awaits! Hither he rides!
Cold fall the dews, chill rise the tides,
To this still Song of Deicides!

IX.

ROSES.

'SAD, and sweet, and wise,
 Here a child reposes,
Dust is on his eyes,
 Quietly he lies,—
  Satan, strew Roses!'

Weeping low, creeping slow,
  Came the Weary-wingèd!
Roses red over the dead
  Quietly he flingèd.

'I am old,' he thought,
  'And the world's day closes;
Pale and fever-fraught,
  Sadly have I brought
These blood-red Roses.'

By his side the mother came
  Shudderingly creeping;
The Devil's and the woman's heart
  Bitterly were weeping.

'Swift he came and swift he flew,
  Hopeless he reposes;
Waiting on is weary too,—
  Wherefore on his grave we strew
Bitter, withering Roses.'

The Devil gripped the woman's heart,
  With gall he staunched its bleeding;
Far away, beyond the day,
  The Lord heard interceding.

'Lord God, One in Three!
  Sure Thy anger closes;
Yesterday I died, and see
  The Weary-wingèd over me
Bitterly streweth Roses.'

The voice cried out, 'Rejoice! rejoice!
  There shall be sleep for evil!'
And all the sweetness of God's voice
  Passed strangely through the Devil.

x.
HERMAPHRODITUS.

THIS is a section of a Singer's Brain—
How delicately run the granular lines!
By what strange chemic could I touch this
    thing,
That it again might quicken and dissolve,
Changing and blooming, into glittering
    gleams
Of fancy; or what chemic could so quicken
The soft soil backward that it might put
    forth
Green vegetable shoots,—as long ago?
Upon what headland did it blow of old

And ripen hitherward! Surely 'twas a place
Flowery and starry!
    Cast it back to the grave!
Look down no more, but raise thine eyes
    and see
Who standeth glorious in the brightening
    Dawn!

Behold him, on the apex of the cone,
The perfect blossom of miraculous life,
Hermaphroditus. With how subtle shade
Male into female beauty mingleth—thews
Of iron coated o'er with skin of silk;—
There, on the crown he stands, the perfect
    one,
Witching the world with sterile loveliness,—
Beyond him, darkness and the unknown
    change,
The next uncurtain'd and still higher scene
That is to follow. Are those pinions,—
    peeping
Under the delicate-flesh'd white shoulder-
    blades?

xi.
AFTER.

I SEE, as plain as eyes can see,
From this dark point of mystery,
Death sitting at his narrow Gate,—
While all around, disconsolate,
The wretched weep, the weary wait.
  God pity us who weep and wait!

But, better still, if sadder, I
From this dark corner can descry
What is well-veil'd from human view:
Beyond the Gate I can pursue
The flight of those who have passed thro'.
  God pity us who have passed thro'!

In at the portal, one by one,
They creep, they crawl, with shivering
    moan—
Nobles and Beggars, Priests and Kings;
Out at the further gate each springs
A Spirit,—with a pair of wings!
  God pity us now we have wings!

All round the starry systems stir,
Each silent as a death-chamber;
There is no sound of melody,
Only deep space and mystery;

U

And each hath wings to wander free.
God pity us who wander free!

Some cannot use their wings at all ;
Some try a feeble flight and fall ;
A few, like larks in earthly skies,
With measured beat of wings uprise,
And make their way to Paradise.
God help us on to Paradise!

If ever in their flight through space
They chance to reach that resting-place,
I do not think these creatures dim
Will find the Lord of Cherubim
Exactly what they picture Him.
May God be what we picture Him!

Out of the fiery Sun is thrown
To other worlds the meteor-stone ;
Back to the Sun, in season right,
The meteor-stone doth take its flight.
Lost in that melancholy light.
We fade in melancholy light.

I see, as plain as eyes can see,
From this dark point of mystery,
Those fledgling Spirits everywhere ;
They sing, they lessen, up the air ;
The go to God—Christ help them there!
We go to God—Christ help us there!

XII.

HIS PRAYER.

IN the time of transfiguration,
Melt me, Master, like snow ;
Melt me, dissolve me, inhale me
Into Thy wool-white cloud ;
With a warm wind blow me upward
Over the hills and the seas,
And upon a summer morning
Poise me over the valley
Of Thy mellow, mellow realm ;
Then, for a wondrous moment,
Watch me from infinite space
With Thy round red Eyeball of sunlight,
And melt and dissolve me downward
In the beautiful silver Rain
That drippeth musically,
With a gleam like Starlight and Moonlight,
On the footstool of Thy Throne.

VIII.

THE VISION OF THE MAN ACCURST.

How in the end the Judgment dread
Shall by the Lord thy God be said,—
While brightly in a City of Rest
Shall flash the fountains of the Blest,
And gladdening around the Throne
All mortal men shall smile,—save one. . . .
Children of Earth, hear, last and first,
The Vision of the Man Accurst.

JUDGMENT was over ; all the world re
 deem'd
Save one Man,—who had sinned all sins
 whose soul
Was blackness and foul odour. Last of all
When all was lamb-white, through the
 summer Sea
Of ministering Spirits he was drifted
On to the white sands ; there he lay and
 writhed,
Worm-like, black, venomous, with eyes
 accurst
Looking defiance, dazzled by the light
That gleam'd upon his clench'd and blood
 stain'd hands ;
While, with a voice low as a funeral bell,
The Seraph, sickening, read the sable
 scroll,
And as he read the Spirits ministrant
Darken'd and murmur'd, 'Cast him forth
 O Lord!'
And, from the Shrine where unbeheld He
 broods,
The Lord said, ''Tis the basest mortal
 born—
Cast him beyond the Gate!'

   The wild thing laugh'd
Defiant, as from wave to wave of light
He drifted, till he swept beyond the Gate,
Past the pale Seraph with the silvern eyes ;
And there the wild Wind, that for ever
 beats
About the edge of brightness, caught him
 up,
And, like a straw, whirl'd round and lifted
 him,
And on a dark shore in the Underworld
Cast him, alone and shivering ; for the
 Clime

Was sunless, and the ice was like a sheet
Of glistening tin, and the faint glimmering
  peaks
Were twisted to fantastic forms of frost,
And everywhere the frozen moonlight
  steam'd
Foggy and blue, save where the abysses
  loom'd
Sepulchral shadow. But the Man arose,
With teeth gnash'd beast-like, waved wild
  feeble hands
At the white Gate (that glimmer'd far away,
Like to the round ball of the Sun beheld
Through interstices in a wood of pine),
Cast a shrill curse at the pale Judge within
Then groaning, beast-like crouch'd.

              Like golden waves
That break on a green island of the south,
Amid the flash of many plumaged wings,
Passed the fair days in Heaven. By the
  side
Of quiet waters perfect Spirits walked,
Low singing, in the star-dew, full of joy
In their own thoughts and pictures of those
  thoughts
Flash'd into eyes that loved them; while
  beside them,
After exceeding storm, the Waters of Life
With soft sea-sound subsided. Then God
  said,
'Tis finished—all is well!' But as He
  spake
A voice, from out the lonely Deep beneath,
  Mock'd!
           Then to the Seraph at the Gate,
Who looketh on the Deep with steadfast
  eyes
For ever, God cried, 'What is he that
  mocks?'
The Seraph answered, ''Tis the Man
  accurst!'
And, with a voice of most exceeding peace,
God ask'd, 'What doth the Man?'

              The Seraph said:
'Upon a desolate peak, with hoar-frost
  hung,
Amid the steaming vapours of the Moon,
He sitteth on a throne, and hideously
Playeth at judgment; at his feet, with eyes
Slimy and luminous, squats, a monstrous
  Toad;
Above his head pale phantoms of the Stars
Fulfil cold ministrations of the Void,
And in their dim and melancholy lustre
His shadow, and the shadow of the Toad
Beneath him, linger. Sceptred, thron'd,
  and crown'd,
The foul judgeth the foul, and sitting grim,
  Laughs!'
       With a voice of most exceeding peace
The Lord said, 'Look no more!'

              The Waters of Life
Broke with a gentle sea-sound gladdening—
God turn'd and blest them; as He blest the
  same,
A voice from out the lonely Void beneath,
  Shriek'd!

           Then to the Seraph at the Gate,
Who looketh on the Deep with steadfast
  eyes
For ever, God cried, 'What is he that
  shrieks?'
The Seraph answered, ''Tis the Man
  accurst!'
And, with a voice of most exceeding peace,
God ask'd, 'What doth the Man?'

              The Seraph said:
'Around him the wild phantasms of the
  fog
Moan in the rheumy hoar-frost and cold
  steam.
Long time, crown'd, sceptred, on his
  throne he sits
Playing at judgment; then with shrill voice
  cries—
'"Tis finished, thou art judged!" and,
  fiercely laughing,
He thrusteth down an iron heel to crush
The foul Toad, that with dim and luminous
  eyes
So stareth at his Soul. Thrice doth he lift
His foot up fiercely—lo! he shrinks and
  cowers—'
Then, with a wild glare at the far-off Gate,
Rushes away, and, rushing through the dark,
  Shrieks!'

       With a voice of most exceeding peace
The Lord said, 'Look no more!'

THE BOOK OF ORM.

     The Waters of Life,
The living, spiritual Waters, broke,
Fountain-like, up against the Master's
 Breast,
Giving and taking blessing. Overhead
Gather'd the shining legions of the Stars,
Led by the ethereal Moon, with dewy eyes
Of lustre: these have been baptised in fire,
Their raiment is of molten diamond,
And 'tis their office, as they circling move
In their blue orbits, evermore to turn
Their faces heavenward, drinking peace
 and strength
From that great Flame which, in the core
 of Heaven,
Like to the white heart of a violet burns,
Diffusing rays and odour. Blessing all,
God sought their beauteous orbits, and
 behold!
The Eyes innumerably glistening
Were turned away from Heaven, and with
 sick stare,
Like the blue gleam of salt dissolved in fire,
They searched the Void, as human faces
 look
On horror.

    To the Seraph at the Gate,
Who looketh on the Deep with steadfast
 eyes,
God cried, 'What is this thing whereon
 they gaze?'
The Seraph answered, 'On the Man
 accurst.'
And, with a voice of most exceeding peace,
God ask'd, 'What doth the Man?'

      The Seraph said:
'O Master! send Thou forth a tongue of
 fire
To wither up this worm! Serene and cold,
Flooded with moon-dew, lies the World,
 and there
The Man roams; and the image of the
 Man
In the wan waters of the frosty sphere
Falleth gigantic. Up and down he drifts,
Worm-like, black, venomous, with eyes
 accursed,
Waving his bloody hands in fierce appeal,
So that the gracious faces of Thy Stars
Are troubled, and the stainless tides of
 light

Shadow pollution. With wild, ape-like
 eyes,
The wild thing whining peers through
 horrent hair,
And rusheth up and down, seeking to find
A face to look upon, a hand to touch,
A heart that beats; but all the World is
 void
And beauteous. All alone in the Cold
 Clime,
Alone within the lonely universe,
Crawleth the Man accurst!'

       Then said the Lord,
'Doth he repent?' And the fair Seraph
 said,
'Nay he blasphemeth! Send Thou forth
 Thy fire!'
But with a voice of most exceeding peace,
Out of the Shrine where unbeheld He
 broods,
God said, 'What I have made, a living
 Soul,
Cannot be unmade, but endures for ever.'
Then added, 'Call the Man!'

       The Seraph heard,
And in a low voice named the lost one's
 name;
The wild Wind that for ever beats the Gate
Caught up the word, and fled through the
 cold Void.
'Twas murmur'd on, as a lorn echo fading,
From peak to peak. Swift as a wolf the
 Man
Was rushing o'er a waste, with shadow
 streaming
Backward against a frosty gleaming wind,
When like a fearful whisper in his ear
'Twas wafted; then his blanch'd lips shook
 like leaves
In that chill wind, his hair was lifted up,
He paused, his shadow paused, like stone
 and shadow,
And shivering, glaring round him, the Man
 moaned,
'Who calls?' and in a moment he was
 'ware
Of the white light streaming from the far
 Gate,
And looming, blotted black against the
 light,
The Seraph with uplifted forefinger,
Naming his name!

And ere the Man could fly,
The wild Wind in its circuit swept upon him,
And, like a straw, whirled him and lifted him,
And cast him at the Gate,—a bloody thing—
Mad, moaning, horrible, obscene, unclean ;
A body swollen and stainèd like the wool
Of sheep that in the rainy season crawl
About the hills, and sleep on foul damp beds
Of bracken rusting red. There, breathing hard,
Glaring with fiery eyes, panted the Man,
With scorch'd lips drooping, thirsting as he heard
The flowing of the Fountains far within.

Then said the Lord, ' Is the Man there ? ' and ' Yea,'
Answered the Seraph pale. Then said the Lord,
'What doth the Man?' The Seraph, frowning, said :
' O Master, in the belly of him is fire,
He thirsteth, fiercely thrusting out his hands,
And threateneth, seeking water ! ' Then the Lord
Said, ' Give him water—let him drink ! '

The Seraph,
Stooping above him, with forefinger bright
Touched the gold kerbstone of the Gate, and lo !
Water gush'd forth and gleamed ; and lying prone
The Man crawl'd thither, dipt his fever'd face,
Drank long and deeply ; then, his thirst appeased,
Thrust in his bloody hands unto the wrist,
And let the gleaming Fountain play upon them,
And looking up out of his dripping hair,
Grinned mockery at the giver.

Then the Lord
Said low, ' How doth the Man ? ' The Seraph said :
' It is a snake ! He mocketh all Thy gifts,
And, in a snake's voice half-articulate,
Blasphemeth ! ' Then the Lord : ' Doth the Man crave
To enter in ? ' ' Not so,' the Seraph said,
' He saith——' ' What saith he ? ' ' That his Soul is filled
With hate of Thee and of Thy ways ; he loathes
Pure pathways where the fruitage of the Stars
Hangeth resplendent, and he spitteth hate
On all Thy Children. Send Thou forth Thy fire !
In no wise is he better than the beasts,
The gentle beasts, that come like morning dew
And vanish. Let him die ! ' Then said the Lord :
' What I have made endures ; but 'tis not meet
This thing should cross my perfect work for ever.
Let him begone ! ' Then cried the Seraph pale :
' O Master ! at the frozen Clime he glares
In awe, shrieking at Thee ! ' ' What doth he crave ?
' Neither Thy Heaven nor by Thy holy ways.
He murmureth out he is content to dwell
In the Cold Clime for ever, so Thou sendest
A face to look upon, a heart that beats,
A hand to touch—albeit like himself,
Black, venomous, unblest, exiled, and base ;
Give him this thing, he will be very still,
Nor trouble Thee again.'

The Lord mused.

Still,
Scarce audible trembled the Waters of Life—
Over all Heaven the Snow of the same Thought
Which rose within the Spirit of the Lord
Fell hushedly ; the innumerable Eyes
Swam in a lustrous dream.

Then said the Lord :
' In all the waste of worlds there dwelleth not
Another like himself—behold he is
The basest Mortal born. Yet 'tis not meet
His cruel cry, for ever piteous,
Should trouble my eternal Sabbath-day.
Is there a Spirit here, a human thing,

Will pass this day from the Gate Beautiful
To share the exile of this Man accurst,—
That he may cease the shrill pain of his cry,
And I have peace?'

     Hushedly, hushedly,
Snow'd down the Thought Divine—the
 living Waters
Murmured and darkened. But like mourn-
 ful mist
That hovers o'er an autumn pool, two
 Shapes,
Beautiful, human, glided to the Gate
And waited.
   'What art thou?' in a stern voice
The Seraph said, with dreadful forefinger
Pointing to one. A gentle voice replied,
'I will go forth with him whom ye call curst!
He grew within my womb—my milk was
 white
Upon his lips. I will go forth with him!'
'And *thou*?' the Seraph said. The second
 Shape
Answered, 'I also will go forth with him;
I have kist his lips, I have lain upon his
 breast,
I bare him children, and I closed his eyes;
I will go forth with him!'

     Then said the Lord,
'What Shapes are these who speak?' The
 Seraph answered:
'The woman who bore him and the wife he
 wed—
The one he slew in anger—the other he
 stript,
With ravenous claws, of raiment and of
 food.'
Then said the Lord, 'Doth the Man hear?'
'He hears,'
Answer'd the Seraph; 'like a wolf he lies,
Venomous, bloody, dark, a thing accurst,
And hearkeneth, with no sign!' Then said
 the Lord:
'Show them the Man,' and the pale Seraph
 cried,
'Behold!'

    Hushedly, hushedly, hushedly,
In heaven fell the Snow of Thought Divine,
Gleaming upon the Waters of Life beneath,
And melting,—as with slow and lingering
 pace,

The Shapes stole fo
And saw the thing
 and lived,
And stooped above
 a hand
And touch'd him,
 shrank and spa
Hiding his face.

    'Have
The Lord said; an
 'Yea;'
And the Lord said
 Man?'

'He lieth like a log
And as he lieth, lo
His head into her la
And smoothes his
 brow,
And croons in a lo
And lo! the other
Half-shrinking in th
Yet hungering with
 ately
Kissing his bloody

'Will they go fort
 replied,
'He grew within m
 white
Upon his lips. I w
And a voice cried,
 him;
I have kist his lip
 breast,
I bare him children,
I will go forth with

Snowed down the
 Waters of Life
Flow'd softly, sadly
A piteous human cr
Thrill'd to the heart

And in a voice of
The Lord said (w
 Divine
The Waters of Lif
 dening):
'The Man is saved

Political Mystics.

(1871.)

Shades of the living Time,
Phantoms men deem real,
Rise to a runic rhyme,
Cloak'd from head to heel!
One by one ye pass
As in a magician's glass,
One by one displace
The hood which veils the face;
And ever we recognise,
With terrible deep-drawn breath,
Christ's inscrutable eyes,
And the bloodless cheeks of Death!

TITAN AND AVATAR.

A 'CHORAL MYSTIC.

I.

ODE OF NATIONS.

'TWAS the height of the world's night, there
  was neither warmth nor light,
And the heart of Earth was heavy as a
  stone';
Yet the nations sick with loss saw the surge
  of heaven toss
Round the meteor of the Cross; and with
  a moan
All the people desolate gazed thereon and
  question'd fate,
And the wind went by and bit them to the
  bone.

Hope was fled and Faith was dead, and the
  black pall overhead
Hung like Death's, for doom was heavy
  everywhere,—
When there rose a sudden gleam, then a
  thunder, then a scream,
Then a lightning, stream on stream aslant
  the air!
And a dreadful ray was shed around the
  Cross, and it grew red,
And the pallid people leapt to see the
  glare.

Fire on the heights of France! Fire on the
  heights of France!
  Fire flaming up to heaven, streak on
    streak!

How on France Kings look't askance! how
  the nations join'd in dance!
To see the glory glance from peak to
  peak!
How the chain'd lands curst their chance,
  as they bent their eyes on France!
Earth answer'd, and her tongues began
  to speak.

Now hark!—who lit the spark in the
  miserable dark?
O Washington, men miss thee and
  forget.
Where did the light arise, in answer to
  man's cries?
In the West; in those far skies it rose
  and set.
Who brought it in his breast from the
  liberated West?
Speak his name, and kneel and bless
  him: Lafayette.

O Sire, that madest Fire! How with
  passionate desire
Leapt the nations while it gather'd and
  up-streamed;
Then they fed it, to earth's groans, with
  Man's flesh and blood and bones,
And with Altars and with Thrones; and
  still it screamed.
Then they cast a King thereon—but a
  flash, and he was gone.
Then they brought a Queen to feed it:—
  how it gleam'd!

Then it came to pass, Earth's frame seem'd dissolving in the flame,
Then it seem'd the Soul was shaken on its seat,
And the pale Kings with thin cries look'd in one another's eyes,
Saying, 'Hither now it flies, and O how fleet!
Sound loud the battle-cry, we must trample France or die,
Strike the Altar, cast it down beneath our feet.'

Forth they fared. The red fire flared on the heights of France, and glared
On the faces of the free who kept it fed ;
Came the Kings with blinded eyes, but with baffled prayers and cries
They beheld it grow and rise, still bloody-red ;
When lo! the Fire's great heart, like a red rose cloven apart
Open'd swiftly, to deep thunder overhead.

And lo, amid the glow, while the pale Kings watched woe,
Rose a single SHAPE, and stood upon the pyre.
Its eyes were deeply bright, and its face, in their sad sight,
Was pallid in a white-heat of desire,
And the cheek was ashen hued ; and with folded arms it stood
And smiled bareheaded, fawn'd on by the Fire!

Forehead bare, the Shape stood there, in the centre of the glare,
And cried, 'Away ye Kings, or ye shall die.'
And it drave them back with flame, o'er the paths by which they came,
And they wrung their hands in shame as they did fly.
As they fled it came behind fleeter-footed than the wind,
And it scatter'd them, and smote them hip and thigh.

All amazed, they stood and gazed, while their crying kingdoms blazed,
With their fascinated eyes upon the Thing ;—

When lo, as clouds dilate, it grew greater and more great,
And beneath it waited Fate with triple sting ;
All collossus-like and grand, it bestrode the sea and land,
And behold the crownèd likeness of a KING !

Then the light upon the height, that had burned in all men's sight
Was absorb'd into the creature where he smiled.
O his face was wild and wan—but the burning current ran
In the red veins of the Man who was its child :—
To the sob of the world's heart did the meteor-light depart,
Earth darken, and the Altar fall defiled.

The aloud the Phantom vow'd, 'Look upon me, O ye proud !
Kiss my footprints ! I am reaper, ye are wheat !
Ye shall tremble at my name, ye shall ea my bread in shame,
I will make ye gather tame beneath my Seat.'

And the gold that had been bright on the hair of Kings at night,
Ere dawn was shining dust about his feet.
At this hour behold him tower, in the darkness of his power,
Look upon him, search his features, O ye free !
Is there hope for living things in this fiery King of Kings,
Doth the song that Freedom sings fit such as he?
Is it night or is it day, while ye bleed beneath his sway?
It is night, deep night on earth and air and sea.

Still the height of the world's night. There is neither warmth nor light,
And the heart of Earth is heavy as a stone ;
And within the night's dark core where the sad Cross gleam'd before
Sits the Shape that Kings adore, upon a Throne ;

And the nations desolate crawl beneath and
   curse their fate,
And the wind goes by and bites them to
   the bone.

O Sire that mad'st the Fire, and the Shape
   that dread and dire
Came from thence, the first and last born
   of the same,
To Thee we praying throng, for Thou alone
   art strong,
To right our daily wrong and bitter
   shame:
From the aching breast of earth, lift the red
   Fire and its birth!
Consume them—let them vanish in one
   flame!

II.
THE AVATAR'S DREAM.
(Buonaparte loquitur, at Erfurt.)

THE cup is overflowing. Pour, pour yet,
My Famulus—pour with free arm-sweep
   still,
And when the wine is running o'er the brim,
Sparkling with golden bubbles in the sun,
I will stoop down and drink the full great
   draught
Of glory, and as did those heroes old
Drinking ambrosia in the happy isles,
Dilate at once to perfect demigod.
Meantime, I feast my eyes as the wine runs
And the cup fills. Fill up, my Famulus!
Pour out the precious juice of all the earth,
Pour with great arm-sweep, that the world
   may see.

O Famulus—O Spirit—O good Soul,
Come close to me and listen—curl thyself
Up in my breast—let us drink ecstasy
Together; for the charm thou taughtest
   me
I working like slow poison in the veins
Of the great Nations: each, a wild-beast
   tamed,
Looks mildly in mine eyes and from my
   hand
Eats gently; and this day I speak the
   charm
To Russia, and, behold! the crafty eyes
Blink sleepily, while on the fatal lips
Hovers the smile of appetite half-fed,

Half-hungry: he being won, all else is won,
And at our feet, our veritable slave,
Lies Europe. Whisper now, Soul of my
   Soul,
Since we have won this Europe with the
   sword,
How we shall portion it to men anew.

First, in the centre of the West, I set
My signet like a star, and on a rock
Base the imperial Throne: seated whereon,
The royal crown of France upon my head,
At hand the iron crown of Lombardy,
And in my sceptre blended as a sign
The hereditary gems of Italy,
Spain, Holland, I shall see beneath my feet
My Puppets sit with strings that reach my
   hand:
Murat upon the throne of Italy,
Jerome upon new-born Westphalia,
Louis the lord of Holland, and perchance
A kinsman in the Prussian dotard's place;
And, lower yet, still puppets to my hand,
Saxony, Würtemberg, Bavaria,
The petty principalities and powers,
All smiling up in our hot thunderous air;—
And all the thrones, the kingdoms, and the
   powers
That break to life beneath them, murmur-
   ing
'Hail, King of Europe—Emperor of the
   West.'

Thus far. Still farther? Driven to the East,
First by fond cunning, afterwards by blows,
The Russian's eyes bloodshot with greed
   will watch,
While still our flood-tide inexhaustible
Of Empire washes to the Danube, rolls
Into the Baltic, and with one huge wave
Covers the plains of Poland. Then at last
The mighty Empires of the East and West
Shall clash together in the final blow,
And that which loses shall be driven on
To lead the heathen on in Asia,
And that which hurls the other to, such
   doom
Shall be the chosen Regent of the World.
Shall this be so, O Spirit? Pour, O pour—
Yea, let me feast mine eyes upon the wine,
Albeit I drink not. See!—Napoleon,
Waif from the island in the southern sea,

Sun to whom all the Kings o' the earth are stars,
Sword before which all earthly swords are straws,
Child of the Revolution, Crown and Head,
Heart, Soul, Arm, King, of all Humanity!

O Famulus—in God's name keep my soul
From swooning to vain-glory. I believe
God (not the other) sends thee, that thy mouth
May fill me with a message for the race,
And purge the peevish and distemper'd world
Of her hereditary plague of Kings.
For Man, I say, all in due season grow
Back to the likeness hat he wore at first,
One mighty nation pling the green earth,
One equal people with one King and head,
One Kingdom with one Temple, and therein
No priest, no idol, no ark sacrifice,
But spheric music and the dreamy light
Of heaven's mild azure and the changeless stars.
The curse of earth hath been the folly of peace
Under vain rulers, so dividing earth,
That twenty thousand kings of Lilliput
Strutted and fretted heaven and teased the time,
Kept nature's skin for ever on the sting
Like vermin, and perplex'd Humanity
With petty pangs and peevish tyranny,
While the soul sickened of obscure disease,
And the innumerable limbs of state
Moved paralysed, most inert, or dead.
Came Revolution like avenging fire;
And in the red flash miserable men
Beheld themselves and wondered—saw their Kings
Still strutting Lilliputian in the glare,—
And laugh'd till heaven rung,—gave one fierce look
To heaven, and rose. Outraged Columbia
Breath'd o'er the sea, and scorch'd the insolent cheek
Of Albion. Albion paled before the flame.
The darken'd embers faded in the West,
And all was still again; when one mad morn
Men wakening, saw the heights of France afire!

Earth shook to her foundation, and the light
Illumed the hemispheres from west to east,
And men that walk beneath and under us,
Holding their heads to other stars, beheld
The glory flaming from the underworld.
The little Kings of Europe, lily-pale,
Scream'd shrill to one another. Germany
In her deep currents of philosophy
Mirror'd the fiery horror. Russia groaned,
Sheeted in snows that took the hue of blood
Under the fierce reflection. Italy,
Spain and the Tyrol, wild Helvetia,
Caught havoc; and even on the white English crags
A few strong spirits, in a race that binds
Its body in chains and calls them Liberty,
And calls each fresh link Progress, stood erect
With faces pale that hunger'd to the light.
Then, like a hero in his anguish, burnt
Poor gentle Louis, whom the stars destined
To be a barber and who was a King,
And as he flamed and went like very straw,
Earth shriek'd and fever'd France grew raving mad.

Pass o'er the wild space of delirium,
When France upon her stony bed of pain
Raved, screamed, blasphemed, was medicined with blood,
Forgot all issues and the course of time;
And come to that supremer, stiller hour
When, facing these fierce wasps of Kings who flocked
To sting the weary sufferer to death,
I rose and stood behind her, drove them back,
So I with a sword-sweep. Those were merry days,
My Spirit! These were spring days, winds of war
Sharp-blowing, but the swallow on the way
Already bringing summer from the south!
Then one by one I held these little Kings
Between my fingers and inspected them
Like curious insects, while with buzz and hiss
Their tiny stings were shooting in and out;
And how I laugh'd
To think such wretched vermin had so long
Tortured unhappy Man, and to despair

Driven him and his through infinite ways of woe!
When, with one sweep of his great arm, one blow
Of his sharp palm, he might annihilate
Such creatures by the legion and in sooth
Exterminate the breed! O Spirit of Man!
A foolish Titan! foolish now as then,
Guided about the earth like a blind man
By any hand that leads,
And then and now unconscious of a frame
Whose strength, into one mighty effort gathered,
Might shake the firmament of heaven itself!
. . . Well, we have done this service. We have freed
Earth from its pest of Kings, so that they crawl
Powerless and stingless; we have medicined
Desperate disease with direful remedies;
And lo, the mighty Spirit of mankind
Hath stagger'd from the sick-bed to his feet,
And feebly totters, picking darken'd steps,
And while I lead him on scarce·sees the sun,
But questions feebly 'Whither?' Whither? Indeed
I am dumb, and all Earth's voices are as dumb—
God is not dumber on His throne. In vain
I would peer forward, but the path is black.
Ay,—whither?

O what peevish fools are mortals,
Tormented by a raven on each shoulder,
'Whither?' and 'wherefore?' Shall I stand and gape
At heaven, straining eyes into the tomb,
Like some purblind philosopher or bard
Asking stale questions of the Infinite
Dumb with God's secret? questioning the winds,
The waves, the stars, all things that live and move,
All signs, all augurs? Never yet hath one
Accorded answer. 'Whither?' Death replies
With dusky smile. 'Wherefore?' The echoes laugh
Their 'wherefore? wherefore?' Of the time unborn,
And of the inevitable Law, no voice
Bears witness. The pale Man upon the Cross
Moan'd,—and beheld no further down the Void
Than those who gather'd round to see Him die.

Ay,—but the Soul, being weather-wise, can guess
The morrow by the sunset, can it not?
And there are signs about the path whereon
I guide the foolish Titan, that imply
Darkness and hidden dangers. All these last
I smile at; but, O Soul within my Soul,
'Tis he, the foolish Titan's self, I fear:
For, though I have a spell upon him now,
And say it, and he follows, any morn
(Awakening from his torpor as he woke
One bloody morn in Paris and went wild),
He may put out his frightful strength again,
And with one mighty shock of agony
Bring down the roof of Empire on my head.
He loves me now, and to my song of war
Murmurs deep undertone, and as he goes
Fondles the hand that leads; but day by day
Must I devise new songs and promises,
More bloody incantation, lest he rouse
And rend me. Oftentimes it seems *he* leads,
I follow,—he the Tyrant, I the Slave,—
And it, perchance, were better had I paused
At Amiens, nor with terrible words and ways
Led him thus far, still whispering in his ear
That he at last shall look on 'Liberty.'

Liberty? Have I lull'd him with a Lie?
Or shall the Titan Spirit of man be led
To look again upon the face of her,
His first last love, a spirit woman-shaped,
Whom in the sweet beginning he beheld,
Adored, loved, lost, pursued, whom still in tears
He yearns for; in whose name alone all Kings
Have led and guided him a space and throve,
Denying whom all Kings have died in turn,

Whose memory is perfume, light and dream,
Whose hope is incense, music, bliss, and tears,
To him whose great heart with immortal beat
Measures the dark march of Humanity.
I do believe this Shape he saw and loved
Was but a Phantasm, unsubstantial, strange,
A vision never to be held and had,
A spectral woman ne'er to be enjoyed ;
But such a thought whisper'd into his ear
Were rank as blasphemy cried up at God.
The name is yet a madness, a supreme
Ecstasy and delirium ! All things
That cry it, move the tears into the eyes
Of the sad Titan. Echoed from the heights
Of France, it made him mad, and in his rage
He tore at Earth's foundations. Evermore
He turns his suffering orbs upon the dark,
Uplifts his gentle hands to the chill stars,
Pauses upon the path, and in the ear
Of him who leadeth cries with broken voice,
' How long, how long, how long ? '

    And unto him,
This Titan, I, supreme of all the earth,
Am but a pigmy (let me whisper it !)
And I have won upon him with strange lies,
And he has suffered all indignities,
Bonds, chains, a band to blindfold both his eyes,
Patient and meek, since I have sworn at last
To lead him to the trysting-place where waits
His constant love and most immortal Bride.
Still in mine ears he murmureth her name,
And follows. I have le him on through fire,
Blood, darkness, tears, and still he hath been tame,
Though ofttimes shrinking from things horrible,
And on and on he follows even now,
Blindfold, with slower and less willing feet—
I fear with slower and less willing feet—
And still I ead, through lurid light from heaven,
Whither I know not. 'Whither !' Oftentimes
My great heart fails, lest on some morn we reach
That portal o'er which flaming Arch is writ,
' All hope abandon ye who enter here ! '
And he, perceiving he hath been befool'd,
Will cast me from him with his last fierce breath
Down through the gate into some pit of doom.

Meantime he follows smiling. O Famulus !
Could I but dream that she, the Shape he seeks,
Whom men name Liberty, and gods name Peace,
Were human, could inhale this dense dark air,
Could live and dwell on earth, and rear the race,
'Twere well,—for by Almighty God I swear
I would find out a means to join their hands
And bless them, and abide their grateful doom.
But she he seeks I know to be a dream,
A vision of the rosy morning mist,
A creature foreign to the earth and sea,
Ne'er to be look'd upon by mortal soul
Out of the mortal vision. Wherefore still
I fear this Titan. I can never appease
His hungry yearning wholly. He will bear
No future chains, no closer blindfolding,
And if a fatal whisper reach his ear,
I and all mine are wholly wreck'd and lost.
Yet is this Titan old so weak of wit,
So senile-minded though so huge of frame,
So deaf to warning voices when they cry,
That, should no angel light from heaven an speak
The mad truth in his ear, he will proceed
Patiently as a lamb. He counteth not
The weary years ; his eyes are shut indeed
With a half-smile, to see the mystic Face
Pictured upon his brain ; only at times
He lifteth lids and gazeth wildly round,
Clutching at the cold hand of him' that guides,—
But with a whisper he is calm'd again,
Relapsing back into his gentle dream.

O he is patient, and he will await
Century after century in peace,
So that he hears sweet songs of her he
   seeks,
So that his guides do speak to him of her,
So that he thinks to clasp her in the end.

The end? Sweet sprite, the end is what I
   fear—
If I might live for ever, Famulus !—
Why am I not immortal and a god?
I have caused tears enough, as bitter tears
As ever by the rod divine were struck
Out of this rock of earth. O for a spell
Wherewith to cheat old Death, whose feet
   I hear
Afar off, for I hate the bony touch
Of hands that change the purple for the
   shroud !
Yet I could go in peace (since all must go)
So that my seed were risen and in its eyes
I saw assurance of imperial thoughts,
Strength, and a will to grasp the thunder-
   bolt
I leave unhurl'd beside the Olympian
   throne.
Ah God, to die, and into the dark gloom
Drag that throne with me, to the hollow
   laugh
Of the awakening Titan ! All my peers
Are ciphers, all my brethren are mere
   Kings
Of the old fashion, only strengthen'd now
By my strong sunshine ; reft of that, they
   die,
Like sunflowers in the darkness. Death,
   old Death,
Touch me this day, or any dark day soon,
And I and mine are like the miser's hoard,
A glorious and a glittering pile of gold
Changed to a fluttering heap of wither'd
   leaves.

This must not be. No, I must have a
   child,
I must be firm and from my bed divorce
The barren woman. Furthermore, to link
My throne with all the lesser thrones of
   earth,
I must wed the seed of Kings. Which seed,
   which child?
Which round ripe armful of new destiny?
Which regal mould for my imperial issue?

Thine, fruitful house of Hapsburg? Russia,
   thine?
The greater, not the lesser. I must wed
Seed of the Czar, and so with nuptial rites
Unite the empires of the East and West.

Fill, fill, my Famulus, the golden cup
I thirst for ; all the peril as I gaze
Hath faded. I no more with fluttering lips
Cry ' Whither?' but with hands outstretch'd
   I watch
Rubily glistening glory. It shall thrive !
King of the West, sowing the seed of
   Kings
First of the Empire of the Golden Age,
The sleeping Titan, and the quiet Sea ;
Light of the Lotus and all mortal eyes,
Whose orbit nations like to heliotropes
Shall follow with lesser circle and sweet
   sound !

III.

THE ELEMENTAL QUEST.

SEMI-CHORUS I.

FORM of her the Titan full of patience
Sees amid the darkness of the nations ;
Voice of her whose sound in the beginning
Came upon him desolate and sinning ;
Face and fairest form of her whose gleam-
   ing
Soothes his gentle spirit into dreaming ;
Spirit ! whom the Titan sees above him !

SEMI-CHORUS II.

Gentle eyes that shine and seem to love
   him !
Tender touch, the thrill of her sweet fingers,
Thrill that reach'd his soul and burns and
   lingers ;
Breath of her, and scent of her, and bliss
   of her ;
Dream of her, and smile of her, and kiss of
   her !
Come again, and speak, and bend above
   him,
Spirit that came once and seemed to love
   him.

THE TITAN.

How long, how long?

SEMI-CHORUS I.

Courage, great heart and strong,
Break not, but beat low chime

To the dark flow of Time;
Follow the path foot-worn,
Sad night and dewy morn,
Under the weary sun
Follow, O mighty one;
Under dim moon and star!

THE TITAN.

Whither? How far, how far?

SEMI-CHORUS I.

Spirit of the fathomless abysses,
Spirit that he looked upon and misses,
Free and fair and perfect, more than human,
Bringing love and peace-gifts like a woman;
Come unto him, lessen to his pleading.

SEMI-CHORUS II.

Mark his patience, hear his gentle interceding;
O'er mountain upon mountain left behind thee,
He hath cheerly climb'd in vain to find thee:
Wild waters he hath cross'd, wild sea and river,
All countries he hath traversed, faithful ever,
Ever hoping, ever waiting, never seeing.

CHORUS.

Spirit seen in some long darken'd being,
Spirit that he saw at the world's portal,
Saw, and knew, and loved, and felt immortal,
Spirit that he wearies for and misses,
Answer from the fathomless abysses!

THE TITAN.

How long, how long?

SEMI-CHORUS I.

Courage, O Titan strong!
Courage, from place to place
Still follow the voice and the face!

THE TITAN.
Whither?

A VOICE AFAR.
O hither!

THE TITAN.
Whither?

SEMI-CHORUS I.

Voice of her he follows in dumb pleasure,
Camest thou from the earth or from the azure;
Camest thou from the pastures on the mountains,
From the ocean, from the rivers, from the fountains,
From the vapours blowing o'er him while he hearkens,
From the ocean hoar that beats his feet and darkens,
From the star that on the sea-fringe melts and glistens?

SEMI-CHORUS II.

O homeless voice, he maddens as he listens,
O voice divine, his wild lips part asunder;
He speaketh, and his words are a low thunder.

THE TITAN.
Whither, O whither?

VOICE AFAR.
Hither!

THE TITAN.

Whither? Wherefore, while I wait in patience,
Mock her voice, O voices of the nations;
    Wherefore by night and day,
    Where'er my slow feet stray,
Trouble all hours with wild reverberations?

Mountain winds, ye name her name unto me!
Flowing rivers glance and thrill it through me!
    Earth, water, air, and sky,
    Name her as I go by!
With her dim ghost the floating clouds pursue me.

All of these have seen her face and love her,
Earth beneath and heaven that bends above her;
    The rain-wreck and the storm
    Mimic the one fair form,
The whirlwind knows her name and cries it over.

Flowers are sown by her bright foot, wherever
They are flashing past by mere and river ;
   Birds in the forest stir,
   Singing mad praise of her ;
All green paths know her, though she flies
   for ever.

CHORUS.

Joy of wind and wave and cloud and
   blossom,
Pause at last, and fall upon his bosom !

THE TITAN.

None behold her twice, but having conn'd
   her
While she flashes past with feet that
   wander,
   Remember the blest gleam,
   And grow by it, and dream,
And fondle the sweet memory, and ponder.

All have known her, and yet none possess
   her ;
None behold her, yet all things caress her ;
   The warmth of her white feet,
   Where it doth fall so sweet,
Abides for ever there, and all things bless
   her.

Faster than the prophesying swallow,
Fast by wood and sea and hill and hollow,
   Sought by all things that be,
   But most of all by me,
She flieth none know whither, and I follow.

SEMI-CHORUS I.

O wherefore, radiant one,
Under the moon and sun,
Glimmer away?

VOICE AFAR.

Here on the heights I stay ;
Come hither.

THE TITAN.

Whither?

VOICE AFAR.

           O hither !

CHORUS.

Form of her the Titan full of patience
Sees amid the darkness of the nations ;
Voice of her whose song in the beginning
Came upon him desolate and sinning ;
Face and fairest form of her whose gleaming
Soothes his gentle spirit into dreaming ;
Touch of her, the thrill of her quick fingers,
Thrill that reach'd his soul and burns and
   lingers ;
Soul beyond his soul, yet ever near it,
His heart's home, and haven of his spirit ;
Joy of wind and wave and cloud and
   blossom,
Pause at last, and fall upon his bosom !

IV.

THE ELEMENTAL DOOM.

CHORUS OF SPIRITS.

STRANGE hands are passing across our
   eyes,
Before our souls strange visions rise
   And dim shapes flash and flee.
The mists of dream are backward roll'd—
As from a mountain, we behold
   What is, and yet shall be.

A VOICE.

Speak, while the depths of dream unfold,
   What is it that ye see ?

SEMI-CHORUS I.

'Tis vision. Lo, before us stands,
Casting his shade on many lands,
The mighty Titan, by the sea
Of tempest-tost humanity ;
And to the earth, and sea, and sky,
He uttereth a thunder-cry
   Out of his breaking heart,
And the fierce elements reply,
   And earth is cloven apart.

SEMI-CHORUS II.

Like sparks blown from a forge, the spheres
Drift o'er us ;—all our eyes and ears
   Are full of fire and sound.
With blood about him blown like rain,
We see how on a darken'd plain
   Stands the Avatar, crown'd.
Silent he waits, and white as death,
   Looks in the Titan's eyes.
They stand—the black sky holds its breath—
   The deep Sea stills its cries,
The mad storm hushes driving past,

The sick stars pause and gaze—the blast,
The wind-rent rain, the vapours dark,
Like dead things crouch, and wait, and hark;
And lo ! those twain alone and dumb
Loom desolate and strange.

SEMI-CHORUS I.

Is the time come?

SEMI-CHORUS II.

The time is come.

CHORUS.

Titan, to thy revenge !

SEMI-CHORUS I.

O look and listen !
His great eyes glisten,
Like an oak the storm rendeth
He swayeth and bendeth,
With lips torn asunder
He shakes, but no thunder
Comes thence.

SEMI-CHORUS II.

While still nigh him,
With smiles that defy him,
The crown'd one is standing,—
His pale look commanding
A tigress, that crouching
Beneath him and touching
His feet with low cries,
Waits, fiercely betraying
Blood's thirst yet obeying
His eyes !

CHORUS.

Is he doom'd?

A VOICE.

He is doom'd.

CHORUS.

Oh, by whom ?

VOICE.

By the child yet unborn in the womb,
By the dead laid to sleep in the tomb,
He is doom'd, he is doom'd.

CHORUS.

Speak his doom !

THE TITAN.

Napoleon ! Napoleon !

THE AVATAR.

Who cries ?

THE TITAN.

I, child of the earth and the skies,
I, Titan, the mystical birth,
Whose voice since the morning of earth
Hath doom'd such as thou in the end,
Speak thy doom !

THE AVATAR.

Speak ! I smile and attend.

THE TITAN.

Because thou hast with lies and incantations,
With broken vows and false asseverations,
For thine own ends accurst,
Betrayed me from the first,
I speak, and doom thee, in the name of nations.

Because I have wander'd like a great stream flowing
From its own channel and through strange gulfs going,
So that for years and years
I must retrace in tears
The black and barren pathway of thy showing.

Because one further step after thy leading
Had hurl'd me down to doom past interceding,
So that I never again,
In passion or in pain,
Might look upon the face I follow pleading.

Because thou hast led me blind, knee-deep through slaughter,
Through fields of blood that wash'd our way like water,
Because in that divine
Name I adore, and mine,
Thou hast bruised Earth, and to desolation brought her.

Because thou hast been a liar and blasphemer,
Deeming me triply dotard and a dreamer,

Because thy hand at length
Would strike me in my strength,
Me, deathless! me, diviner and supremer!

Because all voices of the earth and azure,
All things that breathe, all things curst for
thy pleasure,
All poor dead men who died
To feed thy bitter pride,
All living, all dead, cry—mete to him our
measure!

Because thou hast slain Kings, and as a
token
Stolen their crowns and worn them, having
spoken
My curse against the same ;
Because all things proclaim
That thou didst swear a troth, and that 'tis
broken.

By her whom thou didst swear under God's
heaven
To find ; by her who being found was
driven
O'er earth, air, sky, and sea,
Through desolate ways, by thee,
With voice appealing and with raiment
riven!

Because thou hast turned upon and violated
Her soul to whom thou first wert conse-
crated,
Because, thro' thy soul's lie
And life's delusion, I
Must wait more ages, who have wept and
waited

Since the beginning. By the soul of
Patience,
Sick of thy face and its abominations,
I speak on thine and thee
The doom of Destiny,
Hear it, and die, hear in the name of
nations !

SEMI-CHORUS I.
Is he doom'd ?

SEMI-CHORUS II.
He is doom'd. 'Tis the end.

THE TITAN.
Napoleon!

THE AVATAR.
Speak ! I attend.

THE TITAN.
Utter the doom thou dost crave.

THE AVATAR.
'Tis spoken. A shroud and a grave.

THE TITAN.
O voices of earth, air, and sky,
Hear ye his doom, and reply.

HUMAN VOICES.
Death is sleep. Let him wake and not die.

THE TITAN.
Because by thee all comfort hath been
taken,
So that the Earth rocks still forlorn and
shaken,
Staring at the sad skies
With sleepless aching eyes,
Thou shalt *not* die, but wait and watch and
waken.

This is thy doom. Lone as a star thy being
Shall see the waves break and the drift-cloud
fleeing,
Hear the wind cry and grow,
Watch the great waters flow,
And seeing all, shine hid from all men's
seeing.

Here on this Isle amid a sea of sorrow
I cast thee down. Black night and weary
morrow,
Lie there alone, forgot,
So doom'd and pitied not ;
Let all things watch thy face, and thy face
borrow

The look of these mad elements that ever
Strike, scream, and mingle, sever and dis-
sever ;
Gather from air and sea
The thirst of all things free,
The up-looking want, the hunger ceasing
never.

All shall forget thee. Thou shalt hear the
nations
Flocking with music light and acclamations

X

To kiss his royal feet
Who sitteth in thy Seat,
Surrounded by the slaves of lofty stations.

A rock in the lone Sea shall be thy pillow.
In the wide waste of gray wave and green
  billow,
The days shall rise and set
  In silence, and forget
To sun thee,—a black shape beneath a
  willow

Watching the weary waters with heart
  bleeding ;
Or dreaming cheek upon thy hand ; or
  reading
The book upon thy knee ;
  And ever as the sea
Moans, raising eyes to the still heavens,
  and pleading :

Till like a wave worn out with silent break-
  ing
Or like a wind blown weary ; thou, for-
  saking
Thy tenement of clay,
  Shalt wear and waste away,
And grow a portion of the ever-waking .

Tumult of cloud and sea. Feature by
  feature
Losing the likeness of the living creature,
  Returning back thy form
To its elements of storm,
Thou shalt dissolve in the great wreck of
  Nature.

            SEMI-CHORUS I.
Is it done?
            SEMI-CHORUS II.
              It is done.
            SEMI-CHORUS I.
                Look again.
            SEMI-CHORUS II.
I see on the rock in the main
The Shape sitting dark by the sea,
And his shade, and the shade of the tree,
Where he sitteth, are pencil'd jet-black
On the luminous sky at his back ;
But lo ! while I gaze, from the sky
Like phantoms they vanish and die :—
All is dark.

            SEMI-CHORUS I.
                Look again.

            SEMI-CHORUS II.
              Hark, O hark !

            SEMI-CHORUS I.
A shrill cry is piercing the dark—
Like the multitudinous moan
Of the waves as they clash, comes a groan
From afar—

            THE TITAN.
        What is this, O ye free ?

            SEMI-CHORUS II.
He has gone like a wave of the sea—
Day dieth, the light falleth red,—
O Titan, behold he is dead ! . . .

              CHORUS.
Strange hands are passed across our eyes,
Before our souls strange visions rise,
  And dim shapes flash and flee ;
The mists of dream are backward rolled—
As from a mountain we behold
  That Island in the sea.

            SEMI-CHORUS I.
Now bow thy face upon thy breast,
O Titan, and bemoan thy quest !
O look not thither with thine eyes,
But lift them to the constant skies !

              THE TITAN.
What do ye see that thus to me
Ye turn and smile so bitterly ?

            SEMI-CHORUS I.
'Tis vision. On that island bare
Sits one with face divinely fair,
  And pensive smiling lips ;
And on her lap the proud head lies.—
Pale with the seal on its proud eyes
  Of Death's divine eclipse ;
All round is darkness of the sea,
And sorrow of the cloud.

            SEMI-CHORUS II.
                Yet she
Is making with her heavenly face
Sweetness like sunlight ; and the place

Grows luminous ; and the world afar
Looks thither as to some new star,
All wondering ; and with lips of death
Men name one name beneath their breath,
Not cursing as of yore, for now
All the inexorable brow
Is mouldering marble.

SEMI-CHORUS I.

Hark, O hark !
A silver voice divides the dark !

A VOICE.

Hither, O hither !

ANOTHER VOICE.

Whither ?

FIRST VOICE.

O sweet is sleep if sleep be deep,
And sweetest far to eyes that weep ;
He who upon my breast doth creep
Shall close his weary eyes and sleep.

Yet he who seeks me shall not find,
And he who chains me shall not bind ;
For fleeter-footed than the wind
I still elude all human kind.

But when, soul-weary of the chase,
Falleth some man of mortal race,
I pause—I find him in his place,
I pause—I bless his dying face !

Whatsoever man he be,
I take his head upon my knee,
I give him words and kisses three,
Kissing I whisper, ' Thou art free !

O free is sleep if sleep be deep !—
I soothe them sleeping, and I heap
Greenness above them, and they weep
No longer, but are free, and sleep.

O royal face and royal head !
O lips that thunder'd ! O eyes red
With nights of watch ! O great soul dead !
Thy blood is water, thy heart lead !

They doom'd thee in my name, but see !
I doom thee not, but set thee free ;
Balm for all hearts is shed by me,
And for all spirits, liberty.

He finds me least who loves me best,
His Soul in an eternal quest
Wails still, while one by one are prest
Tyrants that hate me, to my breast.

The sad days fly—the slow years creep,
And he alone doth never sleep,
Would he might slumber and not weep.
O free is sleep, if sleep be deep.

THE TITAN.

Irene !.

THE FOOL OF DESTINY.

A CHORIC DRAMA.

Scene.—THE CHÂTEAU OF WILHELMS-
HÖHE, IN CASSEL.
*German Citizens walking in the Gardens
without.*

FIRST CITIZEN.

How fine it is to lounge in talk
Together, down this long green walk
While russet trees to left and right
Snaring the rosy shafts of light
Shade them to silver, till they glow
There on the roof of the château
Gleaming bright ruby !

SECOND CITIZEN.

Not too near—
The place is private.

FIRST CITIZEN.

Didst thou hear
The news ? Another glorious blow
For Fatherland !

SECOND CITIZEN.

To-night at five
I saw the courier arrive,
Bringing the news to him who waits
Yonder.—O he may thank the fates
He sits so snug, the man of sin !—
How cunningly, before the end,
The Snake contrived to save his skin !

FIRST CITIZEN.

Thou art too hard upon him, friend.
He saw that all his cards were played,

And so, to save more bloodshed, strayed
Into the cage.

SECOND CITIZEN.
                A cage, indeed !
Where from a gold plate he may feed
Of all earth's dainties, while afar
France, 'neath the tramping feet of War,
Bleeds like a winepress. There he lolls,
Butcher of bodies and of souls,
Smiling, and sees the storm blow by !

FIRST CITIZEN.
What could he do?

SECOND CITIZEN.
                Could he not die?

FIRST CITIZEN.
Die? Sentiment ! If I were he
I'd bless the stars which set me free
From that foul-hearted Whore's embrace,
France, with her fickle painted face.
Better in Germany to dine,
Smoke one's cigar, and sip one's wine ;
And in good time, like most, no doubt,
Who have worn their wicked members out,
Repent, and be absolved, and then
Die in one's bed, like smaller men !

SECOND CITIZEN.
Thou cynic !

FIRST CITIZEN'S WIFE.
                Dost thou think that he
Is happy ?
FIRST CITIZEN.
        Why not? . . . Possibly,
My dear, 'tis something after all
To know the worst that can befall ;
To know, whatever joy or sorrow
Fate is preparing for the morrow,
It cannot make more dark the lot
One bears to-night. Happy ! Why not?
Happy as most of our poor kind.

WIFE.
He hath so much upon his mind !

FIRST CITIZEN.
A woman's thought ;—but hark to me,
And take this for philosophy—

Beyond a given amount of pain,
The spirit suffers not a grain.
What stuff we humble folk are taught
Of monarchs and their weight of thought !
Why, thou and I, and Jack and Jill,
Feel just as much of good and ill,
Of life and strife, of thought and care,
As he who sitteth musing there !

SECOND CITIZEN.
I saw him walking, yesterday.
He is much aged of late, they say—
He stoops much, and his features are
Gray as the ash of the cigar
He smokes for ever.

FIRST CITIZEN (*to wife*).
                Come, my dear,
Let's home ! 'Tis growing chilly here ;
So !—take my arm. Yes, I contend
It matters little in the end
If one be Beggar, Priest, or King—
The whip's for all—the pang, the sting !
Dost thou remember—canst forget ?
When all our goods were seized for deb',
In Friedberg? Claim was heap'd on claim—
Blow came on blow—shame follow'd shame ;
And last to crown our dire distress,
Thy brother Hans' hard-heartedness.
Think you *I* felt a whit less sad,
Less thunderstruck, less fierce, less mad,
Than yonder melancholy Man,
When, through the dark cloud of Sedan,
He, as a star that shoots by night,
Swept from his sphere of lonely light,
And at the feet of Wilhelm lay
Glow-worm-like, in the garish day
Of conquest ? Well, well ! wait and see—
I rose again, and so may he.
The world is but a Play, tho' ye
Dear creatures take it seriously !
I cannot pity from my heart
The player of the Monarch's part,
For at the worst he never knows
The famish'd Body's bitter throes.
I pity more with all my soul
The filler of the Soldier's rôle,
Who feels the ball, and with a groan
Sinks in the bloody ranks unknown,
And while the far-off cannon cries,
Kisses his sweetheart's hair, and dies.
                                [*Exeunt.*

THE FOOL OF DESTINY.

NAPOLEON. A PHYSICIAN.

PHYSICIAN.

The sickness is no sickness of the flesh,
No ailment such as common mortals feel,
But spiritual: 'tis thy fiery thought
Drying the wholesome humour of the veins,
Consuming the brain's substance, and from thence,
As flame spreads, through each muscle, vein, and nerve,
Reaching the vital members. If your Highness
Could stoop from the tense strain of great affairs
To books and music, or such idle things
As wing the weary hours for lesser men !
Turn not thine eyes to France ; receive no news :
Shut out the blinding gleam of battle : rest
From all fierce ache of thought ; and for a time
Let the wild world go by.

NAPOLEON.

Enough, old friend :
Thine is most wholesome counsel. I will seek
To make this feverish mass of nerve and thew,
Th's thing of fretful heart-beats,
Fulfil its functions more mechanically.
Farewell.

PHYSICIAN.

Farewell, Sire. Brighter waking thoughts,
And sweeter dreams, attend thee ! [*Exit*.

NAPOLEON.

All things change
Their summer livery for the autumn tinge
Of wind-blown withering leaves. That man is faithful,—
I have been fed from his cold palm for years,
And I believe, so strongly use and wont
Fetter such natures, he would die to serve me ;
Yet do I see in his familiar eyes
The fatal pain of pity. I have lain
At Death's door divers times, and he hath slowly,
With subtle cunning and most confident skill,

Woo'd back my breath, but never even then,
Though God's Hand held me down, did he regard me
With so intense a gaze as now, when smitten
By the mail'd hand of Man. I am not dead !
Not dying ! only sick,—as all are sick
Who feel the mortal prison-house too weak
For the free play of Soul ! I eat and drink—
I laugh—I weep, perchance—I feel—
I think—
I still preserve all functions of a man—
Yet doth the free wind of the fickle world
Blow on me with as chilly a respect
As on a nameless grave. Is there so sad
A sunset on my face, that all beholding
Think only of the morrow ?—other minds,
Other hearts, other hands ? Almighty God,
If I dare pray Thee by that name of God,
Strengthen me ! blow upon me with Thy breath !
Let one last memorable flash of fire
Burst from the blackening brand !—
Yes, sick—sick—sick :
Sick of the world ; sick of the fitful fools
That I have played with ; sick, forsooth, of breath,
Of thought, of hope, of Time. I staked my Soul
Against a Crown, and won. I wore the Crown,
And 'twas of burning fire. I staked my Crown
Against a Continent, and lost. I am here ;
Fallen, unking'd, the shadow of a power.
Yet not heart-broken—no, not heart-broken—
But surely with more equable a pulse
Than when I sat on yonder lonely Seat
Fishing for wretched souls, and for my sport,
Although the bait was dainty to the taste,
Hooking the basest only. I am nearer
To the world's heart than then ; 'tis bitter bread,
Most bitter, yea, most bitter ; yet I eat
More freely, and sleep safer. I could die now :
And yet I dare not die.

Maker of men!
Thou Wind before whose strange breath
  we are clouds
Driving and changing!—Thou who dost
  abide
While all the laurels on the brows of Kings
Wither as wreaths of snow!—Thou Voice
  that dwellest
In the high sleeping chambers of the great,
When council and the feverish pomp are
  hush'd,
And the dim lamp burns low, and at its
  side
The sleeping potion in a cup of gold :—
Hear me, O God, in this my travail hour!
From first to last, Thou knowest—yea,
  Thou knowest—
I have been a man of peace : a silent man,
Thought-loving, most ambitious to appease
Self-chiding fears of mental littleness,
A planner of delights for foolish men—
In all, a man of peace. I struck one blow,
And saw my hands were bloody ; from that
  hour
I knew myself too delicately wrought
For crimson pageants ; yea, the sight of
  pain
Sicken'd me like a woman. Day and night
I felt that stain on my immortal soul,
And gloved it from the world, and diligently
Wrought the red sword of empire to a
  scythe
For the swart hands of husbandmen to reap
Abundant harvest.—Nay, but hear me
  swear,
I never dreamed such human harvests blest
As spring from that red rain which pours
  this day
On the fair fields I sowed. Never, O God,
Was I a butcher or a thing of blood ;
Always a man of peace :—in mine ambition
Peace-seeking, peace-engendering;—till that
  day
I saw the half-unloosen'd hounds of War
Yelp on the chain and gnash their bloody
  teeth,
Ready to rend mine unoffending Child,
In whose weak hand the mimic toy of
  empire
Trembled to fall. Then feverishly I
  wrought
A weapon in the dark to smite those
  hounds
From mine imperial seat ; and as I wrought
One of the fiends that came of old to Cain
Found me, and since I thirsted gave to me
A philtre, and in idiocy I drank :
When suddenly I heard as in a dream
Trumpets around me silver-tongued, and
  saw
The many-colour'd banners gleam in the
  sun
Above the crying legions, and I rode
Royal before them, drunk with light and
  power,
My boy beside me blooming like a rose
To see the glorious show. Yet God, my
  God,
Even then I swear the hideous lust of life
Was far from me and mine ; nay, I rode
  forth,
As to a gay review at break of day,
A student dazzled with the golden glare,
Half conscious of the cries of those he ruled,
Half brooding o'er the book that he had
  left
Open within his chamber. 'Blood may
  flow,'
I thought, 'a little blood—a few poor
  drops,—
A few poor drops of blood : but they shall
  prove
Pearls of great price to buy my people
  peace ;
The hounds of War shall turn from our
  fair fields,
And on my son a robe like this I wear
Shall fall, and make him royal for all time !
O fool, fool, fool ! What was I but a
  child,
Pleased beyond understanding with a toy,
Till in mine ears the scream of murther'd
  France
Rang like a knell. I had slain my best
  beloved !
The curse of blood was on mine hands
  again !
My gentle boy, with wild affrighted gaze,
Turn'd from his sire, and moaned ; the
  hounds of War
Scream'd round me, glaring with their
  pitiless eyes
Innumerable as the eyes of heaven ;
I felt the sob of the world's woe ; I saw
The fiery rain fill all the innocent air ;
And, feeble as a maid who hides her face

In terror at a sword-flash, conscience-
   struck,
Sick, stupefied, appalled, and all alone,
I totter'd, grasped the empty air,—and
   fell !
   CHORUS OF SPIRITS.
Vast Sea of Life that, 'neath the arc
   Of yonder glistening sky,
Rollest thy waters deep and dark,
   While windy years blow by :
On thy pale shore this night we stand,
And hear thy wash upon the sand.

Calm is thy sheet and wanly bright,
   Low is thy voice and deep ;
There is no child on earth this night
   Wrapt in a gentler sleep ;
Crouch'd like a hound thou liest now,
With eye upcast and dreadful brow.

O Sea, thy breast is deep and blest
   After a dreadful day ;
And yet thou listenest in thy rest
   For some sign far away ;
Watching with fascinated eyes
The uplifted Finger in the skies !

A hundred years thy still tides go
   And touch the self-same mark—
Thus far, no farther, may they flow
   And fall in light and dark ;
The mystic water-line is drawn
By moonlit night and glimmering dawn.

Sure as a heart-beat year by year,
   Though winds and thunders call,
Be it storm or calm, the tides appear,
   Touch the long line and fall,
Liquid and luminously dim ;
And men build dwellings on their brim.

O well may this man wring his hands,
   And utter a wild prayer.
He built above thy lonely sands
   A Feast-house passing fair ;
It rose above thy sands, O Sea,
   In a fair nook of greenery.

For he had watched thee many days,
   And mark'd thy weedy line,
And far above the same did raise
   His Temple undivine.
Throng'd with fair shapes of sin and guilt
It rose most magically built.

Not to the one eternal Light,
   Lamp of both quick and dead,
Did he uprear it in thy sight,
   But with a smile he said :
' To the unvarying laws of Fate,
This Temple fair I dedicate.

' To that sure law by which the Sea
   Is driven to come and go
Within one mystic boundary,
   And can no further flow ;
So that who knoweth destiny
May safely build, nor fear the Sea !'

O fool ! O miserable clod !
   O creature made to die !
Who thought to mark the might of God
   And mete it with his eye ;
Who measured God's mysterious ways
By laws of common nights and days.

O worm, that sought to pass God by,
   Nor feared that God's revenge :
The law within the law, whereby
   All things work on to change ;
Who guessed not how the still law's course
Accumulates superfluous force ;—

How for long intervals and vast
   Strange secrets hide from day,
Till Nature's womb upheaves to cast
   The gather'd load away ;
How deep the very laws of life
Deposit elements of strife.

O many a year in sun and shower
   The quiet waters creep !—
But suddenly on some dark hour
   Strange trouble shakes the deep :
Silent and monstrous thro' the gloom
Rises the Tidal Wave for doom.

Then woe for all who, like this Man,
   Have built so near the Sea,
For what avails the human plan
   When the new force flows free ?
Over their bonds the waters stream,
And Empires crash and despots scream.

O, is it earthquake far below
   Where the still forces sleep ?
Doth the volcano shriek and glow,
   Unseen beneath the deep ?
We know not ; suddenly as death
Comes the great Wave with fatal breath.

God works His ends for ever thus,
  And lets the great plan roll
He wrought all things miraculous,
  The Sea, the Earth, the Soul ;
And nature from dark springs doth draw
  Her fatal miracles of law.

O well may this Man wring his hands,
  And utter a wild prayer ;
He built above the shifting sands
  A Feast-house passing fair.
Long years it stood, a thing of shame :
At last the mighty moment came.

Crashing like grass into its grave,
  Fell down the fair abode ;
The despot struggled in the wave,
  And swimming screamed to God.
And lo, the waters with deep roar
Cast the black weed upon the shore.

Then with no warning, as they rose,
  Shrunk back to their old bounds :
Tho' still with deep volcanic throes
  And sad mysterious sounds
They quake. The Man upon their brim
Sees wreck of Empire washed to him.

Vast Sea of life, that 'neath the arc
  Of yonder glistening sky,
Spreadest thy waters strange and dark
  While windy years blow by,
Creep closer, kiss his feet, O Sea,
Poor baffled worm of Destiny !

Fain would he read with those dull eyes
  What never man hath known,
The secret that within thee lies
  Seen by God's sight alone ;
Thou watchest Heaven all hours ; but he,
Praying to Heaven, watches thee.

So will he watch with weary breath,
  Musing beside the deep,
Till on thy shore he sinks in death,
  And thy still tides upcreep,
Raise him with cold forgiving kiss,
And wash his dust to the Abyss.

NAPOLEON. A BISHOP.

NAPOLEON.

Speak out thy tidings quickly,
How fares it with the Empress and my son ?

BISHOP.

Well, Sire. They bid thee look thy fate in
  the face,
And be of cheer.

NAPOLEON.

Where didst thou part with them ?

BISHOP.

In England, Sire, where they have found a
  home
Among the frozen-blooded islanders,
Who yesterday called blessings on thy
  brow,
And now rejoice in thy calamity.
Thus much thy mighty lady bade me say,
If I should find thee private in thy woe :—
With thy great name the streets are gar-
  rulous :
Mart, theatre, and church, palace and
  prison,
Down to the very commons by the road
Where Egypt's bastard children pitch their
  tents,
Murmur 'Napoleon' ; but, alas ! the sound
Is an echo that with no refrain,
No loving echo in a living voice,
Dies a cold death among the mountain
  snow.

NAPOLEON.

Old man, I never looked for friendship
  there,
I never loved that England in my heart ;
Tho' 'twas by such a sampler I believed
To weave our France's fortunes thriftily
With the gold tissues of prosperity.

BISHOP.

Ah, Sire, if I dare speak—

NAPOLEON.
                Speak on.
BISHOP.
                    Too much
Thine eyes to that cold isle of heretics
Turn'd from thy throne for use and pre-
  cedent ;
Too little did they look, and that too late,
On that strong rock whereon the Lord thy
  God
Hath built His Holy Church.

NAPOLEON.
                    Something of this
I have heard in happier seasons.

                BISHOP.
                            Hear it now
In the dark day of thine adversity.
O Sire, by him who holds the blessed Keys,
Christ's Vicar on the earth for blinded men,
I do conjure thee, hearken—with my mouth,
Though I am weak and low, the Holy
    Church
Cries to her erring son!

                NAPOLEON.
                    Well, well, he hears.

                BISHOP.
Thou smilest, Sire. With such a smile, so
    grim,
So bitter, didst thou mock our blessed
    cause
In thy prosperity.

                NAPOLEON.
                    False, Bishop, false!
I made a bloody circle with my sword
Round the old Father's head, and so
    secured him
Safe on his tottering Seat against the world,
When all the world cried that his time was
    come.
What then? He totter'd on. I could not
    prop
His Seat up with my sword, that Seat being
    built,
Not on a rock, but sand.

                BISHOP.
                    The world is sick
And old indeed, when lips like thine blas-
    pheme.
Whisper such words out on the common
    air,
And, as a child,
Blow thy last hopes away.

                NAPOLEON.
                    Hopes, hopes! What hopes?
What knowest thou of hopes?

                BISHOP.
                    Thy throne was rear'd
(Nay hear me, Sire, in patience to the end)
Not on the vulgar unsubstantial air
Which men call Freedom, not on half con-
    sent
Of unbelievers — tho', alas! thou hast
    stoop'd
To smile on unbelievers—not on lives
That saw in thee one of the good and
    wise,
Not wholly on the watchword of thy name;
But first on this—the swords thy gold could
    buy,
And most and last, upon the help of those
Who to remotest corners of our land
Watch o'er the souls of men, sit at their
    hearths,
Lend their solemnity to birth and death,
Guide as they list the motions of the mind,
And as they list with darkness or with light
Appease the spiritual hunger. Where
Had France been, and thou, boasted Sun
    of France,
For nineteen harvests, save for those who
    crept
Thine agents into every cottage-door,
Slowly diffusing thro' each vein of France
The sleepy wine of empire? Like to slaves
These served thee, used thy glory for a
    charm,
Hung up thine image in a peasant's room,
Beside our blessed Saints, and cunningly,
As shepherds drive their sheep unto the fold,
Gather'd thy crying people where thy hand
Might choose them out for very butchery.
Nay, more; as fearful men may stamp out
    fire,
They in the spirits of thy people killed
The sparks of peril left from those dark
    days,
When France being drunk with blood and
    mad with pain
Sprang on the burning pyre, and with her
    raiment
Burning and streaming crimson in the wind,
Curst and denied her God. They made
    men see,
Yea, in the very name of Liberty,
A net of Satan's set to snare the soul
From Christ and Christ's salvation: in their
    palms
They welded the soft clay of popular
    thought
To this wish'd semblance yet more cun-
    ningly;

Till not a peasant heir of his own fields,
And not a citizen that own'd a house,
And not a man or woman who had saved,
But when some wild voice shriek'd out
'Liberty!'
Trembled as if the robber's foot were set
Already on his threshold, and in fear
Clutch'd at his little store. These things did they,
Christ's servants serving thee; they were as veins
Bearing the blood through France from thee its heart
Throbbing full glorious in the capital.
And thou, O Sire, in thine own secret mind
Knowest what meed thou hast accorded them,
Who, thy sworn liegemen in thy triumph-hour,
Are still thy props in thy calamity.

NAPOLEON.

Well; have you done?

BISHOP.
          Not yet.

NAPOLEON.
               What more?

BISHOP.
           Look round
This day on Europe, look upon the World,
Which like a dark tree o'er the river of Time
Hangeth with fruit of races, goodly some,
Some rotten to the core. Out of the heart
Of what had seem'd the sunset of the west,
Rises the Teuton, silent, subtle, and sure,
Gathering his venom slowly like a snake
Wrapping the sleepy lands in fold by fold;
Then springing up to stab his prey with fangs
Numerous as spears of wheat in harvest time.
O, he is wise, the Teuton, he is deep
As Satan's self in perilous human lore,
Such as the purblind deem philosophy!
But, be he cunning as the Tempter was,
Christ yet shall bruise his head; for in himself
He bears, as serpents use,
A brood of lesser snakes, cunning things too
But lesser, and of these many prepare
Such peril as in his most glorious hour
May strike him feebler than the wretched worms

That crawl this day on the dead lambs of France.
Meantime, he to his purpose moves most slow,
And overcomes. Note how, upon her rock
The sea-beast Albion, swollen with idle years
Of basking in the prosperous sunshine, rolls
Her fearful eyes, and murmurs. See how wildly
The merciless Russian paceth like a bear
His lonely steppes of snow, and with deep moan
Calling his hideous young, casts famished eyes
On that worn Paralytic in the East,
Whom thou of old didst save. Call thou to these
For succour; shall they stir? Will the sea-beast
Budge from her rock? Will the bear leave his wilds?
Then mark how feebly in the wintry cold
Old Austria ruffles up her plumage, Sire,
Covering the half-heal'd wound upon her neck;
See how on Spain her home-bred vermin feed,
As did the worms on Herod; Italy
Is as a dove-cote by a battle-field,
Abandoned to the kites of infamy,
Belgium, Denmark, and Helvetia,
Like plovers watching while the wind-hover
Strikes down one of their miserable kind,
Wheeling upon the wind cry to each other;
And far away the Eagle of the West,
Poised in the lull of her own hurricane,
Sits watching thee with eyes as blank of love
As those grey seas that break beneath her feet.

NAPOLEON.

This is cold comfort, yet I am patient
Well?
To the issue! Dost thou keep behind t
salve
Whose touch shall heal my wounds? or d
thou only,
As any raven on occasion can,
Croak out the stale truth, that the day
lost,
And that the world's slaves knee the con
queror?

BISHOP.
Look not on these, thy crownèd peers, for aid,
But inward. Read thy heart.

NAPOLEON.
It is a book
I have studied somewhat deeply.

BISHOP.
In thine heart,
Tho' the cold lips might sneer, the dark brow frown,
Wert thou not ever one believing God?

NAPOLEON.
I have believed, and do believe, in God.

BISHOP.
For that, give thanks to God. He shall uplift thee.

NAPOLEON.
How?

BISHOP.
By the secret hands of His great Church.
Even now in darkness and on tilths remote
They labour in thy service; one by one
They gather up the fallen reins of power
And keep them for thy grasp; so be thou sure,
When thou hast woven round about thy soul
The robe of holiness, and from the hands
Of Holy Church demandest thy lost throne,
It shall be hers to give thee.

NAPOLEON.
In good truth,
I scarce conceive thee. What, degenerate Rome,
With scarce the power in this strong wind of war
To hold her ragged gauds about her limbs;
Rome, reft of the deep thunder in her voice,
The dark curse in her eye; Rome, old, dumb, blind,—
Shall Rome give Kingdoms?—Why, she hath already
Transferred her own to Heaven.

BISHOP.
Canst thou follow
The coming and the going of the wind,
Fathom the green abysses of the sea?
For such as these, is Rome:—the voice of God
Sounding in darkness and a silent place;
The morning dew scarce seen upon the flowers,
Yet drawn to heaven and grown the thunderbolt
That shakes the earth at noon. When man's wild soul
Clutches no more at the white feet of Christ;
When death is not, nor spiritual disease;
When atheists can on the black mountain tops
Walk solitary in the light of stars,
And cry, ' God is not '; when no mothers kneel
Moaning on graves of children; when no flashes
Trouble the melancholy dark of dream;
When prayer is hush'd, when the Wise Book is shut—
Then Rome shall fall indeed: meantime she is based
Invulnerable on the soul of man,
Its darkest needs and fears; she doth dispense
What soon or late is better prized than gold,—
Comfort and intercession; for all sin
She hath the swiftest shrift, wherefore her clients
Are those that have sinned deeply, and of such
Is half the dreadful world; all these she holds
By that cold eyeball which hath read their souls,
So that they look upon her secretly
And tremble,—while in her dark book of Fate
E'en now she dooms the Teuton.

Enter a MESSENGER.

NAPOLEON.
Well, what news?

MESSENGER.
'Tis brief and sad. The mighty Prussian chiefs,
Gathering their fiery van in silence, close
Toward the imperial City—in whose walls
Treason and Rage and Fear contend together

Like hunger-stricken wolves; and at their cry,
Echoed from Paris to the Vosges, France,
Calling her famish'd children round her knees,
Looks at the trembling nations. All is still,
Like to that silence which precedes the storm,
And shakes the forest leaves without a breath;
But surely as the vaporous storm is woven,
The German closes round the heart of France
His hurricane of lives.

NAPOLEON.

(*To Bishop*) The Teuton thrives
Under the doom we spake of.
(*To Messenger*) Well, speak on!

MESSENGER.

Meantime, like kine that see the gathering clouds
And shelter 'neath the shade of rocks and trees,
Thy timorous people fly before the sound
Of the approaching footsteps, seeking woods
For shelter, snaring conies for their food,
And sleeping like the beasts; some fare in caves,
Fearing the wholesome air, hushing the cries
Of infants lest the murderous foe should hear;
Some scatter west and south, their frighted eyes
Cast backward, with their wretched household goods;
And where these dwelt, most blest beneath thy rule,
The German legions thrive, let loose like swine
Amid the fields of harvest, in their track
Leaving the smoking ruin, and the church
Most desecrated to a sleeping-sty;—
So that the plenteous lands that rolled in gold
Round thy voluptuous City, lie full bare
To shame, to rapine, to calamity.

NAPOLEON.

O for one hour of empire, that with life
I might consume this sorrow! 'Tis a spell
By which we are subdued!

MESSENGER.

Strasbourg still stands,
Stubborn as granite, but the citadel
Is falling. Within, Famine and Horror nest,
And rear their young on ruin. [*Exit.*

Enter a MESSENGER.

NAPOLEON.

How, peal on peal!
Like the agonising clash of bells when flame
Hath seized on some fair city. News, more news?
Dost thou too catch the common trick o' the time,
And ring a melancholy peal?

MESSENGER.

My liege,
Strasbourg still stands.

NAPOLEON.

And then?

MESSENGER.

Pent up in Metz,
Encircled by a river of strong lives,
Bazaine is faithful to the cause and thee,
And from his prison doth proclaim himself,
And all the host of Frenchmen at his back,
Thy liegemen to the death.

NAPOLEON.

Why, that last peal
Sounds somewhat blither. Well?

MESSENGER.

From his lone isle
The old Italian Red-shirt in his age
Hath crawl'd, tho' sickly and infirm, to France,
And slowly there his leonine features breed
Hope in the timid people, who——

NAPOLEON.

Enough! [*Exit Messenger.*
That tune is flat and tame.

Enter a MESSENGER.

What man art thou
Speak!

MESSENGER.

Better I had died at Weissenburg,
Where on the bloody field I lay for dead,

Than live to bring this woe. Ungenerous
France,
Forgetful of thy gracious years of reign,
Pitiless as a sated harlot is
When ruin overtaketh him whose hand
Hath loaded her with gems, shameless and
mad,
France, like Delilah, now betrays her lord.
The streets are drunken—from thy palace-
gate
They pluck the imperial eagles, trampling
them
Into the bloody mire; thy flags and pennons,
Torn from their vantage in the wind, are
wrapt
In mockery round the beggar's ragged
limbs;
And thine imperial images in stone,
Dash'd from their lofty places, strew the
ground
In shameful ruin. All the ragged shout,
While Trochu from the presidential seat
Proclaims the empire dead, and calleth up
A new Republic, in whose chairs of office
Thine enemies, scribblers and demagogues,
Simon, Gambetta, Favre, and linked with
these
The miserable Rochefort, trembling grasp
The reins of power, unconscious of the scorn,
That doth already doom them. To their
feet
Come humming back, vain-drunken, all the
wasps
Whom in thine hour of glory thou didst
brush
With careless arm-sweep from thy festal cup;
Shoulder'd by mobs the pigmy Blanc de-
claims,
The hare-brain'd Hugo shrieks a maniac
song
In concert, and the scribblers, brandishing
Their pens like valiant lilliputians
Against the Teuton giant, frantically
Scream chorus. Coming with mock-humble
eyes
To the Republic, this sham shape of straw,
This stuff'd thing of a harlot's carnival,
The dilettante sons of Orleans, kneeling,
Proffer forsooth their swords, which being
disdain'd
They sheathe chapfallen and with bows
withdraw
Back to their pictures and perfumery.

NAPOLEON.
Why, thine is news indeed! Nor do I
weep
For mine own wrong, but for the woes of
France,
Whose knell thou soundest. With a tongue
of fire
Our enemy shall like the ant-eater
Devour these insect rulers suddenly.
(*Aside*) Now, may the foul fiend blacken
all the air
Above these Frenchmen, with revolt and
fear
Darken alike the wits of friends and foes,
With swift confusion and with anarchy
Disturb their fretful counsels, till at last,
Many-tongued, wild-hair'd, mad, and hor-
rible
With fiery eyes and naked crimson limbs,
Upriseth the old Spectre of the Red,
And as of yore lifts up the shameful knife
To stab unhappy France; then, in her
need,
Fearful and terror-stricken, France shall
call
On him who gave her nineteen plenteous
years—
And he may rise again. [*Exeunt.*

CHORUS OF SPIRITS.
Who in the name of France curses French
souls this day?
How! shall the tempter curse? Silence;
and turn away;
Turn we our faces hence white with a wild
desire,
Westward we lift our gaze till the straining
balls flash fire.
Westward we look to France, sadly we watch
and mark:—
Far thro' the pitch-black air, like breaking
foam in the dark,
Cometh and goeth a light across the
stricken land,
And we hear a distant voice like the wash
of waves on the sand.

VOICES.
Set the cannon on the heights, and under
Let the black moat gape, the black graves
grow!
Now let thunder
Answer back the thunder of the foe!

France has torn her cerements asunder,
France doth live, to strike the oppressor low.

CHORUS.

O hark! O hark! a voice arises wild and strong,
Loud as a bell that rings alarm it lifts the song.
See! see! the dark is lit, fire upon fire upsprings,
Loudly from town to town the fiery tiding rings.
Now the red smithies blaze and the blue steel is sped,
They twist bright steel for guns, they cast the fatal lead;
Cannon is drawn to the gate,—and lo, the bravest stand
Bare to the shoulder there, smoke-begrim'd, fuse in hand;
Now to the winds of heaven the Flag of Stars they raise,
While those sing martial songs who are too frail for frays.
France is uprisen again! France the sworn slayer of Kings!
With bleeding breast and bitter heart at the Teuton's throat she springs.

VOICES.

Now like thunder
Be our voice together while we cry!
Kings shall never hold our spirits under,
Kings shall cast their crowns aside and fly;
Latin, Sclav, or Teuton, they shall wonder;
The soul of man hath doom'd them—let them die.
We have slain Kings of old, they were our own to slay,
But now we doom all Kings until the Judgment day,
Raise ye the Flag of Stars! Tremble, O Kings, and behold!
Raise ye the Flag of man, while the knell of anarchs is tolled.
This is a festal day for all the seed of Eve;
France shall redeem the world, and heal all hearts that grieve;
France with her sword this day shall free all human things,
With blood drain'd from her heart our France shall write the doom of Kings.

CHORUS.

Silence and hearken yet! O but it is a cry
Heard under heaven of old, tho' the terrible day blew by,
The red fire flames to heaven, and in the crimson glow
Black shapes with prayers and cries, are gliding to and fro.

VOICES.

Fill each loophole with a man! and finding
Each a foe, aim slowly at the brain,
While the blinding
Lightnings flash, and the great guns refrain.
To the roofs! and while beneath the foe are winding,
Dash ye stones and missiles down like rain.
Watch for the gray-beard King: to drink his blood were great.
Watch for the Cub thereto—aim at his brain full straight.
Watch most for that foul Knave who crawls behind the crown,
Who smiles befooling all with crafty eyes cast down;
Sweeter than wine indeed his wretched blood would flow,
Curst juggler with our souls, he who hath wrought this woe.
France hath uprisen again! Let the fierce shaft be sped
Till all the foul satanic things that flatter Kings be dead!

CHORUS.

Echo the dreadful prayer, let the fierce shaft be sped,
Till all the foul satanic things that flatter Kings be dead!

VOICES.

Send the light balloon aloft with singing,
Let our hopes rise with it to the sky,
Let our voices like one fount upspringing
Tell the mighty realm that hope is nigh!
See, in answer, from the distance winging
Back unto our feet the swift doves fly!

CHORUS.

We see the City now, dark square and
    street and mart,
The muffled drum doth sound réveille in its
    heart,
The chain'd balloon doth swing, while men
    stand murmuring by,
Then with elastic bound upleaps into the
    sky.
We see the brightening dawn, the dimly
    dappled land,
The shapes with arms outstretch'd that on
    the housetops stand,
The eyes that turn to meet with one quick
    flash of fear
The birds that sad and slow wing nearer
    and more near.
O courage! all is well—yea, let your hearts
    be higher,
North, south, east, west, the souls of
    Frenchmen are as fire,
The reaper leaves the wheat, the workman
    leaves his loom,
Tho' the black priest may frown, who heeds
    his look of gloom?
Flash the wild tidings forth! ring them from
    town to town,
Till like a storm of scythes ye rise, and the
    foe like wheat go down.

VOICES.

See! how northward the wild heavens
    lighten,
Red as blood the fierce aurora waves,
Let it bathe us strong in blood and brighten
Sweet with resurrection on our graves,
Lighten, lighten,
Scroll of God!—unfold above and brighten,
Light the doom of monarchs and their
    slaves.
This is a day indeed—be sure that God can
    see.
Raise the fierce cry again, 'Liberty!
    Liberty!'
Courage! No man dies twice, and he
    shall live in death,
Who for the Flag of Stars strikes with his
    latest breath.
Nay, not a foe shall live to tell if France be
    slain:
If the wild cause be lost, only the grave
    shall gain.

Teuton and Frank in fierce embrace shall
    strew the fatal sod,
And they shall live indeed who died to
    save their souls for God.

CHORUS.

O Spirits, turn and look no more and hark
    not to their cry;
A Hand is flashed before our eyes, a Shape
    goes sadly by.
And as it goes, it looks on us with eyes that
    swim in tears,
And bitter as the death-cry sounds the echo
    in our ears.
O look no more and seek no more to read
    the days unborn,
'Tis storm this night on the world's sea,
    and 'twill be storm at morn.
The Lord hath sent His breath abroad, and
    all the waves are stirr'd:
Amid the tempest Liberty flies like a white
    sea-bird,
And, while the heavens are torn apart and
    the fierce waters gleam,
Doth up and down the furrow'd waves dart
    with a sea-bird's scream.
O bow the head, and close the eyes, and
    pray a quiet prayer,
But let the bitter curse of Man go by upon
    the air.

NAPOLEON. AN OFFICER.

NAPOLEON.

Is there no hope for France?

OFFICER.

          None. Yet I know not!
A nation, thus miraculously strengthen'd,
And acting in the fiercest wrath of love,
Hath risen ere this above calamity,
Yea out of anguish conjured victory.
If strength and numbers, if the mighty
    hands
Of the Briareus, shall decide the day,
Then surely as the sun sets France must
    fall;
If love or prayer can make a miracle
And bring an angel down to strike for her,
Then France may rise again.

NAPOLEON.

Have we not proved
Her children cowards? Yea, by God!
Like dogs
That rend the air with wrath upon the
    chain,
And being loosen'd slink before the thief,
They fail'd me—those who led and those
    who follow'd;
Scarce knowing friend from foe, while inch
    by inch
The Germans ate their ranks as a slow fire
Devoureth wind-blown wheat. I cannot
    trust
In France or Frenchmen.

OFFICER.
    Sire——

NAPOLEON.
    Why dost thou hang
Thy head, old friend, and look upon the
    ground?
Nay, if all Frenchmen had but hearts like
    thine,
Then France were blest in sooth, and I, its
    master,
Were safe against the swords of all the
    world.

OFFICER.
Sire, 'twas not that I meant—my life is
    yours
To give or take, to blame or praise; I
    blush'd
Not for myself, but France.

NAPOLEON.
    Then hadst thou cause
For crimson cheeks indeed.

OFFICER.
    Sire, as I live,
Thou wrongest her! The breast whereon
    we grew
Suckled no cowards. For one dizzy hour
France totter'd, and look'd back; but now
    indeed
She hath arisen to the very height
Of her great peril.

NAPOLEON.
    'Tis too late. She is lost;
She did betray her master, and shall die.

OFFICER.
Not France betrayed thee, Sire; but rather
    those
Whom thy most noble nature, royally
    based
Above suspicion and perfidious fear,
Welcom'd unto thy council; not poor
    France,
Whose bleeding wounds speak for her loud
    as tongues,
Bit at the hand that raised her up so high;
Not France, but bastard Frenchmen, doubly
    damn'd
Alike by her who bare them, and by thee
Who fed them. These betrayed thee to
    thy doom,
And falling clutch'd at thine imperial crown,
Dragging it with them to the bloody dust;
But these that held her arms like bands of
    lead
Being torn from off her, France, unchain'd
    and free,
Uplifts her pale front to the stars, and
    stands
Serene in doom and danger, and sublime
In resurrection.

NAPOLEON.
    How the popular taint
Corrupts the wholesome matter of thy mind!
This would be treason, friend, if we were
    strong—
Now 'tis less perilous: the commonest
    wind
Can blow its scorn upon the fallen.

OFFICER.
    Sire,
Behold me on my knees, tears in mine eyes,
And sorrow in my heart. My life is thine,
My life, my heart, my soul are pledged to
    thine;
And triply now doth thy calamity
Hold me thy slave and servant. If I pray,
'Tis that thou mayst arise, and thou shalt
    rise;
And if I praise our common mother, France,
Who for the moment hath forgot her lord,
'Tis that my soul rejoices for thy sake,
That when thou comest to thine own again
Thy realm shall be a realm regenerate,
Baptised a fair thing worthy of thy love
In its own blood of direful victory.

NAPOLEON.

Sayest thou?—Rise!—Friend, thou art little skilled
In reading that abstruse astrology
Whereby our cunning politicians cast
The fate of Kings. France robed in victory
Is France for ever lost to our great house.
France fallen, is France that with my secret hand
I may uplift again. But tell thy tale
Most freely: let thy soul beat its free wings
Before me as it lists. Come! as thou sayest,
France is no coward;—she hath at last arisen;
Nay, more—she is sublime. Proceed.

OFFICER.

My liege,
God, ere He made me thy most loving servant,
Made and baptised me, Frenchman; and my heart,
A soldier's heart, yearns out this day in pride
To her who bare me, and, both great and low,
My brethren. Courage is a virtue, Sire,
Even in a wretched cause. In Strasbourg still
Old Uhrich with his weight of seventy years
Starves unsubdued, while the dull enemy
Look on in wonder at such strength in woe;
Bazaine still keeps the glittering hosts at bay,
And holds them with a watchful hand and eye;
The captain of the citadel at Laon,
Soon as the foeman gather'd on his walls,
Illumed the hidden mine, and Frank and Teuton,
With that they strove for, strew'd the path in death;
From Paris to the Vosges, loud and wild
The tocsin rings to arms, and on the fields
The fat ripe ear empties itself unreapt,
While every man whose hand can grasp a sword
Flocks to the petty standard of his town;
The many looms of the great factory
Stand silent, but the fiery moulds of clay
Are fashioning cannon, and the blinding wheels
Are sharpening steel. In every market-place
Peasant and prince are drilling side by side;
Roused from their wine-fed torpor, changed from swine
To men, the very country burghers arm,
Nay, what is more to them than blood, bleed gold,
Bounteously, freely. I have heard that priests,
Doffing the holy cassock secretly,
Shouting uplift the sword, and crying Christ
To aid them strike for France. Only the basest,
Only the scum, shrink now; for even women,
Catching the noble fever of the time,
Buckle the war-belts round their lovers' waists,
And clapping hands, with mingled cries and sobs,
Urge young and old against the enemy.

NAPOLEON.

Of so much thunder may the lightning spring!
I know how France can thunder, and I have felt
How women's tongues can urge. But what of Paris?
What of the City of Light? How doth it bear
The terror and the agony?

OFFICER.

Most bravely,
As doth become the glorious heart of France:
Strong, fearless, throbbing with a martial might,
Dispensing from its core the vital heat
Which filleth all the members of the land;
Though even now the sharp steel pricks the skin,
To stab it in its strength.

NAPOLEON.

Who holds the reins
Within the gates?

Y

OFFICER.

Trochu.

NAPOLEON.

Still? Why, how long
Have the poor fools been constant? Favre
also?
Gambetta? Rochefort? All these gentle-
men
Still flourish? And Thiers? Hath the
arch-schemer
A seat among the gods, a place of rank
With the ephemera?

OFFICER.

Not so, my liege.

NAPOLEON.

Well, being seated on Olympus' top,
What thunderbolts are France's puny Joves
Casting abroad? Or do they sit and quake
For awe of their own voices, which in
France,
As in the shifting glaciers of the Alps,
May bring the avalanche upon their heads?

OFFICER.

The men, to do them justice, use their
power
Calmly and soldierly, and for a time
Forget the bitter humours of the senate
In the great common cause. Paris is
strong,
And full of noble souls.

NAPOLEON.

Paris must fall.

OFFICER.

Not soon, my liege—for she is belted round
And arm'd impregnable on every side.
Hunger and thirst may slay her, not the
sword;
And ere the foeman's foot is heard within,
Paris will spring upon her funeral pyre
And follow Hope to heaven. Last week I
walk'd
Reading men's faces in the silent streets,
And, as I am a soldier, saw in none
Fear or capitulation: very harlots
Cried in their shame the name of Liberty,
And, hustled from the gates, shriek'd out a
curse

Upon the coming T
And dreadful; but
Drilled in the squar
vard groups
Whisper'd together,
At white heat; in tl
Dim lit by lamps,
mothers,
Silently working for
And husbands; in
sat
And wrought, while
Rung on the paver
eyes
They turn'd to see
Kneel at his orison:
Ere the moon ros
death:
Yet as a lion sleeps,
Hearing each murn
Crouching and rea
dawn
I saw the country c
And the scared c
wild eyes
And open mouths,
bringing
Horrible tidings of
Who had devoured
homes.
Then suddenly like
The rumour that th
And climbing a cat
I saw the pitch-blac
Gleam phosphores
sea,
And heard at inter
Like far-off thunde
Clashing on some
storm,
Come smother'd fr
yet,
I haunted the great
While silently the
Around about it by
Still, as I am a sol
That look'd capitu
The knitted eyel
teeth,
The stealthy hand
sword.
The eye that glan
doth

Towards the battlements. Then (for at last
A voice was raised against my life) I sought
Trochu, my schoolfellow and friend in
   arms,
And, though his brow darkened a moment's
   space,
He knew me faithful and reached out his
   hand
To save me. By his secret help I found
A place in a balloon, that in the dusk
Ere daylight rose upon a moaning wind
And drifted southward with the drifting
   clouds;
And as the white and frosty daylight grew,
And opening crimson as a rose's leaves
The clouds to eastward parted, I beheld
The imperial City, gables, roofs, and spires,
White and fantastic as a city of dream,
Gleam orient, while the muffled drums
   within
Sounded réveille; then a red flash and
   wreath
Of vapour broke across the outer line,
Where the back fortifications frowning rose
Ring above ring around the imperial-gates,
And flash on flash succeeded with a sound
Most faint and lagging wearily behind.
Still all without the City seemed as husht
As sleep or death. But as the reddening
   day
Scattered the mists, the tiny villages
Loomed dim; and there were distant
   glimmerings,
And far-off muffled sounds; yet scarce a
   sign
Showed the innumerable enemy,—
Who snugly housed and canopied with
   stone
Lay hidden in their strength; only the
   watch-fire
Gleam'd here and there, only from place to
   place
Masses of shadow seem'd to move, and
   light
Was glimmered dimly back from hidden
   steel;
And, woefullest sight of all, miles to the
   west,
Along the dark line of the foe's advance,
On the straight rim where earth and heaven
   meet,
The forests blazed, and to the driving
   clouds

Cast blood-red phantoms growing dim in
   day.
Meantime, like one whirl'd in a dizzy
   dream,
Onward we drove below the driving cloud,
And from the region of the burning fire
And smouldering hamlet rose still higher,
   and saw
The white stars like to tapers burning out
Above the region of the nether storm,
And the illimitable ether growing
Silent and dark in the deep wintry dawn.

Enter a MESSENGER.

MESSENGER.

Most weighty news, my liege, from Italy.

NAPOLEON.

Yes?

MESSENGER.

Rome is taken. The imperial walls
Yawn where the cannon smote; in the red
   street
Romans embracing shout for Liberty;
From Florence to Messina bonfires blaze,
And rockets rise and wild shouts shake the
   air;
And with the thunder in his aged ears,
Surrounded by his cold-eyed Cardinals,
Clutching his spiritual crown more close,
Trembling with dotage, sits the grey-haired
   Pope
Anathematising in the Vatican. [*Exit.*

OFFICER.

Woe to the head on whom his curse shall
   fall,
For in the day of judgment it shall be
Better with Sodom and Gomorrah. Wait!
This is the twilight; red will rise the dawn.

NAPOLEON.

Peace, friend; yet if it ease thy heart,
   speak on.
I would to God, I did believe in God
As thou dost. Twilight surely—'tis indeed
A twilight—and therein from their fair
   spheres
Kings shoot like stars. How many nights
   of late
The heavens have troubled been with fiery
   signs,

Y 2

With characters like monstrous hieroglyphs,
And the aurora, brighter than the day
And red as blood, has burst from west to east.

OFFICER.

I do believe the melancholy air
Is full of pain and portent.

NAPOLEON.
     Would to God
I had more faith in God, for in this work
I fail to trace His hand; but rather feel
The nether-shock of earthquake everywhere
Shaking old thrones and new, those rear'd on rock
As well as those on sand. All darkens yet,
And in that darkness, while with cheeks of snow
The affrighted people gaze at one another,
The Teuton still, mouthing of Deity,
Works steadfastly to some mysterious end.
My heart was never Rome's so much as now,
Now, when she shares my cup of agony.
Agony! Is this agony? then indeed
All life is agony.

OFFICER.
    Your Imperial Highness
Is suffering! Take comfort, Sire.

NAPOLEON.
     It is nought—
Only a passing spasm at the heart—
'Tis my disease, comrade; 'tis my disease!
So leave me: it is late; and I would rest.

OFFICER.

God in his gracious goodness give thee health!

NAPOLEON.

Pray that He may; for I am deeply sick—
Too sick for surgery—too sick for drugs—
Too sick for man to heal. 'Tis a complaint
Incident to our house; and of the same
Mine imperial uncle died. [*Exit Officer.*
     France in the dust,
With the dark Spectre of the Red above her!
Rome fallen! Aye me, well may the face of heaven
Burn like a fiery scroll. Had I but eyes
To read whose name is written next for doom!
The Teuton's? Oh the Serpent, that has bided
His time so long, and now has stabbed so deep!
Would I might bruise his head before I die!
       [*Exit.*

Night. NAPOLEON *sleeping.* CHORUS *of* SPIRITS.

A VOICE.

What shapes are ye whose shades darken his rest this night?

CHORUS.

Cold from the grave we come, out of the dark to the light.

A VOICE.

Voices ye have that moan, and eyes ye have that weep,
Ah! woe for him who feels such shadows round his sleep!

CHORUS.

Tho' thou wert buried and dead,
 Still would we seek thee and find thee,
Ever there follows the tread
 Of feet from the tomb behind thee;
Sleep, shall thy soul have sleep?
 Nay, but be broken and shaken.
Gather around him and weep,
 Trouble him till he awaken.

A VOICE.

Who, in imperial raiment, darkly frowning stand,
Laurel-leaves in their hair, sceptred, yet sword in hand?

ANOTHER VOICE.

Who in their shadow looms, woman-eyed, woe-begone,
And bares his breast to show the piteous wounds thereon?

CHORUS.

Peace, they are Kings, they are crowned;
 Kings, tho' their realms have departed,
Realms of the grave they have found,
 And they walk in the same heavy-hearted.
Sleep? did their souls have sleep?
 Nay, for like his was their being.

Gather around him and weep,
Awake him to hearing and seeing.

SPIRIT OF CÆSAR.

Greater than thou I fell. Die ; for thy day
 is o'er.
Thou reap the world with swords? *thou*
 wear the robe I wore?
Up like the bird of Jove, I rose from height
 to height,
Poised on the heavenly air, eyes to the
 blood-red light ;
Swift came the flash of wrath, one long-
 avenging glare—
Down like a stone I fell, down thro' the
 dizzy air ;
Dark burnt the heaven above, red ran the
 light of day,
In the great square of Rome, bloody I fell,
 and lay.

CHORUS.

Kings of the realms of fear,
 Each the sad ghost of the other,
One by one step near,
 Look in the eyes of a brother.
Hush ! draw nearer and speak—
And ere he waketh each morrow
Blow on his bloodless cheek
With the chilly wind of your sorrow.

SPIRIT OF BUONAPARTE.

Greater than thou I fell. Die, Icarus, and
 give place.
Thou take from my cold grave the glory and
 the grace !
Out of the fire I came, onward thro' fire I
 strode ;
Under my path earth burnt, o'er it the pale
 stars glow'd ;
Sun of the earth, I leapt up thro' the won-
 dering sky,
Naming my name with God's, Kings knelt
 as I went by.
Aye ; but my day declined ;—to one glad
 cry of the free
My blood-red sunset died on the eternal Sea.

A VOICE.

What spirit art thou, with cold, still smile
 and face like snow?

SPIRIT.

Orsini ; and avenged. Too soon I struck
 the blow.

A VOICE.

And thou, with bleeding breast and eyes
 that roll in pain ?

SPIRIT.

I am that Maximilian, miserably slain.

A VOICE.

And ye, O shadowy things, featureless
 wild, and stark ?

VOICES.

We are the nameless ones whom he hath
 slain in the dark.

A VOICE.

Ye whom this man hath doom'd, Spirits,
 are ye all there ?

CHORUS.

Not yet ; they come, they come—they
 darken all the air.

A VOICE.

O latest come, and what are ye ? Why do
 ye moan and call ?

CHORUS.

O hush ! O hush ! they come to speak the
 bitterest curse of all.

SPIRITS.

With Sin and Death our mothers' milk
 was sour,
The womb wherein we grew from hour
 to hour
Gather'd pollution dark from the polluted
 frame—
Beside our cradles naked Infamy
Caroused, and Lust sat smiling hide-
 ously—
We grew like evil weeds apace, and knew
 not shame.
With incantations and with spells most
 rank,
The fount of Knowledge where we might
 have drank,
And learnt to love the taste, was hidden
 from our eyes ;
And if we learn'd to spell out written
 speech,
Thy slaves were by, and we had books to
 teach
Falsehood and Filth and Sin, Blasphemies,
 Scoffs, and Lies.

We drank of poison, ev'n as flowers drink
   dew ;
We ate and drank of poison till we grew
Noxious, polluted, black, like that whereon
   we fed ;
   We never felt the light and the free
      wind—
   Sunless we grew, and deaf, and dumb,
      and blind—
How should we dream of God, souls that
   were slain and dead ?
   Love with her sister Reverence passed
      our way
As angels pass, unseen, but did not stay—
We had no happy homes wherein to bid
   them dwell ;
We turn'd from God's blue heaven with
   eyes of beast,
We heard alike the atheist and the priest,
And both these lied alike to smooth our
   hearts for Hell.
Of some, both Soul and Body died ; of
   most,
The Body fatten'd on, while the poor
   ghost,
Prison'd from the sweet day, was withering
   in woe ;
Some robed in purple quaff'd their fatal
   cup,
Some out of rubied goblets drank it
   up—
We did not know God was ; but now, O
   God, we know.
   Lambs of thy flock, but oh ! not white
      and fair ;
   Beasts of the field, tamed to thy hand, we
      were ;
   Not men and women—nay, not heirs to
      light and truth :
   Some fattening ate and fed ; some lay at
      ease ;
   Some fell and linger'd of a long disease ;
   But all look'd on the ground—beasts of the
      field forsooth.

   Ah woe, ah woe, for those thy sceptre
      swayed,
   Woe most for those whose bodies, fair
      arrayed,
   Insolent, sat at ease, smiled at thy feet of
      pride ;
   Woe for the harlots with their painted
      bliss !

Woe for the red wine-oozing lips they kiss !
Woe for the Bodies that lived, woe for the
   Souls that died !

SEMI-CHORUS I.

Tho' thou wert buried and dead,
   Still would they seek thee and find thee.
Ever there follows the tread
   Of feet from the grave behind thee.

SPIRIT OF HORTENSE.

Woe ! woe ! woe !

SEMI-CHORUS II.

Ye who saw sad light fall,
   Thro' the chink of the dungeon gleaming,
And watch'd your shade on the wall
   Till it took a sad friend's seeming ;
Ye who in speechless pain
   Fled from the doom and the danger,
And dragging a patriot's chain
   Died in the land of the stranger ;
Men who stagger'd and died,
   Even as beasts in the traces,
Women he set aside
   For the trade of polluting embraces,
Say, shall his soul have sleep,
   Or shall it be troubled and shaken ?

CHORUS.

Gather around him and weep,
   Trouble him till he awaken.

NAPOLEON (*awakening*).

Who's there ? Who speaks ?—All silent.
   O how slowly
Moveth the dark and melancholy night !
I cannot rest—I am too sick at heart—
I have had ill dreams. The inevitable Eyes
Are watching, and the weary void of sleep
Hath voices strangely sad.
   [*He rises, and paces the chamber.*
         O those dark years
Of Empire ! He who tames the tiger, and
   lies
Pillow'd upon its neck in a lone cave,
Is safer. Who could sleep on such a bed ?
Mine eyes were ever dry of the pure dew
God scatters on the lids of happy men ;
Watching with fascinated gaze the orbs,
Ring within ring of blank and bestial light,
Where the wild fury slept : seeking all arts
To soothe the savage instinct in its throes
Of passionate unrest. One co'd hand held

Sweet morsels for the furious thing to lap,
And with the other, held behind my back,
I clutch'd the secret steel: oft, lest its teeth
Should fasten on its master, cunningly
Turning its wrath against the shapes that moved
Outside its splendid lair! until at last,
Let forth to the mad light of War, it sprang
Shrieking and sought to rend me. O thou beast!
Art thou so wild this day? and dost thou thirst
To fix on thine imperial ruler's throat?
Why, have I bidden thee 'down,' and thou hast crouch'd
Tamely as any hound! Thou shalt crouch yet,
And bleed with shamefuller stripes!

Let me be calm,
Not bitter. 'Tis too late for bitterness.
Yet I could gnaw my heart to think how France
Hath fail'd me! nay, not France, but rather those
Whom to high offices and noble seats
In France's name I raised. I bought their souls—
What soul can power not buy?—and, having lost
The blessed measure of all human truth,
Being soulless, these betrayed me; yea, became
A brood of lesser tigers hungering
With their large eyes on mine. I did not build
My throne on sand; no, no,—on Lies and Liars,
Weaker than sand a thousandfold!
                                    In this
I did not work for evil. Tho' my means
Were dark and vile perchance, the end I sought
Was France's weal, and underneath my care
She grew as tame as any fatted calf.
I never did believe in that stale cry
Raised by the newsman and the demagogue,
Though for mine ends I could cry 'Liberty!'
As loud as any man. The draff of men
Are as mere sheep and kine, with heads held down
Grazing, or resting blankly ruminant.
These must be tended, must be shepherded.

But Frenchmen are as wild things scarcely tamed,
Brute-like yet fierce, mad too with some few hours
Of rushing freely with an angry roar.
These must be awed and driven. By a scourge
Dripping with sanguine drops of their own blood,
I awed them: then I drove them: then in time
I tamed them. Fool! deeming them wholly mine,
I sought to snatch a little brief repose;
But with a groan they found me, and I woke;
And since they seem'd to suffer pain I said
'Loosen the yoke a little,' and 'twas done,
And they could raise their heads and gaze at me
And the wild hunger deepen'd in their eyes,
While fascinated on my throne I sat
Forcing a melancholy smile of peace.
O had I held the scourge in my right hand,
Tighten'd the yoke instead of loosening,
It had not been so ill with me as now!
But Pity found me with her sister Fear,
And lured me. He who sitteth on a throne
Should have no counsellors who come in tears;
But rather that still voice within his brain,
Imperturbable as his own cold eyes
And viewless as his coldly-flowing blood;
Rather a heart as strong as the great heart
Driving the hot life through a lion's thews;
Rather a will that moves to its desire
As steadfast as the silent-footed cloud.
What peevish humour did my mother mix
With that immortal ichor of our race
Which unpolluted fill'd mine uncle's veins?
He lash'd the world's Kings to his triumph-car
And sat like marble while the fiery wheels
Dript blood beneath him: tho' the live earth shriek'd
Below him, he was calm, and like a god
Cold to the eloquence of human tears,
Cold to the quick, cold as the light of stars,
Cold as the hand of Death on the damp brow,
Cold as Death brooding on a battle-field
In the white after-dawn,—from west to east
Royal he moved as the red wintry sun,

He never flatter'd Folly at his feet;
He never sought to syrup Infamy;
He, when the martyrs curst him, drew around him
The purple of his glory and passed on
Indifferently like Olympian Jove.
There was no weak place in the steel he wore,
Where women's tongues might reach his mighty heart
As they have reach'd at mine. O had I kept
A heart of steel, a heart of adamant;
Had I been deaf to clamour and the peal
Of peevish fools; had I for one strong hour
Conjured mine uncle's soul to mix with mine,
Sedan had never slain me! I am lost
By the damn'd implements mine own hands wrought—
Things that were made as slavish tools of peace,
Never as glittering weapons meet for war.
He never stoop'd to use such peaceful tools;
But, for all uses,
Made the sword serve him—yea, for sceptre and scythe;
Nay more, for Scripture and for counsellor!

Yet he too fell. Early or late, all fall.
No fruit can hang for ever on the tree.
Daily the tyrant and the martyr meet
Naked at Death's door, with the fatal mark
Both brows being branded. Doth the world then slay
Only its anarchs? Doth the lightning flash
Smite Cæsar and spare Brutus? Nay, by heaven!
Rather the world keeps for its paracletes
Torture more subtle and more piteous doom
Than it dispenses to its torturers.
Tiberius, with his foot on the world's neck,
Smileth his cruel smile and groweth grey,
Half dead already with the weight of years
Drinking the death he is too frail to feel,
While in his noon of life the Man Divine
Hath died in anguish at Jerusalem.
    [*He opens a Life of Jesus and reads.
    A long pause.*

Here too the Teuton works, crafty and slow,
Anatomising, gauging, questioning,
Till that fair Presence which redeem'd the world
Dwindles into a phantom and a name.
Shall he slay Kings, and spare the King of Kings?
In her fierce madness France denied her God,
But still the Teuton doth destroy his God
Coldly as he outwits an enemy.
Yet doth he keep the Name upon his lips,
And coldly dedicating the dull deed
To the abstraction he hath christen'd 'God,'
To the creation of his cogent brain,
Conjures against the blessed Nazarene,
That pallid apparition masculine,
That shining orb hemm'd in with clouds of flesh;
Till, darken'd with the woe of his own words,
The fool can turn to Wilhelm's wooden face
And Bismarck's crafty eyes, and see therein
Human regeneration, or at least
The Teuton's triumph mightier than Christ's.
Lie there, Iconoclast! Thou art thrice a fool,
Who, having nought to set within its place
But civic doctrine and a naked sword,
Would tear from out its niche the piteous bust
Of Him whose face was Sorrow's morning star.
    [*Takes up a second Book, and reads.*

Mark, now, how speciously Theology,
Leaving the broken fragments of the Life
Where the dull Teuton's hand hath scatter'd them,
Takes up the cause in her high fields of air.
'Darkness hath lain upon the earth like blood,
And in the darkness human things had shriek'd
And felt for God's soft hand, and agonised.
But overhead the awful Spirit heard,
Yet stirr'd not on His throne. Then lastly, One
Dropt like a meteor stone from suns afar,
And stirred and stretch'd out hands, and lived, and knew
That He indeed had dropt from suns afar,
That He had fallen from the Father's breast
Where He had slumber'd for eternities.
Hither in likeness of a Man He came—

He, Jesus, wander'd forth from heaven and
    said,
"Lo, I, the deathless one, will live and
    die!
Evil must suffer—Good ordains to suffer—
Our point of contact shall be suffering,
There will we meet, and ye will hear my
    voice;
And my low tones shall echo on thro' time,
And one salvation proved in fatal tears
Be the salvation of Humanity."'

Ah old Theology, thou strikest home!
'Evil *must* suffer—Good *ordains* to suffer'—
Sayst thou? Did He then quaff His cup
    of tears
Freely, who might have dash'd it down, and
    ruled?
The world was ready with an earthly crown,
And yet He wore it not. Ah, He was wise.
Had He but sat upon a human throne,
With all the kingdom's beggars at His feet,
And all its coffers open at His side,
He had died more shameful death, yea, He
    had fallen
Even as the Cæsars. Rule the world with
    Love?
Tame savage human nature with a kiss?
Turn royal cheeks for the brute mob to
    smite?
He knew men better, and He drew aside,
Ordain'd to do and suffer, not to reign.

My good physician bade me search in
    books
For solace. Can I find it? Verily,
From every page of all man's hand hath
    writ
A dark face frowns, a voice moans 'Vanity!'
There is one Book—one only—that for ever
Passeth the understanding and appeaseth
The miserable hunger of the heart—
Behold it—written with the light of stars
By God in the beginning.
            [*Looks forth. A starry night.*

            I believe
God is, but more I know not, save but
    this—
He passeth not as men and systems pass,
For while all change the Law by which they
    change
Survives and is for ever, being God.

Our sin, our loss, our misery, our death,
Are but the shadows of a dream: the hum
Within our ears, the motes within our eyes;
Death is to us a semblance and an end,
But is as nothing to that Central Law
Whereby we cannot die.

            Yonder blue dome,
Gleaming with meanings mystically wrought,
Hath been from the beginning, and shall be
Until the end. How many awe-struck eyes
Have look'd and spelt one word—the name
    of God,
And call'd it as they listed, Law, Fate,
    Change,
And marvell'd for its meaning till they died,
And others came and stood upon their
    graves
And read in their turn, and marvelling gave
    place.
The Kings of Israel watch'd it with wild
    orbs,
Madden'd, and cried the Name, and drew
    the sword.
Above the tented plain of Troy it bent
After the sun of day had set in blood.
The superstitious Roman look'd by night
And trembled. All these faded phantom-
    like,
And lo! where it remaineth, watch'd with
    eyes
As sad as any of those this autumn night,—
The Higher Law writ with the light of
    Stars
By God in the beginning. . . .

            Let me sleep!
Or I shall gaze and gaze till I grow wild
And never sleep again. Too much of God
Maketh the heart sick. Come then forth,
    thou charm,   .
Thou silent spell wrung from the blood-red
    flower,
With power to draw the curtains of the soul
And shut the inevitable Eyes away.

Dead mother, at thy knees I said a prayer—
Lead me not into temptation, and, O God,
Deliver me from evil. Is it too late
To murmur it this night? This night, O
    God,
Whate'er Thou art and wheresoe'er Thou
    art,

This night at least, when I am sick and fallen,
Deliver me from evil!

CHORUS.

Under the Master's feet the generations
Like ants innumerably come and go:
He leans upon a Dial, and in patience
Watches the hours crawl slow.

In His bright hair the eternal stars are burning,
Around His face Heaven's glories burn sublime:
He heeds them not, but follows with eyes yearning
The Shadow men call Time.

Some problem holds Him, and He follows dreaming
The lessening and lengthening of the shade.—
Under His feet, ants from the dark earth streaming,
Gather the men He made.

He heeds them not nor turns to them His features—
They rise, they crawl, they strive, they run, they die;
How should He care to look upon such creatures,
Who lets great worlds roll by?

He shall be nowise heard who calls unto Him,
He shall be nowise seen who seeks His face;
The problem holds Him—no mere man may woo Him,
He pauseth in His place.

So hath it been since all things were created,
No change on the immortal Face may fall,
Having made all, God paused, and fascinated,
Watch'd Time, the shade of all.

Call to the Maker in thine hour of trial,
Call with a voice of thunder like the sea:
He watches living shadows on a Dial,
And hath no ears for thee,

He watches on—He feels the still hours fleeing,
He heeds thee not, but lets the days drift by;
And yet we say to thee, O weary being,
Blaspheme not, lest thou die.

Rather, if woe be deep and thy soul wander,
Ant among ants that swarm upon a sod,
Watching thy shadow on the grass-blade, ponder
The mystery with God.

So may some comfort reach thy soul wayfaring,
While the days run and the swift glories shine,
And something God-like shall that soul grow, sharing
The attitude divine.

Silent, supreme, sad, wondering, quiescent,
Seeking to fathom with the spirit-sight
The problem of the Shadow of the Present
Born of eternal Light.

THE TEUTON MONOLOGUE.
(1870.)

To stand this night alone with Destiny,
Alone in all the world beneath the stars,
And hold the string that makes the puppets dance,
Is something; but to feel the steadfast will
Deepen, the judgment clear itself, the gaze
Grow keener, all the purpose that was dim
Brighten distinct in the serene still light
Of conquest—that is more; more than all power,
More than lip-homage, more than crowns and thrones,
More than the world; for it is life indeed.
O how the dreams and hopes and plans cohere!
How the great phalanx broadens! Like a wave
It washes Europe, and before its sweep
The lying idols, based on quicksand, shift,
Totter, and fall: strewn with the wreck'd and dead,
It shrieks and gathers up a flashing crest
In act to drown the lingering life of France.

Tide of the Teuton, is it wonderful
The grand old King sees in thy victory
The strength and wrath of God?

                   Here then I pause,
And (let me whisper it to mine own heart)
I tremble. I have played with fire; behold,
It hath devour'd God's enemy and mine;
And tamely at my bidding croucheth now
With luminous eyes half closed. This fire
   is Truth,
And by it I shall rise or fall. This fire
Is very God's—I know it; and thus far
God to my keeping hath committed it.
What next? and next? There at my feet
   lies France,
Bound, stricken, screaming,—yonder, good
   as dead.
Pluckt of his fangs, the imperial Adder
   crawls,
Tame as a mouse. I have struck down
   these twain,
The Liar, and the creature of the Liar;
I have slain these twain with an avenging
   flame;
And while I stand victorious comes a Voice
Out of the black abysses of the earth
Whereat I pause and tremble. 'Tis so
   easy
To cast down Idols! The tide so pitilessly
Washes each name from the waste sands of
   time!
'Twas yestermorn the Man of Mysteries
   fell—
Whose turn comes next? . . .
From Italy to the blue Baltic rolls
A voice, a wind, a murmur in the air,
A tone full of the sense of wind and waters
And the faint whispers from ethereal fields,
A cry of anguish and of mystery
Echoed by the Volcano in whose depths
The monarchs one by one have disappeared.
And men who hear it answer back one
   word,
'Liberty!'—Cities echo through their
   streets;
The word is wafted on from vale to vale:
Heart-drowsy Albion answers with a cheer,
Feeble yet clear; the great wild West
   refrains;
Italy thunders, and Helvetia
Blows the wild horn high up among her
   hills;

France, wounded, dying, stretch'd beneath
   my feet,
Gnaws at her bonds and shrieks in mad
   accord
(For she indeed first gave the thing a name),
And even the wily Russian, with his yoke
Prest on innumerable groaning necks,
Sleek like the serpent, smooths his frosty
   cheek
To listen, fiercely smiling hisses back
The strange word 'Liberty!' between his
   teeth,
And shivers with a bitterer sense of cold
Than ever seized him in that lonely realm
O'er which he paceth hungry and alone.
What is this thing that men call 'Liberty'?
Not force, not tumult, not the wind and
   rain
And tempest, not the spirit of mere Storm,
Not Earthquake, not the Lightning, not
   swift Fire,
Not one of these; but mightier far than
   these,—
The everlasting principle of things,
Out of whose silence issue all, the rock
Whereon the mountain and the crater stand,
The adamantine pillars of the Earth,
Deep-based beneath the ever-varying air
And under the wild changes of the Sea,
The Inevitable, the Unchangeable,
The secret law, the impulse, and the
   thought,
Whereby men live and grow.

                   Then I, this night
As ever, dare with a man's eyes and soul
Hold by this thing whereof the foolish rave,
And cry, 'In God's name, peace, ye winds
   and waves,
Ye froths and bubbles on the sea, ye voices
Haunting the fitful region of the air!
God is above ye all, and next to God
The Son and Holy Spirit, and beneath
These twain the great anointed Kings of
   Earth,
And underneath the Kings the Wise of
   Wit,
And underneath the Wise the merely
   Strong,
And least of all, clay in the hands of all,
The base, the miserable, and the weak.'
What, then, is this that ye name 'Liberty'?
There is evermore a higher. Not like waves

Beating about in a waste sea are men,
But great, small, fair, foul, strong, weak, miserable ;—
And Liberty is law creating law
Wherein each corporal member of the world
Filleth his function in the place ordain'd.
Child at the knee, look in thy mother's face!
Boy-student, reverence the philosopher!
Clown, till the earth, and let the market thrive!
Citizen, doff to beauty and to grace,
To antique fame and holy ancestry!
Nobles, blood purified from running long,
Circle of sanctity, surround the King!
King, stand on the bare height and raise thine eyes,
For there sits God above thee, reverencing
The perfect Mirror of the soul of things,
Wherein He gazes calmly evermore,
And knows Himself divine!

               Thus stands for ever
The eternal Order like a goodly Tree,
The root of which is deep within the soil.
And lo! the wind and rain are beating on it,
And lightning rends its branches; yet anon
It hangs in gorgeous blossom still-renewed,
And shoots its topmost twig up through the cloud
To touch the changeless stars.   Herr Democrat
Comes with his blunt rough axe, and at its root
Strikes shrieking; the earth's parrots echo him;
Blow follows blow; the air reverberates;
But the Tree stands. Come winds and waves and lightnings,
Come axe-wielders, come ye iconoclasts,
And spend your strength in vain. What! ye would stretch
This goodly trunk, this very Iggdrasil,
Down to the dusty level of your lives,
Would strew the soil with the fair blooms thereof,
Would tear away the succulent leaves and make
A festal chaplet for Silenus' hair,
A drunken garland for the Feast of Fools.
See, yonder blow the branches where the Great

Tremble like ripen'd fruit; yonder the Holy
Gleam in the silvern foliage, sweet and fair;
There just beneath the cloud, most dim in height,
The flowers of monarchy open their buds
And turn their starry faces upward still.
Strike at the root, my little democrat,
Down with them! Down with the whole goodly Tree!
Down even with that fair shoot beyond the cloud,
Down with the unseen bloom of perfect height,
Down with the blossom on the topmost twig,
Down with the light of God!

               I compare further
This Order to a Man, body and brain,
Heart, lungs, eyes, feet to stand on, hands to strike.
The King is to the realm what conscience is
To manhood: the true statesman is the brain;
And under these subsist, greater and less,
The members of the body politic.
Behold now, this alone is majesty:
The incarnate Conscience of the people, fixed
Beyond the body, higher than the brain,
Yet perfect fruit of both,—the higher sense
That flashes back through all the popular frame
The intuitions and the lights divine
Whereby the world is guided under God.
Nor are all Kings ancestral, though these same
Are highest. Yonder in the stormy West
The plain man Lincoln rose to majesty,
Incarnated the conscience and the will
Of the strong generation, moved to his end,
Struck, triumph'd in the name of Conscience, fell,
And like a sun that sets in bloody light,
In dying darken'd half earth's continents.
. . . What, art thou there, old Phantom of the Red?
Urge on thy dreadful legions, for in truth
There is no face in France this day with light
So troublous to the eyes of victory.
O brave one, wert *thou* France's will and soul,

Why we might tremble. Let there rise a
    land,
As strong in conscience and as stern in soul
As we have been to follow a living truth,
And it might slay us even as we have slain
Imperial France and the Republic. Now
Supreme we stand, our symbol being the
    Sword,
Our King the hand that wields; in that
    one hand
I strike, all strike, yea every Teuton strikes.
Reason and conscience knitted in accord
Are deathless, and must overcome the
    world.
The higher law will shape them. I believe
There is evermore a higher !

THE REPLY.

BLUE arc of heaven whose lattices
    Are throng'd with starry eyes;
Vast dome that over land and seas
    Dost luminously rise,
With mystic characters enwrought
More strange than all poetic thought !

Hear, Heaven, if thou canst hear ! and see,
    O stars, if see ye can !
Mark, while your speechless mystery
    Flows to a Voice in man:
He stands erect this solemn hour
In reverent insolence of power.

Order divine, whose awful show
    Dazzles all guess or dream ;
Sequence unseen, whose mystic flow
    Fulfils the immortal scheme ;
Thou Law whereby all stand or stir,—
Here breathes your last interpreter !

Because one foolish King hath slain
    Another foolish King ;
Because a half-born nation's brain
    With dizzy joy doth ring ;
Because at the false Shepherd's cry
The silly sheep still throng to die ;

Because purblind Philosophy
    Out of her cobweb'd cave
Croaks in a voice of senile glee
    While empty patriots rave ;
Because humanity is still
The gull of any daring will ;

Because the Tinsel Order stands
    A little longer yet ;
Because in each crown'd puppet's hands
    A laurel-sprig is set,
While the old lame device controls
The draff of miserable souls ;

Because man's blood again bathes bright
    The purple and the throne,
And gray fools gladden at the sight,
    And maiden choirs intone ;
Because once more the puppet Kings
Dance, while Death's lean hand pulls the
    strings ;

Because these things have been and are,
    And oft again may be,
Doth this man swear by sun and star,
    And oh our God by Thee,
Framing to cheat his own shrewd eyes
His fair cosmogony of lies.

O Lord our God whose praise we sing,
    Behold he deemeth Thee
A little nobler than the King,
    And greater in degree,
Set just above the monarch's mind,
Greater in sphere but like in kind !

O calm Intelligence divine,
    Transcending life and death,
He deems these bursting bubbles Thine,
    Blown earthward by Thy breath,—
He marks Thee sitting well content,
Like some old King at tournament.

The lists are set ; upon the sod
    The gleaming columns range ;
The sign is given by Thee, O God,
    From Thy Pavilion strange :
The trumpets blow, the champions meet,
One screams—Thou smilest on Thy seat.

Behold, O God, the Order blest
    Of Thy great chivalry !
See tinsel crown and glittering crest,
    Cold heart and empty eye !
The living shout, the dying groan,
All reddens underneath Thy throne !

Accept Thy chosen ! great and good,
    Vouchsafe them all they seek !
Deepen their purple in man's blood !
    Trumpet them with man's shriek !
Paint their escutcheons fresh, O Sire ;
With heart's blood bright and crimson fire !

And further, from the fire they light
    Protect them with Thy hand,
Beyond the bright hill of the fight
    Let them in safety stand ;
For 'twere not well a random blow
Should strike Thy next-of-kin below.

O God ! O Father ! Lord of All !
    Spare us, for we blaspheme,
See,—for upon our knees we fall,
    And hush our mocking scream—
Let us pray low ; let us pray low ;
Thy will be done ; Thy Kingdom grow !

Blue arc of heaven whose lattices
    Are throng'd with starry eyes,
Still dome that over earth and seas
    Doth luminously rise ;
Fair Order mystically wrought,
More strange than all poetic thought.

He fears ye all, this son of man,
    To his own soul he lies,
Lo ! trembling at his own dark plan
    He contemplates the prize :
He has won all, and lo ! he stands
Clutching the glory in his hands !

To one, to all, on life's dark way,
    Sooner or late is brought
The silent solemnising ray
    Illuminating thought ;
It shines, they stand on some lone spot,
Its light is strange, they know it not.

Sleeps, like a mirror in the dark,
    The Conscience of the Soul,
Unknown, where never eye may mark,
    While days and seasons roll ;
But late or soon the walls of clay
Are loosening to admit the day.

Light comes—a touch—a streak—a beam—
    Child of the unknown sky—
And lo ! the Mirror with a gleam
    Flashes its first reply :
Light brighteneth : and all things fair
Flow to the glass and tremble there.

O Lord our God, Thou art the Light,
    We shine by Thee alone ;
Tho' Thou hast made us mirrors bright,
    The gleam is not our own ;
Until Thy ray shines sweet and plain
All shall be dark as this man's brain.

Thro' human thought as thro 'a cave
    Creep gently, Light, this hour ;
Tho' now 'tis darker than the grave,
    There lies the shining power ;
Come ! let the Soul flash back to Thee
The million lights of Deity !

THE CITY OF MAN.

COMFORT, O free and true !
    Soon shall there rise for you
A City fairer far than all ye plan ;
    Built on a rock of strength,
    It shall arise at length,
Stately and fair and vast, the City meet for Man !

Towering to yonder skies
    Shall the fair City rise,
Dim in the dawning of a day more pure :
    House, mart, and street, and square,
    Yea, and a Fane for prayer—
Fair, and yet built by hands, strong, for it shall endure.

In the fair City then
    Shall walk white-robëd men,
Wash'd in the river of peace that watereth it ;
    Woman with man shall meet
    Freely in mart and street—
At the great council-board woman with man shall sit.

Hunger and Thirst and Sin
    Shall never pass therein ;
Fed with pure dews of love, children shall grow.
    Fearless and fair and free,
    Honour'd by all that see,
Virgins in golden zones shall walk as white as snow.

There, on the fields around,
    All men shall till the ground,
Corn shall wave yellow, and bright rivers stream ;
    Daily, at set of sun,
    All, when their work is done,
Shall watch the heavens yearn down and the strange starlight gleam.

In the fair City of men
    All shall be silent then,
While, on a reverent lute, gentle and low,
    Some holy Bard shall play
    Music divine, and say
Whence those that hear have come, whither in time they go.

No man of blood shall dare
Wear the white mantle there ;
No man of lust shall walk in street or
 mart ;—
Yet shall the Magdalen
Walk with the citizen ;
Yet shall the sinner stand gracious and pure
 of heart.

Now, while days come and go,
Doth the fair City grow,
Surely its stones are laid in sun and moon.
Wise men and pure prepare
Ever this City fair.
Comfort, O ye that weep ; it shall arise full
 soon.

When, stately, fair, and vast,
It doth uprise at last,
Who shall be King thereof, say, O ye
 wise ?—
When the last blood is spilt,
When the fair City is built,
Unto the throne thereof the Monarch shall
 arise.

Flower of blessedness,
Wrought out of heart's distress,
Light of all dreams of saintly men who died,

He shall arise some morn
One Soul of many born,
Lord of the realms of peace, Heir of the
 Crucified !

O but he lingereth,
Drawing mysterious breath
In the dark depths where he was cast as seed.
Strange was the seed to sow,
Dark is the growth and slow ;
Still hath he lain for long—now he grows
 quick indeed.

Quicken, O Soul of Man !
Perfect the mystic plan—
Come from the flesh where thou art darkly
 wrought ;
Wise men and pure prepare
Ever thy City fair—
Come when the City is built, sit on the
 Throne of Thought.

Earth and all things that be,
Wait, watch, and yearn for thee,
To thee all loving things stretch hands
 bereaven ;—
Perfect and sweet and bright,
Lord of the City of Light,
Last of the flowers of Earth, first of the
 fruits of Heaven !

Songs of the Terrible Year.

(1870.)

*** These 'Songs,' inasmuch as they formed a portion of the 'Drama of Kings,' preceded by a long period the publication of Victor Hugo's series under the same admirable title. The 'Drama of Kings' was written under a false conception, which no one discarded sooner than the author ; but portions of it are preserved in the present collection, because, although written during the same feverish and evanescent excitement, they are the distinct lyrical products of the author's mind, and perfectly complete in themselves.—R. B.

ODE TO THE SPIRIT OF AUGUSTE COMTE.

(1871.)

Spirit of the great brow !
Fire hath thy City now :
She shakes the sad world with her troubled
 scream !
O spirit who loved best
This City of the West,
Hark ! loud she shattered' cries — great
 Queen of thy great Dream.

But, as she passes by
. To the earth's scornful cry,
What are those Shapes who walk behind so
 wan ?—
Martyrs and prophets born
Out of her night and morn :
Have we forgot them yet ?—these, the great
 friends of Man.

We name them as they go,
Dark, solemn-faced, and s'ow—

Voltaire, with saddened mouth, but eyes
    still bright,
Turgot, Malesherbes, Rousseau,
Lafayette, Mirabeau—
These pass and many more, heirs of large
    realms of Light.

Greatest and last pass *thou!*
Strong heart and mighty brow,
Thine eyes surcharged with love of all
    things fair;
Facing with those grand eyes
The light in the sweet skies,
While thy shade earthward falls, darkening
    my soul to prayer.

Sure as the great sun rolls,
The crown of mighty souls
Is martyrdom, and lo! thou hast thy
    crown.
On her pale brow there weighed
Another such proud shade—
O, but we know you both, risen or stricken
    down.

Sinful, mad, fever-fraught,
At war with her own thought,
Great-soul'd, sublime, the heir of constant
    pain,
France hath the dreadful part
To keep alive Man's heart,
To shake the sleepy blood into the slug-
    gard's brain;

Ever in act to spring,
Ever in suffering,
To point a lesson and to bear the load,
Least happy and least free
Of all the lands that be,
Dying that all may live, first of the slaves
    of God.

To try each crude desire
By her own soul's fierce fire,
To wait and watch with restless brain and
    heart,
To quench the fierce thirst never,
To feel supremely ever,
To rush where cowards crawl—this is her
    awful part.

Ever to cross and rack,
Along the same red track,
Genius is led, and speaks its soul out plain;

Blessed are those that give—
They die that man may live,
Their crown is martyrdom, their privilege is
    pain.

Spirit of the great brow!
I see thee, know thee now—
Last of the flock who die for man each day.
Ah, but *I* should despair
Did I not see up there
A Shepherd heavenly-eyed on the heights
    far away.

No cheat was thy vast scheme
Tho' in thy gentle dream
Thou saw'st no Shepherd watching the wild
    throng—
Thou, walking the sad road
Of all who seek for God,
Blinded became at last, looking at Light so
    long.

Yet God is multiform,
Human of heart and warm,
Content to take what shape the Soul loves
    best;
Before our footsteps still,
He changeth as we will—
Only, – with blood alone we gain Him, and
    are blest.

O, latest son of her,
Freedom's pale harbinger,
I see the Shepherd whom thou could'st not
    find;
But on thy great fair brow,
As thou didst pass but now,
Bright burnt the patient Cross of those who
    bless mankind.

And on her brow, who flies
Bleeding beneath the skies,
The mark was set that will not let her rest—
Sinner in all men's sight,
Mocker of very Light,
Yet is she chosen thus, martyr'd—and shall
    be blest.

Go by, O mighty dead!
My soul is comforted;
The Shepherd on the summit needs no
    prayers;
Best worshipper is he
Who suffers and is free—
That Soul alone blasphemes which trembles
    and despairs.

This is the perfect State,
Early in arms and late;
   Blessed at home;—
Ready at Freedom's cry
Forward to fare and die,
   Over the foam.
Loving States great and small,
Loving home best of all,
Yet at the holy call
   Springing abroad:
This is the royal State,
Perfect and adequate,
Equal to any fate,
   Chosen of God!

THE TWO VOICES.

(January 1871.)

I.

FIRST VOICE.

Fly to me, England! Hie to me,
  Now in mine hour of woe;
Haste o'er the sea, ere I die, to me;
Swiftly, my Sister! stand nigh to me.
Help me to strike one blow!
Over the land and the water,
  Swifter than winds can go,
Up the red furrow of slaughter,
  Down on the lair of the foe!
Now, when my children scream madly and
  cling to me;
Now, when I droop o'er the dying they
  bring to me;
Come to me, England! O speak to me,
  spring to me!
Hurl the assassin low!

II.

SECOND VOICE.

Woe to thee? I would go to thee
  Faster than wind can flee;
Doth not my fond heart flow to thee?
Would I might rise and show to thee
  All that my love would be!
But behold, they bind me and blind me;
  Cowards, yet born of *me*;
They fasten my hands behind me,
  I am chain'd to a rock in the sea.
Alas, what availeth my grief while I sigh for
  thee?
Traitors have trapt me—I struggle—I cry
  for thee—
Come to thee, Sister? Yea, were it to die
  for thee!—
O that my hands were free!

III.

FIRST VOICE.

Pray for me, Sister! say for me
  Prayers until help is nigh;
Send thy loud voice each way for me,
Trouble the night and the day for me,
  Waken the world and the sky:
Say that my heart is broken,
  Say that my children die;
With blood and tears for thy token,
  Plead till the nations reply.
Plead to the sea, and the earth, and the air
  for me!
Move the hard heart of the world till it care
  for me—
Come to me, England!—at least say a
  prayer for me,
Waken the winds with a cry!

IV.

SECOND VOICE.

Doom on me, Hell's own gloom on me,
  Blood and a lasting blame!
Already the dark days loom on me,
Cold as the shade of the tomb on me;
  I am call'd by the coward's name.
Shall I hark to a murder'd nation?
  Shall I sit unarm'd and tame?
Then woe to this generation,
  Tho' out of my womb they came.
Betrayed by my children, I wail and I call
  for thee;
Not tears, but my heart's blood, O Sister,
  should fall for thee.
My children are slaves, or would strike one
  and all for thee:
Shame on them, shame! shame! shame!

V.

FIRST VOICE.

Pain for thee! all things wane for thee
  In truth, if this be so,

Fatal will be the stain for thee,
Dying, I mourn and 'plain for thee,
Since thou art left so low :
For Death can come once only,
Tho' bitterly comes the blow ;
But Shame abideth, and lonely
Feels a sick heart come and go.
Homeless and citiless, yet I can weep for
thee ;
Fast comes the morrow with anguish most
deep for thee ;
Dying, I mourn for the sorrow they heap
for thee :
Thine is the bitterest woe.

VI.

SECOND VOICE.

Mourn me not, Sister ! scorn me not !
Pray yet for mine and me ;
Tho' the old proud fame adorn me not,
The sore grief hath outworn me not :
Wait ; I will come to thee.
I will rend my chains asunder,
I will tear my red sword free,
I will come with mine ancient thunder,
I will strike the foe to his knee.
Yea ! tho' the knife of the butcher is nigh
to thee ;
Yea ! while thou screamest and echoes
reply to thee ;
Comfort, O France ; for in God's name, I
fly to thee—
Sword in hand, over the sea !

ODE BEFORE PARIS.

(December 1870.)

CITY of loveliness and light and splendour,
City of Sorrows, hearken to our cry ;
O Mother tender,
O Mother marvellously fair,
And fairest now in thy despair,
Look up ! O be of comfort ! Do not
die !
Let the black hour blow by.

Cold is the night, and colder thou art lying.
Gnawing a stone sits Famine at thy feet
Shivering and sighing ;
Blacker than Famine, on thy breast,
Like a sick child that will not rest,
Moans Pestilence ; and hard by, with
fingers fleet,
Frost weaves his winding-sheet.

Snow, snow ! the wold is white as one cold
lily.
Snow :. it is frozen round thee as hard
as lead ;
The wind blows chilly ;
Thou liest white in the dim night,
And in thine eyes there is no light,
And the Snow falleth, freezing on thy
head,
And covering up thy dead.

Ah, woe ! thy hands, no longer flower-
bearing,
Press stony on thy heart ; and that
heart bleeds ;
Thine eyes despairing
Watch while the fierce Fire clings and
crawls
Through falling roofs and crumbling
walls.
Ah, woe ! to see thee thus, the wild
soul pleads,
The wild tongue intercedes.

O, we will cry to God, and pray and plead
for thee ;
We, with a voice that troubles heaven
and air,
Will intercede for thee :
We will cry for thee in thy pain,
Louder than storm and 'wind and
rain ;
What shape among the nations may
compare
With thee, most lost, most fair ?

Yea, thou hast sinned and fallen, O City
splendid,
Yea, thou hast passed through days of
shamefullest woe—
And lo ! they are ended—
Famine for famine, flame for flame,
Sorrow for sorrow, shame for shame,
Verily thou hast found them all ;—and
lo !
Night and the falling snow.

Let Famine eat thy heart, let Fire and
    Sorrow
Hold thee, but turn thy patient eyes
    and see
        The dim sweet morrow.
Better be thus than what thou wast,
Better be stricken and overcast,
Martyr'd once more, as when to all
    things free
Thy lips cried 'Liberty!'

Let the Snow fall! thou shalt be sweeter
    and whiter;
Let the Fire burn! under the morning
    sky
        Thou shalt look brighter.
Comfort thy sad soul through the
    night;
Turn to the east and pray for light;
Look up! O be of comfort! Do not
    die!
Let the black hour blow by!

A DIALOGUE IN THE SNOW.

(Before Paris, December 1870.)

DESERTER.

O, I am spent! My heart fails, and my
    limbs
Are palsied. Would to God I were dead!

SISTERS OF MERCY.

Stand! What art thou, who like a guilty
    thing
Creepest along the shadow, stooping low?

DESERTER.

A man. Now stand aside, and let me pass.

SISTERS.

Not yet. Whence fleest thou? Whither
    dost thou go?

DESERTER.

From Famine and Fire. From Horror.
    From Frost and Death.

SISTERS.

O coward! traitor to unhappy France!
Stand forward in the moon, that it may light
The blush of shame upon thy guilty cheek!

Lo, we are women, yet we shiver cold
To look upon so infamous a thing.

DESERTER.

Nay, look your fill, I care not—stand and
    see.

SISTERS.

O horror! horror! who hath done this deed?

DESERTER.

What say ye? am I fair to look upon?

SISTERS.

The dead are fairer. O unhappy one!

DESERTER.

Why do ye shudder? Am I then so foul?

SISTERS.

There is no living flesh upon thy bones.

DESERTER.

Famine hath fed upon my limbs too long.

SISTERS.

And thou art rent as by the teeth of hounds.

DESERTER.

Fire tore me, and what blood I have I bleed.

SISTERS.

Thine eyes stare like the blank eyes of a
    corpse.

DESERTER.

They have look'd so close on horror and so
    long,
I cannot shut them from it till I die.

SISTERS.

Thou crawlest like a man whose sick limbs
    fail.

DESERTER.

Ha! Frost is there, and numbs me like a
    snake.

SISTERS.

God help thee, miserable one; and yet,
Better if thou hadst perish'd in thy place
Than live inglorious, tainted with thy
    shame.

DESERTER.

Shame? I am long past shame. I know
    her not.

SISTERS.
Is there no sense of honour in thy soul?

DESERTER.
Honour? Why see, she hath me fast
  enough:
These are her other names, Fire, Famine,
  and Frost,—
Soon I shall hear her last and sweetest,—
  Death.

SISTERS.
Hast thou no care for France, thy martyr'd
  land?

DESERTER.
What hath she given me? Curses and blows.

SISTERS.
O miserable one, remember God!

DESERTER.
God? Who hath look'd on God? Where
  doth He dwell?
O fools, with what vain words and empty
  names
Ye sicken me. Honour, France, God! All
  these—
Hear me—I curse. Why, look you, there's
  the sky,
Here the white earth, there, with its bleed-
  ing heart,
The butcher'd City; here half dead stand I.
A murder'd man, grown grey before my
  time,
Forty years old—a husband, and a father—
An outcast flying out of Hell. Who talks
To me of 'honour'? The first tears I wept
When standing at my wretched mother's
  knee,
Because her face was white, and she wore
  black.
That day the bells rang out for victory.
Then, look you, after that my mother sat
Weeping and weary in an empty house,
And they who look'd upon her shrunken
  cheeks
Fed her with 'honour.' 'Twas too gentle
  fare,—
She died. Nay, hearken! Left to seek for
  bread,
I like a wild thing haunted human doors
Searching the ash for food. I ate and lived.
I grew. Then, wretched as I was, I felt

Strange stirs of m
  bones,
Dim yearnings, fier
  face
Could still them as
  the sea.
Oh, but I was a lo
And yet she loved
  hands
To God, and blest
Mark that:—I bl
  stood,
Bright in new man
  a hand
Fell on my shoul
  name,'
A voice cried, 'Fo
  held
Cold steel:—I folk
  face
Fade to a bitter cry
Curs'd, jeer'd at, s
  a dream,
And, driven into th
Struck like a blinde
Blows for I knew
  years came
Like ulcers on my
  went.
Then I crept back,
To seek her, and I
  had died,
Poor worm, of hun
  bread,
And 'France' had
  had pray'd to
He had given her
  died,
The bells rang for
              s
O do not weep!

              DE
Now mark, I was t
Too long and dee
  My heart
Heal'd, and as v
  Once again
I join'd the wolves
  earth
Rush tearing at m
  hearts.

That passed, and I was free. One morn I
    saw
Another woman, and I hunger'd to her,
And we were wedded. Hard days follow'd
    that ;
And children—she was fruitful—all your
    worms
Are fruitful, mark—that is God's blessing
    too !
Well, but we throve, and farm'd a bit of land
Out yonder by the City. I learn'd to love
The mother of my little ones. Time sped ;
And then I heard a cry across the fields,
The old cry, ' Honour,' the old cry, ' For
    France !'
And like a wolf caught in his lair I shrunk
And shudder'd. It grew louder, that curst
    cry !
Day follow'd day, no bells rung victory,
But there were funeral faces everywhere ;
And then I heard the far feet of the foe
Trampling the field of France and coming
    nearer
To that poor field I sow'd. I would have
    fled,
But that they thrust a weapon in mine hands
And bade me stand and strike ' for France.'
    I laugh'd !
But the wolves had me, and we screaming
    drew
Into the City. Shall I gorge your souls
With horror ? Shall I croak into your ears
What I have suffer'd there, what I have
    seen ?
I was a worm, ever a worm, and starved
While the plump coward cramm'd. Look
    at me, women,
Fire, Famine, and Frost have got me ; yet
    I crawl,
And shall crawl on ; for hark you, yester-
    night,
Standing within the City, sick at heart,
I gazed up eastward, thinking of my home
And of the woman and children desolate,
And lo ! out of the darkness where I knew
Our hamlet lay there shot up flames and
    cast
A bloody light along the arc of heaven ;
And all my heart was sicken'd unaware
With hunger such as any wild thing feels
To crawl again in secret to the place
Whence the fierce hunter drove it, and to
    see

If its young live ; and thither indeed I fare ;
And yonder flame still flareth, and I crawl,
And I shall crawl unto it though I die ;
And I shall only smile if they be dead,
If I may merely see them once again,—
For come what may, my cup of life is full,
And I am broken from all use and will.

SISTERS.

Pass on, unhappy one ; God help thee
    now !

DESERTER.

If ye have any pity, give me bread.

SISTERS.

Lean on us ! Oh thou lost one, come this
    way.

THE PRAYER IN THE NIGHT.

STARS in heaven with gentle faces,
Can ye see and keep your places?
Flowers that on the old earth blossom,
Can ye hang on such a bosom?
Canst thou wander on for ever
Through a world so sad, O River?
O ye fair things 'neath the sun,
Can ye bear what Man hath done?

This is Earth. Heaven glimmers yonder.
Pause a little space and ponder !

Day by day the fair world turneth
Dewy eyes to heaven and yearneth,
Day by day the mighty Mother
Sees her children smite each other :
She moans, she pleads, they do not hear
    her—
She prays—the skies seem gathering near
    her—
Yearning down diviner, bluer,
Baring every star unto her,—
Each strange light with swinging censer
Sweeter seeming and intenser,—
Yet she ceaseth not her cry,
Seeing how her children die.

On her bosom they are lying,
Clinging to her, dead and dying—
Dead eyes frozen in imploring
Yonder heaven they died adoring,

Dying eyes that upward glimmer
Ever growing darker, dimmer ;
And her eyes, too, thither turning,
Asking, praying, weeping, yearning,
Search the blue abysses, whither
He who made her, brought her hither,
Gave her children, bade them grow,
Vanished from her long ago.

Ah, what children ! Father, see them !
Never word of *hers* may free them—
Never word of love may win them.
For there burneth fierce within them
Fire of thine ; soul-sick and sinning,
As they were in the beginning,
Here they wander. Father, see !
Generations born of *Thee !*

Blest was Earth when on her bosom
First she saw the double blossom,
Double sweetness, man and woman,
One in twain, divine and human,
Leaping, laughing, crying, clinging,
To the sound of her sweet singing—
Flesh like lily and rose together,
Eyes as blue as April weather,
Golden hair with golden shadows,
In the face the light of meadows,
In the eyes the dim soul peeping
Like the sky in water sleeping.
' Guard them well !' the Father said,
Set them in her arms,—*and fled.*

Countless worlds around Him yearning,
Vanish'd He from her discerning ;—
Then she drooped her fair face, seeing
On her breast each gentle being :
And unto her heart she prest them,
Raised her look to heaven and blest them ;
And the fountains leapt around her,
Leaves and flowers shot up and crown'd her,
Flowers bloom'd and streams ran gleaming.
Till with bliss she sank to dreaming ;—
And the darkness for a cover
Gently drew its veil above her,
And the new-born smiled reposing,
And a million eyes unclosing
Yearn'd through all the veil to see
That new fruit of mystery.

Father ! come from the abysses ;
Come, Thou light the Mother misses ;
Come ; while hungry generations
Pass away, she sits in patience.
Of the children Thou didst leave her,
Millions have been born to grieve her.
See ! they gather, living, dying,
Coming, going, multiplying ;
And the Mother, for the Father,
Though like waves they rise and gather,
Though they blossom thick as grasses,
Misses every one that passes,
Flashes on them peace and light
Of a love grown infinite.

Father ! see them : hath each creature
Something in him of Thy nature ?
Born of Thee and of no other,
Born to Thee by a sweet Mother,
Man strikes man, and brother brother.
Hearts of men from Thy heart fashioned
Bleed and anguish bloody-passion'd ;
Beast-like roar the generations ;
Tiger-nations spring on nations ;
Though the stars yearn downward nightly,
Though the days come ever brightly,
Though to gentle holy couches
Death in angel's guise approaches,
Though they name Thee, though they woo Thee,
Though they dream of, yearn unto Thee,
Ill they guess the guise Thou bearest,
Ill they picture Thee, Thou Fairest ;—
Come again, O Father wise,
Awe them with those loving eyes !

Stars in heaven with tender faces,
Can ye see and keep your places ?
Flowers that on the Earth will blossom,
Can ye deck so sad a bosom ?
Canst thou singing flow for ever
Through a world so dark, O River ?
Father, canst Thou calmly scan
All that Man hath made of Man ?

THE SPIRIT OF FRANCE.

WHO passeth there
Naked and bare,
A bloody sword upraising ?
Who with thin moan
Glides past alone,
At the black heaven gazing ?

Limbs thin and stark,
Eyes sunken and dark,
The lightning round her leaping?
What shape floats past
Upon the blast,
Crouching In pain and creeping?
Behold! her eyes to heaven are cast,
And they are red with weeping.

Say a prayer thrice
With lips of ice:
'Tis she—yea, and no other;
Look not at me
So piteously,
O France—O martyr mother!
O whither now,
With branded brow
And bleeding heart, art flying?
Whither away?
O stand! O stay!
Tho' winds, waves, clouds are crying—
Dawn cometh swift—'twill soon be day—
The Storm of God is dying.

She will not speak,
But, spent and weak,
Droops her proud head and goeth;
See! she crawls past,
Upon the blast,
Whither no mortal knoweth—
O'er fields of fight,
Where glimmer white
Death's steed and its gaunt rider—
Thro' storm and snow
Behold her go,
With never a friend beside her—
O Shepherd of all winds that blow,
To Quiet Waters guide her!

There, for a space,
Let her sad face
Fall in a tranquil mirror—
There spirit-sore
May she count o'er
Her sin, her shame, her error,—
And read with eyes
Made sweet and wise
What her strong God hath taught her,
With face grown fair
And bosom bare
And hands made clean from slaughter—
O Shepherd, seek and find her there,
Beside some Quiet Water!

THE APOTHEOSIS OF THE SWORD.

(Versailles, 1871.)

PRIEST.

HARK to the Song of the Sword!
In the beginning, a Word
Came from the lips of the Lord;
And He said, 'The Earth shall be,
And around the Earth and Sea,
And over these twain the Skies;
And out of the Earth shall rise
Man, the last and the first;
And Man shall hunger and thirst,
And shall eat of the fruits in the sun,
And drink of the streamlets that run,
And shall find the wild yellow grains,
And, opening earth, in its veins
Sow the seeds of the same; for of bread
I have written that he shall be fed.'
Thus at the first said the Lord.

CHOIR.
Hark to the Song of the Sword!

PRIEST.
Then Man sowed the grain, and to bread
Kneaded the grain, and was fed,
He and his household indeed
To the last generation and seed:
Then the children of men, young and old,
Sat by the waters of gold,
And ate of the bread and the fruit,
And drank of the stream, but made suit
For blessing no more than the brute.
And God said, ' 'Twere better to die
Than eat and drink merely, and lie
Beast-like and foul on the sod,
Lusting, forgetful of God!'
And he whispered, 'Dig deeper again,
Under the region of grain,
And bring forth the thing ye find there
Shapeless and dark; and prepare
Fire,—and into the same
Cast what ye find—let it flame—
And when it is burning blood-bright,
Pluck it forth, and with hammers of might
Beat it out, beat it out, till ye mark
The thing that was shapeless and dark
Grown beautiful, azure, and keen,
Purged in the fire and made clean,

Beautiful, holy, and bright,
Gleaming aloft in the light ;—
Then lift it, and wield ! ' said the Lord.

CHOIR.

Hark to the Song of the Sword !

PRIEST.

Then Man with a brighter desire
Saw the beautiful thing from the fire,
And the slothful arose, and the mean
Trembled to see it so keen,
And God, as they gather'd and cried,
Thunder'd a World far and wide :
' This Sword is the Sword of the Strong !
It shall strike at the life's blood of wrong ;
It shall kill the unclean, it shall wreak
My doom on the shameful and weak ;
And the strong with this sign in their hands
Shall gather their hosts in the lands,
And strike at the mean and the base,
And strengthen from race on to race ;
And the weak shall be wither'd at length,
For the glory of Man is his strength,
And the weak man must die,' saith the Lord.

CHOIR.

Hark to the Song of the Sword !

PRIEST.

Sire, whom all men of thy race
Name as their hope and their grace ;
King of the Rhine-water'd land.
Heart of the state and its hand,
Thou of the purple and crown,
Take, while thy servants bow down,
The Sword in thy grasp.

KAISER.
     It is done.

PRIEST.

Uplift ! let it gleam in the sun—
Uplift in the name of the Lord !

CHOIR.

Hail to the King and the Sword !

KAISER.

Lo ! how it gleams in the light,
Beautiful, bloody, and bright—
Such in the dark days of yore
The monarchs of Israel bore ;
Such by the angels of heaven
To Charles the Mighty was given—
Yea, I uplift the Sword,
Thus in the name of the Lord !

THE CHIEFS.

Form ye a circle of fire
Around him, our King and our Sire—
While in the centre he stands,
Kneel with your swords in your hands,
Then with one voice deep and free
Echo like waves of the sea—
 ' In the name of the Lord ! '

CHANCELLOR.

Sire, while thou liftest the Sword,
Thus in the name of the Lord,
I too, thy slave, kneel and blend
My voice with the hosts that attend—
Yea, and while kneeling I hold
A scroll writ in letters of gold,
With the names of the monarchs who bow
Thy liegemen throned lower than thou ;
Moreover, in letters of red,
Their names who ere long must be led
To thy feet, while thou liftest the Sword,
Thus in the name of the Lord.

VOICES WITHOUT.

Where is he ?—he fades from our sight !
Where the Sword ?—all is blacker than night.
Is it finish'd, that loudly ye cry ?
Doth he sheathe the great Sword while we die ?
O bury us deep, most deep ;
Write o'er us, wherever we sleep,
' In the name of the Lord ! '

KAISER.

While I uplift the Sword,
Thus in the name of the Lord,
Why, with mine eyes full of tears,
Am I sick of the song in mine ears ?
God of the Israelite, hear ;
God of the Teuton, be near ;
Strengthen my pulse lest I fail,
Shut out these slain while they wail—
For they come with the voice of the grave
On the glory they give me and gave.

CHORUS.

In the name of the Lord ? Of what Lord ?
Where is He, this God of the Sword ?
Unfold Him ; where hath He his throne ?
Is he Lord of the Teuton alone ?

Doth He walk on the earth? Doth He tread
On the limbs of the dying and dead?
Unfold Him! We sicken, and long
To look on this God of the strong!

PRIEST.

Hush! In the name of the Lord,
Kneel ye, and bless ye the Sword!
Bless it with soul and with brain,
Bless it for saved and for slain,
For the sake of the dead in the tomb,
For the sake of the child in the womb,
For the sake of these Kings on the knee,
For the sake of a world it shall free!
Bless it, the Sword! bless the Sword!
Yea, in the name of the Lord!

CHIEFS.

Deepen the circle of Fire
Around him, our King and our Sire!
While in our centre he towers,
Kneeling, ye spirits, ye powers,
Bless it and bless it again,
Bless it for saved and for slain,
Bless ye the beautiful Sword,
Aloud in the name of the Lord!

KAISER.

In the name of the Lord!

ALL.

In the name of the Lord!

THE CHAUNT BY THE RHINE.

(1871.)

Te verò appello sanctissimum FLUMEN,
tibique futura prædico: torrenti sanguine plenus
ad ripas usque erumpes, undæque divinæ non
solum polluentur sanguine, sed totæ rumpentur,
et viris multo major erit numerus sepultorum.
Quid fles, O Asclepi?—THE ASCLEPIAN DIA-
LOGUE.

FIRST VOICE.

(From Germany.)

Flash the sword!—and even as thunder
Utter ye one living voice,—
While the watching nations wonder,
Hills of Fatherland, rejoice:
Echo!—echo back our prayers and accla-
mations!

SECOND VOICE.

(From France.)

France, O Mother! lie and hearken,
Make no bitterer sign of woe,
Here within thee all things darken,
All things brighten with thy foe:
Hush thy weeping; still thy bitter lamen-
tations.

FIRST VOICE.

Flash the sword!—A voice is flowing
From the Baltic bound in white,
Though 'tis blowing chill and snowing,
Blue-eyed Teutons see the light.
And the far white hills of Norway hear the
crying.

SECOND VOICE.

Thou too hearkenest, Mother dearest,
Thou too hearkenest through thy tears,
And thou tremblest as thou hearest,
For 'tis thunder in thine ears;
And thou gazest on the dead and on the
dying.

FIRST VOICE.

Lübeck answers and rejoices,
Though her dead are brought to her;
Potsdam thunders; there are voices
In the fields of Hanover;
And the spirits of the lonely Hartz awaken.

SECOND VOICE.

And in France's vales and mountains
Hands are wrung and tears are shed;
Women sit by village fountains,
And the water bubbles red.
O comfort, O be of comfort—ye forsaken!

FIRST VOICE.

O'er Bavarian woods and rivers,
Where the Brunswick heather waves,
On the glory goes and quivers
Through the Erzgebirge caves;
And the swords of Styria gleam like moonlit
water.

SECOND VOICE.

There is silence, there is weeping,
On the bloody banks of Seine,
And the unburied dead are sleeping
In the fields of trampled grain;
While the roadside Christs stare down on
fields of slaughter.

FIRST VOICE.

Flash the sword! Where need is sorest,
  Sitting in the lonely night,
While the wind in the Black Forest
  Moans, the woodman sees the light;
And the hunters wind the horn and hail each other.

SECOND VOICE.

Strasbourg sits among her ashes
  With a last despairing cry;
East and west red ruin flashes
  With a red light on the sky.
Not a word! Sit yet and hearken, O my Mother!

FIRST VOICE.

Flash the sword! The glades of Baden
  Echo; Jena laughs anon;
Dresden old and Stuttgart gladden,
  There is mirth in Ratisbon:—
And underneath the Linden there is leaping.

SECOND VOICE.

In thine arms the horror tarries,
  And the sword-flash gleams on thee,
Hide thy funeral face, O Paris,
  Do not hearken; do not see;
Electra, clasp thine urn, and hush thy weeping.

FIRST VOICE.

Hamburg kindles, and her women
  Sadly smile remembering all;
There are bitter smiles in Bremen,
  Where Vandamme's fierce feet did fall;
But the Katzbach, O the Katzbach laugheth loudly!

SECOND VOICE.

Comfort, Mother! hear not, heed not;
  Let the dead bury the dead!
Fold thy powerless hands and plead not,
  They remember sorrows fled,
And their dead go by them, silently and proudly.

FIRST VOICE.

O that Fritz's soul could hear it
  In the walks of Sans Souci!
O to waken Lützow's spirit,
  Blücher's too, the grim and free;
And the Jäger, the wild Jäger, would they listen'd!

SECOND VOICE.

Comfort, Mother! O cease weeping!
  Let the past bury the past:
Faces of the slain and sleeping
  Gleam along upon the blast.
Yea, 'twas 'Leipsic' that they murmur'd as they glisten'd.

FIRST VOICE.

All the land of the great River
  Slowly brightens near and far;
Lost for once, and saved for ever,
  Körner's spirit like a star
Shooteth past, and all remember the beginning.

SECOND VOICE.

They are rising, they are winging,
  Spirits of her singers dead;
'Tis an old song they are singing,
  Fold thy hands and bow thy head,
But they sing for *thee* too, gentle to thy sinning.

FIRST VOICE.

And the River to the ocean
  Rolls; and all its castles dim
Gleam; and with a shadowy motion,
  Like a mist upon its brim,
Rise the Dead,—and look this way with shining faces.

SECOND VOICE.

Thine, too, rise!—and darkly cluster,
  Moaning sad around thee now,
In their eyes there is no lustre,
  They are cold as thy cold brow—
Let them vanish; let them sleep in their dark places.

FIRST VOICE.

Flash the sword! In the fair valleys
  Where the scented Neckar flows,
Fair-hair'd Teutons lift the chalice,
  And the winter vineyard grows,
And the almond forests tremble into blossom.

SECOND VOICE.

On thy vineyards the cold daylight
  Gleams, and they are deadly chill;
Women wander in the grey light,
  And the lean trees whistle shrill;
Hold thine urn, O martyr Mother, to thy bosom.

FIRST VOICE.

Flash the sword! Sweet notes of pleasure
  O'er the Rhenish upland swell,
And the overhanging azure
  Sees itself in the Moselle.
All the land of the great River gleams and
    hearkens!

SECOND VOICE.

Dost thou hear them? dost thou see them?
  There 'tis gladness, here 'tis pain ;
One great Spirit comes to free them,
  But he holds thee with a chain.
All the land of the great City weeps and
    darkens!

FIRST VOICE.

River of the mighty people,
  Broaden to the sea and flow,
Mirror tilth and farm and steeple,
  Darken with boats that come and go.
Smile gently, like a babe that smiles and
    prattles.

SECOND VOICE.

Yea! and though thou flow for ever,
  Bright and bloodless as to-day,
Scarcely wilt thou wash, O River,
  Thy dark load of dead away,
O bloody River! O field of many battles!

FIRST VOICE.

On with great immortal waters
  Brightening to a day divine,
Through the fields of many slaughters
  Freely roll, O German Rhine.
Let the Teuton drink thy wine and wax the
    stronger.

SECOND VOICE.

On and on, O mighty River,
  Flow through lands of corn and vine—
Turn away, O France, for ever,
  Look no more upon the Rhine ;
On the River of many sorrows look no
    longer.

FIRST VOICE.

Lo! the white Alps for a token
  With the wild aurora gleam,
And the Spectre of the Brocken
  Stands aloft with locks that stream,—
All the land of the great River can behold it!

SECOND VOICE.

Hide thine eyes and look not thither!
  For, in answer to their cries,
Fierce the Phantasm gazeth hither
  With an Avenging Angel's eyes ;
It is fading, and the mists of storm enfold it!

Saint Abe and his Seven Wives.

A TALE OF SALT LAKE CITY.

DEDICATION: TO OLD DAN CHAUCER.

Maypole dance and Whitsun ale,
Sports of peasants in the dale,
Harvest mirth and junketting,
Fireside play and kiss-in-ring,
Ancient fun and wit and ease,—
Gone are one and all of these :
All the pleasant pastime planned
In the green old Mother-land :
Gone are these and gone the time
Of the breezy English rhyme,
Sung to make men glad and wise
By great Bards with twinkling eyes:

Gone the tale and gone the song
Sound as nut-brown ale and strong,
Freshening the sultry sense
Out of idle impotence,
Sowing features dull or bright
With deep dimples of delight!

Thro' the Mother-land I went,
Seeking these, half indolent :
Up and down, I saw them not ;
Only found them, half-forgot,
Buried in long-darken'd nooks
With thy barrels of old books,
Where the light and love and mirth
Of the morning days of earth

Sleeps, like light of sunken suns
Brooding deep in cob-webb'd tuns!
Everywhere I found instead,
Hanging her dejected head,
Barbing shafts of bitter wit,
The pale Modern Spirit sit—
While her shadow, great as Gog's,
Cast upon the island fogs,
In the midst of all things dim
Loom'd, gigantically grim.

Honest Chaucer, thee I greet
In a verse with blithesome feet,
And, tho' modern bards may stare,
Crack a passing joke with Care!
Take a merry song and true
Fraught with inner meanings too!
Goodman Dull may croak and scowl :—
Leave him hooting to the owl!
Tight-laced Prudery may turn
Angry back with eyes that burn,
Reading on from page to page
Scrofulous novels of the age!
Fools may frown and humbugs rail,
Not for them I tell the Tale;
Not for them, but souls like thee,
Wise old English JOLLITY!

Newport, October, 1871.

APPROACHING UTAH.—THE BOSS'S TALE.

I.

PASSING THE RANCHE.

'GRRR!" shrieked the boss, with teeth clench'd tight,
Just as the lone ranche hove in sight,
And with a face of ghastly hue
He flogg'd the horses till they flew,
As if the devil were at their back,
Along the wild and stony track.
From side to side the waggon swung,
While to the quaking seat I clung.
Dogs bark'd; on each side of the pass
The cattle grazing on the grass
Raised heads and stared; and with a cry
Out the men rush'd as we roll'd by.
'Grrr!' shriek'd the boss; and o'er and o'er
He flogg'd the foaming steeds and swore;
Harder and harder grew his face
As by the ranche we swept apace,
And faced the hill, and past the pond,
And gallop'd up the height beyond,
Nor tighten'd rein till field and farm
Were hidden by the mountain's arm

A mile behind; when, hot and spent,
The horses paused on the ascent,
And mopping from his brow the sweat,
The boy glanced round with teeth still set,
And panting, with his eyes on me,
Smil'd with a look of savage glee.

Joe Wilson is the boss's name,
A Western boy well known to fame.
He goes about the dangerous land
His life for ever in his hand;
Has lost three fingers in a fray,
Has scalp'd his Indian too they say;
Between the white man and the red
Four times he hath been left for dead;
Can drink, and swear, and laugh, and brawl,
And keeps his big heart thro' it all
Tender for babes and women.
                                    He
Turned, smiled, and nodded savagely;
Then, with a dark look in his eyes
In answer to my dumb surprise,
Pointed with jerk of the whip's heft
Back to the place that we had left,
And cried aloud,
                      ' I guess you think
I'm mad, or vicious, or in drink.
But theer you're wrong. I never pass
The ranche down theer and bit of grass,
I never pass 'em, night nor day,
But the fit takes me just that way!
The hosses know as well as me
What's coming, miles afore we see
The dern'd old corner of a place,
And they git ready for the race!
Lord! if I *didn't* lash and sweer,
And ease my rage out passing theer,
Guess I should go clean mad, that's all.
And thet's the reason why I call
This turn of road where I am took
Jest Old Nick's Gallop!'
                                Then his look
Grew more subdued yet darker still;
And as the horses up the hill
With loosen'd rein toil'd slowly, he
Went on in half soliloquy,
Indifferent almost if I heard,
And grimly grinding out each word.

II.

JOE WILSON GOES A-COURTING.

'There was a time, and no mistake,
When thet same ranche down in the brake

Was pleasanter a heap to me
Than any sight on land or sea.
The hosses knew it like their master,
Smelt it miles orf, and spank'd the faster!
Ay, bent to reach thet very spot,
Flew till they halted steaming hot
Sharp opposite the door, among
The chicks and children old and young;
And down I'd jump, and all the go
Was 'Fortune, boss!' and 'Welcome,
  Joe!'
And Cissy with her shining face,
Tho' she was missus of the place,
Stood larfing, hands upon her hips;
And when upon her rosy lips
I put my mouth and gave her one,
She'd cuff me, and enjy the fun!
She was a widow young and tight,
Her chap had died in a free fight,
And here she lived, and round her had
Two chicks, three brothers, and her dad,
All making money fast as hay,
And doing better every day.
Waal! guess tho' I was peart and swift,
Spooning was never much my gift;
But Cissy was a gal so sweet,
So fresh, so spicy, and so neat,
It put your wits all out o' place,
Only to star' into her face.
Skin whiter than a new-laid-egg,
Lips full of juice, and sech a leg!
A smell about her, morn and e'en,
Like fresh-bleach'd linen on a green;
And from her hand when she took mine,
The warmth ran up like sherry wine;
And if in liquor I made free
To pull her larfing on my knee,
Why, there she'd sit, and feel so nice,
Her heer all scent, her breath all spice!
See! women hate, both young and old,
A chap that's over shy and cold,
And fire of all sorts kitches quick,
And Cissy seem'd to feel full slick
The same fond feelings, and at last
Grew kinder every time I passed;
And all her face, from eyes to chin,
Said 'Bravo, Joe! You're safe to win!'
And tho' we didn't fix, d'ye see,
In downright *words* that it should be,
Ciss and her fam'ly understood
That she and me would jine for good.
Guess I was like a thirsty boss
Dead beat for days, who comes across

A fresh clear beck, and on the brink
Scoops out his shaky hand to drink;
Or like a gal or boy of three,
With eyes upon a pippin-tree;
Or like some Injin cuss who sees
A bottle of rum among the trees,
And by the bit of smouldering log,
Where squatters camp'd and took their grog
The night afore. Waal!' (here he ground
His teeth again with savage sound)
'Waal, stranger, fancy, jest for fun,
The feelings of the thirsty one,
If, jest as he scoop'd out his hand,
The water turn'd to dust and sand!
Or fancy how the lad would scream
To see thet fruit-tree jest a dream!
Or guess how thet poor Injin cuss,
Would dance and swear, and screech and
  fuss,
If when he'd drawn the cork and tried
To get a gulp of rum inside,
'Twarn't anything in thet theer style,
But physic stuff or stinking ile!
Ah! you've a notion now, I guess,
Of how all ended in a mess,
And how when I was putting in
My biggest card and thought to win,
The Old One taught her how to cheat,
And yer I found myself, clean beat!'

III.

SAINT AND DISCIPLE.

Joe Wilson paused, and gazed straight
  down,
With gritting teeth and bitter frown,
And not till I entreated him
Did he continue,—fierce and grim,
With knitted brow and teeth clench'd tight.

'Along this way one summer night,
Jest as I meant to take the prize,
Passed an APOSTLE—dern his eyes!—
On his old pony, gravel-eyed,
His legs a-dangling down each side,
With twinkling eyes and wheedling smile,
Grinning beneath his broad-brimm'd tile,
With heer all scent and shaven face,
He came a-trotting to the place.
My luck was bad, I wasn't near,
But busy many a mile from yer;
And what I tell was told to me
By them as were at hand to see.

'Twarn't every day, I reckon, they
Saw an Apostle pass their way !
And Cissy, being kind o' soft,
And empty in the upper loft,
Was full of downright joy and pride
To hev thet saint at her fireside—
One of the seventy they call
The holiest holy—dern 'em all !
O he was 'cute and no mistake,
Deep as Salt Lake, and wide awake !
Theer at the ranche three days he stayed,
And well he knew his lying trade.
'Twarn't long afore he heard full free
About her larks and thet with me,
And how 'twas quite the fam'ly plan
To hev me for her second man.
At fust thet old Apostle said
Little, but only shook his head ;
But you may bet he'd no intent
To let things go as things had went.
Three nights he stayed, and every night
He squeezed her hand a bit more tight ;
And every night he didn't miss
To give a loving kiss to Ciss ;
And tho' his fust was on her brow,
He ended with her mouth, somehow.
O, but he was a knowing one,
The Apostle Hiram Higginson !
Grey as a badger's was his heer,
His age was over sixty year
(Her grandfather was little older),
So short, his head just touch'd her
    shoulder ;
His face all grease, his voice all puff,
His eyes two currants stuck in duff :—
Call thet a man !—then look at *me* !
Thretty year old and six foot three,
Afear'd o' nothing morn nor night,
The man don't walk I wouldn't fight !
Women is women ! Thet's their style—
Talk *reason* to them and they'll bile ;
But baste 'em soft as any pigeon,
With lies and rubbish and religion ;
Don't talk of flesh and blood and feeling,
But Holy Ghost and blessed healing ;
Don't name things in too plain a way,
Look a heap warmer than you say,
Make 'em believe they're serving true
The Holy Spirit and not you,
Prove all the world but you's damnation,
And call your kisses jest salvation ;
Do this, and press 'em on the sly,
You're safe to win 'em. Jest you try !

' Fust thing I heerd of all this game,
One night when to the ranche I came,
Jump'd down, ran in, saw Cissy theer,
And thought her kind o' cool and queer ;
For when I caught her with a kiss,
'Twarn't that she took the thing amiss,
But kept stone cool and gev a sigh,
And wiped her mouth upon the sly
On her white milkin'-apron. "Waal,"
Says I, "you're out o' sorts, my gel !"
And with a squeamish smile for me,
Like folks hev when they're sick at sea,
Says she, "O, Joseph, ere too late,
I am awaken'd to my state—
How pleasant and how sweet it is
To be in sech a state of bliss !"
I stared and gaped, and turned to Jim
Her brother, and cried out to him,
"Hullo, mate, what's the matter here ?
What's come to Cissy ? Is she *queer* ?"
Jim gev a grin and answered, " Yes,
A trifle out o' sorts, I guess."
But Cissy here spoke up and said,
" It ain't my stomach, nor my head,
It ain't my flesh, it ain't my skin,
It's holy *spirits* here within !"
"Waal," says I, meanin' to be kind,
"I must be off, for I'm behind ;
But next time that I pass this way
We'll fix ourselves without delay.
I know what your complaint is, Ciss,
I've seen the same in many a miss,
Keep up your spirits, thet's your plan,
You're lonely here without a man,
And you shall hev as good a one
As e'er druv hoss beneath the sun !"
At that I buss'd her with a smack,
Turn'd out, jump'd up, and took the track,
And larfing druv along the pass.

' Theer ! Guess I was as green as grass ! '

IV.

THE BOOK OF MORMON.

' 'Twas jest a week after thet day
When down I druv again this way.
My heart was light ; and 'neath the box
I'd got a shawl and two fine frocks
For Cissy. On in spanking style
The hosses went mile arter mile ;
The sun was blazing golden bright,
The sunflowers burning in the light,

The cattle in the golden gleer
Wading for coolness everywheer
Among the shinin' ponds, with flies
As thick as pepper round their eyes
And on their heads. See! as I went
Whistling like mad and waal content,
Altho' 'twas broad bright day all round,
A cock crow'd, and I thought the sound
Seem'd pleasant. Twice or thrice he crow'd,
And then up to the ranche I rode.
Since then I've often heerd folk say
When a cock crows in open day
It's a *bad sign*, announcin' clear
Black luck or death to those thet hear.

'When I drew up, all things were still.
I saw the boys far up the hill
Tos in' the hay ; but at the door
No Cissy stood as oft afore.
No, not a soul there, left nor right,
Her very chicks were out o' sight.
So down I jump'd, and "Ciss!" I cried,
But not a sign of her outside.
With thet into the house I ran,
But found no sight of gel or man—
All empty. Thinks I, "This is queer!"—
Look'd in the dairy—no one theer ;
Then loiter'd round the kitchen track
Into the orchard at the back:
Under the fruit-trees' shade I pass'd, . . .
Thro' the green bushes, . . . and at last
Found, as the furthest path I trode,
The gel I wanted. Ye . . . s! by —— !

' The gel I wanted—ay, I found
More than I wanted, you'll be bound !
Theer, seated on a wooden cheer,
With bows and ribbons in her heer,
Her hat a-swinging on a twig
Close by, sat Ciss in her best rig,
And at her feet that knowing one,
The Apostle Hiram Higginson !
They were too keen to notice me,
So I held back behind a tree
And watch'd 'em. Never night nor day
Did I see Cissy look so gay,
Her eyes all sparkling blue and bright,
Her face all sanctified delight.
She hed her gown tuck'd up to show
Embrider'd petticoat below,
And jest a glimpse, below the white,
Of dainty leg in stocking tight
With crimson clocks ; and oh her knee
She held an open book, which he,

Thet dern'd Apostle at her feet,
With her low milking-stool for seat
Was reading out all clear and pat
Keeping the place with finger fat ;
Creeping more close to book and letter
To feel the warmth of his text better
His crimson face like a cock's head
With his emotion as he read,
And now and then his eyes he'd clos
Jest like a cock does when he crow s
Above the heads of thet strange two
The shade was deep, the sky was blue,
The place was full of warmth and smell,
All round the fruit and fruit-leaves fell,
And that Saint's voice, when all was still,
Was like the groanin' of a mill.

' At last he stops for lack of wind,
And smiled with sarcy double-chinn'd
Fat face at Cissy, while she cried,
Rocking herself from side to side,
"O Bishop, them are words of bliss !"
And then he gev a long fat kiss
On her warm hand, and edged his stool
Still closer. Could a man keep cool
And see it ? Trembling thro' and thro'
I walked right up to thet theer two,
And caught the dern'd old lump of duff
Jest by the breeches and the scruff,
And chuck'd him off, and with one kick
Sent his stool arter him right slick—
While Cissy scream'd with frighten'd face,
"Spare him ! O spare that man of grace !"

' "Spare him !" I cried, and gev a shout,
"What's this yer shine you air about—
What cuss is this that I jest see
With that big book upon your knee,
Cuddling up close and making sham
To read a heap of holy flam ?"
Then Cissy clasp'd her hands, and said,
While that dern'd Saint sat fierce and red,
Mopping his brow with a black frown,
And squatting where I chuck'd him down,
" Joe Wilson, stay your hand so bold,
Come not a wolf into the fold ;
Forbear to touch that holy one —
The Apostle Hiram Higginson."
"Touch him !" said I ; "for half a pin
I'd flay and quarter him and skin !
Waal may he look so white and skeer'd,
For of his doings I have heerd ;
Five wives he hev already done,
And him—not half the man for one !"

A A

'And then I stoop'd and took a peep
At what they'd studied at so deep,
And read, for I can read a bit,
"The Book of Mormon"—what was writ
By the first Saint of all the lot,
Mad Joseph, him the Yankees shot.
"What's the contents of this yer book?"
Says I, and fixed her with a look.
"O Joe," she answered, "read aright,
It is a book of blessed light—
Thet holy man expounds it clear;
Edification great is theer!"
Then, for my blood was up, I took
One kick at thet infernal book,
And tho' the Apostle guv a cry,
Into the well I made it fly,
And turning to the Apostle cried,
"Tho' thet theer Scriptur' is your guide,
You'd best depart without delay,
Afore you sink in the same way!
And sure as fate you'll wet your skin
If you come courting yer agin!"

'At first he stared and puff'd and blew,—
"Git out!" I cried, and off he flew,
And not till he was out o' reach
Shook his fat fist and found his speech.
I turned to Cissy. "Cicely Dunn,"
Ses I, "is this a bit of fun
Or eernest?" Reckon 'twas a sight
To see the way she stood upright,
Rolled her blue eyes up, tried to speak,
Made fust a giggle, then a squeak,
And said half crying, " I despise
Your wicked calumnies and lies,
And what you would insinuate
Won't move me from my blessed state.
Now I perceive in time, thank hiven,
You are a man to anger given,
Jealous and vi'lent. Go away!
And when you recollect this day,
And those bad words you've said to me,
Blush if you kin. Tehee! tehee!"
And then she sobbed, and in her cheer
Fell crying: so I felt quite queer,
And stood like a dern'd fool, and star'd
Watchin' the pump a-going hard;
And then at last, I couldn't stand
The sight no more, but slipt my hand
Sharp into hers, and said quite kind,
"Say no more, Cissy—never mind;
I know how queer you women's ways is—
Let the Apostle go to blazes!"

Now thet was plain and fair. With this
I would have put my arm round Ciss.
But Lord! you should have seen her face,
When I attempted to embrace;
Sprang to her feet and gev a cry,
Her back up like a cat's, her eye
All blazing, and cried fierce and clear,
"You villain, touch me if you deer!"
And jest then in the distance, fur
From danger, a voice echoed her,—
The dern'd Apostle's, from some place
Where he had hid his ugly face,—
Crying out faint and thick and clear,
"Yes, villain, touch her if you deer!"

'So riled I was, to be so beat,
I could have struck her to my feet.
I didn't tho', tho' sore beset—
I never struck a woman yet.

'But off I walked right up the pass,
And found the men among the grass,
And when I came in sight said flat,
"What's this yer game Cissy is at?
She's thrown me off, and taken pity
On an Apostle from the City.
Five wives already, too, has he—
Poor cussed things as e'er I see—
Does she mean *mischief* or a *lark*?"
Waal, all the men at thet look'd dark,
And scratch'd their heads and seem'd i
  doubt.
At last her brother Jim spoke out—
"Joe, don't blame *us*—by George, it's true
We're chawed by this as much as you;
We've done our best and tried and tried,
But Ciss is off her head with pride.
And all her thoughts, both night and day,
Are with the Apostles fur away.
'O that I were in bliss with them
Theer in the new Jerusalem!'
She says; and when we laugh and sneer,
Ses we're jest raging wolves down here.
She's a bit dull at home d'ye see,
Allays liked heaps of company,
And now the foolish critter paints
A life of larks among the Saints.
We've done our best, don't hev a doubt,
To keep the old Apostle out:
We've trained the dogs to seize and bite him
We've got up ghosts at night to fright him
Doctor'd his hoss and so upset him,
Put tickle-grass in bed to fret him,

Jalap'd his beer and snuffed his tea too,
Gunpowder in his pipe put free too ;
A dozen times we've well-nigh kill'd him.
We've skeer'd him, shaken him, and spill'd
 him ;
In fact, done all we deer," said Jim,
"Against a powerful man like him ;
But all in vain we've hed our sport ;
Jest like a cat that *can't* be hurt,
With nine good lives if he hev one,
Is this same Hiram Higginson !"'

V.

JOE ENDS HIS STORY—FIRST GLIMPSE
 OF UTAH.

Joe paused, for down the mountain's brow,
His hastening horses trotted now.
Into a canyon green and light,
Thro' which a beck was sparkling light,
Quickly we wound. Joe Wilson lit
His cutty pipe, and suck'd at it
In silence grim ; and when it drew,
Puff after puff of smoke he blew,
With blank eye fixed on vacancy.
At last he turned again to me,
And spoke with bi ter indignation
The epilogue of his narration.

'Waal, stranger, guess my story's told,
The Apostle beat and I was bowl'd.
Reckon I might have won if I
Had allays been at hand to *try* ;
But I was busy out of sight,
And he was theer, morn, noon, and night,
Playing his cards, and waal it weer
For him I never caught him theer.
To cut the story short, I guess
He got the Prophet to say "yes,"
And Cissy without much ado
Gev her consent to hev him too ;
And one fine morning off they druv
To what he called the Abode of Love—
A dern'd old place, it seems to me,
Jest like a dove-box on a tree,
Where every lonesome woman-soul
Sits shivering in her own hole,
And on the outside, free to choose,
The old cock-pigeon struts and coos.
I've heard from many a one that Ciss
Has found her blunder out by this,
And she'd prefer for company
A brisk young chap, tho' poor, like me,
Than the sixth part of him she's won—
The holy Hiram Higginson.
I've got a peep at her since then,
When she's crawl'd out of thet theer
 den,
But she's so pale and thin and tame
I shouldn't know her for the same.
No flesh to pinch upon her cheek,
Her legs gone thin, no voice to speak,
Dabby and crush'd, and sad and flabby,
Sucking a wretched squeaking baby ;
And all the fun and all the light
Gone from her face, and left it white.
Her cheek 'll take a feeble flush,
But hesn't blood enough to blush ;
Tries to seem modest, peart and sly,
And brighten up if I go by,
But from the corner of her eyes
Peeps at me quietly, and sighs.
Reckon her luck has been a stinger !
She'd bolt if I held up my finger ;
But tho' I'm rough, and wild, and free,
Take a *Saint's* leavings—no not me !
You've heerd of Vampires—them that rise
At dead o' night with flaming eyes,
And into women's beds 'll creep
To suck their blood when they're asleep.
I guess these Saints are jest the same,
Sucking the life out is their game ;
And tho' it ain't in the broad sun
Or in the open streets it's done,
There ain't a woman they clap eyes on
Their teeth don't touch, their touch don't
 pison ;
Thet's their dern'd way in this yer spot—
Grrr ! git along, hoss ! dern you, trot !'

From pool to pool the wild beck sped
Beside us, dwindled to a thread.
With mellow verdure fringed around
It sang along with summer sound :
Here gliding into a green glade ;
Here darting from a nest of shade
With sudden sparkle and quick cry,
As glad again to meet the sky ;
Here whirling off with eager will
And quickening tread to turn a mill ;
Then stealing from the busy place
With duskier depths and wearier pace
In the blue void above the beck
Sailed with us, dwindled to a speck,
The hen-hawk ; and from pools below
The blue-wing'd heron oft rose slow,

A A 2

And upward pass'd with measured beat
Of wing to seek some new retreat.
Blue was the heaven and darkly bright,
Suffused with throbbing golden light,
And in the burning Indian ray
A million insects hummed at play.
Soon, by the margin of the stream,
We passed a driver with his team
Bound for the City ; then a hound
Afar off made a dreamy sound ;
And suddenly the sultry track
Left the green canyon at our back,
And sweeping round a curve, behold !
We came into the yellow gold
Of perfect sunlight on the plain ;
And Joe abruptly drawing rein,
Said quick and sharp, shading his eyes
With sunburnt hand, 'See, theer it lies—
Theer's *Sodom !*'

             And even as he cried,
The mighty Valley we espied,
Burning below us in one ray
Of liquid light that summer day ;
And far away, 'mid peaceful gleams
Of flocks and herds and glistering streams,
Rose, fair as aught that fancy paints,
The wondrous City of the Saints !

THE CITY OF THE SAINTS.

O Saints that shine around the heavenly Seat !
What heaven is this that opens at my feet ?
What flocks are these that thro' the go'den gleam
Stray on by freckled fields and shining stream ?
What glittering roofs and white kiosks are these
Up-peeping from the shade of emerald trees ?
Whose City is this that rises on the sight
Fair and fantastic as a city of light
Seen in the sunset ? What is yonder sea
Opening beyond the City cool and free,
Large, deep, and luminous, looming thro' the heat,
And lying at the darkly shadowed feet
Of the Sierras, which with jagged line
Burning to amber in the light divine,
Close in the Valley of the happy land,
With heights as barren as a dead man's hand ?

O pilgrim, halt ! O wandering heart, give praise !
Behold the City of these Latter Days !
Here may'st thou leave thy load and be forgiven,
And in anticipation taste of Heaven !

I.

AMONG THE PASTURES—SUMMER
EVENING DIALOGUE.

Bishop Pete. Bishop Joss. Stranger.

BISHOP PETE.

AH, things down here, as you observe, are getting more pernicious,
And Brigham's losing all his nerve, altho' the fix is vicious.
Jest as we've rear'd a prosperous place and fill'd our holy quivers,
The Yankee comes with dern'd long face to give us all the shivers !
And on his jaws a wicked grin prognosticates disaster,
And, jest as sure as sin is sin, he means to be the master.
' Pack up your traps,' I hear him cry, ' for here there's no remainin','
And winks with his malicious eye, and progues us out of Canaan.

BISHOP JOSS.

It ain't the Yankee that *I* fear, the neighbour, nor the stranger—
No, no, it's closer home, it's *here*, that I perceive the danger.
The wheels of State has gather'd rust, the helm wants hands to guide it,
'Tain't from without the biler'll bust, but 'cause of steam inside it ;
Yet if we went falootin' less, and made less noise and flurry,
It isn't Jonathan, I guess, would hurt us in a hurry.
But there's sedition east and west, and secret revolution,
There's canker in the social breast, rot in the constitution ;
And over half of us, at least, are plunged in mad vexation,
Forgetting how our race increased, our very creed's foundation.
What's our religion's strength and force, its substance, and its story ?

STRANGER.

Polygamy, my friend, of course ! the law of love and glory !

BISHOP PETE.

Stranger, I'm with you there, indeed :—it's
  been the best of nusses ;
Polygamy is to our creed what meat and
  drink to *us* is.
Destroy that notion any day, and all the
  rest is brittle,
And Mormondom dies clean away like one
  in want of vittle.
It's meat and drink, it's life, it's power! to
  heaven its breath doth win us!
It warms our vitals every hour! it's Holy
  Ghost within us!
Jest lay that notion on the shelf, and all
  life's springs are frozen!
I've half a dozen wives myself, and wish I
  had a dozen!

BISHOP JOSS.

If all the Elders of the State like *you* were
  sound and holy,
P. Shufflebotham, guess our fate were far
  less melancholy.
You air a man of blessed toil, far-shining
  and discerning,
A heavenly lamp well trimm'd with oil,
  upon the altar burning.
And yet for every one of us with equal re-
  solution,
There's twenty samples of the Cuss, as
  mean as Brother Clewson.

STRANGER.
St. Abe?

BISHOP JOSS.

Yes, *him*—the snivelling sneak—his very
  name provokes me,—
Altho' my temper's milky-meek, he sours
  me and he chokes me.
To see him going up and down with those
  meek lips asunder,
Jest like a man about to drown, with lead
  to sink him under,
His grey hair on his shoulders shed, one
  leg than t'other shorter,
No end of cuteness in his head, and him—
  as weak as water!

BISHOP PETE.

And yet how well I can recall the time
  when Abe was younger—
Why not a chap among us all went for the
  notion stronger.
When to the mother-country he was sent
  to wake the sinning,
He shipp'd young lambs across the sea by
  flocks—he was so winning ;
O but he had a lively style, describing
  saintly blisses!
He made the spirit pant and smile, and
  seek seraphic kisses!
How the bright raptures of the Saint fresh
  lustre seemed to borrow,
While black and awful he did paint the
  one-wived sinner's sorrow!
Each woman longed to be his bride, and by
  his side to slumber—
'The more the blesseder!' he cried, still
  adding to the number.

STRANGER.

How did the gentleman contrive to change
  his skin so quickly?

BISHOP JOSS.

The holy Spirit couldn't thrive because the
  Flesh was sickly!
Tho' day by day he did increase his flock,
  his soul was shallow,
His brains were only candle-grease, and
  wasted down like tallow.
He stoop'd a mighty heap too much, and
  let his household rule him,
The weakness of the man was such that
  any face could fool him.
Ay! made his presence cheap, no doubt,
  and so contempt grew quicker,—
Not measuring his notice out in smallish
  drams, like liquor.
His house became a troublous house, with
  mischief overbrimmin',
And he went creeping like a mouse among
  the cats of women.
Ah, womenfolk are hard to rule, their tricks
  is most surprising,
It's only a dern'd spoony fool goes *senti-
  mentalising!*
But give 'em now and then a bit of notice
  and a present,
And lor, they're just like doves, that sit on
  one green branch, all pleasant!
But Abe's love was a queer complaint, a
  sort of tertian fever,
Each case he cured of thought the Saint a
  thorough-paced deceiver ;

And soon he found, he did indeed, with all
    their whims to nourish,
That Mormonism ain't a creed where
    fleshly follies flourish.

BISHOP PETE.

Ah, right you air! A creed it is demandin'
    iron mettle!
A will that quells, as soon as riz, the biling
    of the kettle!
With wary eye, with manner deep, a spirit
    overbrimmin',
Like to a shepherd 'mong his sheep, the
    Saint is 'mong his women;
And unto him they do uplift their eyes in
    awe and wonder;
His notice is a blessed gift, his anger is
    blue thunder.
No n'ises vex the holy place where dwell
    those blessed parties;
Each missus shineth in her place, and
    blithe and meek her heart is!
They sow, they spin, they darn, they hem,
    their blessed babes they handle,
The Devil never comes to *them*, lit by that
    holy candle!
When in their midst serenely walks their
    Master and their Mentor,
They're hush'd, as when the Prophet stalks
    down holy church's centre!
They touch his robe, they do not move,
    those blessed wives and mothers,
And, when on one he shineth love, no envy
    fills the others;
They know his perfect saintliness, and
    honour his affection —
And, if they did object, I guess he'd settle
    that objection!

BISHOP JOSS.

It ain't a passionate flat like Abe can
    manage things in *your* way!
They teased that most etarnal babe, till
    things were in a poor way.
I used to watch his thorny bed, and bust
    my sides with laughter.
Once give a female hoss her head you'll
    never stop her after.
It's one thing getting seal'd, and he was
    mighty fond of Sealing,
He'd all the human heat, d'ye see, without
    the saintly feeling.

His were the wildest set of gals that ever
    drove man silly,
Each full of freaks and fal-de-lals, as frisky
    as a filly.
One pull'd this way, and t'other that, and
    made his life a mockery,
They'd all the feelings of a cat scampaging
    'mong the crockery.
I saw Abe growing pale and thin, and well
    I knew what ail'd him—
The skunk went stealing out and in, and
    all his spirit failed him;
And tho' the tanning-yard paid well, and
    he was money-making,
His saintly home was hot as Hell, and, ah!
    how he was baking!
Why, now and then at evening-time, when
    his day's work was over,
Up this here hill he used to climb and squat
    among the clover,
And with his fishy eye he'd glare across the
    Rocky Mountains,
And wish he was away up there, among
    the heavenly fountains!
I had an aunt, Tabitha Brooks, a virgin
    under fifty,
She warn't so much for pretty looks, but
    she was wise and thrifty:
She'd seen the vanities of life, was good at
    'counts and brewin'—
Thinks I, ' Here's just the sort of Wife to
    save poor Abe from ruin.'
So, after fooling many a week, and showing
    him she loved him,
And seeing he was shy to *speak*, whatever
    feelings moved him,
At last I took her by the hand, and led her
    to him straightway,
One day when we could see him stand jest
    close unto the gateway.
My words were to the p'int and brief: says
    I, ' My brother Clewson,
There'll be an end to all your grief, if
    you've got resolution.
Where shall you find a house that thrives
    without a head that's ruling?
Here is the paragon of wives to teach those
    others schooling!
She'll be to you not only wife, but careful
    as a mother—
A little property for life is hers; you'll
    share it, brother,

I've seen the question morn and eve within
  your eyes unspoken,
You're slow and nervous I perceive, but
  now—the ice is broken.
Here is a guardian and a guide to bless a
  man and grace him;'
And then I to Tabitha cried, 'Go in, old
  gal—embrace him!'

STRANGER.

Why, that was acting fresh and fair;—but
Abe, was he as hearty?

BISHOP JOSS.

We . . ll! Abe was never anywhere
  against a *female* party!
At first he seemed about to run, and then
  we might have missed him;
But Tabby was a tender one, she collar'd
  him and kissed him,
And round his neck she blushing hung,
  part holding, part caressing,
And murmur'd, with a faltering tongue,
  'O, Abe, I'll be a blessing.'
And home they walk'd one morning, he
  just reaching to her shoulders,
And sneaking at her skirt, while she stared
  straight at all beholders.
Swinging her bonnet by the strings, and
  setting her lips tighter,
In at his door the old gal springs, her grim
  eyes growing brighter;
And, Lord! there was the devil to pay,
  and lightning and blue thunder,
For she was going to have her way, and
  hold the vixens under;
They would have torn old Abe to bits, they
  were so anger-bitten,
But Tabby saved him from their fits, as a
  cat saves her kitten.

STRANGER.

It seems your patriarchal life has got its
  botherations,
And leads to much domestic strife and
  infinite vexations!
But when the ladies couldn't lodge in peace
  one house-roof under,
I thought that 'twas the saintly dodge to
  give them homes asunder?

BISHOP JOSS.

And you thought right; it is a plan by
  many here affected—
Never by *me*—I ain't the man—I'll have
  my will respected.
If all the women of *my* house can't fondly
  pull together,
And each as meek as any mouse, look out
  for stormy weather!—
No, no, I don't approve at all of humour-
  ing my women,
And building lots of boxes small for each
  one to grow grim in.
I teach them jealousy's a *sin*, and solitude's
  just bearish,
They nuss each other lying-in, each other's
  babes they cherish;
It is a family jubilee, and not a selfish
  pleasure,
Whenever one presents to me another infant
  treasure!
All ekal, all respected, each with tokens of
  affection,
They dwell together, soft of speech, beneath
  their lord's protection;
And if by any chance I mark a spark of
  shindy raising,
I set my heel upon that spark,—before the
  house gets blazing!
Now that's what Clewson should have done,
  but couldn't, thro' his folly,
For even when Tabby's help was won, he
  wasn't much more jolly.
Altho' she stopt the household fuss, and
  husht the awful riot,
The old contrairy stupid Cuss could not
  enj'y the quiet.
His house was peaceful as a church, all
  solemn, still, and saintly;
And yet he'd tremble at the porch, and
  look about him faintly;
And tho' the place was all his own, with
  hat in hand he'd enter,
Like one thro' public buildings shown, soft
  treading down the centre.
Still, things were better than before, though
  somewhat trouble-laden,
When one fine day unto his door there
  came a Yankee maiden.
'Is Brother Clewson in?' she says; and
  when she saw and knew him,

The stranger gal to his amaze scream'd out
  and clung unto him,
Then in a voice all thick and wild, exclaim'd
  that gal unlucky,
'O Sir, I'm Jason Jones's child—he's *dead*
  —stabb'd in Kentucky!
And father's gone, and O I've come to *you*
  across the mountains.'
And then the little one was dumb, and
  Abe's eyes gushed like fountains. . . .
He took that gal into his place, and kept
  her as his daughter—
Ah, mischief to her wheedling face and the
  bad wind that brought her!

BISHOP PETE.

I knew that Jones;—used to faloot about
  Emancipation—
It made your very toe-nails shoot to hear
  his declamation,
And when he'd made all bosoms swell with
  wonder at his vigour,
He'd get so drunk he couldn't tell a white
  man from a nigger!
Was six foot high, thin, grim, and pale,—
  his troubles can't be spoken—
'Tarred, feathered, ridden on a rail, left
  beaten, bruised, and broken;
But nothing made his tongue keep still, or
  stopt his games improper,
Till, after many an awkward spill, he came
  the final cropper.

BISHOP JOSS.

. . . That gal was fourteen years of age,
  and sly with all her meekness;
It put the fam'ly in a rage, for well they
  knew Abe's weakness.
But Abe (a cuss, as I have said, that any
  fool might sit on)
Was stubborn as an ass's head, when once
  he took the fit on!
And, once he fixed the gal to take, in spite
  of their vexation,
Not all the rows on earth would break his
  firm determination.
He took the naggings as they came, he
  bowed his head quite quiet,
Still mild he was and sad and tame, and
  ate the peppery diet;
But tho' he seemed so crush'd to be, when
  this or that one blew up,

He stuck to Jones's Legacy and school'd
  her till she grew up.
Well! there! the thing was said and done,
  and so far who could blame him?
But O he was a crafty one, and sorrow
  couldn't shame him!
That gal grew up, and at eighteen was
  prettier far and neater—
There were not many to be seen about these
  parts to beat her;
Peart, brisk, bright-eyed, all trim and tight,
  like kittens fond of playing,
A most uncommon pleasant sight at pic-nic
  or at praying,
Then it became, as you'll infer, a simple
  public duty,
To cherish and look after her, considering
  her beauty;
And several Saints most great and blest
  now offer'd their protection,
And I myself among the rest felt something
  of affection.
But O the selfishness of Abe, all things it
  beats and passes!
As greedy as a two-year babe a grasping at
  molasses!
When once those Shepherds of the flock
  began to smile and beckon,
He screamed like any fighting cock, and
  raised his comb, I reckon!
First one was floor'd, then number two, she
  wouldn't look at any;
Then *my* turn came, although I knew the
  maiden's faults were many.
'My brother Abe,' says I, ' I come untoe
  your house at present
To offer sister Anne a home which she will
  find most pleasant.
You know I am a saintly man, and all my
  ways are lawful '—
And in a minute he began abusing me most
  awful.
'Begone,' he said, 'you're like the rest,—
  wolves, wolves with greedy clutches!
Poor little lamb, but in my breast I'll shield
  her from your touches!'
'Come, come,' says I, 'a gal can't stay a
  child like that for ever,
You'll *hev* to seal the gal some day;' but
  Abe cried fiercely, 'Never!'
Says I, 'Perhaps it's in your view *yourself*
  this lamb to gather?'

And ' If it is, what's that to *you*?' he cried;
    ' but I'm her father!
You get along, I know your line, it's crush-
    ing, bullying, wearing,
You'll never seal a child of mine, so go, and
    don't stand staring!'
This was the man once mild in phiz as any
    farthing candle—
A hedgehog now, his quills all riz, whom
    no one dared to handle!
But O! little guessed his deal, nor tried to
    circumvent it,
I never thought he'd dare to *seal* another;
    but he meant it!
Yes, managed Brigham on the sly, for fear
    his plans miscarried,
And long before we'd time to cry, the two
    were sealed and married.

BISHOP PETE.

Well, you've your consolation now—he's
    punish'd clean, I'm thinking,
He's ten times deeper in the slough, up to
    his neck and sinking.
There's vinegar in Abe's pale face enough
    to sour a barrel,
Goes crawling up and down the place,
    neglecting his apparel,
Seems to have lost all heart and soul, has
    fits of absence shocking—
His home is like a rabbit's hole when
    weasels come a-knocking.
And now and then, to put it plain, while
    falling daily sicker,
I think he tries to float his pain by copious
    goes of liquor.

BISHOP JOSS.

Yes, that's the end of selfishness, it leads to
    long vexation—
No man can pity Abe, I guess, who knows
    his situation;
And, Stranger, if this man you meet, don't
    take *him* for a sample,
Although he speaks you fair and sweet, he's
    set a vile example.
Because you see him ill at ease, at home,
    and never hearty,
Don't think these air the tokens, please, of
    a real saintly party!
No, he's a failure, he's a sham, a scandal
    to our nation,

Not fit to lead a single lamb, unworthy of
    his station;
No! if you want a Saint to see, who rules
    lambs when he's got 'em,
Just cock your weather-eye at *me*, or Brother
    Shufflebotham.
We don't go croaking east and west, afra'd
    of women's faces,
We bless and we air truly blest in our
    domestic places;
We air religious, holy men, happy our folds
    to gather,
Each is a loyal citizen, also a husband—
    rather.
But now with talk you're dry and hot, and
    weary with your ride here,
Jest come and see *my* fam'ly lot,—they're
    waiting tea inside here.

II.
WITHIN THE CITY.
ST. ABE AND THE SEVEN.

Sister Tabitha, thirty odd,
Rising up with a stare and a nod;
Sister Amelia, sleepy and mild,
Freckled, Dudu-ish, suckling a child;
Sister Fanny, pert and keen,
Sister Emily, solemn and lean,
Sister Mary, given to tears,
Sister Sarah, with wool in her ears;—
All appearing like tapers wan
In the mellow sunlight of Sister Anne.

With a tremulous wave of his hand, the
Introduces the household quaint,
And sinks on a chair and looks around,
As the dresses rustle with snakish sound.
As curtsies are bobb'd, and eyes cast
Some with a simper, some with a frown,
And Sister Anne, with a fluttering breast,
Stands trembling and peeping behind the
    rest.

Every face but one has been
Pretty, perchance, at the age of eighteen
Pert and pretty, and plump and bright
But now their fairness is faded quite,
And every feature is fashion'd here
To a flabby smile, or a snappish sneer.
Before the stranger they each assume
A false fine flutter and feeble bloom,

And a little colour comes into the cheek
When the eyes meet mine, as I sit and speak;
But there they sit and look at me,
Almost withering visibly,
And languidly tremble and try to blow—
Six pale roses all in a row!

Six? ah, yes; but at hand sits one,
The seventh, still full of the light of the sun.
Though her colour terribly comes and goes,
Now white as a lily, now red as a rose,
So sweet she is, and so full of light,
That the rose seems soft, and the lily bright.
Her large blue eyes, with a tender care,
Steal to her husband unaware,
And whenever he feels them he flushes red,
And the trembling hand goes up to his head!
Around those dove-like eyes appears
A redness as of recent tears.
Alone she sits in her youth's fresh bloom
In a dark corner of the room,
And folds her hands, and does not stir,
And the others scarcely look at her,
But crowding together, as if by plan,
Draw further and further from Sister Anne.

I try to rattle along in chat,
Talking freely of this and that—
The crops, the weather, the mother-land,
Talk a baby could understand;
And the faded roses, faint and meek,
Open their languid lips to speak.
But in various sharps and flats, all low,
Gave a lazy 'yes' or a sleepy 'no.'
Yet now and then Tabitha speaks,
Snapping her answer with yellow cheeks,
And fixing the Saint who is sitting by
With the fish-like glare of her glittering eye,
Whenever the looks of the weary man
Stray to the corner of Sister Anne.

Like a fountain in a shady place
Is the gleam of the sadly shining face—
A fresh spring whither the soul might turn,
When the road is rough, and the hot sands burn;
Like a fount, or a bird, or a blooming tree,
To a weary spirit is such as she!
And Brother Abe, from his easy chair,
Looks thither by stealth with an aching care,
And in spite of the dragons that guard the brink
Would stoop to the edge of the fount, I think,
And drink! and drink!

'Drink? Stuff and fiddlesticks,' you cry.
Matron reader with flashing eye:
'Isn't the thing completely *his*,
His wife, his mistress, whatever you please?
Look at her! Dragons and fountains!
Absurd!'
Madam, I bow to every word;
But truth is truth, and cannot fail,
And this is quite a veracious tale.
More like a couple of lovers shy,
Who flush and flutter when folk are by,
Were man and wife, or (in another
And holier parlance) sister and brother.
As a man of the world I noticed it,
And it made me speculate a bit,
For the situation was to my mind
A phenomenon of a curious kind—
A person in love with his *wife*, 'twas clear,
But afraid, when another soul was near,
Of showing his feelings in any way
Because—there would be the Devil to pay!

The Saint has been a handsome fellow,
Clear-eyed, fresh-skinn'd, if a trifle yellow,
And his face, though somewhat soft and plain,
Ends in a towering mass of brain.

His locks, though still an abundant crop,
Are thinning a little at the top,
But you only notice here and there
The straggling gleam of a silver hair.
A man by nature rol'ed round and short,
Meant for the Merry Andrew's sport,
But sober'd down by the wear and tear
Of business troubles and household care:
Quiet, reticent, gentle, kind,
Of amorous heart and extensive mind,
A Saint devoid of saintly sham,
Is little Brother Abraham.

Brigham's right hand he used to be—
Mild though he seems, and simple, and free;
Sound in the ways of the world, and great
In planning potent affairs of state;
Not bright, nor bumptious, you must know,
Too retiring for popular show,
But known to conceive on a startling scale
Gigantic plans that never fail;
To hold with a certain secret sense
The Prophet under his influence,
To be, I am led to understand,
The Brain, while the Prophet is the Hand,
And to see his intellectual way

Thro' moral dilemmas of every day,
By which the wisest are led astray.

Here's the Philosopher!—here he sits,
Here, with his vaguely wandering wits,
Among the dragons, as I have said,
Smiling, and holding his hand to his head.
What mighty thoughts are gathering now
Behind that marble mass of brow?
What daring schemes of polity
To set the popular conscience free,
And bless humanity, planneth he?
His talk is idle, a surface-gleam,
The ripple on the rest of the stream,
But his thoughts—ah, his *thoughts*—where
   do they fly,
While the wretched roses under his eye
Flutter and peep? and in what doth his plan
Turn to the counsel of Sister Anne?
For his eyes give ever a questioning look,
And the little one in her quiet nook
Flashes an answer, and back again
The question runs to the Brother's brain,
And the lights of speculation flit
Over his face and trouble it.

Follow his eyes once more, and scan
The fair young features of Sister Anne:
Frank and innocent, and in sooth
Full of the first fair flush of youth.
Quite a child—nineteen years old;
Not gushing, and self-possessed, and bold,
Like our Yankee women at nineteen,
But low of voice, and mild of mien—
More like the fresh young fruit you see
In the mother-land across the sea—
More like that rosiest flower on earth,
A blooming maiden of English birth,
Such as we find them yet awhile
Scatter'd about the homely Isle,
Not yet entirely eaten away
By the canker-novel of the day,
Or curling up and losing their scent
In a poisonous dew from the Continent.

There she sits, in her quiet nook,
Still bright tho' sadden'd; and while I look,
My heart is filled and my eyes are dim,
And I hate the Saint when I turn to him!
Ogre! Blue Beard! Oily and sly!
His meekness a cheat, his quiet a lie!
A roaring lion he'll walk the house
Tho' now he crouches like any mouse!

Had not he pluck'd enough and to spare
Of roses like these set fading there,
But he must seek to cajole and kiss
Another yet, and a child like this?
A maid on the stalk, just panting to prove
The honest joy of a virgin love;
A girl, a baby, an innocent child,
To be caught by the first man's face that
   smiled!
Scarce able the difference to fix
Of polygamy and politics!
Led to the altar like a lamb,
And sacrificed to the great god *Sham*!
Deluded, martyr'd, given to woe,
Last of seven who have perish'd so;
For who can say but the flowers I see
Were once as rosy and ripe as she?

Already the household worm has begun
To feed on the cheeks of the little one;
Already her spirit, fever-fraught,
Droops to the weight of its own thought;
Already she saddens and sinks and sighs,
Watched by the jealous dragonish eyes.
Even Amelia, sleepy and wan,
Sharpens her orbs as she looks at Anne;
While Sister Tabby, when she can spare
Her gaze from the Saint in his easy-chair,
Fixes her with a gorgon glare.

All is still and calm and polite,
The Sisters bolster themselves upright,
And try to smile, but the atmosphere
Is charged with thunder and lightning here.
Heavy it seems, and close and warm,
Like the air before a summer storm;
And at times,—as in that drowsy dream
Preluding thunder, all sounds will seem
Distinct and ominously clear,
And the far-off cocks seem crowing near;—
Ev'n so in the pauses of talk, each breast
Is strangely conscious of the rest,
And the tick of the watch of Abe the Saint
Breaks on the air, distinct though faint,
Like the ticking of his heart!

   I rise
To depart, still glancing with piteous eyes
On Sister Anne; and I find her face
Turn'd questioning still to the same old
   place—
The face of the Saint. I stand and bow,
Curtsies again are bobbing now,

Dresses rustling . . . I know no more
Till the Saint has led me to the door,
And I find myself in a day-dream dim,
Just after shaking hands with him,
Standing and watching him sad and slow
Into the dainty dwelling go,
With a heavy sigh, and his hand to his head.

. . . Hark, *distant thunder*!—'tis as I said :
The air was far too close ;—at length
The Storm is breaking in all its strength.

III.

PROMENADE—MAIN STREET, UTAH.

THE STRANGER.

Along the streets they're thronging, walking,
Clad gaily in their best and talking,
Women and children, quite a crowd ;
The bright sun overhead is blazing,
The people sweat, the dust they're raising
Arises like a golden cloud.
Still out of every door they scatter,
Laughing and light. Pray what's the matter,
That such a flock of folks I see?

A LOUNGER.

They're off to hear the Prophet patter,
This yer's a day of jubilee.

VOICES.

Come along, we're late I reckon. . .
There's our Matt, I see him beckon. . .
How d'ye do, marm? glad to meet you. . .
Silence, Hiram, or I'll beat you. . .
Emm, there's brother Jones a-looking. . .
Here's warm weather, how I'm cooking!

STRANGER.

Afar the hills arise with cone and column
Into a sky of brass serene and solemn ;
And underneath their shadow in one haze
Of limpid heat the great salt waters blaze,
While faint and filmy through the sultry veil
The purple islands on their bosom sail
Like floating clouds of dark fantastic air.
How strangely sounds (while 'mid the Indian glare
Moves the gay crowd of people old and young)
The bird-like chirp of the old Saxon tongue!
The women seem half weary and half gay,
Their eyes droop in a melancholy way,—
I have not seen a merry face to-day.

A BISHOP.

Thet's a smart hoss you're riding, brother !
How are things looking, down with you?

SECOND BISHOP.

Not over bright with one nor 'tother,
Taters are bad, tomatoes blue.
You've heer'd of Brother Simpson's losses?—
Buried his wife and spiled his hay.
And the three best of Hornby's hosses
Some Injin cuss has stol'n away.

VOICES.

Zoë, jest fix up my gown. . .
There's my hair a-coming down. . .
Drat the babby, he's so crusty—
It's the heat as makes him thusty. . .
Come along, I'm almost sinking. . .
There's a stranger, and he's winking.

STRANGER.

That was a fine girl with the grey-hair'd lady,
How shining were her eyes, how true and steady,
Not drooping down in guilty Mormon fashion,
But shooting at the soul their power and passion.
That's a big fellow, six foot two, not under,
But how he struts, and looks as black as thunder,
Half glancing round at his poor sheep to scare 'em—
Six, seven, eight, nine,—O Abraham, what a harem !
All berry brown, but looking scared as may be,
And each one but the oldest with a baby.

A GIRL.

Phœbe !

ANOTHER.

Yes, Grace !

FIRST GIRL.

Don't seem to notice, dear,
That Yankee from the camp again is here,
Making such eyes, and following on the sly,
And coughing now and then to show he's nigh.

SECOND GIRL.

Who's that along with him—the little scamp
  Shaking his hair and nodding with a smile?

FIRST GIRL.

Guess he's some new one just come down to camp.

SECOND GIRL.

Isn't he handsome?

FIRST GIRL.

  No; the first's my style!

STRANGER.

If my good friends, the Saints, could get their will,
These Yankee officers would fare but ill;
Wherever they approach the folk retire,
As if from veritable coals of fire;
With distant bow, set lips, and half-hid frown,
The Bishops pass them in the blessed town;
The women come behind like trembling sheep,
Some freeze to ice, some blush and steal a peep.
And often, as a band of maidens gay
Comes up, each maid ceases to talk and play,
Droops down her eyes, and does not look their way;
But after passing where the youngsters pine,
All giggle as at one concerted sign,
And tripping on with half-hush'd merry cries,
Look boldly back with laughter in their eyes!

VOICES.

Here we are, . . how folk are pushing! . .
Mind the babby in the crushing. . .
Pheemy! . . Yes, John! . . Don't go staring
At that Yankee—It's past bearing.
Draw your veil down while he passes,
Reckon you're as bold as brass is.

ABE CLEWSON.

(Passing with his hand to his head, attended by his Wives.)

Head in a whirl, and heart in a flutter,
Guess I don't know the half that I utter.
Too much of this life is beginning to try me,
I'm like a dern'd miller the grind always nigh me;
Praying don't soothe me nor comfort me any,
My house is too full and my blessings too many—
The ways o' the wilderness puzzle me greatly.

SISTER TABITHA.

Do walk like a Christian, and keep kind o' stately!
And jest keep an eye on those persons behind you,
You call 'em your Wives, but they tease you and blind yon;
Sister Anne's a disgrace, tho' you think her a martyr,
And she's tuck'd up her petticoat nigh to her garter.

STRANGER.

What group is this, begrim'd with dust and heat,
Staring like strangers in the open street?
The women, ragged, wretched, and half dead,
Sit on the kerbstone hot and hang the head,
And clustering at their side stand children brown,
Weary, with wondering eyes on the fair town.
Close by in knots beside the unhorsed team
The sunburn'd men stand talking in a dream,
For the vast tracts of country left behind
Seem now a haunting mirage in the mind.
Gaunt miners folding hands upon their breasts,
  Big-jointed labourers looking ox-like down,
And sickly artizans with narrow chests
  Still pallid from the smoke of English town.
Hard by to these a group of Teutons stand,
Light hair'd, blue-eyed, still full of Fatherland,
With water-loving Northmen, who grow gay
To see the mimic sea gleam far away.
Now to this group, with a sharp questioning face,
Cometh a holy magnate of the place
In decent black; shakes hands with some; and then

Begins an eager converse with the men:
All brighten; even the children hush their cries,
And the pale women smile with sparkling eyes.

BISHOP.

The Prophet welcomes you, and sends
His message by my mouth, my friends;
He'll see you snug, for on this shore
There's heaps of room for millions more! ..
Scotchman, I take it? .. Ah, I know
Glasgow—was there a year or so. . .
And if *you* don't from Yorkshire hail,
I'll—ah, I thought so; seldom fail.
Make yourselves snug and rest a spell,
There's liquor coming—meat as well.
All welcome! We keep open door—
Ah, *we* don't push away the poor;
Tho' he's a fool, you understand,
Who keeps poor long in this here land.
The land of honey you behold—
Honey and milk – silver and gold!

AN ARTIZAN.

Ah, that's the style—Bess, just you hear it;
Come, come, old gal, keep up your spirit:
Silver and gold, and milk and honey,
This is the country for our money!

A GERMAN.

Es lebe die Stadt! es lebe dran!
Das heilige Leben steht mir an!

A NORTHMAN.

Taler du norske?

BISHOP.

(*Shaking his head, and turning with a wink to the English.*)

No, not me!
Saxon's the language of the free!
The language of the great Evangels!
The language of the Saints and Angels!
The only speech that Joseph knew!
The speech of him and Brigham too!
Only the speech by which we've thriven
Is comprehended up in Heaven! ..
Poor heathens! but we'll make 'em spry,
They'll talk like Christians by-and-by.

STRANGER. (*Strolling out of the streets.*)

From east, from west, from every worn-out land,
Yearly they stream to swell this busy band.
Out of the fever'd famine of the slums,
From sickness, shame, and sorrow, Lazarus comes,
Drags his sore limbs o'er half the world and sea,
Seeking for freedom and felicity.
The sewer of ignorance and shame and loss,
Draining old Europe of its dirt and dross,
Grows the great City by the will of God;
While wondrously out of the desert sod,
Nourished with lives unclean and weary hearts,
The new faith like a splendid weed upstarts.
A splendid weed! rather a fair wild-flower,
Strange to the eye in its first birth of power,
But bearing surely in its breast the seeds
Of higher issues and diviner deeds.
Changed from Sahara to a fruitful vale
Fairer than ever grew in fairy tale,
Transmuted into plenteous field and glade
By the slow magic of the white man's spade,
Grows Deseret, filling its mighty nest
Between the eastern mountains and the west,
While—who goes there? What shape antique looks down
From this green mound upon the festive town,
With tall majestic figure darkly set
Against the sky in dusky silhouette?
Strange his attire: a blanket edged with red
Wrapt royally around him; on his head
A battered hat of the strange modern sort
Which men have christened 'chimney pots' in sport;
Mocassins on his feet, fur-fringed and grand,
And a large green umbrella in his hand.
Pensive he stands with deep-lined dreamy face,
Last living remnant of the mighty race
Who on these hunting-fields for many a year
Chased the wild buffalo, and elk, and deer
Heaven help him! In his mien grief and despair
Seem to contend, as he stands musing there;
Until he notices that I am nigh,
And lo! with outstretched hands and glistening eye
Swift he descends—Does he mean mischief? No;
He smiles and beckons as I turn to go.

INDIAN.

Me Medicine Crow. White man gib drink to me.
Great chief; much squaw; papoose, sah, one, two, three!

STRANGER.

With what a leer, half wheedling and half winking,
The lost one imitates the act of drinking;
His nose already, to his woe and shame,
Carbuncled with the white man's liquid flame!
Well, I pull out my flask, and fill a cup
Of burning rum—how quick he gulps it up;
And in a moment in his trembling grip
Thrusts out the cup for more with thirsty lip.
But no!—already drunken past a doubt,
Degenerate nomad of the plains, get out!

[*A railway whistle sounds in the far distance.*

Fire-hearted Demon tamed to human hand,
Rushing with smoky breath from land to land,
Screaming aloud to scare with rage and wrath
Primæval ignorance before his path,
Dragging behind him as he runs along
His lilliputian masters, pale and strong,
With melancholy sound for plain and hill
Man's last Familiar Spirit whistles shrill.

Poor devil of the plains, now spent and frail,
Hovering wildly on the fatal trail,
Pass on!—there lies thy way and thine abode,
Get out of Jonathan thy master's road.
Where? anywhere!—he's not particular where,
So that you clear the road, he does not care;
Off, quick! clear out! ay, drink your fill and die;
And, since the Earth rejects you, try the Sky!
And see if He, who sent your white-faced brother
To hound and drive you from this world you bother,
Can find a corner for you in another!

IV.

WITHIN THE SYNAGOGUE.
SERMONIZETH THE PROPHET.

THE PROPHET.

Sisters and brothers who love the right,
   Saints whose hearts are divinely beating,
Children rejoicing in the light,
   I reckon this is a pleasant meeting.
Where's the face with a look of grief?—
   Jehovah's with us and leads the battle;
We've had a harvest beyond belief,
   And the signs of fever have left the cattle;
All still blesses the holy life
   Here in the land of milk and honey.

FEMININE WHISPERS.

Brother Shuttleworth's seventeenth wife,...
Her with the heer brushed up so funny!

THE PROPHET.

Out of Egypt hither we flew,
   Through the desert and rocky places;
The people murmur'd, and all look'd blue,
   The bones of the martyr'd filled our traces.
Mountain and valley we crawl'd along,
   And every morning our hearts beat quicker.
Our flesh was weak, but our souls were strong,
   And we'd managed to carry some kegs of liquor.
At last we halted on yonder height,
   Just as the sun in the west was blinking.

FEMININE WHISPERS.

Isn't Jedge Hawkins's last a fright?...
I'm suttin that Brother Abe's been drinking!

THE PROPHET.

That night, my lambs, in a wondrous dream,
   I saw the gushing of many fountains;
Soon as the morning began to beam,
   Down we went from yonder mountains,
Found the water just where I thought,
   Fresh and good, though a trifle gritty,
Pitch'd our tents in the plain, and wrought
   The site and plan of the Holy City.
' Pioneers of the blest,' I cried,
   ' Dig, and the Lord will bless each spadeful.

FEMININE WHISPERS.

Brigham's sealed to another Bride...
How worn he's gittin'! he's aging dreadful.

THE PROPHET.

This is a tale so often told,
   The theme of every eventful meeting;
Yes! you may smile and think it old;
   But yet it's a tale that will bear repeating.

That's how the City of Light began,
   That's how we founded the saintly nation,
All by the spade and the arm of man,
   And the aid of a special dispensation.
'Work' was the word when we begun,
   'Work' is the word now we have plenty.

       FEMININE WHISPERS.

Heard about Sister Euphemia's son? . . .
   Sealing already, though only twenty!

       THE PROPHET.

I say just now what I used to say,
   Though it moves the heathens to mock
       and laughter,
From work to prayer is the proper way—
   Labour first, and Religion after.
Let a big man, strong in body and limb,
   Come here inquiring about his Maker,
This is the question I put to him,
   'Can you grow a cabbage, or reap an
       acre?'
What's the soul but a flower sublime,
   Grown in the earth and upspringing
       surely?

       FEMININE WHISPERS.

O yes! she's hed a most dreadful time!
   Twins, both thriving, though she's so
       poorly.

       THE PROPHET.

Beauty, my friends, is the crown of life,
   To the young and foolish seldom granted;
After a youth of honest strife
   Comes the reward for which you've
       panted.
O blessed sight beyond compare,
   When life with its halo of light is
       rounded,
To see a Saint with reverend hair
   Sitting like Solomon love-surrounded!
One at his feet and one on his knee,
   Others around him, blue-eyed and dreamy!

       FEMININE WHISPERS.

All very well, but as for *me*,
   My man had better!—I'd *pison* him,
       Phœmy!

       THE PROPHET.

There in the gate of Paradise
   The Saint is sitting serene and hoary,
Tendrils of arms, and blossoms of eyes,
   Festoon him round in his place of glory;
Little cherubs float thick as bees
   Round about him, and murmur 'father!'
The sun shines bright and he sits at ease,
   Fruit all round for his hand to gather.
Blessed is he and for ever gay,
   Floating to Heaven and adding to it!

       FEMININE WHISPERS.

Thought I should have gone mad that day
   He brought a second; I made him rue it!

       THE PROPHET.

Sisters and Brothers by love made wise,
   Remember, when Satan attempts to quell
       you,
If this here Earth isn't Paradise
   You'll never see it, and so I tell you.
Dig and drain, and harrow and sow,
   God will bless you beyond all measure;
Labour, and meet with reward below,
   For what is the end of all labour?
       Pleasure!
Labour's the vine, and pleasure's the grape,
   The one delighting, the other bearing.

       FEMININE WHISPERS.

Higginson's third is losing her shape.
   She hes too many—it's dreadful wearing.

       THE PROPHET.

But I hear some awakening spirit cry,
   'Labour is labour, and all men know it;
But what is p'easure?' and I reply,
   Grace abounding and Wives to show it!
Holy is he beyond compare
   Who tills his acres and takes his blessing,
Who sees around him everywhere
   Sisters soothing and babes caressing.
And *his* delight is Heaven's as well,
   For swells he not the ranks of the chosen?

       FEMININE WHISPERS.

Martha is growing a handsome gel. . . .
   Three at a birth?—that makes the dozen.

       THE PROPHET.

Learning's a shadow, and books a jest,
   One Book's a Light, but the rest are
       human.
The kind of study that I think best
   Is the use of a spade and the love of a
       woman.
Here and yonder, in heaven and earth,
   By big Salt Lake and by Eden river,

The finest sight is a man of worth,
 Never tired of increasing his quiver.
He sits in the light of perfect grace
 With a dozen cradles going together !

FEMININE WHISPERS.

The babby's growing black in the face !
 Carry him out—it's the heat of the weather !

THE PROPHET.

A faithful vine at the door of the Lord,
 A shining flower in the garden of spirits,
A lute whose strings are of sweet accord,
 Such is the person of saintly merits.
Sisters and brothers, behold and strive
 Up to the level of his perfection ;
Sow, and harrow, and dig, and thrive,
 Increase according to God's direction.
This is the Happy Land, no doubt,
 Where each may flourish in his vocation. . . .
Brother Bantam will now give out
 The hymn of love and of jubilation.

V.

THE FALLING OF THE THUNDERBOLT.

Deep and wise beyond expression
Sat the Prophet holding session,
And his Elders, round him sitting
With a gravity befitting,
Never rash and never fiery,
Chew'd the cud of each inquiry,
Weigh'd each question and discussed it,
Sought to settle and adjust it,
Till, with sudden indication
Of a gush of inspiration,
The grave Prophet from their middle
Gave the answer to their riddle,
And the lesser lights all holy,
Round the Lamp revolving slowly,
Thought, with eyes and lips asunder,
'*Right*, we reckon he's a wonder !'

Whether Boyes, that blessed brother,
Should be sealed unto another,
Having, tho' a Saint most steady,
Very many wives already?
Whether it was held improper,
If a woman drank, to drop her?
Whether unto Brother Fleming

Formal praise would be beseeming,
Since from three or four potatoes
(Not much bigger than his great toes)
He'd extracted, to their wonder,
Four stone six and nothing under?
Whether Bigg be reprimanded
For his conduct underhanded,
Since he'd packed his prettiest daughter
To a heathen o'er the water?
How, now Thompson had departed,
His poor widows, broken-hearted,
Should be settled? They were seven,
Sweet as cherubs up in heaven ;
Three were handsome, young, and pleasant,
And had offers on at present—
Must they take them ? . . . These and other
Questions proffer'd by each brother,
The great Prophet ever gracious,
Free and easy, and sagacious,
Answer'd after meditation
With sublime deliberation ;
And his answers were so clever
Each one whisper'd, ' Well, I never ! '
And the lesser lights all holy,
Round the Prophet turning slowly,
Raised their reverend heads and hoary,
Thinking, ' To the Prophet, glory !
Hallelujah, veneration !
Reckon that he licks creation ! '

Suddenly as they sat gleaming,
On them came an unbeseeming
Murmur, tumult, and commotion,
Like the breaking of the ocean ;
And before a word was utter'd,
In rush'd one with voice that fluttered,
Arms uplifted, face the colour
Of a bran-new Yankee dollar,
Like a man whose wits are addled,
Crying—'*Brother Abe's skedaddled !*'

Then those Elders fearful-hearted
Raised a loud cry and upstarted,
But the Prophet, never rising,
Said, ' Be calm ! this row's surprising ! '
And as each Saint sank unsinew'd
In his arm-chair he continued :
' Goodman Jones, your cheeks are yellow,
Tell thy tale, and do not bellow !
What's the reason of your crying—
Is our brother *dead ?*—or *dying ?* '

As the Prophet spake, supremely
Hushing all the strife unseemly,

B B

Sudden in the room there entered
Shapes on whom all eyes were centred—
Six sad female figures moaning,
Trembling, weeping, and intoning,
' We are widows broken-hearted—
Abraham Clewson has departed ! '

While the Saints again upleaping
Joined their voices to the weeping,
For a moment the great Prophet
Trembled, and look'd dark as Tophet.
But the cloud pass'd over lightly.
' Cease ! ' he cried, but sniffled slightly,
' Cease this murmur and be quiet—
Dead men won't awake with riot.
'Tis indeèd a loss stupendous—
When will Heaven his equal send us?
Speak, then, of our brother cherish'd,
Was it *fits* by which he perish'd?
Or did Death come even quicker,
Thro' a bolting horse or kicker ? '

At the Prophet's question scowling,
All the Wives stood moaning, howling,
Crying wildly in a fever,
' O the villain ! the deceiver ! '
But the oldest stepping boldly,
Curtseying to the Session coldly,
Cried in voice like cracking thunder,
' Prophet, don't you make a blunder !
Abraham Clewson isn't dying—
Hasn't died, as you're implying ;
No ! he's not the man, my brothers,
To die decently like others !
Worse ! he's from your cause revolted—
Run away ! skedaddled ! bolted ! '

Bolted ! run away ! skedaddled !
Like to men whose wits are addled,
Echoed all those Lights so holy,
Round the Prophet shining slowly
And the Prophet, undissembling,
Underneath the blow sat trembling,
While the perspiration hovered
On his forehead, and he covered
With one trembling hand his features
From the gaze of smaller creatures.
Then at last the high and gifted
Cough'd and craved, with hands uplifted,
Silence. When 'twas given duly,
' This,' said he, ' 's a crusher truly !
Brother Clewson fall'n from glory !
I can scarce believe your story.

O my Saints, each in his station,
Join in prayer and meditation ! '

Covering up each eyelid saintly
With a finger-tip, prayed faintly,
Shining in the church's centre,
Their great Prophet, Lamp, and Mentor ;
And the lesser Lights all holy,
Round the Lamp revolving slowly,
Each upon his seat there sitting,
With a gravity befitting,
Bowed their reverend heads and hoary,
Saying, ' To the Prophet glory !
Hallelujah, veneration !
Reckon that he licks creation ! '

Lastly, when the trance was ended,
And, with face where sorrow blended
Into pity and compassion,
Shone the Light in common fashion ;
Forth the Brother stept who brought them
First the news which had distraught them,
And, while stood the Widows weeping,
Gave into the Prophet's keeping
A seal'd paper, which the latter
Read, as if 'twere solemn matter—
Gravely pursing lips and nodding,
While they watch'd in dark foreboding,
Till at last, with voice that quivered,
He these woeful words delivered :—

' Sisters, calm your hearts unruly,
'Tis an awful business truly ;
Weeping now will save him never,
He's as good as lost for ever ;
Yes, I say with grief unspoken,
Jest a pane crack'd, smash'd, and broken
In the windows of the Temple —
Crack'd 's the word—so take example !
Had he left ye one and all here,
On our holy help to call here,
Fled alone from *every* fetter,
I could comprehend it better !
Flying, not with some strange lady,
But with her he had already,
With his own seal'd Wife eloping—
It's a case of craze past hoping !
List, O Saints, each in his station,
To the idiot's explanation ! '

Then, while now and then the holy
Broke the tale of melancholy
With a grunt contempt expressing,
And the Widows made distressing

(left column, cut off)	
tion	And to Tabitha give for me a tender kiss of healing—
narration,	Guilt wrings my soul—I seem to see that well-known face appealing !
affliction	
iction.	And now,—before my figure fades for ever from your vision,
T. ABE TO THE ISTS.	Before I mingle with the shades beyond your light Elysian,
the Light !—don't you,	*Now*, while your faces all turn pale, and you raise eyes and shiver,
of darkest night I d bless you !'	Let me a round unvarnish'd tale (as Shakspere says) deliver ;
g tear, nor even a	And let there be a warning text in my most shameful story,
y sphere, I yield to	When some poor sheep, perplext and vext, goes seeking too much glory.
cot into the depths	O Brigham, think of my poor fate, a scandal to beholders,
ring and mute, my ou ;	And don't again put too much weight before you've tried the shoulders !
ssed care my well-	Though I'd the intellectual gift, and knew the rights and reasons ;
y and to spare to d houses,	Though I could trade, and save, and shift, according to the seasons ;
irm and fold, yea, iven :	Though I was thought a clever man, and was at spouting splendid,—
n sold, and to my	Just think how finely I began, and see how all has ended !
em at their worth merit,	In *principle* unto this hour I'm still a holy being—
me in the earth, a	But oh, how poorly is my power proportion'd to my seeing !
good-bye, and see g ;	You've all the logic on your side, you're right in each conclusion,
ck and fly without	And yet how vainly have I tried, with eager resolution !
, by careful educa-	My will was good, I felt the call, although my strength was meagre,
p a man of strength	There wasn't one among you all to serve the Lord more eager !
' men, and say I'm	I never tired in younger days of drawing lambs unto me,
now and then, I tter !	My lot was one to bless and praise, the fire of faith thrill'd through me.
fill with holy con-	And *you*, believing I was strong, smiled on me like a father,—
her still a-reading	Said, 'Blessèd be this man, though young, who the sweet lambs doth gather !'
r tears—she's free	At first it was a time full blest, and all my earthly pleasure
ve my fears she's r ;	Was gathering lambs unto my breast to cherish and to treasure ;

Ay, one by one, for heaven's sake, my
    female flock I found me,
Until one day I did awake and heard them
    bleating round me,
And there was sorrow in their eyes, and
    mute reproach and wonder,
For they perceived to their surprise their
    Shepherd was a blunder.
O Brigham, think of it and weep, my firm
    and saintly Master—
*The Pastor trembled at his Sheep, the Sheep
    despised the Pastor !*

O listen to the tale of dread, thou Light
    that shines so brightly—
Virtue's a horse that drops down dead if
    overloaded slightly !
She's all the *will*, she wants to go, she'd
    carry every tittle ;
But when you see her flag and blow, just
    ease her of a little !
One wife for me was near enough, *two*
    might have fixed me neatly,
Three made me shake, *four* made me puff,
    five settled me completely,—
But when the *sixth* came, though I still was
    glad and never grumbled,
I took the staggers, kick'd, went ill, and
    in the traces tumbled !

Ah, well may I compare my state unto a
    beast's position —
Unfit to bear a saintly weight, I sank and
    lost condition ;
I lack'd the moral nerve and thew, to fill so
    fine a station—
Ah, if I'd had a head like you, and your
    determination !
Instead of going in and out, like a superior
    party,
I was too soft of heart, no doubt, too open,
    and too hearty.
When I *began* with each young sheep I was
    too free and loving.
Not being strong and wise and deep, I set
    her *feelings* moving ;
And so, instead of noticing the gentle flock
    in common,
I waken'd up that mighty thing—the Spirit
    of a Woman.
Each got to think me, don't you see,—so
    foolish was the feeling,—
Her own especial property, which all the
    rest were stealing !

And, since I cou
    whole of my a
All came to grief,
    delicate to me
Bless them ! they
    they erred in t
I lack'd the proper
    mere emotion
The solemn air ser
    so tranquillisir
That on the fema
    the same from
But holds them do
    and, if some v
Comes like a col(
    into *ice* transf

And there, betwe
    difficulty grow
Since most men a
    passionate anc
They cannot in yo
    guest from He
Within this tenem
    Soul is given ;
They cannot like a
    and strong int
Eating and drinkir
    gazing thro' it
No, every mortal's
    very few are,
So weak they are,
    holy men like
Instead of keeping
    Spirit, brother
And making one
    nigger of the c
They muddle and
    mix, and twist
So that it takes a c
    either single.
The Soul gets n
    beyond all sep
The Body holds
    sensation ;
The poor bewilder
    in nature dout
Half light and sou!
    given up to tro
He thinks the insti
    ings of the Sp
And when the Sp
    the Flesh to he

he slave of every passing whim, the dupe
 of every devil,
ispired by every female limb to love, and
 light, and revel,
\upu'sive, timid, weak, or strong, as Flesh
 or Spirit makes him,
he lost one wildly moans along till mis-
 chief overtakes him ;
nd when the Soul has fed upon the Flesh
 till life's spring passes,
inds strength and health and comfort
 gone—the way of last year's grasses,
nd the poor Soul is doom'd to bow, in
 deep humiliation,
/ithin a place that isn't now a decent
 habitation.

o I keep the Soul and Flesh apart in pious
 resolution,
on't let weak flutterings of the heart lead
 you to *my* confusion !
ut let the Flesh be as the *horse*, the Spirit
 as the *rider*,
nd use the snaffle first of course, and ease
 her up and guide her ;
nd if she's going to resist, and won't let
 none go past her,
ist take the *curb* and give a twist, and
 show her you're the Master.
he Flesh is but a temporal thing, and
 Satan's strength is in it,
se it, but conquer it, and bring its vice
 down every minute !
ito a woman's arms don't fall, as if you
 meant to *stay* there,
ust come as if you'd made a call, and
 idly found your way there ;
on't praise her too much to her face, but
 keep her calm and quiet,—
ost female illnesses take place thro' far
 too warm a diet ;
nto her give your fleshly kiss, calm, kind,
 and patronising,
hen—soar to your own sphere of bliss,
 before her heart gets rising !
on't fail to let her see full clear, how in
 your saintly station
he Flesh is but your nigger here obeying
 your dictation ;
nd tho' the Flesh be e'er so warm, your
 Soul the weakness smothers
f loving any female form much better than
 the others !

O Brigham, I can see you smile to hear
 the Devil preaching ;—
Well, I can praise your perfect style, tho'
 far beyond my reaching.
Forgive me, if in shame and grief I vex you
 with digression,
And let me come again in brief to my own
 dark confession.

The world of men divided is into *two
 portions*, brother,
The first are Saints, so high in bliss that
 they the Flesh can smother ;
God meant them from fair flower to flower
 to flutter, smiles bestowing,
Tasting the sweet, leaving the sour, just
 hovering,—and going.
The second are a different set, just *halves*
 of perfect spirits,
Going about in bitter fret, of uncompleted
 merits,
Till they discover, here or there, their
 other half (or woman),
Then these two join, and make a Pair, and
 so increase the human.
The second Souls inferior are, a lower spirit-
 order,
Born 'neath a less auspicious star, and taken
 by soft sawder ;—
And if they do not happen here to find th ir
 fair Affinity,
They come to grief and doubt and fear, and
 end in asininity ;
And if they try the blessed game of those
 superior to them,
They're very quickly brought to shame,—
 their passions so undo them.
In some diviner sphere, perhaps, they'll
 look and grow more holy,—
Meantime they're vessels Sorrow taps and
 grim Remorse sucks slowly.

Now, Brigham, *I* was made, you see, one
 of those *lower* creatures,
Polygamy was not for me, altho' I joined
 its preachers.
Instead of, with a wary eye, seeking the one
 who waited,
And sticking to her, wet or dry, because
 the thing was fated,
I snatch'd the first whose beauty stirred my
 soul with tender feeling !
And then another ! then a third ! and so
 continued Sealing !

And duly, after many a smart, discovered,
  sighing faintly,
I *hadn't* found my missing part, and *wasn't*
  strong and saintly !
O they were far too good for me, altho' their
  zeal betrayed them ;—
Unfortunately, don't you see, heaven for
  some other made them :
Each would a downright blessing be, and
  Peace would pitch the tent for her,
If ' she ' could only find the ' he ' originally
  meant for her !

Well, Brother, after many years of bad
  domestic diet,
One morning I woke up in tears, still weary
  and unquiet,
And (speaking figuratively) lo ! beside my
  bed stood smiling
The Woman, young and virgin snow, but
  beckoning and beguiling.
I started up, my wild eyes rolled, I knew
  her, and stood sighing,
My thoughts throng'd up like bees of gold
  out of the smithy flying.
And as she stood in brightness there,
  familiar, tho' a stranger,
I looked at her in dumb despair, and
  trembled at the danger.

But, Brother Brigham, don't you think
  the Devil could so undo me,
That straight I rushed the cup to drink too
  late extended to me.
No, for I hesitated long, ev'n when I found
  she loved me,
And didn't seem to think it wrong when
  love and passion moved me.
O Brigham, you're a Saint above, and know
  not the sensation
The ecstasy, the maddening love, the
  rapturous exultation,
That fills a man of lower race with wonder
  past all speaking,
When first he finds in one sweet face the
  Soul he has been seeking !
When two immortal beings glow in the first
  fond revealing,
And their inferior natures know the luxury
  of feeling !
But ah, I had already got a quiver-full of
  blessing,
Had blundered, tho' I knew it not, six
  times beyond redressing,

And surely it was t
  lot was lonely
My house was lik
  tho' with ' mis

And so I *should* l
  wretchedest of
Rather than put c
  belovèd featur
But that it happe:
  the secret's flit
Was left in this g
  my care comn
Her father, Jason
  whose faults w
' O, be a father, A
  daughter Ann
And so I promised
  to this city,
And set my fool
  mingled love a
And as she prett
  throve 'neath
*I saw the Saints
  tokens of affect*
O, Brigham, pray
  and love coml
I hated every sair
  clining !
Sneered at their m
  went wild and
And saw Polygan
  for the maide:
Why *not*, you sa
  from your hig
But I'm of an infe
  Elysian.
I tore my hair, wh
  her to distract
I saw the dange
  trembled at th
At last I came to
  my tender fee
You said, ' Your
  this is a case
And since you ha
  made no hein
Why, brother Ab
  mind you kee
Well ! then I wer
  most heart un
Told her my feeli
  ing next to nc

Explain'd the various characters of those I
    had already,
The various tricks and freaks and stirs
    peculiar to each lady,
And, finally, when all was clear, and hope
    seem'd to forsake me,
'There! it's a wretched chance, my dear—
    you leave me, or you take me.'
Well, Sister Annie look'd at me, *her* inmost
    heart revealing
(Women are very weak, you see, inferior,
    full of feeling),
Then, thro' her tears outshining bright,
    'I'll never, never leave you!
'O Abe,' she said, 'my love, my light, why
    should I pain or grieve you?
I do not love the way of life you have so
    sadly chosen,
I'd rather be a single wife than one in half
    a dozen;
But now you cannot change your plan,
    tho' health and spirit perish,
And I shall never see a man but you to love
    and cherish.
Take me, I'm yours, and O, my dear, don't
    think I miss your merit,
I'll try to help a little here your true and
    loving spirit.'
'Reflect, my love,' I said, 'once more,'
    with bursting heart, half crying,
'Two of the girls cut very sore, and most
    of them are trying!'
And then that gentle-hearted maid kissed
    me and bent above me,
'O Abe,' she said, 'don't be afraid,—I'll
    try to make them *love* me!'
Ah well! I scarcely stopt to ask myself, till
    all was over,
How precious tough would be her task who
    made those dear souls love her!
But I was seal'd to Sister Anne, and straight-
    way, to my wonder,
A series of events began which show'd me
    all my blunder.

  Brother, don't blame the souls who erred
    thro' their excess of feeling—
So angrily their hearts were stirred by my
    last act of sealing;
But in a moment they forgot the quarrels
    they'd been wrapt in,
And leagued together in one lot, with
    Tabby for the Captain.

Their little tiffs were laid aside, and all
    combined together,
Preparing for the gentle Bride the blackest
    sort of weather.
It wasn't *feeling* made them flout poor
    Annie in that fashion,
It wasn't love turn'd inside out, it wasn't
    jealous passion,
It wasn't that they cared for *me*, or any
    other party,
Their hearts and sentiments were free,
    their appetites were hearty.
But when the pretty smiling face came
    blossoming and blooming,
Like sunshine in a shady place the fam'ly
    Vault illuming,
It naturally made them grim to see its sunny
    colour,
While like a row of tapers dim by daylight,
    they grew duller.
She tried her best to make them kind, she
    coaxed and served them dumbly,
She watch'd them with a willing mind,
    deferred to them most humbly;
Tried hard to pick herself a friend, but
    found her arts rejected,
And fail'd entirely in her end, as one might
    have expected,
But, Brother, tho' I'm loth to add one word
    to criminate them,
I think their conduct was too bad,—it
    almost made me hate them.

Ah me, the many nagging ways of women
    are amazing,
Their cleverness solicits praise, their cruelty
    is crazing!
And Sister Annie hadn't been a single day
    their neighbour,
Before a baby could have seen her life would
    be a labour,
But bless her little loving heart, it kept its
    sorrow hidden,
And if the tears began to start, suppressed
    the same unbidden.
She tried to smile, and smiled her best, till
    I thought sorrow silly,
And kept in her own garden nest, and lit
    it like a lily.
O I should waste your time for days with
    talk like this at present,
If I described her thousand ways of making
    things look pleasant!

But, bless you, 'twere as well to try, when
    thunder's at its dire work,
To clear the air, and light the sky, by
    pennyworths of firework.
These gentle ways to hide her woe and make
    my life a blessing,
Just made the after darkness grow more
    gloomy and depressing.
Taunts, mocks, and jeers, coldness and
    sneers, insult and trouble daily,
A thousand stabs that brought the tears, all
    these she cover'd gaily ;
But when her fond eyes fell on *me*, the
    light of love to borrow,
And Sister Anne began to see *I knew* her
    secret sorrow,
All of a sudden like a mask the loving
    cheat forsook her,
And reckon I had all my task, for *illness*
    overtook her.
She took to bed, grew sad and thin, seem'd
    like a spirit flying,
Smiled thro' her tears when I went in, but
    when I left fell crying ;
And as she languish'd in her bed, as weak
    and wan as water,
I thought of what her father said, ' Take
    care of my dear daughter ! '
Then I look'd round with secret eye upon
    her many Sisters,
And close at hand I saw them lie, ready
    for use—like blisters ;
They seemed with secret looks of glee, to
    keep their wifely station ;
They set their lips and sneer'd at me, and
    watch'd the situation.
O Brother, I can scarce express the agony
    of those moments,
I fear your perfect saintliness, and dread
    your cutting comments !
I prayed, I wept, I moan'd, I cried, I
    anguish'd night and morrow,
I watch'd and waited, sleepless-eyed, beside
    that bed of sorrow.

At last I knew, in those dark days of sorrow
    and disaster,
Mine wasn't soil where you could raise a
    Saint up, or a Pastor ;
In spite of careful watering, and tilling
    night and morning,
The weeds of vanity would spring without
    a word of warning.

I was and ever must subsist, labell'd on
    every feature,
A wretched poor *Monogamist*, a most in-
    ferior creature—
Just half a soul, and half a mind, a blunder
    and abortion,
Not finish'd half till I could find the other
    missing portion !
And gazing on that missing part which I at
    last had found out,
I murmur'd with a burning heart, scarce
    strong to get the sound out,
' If from the greedy clutch of Fate I save
    this chief of treasures,
I will no longer hesitate, but take decided
    measures !
A poor monogamist like me can *not* love
    half a dozen,
Better by far, then, set them free, and take
    the Wife I've chosen !
Their love for me, of course, is small, a
    very shadowy tittle,
They will not miss my face at all, or miss
    it very little.
I can't undo what I have done, by my for-
    lorn embraces,
And call the brightness of the sun again
    into their faces ;
But I *can* save one spirit true, confiding and
    unthinking,
From slowly curdling to a shrew or into
    swinedom sinking.'
These were my bitter words of woe, my
    fears were so distressing,
Not that I would reflect—O no !—on any
    living blessing.

Thus, Brother, I resolved, and when she
    rose, still frail and sighing,
I kept my word like better men, and bolted,
    —and I'm flying.
Into oblivion I haste, and leave the world
    behind me,
Afar unto the starless waste, where not a
    soul shall find me.
I send my love, and Sister Anne joins cor-
    dially, agreeing
I never was the sort of man for your high
    state of being ;
Such as I am, she takes me, though ; and
    after years of trying,
From Eden hand in hand we go, like our
    first parents flying ;

And like the bright sword that did chase
   the first of sires and mothers,
Shines dear Tabitha's flaming face, sur-
   rounded by the others :
Shining it threatens there on high, above
   the gates of Heaven,
And faster at the sight we fly, in naked
   shame, forth-driven.
Nothing of all my worldly store I take,
   'twould be improper,
I go a pilgrim, strong and poor, without a
   single copper.
Unto my Widows I outreach my property
   completely.
There's modest competence for each, if it
   is managed neatly.
That, Brother, is a labour left to your
   sagacious keeping ;—
Comfort them, comfort the bereft ! I'm
   good as dead and sleeping !
A fallen star, a shooting light, a portent
   and an omen,
A moment passing on the sight, thereafter
   seen by no men !
I go, with backward-looking face, and spirit
   rent asunder.
O may you prosper in your place, for you're
   a shining wonder !
So strong, so sweet, so mild, so good !—by
   Heaven's dispensation,
Made Husband to a *multitude* and Father
   to a *nation!*
May all the saintly life ensures increase
   and make you stronger !
Humbly and penitently yours,
      A. CLEWSON (*Saint no longer*)

THE FARM IN THE VALLEY—
SUNSET.

(1871.)

STILL the saintly City stands,
Wondrous work of busy hands ;
Still the lonely City thrives,
Rich in worldly goods and wives,
And with thrust-out jaw and set
Teeth, the Yankee threatens yet—
Half admiring and half riled,
Oft-by bigger schemes beguiled,
Turning off his curious stare
To communities elsewhere,
Always with unquiet eye
Watching Utah on the sly.

  Long the City of the Plain
Left its image on my brain :
White kiosks and gardens bright
Rising in a golden light ;
Busy figures everywhere
Bustling bee-like in the glare ;
And from dovecotes in green places,
Peep'd out weary women's faces,
Flushing faint to a thin cry
From the nursery hard by,
And the City in my thought
Slept fantastically wrought,
Till the whole began to seem
Like a curious Eastern dream,
Like the pictures strange we scan
In the tales Arabian :
Tales of magic art and sleight,
Cities rising in a night,
And of women richly clad,
Dark-eyed, melancholy, sad,
Ever with a glance uncertain,
Trembling at the purple curtain,
Lest behind the black slave stand
With the bowstring in his hand ;—
Happy tales, within whose heart
Founts of weeping eyes upstart,
Told, to save her pretty head,
By Scheherazad in bed !

All had faded and grown faint,
Save the figure of the Saint
Who that memorable night
Left the Children of the Light,
Flying o'er the lonely plain
From his lofty sphere of pain
Oft his gentle face would flit
O'er my mind and puzzle it,
Ever waking up meanwhile
Something of a merry smile,
Whose quick light illumined me
During many a reverie,
When I puffed my weed alone.

Faint and strange the face had grown,
Tho' for five long years or so
I had watched it come and go,
When, on busy thoughts intent,
I into New England went,
And one evening, riding slow
By a River that I know,

(Gentle stream! I hide thy name,
Far too modest thou for fame!)
I beheld the landscape swim
In the autumn hazes dim,
And from out the neighbouring dales
Heard the thumping of the flails.

All was hush'd; afar away
(As a novelist would say)
Sank the mighty orb of day,
Staring with a hazy glow
On the purple plain below,
Where (like burning embers shed
From the sunset's glowing bed,
Dying out or burning bright,
Every leaf a blaze of light)
Ran the maple swamps ablaze;
Everywhere amid the haze,
Floating strangely in the air,
Farms and homesteads gather'd fair:
And the River rippled slow,
Thro' the marshes green and low,
Spreading oft as smooth as glass
As it fringed the meadow grass,
Making 'mong the misty fields
Pools like golden gleaming shields.

Thus I walked my steed along,
Humming a low scrap of song,
Watching with an idle eye
White clouds in the dreamy sky
Sailing with me in slow pomp.
In the bright flush of the swamp,
While his dogs bark'd in the wood,
Gun in hand the sportsman stood;
And beside me, wading deep,
Stood the angler half asleep,
Figure black against the gleam
Of the bright pools of the stream;
Now and then a wherry brown
With the current drifted down
Sunset-ward, and as it went,
Made an oar-splash indolent;
While with solitary sound,
Deepening the silence round,
In a voice of mystery
Faintly cried the chickadee.

  Suddenly the River's arm
Rounded, and a lonely Farm
Stood before me blazing red
To the bright blaze overhead;
In the homesteads at its side,

Cattle lowed and voices cried,
And from out the shadows dark
Came a mastiff's measured bark.
Fair and fat stood the abode
On the path by which I rode,
And a mighty orchard, strown
Still with apple-leaves wind-blown,
Raised its branches gnarl'd and bare
Black against the sunset air,
And with greensward deep and dim,
Wander'd to the River's brim.

Close beside the orchard walk
Linger'd one in quiet talk
With a man in workman's gear.
As my horse's feet drew near,
The labourer nodded rough 'good-day,
Turned his back and loung'd away.
Then the first, a plump and fat
Yeoman in a broad straw hat,
Stood alone in thought intent,
Watching while the other went,
And amid the sunlight red
Paused, with hand held to his head.

In a moment, like a word
Long forgotten until heard,
Like a buried sentiment
Born again to some stray scent,
Like a sound to which the brain
Gives familiar refrain,
Something in the gesture brought
Things forgotten to my thought;
Memory, as I watched the sight,
Flashed from eager light to light.
Remember'd and remember'd not,
Half familiar, half forgot,
Stood the figure, till at last,
Bending eyes on his, I passed,
Gazed again, as loth to go,
Drew the rein, stopt short, and so
Rested, looking back; when he,
The object of my scrutiny,
Smiled and nodded, saying, ' Yes!
Stare your fill, young man! I guess
You'll know me if we meet again!'

In a moment all my brain
Was illumined at the tone,
All was vivid that had grown
Faint and dim, and straight I knew him,
Holding out my hand unto him,
Smiled, and called him by his name.

Wondering, hearing me exclaim,
Abraham Clewson (for 'twas he)
Came more close and gazed at me.
As he gazed, a merry grin
Brighten'd down from eyes to chin:
In a moment he, too, knew me,
Reaching out his hand unto me,
Crying 'Track'd, by all that's blue!
Who'd have thought of seeing *you*?'

Then, in double quicker time
Than it takes to make the rhyme,
Abe, with face of welcome bright,
Made me from my steed alight;
Call'd a boy, and bade him lead
The beast away to bed and feed;
And, with hand upon my arm,
Led me off into the Farm,
Where, amid a dwelling-place
Fresh and bright as her own face,
With a gleam of shining ware
For a background everywhere,
Free as any summer breeze,
With a bunch of huswife's keys
At her girdle, sweet and mild
Sister Annie blush'd and smiled,—
While two tiny laughing girls,
Peeping at me through their curls,
Hid their sweet shamefacëdness
In the skirts of Annie's dress.

. . . . .

That same night the Saint and I
Sat and talked of times gone by,
Smoked our pipes and drank our grog
By the slowly smouldering log,
While the clock's hand slowly crept
To midnight, and the household slept.
'Happy?' Abe said with a smile,
'Yes, in my *inferior* style,
Meek and humble, not like them
In the New Jerusalem.'
Here his hand, as if astray,
For a moment found its way
To his forehead, as he said,
'Reckon they believe I'm dead!
Ah, that life of sanctity
Never was the life for me.
Couldn't stand it wet nor dry,
Hated to see women cry;
Couldn't bear to be the cause
Of tiffs and squalls and endless jaws;
Always felt amid the stir
Jest a whited sepulchre;

And I did the best I could
When I ran away for good.
Yet, for many a night, you know
(Annie, too, would tell you so),
Couldn't sleep a single wink,
Couldn't eat, and couldn't drink,
Being kind of conscience-cleft
For those poor creatures I had left.
Not till I got news from there,
And I found their fate was fair,
Could I set to work, or find
Any comfort in my mind.
Well (here Abe smiled quietly),
Guess they didn't groan for me!
Fanny and Amelia got
Sealed to Brigham on the spot;
Emmy soon consoled herself
In the arms of Brother Delf;
And poor Mary one fine day
Packed her traps and tript away
Down to Fresco with Fred Bates,
A young player from the States;
While Sarah, 'twas the wisest plan,
Pick'd herself a single man—
A young joiner fresh come down
Out of Texas to the town—
And he took her with her baby,
And they're doing well as maybe.'

Here the Saint with quiet smile,
Sipping at his grog the while,
Paused as if his tale was o'er,
Held his tongue and said no more.
'Good,' I said, 'but have you done?
You have spoke of all save one—
All your Widows, so bereft,
Are most comfortably left,
But of one alone you said
Nothing. Is the lady *dead*?'

Then the good man's features broke
Into brightness as I spoke,
And with loud guffaw cried he,
'What, Tabitha? Dead! Not she.
All alone and doing splendid—
Jest you guess, now, how she's ended!
Give it up? This very week
I heard she's at Oneida Creek,
All alone and doing hearty,
Down with Brother Noyes's party
Tried the Shakers first, they say,
Tired of them and went away,
Testing with a deal of bother
This community and t'other,

Till she to Oneida flitted,
And with trouble got admitted.
Bless you, she's a shining lamp,
Tho' I used her like a scamp,
And she's great in exposition
Of the Free Love folk's condition,
Vowing, tho' she found it late,
'Tis the only happy state. . . .

'As for me,' added the speaker,
'I'm lower in the scale, and weaker;
Polygamy's beyond my merits,
Shakerism wears the spirits,
And as for Free Love, why you see
(Here the Saint wink'd wickedly)
With my whim it might have hung
Once, when I was spry and young;

But poor Annie's love alone
Keeps my mind in proper tone,
And tho' my spirit mayn't be strong,
I'm lively—as the day is long.'

As he spoke, with half a yawn,
Half a smile, I saw the dawn
Creeping faint into the gloom
Of the quickly-chilling room.
On the hearth the wood-log lay,
With one last expiring ray;
Draining off his glass of grog,
Clewson rose and kick'd the log;
As it tumbled into ashes,
Watched the last expiring flashes,
Gave another yawn and said,
'Well! I guess it's time for bed!'

White Rose and Red.
A LOVE STORY.

DEDICATION.

To WALT WHITMAN and ALEXANDER GARDINER, with all friends in Washington,
I dedicate this Poem.

INVOCATION.

'KNOW'ST THOU THE LAND?'

I.

KNOW'ST thou the Land, where the lian-flower
Burgeons the trapper's forest bower,
Where o'er his head the acacia sweet
Shaketh her scented locks in the heat,
Where the hang-bird swings to a blossom-cloud,
And the bobolink sings merry and loud?
Know'st thou the Land?
    O there! O there,
Might I with thee, O friend of my heart,
 repair!

II.

Know'st thou the Land where the golden Day
Flowers into glory and glows away,
While the Night springs up, as an Indian girl
Clad in purple and hung with pearl!
And the white Moon's heaven rolls apart,
Like a bell-shaped flower with a golden heart,—
Know'st thou the Land?
    O there! O there,
Might I with *thee*, O Maid of my Soul,
 repair!

III.

Know'st thou the Land where the woods are free,
And the prairie rolls as a mighty sea,
And over its waves the sunbeams shine,
While on its misty horizon-line
Dark and dim the buffaloes stand,
And the hunter is gliding gun in hand?
Know'st thou it well?
    O there! O there,
Might I, with those whose Souls are free,
 repair!

IV.

Know'st thou the Land where the sun-birds
    song
Filleth the forest all day long,
Where all is music and mirth and bloom,
Where the cedar sprinkles a soft perfume,
Where life is gay as a glancing stream,
And all things answer the Poet's dream?
Know'st thou the Land?
                  O there! O there,
Might I, with him who loves my lays,
    repair!

V.

Know'st thou the Land where the swampy
    brakes
Are full of the nests of the rattlesnakes,
Where round old Grizzly the wild bees
    hum,
While squatting he sucks at their honey-
    comb,
Where crocodiles crouch and the wild cat
    springs,
And the mildest ills are mosquito stings?
Know'st thou the Land?
                  O there! O there,
Might I, with adverse Critics, straight
    repair!

VI.

Know'st thou the Land where wind and
    sun
Smile on all races of men—save one:
Where (strange and wild as a sunset proud
Streak'd with the bars of a thunder-cloud)
Alone and silent the Red Man lies,
Sees the cold stars coming, and sinks, and
    dies?
Know'st thou the Land?
                  O there! O there,
Might I to wet his poor parch'd lips repair!

VII.

Lock up thy gold, and take thy flight
To the mighty Land of the red and white;
A ditty I love I would have thee hear,
While daylight dies, and the Night comes
    near
With her black feet wet from the western sea,
And the Red Man dies, with his eyes on
    thee!
Fast to that Land, ere his last footprints there
Are beaten down by alien feet, repair!

PART I.
THE CAPTURE OF EUREKA HART.

I.
NATURA NATURANS.

DAWN breaking. Thro' his dew-veil smiles
    the sun,
And under him doth run
On the green grass and in the forest brake
Bright beast and speckled snake;
Birds on the bough and insects in the ray
Gladden; and it is day.

What is this lying on the thymy steep,
    Where yellow bees hum deep,
And the rich air is warm as living breath?
    What soft shape slumbereth
Naked and dark, and glows in a green nest,
    Low-breathing in bright rest?
Is it the spotted panther, lying there
    Lissome and light and fair?
Is it the snake, with glittering skin coil'd
    round
And gleaming on the ground?
Is it some wondrous bird whose eyric lies
    Between the earth and skies?
'Tis none of these, but something stranger
    far—
    Strange as a fallen star!
A mortal birth, a marvel heavenly-eyed,
    With dark pink breast and side!
And as she lies the wild deer comes most
    meek
    To smell her scented cheek,
And creeps away; the yeanling ounce lies
    near,
    And watches with no fear;
The serpent rustles past, with touch as light
    As rose-leaves, rippling bright
Into the grass beyond; while yonder, on high,
    A black speck in the sky,
The crested eagle hovers, with sharp sight
    Facing the flood of light.

What living shape is this who sleeping lies
    Watch'd by all wondering eyes
Of beast and speckled snake and flying bird?
    Softly she sleeps, unstirr'd
By wind or sun; and since she first fell there
    Her raven locks of hair

Have loosen'd, shaken round her in a
   shower,
Whence, like a poppy flower
With dark leaves and a tongue to brightness
   tipt,
She lies vermilion-lipt.
Bare to the waist, her head upon her arm,
   Coil'd on a couch most warm
Of balsam and of hemlock, whose soft scent
   With her warm breath is blent.
Around her brow a circlet of pure gold,
   With antique letters scroll'd,
Burns in the sun-ray, and with gold also
   Her wrists and ankles glow.
Around her neck the threaded wild cat's
   teeth
Hang white as pearl; beneath
Her bosoms heave, and in the space between,
   Duskly tattoo'd, is seen
A figure small as of a pine-bark brand
   Held blazing in a hand. *
Her skirt of azure, wrought with braid and
   thread
In quaint signs yellow and red,
Scarce reaches to her dark and dimpled knee,
   Leaving it bare and free.
Below, mocassins red as blood are wound,
   With gold and purple bound;—
So that red-footed like the stork she lies,
   With softly shrouded eyes,
Whose brightness seems with heavy lustrous
   dew
To pierce the dark lids thro'.
Her eyelids closed, her poppied lips apart,
   And her quick eager heart
Stirring her warm frame, as a bird unseen
   Stirs the warm lilac-sheen,
She slumbers,—and of all beneath the skies
   Seemeth the last to rise.

She stirs—she wakens—now, O birds, sing
   loud
Under the golden cloud!
She stirs—she wakens—now, O wild beast,
   spring.
Blooms grow, breeze blow, birds sing!
She wakens in her nest and looks around,
   And listens to the sound;
Her eyelids blink against the heavens' bright
   beam,
Still dim and dark with dream,
Her breathing quickens, and her cheek
   gleams red,

And round her shining head
Glossy her black hair glistens. Now she
   stands,
And with her little hands
Shades her soft orbs and upward at the sky
   She gazeth quietly;
Then at one bound springs with a sudden
   song
The forest-track along.

Thro' the transparent roof of twining leaves,
   Where the deep sunlight weaves
Threads like a spider's-web of silvern
   white,
Faint falls the dreamy light
Down the gray bolls and boughs that
   intervene,
On to the carpet green
Prinkt with all wondrous flowers, on emerald
   brakes
Where the still speckled snakes
Crawl shaded; and above the shaded
   ground,
Amid the deep-sea sound
Of the high branches, bright birds scream
   and fly
And chattering parrots cry;
And everywhere beneath them in the bowers
   Float things like living flowers,
Hovering and settling; and here and there
   The blue gleams deep and fair
Thro' the high parted boughs, while serpent-
   bright
Slips thro' the golden light,
Startling the cool deep shades that brood
   around,
And floating to the ground,
With multitudinous living motes at play
   Like dust in the rich ray.

Hither for shelter from the burning sun
   Hath stolen the beauteous one,
And thro' the ferns and flowers she runs,
   and plucks
Berries blue-black, and sucks
The fallen orange. Where the sunbeams
   blink
She lieth down to drink
Out of the deep pool, and her image sweet
   Floats dim below her feet,
Up-peering thro' the lilies yellow and
   white
And green leaves where the bright

Great Dragon-fly doth pause. With burning
   breath
She looks and gladdeneth.
She holds her hands, the shape holds out
   hands too;
She stoops more near to view,
And it too stoopeth looking wild and sly;
Whereat, with merry cry,
She stareth up, and fluttering onward flies
With gladness in her eyes..

But who is this who all alone lies deep
In heavy-lidded sleep?
A dark smile hovering on his bearded lips,
   His hunter's gun he grips,
And snores aloud where snakes and lizards
   run,
   His mighty limbs i' the sun
And his fair face within the shadow. See!
   His breath comes heavily
Like one's tired out with toil; and when in
   fear
   The Indian maid comes near,
And bendeth over him most wondering,
   The bright birds scream and sing,
The motes are madder in the ray, the snake
   Glides luminous in the brake,
The sunlight flashes fiery overhead,
   The wood-cat with eyes red
Crawleth close by, with her lithe crimson
   tongue
   Licking her clumsy young,
And, deep within the open prairie nigh,
   Hawks swoop and struck birds cry!

Dark maiden, what is he thou lookest on?
   O ask not, but begone!
Go! for his eyes are blue, his skin is white,
   And giant-like his height.
To him thou wouldst appear a tiny thing,
   Some small bird on the wing,
Some small deer to be kill'd ere it could fly,
   Or to be *tamed*, and die!—
O look not, look not, in the hunter's face,
   Thou maid of the red race,
He is a tame thing, thou art weak and wild,
   Thou lovely forest-child!
How should the deer by the great deer-
   hound walk,
   The wood-dove seek the hawk?—
Away! away! lest he should wake from rest,
   Fly, sun-bird, to thy nest!

Why doth she start, and backward softly
   creep?
He stirreth in his sleep—
Why doth she steal away with wondering
   eyes?
He stretches limbs, and sighs.
Peace! she hath fled—and he is all alone,
   While, with a yawn and groan,
The man sits up, rubs eyelids, grips his gun,
   Stares heavenward at the sun,
And cries aloud, stretching himself anew:
   '*Broad day,*—by all that's blue!'

II.

EUREKA.

ON the shores of the Atlantic,
Where the surge rolls fierce and frantic,
Where the mad winds cry and wrestle
With each frail and bird-like vessel,—
Down in Maine, where human creatures
Are amphibious in their natures,
And the babies, sons or daughters,
Float like fishes in the waters,—
Down in Maine, by the Atlantic,
Grew the Harts, of race gigantic,
And the tallest and the strongest
Was Eureka Hart, the youngest.

Like a bear-cub as a baby,
Rough, and rear'd as roughly as may be,
He had rudely grown and thriven
Till, a giant, six foot seven,
Bold and ready for all comers,
He had reach'd full thirty summers.
All his brethren, thrifty farmers,
Had espoused their rural charmers,
Settling down once and for ever
By the Muskeosquash River:
Thrifty men, devout believers,
Of the tribe of human *beavers*;
Life to them, with years increasing,
Was an instinct never-ceasing
To build dwellings multifarious
In the fashion called gregarious,
To be honest in their station,
And increase the population
Of the beavers! They, moreover,
Tho' their days were cast in clover,
Had the instinct of *secreting*;
Toiling hard while time was fleeting,
To lay by in secret places,
[Like the bee and squirrel races,]

Quiet stores of yellow money,
[Which is human nuts and honey.]

Tho' no flowers of dazzling beauty
In their ploughshare line of duty
Rose and bloom'd, still, rural daisies,
Such as every village raises,
From the thin soil of their spirits
Grew and throve. Their gentle merits,
Free of any gleam of passion,
Flower'd in an instructive fashion.
Quite convinced that life was fleeting
Every week they went to meeting,
Met and prayed to God in dozens,
Uncles, nephews, nieces, cousins,
Joining there in adoration,
All the beaver population !
From this family one creature,
Taller and more fair of feature,
Err'd and wander'd, slightly lacking
In the building, breeding, packing,
Tribal-instinct ; and would never
Settle down by wood or river,
Build a house or take a woman
In the pleasant fashion common
To his race ; evincing rather
Traces of some fiercer father,
Panther-like, to hunting given
In the eye of the blue heaven !
When beneath the mother's bosom
His great life began to blossom,
Haply round her winds were crying,
O'er her head the white clouds flying,
At her feet the wild waves flowing,
All things moving, coming, going,
And the motion and vibration
Reach'd the thing in embryoation,
On its unborn soul conferring
Endless impulse to be stirring,—
To be ever wandering, racing,
Bird-like, wave-like, chased or chasing !
Born beside the stormy ocean,
'Twas the giant's earliest notion
To go roaming on the billow,
With a damp plank for a pillow.
In his youth he went as sailor
With the skipper of a whaler ;
But in later life he better
Loved to feel no sort of fetter,
All his own free pathway mapping
In the forest,—hunting, trapping.
By great rivers, thro' vast valleys,
As thro' some enchanted palace

Ever bright and ever changing,
Many years he went a-ranging,—
Free as any wave, and only
Lonely as a cloud is lonely,
Floating in a void, surveying
Endless tracts for endless straying.

Pause a minute and regard him !
Years of hardships have not marr'd him.
Limbs made perfect, iron-solder'd,
Narrow-hipp'd and mighty-shoulder'd,
Whisker'd, bearded, strong and stately,
With a smile that lurks sedately
In still eyes of a cold azure,
Never lighting to sheer pleasure,
Stands he there, 'mid the green trees
Like the Greek god, Herakles.

Stay, nor let the bright allusion
Lead your spirit to confusion.
Tho' a wanderer, and a creature
Almost as a god in feature,
This man's nature was as surely
Soulless and instinctive purely,
As the natures of those others,
His sedater beaver-brothers ;
Nothing brilliant, bright, or frantic,
Nothing maidens style romantic,
Flash'd his slow brain morn or night
Into spiritual light !

As waves run, and as clouds wander,
With small power to feel or ponder,
Roam'd this thing in human clothing,
Intellectually—nothing !
Further in his soul receding,
Certain signs of beaver-breeding
Kept his homely wits in see-saw ;
Part was Jacob, part was Esau ;
No revolter ; a believer
In the dull creed of the beaver ;
Strictly moral ; seeing beauty
In the ploughshare line of duty ;
Loving nature as beasts love it,
Eating, drinking, tasting of it,
With no wild poetic gleaming,
Seldom shaping, never dreaming ;
Beaver with a wandering craze,
Walked Eureka in God's ways.

Now ye know him, now ye see him ;
Nought from beaver-blood can free him ;
Yet stand by and shrewdly con him,
While a wild light strikes upon him,

While a gleam of glory finds him,
Flashes in his eyes and blinds him,
Shapes his mind to its full measure,
Raising him, in one mad pleasure,
'Spite the duller brain's control,
To the stature of a SOUL!

III.
THE CAPTURE.

The wild wood rings, the wild wood gleams,
The wild wood laughs with echoes gay;
Thro' its green heart a bright beck streams,
Sparkling like gold in the sun's beams,
But creeping, like a silvern ray,
Where hanging boughs make dim the day.
Hush'd, hot, and Eden-like all seems,
And onward thro' the place of dreams
Eureka Hart doth stray.

Strong, broad-awake, and happy-eyed,
With the loose tangled light for guide,
He wanders, and at times doth pass
Thro' open glades of gleaming grass,
With spiderwort and larkspur spread,
And great anemones blood-red;
On every side the forest closes,
The myriad trees are interlaced,
Starr'd with the white magnolia roses,
And by the purple vines embraced,
Beneath on every pathway shine
The fallen needles of the pine;
Around are dusky scented bowers,
Bridged with the glorious lian-flowers.
Above, far up thro' the green trees,
The palm thrusts out its fan of green,
Which softly stirs in a soft breeze,
Far up against the heavenly sheen.

And all beneath the topmost palm
Is sultry shade and air of balm,
Where, shaded from the burning rays,
Scream choirs of parroquets and jays;
Where in the dusk of dream is heard
The shrill cry of the echo-bird;
And on the grass, as thick as bees,
Run mocking-birds and wood-doves small
Pecking the blood-red strawberries,
And fruits that from the branches fall;
All rising up with gleam and cry,
When the bright snake glides hissing by,
Springs from the grass, and, swift as light,
Slips after the chameleons bright

From bough to bough, and here and there
Pauses and hangs in the green air,
Festoon'd in many a glistening fold,
Like some loose chain of gems and gold.

Smoke from a mortal pipe is blent
With cedar and acacia scent:
Phlegmatically relishing,
Eureka smokes; from every tree
The wood-doves brood, the sun-birds sing,
The forest doth salute its King,
The monarch Man,—but what cares he?
His eyes are dull, his soul in vain
Hears the strange tongues of his domain,
No echo comes to the soft strain
From the dull cavern of his brain.

But hark! what quick and sparkling cry
Darts like a fountain to the sky?
How, human voices! strangely clear,
They burst upon the wanderer's ear.
He stops, he listens—hark again,
Wild rippling laughter rises plain!

O'er his fair face a look of wonder
Is spreading—' Injins here—by thunder!'
He cocks his gun, and stands to hear,
Sets his white teeth together tight,
Then, silent-footed as the deer,
Creeps to the sound. The branches bright
Thicken around him; with quick flight
The doves and blue-birds gleam away,
Shooting in showers from spray to spray.
A thicket of a thousand blooms,
Green, rose, white, blue, one rainbow glow,
Closes around him; strange perfumes,
Crush'd underfoot in the rich glooms,
Load the rich air as he doth go;
The harmless snakes around him glow
With emerald eyes; lithe arms of vine
Trip him and round his neck entwine,
Bursting against his stained skin
Their grapes of purple glossy-thin.
But still the rippling laughter flows
Before him as he creeps and goes,
Till suddenly, with a strange look,
He crouches down in a green nook,
Crouches and gazes from the bowers,
Curtain'd and cover'd up in flowers.

O, what strange sight before him lies?
Why doth he gaze with sparkling eyes
And beating heart? Deep, bright, and cool,
Before him gleams a crystal pool,

C C

Fed by the beck: and o'er its brim
Festoons of roses mirror'd dim
Hang drooping low on every side;
   And glorious moths and dragon-flies
Hover above, and gleaming-eyed
   The stingless snake hangs blossom-wise,
In loose folds sleeping. Not on these
Gazes Eureka thro' the trees:
Snake never made such smiles to grace
His still blue eyes and sun-tann'd face,
And never flower, howe'er so fair,
Would fix that face to such a stare.
And yet like gleaming water-snakes
   They wind and wanton in the pool.
Above their waists in flickering flakes
The molten sunlight slips and shakes;
   Beneath, their gleaming limbs bathe cool.
One floats above with laughter sweet,
And splashes silver with her feet;
One clinging to the drooping boughs
   Leans back, and lets her silken hair
Rain backward from her rippling brows,
   While on her shoulders dark and bare
Blossoms fall thick and linger there
Nestling and clinging. To the throat
Cover'd, one dark-eyed thing doth float,
Her face a flower, her locks all wet,
Tendrils and leaves around it set;
O sight most strangely beautiful,
Three Indian Naiads in a pool!

Eureka, be it understood,
Though beaver-born, is flesh and blood,
And what he saw in day's broad gold
Was stranger far a thousand fold,
Than that wild scene bold Tam O'Shanter
In Scotland saw one winter night,
(Ah with the Scottish Bard to canter,
On Pegasus to Fame instanter,
   Singing one song so trim and tight!)
He look'd, and look'd, like Tam; like him.
On the most fair of face and limb
Fixing most long his wondering eye;
For I like greater bards should lie,
If I averr'd that all and one
Who sported there beneath the sun,
Were gloriously fair of face;
But they were women of red race,
Clad in the most bewitching dress,
Their own unconscious loveliness;
And tho' their beauty might not be
   Perfect and flawless, they were fine,

Bright-eyed, red-lipp'd, made strong and
   In many a cunning curve and line
A sculptor would have deem'd divine.
Not so the rest, who all around
With fierce eyes squatted on the ground,
Nodding approval:—squaws and crones
Clapping their hands with eager groans.
These were the witches, I might say,
Of this new tropic Alloway.
[As for the Devil—even *he*
   Was by the Serpent represented
Swinging asleep from a green tree,—
   Reflected, gloriously painted,
In the bright water where the three
Laugh'd and disported merrily.]

But chiefly poor Eureka gazed,
Trembling, dumb-stricken, and amazed,
On the most beautiful of all,
   Who standing on the water-side,
A perfect shape queenly and tall
   Stood in the sun erect, and dried
Her gleaming body head to feet
In one broad ray of golden heat.
Naked she stood, but her strange sheen
Of beauty clad her like a queen,
And beaming rings of yellow gold
Were round her wrists and ankles roll'd,
And on her skin Eureka scann'd
A symbol bright as of a brand
Held burning in a human hand.

Smiling, she spake in a strange tongue,
And eager laughter round her rung,
While wading out all lustrous-eyed
She sat upon the water-side,
And pelted merrily the rest
With blossoms bright and flowers of jest

Ah, little did Eureka guess,
While wondering at her loveliness,
The same fair form had softly crept
And look'd upon him while he slept,
And thought him (*him!* the man of Mai
Civilizee with beaver-brain!)
Beauteous, in passion's first wild beam,
Beyond all Indian guess or dream!

Eureka Hart, though tempted more
Than e'er was mortal man before,
Did not like Tam O'Shanter break
   The charm with mad applause or call
Too wise for such a boor's mistake,
   He held his tongue, observing all;

But while the hunter forward leant,
Sharing the glorious merriment,
He moved a little unaware
    The better to behold the sport,
And lo! upon the heavy air
Off went his gun with sharp report,
And while the bullet past his ear
    Whizz'd quick, he stagger'd with the shock,
And with one scream distinct and clear
Rose the red women in a flock.
The naked bathers stood and scream'd,
The brown squaws cried, their white teeth gleam'd;
And ere he knew, with startled face
He stagger'd to the open space;
The sharp vines tript him, and, confounded,
He stumbled, grasping still his gun,—
And, by the chattering choir surrounded,
    Half dazed, lay lengthways in the sun.

As when a clumsy grizzly bear
Breaks on a dove-cot unaware,
As when some snake, unwieldy heap,
Drops from a pine-bough, half asleep,
Plump in the midst of grazing sheep;—
Even so into the women-swarm
Suddenly fell the giant's form!
They leapt, they scream'd, they closed, they scatter'd,
Some fled, some stood, all call'd and chatter'd,
And to the man in his amaze
Innumerable seem'd as jays
And parroquets in the green ways.
Had they been men, despite their throng,
In sooth he had lain still less long;
But somehow in the stars 'twas fated,
He for a space was *fascinated*!
And ere he knew what he should do,
All round about him swarm'd the crew,
Sharp-eyed, quick-finger'd, and, despite
His struggling, clung around him tight;
Half choked, half smother'd by embraces,
In a wild mist of arms and faces,
He stagger'd up; in vain, in vain!
Hags, squaws, and maidens in a chain
Clung round him, and with quicker speed
Than ye this running rhyme can read,
With tendrils tough as thong of hide,
Torn from the trees on every side,
In spite of all his strength, the band
Had bound the Giant foot and hand.

IV.
THRO' THE WOOD.

Through the gleaming forest closes,
Where on white magnolia-roses
Light the dim-draped queen reposes,
    Lo, they lead the captive Giant.

Shrieking shrill as jays around him,
They have led him, they have bound him,
With a wreath of vine-leaves crown'd him,
    Which he weareth, half defiant.

If their ears could hear him swearing!
Of his oaths he is not sparing,
While, with hands sharp-claw'd for tearing,
    Hags and beldams burn to rend him.

If the younger, prettier creatures
Heard that tallest of beseechers,
While he pleads with frantic features!
    But they do *not* comprehend him.

In their Indian tongue they're crying,
From the forest multiplying,
Mocking, murmuring, leaping, flying,
    While he shouts out, 'D—— the women!'

All his mighty strength is nothing:
Like a ship, despite his loathing,
Mid these women scant of clothing
    He is tossing, struggling, screaming.

Crown'd like Bacchus on he passes,
O'er deep runlets, through great grasses,
While [like flies around molasses]
    Fair and foul are round him humming!

Half a day they westward wander,
Stopping not to rest or ponder;
Then the forest ends; and yonder
    Wild dogs bark to hear them coming.

Cluster'd in an open clearing
Stand the wigwams they are nearing,
Bark the dogs, a strange foot fearing,
    Low the cattle,—straight before them.

Out into the sunlight leaping,
There they see the wigwams sleeping,
With a blue smoke upward creeping,
    And the burning azure o'er them!

All is still, save for the screaming
Children from the wigwams streaming,
All is still and sweet to seeming,
    Not a man's face forward thrusting.

Thinks Eureka, ' This looks stranger—
Ne'er a man—then double danger ;
Many a year I've been a ranger,—
    Woman's mercy put no trust in !'

As he speaks in trepidation,
All his heart in palpitation,
He is fill'd with admiration
    At a vision wonder-laden.

From the largest wigwam, slowly,
While the women-band bow lowly,
Comes an old man white and holy,
    Guided gently by a maiden !

V.

THE RED TRIBE.

Ninety long years had slowly shed
Their snows upon the patriarch's head,
And on a staff of ash he leant,
Shaking and bending as he went.
His face, sepulchral, long, and thin,
Was shrivell'd like a dried snake's skin,
And on the cheeks and forehead dark
Tattoo'd was many a livid mark,
And in the midst his eyeballs white
Roll'd blankly, seeing not the light ;
And when he listen'd in his place
    You saw at once that he was *blind*,
For with a visionary grace
    Dim mem'ries moved from his own mind,
And the wild waters of his face
    Waved in a wondrous wind.

From an artistic point of sight,
The aged man was faultless quite ;
Albeit the raiment he did wear
Was somewhat hybrid ; for example,
A pair of pantaloons threadbare
Match'd strangely with his Indian air,
And blanket richly wrought and ample ;
And, though perchance not over clean,
He had a certain gentle mien
Kindly and kingly ; and a smile
Complacent in the kingly style,
Yet fraught with strangely subtle rays,
The lingering light of other days :—
Brightness and motion such as we
Trace in the trouble of the Sea,
When the long stormy day is sped,
And in the last light dusky-red
The waves are sinking, one by one.

But she who led him !—In the sun
She gleam'd beside him, like a rose
That by a dark sad water grows
And trembles. In a moment's space
Eureka recognised the face !
'Twas hers, who stood most beautiful,
Queen of those bathers in the pool !
But her bright locks were braided now
Around her clear and glistening brow,
And on her limbs she wore a dress
Less rich than her own loveliness.
From the artistic point of view,
The maiden's dress was faultless too,
But, look'd at closely, not so rare
As white-skinn'd maid would wish to wear
'Twas coarsest serge of sullen dye,
Albeit embroider'd curiously ;
And the few ornaments she wore
Were trifles valueless and poor ;—
Their merit, let us straight confess,
And all the merit of her dress,
Was that they form'd for eyes to see
Nimbus enough of drapery
And ornament, just to suggest
The costume that became her best—
Her own brave beauty. She just wore
Enough for modesty—no more.
She was not, as white beauties seem,
Smother'd, like strawberries in cream,
With folds of silk and linen. No !
The Indians wrap their babies so,
And *we* our women ; who, alas !
Waddle about upon the grass,
Distorted, shapeless, smother'd, choking,
Hideous, and horribly provoking,
Because we long, without offence,
To tear the mummy-wrappings thence,
And show the human form enchanting
That 'neath the fatal folds is panting !

She was a shapely creature, tall,
And slightly form'd, but plump withal,—
Shapely as deer are—finely fair
As creatures nourish'd by warm air,
And luscious fruits that interfuse
Something of their own glorious hues,
And the rich odour that perfumes them,
Into the body that consumes them.
She had drank richness thro' and thro'
As the great flowers drink light and dew ;

THE CAPTURE OF EUREKA HART.

And she had caught from wandering streams
Their restless motion ; and strange gleams
From snakes and flowers that glow'd around
Had stolen into her blood, and found
Warmth, peace, and silence ; and, in brief,
Her looks were bright beyond belief
Of those who meet in the green ways
The rum-wreck'd squaws of later days.

[I would be accurate, nor essay
Again in Cooper's pleasant way
A picture highly wrought and splendid
Of the red race whose pride has ended.
Nor here by contrast err : indeed,
The red man is of Esau's seed,
Hath Esau's swiftness, and, I guess,
Much, too, of Esau's loveliness.
A thousand years in the free wild
He fought and hunted, leapt and smiled ;
A million impulses and rays
Shot thro' his spirit's tangled ways,
Working within his dusky frame
As in a storm-cloud worketh flame;
Shaping his strength as years did roll
Into the semblance of his soul.
Slowly his shape and spirit caught
The living likeness wonder-fraught,
The golden, many coloured moods
Of those free plains and pathless woods ;
Those blooms that burst, those streams that
    run
One changeless rainbow in the sun !
Unto the hues of this rich clime
His nature was subdued in time ;
And he became as years increased
A glorious animal, at least.]

Soon like a mist did disappear
Eureka Hart's first foolish fear,
For courteously the chief address'd him,
  In English speech distinct tho' broken,
Bade them unloose and cease to pest him,
  And further, smiling and soft spoken,
Inquired his country and his name,
Whither he fared and whence he came.
Eureka, from the withes released,
Shook himself like a bright-eyed beast,
And mutter'd ; then, meeting the look
Of that bright naïad of the brook,
Blush'd like a shamefaced boy, while she
Stood gazing on him silently,
With melancholy orbs whose flame
Confused his soul with secret shame.

In a brief answer and explicit,
He told the cause of his strange visit.
The old chief smiled and whisper'd low
  Into the small ear of the maiden :
Her large eyes fell, and with a glow
  Of dark, deep rose her face was laden.
Then, like a sound of many waters,
Innumerable screams and chatters,
The voices of the women-band
  Broke out in passion and in power ;
But, at the raising of his hand,
  Ceased, like the swift cease of a shower.

Full soon Eureka saw and knew
That the Dark Dame who favours few
Had brought him to a friendly place,
Where, far from cities, a mild race
Of happy Indians spent their days
'Mid pastures and well-water'd ways.
An ancient people strong and good,
With something sacred in their blood ;
Scatter'd and few, to strangers kind ;
Wise in the ways of rain and wind ;
Peaceful when pleased, bloody when roused,
They dwelt there comfortably housed ;
And in those gardens ever fair,
Hunted and fish'd with little care.
Just then their braves were roaming bound
On an adjacent hunting-ground ;
And all the population then
Were women wild and aged men.—
But he, that old man blind and tall,
Was a great King, and Chief of all ;
And she who led him was by birth
His grandchild, dearest thing on earth
To his dusk age ; and dear tenfold
  Because no other kin had she,—
Since sire and mother both lay cold
  Under Death's leafless Upas-tree.

Enough ! here faltereth my first song :
  Eureka, still in secret captured,
In that lost Eden lingers long,
  And his big bosom beats enraptured.
Long days and nights speed o'er him there ;
What binds him *now* ? a woman's hair !
What doth he see ? a woman's eyes
  Above him luminously rise !
What doth he kiss ? a woman's mouth
Sweeter than spice-winds of the south !
By golden streams he lies full blest,
And Red Rose blossoms on his breast.

O love! love! love! whose spells are shed
On bodies black, white, yellow, red—
Flame of all matter,—flower of clay,—
Star of pangenesis ;—but stay !
A theme of so divine a tone
Must have a canto of its own !

PART II.
RED ROSE.

I.
ERYCINA RIDENS.

O LOVE ! O spirit of being !
  O wonderful secret of breath,
Sweeter than hearing or seeing,
  Sadder than sorrow or death.

Earth with its holiest flavour,
  Life with its lordliest dower,
The fruit's strange essence and flavour,
  Bloom and scent of the flower.

[Thus might a modern poet,
  O Aphrodite, uptake
His fanciful flute and blow it,
  And wail the echoes awake !]

O love, love, Aphrodite,
  Cytherea divine,
I hold you fever'd and flighty,
  And seek a pleasanter shrine.

Yet hither, O spirit fervent,
  Just to help me along,
Forget I am not thy servant,
  And blow in the sails of my song.

For lo ! 'tis a situation
  Caused by thyself, 'twould seem ;
The old, old foolish sensation,
  Two lovers lost in a dream.

O the wonder and glory,
  Bright as Creation's burst !
O the ancestral story,
  Old as Adam the first !

Flame, and fervour, and fever,
  Flashing from morning to night,
Alliteration for ever
  Of love, and longing, and light.

How should the story vary?
  How the song be new?
Music and meaning marry?
  'Tis love, love, love, all thro' !

As it was in the beginning,
  Is, and ever shall be !
Loving, and love for the winning,
  Love, and the soul set free.

[An invocation like this is
  Need not be over-wise ;
Who shall interpret kisses?
  What is the language of eyes?]

Again a man and a woman
  Feeling the old blest thing,
Better than voices human
  A bird on the bough could sing.

Only a sound is wanted,
  Merry, and happy, and loud,—
Such as the lark hath panted
  Up in the golden cloud.

Lips, and lips to kiss them ;
  Eyes, and eyes to behold ;
Hands, and hands to press them ;
  Arms, and arms to enfold.

The love that comes to the palace,
  That comes to the cottage door ;
The ever-abundant chalice
  Brimming for rich and poor ;

The love that waits for the winning,
  The love that ever is free,
That was in the world's beginning,
  Is, and ever shall be !

II.
LOG AND SUNBEAM.

As a pine-log prostrate lying,
  Slowly thro' its knotted skin
Feels the warm revivifying
  Spring-time thrill and tremble in ;
As a pine-log, strong and massive,
Feels the light and lieth passive,
While a Sunbeam, coming daily,
Creeps upon its bosom gaily ;
Warms the bark with quick pulsations,
Warms and waits each day in patience,
While the green begins to brighten,
And the sap begins to heighten,—

Till at last from its hard bosom
Suddenly there slips a blossom
Green as emerald!—then another!
    Then a third! then more and more!
Till the soft green bud-knots smother
    What was sapless wood before;
Till the thing is consecrated
    To the spirit of the Spring,
Till the love for all things fated
    Burns and beautifies the thing;—
And the wood-doves sit and con it,
    And the squirrels from on high
Fluttering drop their nuts upon it,
    And the bee and butterfly
Find it pleasant to alight there,
    And taps busy morn and night there
Many a bird with golden beak;
    Till, since all has grown so bright there,
It would cry (if Logs could speak),
'Sunbeam, sunbeam, I'm your debtor!
    I was fit for firewood nearly,
I'm considerably better,
    And I *love* you, Sunbeam, dearly!'

. . . Thou, Eureka, wast the wood!
    She, the Sunbeam of the Spring,
Vivifying thy dull blood
    Past thy mind's imagining!
Till the passion of her loving,
    Seething forth with ardours frantic,
Brought the buds forth, set thee moving,
    Made thee almost look romantic.

'O would some power the giftie gie us
    To see oursels as others see us!'
Sang the wise ploughman in his power.
    And yet, Eureka, had sweet Heaven
To thee her wondrous 'giftie' given
    To see thyself as seen that hour,
To know thy features as *she* knew them,
    To see thy shape as *she* perceived it;
To see thine eyes, and thro' and thro' them,
    Into thy Soul as she conceived it;
Either thy blood had run mad races,
    And driven thee to some maniac action;
Or (what more likely in the case is)
    Thy wits had frozen to stupefaction!

For never god in olden story,
    When the gods had honour due,
Gather'd brighter guise and glory,
    In an adoring mortal's view.
Let me own it, though thy nature
    Was sedate and beaver-bred,

As a god thou wert in stature,
    Fair of face and proud of tread;
And thine eyes were luminous glasses,
    And thy face a glorious scroll,
And the radiant light that passes
    O'er the dumb flowers and the grasses,
Caught thy gaze and *look'd* like Soul;
    And the animal vibration
Throbbing in thee at her touch,
    The wild earthly exaltation,
Beasts and birds can feel as much,
    Radiating and illuming
Every fibre of thy flesh,
    Made thee beautiful and blooming,
Great and glorious, fair and fresh;
    Fit it seem'd for love to yearn to,
For a fairer Soul than thine,
    Morning, noon, and night to burn to,
In a flash that felt divine.
Her tall white chief, whom God had brought her
    From the far-off Big-Sea Water!
Her warrior of the pale races,
    With wise tongues and paintless faces;
More than mortal, a great creature,
    Soft of tongue, and fine of feature;
As the wind that blew above her
    O'er the hunting-fields of azure,
As the stately clouds that hover
    In the air that pants for pleasure,
Full of strength and motion stately,
    Were thy face and form unto her;
And thy blue eyes pleased her greatly,
    And thy clear voice trembled thro' her;
And for minute after minute
    She did pore upon thy face,
Read the lines and guess within it
    The great spirit of thy race;
And thou seemedst altogether
    A great creature, fair of skin,
Born in scenes of softer weather,
    Nobler than her savage kin!

As a peasant maiden homely
    Might regard some lordly wooer,
Find each feature trebly comely
    From the pride it stoops unto her;
Thus, Eureka, she esteem'd thee
    Fairer for thy finer blood;
She revered thee, loved thee, deem'd thee
    Wholly beautiful and good!
And her day-dream ne'er was broken,
    As some mortal day-dreams are,

By a word or sentence spoken
  In thy coarse vernacular.
For she could not speak a dozen
  Words as used by the white nation !
And thy speech seem'd finely chosen,
  Since she made her own translation,
Scarce a syllable quite catching,
  Yet, upon thy bosom leaning,
Out of ever sentence snatching
  Music with its own sweet meaning.

Powers above ! the situation's
  Psychological, I swear !
How express the false relations
  Of this strange-assorted pair ?
Happy, glorious, self-deluded,
  On the handsome face she brooded,
Ne'er by word or gesture driven
  From her day-dream sweet as heaven.
In her native language for him
  She had warrior's names most sweet :
And she loved and did adore him,
  Falling fawn-like at his feet ;
More, the rapturous exultation
  Struck *him* ! blinded *him*, in turn !
Till with passionate sensation
  Body and brain began to burn ;—
And he yielded to the bursting,
  Burning, blinding, hungering, thirsting,
Passion felt by beasts and men !
  And his eyes caught love and rapture,
And he held her close in capture,
  Kissing lips—that kiss'd again !

III.
NUPTIAL SONG.

Where were they wedded ? In no Temple
  of ice
Built up by human fingers ;
The floor was strewn with flowers of fair
  device,
  The wood-birds were the singers.

Who was the Priest ? The priest was the
  still Soul,
  Calm, gentle, and low-spoken ;
He read a running brooklet like a scroll,*
  And trembled at the token.

What was the service ? 'Twas the service read
  When Adam's faith was plighted !
The tongue was silent, but the lips rose-red
  In silence were united.

Who saw it done ? The million starry eyes
  Of one ecstatic Heaven.
Who shared the joy ? The flowers, the
  trees, the skies
  Thrill'd as each kiss was given.

Who was the Bride ? A spirit strong and
  true,
  Beauteous to human seeing,—
So't elements of flesh, air, fire, and dew,
  Blent in one Rose of being.

What was her consecration ? Innocence !
  Pure as the wood-doves round her,
Nothing she knew of rites—the strength
  intense
  Of God and Nature found her.

As freely as maids give a lock away,
  She gave herself unto him.
What was the Bridegroom ? Clay, and
  common clay,
  Yet the wild joy slipt through him.

Hymen, O Hymen ! By the birds was shed
  A matrimonial cadence !
Da nuces! Squirrels strew'd the nuts, in-
  stead
  Of rosy youths and maidens !

Eureka, yea, Eureka was to blame—
  He was an erring creature :
Uncivilised by one wild flash of flame
  He waver'd back on Nature.

He kiss'd her lips, he drank her breath in
  bliss,
  He drew her to his bosom :
As a clod kindles at the Spring's first kiss
  His being burst to blossom !

Who rung the bells ? The breeze, the
  merry breeze,
  Set all in bright vibration :
Clear, sweet, yet low, there trembled
  through the trees
  The nuptial jubilation !

IV.
ARRETEZ !

O'er this joy I dare not linger :
Stands a Shape with lifted finger
Crying in a low voice, 'Singer !
  Far too much of Eve and Adam.

'Details of this dark connection
I desire not for inspection!'
And the Bard, with genuflexion,
Answers, ' I obey thee, Madam!'

Stands the Moral Shape reproving,
While I linger o'er this loving;
Cries the voice, ' Pass on! be moving!
We are virtuous, here to nor'ward!'

Constable, I force cessation
To my flood of inspiration;
Such a theme for adumbration!
I resign it, and move forward.

V.
THE FAREWELL.

Love, O love! thou bright and burning
Weathercock for ever turning;
Gilded vane, fix'd for our seeing
On the highest spire of being;
Symbol, indication; reeling
Round to every wind of feeling;
Only pointing some sad morrow,
In one sudden gust of sorrow,
Sunset-ward, where redly, slowly,
Passion sets in melancholy.

In the wood-ways, roof'd by heaven,
Were the nuptial kisses given;
In the dark green, moonbeam-haunted
Forest; in the bowers enchanted
Where the fiery specks are flying,
And the whip-poor-will is crying;
Where the heaven's open blue eye
Thro' the boughs broods dark and dewy,
And the white magnolia glimmers
Back the light in starry tremors;
Where the acacia in the shady
Silence trembles like a lady
Scented sweet and softly breathing;
There, amid the brightly wreathing,
Blooming branches, did they capture
Love's first consecrated rapture.

Pure she came to him, a maiden
Innocent as Eve in Eden,
Tho' in secret; for she dreaded
Wrath of kinsmen tiger-headed,
In whose vision, fierce and awful,
Love for white men was unlawful.
Yet in this her simple reason
Knew no darker touch of treason

Than dost thou, O white and dainty
English maid of sweet-and-twenty,
When from guardian, father, brother,
[Harsh protectors, one or t'other,]
Off you trip, self-handed over
To your chosen lord and lover,
Tears of love and rapture shedding
In the hush of secret wedding.

Now from these lost days Elysian,
Modestly I drop my vision!
Rose the wave supreme and splendid,
To a tremulous crest, and ended,
Falling, falling, one sad morrow,
In a starry spray of sorrow.

Whether 'twas by days or hours,
Weeks or months, in those bright bowers,
They their gladness counted,—whether
Like the one day's summer weather
At the pole, their bliss upstarted,
Brighten'd, blacken'd, and departed,—
I relate not; all my story
Is, that soon or late this glory
Fell and faded. After daylight
Came an eve of sad and gray light;
There were tears—wild words were spoken,
Down the cup was dash'd, and broken.

First came danger,—eyeballs fiery
Watch'd the pair in fierce inquiry;
Secret footsteps dodged the lovers;
As a black hawk slowly hovers
O'er the spot amid the heather
Where the gray birds crouch together,
Hung Suspicion o'er the places
Where they sat with flaming faces.
Next came—what d'ye call the dreary
Heavy-hearted thing and weary,
In old weeds of joy bedizen'd?
By the shallow French 'tis christen'd
Ennui! Ay, the snake that grovels
In a host of scrofulous novels,
Leper even of the leprous
Race of serpents vain and viprous,
Bred of slimy eggs of evil,
Sat on by the printer's devil,
Last, to gladden absinthe-lovers,
Born by broods in paper covers!

After the great wave of madness,
Ennui came; and tho' in gladness
Still the Indian maiden's nature
Clung round the inferior creature,

Though with burning, unconsuming,
Deathless love *her* heart was blooming,
He grew weary, and his passion
In a dull evaporation
Slowly lessen'd, till caressing
Grew distracting and distressing.
Conscience waken'd in a fever,
Just a day too late, as ever;
He remember'd, one fine day,
His relations far away.

All the beavers! the deceiver!
After all, he *was* a beaver
Born and bred, tho' the unchanging
Dash of wild blood kept him ranging;
Beaver-conscience, now awaken'd,
Since the first true bliss had slacken'd,
Whisper'd with a sad affection,
'Fie! it is a strange connection!
Is it worthy? Can it profit?
Sits the world approving of it?'
While another whisper said,
'*You*'re a white man! She is red!'
Ne'ertheless he seem'd to love her,
Watch'd her face and bent above her,
Fondly thinking, 'Now, I wonder
If the world would blame my blunder?
If her skin were only whiter,
If her manners were politer,
I would take her with me nor'ward,
Wed her, cling to her thenceforward,
Clothe her further, just a tittle,
Live respectable and settle!'
She was silent, as be brooded
Handsome-faced and beaver-mooded,
Thinking, 'Now my chief is seeming
Where the fires of fight are streaming!
O, how great and grand his face is,
Lit with light of the pale races!'
And she bent her brows before him,
Kiss'd his hands, and did adore him,
And she waited in deep duty;
While her eyes of dazzling beauty,
Like two jewels ever streaming
  Broken yet unceasing rays,
Watch'd him as in beaver-dreaming
  He would walk in the green ways.

Still he seem'd to her a splendid
Creature, but his trance had ended;
More and more, thro' ever seeing
Red skins round him, he lost patience,
More and more the hybrid being
  Sigh'd for civilised relations;

For Eureka Hart, tho' wholly
Of a common social mind,
Narrow-natured, melancholy,
Hated *ties* of any kind;—
Yet if any tie could hold him
To a place or to a woman,
'Twould be one the world had told him
Was respectable and common.
Here, then, hemm'd in by a double
Dark dilemma, he found trouble,
And with look a Grecian painter
Would have given to a god,
Feeling passion still grow fainter,
Thought, 'I reckon things look odd!
Wouldn't Parson Pendon frown,
If he knew, in Drowsietown?'

As he spoke he saw the village
Rising up with tilth and tillage,
Saw the smithy, like an eye
Flaming bloodshot at the sky,
Saw the sleepy river flowing,
  Saw the swamps burn in the sun,
Saw the people coming, going,
  All familiar, one by one.
'There the plump old Parson goes,
Silver buckles on his toes.
Broad-brimm'd beaver on his head,
Clean-shaved chin, and cheek as red
As ripe pippins, kept in hay,
Polish'd on Thanksgiving day;
Black coat, breeches, all complete,
On the old mare he keeps his seat,
Jogging on with smiles so bright
To creation left and right.
There's the Widow Abner smiling
  At her door as he goes past,
Guess she thinks she looks beguiling,
  But he cuts along more fast.
There's Abe Sinker drunk as ever,
  There's the pigs all in the gutter,
There's the miller by the river,
  Broad as long and fat as butter.
See it all, so plain and pleasant,
  Just like life their shadows pass,
Wonder how they are at present?
  Guess they think *I*'m gone to grass!'
While this scene he contemplated,
  Sighing like a homeless creature,
Round him, brightly concentrated,
  Glow'd the primal fire of Nature!
Rainbow-hued and rapturous-colour'd,
  With one burning brilliant look

Flaming fix'd upon the dullard,
  Nature rose in wild rebuke !
Shower'd her blossoms round him, o'er him,
  Breathed warm breath upon his face,
Flash'd her flowers and fruits before him,
  Follow'd him from place to place ;
With wild jasmine and with amber
  She perfumed his sleeping chamber,
Hung around him happy hours
  With her arms of lustre-flowers,
Held to his in blest reposes
  Her warm breasts of living roses ;
Bade a thousand dazzling, crying,
  Living, creatures do him honour,
Stood herself, naked and sighing,
  With an aureole upon her ;
Then, with finger flashing brightly
  Pointing to her prime creation,—
Fruits and flowers and scents blent lightly
  In one dazzling adumbration,—
Cried unto him over and over,
  'See my child ! O love her, love her !
I eternal am, no comer
  In a feeble flush of summer,
Like the hectic colour flying
  Ot a maid love-sick and dying ;
Here no change, but ever burning
  Quenchless fire, and ceaseless yearning :
Endless exquisite vibration
  Sweet as love's first nuptial kiss,
One soft sob of strange sensation
  Flowering into shapes of bliss ;
And the brightest, O behold her
  With a changeless warmth like mine—
Love her ! In thy soul enfold her !
  Blend with *us*, and be divine !'
All in vain that fond entreating !
  Still Eureka's beaver-brain
Thought—'This climate's rather heating—
  Weather's cooler up in Maine !'

Yet no wonder Nature loved him,
  Sought to take his soul by storm,
Gloried when her meaning moved him,
  Clung in fondness round his form ;
For, in sooth, tho' unimpassion'd,
  Gloriously the man was fashion'd :
One around whose strength and splendour
  Women would have pray'd to twine,
As the Ilian loves to blend her
  Being with the beech or pine.
And his smile when she was present
  Was seraphic, full of spirit,

And his voice was low and pleasant,
  And her soul grew bright to hear it !
And when tall he strode to meet her,
  And his handsome face grew sweeter,
In her soul she thought, 'O being,
  Fair and gracious and deep-seeing,
White man, great man, far above me,
  What am *I*, that thou shouldst love me ?'

She had learnt him with lips burning
  (O for such a course of learning !)
Something of her speech,—'twas certain
  Quite enough to woo and flirt in ;
Words not easy of translation
  They transfused into sensation,
Soon discovering and proving,
  As a small experience teaches,
'Bliss' and 'kiss,' and other loving
  Words, are common to *all* speeches !
Ah, the rapture ! ah, the fleeting
  Follies of each fond, mad meeting !
Smiling with red lips asunder,
  Clapping hands at each fond blunder,
She instructed him right gaily
  In her Indian *patois* daily,
Sweetly from his lips it sounded,
  Help'd with those great azure eyes,
Till upon his heart she bounded
  Panting praise with laughs and cries.
'Twas a speech antique and olden,
  Full of gurgling notes, it ran
Like some river rippling golden
  Down a vale Arcadian ;
Like the voices of doves brooding ;
  Like a fountain's gentle moan ;
Nothing commonplace intruding
  On its regal monotone :
Sounds and symbols interblending
  Like the heave of loving bosoms ;
Consonants like strong boughs bending,
  Snowing vowels down like blossoms !
Faltering in this tongue, he told her,
  Sitting in a secret place,
While with bright head on his shoulder,
  Luminous-eyed, she watch'd his face,
How, tho' every hour grown fonder,
  Tho' his soul was still aflame,
Still, he sigh'd once more to wander
  To the clime from whence he came ;
Just once more to look upon it,
Just for one brief hour to con it,
Just to see his kin and others
  In the Town where they did dwell.

Just to say to his white brothers
  One farewell, a last farewell.
Then to hasten back unto her,
  And to live with her and die. . . ,
Sharp as steel his speech stabb'd thro' her,
  Cold she sat without a cry,
On her heart her small hand pressing,
  Breathing like a bird in pain,
Silent, tho' he smiled caressing,
  Kiss'd, but kissing not again.

Then she waken'd, like one waking
  From a trance, and with heart aching
Clung around him, as if dreading
  Lest some hand should snatch him thence!
Then, upon his bosom shedding
  Tears of ecstacy intense,
By her gods conjured him wildly
  Never, never to depart!
O how meekly, O how mildly,
  Answer'd back Eureka Hart!

But by slow degrees he coax'd her,
  Night by night, and day by day,
With such specious spells he hoax'd her
  That her first fear fled away.
Slow she yielded, still believing
  Not for long he'd leave her lonely;
For he told her, still deceiving,
  'Twas a *little journey* only.
Poor, dark bird! nought *then* knew she
  Of this world's geography!

Troubled, shaken, half-demented,
  Broken-hearted—she assented.
Since, by wind, and wave, and vapour,
  By the shapes of earth and skies;
By the white moon's ghostly taper,
  By the stars that like dead eyes
Watch it burning; by the mystic
  Motion of the winds and woods;
By all dark and cabalistic
  Shapes of tropic solitudes;
By the waters melancholy;
  By God's hunting-fields of blue;
By all things that she deem'd holy
  He had promised to be true!
Just to pay a flying visit
  To connections close at hand,
Then to haste with love undying
  Back unto that happy land.
'Twas enough! the Maid assented,
  Thinking sadly, in her pain,

' He will never be contented
  Till he sees them once again.
Thither, thither let him wander;
  When once more I feel his kiss,
His proud spirit will be fonder
  Since my love hath granted this!'

'Go!' she cried, and her dark features
  Kindled like a dying creature's,
And her heart rose, and her spirit
  Cried as if for God to hear it—
Wildly in her arms she press'd him
  To her bosom broken-hearted—
Call'd upon her gods, and blest him!
  And Eureka Hart departed.

VI.

THE PAPER.

Here should my second canto end—yet stay
Listen a little ere ye turn away.

By night they parted; and she cut by night
One large lock from his forehead, which
  with bright,
Warm lips she kiss'd; then kiss'd the lock
  of hair,
With one quick sob of passionate despair;
And he, with hand that shook a little now,
Still with that burning seal upon his brow,
While in that bitter agony they embraced,
He in her little hand a paper placed,
Whereon, at her fond prayer, he had writ
  plain,
'*Eureka Hart, Drowsietown, State of
  Maine.*'
'For,' thought he, 'I have promised soon
  or late
Hither to come again to her, my mate;
And I will keep my promise, sure, some day,
Unless I die or sicken by the way.
But no man knows what pathway he may
  tread,—
To-morrow—nay, ere dawn—I may be
  dead!
And she shall know, lest foul my fortune
  proves,
The name and country of the man she loves;
And since she wishes it, to cheer her heart,
It shall be written down ere I depart.'
And so it was; and while his kiss thrill'd
  thro' her,
With that loved lock of hair he gave it to
  her.

Aye, so it was; for in the woods at dawn
He from his pouch had an old letter drawn,
One leaf of which was blank, and this he
    took,
And smiling at the woman's wondering look,
While quietly she murmur'd, ''Tis a charm!'
In hunter's fashion he had prick'd his arm,
And, having pen nor ink, had ta'en a spear
Of thorn for stylus, and in crimson clear,
His own heart's blood, had writ the words
    she sought.
And in that hour deep pity in him wrought,
And he believed that he his vows would
    keep,
Nor e'er be treacherous to a love so deep.
'See!' said he, as the precious words he
    gave,
'Keep this upon thy bosom, and be brave.
As sure as that red blood belong'd to me,
I shall, if I live on, return to thee.
If death should find me while thou here
    dost wait,
Thou canst at least make question of my fate
Of any white man whose stray feet may fare
Down hither, showing him the words writ
    there.'
All this he said to her with faltering voice
In broken Indian, and in words less choice;
And quite persuaded of his good intent,
Shoulder'd his gun with a gay heart, and
    went.

And in that paper, while her fast tears fell,
She wrapt the lock of hair she loved so well,
And thrust it on her heart; and with sick
    sight,
Watch'd his great figure fade into the night;
Then raised her hands to her wild gods,
    that sped
Above her in a whirlwind overhead,
And the pines rock'd in tempest, and her form
Bent broken with the breathing of the storm.

O little paper! Blurr'd with secret tears!
O blood-red charm! O thing of hopes and
    fears!
Between two worlds a link, so faint, so slight,
The two worlds of the red man and the
    white!
Lie on her heart and soothe her soul's sad
    pain!

'EUREKA HART, DROWSIETOWN, STATE
    OF MAINE.'

PART III.

WHITE ROSE.

I.

DROWSIETOWN.

O so drowsy! In a daze
Sweating 'mid the golden haze,
With its smithy like an eye
Glaring bloodshot at the sky,
And its one white row of street
Carpetted so green and sweet,
And the loungers smoking still
Over gate and window-sill;
Nothing coming, nothing going,
Locusts grating, one cock crowing,
Few things moving up or down,
All things drowsy—Drowsietown!

Thro' the fields with sleepy gleam,
Drowsy, drowsy steals the stream,
Touching with its azure arms
Upland fields and peaceful farms,
Gliding with a twilight tide
Where the dark elms shade its side;
Twining, pausing sweet and bright
Where the lilies sail so white;
Winding in its sedgy hair
Meadow-sweet and iris fair;
Humming as it hies along
Monotones of sleepy song;
Deep and dimpled, bright nut-brown,
Flowing into Drowsietown.

Far as eye can see, around,
Upland fields and farms are found,
Floating prosperous and fair
In the mellow misty air:
Apple-orchards, blossoms blowing
Up above,—and clover growing
Red and scented round the knees
Of the old moss-silvered trees.
Hark! with drowsy deep refrain,
In the distance rolls a wain;
As its dull sound strikes the ear,
Other kindred sounds grow clear—
Drowsy all—the soft breeze blowing,
Locusts grating, one cock crowing,
Cries like voices in a dream
Far away amid the gleam,
Then the waggons rumbling down
Thro' the lanes to Drowsietown.

Drowsy? Yea!—but idle? Nay!
Slowly, surely, night and day,
Humming low, well greased with oil,
Turns the wheel of human toil.
Here no grating gruesome cry
Of spasmodic industry ;
No rude clamour, mad and mean,
Of a horrible machine !
Strong yet peaceful, surely roll'd,
Winds the wheel that whirls the gold.
Year by year the rich rare land
Yields its stores to human hand—
Year by year the stream makes fat
Every field and meadow-flat—
Year by year the orchards fair
Gather glory from the air,
Redden, ripen, freshly fed,
Their bright balls of golden red.
Thus, most prosperous and strong,
Flows the stream of life along
Six slow days! wains come and go,
Wheat-fields ripen, squashes grow,
Cattle browse on hill and dale,
Milk foams sweetly in the pail,
Six days : on the seventh day
Toil's low murmur dies away—
All is husht save drowsy din
Of the waggons rolling in,
Drawn amid the plenteous meads
By small fat and sleepy steeds.
Folk with faces fresh as fruit
Sit therein or trudge afoot,
Brightly drest for all to see,
In their seventh-day finery :
Farmers in their breeches tight,
Snowy cuffs, and buckles bright ;
Ancient dames and matrons staid
In their silk and flower'd brocade,
Prim and tall, with soft brows knitted,
Silken aprons, and hands mitted ;
Haggard women, dark of face,
Of the old lost Indian race ;
Maidens happy-eyed and fair,
With bright ribbons in their hair,
Trip along, with eyes cast down,
Thro' the streets of Drowsietown.
Drowsy in the summer day
In the meeting-house sit they ;
'Mid the high-back'd pews they doze,
Like bright garden-flowers in rows ;
And old Parson Pendon, big
In his gown and silver'd wig,
Drones above in periods fine
Sermons like old-flavour'd wine—
Crusted well with keeping long
In the darkness, and not strong.
O! so drowsily he drones
In his rich and sleepy tones,
While the great door, swinging wide,
Shows the bright green street outside,
And the shadows as they pass
On the golden sunlit grass.
Then the mellow organ blows,
And the sleepy music flows,
And the folks their voices raise
In old unctuous hymns of praise,
Fit to reach some ancient god
Half asleep with drowsy nod.
Deep and lazy, clear and low,
Doth the oily organ grow !
Then with sudden golden cease
Comes a silence and a peace ;
Then a murmur, all alive,
As of bees within a hive ;
And they swarm with quiet feet
Out into the sunny street ;
There, at hitching-post and gate
Do the steeds and waggons wait.
Drawn in groups, the gossips talk,
Shaking hands before they walk :
Maids and lovers steal away,
Smiling hand in hand, to stray
By the river, and to say
Drowsy love in the old way—
Till the sleepy sun shines down
On the roofs of Drowsietown.
In the great marsh, far beyond
Street and building, lies the Pond,
Gleaming like a silver shield
In the midst of wood and field ;
There on sombre days you see
Anglers old in reverie,
Fishing feebly morn to night
For the pickerel so bright.
From the woods of beech and fir,
Dull blows of the woodcutter
Faintly sound ; and haply, too,
Comes the cat-owl's wild 'tuhoo!'
Drown'd by distance, dull and deep,
Like a dark sound heard in sleep ;—
And a cock may answer, down
In the depths of Drowsietown.

Such is Drowsietown—but nay !
Was, not *is*, my song should say—

Such *was* summer long ago
In this town so sleepy and slow.
Change has come: thro' wood and dale
Runs the demon of the rail,
And the Drowsietown of yore
Is not drowsy any more!

O so drowsy! In the haze
Of those long dead summer days,
Underneath the still blue sky
I can see the hamlet lie—
Like a river in a dream
Flows the little nut-brown stream;
Yet not many a mile away
Flashes foam and sprinkles spray,
Close at hand the green marsh flows
Into brackish pools and sloughs,
And with storm-wave fierce and frantic
Roars the wrath of the Atlantic.

Waken Drowsietown?—The Sea?
Break its doze and reverie?
Nay, for if it hears at all
Those unresisting waters call,
They are far enough, I guess,
Just to soothe and not distress.
When the wild nor'wester breaks,
And the sullen thunder shakes,
For a space the Town in fear,
Dripping wet with marsh and mere,
Quakes and wonders, and is found
With its ear against the ground
Listening to the sullen war
Of the flashing sea afar!
But the moment all is done
On its tear-drops gleams the sun,
Each rude murmur dies; and lo!
In a sleepy sunny glow,
'Mid the moist rays slanting down,
Once more dozes Drowsietown.

As the place is, drowsy-eyed
Are the folks that there abide;
Strong, phlegmatic, calm, revealing
No wild fantasies of feeling;
Loving sunshine; on the soil
Basking in a drowsy toil.
Mild and mellow, calm and clear,
Flows their life from year to year—
Each fulfils his drowsy labour,
Each the picture of his neighbour,
Each exactly, rich or poor,
What his father was before—

O so drowsy! In a gleam,
Far too steady to be Dream,
Flows their slow humanity
Winding, stea'ing, to the Sea.

Sea? What Sea? The Waters vast,
Whither all life flows at last,
Where all individual motion
Lost in one imperious ocean
Fades, as yonder river doth
In the great Sea at its mouth.
Ah! the mighty wondrous Deep,
'Tis so near;—yet half asleep,
Deaf to all its busy hum,
These calm people go and come;—
Quite forgetting it is nigh,
Save when hurricanes go by
With a ghostly wail o'erhead
Shrieking shrill—'Bury your dead!'
For a moment, wild-eyed, caught
In a sudden gust of thought,
Panting, praying, wild of face,
Stand the people of the place;
But, directly all is done,
They are smiling in the sun—
Drowsy, yet busy as good bees
Working in a sunny ease,
To and fro, and up and down,
Move the folks of Drowsietown.

II.

AFTER MEETING.

DEACON JONES.

Well, winter's over altogether;
  The loon's come back to Purley Pond;
It's all green grass and pleasant weather
  Up on the marsh and the woods beyond.
It's God Almighty's meaning clear
  To give us farmers a prosperous year;
Tho' many a sinner that I could mention
Is driving his ploughshare nowadays
Clean in the teeth of the Lord's intention,
  And spiling the land he ought to raise.

DEACON HOLMES.

I've drained the marsh by Simpson's building,
  Cleared out the rushes, and flag, and weed,
The ground's all juicy, and looks like yielding,
  And I'm puttin' it down in pip-corn seed.

How's Father Abel? Comin' round?
Glad the rheumatics have left him now.

DEACON JONES.

Summer's *his* med'cine; he'll soon be sound,
And spry as a squirrel on a bough.

BIRD CHORUS.

 Chickadee! chickadee!
 Green leaves on every tree!
 Over field, over foam,
 All the birds are coming home.
 Honk! honk! sailing low,
 Cried the gray goose long ago.
 Weet! weet! in the light
 Flutes the phœbe-bird so bright.
 Chewink, veery, thrush o' the wood,
  Silver treble raise together;
 All around their dainty food
  Ripens with the ripening weather.
 Hear, O hear!
 In the great elm by the mere
 Whip-poor-will is crying clear.

MOTHER ABNER.

And so it is! And so the news is true!
And your Eureka has returned to you;
I saw him in the church, and took a stare.
A Hart, aye every inch, the tallest there.
You'll hold the farm-land now, and keep
 things clear;
You wanted jest a man—Eureka's here.

WIDOW HART.

Well, I don't know. Eureka ain't no hand
At raising crops or looking after land;
It's been a bitter trial to me, neighbour,
To see his wandering ways and hate o'
 labour.
He's been abroad too much to care jest now
For white men's ways, and following the
 plough.

MOTHER ABNER.

He's a fine figure and a handsome face;
There ain't his ekal this day in the place.
And if he'd take a wife and settle down,
There's many a wench would jump in
 Drowsietown.
Ah! that's the only way to tie your son,
And now he's got the farm 'tis easy done;
There's Jez'bel Jones, and there's Euphe-
 mia Clem,
And Sarah Snowe,—they're all good
 matches, them.
And there's—why, there he goes, right
 down the flat,
Looks almost furrin' in that queer straw
 hat;
And who's that with him in the flower'd
 chintz dress?
Why, Phœbe Anna Cattison, I guess!
That little mite! How tiny and how prim
Trips little Phœbe by the side of him!
And when she looks up in his face, tehee!
It's like a chipmunk looking up a tree!

THE RIVER SINGS.

 O willow loose lightly
  Your soft long hair!
 I'll brush it brightly
  With tender care;
 And past you flowing
  I'll softly uphold
 Great lilies blowing
  With hearts of gold.
 For spring is beaming,
  The wind's in the south,
 And the musk-rat's swimming,
  A twig in its mouth,
 To built its nest
  Where it loves it best,
 In the great dark nook
  By the bed o' my brook.
 It's spring, bright spring,
  And blue-birds sing!
 And the fern is pearly
  All day long,
 And the lark rises early
  To sing a song.
The grass shoots up like fingers of fire,
And the flowers awake to a dim desire,
So willow, willow, shake down, shake down
 Your locks so silvern and long and slight;
For lovers are coming from Drowsietown,
And thou and I must be merry and
 bright!

PHŒBE ANNA.

This is the first fine day this year:
The grass is dry and the sky is clear;
The sun's out shining; up to the farm
It looks like summer; so bright and warm;
There's apple blooms on the boughs al-
 ready,
Long as your finger the corn-blades
 shoot,

And father thinks, if the sun keeps steady,
'Twill be a wonderful fall for fruit.
How do you like being here at home again?
Reckon you'd rather pack up and roam
  again!

EUREKA.

I'm sick o' roaming, I hate strange places;
  I've slep' too long in the woods and
  brakes;
It's pleasure seeing white folks' faces
  After the b'ars, and the birds, and the
  snakes.
This yer life is civilisation,
T'other's a heathen dissipation!
One likes to die where his father before him
Died, with the same sky shinin' o'er him.
I've been a wastrel and that's the truth,
  Earning nought but a sneer and a frown;
I've wasted the precious days o' youth,
  Instead of stopping and settling down.

PHŒBE ANNA.

But now the farm is your own to dwell in,
  You'll ne'er go back to the wilderness?

EUREKA.

Vaal! that's a question! There's no
  tellin';
  I ain't my own master quite, I guess.
Think I shall *have* to go some day,
And fix some business far away.
I—there's your mother beckonin' yonder,
  Looks kind o' huffish, you'd better run;
(*Alone, sotto voce*) That girl's a sort of a
  shinin' wonder,
The prettiest pout beneath the sun.

BIRD CHORUS.

Chickadee! chickadee!
  Green leaves on every tree;
  Winter goes, spring is here;
  Little mate, we loved last year.
Cheewink, veery, robin red,
  Shall we take another bride?
We have plighted, we are wed.
  Here we gather happy-eyed.
Little bride, little mate,
Shall I leave you desolate?
Men change; shall we change too?
Men change; but we are true.
If I cease to love thee best,
May a black boy take my nest.

EUREKA.

Soothin' it is, after so many a year,
To hear the Sabbath bells a-ringing clear,
The air so cool and soft, the sky so blue,
The place so peaceful and so well-to-do. . . .
Wonder what *she* is doing this same day?
Thinkin' o' me in her wild Injin way,
Listenin' and waitin', dreaming every
  minute
The door will open, and this child step in it.
Poor gal! I seem to feel her eyes so bright
A-followin' me about, morn, noon, and
  night!
Sometimes they make me start and thrill
  right thro'—
She was a splendid figure, and that's true!
Not jest like Christian women, fair and
  white,
A heap more startlin' and a deal more
  bright;
And as for looks, why many would prefer
That Phœbe Ann, or some white gal like
  her!
Don't know! *I've* got no call to judge;
  but see!
The little white wench is so spry and free!
And tho' she's but a mite, small as a mouse,
She'd look uncommon pretty in a house.
No business, tho', of mine—I've made my
  bed,
And I must lie in it, as I have said.
Ye . . . s, I'll go back—and stay—or bring
  her here,
But there's no call to hurry yet, that's clear.
She'll fret and be impatient for a while,
And go on in the wild mad Injin style;
But she can't know, for a clear heathen's
  sake,
The sort o' sacrifice I'm fix'd to make.
Some wouldn't do it; Parson there would
  say
It's downright throwing next world's chance
  away;
But I've made up my mind—It's fix'd at
  present;
And—there, let's try to think of something
  pleasant!

THE CAT-OWL.

Boohoo! boohoo!
  White man is not true;
  I have seen such wicked ways
  That I hide me all the days,

D D

And come from my hole so deep
While the white man lies asleep.
A misanthrope am I,
  And, tho' the skies are blue,
I utter my warning cry—
  Boohoo!
Boohoo! boohoo! boohoo!

THE LOON.
(Chuckling to himself on the pond.)

Ha! ha! ha! back again,
Thro' the frost and fog and rain;
Winter's over now, that's plain.
Ha! ha! ha! back again!
  And I laugh and scream,
    For I love so well
  The bright, bright bream,
    And the pickerel!
  And soft is my breast,
    And my bill is keen,
  And I'll build my nest
    'Mid the sedge unseen.
I've travell'd—I've fish'd in the sunny south,
In the mighty mere, at the harbour mouth;
I've seen fair countries, all golden and gay;
  I've seen bright pictures that beat all wishing;
I've found fine colours far away—
But give me Purley Pond, for fishing;
Of all the ponds, north, south, east, west,
This is the pond I love the best;
For all is quiet, and few folk peep,
  Save some of the innocent angling people;
And I like on Sundays, half asleep,
All alone on the pool so deep,
  To rock and hear the bells from the steeple.
And I laugh so clear that all may hear
The loon is back, and summer is near.
Ha! ha! ha! so merry and plain
I laugh with joy to be home again.
(A shower passes over; all things sing.)

  The swift is wheeling and gleaming,
    The brook is brown in its bed,
  Rain from the cloud is streaming,
    And the Bow bends overhead.
The charm of the winter is broken! the last of the spell is said!

The eel in the pond is quick'ning,
  The grayling leaps in the stream—
What if the clouds are thick'ning?
  See how the meadows gleam!
The spell of the winter is shaken; the world awakes from a dream!

  The fir puts out green fingers,
    The pear-tree softly blows,
  The rose in her dark bower lingers,
    But her curtains will soon unclose,
The lilac will shake her ringlets over the blush of the rose.

  The swift is wheeling and gleaming,
    The woods are beginning to ring,
  Rain from the cloud is streaming;—
    There, where the Bow doth cling,
Summer is smiling afar off, over the shoulder of Spring!

III.
PHŒBE ANNA.

Dimpled, dainty, one-and-twenty,
  Rosy-faced and round of limb,
Warm'd with mother-wit in plenty,
  Prudent, modest, spry yet prim,
Lily-handed, tiny-footed,
  With an ankle clean and neat,
Neatly gloved and trimly booted,
  Looking nice and smelling sweet!
Self-possess'd, subduing beauty
  To a sober sense of duty,
Chaste as Dian, plump as Hebe,
Such I guess was little Phœbe.
O how different a creature
  From that other wondrous woman!
Not a feeling, not a feature,
  Had these two fair flowers in common.
One was tall and moulded finely,
  Large of limb, and grand of gaze,
Rich with incense, and divinely
  Throbbing into passionate rays,—
Lustrous-eyed and luscious-bosom'd,
  Beautiful, and richly rare,
As a passion-flower full blossom'd,
  Born to Love and Love's despair.
Such was Red Rose; and the other?
  Tiny, prudish, if you please,
Meant to be a happy mother,
  With a bunch of huswife's keys.
Prudent, not to be deluded,
Happy-eyed and sober-mooded,
Dainty, mild, yet self-reliant,
  She, as I'm a worthy singer,

Wound our vacillating giant
    Round her little dimpled finger.

Bit by bit, a bashful wooer,
    Fascinated unaware,
Did Eureka draw unto her,
    Tame as any dancing bear.
Not a finger did she stir,
    Yet he glow'd and gazed at her!
Not a loving look she gave,
    Yet he watch'd her like a slave!
He, who had been used to having
    Pleasures past all human craving,
Who had idly sat and taken
    Showers of kisses on him shaken,
Who had fairly tired of passion
    Ever felt in passive fashion,
Now stood blushing like a baby
    In the careless eyes of Phœbe!

Fare ye well, O scenes of glory,
    One bright sheet of golden sheen!
Love, the spirit of my story,
    Wakens in a different scene.
Down the lanes, so tall and leafy,
    Falls Eureka's loving feet,
Following Phœbe's, but in chief he
    In the kitchen loves to sit,—
Loves to watch her, tripping ruddy
    In the rosy firelight glow,
Loves to watch, in a brown study,
    The warm figure come and go.

Half indifferent unto him,
    Far too wise to coax and woo him,
Ill-disposed to waste affection,
    Full of modest circumspection.
Quite the bright superior being,
    Tho' so tiny to the seeing,
With a mind which penetrated,
    In a sly and rosy mirth,
Thro' the face, and estimated
    Grain by grain the spirit's worth,
Phœbe Anna, unenraptured,
    Led the creature she had captured.

What is Love? A shooting star,
    Flying, flashing, lost afar.
What is Man? A fretful boy,
    Ever seeking some new toy.
What is Memory? Alas!
    'Tis a strange magician's glass,
Where you pictures bright may mark
    If you hold it *in the dark*.

Thrust it out into the sun,
    All the picturing is done,
And the magic dies away
    In the golden glow of day!

Coming back to civilisation,
    Petted, fêted, shone on daily,
Was a novel dissipation,
    And Eureka revell'd gaily.
Friendly faces flash'd around him,
    Church-bells tinkled in his ear,
Cosy cronies sought and found him,
    Drowsietown look'd bright and clear.
Parson Pen'don and his lady
    (Respectability embodied)
Welcom'd the stray sheep already,
    Matrons smiled, and deacons nodded.
Uncle Pete had left him lately
    Malden Farm and all its store,
And he found himself prized greatly
    As a worthy bachelor.
All his roaming days seem'd over!
    Like a beast without a load,
Grazing in the golden clover,
    In the village he abode!
And he loved the tilth and tillage,
    All the bustle of the village—
Loved the reaping and the sowing,
    Loved the music of the mill,
Loved to see the mowers mowing,
    And the golden grasses growing,
    Breast-deep, near the river still.
Civilisation altogether
    Seem'd exactly to his notion!
Life was like good harvest weather,
    Faintly flavoured with devotion.
Ruefully he cogitated,
    With the peaceful spire in sight:—
'Waal, I guess the thing was fated,
    And it's hard to set it right.
Seems a dream, too! now, I wonder
    If it seems a dream to *her*!
After that first parting stunn'd her,
    For a time she'd make a stir;
P'raps, tho', when the shock was over,
    Other sentiments might move her!
First she'd cry, next, she'd grow fretful,
    Thirdly, riled, and then forgetful.
After all that's done and said,
    Injin blood is Injin ever!
I'm a white skin she's a red;
    Providence just made us sever.

Parson says that sort of thing
  Isn't moral marrying!
Tho' the simple creature yonder
  Had no better education—
Ignorance jest made her fonder,
  And *I* yielded to temptation.
Here's the question: I've been sinning—
Wrong, clean wrong, from the beginning;
Can I make my blunder better
  By repeating it again?
When mere Nature, if I let her,
  Soon can cure the creature's pain;
She'll forget me fast enough—
  And she's no religious feeling;
Injin hearts are always tough,
  And their wounds are quick of healing.
Heigho!'—here he sighed; then seeing
  Phœbe Ann trip by in laughter,
Brightening up, the bother'd being
  Shook off care, and trotted after!

Had this final complication
  Not been added to the rest;
Had not Fate with new temptation
  Drugg'd the conscience of his breast,
Possibly his better nature
  Might have triumph'd o'er the treason;
But the passions of the creature
  Rose in league with his false reason;
On the side of civilisation
  Rose the pretty Civilisee:
In a flush of new sensation,
  Conscience died, and Shame did flee.
That bright picture, many-colour'd,
  Nature had flash'd before the dullard;
That wild ecstasy and rapture
  She had tamed unto his capture—
That grand form, intensely burning
  To a lightning-flash of yearning—
That fair face transfigur'd brightly
  Into starry rapture nightly—
Those large limbs of living lustre,
  Moving with a flower-like grace—
Those great joys which hung in cluster,
  Like ripe fruit in a green place—
All had faded from his vision,
  And instead, before his sight,
Tript the pretty-faced precisian,
  Deep and dimpled, warm and white!

In her very style of looking
There was cognisance of cooking!
From her very dress were peeping
Indications of housekeeping!
You might gather in a minute,
  As she lightly passed you by,
She could (with her whole heart in it!)
  Nurse a babe or make a pie.
Yet her manner and expression
  Shook the foolish giant's nerve,
With their quiet self-possession
  And their infinite reserve.
In his former time the wooing
  Had been all the *female's* doing;
He had waited while the other
  Did his soul with raptures smother!
But 'twas quite another matter,
  Here in civilisation's school!
And his heart went pitter-patter,
  And he trembled like a fool.
Thro' the church the road lay to her;—
  That was written on her face,
Lawfully the man must woo her
  In the manner of her race.
So by slow degrees he enter'd
  Courtship's Maze so mystic-centred!
Round and round the pathways wander'd,
  Made his blunders, puzzled, ponder'd;
Laugh'd at, laughing, scorn'd, imploring,
Mad, enraged, distraught, adoring;
This way, that way, turning, twisting;
Yielding oft, and oft resisting:
Gasping while the voice of Cupid
Madden'd him with 'Hither, stupid!'
Seeking ever for the middle
Of the green and golden riddle—
Oft, just as he cried, 'I've got it!'
Finding *culs de sac*, and not it!
Till at last his blunders ended
On a summer morning splendid,
When with vision glad and hazy,
  Seeing Phœbe blushing falter,
In the centre of the Maze, he
  Found himself before—an Altar!

IV.

NUPTIAL SONG.

Where were they wedded? In the holy
    house
  Built up by busy fingers.
All Drowsietown was quiet as a mouse
  To hear the village singers.

Who was the Priest? 'Twas Parson Pendon,
    dress'd
  In surplice to the knuckles,

Wig powder'd, snowy cambric on his breast,
Silk stockings, pumps, and buckles.

What was the service? 'Twas the solemn,
    stale,
Old-fashioned, English measure :
' Wilt thou this woman take? and thou this
    male?'
' I will '—' I will '—with pleasure.

Who saw it done? The countless rustic
    eyes
Of folk around them thronging.
Who shared the joy? The matrons with
    soft sighs,
The girls with bright looks longing.

Who was the bride? Sweet Phœbe, dress'd
    in clothes
As white as she who wore 'em,
Sweet-scented, self-possess'd,—one bright
    White Rose
Of virtue and decorum.

Her consecration? Peaceful self-control,
And modest circumspection—
The sweet old service softening her soul
To formulised affection.

Surveying with calm eyes the long, straight
    road
Of matrimonial being,
She wore her wedding clothes, trusting in
    God,
Domestic, and far-seeing.

With steady little hand she sign'd her name,
Nor trembled at the venture.
What did the Bridegroom? Blush'd with
    sheepish shame,
Endorsing the indenture.

O Hymen, Hymen ! In the church so calm
Began the old sweet story,
The parson smiled, the summer fields
    breathed balm,
The crops were in their glory.

Out from the portal came the wedding crew,
All smiling, palpitating ;—
And there was Jacob with the cart, bran
    new,
And the white pony, waiting.

The girls waved handkerchiefs, the village
    boys
Shouted, around them rushing,
And off they trotted thro' the light and
    noise,
She calm, the giant blushing.

Down the green road, along by glade and
    grove,
They jog, with rein-bells jingling,
The orchards pink all round, the sun above,
She cold, Eureka tingling.

And round her waist his arm becomes
    entwined,
But still her ways are coolish—
' There's old Dame Dartle looking ! Don't
    now ! Mind
The pony ! Guess you're foolish !'

Who rang the bells? The ringers with a
    will
Set them in soft vibration.
Hark ! loud and clear, there chimes o'er
    vale and hill
The nuptial jubilation.

PART IV.
THE GREAT SNOW.

I.

THE GREAT SNOW.

'TWAS the year of the Great Snow.

First the East began to blow
Chill and shrill for many days,
On the wild wet woodland ways.
Then the North, with crimson cheeks,
Blew upon the pond for weeks,
Chill'd the water thro' and thro',
Till the first thin ice-crust grew
Blue and filmy ; then at last
All the pond was frosted fast,
Prison'd, smother'd, fetter'd tight,
Let it struggle as it might.
And the first Snow drifted down
On the roofs of Drowsietown.

First the vanguard of the Snow ;
Falling flakes, whirling slow,
Drifting darkness, troubled dream ;
Then a motion and a gleam ;

Sprinkling with a carpet white
  Orchards, swamps, and woodland ways,
Thus the first Snow took its flight,
  And there was a hush for days.

'Mid that hush the Spectre dim,
Faint of breath and thin of limb,
HOAR-FROST, like a maiden's ghost,
Nightly o'er the marshes crost
In the moonlight: where she flew,
  At the touch of her chill dress
Cobwebs of the glimmering dew
  Froze to silvern loveliness.

All the night, in the dim light,
Quietly she took her flight;
Thro' the streets she crept, and stayed
In each silent window shade,
With her finger moist as rain
Drawing flowers upon the pane;—
On the phantom flowers so drawn
  With her frozen breath breath'd she;
And each window-pane at dawn
  Turn'd to crystal tracery!

Then the Phantom Fog came forth,
Following slowly from the North;
Wheezing, coughing, blown, and damp,
He sat sullen in the swamp,
Scowling with a blood-shot eye;
As the canvas-backs went by;
Till the North-wind, with a shout,
Thrust his pole and poked him out;
And the Phantom with a scowl,
  Black'ning night and dark'ning day,
Hooted after by the owl,
  Lamely halted on his way.

Now in flocks that ever increase
Honk the armies of the geese,
'Gainst a sky of crimson red
Silhouetted overhead.
After them in a dark mass,
Sleet and hail hiss as they pass,
Rattling on the frozen lea
With their shrill artillery.
Then a silence: then comes on
Frost, the steel-bright Skeleton!
Silent in the night he steals,
With wolves howling at his heels,
Seeing to the locks and keys
On the ponds and on the leas.
Touching with his tingling wand
Trees and shrubs on every hand,

Till they change, transform'd to sight,
Into dwarfs and druids white,—
Icicle-bearded, frosty-shrouded
Underneath his mantle clouded;
And on many of their shoulders,
Chill, indifferent to beholders,
Sits the barr'd owl in a heap,
Ruffled, dumb, and fast asleep.
There the legions of the trees
Gather ghost-like round his knees;
While in cloudy cloak and hood,
Cold he creeps to the great wood:—
Lying there in a half-doze,
While on finger-tips and toes·
Squirrels turn their wheels, and jays
Flutter in a wild amaze,
And the foxes, lean and foul,
Look out of their holes and growl.
There he waiteth, breathing cold
On the white and silent wold.

In a silence sat the Thing,
Looking north, and listening!
And the farmers drave their teams
Past the woods and by the streams,
Crying as they met together,
With chill noses, '*Frosty weather!*'
And along the iron ways
Tinkle, tinkle, went the sleighs.
And the wood-chopper did hie,
Leather stockings to the thigh,
Crouching on the snow that strew'd
Every corner of the wood.
Still Frost waited, very still;
Then he whistled, loud and shrill;
Then he pointed north, and lo!
The main Army of the Snow.

Black as Erebus afar,
Blotting sun, and moon, and star,
Drifting, in confusion driven,
Screaming, straggling, rent and riven,
Whirling, wailing, blown afar
In an awful wind of War,
Dragging drifts of death beneath,
  With a melancholy groan,
While the fierce Frost set his teeth,
  Rose erect, and waved them on!

All day long the legions passed
On an ever-gathering blast;
In an ever-gathering night,
Fast they eddied on their flight,

With a tramping and a roar,
Like the waves on a wild shore ;
With a motion and a gleam,
Whirling, driven in a dream ;
On they drave in drifts of white,
Burying Drowsietown from sight,
Covering ponds, and woods and roads,
Shrouding trees and men's abodes ;
While the great Pond loaded deep,
Turning over in its sleep,
Groaned ;—but when night came, forsooth,
  Grew the tramp unto a thunder ;
Wind met wind with wail uncouth,
Frost and Storm fought nail and tooth,
  Shrieking, and the roofs rock'd under.
Scared out of its sleep that night,
Drowsietown awoke in fright ;
Chimney-pots above it flying,
  Windows crashing to the ground,
Snow-flakes blinding, multiplying,
  Snow-drift whirling round and round ;
While, whene'er the strife seemed dying,
The great North-wind, shrilly crying,
  Clash'd his shield in battle-sound l. .

Multitudinous and vast,
Legions after legions passed.
Still the air behind was drear
With new legions coming near ;
Still they waver'd, wander'd on,
Glimmer'd, trembled, and were gone.
While the drift grew deeper, deeper,
  On the roofs and at the doors, .
While the wind-awoke each sleeper
  With its melancholy roars.
Once the Moon looked out, and lo !
Blind against her face the Snow
Like a wild white grave-cloth lay,
Till she shuddering crept away.
Then thro' darkness like the grave,
On and on the legions drave.

When the dawn came, Drowsietown
  Smother'd in the snow-drift lay.
Still the swarms were drifting down
  In a dark and dreadful day.
On the blinds the whole day long
  Thro' the red light shadows flitted.
At the inn in a great throng
  Gossips gather'd drowsy-witted.
All around on the white lea
Farm-lamps twinkled drearily ;
Not a road was now revealed,
  Drift, deep drift, at every door ;

Field was mingled up with field,
  Stream and pond were smother'd o'er,
Trees and fences fled from sight
  In the deep wan waste of white.

Many a night, many a day,
Pass'd the wonderful array,
Sometimes in confusion driven,
By the dreadful winds of heaven ;
Sometimes gently wavering by
With a gleam and smothered sigh,
While the lean Frost still did stand
Pointing with his skinny hand
Northward, with the shrubs and trees
Buried deep below his knees.
Still the Snow passed ; deeper down
In the snow sank Drowsietown.
Not a bird stayed, big or small,
Not a team could stir at all.
Round the cottage window-frame
Barking foxes nightly came,
Scowling in a spectral ring
At the ghostly glimmering.
Old Abe Sinker at the Inn
Heap'd his fire up with a grin,
For the great room, warm and bright,
Never emptied morn or night.
Old folks shiver'd with their bones
Full of pains and cold as stones.
Nought was doing, nought was done,
From the rise to set of sun.
Yawning in the ale-house heat,
Shivering in the snowy street,
Like dream-shadows, up and down,
  With their footprints black below,
Moved the folk of Drowsietown,
  In the Year of the Great Snow !

II.

THE WANDERER.

Snowing and blowing, roaring and rattle,
Frost, snow, and wind are all busy at battle !
O what a quaking, and shaking, and call-
  ing,
Whitely, so whitely, the snow still is falling ;
Stone-dead the earth is, shrouded all over,
White, stiff, and hard is the snow-sheet
  above her,
Deep, deep the drift is ; and tho' it is snow-
  ing,
Blacker, yet blacker, the heavens are
  growing.

Oh, what a night! gather nearer the fire!
Pile the warm pine-logs higher and higher;
Shut the black storm out, close tight the shutters,
Hark! how without there it moans and it mutters,
Tearing with teeth, claws, and fingers tremendous,
Roof, wall, and gable!—now Angels defend us!
There was a roar!—how it crashes and darkens!
No wonder that Phœbe stops, trembles, and hearkens.

For black as the skies are, tho' hueless and ghastly,
Stretches the wold, 'mid the snow falling fastly,
Here in the homestead by Phœbe made cosy,
All is so pleasant, so ruddy, and rosy.
All by herself in the tile-paven kitchen,
In white huswife's gown, and in apron bewitching,
Flits little Phœbe, so busily making
Corn bread and rye bread for Saturday's baking.
See! in the firelight that round her is gleaming,
How she is glowing, and glancing, and beaming,
While all around her, in sheer perspiration
Of an ecstatic and warm admiration,
Plates, cups, and dishes, delightedly glowing,
Watch her sweet shade as 'tis coming and going,
Catch her bright image as lightly she passes,
Shine it about in plates, dishes, and glasses!
Often in wonder all trembling and quaking,
To feel how the homestead is swaying and shaking,
All in a clatter they cry out together,
'The roof will be off in a minute! What weather!'

. . . . A face in the darkness, a foot on the Snow,
I it there? Dost thou hear? Doth it come? Doth it go?
Hush! only the gusts as they gather and grow.

O Phœbe is busy!—with little flour'd fingers,
Like rosebuds in snow, o'er her labour she lingers;
And oft when the tumult is loudest she listens,
Her eyes are intent, and her pretty face glistens
So warm in the firelight. Despite the storm's crying,
Sound, sound in their slumbers the farm-maids are lying;
The clock with its round face perspiring and blinking,
Is pointing to bed-time, and sleepily winking.
The sheep-dog lies basking, the grey cat is purring,
Only the tempest is crying and stirring.
The minutes creep on, and the wind still is busy,
And Phœbe still hearkens, perplex'd, and uneasy.

. . . . A face in the wold where the snow-drift lies low.
A footfall by night?—or the winds as they blow?
O hush! it comes nearer, a foot on the Snow.

Phœbe's fond heart is beginning to flutter,
She harks for a footfall, a tap on the shutter;
She lists for a voice while the storm gathers shriller,
The drift's at the door, and the frost groweth chiller.
She looks at the clock, and she starteth back sighing,
While the cuckoo leaps out from his hole in it, crying
His name ten times over; past ten, little singer!
'O what keeps Eureka? and where can he linger?'
The snow is so deep, and the ways are so dire,
She thinks; and a footfall comes nigher and nigher.

. . . . A face in the darkness, a face full of woe,
A face and a footfall—they come and they go,

Still nearer and nearer—a foot on the
  Snow!

Eureka's abroad in the town,—but 'tis later
Than Drowsietown's bed-time. Still greater
  and greater
The fears of poor Phœbe each moment are
  growing;
And sadder and paler her features are
  glowing.
She steps to the door—lifts the latch—with
  wild scolding
The door is dashed open, and torn from
  her holding,
While shivering she peers on the blackness,
  vibrating
With a trouble of whiteness within it pulsat-
  ing!
The wind piles the drift at the threshold
  before her,
The snow swarms upon her, around her,
  and o'er her,
But melts on the warmth of her face and
  her hands.
A moment in trouble she hearkens and
  stands.

All black and all still, save the storm's wild
  tabor!
And she closes the door, and comes back
  to her labour.
In vain—she grows paler—her heart sinks
  within her,
The cuckoo bursts out in a flutter (the
  sinner),
And chimes the half-hour—she sits now
  awaiting.
Her heart forebodes evil, her mind still
  debating;
The drift is so deep—could a false step
  within it
Have led to his grave in one terrible
  minute?
'Could his foot have gone wand'ring away
  in the wold there,
While frozen and feeble he sank in the cold
  there?
'Tis his foot! . . . Nay, not yet! . . .
  There he's tapping, to summon
His wife to the door! Nay, indeed, little
  woman!
'Tis his foot at the door!—and he listens to
  hear her!

Nay, not yet; yet a footfall there *is*, com-
  ing nearer.

A face in the darkness, a foot on the Snow,
Nearer it comes to the warm window-glow;
O hush! thro' the wind, a foot-fall on the
  Snow.

Now heark, Phœbe, heark!—But she hearks
  not; for dreaming,
Her soft eyes are fixed on the fire's rosy
  gleaming;
Hands crossed on her knees she rocks to
  and fro;
O heark! Phœbe, heark! 'tis a foot on the
  Snow.
O heark! Phœbe, heark! and flit over the
  floor,
'Tis a foot on the Snow! 'tis a tap at the
  door!
Low, faint as hail tapping. . . Upstarting,
  she hearkens.
It ceases. The firelight sinks low, the
  room darkens.
She listens again. All is still. The wind
  blowing,
The thrill of the tempest, the sound of the
  snowing.
Hush again! something taps—a low mur-
  mur is heard.
'Come in,' Phœbe cries; but the latch is
  not stirred.

Her heart's failing fast; superstitious and
  mute
She stands and she trembles, and stirs not
  a foot.
She hears a low breathing, a moaning, a
  knock,
Between the wind's cry and the tick of the
  clock:
Tap! tap! . . with an effort she shakes
  off her fear,
Makes one step to the door; again pauses
  to hear.
The latch stirs; in terror and desperate
  haste
She opens the door, shrinking back pallid-
  faced,
And sees at the porch, with a thrill of
  affright,
'Mid the gleaming of snow and the dark-
  ness of night,
A shape like a Woman's, a tremulous form

White with the snow-flakes and bent with
 the storm !
Great eyes looking out through a black
 tatter'd hood,
With a gleam of wild sorrow that thrills
 through the blood,
A hand that outreaches, a voice sadly strung,
That speaks to her soul in some mystical
 tongue !

The face in the darkness, the foot on the Snow,
They have come, they are here, with their
 weal and their woe :
O long was the journey ! the wayfarer slow !

Now Phœbe hath courage, for plainly the
 being
She looks on is mortal, though wild to the
 seeing—
Tall, spectral, and strange, yet in sorrow so
 human—
And the eyes, though so wild, are the eyes
 of a woman.
Her face is all hid ; but her brow and her
 hands,
And the quaint ancient cloak that she
 wears as she stands,
Are those of the red race who still wander
 scatter'd—
The gipsies of white towns, dishonour'd,
 drink-shatter'd.
And strange, too, she seems by her tongue ;
 yet her words are
As liquid and soft as the notes of a bird are.
All this in a moment sees Phœbe ; then lo !
She sees the shape staggering in from the
 snow,
Revealing, as in to the fire-gleam she goes,
A face will with famine, and haggard with
 woes,
For her hood falls away, and her head
 glimmers bare,
And loosen'd around falls her dank drip-
 ping hair,
And her eyes gleam like death—she would
 fall to the earth,
But the soft little hands of kind Phœbe
 reach forth,
And lead her, half swooning, half con-
 scious, until
She sinks in a chair by the fire and is still ;
Still, death-like,—while Phœbe kneels down
 by her chair,

And chafes her chill hands with a motherly
 care.

The face is upon her, it gleams in the glow,
She hears a voice warning, still dreadful
 and low,
Far back lies the footprint, a track in the
 Snow.

The woman was ghost-like, yet wondrously
 fair
Through the gray cloud of famine, the dews
 of despair,
Her face hunger'd forth—'twas a red
 woman's face,
Without the sunk eyeball, the taint of the
 race ;
With strange gentle lines round the mouth
 of her, cast
By moments of being too blissful to last.
Her cloak fallen wide, as she sat there
 distraught,
Revealed a strange garment with figures
 enwrought
In silk and old beads—it had once been
 most bright—
But frayed with long wearing by day and
 by night.
Mocassins she wore, and they, too, had
 been gay,
And now they were ragged and rent by the
 way ;
And bare to the cold was one foot, soft and
 red,
And frozen felt both, and one trickled and
 bled.

The face of the stranger, 'tis worn with its
 woe,
It comes to thee, Phœbe, but when shall it
 go ?
Far back go the footprints ; see ! black in
 the Snow.

But look ! what is that ? lo ! it lies on her
 breast,
A small living creature, an infant at rest !
So tiny, so shrivell'd, a mite of red clay,
Warm, mummied, and wrapt in the Indian
 way.
It opens its eyes, and it shrivels red cheeks ;
It thrusts out its hand to the face, and it
 speaks

With a cry to the heart of the mother; and
  lo!
She stirs from her swoon, and her famish'd
  cheeks glow,
She rolls her wild eyes at the cry of distress,
And her weak hands instinctively open her
  dress
That the babe may be fed; and the touch
  of the child
When it comes to her bosom, warm, milky,
  and mild,
Seems blissful—she smiles—O, so faintly!
  —Is blest
To feel its lips draw at the poor weary breast.
She closes her eyes, she is soothed, and her
  form
Within the great firelight grows happy and
  warm.
She hears not the wind, and she seems in a
  dream,
Till her orbs startle open amid the glad
  gleam;
Her looks fall on Phœbe, who trembles for
  pity;
She holds out her hands with a cry of
  entreaty;
Her thoughts flow together—she knows the
  bright place,
She feels the sweet firelight, she sees the
  kind face—
For Phœbe unloosens her poor dripping
  cloak,
And its damp rises up in the kitchen like
  smoke;
And Phœbe, with tender and matronly
  grace,
Is wiping the snow and the wet from her
  face.
She looks, sinks again, speaks with quick
  birdlike cries,
In her own thrilling speech; but her voice
  breaks and dies,
And her tears, through shut eyelids, ooze
  slowly and blindly
On the white little hands that are touching
  her kindly.

A face in the darkness, a face full of woe,
Deep, deep, are the white ways, and bleak
  the winds blow;
O, long was the journey, the wayfarer slow,
O, look! black as death, stretch the prints
  in the Snow.

III.
RETROSPECT: THE JOURNEY.

A footprint—trace it back. O God!
The bleeding feet, the weary road.
Fly, Fancy, as the eagle flies,
With beating heart and burning eyes,
Fly on the north-wind's breath of power,
Beat mile by mile, and hour by hour,
Southward, still southward: shouldst thou
  tire,
Rest with the solar sphere of fire,
Then rise again and take thy flight
Across the continent in white,
And track, still track, as thou dost go
This bleeding footprint in the snow!
Fly night by night, or day by day,
Count the long hours, watch the wild way;
Then see, beneath thee sailing swift
The white way melteth, and the drift
Gathers no longer; and instead
Of snow a dreary rain is shed,
On grassy ways, on dreary leas,
And sullen pools that do not freeze.
Now must thy keen eye look more near
To trace the bloody footprint here;
But see! still see! it can be traced
On the wet pastures of the waste;
On! on, still on! still southward sail,
While tall trees shake in the shrill gale,
And great streams gather, and things green
Begin to show thro' the dim sheen.
Here thro' a mighty wood the track
Errs like a silk thread slowly back,
And here birds singing go and come,
Tho' far away the world is dumb.
A river, and the track is lost.
But when the stream is safely cross'd
Again, upon the further brim,
The drop of blood, the footprint dim!
O wingèd thought, o'er half a world
Thou sailest with great wings unfurl'd,
From white to dark, from dark to bright,
From north to south, thou takest flight,
Passing with constant waft of wing
From winter climes to climes of spring,
Swiftly thou goest, and still thy gaze
Follows the footprint thro' wild ways;
Swiftly thou speedest south—O God!
A thousand leagues of weary road!

A thousand leagues! O see, the track,
Clear to the soul's eye, wavers back

Dim yet unbroken, linking slow
Winter with spring, sunshine with snow,
The dead leaf with the leaf still blowing,
The frozen stream with the stream flowing:
Linking and binding silently
Forgetfulness with memory,
Love living with love long at rest,
A burning with a frozen breast,
A Sunbeam Soul all light and seeing
With a mere Beaver of a being.

Turn back, my Spirit, turn and trace
The woman from her starting place,
Whence with fix'd features and feet free
She plunged into the world's great Sea,—
A fair sweet swimmer, strong of limb,
Most confident in God, and *him*,
And found herself by wild winds blown,
In a great waste, alone, alone!

Long with the patience of her race,
Had Red Rose waited for the face
That came not, listen'd for the voice
That made her soul leap and rejoice.
They came not: all was still. For days,
She like a fawn in the green ways
Wander'd alone; and night by night
She watch'd heaven's eye of liquid light
With eyes as luminous as theirs,
'Mid tremulous sighs and panted prayers.
He came not: all was still: her tread
Grew heavier on the earth, her head
Hung sadder, and her weeping eyes
Look'd more on earth than on the skies:
Like a dead leaf she droop'd in woe,
Until one day, with a quick throe,
She turn'd to crimson as she wept,
And lo! within her something leapt!

Flesh of her flesh, the blossom broke,
 Blood of her blood, she felt it stir,
Within her life another woke
 With still small eyes, and look'd at her!
And with a strange ecstatic pain,
She breathed, and felt it breathe again.
She seem'd to see it night and day,
Coming along from far away
Down a green path, and with fierce flame
She rush'd to meet it as it came,
But as she rush'd the shape did seem
Suddenly to dissolve in dream,
And daily she stood hungering sore,
Till far off it arose once more,

But as the life within her grew
A horror took away her breath,
Lest when her cruel kinsmen knew
Her secret, they should deal her death.
For now the aged Chief, with whom
Her happy life had broke to bloom,
Along the dark deep path had wound
That leads to God's great hunting-ground;
And a young brave of the red band
Was proudly wooing for her hand;—
Not in white fashion fervently,·
Not with wild vows and on his knee;
Rather a proud majestic wooer
Who felt his suit an honour to her,
And who his formal presents sent
In calm assumption of consent,
And never dream'd the maid would dare
To turn her tender eyes elsewhere;—
Nor dared she openly disdain
A suit so solemn and so plain;
But with a smile half agonized
She (as we whites say) temporized!

She found two friendly women, who,
Tho' hags in form, were kind and true,
And with their aid, when the hour came,
She bare her child and hid her shame.
As Eve bare Cain, upon a bed
Of balsam and of hemlock, spread
By those kind hands, in the deep woods,
Amid the forest solitudes,
With myriad creatures round her flying,
And every creature multiplying;
In the warm greenwood, hid from sight,
She held her babe to the glad light,
And brighten'd. ·As she linger'd there,
She had a dream most sadly fair:
She seem'd upon a river-side,
Gazing across a crystal tide,
And o'er the tide in dying swells
There came a burthen as of bells
Out of a mist; then the mist clear'd,
And on the further bank appear'd
A dim shape fondly beckoning—
Her warrior tall, her heart's white King!
She cried, and woke; the dream was nought;
But ever after her wild thought
Yearn'd with an instinct mad and dumb
To seek him, since he did not come.
She thought, 'My warrior beckons me!
He would be here if he were free.
And if I stay my kinsmen wild
Will surely slay me and the child;

But there, with *him* in that fair place,
Where he is chief of his own race,
All will be well ; for he is good,
Of milder race and gentler blood ;
And tho' I die upon the way
'Twill not be worse than if I stay,
Butcher'd and shamed in all men's sight
When my sad secret comes to light.
'Tis well ! th's paper in my hand
Will guide my footsteps thro' the land,
And when I strengthen I will fly,
And I will find my lord, or die !'
'Twas thought, 'twas done ; at dead of night,
She clasp'd her infant and took flight.

One guide she had—the luminous star,
On the horizon line afar ;
For thither oft Eureka's hand
Had pointed, telling her his land
Lay thitherward : gazing thereon,
That night she busied to be gone,
It seem'd a lamp that he had placed
To guide her footsteps o'er the waste.
She gather'd food, then to her back
Attach'd the babe, and took the track,
Waving her hands in wild ' adieu'
To those kind women dark of hue,
Who crouching on a dark ascent
Moan'd low, and watch'd her as she went.
There shone the star liquid and clear,
His voice seem'd calling in her ear,
The night was warm as her desire,
And forth she fled on feet of fire.

One guide ; she had another too :
A crumpled paper coarse to view,
Wherein she had kept with tender care
A little lock of precious hair,
And on the paper this was written plain :
'EUREKA HART, DROWSIETOWN, STATE
OF MAINE.'

O poor dark bird, nought still knew she
Of this wild world's geography !
Less than the swallow sailing home,
Less than the petrel 'mid the foam,
Less than the mallard winging fast,
O'er solitary fens and vast,
To seek his birthplace far away
In regions of the midnight day.
She only knew that somewhere *there*,
In some strange land afar or near,
Under that star serene and fair,
He waited ; and her soul could hear

His summons ; even as a dove
Her soul's wild pinions she unfurl'd,
And sought in constancy and love
Her only refuge in the world !

A footprint—trace it on !—
For days
Her path was on great pasture ways :
League after league of verdurous bloom
Of star-like flowers and faint perfume,
And from her coming leapt in fear
The antelope and dappled deer ;
And everywhere around her grew
Ripe fruit and berries that she knew,
While glistening in the golden gleam
Glanced many a mere and running stream.
A happy land of flocks and herds,
And many-colour'd water-birds !
Oft, sailing with her as she went,
The eagle eddied indolent
On soft swift wing ; and with his wild
Dark dewy eye glanced at her child,
Nor till she scream'd and arms upthrew,
Turn'd, and on sullen wing withdrew.
But sweet it was by night to rest
And give her little babe the breast,
And O each night with eyes most dim
She felt one night more near to *him* :
And all the pains of the past day,
With all the perils of the way,
Seem'd as a dream ; and lo ! afar
She saw the smiling of the Star.

'Twere but a weary task to trace
Her footprint on from place to place,
From day to day ; to sing and tell
What daily accidents befell,
What dangers threaten'd her, what eyes
Watch'd her go by in wild surprise,
What prospects blest her, where and when
She look'd on life and met with men.
Enough to say, tho' light and dark,
Straight, as an arrow to its mark,
The woman flew ; wise in the ways
Of her own race, she hid from gaze
When flitting forms against the sky
Warn'd her that Indians might be nigh ;
And when the wild beast dreadful-eyed
Approach'd her, with shrill shriek she cried,
Until the bloody coward shook
Before the red rage of her look.
And tho' the prospect changed all days,
It did not change to *her* ; whose gaze

Saw these things only: the white star
On the horizon line afar,
And the quick beckoning of a hand
Out of another, sweeter land.

The long sad road—the way so dreary
The very *Fancy* falters weary !
The very soul is dazed, and shows
Only a gleam of wild tableaux :
In midst of each that shape of woe
Still straggling northward—slow, slow, slow.

. . . A river deep. She cannot find
A wading-place to suit her mind ;
But on the bank sets quietly,
Amid the sunflowers tall as she,
Her little babe : then slips her dress
And stands in mother-nakedness ;
Then in a bundle on her head
She ties her raiment yellow and red,
And swimming o'er the waters bright,
With glistening limbs of liquid light,
Sets down her burden dry, and then,
With swift stroke sailing back again,
Seeks the small babe where it doth lie,
And with her right hand holds it high,
While with the other slow she swims,
Trailing her large and liquid limbs ;
Then dripping wades to the far shore,
And clothes her loveliness once more . . .

. . . On a lone plain she now is tread,
Where troglodytes dwell underhead
Wild settlers peering from big eyes
Like dead men moving in on the skies
Rise round her as she cup'd in woe, are
With hungry eyes thro' lick the hair ;
But they are gentle, and they give
Herbs and black bread that she may live,
And in their caves the weary one
Rests till the rising of the sun ;
Then the wild shapes around her stand
Reading the paper in her hand,
And point her northward ; and she flies
Fleet-footed, while with wandering eyes
They stand and watch her shape fade dim
Across the dark horizon-rim . . .

. . . She stands on a great river's bank,
'Mid noxious weeds and sedges dank ;
And on the yellow river's track,
Jagged with teeth like snags jet black,
The ferryman in his great boat,
A speck on the broad waste, doth float,

Approaching to the water's side,
But lengthways drifting with the tide.
She leaps into the boat, and o'er
The waste to the dark further shore,
Slowly they journey ; as he rows
The paper to the man she shows,
Who reads ; and as she springs to land,
He too points northward with his hand . . .

. . . See, with a crimson glare of light,
A log-town burneth in the night !
And flying forth with all their goods
Into the sandy solitudes,
The people wild, with bloodless cheeks,
Glare at a wanderer who speaks
In a strange tongue ; but as they fly
Are dumb, and answer not her cry . . .

. . . Now thro' a land by the red sun
Scorch'd as with fire, the lonely one
Treads slowly ; and ere long she hears
The sharp cry of shrill overseers,
Driving black gangs that toiling tramp
Thro' cotton fields and sugar swamp.
Here first the hand of man is raised
To harm her—for with eyes amazed
She nears a City, and is cast
Into a slave-pen foul and vast,
Seized as an Ethiop slave. From thence
She in an agony intense
Is thrust ; but not ere eager eyes
Have mark'd her beauty as a prize.
But God is good, and one blest day
She hears upon the burning way
An aged half-caste burnt and black
Speak in her tongue and answer back.
These twain wring hands upon the road,
And in the stranger's poor abode
She sleeps that night ; but with the sun
She wakens, and is pointed on . . .

. . . Now in a waggon great she lies,
And shaded from the brazen skies,
Slowly she jogs, and all at rest
She gives her little babe the breast.
Happy she rests ; hears in her dream
The driver's song, the jingling team.
With jet black cheek and bright red lip,
The negro drives and cracks his whip,
Singing plantation hymns to God,
And grinning greetings with a nod . . .

. . . Now, toiling on a dusty way,
She begs her bread from day to day,

And some are good to her and mild,
And most are soften'd by the child.
Once, as she halts at a great door,
Hungry and weary, sick and sore,
A lovely lady white as milk
Glides past her in her rustling silk ;
Then pauses, questioning, and sees
The sleeping babe upon her knees,
And takes the paper from her hand,
And reading it doth understand ;
Then stoops to *kiss* the child with cold
Kind lips, and gives the mother gold . . .

. . . Now in a mighty boat, among
A crowd of people strange of tongue,
She saileth slow, with wandering sight,
On a vast river day and night ;
All day the prospect drifteth past—
Swamp, wood, and meadow, fading fast,—
With lonely huts, and shapes that stand
On the stream's bank, and wave the hand ;
All night with eyes that look aloft,
Or close in sleep, she sails ; but oft
The blackness takes a deeper frown,
And the wild eyeballs of a town
Flash open as the boat goes by,
And she awakens with a cry . . .

On, on, and on—O the blind quest,
The throbbing heart, the aching breast !
And O the faith, more steadfast far
Than aught on earth, or any star ;
The faith that never ceased to shine,
The strength of constancy divine,
The will that warm'd her as she went
Across a mighty continent,
Unknown, scarce help'd, from land to land,
With that poor paper in her hand !

The vision falls. The figure fades
Amid the lonely forest glades,
Fringing the mighty inland seas.
I see her still ; and still she flees
Onward, still onward ; tho' the wind
Blows cold, and nature looks unkind :
The dead leaves fall and rot ; the chill
Damp earth-breath clings to vale and hill,
The birds are sailing south ; and hark !
As she fares onward thro' the dark,
The honking wild geese swiftly sail
Amid a slowly gathering gale.
All darkens ; and around her flow
The cold and silence of the Snow.

There, she is lost ; in that white gleam
She fadeth, let her fade, in dream !
Poor bird of the bright summer, now
She feels the kisses on her brow
Of Frost and Fog ; and at her back
Another Shadow keeps the track.
'Tis winter now ; and birds have flown
Southward, to seek a gladder zone ;
One, only one, doth northward fare,
And dreams to find her summer *there.*
God help her ! look not ! let her go
Into the realm of the Great Snow !

IV.
THE JOURNEY'S END.

Back in a swoon, with haggard face,
Falleth the woman of wild race,
Dumb, cold as stone, her weary eyes
Fix'd as in very death she lies—
While little Phœbe trembling stands,
Wetting her lips, chafing her hands,
Trembling, almost afraid to stir
For wonder, as she looks at her :
So weird, so wild a shape, she seems
Like some sad spirit seen in dreams ;
Beauteous of face beyond belief,
And yet so worn with want and grief.

The clock ticks low within. Without
The wind still wanders with shrill shout.
The cuckoo strikes the hour—*midnight* !
And Phœbe starteth in affright.

'O what can keep Eureka still ? '
She thinks, and listens with a thrill
For his foot's sound. It doth not come.
The clock ticks low. All else is dumb.
And still the woman lieth there,
Down drooping in the great arm-chair,
With hanging hands, chin on her breast,
And 'neath her cloak the babe at rest.
She doth not breathe, she doth not moan,
But lieth like a thing of stone.
' O God,' thinks Phœbe, deadly white,
' If she be dead ! ' and faint with fright,
Chafeth the fingers marble cold
That seem to stiffen in her hold.
She cannot stir, she cannot move,
To wake the maids who sleep above ;
Her heart is fluttering in its fear,
' Eureka ! O that he were here ! '

[*He* hurries not ! Perchance some sense
Of danger may detain him hence.

He would not hasten, if he knew
The curious sight he has to view.
Few mortal husbands, red or white,
Would care to wear his shoes this night.]

'What can she be?' thinks little Phœbe,
'Some Indian tramp—a beggar maybe—
And yet she's got a different mien
To such of these as I have seen.
Her face is like a babe's—she's young,
And she can speak no other tongue
Than Indian. When she spoke her words
Came like the gurgling notes of birds.
Poor thing! and out on such a night,
When all the world is wild and white
With the Great Snow. And O, to see
The little babe upon her knee!
I wonder now, if I should take it
From her cold bosom, I should wake it—
Poor little child!' And as she spake
Those words she saw the baby wake,
Sweet-smiling in the fire's red streaks,
With beaded eyes and rosy cheeks.
Then Phœbe started. 'Why,' thought she,
'The babe is near as fair as me!
With just one dark flush on its face
To show the taint of Indian race.
That's strange! Poor little outcast mite!
I guess his *father's* skin is white.'
Then, for a moment, Phœbe's mien
Wore an expression icy-keen,
As now in scrutiny amazed
The sleeping woman's hand she raised,
And dropt it quickly, murmuring—
'She is no wife! she wears no ring!'
So for a space her features took
Pure matronhood's Medusa-look,—
That look, so pitiless and lawful,
Which oft makes little women awful;
And which weak women, when they fall,
Dread in their sisters worst of all!
But bless thee, Phœbe, soon the child
Soften'd thy face and made it mild;
To see it lie so bright and pretty,
Thy woman's eyes were moist for pity,
And soon thy tears began to flow—
'Poor soul! and out in the Great Snow!'

E'en as she spake the stranger stirr'd.

The cold lips trembled with no word.
The fingers quiver'd, the great eyes
Open'd in stupefied surprise,
A deep sigh tore her lips apart,
And with a thickly-throbbing heart
She gazed around. The ruddy light,
The cosy kitchen warm and bright,
The clock's great shining face, the human
Soft kindly eyes of the white woman,
Came like a dream—her eyes she closed
A moment with a moan, and dozed.
Then suddenly her soul was 'ware
Of the wild quest that brought her there!
She open'd eyes—a flush of red
Flash'd to her cheeks so chill and dead—
She murmur'd quick with quivering lips,
And, trembling to the finger tips,
Thrust her chill hand into her breast,
Under the ragged cloak, in quest
Of something precious hidden there!—
'Tis safe,—she draws it forth with care;
A wretched paper, torn and wet,
  Thumb-mark'd with touch of many a hand,
'Tis there—'tis safe—she has it yet,
Her heart's sole guide, the amulet,
That led her lone feet thro' the land!
But first, unto her lips of ice
She holds it eagerly, and thrice
She *kisses* it ; then, with wild eyes
And unintelligible cries,
Holds it to Phœbe. 'Read!' cries she,
In her own tongue, distractedly;
And little Phœbe understands,
And takes the paper in her hands,
And on the hearth she stoopeth low,
To read it in the firelight glow.

Now courage, Phœbe! steel thy spirit!
A blow is coming—thou must bear it!

Slowly, so vilely it is writ,
Her unskill'd eyes decipher it;
So worn it is with snow and rain,
That scarce a letter now is plain,
And every red and ragged mark
Is smudged with handling, dim, and dark.

' E-U-R-E '—in letters blurr'd
She spells. '*Eureka!*' that's the word.
But why does little Phœbe start
As she reads on? '*Eureka Hart!*'—
His name, her husband's name; and now
The red blood flames on cheek and brow!
She stops—she quivers—glares wild-eyed
At the red woman at her side,

Who watches *her* with one sick gaze
Of wild entreaty and amaze :
Then she spells on—her features turn
To marble, though her bright eyes burn,
For all the bitter truth grows plain.
'EUREKA HART, DROWSIETOWN, STATE
   OF MAINE.'

First lightning flash of fierce surprise !
It burns her cheek, and blinds her eyes.
Again she looks on the strange creature's
Tall, ragged form and beauteous features.
Next lightning flash, and muffled thunder—
'The baby's skin is white—no wonder !'
And she perceives, as plain as may be,
All the event—down to the baby !
Last flash, the whole dark mystery light-
   ing,—
'Why, it's Eureka's own handwriting !'

Ay, little wife !—and these dim stains
Are life-blood from Eureka's veins ;
In blood the words were writ by him,
And see ! how faded and how dim !

The woman took her hand. She shook
The touch away with tiger-look,
And trembling gazed upon her. So.
She stagger'd underneath the blow,
Watch'd by the stranger's luminous eyes
In mingled stupor and surprise ;
Ah ! little did the stranger guess
The situation's bitterness,
But in her own wild tongue did say,
'Where is my love ? show me the way !'

A hand upon the latch. Both start,—
   The door swings wide—the drift sweeps
     in.
Footsteps : and lo ! Eureka Hart,
Snow-cover'd, muffled to the chin.

V.
FACE TO FACE.

Warmly muffled to the chin there,
   Blind with snow-drift, stamping, waiting,
Dazzled by the light within there,
   Stood the giant oscillating.
Then he closed the door, and turning
His great back against it, smiled !
Slightly tipsy, not discerning
   The red woman and her child.

By the great eyes dimly blinking,
   Feebly leering at his mate,
Phœbe saw he had been drinking,
   While he hiccup'd, 'Guess I'm late !'
So he stood ; when, wildly ringing,
   Rose a scream upon the air,
'Twas the Indian woman, springing,
   Gasping, gazing, from her chair.

Round her face the black hair raining,
   To her heart the baby straining,
Gasping, gazing, half believing
   'Twas some phantom soul-deceiving,
Bound as by a spell she linger'd,
Pointing at him fiery-finger'd ;
And the giant mighty-jointed,
Groan'd and stagger'd as she pointed,
Thinking, while his heart beat quicker,
'Twas some phantom born of liquor ! . . .
While he rubb'd his eyes and mutter'd,
   While he roll'd his eyes distress'd,
O'er the floor a thin form flutter'd,
   Cried, and sank upon his breast !

Phœbe screams. Stagger'd and blinded,
Stands the creature beaver-minded,
While upon his heart reposes
Cheeks he knows full well—Red Rose's !
Half repulsing and half holding,
While her arms are round him folding,
Gaunt he stands in pain afflicted,
An impostor self-convicted !
While her great eyes, upward-looking,
Not reproaching, not rebuking,
Trusting, loving, lustre-pouring,
Happy now, and still adoring,
Burn on his ; and her dark passion
Masters her in the old fashion,
Thrills the frail thin figure, burning
With a lightning flash of yearning,
Lights the worn cheeks and the faded
Forehead with her dark locks shaded,
Thrills, transfigures, seems to lend her
All the soul of her old splendour ;—
So that all the rags upon her,
All the anguish and dishonour,
All the weary days of wandering,
All the weeping, plaining, pondering,
All the sorrow, all the striving
Ne'er a man could face surviving,
All the Past, burns iridescent
In one Rainbow of the Present.
See ! she feasts on every feature
Madly, like a famish'd creature,

E E

Reads each line in rapture, reeling
With the frantic bliss of feeling ;
Kindling now her arms are round him,
Murmuring madly, she hath found him,
He is folded close unto her,
And the bliss of God thrills thro' her !

Her white Chief, whom God had brought her
From the shining Big Sea Water,
Her great Chief of the pale races,
With wise tongues and paintless faces !
More than mortal in her seeing,
Glorious, grand, a god-like being !
Nor, tho' Phœbe stands there, looking
Most distractedly rebuking,
Doth this child of the red nation
Comprehend the situation !
Not a thought hath she to move her,
Save that all the quest is over !
He is living, he is near her,
Grander, greater, braver, dearer !
No reproach in her fixed gaze is
While her eyes to his she raises—
Only hungering and thirsting
Of a heart with pleasure bursting ;
Only a supreme sensation
Of ecstatic admiration,
Melting in one soul-flush splendid
Years of heart-ache past and ended.

Her white Warrior, her fair Master !
Hers, all hers, despite disaster !
Hers, her own, that she may cry for,
Cling to, smile to, trust in, die for !
Is she *blind*? Hath the glad wonder
Struck her to the soul and stunn'd her?
Sees she not on every feature
The sick horror of the creature ?
Sober now, and looking ghastly,
Trembling while his breath comes fastly,
With the cold sweat on his forehead,
Shrinking as from something horrid,
Paralysed with guilt, despairing,
Not at *her* but Phœbe glaring,
Speechless, helpless, and aghast,
Stands the giant, pinion'd fast.

Yes, her eyes are blindly gleaming
Thro' the warm tears wildly streaming—
Yes, her soul *is* blind (God guide her !) ;
Hunger, thirst, and grief have tried her,
She is feeble, not perceiving
Cause for bitterness or grieving ;

She is foolish, never guessing
That her visit is distressing,
She is mad, mad, mad, presuming
He has waited for her coming !

No, she will *not* see the horror
Fate hath been preparing for her—
All the little strength remaining
She will wildly spend in straining,
In a rapturous confusion,
To her breast the old delusion.
Hark ! her lips speak, words are springing
Like the notes of a bird singing,
Like a fountain sunward throbbing
With a silvern song of sobbing ;
Not a word is clear, but all
Rise in rapture, blend, and fall !

Suddenly the rapture falters,
Her hands loosen, her face alters,
Drawing from him softly, quickly,
While he staggers white and sickly,
She, with grace beyond all beauty,
 Doth her ragged cloak unloose,
Then, with looks of loving duty,
 Shows Eureka—the papoose !

Tiny, pink-cheek'd, blushing brightly,
Like a mummy roll'd up tightly ;
Puffing cheeks, and fat hands spreaning [1]
In an ecstasy unmeaning ;
Blinking, his pink cheeks in gathers,
With *blue* eyes just like his father's !
In his pretty face already
Just the image of his daddy !
Stolid, stretching hands to pat him,
Lies the baby, smiling at him !

Still stands little Phœbe, panting,
This, and only this, was wanting ;
Now, with all her courage rallied,
She between them—panting, pallid—
Stands ; and, keen-eyed as an eagle,
 Tho' as fluttering as a linnet,
Folds her virtue, like a regal
 Robe, around her ; frowning in it.
Yet so wildly doth she flutter,
Not a sentence can she utter ;
Stately, speechless, with eyes blazing,
Stands the little White Rose, gazing !

---

[1] The Printer's Devil queries this, but h
does not know the Old Poets. See (*e.g.*) Micha
Drayton's *Moses' Birth and Miracles*—'An
spreans the pretty hands.'

Suddenly, with acclamation,
On that group of desperation
Bursts the Storm !—With one wild rattle
Of the elements at battle,
With one horrid roar and yelling,
Tearing, tugging at the dwelling,
Strikes the Wind ; the latch is lifted,
    With a crash wide swings the door ;
In the blinding Snow is drifted,
    With a melancholy roar !
'Tis the elements of Nature
Flocking round the weary creature,
Crying to her, while they blind her,
'Come to *us* ! for we are kinder !
Cross the cruel, fatal portal
Of the miserable mortal ;
Come, our hands are cold but loving !
Back into the midnight moving,
In some spot of silence creeping,
Find a quiet place for sleeping.
We, the Winds, will dig it straightway,
Far beyond the white man's gateway.
I, the Snow, will place above it
My soft cheek, and never move it ;
With my beauty, white and chilly,
Lying o'er thee like a lily,
Dress'd for sleep in snowy clothing
Thou shalt slumber, hearing nothing.
We will freeze thine ears from hearing
His hard foot when it is nearing ;
We will close thine ears from conning
His that look upon thee shunning.
We will keep thee, we will guard thee,
Till the kiss of God reward thee.
Come, O come !' Thus, unavailing,
Sounds the elemental wailing.

Peace, O Winds, your weary voices
Teach her nothing : she rejoices !
Hush, O Snow, let your chill hands not
Touch her cheek ; she understands not ;
Hush ! But God, who is that other,
    Standing beckoning unto her?
Winds and Snows, 'tis your pale brother,
    And his chilly breath thrills thro' her.
Ay, the Shadow there is looming
Thro' the tempest and the glooming !
O'er each path her feet have chosen—
Mountains, valleys, rivers frozen ;
Creeping near, with eyes that glisten,
When her cold foot flagg'd, to listen ;
As a bloodhound, ever flitting,
Night-time, day-time, never quitting ;

Sure of scent, with thin foot trailing
In the snowdrift, never failing,
He has follow'd, follow'd slow,
That red footprint in the Snow !
Now he finds her white and wan,—
"'Tis the Winter, Peboan.[1]

Spare her ! Who would bid him spare her?
Let him trance her and upbear her
In his arms, and softly place her
Where no cruel foot can trace her.
Let her die ! See, his eyes con her,
And his icy hand is on her ;
Thro' her form runs the quick shiver,
Light as leaves her eyelids quiver,
And with quick, spasmodic touches,
The belovèd form she clutches ;
From the cruelty of man,
Take her gently, Peboan !

Phœbe shivers. To her reaching,
With an agony beseeching,
Red Rose holds the babe ; one moment,
With a shrug of bitter comment,
Phœbe shrinks ; then, being human,
    Frighten'd, thinking Death is there,
Quietly the little woman
    Takes the burden unaware.
Not a breath too soon ; for, rocking
    In the roaring of the storm,
With the snow flakes round her flocking,
    And the wild wind round her form,
With a cry of anguish, prone
Falls the wanderer, cold as stone !

VI.
PAUGUK.

O poor Red Rose ! rent by the storm !
The flame still flickered in her form.

Moveless she lay ; but in her breast
The tumult was not quite at rest.

They raised her up, and, with soft tread,
They bore her slowly to a bed.

And little Phœbe's heart did ache,
Despite her wrongs, for pity's sake ;

And little Phœbe's own kind hands
(God bless them !) loos'd the wand'rer's
    bands,

[1] See the American-Indian Mythology. 'Peboan' is the personification of extreme Cold.

Took softly off the dripping dress,
With eyes that wept for kindliness,

Wrung the wet hair, and smoothed it right,
And clad the Red Rose all in white.

There, all in white, on a white bed,
The Red Rose hung her heavy head.

Around her was a roar, a gleam,
And she was struggling in a dream.

Faces round her went and came,
Her great eyes flash'd with fading flame.

For all the time, fever'd and sore,
She did her journey yet once more ;

Once again her Soul's feet trod
The pathless wild, the weary road ;

Once again she sail'd along
The mighty meres and rivers strong ;

Once again, with weary tread,
She stagger'd on, and begged her bread ;

Once again she falter'd slow
Into the realm of the Great Snow.

Oh, the roaring in her brain !
Oh, the wild winds that moan again !

Against her, as she clasps her child,
The hail is driven, the drift is piled.

She sees a light that shines afar ;
It beckons her—a hand, a Star.

She hears a voice afar away ;
It calls to her ; she must not stay.

Around her clouds of tempest roll,
And, oh ! the storm within her soul !

But now and then, amid the snow,
There comes a silence and a glow ;

And white she lies, in a white room,
And some one watches in the gloom.

Close by the bed where she doth rest,
Sits, with the babe upon her breast,

A little woman, waiting there,
Despite her wrongs, so kind, so fair !

E'en as she wakens, wild and weak,
Red Rose sits up, and tries to speak,

And reaching out, with a thin moan,
She takes a white hand in her own ;

But swoons once more, and hears again
The tempest roaring in her brain !

Now as she dreams, with fever'd cries,
Phœbe looks on with quiet eyes ;

And Phœbe and her maidens go
Softly and lightly to and fro.

Downstairs by the great fire of wood,
Alone, Eureka Hart doth brood ;

And when his little wife descends
He scowls, and eyes his finger-ends.

She scarcely looks into his face,
But orders him about the place ;

And at her will he flies full meek,
With red confusion on his cheek.

Her eyes are swoll'n with tears ; to him
Her face is pitiless and grim.

But as she reascends the stairs
Her pale cheek flushes unawares.

In pity half, and half in' scorn,
She sees again that shape forlorn.

She cannot love her ; yet her heart
Flutters, and takes the wand'rer's part.

Her thoughts are angry, weak and wild,
Yet carefully she tends the child.

Often she prays, with heart astir,
The white man's God to strengthen her.

And thus, despite her heart's distress,
She doth a deed of blessedness.

Silent for days by that bedside
She waiteth, watching, weary-eyed :

Not all alone ; by her unseen,
Sitteth another, strange of mien.

He squatteth in the corner there,
And looketh on through his thin hair.

Clad in fantastic Indian weeds,
With calumet and skirt of beads,

Gaunt, haggard, hungry, woebegone,
Waiteth Pauguk,[1] the Skeleton !

For wintry Peboan hath fled,
Leaving this shadow in his stead.

[1] In the same mythology, Pauguk is, as represented in the poem, the Indian spirit of Death.

And there he waits, unseen, unheard;
And as a serpent on a bird

Fixeth his glittering gaze, Pauguk
Watcheth the bed with hungry look.

VII.
THE MELTING OF THE SNOW.

A sound of streamlets flowing, flowing;
A cry of winds so bleakly blowing;
A stir, a tumult ever growing;
Deep night; and the Great Snow was going.

Underneath her death-shroud thick,
Like a body buried quick,
Heaved the Earth, and thrusting hands
Crack'd the ice and brake her bands.
Heaven, with face of watery woe,
Watched the resurrection grow.
All the night, bent to be free,
In a sickening agony,
Struggled Earth. With silent tread
From his cold seat at her head
Rose the Frost, and northward stole
To his cavern near the pole.
When the bloodshot eyes of Morn
Opened in the east forlorn,
'Twas a dreary sight to see
Blotted waste and watery lea,
All the beautiful white plains
Blurr'd with black'ning seams and stains,
All the sides of every hill
Scarr'd with thaw and dripping chill,
All the cold sky scowling black
O'er the soaking country track;
There a sobbing everywhere
In the miserable air,
And a thick fog brooding low
O'er the black trail of the snow;
While the Earth, amid the gloom
Still half buried in her tomb,
Swooning lay, and could not rise,
With dark film upon her eyes.

In the farmhouse (where a light
Glimmer'd feebly day and night
From the sick-room) Red Rose heard
Earth's awakening, and stirr'd,
Gazed around her, and descried
Phœbe sitting at her side,
Knitting, while the little child,
Sleeping on the pillow, smiled.

Little Phœbe's face was still,
Calm with quiet strength and will.
And the lamplight round her flitted
Faintly, feebly, as she knitted.
Full confession had she brought
From Eureka's soul distraught.
What he hid, in desperation,
She supplied, by penetration.
So she traced from the beginning
All the story of the sinning.
Had her spirit felt perchance
Just a little more romance;
Had the giant in her sight
Seem'd a paragon more bright;
Had the married love she bore
Been a very little more—
Why, perchance poor Phœbe's heart
Might have taken the man's part,
Heaping fiercely, as is common,
All its hate upon the woman.
Not so Phœbe! cold and pale
Did she listen to the tale;
Ne'er relenting, scarcely heeding,
Heard the man's excusing, pleading;
Felt her blood boil, and her face
Crimson for a moment's space,
Thinking darkly, in dismay,
'What will Parson Pendon say?'
But at last the little soul
Back to the sick chamber stole;
Saw the wanderer lying there,
Wildly, marvellously fair;
Saw the little baby too
Blinking with big eyes of blue;
And she murmured, with a sigh,
'She's deceived, as well as I.
Hers is far the bitterest blow,
'Cause she seems to love him so.'
So thought Phœbe, calmly sitting
By the bedside at her knitting,
While the fog hung thick and low
O'er the black trail of the Snow.

Thus she did her duty there,
Tending with a bitter care
Her sick rival; spite her pain,
Able, with a woman's brain,
To discern as clear as day
On whose side the sinning lay;
Able to compassionate
Her deluded rival's fate,
All the weariness and care
Of the fatal journey there;

Able to acknowledge (this
Far the most amazing is)
On how dull and mean a thing
Wasted was this passioning;
On how commonplace a chance
Hung the wanderer's romance;
Round how mere a Log did twine
The wild tendrils of this vine.

Screen'd thus from the wintry blast,
Droopt the Red Rose, fading fast;
While the White Rose, hanging near,
Trembled in a pensive fear.
So the snow had nearly fled,
And upon her dying bed
Earth was quick'ning; damp and chill
Streamed the fog on vale and hill.
Like a slimy crocodile
Weltering on banks o' Nile,
Everywhere, with muddy maw,
Crawl'd the miserable Thaw.
On the pond and on the stream
Loosen'd lights began to gleam,
And before the snow could fleet
Drizzly rains began to beat.

Here and there upon the plain,
'Mid the pools of thaw and rain,
Linger'd in the dismal light
Patches of unmelted white.
As these melted, very slowly,
In a quiet melancholy,
Vacant gleams o' the clouded blue
Through the dismal daylight flew,
And the wind, with a shrill clang,
Went into the west, and sang.

A sound of waters ever flowing;
A stir, a tumult, ever growing;
A gleam o' the blue, a west wind blowing;
Warmth, and the last snow wreath was
  going.

Not alone! ah! not alone!

Waking up with fever'd moan,
Red Rose started and looked round,
Listening for a voice, a sound,
And the skeleton, Pauguk,
Crouching silent in his nook,
Panted, like a famish'd thing,
In the very act to spring.

'Twas at sunset; on the bed
Crimson shafts of light were shed,
And the face, famish'd and thin,
Flash'd to sickly flame therein,
While the eyes, with fevered glare,
Sought a face they saw not there.
Then she moan'd, and with a cry,
Beckoning little Phœbe nigh,
Whisper'd; but the words she said
Perish'd uninterpreted.
Still, in bitterest distress,
Clinging to poor Phœbe's dress,
With wild gestures, she in vain
Tried to make her meaning plain.
Then did little Phœbe see
How the face changed suddenly!
For invisible Pauguk,
Creeping swiftly from his nook,
Stood erect, and hung the head
O'er the woman on the bed.
Still the woman, glaring round,
Listen'd for a voice, a sound,
Crying wildly o'er and o'er,
With her great eyes on the door.

Pale, affrighted, and aghast,
Phœbe understood at last—
Knew the weary wanderer cried
To behold *him* ere she died;
So, without a word of blame,
Phœbe called him, and he came.

The sun was set, the night was growing,
Softly the wind o' the west was blowing,
The gates of heaven were overflowing;
With the last snow Red Rose was going.

VIII.
THE LAST LOOK.

To the bedside, white and quaking,
  Came Eureka, with a groan,
Conscience-stricken now, and taking
  Her thin hand into his own.
At the touch she kindled, rallied,
  With a look of gentle grace;
Clung about him deathly pallid,
  And, uplooking in his face,
Smiled! Ah, God! that smile of parting
From her soul's dim depths upstarting!
'Twas a smile of awful beauty,
Full of fatal love and duty;
Such a smile as haunts for ever
Any being but a beaver.
Ev'n Eureka's stolid spirit
Was half agonized to bear it.

Smiling thus, and softly crooning
Words he could not understand,
Sank she on the pillow, swooning,
Clutching still her hero's hand.

Silent Spirits, shapes that love her,
Is she resting? is all over?
Nay; for while Eureka, quaking,
Heart-sick, soul-sick to behold her,
From the bed her worn form taking,
Leans her head upon his shoulder;
Once again, the spirit flying,
With a last expiring ray,
Waves a message, dimly dying,
From its tenement of clay.
Those great eyes upon him looking,
Not reproaching, not rebuking,
Brighten into bliss—perceiving
Nought of shame or of deceiving:
Only for the last time seeing
Her great Chief, a god-like being;
Only happy, all at rest,
To be dying—on his breast.

See! her hand points upward, slowly,
With an awful grace and holy,
And her eyes are saying clearly,
'Master, lord, beloved so dearly,
We shall meet, with souls grown fonder,
In God's happy prairies yonder;
Where no Snow falls; where, for ever,
Flows the shining Milky River,
On whose banks, divinely glowing,
Shapes like ours are coming, going,
In the happy star-dew moving,
Silent, smiling, loved, and loving!
Fare thee well, till then, my Master!'
Hark, her breath comes fainter, faster,
While, in love man cannot measure,
Kissing her white warrior's hand,
She sinks, with one great smile of pleasure—
Last flash upon the blackening brand!

EPILOGUE.

IN a dark corner of the burial-place,
Where sleep apart the creatures of red race,
Red Rose was laid, cold, beautiful, and dead,
With all the great white Snow above her bed.
And soon the tiny partner of her quest,
The little babe, was laid upon her breast;
For, though the heart of Phœbe had been kind,
And sought to save the infant left behind,
It wither'd when the mother's kiss withdrew—
The Red Rose faded, and the Blossom too.
There sleeps their dust, but 'neath another sky,
More kind than this, their Spirits sleeping lie.

Sleeping, or waking? *There*, with eyes tear-wet,
Is her soul homeless? doth she wander yet,
Silent by those still pathways, with bent head,
Still listening, listening, for her warrior's tread?
It came not, comes not—tho' the ages roll,
Still with that life-long hunger in her soul,
She must wait on, and thousand others too,
If waking Immortality be true.
But, no; God giveth his belovèd sleep;
Rose of the wilderness, may thine be deep!
Not 'near the white man's happy Deathdomains,
But in the red man's mighty hunting-plains;
Amid the harmless shades of flocks and herds,
Amid the hum of bees, the song of birds,
With fields and woods all round, and skies above
Dark as thine eyes, and deathless as thy love!

Here ends my tale; what further should I state?
Save that poor Phœbe soon forgave her mate,
As small white wives forgive; with words outspoken
The peace was patch'd almost as soon as broken;
For Phœbe argued, after a good cry,
' 'Tis a bad job; but break my heart—not I!
All the men do it—that's a fact confess'd,
And my great stupid's only like the rest.
But what's the good of fretting more than need?
I've got the cows to mind, the hens to feed.
I 'spose it's dreadful, but 'tis less a sin
Than if the wench had a white woman's skin!'

Oft at his head her mocking shafts she aim'd,
While by the hearth he hung the head ashamed,
Pricking his moral hide right thro' and thro',
As virtuous little wives so well can do,
Till out he swagger'd, cursing, sorely hit,
And puzzled by the little woman's wit.
Indeed, for seasons of domestic strife,
She kept this rod in pickle all her life.

As for Eureka, why, he felt, of course,
Some conscience-prick, some tremor of remorse,
Not deep enough to cause him many groans,
Or keep the fat from growing on his bones.

He throve, he prosper'd, was esteem'd by all,—
At fifty, he was broad as he was tall;
Loved much his pipe and glass, and at the inn
Spake oft—an oracle of double chin.
Did he forget her? Never! Often, while
He sat and puff'd his pipe with easy smile,
Surveying fields and orchards from the porch,
And far away the little village church,
While all seem'd peaceful—earth, and air, and sky,—
A twinkle came into his fish-like eye;
'Poor critter!' sigh'd he, as a cloud he blew,
'She was a splendid figure, and that's true!'

Faces on the Wall.

(1876.)

LONE HOUSE.

LONE HOUSE amid the Main, where I abide,
Faces there are around thy walls; I see
With constant features, fair and faithful-eyed,
In solemn silence these admonish me.
They are the Faces of the strong and free;
Prophets who on the car of Tempest ride;
Martyrs who drift amid the waters wide
On some frail raft, and pray on bended knee.
Stay with me, Faces! make me free and strong!
On other walls let flush'd Bacchantes leer;
In quainter rooms of snugger sons of song
Let old fantastic tapestries appear.
Lone House! for comfort, when the nights are long,
Let none but future-seeking eyes be here!

STORM AND CALM.

THE lone House shakes, the wild waves leap around,
Their sharp mouths foam, their frantic hands wave high;
I hear around me a sad soul of sound,—
A ceaseless sob,—a melancholy cry.
Above, there is the trouble of the sky.
On either side stretch waters with no bound.
Within, my cheek upon my hand, sit I,
Oft startled by sick faces of the drown'd.
Yet are there golden dawns and glassy days
When the vast Sea is smooth and sunk in rest,
And in the sea the gentle heaven doth gaze,
And, seeing its own beauty, smiles its best;
With nights of peace, when, in a virgin haze,
God's Moon wades thro' the shallows of the West.

WITHOUT AND WITHIN.

The Sea without, the silent room within,
   The Mystery above, the Void below !
I watch the storms die and the storms begin ;
   I see the white ships ghost-like come
     and go ;
   I wave a signal they may see and know,
As, crowding up on deck with faces thin,
   The seamen pass,—some sheltered creek to
     win,
   Or drift to whirling pools of pain and woe.
What prospect, then, on midnights dark
     and dead,
   When the room rocks and the wild water
     calls ?—
Only to mark the beacon I have fed,
   Whose cold streak glassily on the black
     sea falls ;
Only, while the dim lamp burns overhead,
   To watch the glimmering Faces on the
     walls.

NAPOLEON.

Look on that picture, and on this. . . .
   Behold
The Face that frown'd the rights of
     realms away ;
The imperial forehead, filleted with gold ;
   The arrogant chin, the lips of frozen clay.
This is the later Cæsar, whose great day
Was one long sunset in blood-ruby rolled,
   Till, on an ocean-island lone and gray,
It sank unblest, forgotten, dead, and cold.
Yea, this is he who swept from plain to
     plain,
   Watering the harvest-fields with crimson
     rain ;
This is the Eagle who on garbage fed.
Turn to the wall the pitiless eyes. Art,
     Thought,
Law, Science, owed the monster less than
     nought ;
And Nature breath'd again when he was
     dead.

ABRAHAM LINCOLN.

Turn ; and, behold the sad Soul of the West
   Passing behind a Rainbow bloodily !
Conscience incarnate, steadfast, strong,
     and free,
Changeless thro' change, blessing and ever
     blessed.

Sad storm-cloud with God's Iris on his
     breast,
Across the troubled ocean travelled he,—
Sad was his passing ! gentle be his rest !
God's Bow sails with him on another sea !

At first no larger than a prophet's hand,
   Against the dense insufferable blue
Cloud-like he came ; and by a fierce wind
     fanned,
   Didst gather into greatness ere we knew,
Then, flash by flash, most desolately grand,
   Passed away sadly heavenward, dropping
     dew !

WALT WHITMAN.

Friend Whitman ! wert thou less serene
     and kind,
Surely thou mightest (like our Bard sub-
     lime,
Scorn'd by a generation deaf and blind),
   Make thine appeal to the avenger, Time ;
For thou art none of those who upward
     climb,
   Gathering roses with a vacant mind,
Ne'er have thy hands for jaded triflers
     twined
   Sick flowers of rhetoric and weeds of
     rhyme.
Nay, thine hath been a Prophet's stormier
     fate.
While Lincoln and the martyr'd legions
     wait
   In the yet widening blue of yonder sky,
On the great strand below them thou art
     seen,—
Blessing, with something Christ-like in thy
     mien,
A sea of turbulent lives that break and
     die !

O FACES!

O Faces! that look forward, eyes that
     spell
   The future time for signs, what see ye
     there ?
On what far gleams of portent do ye dwell ?
   Whither, with lips like quivering leaves
     and hair
Back-blowing in the whirlwind, do ye stare
So steadfast and so still ? Oh speak and tell !

Is the soul safe? shall the sick world be
  well?
Will morning glimmer soon, and all be
  fair?
O Faces! ye are pale, and somewhat sad,
  And in your eyes there swim the fatal
    tears;
But on your brows the dawn gleams cold
  and hoar.
I, too, gaze forward, and my heart grows
  glad;
I catch the comfort of the golden years;
I see the Soul is safe for evermore!

TO TRIFLERS.

Go, triflers with God's secret. Far, oh far
  Be your thin monotone, your brows
    flower-crown'd,
Your backward-looking faces; for ye mar
  The pregnant time with silly sooth of
    sound,
  With flowers around the feverish temples
    bound,
And withering in the close air of the feast.
Take all the summer pleasures ye have
  found,
While Circe-charm'd ye turn to bird and
  beast.
Meantime I sit apart, a lonely wight
On this bare rock amid this fitful Sea,
  And in the wind and rain I try to light
A little lamp that may a Beacon be,
  Whereby poor ship-folk, driving thro' the
    night,
May gain the Ocean-course, and think
  of me!

THE WANDERERS.

GOD'S blessing on poor ship-folk! Peace
  and prayer
Fall on their eyelids till they close in
  sleep!
God send them gentle winds and summer
  air,
For the great sea is treacherous and
  deep.
Light me up lamps on every ocean-
  steep,—
Beacon the shallows with a loving care.

Ay me! the wind cries and the wild
  waves leap,
And on they drive—God knows—*they* know
  not—where.
Come Poets! come, O Prophets! yea,
  disown
The phantasies and phantoms ye pursue!
Lights! lights! with fatal snares the sea
  is sown.
Guide the poor ship-folk lone beneath the
  blue.
Nay, do not light for Lazarus alone,
But light for Dives and the Devil too.

THE WATCHER OF THE BEACON.

LONE is his life who, on a sea-tower blind,
  Watcheth all weathers o'er the beacon-
    light.
Ah! woe to him if, mad with his own mind,
  He groweth sick for scenes more sweet
    and bright;
For round him, in the dreadful winter
  night,
The snow drifts, and the waves beat, and
  the wind
Shrieks desolately, while with feeble sight
He readeth some old Scripture left behind
  By those who sat before him in that
    place,
And in their season perish'd, one and
  all. . . .
Wild raves the wind: the Faces on the
  wall
Seem phantoms: features dark and dim
  to trace.
He starteth up—he tottereth—he would fall,
  When, lo! the gleam of one Diviner
    Face!

'AND THE SPIRIT OF GOD MOVED UPON THE WATERS.'

O FACES! fade upon the wall, and leave
  This only, for the watcher to implore.
Dim with the peace that starry twilights
  weave,
It riseth, and the storm is hush'd and
  o'er.

Trembling I feed my feeble lamp once
    more,
Tho' all be placid as a summer eve.
See there it moves where weary waters
    grieve,—
O mariners! look yonder and adore!
Spirit, grow brighter on my nights and
    days;

Shine out of heaven; my guide and comfort
    be:
Pilot the wanderers through the ocean
    ways;
Keep the stars steadfast, and the waters free;
Lighten thy lonely creature while he
    prays:
Keep his Soul strong amid the mighty Sea!

Balder the Beautiful.

A SONG OF DIVINE DEATH.

ὦ Θάνατε Παιδν!

'For as in Adam all die, even so in Christ shall all be made alive. . . . But some man will say,
How are the dead raised up? and with what body do they come? Thou fool, that which thou
sowest is not quickened, except it die. . . . Behold, I show you a mystery; we shall not all sleep,
but we shall all be changed.'—PAUL, COR. 1st Ep. chap. xv.

NOTE.

It may be well for readers of the following poem to dismiss from their minds all recollection of
the *Eddas*, Ewald's *Balder*, Oehlenschläger's *Balder hūn Gode*, and even Mr. Arnold's *Balder
Dead*. With the hero of these familiar works my Balder has little in common; he is neither the
shadowy god of the *Edda*, nor the colossal hero of Ewald, nor the good principle of Oehlenschläger,
nor the Homeric demigod of Mr. Arnold. In the presentation of both the Father and Son, I have
reverted to the lines of the most primitive mythology: discovering in the one the northern Messiah
as well as the northern Apollo, in the other (instead of the degraded Odin of later superstition) the
Alfadur, or temporarily omnipotent godhead, who, despite his darker features, has affinity with both
the Zeus of the Eleusinian mysteries and the Jehovah of the Bible. It is unnecessary, however,
further to explain the spirit of a poem which each competent reader will interpret in his own way,
and which, if it fulfils its purpose at all, should have many meanings for many minds.

A portion of *Balder the Beautiful* has already been printed in the pages of the *Contemporary
Review*.

PROEM TO ——.

A SONG OF A DREAM.

O WHAT is this cry in our burning ears,
    And what is this light on our eyes, dear
        love?
The cry is the cry of the rolling years,
    As they break on the sun-rock, far above;
And the light is the light of that rock of gold
    As it burneth bright in a starry sea;
And the cry is clearer a hundredfold,
    And the light more bright, when I gaze
        on thee.
My weak eyes dazzle beneath that gleam,
My sad ears deafen to hear that cry:
I was-born in a dream, and I dwell in a
    dream,
    And I go in a dream to die!

O whose is this hand on my forehead bare,
    And whose are these eyes that look in
        mine?
The hand is the Earth's soft hand of air,
    The eyes are the Earth's—thro' tears they
        shine;
And the touch of the hand is so soft, so light,
    As the ray of the blind orbs blesseth me;
But the touch is softest, the eyes most bright,
    When I sit and smile by the side of thee.
For the mortal Mother's blind eyes beam
    With the long-lost love of a life gone by,
On her breast I woke in a beauteous dream,
    And I go in a dream to die!

O what are the voices around my way,
    And what are these shadows that stir
        below?

The voices of waifs in a world astray,
  The shadows of souls that come and go.
And I hear and see, and I wonder more,
  For their features are fair and strange as mine,
But most I wonder when most I pore
  On the passionate peace of this face of thine.
We walk in silence by wood and stream,
  Our gaze upturned to the same blue sky :
We move in a dream, and we love in a dream,
  And we go in our dream to die !

O what is this music of merry bells,
  And what is this laughter across the wold?
'Tis the mirth of a market that buys and sells,
  'Tis the laughter of men that are counting gold.
I walk thro' Cities of silent stone,
  And the public places alive I see ;
The wicked flourish, the weary groan,
  And I think it real, till I turn to thee !
And I smile to answer thine eyes' bright beam,
  For I know all's vision that darkens by :
That they buy in a dream, and they sell in a dream,
  And they go in a dream to die.

O what are these shapes on their thrones of gold,
  And what are those clouds around their feet?
The shapes are kings with their hearts clay-cold,
  The clouds are armies that ever meet ;
I see the flame of the crimson fire,
  I hear the murdered who moan 'Ah me!'—
My bosom aches with its bitter ire,
  And I think it real, till I turn to thee !
And I hear thee whisper, 'These shapes but seem—
  They are but visions that flash and fly,
While we move in a dream, and love in a dream,
  And go in our dream to die !'

O what are these Spirits that o'er us creep,
  And touch our eyelids and drink our breath ?
The first, with a flower in his hand, is Sleep ;
  The next, with a star on his brow, is Death.
We fade before them whene'er they come,
  (And never single those spirits be !)
A little season my lips are dumb,
  But I waken ever,—and look for thee.
Yea, ever each night when the pale stars gleam
  And the mystical Brethren pass me by,
This cloud of a trance comes across my dream,
  As I seem in my dream to die !

O what is this grass beneath our feet,
  And what are these beautiful underblooms?
The grass is the grass of the churchyard, Sweet,
  The flowers are flowers on the quiet tombs.
I pluck them softly, and bless the dead,
  Silently o'er them I bend the knee,
But my tenderest blessing is surely said,
  Tho' my tears fall fast, when I turn to thee.
For our lips are tuned to the same sad theme,
  We think of the loveless dead, and sigh ;
Dark is the shadow across our dream,
  For we go in that dream to die !

O what is this moaning so faint and low,
  And what is this crying from night to morn ?
The moaning is that of the souls that go,
  The crying is that of the souls new-born.
The life-sea gathers with stormy calls,
  The wind blows shrilly, the foam flies free.
The great wave rises, the great wave falls,
  I swim to its height by the side of thee !
With arms outstretching and throats that scream,
  With faces that flash into foam and fly,
Our beings break in the light of a dream,
  As the great waves gather and die.

O what is this Spirit with silvern feet,
  His bright head wrapt in a saffron veil?
Around his raiment our wild arms beat,
  We cling unto them, but faint and fail.

'Tis the Spirit that sits on the twilight s'
    And soft to the sound of the waves s'
        he,
He leads the chaunt from his crystal ca
    And I join in the mystical chaunt
        thee,
And our beings burn with the heav
        theme,
For he sings of wonders beyond the sky
Of a god-like dream, and of gods in a dre
Of a dream that cannot die !

O closer creep to this breast of mine ;
    We rise, we mingle, we break, dear love !
A space on the crest of the wave we shine,
    With light and music and mirth we move ;
Before and behind us (fear not, sweet !)
    Blackens the trough of the surging sea—
A little moment our mouths may meet,
    A little moment I cling to thee ;
Onward the wonderful waters stream,
    'Tis vain to struggle, 'tis vain to cry—
We wake in a dream, and we ache in a
        dream,
And we break in a dream, and die !

But who is this other with hair of flame,
    The naked feet, and the robe of white ?
A Spirit, too, with a sweeter name,
    A softer smile, a serener light.
He wraps us both in a golden cloud,
    He thrills our frames with a fire divine,
Our souls are mingled, our hearts beat loud,
    My breath and being are blent with thine:
And the sun-rock flames with a flash
        supreme,
    And the starry waves have a stranger cry—
We climb to the crest of our golden dream,
    For we dream that we cannot die !

Aye ! the cry rings loud in our burning ears,
    And the light flames bright on our eyes,
        dear love,
And we know the cry of the rolling years
    As they break on the sun-rock far above ;
And we know the light of the rock of gold,
    As it burneth bright in a starry sea,
And the glory deepens a thousandfold
    As I name the immortal gods and thee !
We shrink together beneath that gleam,
    We cling together before that cry ;
We were made in a dream, and we fade in
        a dream,
And if death be a dream, we die !

The smile of the sunshine,
    The sob of the shower,
The beam of the moonshine,
    The gleam of the star.
'Mid shining of faces
    And waving of wings,
With gifts from all places
    Came beautiful things ;
By night-time and day-time
    No life was forlorn,
'Twas leaf-time, 'twas May-time,
    And Balder was born.

Yet the spell had been woven
    Long ages ago,
That the clouds should be cloven,
    The Father undone,
    The light of the sunshine

THE BIRTH OF BALDER.

I.

BALDER'S BIRTH-SONG.

THERE blent with his growing
    The leaf and the flower,
The wind lightly blowing
    Its balm from afar,
The smile of the sunshine,
    The sob of the shower,
The beam of the moonshine,
    The gleam of the star.
'Mid shining of faces
    And waving of wings,
With gifts from all places
    Came beautiful things ;
The blush from the blossom,
    The bloom from the corn,
Blent into his bosom,
    Ere Balder was born.

As a rainbow in heaven
    Was woven the rune,
The colours were seven
    Most dim and divine :
Thro' regions of thunder
    Serene swam the moon,
With white rays of wonder
    Completing the sign.
The snow-star was gleaming
    Cold, silent, and clear,
Its bright image beaming
    Deep down in the mere ;
The night grew profounder,
    The earth slept forlorn,

The voices of waifs in a world astray,
  The shadows of souls that come and go.
And I hear and see, and I wonder more,
  For their features are fair and strange as
     mine,
But most I wonder when most I pore
  On the passionate peace of this face of
     thine.
We walk in silence by wood and stream,
  Our gaze upturned to the same blue sky:
We move in a dream, and we love in a
     dream,
  And we go in our dream to die!

O what is this music of merry bells,
  And what is this laughter across the wo¹
 'Tis the mirth of a market shared not,
    Ere Balder was born.

    There, hid from the Father,
      She brooded below,
    In realms where pines gather
      Ice-robed and ice-crown'd,
    And the great trees were drooping,
      Struck down by the snow,
    With chilly arms stooping
      To touch the white ground.
    While whirlwinds were weaving
      Their raiment of cloud,
    She sat there conceiving,
      Dark, brooding, and bow'd ;
    But where the boughs thicken'd
      A bird sang one morn,—
    And she kindled and quicken'd,
      Ere Balder was born.

    Then by that great water,
      Within the dark woods,
    The dawn broke, and brought her
      A glimmer of Spring!
    The gray geese came crying
      Far over the floods,
    The black crane pass'd, flying
      With slow waft of wing.
    And when the moon's silver
      Was shed on the mere,
    The cry of the culver
      Was heard far and near,
    And the owls to each other
      Made answers forlorn,—
    And she smiled, the sad Mother,
      Ere Balder was born.

    Then the peace and the splendour
      Of powers of the night,
    And the strength that grows tender
      Where dusk rivers run.
    The beam of the moonshine,
      The soft starry light,
    And the first smile of sunshine,
      Were woven in one.
    And they mingled within her
      With motions of earth
    To strengthen and win her
      To mystical birth ;—
    By the pangs of a woman
      The goddess was torn,
    Ere, with heart of the human,
      God Balder was born.

    The wind-gods were blowing
      Their trumpets of might,
    The skies were still snowing,
      And dark was the wold,—
    With a rock for her pillow
      Lay Frea that night,
    Beneath a great willow
      All leafless and cold—
    But the earth to strange motion
      Was stirring around,
    And the ice of the ocean
      Had split with shrill sound ;—
    When coldly upspringing
      Arose the red morn,
    To a sound as of singing
      Bright Balder was born!

    His hair was as golden
      As lily-hearts be,
    When, softly unfolden,
      From black tarns they rise,—
    The lights of the azure,
      The shades of the sea,
    Blent into the pleasure
      Of beautiful eyes ;
    Like the aspen that lingers
      Where waters run fleet
    Was the touch of his fingers,
      The thrill of his feet ;
    White, white as the blossom
      That blows on the thorn,
    On Frea's fair bosom
      Bright Balder was born.

    While soften'd and sadden'd
      With love shone her face,

THE BIRTH OF BALDER.

Uplooking he gladden'd
   And clung to her breast,
For a light as of summer
   Swept over the place,
When the shining new-comer
   Awoke from his rest !
And the willow and alder
   Thrill'd out unto bloom,
And the lilac brought Balder
   Its light and perfume,
While the merle sable-suited
   Sang merry by morn,
And with bill of gold fluted
   That Balder was born !

At the notes of the singer
   The sun glimmer'd gay,
And touch'd with bright finger
   The child as he stirred !
For the snow from the mountains
   Was melting away,
And the sound of the fountains
   Upleaping was heard ;
And the black soil was broken
   To radiance of flowers,
While the Bow for a token
   Gleam'd down thro' the showers ;
Deep under the fallow
   Now sprouted the corn,
And swift flash'd the swallow,
   For Balder was born !

Yea, again up in heaven
   Was rainbow'd the rune,
And the colours were seven
   Most dim and divine :
Sweet creatures work'd under
   The sun and the moon,
Completing the wonder
   With whisper and sign.
With eyes brightly gleaming
   The squirrel came near,
In flocks swam the lemming
   Across the great mere,
And the gold-speckled spider
   Found Frea that morn,
And was busy beside her
   When Balder was born.

And with him came waking
   The leaf and the flower,
The wind lightly shaking
   Its balm from afar,

The smile of the sunshine,
   The sob of the shower,
The beam of the moonshine,
   The gleam of the star.
'Mid shining of faces
   And waving of wings,
With gifts from all places
   Came beautiful things ;
By night-time and day-time
   No life was forlorn,
'Twas leaf-time, 'twas May-time,
   And Balder was born.

Yet the spell had been woven
   Long ages ago,
That the clouds should be cloven,
   The Father undone,
When the light of the sunshine,
   The white of the snow,
And the starshine and moonshine,
   Were mingled in one ;
When the wind and the water,
   The star and the flower,
Found a goddess, and brought her
   Their strength for a dower ;
Yea, in runes it was written,
   With letters forlorn,
That the gods should be smitten
   When Balder was born.

Then roar'd the mad thunder
   From regions afar,
And the world darken'd under
   That wrath of the skies.
But the new-born, upleaping
   As bright as a star,
Awoke from his sleeping
   With love in his ears ;—
And the dark rain ceased falling,
   With slow silvern thrills,
And the cuckoo came, calling
   Aloud on the hills,
And the glad Earth uplifted
   Her face to the morn,
And past the storm drifted,
   For Balder was born.

. . . In the sedge of the river
   The swan makes its nest ;
In the mere, with no quiver,
   Stands shadow'd the crane ;
Earth happy and still is,
   Peace dwells in her breast,

And the lips of her lilies
  Drink balm from the rain;
The lamb in the meadow
  Upsprings with no care,
Deep in the wood's shadow
  Is born the young bear;
The ash and the alder,
  The flowers and the corn,
All waited for Balder,—
  And Balder is born!

II.

HIS GROWTH AND GODHEAD.

Lovely as light and blossoms are,
  And gentle as the dew,
A white god stainless as a star,
  Deep-hidden, Balder grew.

For in the time when violets grow,
  And birds sing thro' the showers,
Pale Frea left the child below,
  Upon a bank of flowers.

And heavenward now on weary feet
  The mighty goddess flies,
And kneeleth at the Father's seat,
  And gazeth in his eyes.

Around her in those shadowy halls
  The great gods darkly tread.
'Where is thy child?' each cold voice calls;
  Calmly she answereth, 'Dead.

'The arrows of the gods are keen,
  An infant's heart is mild;
Buried within the forest green,
  Now slumbereth my child.

'The robin strewed him o'er with leaves,
  And closed his eyes of blue,
And overhead the spider weaves
  Her rune of silk and dew.'

Pale at the mighty banquet board
  The Mother sat in pain:
The great gods smiling, with no word,
  Drank deep, and breathed again. . . .

But down within the forest dim
  The child divine lies quick!
The slanted sunlight comes to him
  Thro' branches woven thick.

He drinks no nurture of the breast,
  No mother's kiss he knows;
Warm as a song bird in its nest
  He feels the light, and grows.

Around him flock all gentle things
  Which range the forest free:
Each shape that blooms, each shape that sings,
  Looks on him silently.

The light is melted on his lips
  And on his eyes of blue,
And from the shining leaves he sips
  The sweetness of the dew.

And slowly like an earthborn child
  He learns to walk and run—
A forest form, with laughter wild,
  He wanders in the sun.

And now he knows the great brown bear,
  And sitteth with its young,
And of their honey takes his share,
  Sucking with thirsty tongue.

Around him as he comes and goes
  There clings a golden mist,
And in his bright hair blooms a rose,
  And a bird sings on his wrist!

And wheresoe'er he sets his feet
  Fair ferns and flowers spring,
And honeysuckles scented sweet
  Grow where his fingers cling.

He calls, and wood-doves at the cry
  Come down to be caress'd;
Curl'd in his arms the lynx will lie,
  Its lips against his breast.

O look into his happy eyes,
  As lustrous as the dew!
A light like running water lies
  Within their depths of blue;

And there the white cloud's shadow dim
  Stirs, mirror'd soft and gray,
And far within the dream-dews swim
  With melancholy ray.

Ev'n thus in beauteous shape he grows,
  Unknown, unseen, unheard,
And night by night he takes repose
  Like any flower or bird.

He drinks the balmy breath of Earth,
He feels the light and rain,
Till, like a thing of mortal birth,
He shares her peace or pain.

A wild white shape with wondering eyes
He walks by wood and stream,
And softly on his spirit lies
The burthen of a dream.

His hair is like the midnight sun's,
All golden-red and bright ;
But radiance as of moonrise runs
Upon his limbs of white.

And now the wood without a sound
Hushes its leaves in dread ;
Beauty and mystery surround
The silence of his tread.

Quietly as a moonbeam creeps
He moves from place to place ;
Soft steals the starlight, as he sleeps,
To breathe upon his face.

The ground grows green beneath his feet,
While, trembling on the stem,
The pale flowers drink again, full sweet,
The breath he draws from them.

Now brightly gleams the soft green sod,
The golden seeds are sown ;
O pale white lily of a god,
Thou standest now full blown !

II.

THE FINDING OF BALDER.

I.

FREA IN THE WOOD.

BLUE night. Along the lonely forest way
The goddess, mighty-limb'd and marble white,
Tall in the shadow of the pines that waved
Their black arms in the moonrise overhead,
Stole silent-footed. Round her naked feet
The dews were luminous, and the breath of flowers
Rose from the scented path of grass and fern,
And all was stiller than a maiden's dream.

From grove to grove she went, like one that knew
Each shadow of that silent forest old,
And ever as she went the tangled light
That trembled on her thro' the woven boughs
Grew deeper and more dewy, until at last
She knew by chilly gleams upon the grass
That dawn was come. Still did that umbrage deep
Remain in dimness, tho' afar away
The hills were kindling with dull blood-red fires ;
But when the trumpet of the day was blown
From the great golden gateways of the sun,
When leaf by leaf the crimson rose o' the east
Open'd, and leaf by leaf illumed in turn
Glitter'd the snowy lily of the north,
She left the shelter of those woods, and stood
Under the shining canopy of heaven.

Before her lay a vast and tranquil lake,
And wading in its shallows silently
Great sto.ks of golden white and light green cranes
Stood sentinel, while far as eye could see,
Swam the wild water-lily's oilèd leaves.
Still was that place as sleep, yet evermore
A stir amid its stillness ; for behold,
At every breath of the warm summer wind
Blown on the beating bosom of the lake,
The white swarms of the new-born lily-flowers,
A pinch of gold-dust in the heart of each,
Rose from the bubbling depths, and open'd up,
And floated luminous with cups of snow.
Across that water came so sweet an air,
It fell upon the immortal mother's brow
Like coolest morning dew, and tho' she stood
Beneath the open arch of heaven, the light
Stole thro' the gauze of a soft summer mist
Most gentle and subdued. Then while she paused
Close to the rippling shallows sown with reeds,
Those cranes and storks arose above her head
In one vast cloud of flying green and gold ;
And from the under-heaven innumerable
The lilies upward to the surface snow'd,

F F

Till all the waters glitter'd gold and white;
And lo! the sun swept shining up the east,
And thro' the cloud of birds, and on the lake,
Shot sudden rays of light miraculous,—
Until the goddess veil'd her dazzled eyes,
And with the heaving whiteness at her feet
Her bosom heaved, till of that tremulous life
She seem'd a throbbing part!

             Tall by the marge
The goddess tower'd, and her immortal face
Was shining as anointed; then she cried,
'Balder!' and like the faint cry of a bird
That passeth overhead, the sound was borne
Between the burning ether and the earth.
Then once again she called, outstretching arms,
'Balder!' Upon her face the summer light
Trembled in benediction, while the voice
Was lifted up and echoed till it died
Far off amid the forest silences.

A space she paused, smiling and listening,
Gazing upon the lilies as they rose
Large, luminously fair, and new-baptized;
And once again she would have call'd aloud,
When far across the waters suddenly
There shone a light as of the morning star;
Which coming nearer seem'd as some bright bird
Floating amid the lilies and their leaves,
And presently, approaching closer still,
Assumed the likeness of a shining shape,
Who, with white shoulders from the waters reaching,
And sunlight burning on his golden hair,
Swam like a swan. Upon his naked arms
The amber light was melted, while they clove
The crystal depths and softly swept aside
The glittering lilies and their clustering leaves,
And on the forehead of him burnt serene
A light as of a pearl more wonderful
Than ever from the crimson seas of Ind
Was snatch'd by human hand; for pearl it seem'd,
Tho' blood-red, and as lustrous as a star.
Him Frea breathless watch'd, for all the air
Was golden with his glory as he came;
And o'er his head the bird-cloud hover'd bright
With murmurs deep; and thro' the lake he swam
With arm-sweeps swift, till in the shallows bright,
Still dripping from the kisses of the waves,
He rose erect in loveliness divine.
The lustre from his ivory arms and limbs
Stream'd as he stood, and from his yellow hair
A glory rain'd upon his neck and breast,
While burning unextinguish'd on his brow
Shone that strange star.

             Then as he shining rose,
And on her form the new effulgence fell,
The goddess, with her face beatified,
Yet gentle as a mortal mother's, cried
'Balder! my Balder!'—and while from all the woods,
And from the waters wide, and from the air
Still rainbow'd with the flashing flight of birds,
Innumerable echoes answer'd, 'Balder!'—
Clad in his gentle godhead Balder stood,
Bright, beautiful, and palpably divine.

II.

THE SHADOW IN THE WOOD.

'Mother!' he said, and on that mother's face
Fixing the brightness of his starry eyes,
He kiss'd her, smiling. E'en as sunlight falls
Upon the whiteness of some western cloud,
Irradiating and illuming it,
His beauty smote her sadness: silently
She trembled; and her large immortal orbs
Were raised to heaven. For a space she stood
O'er-master'd by that splendour, but at last,
While softly from her forehead and her cheeks
The loving rapture ebb'd, and once again
Her face grew alabaster calm and cold,
Her soul found speech.

             'O Balder! best beloved!
God of the sunlight and the summer stars,
White Shepherd of the gentle beasts and birds,
Benign-eyed watcher of all beauteous things,

Thou know'st me! thou rememberest! thou art here,
Supreme, a god, my Son!—Within thine eyes
Immortal innocence and mortal peace
Are blent to love and gentleness divine;
And tho' I left thee in these woods a babe,
Fair and unconscious as a fallen flower,
And tho' I have not watch'd thy beauty grow,
I come again to seek thee, and behold
Thou know'st me—thou rememberest! thou art here,
Supreme, a god, my Son! Blest be those powers
To whose lone keeping I committed thee!
The heavens have shone upon thee, and the boughs
Have curtain'd thee for slumber, and the rain
Hath smooth'd thy soft limbs with its silvern fingers,
And gently ministrant to thee have been
The starlight and the moonlight and the dew,
And in their seasons all the forest flowers;
And from the crimson of divine deep dawns
And from the flush of setting suns, thy cheeks
Have gather'd such a splendour as appals
The vision, even mine. Balder! beloved!
Speak to me! tell me how thy soul hath fared
Alone so long in these green solitudes.'

She ceased, and Balder smiled again, and took
Her hand and held it as he answer'd her;
And ne'er was sound of falling summer showers
On boughs with lilac laden and with rose,
Or cuckoo-cries o'er emerald uplands heard,
Or musical murmurs of dark summer dawns,
More sweet than Balder's voice. 'O Mother, Mother,'
It answer'd, 'when I saw thee from afar,
Silent, stone-still, with shadow at thy feet,
I knew thee well, for nightly evermore
I have seen thy shape in sleep.' And while the face
Of the great goddess kindled once again
With its maternal love ineffable, .
He added, 'Thou shalt read me all my dream!

For in a dream here have I grown and thriven,
With such dim rapture as those lilies feel
Awakening and uprising mystically
From darkness to the brightness of the air;
And growing in a dream I have beheld
All things grow gladder with me, sun and star,
Strange fronds, and all the wonders of the wood;
Till round me, with me, soul and part of me,
This world hath kindled like an opening rose.
And happy had I been as any bird
Singing full-throated in the summer light,
But for some dark and broken images
Which come to me in sleep—yea come each night
When from the starlight and the silvern moon
I fade with closèd eyes. But thou art here,
And in the love of thy celestial looks
I read the answer to the mystery
Of my dim earthly being.'

As he spake,
Across the goddess' face and thro' her frame
There pass'd the wind of an old prophecy,
Bending her downward as a storm-swept bough.
'In sleep! what shapes have come to thee in sleep?'
She cried, and Balder answer'd, 'It were long
To tell thee all, my Mother! but meseems
I have dream'd nightly of mysterious forms
White-brow'd like thee and very beautiful—
Strange spirits, each more bright than is a star,
In robes of linen and of whitest wool,
And some all raimentless as leaf or flower,
And in their nakedness the more divine.'
Then Frea smiled and answer'd, 'That is well—
'These, Balder, are thy sisters and my kin,
Less beautiful than thou, yet very fair.'
And Balder said, 'Ofttimes mine eyes have seen
Great shapes caparison'd in burning gold,
Tall as the tallest pine within these woods,
Who flash'd red brands together, or upheld
Bright cups of ruby, gazing on each other!'

And Frea smiled and said, 'That too is well—
Those, Balder, are thy brethren and thy peers,
Great gods, yet less than thou.' Then Balder's voice
Sank lower, saying, 'Three times in my sleep
I have seen my Father!'

Frea's cheek was blanch'd,
And pressing one white hand upon her heart,
'How seem'd he in thy sleep?' the goddess sigh'd,
'Frown'd he or smiled he? speak!' And Balder said,
In solemn whispers, sinking ever lower,
'My soul perceived a darkness and a sound
Of many voices wailing, and I seem'd
As one that drifts upon a sunless water,
Amid the washing of a weary rain—
Wet were my locks and dripping, and my limbs
Hung heavily as lead—while wave by wave
I floated to some vapour-shrouded shore.
At last, wash'd in upon the slippery weeds,
I saw before me on a mountain top
One brooding like a cloud; and as a cloud
At first he seem'd, yet ever as I look'd
Grew shapen to an image terrible,
With eyes eternal gazing down at mine.
And as I rose a voice came from the cloud
Like far-off muffled thunder, crying "Balder!
Come hither, my son Balder!"—when in fear
I scream'd and woke, and saw the daylight dance
Golden upon the forests and the meres.'

He ceased; and utter pity fill'd his soul
To see across his beauteous Mother's face
The scorching of unutterable pain;
Then thrice the troubled goddess raised her eyes
And gazed up northward where the rose-red shafts
Of dawn were trembling on the cloud-capt towers
Of Asgard; thrice the sorrow master'd her;
But soon her strong soul conquer'd, and she forced
A strange sad look of calm. 'If that be all,
Take courage—and I do conjure thee now,
Fear not thy Father. If that Father ever
Hath cherish'd dread of thee, the loveliness
Of thy completed godhead shall disarm
His wrath,—yea, win his love.' Her gentle hand
Clasp'd his with more than mortal tenderness,
And in his eyes she gazed again and drank
The solace of his beauty while the dawn
Encrimson'd both and all the heavens and air,
But Balder trembled shrinking to her side,
And cried, with quick eyes glancing all around,
'Mother, that is not all!'

'O speak no more,'
The goddess said, 'if aught else terrible
Thine eyes have vision'd or thy sense hath dream'd,
Speak, speak, no more!' but Balder answer'd, 'Mother!
A weight is on my heart, and I must speak.
Last night I dream'd the strangest dream of dreams!
Methought I in the summer woodland walk'd
And pluck'd white daffodils and pansies blue,
And as I went I sang such songs as sing
The spirits of the forest and the stream;
And presently the golden light went in,
But balmy darkness follow'd, for the rain
Patter'd with diamond dews innumerable
On the green roof of umbrage overhead.
I stood and waited, listening. Then methought
I heard a voice from far away—*thy* voice
It seem'd, my Mother—murmur three times
"Balder!"
And as it ceased, there pierced the wood's green heart
A shriek so sharp and shrill that all my blood
Turn'd cold to listen! Suddenly I felt
My brow was damp with chilly drops of rain,
And looking up I saw that every leaf
Had wither'd from the branches overhead,
Leaving them black against a sunless heaven
Of dark and dreary gray. Again I heard

Thy voice moan " Balder," and methought
  the boughs
Toss'd their wild arms above and echoed
  " Balder,"
When lo, the black and miserable rain
Came slower and slower, wavering through
  the dark,
Till every drop was as a flake of white
Falling upon the ground as light as wool!
And terror seized me, and I felt my heart
Cold as a stone, and from my hands the
  flowers
Dropt, wither'd, with that whiteness on the
  ground.
I tried to stir, and could not stir; I sought
To shake the chilly flakes from off my neck,
But could not; and each time I sought to
  cry,
My cries were frozen in my throat. Now
  mark!
O mark, my mother, for these things are
  strange!
As thus I stood, mine eyes were 'ware of
  ONE,
A Shape with shadowy arms outspread like
  wings,
Which, hovering o'er me even as a hawk,
Fix'd on my face its fatal luminous eyes.
O Mother, that wan shape! The forest holds,
In form of beast or bird or glittering snake,
No likeness of its awful lineaments!
For ever as its features seem'd to take
Clearness and semblance, they did fade
  away
Into a swooning dimness; and it seem'd
Now shapen and now shapeless, blowing
  amid
The wonder of that wan and sunless shower.
Yet ever as I gazed it gazed again,
And ever circling nearer seem'd in act
To swoop upon me with cold claws and
  clutch
The heart that flutter'd wildly in my breast.
At last that look became too much to bear:
Answering at last *thy* scream, I scream'd
  aloud;
And as I scream'd, I woke—and saw again
The sunlight on the forests and the meres.'

Now ev'n as Balder spake the goddess' face
Was like a shrouded woman's: once again
She gazed at heaven, and her eyes were
  glazed

With agony and despair, for now she knew
That shape which Balder had beheld in
  dream
Was he whom mortal man have christen'd
  Death.
At last she spake, and all her proud soul
  flash'd,
Rebuking its own terror. 'Unto all,
Yea even unto gods upon their thrones,
Such shadows come in sleep; thy Father
  even
Hath had his visions, and I too have mine;
But be of comfort since thou art my Son,
For he who hover'd o'er thee in thy dream
Is impotent against the strength of gods.
Haunter is he of this sad nether sphere,
And on the little life of bird and beast,
And on the life of flowers and falling leaves,
His breath comes chill, but to the Shapes
  divine
He is as wind that bloweth afar below
The silence of the peaks.'

                          Ev'n as she spake,
On her bright Balder gazed not, but with
  eyes
Fix'd as in fascination, cried aloud
'Look! look!'—and pointed.

                        Close to that bright spot
Whereon they stood in the full flame of
  day,
The forest open'd, flashing green and gold,
Sparkling with quick and rapturous thrill of
  leaves
And rainbow-flush of flowers. Upon a
  bough
That reach'd its heavy-laden emerald arm
Into the summer light beyond the shade,
There clung, with panting breast and
  fluttering wings,
A trembling ringdove whose soft iris'd eyes
Were fix'd like Balder's on some shape of
  dread
Just visible in the shadow, lying low
Under the scented umbrage of the wood.
A Form, yet indistinct as the green sheen;
A Face, yet featureless; a head with eyes
Now faint as drops of dew, now strangely
  bright
As lustrous gems. Crouch'd on the under-
  grass,
It watch'd in serpent fashion every thrill

Of that bright bird; while all around, the air
Was mad and merry with the summer song
Of choirs that sat alive on leafy boughs,
Singing aloud!

Then came a hush, wherein
Every faint pulse of life in those great woods
Was heard to beat; and then the fated bird
Cooing and quivering fluttered from the bough,
And 'mid the summer sheen beyond the shade,
With one last dying tremor of the wings,
Lay stricken still. . . . Among the darkening leaves
There was a stir, as creeping thro' the gloom,
Scarce visible, fixing eyes on that dead dove,
Forth from his lair the form began to crawl.
And Balder sicken'd, and his sense grew cold.
But with a queenly gesture Frea rose,
And pointed with her white imperious hand
Into the forest. Suddenly the shape
Was 'ware of that pale goddess and her son
More beauteous and insufferably bright.
A moment in the dimness of his lair
He paused, uprearing, as in act to spring,
A head half human, with a serpent's eyes;
Then, conscious of some presence that he feared,
All swift and silent, like a startled snake,
He faded back into the shadowy woods.

II.

FULL GODHEAD.

O whither are they wending side by side
Thro' that green forest wide?
Down the deep dingles, amid ferns and flowers,
They wander hours and hours.
Bright-lock'd, with limbs of alabaster white,
Now gleaming in the light,
Now 'mong the dusky umbrage of the glade
Deep'ning to amber shade,
Their eyes on one another, whither away
Do these Immortals stray?

She murmurs, 'Thou shalt mark all things that be;
The rivers and the sea,
The mountains that for ever crimson'd lie
Against the arctic sky,
The meteors that across the pale pole flit,
Strangely illuming it;
And thou shalt look on gods, thy kin and mine,
Since *thou* too art divine.'
Divine!—The forest glimmers where he goes
To crimson and to rose!
And wheresoe'er he comes no creature fears;
Each lingers, sees, and hears.
The boughs bend down to touch his yellow hair;
Around his white feet bare
The grass waves amorous; on his shoulder white
The singing birds alight,
Singing the sweeter; and in spaces clear
The brown-eyed dappled deer
With tremulous ear and tail around him stand,
Licking his outstretch'd hand
With warm rough tongues. He sings—all things around
Are husht to hear the sound!
He smiles—all things are smiling—wood and stream
With some new glory gleam,
Dark branches blossom, and the greensward nigh
Is sunnier than the sky!

She murmurs, 'They have cherish'd thee indeed,
In answer to thy need.
Ere thou wast born, into thy veins they grew,
Earth, sunlight, air, and dew,
The flower, the leaf, star's glimmer and bird's song;
And these have made thee strong
With other strength than ours; for ne'er till now,
On any immortal brow
Have I beheld such living splendour shine
As lies this hour on thine.
O sunbeam of the gods! O fairer far
Than ev'n Immortals are!
Divinest, gentlest, by the glad Earth given
To be a lamp in heaven!'

Divine!—The boughs shook down their
   shafts of green
And gleam'd to golden sheen ;
The silvern snake stole from the dark tree-
   root
And twined round Balder's foot
With happy eyes ; the tiger-moth and bee
   About him hover'd free ;
With yellow aureole his head was crown'd,
   And his bright body around
There swam a robe of sunshine scented
   sweet,
Clothing him head to feet.

She crieth, ' Could the Father see thee there,
   While on thy silken hair
The soft light trembles like a shining hand!
   Couldst thou before him stand,
Flowers round thy feet, a dove upon thy
   wrist,
Earth-blest and heaven-kist,
Would he not smile? would he not scorn
   full soon
The wearily woven rune
Which said that sorrow should be born
   when *thou*
Didst break with orient brow
The night-cloud of the Earth? O Son! my
   Son!
The crimson thread is spun,
The snow-white bud is blown, and now,
   behold-!
The branch with fruit of gold
Hath grown full straight and swings i' the
   summer shine
Ineffably divine.'

He questions, ' Whither go we?' She
   replies,
' To that dim Land which lies
Ev'n as a cloud around the Father's feet!'
He smiles, his pulses beat
With brighter rapture. 'Shall mine eyes
   then see
My Father?' crieth he ;
' Where dwells he? and my brethren, where
   dwell they?'
She answereth, ' Far away!'
Then, her face darken'd by some dreamy
   dread,
She moves with sadder tread.

The shadows grow around them as they stray
   From glade to glade ; their way

Winds still 'mong flowers and leaves, where
   day and night,
Both sleepless and both bright,
One golden and one silvern, come and go.
Nor, when dark twilights sow
Their asphodels in the broad fields of blue,
   And a cold summer dew
Gleams on the grass, and moths with fiery
   eyes
Flit, and the night-jar cries,
Doth Balder glimmer less divine. Ah, nay!
   Dim things that know not day
Find him and love him ; drinking his pure
   breath
The white owl hovereth ;
About his footprints in the faint moon-ray
   Wild lynxes leap and play ;
The ringdoves on the branches brood ; meek
   hares
Creep from their grassy lairs
To look upon him. So he goeth by
   Of all things that descry
Beloved, and missed ; around him like a
   veil
The moonbeams cluster pale,
And all the eyes of heaven with soft dews
   swim,
As they gaze down on him.

But now they leave the mighty woods, and
   pass
Thro' valleys of deep grass,
Sprinkled with saxifrage and tormentil ;
   And many a mountain rill
Leaps by them, singing. Far away, on
   high,
They mark against the sky
Blue-shadow'd mountains crown'd with
   sparkling snow ;
And thitherward they go.

Thro' lonely mountain valleys in whose
   breast
The white grouse makes its nest,
And where in circles wheel the goshawk
   keen
And fleet-wing'd peregrine ;
Past torrents gashing the dark heathery
   height
With gleams of hoary white,
Their shining feet now fall, and where they
   fare
Faint rainbows fill the air

And span the streams; with sound of rip-
    pling rain
  The cataracts leap amain,
The deer cry from the heights, and all around
  Is full of summer sound.

Silent, upon the topmost peak they come,
    By precipices dumb
And melancholy rocks girt round; and so
    They reach the realms of snow.
Far o'er their heads a hooded eagle wings
    In ever-widening rings,
Till in the blinding glory of the day
    A speck he fades away.
Then Balder's eyes gaze down. Stretch'd
    far beneath,
  Forest and field and heath,
Netted with silvern threads of springs and
    streams,
  Shine in the summer beams—
And valley after valley farther on
  Fades dim into the sun.

He crieth, 'Far away methinks I mark
    A mighty Forest dark,
Crown'd by a crimson mist; yonder it lies,
    Stretching into the skies,
And farther than its darkness nought I see.'
    And softly answereth she,
'O Balder! 'tis the Ocean. Vast and
    strange,
  It changeth without change,
Washing with weary waves for evermore
    The dark Earth's silent shore.'
And Balder spake not, but he gazed again
    Thro' the soft mist of rain
Which curtain'd that new wonder from his
    sight.

At last, when day and night
Have passed, they cross a purple cape and
    stand
  On shores of golden sand,
And pausing silent, see beneath the sky
    The mighty Ocean lie.

IV.

THE MAN BY THE OCEAN.

Calmly it lieth, limitless and deep,
    In windless summer sleep,
And from its fringe, cream-white and set
    with shells,
  A drowsy murmur swells,

While in its shallows, on its yellow sands,
    Smiling, uplifting hands,
Moves Balder, beckoning with bright looks
    and words
  The snow-white ocean birds.
He smiles—the heavens smile answer! All
    the sea
  Is glistering glassily.
Far out, blue-black amid the waters dim,
    Leviathan doth swim,
Spouts fountain-wise, roars loud, then sink-
    ing slow,
  Seeks the green depths below.
All silent. All things sleeping in the light,
  And all most calmly bright!

He walks the weed-strewn strand, and
    where the waves
  Creep into granite caves,
Green-paven, silver-fretted, roof'd with rose,
    He like a sunbeam goes,
And ocean-creatures know him. The black
    seal
  Out of the darkness steal
With gentle bleat, or with their lambs arise,
    Their dark and dewy eyes
Uplooking into his; the cormorants green,
    Which ranged in black rows preen
Their dusky plumage, at his footstep's sound
    Turn snake-like necks around,
But rise not; o'er his head the white terns fly
    With shrill unceasing cry;
And out of caverns come the rock-doves
    fleet,
  Alighting at his feet!
Across the waters darts a shaft supreme
    Of strange and heavenly gleam,
That doth his consecrated form enfold
    Like to a robe of gold,—
While all the Ocean gladdeneth anew,
    Stretch'd bright beneath the blue.

But what is this he findeth on his way,
    Here, where the golden ray
Falleth on sands 'neath crimson crags that
    rise
  Dark 'gainst the great blue skies?
What is this shape that, breathing soft and
    deep,
  Lies on its side asleep,
Here on the strand where drifted sea-weeds
    cling?
  Is it some ocean thing,

Crept from the emerald darkness of the brine
   To bask i' the summer shine?
Is it some gentle monster whose green home
   Lies far below the foam?
Softly he sleeps, while on his closèd eyes
   The summer sunlight lies;
Around his face, that seemeth wildly fair,
   Hang tawny locks of hair,
On dusky shoulders falling loosely down;
   And lo, his cheeks are brown
With kisses of the sun, and round his limbs
   A light like amber swims
Divinely clear; and by his side is thrown
   A spear of walrus-bone,
A bear-skin blanket, and a seal-hide thong;
   So sleeps he, brown and strong;
And nought that lieth upon land or sea
   Seemeth more strange than he,
Like some wild birth of ocean wash'd to
      land,
   And cast upon the sand
With many a drifting weed and waif beside.

'O Mother!' Balder cried,
Suddenly falling on his bended knee,
   'What shape is this I see?
It sleeps—it breathes—it lives!' And Frea
      said,
   Scarce turning her proud head,
'It is a mortal man not worth thy care!
   Ev'n as the birds of the air
They are born, they gladden, and they come
      and go.'
   But Balder, stooping low,
Passing soft fingers o'er the sleeper's side,
   And smiling sweetly, cried,
'Awake, awake!' and gently from the
      strand
   He raised one strong brown hand.
'Hush!' said the pallid goddess, sighing
      deep,
   'Lest he awake from sleep,
And touch him not, lest from his mortal
      breath
   Thou know'st the taint of Death.'
'Death!' Balder echoed with a quick sharp
      pain;
   And Frea spake again,
'Nought on this nether sphere which foster'd
      thee,
   But drinks mortality;
Fade not the leaf, the lily, and the rose?
   Yea, and the oak-tree knows

Only its season;—in their seasons all
   Are fashion'd, fade, and fall—
Birds on the boughs, and beasts within the
      brake,
   Yea, ev'n the hawk and snake,
Are born to perish; and this creature shares
   An earthly lot like theirs.'
She paused; for suddenly in the bright
      sun-ray
   God Balder's cheeks grew gray
And sunken—his eyes dim;—a moment's
      space
   Across his troubled face
Pass'd darkness. Frea quail'd. A moment
      more,
   And that strange shade pass'd o'er,
And Balder's looks again grew beautiful.

O'erhead, as white as wool,
The calm clouds melted in the burning
      blue;
   Beneath, the great seas grew
Stiller and calmer, while the immortal one
   Stood dreaming in the sun,
On that dark sleeper fixing eyes grown
      bright
   With heavenly love and light.

'O come!' the goddess cried, and took his
      hand.
   Along the shining strand
They pass'd, but evermore god Balder's face
   Turn'd backward to the place
Where he had left the weary wight asleep.

Then, as beside the Deep
They wander'd slowly onward, Frea told
   Strange tales and legends old
Of living men, and how they came to be,
   And how they bend the knee
To gods they know not, till beneath the sun
   They die, and all is done.

And ever her finger pointed as she spoke
   To wreaths of light-blue smoke
Upcurling heavenward o'er the sleeping seas
   From fishing villages.
Love in his heart and wonder on his brow,
   Bright Balder hearken'd now
In silence. 'Far beyond those lonely woods
   And these sea-solitudes,
Peopling the dark Earth, living forms like
      these
   Gather as thick as bees:—

Shapen like gods, yet perishable; born
  For ever night and morn,
And night and morn for ever vanishing.
  An old dark doom doth cling
Around them and all kindred things that
    bloom
  Out of the green world's womb.
Heed them not *thou!* To gods they are no
    more
Than singing birds that soar
A little flight, and fall. Tho' for a space,
  Rear'd in a lowly place,
Thou hast known, as mortals know, Earth's
    shade and shine,
  Another lot is thine!—
To sit among the gods, on heights supreme,
  Beyond Man's guess or dream!'

III. THE HEAVENWARD JOURNEY.

I.

THE GODDESSES.

There is a valley by the northern sea,
O'ershadow'd softly by eternal hills
And canopied by the ethereal blue.
Above it silently for ever gleam
Cold peaks of ice and snow, and over these
The wind goes, and the shadows of the
    wind;
While far below, the hollows of the vale
Are strewn most deep with heather and with
    thyme,
And weeping willows hang their silken hair
O'er dusky tarns with summer lilies sown;
And from these tarns smooth tracts of
    greensward slope
Until they blend with silvern sands that kiss
The foam-white lips of the still sleeping sea.

Into that valley by a secret way,
The goddess guided her immortal son.
Long had they wander'd, o'er the realms of
    snow,
Thro' forests vast, down desolate ravines;
And still, where'er they stept, before their
    feet
A wind of brightness like a river ran,
And rippled softly into grass and flowers,—

So that they walked on rainbows with no
    rain,
And under heaven made heaven beneath
    their feet.
At last their path wound upward, while
    again
They trod the white snows of the topmost
    peaks,
And saw beneath them, faint and far away,
The secret valley: purple woods of pine,
Crags of wild umbrage lit by flashing falls,
Smooth emerald lawns; and beyond all,
    the sea.

And lo! as Balder gazed, that valley fair
Grew fairer—on its sleep his brightness fell
As benediction—and in saffron light
It swam below him like a sunset cloud.
Down from the lonely heights whereon he
    stood
A snow-white cataract, like a naked god
With plumes of silver plunging from a peak
Into a purple ocean, headlong flash'd;
Then, lost among the dark green pine-tree
    tops,
Sounded unseen, mingling its far-off voice
With the deep murmur of the wind-swept
    boughs.
From rocky shelf to shelf, with golden moss
Enwrought and fringèd with dwarf willow
    trees,
They now descended in the torrent's track,
And plunging swiftly downward found a path
Thro' the cool darkness of the shadowy
    woods;
But as they went the dusky forest way
Grew brighter, ever flash'd to softer green
The green leaves, and the sward to sunnier
    hues,
Till from the leafy umbrage they emerged,
And Balder saw a vision fairer far
Than ever poet fabled in a dream.

Beside those waters, on those emerald
    lawns
Basking in one eternal summer day,
Lay goddesses divine with half-closed eyes
Gazing out seaward on the crimson isles
Sown in the soft haze of the summer deep.
And there they wove white runes to win the
    hearts
Of gods and men, while o'er their happy
    heads

Eternity hung steadfast as a star.
Some stretch'd upon the scented greensward
   lay
Moveless and wonderfully robed in white ;
Some sitting silent by the dusky tarns
Look'd upward, with their faces dim as
   dream ;
Some musing stood, their eyes upon the sea,
Their thoughts afar; and many up and
   down
Along the quiet greensward paced and
   mused,
There was no laughter as of maiden voices,
No sound like human singing: all was
   still—
Still as a heartbeat, silent as a sleep.

But when from the green shadow of the
   woods
Immortal Balder in his beauty came,
And stood irresolute in light divine
Gazing upon that wonder of white life,
There was a cry of startled handmaidens
Flocking round goddesses most marble pale.
All to their feet had risen, and one supreme
Tall shape with mailèd plates upon her
   breast,
A skirt blood-red, and in her hand a spear,
Stood, while pale virgins crouch'd around
   her feet,
Confronting Balder with black eyes of fire.
Lithe was she as a serpent, lithe and tall,
Her dark skin glimmering bronzèd in the
   sun,
Her eyebrows black drawn down, and as
   the beam
Of Balder's beauty struck upon her frame,
She raised her spear, and seem'd in act to
   strike ;
But Frea, coming stately from the shade,
Cried, ' Hold ! ' and Rota (for 'twas she
   whose soul
Delights in sowing strife 'mong weary men)
Paused frowning, and the virgins at her feet
Look'd up amazed.

    ' Whom bring'st thou here ? ' she cried—
' What shape is this, with pale blue human
   eyes,
Yet more than human brightness, venturing
Where never foot of earthborn thing hath
   fared ? '
And Frea answer'd gently, ' Harm him not !

Nor give him chilly greeting, sister mine—
Kin is he to immortal gods and thee—
'Tis Balder ! my son Balder ! ' At the word
The wind of that old prophecy arose
And for a moment like a fever'd breath
Faded across those lawns and sleeping
   pools ;
And blown from group to group of white-
   robed forms,
From goddess on to goddess, echoed low
The name of ' Balder,' till it reached the
   sands,
And on the far-off foam did die away
In low sad echoes of the mighty main.

Then Balder with a heavenly look advancing
Shone on the place, and Rota dropt her
   spear,
Still darkening, as in wonder and in scorn
She gazed upon him, crying, ' Then he
   lives !
Woe to the race of Asa since he lives !
Why comes he here ? ' And Balder, with
   a voice
As sweet as fountains falling, made reply,
' I seek my sisters and my kin divine,
And *thou* art of them ! ' and he reach'd out
   hands,
Smiling !

    As Rota stood irresolute,
Half-angry, half-disarm'd by his sweet eyes,
Another shape most fair and wonderful
In snow-white robe array'd thro' which her
   limbs
Shone with a rosy and celestial ray,
Cried ' Balder ! ' in a voice so strange and
   deep
It fell upon the fountains of his heart
Like sudden light ; and two serene large
   eyes
Shone clear as clearest stars before his
   sight.
' Who speaketh ? ' Balder cried, and the
   deep voice
Made answer, ' O thou foster-child of earth,
With eyes like tender harebells, and with
   flesh
Bright as the body of a mortal man,
Dost thou not know me ?—I am Gefion,
Whose touch could make thee fruitful as a
   tree
That drops ripe fruit at every kiss o' the
   wind.'

And Balder would have answer'd eagerly,
But Frea now uplifting a white hand
With queenly gesture, raised her voice and
    said,
'O sisters! goddesses! O lilies fair
Blown in the still pools of eternity!
Be silent for a space, and for a space
Gaze on my son whom to your bowers I
    bring
For benediction; now, behold, he lives,
Immortal as yourselves and beautiful
As any star that in the heaven of heavens
Hangs luminous, a lamp for mortal eyes.
Him in the secret furrows of the Earth
I cast like seed, while far away the storm
Flash'd to a portent, and I wove my rune:
That neither wind nor snow nor any touch
Of god or goddess might disturb his growth
From season unto season, while he rose
Ev'n as a flower from the sweet-soilèd earth.
There came unto his making leaf and flower,
The soft rain and the shadow of the rain,
The sundew and the moondew, and the
    gleam
Of starlight, and the glowlight on the grass.
To secret things my hands committed him,
And strangely he hath thriven since that
    hour,
Ev'n as a leaf is fashion'd, ev'n as the hair
Of the long grass is woven, wondrously!
And thus, his brow bright with the balms
    of Earth,
He stands complete, his Father's child, my
    son.
O look upon him! See his happy eyes!
And tell me that ye love him, and in turn
Will bless him, shielding him upon your
    breasts
If ever evil hour to him should come.
Oh, that sad rune we fear'd of old is false!
For gentle is he as the gentle things
Which foster'd him, too blest and beautiful
To be a terror or a grief to gods.'

She ceased; and Gefion thro' her loosen'd
    hair
Smiled, and stern Rota's look grew tenderer.
Then, stretch'd her listless length upon the
    grass,
Her dark face glowing brightly in the sun,
Upon one elbow leaning, sun-tanned Eir
Raised with quick wicked laugh her root
    and knife,

Saying, 'O Frea, had I found him there
Fall'n like a flower in the dark arms of
    Earth,
This knife had made an end; but since he
    stands
Full-grown and fair, immortal, and thy son,
I bid him welcome!'—As she spake, the
    eyes
Of Balder fell upon the root and knife,
And lo, the knife gleam'd as a brand of
    gold,
While the black root, moist with the dews
    of earth,
Trembled, and blossom'd into light green
    leaves!
Then trembling, Eir arose, and stood her
    height,
While gazing full into her troubled eyes,
Bright Balder moved to embrace her
    silently.

But as he gently came there interposed
A wonder of new brightness,—such a shape,
So perfect in divine white loveliness,
As never mortal yet beheld and lived.
And Balder trembled, and his bosom heaved
With an exceeding sweetness strange and
    new,
While close to his there came a shining
    face,
Still as a sunbeam, dimmer than a dream.
And Freya, for 'twas she whose touch is
    life
To happy lovers and to loveless men
Is sickness and despair, said, breathing
    warm,
While on her alabaster arms love's light
Was flushing faint as thro' a rose's leaves,
'Let all my sisters greet thee as they will,
I *love* thee, Balder! since of lovely things
Thou art the brightest and the loveliest!'
And lo! ere he was ware of her intent,
Unto his cheek she prest a warm red mouth
Kings of great empires would have swoon'd
    to touch,
And poets heavenly-dower'd would have
    died
To dream of kissing. Then thro' Balder
    ran
A new miraculous rapture such as feels
The dark Earth when the scented Summer
    leaps
Full-blossom'd as a bridegroom to her arms;

Such as musk-roses know when blown apart
By sunbeams in mid-June ; and Balder's
   sense
Swoon'd, and he seem'd strewn o'er with
   fruit and flowers,
And on his lids were touches like warm
   rain,
And on his nostrils and his parted lips
Delicious balm and spicy odours fell,
And all his soul was like a young maid's
   frame
Bathed in the warmth of love's first virgin
   dream.

Then, as he trembled thro' and thro' his
   form
With the last flush of that celestial fire,
The goddesses around him flocking came,
All giving welcome. Some into his eyes
Gazed in such awe as pallid virgins feel
For some mysterious splendour masculine
They seek yet fear and shrink from as they
   touch.
For Balder's loveliness in that bright place
Was as the soft sheen of the summer moon
Arising silvern in the cloudless west
Above the sunset seas of orange gold ;
And there was trouble in his human eyes
Most melancholy sweet,—trouble like tears,
Of starlight, or the tremor of the dew.

II.

THE FRUIT OF LIFE.

They led him to a bank with moss inlaid,
Close to the tranquil mirror of the sea,
And thither came pale ocean handmaidens
Singing to lutes of amber and of pearl,
While 'Love him, love him,' cried the god-
   desses,
' O love him, love him, he is beautiful ! '
But Frea lifted up her hand, and cried,
' Love is not all—swear against all things ill
To watch him and protect him ; '—and they
   cried,
' We swear ! we swear ! ' Then bending
   over him
With bright black eyeballs burning into his,
Pale Rota touched his forehead with her
   spear,
Crying. ' Live on ! No touch of time shall
   cause
One wrinkle on thy smooth unruffled brow ! '

And Eir, low-laughing, held with tender
   teeth,
Not bruising the fair skin, his naked arm,
And murmur'd, ' Strength and subtle force
   be thine,
Drunk from my breath into thy deepest
   veins.'
And Gefion, with her large, sad, heavenly
   eyes
Upgazing in his face, and one white hand
Laid softly on his side, cried, ' As a tree
Be fruitful ! Wheresoe'er thou wanderest,
Fruitage go with thee and a thousand
   flowers ! '
But Freya kiss'd him calmly on the brow,
And whisper'd to him lower than the rest,
' O Balder ! my soul's gift is best of all—
They bring thee life, but I have given thee
   love.'

And Balder sank into a dream. Much joy
Made his sense drowsy, and with happy
   eyes
He saw that mist of light and loveliness
Enclose him, while he seem'd as one who
   swims
Among the shallows of an orient sea.
A voice like music woke him, and he saw
Standing before him in light azure robes
A shape that 'midst those others seem'd as
   dim
And unsubstantial as a summer shade.
Tall was she, and her wondrous sheen of
   hair
Rain'd downward like the silvern willow's
   leaves,
And on her mystic raiment blue as heaven
There glimmer'd dewy drops like shining
   stars.
Pale was she, with the pallor of wan waters
That wash for evermore the cold white feet
Of spectral polar moons ; and when she
   spake,
'Twas low as sea-wash on the starlit sands
And strange and far-away as sounds in
   sleep.
' Balder ! ' she sigh'd ; and like a man who
   hears,
Upstarting on his bed, some wondrous cry,
Balder upstarted wildly listening.
' Balder ! O brother Balder, whose fair face,
Ere yet I gazed upon it shining here,
I knew thro' dark eternities of dream,

See what *I* give thee! see what gentle gift
Thy sister Ydun brings thee; more divine
Than life's sweet breath, or the fair flame
   of love.'

So saying, from her veiled breast she drew
Mystical apples like to diamond seeds,
So small to seeming that a score might lie
In the pink hollow of an infant's hand.
Each shone complete and pure as mother-
   o'-pearl
Touch'd with prismatic gleams of wondrous
   light,
And unto each on the scarce visible stem
There clung two perfect little leaves of gold.
This secret fruit the gods and goddesses
For ever feed on, evermore renewed;
And in a garden desolate and dim
Wash'd by the wild green sea of human
   graves,
Pale Ydun plucks it, and none other may.
'Eat!' Ydun murmur'd—'Balder, eat and
   live—
This fruit shall slay the lingering taint of
   Earth
Within thee, and preserve thee all divine.'

   Then Balder reaching out his open'd
      hand
Did take the fruit, and eating of the same,
Which melted on his tongue like flakes of
   snow,
He felt thro' all his limbs the rapturous
   thrill
Of some supreme and unfamiliar life.
So leaving all those luminous shapes behind,
He took the hand of Ydun, kissing her
As moonlight kisses dew; and side by side
They wended down across the yellow
   sands,—
And many hours they wander'd whispering
   low
Close to the bright edge of that sleeping Sea.

III.

THE CITY OF THE GODS.

So Balder knew what mystical delights,
What slumberous idleness and peace su-
   preme
Belong to the immortal goddesses;
And not a goddess in those golden walks
But loved the human light in Balder's face.

At last thund'rous out of heaven with no
   words.
When Frea cried, 'Thou hearest! Hark, he
To say 'tis—
A weary that murmur out into the dark,
Among shall guide thee to the Father's feet.'
And Bald
   groves, softly smiling, with no fear,
His soul pass'd on; and as one gropes his way
Ev'n Freyr'd guided by the ocean's voice,
And Gefid slowly forth into the night.
And only
His spirit
And Bald   v.
To dwell BALDER'S RETURN.
   bowes
But to far down to the earth she waited, crouch-
Ev'n as a cold ashes of the sunken City,
But still osing round her like to prison walls
   with impenetrable darkness grew.
And so fr it shed a heavy, weary rain,
They pa ng upon her, chilling soul and sense,
   and a corpse's lips; and all the while,
Thro' oth listens from its folded wings,
   n'd!

And from
Of Balder   But the only sound she heard
Forgotten, ow murmur of that weary rain,
Of those gr ead wet fingers o'er the shudder-
From that eavens,
All forms rily drew down the rainy lids
Like shade gentle eyes of all the stars.
Yea even
And gazed lay and hearken'd, till her soul
   sea all count of time and faded back
Smiling all n sad, dumb eternity. . . .
And only
Writing hi stirred like one that wakes from
And weavir
   had ceased, the darkness to the
. . . But
   realms, and her eyes beheld afar,
Still northwa   orthern night,
   nothing live.   eturning feet.
The goddess guide
Into their faces flash   eart is heavy;
So that the streams w
   heights   ly as he moves;
Took deeper darkness brooding at his back,
The stars w r, and his coming far away
   gold. s moonlight when the moon is
Then Frea
'Behold the ghts of March; and when again

He pass'd across the ashes of the City,
And she who bare him could behold his face,
'Twas spectral white, and in his heavenly
   eyes
There dwelt a shadowy pain. Ev'n as a man
Who passing thro' the barrows of the slain
Hath seen the corpses sit at dead of night
Gazing in silence from their own green
   graves ;
Or as a maiden who hath seen a wraith
And knoweth that her shroud is being
   woven,
Came Balder out of heaven : still divine,
And beautiful, but ah ! how sorrowful ;
Still bright, but with a light as sadly fair,
Compared to that first splendour of the
   dawn,
As moonshine is to sunshine ; on his brow
The shade of some new sorrow, in his eyes
The birth of some new pity ; as a god,
Yet ghost-like, with deep glamour in his
   gaze,
Slowly, with faltering footsteps, Balder
   came.

Then Frea rose in silence, very pale,
For on her soul beholding Balder's face
Some desolate anticipation fell,
And turn'd her eyes on his, stretching her
   hands
To hold him and to embrace him, keen to
   hear
His message ; but he spake not when her
   arms
Were wound about him and upon his brow.
Her soft kiss fell ; vacant his sad eyes
   seem'd,
As if they gazed on something far away.
Then Frea sobbed in agony of heart,
'Son, hast thou seen thy brethren?' and
   again,
'Son, hast thou seen thy Father?' Yet a
   space
His lips were silent, and his eyes were
   blank,
But when again and yet again her tongue
Had framed the same fond question, Balder
   said,
In a low voice and a weary, ' I have seen
My brethren and my Father !' Like a man
Smit thro' and thro' with sudden sense of
   cold,
He shiver'd.

Then the goddess, mad to see
The light of agony on that well-loved face,
Clung to him wailing, 'Balder ! my Son
   Balder !
Why is thy look so sick, thy soul so weary?
What hast thou done and seen ? what sight
   of heaven
Hath made thee sad?'—and Balder answer'd
   low,
'O Mother ! I have dream'd another
   dream—
I have seen my brethren in a dream—have
   seen
My brethren and my Father ; and it seems
From that strange trance I have not waken'd
   yet,
But that I still am darkling in my dream,
The breath of gods about me, and the eyes
Of gods upon me ! Patience—question
   not—
The light is coming, and my soul is waking—
My dream grows clear, and I shall soon
   remember
All that mine eyes have seen, mine ears
   have heard.'

Then on that City's ashes side by side
Sat son and mother, two colossal shapes,
Silent, in shadow ; but the eyes of heaven
Were opening above, and to the south
They saw the white seas flash with glittering
   bergs
In fitful glimmers to the windy night.
And when a little space had pass'd away
The god spake softly, saying, 'All is clear,
My sorrow and my dream ; and Mother,
   now
I know those things which seem'd so sad
   and dark.
Ah ! woe is me that I was ever born
To be a terror and a grief to gods !'

Then Frea cried, 'O Balder, unto whom
Can all the promise of thy beauty bring
Terror or grief? Nay, 'twas with looks
   serene
To win the heart of heaven, that its wrath
Might never turn against thee, and to mock
With glory of thy human gentleness
The prophecy of that ancestral rune,
I bade thee go up beauteous and alone
Before the darkness of the Father's face.
Yet thou returnes barren of such joy

G G

As thou a god shouldst snatch from gods
    thy kin,
First in thy plenitude beholding them ;
And on thy brow is sadness, not such peace
As comes from consecration of a kiss
Given by a Father to a son beloved
    In whom he is well pleased ! '

                  Then once again
Like a man smitten to the bone with cold,
Bright Balder shiver'd, and his beautiful face
Grew gray as any mortal's fix'd in death ;
And suddenly he cried, ' O come away !
Come back to those green woods where I
    was born.
The ways of heaven are dreary, and the
    winds
Of heaven blow chilly, and I fain would find
A refuge and a home ! '

                  But Frea moan'd,
Turning her fair face northward in quick
    wrath,
'Ay me thy dream—I read it, from mine own
Most bitterly awaking. Woe to them !
Woe to the Father and the gods thy kin !
Out of thy mansion have they cast thee forth,
Denying thee thy birthright and thy seat
Up yonder at thy heavenly Father's side ! '
But Balder, in a feeble voice and low,
Said, ' They denied me nought, those
    Shapes I saw
Strangely as in a sleep ; nay, but meseem'd
They pointed at me with their spectral hands
And waved me back, some with their raiment hems
Hiding their faces ; in their eyes I saw
Not love but protestation absolute ;
And when I rose and named my Father's
    name,
It seem'd creation rock'd beneath my feet
And all the cloudy void above my head
Trembled ; and when I named my name, a
    voice
Shriek'd " Balder ! " and the naked vaults of
    heaven
Prolong'd in desolation and despair
The echoes of the word till it became
As thunder ! Then meseem'd I saw a hand,
Gripping the fiery lightning suddenly,
Strike at my head as if to smite me down ;
But tho' my frame was wrapt about with fire,
I stood unscathed ; and as I paused I saw,

Confused as stormy shadows in the sea,
Thrones gleaming, faces fading, starry
    shapes
Coming and going darkly ; and each time
I call'd upon my Father, that great hand
Flash'd down the fierce darts of the crimson
    levin,
And from that darkness which I knew was he
A voice came, and a cry that seem'd a curse,
Until my soul was sicken'd and afraid.
Then, for my heart was heavy, yearning still
To look upon him and to feel at last
The welcome of his consecrating kiss,
I fell upon my knees, folded my hands
Together, and I blest him ;—when methought
The voice wail'd, and the cry that seem'd a
    curse
Re-echoed. Then came blackness more
    intense ;
And for a space my sense and sight seem'd
    lost,
And when I woke I stood beside thee here,
Holding thy hand and looking in thine
    eyes.'

Then Frea wail'd, ' 'Tis o'er ! my hope is
    o'er !
Thy Father loves thee not, but casts thee
    forth—
Where wilt thou find a place to rest thy
    feet ? '
But Balder answer'd, ' Where the cushat
    builds
Her nest amid green leaves, and where
    wild roses
Hang lamps to light the dewy feet of dawn,
And where the starlight and the moonlight
    slumber,
Ev'n there, upon the balmy lap of Earth,
Shall I not sleep again ? O Mother,
    Mother !
Pray to my Father that his soul may learn
To love me in due season, while again
Earthward we fare ; and Mother, bless thou
    me,
Me whom my heavenly Father blesseth not,
With ministering hands before we go ! '

Then Frea cried, blessing and kissing
    Balder,
' Go *thou*,—the green Earth loves thee, and
    thy face

Is as a lamp to all the gentle things
Which mingled in thy making—Go
  down,
But I will journey upward till I find
The footstool of the Father. Night and
With prayers, with intercession of deer
With ministering murmurs, I will
Low-lying like a cloud around his
Thy cause, and the green Earth
  foster'd thee :
That in a later season love may come
In answer, and the Father fear no
To seat thee 'mong Immortals at
Go down, my child, my sunbeam,
  born,
My Balder, who art still deem'd beauti.
Save only in the heavenly Father's sight !
And when all things have blest thee ; when
  all forms
Have gladden'd in thy glory; when all
  voices,
The mountains and the rivers and the seas,
The white clouds and the stars upon their
  thrones,
Have known thy face and syllabled thy
  name ;
Come back again under the arch of heaven,
Not as a suppliant but a conqueror,
And take thy throne !'

           The darkness far away
Groan'd: and the great void answer'd ;
  overhead
Cluster'd the countless spheres of night,
  like eyes
Downgazing ; but beneath the goddess' feet
Shot up dim gleams of dawn.

           Then bright as day
Grew Balder, while his face, composed to
  peace,
Turn'd earthward ; and he stretch'd out
  eager arms
To that belovèd land where he was born.
'Farewell !' he said, and softly kiss'd the
  mother ;
Then, while the goddess glided like a cloud
Up heavenward, down to the dim Earth he
  pass'd
Slowly, with luminous feet.

        . . . And when he came
To that cold realm which belts the Frozen
  Sea,

And all things grow loving,
  And all things grow bright :
Buds bloom in the meadows,
  Milk foams in the pail,
There is scent in the shadows,
  And sound in the light :
O listen ! he passes
  Thro' valleys of flowers,
With springing of grasses
  And singing of showers.
Earth wakes—he has called her,
  Whose voice she holds dear ;
She was waiting for Balder,
  And Balder is here !

         II.

'Mid mountains white by rainbows

BALDER'S RETURN TO EARTH.

I.

'BALDER IS HERE.'

O who cometh sweetly
  With singing of showers?—
The wild wind runs fleetly
  Before his soft tread,
The sward stirs asunder
  To radiance of flowers,
While o'er him and under
  A glory is spread—
A white cloud above him
  Moves on thro' the blue,
And all things that love him
  Are dim with its dew :
The lark is upspringing,
  The merle whistles clear,
There is sunlight and singing,
  For Balder is here !

He walks on the mountains,
  He treads on the snows ;
He loosens the fountains
  And quickens the wells ;
He is filling the chalice
  Of lily and rose,
He is down in the valleys
  And deep in the dells—
He smiles, and buds spring to him,
  The bright and the dark ;
He speaks, and birds sing to him,
  The finch and the lark,—

As thou a god shouldst snatch from gods
    thy kin,
First in thy plenitude beholding them ;
And on thy brow is sadness, not such peace
As comes from consecration of a kiss
Given by a Father to a son beloved
In whom he is well pleased ! '

                   Then once again
Like a man smitten to the bone with cold,
Bright Balder shiver'd, and his beautiful face
Grew gray as any mortal's fix'd in death ;
And suddenly he cried, ' O come away !
Come back to those green woods where I
    was born.
The ways of heaven are dreary, and the
    winds
Of heaven blow chilly, and I *found* him,
    The leaves whisper near—
' He is ours—we have found him—
    Bright Balder is here ! '

    The forest glows golden
      Where'er he is seen,
    New flowers are unfolden,
      New voices arise ;
    Flames flash at his passing
      From boughs that grow green,
    Dark runlets gleam, glassing
      The stars of his eyes.
    The Earth wears her brightest
      Wherever he goes,
    The hawthorn its whitest,
      Its reddest the rose ;
    The days now are sunny,
      The white storks appear,
    And the bee gathers honey,
      For Balder is here.

He is here on the heather,
    And here by the brook,
And here where together
    The lilac boughs cling ;
He is coming and going
    With love in his look,
His white hand is sowing
    Warm seeds, and they spring !
He has touch'd with new silver
    The lips of the stream,
And the eyes of the culver
    Are bright from his beam,
He has lit the great lilies
    Like lamps on the mere ;

All happy and still is,
    For Balder is here.

Still southward with sunlight
    He wanders away—
The true light, the one light,
    The new light, is he !
And with music and singing
    The mountains are gay,
Until the peace he is bringing
    Spreads over the sea.
To look on night, while stars twinkling
    Gleam down on the glade,
His white hands are sprinkling
    With harebells the shade ;
And when day hath broken,
    All things that dwell near
Will know, by that token,
    That Balder is here.

In the dark deep dominions
    Of pine and of fir,
Where the dove with soft pinions
    Sits still on her nest,
He sees her, and by her
    The young doves astir,
And smiling sits nigh her,
    His hand on her breast ;
The father-dove lingers
    With love in its eyes,
Alights on his fingers,
    And utters soft cries,
And the sweet colours seven
    Of the rainbow appear
On its neck, as in heaven,
    Now Balder is here.

He sits by a fountain
    Far up near the snow,
And high on the mountain
    The wild reindeer stand ;
On crimson moss near to him
    They feed walking slow,
Or come with no fear to him,
    And eat from his hand.
He sees the ice turning
    To columns of gold,
He sees the clouds burning
    On crags that were cold ;
The great snows are drifting
    To cataracts clear,
All shining and shifting,
    For Balder is here.

O who sitteth singing,
  Where sunset is red,
And wild ducks are winging
  Against the dark gleam?
It is he, it is Balder,
He hangeth his head
Where willow and alder
  Droop over the stream;
And the purple moths find him
  And hover around,
And from marshes behind him
  He hears a low sound:
The frogs croak their greeting
  From swamp and from mere,
And their faint hearts are beating,
  For Balder is here.

The round moon is peeping
  Above the low hill;
Her white light, upcreeping
  Against the sun's glow,
On the black shallow river
  Falls silvern and chill,
Where bulrushes quiver
  And wan lilies grow.
The black bats are flitting,
  Owls pass on soft wings,
Yet silently sitting
  He lingers and sings—
He sings of the Maytime,
  Its sunlight and cheer,
And the night like the daytime
  Knows Balder is here.

He is here with the moonlight,
  With night as with day,
The true light, the one light,
  The new light, is he;
The moon-bows above him
  Are melted away,
And the things of night love him,
  And hearken and see.
He sits and he ponders,
  He walks and he broods,
Or singing he wanders
  'Neath star-frosted woods;
And the spheres from afar, light
  His face shining clear:
Yea, the moonlight and starlight
  Feel Balder is here.

He is here, he is moving
  On mountain and dale,
And all things grow loving,
  And all things grow bright:
Buds bloom in the meadows,
  Milk foams in the pail,
There is scent in the shadows,
  And sound in the light:
O listen! he passes
  Thro' valleys of flowers,
With springing of grasses
  And singing of showers.
Earth wakes—he has called her,
  Whose voice she holds dear;
She was waiting for Balder,
  And Balder is here!

II.

'Mid mountains white by rainbows
    spanned,
  Upon his knees he sank,
And melted in his hollow'd hand
  The stainless snows, and drank.

And far beneath in mists of heat
  Great purple valleys slept,
And flashing bright beneath his feet
  The loosen'd cataracts leapt.

Down to those happy vales he drew
  Where men and women dwell,
And white snow melted, green grass grew,
  Where'er his footprints fell.

Then night by night and day by day
  His deepest joy was found
In watching happy things of clay
  And hearing human sound.

All human eyes to him were sweet,
  He loved the touch of hands,
He kissed the print of human feet
  Upon the soft sea-sands.

Most silently he went and came,
  With mild and blissful mien,
Bright as a beam his face would flame
  Amid the forests green.

To timid mortals passing by
  He seemed a vision fair,
But little children oft drew nigh,
  And let him smooth their hair;

And witless men would come to him
  With wild and eldritch cries,
And lying in the moonbeams dim
  Would gaze into his eyes!

His voice was in the lonely wood,
   And by the nameless stream,—
He shed in silent solitude
   The peaceful rays of dream.

From vale to vale he went, and blest
   The wild beast and the bird,—
While deep within the glad Earth's breast
   The founts of being stirred. . . .

He sat down in a lonely land
   Of mountain, moor, and mere,
And watch'd, with chin upon his hand,
   Dark maids that milk'd the deer.

And while the sun set in the skies,
   And stars shone in the blue,
They sang sweet songs, till Balder's eyes
   Were sad with kindred dew.

He passed along the hamlets dim
   With twilight's breath of balm,
And whatsoe'er was touch'd by him
   Grew beautiful and calm.

The old man sitting on the grass
   Look'd up 'neath hoary hair,
And felt some heavenly presence pass
   And gladden'd unaware!

He came unto a hut forlorn
   As evening shadows fell,
And saw the man among the corn,
   The woman at the well.

And entering the darken'd place,
   He found the cradled child;
Stooping he lookt into its face,
   Until it woke and smiled!

Then Balder passed into the night
   With soft and shining tread,
The cataract called upon the height,
   The stars gleam'd overhead.

He raised his eyes to those cold skies
   Which he had left behind,—
And saw the banners of the gods
   Blown back upon the wind.

He watch'd them as they came and fled,
   Then his divine eyes fell.
'I love the green Earth best,' he said,
   'And I on Earth will dwell!'

III.
ALL THINGS BLEST BY BALDER.

So when his happy feet had wander'd far,
When all the birds had brighten'd and his hand
Had linger'd on the brows of all the beasts,
He came among the valleys where abode
Mortals that walk erect upon the ground.
First, southward passing, he beheld those men
Who, where the snow for ever lieth, dwell
In caverns of the ground and swathe their limbs
In skins of beasts: these felt his glory pass,
But knew it not, because their eyes were dim
With many nights of darkness. Round their doors
Sorrel blood-red he cast and saxifrage,
And singing passed away! Then roam'd he on,
Past porphyry and greenstone crags that line
Limitless oceans of unmelting ice,
Until he enter'd valleys kindlier
That redden'd into ruby as he came;
And in among the countless deer he stole,
Marking their horns with golden moss, and singing
A strange soft song their souls could understand.

Then as the Earth grew fairer, presently
He came beneath the shade of forest leaves,—
And deep among the emerald depths he found
Those mortal men who dwell in woods and build
Their dwellings of the scented boughs of trees.
And often, with his cheek upon his hand,
Balder would sit and watch the smoke of fire
Upcurling thro' the branches heavenward,
While to and fro in sunshine passed the shapes
Of men and women. Most he loved to mark
Those forms which gods made fairest, and to hear
Those voices gods make sweetest; but his hand,

Falling unseen, was gentlest on the hair
Of children and of hoary aged men.

Then Balder said, 'The Earth is fair, and fair,
Yea fairer than the stormy lives of gods,
The lives of gentle dwellers on the Earth;
For shapen are they in the likenesses
Of goddesses and gods, and on their limbs
Sunlight and moonlight mingle, and they lie
Happy and calm in one another's arms
O'er-canopied with greenness; and their hands
Have fashion'd fire that springeth beautiful
Straight as a silvern lily from the ground,
Wondrously blowing; and they measure out
Glad seasons by the pulses of the stars.
O Spirit whom I know not, tho' I fear
Thy shadow on my soul where'er I go,
Almighty Father, tho' thou lov'st me not,
I love thy children! I could sit all hours,
Just looking into their still heavenly eyes,
Holding their hands! Most dear they are to me,
Because they are my brethren;—beautiful,
My brethren and thy children!'

     O'er his head
The blue sky darken'd, and a thund'rous voice
Murmur'd afar off,—and in great black drops
Came out of heaven the blind and desolate rain.
But Balder gazing upward reach'd out arms
And bless'd it as it fell; and lo, it grew
Silvern and lovely as an old man's hair!
And scents came out of the rich-soilèd earth,
And all the boughs were glad and jewel-hung,
Till very softly, very silently,
The shower ceased, with kisses tremulous
On Balder's lifted hands!

     Even so he turn'd
The saddest things to beauty. With his face
Came calm and consecration; and the Earth
Uplifting sightless eyes in a new joy,
Answer'd the steadfast smile of the still heavens
With one long look of peace. In those strange days
The wild wind was his playmate,—yea, the blast
New-loosen'd by the very hands of gods
Leapt to him like a lamb, and at his smile
Fell at his feet, and slept. Then out of heaven
Came lightnings, from whose terror every face
Of humankind was hidden,—meteors, flames,
Forms of the fiery levin, such as wait
For ever at the angry beck of gods.
But Balder stood upon a promontory,
And saw them shining o'er the open sea,
And on the fields of ether crimson'd red;
And lo, he lifted up a voice and cried,
'O beautiful wild children of the fire,
Whence come ye? whither go ye? Be at peace,
Come hither!' and like soft white stingless snakes
That crawl on grass, the fiery meteors came,
Licking his feet in silence, looking up
With luminous eyes!

    Ev'n as he conquer'd these,
Heaven's fiery messengers, he tamed the hearts
Of human things, and in the sun they sat
Weaving green boughs, or wooing in the shade,
Or leading home the white and virgin bride.
For as the holy hunger and desire
Came quickening in the hearts of birds and beasts,
Ev'n so woke love within the hearts of men;
And out of love came children; and the Earth
Was merry with new creatures thronging forth
Like ants that quicken on the sun-kist sod.

IV.
THE CRY FROM THE GROUND.

And Balder bends above them, glory-crown'd,
Marking them as they creep upon the ground,
Busy as ants that toil without a sound,
 With only gods to mark.

But list! O list! what is that cry of pain,
Faint as the far-off murmur of the main?
Stoop low and hearken, Balder! List again!
'Lo! Death makes all things dark!'

Ay me, it is the earthborn souls that sigh,
Coming and going underneath the sky;
They move, they gather, clearer grows their cry—
O Balder, bend, and hark!

The skies are still and calm, the seas asleep,
In happy light the mortal millions creep,
Yet listen, Balder!—still they murmur deep,
'Lo! Death makes all things dark.'

[Oh, listen! listen!] 'Blessed is the light,
We love the golden day, the silvern night,
The cataracts leap, the woods and streams are bright,
We gladden as we mark.

'Crying we come, but soon our cheeks are dried—
We wander for a season happy-eyed,
And we forget how our gray sires have sigh'd,
"Lo! Death makes all things dark."

'For is the sun not merry and full of cheer?
Is it not sweet to live and feel no fear?
To see the young lambs leaping, and to hear
The cuckoo and the lark?

'Is toil not blest, is it not blest to be?
To climb the snows, to sail the surging sea,
To build our saeters where our flocks roam free?
But Death makes all things dark.

'Is love not blest, is it not brave and gay
With strong right hand to bear one's bride away,
To woo her in the night time and the day
With no strange eyes to mark?

'And blest are children, springing fair of face
Like gentle blossoms in the dwelling-place;
We clasp them close, forgetting for a space
Death makes the world so dark.

'And yet though life is glad and love divine,
This Shape we fear is here i' the summer shine,—
He blights the fruit we pluck, the wreath we twine,
And soon he leaves us stark.

'He haunts us fleetly on the snowy steep,
He finds us as we sow and as we reap,
He creepeth in to slay us as we sleep,—
Ah! Death makes all things dark!

'Yea, when afar over our nets hang we,
He walks unto us even on the sea;
The wind blows in his hair, the foam flies free
O'er many a sinking bark!

'Pity us, gods, and take this god away,
Pity us, gods, who made us out of clay,
Pity us, gods, that our sad souls may say,
"Bright is the world, which Death a space made dark."'

V.

THE SHADOW ON THE EARTH.

Now all his peace was poison'd and he found
No solace in the shining eyes of day,
Starlight and moonlight now seem'd sorrowful,
And in his soul there grew the sense of tears.
For wheresoe'er he wander'd, whatsoe'er
He gazed on, whether in the light or dark,
Was troubled by a portent.
          Evermore,
Listening to nature's sad unceasing moan,
Balder remember'd that pale haunting Shape
Which he had seen in those primæval woods
Where he was foster'd by the happy Earth;
And those sad tales the mother-goddess told
Of mortal men, and how they waste and wane,
Came back upon his life with fearful gleams.
Yea, Balder's heart was heavy. All in vain
He wove wild runes around the flowers and trees,
And round the necks of beasts and gentle birds;
For evermore the cold hand found them out,
And evermore they darkly droop'd and died.

This direful thing was on the helpless
    Earth,
Unprison'd, unconfined. Before his face
It faded, and before his eager touch
Melted and changed, but evermore again
It gather'd into dreadful lineaments,
And passed with arms outreaching on its
    way.

Then Balder lifted up his trembling hands
To heaven, crying, 'FATHER!' and no
    sound
Came from the frozen void; and once again,
'O Mother, Mother!' but pale Frea lay
Stone-still in anguish at the Father's feet,
And dared not answer; and he cried once
    more,
'Gods, gods, immortal gods!' when sud-
    denly
He saw across the open arctic heaven
The hosts of Asgard, ev'n as sunset clouds
That drift confusedly in masses bright,
Trooping, with blood-red rays upon their
    heads,
To fight against the meteor snakes that flash
Far northward in the white untrodden
    wastes.
They passed, they saw not, but he heard
    their feet
Afar as muffled thunder, and he cried,
'O Slayers of the snake, immortal gods,
Come hither and slay the slayer, that the
    world
May rest in peace!'

              If ever his faint cry
Reach'd to their ears, the dark gods only
    smiled,
With smiles like sullen lightning on the lips
Of tempest; and he found no comfort there.
Nor from the mouths of flower, or bird, or
    tree,
Sea-fern, or sighing shell upon the shore,
Came any answer when he question'd low,
'What is this thing ye fear? who sent it
    hither,
This shape which moaning mortals christen
    Death?'
But from the darkness of his own heart's
    pity,
And from all things in unison—the gloom
Of midnight, and the trouble of the clouds,
From sunless waters, solitary woods,

There came a murmur, 'None can answer
    thee,
Save him thou followest with weary feet!'

Wherefore he wander'd on, and still in
    vain
Sought Death the slayer. Into burial-places,
Heapen with stones and seal'd with slime
    of grass,
He track'd him, found him sitting lonely
    there
Like one that dreams, his dreadful pitiless
    eyes
Fix'd on the sunset star. Or oftentimes
Beheld him running swiftly like a wolf
Who scents some stricken prey along the
    ground.
Or saw him into empty huts crawl slow,
And while the man and woman toiled i' the
    field,
Gaze down with stony orbs a little space
Upon the sickly babe, which open'd eyes,
And laugh'd, and spread its little faded
    hands
In elfin play. Nay, oft in Balder's sight
The form seem'd gentle, and the fatal
    face
Grew beautiful and very strangely fair.
Yet evermore while his swift feet pursued,
Darkling it fled away, and evermore
Most pitiful rose cries of beasts and birds,
Most desolate rose moans of stricken men,
Till Balder wept for sorrow's sake, and
    cried,
'Help me, my Father!'

              Even as he spake,
A gray cloud wept upon the Earth, which
    wore
A gentle darkness; and the wastes and
    woods,
The mountains trembling in their hoary
    hair,
The mighty continents and streams and seas,
Uplifted a low voice of mystery
And protestation. Then a wingèd wind
Caught up the sound and bore it suddenly
To the great gates of Asgard, so that all
Within the shadowy City heard; and He
Who sitteth far beyond upon his throne,
Immortal, terrible, and desolate,
Heard, but was silent; and no answer came,
No help or answer, from the lips of heaven.

VI.

ON THE HEIGHTS—EVENING.

MOUNTAIN GIRL.

Art thou a god? thy brow is shining so!
O thou art beautiful! What is thy name?

BALDER.

Balder.

GIRL.

Now let me look into thy face.

BALDER.

Look,

GIRL.

How I love thee!

BALDER.

And *thy* name?

GIRL.

Snow-blossom.
That is my mother standing at the door,
Shading her face and gazing up the hill.
I keep my mother's reindeer, and each night
Milk them, and drive them to their pasturage.
How clear thine eyes are! They are like that star
Up yonder, twinkling on the snow!

BALDER.

Come hither!
Thou hast bright hair like mine, and starry eyes,
Snow-blossom, and a voice like falling water;
Thy flesh is like the red snow and the white
Mingled together softly, and thy breath
Is scented like the fragrant thyme in flower.
Mine eyes have look'd on many shapes like thine—
Yet thou art fairest.

GIRL.

I am call'd Snow-blossom
Because I am not brown like other maids,
And when a little child I was so white!

BALDER.

Snow-lily!

GIRL.

They are calling—I must go—
Come down with me, and by our saeter's fire
Slumber this night, and ere thou liest down
I'll sing to thee the strange old songs I know
Of Death, and of the battle-fields of gods,
And of the wondrous City where they dwell
Yonder afar away!

BALDER.

What knowest *thou*
Of Death or gods?

GIRL.

Only last winter tide
I saw my father die: he drew one breath,
Then went to sleep; but when we touch'd his hands
They had no warmth, and his twain eyes were glazed,
Gazing at something that we saw not. Then
We wrapt him warm in skins and in his hands
We set his seal-spear and his seal-hide thong,
And placed him sitting in the sunless earth,
Crouch'd resting on the ground with knees drawn up
As many a night he sat beside the fire.
And that the fierce white bear might find him not,
We wall'd him up with earth and mighty stones,
Seal'd tight with snow and water: then we said
A prayer to the good gods, and left him there
Where they might find him.

BALDER.

Hast thou seen that Death
Which smote thy father?

GIRL.

Nay!—no mortal thing
Sees him and lives. He walks about the Earth
At his good will, and smites whate'er he lists,
Both young and old. There is no spirit at all
More strong than he!

BALDER.

Is he a god?

GIRL.

I know not.

BALDER.

And will thy father waken?

GIRL.

When the gods
Find out his grave, and open up the stones,
Then he will waken, and will join the hosts
Of Hermod and of Thor; for he was brave,
My father: he could keep his own, and ere
He took my mother, with his spear he slew
Her father and her brother, who were wroth
Because they hated him; and evermore
When he shed blood, he made his offering
To Hermod and the rest.

BALDER.

And thou, Snow-blossom,
Thou in thy turn wilt wed a mighty man,
And bear strong children?

GIRL.

Yes!—a man of strength,
Fair like my father. I would have him fierce
As bears are, bearded, a seal-strangler, swift,
And a great hunter with a boat and dogs.
But I would have him very cunning too,
Knowing old songs and wise at weaving runes,
That in the season when the sun is fled
We might be merry thro' the long cold nights
Waiting for summer!

BALDER.

Hark!

GIRL.

It is my mother
Calling again! Wilt thou not come?

BALDER.

Go thou!
I shall fare further o'er the summer hills.
Snow-blossom! Let me kiss thee ere thou goest!

GIRL.

Yes!

BALDER.

Now farewell!...
How lightly down the height
She leapeth with the leaping cataract,
And now she turns and waves her little hand,
And plunging down she fades. And in the world

Dwell countless thousands beautiful as she,
Happy and virgin, drinking with no pain
The vital air of heaven! O pink flesh
Over the warm nest of a singing heart
Heap'd soft as blossoms! O strange starry eyes
Of mortals, beautiful as mine! O flame
Out of soft nostrils trembling, like the light
From lips of flowers! O wonder of Earth's life,
Why is it that the great gods chase thee down?
Why is it that thou fallest evermore
When thou art fairest? Up and down the world
Each creature walks, and o'er each red mouth hangs
Breath like a little cloud, faint smoke of breath
Blown from the burning of the fire within.
Great gods, if as they say ye fashion'd them,
Why do ye suffer this wild wind of doom
To wither what ye made so wonderful?

The vale is dark, the snow-fields on the height
Are purpled with the midnight....
Steadfastly
One lamp shines in the valley, and above
The still star shines an answer. Slumber well,
Snow-blossom! May no shadow of the gods
Come near to trouble thee in thy repose!
Sleep like immortal raiment wrap thee round,
To charm away the rayless eyes of Death!

VII.
The Vow of Balder.

Bright Balder cried, 'Curst be this thing
  Which will not let man rest,
Slaying with swift and cruel sting
  The very babe at breast!

'On man and beast, on flower and bird,
  He creepeth evermore;
Unseen he haunts the Earth; unheard
  He crawls from door to door.

'I will not pause in any land,
  Nor sleep beneath the skies,
Till I have held him by the hand
  And gazed into his eyes!'

V.

BALDER'S QUEST FOR DEATH.

I.

HE sought him on the mountains bleak and bare
  And on the windy moors;
He found his secret footprints everywhere,
  Yea, ev'n by human doors.

All round the deerfold on the shrouded height
  The starlight glimmer'd clear;
Therein sat Death, wrapt round with vapours white
  Touching the dove-eyed deer.

And thither Balder silent-footed flew,
  But found the phantom not;
The rain-wash'd moon had risen cold and blue
  Above that lonely spot.

Then as he stood and listen'd, gazing round
  In the pale silvern glow,
He heard a wailing and a weeping sound
  From the wild huts below.

He mark'd the sudden flashing of the lights,
  He heard cry answering cry—
And lo! he saw upon the silent heights
  A shadowy form pass by.

Wan was the face, the eyeballs pale and wild,
  The robes like rain wind-blown,
And as it fled it clasp'd a naked child
  Unto its cold breast-bone.

And Balder clutch'd its robe with fingers weak
  To stay it as it flew—
A breath of ice blew chill upon his cheek,
  Blinding his eyes of blue.

'Twas Death! 'twas gone!—All night the shepherds sped,
  Searching the hills in fear;
At dawn they found their lost one lying dead
  Up by the lone black mere;

And lo! they saw the fatal finger-mark,
  Which reacheth young and old,
Seal'd, livid still, upon its eyelids dark
  And round its nipples cold.

Then Balder moan'd aloud and smote his breast,
  'O drinker of sweet breath,
Curst be thy cruel lips! I shall not rest
  Until I clasp thee, Death!'

He track'd the footprints in the morning gray
  From rocky haunt to haunt.
Far up the heights a wolf had crost Death's way;
  It lay there, lean and gaunt.

He reach'd the highest snows and found them strewn
  With bleaching bones of deer. . . .
Night came again,—he listen'd 'neath the moon
  Shining most cold and clear.

Beneath him stretch'd vast valleys green and fair,
  Still in the twilight shine,
With great waste tarns and cataracts hung in air,
  And woods of fir and pine;

And on the tarns lay dim red dreams of day
  The midnight sun cast there,—
Sunlight and moonlight blending in one ray
  Of mother-o'-pearl most fair.

He wander'd down thro' woods that fringed the snows,
  Down cliffs with ivy crown'd,
He passed by lonely tarns whence duskly rose
  Great cranes, and hover'd round.

He paused upon a crimson crag, and lo!
  Deep down at the crag's foot,
The Shape he sought, in shadow, far below,
  With folded wings, sat mute!

Ev'n as a vulture of the east it seem'd,
  Brooding on something dead;
Dark was the form on which its cold eyes gleam'd,
  And still and heavy as lead.

Then Balder swung himself from tree to
    tree,
    And reach'd the fatal place! . . .
The phantom fled as silent wild things flee,
    But a white human face
Gleam'd from the ground; and Balder's
    glory shone
    On a wild cowherd's hair!
Too late—his cheeks were chill—his breath
    was gone—
    His bosom torn and bare.

The Shape unseen had cast him o'er the
    steep,
    Down, down, the abysses dim,—
Then, as an eagle followeth a sheep,
    Had flutter'd after him!

His bearskin dress was bloody; in his grip
    He clutch'd a cowherd's horn;
His eyes were glazed, and on his stainèd lip
    Death's kisses lay forlorn.

But Balder touch'd him and his face grew
    fair,
    Shining beneath the skies,
Yea, Balder crost his hands, and smooth'd
    his hair,
    And closed his piteous eyes. . . .

Not resting yet, the bright god wander'd
    soon
    Down by the torrent's track;
And lo! a sudden glory hid the moon,
    And dawn rose at his back.

II.

Dawn purple on the peaks, and pouring in
    floods
    Into the valleys fair,
Encrimsoning the lakes and streams and
    woods,
    Illuming heaven and air.

And every creature gladden'd, and the
    Earth
    Turn'd on her side and woke:
There came sweet music; sunny gleams of
    mirth
    Across the landscape broke.

And when a thousand eyes of happy things
    Had open'd all around,
And when each form that blooms, each
    form that sings,
    Saw Balder glory-crown'd,

Standing like marble bathed in liquid flame,
    Perfect of face and limb,
Infinite voices syllabled his name,
    And Earth smiled up at him!

All shapes that knew him (and all shapes
    that be
    Knew Balder's face that hour)
Grew glorified—the torrent and the tree,
    The white cloud and the flower.

The meres flash'd golden mirrors for his
    face;
    The forests saw and heard;
The cataracts brighten'd; in its secret place
    The sunless runlet stirred.

A light of green grass ran before his feet,
    His brow was bright with dew,
Where'er he trod there sprang a flower full
    sweet,
    Rose, crimson, yellow, or blue.

But Balder's face was pale, altho' his frame
    Its natal splendour wore;
Altho' the green Earth gladden'd as he
    came,
    God Balder's soul was sore.

'O happy Earth! O happy beams of day!
    O gentle things of breath!
Blest were ye, if some hand divine might
    slay
    The slayer, even Death!'

He spake, and he was answer'd. By his side
    A crimson river ran,
Out of the cloven mountains spreading wide
    It water'd vales for man.

Amid its shallows flowers and sedge did
    twine,
    But in the midst 'twas deep,
And on its sides fed flocks of goats and kine
    O'er meadows soft as sleep.

Suddenly, while upon its marge he stood,
    His heart grew cold as clay,—
For lo! the phantom! sailing down the
    flood,
    Dim in the dawn of day! . . .

'Mid drifted foxglove-bells and leaves of green
Uptorn and floating light,
There came, with face upturn'd, now hid, now seen,
A maiden dark as night—
Her raven hair was loosen'd, her soft breath
Had fled and left no stir,
Her eyes were open, looking up at Death,
Who drifted down with her.

Beside her, tangled 'mid the foxglove-bells,
A shepherd's crook was cast,
While softly on the waters silvern swells
Her form was floating past.

And lo! with eyes of feverish fatal light
Fix'd on her face in dream,
Death clung unto her 'mid the eddies bright
Upon the shining stream.

And Balder wail'd; and wafted down that way,
Death saw his shape and knew,—
Then, like a falcon startled from its prey,
Rose, vanishing from view!

III.

THE FIGHT OF SHIPS.

Now Balder came across the great sea-shore,
And saw far out upon the windless waves
A fight of water-dragons fierce as fire,
Wingèd and wild and wrought about with gold.
And dragon unto dragon clash'd and clung,
And each shriek'd loud, and teeth in teeth were set,
Until the sea was crimson'd, and one sank
In its own blood. So like to living things
They seem'd, but ships they were within whose wombs
Throbbed many savage hearts. And suddenly,
Amid that clangour of sharp steel and shriek
Of living voices, 'mid the thick o' the fight,
When in the stainèd waters all around
Men to the brain were cloven as they swam,
Balder saw dimly, hovering on wings,
Ev'n as the kestrel hovers poised and still
With glittering eyes searching the nether ground,
The Shape he sought. As the bright dragons rush'd
This way and that with rapid sweep of oars,
And as the tumult passed from wave to wave,
It follow'd, as the falcon followeth
Some fearful quarry creeping on the ground.
And when the sunset came, and the great din
Was hush'd, and torn apart from one another
The dragons darken'd on a fiery sea,
The Shape, illumined with a crimson gleam,
Still linger'd o'er them very quietly,
Scenting the slain that drifted like to weeds
On the red waters, shoreward.

     Then aloud
Cried Balder, 'FATHER!' uttering from his heart
A bitter moan, and as he spake he saw,
All congregating on the brazen walls
Of sunset, with their wild eyes looking down,
Feeding upon the carnage of the fight,
The gods his kin; and like to evening clouds,
Crimson and golden in the sunset flame,
They would perchance have seem'd to human eyes,
But his perceived them clearly and discern'd
The rapture in their faces as they gazed.
Yet ne'ertheless he cried, 'Come down, ye gods,
And help me, that upon this fatal thing
I lay my hand!' They laugh'd reply, and lo!
He saw their banners raised i' the wind, their brands
Flashing and moving.

     'FATHER!'

     No reply;
But quiet as a curtain fell the night,
Solemn, without a star.

     Then by the sea
Silent walk'd Balder, and all sounds were still
Beyond him on the bosom of the deep.
And where he went along the moonless sands
He made a brightness such as ocean shells
Keep in their iris'd ears; and the soft sea
Came singing round his silvern feet; and doves

Came out of caves and lit upon his hands.
Then Balder thought, ' He answer'd, and
    has sent
The darkness as a token!' and ev'n then
He *blest* his father.

   . . . What is this that flames,
Lurid and awful, out upon the sea?
What dusky radiance, tho' the world is dark,
Shoots like a comet yonder upon the sky?
Seized in the fangs of fire, a dragon-ship
Consumes and shrieks, and as it burns
    illumes
The water under and the thunderous rack
Blackening above; and Balder as he stands
Pallid upon a headland, on his face
Catches the red reflection of the ray;
Ocean and sky are crimson'd, and he sees
Black shapes that hither and thither, waving
    arms,
Dart 'midst the flame on the consuming
    decks
And plunge with shrill scream down into
    the sea.

What care to call on the Immortals now?
He looks, one hand prest hard in agony
Upon his aching heart, and he discerns,
Brooding above that brightness, poised i'
    the air,
Down gazing, half illumed, half lost in
    light,
The Phantom! As the ship consumes and
    fades,
And as the last cry rises on the air,
The Shape sinks lower with no waft of
    wing.
And when in dumb and passionate despair,
Balder looks northward once again, he sees
The cloud-rack parted, the cold north on
    fire,
And all the gods, with cruel cheeks aflame
And bright eyes glittering like cluster'd
    stars,
Thronging against the blacken'd bars of
    Heaven.

IV.
YDUN.

Then Balder lifted up his voice and cried,
'Curst be this thing and you who sent it
    hither,
Tho' ye be gods, immortal, and my kin;
For now I loathe you, deeming lovelier far

The black hawk, and the fox upon the
    ground,
Who slay sweet lives not knowing what
    they do;
But ye, O gods, are wise, yet Death's sick
    scent
Is pleasant to your nostrils.' Loudly afar
A laugh of thunder answer'd, and the shapes
Still congregated in the glistening north
Flash'd like the pale aurora one white
    gleam
Of earthward-looking eyes, and in the midst
A hoary Face like to a moonlit cloud,
Silent, and staring down with orbs of stone.
And on this last did Balder gaze, and lo!
He shiver'd cold, his cheek divine was
    blanch'd,
And with no further word he turn'd away.

   . . . So walk'd he by the Ocean, till that
    gleam
Far out upon the crimson waters died;
Till night grew deeper and all sounds were
    still'd.

And all that night his human heart was
    turn'd
Against the gods his kin, against the god
His father; for he thought, ' He made this
    thing,
He sent it hither to the happy Earth;
And when it slays they gladden in the halls
Of Asgard, and no pity fills their hearts
For gentle stricken men.' Long hours he
    paced
The cold sands of the still black sea; and
    where
His foot fell moonlight lay and live sea-
    snails
Crept glimmering with pink horns; and
    close to shore
He saw the legions of the herring flash,
Swift, phosphorescent, on the surface shin-
    ing
Like bright sheet-lightning as they came
    and went.
At intervals, from the abyss beyond,
Came the deep roar of whales.

                     Betimes he stood
Silent, alone, upon a promontory
And now about him like white rain there fell
The splendour of the moonlight. All around
The calm sea rolled upon the rocks or drew

Dark surges from the caverns, issuing thence
Troubled and churn'd to boiling pools of
 foam.
Erect he stood, uplifting his white hands;
For round him on the slippery weed-hung
 reefs,
Outcreeping from the blackness of the sea,
In legions came the flocks of gentle seals
And gray sea lions with their lionesses.
And o'er the rocks they clomb till all the place
Was blacken'd, and the rest upon the sea,
Their liquid eyeballs in the moonlight
 burning,
Swam round and round with necks out-
 stretch'd to gaze;
And those beneath him touch'd his shining
 feet,
And when he raised his hand and blest
 them all,
Uplifted heads like happy flocks of sheep
Bleating their joy!

    Ev'n then he heard a voice
Cry 'Balder!' thrice, and turning he beheld
Standing above him on the promontory
A spirit he remember'd; for her hair
Swept downward like the silvern willow's
 leaves,
And on her mystic raiment blue as heaven
There glimmer'd dewy drops like heavenly
 stars.
And as he turn'd unto her he perceived
Her deathlike pallor, and he straightway
 knew
He look'd on Ydun, who had given to him
Those mystic apples which immortal forms
For ever feed on evermore renew'd.

And Ydun said, 'O Balder, I could hear
Thy lone cry yonder in the silent realms
Where, gathering golden asphodels in
 meads
Of starlight under the dark Tree, I stray'd;
And all my heart was troubled for thy sake,
My brother, and I came across the worlds
To seek thee, bringing in my veilèd breast
More fruits to heal thee and to make thee
 strong
Despite the gods who love thee not, thy kin;
For I who bring them love thee, knowing
 well
There stands no shape in the celestial halls
So beautiful as thou!'

    And as she spake
She drew the apples forth and proffer'd
 them
To Balder's lips; but on those lips there
 lay
An ashen tinge as of mortality.
And taking not the gift he answer'd low,
'O Ydun, let me give thy gift to men,
That *they* may eat and live!'

    But Ydun said,
While on his cheek he felt her breath come
 cold
As frosty moonlight,—'Name them not,
 but eat—
Eat *thou*, and live. O Balder, men were
 born
To gather earthly fruit a little space,
And then, grown old with sudden lapse of
 years,
To wither up and die; and fruit like this
Could never light on any human lip
The flame-like breath of immortality.
Flesh are they, and must fall; spirits are we,
And fed with life diviner, we endure.'

Then Balder said, 'Dost thou not weep for
 them?
Poor mortals with their shadows on the
 ground,
Yet kin to thee and me! He made them
 fair
As we are, tho' they sicken and are slain;
Yea, by a god accurst that haunts the world
Their hearts are set asunder, and their teeth
Devour each other. Lo! the beautiful
 Earth
Is desolate of children, strewn with dead,
Sick with a ceaseless moan of stricken
 things
For ever coming and for ever going,—
Like wild waves darkly driven on a sea
Eternally distress'd.'

    Coldly replied
The goddess, 'Take no heed for things of
 clay,—
For 'twere as well to weep for stricken
 birds,
Or flowers that in their season fade and
 fall,
Or beasts that mortals slay for food or
 cast
Upon thy Father's shrines for sacrifice,

As mourn for that dark dust beneath thy
    feet
Which thou call'st men. O Balder, take
    no heed—
Be wise—such pity ill beseems a god!'

But Balder wrung his hands and wail'd aloud
In a sad human voice, ' Not pity *those*?
Hath a bird fallen in my sight and fail'd
To win some meed of tears? Doth a beast
    die,
I would not wind in my immortal arms,
And kiss into a new and lovelier life?
And on the dead leaves shed i' the weary
    woods
Do I not strew my tears divine, like dew?
O Ydun, listen, for thou know'st me not.
The taint of clay is on me and I lack
The large cold marble heart befitting gods.
I drank strange mercy from the dark Earth's
    breast
When she my foster-mother suckled me
Close to her leafy heart; I am not wise,
Ay me, I am not wise, if not to love
The happy forms below me, and the faces
That love my voice and gladden in my
    smile,
Be wisdom; I am of them; I have learn'd
The pathos of the setting sun, the awe
Of moonlight and of starlight; nay, I
    dream
That shape which sets its icy hand on all
Will find me in my season like the rest.
They are my brethren, wanderers in the
    world,
Yet fatherless and outcast like myself,
And exiled from their home!'

                    But Ydun said,
'That shape which sets its icy hand on all
Need never trouble thee, if thou wilt eat,
Eat as I bid, and live;—nay, Death himself,
Tame as a hound some little child may lead,
Hath fed from out my hand and from my
    fruits
Drank immortality; and lo, he walks
Immortal among mortals, on Earth's ways
Shedding the sad leaves of humanity.
For this is written, they must die; and those
Who die in battle or with bloody hands
The gods redeem and snatch to deathless
    days
Of terror in Valhalla; but the rest,

Weak maiden-hearted men and women
    pale,
And children, dying bloodless, find below
A nameless and an everlasting sleep.'

'O Ydun,' Balder cried, 'I have search'd
    the Earth,
And have not found him, tho' my spirit pants
To look into his face and question him,
That Death of whom you speak, that fan-
    tasy,
Immortal, and a god; but evermore
His form eludes me in the light and dark,
And evermore beneath my feet I find
Only some gentle shape that he hath slain.'

Then Ydun smiled as pallid starlight smiles
On marble, and she answer'd, ' Eat, then
    eat!
And by the gods of Asgard I will swear
To lead thee to him and to read a rune
Which whisper'd in his ear shall make him
    meek
And weak as any lamb to do thy will;'
And as she spake she held the apples forth
And proffer'd them again to Balder's lips.

Then hungry for her promise Balder ate,
And in his mouth the mingled red and white
Melted as snow, and suddenly he seem'd
Grown into perfect glory like the moon
Springing all silvern from a summer cloud.

VI.
BALDER AND DEATH.

I.

THE ALTAR OF SACRIFICE.

'LOOK!' Ydun said; and pointed.
                      Far in the night
She had led Balder,—o'er the darken'd
    dales,
And by the silence of black mountain tarns,
And thro' the slumber of primæval woods,—
Till she had come unto an open plain
Cover'd with ragged heath and strewn with
    stones,
As with the broken fragments of some world
Upheaven, rent by earthquake. And the
    waste
All round was lonely and illimitable,
A tract of stone and heath without a tree,

H H

Save where against the blood-red northern
    sky
A mountain like the great white hand of
    Earth
Pointed at highest heaven. Far out beyond
The shadow of the snowy mountain, rose
Columns gigantic of red granite rock
Scarr'd with the tempest, hung with slimy
    moss,
And looming in the cold and spectral light
Like living shapes of gods; and some by
    storm
Were cast upon the ground and lay full
    length
Like giants slain, but most stood poised on
    end,
Not tottering, with their shadows wildly cast
Southward, along the sward. High in the
    midst
Stones fashion'd as an altar were upraised,
And on the altar was a coffin'd space
Wherein a man full-grown might lie his
    length
And with his pleading eyes upon the stars
Make ready for the sacrificial knife.

'Look!' Ydun said; and Balder look'd;
    and saw,
Crouching upon the altar, one that loom'd
Like to a living shape. And Ydun said,
'That is thy Father's altar, and thereon
Blood-offering brighter than the life of
    lambs
Is scatter'd by his priests; at sunset here
A virgin died, and all the desert air
Is sweeter for her breath; and those black
    birds
That hover o'er the altar moaning low
Are hungry to come near her and to feed,—
But he who lieth yonder hath not fed
His own immortal hunger. There he broods
Still as a star above her, with one hand
Placed on her lifeless breast!'

                    Then Balder felt
His godhead shrink within him like a flame
A cold wind bloweth, and for pity's sake
His eyes divine were dim; but, creeping
    close,
Within the shadow of a shatter'd column,
He gazed and gazed. And lo, the sight he
    saw
Was full of sorrow only eyes divine

Could see and bear. Upon the altar-stone
Lay stretch'd naked and most marble white
That gentle virgin, with the slayer's mark
Across her throat, her red mouth open wide,
And two great sightless orbs upraised to
    heaven,
And he who clung unto her, like a hawk
With wings outstretch'd, and dim dilated
    eyes
Feeding upon the sorrow of her face,
Was he whom Balder o'er the world had
    sought
And had not found. Ne'er yet, by sea or
    shore,
Not ev'n within the silence of the woods
When his sad eyes beheld him first of old,
Had Balder to that spirit terrible
E'er crept so nigh or seen its shape so well.
Shadow it seem'd, and yet corporeal,
But thro' the filmy substance of its frame
The blood-red light of midnight penetrated;
And dreadfully with dreadful loveliness
The features changed their shining linea-
    ments,
Now lamb-like, wolf-like now, now like a
    maid's
Scarce blossom'd, now deep-wrinkled like a
    man's,
Now beautiful and awful like a god's,—
But never true to each similitude
Longer than one quick heart-beat.

                    Thus it hung,
So fascinated by the form it watch'd,
It saw not, heard not, stirr'd not, though
    the birds
Shriek'd wildly overhead. Ev'n as one cast
Into a trance mesmeric, it prolong'd
The famine of its gaze until its face
Was fiẍed as a star. Then Ydun crept
Close unto Balder, whispering, 'Remember
That rune I read thee! touch him in his
    trance,
And name him by his mystic human name,
And as I live his lips shall answer thee
In human speech!' So speaking, Ydun
    smiled
And vanish'd, leaving Balder all alone
To look and watch and wait. . . .

                    . . . Then on his soul,
Beholding that great trance of Death, there
    came

Most fatal fascination. For a space
He could not stir. Upon the sacred grove
Lay darkness; only on the altar stone
The naked victim glimmer'd beautiful,
And terrible above her linger'd Death;—
When suddenly beyond the snow-white peak
Rose round and luminous and yellow as gold
The full-orb'd moon; by slow degrees its beams
Stole down the shrouded mountains, till they fell
Prone on the altar, turning all things there
To brightness:—so that Death himself was changed
From purple into silvern;—that dead maid
To silvern too from marble;—the great grove,
With all the columns looming black therein,
New-lit with lunar dawn. Then as the light
Touch'd and illumed him, for a moment Death
Stirr'd, ev'n as one that stirreth from a sleep,
And trembled, looking upward; and behold!
His face grew beautiful thro' golden hair,
His eyes dim heavenly blue, and all his looks
Strange and divinely young! . . .

. . . Then, ere that trance
Was wholly shaken from him, Balder rose,
And crept unto the altar with no sound;
And ere the shape could stir or utter cry,
He clutch'd him with one quick and eager hand;
And tho' his hand was frozen as it touch'd,
Ere Death could fly he gazed into his eyes
And named him by his mystic human name.
. . . And Death gazed back with looks so terrible,
They would have wither'd any living man;
But Balder only smiled and wove his rune,—
And in a little space the shape was charm'd,
Looking and listening in a nameless fear.

II.

BALDER AND DEATH.

'O Death, pale Death, thro' many a lonely land
My feet have follow'd thee;
Sisters and brothers stricken by thy hand
Oft have I stoop'd to see;

'To kiss the little children on their biers
So innocent and sweet,
To bless the old men wearied out with years
Wrapt in thy winding-sheet.

'To look into thine eyes, to drink thy breath,
I have cried with a weary cry:
Prayers I have said to the great gods, O Death,
While thou hast darken'd by.

'Thy mark is on the flower and on the tree,
And on the beast and the bird,
Thy shade is on the mountains, even the sea
By thy sad foot is stirred.

'Slayer thou art of all my soul deems fair,
Thou saddenest the sun,—
Of all things on the earth and in the air,
O Death, thou sparest none.

'And therefore have I sought with prayers and sighs
To speak with thee a space!'
Bright Balder in the hollow rayless eyes
Look'd with a fearless face.

The phantom darken'd 'neath the clay-cold moon
And seem'd to shrink in woe,
But Balder named his name and wove the rune,
And would not let him go.

'O Death! pale Death! thou hast a lovelier name,
Who gave that name to thee?
By the high gods, by that from which they came,
Thy mouth must answer me!'

Death answer'd not, but mystically bright,
His shadowy features grew,
And on his brow the chilly lamps of night
Sprinkled their glistening dew;

And Balder wonder'd, for those lights above
Seem'd shining down on him,
And Death's pale face grew as the face of Love,
Yet more divinely dim.

'O Death, pale Death!
Who gave thee that sweet name,
Yet sent thee down to slay poor things of breath,
And turn men's hearts to flame?

H H 2

'Who gave thee life and cast thy lot below
  With those sad slaying eyes?'
Death pointed with a hand as white as snow
  Up to the moonlit skies.

'Who sent thee here where men and beasts
  have birth?'
  Death trembled and was still.
'What drew thee down on my beloved
  Earth,
  To wither up and kill?'

Death answer'd not, but pointed once again
  Up thro' the starry shine;
And Balder question'd with a quick new
  pain,
'My kin? the gods divine?'

Death answer'd not, but gazed on Balder
  now
With strange and questioning gleam—
His eyes were soft in sorrow and his brow
  Was wonderful with dream.

'Speak to me, brother, if thou art not dumb;
  Speak to my soul, O Death!'
The thin lips flutter, but no answer hath
  come,
  No sigh, no sound, no breath.

Yet on the brow of Death there lives a light
  Like starlight shed on snow,
The fatal face grows beautiful and bright
  With some celestial woe.

And round the shadowy cheeks there softly
  swim
  Thin threads of silken hair,
And Balder sees the form world-worn and
  dim
  Hath once been young and fair.

And as they sit together in the night,
  Hand in hand, mingling breath,
The fingers white of the cold starry light
  Smooth the sad hair of Death.

III.
'O DEATH, PALE DEATH.'

'O Death! pale Death!
  Thy hair is golden, not gray—
In the dark mirrors of thine eyes, O Death,
  Lie glimmering dreams of day.

'O gentle Death!
  Thy hand is warm, not chill,—
Thy touch is soft and living, and thy breath
  Sweet, with no power to kill.

'I love thee, Death, for that great heavenly
  brow
  Still dark from love's eclipse—
And lo! a hundredfold I hunger now
  To hear thy living lips.

'O gentle Death!
  Speak, that mine ears may hear.'
Then like a fountain rose the voice of Death,
  Low, sweet, and clear!

IV.
DEATH SINGS.

'I know not whence my feet have come,
  Nor whither they must go—
Lonely I wander, dark and dumb,
  In summer and in snow.

'For on mine eyes there falls a gleam,
  That keeps them dim and blind,
Of strange eternities of dream
  Before me and behind;

And ever, ever as I pace
  Along my lonely track,
The light retires before my face,
  Advancing at my back;

'But ever, ever if I turn
  And would my steps retrace,
Close to my back that light doth burn,
  But flies before my face.

'I close mine eyes, I fain would sleep,
  I rest with folded wing,
Or on my weary way I creep
  Like any harmless thing.

'Yet day by day, from land to land,
  From gentle fold to fold,
I pass, and lo, my cruel hand
  Leaves all things calm and cold.

'Man marketh with his bitterest moan
  My shadow sad and dim;
Of all things hateful, I alone
  Am hatefullest to him!

'Ay me, a brand is on my brow,
  A fire is in my breast,—

Ever my bitter breath doth bow
 Those flowers I love the best.

'I crouch beside the cradled child,
 I look into its eyes,
I love to watch its slumber mild
 As quietly it lies.

'I dare not touch it with my hand,
 Or creep too close to see,
Yet for a little space I stand
 And mark it, silently,

'Ah, little dream pale human things,
 At rest beneath the skies,
How, as they sleep, with gentle wings
 I shade their cheeks and eyes!

'The maiden with her merry laugh,
 The babe with its faint cry,
The old man leaning on his staff,
 Are mine, and these must die.

'I touch them softly with my hand,
 They turn as still as stone,
Then looking in their eyes I stand
 Until their light hath flown.

'I set faint gleams around their lips,
 I smooth their brows and hair,
I place within their clay-cold grips
 The lilies of despair.

'And verily when they bear them forth
 I follow with the rest;
But when their bones are in the earth
 My gentle task is best.

'For there I sit with head bent low
 For many a dreamy day,
And watch the grass and flowers grow
 Out of the changing clay.

'O think of this and blame not me,
 Thou with the eyes divine—
A Shadow creeps from sea to sea,
 Stranger than thine or mine.

'Who made the white bear and the seal?
 The eagle and the lamb?
As these am I—I live and feel—
 ONE made me, and I am,'

V.

Then Balder lifted up his voice and cried,
Placing his fingers on Death's heavenly hair,
'Lo, I absolve thee!' and the Spirit crouch'd
In silence, looking up with wondering gaze
At that immortal brightness blessing him
With holy imposition of white hands.
For beautiful beyond all dream, and bright
Beyond all splendour of the summer Earth,
Divine, with aureole around his head,
God-like, yet fairer far than any god,
Stood Balder, like a thing that could not die!
Upon his face the countless eyes of heaven
Gazed, with their own exceeding lustre dim ;
And moonlight hung around him like a veil
Through which his glory trembled paramount ;
And dim sheen showering from a thousand worlds,
Mingling with moisture of the nether-air,
Touch'd his soft body with baptismal dews.

Then far away in the remotest north,
Cloud-like and dark and scarce distinguishable,
The clustering faces of the gods look'd down.
And Balder cried, 'Lo, I have ranged the Earth,
And found it good ; yea, hills and vales and streams,
Forests and seas, all good and beautiful ;
And I have gazed in eyes of birds and beasts,
And in the gentle orbs of mortal men,
And seen in all the light of that dim dream
Which grew within my soul when I was born.
Only this thing is bitter, O ye gods,
Most dark and bitter : that eternal Death
Sits by his sad and silent sea of graves,
Singing a song that slays the hopes of men.
Yet lo, I gaze into the eyes of Death,
And *they* are troubled with that self-same dream.

'O gods, on you I cry not, but I cry
On him, the Father, who has fashion'd Death
To be the sorrow of created things,
And set this ceaseless hunger in his heart
To wither up and kill. Oh, I have wept
Till all my heart is weary, and no voice
Makes answer. By thy servant Death, O God,
By him whom I have sought and found in pain,

Listen!—Uplift this shadow from the Earth,
And gladly will I die as sacrifice,
And all the gentle things I love shall live.

Far, far away in the remotest north
A white face in the darkness of a cloud
Gleam'd. Thither, crouching low at
    Balder's feet,
Death pointed with his skeleton finger fix'd,
Silent. Then, even as a snow-white lamb
That on the altar cometh with no fear
But looks around with eager innocent eyes,
God Balder on the stone of sacrifice
Leapt, reaching arms up heavenward!

       . . . And he pray'd.

VI.

THE LAST PRAYER.

'Father in heaven, my dream is over,
  Father in heaven, my day is dark,—
I sat in the sun and I sang like a lover
  Who sings sweet songs for a maid to mark;
And the light was golden upon my hair,
And the heavens were blue and the Earth
    was fair,
And I knew no touch of a human care,
  And I bless'd thy name, my Father!
I sang, and the clarion winds blew clear,
And the lilies rose like lamps on the mere,
And all the night in the balmy light
  I lifted up my hands snow-white,
  And the stars began to gather!

'Father, Father, which art in heaven,
  Lord of men and master of Earth.
The rune was woven of colours seven,
  And out of thy being I had birth;
As a snowdrop wakes on the naked ground,
And opens its eye without a sound
While the winds are murmuring around,
  I woke on the green Earth's bosom;
And I heard a cry, as the storks went by
Sailing northward under the sky,
And a cry from the mountains answer'd loud,
And the cataract leapt like a corpse from
    its shroud,
  And the sward began to blossom.

'White clouds passed over with low sweet
    thunder,
  Shaking downward the silvern dew,
The soft sods trembled and fell asunder,
  And the emerald flame of the grass
    gleam'd thro',

And the fire of the young boughs overhead
Ran green and amber, golden and red,
And the flashing lamps of the leaves were fed
  At the torch of the flaming sunshine:
Beautiful, wrapt in a blissful dream,
Lay mere and mountain, meadow and
    stream;
And beautiful, when the light was low,
Creeping white through the after-glow,
  The starshine and the moonshine!

'Father, Father, hearken unto me,
  Then work thy will on the world and me—
I walk'd the world, and the glad world
    knew me,
  And my feet were kissed by thy slave the
    Sea.
And ever with every happy hour,
My love grew deeper for tree and flower,
For the beast in the brake, for the bird in
    the bower,
  And the deer on the white high places.
But ere my golden dream was done,
I saw thy Shadow across the sun,
I saw thy Shadow that all men see,
On beast and bird, on flower and tree,
  And the flower-sweet human faces!

'The flower-sweet faces of mortal races
  Blossoming sadly under the sky!
I saw my dream on those fading faces,
  I heard my voice in their failing cry.
Out of the soil and into the sun
Their souls were stirring as mine had done,
Their dooms were written, their threads
    were spun,
  By the hands of the immortals;
They rose in a dream and they lookt around,
They saw their shadows upon the ground,
And wherever they went beneath the blue
The darker Shadow thy Spirit threw
  From the great sun's shining portals.

'Thou hadst taken clay and hadst made it
    human,
  Blown in its nostrils and lent it breath,
Thou hadst kindled the beauty of man and
    woman,
  To hunt them down with thy bloodhound,
    Death.
They did not crave to be born or be,
Yet thou gavest them eyes that their souls
    might see,

And thou hatest them as thou hatest me
   And the Earth thy godhead bearing.
They shrink and tremble before thy hand,
They ask and they do not understand,
They bid thee pity who pitiest none,
   And they name thy name, as I, thy Son,
   Now name it, still despairing.

' Father, Father, which art in heaven,
   Why hast thou fashion'd my brethren so?
Form'd of fire, with the dust for leaven,
   As thou hast made them, they come and go.
Yet ever thy hand is on their hair
To seize and to slay them unaware,
And ever their faces are pale with prayer
   As round thy fanes they gather. . . .
Thou askest blood and they give thee life
   With sweep of the sacrificial knife ;
Thou seekest praise and they give thee pain,
   And their altars smoke with the crimson rain
   Thou lovest, O my Father !

' Father, Father, 'tis sad to falter
   Out of the light and into the dark,
Like a wreath of smoke from a burning altar
   To fade and vanish where none may mark.
But O my Father, 'tis blest to be
A part of the joy of the land and sea,
To upleap like a lamb, to be glad and free
   As the stream of a running river.
Could'st thou not spare them a longer space
With sweeter meed of a surer grace?
Could'st thou not love the light that lies
   On happy fields and in human eyes,
   And let it shine for ever?

' I hear thy voice from the void of heaven,
   It thunders back and it answers " Nay "—
The rune was woven of colours seven
   For me, thy Son, and for things of clay.
Then mark me now as I rise and swear,
By the beasts in the brake, by the birds in the air,
By Earth, by all those forces fair
   Which mingled in my making ;
By men and women who stand supreme
Proud and pale with mine own soul's dream,
I will drink the cup their lips partake !
I will share their lot, while their sad hearts break
   As mine, thy Son's, is breaking !

' Father in heaven, my heart is human,
   I cast a shade like a human thing,
Grant me the doom of man and woman ;
   From the Earth I came, to the Earth I cling.
Behold who standeth at my side !
Even Death, thy servant heavenly eyed—
I will die, as the children of men have died,
   To the sound of his sad singing.
Behold, I look in the face of Death,
I look in his eyes and I drink his breath ;
The chill light brightens upon his brow,
He creepeth close and he smileth now,
   His cold arms round me flinging.

' Father, Father, bend down and hearken,
   And place thy hand upon my hair ;
Ere yet I wither, ere yet I darken,
   Hear me murmur a last low prayer.
As the blood of a sacrifice is shed,
Let me die in my brethren's stead—
Let me die ; but when I am dead,
   Call back thy Death to heaven !
Ay me, my Father, if this may be,
I will go with a prayer for him and thee,
I will pass away without a cry,
Blessing and praising thee under the sky,
   Forgiving and forgiven.

' . . . . Father, Father, my dream is over—
   He folds me close, and I cannot see ;
Yet I shall sleep like a quiet lover
   If my boon is granted and this may be.
O sweet it is if I may rest
Asleep on my foster-mother's breast,
If over my grave the flowers blow best
   And happy mortals gather.
Yet Father, tho' darkness shrouds my face,
Remember me for a little space,
Remember, remember, and forgive
Thy Son who dies that men may live. . . .
   Accept me, O my Father !'

VII.

THE FIRST SNOWFLAKE—FALLING OF THE SNOW.

He ceased ; no voice replied ; but round his frame
Cold arms were woven, and his golden head
Droop'd like a lily on the breast of Death. . . .
Then suddenly a darkness like a veil

Was drawn across the silent void of Heaven,
Starlight and moonlight faded mystically,
And save for Balder's face, that as a star
Still flash'd in pallor on the face of Death,
There was no light at all. . . .

                Then Balder cried,
'Lo, he hath answer'd; I am thine, O Death;
Now let me look into thy loving eyes,
And ere I rest, sing low to me again.'
Shivering he spake, and sank upon the ground;
But Death stoop'd down above him as he lay,
And took the shining head into his lap,
And smooth'd with fingers cold the silken hair,
And murmur'd Balder's name with singing lips
Soft as the whisper of a wind in June.
'O Death, white Death, all is so cold and dark,
I cannot see the shining of thy face!'
Then touching Balder's lips, Death answer'd low,
'Thy day is ended—thou wilt see no more—
Sleep, sleep!' . . .

    . . . But what is this that wavers slowly
Out of that purple blackness overhead?
Is it a blossom from the silvern boughs
O'ershadowing the azure pools of heaven?
Or feather from the plume of some sweet star
That ever moveth magically on
From mansion unto mansion of the sky?
Soft as a bloom from the white hawthorn spray
It wavers earthward thro' the starless dark,
Unseen, unfelt, until it gains the light
Which Balder breathes around him as he lies.
There, as a white moth hovers in the moon,
It floats and gleams, then sinking softly down,
Falls as a seal on Balder's shining brow
And melts away.

      '. . . O Death, upon mine eyes,
And on my brow, I feel a touch like dew,
Like cold dew shaken from a morning cloud.
Look heavenward—seest thou aught of the great gods,
Or God my Father?' But the form replied,
'On heaven and in the air 'tis night, deep night;

No shape is seen, no star, nor any light.
Sleep, Balder, sleep!'

                Then bending low he kissed
The lips of Balder, yea with kisses calm
He drew sweet Balder's breath, and lo! he shone
Brighter and brighter with the life he drank.
But Balder darken'd ever and grew cold.
'O Death, I feel thee smiling in a dream
Serene and still and very beautiful—
But ah, thy lips are chill!' and Death moan'd low,
Winding his thin arms tight round Balder's frame,
'Sleep, sleep!'

    . . . O what are these that waver slowly
Out of the purple blackness overhead?
Soft as that first white blossom blown from heaven,
Faltering downward thro' the rayless dark,
They come, they gather, falling flake on flake
With silvern lapse and silent interchange,
Hovering in soft descent as if they lived.
Upon the drooping head of Death they fall
Like lightly shaken leaves, and looking up
He sees the black air troubled into life
Of multitudinous waifs that wander down.
There is no sound—only the solemn hush
Of mystic motions and invisible wings;
There is no lamp, no star; but lo! the air
Is glimmering dimly with the faint wan light
Shed from the blossoms as they melt and fade.

'Under green boughs, under green boughs, O Death,
Thou hast borne me, and I see not, but I hear
The tremor of the soft trees overhead,
A sound like fountains flowing, and a touch
Like cool leaves shaken on mine eyes and hair!'

And Balder stirred his gentle head and smiled—
Then drew one last long breath, and sank to sleep.

'Tis over now—the gods may gaze in peace—
Balder is dead!

             Ay me, the light hath passed
From that once glorious head: still as a stone

It lies, not shining, in the lap of Death ;
The hair is white, the eyes are glazed and
    dim,
There is no red upon the loving lips,
And in its cage the singing heart lies cold.
Ah, Death, pale Death, thy kisses come in
    vain.
Close thou his lids, and by his side stretch
    down
The cold white marble arms, and at his head
Watch like a mourner, for a little space.

Death sits and gazes on ; but lo, his looks
Are pale as Balder's. . . . All the light he
  . wore
Hath faded, and his orbs are rayless now.
Lifeless he looms in vigil while his eyes
Turn upward and his thin cold hand still lies
Ev'n as a frozen stone on Balder's heart.
Thicker and thicker from the folds of heaven
The floating blooms are shaken ; lo, the waste
Is with a glittering whiteness carpeted,—
While still o'erhead in ever-gathering clouds,
Drifting from out the vapours of the dark,
The white flakes fall.

    O wonder of the snow !
The world's round ball is wrapt in crystal
    now,
And out of heaven there comes a freezing
    breath ;
And nothing stirs or lives ; and in his shroud
Woven by frost's swift fingers, Balder lies,
And that fair face which made creation glad
Is fixed as a rayless mask of ice.

Crouch at his head, O Death ! and hour by
    hour
Watch the still flakes of heaven wavering
    down,
Till thou, and that which lieth at thy feet,
And all the world, are clad in wondrous
    white !

VII.
THE COMING OF THE OTHER.

I.

How long he lay in that strange trance of
    night
Might Balder never know ;
Silently fell the waifs of stainless white,
And deeper grew the snow.

While out of heaven the falling flakes were
    shed,
The dark hours grew to days ;
And round and round a red moon overhead
Went circling without rays.

There were no stars, only that cheerless thing
Treading the wintry round ;
There was no light, save snow-flowers
    glimmering
Without a sound.

Darkness of doom is shed on Balder's eyes,
But whiteness shrouds the wold ;
And still at Balder's head the phantom lies
Silent and calm and cold.

And chill is Balder as some naked man
Made marble by the frost ;
His veins are ice ; upon his bosom wan
His two thin hands are crost.

But as within some clammy wall of stone
The death-watch keeps its chime,—
The cold heart in that crouching skeleton
Ticks out the time.

All round, a world of snow, and snows
    that fall,
Flake upon flake, so white ;
An empty heaven fluttering like a pall,
Lit by that one red light.

All round, the solemn slumber of the snow,
No sigh, no stir, no breath,—
But in the midst, scarce audible, slow, low,
The throbbing pulse of Death. . . .

The hours creep on, the dreary days are shed,
Measured by that slow beat ;
And all the while god Balder lieth dead,
Wrapt in his winding-sheet.

II.
THE LIGHT ON THE SNOW.

O Death, Death, press thy hand so lean
    and bare
Upon thy beating heart !
O Death, raise up thy head and scent the air
With nostrils cold apart !

Awaken from thy trance, O Death, and rise,
And hearken with thine ears ! . . .

Death stirs, and like a snake with glistening eyes
His luminous head uprears. . . .

Awaken! listen! Far across the night,
And down the drifts of snow,
There stirs a lonely light,—a blood-red light
That moveth to and fro.

Small as a drop of dew, most dim to sight,
It glimmereth afar. . . .
O Death, it cometh hither,—growing bright
And luminous as a star.

O Death, pale Death,
What do thine eyes behold?
What lonely star flasheth afar
Across the wintry wold?

The world is folded in its shroud of white;
The skies are smother'd deep;
There is no lamp at all in heaven, to light
Dead Balder's sleep.

There is no lamp at Balder's head, no star
Outlooking from the cloud;
White is the snow-drift woven near and far,
And white is Balder's shroud.

O death, pale Death, across the lone white land
No heavenly rays are shed,—
Yet still thou gazest, clutching Balder's hand,
At yonder gleam blood-red. . . .

It crawleth as a snail along the ground,
Still far and faint to see,
O Death, it creepeth surely, with no sound,
Across the night, to thee.

O gentle Death,
Why dost thou crouch so low?
A star it seems, a star that travelleth
From snow to snow.

Nearer it cometh, and across the night
Its beams fall crimson red,
The drifts beneath it glimmer and grow bright
Like cheeks lamp-lit and dead.

O gentle Death,
Hither it cometh slow;—
A Shadow creepeth with the same, O Death
From snow to snow.

III.
THE FACE AND THE VOICE.

Nearer and nearer o'er the waste of white
It steals, and doth not fade:
A light, and in the glimmer of the light
A form that casts a shade.

Nearer and nearer, till Death's eyes behold
A semblance strange and gray,
A silent shape that stoopeth and doth hold
The lamp to light its way.

Bent is he as a weary snow-clad bough,
Gaunt as a leafless tree,
But glamour of moonlight lies upon his brow,
Most strange to see!

And in one hand a silvern lanthorn swings
Fill'd with a crimson light,
And round his frame wind-blown and shivering clings
A robe of starry white. . . .

O Death, pale Death,
Well may thy cold heart beat!
The form that comes hath piercëd hands, O Death,
And bloody piercëd feet.

Slowly he crawleth under the cold skies,
His limbs trail heavy as lead,
Pale fixëd blue his eyes are, like the eyes
Of one that sleeps stone-dead.

Ay me, for never thro' so wan a wold
Walk'd one so sadly fair—
The wild snows drift, the wind blows shrill and cold,
And those soft feet are bare. . . .

O who is this that walketh the wintry night,
With naked hands and feet!
O who is this that beareth a blood-red light,
And weareth a winding-sheet!

The night is still, no living thing makes moan;
Silent the cold skies loom;—
But hark! what voice is this, so faintly blown
Across the gloom?

'Balder! Balder!'
  Hush! that cry!
The form stands white i' the chilly night,
  Holding its lamp on high.

'Balder! Balder!
  Where art thou?'
The snow smooths still with fingers chill
  Dead Balder's brow.

O gentle Death,
  What voice is this that cries?
What sad shape stands with lifted hands
  Alone under the skies?

'Balder! O Balder!
  Answer me!'
He stands and softly sighs,
  And vacant are his eyes
As if they cannot see!

Yet in the weary gloom full faint they glow,
  And fix themselves at last—
He sees dead Balder sleeping in the snow,
  And thither he fleeteth fast!

He comes now swifter than a bark
  Which bitter tempests blow,—
Dreadful he flashes down the dark,
  With black prints on the snow!

'Wake, Balder! wake!'
  His voice calls now—
The shrill cry circles like a snake
  Round Balder's brow!

Oh, who is this that walketh the wintry night
  With naked hands and feet?
O who is this that beareth a blood-red light
  And weareth a winding-sheet?

There is a gleam upon his brow and hair
  Ev'n as of luminous hands;
Swiftly he comes to Balder's side, and there
  He stands!

And Death crawls moaning from his snowy
    seat
  To grasp his raiment hem,
And toucheth with his mouth the piercèd
    feet,
  Yea, softly kisseth them.

O Death! pale Death!
  He gazeth down on thee—
His smile is like no smile of thing of breath,
  Yet is it sweet to see.

He lifts the lamp—and lo! its red rays
    glance
  On Balder's sleeping eyes—
'Balder! O Balder! from thy trance
  Arise!' . . . .

Strange flash'd the wondrous ray
  Aslant the silent snows;
Death wail'd—and slowly, gaunt and gray,
  Dead Balder rose!

IV.

'WAKE, BALDER! WAKE!'

Silent rose Balder, ev'n as one
  Who wakens from a swoon,
Turning his head from side to side
  In the red wintry moon.

Wrapt in his winding-sheet of snow
  He loom'd in the dim light,
And marble-pale his cold cheeks gleam'd
  Under his locks of white.

'Wake, Balder! wake!' the strange voice
    cried;
Dead Balder woke and heard,
And turn'd his face to his who spake,
  Shiv'ring, but said no word.

'Wake, Balder! wake!' the strange voice
    cried;
And Balder woke and knew,—
And lo! upon his lips and hair
  A golden glimmer grew!

O who art thou with blessed voice,
  Who biddest my heart beat?
And wherefore hast thou waken'd me
  From sleep so heavenly sweet?'

Then answer'd back that tall still form,
  In a clear voice and low,
Stretching his arms and brightening,
  White-robed, and pale as snow.

'I am thine elder Brother
  Come from beyond the sea;
For many a weary night and day
  I have been seeking thee!'

Oh, Balder's cheeks are shining bright,
  And smiles are on his face—
'I dream'd, and saw one with a lamp
  Passing from place to place.

' And ever, as he wander'd on,
  Softly he cried to me—
Art thou mine elder Brother?
  Then shall my lips kiss thee ! '

' I am thine elder Brother,
  Come from beyond the sea ;
Balder, my brother Balder,
  Kiss thou me ! '

Death moans, and crouching on the snow
  Uplooketh with eyes dim,
For Balder on his brother's breast
  Hath fallen, kissing him.

' Thou art mine elder Brother,
  The risen Balder cries ;
' I know thee by thy gentle voice
  And by thy tearful eyes.

' Thou art mine elder Brother,
  Most heavenly sad and sweet,
Yet wherefore hast thou piercèd hands
  And naked piercèd feet?

' O wherefore are thy cheeks so chill,
  Thy lips so cold and blue,
And wherefore com'st thou in thy shroud,
  As if arisen too ? '

The white Christ smiled in Balder's face,
  But softly his tears ran—
' Like thee I lived, like thee I loved,
  And died, like thee, for Man.'

V.
THE BIRTH AND DEATH.

The white Christ cried, and on the air
  His voice like music rang,
And Balder listen'd silently
  As if an angel sang.

' Out of the dark Earth was I born,
  Under the shining blue,
And to a human height I rose,
  And drank the light, and grew.

' The land was beauteous where I dwelt,
  A still and silent land,
Where little pools of heaven fall
  And gleam 'mid wastes of sand.

' I loved the bright beasts of the earth,
  And birds both great and small ;
I loved all God made beautiful,
  But mortals most of all.

' For on their faces framed of clay,
  And in their eyes divine,
I saw the shadow of the dream
  Which nightly sadden'd mine.

' But when I knew their days were dark,
  And all their spirits sore,
Because of this same silent Death
  Creeping from door to door,

' I raised my hands to heaven and cried
  On him that fashion'd me,
My Father dear who dwells in heaven,
  And suffers Death to be.

' And sweet and low this answer came
  Out of the quiet sky—
*All that is beautiful shall abide,
  All that is base shall die !*

' *Take thou thy cross and bear it well,
  And seek my servant Death :
Thou too shalt wither like a flower
  Before his bitterest breath.*

' *Yea, thou shalt slumber in his arms
  Three nights and days, and then,
With that cold kiss upon thy lips,
  Awaken once again !*

' *And when thou wakenest at last
  Thy work is yet undone,
For thou shalt roam the Earth, and seek
  Thy Brethren one by one !*

' *Yea, one by one unto thy heart
  Thy kin shall gather'd be,
Each pallid from the kiss of Death
  And beautiful like thee !* '

' O Balder, when my dark day came,
  And in despair I died,
The same sad Death sang low to me,
  Who croucheth at thy side !

' And all my living breath was gone
  For three long nights and days,
And by my side the phantom knelt
  Like one that waits and prays.

' But when my Father's voice again
  Came faint and low to me,
I rose out of my grave, and saw
  Earth sleeping silently.

'He who had hush'd me in his arms
  Was busy other-where. . . .
I stood and watch'd my Father's eyes
  Shine down thro' azure air.

'Then softly, with a happy smile,
  Along the land I crept,
And found the men that I had loved,
  Who waited, lived, and wept.

'And lo, I blessed them one and all,
  And cried with a human cry,
"All that is beautiful shall abide,
  All that is base shall die."

'But when my loving task was done,
  My soul took better cheer,
And wandering thro' the world unseen
  I sought my Brethren dear.

'All in my robe of snowy white
  From realm to realm I trod,
Seeking my Brethren who had died,
  The golden Sons of God!'

VI.
THE PARACLETES.

'I wander'd east, thro' shining realms
  Of bright and brazen day,
And there, by a great river's side,
  I saw a Brother pray.

'For past his feet the corpses drave
  Along the yellow tide,
Chased by the emerald water-snakes
  And vultures crimson-eyed.

'And from the banks there rose a wail
  Of women for their dead ;
They wept and tore their linen robes,
  And plunged 'neath wheels of dread.

'Upon his brow he wore a crown,
  But his black feet were bare,
And in his bright and brooding eyes
  There dwelt a piteous care.

'From his red lips there came a sound
  Like music of a psalm,
And those who listen'd ceased their tears
  And grew divinely calm.

'On his own grave he sat and smiled,
  A spirit dark and sweet,
And there were flowers upon his head
  And fruits around his feet. . . .

'I wander'd west where eagles soar
  Far o'er the realms of rains,
And there, among pale mountain peaks,
  One hung in iron chains.

'His head was hoary as the snow
  Of that serene cold clime,
Yet like a child he smiled, and sang
  The cradle song of Time.

'And as he sang upon his cross,
  And in no human tones,
The cruel gods who placed him there
  Were shaken on their thrones.

'I kiss'd him softly on the lips,
  And sighing set him free—
He wanders now in the green world,
  Divine, like thee and me. . . .

'Then faring on with foot of fire
  I cross'd the windy main,
And reach'd a mighty continent
  Wash'd green with dew and rain.

'There swift as lightning in the sun
  Ran beauteous flocks and herds,
And there were forests flashing bright,
  And many-colour'd birds.

'And there the red-skin'd hunters chased
  The deer and wild black kine,—
And lo! another gentle god
  Was sitting in a shrine!

'His skin enwrought, as if he lived,
  With mystic signs, sat he ;
Shaven his forehead, and his face
  Was painted terribly.

'Yet was he gentle as the dew,
  And gracious as the rain :
With healing gifts he made men glad
  Upon that mighty plain. . . .

'I wander'd south, where rivers roll'd
  Yellow with slime and sand,
And, black against an orange sky,
  I saw another stand.

'Two cymbals held he as he stood,
  And clash'd them with shrill wail :
The clash was as the thunder's voice,
  Heard 'mid the drifting gale.

'Black was his skin as blackest night,
　Naked as night each limb,
Yet in his eyeballs, on his cheeks,
　The heavenly dew did swim. . . .

'O Balder, these thy Brethren were
　Surely as they were mine.
I wander north, and thee I find
　The best and most divine!

'Yea, each of these was offer'd up
　As thou hast been, and I;
Their blood was drifted ev'n as smoke
　Up to the silent sky.

'All these loved Man and the green Earth
　As thou hast done, and I;
And each of these by stronger gods
　Was smitten down to die.

'Yet ever when I came, and spake
　The word and made the sign,
Their souls grew clothed in gentleness
　And rose again with mine!

'Yea, for the love of living men
　They stood renew'd in breath,
And smote the great gods from their thrones
　With looks made strong thro' Death.

'With faces fair they rose and wrought
　Against the gods with me,
To make the green Earth beautiful
　From shining sea to sea.

'Yea, Balder, these thy Brethren were,
　Surely as they were mine:
My Father's blessing on thy lips,
　For *thou*, too, art divine!'

VII.

Beneath his feet the pale Death crouch'd
　Ev'n as a lean white bear,
Watching with dark and dreamful eyes
　That face so strangely fair.

But paler, sadder, wearier,
　Stood Balder in his shroud,
While overhead a star's still hand
　Parted the drifting cloud;

And from the lattices of heaven
　The star look'd down on him;
But Balder saw not, and his eyes
　With tearful dews were dim.

'O Brother, on my sense still lies
　The burthen of my sleep,
A weight is on me like the weight
　Of winter on the Deep.

'For I remember as I wake
　Mine old glad life of dream—
The vision of the bridal Earth,
　The glory and the gleam!

'Oh, beautiful was the bright Earth,
　And round her purple bed
The torches of great rivers burnt
　Amber and blue and red!

'And beautiful were living men,
　Wandering to and fro,
With sun and moon and stars for lights,
　And flowers and leaves below.

'But evermore this phantom Death
　Was darkening the sun,
Seeking the sweetest to destroy.
　Sparing and pitying none.

'And lo, I live, and at my feet
　Death cold and silent lies,—
While in thine own dear Father's name
　Thou biddest me arise.

'O wherefore should I rise at all
　Since all is black above,
And trampled 'neath the feet of gods
　Lie all the shapes I love?

'Ay me, the dead are strewn with snows,
　They sleep and cannot see,
With no soft voice to waken *them*
　As thine has waken'd me!

'And wherefore should my soul forget
　What cruel kin were mine,
Tho' in another Father's name
　Thou greetest me divine?'

The white Christ gazed in Balder's face,
　And held his hand, and cried,
'Divine thou art and beautiful,
　And therefore *must* abide!

'And in mine own dear Father's name
　I greet and bid thee rise,
And we shall stand before his throne
　And look into his eyes.'

But Balder moan'd, 'Who made the Earth,
  And all things foul or fair?
Who made the white bear on the berg,
  The eagle in the air?

'Who made the lightning's forkèd flame,
  Who thunder's blacken'd brand?
Who fashion'd Death, with fatal eyes,
  Chill breath, and clammy hand?'

Death stirred and clung to Balder's feet
  And utter'd forth a cry—
A thousand starry hands drew back
  The curtains of the sky!

And countless eyes look'd calmly down
  Thro' azure clear and cold,
And lo! the round red moon became
  A shining lily of gold!

Then on the wilderness of snow
  A lustrous sheen was shed,
And splendour as of starlight grew
  Around the white Christ's head.

And Christ cried, gazing down on Death,
  Making a mystic sign,
'Now blessings on my servant Death,
  For *he* too is divine.

'O Balder, he who fashion'd us,
  And bade us live and move,
Shall weave for Death's sad heavenly hair
  Immortal flowers of love.

'Ah! never fail'd my servant Death,
  Whene'er I named his name,—
But at my bidding he hath flown
  As swift as frost or flame.

'Yea, as a sleuth-hound tracks a man,
  And finds his form, and springs,
So hath he hunted down the gods
  As well as human things!

'Yet only thro' the strength of Death
  A god shall fall or rise—
A thousand lie on the cold snows,
  Stone still, with marble eyes.

'But whosoe'er shall conquer Death,
  Tho' mortal man he be,
Shall in his season rise again,
  And live, with thee, and me!

'And whosoe'er loves mortals most
  Shall conquer Death the best,
Yea, whosoe'er grows beautiful
  Shall grow divinely blest.'

The white Christ raised his shining face
  To that still bright'ning sky.
'Only the beautiful shall abide,
  Only the base shall die!'

VIII.

But Balder moan'd, 'O beauteous Earth
  Now lying cold and dead,
Bright flash'd the lamps of flowers and
    stars
  Around thy golden head!

'And beautiful were beast and bird,
  And lamb and speckled snake,
And beautiful were human things
  Who gladden'd for my sake.

'But lo! on one and all of those
  Blew the cold blighting breath,
Until I died that they might live
  And bought their life with death.

'Behold, I live, and all is dark,
  And wasted is my pain,
For glimmering at my feet I see
  The fatal eyes again.

'Why stays he here upon the Earth?
  Why lingers he below?
The empty heavens wait for him,—
  'Tis ended—let him go!'

Death look'd up with a loving face,
  And smiled from the white ground;—
The stars that sat upon their thrones
  Seem'd singing with low sound.

The white Christ cried, 'The green Earth
    lives!
  She sleeps, but hath not died!
She and all fair things thou hast named
  Shall quicken and abide!

'O Balder, those great gods to whom
  Thy radiant life was given,
Were far too frail to keep their plight
  And summon Death to heaven.

'There is no god of all thy kin
  Dare name that name aloud:

When his cold hand was on thy heart,
　Each crouch'd within his cloud.

'Thou couldst not buy the boon of those,
　They were too weak and poor;
Fain would they buy a boon of *thee*,
　Now thy strange sleep is o'er!

'Yet now for evermore fulfilled
　Is thine ancestral rune,
For thou indeed hast conquer'd Death
　And won thy gentle boon.

'Yea, thou hast died as fair things die
　In earth, and air, and deep,
Yet hast thou risen thrice beautiful
　Out of thy solemn sleep.

'For life thrice seal'd and sanctified
　Is on thy lips and eyes;
And whatsoe'er grows fair like thee
　By love shall also rise.

'Lo! out of beauty cast away
　Another beauty grows:
What Death reaps in the fields of life
　In fairer fields he sows.

'And thro' a thousand gates of gloom,
　With tracts of life between,
The creatures that the Father made
　Creep on, now hid, now seen;

'And duly out of every doom
　A sweeter issue flows,
As out of dreary dooms of gods
　At last thy glory rose!

'So fairer yet, and ever fair,
　Thy soul divine shall gleam,
A spirit springing from a tomb
　And rainbow'd into dream!

'O kiss me, Brother, on the mouth,
　Yea, kiss me thrice again;
For when I feel thy kiss, I feel
　The sun, and the wind, and the rain!

'The dead Earth wakens 'neath thy feet,
　Flame kindles thro' the sod. . . .
O kiss me with thy human lips,
　Thou brightest born of God!'

VIII.
THE TWILIGHT OF THE GODS.

I.

'BALDER! Balder!'

　　　　And Balder said,
Turning round his gentle head,
'I hear!'

　'And thou, my servant Death,
Kneeling low with hushèd breath,
While my hand is on thy hair!'

Death made answer, kneeling there,
'I hear!'

　'At last the cold snows cease,
The white world is hush'd in peace,
The sky is clear, the storm has gone,
Stars are rising to light us on—
In the north the moon grows gray,—
Take my hand and come away!'

　'Whither, O Whither?'

'To the City strange wherein
Dwell the mighty gods thy kin;—
O Balder, lead me thither!'

'Across the darkness and the day,
Long and dreary is the way—
O'er chill wastes of misery,
Past the silent Frozen Sea,
Where the white bears lean and old
Run and shiver in the cold—
Where the vast ice-mountains rise
Violet-blue against the skies,
Then across the wondrous Bow
　Only gods and ghosts may tread,—
Beyond the sea, above the snow,
　Where the sunfire fadeth red;
There the night lies and no day—
Long and weary is the way—
O Brother, fare not thither!'

'Broken is the wintry night,
Rising yonder is the light;
Half our task is yet to do—
Come! and thou, Death, follow too—
O Balder, lead me thither!'

Far away across the gloom,
Rose-red like a rose in bloom,

Flashing, changing, ray by ray,
Glorious as the ghost of day,
Gleam'd in one vast aureole
Shifting splendours of the pole.
All across the vault of blue
Shooting lights and colours flew,
And the milky way shone there
Like a bosom white and bare,
Throbbing, trembling, softly moved
By some heart that lived and loved.
Night was broken, and grew bright.
All the countless lamps of light
Swinging, flashing, near and far,
Cast their glittering rays below,—
While the silvern polar star
Throbb'd close down upon the snow. . . .

'Take my hand, and let us go!'

II.

And so those twain have passed across the night,
 O'er frozen wilds of white,
With eyes still fixed upon the polar star
 That burneth bright afar;
And Death behind them, creeping like a hound,
 Still follows with no sound.

O wonders of the cold untravell'd Waste
 Whereon their swift feet haste!
The night is troubled; on the black pole's pyres
 Flash fierce electric fires,
And shadows come and go, phantoms move forth
 Gigantic in the north.
Upon the snow a green light glimmereth,
 With phosphorescent breath
Flashing and fading; and from unseen lairs
 Creep hoary ghost-like bears,
Crawling across their path without a cry.

 At last against the sky
They see the lonely arctic mountains loom,
 Touch'd with a violet bloom
From peak to base and wearing on their heights
 Strange ever-shifting lights,
Yellow and azure and dark amethyst;
 But westward they are kissed
By the bright beams of a great moon of gold

Dead-white and calm and cold
Sleeps the great waste, while ever as they go,
 With shadows on the snow.
Their shapes grow luminous and silvern fair,
 And in the hush'd chill air
The stars of heaven cluster with quick breath
 To gaze on them and Death.
Now thro' the trembling sheen of the still sky
 Blue fires and emerald fly
With wan reflections on the sheeted white
 Outspread beneath the night,
And passing thro' them, Christ and Balder seem
 As spectres in a dream,
Until at last their feet come silently
 To the great arctic sea.

Moveless and boundless, stretching blindly forth
 Into the purple north,
Rise mountainous waves and billows frozen all
 As if i' the act to fall,
And tho' they stir not, yet they seem to roll
 In silence to the pole.
So, lit by countless stars, that Ocean old
 Wrapt in the vapours cold
Of its own breath, beneath the lamps of night
 Gleams blue and shadowy white!
Then Balder crieth,—and around his brow
 New glory glimmereth now,—
'Ay me, remote from men are the abodes
 Of the immortal gods;
Beyond the ocean of the ice; afar
 Under the sleepless star;
And o'er the flood of the wild waters spanned,
 From lonely land to land,
By the great bridge of the eternal Bow.'

 The white Christ answereth low,
'Tho' it were further than the furthest light
 That glimmereth this night,
Thither our souls are bound, our feet must go!'

III.

THE BRIDGE OF GHOSTS.

Their feet have passed the frozen Deep
 Whose waves in silence roll,
And now they reach that ocean black
 Which beats the inmost pole.

Before them, on the northern sky
 Rose-red and far withdrawn,

Mingled with meteors of the night,
 Gleam golden dews of dawn ;
And cast across that liquid sea
 Which surges black below,
They see the pathway of the gods,
 A many-colour'd Bow.

[There comes from off its heights a wind
 That blows for endless time,
As swift as light, as keen as frost,
 It strikes down souls that climb.]

'O brother, place thy hand in mine,'
 The gentle Balder said ;
The rayless waters roar'd beneath,
 The Bridge flash'd overhead.

Then hand in hand against the wind
 They falter'd upward slow,
On stairs of crimson and of gold
 Climbing the wondrous Bow.

Like a great rainbow of the earth
 It rose with faint hues seven,
And thro' the purple of the arch
 Glimmer'd the lights of heaven.

When they had reach'd the midmost height,
 In air they stood so high,
To one beneath they would have seem'd
 As stars upon the sky.

The white Christ cried, 'What lonely light
 Burns yonder ruby red?'
'The mansion of the sun-god Fryer
 Stands yonder,' Balder said.

'There ranged in rows with cold hands crost
 The slain in silence lie,
The face of each ablaze like brass
 Against the burning sky.'

Far under, as they linger'd there,
 The dark deep waters roll'd ;
Beyond, the polar mountains flash'd
 With gleams of fiery gold.

Upon the shores rose hills of ice
 Hewn as in marble white,
Inlaid with opal and with pearl
 And crown'd with chrysolite.

From stair to stair the brethren trod,
 And Death crawl'd close behind,
And ever as they walk'd, the Bridge
 Shook wavering in the wind.

And lo! they seem'd as meteor shapes,
 White-robed and shod with flame ;
And to them out of the cold north
 A threatening murmur came.

Down in the sullen sea below
 Now ghostly faces clomb,
Uplooking with wild eyes to theirs
 And waving hands of foam!

So o'er the mighty Bow they moved
 Snow-vestured and star-crown'd,
And Death behind them like a shade
 Follow'd without a sound.

But as they reach'd the shores and stood,—
 The bright Bridge at their back,—
The gods gazed out from the cold north
 And shriek'd, and all grew black!

Deep thunders shook the darken'd heaven,
 Wild lightning flash'd and fled,
The frozen shores of ice and snow
 Trembled beneath their tread.

Round the ice-mountains of the pole
 Dense smokes of tempest rose,
And from their lairs swift whirlwinds leapt
 Wrapt round with drifting snows.

'O Brother, hold me by the hand,
 For lo! the hour is nigh ; —
I see the shadows of the gods,
 Yonder upon the sky!'

IV.

'BEHOLD, I AM RISEN.'

They stood in the snow and they clung
  together,—
 The air was blacken'd, the snow was
  driven ;
There came a tempest of wintry weather
 Out of the open gates of heaven.
The darkness drifted, the dark snows shifted,
 The winnowing fans of the winds were lifted,
 And the realms of the ice were riven ;
The white flakes whirl'd like a wingèd cloud
 Round and over and under ;
The Earth shriek'd loud from her rending
  shroud,
 And the black clouds echoed in thunder!

'O Balder! Balder!'

                And Balder replied,
Feeling not seeing his face who cried,
  'I hear!'

        'And thou other who crouchest there,
Gazing up thro' thy hoary hair,
  Stir not yet till I bid thee go!'

And Death moan'd answer out of the snow,
  'I hear!'

        'At last the hour hath come,
The sky is troubled, the world is shaken,
The sleeping gods on their thrones awaken,
  Altho' their lips are dumb.
I feel a breath from the frozen north,
For the souls of the slain are faring forth,
And their tramp is heard on the frozen ocean,
  And their tread is swift in the vales of snow.
  They come, and the great deep throbs
    below
To the sound of their thund'rous motion.
O Balder, Balder!'

            'I hearken, I hearken!'

'Thro' the flakes that fall and the ways that
    darken,
Over the earth or over the sea,
North is the way that our feet must flee,
Till we find them sitting beyond the pole,
Gods without pity, gods without soul,
  Fresh from the slaying of thee.
North is the way that our feet must go,
Breasting the blasts from the gates of woe,
Till we find them there in their sacred places,
Gods with their terrible bloodless faces,
Writing red-handed for mortal races
  Black runes on the stainless snow!'

. . . Deeper and darker the night is growing,
Faster and faster the clouds are snowing—
Fleeter and fleeter the Brethren fly
  With faces silver'd against the sky,
Till close before them, beyond the pole,
The aurora flashes its fiery scroll,
While the winds of the frozen waste are
    blowing,
  And the ice is riven asunder!
Lo! ghastly blue with a dreary gleam
The bergs of the pole, like ghosts in a dream,
Standing pallid against the heaven,
Flash with the forks of the fiery levin,

And to and fro in the frozen snow,
  Pass manifold shapes of wonder.
Faster, faster, out of the north,
The ghosts of Asgard are hurrying forth,
And their shields of ice and their spears of
    hail
Clash in the heart of the gathering gale,
  As they come upon feet of thunder.

'O Balder! Balder! cling unto me!'

'Lift up thy lamp, for I cannot see—
I shiver deep to the bitter bone,—
While the chilly seeds of the sleet are sown
  In my flesh, and I feel not thee!'

The lamp is lifted: a dreary light
It sheddeth out on the northern night;
It comes and goes like the lighthouse ray
Lost on the soot-black ocean way.
Nought they see and nought they feel,
Only the frost with fingers of steel
Gripping their throats, so fierce, so fast,
Only the breath of the bitter blast
Bending their bodies as trees are bent,
Rending their garments as clouds are rent,
While overhead, with a thund'rous tread,
The black heavens frown to trample them
    down,
And the vials of storm are spent.

'O Balder! Balder! what shadows white
Stand in the tempest's shrieking flight?
There in the darkness I discern
Faces that fade and eyes that burn;
They loom in the flash of the thunder-cloud,
And the tramp of their feet is as surges that
    roar,
Rolling around,
  On some desolate rocky shore.'

Then Balder answer'd with eager cry—
'Cover thy face lest thou droop and die:
'Tis the gods my brethren! I see them plain,
Each sitteth there in a spectral pain;
They search the waste all round for us,
And the light in their eyes is tremulous
  With the wrath that burns the brain!'

. . . Blacker, blacker, the night is growing,
Thicker, faster, the snow is snowing.
Silent amid those frozen peaks
Sit gods with terrible bloodless cheeks,—

Each like a statue of marble stone,
Each alone on a lonely throne,
With the red aurora upon their hair,
They loom in desolate circles there,
 Silent, with folded wings ;
They do not stir though the storm drifts by,
They do not speak though the wild winds
 cry,
Silent they reign in a starry dream,
While the north star flashes its fiery beam,
And the serpent lightning springs. . . .
Silent they sit,—but who is He
Who broods in the centre awfully?
Like a pale blue berg in the frosty light,
Solemn, speechless, hoary white,
Coldly wrapt from head to feet
In a robe of snow like a winding-sheet,
With a crown of starlight on his hair,
He sitteth dreaming with fatal stare,
 Tho' his throne is strangely shaken.
Black is his home, and he sits thereon
Still as a mortal whose breath is gone,
And the waves are frozen around his feet,
And faint, far under, the earthquakes beat,
 Yet he broods, and doth not waken.

'O Balder! Balder! who is he
Who sitteth there so silently?
Who sitteth there so hoary and old,
A god in the midst of gods so cold,
And hears not at all, though the storm
 winds call,
And the ghosts of Asgard gather?'

Then Balder answer'd, 'The gods creep
 here,
Weary with seasons of strife and fear—
They come, they go—but for ever and aye
He stirreth not, be it night or day ;
Still as a stone, he reigneth alone!'

And Balder raising his hands, made moan,
 'BEHOLD I AM RISEN, MY FATHER!'

V.

ALFADUR.

The rune is woven, the spell is spoken,
And lo! the dream of the gods is broken,
And each pale throne is shaken.
They rise, they tremble against the sky,
They shriek an answer to Balder's cry
 And white as death they waken!

Gods they glimmer in frozen mail,
Their faces are flashing marble pale,
They rise erect, and they wave their hands,
They scatter the shifting snows as sands,
 And gaze in the face of the Father! . . .

. . . Blacker, blacker, the night is growing,
Faster, faster, the snow is snowing—
Silently looking thro' the storm,
Towers the one gigantic Form,
And all around with a trumpet sound
 The wintry winds are blowing.
The light of doom is in his eyes, his arms
 spread wide for slaughter,
He sits 'mid gleams of burning skies and
 wails of wind-blown water,
Behind the outline of his cheeks the pale
 aurora flashes,
He broods 'mid moveless mountain peaks
 and looks thro' fiery lashes :
On heaven and earth that round him float
 in whirls of snowy wonder,
He looks, and from his awful throat there
 comes the cry of thunder !

 'BALDER! BALDER!'

 . . . 'He cries on me—
He standeth yonder, and beckoneth!'
'He looketh around, but he cannot see!
Answer him back with a gentle breath,
 Now the air is still!' . . .

 'I am here, I am here!'
. . . The cry went up to the godhead drear,
Like the cry of a lamb in the midst of the
 snow,
When the voices of tempest have sobbed
 their fill,
 And the clouds are still
For a little space, and the winds lie low.
Then rose in answer a wail so loud
It roll'd as thunder from cloud to cloud,
And the gods arose in a wingèd crowd,
As oft 'mid desolate mountain-peaks,
With clangour of wings and hungry shrieks,
 Great flocks of eagles gather,
Tearing asunder their frozen mail,
Smiting their breasts with a woful wail,
Looming with faces spectral pale,
 They gazed in the eyes of the Father!
Then even as mighty eagles spread
Their wings and soar, they arose and fled

Crossing the gleam of the fiery north,
Facing the dark drift hurrying forth,
They flew on flashing pinions ;
As wild clouds scatter'd across the sky,
They wing'd their way with a thunder-cry. . . .
But moveless there, when the rest had flown,
The Father sat on his silent throne,
Dreary, desolate, all alone,
In the midst of the white dominions.

   ' BALDER ! BALDER !'

       ' He looks on me !
He stirreth now, with a sound like the sea,
And he calleth aloud !'

      ' Then move no limb,
But crouch in thy place and answer him ;—
Cry once more full loud and clear,
Now he pauseth again !' . . .

     ' I am here, I am here !'
Again the thunder rolling near,
Again the tumult of wind and ocean ;
Around the throne with a serpent motion
 The meteor snakes appear.
White in the midst He stands, the Spirit of
 God the Master,
Waving his wild white hands, urging his
 snows on faster ;
But ever darker yet the troubled air grows
 o'er him,
And still with fierce face set he searcheth
 night before him,
And then again, all blind, with black robes
 blown asunder,
He gropeth down the wind, and calls aloud
 in thunder,

   'BALDER, BALDER.'

    . . . ' I see him now,
The wrath of heaven is on his brow—
He stands in the circle of meteors white,
His white feet glimmer like cold moonlight—
I can feel his breath !'

      ' Now hold my hand—
Rise erect on thy feet and stand—
Make answer !'

     ' My Father, I am here !'

As an infant's cry, so faint, so clear,
As a young lamb's cry, so soft, so low,
Cometh the voice from the waste of snow,—
And silence deep as the sleep o' ocean,
Stillness with no stir, no motion,
 Follows the sound of the cry. . . .
Terrible, desolate, the Form
Stands and broods in the midst of the storm,
Beneath him wolves of the fierce frost swarm,
 But quiet and hush'd they lie.
With his robe wind-rent and his form wind-
 blown
 He gazeth round and round.
He seeth a snow amid the snow
 And heareth a human sound.

 ' BALDER ! BALDER !'

      ' O Father dear,
Turn thine eyes and behold me here—
Ev'n Balder thy Son !'

       *' I see thee not—
Only a gleam on a darken'd spot,
And the ray of the light in thy hand !'*

       ' Ay me,
No light I carry that thou mayst see.
What wouldst thou, Father ?'

     *' Why hast thou risen ?
We deem'd thee dead, and we slept in peace—
We deem'd thee dead with the snow for prison,
 That the old sad fear might cease.
We deem'd thee dead, and our hearts were
 light,
For never more would thy beauty blight
 The spirit of Me thy Father !'*

Then answer'd Balder, ' O Father dear,
Turn thine eyes, and behold me here—
Why hatest thou me ?'

     *' We hate thee all
For thy summer face, for thy soft footfall,
For thy beauty blended of star and flower,
For thine earthly love, for thine heavenly
 dower ;
For the rune that was written, the rune that
 was read,
We cursed thee all, but our curse was said
Deepest and best when we read that rune
By thy love for men !'*

As the rising moon
Creeping up from a cloudy place,
A glory grew upon Balder's face—
Again he murmur'd, 'O Father dear,
Turn thine eyes and behold me here—
Why hatest thou me?'

    '*We hate thee most*
*By the rune that was written, the rune that
    was lost,*
*By the doom that above thee hung sharp as
    a sword,*
*When thy feet stood there and thy voice
    implored*
For pity of men; and we loved thee least
For loosing the yoke of man and beast,
For making the hearts of mortals tame,
*For calming wild hawk-like men who came
To thy beck as doves; then we loathed to see
The light of thy name upon flower and tree,
The peace of thy name upon hill and vale,
The love of thy name on the faces pale
Of maidens and men; yea, for all these
    things,*
For all thy life and the light it brings,
We have hated and hate thee unto death.'

But Balder answereth back and saith,
'Why hatest thou me?'

    '*For this the most!*
*Because thy coming is as the ghost
Of the coming doom that shall strike us dead.
For the rune was written, the rune was read,
And we knew no rest till we bought our breath
With the gentle boon of thy willing death.
Why hast thou risen? how hast thou risen?
We gave thee the frost and the snow for
    prison,*
We heard thy sigh and we let thee die,
*Yet thou criest again with a human cry
From the gates of life! . . . But I stoop at
    last
To sweep thee hence with my bitterest blast
Out to the heavens of pitiless air,
Where nevermore with a human care
    That face of thine
May trouble the eyes of the gods divine!
Out 'mong the wingèd stars, deep down the
    dark abysses,
Beyond the black tomb's bars, far from the
    green Earth's kisses.*

*As dust thou shalt be cast, as snow thou
    shalt be drifted,*
*Seized by my fiercest blast thou shalt be now
    uplifted.*
*Call on all living things that stir in sun or
    shadow—*
*White flowers, sweet forms with wings, wild
    deer, or lambs o' the meadow;*
*Call on the moonlight now that mingled in
    thy making;*
*To heaven uplift thy brow, where the pale
    spheres are waking;*
*On water, air, and fire, on snow and on
    wind and on forest,*
*Call with a wild desire, now when thy need
    is sorest!*
*Call now on flower or bird to fill the plight
    they gave thee!*
*Call, let thy voice be heard, and see if Earth
    can save thee!'*

Behind the back of the Shadow hoar,
There grew a trouble, a sullen roar,
Roar as of beasts that prepare to come,
Trouble like surges that flash to foam;
Faster and faster the drift whirl'd round,
Deeper and direr grew the sound,
And the four fierce winds are blowing!
Yet brighter, calmer grew Balder's face,
Till a light and a glory fill'd the place,
And he rose his height, like a lily white,
Like a lily white in the heart of the night,
    With the flakes around him snowing!

.

VI.
THE BRETHREN.

'Father, Father, why hatest thou me,
Whom the green Earth loves, and the cir-
    cling sea,
And the pure blue air, and the light of the
    sun,
And the birds of the air, and the flowers
    each one?
Hatest thou me thro' my love for these?
For the swift deep rivers, the fronded trees,
The golden meres and the mountains white,
The cataracts leaping from height to height,
And the deer that feed on the snowy steeps
Where the rainbow hangs and the white
    mist creeps?
Hatest thou me the most of all

For my care of mortals whom thou hast
    made,
My blessing on lovers whose soft footfall
    Soundeth still in the flowery shade?
Father, Father, hatest thou me,
Because of my light on humanity?
Because with a holy anointing balm
I have heal'd their hearts and kept them
    calm;
Because I have sown in forest and grove
The roses of beauty, the lilies of love,
That men might gather, and sweeten away
The taint of the perishable clay?
Father, Father, listen to me—
I will not call upon bird or tree,
I will not call upon lamb or dove,
On the flowers below or the stars above;
I will call aloud, and thine ears shall know,
I will call aloud in the midst of the snow,
On a mortal thing of mortal breath
Who has gazed and smiled in the eyes of
    Death,
Who has loosen'd his shroud and his feet
    made free
To follow and find me over the sea.
 . . . . My brother Jesus, hearest thou me!'

Sweet as a star that opens its lids of silver
    and amber,
Soft as a lily that rises out of a water still,
Pure as a lamp that burns in a virgin's
    vestal chamber
When winds with folded wings sleep on
    the scented sill,
Pale as the moving snow, yet calmer, clearer,
    and whiter,
Holding the light in his hand, and flash-
    ing a ray blood-red,
Robed in a silvern robe that ever grew
    stranger and brighter,
Robed in a robe of the snow, with a
    glory around his head,
Christ now arose! and upstanding held the
    cold hand of his Brother,
Turning his face to the storm like the
    wrath of some beautiful star,—
And the sound of the storm was hush'd,
    and pale grew the face of that Other,
He, Alfadur supreme, most direful of all
    gods that are!

'BALDER! BALDER!'

            'O Father, I listen!'

'What shape is this whose sad eyes glisten
Bright as the lamp he is uplifting?
Round and o'er him snows are drifting,
Yet as a still star shineth he,
Pale and beautiful like thee.
Who is this that standeth there
Even as a mortal man,
Thin and weary and wan,
A lanthorn in his hold,
His feet bloody and bare,
And a ring of brightest gold
    Round his hair?'

'O Father, 'tis he and none other
    Who woke me from my tomb;
The Christ it is, my Brother,
    Tho' born of a woman's womb.
He has conquer'd the grave, for lo!
    He died and he rose again!
He comes to the silence of snow,
    From the beautiful regions of rain;
And his hair is bright with a peaceful light
    As the yellow moon's on a summer night,
And the flesh on his heart is heapen white
    To cool an immortal pain!'

Blacker, blacker the night is growing,
Deeper, deeper the snow is snowing. . . .
As the rigid wave of the ocean-storm
Towereth the gigantic Form,
And he lifts his hand with a cold command,
    And the shrill winds answer blowing!

A ghastly gleam is on his cheeks, his white
    robes roll asunder,
He raises up his arms and shrieks in his
    old voice of thunder,
'The rune was writ, the rune is read—Son,
    thou hast slain thy Father,
The frames are quick that late were dead,
    and from the grave they gather,
The pale One cometh heavenly eyed, as in
    thy dreams, O Mother!
He wakes, he stands by Balder's side as
    brother smiles by brother.
O gods, these live, and must we die? these
    bloom, and must we wither?
Cry with a loud exceeding cry on Death and
    send him hither!
Come, come, O Death! I call on thee—come
    hither, fleeter, faster!
Thou hunter of humanity, thou hound of
    me thy Master!

*Slay thou these twain, that we may live,
  who feed thy throat with slaughter,
And blood to quench thee gods will give,
  shed free as torrent water!
Come thou this night, O Death divine,
  come quickly or come never,
And the great Earth shall all be thine for
  ever and for ever!'*

The snows are blowing, the Earth is crying,
The eagles of storm are shrieking and flying;
Thunder-cloud upon thunder-cloud
Piled, and flashing and roaring aloud,
Roll from the north, and the winds rush forth,
  And the billows of heaven are breaking.
Hand in hand the Brethren stand,
Fair and bright in the midst of the night,
Fair and bright and marble white,
  Quiet as babes awaking. . . .
But who is *he* that stirring slow,
Wrapt in winding-sheet of snow,
Riseth up from the Christ's feet?
His golden hair all white with sleet,
His eyes all dim, his face snow-pale,
He stands erect in the drifting gale!
Tall and terrible loometh he,
Facing the blast like a frozen tree!

'*Death, Death!*' the god shrieks now—
*Death, Death, is it surely thou?
Death, Death!*' and the god laughs loud,
Answer'd by every thunder-cloud,
  While the snows are falling faster,—
'*Death, Death, there is thy prey!—
Take them and tear them and rend them
  away,
As flakes of snow, as drops of spray,
In the name of Me thy Master!*' . . .

Like two lilies crown'd with gold,
Very beauteous to behold,
  Blown in summer weather,
Like two lambs with silvern feet,
Very beauteous and sweet,
Held together with a chain
In some sacrificial fane,
  The Brethren cling together.
Ever fairer still they grow
While the noise of storm sinks low,
And the Father's snow-white hand
Pointeth at them as they stand,
And the silent shape of Death
Creepeth close and shuddereth!

See, O see, the light they wear,
On their heads and o'er their hair,
Falleth on the Phantom now,
Lying softly on his brow. . . .
Death, O Death, can this be *thou?*

VII.
FATHER AND SON.

Now hark, one crieth!
          '*My servant Death,
Kneeling there with hushèd breath,
Listen, ere I bid thee go!*'
Death makes answer out of the snow,
'*I hear!*'

          The Christ hath risen his height,
Large and strange in a lonely light,
And he lifts his hand and makes the sign
Of the blessed cross on his breast divine,
And the thrones of the white gods flash like
  fire,
And sink in earthquake around the Sire,
  Shaken and rent asunder!
Then he lifts his hand and he makes the sign
Once again on his breast divine,
And the mountains of ice around the throne
Are troubled like breakers rolling on
  To the sound of their own thunder!

'Father! Father!' Balder cries,
With arms outstretch'd and weeping eyes,
'Father!'—but lo! the white Christ stands,
Raising yet his holy hands,
And cries, 'O Death, speed on! speed on!
Conquer now and take thy throne—
Now all the gods have taken flight,
Reign thou there one starless night
  In the room of him, the Father!'

Slowly over the icy ground,
Slow and low like a lean sleuth-hound,
Without a breath, without a sound,
  The phantom form is crawling.
He makes no shadow, he leaves no trace,
Snow on snow he creepeth apace,
Nearer, nearer, the fixèd Face
  Veil'd with the flakes still falling.
'Father! Father!' Balder cries . . .
Silent, terrible, under the skies,
Sits the God on his throne, with eyes on his
  Son
  Whose gentle voice is calling!
As the cuckoo calls in the heart of the May
  Singing the flowers together,

As the fountain calls thro' its flashing spray,
As a lamb calls low 'mid a mountain-cloud,
As a spirit calls to a corpse in its shroud,
The Son cries on the Father!

VIII.
TWILIGHT.

The wind is blowing, the skies are snowing,
The ice is rent and the rocks are riven,
But morning light in the north is growing,
Crimson light of the altars of heaven.
Silent, still, amidst the storm,
Sitteth there the formless Form,
Hearkening out of his hoary hair,
Waiting on in a dark despair,
  While the burning heavens flame o'er him! . . .
Suddenly, wild and wing'd and bright,
Towering to heaven in shroud of white,
A phantom upriseth against the light
And standeth vast before him. . . .
Is it a Shadow, or only the snow?
The skies are troubled, the light burns low,
But stars still gather and gather.
Is it a Shadow, or only the snow,
Uprising there in the blood-red glow,
Ever towering higher and higher,
In a robe of whiteness fringed with fire,
Outstretching wings without a cry
From verge to verge of the burning sky,
  With eyes on the eyes of the Father?

Now Balder crieth, 'What shape comes there,
Terrible, troubling the heavens and air?
Is it Norna the arctic swan,
The bright and bodiless Skeleton,
Bird-shaped, with a woman's breasts and eyes,
Whose wings are wide as the world and skies?
Is it Norna, or only the snow,
Moving yonder against the glow,
Ever towering higher and higher,
Ever outspreading pinions dire
And looking down in a dumb desire,
  With eyes on the eyes of the Father!'

It is not Norna, it is not the snow.
The skies are troubled; the light burns low;
  Yet stars still gather and gather.
'Father! Father! awaken, awaken!
One bends above thee with bright hair shaken
Over thy throne like a falling flame;

One toucheth thy cheek and nameth thy name,
In a voice I hear, in a tone I know;
It is not Norna, it is not the snow,
By the face and the voice and the tone.
Vaster than these and vaster than thou,
Touching the stars with a shining brow,
Flickering up to the twinkling shades
Where the wild aurora flashes and fades,
Spreading its wings from east to west,
As an eagle that looks on a hawk in its nest
  It hungereth over thy throne!
Father! my Father!'

    'He cannot hear—
Hide thy face, for the hour is near—
Hush!' . . . .

. . . Who shrieks in the heart of the night? . . .
Terrible, desolate, dumb and blind,
Like a cloud snow-white
Struggling and rent in the claws o' the wind,
The Father hath risen with no sound
'Mid the wild winds wavering around,
  And his stirring deepens the storm.
The ice is shaken beneath his tread,
The meteors burn around his head,
But faster, thicker, out of the skies,
Blotting his shape from Balder's eyes,
  The wild flakes waver and swarm.
Now face to face in the blood-red gleam,
Like clouds in the sunset, like shapes in a dream,
Face to face, with outstretch'd hands
Like lightning forks that illume the lands,
Face to face, and sight to sight,
Like vulture and eagle fierce for fight,
They rise and they rise against the skies,—
Alfadur with his fiery eyes,
  And the other vaster Form!

It is not Norna, but stranger and brighter,
It is not the snow, but wilder and whiter;
Ever greater yet it grows
Wrapt about with whirling snows,
Ever it dilateth on,
Till, a crimson Skeleton,
With his head against the sky
Where the pale lights flicker and die,
Strange, he stands, with orbs of fire
Looking down upon the Sire.
See, O see upon his brow
Strangest lustre liveth now,

On his neck and round his frame
Twines a snake of emerald flame. . . .
Death, O Death, can it be *thou?*

" Father, father! I cannot see—
The heavens are bright, but the world is white,
The wings of the wan Form cover thee—
Around and around, with no sigh, with no sound,
Like the mists of a cloud, like the folds of a shroud,
They enwrap thee,—and hide thee from me!'

IX.

'A CROSS AND A LILY.'

'It is over! O Balder, look up and behold!'

'Not yet, for I sicken—my sense shrinketh cold,
And I fear the strange silence that cometh at last!
All is hush'd—all is dead—the dew now is shed
Warm as tears on my hand, but the tempest hath pass'd,
And the sounds of the tempest are fled!'

'Arise!'

'I am risen!'

'Behold!

'All is white,
But the darkness hath gone, and the stars of the night,
And down from the north streams the dawn flowing free;
But I see not my Father!'

'Again!

'Woe is me!
His throne standeth there white and cold, and thereon
Sits another I know, as a King on a throne,
Yea, sceptred and crownèd . . . and vaster tenfold
He seems than the Spirit who sat there of old,
For his form 'gainst the heavens looms fiery and fair,
And the dew of the dawn burneth bright on his hair;

And we twain unto *him* are as birds in the night
That sit gazing up at a great snowy height
Where the starlight is coming and going like breath.'

'So strange and so changed, yet 'tis he, even Death,—
Best and least, last and first. He hath conquer'd his own.
All gods are as sand round his feet tempest-blown,
And lesser yet greater, more weak yet more wise,
Are we who stand here looking up in his eyes.
All hail now to Death, since the great gods are dead!'

'Woe is me—it was written, and lo! it is read!'

'Come together, and bless him!'

'My Father?'

'The same.
On his throne I will mark with a finger of flame
A cross and a lily for thee and for me!'

They pass o'er the ice, and a sound like the sea
Grows under their footprints; and softly they come
Where Death, with his eyes fix'd on heaven, sitteth dumb;
And they pause at his feet, while far o'er them he looms
With his brow 'mong the stars and the amethyst glooms,
Yea, they pause far beneath, and with finger divine
The white Christ hath made on the snow for a sign
The cross and the lily . . . then rising he stands,
And looketh at Death with uplifting of hands.
Still as a star he shineth, brightly his eyes are burning,
White as a dove he seems in the morning's dewy breath,
Lifting again his face with a smile of loving and yearning,
He looketh gently up at the godlike shape of Death;

And the hair of Death is golden,
  Death is glowing,
While softly around his form h.
  mighty wings,
And vast as the vast blue heaven!
  faint form is growing,
But the face that all men fear
  with beautiful things.
Ev'n so the Brethren wait where th,
  snows are drifted,
Small as two doves that light in
  ness alone,
While bright on the blood-red s'
  luminous head uplifted,
In a dream divine upgazing, D^
  upon his throne.

                    '; I linger,
                   d Singer,
      IX.   ';
                   , a token
  THE LAST BLESS. were broken),
                   face.
        I.
                   nt; slowly
  THE WAKING OF THE im and holy;

'ALL that is beautiful shall a'
  All that is base shall die.' an together. .
Hark! birds are singing far hining weather,
Under the summer sky. .   )ne.

Southward across the shinin UNTRY.
  The blessed Brethren cam
They wore soft raiment of Land of Light
And sandals shod with fl
                        ligh thous
And golden lights and rippling rains
  Were on the frozen sea,
The bergs were melting from their chains,
  The waters flashing free.

The white Christ lifted hands above
  The silent wakening Deep,
And the unseen depths began to move
  With motions soft as sleep.

Then on an isle of ice he stept,
  Leading his Brother mild,
And blest the waters as they slept,
  And lo, they woke and smiled!

Around him on the melting sea
  The glittering icebergs' stirred,
And glimmer'd southward silently,
  Like things that lived and heard,

Poems and Ballads.

(1878–83.)

a ballad in print o' life, for then we are sure they are true. . . . This is a merry ballad, but a very pretty one.
                                   The Winter's Tale.

Nothing is stranger than the rest,
  From the pole to the pole,
The weed by the way, the eggs in the nest,
  The Flesh and the Soul.

Look in mine eyes, O Man I meet
  In this Strange Country!
Lie in mine arms, O Maiden sweet,
  With thy mouth kiss me!

Go by, O King, with thy crownèd brow
  And thy sceptred hand—
Thou art a straggler too, I vow,
  From the same strange Land.

O wondrous Faces that upstart
  In this Strange Country!
O Sou's, O Shades, that become a part
  Of my Soul and me!

What are ye working so fast and fleet,
  O Humankind?
'We are building Cities for those whose feet
  ^ ^ ming behind ;
And black seals with t...
  Upon the berg to rest.

Brighter and fairer all around
  The kindling waters shone;
And softly, swiftly, with no sound,
  The white flocks glided on.

And far away on every side
  The glittering ice-blink grew,—
Millions of bergs like ships that ride
  Upon the waters blue.

O Balder, Balder, wherefore hide
  Thy face from the blue sky!'
The voice was music, but it cried
  Like any human cry.

'On his neck and round his frame
Twines a snake of emerald flame. . . .
Death, O Death, can it be *thou*?

'Father, father! I cannot see—
The heavens are bright, but the world is white,
The wings of the wan Form cover thee—
Around and around, with no sigh, with no sound,
Like the mists of a cloud, like the folds of a shroud,
They enwrap thee,—and hide thee from me!'

IX.

'A CROSS AND A LILY.'

'It is over! O Balder, look up and behold!'

'Not yet, for I sicken—my sense shrinketh cold,
And I fear the strange silence that cometh at last!
All is hush'd—all is dead—the dew now is shed
Warm as tears on my hand, but the tempest hath pass'd,
And the sounds of the tempest are fled!'

'Arise!'

'I am risen!'

'Behold!

All is white,
But the darkness hath gone, and the frown of the night, Death's eclipse,'
He named the goddesses each one,
And blest them with his lips.

And lo! from bright'ning far-off lands
He saw glad spirits gleam,
Gazing to sea, and waving hands,
And singing in a dream;

And we tw[o] way where earth and air
night l their gentle lights,
That sit ga[ze] od one marble form most fair
Where the he cloudless heights.
breath

'So stran[ge] he calm and stainless blue
even] d divinely dim,
Best and his mother's form he knew,
conqu lt her eyes on him!
All gods a[re]
blown, paused, serene and crown'd,
And lesser summer sheen,
wise, racts flash'd their lights around
Are we who ods grew dewy green.
All hail now
are dea[d] ail'd beyond her sight
e summer sea,
'Woe is me gain with hands snow-white
read!' all things that be.

'Come toget[her] r, brighter, as he blest,
a'd Ocean grew,
icebergs rock'd at rest
On his throne waters blue.
flame
A cross and a l elting shores of earth
They pass o'e l flame there ran,
sea ld grew bright, and mirth
Grows under the flocks of Man.
they come ew on earth and heaven,
Where Death, of full day!
sitteth d[own] ight rainbow's colours seven
And th every iceberg lay!

In Balder's hand Christ placed his own,
And it was golden weather,
And on that berg as on a throne
The Brethren stood together!

And countless voices far and wide
Sang sweet beneath the sky—
'All that is beautiful shall abide,
All that is base shall die!'

Miscellaneous Poems and Ballads.
(1878-83.)

Clown. What hast here? Ballads?
Mop. Pray now, buy some: I love a ballad in print o' life, for then we are sure they are true.
Aut. Here's one to a very doleful tune, ... This is a merry ballad, but a very pretty one.
The Winter's Tale.

DEDICATION.
To Harriett.

Here at the Half-way House of Life I linger,
Worn with the way, a weary-hearted Singer,
    Resting a little space;
And lo! the good God sends me, as a token
Of peace and blessing (else my heart were broken),
    The sunbeam of thy face.

My fear falls from me like a garment; slowly
New strength returns upon me, calm and holy;
    I kneel, and I atone. . . .
Thy hand is clasped in mine—we lean together. .
Henceforward, through the sad or shining weather,
    I shall not walk alone.

THE STRANGE COUNTRY.

I have come from a mystical Land of Light
    To a Strange Country:
That came and went like the lighthouse gleam
    On a black night at sea.

'Twas the soul of Judas Iscariot
    Crawl'd to the distant gleam;
And the rain came down, and the rain was blown
    Against him with a scream.

So many days and nights he wandered on,
    Hush'd on by hands behind;
'Tis all the days went by like black, black rain
    And the nights like rushing wind.

In the beating Heart, in the burning Brain,
    In the Flesh and the Blood.

Deep as Death is the daily strife
    Of this Strange Country:
All things thrill up till they blossom in Life,
    And flutter and flee.

Nothing is stranger than the rest,
    From the pole to the pole,
The weed by the way, the eggs in the nest,
    The Flesh and the Soul.

Look in mine eyes, O Man I meet
    In this Strange Country!
Lie in mine arms, O Maiden sweet,
    With thy mouth kiss me!

Go by, O King, with thy crownèd brow
    And thy sceptred hand—
Thou art a straggler too, I vow,
    From the same strange Land.

O wondrous Faces that upstart
    In this Strange Country!
O Souls, O Shades, that become a part
    Of my Soul and me!

What are ye working so fast and fleet,
    O Humankind?
' We are building Cities for those whose feet
    Are coming behind;

' Our stay is short, we must fly again
    From this Strange Country;
But others are growing, women and men,
    Eternally!'

Child, what art *thou*? and what am *I*?
But a breaking wave!
Rising and rolling on, we hie
    To the shore of the grave.

I have come from a mystical Land of Light
    To this Strange Country;
This dawn I came, I shall go to-night,
    Ay me! ay me!

I hold my hand to my head and stand
    'Neath the air's blue arc,

I try to remember the mystical Land,
  But all is dark.

And all around me swim Shapes like mine
  In this Strange Country;—
They break in the glamour of gleams divine,
  And they moan 'Ay me!'

Like waves in the cold Moon's silvern breath
  They gather and roll,
Each crest of white is a birth or a death,
  Each sound is a Soul.

Oh, whose is the Eye that gleams so bright
  O'er this Strange Country?
It draws us along with a chain of light,
  As the Moon the Sea!

THE BALLAD OF JUDAS ISCARIOT.

'Twas the body of Judas Iscariot
  Lay in the Field of Blood;
'Twas the soul of Judas Iscariot
  Beside the body stood.

Black was the earth by night,
  And black was the sky;
Black, black were the broken clouds,
  Tho' the red Moon went by.

'Twas the body of Judas Iscariot
  Strangled and dead lay there;
'Twas the soul of Judas Iscariot
  Look'd on it in despair.

The breath of the World came and went
  Like a sick man's in rest;
Drop by drop on the World's eyes
  The dews fell cool and blest.

Then the soul of Judas Iscariot
  Did make a gentle moan—
'I will bury underneath the ground
  My flesh and blood and bone.

'I will bury deep beneath the soil,
  Lest mortals look thereon,
And when the wolf and raven come
  The body will be gone!

'The stones of the field are sharp as steel,
  And hard and cold, God wot;
And I must bear my body hence
  Until I find a spot!'

'Twas the soul of Judas Iscariot,
  So grim, and gaunt, and gray,
Raised the body of Judas Iscariot,
  And carried it away.

And as he bare it from the field
  Its touch was cold as ice,
And the ivory teeth within the jaw
  Rattled aloud, like dice.

As the soul of Judas Iscariot
  Carried its load with pain,
The Eye of Heaven, like a lanthorn's eye,
  Open'd and shut again.

Half he walk'd, and half he seemed
  Lifted on the cold wind;
He did not turn, for chilly hands
  Were pushing from behind.

The first place that he came unto
  It was the open wold,
And underneath were prickly whins,
  And a wind that blew so cold.

The next place that he came unto
  It was a stagnant pool,
And when he threw the body in
  It floated light as wool.

He drew the body on his back,
  And it was dripping chill,
And the next place he came unto
  Was a Cross upon a hill.

sitteth d____ight rainbow's colours seve
nd th- every iceberg lay!

In Balder's hand Christ placed his ow
  And it was golden weather,
And on that berg as on a throne
  The Brethren stood together!

And countless voices far and wide
  Sang sweet beneath the sky—
'All that is beautiful shall abide,
  All that is base shall die!'

The fourth place that he came unto
  It was the Brig of Dread,
And the great torrents rushing down
  Were deep, and swift, and red.

He dared not fling the body in
  For fear of faces dim,

And arms were waved in the wild water
  To thrust it back to him.

'Twas the soul of Judas Iscariot
  Turned from the Brig of Dread,
And the dreadful foam of the wild water
  Had splashed the body red.

For days and nights he wandered on
  Upon an open plain,
And the days went by like blinding mist,
  And the nights like rushing rain.

For days and nights he wandered on,
  All thro' the Wood of Woe ;
And the nights went by like moaning wind,
  And the days like drifting snow.

'Twas the soul of Judas Iscariot
  Came with a weary face—
Alone, alone, and all alone,
  Alone in a lonely place !

He wandered east, he wandered west,
  And heard no human sound ;
For months and years, in grief and tears,
  He wandered round and round.

For months and years, in grief and tears,
  He walked the silent night ;
Then the soul of Judas Iscariot
  Perceived a far-off light.

A far-off light across the waste,
  As dim as dim night be,
That came and went like the lighthouse gleam
  On a black night at sea.

'Twas the soul of Judas Iscariot
  Crawl'd to the distant gleam ;
And the rain came down, and the rain was blown
  Against him with a scream.

For days and nights he wandered on,
  Push'd on by hands behind ;
And the days went by like black, black rain,
  And the nights like rushing wind.

'Twas the soul of Judas Iscariot,
  Strange, and sad, and tall,
Stood all alone at dead of night
  Before a lighted hall.

And the wold was white with snow,
  And his foot-marks black and damp.

The face sae dear that for mony a year
  I hae pray'd to see again,—
A mither's face has a holy grace
  'Bune a' the faces o' men !

Then I'll enter in wi' silent feet,
  And saftly cry her name—
And I'll see the dim auld een grow sweet
  Wi' a heavenly welcome hame !

And I'll cry, "O mither, I'm here, I'm here !
  Forgie me, O forgie !
And never mair shall ye ken a care !
  Your son shall lea' thee never mair
  To sail on the stormy sea ! " '

II.

They row'd him to the lonely shore
  Beyond the lights of the quay,
And he climb'd the brae to the cottage door
  A hundred yards from the sea.

He saw no light thro' the mirk of night,
  And his heart sank down with dread,
But 'tis late,' thought he, 'and she lies, maybe,
  Soond sleeping in her bed !'

Half-way he paused, for the blast blew keen,
  And the sea roar'd loud below,
And he turn'd his face to the town-lights, seen
  Thro' the white and whirling snow.

The lights of Leith ! the lights of Leith !
  How they flash'd on the night-black bay,
White with sullen roar on the rocky shore
  The waters splash'd their spray !

Then close he came to the lonely cot,
  He paused in deeper dread,—
For the gleam that came from the far-off flame
  Just touch'd the walls with red ;

Thro' the doorway dark did the bleak wind blow,
  The windows were black and bare,
And the house was floor'd with the cruel snow,
  And roof'd with the empty air !

'O mither, mither !' he moan'd aloud,
  'And are ye deid and gane ?

I try to remember the mystical Land,
  But all is dark.

And all around me swim Shapes like mine
  In this Strange Country;—
They break in the glamour of gleams divine
  And they moan 'Ay me!'

Like waves in the cold Moon's silvern breath
  They gather and roll,
Each crest of white is a birth or a death,
  Each sound is a Soul.

Oh, whose is the Eye that gleams so bright
  O'er this Strange Country?
It draws us along with a chain of light,
  As the Moon the Sea!

THE BALLAD OF JUDAS ISCARIOT.

'TWAS the body of Judas Iscariot
  Lay in the Field of Blood;
'Twas the soul of Judas Iscariot
  Beside the body stood.

Black was the earth by night,
  And black was the sky;
Black, black were the broken clouds,
  Tho' the red Moon went by.

'Twas the body of Judas Iscariot
  Strangled and dead lay there;
'Twas the soul of Judas Iscariot
  Look'd on it in despair.

The breath of the World came and went
  Like a sick man's in rest;
Drop by drop on the World's eyes
  The dews fell cool and blest.

Then the soul of Judas Iscariot
  Did make a gentle moan—
'I will bury underneath the ground
  My flesh and blood and bone.

'I will bury deep beneath the soil,
  Lest mortals look thereon,
And when the wolf and raven come
  The body will be gone!

'The stones of the field are sharp as steel,
  And hard and cold, God wot;
And I must bear my body hence
  Until I find a spot!'

They saw the glare from far away,
And, safely steer'd to the land-lock'd bay,
  They cast their anchor down.

''Tis sure a feast in the town o' Leith
  (To his mate the skipper spoke),
'And yonder shadows that come and go,
Across the quay where the bonfires glow,
  Are the merry-making folk.

' In right good time we are home once more
  From the wild seas and rough weather—
Come, launch a boat, and we'll run ashore,
  And see the sport together.'

But the mate replied, while he shoreward gazed
  With sad and gentle eyes,
While the lights of Leith beyond him blazed
  And he heard the landward cries:

''Tis twenty lang year since I first left here,
  In the time o' frost and snaw—
I was only a lad, and my heart was mad
  To be up, and free, and awa'!

'My mither she prayed me no' to gang,
  For she had nae bairn but me—
My father was droon'd, and sleeping amang
  The weeds o' the northern sea.

'I stole awa' in the mirk o' night
  And left my mither asleep,
And ere she waken'd, at morning light,
  I was oot on the roaring deep.

'Aye, twenty lang year hae past sin' syne,
  And my heart has aft been sair
To think o' that puir auld mither o' mine,
  Alane, in a warld o' care.

'When back I cam' frae the salt sea faem
  I was a bearded man,
Ae simmer I dwelt in the hoose at hame,
  Then awa' to the sea I ran.

'And twice sin' syne hae I left the sea
  To seek the hameward track,
And aye my mither had had for me—
Tho' ne'er a gift had my hands to gie—
  A tender welcome back.

'Then, cast awa' in a soothern land,
  And taen to slaverie,
I lang'd for the touch o' a mither's hand
  And the glint o' a mither's e'e.

THE LIGHTS OF LEITH.

But noo that my wandering days are done,
   I hae dree'd a penance sad,
Am coming hame, like the Prodigal Son,
   But wi' siller to mak' her glad!

I hae gowden rings for my mither's hand,
   Bonnie and braw past dream,
And, fit for a leddy o' the land,
   A shawl o' the Indian seam.

And I lang, and lang, to seek ance mair
   The cot by the side o' the sea,
And to find my gray old mither there,
   Waiting and watching for me;

To dress her oot like a leddy grand,
   While the tears o' gladness drap,
To put the rings on her wrinkled hand,
   The siller intil her lap!

And to say "O mither, I'm hame, I'm hame!
   Forgie me, O forgie!
And never mair shall ye ken a care
   Until the day you dee!"'

O bright and red shone the lights of Leith
   In the snowy winter-tide—
Down the cheeks of the man the salt tears ran,
   As he stood by the skipper's side.

'But noo I look on the lights o' hame
   My heart sinks sick and cauld—
Lest I come owre late for her love or blame,
   For oh! my mither was auld!

For her een were dim when I sail'd awa',
   And snaw was on her heid,
And I fear—I fear—after mony a year,
   To find my mither—deid!

Sae I daurna enter the toon o' Leith,
   Where the merry yule-fires flame,
Lest I hear the tidings o' dule and death,
   Ere I enter the door o' hame.

But ye'll let them row me to yonder shore
   Beyond the lights o' the quay,
And I'll climb the brae to the cottage door,
   A hunnerd yards frae the sea.

'If I see a light thro' the mirk o' night,
   I'll ken my mither is there;
I'll keek, maybe, through the pane, and see
   Her face in its snawy hair!

'The face sae dear that for mony a year
   I hae prayed to see again,—
O a mither's face has a holy grace
   'Bune a' the faces o' men!

'Then I'll enter in wi' silent feet,
   And saftly cry her name—
And I'll see the dim auld een grow sweet
   Wi' a heavenly welcome hame!

'And I'll cry, "O mither, I'm here, I'm here!
   Forgie me, O forgie!
And never mair shall ye ken a care!
   Your son shall lea' thee never mair
   To sail on the stormy sea!"'

II.

They row'd him to the lonely shore
   Beyond the lights of the quay,
And he climb'd the brae to the cottage door
   A hundred yards from the sea.

He saw no light thro' the mirk of night,
   And his heart sank down with dread,
'But 'tis late,' thought he, 'and she lies, maybe,
   Soond sleeping in her bed!'

Half-way he paused, for the blast blew keen,
   And the sea roar'd loud below,
And he turn'd his face to the town-lights, seen
   Thro' the white and whirling snow.

The lights of Leith! the lights of Leith!
   How they flash'd on the night-black bay,
White with sullen roar on the rocky shore
   The waters splash'd their spray!

When close he came to the lonely cot,
   He paused in deeper dread,—
For the gleam that came from the far-off flame
   Just touch'd the walls with red;

Thro' the doorway dark did the bleak wind blow,
   The windows were black and bare,
And the house was floor'd with the cruel snow,
   And roof'd with the empty air!

'O mither, mither!' he moan'd aloud,
   'And are ye deid and gane?

Hae I waited in tears thro' the weary years,
 And a' in vain, in vain?'
He stood on the hearth, while the snow swam drear
 Between the roofless walls—
'O mither! mither! come here, come here,—
 'Tis your ain son, Robin, calls!'

On his eager ears, as he stood in tears,
 There came a faint foot-tread—
Then out of the storm crept a woman's form
 With hooded face and head.

Like a black, black ghost the shape came near
 Till he heard its heavy breath—
'What man,' it sighed, 'stands sabbing here,
 In the wearifu' hoose o' death?'

'Come hither, come hither, whae'er ye be,'
 He answer'd loud and clear—
'I am Robin Sampson, come hame frae the sea,
 And I seek my mither dear!'

'O Robin, Robin,' a voice cried sobbing,
 'O Robin, and is it yersel'?
I'm Janet Wylie, lame Janet Wylie,
 Your kissen, frae Marywell!'

'O Robin, Robin,' again she cried,
 'O Robin, and can it be?
Ah, better far had the wind and the tide
 Ne'er brought ye across the sea!'

Wailing she sank on the snow-heap'd hearth,
 And rocked her body in pain—
'O Robin, Robin,' she cried to him sobbing,
 Your mither—your mither—is gane!'

The lights of Leith! the lights of Leith!
 How brightly still they glow!
The faint flame falls on the ruined walls,
 On the hearthstone heap'd in snow!

'O Janet, Janet, kind cousin Janet,
 If ever ye cared for me,
Noo let me bear o' my mither dear,
 And hoo she cam' to dee!'

Wailing she lifted her weeping face,
 And answer'd in soul's despair—
'O Robin, awa' frae the wicked place—
 Awa'—and ask nae mair!'

But he grasp'd her arm with a grip of steel
 And cried 'O Janet, speak!'
'O Robin dear, dinna seek to hear,
 For oh! your heart must breik!'

But he pressed her more, and he pleaded sore,
 Till at last the tale was told,
And he listened on, till the tale was done,
 Like a man death-struck and cold.

III.

'O Robin dear, when ye sail'd awa',
 That last time, on the sea,
We knew her heart was breiking in twa,
 And we thought that she wad dee.

'But after a while she forced a smile—
 "I'll greet nae mair," said she,
"But I'll wait and pray that the Lord, ae day,
 May bring him again to me!

'"The Lord is guid, and Robin my son
 As kind as a bairn can be—
Aye true as steel, and he loes me weel,
 Tho' he's gane across the sea."

'O Robin, Robin, baith late and air'
 She prayed and prayed for thee,
But evermair when the blast blew sair,
 She was langest on her knee!'

The lights of Leith! the lights of Leith!
 That flame o'er sea and skies!
How bright they glow!—while the salt tears flow
 From that bearded mariner's eyes.

'But, Robin, your mither was auld and pair,
 And the season's cauld and keen;
The white, white snaw was on her hair,
 The frost film ower her een.

'And here in the hut beside the sea,
 The pair auld wife did dwell—
Her only kin were my mither and me,
 And we were as pair's hersel'.

'She leeved on a handfu' o' barley meal,
 A drink frae the spring sae cauld—
O Robin, Robin, a heart o' steel
 Might bleed for the weak and auld!

'In twa she was bent, on a staff she leant,
 Wi' ragged duds for claise,
And wearifu' up and doon she went,
 Gath'ring her sticks and straes.

'And the weans wad thrang as she creepit
　　alang,
　And point, and cry sae shrill—
"There's Grannie Sampson," was ever their
　　sang,
　"The wicked witch o' the hill!"

'Ah, mony's the time up the hill she'd climb,
　While the imps wad scream and craw—
At the door she'd stand, wi' her staff in hand,
　And angrily screech them awa'!

'Then wi' feeble feet creeping ben, she'd greet
　That the warld misca'd her sae,
And wi' face as white as the winding-sheet,
　She'd kneel by the bed, and pray.

'O Robin, Robin, she prayed for him
　Wha sail'd in the wild sea-rack,
And the tears wad drap frae her een sae dim,
　As she prayed for her bairn to come
　　back!

'Then whiles . . . when she thought nae
　　folk were near . . .
　(O Robin, she thought nae harm!
But stoop your heid, lest they hear, lest they
　　hear!)
　She tried . . . an auld-farrant *charm*.

'A charm aft tried in the ingleside
　When bairns are blythesome and free,
A charm (come near, lest they hear, lest
　　they hear!)
　To bring her boy hame from the sea!

'And the auld black cat at her elbow sat,
　(The cat you gied her yersel')
And the folk, keeking in thro' the pane, saw
　　a sin,
　And thought she was weaving a spell!'

The lights of Leith! the lights of Leith!
　They flame on the wintry gale!
With sore drawn breath, and a face like
　　death,
　He hearks to the gruesome tale!

'O Robin, Robin, I kenna hoo
　The lee was faither'd first,
But (whisper again, lest they ken, lest they
　　ken!)
　They thought the puir body accurst!

'They thought the spell had been wrought
　　in Hell,
　To kill and curse and blight,

They thought she flew, when naebody knew,
　To a Sabbath o' fiends, ilk night!

'Then ane whose corn had wither'd ae morn,
　And ane whose kye sicken'd doon,
Crept, scared and pale, wi' the leein' tale,
　To the meenisters, up the toon.

'Noo, Robin, jest then, King Jamie the
　　King
　Was oot at sea in his bark,
And the bark nigh sank unner, wi' fire-
　　flaught and thunner,
　And they thought—the Deil was at
　　wark!

'The King cam' to land, and loup'd on the
　　strand,
　Pale as a ghaist and afraid,
Wi' courtiers and clergy, a wild fearfu' band,
　He ran to the kirk, and prayed.

'Then the clergy made oot 'twas witchcraft,
　　nae doot,
　And searchit up and doon,
And . . . foond your auld mither (wae's
　　me!) and twa ither,
　And dragg'd them up to the toon!

'O Robin, dear Robin, hearken nae mair!'
　'Speak on, I'll heark to the ca'!'
'O Robin, Robin, the sea oot there
　Is kinder than cruel men!

'They took her before King Jamie the King,
　Whaur he sat wi' sceptre and croon,
And the cooard courtiers stood in a ring,
　And the meenisters gather'd roon'.

'They bade her tell she had wrought the spell
　That made the tempest blaw;
They strippit her bare as a naked bairn,
　They tried her wi' pincers and heated airn,
　Till she shriek'd and swoon'd awa'!

'O Robin, Robin, the King sat there,
　While the cruel deed was done,
And the clergy o' Christ ne'er bade him spare
　For the sake o' God's ain Son! . . .

The lights of Leith! the lights of Leith!
　Like Hell's own lights they glow
While the sailor stands, with his trembling
　　hands
　Prest hard on his heart in woe!

'O Robin, Robin . . . they doom'd her to
  burn . . .
    Doon yonner upon the quay . . .
This night was the night . . . see the light!
    see the light!
    How it burns by the side o' the sea!'
. . . She paused with a moan. . . . He
    had left her alone,
And rushing through drift and snow,
Down the side of the wintry hill he had flown,
    His eyes on the lights below!

IV.

The lights of Leith! the lights of Leith!
    They flame on the eyes of the crowd,
Around, up and down, move the folk of the
    town,
    While the bells of the kirk peal aloud!
High up on the quay, blaze the balefires,
    and see!
Three stakes are deep set in the ground,
To each stake smear'd with pitch clings the
    corpse of a witch,
    With the fire flaming redly around!

What madman is he who leaps in where
    they gleam,
    Close, close, to the centremost form?
'O mither, O mither!' he cries, with a scream,
    That rings thro' the heart of the storm!

He can see the white hair snowing down
    thro' the glare,
    The white face upraised to the skies—
Then the cruel red blaze blots the thing
    from his gaze,
    And he falls on his face,—and dies.

V.

The lights of Leith! the lights of Leith!
    See, see! they are flaming still!
Thro' the clouds of the past their flame is cast,
    While the Sabbath bells ring shrill!

The lights of Leith! the lights of Leith!
    They'll burn till the Judgment Day!
Till the Church's curse and the monarch's
    shame,
    And the sin that slew in the Blessed Name,
    Are burned and purg'd away!

NOTE.—The foundation of this bal'ad is historical, more particularly the part taken by the enlightened pedant, James VI. of Scotland, who, on his accession to the English throne, procured the infamous statute against witchcraft, which actually remained unrepealed till 1736, and even then was repealed under strong protest from the Scottish clergy! One traveller, as late as 1664, casually notices the fact of having seen nine witches *burning together* at Leith, and in 1678, nine others were condemned in a single day.— R. B.

THE WEDDING OF SHON MACLEAN.

A BAGPIPE MELODY.

To the wedding of Shon Maclean,
  Twenty Pipers together
Came in the wind and the rain
  Playing across the heather;
Backward their ribbons flew,
Blast upon blast they blew,
Each clad in tartan new,
  Bonnet, and blackcock feather:
And every Piper was fou,[1]
  Twenty Pipers together! . . .

He's but a Sassenach blind and vain
Who never heard of Shon Maclean—
The Duke's own Piper, called 'Shon the Fair,'
From his freckled skin and his fiery hair.
Father and son, since the world's creation,
The Macleans had followed this occupation,
And played the pibroch to fire the Clan
Since the first Duke came and the Earth
    began.
Like the whistling of birds, like the humming
    of bees,
Like the sough of the south-wind in the trees,
Like the singing of angels, the playing of
    shawms,
Like Ocean itself with its storms and its calms,
Were the strains of Shon, when with cheeks
    aflame
He blew a blast thro' the pipes of fame.
At last, in the prime of his playing life,
The spirit moved him to take a wife—
A lassie with eyes of Highland blue,
Who loved the pipes and the Piper too,
And danced to the sound, with a foot and a
    leg
White as a lily and smooth as an egg.
So, twenty Pipers were coming together

[1] Pronounce *foo* – *i.e.* 'half seas over,' intoxicated.

THE WEDDING OF SHON MACLEAN.

O'er the moor and across the heather,
    All in the wind and the rain;
Twenty Pipers so brawly dressed
Were flocking in from the east and west,
To bless the bedding and blow their best
    At the wedding of Shon Maclean.

At the wedding of Shon Maclean
    'Twas wet and windy weather!
Yet, thro' the wind and the rain
    Came twenty Pipers together!
Earach and Dougal Dhu,
    Sandy of Isla too,
Each with the bonnet o' blue,
    Tartan, and blackcock feather:
And every Piper was fou,
    Twenty Pipers together!

The knot was tied, the blessing said,
Shon was married, the feast was spread.
At the head of the table sat, huge and hoar,
Strong Sandy of Isla, age fourscore,
Whisker'd, grey as a Haskeir seal,
And clad in crimson from hend to heel.
Beneath and round him in their degree
Gathered the men of minstrelsie,
With keepers, gillies, and lads and lasses,
Mingling voices, and jingling glasses.
At soup and haggis, at roast and boil'd,
Awhile the happy gathering toil'd,—
While Shon and Jean at the table ends
Shook hands with a hundred of their friends.—
Then came a hush. Thro' the open door
A wee bright form flash'd on the floor,—
The Duke himself, in the kilt and plaid,
With slim soft knees, like the knees of a maid.
And he took a glass, and he cried out plain
' I drink to the health of Shon Maclean!
To Shon the Piper and Jean his wife,
A clean fireside and a merry life!'
Then out he slipt, and each man sprang
To his feet, and with 'hooch' the chamber rang!
'Clear the tables!' shriek'd out one—
A leap, a scramble,—and it was done!
And then the Pipers all in a row
Tuned their pipes and began to blow,
    While all to dance stood fain:
Sandy of Isla and Earach More,
Dougal Dhu from Kinflannan shore,
Play'd up the company on the floor
    At the wedding of Shon Maclean.

At the wedding of Shon Maclean,
    Twenty Pipers together
Stood up, while all their train
    Ceased to clatter and blether.
Full of the mountain-dew,
    First in their pipes they blew,
Mighty of bone and thew,
    Red-cheek'd, with lungs of leather:
And every Piper was fou,
    Twenty Pipers together!

Who led the dance? In pomp and pride
The Duke himself led out the Bride!
Great was the joy of each beholder,
For the wee Duke only reach'd her shoulder;
And they danced, and turned, when the reel began,
Like a giantess and a fairie man!
But like an earthquake was the din
When Shon himself led the Duchess in!
And she took her place before him there,
Like a white mouse dancing with a bear!
So trim and tiny, so slim and sweet,
Her blue eyes watching Shon's great feet,
With a smile that could not be resisted,
She jigged, and jumped, and twirl'd, and twisted!
Sandy of Isla led off the reel,
The Duke began it with toe and heel,
    Then all join'd in amain;
Twenty Pipers ranged in a row,
From squinting Shamus to lame Kilcroe,
Their cheeks like crimson, began to blow,
    At the wedding of Shon Maclean.

At the wedding of Shon Maclean
    They blew with lungs of leather,
And blithesome was the strain
    Those Pipers played together!
Moist with the mountain-dew,
Mighty of bone and thew,
Each with the bonnet o' blue,
    Tartan, and blackcock feather:
And every Piper was fou,
    Twenty Pipers together!

Oh for a wizard's tongue to tell
Of all the wonders that befell!
Of how the Duke, when the first stave died,
Reached up on tiptoe to kiss the Bride,
While Sandy's pipes, as their mouths were meeting,
Skirl'd, and set every heart a-beating!

Then Shon took the pipes! and all was still,
As silently he the bags did fill,
With flaming cheeks and round bright eyes,
Till the first faint music began to rise.
Like a thousand laverocks singing in tune,
Like countless corn-craiks under the moon,
Like the smack of kisses, like sweet bells ringing,
Like a mermaid's harp, or a kelpie singing,
Blew the pipes of Shon ; and the witching strain
Was the gathering song of the Clan Maclean !
Then slowly, softly, at his side,
All the Pipers around replied,
And swelled the solemn strain :
The hearts of all were proud and light,
To hear the music, to see the sight,
And the Duke's own eyes were dim that night,
At the wedding of Shon Maclean.

So to honour the Clan Maclean
Straight they began to gather,
Blowing the wild refrain,
' Blue bonnets across the heather !'
They stamp'd, they strutted, they blew ;
They shriek'd ; like cocks they crew ;
Blowing the notes out true,
With wonderful lungs of leather :
And every Piper was fou,
Twenty Pipers together !

When the Duke and Duchess went away
The dance grew mad and the guests grew gay;
Man and maiden, face to face,
Leapt and footed and scream'd apace !
Round and round the dancers whirl'd,
Shriller, louder, the Pipers skirl'd,
Till the soul seem'd swooning into sound,
And all creation was whirling round !
Then, in a pause of the dance and glee,
The Pipers, ceasing their minstrelsie,
Draining the glass in groups did stand,
And passed the sneesh-box [1] from hand to hand.
Sandy of Isla, with locks of snow,
Squinting Shamus, blind Kilmahoe,
Finlay Beg, and Earach More,
Dougal Dhu of Kilflannan shore—
All the Pipers, black, yellow, and green,
All the colours that ever were seen,
All the Pipers of all the Macs,
Gather'd together and took their cracks.[2]

[1] Snuff-box.   [2] Conversed sociably.

Then (no man knows how the thing befell,
For none was sober enough to tell)
These heavenly Pipers from twenty places
Began disputing with crimson faces ;
Each asserting, like one demented,
The claims of the Clan he represented.
In vain grey Sandy of Isla strove
To soothe their struggle with words of love,
Asserting there, like a gentleman,
The superior claims of his own great Clan ;
Then, finding to reason is despair,
He seizes his pipes and he plays an air—
The gathering tune of his Clan—and tries
To drown in music the shrieks and cries !
Heavens ! Every Piper, grown mad with ire,
Seizes *his* pipes with a fierce desire,
And blowing madly, with skirl and squeak,
Begins *his* particular tune to shriek !
Up and down the gamut they go,
Twenty Pipers, all in a row,
Each with a different strain !
Each tries hard to drown the first,
Each blows louder till like to burst.
Thus were the tunes of the Clans rehearst
At the wedding of Shon Maclean !

At the wedding of Shon Maclean,
Twenty Pipers together,
Blowing with might and main,
Thro' wonderful lungs of leather !
Wild was the hullabaloo !
They stamp'd, they scream'd, they crew !
Twenty strong blasts they blew,
Holding the heart in tether :
And every Piper was fou,
Twenty Pipers together !

A storm of music ! Like wild sleuth-hounds
Contending together, were the sounds !
At last a bevy of Eve's bright daughters
Pour'd oil—that's whisky—upon the waters ;
And after another dram went down
The Pipers chuckled and ceased to frown,
Embraced like brothers and kindred spirits,
And fully admitted each other's merits.
All bliss must end ! For now the Bride
Was looking weary and heavy-eyed,
And soon she stole from the drinking chorus,
While the company settled to *deoch-an-dorus*.[3]
One hour—another—took its flight—
The clock struck twelve—the dead of night—

[3] The parting glass ; lit. the *cup at the door*.

And still the Bride like a rose so red
Lay lonely up in the bridal bed.
At half-past two the Bridegroom, Shon,
Dropt on the table as heavy as stone,
But four strong Pipers across the floor
Carried him up to the bridal door,
Push'd him in at the open portal,
And left him snoring, serene and mortal!
The small stars twinkled over the heather,
As the Pipers wandered away together,
But one by one on the journey dropt,
Clutching his pipes, and there he stopt!
One by one on the dark hillside
Each faint blast of the bagpipes died,
 Amid the wind and the rain!
And the twenty Pipers at break of day
In twenty different bogholes lay,
Serenely sleeping upon their way
 From the wedding of Shon Maclean!

HANS VOGEL.

AN EPISODE OF THE FRANCO-PRUSSIAN WAR.

'Ein ächter Deutscher Mann mag keinen Franzen leiden!'—BRANDER in *Faust*.

THE fight is o'er, the day is done,
 And thro' the clouds o'erhead
The fingers of the setting sun
 Are pointing down blood-red,—
Beneath, on the white battlefield,
 Lie strewn the drifts of dead.

No breath, no stir; but everywhere
 The cold Frost crawleth slow,
And Frank and Teuton side by side
 Lie stiffening in the snow,—
While piteously each marble face
 Gleams in the ruby glow.

No sound; but yonder midst the dead
 There stands one steed snow-white,
And clinging to its chilly mane,
 Half swooning, yet upright,
Its rider totters, breathing hard,
 Bareheaded in the light!

Hans Vogel. Spectacles on nose,
 He gasps and gazes round—
He shivers as his eyes survey
 That wintry battle-ground—
Then, parch'd with thirst and chill with cold,
 He sinks, without a sound.

Before his vision as he lies
 There gleams a quaint old Town,
He sees the students in the street
 Swaggering up and down,
While at a casement sits a Maid
 In clean white cap and gown.

Hans Vogel thinks, 'My time hath come!
 Ne'er shall these eyes of mine
Behold poor Ännchen, or the trees
 Of dear old Ehbrenstein!'
He smacks his lips, '*Mein Gott!* for one
 Deep draught of Rhenish wine!'

Then swift as thought his wild eyes gleam
 On something at his side—
He stirs—he glares—he sits erect—
 He grips it, eager-eyed;
A Flask it is, some friend or foe
 Hath dropt there ere he died!

To God he mutters now a prayer,
 Quaking in every limb;
Trembling he holds it to the light!—
 'Tis full unto the brim!
A flask, a brimming flask of wine!
 And God hath sent it him!

Hans Vogel's heart leaps up in joy,
 '*Dem Himmel sei Dank!*' he cries—
Then pursing out his thirsty lips
 Prepares to quaff his prize,—
When lo! a sound—he starts—and meets
 A pair of burning eyes!

Propt on a bed of comrades dead,
 His faint breath swiftly flying,
His breast torn open by a shell,
 A Grenadier is lying:—
Grim as a wolf, with gleaming fangs,
 The Frenchman glareth, dying!

White is his hair, his features worn
 With many a wild campaign,
He rocks his head from side to side
 Like to a beast in pain—
He groans athirst, with open mouth,
 Again and yet again.

Hans Vogel, in the act to drink
 And render God due praise,
Drops down his fever'd hand in doubt
 And pauses in amaze,
For on the flask that Grenadier
 Fixeth his thirsty gaze!

Hans Vogel smiles, '. Here lieth one
  Whose need is more than mine!'
Then, crawling over to his foe,
  'Look, Frenchman, here is wine!
And by the God that made us both
  Shall every drop be thine!'

Hast thou beheld a dying boar,
  Struck bleeding to the ground,
Spring with a last expiring throe
  To rip the foremost hound?
Terrible, fatal, pitiless,
  It slays with one swift bound.

Ev'n so that grizzly wolf of war,
  With eyes of hate and ire,
Stirs as he lies, and on the ground
  Gropes with a dark desire,—
Then lifts a loaded carbine up,
  And lo! one flash of fire!

A flash—a crash! Hans Vogel still
  Is kneeling on his knee,
His heart is beating quick, his face
  Is pale as man's can be;
The ball just grazed his bleeding brow,—
  '*Potstausend!*' murmureth he.

Hans frowns; and raising to his lips
  The flask, begins to quaff;
Then holds it to the fading light
  With sly and cynic laugh.
Deep is his drought—sweet is the wine—
  And he hath drunk the half!

But now he glanceth once again
  Where that grim Frenchman lies—
Gasping still waits that wolf of war
  Like to a beast that dies—
He groans athirst, with open mouth,
  And slowly glazing eyes.

Hans Vogel smiles; unto his foe
  Again now totters he—
So spent now is that wolf of war
  He scarce can hear or see.
Hans Vogel holds his hand, and takes
  His head upon his knee!

Then down the dying Frenchman's throat
  He sends the liquor fine:
'*Half* yet remains, old boy,' he cries,
  While pouring down the wine—
'Hadst thou not play'd me such a trick,
  It might have *all* been thine!'

Hans Vogel speaketh in the tongue
  Of his good Fatherland—
The Frenchman hears an alien sound
  And cannot understand,
But he can taste the warm red wine
  And feel the kindly hand.

See! looking in Hans Vogel's face
  He stirs his grizzly head—
Up, smiling, goes the grim moustache
  O'er cheeks as grey as lead—
With one last glimmer of the eyes,
  He smiles,—and he is dead.

PHIL BLOOD'S LEAP.

A TALE OF THE GOLD-SEEKERS.

'THERE's some think Injins pison . . .' [It
    was Parson Pete who spoke,
As we sat there, in the camp-fire glare, like
    shadows among the smoke.
'Twas the dead of night, and in the light
    our faces burn'd bright red,
And the wind all round made a screeching
    sound, and the pines roared overhead.

Ay, Parson Pete was talking; we called him
    Parson Pete,
For you must learn he'd a talking turn, and
    handled things so neat;
He'd a preaching style, and a winning smile,
    and, when all talk was spent,
Six-shooter had he, and a sharp bowie, to
    p'int his argyment.

Some one had spoke of the Injin folk, and
    we had a guess, you bet,
They might be creeping, while we were
    sleeping, to catch us in the net;
And half were asleep and snoring deep,
    while the others vigil kept,
But devil a one let go his gun, whether he
    woke or slept.]

'There's some think Injins pison, and others
    count 'em scum,
And night and day they are melting away,
    clean into Kingdom Come;
But don't you go and make mistakes, like
    many dern'd fools I've known,
For dirt is dirt, and snakes is snakes, but
    an Injin's flesh and bone!

We were seeking gold in the Texan hold,
  and we'd had a blaze of luck,
More rich and rare the stuff ran there at
  every foot we struck ;
Like men gone wild we t'iled and t'iled,
  and never seemed to tire,
The hot sun beamed, and our faces streamed
  with the sweat of a mad desire.

I was Captain then of the mining men, and
  I had a precious life,
For a wilder set I never met at derringer and
  knife ;
Nigh every day there was some new fray, a
  bullet in some one's brain,
And the viciousest brute to stab and to
  shoot, was an Imp of Hell from Maine.

Phil Blood. Well, he was six foot three,
  with a squint to make you skeer'd,
His face all scabb'd, and twisted and stabb'd,
  with carroty hair and beard ;
Sour as the drink in Bitter Chink, sharp as
  a grizzly's squeal,
Limp in one leg, for a leaden egg had
  nick'd him in the heel.

No beauty was he, but a sight to see, all
  stript to the waist and bare,
With his grim-set jaws, and his panther
  paws, and his hawk's eye all aglare ;
With pick and spade in sun and shade he
  labour'd like darnation,
But when his spell was over,—well! he was
  fond of his recreation!

And being a crusty kind of cuss, the only
  sport he had,
When work was over, seemed to *us* a bit
  too rough and bad ;
For to put some lead in a comrade's head
  was the greatest fun in life,
And the sharpest joke he was known to
  poke was the p'int of his precious knife.

But game to the bone was Phil, I'll own,
  and he always fought most fair,
With as good a will to be killed as kill,
  true grit as any there :
Of honour too, like me or you, he'd a scent,
  though not so keen,
Would rather be riddled thro' and thro',
  than do what he thought mean.

But his eddication to his ruination had net
  been over nice,
And his stupid skull was choking full of
  vulgar prejudice ;
With anything white he'd drink, or he'd
  fight in fair and open fray ;
But to murder and kill was his wicked will,
  if an Injin came his way!

'A sarpent's hide has pison inside, and an
  Injin's heart's the same,
If he seems your friend for to gain his end,
  look out for the sarpent's game ;
Of the snakes that crawl, the worst of all is
  the snake in a skin of red,
A spotted Snake, and no mistake!' that's
  what he always said.

Well, we'd jest struck our bit of luck, and
  were wild as raving men,
When who should stray to our camp one
  day, but Black Panther, the Cheyenne ;
Drest like a Christian, all a-grin, the old
  one joins our band,
And tho' the rest look'd black as sin, he
  shakes *me* by the hand.

Now, the poor old cuss had been good to
  us, and I knew that he was true,—
I'd have trusted him with life and limb as
  soon as I'd trust *you* ;
For tho' his wit was gone a bit, and he
  drank like any fish,
His heart was kind, he was well-inclined,
  as even a white could wish.

Food had got low, for we didn't know the
  run of the hunting-ground,
And our hunters were sick, when, jest in
  the nick, the friend in need was found ;
For he knew the place like his mother's face
  (or better, a heap, you'd say,
Since she was a squaw of the roaming race,
  and himself a cast-away).

Well, I took the Panther into camp, and
  the critter was well content,
And off with him, on the hunting tramp,
  next day our hunters went,
And I reckon that day and the next we
  didn't want for food,
And only one in the camp looked vext—that
  Imp of Hell, Phil Blood.

Nothing would please his contrairy idees !
  an Injin made him rile !
He didn't speak, but I saw on his cheek a
  kind of an ugly smile ;
And I knew his skin was hatching sin, and
  I kept the Panther apart,
For the Injin he was too blind to see the
  dirt in a white man's heart !

Well, one fine day, we a-resting lay at noon-
  time by the creek,
The red sun blazed, and we felt half-dazed,
  too beat to stir or speak ;
'Neath the alder trees we stretched at ease,
  and we couldn't see the sky,
For the lian-flowers in bright blue showers
  hung through the branches high.

It was like the gleam of a fairy-dream, and
  I felt like earth's first Man,
In an Eden bower with the yellow flower of
  a cactus for a fan ;
Oranges, peaches, grapes, and figs, cluster'd,
  ripen'd, and fell,
And the cedar scent was pleasant, blent
  with the soothing 'cacia smell.

The squirrels red ran overhead, and I saw
  the lizards creep,
And the woodpecker bright with the chest
  so white tapt like a sound in sleep ;
I dreamed and dozed with eyes half-closed,
  and felt like a three-year child,
And, a plantain blade on his brow for a
  shade, even Phil Blood look'd mild.

Well, back, jest then, came our hunting
  men, with the Panther at their head,
Full of his fun was every one, and the
  Panther's eyes were red,
And he skipt about with grin and shout, for
  he'd had a drop that day,
And he twisted and twirled, and squeal'd
  and skirl'd, in the foolish Injin way.

To the waist all bare Phil Blood lay there,
  with only his knife in his belt,
And I saw his bloodshot eyeballs stare, and
  I knew how fierce he felt,—
When the Injin dances with grinning glances
  around him as he lies,
With his painted skin and his monkey grin,—
  and leers into his eyes !

Then before I knew what I should do Phil
  Blood was on his feet,
And the Injin could trace the hate in his
  face, and his heart began to beat ;
And, 'Git out o' the way,' he heard them
  say, 'for he means to hev your life !'
But before he could fly at the warning cry,
  he saw the flash of the knife.

'Run, Panther run !' cried each mother's
  son, and the Panther took the track ;
With a wicked glare, like a wounded bear,
  Phil Blood sprang at his back.
Up the side so steep of the cañon deep the
  poor old critter sped,
And the devil's limb ran after him, till they
  faded overhead.

Now, the spot of ground where our luck
  was found was a queerish place, you'll
  mark,
Jest under the jags of the mountain crags
  and the precipices dark ;
Far up on high, close to the sky, the two
  crags leant together,
Leaving a gap, like an open trap, with a
  gleam of golden weather.

A pathway led from the beck's dark bed up
  to the crags on high,
And along that path the Injin fled, fast as a
  man could fly.
Some shots were fired, for I desired to keep
  the white beast back ;
But I missed my man, and away he ran on
  the flying Injin's track.

Now all below is thick, you know, with
  'cacia, alder, and pine,
And the bright shrubs deck the side of the
  beck, and the lian flowers so fine.
For the forest creeps all under the steeps,
  and feathers the feet of the crags
With boughs so thick that your path you
  pick, like a steamer among the snags.

But right above you, the crags, Lord love
  you ! are bare as this here hand,
And your eyes you wink at the bright blue
  chink, as looking up you stand.
If a man should pop in that trap at the top,
  he'd never rest arm or leg,
Till neck and crop to the bottom he'd drop—
  and smash on the stones like an egg !

'Come back, you cuss! come back to us!
 and let the critter be!'
I screamed out loud, while the men in a
 crowd stood grinning at them and
 me...
But up they went, and my shots were spent,
 and at last they disappeared,—
One minute more, and we gave a roar, for
 the Injin had leapt, and *cleared!*

A leap for a deer, not a man, to clear,—and
 the bloodiest grave below!
But the critter was smart and mad with fear,
 and he went like a bolt from a bow!
Close after him came the devil's limb, with
 his eyes as dark as death,
But when he came to the gulch's brim, I
 reckon he paused for breath!

For breath at the brink! but—a white man
 shrink, when a red had passed so neat?
I knew Phil Blood too well to think he'd
 turn his back dead beat!
He takes one run, leaps up in the sun, and
 bounds from the slippery ledge,
And he clears the hole, but—God help his
 soul! just touches the tother edge!

One scrambling fall, one shriek, one call,
 from the men that stand and stare,—
Black in the blue where the sky looks thro',
 he staggers, dwarf'd up there;
The edge he touches, then sinks, and
 clutches the rock—our eyes grow dim—
I turn away—what's that they say?—he's a-
 hanging on to the brim!

... On the very brink of the fatal chink a
 ragged shrub there grew,
And to that he clung, and in silence swung
 betwixt us and the blue,
And as soon as a man could run I ran the
 way I'd seen them flee,
And I came mad-eyed to the chasm's side,
 and—what do you think I see?

All up? Not quite. Still hanging? Right!
 But he'd torn away the shrub;
With lolling tongue he clutch'd and swung —
 to what? ay, that's the rub!
I saw him glare and dangle in air,—for the
 empty hole he trode,—
Help'd by a *pair of hands* up there!—The
 Injin's? Yes, by God!

Now, boys, look here! for many a year I've
 roam'd in this here land—
And many a sight both day and night I've
 seen that I think grand;
Over the whole wide world I've been, and
 I know both things and men,
But the biggest sight I've ever seen was the
 sight I saw jest then.

I held my breath—so nigh to death Phil
 Blood swung hand and limb,
And it seem'd to us all that down he'd fall,
 with the Panther after him,
But the Injin at length put out his strength—
 and another minute past,—
—Then safe and sound to the solid ground
 he drew Phil Blood, at last!!!

Saved? True for you! By an Injin too!—
 and the man he meant to kill!
There all alone, on the brink of stone, I see
 them standing still;
Phil Blood gone white, with the struggle
 and fright, like a great mad bull at bay,
And the Injin meanwhile, with a half-skeer'd
 smile, ready to spring away.

What did Phil do? Well, I watched the two,
 and I saw Phil Blood turn back,
Bend over the brink and take a blink right
 down the chasm black,
Then stooping low for a moment or so, he
 sheath'd his bowie bright,
Spat slowly down, and watch'd with a frown,
 as the spittle sank from sight!

Hands in his pockets, eyes downcast, silent,
 thoughtful, and grim,
While the Panther, grinning as he passed,
 still kept his eyes on him,
Phil Blood strolled slow to his mates below,
 down by the .ountain track,
With his lips set tight and his face all white,
 and the Panther at his back.

I reckon they stared when the two appeared!
 but never a word Phil spoke,
Some of them laughed and others jeered,—
 but he let them have their joke;
He seemed amazed, like a man gone dazed,
 the sun in his eyes too bright,
And for many a week, in spite of their chee
 he never offered to fight.

And after that day he changed his play, and
  kept a civiller tongue,
And whenever an Injin came that way, his
  contrairy head he hung ;
But whenever he heard the lying word, '*It's
  a LIE !*' Phil Blood would groan ;
'*A Snake is a Snake, make no mistake!
  but an Injin's flesh and bone!*'

THE FAËRY REAPER.

IRELAND.

'TIS on Eilanowen,
  There's laughter nightly !
For the Fays are sowing
  Their golden grain :
It springs by moonlight
  So stilly and brightly,
And it drinks no sunlight,
  Or silver rain ;—
Tho' the shoots upcreeping
  No man may see,
When men are reaping
  It reapt must be ;
But to reap it rightly,
  With sickle keen,
They must lead there nightly
  A pure colleen !

Yes, pure completely
  Must be that maiden,
Just feeling sweetly
  Her love's first dream.
Should one steal thither
  With evil laden,
The crop would wither
  In the pale moon's beam !
For midnights seven,
  While all men sleep,
'Neath the silent heaven
  The maid must reap ;
And the sweeter and whiter
  Of soul is she,
The better and brighter
  Will that harvest be !

. . . In Lough Bawn's bosom
  The isle is lying,
Like a bright green blossom
  On a maiden's breast—
There the water-eagle [1]

[1] The osprey (*Pandion*).

O'erhead is flying,
  And beneath the sea-gull
    Doth build its nest.
And across the water
  A farm gleams fair,
And the farmer's daughter
  Dwelt lonely there :—
And on Eilanowen
  She'd sit and sing,
When the Fays were sowing
  Their seeds in spring,

She could not hear them,
  Nor see them peeping ;
Tho' she wandered near them
  The spring-tide thro',
When the grouse was crowing,
  The trout was leaping,
And with hare-bells blowing
  The banks were blue.
But not by moonlight
  She dared to stay,
Only by sunlight
  She went that way.
And on Eilanowen
  They walked each night,
Her footprints sowing
  With lilies white !

When the sun above her
  Was brightly blazing,
She'd bare (God love her !)
  Each round white limb.
Unseen, unnoted,
  Save fay-folk gazing,
Dark hair'd, white throated,
  She'd strip to swim !
Out yonder blushing
  A space she'd stand,
Then falter flushing
  Across the strand,—
Till the bright still water
  Would sparkle sweet,
As it kissed and caught her
  From neck to feet !

There, sparkling round her
  With fond caresses,
It clasp'd her, crowned her,
  My maiden fair!
Then, brighter glowing
  From its crystal kisses,
The bright drops flowing
  From her dripping hair,

Outleaping, running
  Beneath the sky,
The bright light sunning
  Her limbs, she'd fly,—
And 'mid tinkling laughter
  Of elfin bowers,
The Fays ran after
  With leaves and flowers!

Could the Fays behold her,
  Nor long to gain her?
From foot to shoulder
  None pure as she!
They cried 'God keep her,
  No sorrow stain her!
The Faëry Reaper
  In troth she'll be!' . . .
With stalks of amber
  And silvern ears,
From earth's dark chamber
  The grain appears.
'Tis harvest weather!
  The moon swims high!
And they flock together
  With elfin cry!

Now, long and truly
  I'd loved that maiden;
And served her duly
  With kiss and sign;
And that same season
  My soul love-laden
Had found new reason
  To wish her mine.
For her cheek grew paler,
  Her laughter less,
And what might ail her
  I could not guess.
Each harvest morrow
  We kissing met,
And with weary sorrow
  Her eyes seem'd wet.

'Oh, speak, *Mavourneen*,
  What ails ye nightly?
For sure each morning
  'Tis sad ye seem!'
Her eyes not weeping
  Looked on me brightly:—
'Each night when sleeping
  I dream a Dream.
'Tis on Ellanowen
  I seem to be,

And bright grain growing
  I surely see;
A golden sickle
  My fingers keep,
And my slow tears trickle
  On what I reap!

'The moon is gleaming,
  The faëries gather,
Like glow-worms gleaming,
  Their eyes flash quick;
I try while reaping
  To name " Our Father!"
But round me leaping
  They pinch and prick—
On the stalks of amber,
  On the silvern ears,
They cling, they clamber,
  Till day appears!
And here I'm waking
  In bed, once more,
My bones all aching,
  My heart full sore!'

I kissed her, crying
  'God bless your reaping!
For sure no sighing
  Can set you free.
They'll bless your wedding
  Who vex your sleeping;
So do their bidding,
  Ma cushla chree!
But oh, remember!
  Your fate is cast,
And ere December
  Hath fairly past,
The Faëry Reaper
  Must be a Bride,
Or a sad cold sleeper
  On the green hill-side!'

'Sure wedding's better
  Than dying sadly!'
She smiled, and set her
  Soft hand in mine.
For three nights after
  She labour'd gladly,
'Mid fairy laughter,
  And did not pine;
And when the seven
  Long nights were run,
Full well 'neath Heaven
  That work was done:

Their sheaves were slanted,
Their harvest made,
And no more they wanted
A mortal's aid.

'Tis on Eilanowen
There's laughter nightly,
When the Fays are sowing
Their golden grain !
God bless that laughter ;
That grain blow brightly !
For luck came after
My Mary's pain.
And when sweet Mary
Was wed to me,
Sure the folk of faëry
Were there to see :—
The white board spreading,
Unheard, unseen,
They blest the wedding
Of a pure colleen !

THE 'MIDIAN-MARA.'[1]

I.

THERE'S a sad sea-maiden
Sighs day and night ;
For lack of Eden
Her eyes weep sore ;
If you come upon her
By pale moonlight,—
Farewell to honour
For evermore !
Tho' her hair is redder
Than blood fresh spilt,
'Tis you must wed her
And share her guilt ;
'Tis you, more pity !
Must buried be
In her shining City
Beneath the Sea.

II.

But shouldest thou view her
When shines the sun,
And softly unto her
On tiptoe creep,
You'll find her dozing
As I have done,
Naked reposing
In a sunny sleep ;

Then be quickly ready
To seize her hair,
And to name Our Lady
As she wakens there ;
And tho' clouds may thunder
O'er the waters wide,
To the walls of wonder
She'll be your guide.

III.

In the year of hunger,[2]
That's long gone by,
When I was younger
Who now am old,
By the Ocean dreary
Like a *taisch*[3] went I,
Thin, weak and weary,
With want and cold.
O sweetly gleaming
Was the Sea that hour,
And the sun was streaming
Thro' a golden shower ;
As I wandered sighing
For the famished Land,
I beheld her lying
On the yellow strand !

IV.

Like the silver shining
Was the Maiden's skin,
The red locks twining
To the breasts of white,
Her cheeks were hueless
And chill and thin,
Her lips were dewless,
But her eyes were bright.
Behind her creeping
I held her hair,—
As she scream'd upleaping
I said the prayer ;—
'O *Midian-Mara* !
I hold thee mine :
Thy help I borrow,
By the Cross's sign !'

V.

Hast thou ever noted
A wounded seal,
As it bleats shrill-throated
Before it dies ?
As a seal's eyes turning
On them that kill,

---

[1] *Anglicè*, 'The Mermaid.' [2] The year of Irish famine. [3] Ghost or spirit.

With a dying yearning,
   Were the maiden's eyes.
With those orbs of azure
   She gazed on me :—
'O what's thy pleasure,
   Gilli ma chree ?'
And her tears fell brightly
   Upon the sands,
As she trembled whitely
   With wringing hands.

VI.

'O take me straightway,'
   To her said I,
'To the City's gateway
   That well ye know—
'Tis the hunger kills me,
   And that's no lie,
And a longing fills me
   From earth to go.'
She ceased her crying,
   And sadly said,
With the white gulls flying
   Above her head,
'Is it there, *mavourneen*,'
   Ye'd wish to stand,
That were bred and born in
   A Christian land?'

VII.

I knew her nature
   Was sly and deep,
Tho' the wicked creature
   Had a heavenly face ;
And I looked below me
   At the waves asleep,
As I answered, 'Show me
   That very place !
'Tis You must charm me
   To take the track,
And no hand shall harm me
   Till I come back.'
As I spake, deep thunder
   Was heard that day,
And I saw, far under,
   Where the City lay !

VIII.

'Neath the green still ocean,
   Far, far, below,
With a mystic motion
   That can't be told,
I saw it gleaming
   On a strand of snow,
Its bright towers beaming
   All glass and gold !
And a sound thrilled thro' me
   Like the sound of bells,
Upwafted to me
   On the ocean swells ;
And I saw far under,
   Within those same,
White shapes of wonder
   That went and came !

IX.

'O Mary, mother,
   That savest me,
'Tis the place, no other,
   Where I would go ;
For 'tis sweet and pleasant,
   Set 'neath the Sea
In the bright white crescent
   Of the strand below.
'Tis the hunger in me
   That works its will,
Lest the devil win me
   To steal or kill.'
I held her tighter,
   And prayed anew :—
As I spoke, still brighter
   That vision grew.

X.

Still glassy and shining
   Those walls of flame,
With the sea-weeds twining
   Around their feet ;
More large the place's
   Great towers became,
Till I saw the faces
   In the golden street.
I saw and knew them
   (The Lord's my guide !)
As the water drew them
   From side to side ;
I saw the creatures,
   And I knew them then—
The wool-white features
   Of drownèd men !

XI.

Upright they drifted,
   All wet and cold,
By the sea-wash lifted
   Like the red sea-tang,

While in wild sad cadence,
  From the towers of gold,
The pale sea-maidens
  Struck harps and sang
'*O shule, shule,
  O shule, aroon!*' [1]
I tell thee truly,
  I heard them croon;
Then I heard that thunder
  Roll deep once more,
And I swooned for wonder
  On the yellow shore!

XII.

When I raised in sorrow
  My fearful face,
The *Midian-Mara*
  Was fled from me;
Without repining
  I left the place,
As the Moon rose shining
  Beyond the sea.
And my feet went faster
  To see her light,
For I feared disaster
  If I stayed that night . . .
When God took pity,
  And brought me bread,
I forgot that City
  Of the drownëd dead.

O'CONNOR'S WAKE.

AN IRISH FIDDLE TUNE.

To the wake of O'Connor
  What boy wouldn't go?
To do him that honour
  Went lofty and low.
Two nights was the waking,
  Till day began breaking,
  And frolics past spaking,
    To please him, were done;
  For himself in the middle,
  With stick and with fiddle,
Stretch'd out at his ease, was the King of
    the Fun.

With a dimity curtain overhead,
And the corpse-lights shining round his bed,
Holding his fiddle and stick, and drest
Top to toe in his Sunday best,

[1] '*Come, come, my darling, come!*'

For all the world he seem'd to be
Playing on his back to the companie.
On each of his sides was the candle-light;
On his legs the tobacco-pipes were piled;
Cleanly wash'd, in a shirt of white,
His grey hair brush'd, his beard trimm'd
    right,
He lay in the midst of his friends, and
    smiled.
At birth and bedding, at fair and feast,
Welcome as light or the smile of the priest,
Ninety winters up and down
O'Connor had fiddled in country and town.
Never a fiddler was clever as he
At dance or jig or *pater-o'-pee*;
The sound of his fiddle no word could
    paint—
'Twould fright the devil or please a saint,
Or bring the heart, with a single skirl,
To the very mouth of a boy or girl.
He played—and his elbow was never done;
He drank—and his lips were never dry;
Ninety winters his life had run,
But God's above, and we all must die.
As she stretch'd him out, quoth Judy
    O'Roon—
'Sure life's like his music, and ended soon—
  There's dancing and crying,
  There's kissing, there's sighing,
  There's smiling and sporting,
  There's wedding and courting,—
But the skirl of the wake is the end of the
    tune!'

'*Shin suas, O'Connor,*'[2]
  Cried Kitty O'Bride—
  Her best gown upon her,
    Tim Bourke by her side—
  All laughed out to hear her,
  While Tim he crept near her,
  To kiss her and cheer her
    At the back o' the door;
  But the corpse in the middle,
  With stick and with fiddle,
All done with diversion, would never play
    more!

On the threshold, as each man entered there,
He knelt on his knee and said a prayer,
But first before he took his seat
Among the company there that night,
He lifted a pipe from O'Connor's feet,
And lit it up by the bright corpse-light.

[2] '*Play up, O'Connor!*'

Chattering there in the cloud of smoke,
They waked him well with song and joke ;
The gray old men and the *cauliaghs*[1] told
Of all his doings in days of old ;
The boys and girls till night was done,
Played their frolics and took their fun,
And many a kiss was stolen sure
Under the window and behind the door.
Andy Hagan and Kitty Delane
   Hid in a corner and courted there,
'*Monamondioul !*' cried old Tim Blane,
   Pointing them out, ' they're a purty pair ! '
But when they blushed and hung the head,
' Troth, never be shamed ! ' the old man said ;
' Sure love's as short as the flowers in June,
And life's like music, and ended soon—
   There's wooing and wedding,
   There's birth and there's bedding,
   There's grief and there's pleasure
   To fill up the measure,—
But the skirl of the wake is the end of the tune ! '

   At the wake of O'Connor
   Great matches were made,
   To do him more honour
   We joked and we played—
   Two nights was the waking,
   Till day began breaking,
   The cabin was shaking
   Before we were done,
   And himself in the middle,
   With stick and with fiddle,
As large as in life, was the King of the Fun !

' Well, I remember,' said Tony Carduff,
Drawing the pipe from his lips with a puff,
' Well, I remember at Ballyslo',—
And troth and it's thirty years ago,—
In the midst of the fair there fell a fight,
And who but O'Connor was in the middle?
Striking and crying with all his might,
   And with what for weapon ? the ould black fiddle !
That day would have ended its music straight
If it hadn't been strong as an iron pot ;
Tho' the blood was on it from many a pate,
Troth, divil a bit of harm it got ! '
Cried Michael na Chauliuy,[2] ' And troth that's true—

[1] Old women.
[2] ' Michael the Ferryman ;' lit. 'belonging to the ferry.'

Himself and the fiddle were matched by few,
They went together thro' every weather,
Full of diversion and tough as leather,—
I thought he'd never think of dying,
But Jesus keep us !—there's he's lying.'
Then the *cauliaghs* squatting round on the floor
Began to *keenagh*[3] and sob full sore ;
' God be good to the ould gossoon !
Sure life's like music, and ended soon.
   There's playing and plighting,
   There's frolic and fighting,
   There's singing and sighing,
   There's laughing and crying,—
But the skirl of the wake is the end of the tune ! '

   At the wake of O'Connor,
   The merry old man,
   To wail in his honour
   The *cauliaghs* began ;
   And Rose, Donnell's daughter
   From over the water,
   Began (sure saints taught her !)
   The sweet *drimindhu* ;[4]
   All was still ;—in the middle,
   With stick and with fiddle,
O'Connor, stretched silent, seem'd hearkening too !

Oh, 'twas sweet as the crooning of fairies by night,
Oh, 'twas sad,—as you listened, you smiled in delight,
With the tears in your eyes ; it was like a shower falling,
When the rainbow shines thro' and the cuckoo is calling ;
You might feel through it all, as the sweet notes were given,
The peace of the Earth and the promise of Heaven !
In the midst of it all the sweet singer did stand,
With a light on her hair, like the gleam of a hand ;
She seem'd like an angel to each girl and boy,
But most to Tim Cregan, who watch'd her in joy,

[3] To cry, as during the coronach at a funeral.
[4] A melancholy ditty.

L L

And when she had ended he led her away,[1]
And whisper'd his love till the dawning o
    day.
After that, cried Pat Rooney, the rogue of
    a lad,
' I'll sing something merry—the last was
    too sad ! '
And he struck up the song of the Piper of
    Clare.
How the bags of his pipes were beginning
    to tear,
And how, when the cracks threaten'd fairly
    to end them,
He cut up his own leather *breeches* to mend
    them !
How we laugh'd, young and old ! ' Well,
    beat *that* if you can,'
Cried fat Tony Bourke, the potheen-making
    man—
'Who sings next?' Tony cried, and at
    that who came in,
Dancing this way and that way in midst of
    the din,
But poor Shamus the Fool ? and he gave a
    great spring—
' By the cross,' merry boys, 'tis mysilf that
    can sing ! '
Then he stood by the corpse, and he folded
    his hands,
And he sang of the sea and the foam on
    the sands,
Of the shining *skiddawn*[1] as it flies to and
    fro,
Of the birds of the waves and their wings
    like the snow.
Then he sank his voice lower and sang with
    strange sound
Of the caves down beneath and the beds of
    the drown'd,
Till we wept for the boys who lie where the
    wave rolls,
With no kinsmen to stretch them and wake
    their poor souls.
When he ceased, Shamus looked at the
    corpse, and he said,
' Sure a dacenter man never died in his bed ! '
And at that the old *cauliaghs* began to croon :
' Sure life's like his music, and ended as
    soon—
    There's dancing and sporting,
    There's kissing and courting,
    There's grief and there's pleasure

[1] Herring.

    To fill up the measure,—
But the skirl of the wake is the end of the
    tune.'

' A health to O'Connor ! '
    Fat Anthony said :
' We'll drink in the honour
    Of him that is dead.'
A two-gallon cag, then,
    Did Anthony drag then
From out his old bag then,
    While all there grew keen.
'Twas sweet, strong, and filling—
    His own best distilling !
Oh, well had the dead man loved Tony's
    potheen ![2]

Then the fun brightened up ; but of all
    that befell
It would take me a long day in summer to
    tell—
Of the dancing and singing, the leaping
    and sporting,
And sweetest of all, the sly kissing and
    courting !
Two nights was the waking ; two long
    winter nights
O'Connor lay smiling in midst of the lights,
In the cloud of the smoke like a cloud of
    the skies,
The blessing upon him, to close his old eyes.
Oh, when the time comes for myself to
    depart,
    May I die full of days like the merry old
    man !
I'll be willing to go with the peace on my
    heart,
Contented and happy, since life's but a
    span ;
And O may I have, when my lips cease to
    spake,
To help my poor soul, such an elegant wake !
The country all there, friends and kinsmen
    and all,
And myself in the middle, with candle and
    pall ! . . .
Came the dawn, and we put old O'Connor
    to rest,
In his coffin of wood, with his hands on his
    breast,
And we followed him all by the hundred
    and more,—

[2] Whisky, illicitly distilled.

The boys all in black, and his friends sigh-
    ing sore.
We left him in peace, the poor sleeping
    gossoon,
Thinking, 'Life's like his music, and ended
    too soon.
There's laughing and sporting,
There's kissing and courting.
There's grief and there's pleasure
To fill up the measure,—
But the wake and the grave are the end of
    the tune!'

  'Good-bye to O'Connor,'
    Cried Barnaby Blake,
  'May the saints do him honour
    For the ould fiddle's sake!
  If the saints love sweet playing—
    It's the thruth that I'm saying—
    His sowl will be straying
      And fiddling an air!
  He'll pass through their middle,
    With stick and with fiddle,
  And they'll give him the *cead mile fealta*¹
    up there!'

NOTE.—The preceding Poem is a literal de-
scription of a wake in the wildest and loneliest
part of Connaught. Several of the characters—
e.g. Shamus the Fool—are well known to the
mountaineers and fishermen of that untrodden
district, where the old Celtic tongue is still
spoken in its purity and the old Celtic customs
are still practised, and where the author, in almost
complete seclusion, passed four happy years.

HIGHLAND LAMENT.

'O MAR tha mi! 'tis the wind that's blowing,
  O mar tha mi! 'tis the sea that's white!
'Tis my own brave boatman was up and
    going,
  From Uist to Barra at dead of night;
Body of black and wings of red
  His boat went out on the stormy sea.
O mar tha mi! can I sleep in my bed?
  O gillie dubh! come back to me!

'O mar tha mi! is it weed out yonder?
  Is it drifting weed or a tangled sail?
On the shore I wait and watch and wander.
  It's calm this day, after last night's gale.

    ¹ 'Hundred thousand welcomes.'

O this is the skiff with wings so red,
  And it floats upturned on the glassy sea
O mar tha mi! is my boatman dead?
  O gillie dubh! come back to me!

'O mar tha mi! 'tis a corpse that's sleeping,
  Floating there on the slippery sands;
His face is drawn and his locks are dreeping,
  His arms are stiff and he's clench'd his
    hands.
Turn him up on his slimy bed,
  Clean his face from the weed o' the sea.
O mar tha mi! 'tis my boatman dead!
  O gillie dubh! won't you look at me?

'O mar tha mi! 'tis my love that's taken!
  O mar tha mi! I am left forlorn!
He'll never kiss and he'll never waken,
  He'll never look on the babe unborn.
His blood is water, his heart is lead,
  He's dead and slain by the cruel sea.
O mar tha mi! I am lone in my bed,
  My gillie dubh is lost to me!'

JAMES AVERY.

AT Portsmouth, in a tavern dark,
  One day of windy weather,
A crew of reckless sailors sat,
  And drank their grog together.

Loud was the talk, and rude the joke,
  So deep the jovial din
They did not mark a lean, wild shape
  Who shivering enter'd in:

A beggar wight, who hugg'd his rags,
  And chatter'd with the cold;
Lean was his shape, his eyeballs dim,
  Wrinkled his cheek, and old.

In a dark corner of the room
  He sat with sorry cheer,
Not list'ning, till a word, a name,
  Fell on his frozen ear.

'James Avery!' and as he spake
  One pointed thro' the pane
At a great playbill on the wall
  Of the damp and oozy lane.

On the dead wall the letters great
  Made tempting bright display:

James Avery, the Pirate King,
　Was posted that night's play.
'Ay!' cried a tar, reading aloud,
　'Well might they call him so!
The Pirate King—I grudge his luck!'
　Then, with an oath, 'I'll go.'

Another cried, 'Ah, that's the life
　To suit a sailor's style!
Ben Conway saw his palace, mates,
　On Madagascar Isle;

'And on a throne, in red and gold,
　Jem sat like any king,
With dark-eyed donnas all around,
　As fresh as flowers in spring!

'They brought him wine in cups of gold,
　And each knelt on her knee—
Each mother-naked, smooth as silk—
　Ah, that's the life for me!'

Then spake a third, 'I sailed with Jem
　On board the "Hurricane";
When he deserted I ne'er thought
　To hear of him again.

'And now it's long since last I heard
　His name, and p'raps he's dead.'
'Not so; he only takes a nap!'
　A grizzly war's-man said.

'He has a fleet of fighting ships,
　Swifter than ours tenfold;
Last spring he took six Indiamen,
　Laden with gems and gold.

'There's not a corner of the main
　But knows the skull and bones—
Up goes the flag! and down comes Jem,
　As sure as Davy Jones.

'But let him have his fling; some day
　We'll catch him at his trade—
Short shrift! a rope! and up he goes,
　And all his pranks are played.'

All laughed; 'But not so fast,' cried one;
　'It's not too late, I vow;
His Majesty would pardon him,
　If he'd surrender now.

'The pardon's in the newspapers,
　In black and white it's there;
If pirate Jem will cease his games,
　They'll spare his life, they swear

All laugh'd again—'Jem's wide awake—
　You don't catch birds with chaff—
Come back to biscuit and salt junk?
　He is too 'cute by half.

'Leave all his gold and precious stones,
　His kingdom, and all that,
Bid all them dark-eyed girls farewell
　For labour,—and the cat?'

Ev'n as they speak, a wretched form
　Springs up before their eyes.
'Give me the paper! let me read!'
　The famished creature cries.

They thrust him back with jeer and laugh,
　So wild and strange is he. . . .
'Why, who's this skeleton?' . . . A voice
　Answers, 'James Avery!'

Louder they laugh—'He's mad! he's mad!'
　They round him in a ring.
'Jem here in rags! no, he's in luck,
　As grand as any king!'

But soon he proves his story true
　With eager words and tones;
Then, as he ends, 'Bread, give me bread!
　I'm starving, mates!' he moans.

'Nay, drink!' they cry; and his lean hands
　Clutch at the fiery cup.
'Here's to the King who pardons me!'
　He cries, and drinks it up.

He tells them of his weary days
　Since that dark hour he fled,
A hunted thing, without a home
　Wherein to lay his head.

Through some mysterious freak of fate,
　His name abroad was spread,
And not a wondrous deed was done
　But that wild name was said;

And all the time James Avery dwelt
　An outcast, gaunt and grim,
Till creeping home that day he heard
　His King had pardoned him.

The wild drink mounted to his brain,
　He revell'd maniac-eyed,
'Come to the playhouse—'twill be sport
　To see thyself!' they cried.

Between them, down the narrow street
　They led his scarecrow form—

The wind blew chill from off the sea,
  Before the rising storm.

They sat and saw the mimic play,
  Till late into the night :—
The happy Pirate, crown'd with gold,
  And clad in raiment bright.

The actor swagger'd on the stage
  And drank of glorious cheer, . . .
James Avery gazed! his hungry laugh
  Was pitiful to hear!

They parted. . . . As the chill white dawn
  Struck down a lonely lane,
It flashed upon the rainy wall
  And made the play-bill plain.

James Avery, the Pirate King!
  The mocking record said—
Beneath, James Avery's famish'd form
  Lay ragged, cold, and dead!

THE DEVIL'S PEEPSHOW.
OLD STYLE.

As thro' the Town of Vanity I trod,
I heard one calling in the name of God,
And turning I beheld a wan-eyed wight,
Clad in a garment that had once been bright,
Who, while a few pale children gathered round,
Did plant his faded Peepshow on the ground.
Trembling the children peep'd; and lingering nigh,
E'en thus I heard the ragged Showman cry :—

I.

Now first your eye will here descry
  How all the world begun :
The earth green-dight, the ocean bright,
  The moon, the stars, the sun.
All yet is dark; but you will mark,
  While round this sphere is spun,
A Hand so bare moves here and there,
  Whence rays of ruby run.
I pull a string, and everything
  Is finish'd bright and new,
Tho' dim as dream all yet doth seem ;
  And this, God wot, is true.

II.

Now this, you see, is Eden Tree,
  In Eden's soil set deep ;
Beneath it lies with closèd eyes
  Strong Adam, fast asleep.
All round, the scene is gold and green,
  And silver rivers creep ;
Him on the grass the wild beasts pass,
  As mild and tame as sheep.
My bell I ring ; I pull a string ;
  And on the self-same spot,
From Adam's side God takes his Bride ;
  And this is true, God wot.

III.

There still doth shine the Tree Divine,
  Flush'd with a purple flame,
And hand in hand our parents stand,
  Naked, but have no shame.
Now Adam goes to take repose
  While musing sits his Dame ;
When, over her, the blest boughs stir,
  To show how Satan came.
A Snake so bright, with horns of light,
  Green leaves he rustles thro',
Fair Eve descries with wondering eyes ;
  And this, God wot, is true.

IV.

Now pray perceive, how over Eve
  The fruits forbidden grow.
With hissing sound the Snake twines round,
  His eyes like rubies glow.
' Fair Eve,' he says (in those old days
  Snakes spoke) and louteth low,
'This fruit you see upon the Tree
  Shall make you see and know. . . .'
My bell I ring ; I pull a string ;
  And on the self-same spot
Fair Eve doth eat the Fruit so sweet ;
  And this is true, God wot.

V.
A CHILD.

Please, why did He who made the Tree,
  Our Father in the sky,
Let it grow there, so sweet and fair,
  To tempt our Parents' eye?

SHOWMAN.

My pretty dear, it is most clear
  He wish'd their strength to try ;
And therefore sent, with wise intent,
  The Serpent swift and sly.
I pull a string, and there (poor thing !)
  Stands Adam eating too!
And now, you mark, all groweth dark ;
  And this, God wot, is true.

VI.

Now, you discern, a voice so stern
  Cries 'Adam, where art *thou?*'
'Tis God the Lord, by all adored,
  Walks there ; and all things bow.
But with his Bride doth Adam hide
  His guilty, burning brow ;
And of fig-leaves each sinner weaves
  A guilty apron now.
My bell I ring ; I pull a string ;
  And from that pleasant spot
A Sword of Flame drives man and dame ;
  And this is true, God wot.

VII.

Now wipe the glass. And we will pass
  To quite another scene :
In a strange land two Altars stand,
  One red, the other green ;
The one of blood right sweet and good,
  The other weeds, I ween !
And there, full plain, stands frowning Cain,
  And Abel spruce and clean.
I pull a string ; and every thing
  Grows dark and sad anew,—
There Abel lies with dying eyes !
  And this, God wot, is true.

VIII.

The wicked Cain has Abel slain
  All with a burning brand ;
And now, sad sight, an Angel bright
  Doth mark him with his hand.

A CHILD.

What specks so red are those that spread
  Behind them as they stand?

SHOWMAN.

The sparks you see the wild eyes be,
  Countless as grains of sand,
Of all those men who have, since then,
  Shed blood in any land !
In grief and pain they look at Cain,
  Aghast on that sad spot ;
And all around blood soaks the ground ;
  And this is true, God wot.

IX.

My bell I ring ; I pull a string :
  Now, Father Noah you mark—
Sleeping he lies, with heavy eyes,
  All full of wine, and stark.
But now, behold ! that good man old
  A Voice in dream doth hark ;
And the Voice cries, 'O Noah, arise !
  And build thyself an Ark.'
Again I ring ; and pull a string ;
  And all is water blue,
Where, floating free, the Ark you see ;
  And this, God wot, is true.

X.

Thus God the Lord, with his great Word,
  Did bid the waters rise,
To drown and kill all things of ill
  He made beneath the skies.
The Lord saved none, but Noah alone,
  His kith and kin likewise ;
Two of each beast, both great and least ;
  Two of each bird that flies.
My bell I ring ; I pull a string ;
  And on the self-same spot,
The water sinks, the bright Bow blinks ;
  And this is true, God wot.

XI.

O day and night, unto your sight
  Such wonders shown might be,
But to conclude this Peepshow good,
  You Heaven and Hell shall see :
The shining things, with spangled wings,
  Who smile and sing so free ;
The crew of shame, who in hell-flame
  Complain eternallie !
My bell I ring ; I pull a string ;
  And you them both may view—
The blest on high, the curst who cry :—
  And this, Got wot, is true.

XII.

A CHILD.

How can they bear, who sit up there
  In shining robes so gay,
From Heaven to peer, without a tear,
  On those who scream and pray?

SHOWMAN.

Why, those who burn had, you must learn,
  As fair a chance as they—
But Adam's fall doth doom them all
  Upon God's judgment day.
I thus conclude with moral good,
  Not soon to be forgot ;
And you must own what I have shown
  Is solemn sooth, Got wot.

XIII.
A LITTLE BOY.

O look at him, that showman grim,
 A frown is on his cheek ;
Come away quick, for I am sick
 Whene'er I hear him speak !

A GIRL.

Along this way, last Holy Day,
 In blessèd Whitsun' week,
There passed a wight, so sweet and bright
 He seemed an Angel meek :
He bare, also, an old Peep-show,
 But prettier far to view,
And loud cried He 'O look and see !
 For all, God wot, is true !'

XIV.
CHILDREN.

And *did* you peep? and did you weep
 To see the pictures wild ?

GIRL.

Ah nay, ah nay, I laughed, full gay,
 I looked and laughed and smiled !
For I discern'd, with bright face turned
 On mine, a little Child ;
And round him, bright burn'd many a light,
 And cakes and sweets were piled ;
And scents most rare fill'd all the air
 All round the heavenly spot,
While loud and wide that Showman cried—
 'This is our Lord, God wot !'

XV.
FIRST CHILD.

'Twas Jesus Child ! so good and mild !
 He grew on Mary's breast !

GIRL.

Sweet were his eyes, his look was wise,
 And his red lips were blest ;
I longed, I wis, those lips to kiss,
 And by his side to rest.
This man's Peepshow is strange, I know,
 But the other was the best !
Now let us go where daisies blow,
 Sweet ferns, and speedwells blue,
And Posies make for Christ His sake,
 For He is bright and true !

XVI.
SHOWMAN (*solus*).

Folk, I'm afraid, are changed ; my trade
 Grows worse each day, I know.
How they did throng when I was young,
 To see this very Show !·
My rivals pass, and lad and lass
 Follow where'er they go,
While up and down, from town to town,
 I creep, most sad and slow.
I too must try some novel cry,
 Lest I be quite forgot :
These pictures old that I unfold
 Have ceased to please, God wot !

DAYBREAK.
FRAGMENT.

BUT now the first faint flickering ray
 Fell from the cold east far away,
The birds awoke and twitter'd, hover'd,
 The dim leaves sparkled in the dew—
Earth slowly her dark head uncover'd
 And held her blind face up the blue,
Till the fresh consecration came
 In yellow beams of orient flame,
Touching her, and she breathed full blest
 With lilies heaving on her breast.
Seas sparkled, dark capes glimmer'd green,
 As Dawn crept on from scene to scene,
Lifting each curtain of the night
 With fingers flashing starry-white.

EUPHROSYNE ; OR, THE PROSPECT.

'FREED from its tenement of clay
 (So the prophetic legend ran),
As pure as dew, as bright as day,
 Shall rise the Soul of Man.'
I read ; and in the shade by me
Sat golden-haired Euphrosyne.

Above our shaded orchard seat
 The boughs stirred scented in the light,
And on the grass beneath our feet
 Lay blossoms pink and white ;
I held the book upon my knee,
Translating to Euphrosyne.

'Twas an old melancholy rune,
  Writ by a Norseman long ago—
Sad with the sense of stars and moon,
  Sea-wash, and frost, and snow—
A vision of futurity!
And wide-eyed heard Euphrosyne.

' Stately and slow the heart shall beat
  To the low throb of Time's soft tide,
While, shaded from the solar heat,
  The Shapes walk heavenly-eyed.'
All round us burnt the starry lea,
And warmly sighed Euphrosyne.

' All shall be innocent and fair,
  Dim as a dream the days shall pass—
No weed of shame shall blossom there,
  No snake crawl on the grass.'—
' How happy such a world will be!'
Sighed beautiful Euphrosyne.

' Flesh shall be fled, sense shall be still,
  The old grey earth buried and dead;
The wicked world, with all things ill—
  Stone, rock, and tree—be fled.'—
' No earth, no world!' softly sighed she,
The little maid, Euphrosyne.

She clasped her hands, she cast her eyes
  Over the landscape bright with May—
Scented and sweet, 'neath cloudless skies,
  Smiled the green world that day—
Loud sang the thrush, low hummed the bee,
And softly sighed Euphrosyne.

' Sickness shall perish, grief and pain
  Be buried with the buried life;
The aching heart, the weary brain,
  At last shall cease their strife.'—
The grey tome trembled on my knee,
But happy sat Euphrosyne.

' The luminous house wherein we dwell,
  The haunted house of shame and lust,
The callow spirit's fleshly shell,
  Shall crumble into dust;
The flower shall fade, the scent fly free!'—
She trembled now, Euphrosyne.

Her warm, white bosom heaved with sighs,
  I felt her light breath come and go,
She drank, with glorious lips and eyes,
  The summer's golden glow;
She felt her life, and sighed ' Ay, me!'
The flower of maids, Euphrosyne.

' And with the flower of flesh shall fade
  The venom'd bloom of earthly love,
No passion-trance of man and maid
  Shall taint the life above;
Flesh shall be fled, sex shall not be!'—
I paused, and watched Euphrosyne.

Her hands were folded round her knees,
  Her eyes were fix'd in a half-dream;
She shared the flame of flowers and trees,
  And drank the summer gleam;
' Kiss sweet, kiss sweet!' upon the tree
The thrush sang, to Euphrosyne.

A little maid of seventeen Mays,
  A happy child with golden hair,
What should she know of Love's wild ways,
  Its hope, its pain, and prayer?
' No *love* in heaven?—how *strange* 'twill be!'
Still musing, sighed Euphrosyne.

' No thoughts of perishable mould
  Shall break the rule of heavenly rest,
But larger light, more still, more cold,
  More beautiful and blest.'—
Her heart was fluttering close to me,
And quickly breathed Euphrosyne.

' There shall be no more *love!*'—but here
  I paused, for from my side she sprang,
And in her bird's voice, loud and clear,
  Of love's young dream she sang—
' Oh, close the foolish book!' cried she,
The happy maid Euphrosyne.

I closed the book, and from my hold
  She took it with her fingers white,
Then down the path of green and gold
  She tripped with laughter light—
' The book, not the glad world, shall be
Deep-buried,' said Euphrosyne.

Within an elm-tree's hollow bole,
  Into the darkness damp and green,
She thrust it, closing up the hole
  With sprays of lilac sheen—
Then, all the radiant flush of glee
Fast faded from Euphrosyne.

Pensively in the summer shine
  Her blue eyes filled with tears of bliss;
She held her little mouth to mine
  In one long heavenly kiss—
' I love the earth, and life, and *thee!*'
She whispered, my Euphrosyne.

Sleep, Book, within thy burial place,
  With flowers and fruit for epitaph !
Kind Heaven, stoop down thy sunny face
  To hear the Earth's glad laugh !
Smile, with your glorious eyes on me,
O child of joy ! Euphrosyne !

STANLEY FARM.

COME, love, and while the landscape glows
  Red in the setting sun,
Let us repair to Stanley Farm,
  Where thou wast wooed and won.

The river runs through a narrow glen,
  And shooting past the mill,
It lingers near the burial-ground
  Where the dark dead lie still.

Then fresh and free it shooteth through
  The bridge at headlong speed ;
But when the village bridge is past,
  It comes to marsh and mead ;

And broadening out with slacken'd pace,
  It fringes green flat land,
Where, blanchèd white by frequent floods,
  Long lines of pollards stand.

And now within its shallow pools,
  The blue-winged hern doth wade,
Still as a stone, with crooked neck
  Above his floating shade.

And water-lilies fringe the brim,
  And all is sedge and reed,
Save one small stream within the midst,
  That winds and winds with speed.

Then down comes Thornby Beck and gains
  The river with a cry,
And on the two together run,
  Under the English sky.

And strong and deep the stream has grown,
  As well as broad and wide,
On reaching Stanley Farm, that sits
  Upon the water's side.

How still it is ! how bright it is,
  These happy summer weeks,
When cattle wade, in the dark blue pools
  Broken to silvern streaks !

But, love, hast thou forgot the Yule,
  'Twenty long years ago ?
The level meads around the stream
  Were white with ice and snow.

The river was frozen white and blue,
  In its cold weedy bed ;
A deep black fog filled all the air,
  And in the fog, o'erhead,

Just hovering close to earth, as small
  As a school-boy's pink balloon,
The wandering sun looked strange and col .
  As the red wintry moon.

The fog was dark, and darkest there
  Above the river's bed,
And from the windows of the farm
  All day the lights gleamed red.

But when the sun's ball rolled from sight,
  The wind began to blow,
The chilly fog was cleft in twain,
  And the moon lit up the snow !

A deep blue flower with a golden heart
  Hung downwards, was the sky,
And white and cold in swathes of snow
  Did mead and hamlet lie.

And ever and anon the wind
  Blew up a cloud so pale,
And held it o'er the yellow moon,
  Like a thin lawny veil.

And through its folds the bright'ning morn
  Gazed, breathing soft and slow,
Till, melted with her breath, the cloud
  Was shriven into snow.

Then ever in the bright'ning beam,
  As each soft cloud stole by,
We saw dark figures on the stream
  Gliding with merry cry.

Men and maidens, old and young,
  The skaters frolicked there ;
Like shapes within a dream, their forms
  Stole through the mystic air.

ON A YOUNG POETESS'S GRAVE.

UNDER her gentle seeing,
  In her delicate little hand,
They placed the Book of Being,
  To read and understand.

The Book was mighty
  Yea, worn and eaten with age ;
Though the letters looked great and golden,
  She could not read a page.

The letters fluttered before her,
  And all looked darkly wild:
Death saw her, and bent o'er her,
  As she pouted her lips and smiled.

Then, weary a little with tracing
  The Book, she look'd aside,
And lightly smiling, and placing
  A Flower in its leaves, she died.

She died, but her sweetness fled not,
  As fly the things of power,—
For the Book wherein she read not
  Is the sweeter for the Flower.

LOVE IN WINTER.
A GENRE PICTURE.

I.

'*O Love is like the roses,*
  And every rose shall fall,
For sure as summer closes
  They perish one and all.
Then love, while leaves are on the tree,
  And birds sing in the bowers:
When winter comes, too late 'twill be
  To pluck the happy flowers.'

It is a maiden singing,
  An ancient girl, in sooth;
The dizzy room is ringing
  With her shrill song of youth;
The white keys sob as fast she tries
  Each shrill and shrieking scale:
'*O love is like the roses!*' cries
  This muslin'd nightingale. . . .

In a dark corner dozing
  I close my eyes and ears,
And call up, while reposing,
  A glimpse from other years;
A genre-picture, quaint and Dutch,
  I see from this dark seat,—
'Tis full of human brightness, such
  As makes remembrance sweet.

II.

Flat leagues of endless meadows
  [In Holland lies the scene],
Where many pollard-shadows
  O'er nut-brown ditches lean;
Grey clouds above that dimly break,
  Mists that pale sunbeams stripe,

With groups of steaming cattle, make
  A landscape 'after Cuyp.'

A windmill, and below it
  A cottage near a road,
Where some meek pastoral poet
  Might make a glad abode;
A cottage with a garden, where
  Prim squares of pansies grow,
And sitting on a garden-chair,
  A Dame with locks of snow.

In trim black truss'd and bodiced,
  With petticoat of red,
And on her bosom modest
  A kerchief white bespread.
Alas! the breast that heaves below
  Is shrivell'd now and thin,
Tho' vestal thoughts as white as snow
  Still palpitate within.

Her hands are mitten'd nicely,
  And folded on her knee;
Her lips, that meet precisely,
  Are moving quietly.
She listens while the dreamy bells
  O'er the dark flats intone—
Now come, now gone, in dying swells
  The Sabbath sounds are blown.

Her cheek a withered rose is,
  Her eye a violet dim;
Half in her chair she doses,
  And hums a happy hymn.
But soft! what wonder makes her start
  And lift her aged head,
While the faint flutterings of her heart
  Just touch her cheek with red?

The latch clicks; thro' the gateway
  An aged wight steps slow—
Then pauses, doffing straightway
  His broad-brim'd gay chapeau!
Swallow-tail'd cot of blue so grand,
  With buttons bright beside,
He wears, and in his trembling hand
  A nosegay, ribbon-tied.

His thin old legs trip lightly
  In breeches of nankeen,
His face is shining brightly,
  So rosy, fresh, and clean—
Wrinkled he is and old and plain,
  With locks of golden-grey,
And leaning on a tassell'd cane
  He gladly comes this way.

Oh, skylark, singing over
　The silent mill hard by,
To this so happy lover
　Sing out with summer cry !
He hears thee, tho' his blood is cold,
She hears, tho' deaf and weak ;
She stands to greet him, as of old,
　A blush upon her cheek.

In spring-time they were parted
　By some sad wind of woe ;
Forlorn and broken-hearted
　Each faltered, long ago ;
They sunder'd,—half a century
Each took the path of pain—
He lived a bachelor, and she
　Was never woo'd again !

But when the summer ended,
　When autumn, too, was dead,
When every vision splendid
　Of youth and hope was fled,
Again these two came face to face
As in the long ago—
They met within a sunless place
　In the season of the snow.

'O love is like the roses,
　Love comes and love must flee !
Before the summer closes
　Love's rapture and love's glee !'
O peace ! for in the garden there
He bows in raiment gay ;
Doffs hat, and with a courtly air
　Presents his fond bouquet.

One day in every seven,
　While church-bells softly ring,
The happy, silent Heaven
　Beholds the self-same thing :
The gay old boy within the gate,
With ribbons at his knee !—
' When winter comes, is love too late ?'
　O Cupid, look and see !

O, talk not of love's rapture,
　When youthful lovers kiss ;
What mortal sight may capture
　A scene more sweet than this ?
Beside her now he sits and glows,
While prim she sits and proud,—
Then, spectacles upon his nose,
　Reads the week's news aloud !

Pure, with no touch of passion,
　True, with no tinge of pain !

Thus, in sweet Sabbath fashion,
　They live their loves again.
She sees in him a happy boy—
　Swift, agile, amorous-eyed ;
He sees in her his own heart's joy—
　Youth, Hope, Love, vivified !

Content there he sits smoking
　His long Dutch pipe of wood :
Gossiping oft and joking,
　As a gay lover should.
And oft, while there in company
　They smile for Love's sweet sake,
Her snuff-box black she hands, and he
　A grave, deep pinch doth take !

There, gravely juvenescent,
　In sober Sabbath joy,
Mingling the past and present,
　They sit, a maid and boy !
' *O love is like the roses !*'—No !
Thou foolish singer, cease !
Love finds the fireside 'mid the snow,
　And smokes the pipe of peace !

WILL O' THE WISP.

A BALLAD WRITTEN FOR CLARI, ON
A STORMY NIGHT.

JUST an inch high
　With a body all yellow,
A bright crimson eye
　And limbs all awry,
Wakes the queer little fellow—
Yes, awakes in the night,
Rubs his eyes in a fright,
Yawns, harks to the thunder,
While the glowworms all set
Round his cradle so wet,
　Stare at him in wonder.
How it blows ! how it rains !
How the thunder refrains !
While the glowworms so wan,
　As they gather together,
Hear the quaint little man
　Squeak faintly, ' What weather !'
　' Who is his father ?
Who is his mother ?'
They cry as they gather,
　And puzzle, and pother—
Such a queer little chap,
Just new-born in a nap !

And such antics are his
  As he springs on his bed,
Such a comical phiz,
  Such a red,
  Shining head !
Hark again,
'Midst the rain
  How the deep thunder crashes !
And the lightning
Is bright'ning
  In fitful blue flashes !
' Here's fun ! here's a din ! '
Cries Will with a grin—
' I'll join in the play—
It's darker than pitch
In this hole of a ditch,
What a place to be born in—I'm off and
  away.'

Out on the heath
  It rains with a will.
The Wind sets his teeth
  And whistles right shrill
All is darkness and sound,
  All is splishing and splashing ;
The pools on the ground
  Glimmer wet in the flashing—
Up and down, round and round,
With a leap and a bound,
  Goes the little one dashing.
' Oh what fun ! ' out he screams
  At the wild blue beams
  As they flicker and pass.
Then he squats down and seems
  With his nose's red gleams
  Like a lamp in the grass ;—
Then 'mid rain washing down, and the
  thunder still busy,
He flies spinning round, till he pauses, half
  dizzy.

How dark and how still,
  In the arm of the hill,
  Lies the hamlet asleep—
While the wind is so shrill,
  And the darkness so deep !
Down the street all is dark,
  And closed is each shutter ;
But he pauses to mark,
  His face like a spark
  In the black polished gutter !
But see ! what a streak
  Gleams out from the inn !

Overhead with a creak,
  And a groan and a squeak,
  Shakes the sign ; while the din
  Comes harsh from within.
Hark !—the jingling of glasses,
  The singers' refrain !
Will stops as he passes
  And peeps through the pane,
  Dripping, slippery with rain,
There they sit and they joke,
  In the grey cloud of smoke,
While the jolly old host,
  With his back to the fire,
  Stands warm as a toast,
  And doth smile and perspire.
Grave, thin, and pedantic,
  The schoolmaster sits,
While, in argument frantic
  With riotous wits,
  The maker of boots
  Still in apron of leather,
Thumps the board and disputes,
  Contradicts and refutes ;
And like sparrows collected, all birds of
  feather,
All smoking long pipes, and all noddin
  together,
The Wiseacres gather, screen'd snug fro
  the weather.

Great, broad, and brown,
  Stands the jug on the board,
  And the ale is poured,
  And they quaff it down.
How it froths, fresh and strong,
  Warm, sweet, full of spice !
Will's beginning to long
  For a sip,—'tis so nice !
So he whispers the Wind,
  Who runs round from the lane,
And they creep in behind,
  And the Wind tries to find
  An entrance in vain.
Then ' The Chimney ! ' cries Will,
While the Wind laughs out shrill,
  And he leaps at one bound
  To the roof up on high,
While the chimneys all round
  Tremble and cry.

One moment he pauses
  Up yonder, and draws his
  Breath deep and strong,

Then dives like a snake,
While the dwelling doth quake,
　To the room where they throng.
Ho, ho! with one blow
Out the lights go,
　Dark and silent is all.
But the fire burns low
　With its ghost on the wall.
' What a night! Ah, here's weather!'
All murmur together
　With voices sunk low,
While softly slips Will
In the jug, drinks his fill,
　And is turning to go,
When a hand, while none mark,
　Lifts the jug in the dark;
'Tis the cobbler so dry
Seeks to drink on the sly!
Tarala! pirouette!
Will springs at his nose,
The jug is upset,
　And the liquor o'erflows.
' What's that?' all exclaim,
Leaping up with a shout,
While the cobbler in shame,
With nose all aflame,
　Cries, ' The *Devil*, no doubt!'
And as fresh lights are brought
　These birds of a feather
Think it quite a new thought
　To nod gravely together,
Crying hot and distraught,
' Well, indeed! this *is* weather!'

Tarala! pirouette!
Out again in the wet!
Like a small dancing spark,
　With his face flashing bright
In the black dripping dark,
　Goes the elf of the night.
Hark! from the church-tower,
Slowly chimeth the hour!
　Twelve times low and deep,
Comes the chime through the shower
　On the village asleep;—
And where ivies enfold
　The belfry, doth sit,
Huddled up from the cold,
The owl grey and old,
　With ' Toowhoo ' and ' Toowhit!'
' Heigho!'—yawns poor Will—
　' Time for bed, by the powers!'
And he lights on a sill,

Among flower-pots and flowers,
And just as he seems
　To slumber inclined,
A white hand forth-gleams
　From within, and the blind
Is drawn back, and oh dear!
　What a beautiful sight!
Clari's face doth appear
　Looking out at the night.
And Clari doth stand,
　With the lamp in her hand,
In her bedgown of white—
Her hair runs like gold on her shoulders,
　and fills
With gleams of gold-shadow her tucks and
　her frills,
And her face is as sweet as a star, and below
Her toes are like rosebuds that peep among
　snow.

Breathless with wonder,
　Quiet and still,
He crouches under
　'The pots on the sill;
Then the blind closes slow,
　And the vision doth fade,
But still to and fro
On the blind moves the shade—
There! out goes the light!
　Will lifts up his head,
All is darker than night,
　She is creeping to bed.
Oh, light be her rest!
She steals into her nest,
　Without a beholder,
And the bed, soft and warm,
Swells up round her form
　To receive and enfold her!

[The wind is increasing,
But the rain is ceasing,
And blown up from the west
　Comes the moon wan and high,
With a cloud on her crest,
　And a tear in her eye.
Distraught and opprest,
　She drifts wearily by!]

' Heigho!' yawns poor Will—
Still crouch'd down on the sill—
　' How sleepy I feel!
There's a cranny up there
To let in the fresh air,—
　Here goes! in I'll steal!'

So said and so done,
   And he enters the room
Where the dainty-limb'd one, like a lily in bloom,
Her face a dim brightness, her breath a perfume,
Sleeps softly. With noiseless invisible tread
The wanderer steals to the side of the bed
Where she lies, oh how fair! so sweet and so warm,
While the white clothes sink round the soft mould of her form;
One hand props her cheek, and one unespied
Lies rising and falling upon her soft side.
Will floats to and fro, and the light that he throws
Just lights this or that as she lies in repose,
Leaving all the rest dark. See! he hops 'mong her hair
And shines like a jewel;—then leans down to stare
In her face,—and his ray as he trembles and spies
Just flashes against the white lids of her eyes;—
While her breath—oh her breath is so sweet and so fine,
Will drinks and turns dizzy—his joy is divine,
And his light flashing down shows the red lips apart,
To free the deep fragrance that steals from her heart

   Just an inch high,
      With a body all yellow,
   A bright crimson eye,
   And limbs all awry,
      Stands the queer little fellow!
And Clari's sweet mouth
   Just a little asunder,
Sweet with spice from the South,
   Fills his spirit with wonder:
Such a warm little mouth!
Such a red little mouth!
The thin bud above and the plump blossom under!
   'Heigho, heart's alive!
   Here's a door, here I'll rest!'
And he takes one quick dive
   And slips into her breast!
And there may he thrive
   Like a bird in a nest!

And Clari turns over
   And flushes and sighs,
Pushes back the warm cover,
   Half opens her eyes,
Then sinking again
   Warm, languid, and bright,
With new bliss in her brain,
   Dreams—such dreams—of delight!
She tosses and turns
   In visions divine;
For within her Will burns
   Like a lamp in a shrine!

. . . And now you've the reason that Cla[ri] is gay,
As a bird on the bough or a brooklet at play
And now you've the reason why Clari [is] bright,
Why she smiles all the day and is glad a[ll] the night;
For the light having entered her boso[m] remains,
Darts fire to her glances and warmth thr[ough] her veins,
Makes her tricksy and merry, yet full of t[he] power
Of the wind and the rain, and the stor[m] and the shower;
Half wise in the ways of the world, an[d] half simple,
As sly as a kiss is, as deep as a dimple,
A spirit that sings like a bird on a tree,—
'I love my love, and my love loves me!'

GIANT DESPAIR.

I.

His Death.

Sad is the plight of Giant Despair,
   In Doubting Castle sick lies he!
The castle is built on a headland bare,
   And looks on the wash of a whirling Se[a]

With the noise in his ears and the gleam [in] his eyes
   Of the breaking waves that beneath hi[m] beat,
Propt on pillows the Giant lies,
   Pillowed, too, are his gouty feet.

In and out the Leeches of Souls
   Run and chatter and prate and pray—

But the great wind wails and the thunder
    rolls:
None may banish his gloom away.
With parchment cheek and lack-lustre eye
    He looketh out on the stormy scene—
Cruel is he and bloody and sly,
    Lustful and bad his life hath been.

O Priests who stand and whisper there,
    While he groans and curses and shrinks
        for fear,
What can ye say to Giant Despair
    To comfort him now his end is near?

Fat and oily and sweet, cries one:—
    Comfort, O comfort! for heaven is sure—
There the believer shall revel in fun,
    And all delight that is plump and pure.

'Nothing delicious the Lord denies,
    Rosy wine he shall drink in bliss'—
'Add, moreover,' another cries,
    'Waists to encircle and lips to kiss.'

With parchment cheek and lack-lustre eye
    The Giant lies and makes no sign:
Women's falsehood has made him sigh,
    He is sick of the very sight of wine.

'Comfort!' another crieth loud,
    'Full of music shall be thy breast,
Thou shalt sit full proud on a rosy cloud,
    Happy and idle, amongst the blest—

'All shall be stainless and sweet and fair;
    All shall be merry from night to morn.'
Giant Despair stirred in his chair,
    Scowled at the speaker and grunted scorn.

Then one said this and one said that,
    And all were full of the world to be:
Yet duller and bitter the Giant sat
    Scowling out at the sullen Sea.

And all the storm of the wind and rain,
    And all the rage of the wrathful wave,
Flowed in and out of the Giant's brain
    As the surge in and out of a dank sea-
        cave.

Forth, at last, stept a shape so grey,
    Crown'd with poppy, and shrouded deep;
He touch'd the Giant with hand of clay.
    And held a goblet—'Drink this, and sleep.

Over thy grave the grass shall grow—
    Roses too, the white and the red—

The generations shall come and go,
    But *thou* shalt slumber,' the spirit said

'Many a year shall blossom and fade,
    Many a life be given and taken,
Ere from thy sleep in the silent shade
    Thou, with a thrill of new life, shalt
        waken.

The Giant smiled. Still loud and strong
    Sounded the sob of the weary Sea.
'My ears are sick!—may my sleep be long!
    For ever and ever, if that may be.'

II.

AFTER

Who on the Giant's tomb
    Sits in the twilight gloom,
        With white hands folded?
Her breath comes fresh and warm;
    Silent she waits, a form
        Divinely moulded.

Maiden she is; with eyes
That search the dark still skies
    She sits in shadow;
Strewn scented at her feet
Are rue and lilies sweet,
    And flowers o' the meadow.

And in her wild black hair
Are wild weeds passing fair,
    Pluck'd from dark places—
Dumb, dead, her sweet lips are,
And fixèd as a star
    Her marble face is.

Under God's starless cope,
Vestured in white sits Hope,
    A musing maiden,
Under a yew sits she,
Watching most silently
    The gates of Eden.

Afar away they shine!
While up those depths divine
    Her eyes are turning—
And one by one on high
The strange lamps of the sky
    Are dimly burning.

Such sounds as fill'd with care
The dark heart of Despair
    Disturb her never,—

Tho' close to her white feet
That mighty Sea doth beat,
Moaning for ever.

She sees the foam-flash gleam,
She hears, in a half dream,
The muffled thunder.
The salt dew fills her hair;
Her thoughts are otherwhere,
Watching in wonder.

There let her sit alone,
Ev'n as a shape of stone
In twilight gleaming;
Despair's pale monument,
There let her sit, content,
Waiting and dreaming.

Ah! which were sweetest, best?
With dead Despair to rest
In sleep unbroken;
Or with that marble Maid
To watch, to sit in the shade,
Waiting a token?

THE MOUNTAIN WELL.

HERE, on the sultry mountain's face,
  Although the heat broods bright around,
The runlet, in a mossy place,
  Drips, drop by drop, without a sound,
Into a basin cool yet bright,
Half-shaded from the golden light.

All is as still as sleep; on high
  The clouds float soft and white as wool;
Fern-fringëd crags and boulders lie
  Sun-parch'd around the dewy pool;
Beneath, the mountain pathway twines,
Above, peaks rise and sunlight shines.

How still it is! nought moves or stirs.
  Afar below, the lake of blue,
With purple islands dark with firs,
  Gleams smooth as glass and dim as dew:
And mountain, isle, and woodland rest
Within the mirror of its breast.

All motionless on yonder stone
  The white grouse crouches in the light;
On high among the crags, alone,
  The eagle sheathes his piercing sight,
Clutching the peak amid the heat,
His shadow black'ning at his feet.

No living thing that flies or creeps
  Comes near the well this noontide hour;
The sunlight scorches crags and steeps,
  The heather shrinks its purple flower;
The wild brook glisters in its bed,
Silent and faded to a thread.

But when the sun is in the west,
  And sheds soft crimson o'er the place,
The grey-hen creeping from her nest,
  Leaving her dull brown eggs a space,
Comes hither, pausing on the brink
With quick sharp eyes, and stoops to drink.

Or from the stones the foumart slim
  Doth hither steal at eve to cool
His bloody mouth; or on the brim
  The blue hare, shadow'd in the pool,
Sits up erect, and thro' the rocks
Springs, at the coming of the fox.

How many a strange and gentle thing
  Hath seen its face reflected here!
How oft at gloaming hath the spring
  Mirror'd the moist eyes of the deer,
While glen and corry, peak and height,
Were redd'ning in the rosy light!

Here stain'd with blood and foamy-lipt,
  The stag of ten hath paused for breath,
His blood in the sad pool hath dript
  Dark, drop by drop, before his death,
While he has watched, with looks of woe,
The hunter toiling from below.

How sweet it lies! how dark and cool!
  Half shaded by the crag on high,
A tiny place, a shallow pool,
  Yet with its own dark depth of sky—
Renewed for ever with no will
By the soft trickling of the hill.

All thro' the dim and dewy night
  It gathers coolness drop by drop,
While in the moon the crags gleam white,
  And on the silent mountain top
The evening star of liquid dew
Gleams like a diamond in the blue.

A never-empty hand, a dim
  Dark eye for dews of love to fill,
A constant cup full to the brim,
  Hast thou, O fount upon the hill.
I stoop and kiss thy lips; and so,
Refresh'd, I bless thee as I go.

THE SONG OF THE SHEALING.[1]

O who sits and sings the sad song of the Shealing,
  Alone on the hill-side, alone in the night!
Dead still through the shadows the moonlight is stealing,
  The dew's on the heather, the mist on the height.
She sitteth in silence, and singeth so slowly;
  She milks the dark kine with her fingers so fair.
White woe of the lost, may her vigil be holy!
  The song of the Shealing is sad on the air.

Dark strewn on the grass are the stones of the Shealing,
  The wild leek and nettle grow black over all;
Here morning to gloaming the black hawk is wheeling,
  And foumart and stoat suckle young in the wall.
It's lonely by daylight, but nightly, ah! nightly,
  She comes from her cave, with her kine, and sits there.
Oh, hearken! she sings, and her face gleams so whitely;
  The song of the Shealing is sad on the air.

O who would not hark to the song of the Shealing!
  I stand in the shadow, I listen and sigh;
The day comes again, happy voices are pealing,
  The blue smoke curls up to the sweet summer sky;
O red in the sunset the kine gather yonder,
  The maidens are milking with rosy feet bare;
The sheep-dog is barking,—I hear it and ponder,—
  The song of the Shealing is sad on the air.

O green was the pasture, and sweet was the Shealing,

And kind were the maidens barefooted and free,
And full of enchantment was Love's tender feeling
  When the moon rose so silently up from the sea.
And on the green knolls walked the loved and the lover,
  Wrapt warm in one plaid, with one thought and one care:
I see them! I hear them! my heart's running over,—
  The song of the Shealing is sad on the air.

O spirit of whiteness, O Ghost of the Shealing!
  Sing on, and sing low in the shade of the hill;
The picture has faded your voice was revealing,
  The white owl looks out through the threshold so chill.
There's a star on Ben Rannoch shines softly above you,
  It sparkles all night on the dew in your hair:
White Soul of the Silence, we hear you and love you,—
  The song of the Shealing is sad on the air.

---

[1] The rude cluster of huts in the midst of the distant pasturage whither the cattle were driven in summer, and where they grazed for many weeks, attended by the women and maidens of the farm.

THE SECRET OF THE MERE.

I BUILT a hut beside the Mere,
  A lowly hut of turf and stone;
Therein I thought from year to year
  To dwell in silence and alone,
Watching the lights of heaven chase
The phantoms on the water's face.

The world of men was far away;
  There was no sound, no speech, no cry;
All desolate the dark Mere lay
  Under the mountains and the sky—
A sullen Mere, where sadly brood
Dark shadows of the solitude.

'It is an evil world,' I said;
  'There is no hope, my doom is dark.'
And in despair of soul I fled
  Where not another eye might mark
My silent pain, my heart's distress,
And all my spirit's weariness.

And when I came unto the Mere,
  It lay and gleam'd through days of gloom.
The livid mountains gather'd drear
  All round, like stones upon a tomb ;
Around its margin rusted red
  The dark earth crumbled 'neath my tread.

I said, 'It is a godless place—
  Dark, desolate, and curst, like me.
Here, through all seasons, shall my face
  Behold its image silently.'
And from that hour I linger'd there
  In protestation and despair.

For mark, the hills were stone and sand,
  Not strewn with scented red or green—
All empty as a dead man's hand,
  And empty lay the Mere between.
No flocks fed there, no shepherd's cry
Awoke the echoes of the sky.

And through a sullen mist I came,
  And beast-like crept unto my lair ;
And many days I crouched in shame
  Out of the sunshine and sweet air.
I heard the passing wind and rain,
Like weary waves within the brain.

But when I rose and glimmer'd forth,
  Ghost-wise across my threshold cold,
The clouds had lifted west and north,
  And all the peaks were touch'd with gold.
I smiled in scorn ; far down beneath
The waters lay as dark as death.

I said, 'Go by, O golden light !
  Thou canst not scatter darkness *here*.
In two sad bosoms there is night,
  In mine and in the lonely Mere ;
Light thou thy lamps, and go thy way.'
It went, and all the heavens grew grey.

And when the lamps of heaven were lit,
  I did not raise mine eyes to see,
But watch'd the ghostly glimmers flit
  On the black waters silently.
I hid my face from heaven, and kept
Dark vigil when the bright sun slept.

And ever when the daylight grew
  I saw with joy the hills were high ;
From dawn to dark, the live day through,
  Not lighting as the sun went by ;
Only at noon one finger-ray
Touch'd us, and then was drawn away.

I cried, 'God cannot find me now ;
  Done now am I with praise or pain.'
Beside the Mere, with darken'd brow,
  I walk'd as desolate as Cain.
I cried, 'Not even God could rear
One seed of love or blessing here !'

'Twas Spring that day ; the air was chill ;
  Above the heights white clouds were roll'd,
The Mere below was blue as steel,
  And all the air was chill and cold,
When suddenly from air and sky
I heard a solitary cry.

Ah me ! it was the same sweet sound
  That I had heard afar away ;
Sad echoes waken'd all around
  Out of the rocks and caverns grey,
And looking upward, weary-eyed,
I saw the gentle bird that cried.

Upon a rock sat that sweet bird,
  As he had sat on pale or tree,
And while the hills and waters heard,
  He named his name to them and me.
I thought, 'God sends the Spring again,
But here at least it comes in vain !'

From rock to rock I saw him fly,
  Silent in flight, but loud at rest ;
And ever at his summer cry
  The mountains gladden'd and seem'd bless'd,
And in the hollows of them all
Faint flames of grass began to crawl !

Some secret hand I could not see
  Was busy where I dwelt alone ;
It touched with tender tracery,
  Faint as a breath, the cliffs of stone ;
Out of the earth it drew soft moss,
And lichens shapen like the Cross.

And lo ! at every step I took
  Some faint life lived, some sweetness stirred,
While loosen'd torrents leapt and shook
  Their shining hair to hear the bird,
And white clouds ran across the blue,
And sweet sights rose, and sweet sounds grew.

I hated every sight and sound ;
  I hated most that happy cry.
I saw the mountains glory-crown'd,
  And the bright heavens drifting by ;

I felt the earth beneath my tread,
Now kindling quick, that late was dead!

Daily I stole unto the Mere,
And black as ever was its sleep.
Close to its margin all was drear;
I heard the weary waters creep.
I laugh'd aloud, ' Though all grow light,
We twain keep dark, in God's despite!

' We will not smile nor utter praise;
He made us dark, and dark we brood.
Sun-hating, desolate of days,
We dwell apart in solitude.
Let Him light lamps for all the land;
We darken and elude His hand.'

Scarce had I spoken in such wise,
When as before I heard the bird,
And lo! the Mere beneath mine eyes
Was deeply, mystically stirred:
A sunbeam broke its gloom apart,
And Heaven trembled in its heart;

There, clustering in that under-gloom,
Like rising stars that open dim,
Innumerable, leaf and bloom,
I saw the water-lilies swim,
Still 'neath the surface dark to sight,
But creeping upward to the light.

As countless as the lights above,
Stirring and glimmering below,
They gather'd; and I watched them move,
Till on the surface, white as snow,
One came, grew glad, and open'd up,
A pinch of gold in its white cup!

Then suddenly within my breast
Some life of rapture open'd too,
And I forgot my bitter quest,
Watching that glory as it grew;
For, leaf by leaf and flower by flower,
The lilies opened from that hour.

And soon the gloomy Mere was sown
With oilèd leaves and stars of white;
The trumpet of the wind was blown
Far overhead, from height to height,
And lo! the Mere, from day to day,
Grew starry as the Milky Way.

I could not bear to dwell apart
With so divine and bright a thing;
I felt the dark depths of my heart
Were stirring, trembling, wakening;

I watched the Mere, and saw it shine,
E'en as the eye of God on mine.

As one that riseth in his tomb,
I rose and wept in soul's distress;
I had not fear'd His wrath and gloom;
But now I fear'd His loveliness.
I craved for peace from God, and then
Crept back and made my peace with men!

MNEMOSYNE; OR, THE RETROSPECT.

STILL were the azure fields, thick strewn
With stars, and trod by luminous feet;
In the low west the wan white Moon
Walked in her winding-sheet—
Holding her taper up, to see
Thy cold fair face, Mnemosyne.

And on that face her lustre fell,
Deepening the marble pallor there,
While by the stream, and down the dell,
Thy slow still feet did fare;
Thy maiden thoughts were far from me,
Thy lips were dumb, Mnemosyne.

I knew thee by a simpler name,
Meet for a maid of English birth,
And though thy beauty put to shame
All beauty born of earth,
Not till that night could my soul see
Thy soul's dark depths, Mnemosyne!

At last thy voice thrilled soft and low—
'Oh, blessed be the silent night!
It brings strange life of long ago
Back to the soul's sad sight—
It trances sense, and thought is free
To tremble through eternity.

'Oh, thinkest thou this life we live,
In this strange haunted planet nurst,
So mystical, so fugitive,
Could be the *last?* or *first?*
Nay, I *remember!*'—Pale stood she,
Fronting the west, Mnemosyne.

The moonlight on her cheek of snow,
The star-dew on her raven hair,
Her eyes in one divine dark glow
On heaven, she waited there—
' Nay, I *remember!*' murmured she,
The earthly maid, Mnemosyne.

And as she spake, it seemed I saw
  Before me, in the mystic light,
That old Greek woman's-shape of awe,
  Large, lustrous-eyed, and white—
The twilight goddess, fair to see,
With heavenly eyes—Mnemosyne!

The haunter of green moonlit tombs,
  The reader of old midnight lore,
The glorious walker through God's glooms,
  Back-looking evermore.
I shook, and almost bent the knee,
Naming the name, 'Mnemosyne!' . . .

'I can *remember!*—all the day
  Memory is dark, the past is dead,
But when the sunshine fades away,
  And in the void o'erhead
Heaven's eyes flash open, I can see
That lost life!' said Mnemosyne.

'Before this mortal sphere I trod,
  I breathed some strange and heavenly air;
Ay, wandered 'mid the glooms of God,
  A living soul, up there!
The old lost life comes back to me
With starry gleams of memory!

'I can *remember!*'—In a trance,
  O love, thou didst upgazing stand,
Nor turned from heaven thy lustrous glance,
  While soft I kissed thy hand,
Whispering that mystic name to thee,
'Mnemosyne! Mnemosyne!'

And all the luminous eyes above
  Concentred one still gaze on thine,
When warm wild words of earthly love
  Poured in thine ears divine,
Till, with thy soft lips kissing me,
Thy soul saw mine, Mnemosyne!

A sense of that forgotten life
  Blew on our cheeks like living breath;
Lifted beyond the world's dark strife,
  Above the gates of Death,
Hand linked in hand, again lived we
That starlight life of ecstasy!

Go by, bright days of golden blooms!
  She shrinks and darkens in your gleam;
Come, starry nights and mystic glooms,
  And deepen that sweet dream!
Let her remember; let her be
Priestess of peace—Mnemosyne!

O child of heaven, the life we live,
  In this strange haunted planet nurst,
So mystical, so fugitive,
  Is *not* the last, or first;
That lost life was, new life shall be—
So keep thy name,—'Mnemosyne!'

VANITY FAIR.

I.

HERE'S a babble
  In Vanity Fair!
Here's a rabble
  Of folk on the stare!
Here's a crying,
Selling and buying,
Groaning and grumbling,
Pushing and stumbling!
Tootle-te-toot!
  Rum-ti-tum-tum!
They blow the flute,
  And they beat the drum.
And yonder in rows
Are the painted shows,
Where zany and clown
  With 'Walk in, walk in!'
Stalk up and down,
  While the people grin.
Hold me tighter, my pretty one,
We'll elbow our way and see the fun.
In we go, where they scramble and scream—
What a rabble! it's like a dream!

  Trip it merrily,
    Pretty one,
  On we stray cheerily
    Full of the fun:
  Punch and Judy;
    Fiddlestring;
  Acrobats moody
    Making a ring;
  Clowns cutting capers
    At every show;
  Bucolic gapers
    Grinning below;
Quiet conjurers quick and sly
Making the public halfpence fly;
Quacks with boluses, nostrums, and pills,
Vending cures for the flesh and its ills;
Every one bawling—(O the din!)
Every voice calling—'Walk in, walk in,'

VANITY FAIR.

'*Stop the thief!*'—how they carry the shout!
How the crowd eddies in and out!
Lean and thin with quivering lip
The rascal writhes in his captor's grip:
He looks all round with a hungry stare;
The mob groans round him and longs to tear—
Off to the gaol the scarecrow bear!
We're virtuous people in Vanity Fair!

    All together,
      Christian and Jew,
    Birds of fine feather,
      And ragged too,
    Dukes and earls,
    And ballet girls,
    Philosophers,
    And patterers;
    The poor from the city,
      The wild sea-rover,
    The beggar witty
      Half-seas over,
    The gipsy pretty
      Red from a romp in the clover.
Right foot, left foot, we trip it and toe it,
You the pretty girl, I your poet,
Rubbing sleeves with great and small,
Jostling along through the heart of them all.
Our hearts are leaping, our heads are dizzy,
The trade's so merry, the mirth so busy,
We squeeze along and we gasp for air,
In the hurry and flurry of Vanity Fair.

        II.

    Clari, my sweetest,
    Trimmest and neatest,
      Why this alarm?
    Why are you sighing,
    Fluttering and crying,
      And gripping my arm?
    'Come away! come away!
      'Tis so sad! 'Tis so loud!
    My soul swoons away,
      To look at the crowd!
    O hark how they cry—
    I am sick, let us fly!'
O Clari, sweet blending of fire and of air,
Come along, come along, out of Vanity Fair.

Out yonder are fields and the sky and the trees—
And the only sounds there are the birds and the breeze,
And the water that throbs in its green woodland nest,
Like the heart that is beating so loud in your breast.

    . . . Breathless, flushing,
    Faint with the crushing,
      Here we are—
    Night is coming,
    Droning and humming
      Sounds Vanity Fair afar;
    And its light, as the night
    Cometh down, is cast bright
      On the sky far away . . .
    How strange feels this stillness!
    Grey and more grey
      Comes the night with its chillness.
Clari, where are we? Outside the Fair,
With the great black earth and the sky and the air.
All alone—Hold me tighter! The noise of the rout
Was dreadful within, but more dreadful without
Seems the silence. O God! see the pale moon arise,
And the hills black as ink in the shade, and the eyes
Of the stars fix'd on ours from the terrible skies.

    What is this looming
      Against the light,
    Silent and glooming
      In the chilly night?
    And what are these clinging,
      Three in a row,
    Dismally, swinging
      When the wind doth blow?
Three black figures against the light,
Their faces white and their legs strapt tight,
Having a swing in the wind this night!
O hold me faster, who is she
That stands at the foot of the cross-shaped tree?
Cowl'd, barefooted, with hooded face,
What doth she in the ghostly place?
Silent she stands, a sad beholder!
Stop, let me touch her on the shoulder.

The moon shines cold
  On the silent place—
O God, I behold
  The dear dead face!
She turns unto me
  Calm and white,
Her eyes thrill through me
  With piteous light.
How cold yet how sweet
  In the night-wind she stands!

See, the poor wounded feet!
  See, the poor pleading hands!
Is it she? Kneel and pray! O my child,
  have no care,
She is near—Hath she fled? Did we dream?
  Was she there?
Ah, cold is the night, and the earth lieth bare,
And, distant and deep, a dull sound fills the air—
The wash of the waters of Vanity Fair.

LONDON : PRINTED BY
SPOTTISWOODE AND CO., NEW-STREET SQUARE
AND PARLIAMENT STREET

[October, 1884.

CHATTO & WINDUS'S
LIST OF BOOKS.

About.—The Fellah: An Egyptian Novel. By EDMOND ABOUT. Translated by Sir RANDAL ROBERTS. Post 8vo, illustrated boards, 2s.; cloth limp, 2s. 6d.

Adams (W. Davenport), Works by:
A Dictionary of the Drama. Being a comprehensive Guide to the Plays, Playwrights, Players, and Playhouses of the United Kingdom and America, from the Earliest to the Present Times. Crown 8vo, half-bound, 12s. 6d. [*Preparing.*
Latter-Day Lyrics. Edited by W. DAVENPORT ADAMS. Post 8vo, cloth limp, 2s. 6d.
Quips and Quiddities. Selected by W. DAVENPORT ADAMS. Post 8vo, cloth limp, 2s. 6d.

Advertising, A History of, from the Earliest Times. Illustrated by Anecdotes, Curious Specimens, and Notices of Successful Advertisers. By HENRY SAMPSON. Crown 8vo, with Coloured Frontispiece and Illustrations, cloth gilt, 7s. 6d.

Agony Column (The) of "The Times," from 1800 to 1870. Edited, with an Introduction, by ALICE CLAY. Post 8vo, cloth limp, 2s. 6d.

Aïdé (Hamilton), Works by:
Carr of Carrlyon. Post 8vo, illustrated boards, 2s.
Confidences. Post 8vo, illustrated boards, 2s.

Alexander (Mrs.).—Maid, Wife, or Widow? A Romance. By Mrs. ALEXANDER. Post 8vo, illustrated boards, 2s.; cr. 8vo, cloth extra, 3s. 6d.

Allen (Grant), Works by:
Crown 8vo, cloth extra, 6s. each.
The Evolutionist at Large. Second Edition, revised.
Vignettes from Nature.
Colin Clout's Calendar.
Nightmares: A Collection of Stories.

Architectural Styles, A Handbook of. Translated from the German of A. ROSENGARTEN, by W. COLLETT-SANDARS. Crown 8vo, cloth extra, with 639 Illustrations, 7s. 6d.

Art (The) of Amusing: A Collection of Graceful Arts, Games, Tricks, Puzzles, and Charades. By FRANK BELLEW. With 300 Illustrations. Cr. 8vo, cloth extra, 4s. 6d.

Artemus Ward:
Artemus Ward's Works: The Works of CHARLES FARRER BROWNE, better known as ARTEMUS WARD. With Portrait and Facsimile. Crown 8vo, cloth extra, 7s. 6d.
Artemus Ward's Lecture on the Mormons. With 32 Illustrations. Edited, with Preface, by EDWARD P. HINGSTON. Crown 8vo, 6d.
The Genial Showman: Life and Adventures of Artemus Ward. By EDWARD P. HINGSTON. With a Frontispiece. Crown 8vo, cloth extra, 3s. 6d.

BOOKS PUBLISHED BY

Ashton (John), Works by:
A History of the Chap-Books of the Eighteenth Century. With nearly 400 Illusts., engraved in facsimile of the originals. Cr. 8vo, cl. ex., 7s. 6d.
Social Life in the Reign of Queen Anne. From Original Sources. With nearly 100 Illusts. Cr.8vo,cl.ex.,7s.6d.
Humour, Wit, and Satire of the Seventeenth Century. With nearly 100 Illusts. Cr. 8vo, cl. extra, 7s. 6d.
English Caricature and Satire on Napoleon the First. 120 Illusts. from Originals. Two Vols., demy 8vo.

Bacteria.—A Synopsis of the Bacteria and Yeast Fungi and Allied Species. By W. B. GROVE, B.A. With 87 Illusts. Crown 8vo, cl. extra, 3s. 6d.

Balzac's " Comedie Humaine " and its Author. With Translations by H. H. WALKER. Post 8vo, cl. limp. 2s. 6d.

Bankers, A Handbook of London; together with Lists of Bankers from 1677. By F. G. HILTON PRICE. Crown 8vo, cloth extra, 7s. 6d.

Bardsley (Rev. C.W.), Works by:
English Surnames: Their Sources and Significations. Third Ed., revised. Cr. 8vo, cl. extra. 7s. 6d. [Preparing.
Curiosities of Puritan Nomenclature. Crown 8vo, cloth extra, 7s. 6d.

Bartholomew Fair, Memoirs of. By HENRY MORLEY. With 100 Illusts. Crown 8vo. cloth extra, 7s. 6d.

Basil, Novels by:
A Drawn Game. Three Vols., cr. 8vo.
The Wearing of the Green. Three Vols., crown 8vo.   [Shortly.

Beaconsfield, Lord: A Biography. By T. P. O'CONNOR, M.P. Sixth Edit., New Preface. Cr.8vo,cl.ex.7s.6d.

Beauchamp. — Grantley Grange: A Novel. By SHELSLEY BEAUCHAMP. Post 8vo, illust. bds., 2s.

Beautiful Pictures by British Artists: A Gathering of Favourites from our Picture Galleries. In Two Series. All engraved on Steel in the highest style of Art. Edited, with Notices of the Artists, by SYDNEY ARMYTAGE, M.A. Imperial 4to, cloth extra, gilt and gilt edges, 21s. per Vol.

Bechstein. — As Pretty as Seven, and other German Stories. Collected by LUDWIG BECHSTEIN. With Additional Tales by the Brothers GRIMM, and 100 Illusts. by RICHTER. Small 4to, green and gold, 6s. 6d.; gilt edges, 7s. 6d.

Beerbohm.—Wanderings in Patagonia; or, Life among the Ostrich Hunters. By JULIUS BEERBOHM. With Illusts. Crown 8vo, cloth extra, 3s. 6d.

Belgravia for 1885. One Shilling Monthly. A Strange Voyage, by W. CLARK RUSSELL, will be begun in the JANUARY Number and continued throughout the year. This Number will contain also the Opening Chapters of a New Story by CECIL POWER, Author of " Philistia," entitled Babylon, and Illustrated by P. MACNAB.
⁎ Now ready, the Volume for JULY to OCTOBER 1884, cloth extra, gilt edges, 7s. 6d.; Cases for binding Vols., 2s. each.

Belgravia Annual. With Stories by F. W. ROBINSON, J. ARBUTHNOT WILSON, JUSTIN H. MCCARTHY, B. MONTGOMERIE RANKING, and others. Demy 8vo, with Illusts., 1s. [Preparing.

Bennett (W.C.,LL.D.),Works by:
A Ballad History of England. Post 8vo, cloth limp, 2s.
Songs for Sailors. Post 8vo, cloth limp, 2s.

Besant (Walter) and James Rice, Novels by. Post 8vo, illust. boards, 2s. each; cloth limp, 2s 6d. each; or crown 8vo, cloth extra, 3s. 6d. each.
Ready-Money Mortiboy.
With Harp and Crown.
This Son of Vulcan.
My Little Girl.
The Case of Mr. Lucraft.
The Golden Butterfly.
By Celia's Arbour.
The Monks of Thelema.
'Twas in Trafalgar's Bay.
The Seamy Side.
The Ten Years' Tenant.
The Chaplain of the Fleet.

Besant (Walter), Novels by:
All Sorts and Conditions of Men: An Impossible Story With Illustrations by FRED. BARNARD. Crown 8vo, cloth extra, 3s. 6d.; post 8vo, illust. boards, 2s ; cloth limp, 2s. 6d.
The Captains' Room, &c. With Frontispiece by E. J. WHEELER. Crown 8vo, cloth extra, 3s. 6d ; post 8vo, illust. bds., 2s ; cl. limp, 2s. 6d.
All In a Garden Fair. With 6 Illusts. by H. FURNISS New and Cheaper Edition. Cr. 8vo, cl. extra, 3s. 6d.
Dorothy Forster. New and Cheaper Edition. With Illustrations by CH. GREEN. Crown 8vo, cloth extra, 3s. 6d.   [Preparing.

The Art of Fiction. Demy 8vo, 1s.

CHATTO & WINDUS, PICCADILLY.

Betham-Edwards (M.), Novels by. Crown 8vo, cloth extra, 3s. 6d. each.; post 8vo, illust. bds., 2s. each.
Felicia. | Kitty.

Bewick (Thos.) and his Pupils. By Austin Dobson. With 95 Illustrations. Square 8vo, cloth extra, 10s. 6d.

Birthday Books:—
The Starry Heavens: A Poetical Birthday Book. Square 8vo, handsomely bound in cloth, 2s. 6d.
Birthday Flowers: Their Language and Legends. By W. J. Gordon. Beautifully Illustrated in Colours by Viola Boughton. In illuminated cover, crown 4to, 6s.
The Lowell Birthday Book. With Illusts., small 8vo, cloth extra, 4s. 6d.

Blackburn's (Henry) Art Handbooks. Demy 8vo, Illustrated, uniform in size for binding.
Academy Notes, separate years, from 1875 to 1883, each 1s.
Academy Notes, 1884. With 152 Illustrations. 1s.
Academy Notes, 1875-79. Complete in One Vol., with nearly 600 Illusts. in Facsimile. Demy 8vo, cloth limp, 6s.
Academy Notes, 1880-84. Complete in One Volume, with about 700 Facsimile Illustrations. Cloth limp, 6s.
Grosvenor Notes, 1877. 6d.
Grosvenor Notes, separate years, from 1878 to 1883, each 1s.
Grosvenor Notes, 1884. With 75 Illustrations 1s.
Grosvenor Notes, 1877-82. With upwards of 300 Illustrations. Demy 8vo, cloth limp, 6s.
Pictures at South Kensington. With 70 Illustrations. 1s.
The English Pictures at the National Gallery. 114 Illustrations. 1s.
The Old Masters at the National Gallery. 128 Illustrations. 1s. 6d.
A Complete Illustrated Catalogue to the National Gallery. With Notes by H. Blackburn, and 242 Illusts. Demy 8vo, cloth limp, 3s.

Illustrated Catalogue of the Luxembourg Gallery. Containing about 250 Reproductions after the Original Drawings of the Artists. Edited by F. G. Dumas. Demy 8vo, 3s. 6d.

The Paris Salon, 1884. With over 300 Illusts. Edited by F. G. Dumas. Demy 8vo, 3s.

Art Handbooks, continued—
The Art Annual, 1883-4. Edited by F. G. Dumas. With 300 full-page Illustrations. Demy 8vo, 5s.

Boccaccio's Decameron; or, Ten Days' Entertainment. Translated into English, with an Introduction by Thomas Wright, F.S.A. With Portrait, and Stothard's beautiful Copperplates. Cr. 8vo, cloth extra, gilt, 7s. 6d.

Blake (William): Etchings from his Works. By W. B. Scott. With descriptive Text. Folio, half-bound boards, India Proofs, 21s.

Bowers'(G.) Hunting Sketches:
Canters in Crampshire. Oblong 4to, half-bound boards, 21s.
Leaves from a Hunting Journal. Coloured in facsimile of the originals. Oblong 4to, half-bound, 21s.

Boyle (Frederick), Works by:
Camp Notes: Stories of Sport and Adventure in Asia, Africa, and America. Crown 8vo, cloth extra, 3s. 6d.; post 8vo, illustrated bds., 2s.
Savage Life. Crown 8vo, cloth extra, 3s. 6d.; post 8vo, illustrated bds., 2s.

Brand's Observations on Popular Antiquities, chiefly Illustrating the Origin of our Vulgar Customs, Ceremonies, and Superstitions. With the Additions of Sir Henry Ellis. Crown 8vo, cloth extra, gilt, with numerous Illustrations, 7s. 6d.

Bret Harte, Works by:
Bret Harte's Collected Works. Arranged and Revised by the Author. Complete in Five Vols., crown 8vo, cloth extra, 6s. each.
Vol. I. Complete Poetical and Dramatic Works. With Steel Portrait, and Introduction by Author.
Vol. II. Earlier Papers - Luck of Roaring Camp, and other Sketches — Bohemian Papers — Spanish and American Legends.
Vol. III. Talks of the Argonauts — Eastern Sketches.
Vol. IV. Gabriel Conroy.
Vol. V. Stories — Condensed Novels, &c.
The Select Works of Bret Harte, in Prose and Poetry. With Introductory Essay by J. M. Bellew, Portrait of the Author, and 50 Illustrations. Crown 8vo, cloth extra, 7s. 6d.
Gabriel Conroy: A Novel. Post 8vo, illustrated boards, 2s.

BOOKS PUBLISHED BY

BRET HARTE'S WORKS, *continued—*
An Heiress of Red Dog, and other Stories. Post 8vo, illustrated boards, 2s.; cloth limp, 2s. 6d.
The Twins of Table Mountain. Fcap. 8vo, picture cover, 1s.; crown 8vo, cloth extra, 3s. 6d.
Luck of Roaring Camp, and other Sketches. Post 8vo, illust. bds., 2s.
Jeff Briggs's Love Story. Fcap. 8vo, picture cover, 1s.; cloth extra, 2s. 6d.
Flip. Post 8vo, illustrated boards, 2s.; cloth limp, 2s. 6d.
Californian Stories (including THE TWINS OF TABLE MOUNTAIN, JEFF BRIGGS'S LOVE STORY, &c.) Post 8vo, illustrated boards, 2s.

Brewer (Rev. Dr.), Works by :
The Reader's Handbook of Allusions, References, Plots, and Stories. Fourth Edition, revised throughout, with a New Appendix, containing a COMPLETE ENGLISH BIBLIOGRAPHY. Cr. 8vo, 1,400 pp., cloth extra, 7s. 6d.
Authors and their Works, with the Dates: Being the Appendices to "The Reader's Handbook," separately printed. Cr. 8vo, cloth limp, 2s.
A Dictionary of Miracles: Imitative, Realistic, and Dogmatic. Crown 8vo, cloth extra, 7s. 6d.; half-bound, 9s.

Brewster (Sir David), Works by:
More Worlds than One: The Creed of the Philosopher and the Hope of the Christian. With Plates. Post 8vo, cloth extra, 4s. 6d.
The Martyrs of Science: Lives of GALILEO, TYCHO BRAHE, and KEPLER. With Portraits. Post 8vo, cloth extra, 4s. 6d.
Letters on Natural Magic. A New Edition, with numerous Illustrations, and Chapters on the Being and Faculties of Man, and Additional Phenomena of Natural Magic, by J. A. SMITH. Post 8vo, cloth extra, 4s. 6d.

Brillat-Savarin.—Gastronomy as a Fine Art. By BRILLAT-SAVARIN. Translated by R. E. ANDERSON, M.A. Post 8vo, cloth limp, 2s. 6d.

Burnett (Mrs.), Novels by :
Surly Tim, and other Stories. Post 8vo, illustrated boards, 2s.
Kathleen Mavourneen. Fcap. 8vo, picture cover, 1s.
Lindsay's Luck. Fcap. 8vo, picture cover, 1s.
Pretty Polly Pemberton. Fcap. 8vo, picture cover, 1s.

Buchanan's (Robert) Works :
Ballads of Life, Love, and Humour. With a Frontispiece by ARTHUR HUGHES. Crown 8vo, cloth extra, 6s.
Selected Poems of Robert Buchanan. With Frontispiece by T. DALZIEL. Crown 8vo, cloth extra, 6s.
Undertones. Cr. 8vo, cloth extra, 6s.
London Poems. Cr. 8vo, cl. extra, 6s.
The Book of Orm. Crown 8vo, cloth extra, 6s.
White Rose and Red: A Love Story. Crown 8vo, cloth extra, 6s.
Idylls and Legends of Inverburn. Crown 8vo, cloth extra, 6s.
St. Abe and his Seven Wives: A Tale of Salt Lake City. With a Frontispiece by A. B. HOUGHTON. Crown 8vo, cloth extra, 5s.
Robert Buchanan's Complete Poetical Works. With Steel-plate Portrait. Crown 8vo, cloth extra, 7s. 6d. [*In the press.*
The Hebrid Isles: Wanderings in the Land of Lorne and the Outer Hebrides. With Frontispiece by W. SMALL. Crown 8vo, cloth extra, 6s.
A Poet's Sketch-Book: Selections from the Prose Writings of ROBERT BUCHANAN. Crown 8vo, cl. extra, 6s.
The Shadow of the Sword: A Romance. Crown 8vo, cloth extra, 3s. 6d.; post 8vo, illust. boards, 2s.
A Child of Nature: A Romance. With a Frontispiece. Crown 8vo, cloth extra, 3s. 6d.; post 8vo, illust. bds., 2s.
God and the Man: A Romance. With Illustrations by FRED. BARNARD. Crown 8vo, cloth extra, 3s. 6d.; post 8vo, illustrated boards, 2s.
The Martyrdom of Madeline: A Romance. With Frontispiece by A.W. COOPER. Cr. 8vo, cloth extra, 3s. 6d.; post 8vo, illustrated boards, 2s.
Love Me for Ever. With a Frontispiece by P. MACNAB. Crown 8vo, cloth extra, 3s. 6d.; post 8vo, illustrated boards, 2s.
Annan Water: A Romance. Crown 8vo, cloth extra, 3s. 6d.
The New Abelard: A Romance. Crown 8vo, cloth extra, 3s. 6d.
Foxglove Manor: A Novel. Three Vols., crown 8vo.

Burton (Robert):
The Anatomy of Melancholy. A New Edition, complete, corrected and enriched by Translations of the Classical Extracts. Demy 8vo, cloth extra, 7s. 6d.
Melancholy Anatomised: Being an Abridgment, for popular use, of BURTON'S ANATOMY OF MELANCHOLY, Post 8vo, cloth limp, 2s. 6d.

Burton (Captain), Works by:
To the Gold Coast for Gold: A Personal Narrative. By RICHARD F. BURTON and VERNEY LOVETT CAMERON. With Maps and Frontispiece. Two Vols., crown 8vo, cloth extra, 21s.

The Book of the Sword: Being a History of the Sword and its Use in all Countries, from the Earliest Times. By RICHARD F. BURTON. With over 400 Illustrations. Square 8vo, cloth extra, 32s.

Bunyan's Pilgrim's Progress.
Edited by Rev. T. SCOTT. With 17 Steel Plates by STOTHARD, engraved by GOODALL, and numerous Woodcuts. Crown 8vo, cloth extra, gilt, 7s. 6d.

Byron (Lord):
Byron's Letters and Journals. With Notices of his Life. By THOMAS MOORE. A Reprint of the Original Edition, newly revised, with Twelve full-page Plates. Crown 8vo, cloth extra, gilt, 7s. 6d.

Byron's Don Juan. Complete in One Vol., post 8vo, cloth limp, 2s.

Cameron (Commander) and Captain Burton.—To the Gold Coast for Gold: A Personal Narrative. By RICHARD F. BURTON and VERNEY LOVETT CAMERON. With Frontispiece and Maps. Two Vols., crown 8vo, cloth extra, 21s.

Cameron (Mrs. H. Lovett), Novels by:
Crown 8vo, cloth extra, 3s. 6d. each; post 8vo, illustrated boards, 2s. each.
Juliet's Guardian.
Deceivers Ever.

Campbell.—White and Black:
Travels in the United States. By Sir GEORGE CAMPBELL, M.P. Demy 8vo, cloth extra, 14s.

Carlyle (Thomas):
Thomas Carlyle: Letters and Recollections. By MONCURE D. CONWAY, M.A. Crown 8vo, cloth extra, with Illustrations, 6s.

On the Choice of Books. By THOMAS CARLYLE. With a Life of the Author by R. H. SHEPHERD. New and Revised Edition, post 8vo, cloth extra, Illustrated, 1s. 6d.

The Correspondence of Thomas Carlyle and Ralph Waldo Emerson, 1834 to 1872. Edited by CHARLES ELIOT NORTON. With Portraits. Two Vols., crown 8vo, cloth extra, 24s.

Chapman's (George) Works:
Vol. I. contains the Plays complete, Including the doubtful ones. Vol. II., the Poems and Minor Translations, with an Introductory Essay by ALGERNON CHARLES SWINBURNE. Vol. III., the Translations of the Iliad and Odyssey. Three Vols., crown 8vo, cloth extra, 18s.; or separately, 6s. each.

Chatto & Jackson.—A Treatise on Wood Engraving, Historical and Practical. By WM. ANDREW CHATTO and JOHN JACKSON. With an Additional Chapter by HENRY G. BOHN; and 450 fine Illustrations. A Reprint of the last Revised Edition. Large 4to, half-bound, 28s.

Chaucer:
Chaucer for Children: A Golden Key. By Mrs. H. R. HAWEIS. With Eight Coloured Pictures and numerous Woodcuts by the Author. New Ed., small 4to, cloth extra, 6s.
Chaucer for Schools. By Mrs. H. R. HAWEIS. Demy 8vo, cloth limp, 2s. 6d.

City (The) of Dream: A Poem. Fcap. 8vo, cloth extra, 6s. [*In the press.*

Cobban.—The Cure of Souls: A Story. By J. MACLAREN COBBAN. Post 8vo, illustrated boards, 2s.

Collins (C. Allston).—The Bar Sinister: A Story. By C. ALLSTON COLLINS. Post 8vo, illustrated bds., 2s.

Collins (Mortimer & Frances), Novels by:
Sweet and Twenty. Post 8vo, illustrated boards, 2s.
Frances. Post 8vo, illust. bds., 2s.
Blacksmith and Scholar. Post 8vo, illustrated boards, 2s.; crown 8vo, cloth extra, 3s. 6d.
The Village Comedy. Post 8vo, illust. boards, 2s.; cr. 8vo, cloth extra, 3s. 6d.
You Play Me False. Post 8vo, illust. boards, 2s.; cr. 8vo, cloth extra, 3s. 6d.

Collins (Mortimer), Novels by:
Sweet Anne Page. Post 8vo, illustrated boards, 2s.; crown 8vo, cloth extra, 3s. 6d.
Transmigration. Post 8vo, illustrated boards, 2s.; crown 8vo, cloth extra, 3s. 6d.
From Midnight to Midnight. Post 8vo, illustrated boards, 2s.; crown 8vo, cloth extra, 3s. 6d.
A Fight with Fortune. Post 8vo illustrated boards, 2s.

Collins (Wilkie), Novels by.
Each post 8vo, illustrated boards, 2s.; cloth limp, 2s. 6d.; or crown 8vo, cloth extra, illustrated, 3s. 6d.
Antonina. Illust. by A. Concanen.
Basil. Illustrated by Sir John Gilbert and J. Mahoney.
Hide and Seek. Illustrated by Sir John Gilbert and J. Mahoney.
The Dead Secret. Illustrated by Sir John Gilbert and A. Concanen.
Queen of Hearts Illustrated by Sir John Gilbert and A. Concanen.
My Miscellanies. With Illustrations by A. Concanen, and a Steel-plate Portrait of Wilkie Collins.
The Woman in White. With Illustrations by Sir John Gilbert and F. A. Fraser.
The Moonstone. With Illustrations by G. Du Maurier and F. A. Fraser.
Man and Wife. Illust. by W. Small.
Poor Miss Finch. Illustrated by G. Du Maurier and Edward Hughes.
Miss or Mrs.? With Illustrations by S. L. Fildes and Henry Woods.
The New Magdalen. Illustrated by G. Du Maurier and C. S. Rands.
The Frozen Deep. Illustrated by G. Du Maurier and J. Mahoney.
The Law and the Lady. Illustrated by S. L. Fildes and Sydney Hall.
The Two Destinies.
The Haunted Hotel. Illustrated by Arthur Hopkins.
The Fallen Leaves.
Jezebel's Daughter.
The Black Robe.
Heart and Science: A Story of the Present Time. Crown 8vo, cloth extra, 3s. 6d.
"I Say No." Three Vols., crown 8vo. 31s 6d.   [*Shortly.*

Colman's Humorous Works:
"Broad Grins," "My Nightgown and Slippers," and other Humorous Works, Prose and Poetical, of George Colman. With Life by G. B Buckstone, and Frontispiece by Hogarth. Crown 8vo, cloth extra, gilt, 7s. 6d.

Convalescent Cookery: A Family Handbook. By Catherine Ryan. Post 8vo, 1s.; cl. limp, 1s. 6d.

Conway (Moncure D.), Works by:
Demonology and Devil-Lore. Two Vols., royal 8vo, with 65 Illusts., 28s.

Conway's (M. D.) Works, *continued*—
A Necklace of Stories. Illustrated by W. J. Hennessy. Square 8vo, cloth extra, 6s.
The Wandering Jew. Crown 8vo, cloth extra, 6s.
Thomas Carlyle: Letters and Recollections. With Illustrations. Crown 8vo, cloth extra, 6s.

Cook (Dutton), Works by:
Hours with the Players. With a Steel Plate Frontispiece. New and Cheaper Edit., cr. 8vo, cloth extra, 6s.
Nights at the Play: A View of the English Stage. New and Cheaper Edition. Crown 8vo, cloth extra, 6s.
Leo: A Novel. Post 8vo, illustrated boards, 2s.
Paul Foster's Daughter. Post 8vo, illustrated boards, 2s.; crown 8vo, cloth extra, 3s. 6d.

Cooper.—Heart Salvage, by Sea and Land. Stories by Mrs. Cooper (Katharine Saunders). Three Vols., crown 8vo.

Copyright. — A Handbook of English and Foreign Copyright in Literary and Dramatic Works. By Sidney Jerrold, of the Middle Temple, Esq., Barrister-at-Law. Post 8vo, cloth limp, 2s. 6d.

Cornwall.—Popular Romances of the West of England; or, The Drolls, Traditions, and Superstitions of Old Cornwall. Collected and Edited by Robert Hunt, F.R.S. New and Revised Edition, with Additions, and Two Steel-plate Illustrations by George Cruikshank. Crown 8vo, cloth extra, 7s. 6d.

Creasy.—Memoirs of Eminent Etonians: with Notices of the Early History of Eton College. By Sir Edward Creasy, Author of "The Fifteen Decisive Battles of the World." Crown 8vo, cloth extra, gilt, with 13 Portraits, 7s. 6d.

Cruikshank (George):
The Comic Almanack. Complete in Two Series: The First from 1835 to 1843; the Second from 1844 to 1853. A Gathering of the Best Humour of Thackeray, Hood, Mayhew, Albert Smith, A'Beckett, Robert Brough, &c. With 2,000 Woodcuts and Steel Engravings by Cruikshank, Hine, Landells, &c. Crown 8vo, cloth gilt, two very thick volumes, 7s. 6d. each.

CRUIKSHANK (G.), *continued*—
The Life of George Cruikshank. By BLANCHARD JERROLD, Author of "The Life of Napoleon III.," &c. With 84 Illustrations. New and Cheaper Edition, enlarged, with Additional Plates, and a very carefully compiled Bibliography. Crown 8vo, cloth extra, 7s. 6d.

Robinson Crusoe. A beautiful reproduction of Major's Edition, with 37 Woodcuts and Two Steel Plates by GEORGE CRUIKSHANK, choicely printed. Crown 8vo, cloth extra, 7s. 6d. A few Large-Paper copies, printed on hand-made paper, with India proofs of the Illustrations, 36s.

Cussans.—Handbook of Heraldry; with Instructions for Tracing Pedigrees and Deciphering Ancient MSS., &c. By JOHN E. CUSSANS. Entirely New and Revised Edition, illustrated with over 400 Woodcuts and Coloured Plates. Crown 8vo, cloth extra, 7s. 6d.

Cyples.—Hearts of Gold: A Novel. By WILLIAM CYPLES. Crown 8vo, cloth extra, 3s. 6d.

Daniel. — Merrie England in the Olden Time. By GEORGE DANIEL. With Illustrations by ROBT. CRUIKSHANK. Crown 8vo, cloth extra, 3s. 6d.

Daudet.—Port Salvation; or, The Evangelist. By ALPHONSE DAUDET. Translated by C. HARRY MELTZER. With Portrait of the Author. Crown 8vo, cloth extra, 3s. 6d.

Davenant.—What shall my Son be? Hints for Parents on the Choice of a Profession or Trade for their Sons. By FRANCIS DAVENANT, M.A. Post 8vo, cloth limp, 2s. 6d.

Davies (Dr. N. E.), Works by:
One Thousand Medical Maxims. Crown 8vo, 1s.; cloth, 1s. 6d.
Nursery Hints: A Mother's Guide. Crown 8vo, 1s.; cloth, 1s. 6d.
Aids to Long Life. Crown 8vo, 2s.; cloth limp, 2s. 6d. [*Shortly.*

Davies' (Sir John) Complete Poetical Works, including Psalms I. to L. in Verse, and other hitherto Unpublished MSS., for the first time Collected and Edited, with Memorial-Introduction and Notes, by the Rev. A. B. GROSART, D.D. Two Vols., crown 8vo, cloth boards, 12s.

De Maistre.—A Journey Round My Room. By XAVIER DE MAISTRE. Translated by HENRY ATTWELL. Post 8vo, cloth limp, 2s. 6d.

De Mille.—A Castle in Spain. A Novel. By JAMES DE MILLE. With a Frontispiece. Crown 8vo, cloth extra, 3s. 6d.

Derwent (Leith), Novels by:
Our Lady of Tears. Cr. 8vo, cloth extra, 3s. 6d.; post 8vo, illust. bds., 2s.
Circe's Lovers. Crown 8vo, cloth extra, 3s. 6d.

Dickens (Charles), Novels by: Post 8vo, illustrated boards, 2s. each.
Sketches by Boz. | **Nicholas Nickleby**
Pickwick Papers. | **Oliver Twist.**

The Speeches of Charles Dickens. (*Mayfair Library.*) Post 8vo, cloth mp, 2s. 6d.

The Speeches of Charles Dickens, 1841-1870. With a New Bibliography, revised and enlarged. Edited and Prefaced by RICHARD HERNE SHEPHERD. Crown 8vo, cloth extra, 6s.

About England with Dickens. By ALFRED RIMMER. With 57 Illustrations by C. A. VANDERHOOF, ALFRED RIMMER, and others. Sq. 8vo, cloth extra, 10s. 6d.

Dictionaries:
A Dictionary of Miracles: Imitative, Realistic, and Dogmatic. By the Rev. E. C. BREWER, LL.D. Crown 8vo, cloth extra, 7s. 6d.; hf.-bound, 9s.
The Reader's Handbook of Allusions, References, Plots, and Stories. By the Rev. E. C. BREWER, LL.D. Fourth Edition, revised throughout, with a New Appendix, containing a Complete English Bibliography. Crown 8vo, 1,400 pages, cloth extra, 7s. 6d.
Authors and their Works, with the Dates. Being the Appendices to "The Reader's Handbook," separately printed. By the Rev. E. C. BREWER, LL.D. Crown 8vo, cloth limp, 2s.
Familiar Allusions: A Handbook of Miscellaneous Information; including the Names of Celebrated Statues, Paintings, Palaces, Country Seats, Ruins, Churches, Ships, Streets, Clubs, Natural Curiosities and the like. By WM. A. WHEELER and CHARLES G. WHEELER. Demy 8vo cloth extra, 7s. 6d.

DICTIONARIES, *continued*—
Short Sayings of Great Men. With Historical and Explanatory Notes. By SAMUEL A. BENT, M.A. Demy 8vo, cloth extra, 7s. 6d.

A Dictionary of the Drama: Being a comprehensive Guide to the Plays, Playwrights, Players, and Playhouses of the United Kingdom and America, from the Earliest to the Present Times. By W. DAVENPORT ADAMS. A thick volume, crown 8vo, half-bound, 12s. 6d. [*In preparation.*

The Slang Dictionary: Etymological, Historical, and Anecdotal. Crown 8vo, cloth extra, 6s. 6d.

Women of the Day: A Biographical Dictionary. By FRANCES HAYS. Cr. 8vo, cloth extra, 6s.

Words, Facts, and Phrases: A Dictionary of Curious, Quaint, and Out-of-the-Way Matters. By ELIEZER EDWARDS. New and Cheaper Issue. Cr. 8vo, cl. ex., 7s. 6d.; hf.-bd., 9s.

Diderot.—The Paradox of Acting. Translated, with Annotations, from Diderot's "Le Paradoxe sur le Comédien," by WALTER HERRIES POLLOCK. With a Preface by HENRY IRVING. Cr. 8vo, in parchment, 4s. 6d.

Dobson (W. T.), Works by:
Literary Frivolities, Fancies, Follies, and Frolics. Post 8vo, cl. lp., 2s. 6d.
Poetical Ingenuities and Eccentricities. Post 8vo, cloth limp, 2s. 6d.

Doran. — Memories of our Great Towns; with Anecdotic Gleanings concerning their Worthies and their Oddities. By Dr. JOHN DORAN, F.S.A. With 38 Illustrations. New and Cheaper Ed., cr. 8vo, cl. ex., 7s. 6d.

Drama, A Dictionary of the. Being a comprehensive Guide to the Plays, Playwrights, Players, and Playhouses of the United Kingdom and America, from the Earliest to the Present Times. By W. DAVENPORT ADAMS. (Uniform with BREWER'S "Reader's Handbook.") Crown 8vo, half-bound, 12s. 6d. [*In preparation.*

Dramatists, The Old. Cr. 8vo, cl. ex., Vignette Portraits, 6s. per Vol.
Ben Jonson's Works. With Notes Critical and Explanatory, and a Biographical Memoir by WM. GIFFORD. Edit. by Col. CUNNINGHAM. 3 Vols.
Chapman's Works. Complete in Three Vols. Vol. I. contains the Plays complete, including doubtful ones; Vol. II., Poems and Minor Translations, with Introductory Essay by A. C. SWINBURNE; Vol. III., Translations of the Iliad and Odyssey.

DRAMATISTS, THE OLD, *continued*—
Marlowe's Works. Including his Translations. Edited, with Notes and Introduction, by Col. CUNNINGHAM. One Vol.
Massinger's Plays. From the Text of WILLIAM GIFFORD. Edited by Col. CUNNINGHAM. One Vol.

Dyer. — The Folk - Lore of Plants. By T. F. THISELTON DYER, M.A., &c. Crown 8vo, cloth extra, 7s. 6d. [*In preparation.*

Early English Poets. Edited, with Introductions and Annotations, by Rev. A. B. GROSART, D.D. Crown 8vo, cloth boards, 6s. per Volume.
Fletcher's (Giles, B.D.) Complete Poems. One Vol.
Davies' (Sir John) Complete Poetical Works. Two Vols.
Herrick's (Robert) Complete Collected Poems. Three Vols.
Sidney's (Sir Philip) Complete Poetical Works. Three Vols.

Herbert (Lord) of Cherbury's Poems. Edited, with Introduction, by J. CHURTON COLLINS. Crown 8vo, parchment, 8s.

Edwardes (Mrs. A.), Novels by:
A Point of Honour. Post 8vo, illustrated boards, 2s.
Archie Lovell. Post 8vo, illust. bds., 2s.; crown 8vo, cloth extra, 3s. 6d.

Eggleston.—Roxy: A Novel. By EDWARD EGGLESTON. Post 8vo, illust. boards, 2s.; cr. 8vo, cloth extra, 3s. 6d.

Emanuel.—On Diamonds and Precious Stones: their History, Value, and Properties; with Simple Tests for ascertaining their Reality. By HARRY EMANUEL, F.R.G.S. With numerous Illustrations, tinted and plain. Crown 8vo, cloth extra, gilt, 6s.

Englishman's House, The: A Practical Guide to all interested in Selecting or Building a House, with full Estimates of Cost, Quantities, &c. By C. J. RICHARDSON. Third Edition. Nearly 600 Illusts. Cr. 8vo, cl. ex., 7s. 6d.

Ewald (Alex. Charles, F.S.A.), Works by:
Stories from the State Papers. With an Autotype Facsimile. Crown 8vo, cloth extra, 6s.
The Life and Times of Prince Charles Stuart, Count of Albany, commonly called the Young Pretender. From the State Papers and other Sources. New and Cheaper Edition, with a Portrait, crown 8vo, cloth extra, 7s. 6d.

Eyes, The.—How to Use our Eyes, and How to Preserve Them. By JOHN BROWNING, F.R.A.S., &c. With 37 Illustrations. Crown 8vo, 1s.; cloth, 1s. 6d.

Fairholt.—Tobacco: Its History and Associations; with an Account of the Plant and its Manufacture, and its Modes of Use in all Ages and Countries. By F. W. FAIRHOLT, F.S.A. With Coloured Frontispiece and upwards of 100 Illustrations by the Author. Crown 8vo, cloth extra, 6s.

Familiar Allusions: A Handbook of Miscellaneous Information; including the Names of Celebrated Statues, Paintings, Palaces, Country Seats, Ruins, Churches, Ships, Streets, Clubs, Natural Curiosities, and the like. By WILLIAM A. WHEELER, Author of "Noted Names of Fiction;" and CHARLES G. WHEELER. Demy 8vo, cloth extra, 7s. 6d.

Faraday (Michael), Works by:
The Chemical History of a Candle: Lectures delivered before a Juvenile Audience at the Royal Institution. Edited by WILLIAM CROOKES, F.C.S. Post 8vo, cloth extra, with numerous Illustrations, 4s. 6d.

On the Various Forces of Nature, and their Relations to each other: Lectures delivered before a Juvenile Audience at the Royal Institution. Edited by WILLIAM CROOKES, F.C.S. Post 8vo, cloth extra, with numerous Illustrations, 4s. 6d.

Fin-Bec.—The Cupboard Papers: Observations on the Art of Living and Dining. By FIN-BEC. Post 8vo, cloth limp, 2s. 6d.

Fitzgerald (Percy), Works by:
The Recreations of a Literary Man; or, Does Writing Pay? With Recollections of some Literary Men, and a View of a Literary Man's Working Life. Cr. 8vo, cloth extra, 6s.
The World Behind the Scenes. Crown 8vo, cloth extra, 3s. 6d.
Little Essays: Passages from the Letters of CHARLES LAMB. Post 8vo, cloth limp, 2s. 6d.

Post 8vo, illustrated boards, 2s. each.
Bella Donna. | Never Forgotten.
The Second Mrs. Tillotson.
Polly.
Seventy-five Brooke Street.
The Lady of Brantome.

Fletcher's (Giles, B.D.) Complete Poems: Christ's Victorie in Heaven, Christ's Victorie on Earth, Christ's Triumph over Death, and Minor Poems. With Memorial-Introduction and Notes by the Rev. A. B. GROSART, D.D. Cr. 8vo, cloth bds., 6s.

Fonblanque.—Filthy Lucre: A Novel. By ALBANY DE FONBLANQUE. Post 8vo, illustrated boards, 2s.

Francillon (R. E.), Novels by:
Crown 8vo, cloth extra, 3s. 6d. each; post 8vo, illust. boards, 2s. each.
Olympia. | Queen Cophetua.
One by One.
Esther's Glove. Fcap. 8vo, picture cover, 1s.
A Real Queen. Cr. 8vo, cl. extra, 3s. 6d.

French Literature, History of. By HENRY VAN LAUN. Complete in 3 Vols., demy 8vo, cl. bds., 7s. 6d. each.

Frere.—Pandurang Hari; or, Memoirs of a Hindoo. With a Preface by Sir H. BARTLE FRERE, G.C.S.I., &c. Crown 8vo, cloth extra, 3s. 6d.; post 8vo, illustrated boards, 2s.

Friswell.—One of Two: A Novel. By HAIN FRISWELL. Post 8vo, illustrated boards, 2s.

Frost (Thomas), Works by:
Crown 8vo, cloth extra, 3s. 6d. each.
Circus Life and Circus Celebrities.
The Lives of the Conjurers.
The Old Showmen and the Old London Fairs.

Fry.—Royal Guide to the London Charities, 1884-5. By HERBERT FRY. Showing their Name, Date of Foundation, Objects, Income, Officials, &c. Published Annually. Crown 8vo, cloth, 1s. 6d.

Gardening Books:
A Year's Work in Garden and Greenhouse: Practical Advice to Amateur Gardeners as to the Management of the Flower, Fruit, and Frame Garden. By GEORGE GLENNY. Post 8vo, cloth limp, 2s. 6d.
Our Kitchen Garden: The Plants we Grow, and How we Cook Them. By TOM JERROLD. Post 8vo, cloth limp, 2s. 6d.
Household Horticulture: A Gossip about Flowers. By TOM and JANE JERROLD. Illust. Post 8vo,cl. lp.,2s.6d.
The Garden that Paid the Rent. By TOM JERROLD. Fcap. 8vo, illustrated cover, 1s.; cloth limp, 1s. 6d.
My Garden Wild, and What I Grew there. By F. G. HEATH. Crown 8vo, cloth extra, 5s.; gilt edges, 6s.

BOOKS PUBLISHED BY

Garrett.—The Capel Girls: A Novel. By EDWARD GARRETT. Post 8vo, illust. bds., 2s.; cr.8vo, cl.ex., 3s. 6d.

Gentleman's Magazine (The) for 1884. One Shilling Monthly. A New Serial Story, entitled "Philistia," by CECIL POWER, is now appearing. "Science Notes," by W. MATTIEU WILLIAMS, F.R.A.S., and "Table Talk," by SYLVANUS URBAN, are also continued monthly.

*** *Now ready, the Volume for* JANUARY *to* JUNE, 1884, *cloth extra, price* 8s. 6d.; *Cases for binding,* 2s. *each.*

German Popular Stories. Collected by the Brothers GRIMM, and Translated by EDGAR TAYLOR. Edited, with an Introduction, by JOHN RUSKIN. With 22 Illustrations on Steel by GEORGE CRUIKSHANK. Square 8vo, cloth extra, 6s. 6d.; gilt edges, 7s. 6d.

Gibbon (Charles), Novels by:
Crown 8vo, cloth extra, 3s. 6d. each; post 8vo, illustrated boards, 2s. each.
Robin Gray.
For Lack of Gold.
What will the World Say?
In Honour Bound.
In Love and War.
For the King.
Queen of the Meadow.
In Pastures Green
Braes of Yarrow.
The Flower of the Forest.
A Heart's Problem.

Post 8vo, illustrated boards, 2s.
The Dead Heart.

Crown 8vo, cloth extra, 3s. 6d. each.
The Golden Shaft.
Of High Degree.
Fancy Free.
Loving a Dream.

By Mead and Stream. Three Vols., crown 8vo.
Found Out. Three Vols., crown 8vo. [*Shortly.*

Gilbert (William), Novels by:
Post 8vo, illustrated boards, 2s. each.
Dr. Austin's Guests.
The Wizard of the Mountain.
James Duke, Costermonger.

Gilbert (W. S.), Original Plays by: In Two Series, each complete in itself, price 2s. 6d. each.
The FIRST SERIES contains—The Wicked World—Pygmalion and Galatea—Charity—The Princess—The Palace of Truth—Trial by Jury.
The SECOND SERIES contains—Broken Hearts—Engaged—Sweethearts—Gretchen—Dan'l Druce—Tom Cobb—H.M.S. Pinafore—The Sorcerer—The Pirates of Penzance.

Glenny.—A Year's Work in Garden and Greenhouse: Practical Advice to Amateur Gardeners as to the Management of the Flower, Fruit, and Frame Garden. By GEORGE GLENNY. Post 8vo, cloth limp, 2s. 6d.

Godwin.—Lives of the Necromancers. By WILLIAM GODWIN. Post 8vo, cloth limp, 2s.

Golden Library, The:
Square 16mo (Tauchnitz size), cloth limp, 2s. per volume.
Bayard Taylor's Diversions of the Echo Club.
Bennett's (Dr. W. C.) Ballad History of England.
Bennett's (Dr.) Songs for Sailors.
Byron's Don Juan.
Godwin's (William) Lives of the Necromancers.
Holmes's Autocrat of the Breakfast Table. With an Introduction by G. A. SALA.
Holmes's Professor at the Breakfast Table.
Hood's Whims and Oddities. Complete. All the original Illustrations.
Irving's (Washington) Tales of a Traveller.
Irving's (Washington) Tales of the Alhambra.
Jesse's (Edward) Scenes and Occupations of a Country Life.
Lamb's Essays of Elia. Both Series Complete in One Vol.
Leigh Hunt's Essays: A Tale for a Chimney Corner, and other Pieces. With Portrait, and Introduction by EDMUND OLLIER.
Mallory's (Sir Thomas) Mort d'Arthur: The Stories of King Arthur and of the Knights of the Round Table. Edited by B. MONTGOMERIE RANKING.
Pascal's Provincial Letters. A New Translation, with Historical Introduction and Notes, by T. M'CRIE, D.D.
Pope's Poetical Works. Complete.
Rochefoucauld's Maxims and Moral Reflections. With Notes, and Introductory Essay by SAINTE-BEUVE.
St. Pierre's Paul and Virginia, and The Indian Cottage. Edited, with Life, by the Rev. E. CLARKE.
Shelley's Early Poems, and Queen Mab. With Essay by LEIGH HUNT.
Shelley's Later Poems. Laon and Cythna, &c.
Shelley's Posthumous Poems, the Shelley Papers, &c.

GOLDEN LIBRARY, THE, *continued—*
Shelley's Prose Works, including A
Refutation of Deism, Zastrozzi, St.
Irvyne, &c.
White's Natural History of Selborne. Edited, with Additions, by
THOMAS BROWN, F.L.S.

Golden Treasury of Thought,
The: An ENCYCLOPÆDIA OF QUOTATIONS from Writers of all Times and
Countries. Selected and Edited by
THEODORE TAYLOR. Crown 8vo, cloth
gilt and gilt edges, 7s. 6d.

Gordon Cumming (C. F.), Works
by:
In the Hebrides. With Autotype Facsimile and numerous full-page Illustrations. Demy 8vo, cloth extra,
8s. 6d.
In the Himalayas and on the Indian Plains. With numerous Illustrations. Demy 8vo, cloth extra, 8s. 6d.
[*Shortly.*

Graham. — The Professor's
Wife: A Story. By LEONARD GRAHAM.
Fcap. 8vo, picture cover, 1s.; cloth
extra, 2s. 6d.

Greeks and Romans, The Life
of the, Described from Antique Monuments. By ERNST GUHL and W.
KONER. Translated from the Third
German Edition, and Edited by Dr.
F. HUEFFER. With 545 Illustrations.
New and Cheaper Edition, demy 8vo,
cloth extra, 7s. 6d.

Greenwood (James), Works by:
The Wilds of London. Crown 8vo,
cloth extra, 3s. 6d.
Low-Life Deeps: An Account of the
Strange Fish to be Found There.
Crown 8vo, cloth extra, 3s. 6d.
Dick Temple: A Novel. Post 8vo,
illustrated boards, 2s.

Guyot.— The Earth and Man;
or, Physical Geography in its relation
to the History of Mankind. By
ARNOLD GUYOT. With Additions by
Professors AGASSIZ, PIERCE, and GRAY;
12 Maps and Engravings on Steel,
some Coloured, and copious Index.
Crown 8vo, cloth extra, gilt, 4s. 6d.

Hair (The): Its Treatment in
Health, Weakness, and Disease.
Translated from the German of Dr. J.
PINCUS. Crown 8vo, 1s.

Hake (Dr. Thomas Gordon),
Poems by:
Maiden Ecstasy. Small 4to, cloth
extra, 8s.

HAKE'S (Dr. T. G.) POEMS, *continued—*
New Symbols. Crown 8vo, cloth
extra, 6s.
Legends of the Morrow. Crown 8vo
cloth extra, 6s.
The Serpent Play. Crown 8vo, cloth
extra, 6s.

Hall.—Sketches of Irish Character. By Mrs. S. C. HALL. With
numerous Illustrations on Steel and
Wood by MACLISE, GILBERT, HARVEY,
and G. CRUIKSHANK. Medium 8vo,
cloth extra, gilt, 7s. 6d.

Halliday.—Every-day Papers.
By ANDREW HALLIDAY. Post 8vo,
illustrated boards, 2s.

Handwriting, The Philosophy
of. With over 100 Facsimiles and Explanatory Text. By DON FELIX DE
SALAMANCA. Post 8vo, cloth limp,
2s. 6d.

Hanky-Panky: A Collection of
Very EasyTricks, Very Difficult Tricks,
White Magic, Sleight of Hand, &c.
Edited by W. H. CREMER. With 200
Illusts. Crown 8vo, cloth extra, 4s. 6d.

Hardy (Lady Duffus). — Paul
Wynter's Sacrifice: A Story. By
Lady DUFFUS HARDY. Post 8vo, illust.
boards, 2s.

Hardy (Thomas).—Under the
Greenwood Tree. By THOMAS HARDY,
Author of "Far from the Madding
Crowd." Crown 8vo, cloth extra,
3s. 6d.; post 8vo, illustrated bds., 2s.

Hawels (Mrs. H. R.), Works by:
The Art of Dress. With numerous
Illustrations. Small 8vo, illustrated
cover, 1s.; cloth limp, 1s. 6d.
The Art of Beauty. New and Cheaper
Edition. Crown 8vo, cloth extra,
with Coloured Frontispiece and Illustrations, 6s.
The Art of Decoration. Square 8vo,
handsomely bound and profusely
Illustrated, 10s. 6d.
Chaucer for Children: A Golden
Key. With Eight Coloured Pictures
and numerous Woodcuts. New
Edition, small 4to, cloth extra, 6s.
Chaucer for Schools. Demy 8vo,
cloth limp, 2s. 6d.

Hawels (Rev. H. R.).—American
Humorists. Including WASHINGTON
IRVING, OLIVER WENDELL HOLMES,
JAMES RUSSELL LOWELL, ARTEMUS
WARD, MARK TWAIN, and BRET HARTE.
By the Rev. H. R. HAWEIS, M.A.
Crown 8vo, cloth extra, 6s.

BOOKS PUBLISHED BY

Hawthorne (Julian), Novels by.
Crown 8vo, cloth extra, 3s. 6d. each;
post 8vo, illustrated boards, 2s. each.
Garth. | Sebastian Strome.
Ellice Quentin. | Dust.
Prince Saroni's Wife.

Mrs. Gainsborough's Diamonds.
Fcap. 8vo, illustrated cover, 1s.;
cloth extra, 2s. 6d.

Crown 8vo, cloth extra, 3s. 6d. each.
Fortune's Fool.
Beatrix Randolph. With Illustrations
by A. FREDERICKS.

Mercy Holland, and other Stories.
Three Vols., crown 8vo. [*Shortly*.

IMPORTANT NEW BIOGRAPHY.
Hawthorne (Nathaniel) and his Wife. By JULIAN HAWTHORNE.
With 6 Steel-plate Portraits. Two
Vols., crown 8vo, cloth extra, 24s.

[Twenty-five copies of an *Edition de Luxe*, printed on the best hand-made paper, large 8vo size, and with India proofs of the Illustrations, are reserved for sale in England, price 48s. per set. Immediate application should be made by anyone desiring a copy of this special and very limited Edition.]

Heath (F. G.). — My Garden Wild, and What I Grew There. By
FRANCIS GEORGE HEATH, Author of
"The Fern World," &c. Crown 8vo,
cl. ex., 5s.; cl. gilt, gilt edges, 6s.

Helps (Sir Arthur), Works by:
Animals and their Masters. Post 8vo, cloth limp, 2s. 6d.
Social Pressure. Post 8vo, cloth limp, 2s. 6d.
Ivan de Biron: A Novel. Crown 8vo, cloth extra, 3s. 6d.; post 8vo, illustrated boards, 2s.

Heptalogia (The); or, The Seven against Sense. A Cap with Seven Bells. Cr. 8vo, cloth extra, 6s.

Herbert. — The Poems of Lord Herbert of Cherbury. Edited, with Introduction, by J. CHURTON COLLINS. Crown 8vo, bound in parchment, 8s.

Herrick's (Robert) Hesperides, Noble Numbers, and Complete Collected Poems. With Memorial-Introduction and Notes by the Rev. A. B.
GROSART, D.D., Steel Portrait, Index of First Lines, and Glossarial Index, &c. Three Vols., crown 8vo, cloth, 18s.

Hesse-Wartegg. (Chevalier Ernst von), Works by
Tunis: The Land and the People. With 22 Illustrations. Crown 8vo, cloth extra, 3s. 6d.
The New South-West: Travelling Sketches from Kansas, New Mexico, Arizona, and Northern Mexico. With 100 fine Illustrations and Three Maps. Demy 8vo, cloth extra, 14s. [*In preparation*.

Hindley (Charles), Works by:
Crown 8vo, cloth extra, 3s. 6d. each.
Tavern Anecdotes and Sayings: Including the Origin of Signs, and Reminiscences connected with Taverns, Coffee Houses, Clubs, &c. With Illustrations.
The Life and Adventures of a Cheap Jack. By One of the Fraternity. Edited by CHARLES HINDLEY.

Hoey. — The Lover's Creed.
By Mrs. CASHEL HOEY. With 12 Illustrations by P. MACNAB. Three Vols., crown 8vo. [*Shortly*.

Holmes (O. Wendell), Works by:
The Autocrat of the Breakfast-Table. Illustrated by J. GORDON THOMSON. Post 8vo, cloth limp, 2s. 6d.; another Edition in smaller type, with an Introduction by G. A. SALA. Post 8vo, cloth limp, 2s.
The Professor at the Breakfast-Table; with the Story of Iris. Post 8vo, cloth limp, 2s.

Holmes. — The Science of Voice Production and Voice Preservation: A Popular Manual for the Use of Speakers and Singers. By GORDON HOLMES, M.D. With Illustrations. Cr. 8vo, 1s.; cl. limp, 1s. 6d.

Hood (Thomas):
Hood's Choice Works, in Prose and Verse. Including the Cream of the Comic Annuals. With Life of the Author, Portrait, and 200 Illustrations. Crown 8vo, cloth extra, 7s. 6d.
Hood's Whims and Oddities. Complete. With all the original Illustrations. Post 8vo, cloth limp, 2s.

Hood (Tom), Works by:
From Nowhere to the North Pole. A Noah's Arkæological Narrative. With 25 Illustrations by W. BRUNTON and E. C. BARNES. Square crown 8vo, cloth extra, gilt edges, 6s.
A Golden Heart: A Novel. Post 8vo, illustrated boards, 2s.

Hook's (Theodore) Choice Humorous Works, including his Ludicrous Adventures, Bons Mots, Puns and Hoaxes. With a New Life of the Author, Portraits, Facsimiles, and Illusts. Cr. 8vo, cl. extra, gilt, 7s. 6d.

Hooper.—The House of Raby: A Novel. By Mrs. GEORGE HOOPER. Post 8vo, illustrated boards, 2s.

Horne.—Orion: An Epic Poem, in Three Books. By RICHARD HENGIST HORNE. With Photographic Portrait from a Medallion by SUMMERS. Tenth Edition, crown 8vo, cloth extra, 7s.

Howell.—Conflicts of Capital and Labour, Historically and Economically considered; Being a History and Review of the Trade Unions of Great Britain, showing their Origin, Progress, Constitution, and Objects, in their Political, Social, Economical, and Industrial Aspects. By GEORGE HOWELL. Cr. 8vo, cloth extra, 7s. 6d.

Hugo. — The Hunchback of Notre Dame. By VICTOR HUGO. Post 8vo, illustrated boards, 2s.

Hunt.—Essays by Leigh Hunt. A Tale for a Chimney Corner, and other Pieces. With Portrait and Introduction by EDMUND OLLIER. Post 8vo, cloth limp, 2s.

Hunt (Mrs. Alfred), Novels by: Crown 8vo, cloth extra, 3s. 6d. each; post 8vo, illustrated boards, 2s. each.
Thornicroft's Model.
The Leaden Casket.
Self Condemned.

Ingelow.—Fated to be Free: A Novel. By JEAN INGELOW. Crown 8vo, cloth extra, 3s. 6d.; post 8vo, illustrated boards, 2s.

Irish Wit and Humour, Songs of. Collected and Edited by A. PERCEVAL GRAVES. Post 8vo, cl. limp, 2s. 6d.

Irving (Washington), Works by: Post 8vo, cloth limp, 2s. each.
Tales of a Traveller.
Tales of the Alhambra.

Janvier.—Practical Keramics for Students. By CATHERINE A. JANVIER. Crown 8vo, cloth extra, 6s.

Jay (Harriett), Novels by. Each crown 8vo, cloth extra, 3s. 6d.; or post 8vo, illustrated boards, 2s.
The Dark Colleen.
The Queen of Connaught.

Jefferies (Richard), Works by:
Nature near London. Crown 8vo, cloth extra, 6s.
The Life of the Fields. Crown 8vo, cloth extra, 6s.

Jennings (H. J.), Works by:
Curiosities of Criticism. Post 8vo, cloth limp, 2s. 6d.
Lord Tennyson: A Biographical Sketch. Crown 8vo, cloth extra, 6s. [*In the press.*

Jennings (Hargrave). — The Rosicrucians: Their Rites and Mysteries. With Chapters on the Ancient Fire and Serpent Worshippers. By HARGRAVE JENNINGS. With Five full-page Plates and upwards of 300 Illustrations. A New Edition, crown 8vo, cloth extra, 7s. 6d.

Jerrold (Tom), Works by:
The Garden that Paid the Rent. By TOM JERROLD. Fcap. 8vo, illustrated cover, 1s.; cloth limp, 1s. 6d.
Household Horticulture: A Gossip about Flowers. By TOM and JANE JERROLD. Illust. Post 8vo, cl. lp., 2s. 6d.
Our Kitchen Garden: The Plants we Grow, and How we Cook Them. By TOM JERROLD. Post 8vo, cloth limp, 2s. 6d.

Jesse.—Scenes and Occupations of a Country Life. By EDWARD JESSE. Post 8vo, cloth limp, 2s.

Jones (Wm., F.S.A.), Works by:
Finger-Ring Lore: Historical, Legendary, and Anecdotal. With over 200 Illusts. Cr. 8vo, cl. extra, 7s. 6d.
Credulities, Past and Present; including the Sea and Seamen, Miners, Talismans, Word and Letter Divination, Exorcising and Blessing of Animals, Birds, Eggs, Luck, &c. With an Etched Frontispiece. Crown 8vo, cloth extra, 7s. 6d.
Crowns and Coronations: A History of Regalia in all Times and Countries. With One Hundred Illustrations. Cr. 8vo, cloth extra, 7s. 6d.

Jonson's (Ben) Works. With Notes Critical and Explanatory, and a Biographical Memoir by WILLIAM GIFFORD. Edited by Colonel CUNNINGHAM. Three Vols., crown 8vo, cloth extra, 18s.; or separately, 6s. each.

Josephus, The Complete Works of. Translated by WHISTON. Containing both "The Antiquities of the Jews" and "The Wars of the Jews." Two Vols., 8vo, with 52 Illustrations and Maps, cloth extra, gilt, 14s.

Kavanagh.—The Pearl Fountain, and other Fairy Stories. By BRIDGET and JULIA KAVANAGH. With Thirty Illustrations by J. MOYR SMITH. Small 8vo, cloth gilt, 6s.

Kempt.—Pencil and Palette: Chapters on Art and Artists. By ROBERT KEMPT. Post 8vo, cloth limp, 2s. 6d.

Kingsley (Henry), Novels by: Each crown 8vo, cloth extra, 3s. 6d.; or post 8vo, illustrated boards, 2s.

Oakshott Castle. | Number Seventeen

Knight.—The Patient's Vade Mecum: How to get most Benefit from Medical Advice. By WILLIAM KNIGHT, M.R.C.S., and EDWARD KNIGHT, L.R.C.P. Crown 8vo, 1s.; cloth, 1s. 6d.

Lamb (Charles):

Mary and Charles Lamb: Their Poems, Letters, and Remains. With Reminiscences and Notes by W. CAREW HAZLITT. With HANCOCK'S Portrait of the Essayist, Facsimiles of the Title-pages of the rare First Editions of Lamb's and Coleridge's Works, and numerous Illustrations. Crown 8vo, cloth extra, 10s. 6d.

Lamb's Complete Works, In Prose and Verse, reprinted from the Original Editions, with many Pieces hitherto unpublished. Edited, with Notes and Introduction, by R. H. SHEPHERD. With Two Portraits and Facsimile of Page of the "Essay on Roast Pig." Cr. 8vo, cloth extra, 7s. 6d.

The Essays of Elia. Complete Edition. Post 8vo, cloth extra, 2s.

Poetry for Children, and Prince Dorus. By CHARLES LAMB. Carefully reprinted from unique copies. Small 8vo, cloth extra, 5s.

Little Essays: Sketches and Characters. By CHARLES LAMB. Selected from his Letters by. PERCY FITZGERALD. Post 8vo, cloth limp, 2s. 6d.

Lane's Arabian Nights, &c.:

The Thousand and One Nights: commonly called, in England, "THE ARABIAN NIGHTS' ENTERTAINMENTS." A New Translation from the Arabic, with copious Notes, by EDWARD WILLIAM LANE. Illustrated by many hundred Engravings on Wood, from Original Designs by WM. HARVEY. A New Edition, from a Copy annotated by the Translator, edited by his Nephew, EDWARD STANLEY POOLE. With a Preface by STANLEY LANE-POOLE. Three Vols., demy 8vo, cloth extra, 7s. 6d. each.

LANE'S ARABIAN NIGHTS, continued—
Arabian Society In the Middle Ages: Studies from "The Thousand and One Nights." By EDWARD WILLIAM LANE, Author of "The Modern Egyptians," &c. Edited by STANLEY LANE-POOLE. Cr. 8vo, cloth extra, 6s.

Lares and Penates; or, The Background of Life. By FLORENCE CADDY. Crown 8vo, cloth extra, 6s.

Larwood (Jacob), Works by:

The Story of the London Parks. With Illustrations. Crown 8vo, cloth extra, 3s. 6d.

Clerical Anecdotes. Post 8vo, cloth limp, 2s. 6d.

Forensic Anecdotes. Post 8vo, cloth limp, 2s. 6d.

Theatrical Anecdotes. Post 8vo, cloth limp, 2s. 6d.

Leigh (Henry S.), Works by:

Carols of Cockayne. With numerous Illustrations. Post 8vo, cloth limp, 2s. 6d.

Jeux d'Esprit. Collected and Edited by HENRY S. LEIGH. Post 8vo, cloth limp, 2s. 6d.

Life In London; or, The History of Jerry Hawthorn and Corinthian Tom. With the whole of CRUIKSHANK'S Illustrations, in Colours, after the Originals. Crown 8vo, cloth extra, 7s. 6d.

Linton (E. Lynn), Works by:

Post 8vo, cloth limp, 2s. 6d. each.

Witch Stories.

The True Story of Joshua Davidson.

Ourselves: Essays on Women.

Crown 8vo, cloth extra, 3s. 6d. each; post 8vo, illustrated boards, 2s. each.

Patricia Kemball.

The Atonement of Leam Dundas.

The World Well Lost.

Under which Lord?

With a Silken Thread.

The Rebel of the Family.

"My Love!"

Ione.

Locks and Keys.—On the Development and Distribution of Primitive Locks and Keys. By Lieut.-Gen. PITT-RIVERS, F.R.S. With numerous Illustrations. Demy 4to, half Roxburghe, 16s.

Longfellow:

Longfellow's Complete Prose Works. Including "Outre Mer," "Hyperion," "Kavanagh," "The Poets and Poetry of Europe," and "Driftwood." With Portrait and Illustrations by VALENTINE BROMLEY. Crown 8vo, cloth extra, 7s. 6d.

Longfellow's Poetical Works. Carefully Reprinted from the Original Editions. With numerous fine Illustrations on Steel and Wood. Crown 8vo, cloth extra, 7s. 6d.

Long Life, Aids to: A Medical, Dietetic, and General Guide in Health and Disease. By N. E. DAVIES, L.R.C.P. Crown 8vo, 2s; cloth limp, 2s. 6d. [*Shortly*.

Lucy.—Gideon Fleyce: A Novel. By HENRY W. LUCY. Crown 8vo, cl. extra, 3s 6d; post 8vo, illust. bds ,2s.

Lusiad (The) of Camoens. Translated into English Spenserian Verse by ROBERT FFRENCH DUFF. Demy 8vo, with Fourteen full-page Plates, cloth boards, 18s.

McCarthy (Justin, M.P.), Works by:
A History of Our Own Times, from the Accession of Queen Victoria to the General Election of 1880. Four Vols. demy 8vo, cloth extra, 12s. each.—Also a POPULAR EDITION, in Four Vols. cr. 8vo, cl. extra, 6s each.
A Short History of Our Own Times. One Vol., crown 8vo, cloth extra, 6s.
History of the Four Georges. Four Vols. demy 8vo, cloth extra, 12s. each. [Vol. I. *in the press.*
Crown 8vo, cloth extra, 3s. 6d. each; post 8vo, illustrated boards, 2s. each.
Dear Lady Disdain.
The Waterdale Neighbours.
My Enemy's Daughter.
A Fair Saxon.
Linley Rochford
Miss Misanthrope.
Donna Quixote.
The Comet of a Season.
Maid of Athens. With 12 Illustrations by F. BARNARD. Crown 8vo, cloth extra, 3s. 6d.

McCarthy (Justin H., M.P.), Works by:
Serapion, and other Poems. Crown 8vo, cloth extra, 6s.
An Outline of the History of Ireland, from the Earliest Times to the Present Day. Cr. 8vo, 1s.; cloth, 1s. 6d.
England under Gladstone. Crown 8vo, cloth extra, 6s.

MacDonald (George, LL.D.), Works by:
The Princess and Curdie. With 11 Illustrations by JAMES ALLEN. Small crown 8vo, cloth extra, 6s.
Gutta Percha Willie, the Working Genius. With 9 Illustrations by ARTHUR HUGHES. Square 8vo, cloth extra, 3s. 6d.
Paul Faber, Surgeon. With a Frontispiece by J. E. MILLAIS. Crown 8vo, cloth extra, 3s 6d.; post 8vo, Illustrated boards, 2s.
Thomas Wingfold, Curate. With a Frontispiece by C. J. STANILAND. Crown 8vo, cloth extra, 3s 6d.; post 8vo, illustrated boards, 2s.

Macdonell.—Quaker Cousins: A Novel. By AGNES MACDONELL. Crown 8vo, cloth extra, 3s. 6d.; post 8vo, illustrated boards, 2s

Macgregor. — Pastimes and Players. Notes on Popular Games. By ROBERT MACGREGOR. Post 8vo, cloth limp, 2s 6d.

Maclise Portrait-Gallery (The) of Illustrious Literary Characters; with Memoirs—Biographical, Critical, Bibliographical, and Anecdotal—illustrative of the Literature of the former half of the Present Century. By WILLIAM BATES, B.A. With 85 Portraits printed on an India Tint. Crown 8vo, cloth extra, 7s. 6d.

Macquoid (Mrs.), Works by:
In the Ardennes. With 50 fine Illustrations by THOMAS R. MACQUOID. Square 8vo, cloth extra, 10s. 6d.
Pictures and Legends from Normandy and Brittany. With numerous Illustrations by THOMAS R. MACQUOID. Square 8vo, cloth gilt, 10s. 6d.
Through Normandy. With 90 Illustrations by T. R. MACQUOID. Square 8vo, cloth extra, 7s. 6d.
Through Brittany. With numerous Illustrations by T. R. MACQUOID. Square 8vo, cloth extra, 7s. 6d.
About Yorkshire. With 67 Illustrations by T. R. MACQUOID, Engraved by SWAIN. Square 8vo, cloth extra, 10s. 6d.
The Evil Eye, and other Stories. Crown 8vo, cloth extra, 3s. 6d.; post 8vo, illustrated boards, 2s.
Lost Rose, and other Stories. Crown 8vo, cloth extra 3s 6d; post 8vo, illustrated boards, 2s.

Mackay.—Interludes and Undertones: or, Music at Twilight. By CHARLES MACKAY, LL.D. Crown 8vo, cloth extra, 6s.

Magician's Own Book (The): Performances with Cups and Balls, Eggs, Hats, Handkerchiefs, &c. All from actual Experience. Edited by W. H. CREMER. With 200 Illustrations. Crown 8vo, cloth extra, 4s. 6d.

Magic No Mystery: Tricks with Cards, Dice, Balls, &c., with fully descriptive Directions; the Art of Secret Writing; Training of Performing Animals, &c. With Coloured Frontispiece and many Illustrations. Crown 8vo, cloth extra, 4s. 6d.

Magna Charta. An exact Facsimile of the Original in the British Museum, printed on fine plate paper, 3 feet by 2 feet, with Arms and Seals emblazoned in Gold and Colours. Price 5s.

Mallock (W. H.), Works by:
The New Republic; or, Culture, Faith and Philosophy in an English Country House. Post 8vo, cloth limp, 2s. 6d.; Cheap Edition, illustrated boards, 2s.
The New Paul and Virginia; or, Positivism on an Island. Post 8vo, cloth limp, 2s. 6d.
Poems. Small 4to, bound in parchment, 8s.
Is Life worth Living? Crown 8vo, cloth extra, 6s.

Mallory's (Sir Thomas) Mort d'Arthur: The Stories of King Arthur and of the Knights of the Round Table. Edited by B. MONTGOMERIE RANKING. Post 8vo, cloth limp, 2s.

Marlowe's Works. Including his Translations. Edited, with Notes and Introduction, by Col. CUNNINGHAM. Crown 8vo, cloth extra, 6s.

Marryat (Florence), Novels by:
Crown 8vo, cloth extra, 3s. 6d. each; or, post 8vo, illustrated boards, 2s.
Open! Sesame!
Written in Fire.

Post 8vo, illustrated boards, 2s. each.
A Harvest of Wild Oats.
A Little Stepson.
Fighting the Air.

Masterman.—Half a Dozen Daughters: A Novel. By J. MASTERMAN. Post 8vo, illustrated boards, 2s.

Mark Twain, Works by:
The Choice Works of Mark Twain. Revised and Corrected throughout by the Author. With Life, Portrait, and numerous Illustrations. Crown 8vo, cloth extra, 7s. 6d.
The Adventures of Tom Sawyer. Post 8vo, illustrated boards, 2s.
An Idle Excursion, and other Sketches. Post 8vo, illustrated boards, 2s.
The Prince and the Pauper. With nearly 200 Illustrations. Crown 8vo, cloth extra, 7s. 6d.
The Innocents Abroad; or, The New Pilgrim's Progress: Being some Account of the Steamship "Quaker City's" Pleasure Excursion to Europe and the Holy Land. With 234 Illustrations. Crown 8vo, cloth extra, 7s. 6d. CHEAP EDITION (under the title of "MARK TWAIN'S PLEASURE TRIP"), post 8vo, illust. boards, 2s.
A Tramp Abroad. With 314 Illustrations. Crown 8vo, cloth extra, 7s. 6d.; Post 8vo, illustrated boards, 2s.
The Stolen White Elephant, &c. Crown 8vo, cloth extra, 6s.; post 8vo, illustrated boards, 2s.
Life on the Mississippi. With about 300 Original Illustrations. Crown 8vo, cloth extra, 7s. 6d.
The Adventures of Huckleberry Finn. With numerous Illusts. Cr. 8vo, cloth extra, 7s. 6d. [*Preparing.*

Massinger's Plays. From the Text of WILLIAM GIFFORD. Edited by Col. CUNNINGHAM. Crown 8vo, cloth extra, 6s.

Mayhew.—London Characters and the Humorous Side of London Life. By HENRY MAYHEW. With numerous Illustrations. Crown 8vo, cloth extra, 3s. 6d.

Mayfair Library, The:
Post 8vo, cloth limp, 2s. 6d. per Volume.
A Journey Round My Room. By XAVIER DE MAISTRE. Translated by HENRY ATTWELL.
Latter-Day Lyrics. Edited by W. DAVENPORT ADAMS.
Quips and Quiddities. Selected by W. DAVENPORT ADAMS.
The Agony Column of "The Times," from 1800 to 1870. Edited, with an Introduction, by ALICE CLAY.
Balzac's "Comedie Humaine" and its Author. With Translations by H. H. WALKER.
Melancholy Anatomised: A Popular Abridgment of "Burton's Anatomy of Melancholy."

MAYFAIR LIBRARY, continued—

Gastronomy as a Fine Art. By Brillat-Savarin.

The Speeches of Charles Dickens.

Literary Frivolities, Fancies, Follies, and Frolics. By W. T. Dobson.

Poetical Ingenuities and Eccentricities. Selected and Edited by W. T. Dobson.

The Cupboard Papers. By Fin-Bec.

Original Plays by W. S. Gilbert. First Series. Containing: The Wicked World — Pygmalion and Galatea — Charity — The Princess — The Palace of Truth — Trial by Jury.

Original Plays by W. S. Gilbert. Second Series. Containing: Broken Hearts — Engaged — Sweethearts — Gretchen — Dan'l Druce — Tom Cobb — H.M.S. Pinafore — The Sorcerer — The Pirates of Penzance.

Songs of Irish Wit and Humour. Collected and Edited by A. Perceval Graves.

Animals and their Masters. By Sir Arthur Helps.

Social Pressure. By Sir A. Helps.

Curiosities of Criticism. By Henry J. Jennings.

The Autocrat of the Breakfast Table. By Oliver Wendell Holmes. Illustrated by J. Gordon Thomson.

Pencil and Palette. By Robert Kempt.

Little Essays: Sketches and Characters. By Chas. Lamb. Selected from his Letters by Percy Fitzgerald.

Clerical Anecdotes. By Jacob Larwood.

Forensic Anecdotes; or, Humour and Curiosities of the Law and Men of Law. By Jacob Larwood.

Theatrical Anecdotes. By Jacob Larwood.

Carols of Cockayne. By Henry S. Leigh.

Jeux d'Esprit. Edited by Henry S. Leigh.

True History of Joshua Davidson. By E. Lynn Linton.

Witch Stories. By E. Lynn Linton.

Ourselves: Essays on Women. By E. Lynn Linton.

Pastimes and Players. By Robert Macgregor.

The New Paul and Virginia. By W. H. Mallock.

The New Republic. By W. H. Mallock.

Puck on Pegasus. By H. Cholmondeley-Pennell.

MAYFAIR LIBRARY, continued—

Pegasus Re-Saddled. By H. Cholmondeley-Pennell. Illustrated by George Du Maurier.

Muses of Mayfair. Edited by H. Cholmondeley-Pennell.

Thoreau: His Life and Aims. By H. A. Page.

Puniana. By the Hon. Hugh Rowley.

More Puniana. By the Hon. Hugh Rowley.

The Philosophy of Handwriting. By Don Felix de Salamanca.

By Stream and Sea. By William Senior.

Old Stories Retold. By Walter Thornbury.

Leaves from a Naturalist's Note-Book. By Dr. Andrew Wilson.

Medicine, Family.—One Thousand Medical Maxims and Surgical Hints, for Infancy, Adult Life, Middle Age, and Old Age. By N. E. Davies, L.R.C.P. Lond. Cr. 8vo, 1s.; cl., 1s. 6d.

Merry Circle (The): A Book of New Intellectual Games and Amusements. By Clara Bellew. With numerous Illustrations. Crown 8vo, cloth extra, 4s. 6d.

Mexican Mustang (On a). Through Texas, from the Gulf to the Rio Grande. A New Book of American Humour. By Alex. E. Sweet and J. Armoy Knox, Editors of "Texas Siftings." 400 Illusts. Cr. 8vo, cloth extra, 7s. 6d.

Middlemass (Jean), Novels by:
Touch and Go. Crown 8vo, cloth extra, 3s. 6d.; post 8vo, illust. bds., 2s.
Mr. Dorillion. Post 8vo, illust. bds., 2s.

Miller.—Physiology for the Young; or, The House of Life: Human Physiology, with its application to the Preservation of Health. For use in Classes and Popular Reading. With numerous Illustrations. By Mrs. F. Fenwick Miller. Small 8vo, cloth limp, 2s. 6d.

Milton (J. L.), Works by:
The Hygiene of the Skin. A Concise Set of Rules for the Management of the Skin; with Directions for Diet, Wines, Soaps, Baths, &c. Small 8vo, 1s.; cloth extra, 1s. 6d.
The Bath in Diseases of the Skin. Small 8vo, 1s.; cloth extra, 1s. 6d.
The Laws of Life, and their Relation to Diseases of the Skin. Small 8vo, 1s.; cloth extra, 1s. 6d.

BOOKS PUBLISHED BY

Moncrieff —. The Abdication; or, Time Tiies All. An Historical Drama. By W. D. SCOTT-MONCRIEFF. With Seven Etchings by JOHN PETTIE, R.A., W. Q. ORCHARDSON, R.A., J. MACWHIRTER, A.R.A., COLIN HUNTER, R. MACBETH, and TOM GRAHAM. Large 4to, bound in buckram, 21s.

Murray (D. Christie), Novels by. Crown 8vo, cloth extra, 3s. 6d. each; post 8vo, illustrated boards, 2s. each.
A Life's Atonement.
A Model Father.
Joseph's Coat.
Coals of Fire.
By the Gate of the Sea.

Crown 8vo, cloth extra, 3s. 6d. each.
Val Strange: A Story of the Primrose Way.
Hearts.
The Way of the World.

North Italian Folk. By Mrs. COMYNS CARR. Illust. by RANDOLPH CALDECOTT. Square 8vo, cloth extra, 7s. 6d.

Number Nip (Stories about), the Spirit of the Giant Mountains. Retold for Children by WALTER GRAHAME. With Illustrations by J. MOYR SMITH. Post 8vo, cloth extra, 5s.

Nursery Hints: A Mother's Guide in Health and Disease. By N. E. DAVIES, L.R.C.P. Crown 8vo, 1s.; cloth, 1s. 6d.

Oliphant. — Whiteladies: A Novel. With Illustrations by ARTHUR HOPKINS and HENRY WOODS. Crown 8vo, cloth extra, 3s. 6d.; post 8vo, illustrated boards, 2s.

O'Connor.—Lord Beaconsfield A Biography. By T. P. O'CONNOR, M.P. Sixth Edition, with a New Preface, bringing the book down to the Death of Lord Beaconsfield. Crown 8vo, cloth extra, 7s. 6d.

O'Reilly.—Phœbe's Fortunes: A Novel. With Illustrations by HENRY TUCK. Post 8vo, illustrated boards, 2s.

O'Shaughnessy (Arth.), Works by:
Songs of a Worker. Fcap. 8vo, cloth extra, 7s. 6d.
Music and Moonlight. Fcap. 8vo, cloth extra, 7s. 6d.
Lays of France. Crown 8vo, cloth extra, 10s. 6d.

Ouida, Novels by. Crown 8vo, cloth extra, 5s. each; post 8vo, illustrated boards, 2s. each.
Held in Bondage.
Strathmore.
Chandos.
Under Two Flags.
Cecil Castlemaine's Gage.
Idalia.
Tricotrin.
Puck.
Folle Farine.
Two Little Wooden Shoes.
A Dog of Flanders.
Pascarel.
Signa.
In a Winter City.
Ariadne.
Friendship.
Moths.
Pipistrello.
A Village Commune.
Bimbi.
In Maremma.

Wanda: A Novel. Crown 8vo, cloth extra, 5s.
Frescoes: Dramatic Sketches. Crown 8vo, cloth extra, 5s [Shortly.
Bimbi: PRESENTATION EDITION. Sq. 8vo, cloth gilt, cinnamon edges, 7s. 6d.
Princess Napraxine. Three Vols., crown 8vo, 31s. 6d.

Wisdom, Wit, and Pathos. Selected from the Works of OUIDA by F. SYDNEY MORRIS. Small crown 8vo, cloth extra, 5s.

Page (H. A.), Works by:
Thoreau: His Life and Aims: A Study. With a Portrait. Post 8vo, cloth limp, 2s. 6d.
Lights on the Way: Some Tales within a Tale. By the late J. H. ALEXANDER, B.A. Edited by H. A. PAGE. Crown 8vo, cloth extra, 6s.

Pascal's Provincial Letters. A New Translation, with Historical Introduction and Notes, by T. M'CRIE, D.D. Post 8vo, cloth limp, 2s.

Patient's (The) Vade Mecum: How to get most Benefit from Medical Advice. By WILLIAM KNIGHT, M.R.C.S., and EDWARD KNIGHT, L.R.C.P. Crown 8vo, 1s.; cloth, 1s. 6d.

Paul Ferroll:
Post 8vo, illustrated boards, 2s. each.
Paul Ferroll: A Novel.
Why Paul Ferroll Killed his Wife.

Paul.—Gentle and Simple. By MARGARET AGNES PAUL. With a Frontispiece by HELEN PATERSON. Cr. 8vo, cloth extra, 3s. 6d.; post 8vo, illustrated boards, 2s.

Payn (James), Novels by.
Crown 8vo, cloth extra, 3s. 6d. each;
post 8vo, illustrated boards, 2s. each.
Lost Sir Massingberd.
The Best of Husbands.
Walter's Word.
Halves. | Fallen Fortunes.
What He Cost Her.
Less Black than we're Painted.
By Proxy. | High Spirits.
Under One Roof. | Carlyon's Year.
A Confidential Agent.
Some Private Views.
A Grape from a Thorn.
For Cash Only. | From Exile.

Post 8vo, illustrated boards, 2s. each.
A Perfect Treasure.
Bentinck's Tutor.
Murphy's Master.
A County Family. | At Her Mercy.
A Woman's Vengeance.
Cecil's Tryst.
The Clyffards of Clyffe.
The Family Scapegrace
The Foster Brothers.
Found Dead.
Gwendoline's Harvest.
Humorous Stories.
Like Father, Like Son.
A Marine Residence.
Married Beneath Him.
Mirk Abbey.
Not Wooed, but Won.
Two Hundred Pounds Reward.

Kit: A Memory. Crown 8vo, cloth extra, 3s. 6d.
The Canon's Ward. With Portrait of Author. Cr.8vo, cloth extra, 3s. 6d.
In Peril and Privation: A Book for Boys. With numerous Illustrations. Crown 8vo, cloth extra, 6s.
(In preparation.

Pennell (H. Cholmondeley),
Works by: Post 8vo, cloth limp, 2s. 6d. each.
Puck on Pegasus. With Illustrations.
The Muses of Mayfair. Vers de Société, Selected and Edited by H. C. PENNELL.
Pegasus Re-Saddled. With Ten full-page Illusts. by G. Du MAURIER.

Phelps.—Beyond the Gates.
By ELIZABETH STUART PHELPS, Author of "The Gates Ajar." Crown 8vo, cloth extra, 2s. 6d.

Pirkis.—Trooping with Crows:
A Story. By CATHERINE PIRKIS, Fcap. 8vo, picture cover, 1s.

Planché (J. R.), Works by:
The Cyclopædia of Costume; or, A Dictionary of Dress—Regal, Ecclesiastical, Civil, and Military—from the Earliest Period in England to the Reign of George the Third. Including Notices of Contemporaneous Fashions on the Continent, and a General History of the Costumes of the Principal Countries of Europe. Two Vols. demy 4to, half morocco profusely Illustrated with Coloured and Plain Plates and Woodcuts, £7 7s. The Vols. may also be had *separately* (each complete in itself) at £3 13s. 6d. each: Vol. I. THE DICTIONARY. Vol. II. A GENERAL HISTORY OF COSTUME IN EUROPE.

The Pursuivant of Arms; or, Heraldry Founded upon Facts. With Coloured Frontispiece and 200 Illustrations. Cr. 8vo, cloth extra, 7s. 6d.

Songs and Poems, from 1819 to 1879. Edited, with an Introduction, by his Daughter, Mrs. MACKARNESS. Crown 8vo, cloth extra, 6s.

Play-time: Sayings and Doings of Baby-land. By EDWARD STANFORD. Large 4to, handsomely printed in Colours, 5s.

Plutarch's Lives of Illustrious Men. Translated from the Greek, with Notes Critical and Historical, and a Life of Plutarch, by JOHN and WILLIAM LANGHORNE. Two Vols. 8vo, cloth extra, with Portraits, 10s. 6d.

Poe (Edgar Allan):—
The Choice Works, in Prose and Poetry, of EDGAR ALLAN POE. With an Introductory Essay by CHARLES BAUDELAIRE, Portrait and Facsimiles. Crown 8vo, cl. extra, 7s. 6d.
The Mystery of Marie Roget, and other Stories Post 8vo, illust.bds.,2s.

Pope's Poetical Works. Complete in One Vol. Post 8vo, cl. limp, 2s.

Power.—Philistia: A Novel. By CECIL POWER. Three Vols, crown 8vo. *[Shortly.*

Price (E. C.), Novels by:
Valentina: A Sketch. With a Frontispiece by HAL LUDLOW. Cr. 8vo, cl. ex., 3s. 6d.; post 8vo,illust.bds.,2s.
The Foreigners. Cr.8vo,cl.ex., 3s.6d.
Mrs. Lancaster's Rival. Crown 8vo, cloth extra, 3s. 6d.

Proctor (Richd. A.), Works by;
Flowers of the Sky. With 55 Illusts. Small crown 8vo, cloth extra, 4s. 6d.
Easy Star Lessons. With Star Maps for Every Night in the Year, Drawings of the Constellations, &c. Crown 8vo, cloth extra, 6s.
Familiar Science Studies. Crown 8vo, cloth extra, 7s. 6d.
Rough Ways made Smooth: A Series of Familiar Essays on Scientific Subjects. Cr. 8vo, cloth extra, 6s.
Our Place among Infinities: A Series of Essays contrasting our Little Abode in Space and Time with the Infinities Around us. Crown 8vo, cloth extra, 6s.
The Expanse of Heaven: A Series of Essays on the Wonders of the Firmament. Cr. 8vo, cloth extra, 6s.
Saturn and Its System. New and Revised Edition, with 13 Steel Plates. Demy 8vo, cloth extra, 10s. 6d.
The Great Pyramid: Observatory, Tomb, and Temple. With Illustrations. Crown 8vo, cloth extra, 6s.
Mysteries of Time and Space. With Illusts. Cr. 8vo, cloth extra, 7s. 6d.
The Universe of Suns, and other Science Gleanings. With Illusts. Cr. 8vo, cloth extra, 7s. 6d. [*Shortly.*
Wages and Wants of Science Workers. Crown 8vo, 1s. 6d.

Pyrotechnist's Treasury (The); or, Complete Art of Making Fireworks. By THOMAS KENTISH. With numerous Illustrations. Cr. 8vo, cl. extra, 4s. 6d.

Rabelais' Works. Faithfully Translated from the French, with variorum Notes, and numerous characteristic Illustrations by GUSTAVE DORÉ. Crown 8vo, cloth extra, 7s. 6d.

Rambosson.—Popular Astronomy. By J. RAMBOSSON, Laureate of the Institute of France. Translated by C. B. PITMAN. Crown 8vo, cloth gilt, with numerous Illustrations, and a beautifully executed Chart of Spectra, 7s. 6d.

Reader's Handbook (The) of Allusions, References, Plots, and Stories. By the Rev. Dr. BREWER. Fourth Edition, revised throughout, with a New Appendix, containing a COMPLETE ENGLISH BIBLIOGRAPHY. Cr. 8vo, 1,400 pages, cloth extra, 7s. 6d.

Richardson. — A Ministry of Health, and other Papers. By BENJAMIN WARD RICHARDSON, M.D., &c. Crown 8vo, cloth extra, 6s.

Reade (Charles, D.C.L.), Novels by. Post 8vo, illust., bds., 2s. each; or cr. 8vo, cl. ex., illust..3s. 6d. each.
Peg Woffington. Illustrated by S. L. FILDES, A.R.A.
Christie Johnstone. Illustrated by WILLIAM SMALL.
It is Never Too Late to Mend. Illustrated by G. J. PINWELL.
The Course of True Love Never did run Smooth. Illustrated by HELEN PATERSON.
The Autobiography of a Thief; Jack of all Trades; and James Lambert. Illustrated by MATT STRETCH.
Love me Little, Love me Long. Illustrated by M. ELLEN EDWARDS.
The Double Marriage. Illust. by Sir JOHN GILBERT, R.A., and C. KEENE.
The Cloister and the Hearth. Illustrated by CHARLES KEENE.
Hard Cash. Illust. by F. W. LAWSON.
Griffith Gaunt. Illustrated by S. L. FILDES, A.R.A., and WM. SMALL.
Foul Play. Illust. by DU MAURIER.
Put Yourself in His Place. Illustrated by ROBERT BARNES.
A Terrible Temptation. Illustrated by EDW. HUGHES and A. W. COOPER.
The Wandering Heir. Illustrated by H. PATERSON, S. L. FILDES, A.R.A., C. GREEN, and H. WOODS, A.R.A.
A Simpleton. Illustrated by KATE CRAUFORD.
A Woman-Hater. Illustrated by THOS. COULDERY.
Readiana. With a Steel-plate Portrait of CHARLES READE.
Singleheart and Doubleface: A Matter-of-fact Romance. Illustrated by P. MACNAB.
Good Stories of Men and other Animals. Illustrated by E. A. ABBEY, PERCY MACQUOID, and JOSEPH NASH.
The Jilt, and other Stories. Illustrated by JOSEPH NASH.

Riddell (Mrs. J. H.), Novels by:
Crown 8vo, cloth extra, 3s. 6d. each; post 8vo, illustrated boards, 2s. each.
Her Mother's Darling.
The Prince of Wales's Garden Party.
Weird Stories. Crown 8vo, cloth extra, 3s. 6d.

Rimmer (Alfred), Works by:
Our Old Country Towns. With over 50 Illusts. Sq. 8vo, cloth gilt, 10s. 6d.
Rambles Round Eton and Harrow. 50 Illusts. Sq. 8vo, cloth gilt, 10s. 6d.
About England with Dickens. With 58 Illusts. by ALFRED RIMMER and C. A. VANDERHOOF. Sq. 8vo, cl. gilt, 10s. 6d.

Robinson (F. W.), Novels by:
Women are Strange. Cr. 8vo, cloth extra, 3s. 6d.; post 8vo, illust. bds., 2s.
The Hands of Justice. Crown 8vo, cloth extra, 3s. 6d.

Robinson (Phil), Works by:
The Poets' Birds. Crown 8vo, cloth extra, 7s. 6d.
The Poets' Beasts. Crown 8vo, cloth extra, 7s. 6d. [*In preparation.*

Robinson Crusoe: A beautiful reproduction of Major's Edition, with 37 Woodcuts and Two Steel Plates by GEORGE CRUIKSHANK, choicely printed. Crown 8vo, cloth extra, 7s. 6d. A few Large-Paper copies, printed on hand-made paper, with India proofs of the Illustrations, price 36s.

Rochefoucauld's Maxims and Moral Reflections. With Notes, and an Introductory Essay by SAINTE-BEUVE. Post 8vo, cloth limp, 2s.

Roll of Battle Abbey, The; or, A List of the Principal Warriors who came over from Normandy with William the Conqueror, and Settled in this Country, A.D. 1066-7. With the principal Arms emblazoned in Gold and Colours. Handsomely printed, 5s.

Rowley (Hon. Hugh), Works by:
Post 8vo, cloth limp, 2s. 6d. each.
Puniana: Riddles and Jokes. With numerous Illustrations.
More Puniana. Profusely Illustrated.

Russell (W. Clark, Author of "The Wreck of the Grosvenor"), Works by:
Crown 8vo, cloth extra, 6s. each.
Round the Galley-Fire.
On the Fok's'le Head: A Collection of Yarns and Sea Descriptions.
[*In the press.*

Sala.—Gaslight and Daylight. By GEORGE AUGUSTUS SALA. Post 8vo, illustrated boards, 2s.

Sanson.—Seven Generations of Executioners: Memoirs of the Sanson Family (1658 to 1847). Edited by HENRY SANSON. Cr. 8vo, cl. ex. 3s. 6d.

Saunders (John), Novels by:
Crown 8vo, cloth extra, 3s. 6d. each; post 8vo, illustrated boards, 2s. each.
Bound to the Wheel.
One Against the World.
Guy Waterman.
The Lion in the Path.
The Two Dreamers.

Saunders (Katharine), Novels by:
Crown 8vo, cloth extra, 3s. 6d. each.
Joan Merryweather.
Margaret and Elizabeth.
Gideon's Rock.
The High Mills.
Heart Salvage, by Sea and Land. Three Vols., crown 8vo.

Science Gossip: An Illustrated Medium of Interchange for Students and Lovers of Nature. Edited by J. E. TAYLOR, F.L.S., &c. Devoted to Geology, Botany, Physiology, Chemistry, Zoology, Microscopy, Telescopy, Physiography, &c. Price 4d. Monthly; or 5s. per year, post free. Each Number contains a Coloured Plate and numerous Woodcuts. Vols. I. to XIV. may be had at 7s. 6d. each; and Vols. XV. to XIX. (1884), at 5s. each. Cases for Binding, 1s. 6d. each.

Scott's (Sir Walter) Marmion. An entirely New Edition of this famous and popular Poem, with over 100 new Illustrations by leading Artists. Elegantly and appropriately bound, small 4to, cloth extra, 16s.

[The immediate success of "The Lady of the Lake," published in 1883, has encouraged Messrs. CHATTO and WINDUS to bring out a Companion Edition of this not less popular and famous poem. Produced in the same style, and with the same careful and elaborate style of illustration, regardless of cost, Mr. Anthony's skilful supervision is sufficient guarantee that the work is elegant and tasteful as well as correct.]

"Secret Out" Series, The:
Crown 8vo, cloth extra, profusely Illustrated, 4s. 6d. each.
The Secret Out: One Thousand Tricks with Cards, and other Recreations; with Entertaining Experiments in Drawing-room or "White Magic." By W. H. CREMER. 300 Engravings.
The Pyrotechnist's Treasury; or, Complete Art of Making Fireworks. By THOMAS KENTISH. With numerous Illustrations.
The Art of Amusing: A Collection of Graceful Arts, Games, Tricks, Puzzles, and Charades. By FRANK BELLEW. With 300 Illustrations.
Hanky Panky: Very Easy Tricks, Very Difficult Tricks, White Magic, Sleight of Hand. Edited by W. H. CREMER. With 200 Illustrations.

"Secret Out" Series, *continued*—

The Merry Circle: A Book of New Intellectual Games and Amusements. By CLARA BELLEW. With many Illustrations.

Magician's Own Book: Performances with Cups and Balls, Eggs, Hats, Handkerchiefs, &c. All from actual Experience. Edited by W. H. CREMER. 200 Illustrations.

Magic No Mystery: Tricks with Cards, Dice, Balls, &c., with fully descriptive Directions; the Art of Secret Writing; Training of Performing Animals, &c. With Coloured Frontispiece and many Illustrations.

Senior (William), Works by:

Travel and Trout in the Antipodes. Crown 8vo, cloth extra, 6s.

By Stream and Sea. Post 8vo, cloth limp, 2s. 6d.

Seven Sagas (The) of Prehistoric Man. By JAMES H. STODDART, Author of "The Village Life." Crown 8vo, cloth extra, 6s.

Shakespeare:

The First Folio Shakespeare.—MR. WILLIAM SHAKESPEARE'S Comedies, Histories, and Tragedies. Published according to the true Originall Copies. London, Printed by ISAAC IAGGARD and ED. BLOUNT. 1623.—A Reproduction of the extremely rare original, in reduced facsimile, by a photographic process—ensuring the strictest accuracy in every detail. Small 8vo, half-Roxburghe, 7s. 6d.

The Lansdowne Shakespeare. Beautifully printed in red and black, in small but very clear type. With engraved facsimile of DROESHOUT'S Portrait. Post 8vo, cloth extra, 7s. 6d.

Shakespeare for Children: Tales from Shakespeare. By CHARLES and MARY LAMB. With numerous Illustrations, coloured and plain, by J. MOYR SMITH. Crown 4to, cloth gilt, 6s.

The Handbook of Shakespeare Music. Being an Account of 350 Pieces of Music, set to Words taken from the Plays and Poems of Shakespeare, the compositions ranging from the Elizabethan Age to the Present Time. By ALFRED ROFFE. 4to, half-Roxburghe, 7s.

A Study of Shakespeare. By ALGERNON CHARLES SWINBURNE. Crown 8vo, cloth extra, 8s.

Shelley's Complete Works, in Four Vols., post 8vo, cloth limp, 8s.; or separately, 2s. each. Vol I. contains his Early Poems, Queen Mab, &c., with an Introduction by LEIGH HUNT; Vol. II., his Later Poems, Laon and Cythna, &c.; Vol. III., Posthumous Poems, the Shelley Papers, &c.: Vol. IV., his Prose Works, including A Refutation of Deism, Zastrozzi, St. Irvyne, &c.

Sheridan:—

Sheridan's Complete Works, with Life and Anecdotes. Including his Dramatic Writings, printed from the Original Editions, his Works in Prose and Poetry, Translations, Speeches, Jokes, Puns, &c. With a Collection of Sheridaniana. Crown 8vo, cloth extra, gilt, with 10 full-page Tinted Illustrations, 7s. 6d.

Sheridan's Comedies: The Rivals, and The School for Scandal. Edited, with an Introduction and Notes to each Play, and a Biographical Sketch of Sheridan, by BRANDER MATTHEWS. With Decorative Vignettes and 10 full-page Illustrations. Demy 8vo, cl. bds., 12s. 6d.

Short Sayings of Great Men. With Historical and Explanatory Notes by SAMUEL A. BENT, M.A. Demy 8vo, cloth extra, 7s. 6d.

Sidney's (Sir Philip) Complete Poetical Works, including all those in "Arcadia." With Portrait, Memorial-Introduction, Essay on the Poetry of Sidney, and Notes, by the Rev. A. B. GROSART, D.D. Three Vols., crown 8vo, cloth boards, 18s.

Signboards: Their History. With Anecdotes of Famous Taverns and Remarkable Characters. By JACOB LARWOOD and JOHN CAMDEN HOTTEN. Crown 8vo, cloth extra, with 100 Illustrations, 7s. 6d.

Sims (G. R.)—How the Poor Live. With 60 Illustrations by FRED. BARNARD. Large 4to, 1s.

Sketchley.—A Match in the Dark. By ARTHUR SKETCHLEY. Post 8vo, illustrated boards, 2s.

Slang Dictionary, The: Etymological, Historical, and Anecdotal. Crown 8vo, cloth extra, gilt, 6s. 6d.

Smith (J. Moyr), Works by:

The Prince of Argolis: A Story of the Old Greek Fairy Time. By J. MOYR SMITH. Small 8vo, cloth extra, with 130 Illustrations, 3s. 6d.

CHATTO & WINDUS, PICCADILLY. 23

Smith's (J. Moyr) Works, *continued*—
Tales of Old Thule. Collected and Illustrated by J. Moyr Smith. Cr. 8vo, cloth gilt, profusely Illust., 6s.
The Wooing of the Water Witch: A Northern Oddity. By Evan Daldorne. Illustrated by J. Moyr Smith. Small 8vo, cloth extra, 6s.

Spalding.—Elizabethan Demonology: An Essay in Illustration of the Belief in the Existence of Devils, and the Powers possessed by Them. By T. Alfred Spalding, LL.B. Crown 8vo, cloth extra, 5s.

Speight.—The Mysteries of Heron Dyke. By T. W. Speight. With a Frontispiece by M. Ellen Edwards. Crown 8vo, cloth extra, 3s. 6d.; post 8vo, illustrated boards, 2s.

Spenser for Children. By M. H. Towry. With Illustrations by Walter J. Morgan. Crown 4to, with Coloured Illustrations, cloth gilt, 6s.

Staunton.—Laws and Practice of Chess; Together with an Analysis of the Openings, and a Treatise on End Games. By Howard Staunton. Edited by Robert B. Wormald. New Edition, small cr. 8vo, cloth extra, 5s.

Sterndale.—The Afghan Knife: A Novel. By Robert Armitage Sterndale. Cr. 8vo, cloth extra, 3s. 6d.; post 8vo, illustrated boards, 2s.

Stevenson (R. Louis), Works by:
Travels with a Donkey in the Cevennes. Frontispiece by Walter Crane. Post 8vo, cloth limp, 2s 6d.
An Inland Voyage. With Front. by W. Crane. Post 8vo, cl. lp., 2s. 6d.
Virginibus Puerisque, and other Papers. Crown 8vo, cloth extra, 6s.
Familiar Studies of Men and Books. Crown 8vo, cloth extra, 6s.
New Arabian Nights. Crown 8vo, cl. extra, 6s., post 8vo, illust. bds., 2s.
The Silverado Squatters. With Frontispiece. Cr. 8vo, cloth extra, 6s.
Prince Otto: A Romance. Crown 8vo, cloth extra, 6s. [*In preparation.*

St. John.—A Levantine Family. By Bayle St. John. Post 8vo, illustrated boards, 2s.

Stoddard.—Summer Cruising in the South Seas. By Charles Warren Stoddard. Illust. by Wallis Mackay. Crown 8vo, cl. extra, 3s 6d.

St. Pierre.—Paul and Virginia, and The Indian Cottage. By Bernardin St Pierre. Edited, with Life, by Rev. E. Clarke. Post 8vo, cl. lp., 2s.

Stories from Foreign Novelists. With Notices of their Lives and Writings. By Helen and Alice Zimmern; and a Frontispiece. Crown 8vo cloth extra, 3s. 6d.

Strutt's Sports and Pastimes of the People of England; including the Rural and Domestic Recreations, May Games, Mummeries, Shows, Processions, Pageants, and Pompous Spectacles, from the Earliest Period to the Present Time. With 140 Illustrations. Edited by William Hone. Crown 8vo, cloth extra, 7s. 6d.

Suburban Homes (The) of London: A Residential Guide to Favourite London Localities, their Society, Celebrities, and Associations. With Notes on their Rental, Rates, and House Accommodation. With Map of Suburban London. Cr. 8vo cl. ex., 7s 6d.

Swift's Choice Works, in Prose and Verse. With Memoir, Portrait, and Facsimiles of the Maps in the Original Edition of "Gulliver's Travels." Cr. 8vo, cloth extra, 7s. 6d.

Swinburne (Algernon C.), Works by:
The Queen Mother and Rosamond. Fcap. 8vo, 5s.
Atalanta in Calydon. Crown 8vo, 6s.
Chastelard A Tragedy. Cr. 8vo, 7s.
Poems and Ballads. First Series. Fcap. 8vo, 9s. Also in crown 8vo, at same price.
Poems and Ballads. Second Series. Fcap. 8vo, 9s. Cr. 8vo, same price.
Notes on Poems and Reviews. 8vo 1s.
William Blake: A Critical Essay. With Facsimile Paintings. Demy 8vo, 16s.
Songs before Sunrise. Cr. 8vo, 10s 6d.
Bothwell: A Tragedy. Cr. 8vo, 12s 6d.
George Chapman: An Essay. Crown 8vo, 7s.
Songs of Two Nations. Cr. 8vo, 6s.
Essays and Studies. Crown 8vo, 12s.
Erechtheus: A Tragedy. Cr. 8vo, 6s.
Note of an English Republican on the Muscovite Crusade. 8vo, 1s.
A Note on Charlotte Bronte. Crown 8vo, 6s.
A Study of Shakespeare. Cr. 8vo, 8s.
Songs of the Springtides. Crown 8vo, 6s.
Studies in Song. Crown 8vo, 7s.
Mary Stuart: A Tragedy. Cr. 8vo, 8s.
Tristram of Lyonesse, and other Poems. Crown 8vo, 9s.
A Century of Roundels. Small 4to, cloth extra 8s.
A Midsummer Holiday, and other Poems. Crown 8vo, 7s.

BOOKS PUBLISHED BY

Symonds.—Wine, Women and Song: Mediæval Latin Students' Songs. Now first translated into English Verse, with an Essay by J. Addington Symonds. Small 8vo, parchment, 6s.

Syntax's (Dr.) Three Tours: In Search of the Picturesque, in Search of Consolation, and in Search of a Wife. With the whole of Rowlandson's droll page Illustrations in Colours and a Life of the Author by J. C. Hotten. Medium 8vo, cloth extra, 7s. 6d.

Taine's History of English Literature. Translated by Henry Van Laun. Four Vols., small 8vo, cloth boards, 30s.—Popular Edition, Two Vols., crown 8vo, cloth extra, 15s.

Taylor (Dr. J. E., F.L.S.), Works by:
The Sagacity and Morality of Plants: A Sketch of the Life and Conduct of the Vegetable Kingdom. With Coloured Frontispiece and 100 Illusts. Crown 8vo, cl. extra, 7s. 6d.
Our Common British Fossils: A Complete Handbook. With numerous Illustrations. Crown 8vo, cloth extra, 7s. 6d. [*Preparing.*

Taylor's (Bayard) Diversions of the Echo Club: Burlesques of Modern Writers. Post 8vo, cloth limp, 2s.

Taylor's (Tom) Historical Dramas: "Clancarty," "Jeanne Darc," "'Twixt Axe and Crown," "The Fool's Revenge," "Arkwright's Wife," "Anne Boleyn," "Plot and Passion." One Vol., crown 8vo, cloth extra, 7s. 6d.
*** The Plays may also be had separately, at 1s. each.

Tennyson (Lord): A Biographical Sketch. By H. J. Jennings. Crown 8vo, cloth extra, 6s.

Thackerayana: Notes and Anecdotes. Illustrated by Hundreds of Sketches by William Makepeace Thackeray, depicting Humorous Incidents in his School-life, and Favourite Characters in the books of his every-day reading. With Coloured Frontispiece. Cr. 8vo, cl. extra, 7s. 6d.

Thomas (Bertha), Novels by. Crown 8vo, cloth extra, 3s. 6d. each; post 8vo, illustrated boards, 2s. each.
Cressida.
Proud Maisie.
The Violin-Player.

Thomas (M.).—A Fight for Life A Novel. By W. Moy Thomas. Post 8vo, illustrated boards, 2s.

Thomson's Seasons and Castle of Indolence. With a Biographical and Critical Introduction by Allan Cunningham, and over 50 fine Illustrations on Steel and Wood. Crown 8vo, cloth extra, gilt edges, 7s. 6d.

Thornbury (Walter), Works by Haunted London. Edited by Edward Walford, M.A. With Illustrations by F. W. Fairholt, F.S.A. Crown 8vo, cloth extra, 7s. 6d.
The Life and Correspondence of J. M. W. Turner. Founded upon Letters and Papers furnished by his Friends and fellow Academicians. With numerous Illusts. in Colours, facsimiled from Turner's Original Drawings. Cr. 8vo, cl. extra, 7s. 6d.
Old Stories Re-told. Post 8vo, cloth limp, 2s. 6d.
Tales for the Marines. Post 8vo, illustrated boards, 2s.

Timbs (John), Works by:
The History of Clubs and Club Life in London. With Anecdotes of its Famous Coffee-houses, Hostelries, and Taverns. With numerous Illustrations. Cr. 8vo, cloth extra, 7s. 6d.
English Eccentrics and Eccentricities: Stories of Wealth and Fashion, Delusions, Impostures, and Fanatic Missions, Strange Sights and Sporting Scenes, Eccentric Artists, Theatrical Folks, Men of Letters, &c. With nearly 50 Illusts. Crown 8vo, cloth extra, 7s. 6d.

Torrens. — The Marquess Wellesley, Architect of Empire. An Historic Portrait. By W. M. Torrens, M.P. Demy 8vo, cloth extra, 14s.

Trollope (Anthony), Novels by: Crown 8vo, cloth extra, 3s. 6d. each; post 8vo, illustrated boards, 2s. each.
The Way We Live Now.
The American Senator.
Kept in the Dark.
Frau Frohmann.
Marion Fay.

Crown 8vo, cloth extra, 3s. 6d. each.
Mr. Scarborough's Family.
The Land-Leaguers.

Trollope (Frances E.), Novels by Like Ships upon the Sea. Crown 8vo, cloth extra, 3s. 6d.; post 8vo, illustrated boards, 2s.
Mabel's Progress. Crown 8vo, cloth extra, 3s. 6d.
Anne Furness. Cr. 8vo, cl. ex., 3s. 6d.

Trollope (T. A.).—Diamond Cut Diamond, and other Stories. By THOMAS ADOLPHUS TROLLOPE. Crown 8vo, cloth extra, 3s. 6d.; post 8vo, illustrated boards, 2s.

Tytler (Sarah), Novels by:
Crown 8vo, cloth extra, 3s. 6d. each; post 8vo, illustrated boards, 2s. each.
What She Came Through.
The Bride's Pass.

Saint Mungo's City. Crown 8vo, cloth extra, 3s. 6d. [*Preparing*.
Beauty and the Beast. Three Vols., crown 8vo, 31s. 6d. [*Shortly*.

Tytler (C. C. Fraser-). — Mistress Judith: A Novel. By C. C. FRASER-TYTLER. Crown 8vo, cloth extra, 3s. 6d.

Van Laun.—History of French Literature. By HENRY VAN LAUN. Complete in Three Vols., demy 8vo, cloth boards, 7s. 6d. each.

Villari.— A Double Bond: A Story. By LINDA VILLARI. Fcap. 8vo, picture cover, 1s.

Walcott.— Church Work and Life in English Minsters; and the English Student's Monasticon. By the Rev. MACKENZIE E. C. WALCOTT, B.D. Two Vols., crown 8vo, cloth extra, with Map and Ground-Plans, 14s.

Walford (Edw., M.A.),Works by:
The County Families of the United Kingdom. Containing Notices of the Descent, Birth, Marriage, Education, &c., of more than 12,000 distinguished Heads of Families, their Heirs Apparent or Presumptive, the Offices they hold or have held, their Town and Country Addresses, Clubs, &c. Twenty-fourth Annual Edition, for 1884, cloth, full gilt, 50s.

The Shilling Peerage (1884). Containing an Alphabetical List of the House of Lords, Dates of Creation, Lists of Scotch and Irish Peers, Addresses, &c. 32mo, cloth, 1s. Published annually.

The Shilling Baronetage (1884). Containing an Alphabetical List of the Baronets of the United Kingdom, short Biographical Notices, Dates of Creation, Addresses, &c. 32mo, cloth, 1s. Published annually.

The Shilling Knightage (1884). Containing an Alphabetical List of the Knights of the United Kingdom, short Biographical Notices, Dates of Creation, Addresses, &c. 32mo, cloth, 1s. Published annually.

Walford's (Edw., M.A.) Works, con.—
The Shilling House of Commons (1884). Containing a List of all the Members of the British Parliament, their Town and Country Addresses, &c. 32mo, cloth, 1s. Published annually.

The Complete Peerage, Baronetage, Knightage, and House of Commons (1884). In One Volume, royal 32mo, cloth extra, gilt edges, 5s. Published annually.

Haunted London. By WALTER THORNBURY. Edited by EDWARD WALFORD, M.A. With Illustrations by F. W. FAIRHOLT, F.S.A. Crown 8vo, cloth extra, 7s. 6d.

Walton and Cotton's Complete Angler; or, The Contemplative Man's Recreation; being a Discourse of Rivers, Fishponds, Fish and Fishing, written by IZAAK WALTON; and Instructions how to Angle for a Trout or Grayling in a clear Stream, by CHARLES COTTON. With Original Memoirs and Notes by Sir HARRIS NICOLAS, and 61 Copperplate Illustrations. Large crown 8vo, cloth antique, 7s. 6d.

Wanderer's Library, The:
Crown 8vo, cloth extra, 3s. 6d. each.
Wanderings in Patagonia; or, Life among the Ostrich Hunters. By JULIUS BEERBOHM. Illustrated.
Camp Notes: Stories of Sport and Adventure in Asia, Africa, and America. By FREDERICK BOYLE.
Savage Life. By FREDERICK BOYLE.
Merrie England in the Olden Time. By GEORGE DANIEL. With Illustrations by ROBT. CRUIKSHANK.
Circus Life and Circus Celebrities. By THOMAS FROST.
The Lives of the Conjurers. By THOMAS FROST.
The Old Showmen and the Old London Fairs. By THOMAS FROST.
Low-Life Deeps. An Account of the Strange Fish to be found there. By JAMES GREENWOOD.
The Wilds of London. By JAMES GREENWOOD.
Tunis: The Land and the People. By the Chevalier de HESSE-WARTEGG. With 22 Illustrations.
The Life and Adventures of a Cheap Jack. By One of the Fraternity. Edited by CHARLES HINDLEY.
The World Behind the Scenes. By PERCY FITZGERALD.
Tavern Anecdotes and Sayings: Including the Origin of Signs, and Reminiscences connected with Taverns. Coffee Houses, Clubs, &c. By CHARLES HINDLEY. With Illusts.

WANDERER'S LIBRARY, THE, *continued—*
 The Genial Showman: Life and Adventures of Artemus Ward. By E. P. HINGSTON. With a Frontispiece.
 The Story of the London Parks. By JACOB LARWOOD. With Illusts.
 London Characters. By HENRY MAYHEW. Illustrated.
 Seven Generations of Executioners: Memoirs of the Sanson Family (1688 to 1847). Edited by HENRY SANSON.
 Summer Cruising in the South Seas. By C. WARREN STODDARD. Illustrated by WALLIS MACKAY.

Warner.—A Roundabout Journey. By CHARLES DUDLEY WARNER, Author of "My Summer in a Garden." Crown 8vo, cloth extra, 6s.

Warrants, &c.:—
 Warrant to Execute Charles I. An exact Facsimile, with the Fifty-nine Signatures, and corresponding Seals. Carefully printed on paper to imitate the Original, 22 in. by 14 in. Price 2s.
 Warrant to Execute Mary Queen of Scots. An exact Facsimile, including the Signature of Queen Elizabeth, and a Facsimile of the Great Seal. Beautifully printed on paper to imitate the Original MS. Price 2s.
 Magna Charta. An exact Facsimile of the Original Document in the British Museum, printed on fine plate paper, nearly 3 feet long by 2 feet wide, with the Arms and Seals emblazoned in Gold and Colours. Price 5s.
 The Roll of Battle Abbey; or, A List of the Principal Warriors who came over from Normandy with William the Conqueror, and Settled in this Country, A.D. 1066-7. With the principal Arms emblazoned in Gold and Colours. Price 5s.

Weather, How to Foretell the, with the Pocket Spectroscope. By F. W. CORY, M.R.C.S. Eng., F.R.Met. Soc., &c. With 10 Illustrations. Crown 8vo, 1s.; cloth, 1s. 6d.

Westropp.—Handbook of Pottery and Porcelain; or, History of those Arts from the Earliest Period. By HODDER M. WESTROPP. With numerous Illustrations, and a List of Marks. Crown 8vo, cloth limp, 4s. 6d.

Whistler v. Ruskin: Art and Art Critics. By J. A. MACNEILL WHISTLER. 7th Edition, sq. 8vo, 1s.

White's Natural History of Selborne. Edited, with Additions, by THOMAS BROWN, F.L.S. Post 8vo, cloth limp, 2s

Williams (W. Mattieu, F.R.A.S.), Works by:
 Science Notes. See the GENTLEMAN'S MAGAZINE. 1s. Monthly.
 Science in Short Chapters. Crown 8vo, cloth extra, 7s. 6d.
 A Simple Treatise on Heat. Crown 8vo, cloth limp, with Illusts., 2s. 6d.
 The Chemistry of Cookery. Crown 8vo, cloth extra, 6s. [*In the press.*

Wilson (Dr. Andrew, F.R.S.E.), Works by:
 Chapters on Evolution: A Popular History of the Darwinian and Allied Theories of Development. Second Edition. Crown 8vo, cloth extra, with 259 Illustrations, 7s. 6d.
 Leaves from a Naturalist's Notebook. Post 8vo, cloth limp, 2s. 6d.
 Leisure-Time Studies, chiefly Biological. Third Edition, with a New Preface. Crown 8vo, cloth extra, with Illustrations, 6s.

Winter (J. S.), Stories by:
 Crown 8vo, cloth extra, 3s. 6d. each, post 8vo, illustrated boards, 2s. each.
 Cavalry Life. | **Regimental Legends.**

Women of the Day: A Biographical Dictionary. By FRANCES HAYS. Crown 8vo, cloth extra, 6s. [*In the press.*

Wood.—Sabina: A Novel. By Lady WOOD. Post 8vo, illust. bds., 2s.

Words, Facts, and Phrases: A Dictionary of Curious, Quaint, and Out-of-the-Way Matters. By ELIEZER EDWARDS. New and cheaper issue, cr. 8vo, cl. ex., 7s. 6d.; half-bound, 9s.

Wright (Thomas), Works by:
 Caricature History of the Georges. (The House of Hanover.) With 400 Pictures, Caricatures, Squibs, Broadsides, Window Pictures, &c. Crown 8vo, cloth extra, 7s. 6d.
 History of Caricature and of the Grotesque in Art, Literature, Sculpture, and Painting. Profusely Illustrated by F. W. FAIRHOLT, F.S.A. Large post 8vo, cl. ex., 7s.6d.

Yates (Edmund), Novels by:
 Post 8vo, illustrated boards, 2s. each.
 Castaway. | **The Forlorn Hope.**
 Land at Last.

NOVELS BY THE BEST AUTHORS.
Now in the press.

WILKIE COLLINS'S NEW NOVEL.
"I Say No." By WILKIE COLLINS. Three Vols., crown 8vo.

Mrs. CASHEL HOEY'S NEW NOVEL
The Lover's Creed. By Mrs. CASHEL HOEY, Author of "The Blossoming of an Aloe," &c. With 12 Illustrations by P. MACNAB. Three Vols., crown 8vo.

SARAH TYTLER'S NEW NOVEL.
Beauty and the Beast. By SARAH TYTLER, Author of "The Bride's Pass," "Saint Mungo's City," "Citoyenne Jacqueline," &c. Three Vols., cr. 8vo.

CHARLES GIBBON'S NEW NOVEL.
By Mead and Stream. By CHARLES GIBBON, Author of "Robin Gray," "The Golden Shaft," "Queen of the Meadow," &c. Three Vols., cr 8vo.

ROBT. BUCHANAN'S NEW NOVEL
Foxglove Manor. By ROBT. BUCHANAN, Author of "The Shadow of the Sword," "God and the Man," &c. Three Vols., crown 8vo.

BASIL'S NEW NOVEL.
"The Wearing of the Green." By BASIL, Author of "Love the Debt," "A Drawn Game," &c. Three Vols., crown 8vo.

JULIAN HAWTHORNE'S NEW STORIES.
Mercy Holland, and other Stories. By J. HAWTHORNE, Author of "Garth," "Beatrix Randolph, &c. Three Vols., crown 8vo.

NEW NOVEL BY CECIL POWER.
Philistia. By CECIL POWER. Three Vols., crown 8vo.

THE PICCADILLY NOVELS.
Popular Stories by the Best Authors. LIBRARY EDITIONS, many Illustrated, crown 8vo, cloth extra, 3s. 6d. each.

BY MRS. ALEXANDER.
Maid, Wife, or Widow?

BY W. BESANT & JAMES RICE.
Ready-Money Mortiboy.
My Little Girl.
The Case of Mr. Lucraft.
This Son of Vulcan.
With Harp and Crown.
The Golden Butterfly.
By Celia's Arbour.
The Monks of Thelema.
'Twas in Trafalgar's Bay.
The Seamy Side.
The Ten Years' Tenant.
The Chaplain of the Fleet.

BY WALTER BESANT.
All Sorts and Conditions of Men.
The Captains' Room.
All in a Garden Fair.
Dorothy Forster.

BY ROBERT BUCHANAN.
A Child of Nature.
God and the Man.
The Shadow of the Sword.
The Martyrdom of Madeline.
Love Me for Ever.
Annan Water.
The New Abelard.

BY MRS. H. LOVETT CAMERON.
Deceivers Ever. | Juliet's Guardian.

BY MORTIMER COLLINS.
Sweet Anne Page.
Transmigration.
From Midnight to Midnight.

MORTIMER & FRANCES COLLINS.
Blacksmith and Scholar.
The Village Comedy.
You Play me False.

BY WILKIE COLLINS.
Antonina.
Basil.
Hide and Seek.
The Dead Secret.
Queen of Hearts.
My Miscellanies.
Woman in White.
The Moonstone.
Man and Wife.
Poor Miss Finch.
Miss or Mrs.?
New Magdalen.
The Frozen Deep.
The Law and the Lady.
The Two Destinies
Haunted Hotel.
The Fallen Leaves
Jezebel's Daughter
The Black Robe.
Heart and Science

BY DUTTON COOK.
Paul Foster's Daughter

BY WILLIAM CYPLES.
Hearts of Gold.

BY ALPHONSE DAUDET.
Port Salvation.

BY JAMES DE MILLE.
A Castle in Spain.

BY J. LEITH DERWENT.
Our Lady of Tears. | Circe's Lovers

PICCADILLY NOVELS, continued—
BY M. BETHAM-EDWARDS.
Felicia. | Kitty.
BY MRS. ANNIE EDWARDES.
Archie Lovell.
BY R. E. FRANCILLON.
Olympia. | One by One.
Queen Cophetua. | A Real Queen.
Prefaced by Sir BARTLE FRERE.
Pandurang Hari.
BY EDWARD GARRETT.
The Capel Girls.
BY CHARLES GIBBON.
Robin Gray.
For Lack of Gold.
In Love and War.
What will the World Say?
For the King.
In Honour Bound.
Queen of the Meadow.
In Pastures Green.
The Flower of the Forest.
A Heart's Problem.
The Braes of Yarrow.
The Golden Shaft.
Of High Degree.
Fancy Free.
Loving a Dream.
BY THOMAS HARDY.
Under the Greenwood Tree.
BY JULIAN HAWTHORNE.
Garth.
Ellice Quentin.
Sebastian Strome.
Prince Saroni's Wife.
Dust. | Fortune's Fool.
Beatrix Randolph.
BY SIR A. HELPS.
Ivan de Biron.
BY MRS. ALFRED HUNT.
Thornicroft's Model.
The Leaden Casket.
Self-Condemned.
BY JEAN INGELOW.
Fated to be Free.
BY HARRIETT JAY.
The Queen of Connaught.
The Dark Colleen.
BY HENRY KINGSLEY.
Number Seventeen.
Oakshott Castle.

PICCADILLY NOVELS, continued—
BY E. LYNN LINTON.
Patricia Kemball.
Atonement of Leam Dundas.
The World Well Lost.
Under which Lord?
With a Silken Thread.
The Rebel of the Family.
"My Love!" | Ione.
BY HENRY W. LUCY.
Gideon Fleyce.
BY JUSTIN McCARTHY, M.P.
The Waterdale Neighbours.
My Enemy's Daughter.
Linley Rochford. | A Fair Saxon.
Dear Lady Disdain.
Miss Misanthrope.
Donna Quixote.
The Comet of a Season.
Maid of Athens.
BY GEORGE MAC DONALD, LL.D.
Paul Faber, Surgeon.
Thomas Wingfold, Curate.
BY MRS. MACDONELL.
Quaker Cousins.
BY KATHARINE S. MACQUOID.
Lost Rose. | The Evil Eye.
BY FLORENCE MARRYAT.
Open! Sesame! | Written in Fire.
BY JEAN MIDDLEMASS.
Touch and Go.
BY D. CHRISTIE MURRAY.
Life's Atonement. | Coals of Fire.
Joseph's Coat. | Val Strange.
A Model Father. | Hearts.
By the Gate of the Sea.
The Way of the World.
BY MRS. OLIPHANT.
Whiteladies.
BY MARGARET A. PAUL.
Gentle and Simple.
BY JAMES PAYN.
Lost Sir Massing- | Carlyon's Year.
berd. | A Confidential
Best of Husbands | Agent.
Fallen Fortunes. | From Exile.
Halves. | A Grape from a
Walter's Word. | Thorn.
What He Cost Her | For Cash Only.
Less Black than | Some Private
We're Painted. | Views.
By Proxy. | Kit: A Memory.
High Spirits. | The Canon's
Under One Roof. | Ward.

CHATTO & WINDUS, PICCADILLY.

PICCADILLY NOVELS, continued—
BY E. C. PRICE.
Valentina. | The Foreigners.
Mrs. Lancaster's Rival.
BY CHARLES READE, D.C.L.
It is Never Too Late to Mend.
Hard Cash. | Peg Woffington.
Christie Johnstone.
Griffith Gaunt. | Foul Play.
The Double Marriage.
Love Me Little, Love Me Long.
The Cloister and the Hearth.
The Course of True Love.
The Autobiography of a Thief.
Put Yourself in His Place.
A Terrible Temptation.
The Wandering Heir. | A Simpleton.
A Woman-Hater. | Readiana.
BY MRS. J. H. RIDDELL.
Her Mother's Darling.
Prince of Wales's Garden-Party.
Weird Stories.
BY F. W. ROBINSON.
Women are Strange.
The Hands of Justice.
BY JOHN SAUNDERS.
Bound to the Wheel.
Guy Waterman. | Two Dreamers.
One Against the World.
The Lion in the Path.
BY KATHARINE SAUNDERS.
Joan Merryweather.
Margaret and Elizabeth.
Gideon's Rock. | The High Mills.

PICCADILLY NOVELS, continued—
BY T. W. SPEIGHT.
The Mysteries of Heron Dyke.
BY R. A. STERNDALE.
The Afghan Knife.
BY BERTHA THOMAS.
Proud Maisie. | Cressida.
The Violin-Player.
BY ANTHONY TROLLOPE.
The Way we Live Now.
The American Senator.
Frau Frohmann. | Marion Fay.
Kept in the Dark.
Mr. Scarborough's Family.
The Land Leaguers.
BY FRANCES E. TROLLOPE.
Like Ships upon the Sea.
Anne Furness.
Mabel's Progress.
BY T. A. TROLLOPE.
Diamond Cut Diamond
By IVAN TURGENIEFF and Other
Stories from Foreign Novelists.
BY SARAH TYTLER.
What She Came Through.
The Bride's Pass.
Saint Mungo's City.
BY C. C. FRASER-TYTLER.
Mistress Judith.
BY J. S. WINTER.
Cavalry Life.
Regimental Legends.

CHEAP EDITIONS OF POPULAR NOVELS.
Post 8vo, Illustrated boards, 2s. each.

BY EDMOND ABOUT.
The Fellah.
BY HAMILTON AÏDÉ.
Carr of Carrlyon. | Confidences.
BY MRS. ALEXANDER.
Maid, Wife, or Widow?
BY SHELSLEY BEAUCHAMP.
Grantley Grange.
BY W. BESANT & JAMES RICE.
Ready-Money Mortiboy.
With Harp and Crown.
This Son of Vulcan. | My Little Girl.
The Case of Mr. Lucraft.
The Golden Butterfly.
By Celia's Arbour.

BY BESANT AND RICE, continued—
The Monks of Thelema.
'Twas in Trafalgar's Day.
The Seamy Side.
The Ten Years' Tenant.
The Chaplain of the Fleet.
BY WALTER BESANT.
All Sorts and Conditions of
The Captains' Room.
BY FREDERICK BOYLE.
Camp Notes. | Savage Life.
BY BRET HARTE.
An Heiress of Red Dog.
The Luck of Roaring Camp.
Californian Stories.
Gabriel Conroy. | Flip.

CHEAP POPULAR NOVELS, continued—
  BY ROBERT BUCHANAN.
The Shadow of the Sword.
A Child of Nature.
God and the Man.
The Martyrdom of Madeline.
Love Me for Ever.
  BY MRS. BURNETT.
Surly Tim.
  BY MRS. LOVETT CAMERON.
Deceivers Ever. | Juliet's Guardian.
  BY MACLAREN COBBAN.
The Cure of Souls.
  BY C. ALLSTON COLLINS.
The Bar Sinister.
  BY WILKIE COLLINS.

Antonina.	Miss or Mrs. ?
Basil.	The New Magda-
Hide and Seek.	len.
The Dead Secret.	The Frozen Deep.
Queen of Hearts.	Law and the Lady.
My Miscellanies.	The Two Destinies
Woman in White.	Haunted Hotel.
The Moonstone.	The Fallen Leaves.
Man and Wife.	Jezebel's Daughter
Poor Miss Finch.	The Black Robe.

  BY MORTIMER COLLINS.
Sweet Anne Page.
Transmigration.
From Midnight to Midnight.
A Fight with Fortune.

MORTIMER & FRANCES COLLINS.
Sweet and Twenty. | Frances.
Blacksmith and Scholar.
The Village Comedy.
You Play me False.
  BY DUTTON COOK.
Leo. | Paul Foster's Daughter.
  BY J. LEITH DERWENT.
Our Lady of Tears.
  BY CHARLES DICKENS.
Sketches by Boz.
The Pickwick Papers.
Oliver Twist.
Nicholas Nickleby.
  BY MRS. ANNIE EDWARDES.
A Point of Honour. | Archie Lovell.
  BY M. BETHAM-EDWARDS.
Felicia. | Kitty.
  BY EDWARD EGGLESTON.
Roxy.

CHEAP POPULAR NOVELS, continued—
  BY PERCY FITZGERALD.
Bella Donna. | Never Forgotten.
The Second Mrs. Tillotson.
Polly.
Seventy-five Brooke Street.
The Lady of Brantome.
  BY ALBANY DE FONBLANQUE.
Filthy Lucre.
  BY R. E. FRANCILLON.
Olympia. | Queen Cophetua.
One by One.
Prefaced by Sir H. BARTLE FRERE.
Pandurang Hari.
  BY HAIN FRISWELL.
One of Two.
  BY EDWARD GARRETT
The Capel Girls.
  BY CHARLES GIBBON.

Robin Gray.	Queen of the Meadow.
For Lack of Gold.	
What will the World Say?	In Pastures Green
In Honour Bound.	The Flower of the Forest.
The Dead Heart.	A Heart's Problem
In Love and War.	The Braes of Yarrow.
For the King.	

  BY WILLIAM GILBERT.
Dr. Austin's Guests.
The Wizard of the Mountain.
James Duke.
  BY JAMES GREENWOOD.
Dick Temple.
  BY ANDREW HALLIDAY.
Every-Day Papers.
  BY LADY DUFFUS HARDY.
Paul Wynter's Sacrifice.
  BY THOMAS HARDY.
Under the Greenwood Tree.
  BY JULIAN HAWTHORNE.
Garth. | Sebastian Strome
Ellice Quentin. | Dust.
Prince Saroni's Wife.
  BY SIR ARTHUR HELPS.
Ivan de Biron.
  BY TOM HOOD.
A Golden Heart.
  BY MRS. GEORGE HOOPER.
The House of Raby.
  BY VICTOR HUGO.
The Hunchback of Notre Dame.

CHATTO & WINDUS, PICCADILLY. 31

CHEAP POPULAR NOVELS, continued—
BY MRS. ALFRED HUNT.
Thornicroft's Model.
The Leaden Casket.
Self-Condemned.

BY JEAN INGELOW.
Fated to be Free.

BY HARRIETT JAY.
The Dark Colleen.
The Queen of Connaught.

BY HENRY KINGSLEY.
Oakshott Castle. | Number Seventeen

BY E. LYNN LINTON.
Patricia Kemball.
The Atonement of Leam Dundas.
The World Well Lost.
Under which Lord?
With a Silken Thread.
The Rebel of the Family.
"My Love!"

BY HENRY W. LUCY.
Gideon Fleyce.

BY JUSTIN McCARTHY, M.P.
Dear Lady Disdain.
The Waterdale Neighbours.
My Enemy's Daughter.
A Fair Saxon.
Linley Rochford.
Miss Misanthrope.
Donna Quixote.
The Comet of a Season.

BY GEORGE MACDONALD.
Paul Faber, Surgeon.
Thomas Wingfold, Curate.

BY MRS. MACDONELL.
Quaker Cousins.

BY KATHARINE S. MACQUOID.
The Evil Eye. | Lost Rose.

BY W. H. MALLOCK.
The New Republic.

BY FLORENCE MARRYAT.
Open! Sesame! | A Little Stepson.
A Harvest of Wild | Fighting the Air.
Oats. | Written in Fire.

BY J. MASTERMAN.
Half-a-dozen Daughters.

BY JEAN MIDDLEMASS.
Touch and Go. | Mr. Dorillion.

CHEAP POPULAR NOVELS, continued—
BY D. CHRISTIE MURRAY.
A Life's Atonement.
A Model Father.
Joseph's Coat.
Coals of Fire.
By the Gate of the Sea.

BY MRS. OLIPHANT.
Whiteladies.

BY MRS. ROBERT O'REILLY.
Phœbe's Fortunes.

BY OUIDA.
Held in Bondage.
Strathmore.
Chandos.
Under Two Flags.
Idalia.
Cecil Castlemaine.
Tricotrin.
Puck.
Folle Farine.
A Dog of Flanders.
Pascarel.
Two Little Wooden Shoes.
Signa.
In a Winter City.
Ariadne.
Friendship.
Moths.
Pipistrello.
A Village Commune.
Bimbi.
In Maremma.

BY MARGARET AGNES PAUL.
Gentle and Simple.

BY JAMES PAYN.
Lost Sir Massingberd.
A Perfect Treasure.
Bentinck's Tutor.
Murphy's Master.
A County Family.
At Her Mercy.
A Woman's Vengeance.
Cecil's Tryst.
Clyffards of Clyffe.
The Family Scapegrace.
Foster Brothers.
Found Dead.
Best of Husbands.
Walter's Word.
Halves.
Fallen Fortunes.
What He Cost Her
Humorous Stories
Gwendoline's Harvest.
Like Father, Like Son.
A Marine Residence.
Married Beneath Him.
Mirk Abbey.
Not Wooed, but Won.
£200 Reward.
Less Black than We're Painted.
By Proxy.
Under One Roof.
High Spirits.
Carlyon's Year.
A Confidential Agent.
Some Private Views.
From Exile.
A Grape from a Thorn.
For Cash Only.

BY EDGAR A. POE.
The Mystery of Marie Roget.

CHEAP POPULAR NOVELS, *continued*—
BY E. C. PRICE.
Valentina.
BY CHARLES READE.
It is Never Too Late to Mend.
Hard Cash.
Peg Woffington.
Christie Johnstone.
Griffith Gaunt.
Put Yourself in His Place.
The Double Marriage.
Love Me Little, Love Me Long.
Foul Play.
The Cloister and the Hearth.
The Course of True Love.
Autobiography of a Thief.
A Terrible Temptation.
The Wandering Heir.
A Simpleton.
A Woman-Hater.
Readiana.
BY MRS. J. H. RIDDELL.
Her Mother's Darling.
Prince of Wales's Garden Party.
BY F. W. ROBINSON.
Women are Strange.
BY BAYLE ST. JOHN.
A Levantine Family.
BY GEORGE AUGUSTUS SALA.
Gaslight and Daylight.
BY JOHN SAUNDERS.
Bound to the Wheel.
One Against the World.
Guy Waterman.
The Lion in the Path.
Two Dreamers.
BY ARTHUR SKETCHLEY.
A Match in the Dark.
BY T. W. SPEIGHT.
The Mysteries of Heron Dyke.
BY R. A. STERNDALE.
The Afghan Knife.
BY R. LOUIS STEVENSON.
New Arabian Nights.
BY BERTHA THOMAS.
Cressida. | Proud Maisie.
The Violin-Player.
BY W. MOY THOMAS.
A Fight for Life.

CHEAP POPULAR NOVELS, *continued*—
BY WALTER THORNBURY.
Tales for the Marines.
BY T. ADOLPHUS TROLLOPE.
Diamond Cut Diamond.
BY ANTHONY TROLLOPE.
The Way We Live Now.
The American Senator.
Frau Frohmann.
Marion Fay.
Kept in the Dark.
By FRANCES ELEANOR TROLLOPE
Like Ships upon the Sea.
BY MARK TWAIN.
Tom Sawyer.
An Idle Excursion.
A Pleasure Trip on the Continent of Europe.
A Tramp Abroad.
The Stolen White Elephant.
BY SARAH TYTLER.
What She Came Through.
The Bride's Pass.
BY J. S. WINTER.
Cavalry Life. | Regimental Legends
BY LADY WOOD.
Sabina.
BY EDMUND YATES.
Castaway. | The Forlorn Hope.
Land at Last.
ANONYMOUS.
Paul Ferroll.
Why Paul Ferroll Killed his Wife.

Fcap. 8vo, picture covers, 1s. each.
Jeff Briggs's Love Story. By BRET HARTE.
The Twins of Table Mountain. By BRET HARTE.
Mrs. Gainsborough's Diamonds. By JULIAN HAWTHORNE.
Kathleen Mavourneen. By Author of "That Lass o' Lowrie's."
Lindsay's Luck. By the Author of "That Lass o' Lowrie's."
Pretty Polly Pemberton. By the Author of "That Lass o' Lowrie's."
Trooping with Crows. By Mrs. PIRKIS.
The Professor's Wife. By LEONARD GRAHAM.
A Double Bond. By LINDA VILLARI.
Esther's Glove. By R. E. FRANCILLON.
The Garden that Paid the Rent. By TOM JERROLD.

J. OGDEN AND CO., PRINTERS, 172, ST. JOHN STREET, E.C.

www.ingramcontent.com/pod-product-compliance
Lightning Source LLC
Chambersburg PA
CBHW031937290426
44108CB00011B/593